A Certain Idea of France

JULIAN JACKSON

A Certain Idea of France

The Life of Charles de Gaulle

ALLEN LANE
an imprint of
PENGUIN BOOKS

ALLEN LANE

UK | USA | Canada | Ireland | Australia
India | New Zealand | South Africa

Allen Lane is part of the Penguin Random House group of companies
whose addresses can be found at global.penguinrandomhouse.com

First published 2018
002

Copyright © Julian Jackson, 2018

The moral right of the author has been asserted

Set in 10.2/13.5 pt Sabon LT Std
Typeset by Jouve (UK), Milton Keynes
Printed and bound in Great Britain by Clays Ltd, Elcograf S.p.A.

A CIP catalogue record for this book is available from the British Library

ISBN: 978–1–846–14351–9

Contents

List of Illustrations

Items in the Archives de Gaulle, Paris, are reproduced by kind permission of the de Gaulle family.

LIST OF PLATES

TEXT ILLUSTRATIONS

Acknowledgements

The research and much of the writing of this book was made possible by the award of a three-year Leverhulme Major Research Fellowship for which I am deeply grateful. The bounty of the Leverhulme Trust to academics at every stage of their career is one of the saving graces of British academia. A sabbatical year from Queen Mary allowed me to complete the manuscript.

At the Archives Nationales in Paris, I am indebted to Nicole Even who catalogued the de Gaulle archives for the period of his Presidency. I also benefited at the Archives Nationales from the help and friendship of Caroline Piketty. Over fifteen years ago, Philippe Oulmont welcomed me at the Fondation Charles de Gaulle, offering assistance and advice – as he has continued to do since his retirement from the Fondation. Claude Marmot, also of the Fondation, shared with me her unrivalled knowledge of the de Gaulle family history, and allowed me to consult the unpublished letters of de Gaulle's brother Jacques to his parents during the Great War.

Among friends and colleagues who have helped in the writing of this book, two deserve special thanks. At Queen Mary, James Ellison shared with me copies of many documents from the National Archives, and from American archives, which he had used for his own work. This act of characteristic generosity saved me weeks of work. He was also kind enough to read the chapters on Gaullist foreign policy, a subject on which he has written with great authority. In Paris, I must thank above all Maurice Vaïsse whose selfless work editing the French diplomatic documents is a major resource to all historians of the period. In addition to this his kindness and help to me has been invaluable.

Robert Gildea, who read the entire manuscript for Penguin, also offered many useful suggestions.

Among others in England, France, the United States and elsewhere who have answered queries or contributed in other ways to the writing of this book (even if they may not remember that they have done), I would like to thank in particular: Grey Anderson, Claire Andrieu, Peter Catterall, Laurent Douzou, Yves de Gaulle, Charlotte Faucher, Martyn Frampton, Gabriel Gorodetsky, Sudhir Hazareesingh, Peter Hennessy, Patrick Higgins, the late Stanley Hoffmann, Colin Jones, Rod Kedward, Andy Knapp, Chantal Morelle, Michael Moriarty, Robert Paxton, Guillaume Piketty, Dominique Parcollet, Robert Service, Todd Shepard, Iain Stewart, Renée Poznanski, Edward Stourton, Robert Tombs, David Valence, Olivier Wieviorka.

My agent Andrew Gordon has been continuously supportive. He was kind enough to read an entire draft of the book and offered many perceptive comments. The team at Penguin has lived up to its reputation. Peter James was a ferociously eagle-eyed copyeditor who saved me from many solecisms, and Cecilia Mackay a brilliantly resourceful picture researcher. Richard Duguid, Rebecca Lee and Ben Sinyor saw the book into print with great professionalism. Stuart Proffitt lived up to his legend: no editor with whom I have worked has ever taken more care with a manuscript.

Finally, my deepest thanks as ever go to Douglas, who has put up with de Gaulle invading our life and spreading over every surface. It is not easy for a tidy interior designer to live with an untidy academic. I wish I could promise him that we are now finished with de Gaulle.

Julian Jackson
February 2018

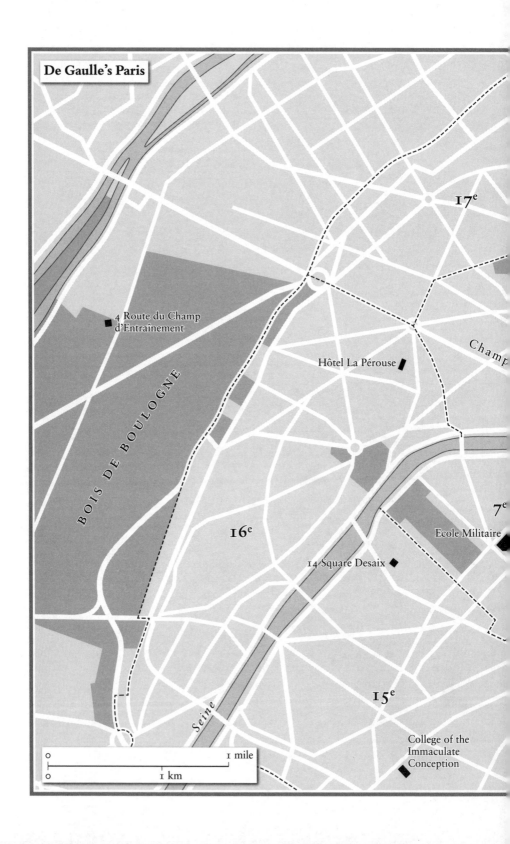

De Gaulle's Paris

17ᵉ

4 Route du Champ
d'Entraînement

Hôtel La Pérouse

Champ

BOIS DE BOULOGNE

7ᵉ

Ecole Militaire

16ᵉ

14 Square Desaix

15ᵉ

College of the
Immaculate
Conception

Seine

0   1 mile
0   1 km

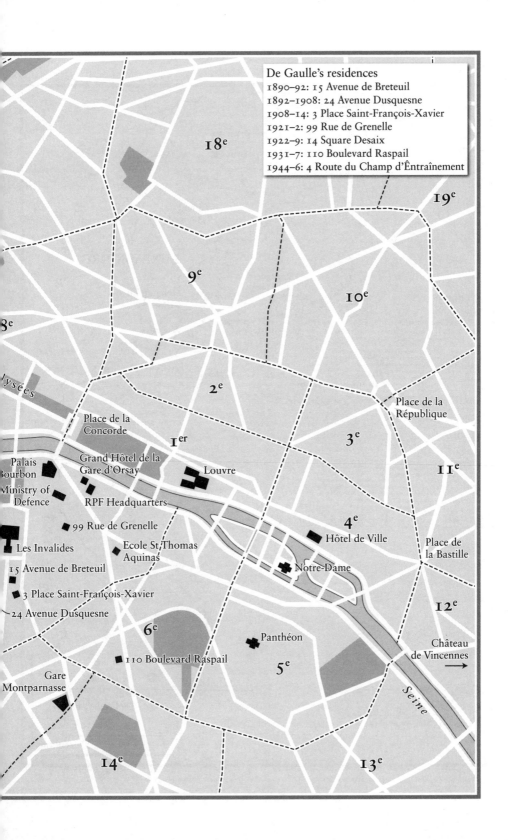

De Gaulle's residences
1890–92: 15 Avenue de Breteuil
1892–1908: 24 Avenue Dusquesne
1908–14: 3 Place Saint-François-Xavier
1921–2: 99 Rue de Grenelle
1922–9: 14 Square Desaix
1931–7: 110 Boulevard Raspail
1944–6: 4 Route du Champ d'Êntraînement

18ᵉ

19ᵉ

9ᵉ

10ᵉ

8ᵉ

lysées

2ᵉ

Place de la
République

Place de la
Concorde

1ᵉʳ

3ᵉ

11ᵉ

Palais
Bourbon

Grand Hôtel de la
Gare d'Orsay

Louvre

Ministry of
Defence

RPF Headquarters

4ᵉ

99 Rue de Grenelle

Hôtel de Ville

Place de
la Bastille

Les Invalides

Ecole St Thomas
Aquinas

Notre-Dame

15 Avenue de Breteuil

12ᵉ

3 Place Saint-François-Xavier

24 Avenue Dusquesne

6ᵉ

Panthéon

Château
de Vincennes
→

110 Boulevard Raspail

5ᵉ

Gare
Montparnasse

Seine

14ᵉ

13ᵉ

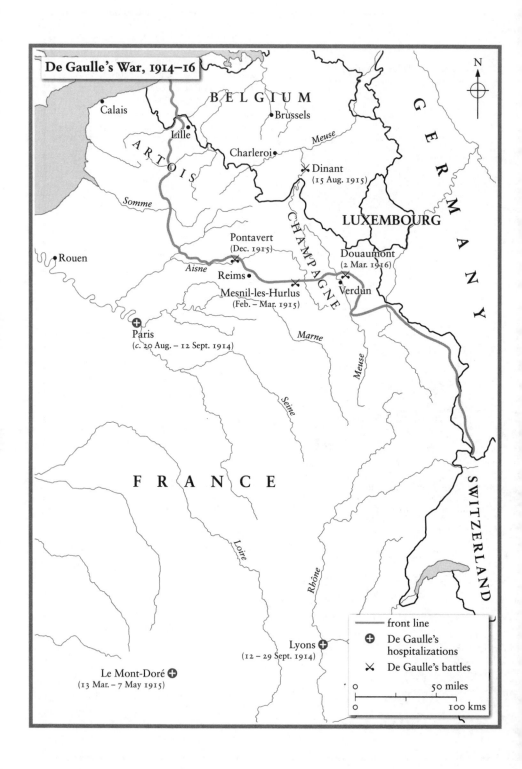

De Gaulle's War, 1914–16

N

Calais

BELGIUM

•Brussels

Lille

A R T O I S

Charleroi•

Meuse

✕ Dinant
(15 Aug. 1915)

LUXEMBOURG

•Rouen

Somme

Pontavert
(Dec. 1915)

✕

C H A M P A G N E

Douaumont
(2 Mar. 1916)

Aisne

Reims •

✕

✕ Verdun

Mesnil-les-Hurlus
(Feb. – Mar. 1915)

G E R M A N Y

Paris
(c. 20 Aug. – 12 Sept. 1914)

Marne

Meuse

Seine

F R A N C E

S W I T Z E R L A N D

Loire

Rhône

front line

De Gaulle's
hospitalizations

Lyons
(12 – 29 Sept. 1914)

✕ De Gaulle's battles

0   50 miles

Le Mont-Doré
(13 Mar. – 7 May 1915)

0   100 kms

Prisoner of War, 1916–18

N

NORTH SEA

DENMARK

SWEDEN

NETHERLANDS

□ Osnabrück
(Mar. – Jun. 1916)

Berlin ●

● Brussels

BELGIUM

● Cologne

Rhine

G E R M A N Y

LUXEMBOURG

Mainz □ ● Frankfurt
(Mar. 1916)

● Metz

Nuremberg
●

Rosenberg □
(Jul. – Nov. 1917)

Wülzburg (May – Nov. 1917)
□

Ingolstadt □
(Sept. 1916 – Jul. 1917
Dec. 1917 – May 1918)

Danube

● Passau

F R A N C E

● Munich

AUSTRIA-HUNGARY

SWITZERLAND

I T A L Y

□ prisons

100 miles

200 kms

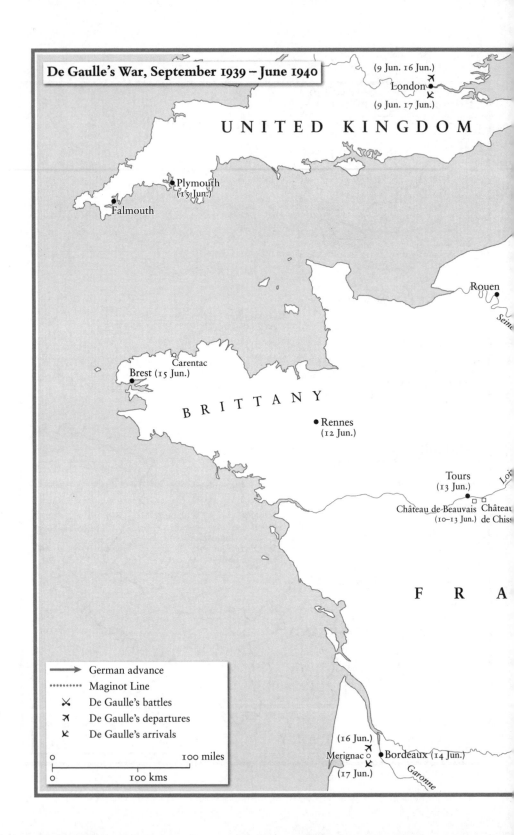

De Gaulle's War, September 1939 – June 1940

(9 Jun. 16 Jun.)
London
(9 Jun. 17 Jun.)

UNITED KINGDOM

Plymouth
(13 Jun.)
Falmouth

Rouen

Seine

Carentac
Brest (15 Jun.)

BRITTANY

Rennes
(12 Jun.)

Tours
(13 Jun.)

Loi

Château de Beauvais   Château
(10–13 Jun.)   de Chiss

F R A

German advance
Maginot Line
De Gaulle's battles
De Gaulle's departures
De Gaulle's arrivals

0   100 miles
0   100 kms

(16 Jun.)
Merignac   Bordeaux (14 Jun.)
(17 Jun.)

Garonne

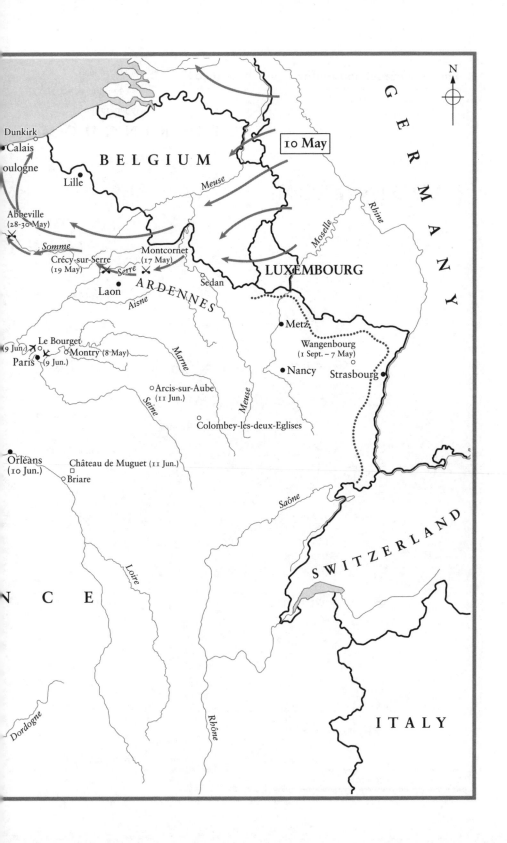

N

10 May

G E R M A N Y

BELGIUM

Dunkirk
Calais
oulogne
Lille
Meuse
Abbeville
(28-30 May)
Somme
Crécy-sur-Serre
(19 May)
Serre
Montcornet
(17 May)
Laon
ARDENNES
Aisne
Sedan

LUXEMBOURG

Moselle

Rhine

Metz

Wangenbourg
(1 Sept. – 7 May)

9 Jun.)
Le Bourget
Montry (8 May)
Paris
(9 Jun.)
Marne
Nancy
Strasbourg

Arcis-sur-Aube
(11 Jun.)
Seine
Meuse
Colombey-les-deux-Eglises

Orléans
(10 Jun.)
Château de Muguet (11 Jun.)
Briare

Saône

N   C   E

SWITZERLAND

Loire

Dordogne

Rhône

ITALY

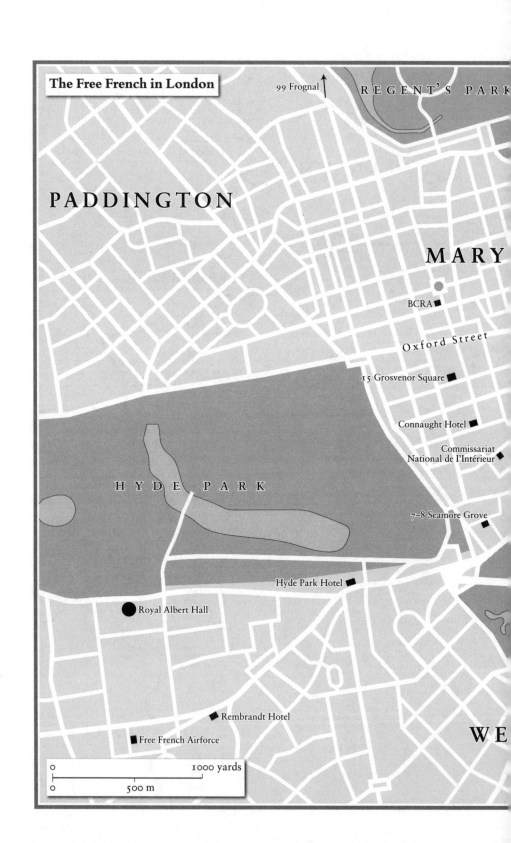

The Free French in London

99 Frognal ↑

REGENT'S PARK

PADDINGTON

MARY

BCRA ■

Oxford Street

15 Grosvenor Square ■

Connaught Hotel ■

Commissariat
National de l'Intérieur ■

HYDE PARK

7–8 Seamore Grove ■

Hyde Park Hotel ■

● Royal Albert Hall

Rembrandt Hotel ■

■ Free French Airforce

WE

0   1000 yards

0   500 m

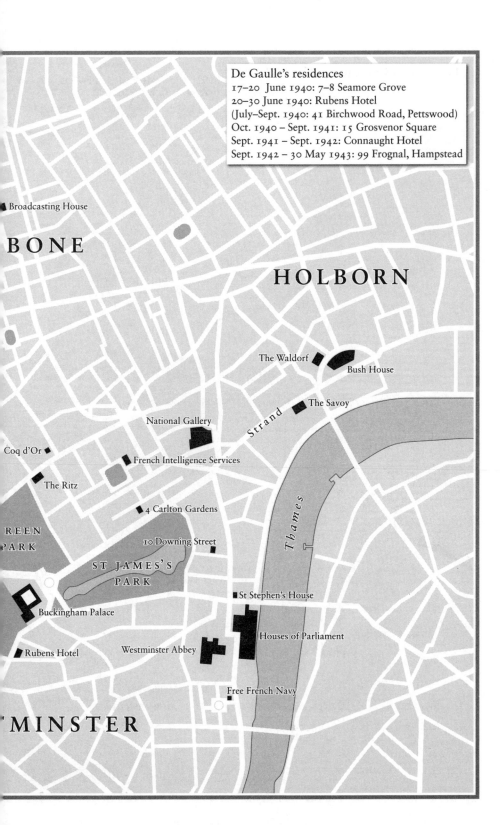

De Gaulle's residences
17–20 June 1940: 7–8 Seamore Grove
20–30 June 1940: Rubens Hotel
(July–Sept. 1940: 41 Birchwood Road, Pettswood)
Oct. 1940 – Sept. 1941: 15 Grosvenor Square
Sept. 1941 – Sept. 1942: Connaught Hotel
Sept. 1942 – 30 May 1943: 99 Frognal, Hampstead

Broadcasting House

BONE

HOLBORN

The Waldorf

Bush House

The Savoy

National Gallery

Strand

Coq d'Or

French Intelligence Services

The Ritz

Thames

4 Carlton Gardens

REEN
PARK

10 Downing Street

ST JAMES'S
PARK

St Stephen's House

Buckingham Palace

Houses of Parliament

Rubens Hotel

Westminster Abbey

Free French Navy

MINSTER

The French Colonies at War, 1940–43

N

FRANCE

Mediterranea

Algiers
Guelma
Tunis
Sétif
Biskra
Casablanca
Tripoli

MOROCCO
Marrakesh

LIBY

ALGERIA
FEZZAN

SPANISH
SAHARA
Murzuk

Dec. 194

MAURITANIA

FRENCH WEST AFRICA

NIGER

Jan. 1941

Dakar
SENEGAL
FRENCH SUDAN
Niger
Lake Tchad

HAUTE
VOLTA
Fort Lamy

GUINEA
Conakry
Freetown
SIERRA LEONE
IVORY
COAST
GOLD
COAST
DAHOMEY
NIGERIA
CAMEROON
Lagos

LIBERIA
Abidjan
Duala

TOGO
BRITISH CAMEROONS

SPANISH GUINEA
Libreville

ATLANTIC OCEAN
GABON

FRENCH
CONGO
Brazzavi
Léopoldville

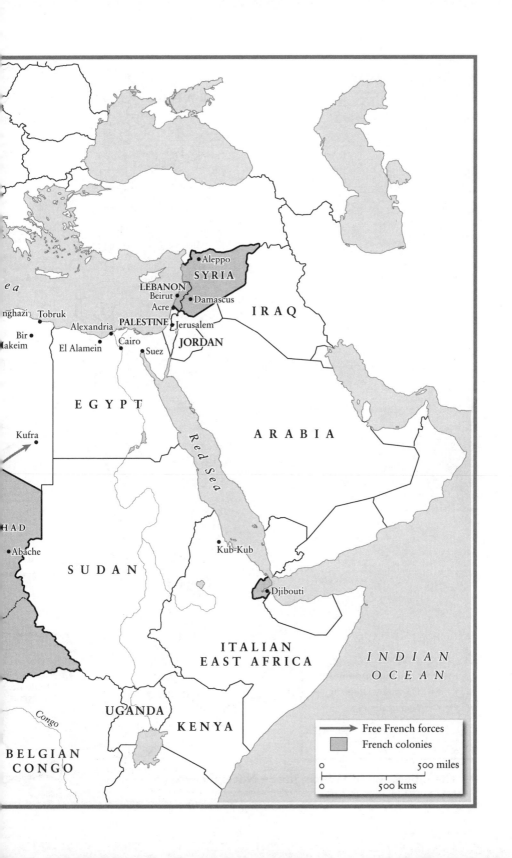

SYRIA

Aleppo

LEBANON
Beirut
Acre • Damascus

IRAQ

nghazi   Tobruk
Bir •
akeim   Alexandria
                                PALESTINE
         El Alamein   Cairo   Jerusalem
                          Suez   JORDAN

Kufra

E G Y P T

A R A B I A

Red Sea

HAD
• Abéché

S U D A N

Kub-Kub •

• Djibouti

U G A N D A

K E N Y A

I T A L I A N
E A S T   A F R I C A

I N D I A N
O C E A N

Congo

BELGIAN
CONGO

⟶ Free French forces
▢ French colonies

o ⟶ 500 miles
o ⟶ 500 kms

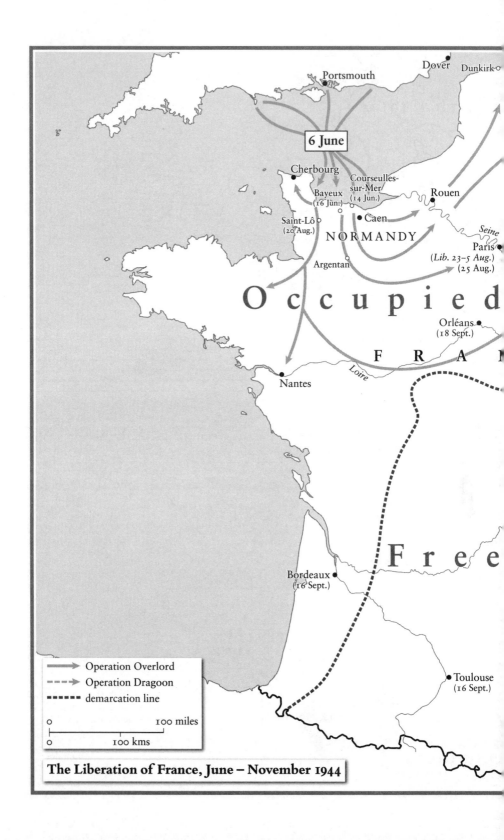

Dover
Dunkirk

Portsmouth

6 June

Cherbourg
Courseulles-
sur-Mer
(14 Jun.)
Rouen
Bayeux
(16 Jun.)
Seine
Saint-Lô
(20 Aug.)
Caen
Paris
(*Lib. 23–5 Aug.*)
NORMANDY
(25 Aug.)
Argentan

O c c u p i e d

Orléans
(18 Sept.)

F R A N

Nantes
Loire

F r e e

Bordeaux
(16 Sept.)

Toulouse
(16 Sept.)

Operation Overlord
Operation Dragoon
demarcation line

0   100 miles
0   100 kms

The Liberation of France, June – November 1944

N

Lille

BELGIUM

GERMANY

ARDENNES

LUXEMBOURG

•Reims

Rhine

•Stuttgart

Z o n e

Strasbourg
(*Lib. 23 Nov.*) •

ALSACE
Colmar •

•Sigmaringen

Langres ○
(*Lib. 13 Sept.*)

Mulhouse
(*Lib. 21 Nov.*) •

C   E

Belfort

Rhine

MORVAN

SWITZERLAND

•Vichy

ITALY

Z o n e

Lyons •
(*Lib 3 Sept.*)
(14 Sept.)

Loire

Rhône

Marseilles
(*Lib 28 Aug.*)
(15 Sept.)

Toulon

15 August

Introduction

DE GAULLE IS EVERYWHERE

In France today, Charles de Gaulle is everywhere: in memories, in street names, in monuments, in bookshops. At the most recent count over 3,600 localities had a public space – street, avenue, square, roundabout – named after him. This puts de Gaulle ahead of Pasteur who comes a close second (3,001) and Victor Hugo who comes third (2,258).[1] The grandest space in Paris, site of Napoleon's Arc de Triomphe, was renamed the Place de l'Etoile-Charles de Gaulle immediately after de Gaulle's death. Walking from there down the Champs-Elysées, one soon reaches a statue of de Gaulle striding resolutely in the same direction. Turning right at the statue, one crosses the Seine to the Hôtel des Invalides, France's army museum, which houses a separate museum exclusively devoted to de Gaulle. Entering this Historial Charles de Gaulle is like crossing the threshold of a sacred Gaullist space.

When an opinion poll in 2010 asked the French to rank the most important figures in their history, 44 per cent placed de Gaulle top (he accumulated 70 per cent of all choices), far ahead of Napoleon in second place with 14 per cent (38 per cent).[2] All politicians, from left to right, invoke de Gaulle's name. At the Presidential elections of 2012 he was cited as an example by both the Socialist François Hollande and his right-wing (supposedly Gaullist) opponent Nicolas Sarkozy – and by pretty well everyone else. Even the extreme-right Front National, whose founder Jean-Marie Le Pen was once a visceral anti-Gaullist, now celebrates de Gaulle's legacy. But no contemporary French politician has more consciously sought inspiration in de Gaulle than Emmanuel Macron whose official photograph as President shows him in front of a table on which one book lies open: the Pléiade edition of de Gaulle's *War Memoirs*.

De Gaulle increasingly floats free of the history of which he was the protagonist. Recent books include a playful squib about a meeting in Ireland between de Gaulle and Jean-Paul Sartre (the two men never met); a fable which imagines de Gaulle coming back from the dead to save trad-itional French egg mayonnaise and defend gay rights; a strip cartoon about de Gaulle on the beach; a 'Dictionary of a lover of de Gaulle' whose author visits Gaullian sites as one might trace the footsteps of a saint.[3]

This extraordinary unanimity around de Gaulle in France could not have been predicted when he left power in 1969. It airbrushes out of his-tory how much, throughout his career, he was a brutally divisive figure. During his thirty years in politics, de Gaulle was the most revered figure of modern French history – and the most hated. He was reviled and ideal-ized, loathed and adored, in equal measure. Other twentieth-century French political figures have been hated but none with such intensity as de Gaulle. For some people hating him gave meaning to their lives; others were driven mad by it. Such was the fate of the conservative politician Henri de Kérillis, who started as a passionate supporter of de Gaulle, broke with him in 1942 and spent his declining years in the United States, a broken and pathetic figure convinced that Gaullist agents were lurking at every street corner ready to inflict violence on him. The strange character of anti-Gaullist pathology is evident from just the titles of the books pub-lished in the years 1964–70 of a former Gaullist resister, André Figueras, who later turned against his former hero: *Charles le dérisoire* (Charles the Contemptible), *Le Général mourra* (The General will Die), *Les Gaullistes vont en enfer* (The Gaullists will Go to Hell), *De Gaulle impuissant* (De Gaulle the Impotent). There is much more in this vein in the Figueras cata-logue. When de Gaulle resigned in 1969, one extreme-right newspaper carried the headline: 'The beast is dead, but the poison lives on.'

Hatred went beyond words. De Gaulle was the target of about thirty serious assassination attempts, two of which – in September 1961 and August 1962 – nearly succeeded. For some anti-Gaullists, the fixation on de Gaulle became so incorporated into their personality that their original reasons for wanting to kill him were eclipsed by the hatred he inspired. This was true, for example, of André Rossfelder who planned the last ser-ious assassination attempt against him in 1964. Like many anti-Gaullist fanatics, he hated de Gaulle for having accepted Algerian independence in 1962. But even after that battle had been lost, Rossfelder still plotted to eliminate him. When asked why, he replied: 'Because he is still there; simply so that I no longer have to go on thinking about the tyrant.'[4] At the other end of the spectrum were those whose reverence for de Gaulle lay some-where between loyalty to a feudal lord and faith in a religious leader. Of the novelist André Malraux, one Gaullist wrote: 'Like all of us he entered into the Gaullian enterprise as one enters into a religion.'[5]

If the lives of the French were so passionately caught up in their relationship with de Gaulle, it was because he was the central actor in France's two twentieth-century civil wars. The first civil war resulted from France's defeat by Germany in 1940 when the government of Marshal Pétain signed an armistice with Hitler. Refusing to accept this decision, de Gaulle departed for London to continue the battle. His act of defiance transformed him into a rebel against the legal government headed by the most revered figure in France: the first shots fired by the soldiers who had rallied to de Gaulle were directed against other French soldiers, not against the Germans. Over the next four years, de Gaulle from London claimed that he, not Pétain, represented the 'true' France. He returned to France in 1944, acclaimed as a national hero, and head of a provisional government until he resigned from power in January 1946.

Another conflict broke out in November 1954 when Algerian nationalists launched their fight for independence from France. The eight-year Algerian War brought de Gaulle back to power in 1958 and culminated in Algerian independence four years later. Although ostensibly a war of decolonization, the conflict had the characteristics of a civil war. Administratively Algeria was part of France, and had been 'French' since 1830, longer than the city of Nice (French since 1859). Those who wanted to hold on to Algeria boasted that the Mediterranean ran through France like the Seine through Paris. Many of the one million Europeans of Algeria had lived there for generations. It genuinely was their home, and for them its loss was even more traumatic than France's defeat by Germany in 1940.

In addition to his central role in these two conflicts, de Gaulle challenged the way that the French thought about their history and politics. After returning to power in 1958, he radically transformed France's political institutions, breaking with the shibboleths of the Republican tradition inherited from the Revolution of 1789. His vision of France's place in the world, encapsulated in the elusive concept of 'grandeur', was admired by some and viewed by others as nationalist posturing. Finally, in May 1968, in the twilight of his career, de Gaulle was the target of the most dramatic revolutionary upheaval in twentieth-century French history.

Some who revered de Gaulle between 1940 and 1944 opposed him over Algeria; some opposed him in both conflicts; some supported him in both; others who had opposed him between 1940 and 1944 supported his return to power in 1958 before turning against him again. The anti-Americanism of his foreign policy of grandeur attracted some on the left who simultaneously opposed his authoritarian style of government. There is truth in de Gaulle's quip 'Everybody is, has been or will be "Gaullist".'[6] But there is also truth in the comment made by an observer on the eve of the 1965 Presidential election: 'Outside the ultra-faithful, everyone has been, is or will be anti-Gaullist. The worst of it is that each of us is both Gaullist and anti-Gaullist and that the division runs through each of our consciences.'[7]

De Gaulle's admirers have included both Henry Kissinger and Osama bin Laden. He has been compared by admirers and detractors to French figures as diverse as Charlemagne, Joan of Arc, Richelieu, Henri IV, Louis XIV, Danton, Saint-Just, Napoleon I, Chateaubriand, Napoleon III, General Boulanger, Léon Gambetta and Georges Clemenceau; and to non-French figures as diverse as Bismarck, Franco, Kerensky, Mussolini, Salazar, Mao, Bolívar, Castro and Jesus Christ. The range of these comparisons reflects de Gaulle's extraordinary contradictions: he was a soldier who spent most of his career fighting the army; a conservative who often talked like a revolutionary; a man of passion who found it almost impossible to express emotions.

'IN THE BEGINNING WAS THE WORD?'

Both the hatred once inspired by de Gaulle and the current adulation create difficulties for a biographer. There is a 'black legend' that has left its traces: half-truths and slurs cling to his memory like barnacles. But escaping from the current hagiography is no less of a problem. Systematic 'demystification' would miss a lot because as Alain Peyrefitte, de Gaulle's Minister of Information during the 1960s, wrote: 'the truth of the General is in his legend.'[8] By this he meant that (as was also true of Napoleon) one of de Gaulle's greatest achievements was the myth that he constructed around himself. This was put in more poetic form by the historian Pierre Nora, who observed that those who write about de Gaulle cannot easily escape the frame of reference de Gaulle himself imposes on those who scrutinize him – 'like a painting by Vermeer where the light that seems to be illuminating the picture in fact comes from the picture itself'.[9]

In de Gaulle's case, the 'light' comes from his own words. In the epigraph to a book he published in 1932, he quoted Goethe's *Faust*: 'In the beginning was the word? No, in the beginning was the deed.' With de Gaulle 'word' and 'deed' are inseparable. The 'deed' that launched him in 1940 was a speech – a speech almost no one actually heard. But subsequent speeches fared better, and for millions of French people between 1940 and 1944 'de Gaulle' existed as a voice heard on the radio. In the 1950s, de Gaulle crafted his legend in his *War Memoirs*. In the 1960s, when he was President of France, it was often said that he governed through the magic of his rhetoric and his mastery of television.

Any biographer of de Gaulle risks being trapped like a fly in the web of his words. Speaking to a journalist in 1966 de Gaulle commented:

> The things that I want to be known, that I consider to be important, I think about them for a long time. I write them down. I learn them by heart . . . This costs me the most terrible effort . . . They are the only things which count in my eyes. And then there are other things I say, that I throw out without having prepared them, without really thinking, without having learnt them, that I say to nobody in particular . . . None of that has any importance or value in my eyes. But you journalists, you report these remarks as well.[10]

De Gaulle vigilantly policed this official record of 'things which count'. Apart from his four volumes of *Memoirs* (three volumes of war memoirs published in the 1950s and one volume covering the years 1958–62 published in 1970), he authorized the publication of five volumes of selected speeches in which he obsessively corrected the placing of every comma. Yet this collection of speeches needs to be treated critically – which we can do by examining just the first six pages. It opens with the most celebrated speech of all: that of 18 June 1940. What we read is certainly the speech de Gaulle *wanted* to deliver but, owing to British pressure, the first two sentences of the speech he actually delivered were different. The next speech in the collection is dated 19 June 1940. The truth, however, is that de Gaulle delivered *no* speech on 19 June – because the British would not allow him to. And the alleged '19 June' speech that is published contains references to events that occurred after 19 June. So it must have been written later but was never delivered. The collection then gives us two speeches de Gaulle *did* deliver on 22 June and 24 June, but it misses out another short one on 23 June that de Gaulle preferred retrospectively to gloss over because it announced the formation of a committee under his leadership that never saw the light of day owing to British opposition. So, in the first six pages of de Gaulle's officially collected speeches, we are offered a speech that *was* delivered but not in the form we read it; a speech that was *never* delivered (and not even written on the day it was supposed to have been delivered); and we lack a speech that was delivered.

After de Gaulle's death, his son began publishing in chronological order ten volumes of letters, notebooks and memoranda from his official archives and family papers. This collection is a vital source for studying de Gaulle, and would presumably also come under the category of 'written' documents accepted by de Gaulle himself as having 'value in my eyes'. But these volumes have problems too. For example, they contain a famous speech de Gaulle made on 6 June 1958 but missing out the final words '*Vive Algérie française*'. Whether or not he wrote these words, no one denies that he uttered them.

In addition to the mass of written texts that have been published, there is a huge corpus of reported conversations. During his lifetime, de Gaulle would give off-the-record interviews to favoured journalists. One of the first sources used for studying him (and still useful today) was a series of books produced in his lifetime by the well-connected journalist Jean-Raymond Tournoux who was a frequent recipient of de Gaulle's confidences and *bons mots*. De Gaulle's son Philippe claimed later that Tournoux was a man who listened at keyholes, but the truth was that in this case he did not need to because the door had been opened wide to him by de Gaulle who found these off-the-record encounters useful for his own purposes.[11] It was Tournoux who first reported de Gaulle's famous *boutade*, 'How can one govern a country which has 258 cheeses?' Such remarks start to take on a life of their own, existing in a kind of ether where one is never sure exactly what was said or whether it was said at all. (The precise number of cheeses, for example, varies wildly in different versions of this comment.) This matters more in the case of Algeria, about which de Gaulle made so many gnomic private comments to different visitors in the 1950s that it becomes difficult to decipher what he really thought.

After de Gaulle's death, most of these unattributed remarks turned out to be 'authentic' because they recur in another important source of 'Gaulliana': the torrent of memoirs, diaries and journals from those who worked in close proximity to him. Of these, the most extensive were the 2,000 pages of conversations – more accurately monologues – published by Alain Peyrefitte, and the 1,500 pages of conversations published by Jacques Foccart, de Gaulle's adviser on African affairs, who saw him almost every day during the 1960s. What status should we attribute to this material? They do not necessarily offer a greater 'truth' than the official written utterances or the off-the-cuff comments to journalists. De Gaulle's conversation was often a performance; 'he plays his scales' as one of his aides put it. But it would be wrong to go to the other extreme of discounting this material just because de Gaulle did not literally 'write' it. All these sources allow us to hear different registers of his voice.

In the book he published on leadership in 1932, de Gaulle wrote that great leaders needed to display mystery, ruse and hypocrisy. On the other hand, Stalin – judging, it is true, by an exacting standard of deviousness – remarked to Churchill that de Gaulle was uncomplicated. De Gaulle elevated mystery into an art of government but was often more transparent than he pretended to be, or wanted to be. It is striking how often, despite de Gaulle's reputation for dissimulation, there is a congruence between his public utterances and his private ones – even if the tone is different. In the last few years, historians have for the first time had access to de Gaulle's archives. But these do not fundamentally change our knowledge. His son had already done a good job of extracting the most important documents for publication. What we do lack is the whole of de Gaulle's private correspondence with his family. Some of this has been published but there is probably much more which might help to elucidate that opaque phenomenon: de Gaulle the private man. To understand de Gaulle's political career, however, we should not expect some extraordinary future revelations. The challenge is to interpret the material that is now available.

DE GAULLE AND HIS BIOGRAPHERS

How have these issues been handled by de Gaulle's biographers? The literature on de Gaulle has reached massive proportions. More has been written about him than about any other figure in modern French history except Napoleon. There is an institution, the Fondation Charles de Gaulle, entirely devoted to studying him. Established just after his death, by 2011 the Fondation had published the proceedings of over forty conferences devoted to him. Some of these examine particular moments of his career; others address themes like 'De Gaulle and Medicine', 'De Gaulle and Science', 'De Gaulle and the Media,' De Gaulle and the Law', 'De Gaulle and Religion', 'De Gaulle and the Young' and so on. De Gaulle, a man, a legend, a symbol is now also an academic industry.

Among innumerable biographies, three stand out. First, the monumental three volumes published by Jean Lacouture between 1985 and 1988. For three decades Lacouture was a brilliant left-wing journalist who spent much of his career covering the Third World as a committed supporter of decolonization. In 1965, during his subject's Presidency, he produced a short biography in which his 'respect' for the de Gaulle of 1940, who had refused defeat, and for the de Gaulle of 1962, who had accepted Algerian independence, was qualified by his hostility to the 'nationalist boasting' of the 'reactionary' de Gaulle of the mid-1960s. Three years later, in a second edition, he ratcheted up his criticism to depict de Gaulle as 'a personality in thrall to hallucinatory xenophobia'. Although de Gaulle's secretariat judged this book too 'unpleasant' to be shown to him, de Gaulle himself was made of sterner stuff. Reading the book he made the priceless comment that 'the author has certainly not grasped the full dimension of the personality.'[12]

That criticism could certainly not be made of the 3,000 pages Lacouture devoted to de Gaulle when returning to the subject twenty years later – in expiation for his earlier irreverence. By then he had developed into a prolific biographer, starting with Nasser and Ho Chi Minh, and moving on to such left-wing French icons as Léon Blum and Pierre Mendès France. This choice of subjects gives a sense of the leftist pantheon into which Lacouture now tried to squeeze de Gaulle. Lacouture was always unapologetic about needing to admire his subjects, but because de Gaulle was not an entirely natural fit, his book reads like a prolonged dialogue between author and subject. Every biographer of de Gaulle has to address the extent to which de Gaulle was influenced in his younger days by ideas of the extreme-right-wing writer Charles Maurras, whose newspaper *Action française* was dedicated to opposing France's parliamentary Republic. Whatever de Gaulle's view of Maurras, one question that needs to be asked of him is: when did he become a 'republican' and what kind of republican did he become? Lacouture irons out the difficulties. For example, in discussing de Gaulle's attitude to Hitler's Germany in the 1930s he tells us that 'in the great debate between dictatorship and democracy de Gaulle did not hesitate over the decision to take'; he was a 'determined adversary of fascism'. In truth, de Gaulle, while certainly never a 'fascist', was not in this period especially worried by fascism – or interested in democracy. He was first and foremost an adversary of *Germany*.[13]

When Lacouture found himself labelled a Gaullist he tetchily responded that he was 'neither a hardcore Gaullist nor a soft Gaullist . . . but a tenacious a-Gaullist'. His way of summing the matter up was to say: 'Montaigne admired the Romans – but from afar, and certainly not with the intention of offering up Cato as a model for his fellow citizens.'[14] 'A-Gaullist' or not, there is no concealing Lacouture's immeasurable admiration and intuitive 'feel' for his subject. But his admiration often tips into myth-making – as in his description of de Gaulle's crucial meeting with Churchill at 10 Downing Street on 17 June 1940:

> Churchill's great predator's eye had recognized the 'man of destiny' and the Constable of France in this hitherto taciturn giant. Already at Briare [when they met a few days earlier] he had scrutinized this face staring out of a Plantagenet chronicle, he girded it with a helmet . . . and admitted it to that round table where the descendants of the Marlboroughs welcomed a select band of knights.[15]

This is splendid purple prose; it is not history. We do not know whether Churchill had such hallucinations since he did not deign to mention that meeting with de Gaulle in his own memoirs. The truth is probably that Churchill, happy to welcome any Frenchman ready to fight on, distractedly made de Gaulle a non-committal promise about being allowed to broadcast, and had him ushered out as fast as possible so that he could turn to more important matters.

Or let us take Lacouture's account of the speech delivered by de Gaulle on 25 August 1944, the day Paris was liberated:

> This figure towering above upturned faces as in an El Greco Ascension, his arms taking the shape of a lyre, the giant's face thrown back as though for a consecration . . . Here de Gaulle truly spoke for the nation; he was the echo of the great Christian orators and of the members of the Convention calling for a mass rising.[16]

The speech is indeed moving, but it was also carefully calculated, and many contemporary listeners were bitterly disappointed and certainly did not think de Gaulle was speaking for them or for the nation.

In the end, despite its panache, there is too much mythologizing in Lacouture for his account of de Gaulle to be satisfying. The second major biography of de Gaulle is by the historian-journalist Paul-Marie de La Gorce. Unlike Lacouture, de La Gorce was happy to call himself a Gaullist but as one of a strange subspecies known as 'left Gaullists'.[17] He wrote a first biography in 1965 while de Gaulle was still President. De Gaulle read the proofs and offered suggestions and commentary. In 1999, thirty years after de Gaulle's death, de La Gorce offered another version running to almost 1,500 pages.[18] While Lacouture wrestles with his subject, de La Gorce has no doubts why he reveres de Gaulle: 'In the work accomplished by General de Gaulle, decolonization will remain undoubtedly the most ineffaceable mark that he brought to the history of the century.'[19] He often confuses the magical power of de Gaulle's rhetoric with the reality of his policies. For the man who came close to declaring war on Britain in 1945 because he wanted to defend the French Empire in Syria; whose government presided over a massacre of Algerian nationalists at Sétif in 1945; who then dragged the French into an unwinnable war to save French Indo-China in 1946; and who, once France had abandoned her African Empire, devised ingenious new ways of hanging on to influence in Africa, the image of prophetic decolonizer needs serious qualification.

The third – and most recent (2002) – biography of de Gaulle could not be more different except in its scale (1,000 pages). Its author, Eric Roussel, made his reputation with a biography of Jean Monnet, famous as an architect of the European Community, a believer in European supranationalism and a committed Atlanticist – all anathema to de Gaulle. Roussel went on to write an admiring biography of de Gaulle's second Prime Minister, and successor, the pragmatic conservative Georges Pompidou. But by the end of de Gaulle's life Pompidou had become so estranged from de Gaulle that some Gaullists dubbed him the 'anti-de Gaulle'.[20] So Roussel's previous choices of biographical subject give a sense of his affinities and point of departure: that of a liberal conservative, European federalist and Atlanti-cist. The contribution made by Roussel's book lies in the extensive use he makes of American, British and Canadian archives and of new French ones. His vision of de Gaulle is less Francocentric than those of Lacouture and de La Gorce. It is the most seriously researched biography of de Gaulle and is fully aware of the 'dimension' of the personality. But, by an accu-mulation of small touches, he paints a subtly negative portrait. Take his treatment of de Gaulle's resignation in January 1946. There has been much speculation about why de Gaulle resigned, and how he expected to return to power. What Roussel offers us on this episode are two pages of charac-teristically deranged remarks by the ardent Gaullist André Malraux to the British Ambassador. Malraux predicted blood in the streets and declared that de Gaulle would return as a dictator to save the west. Since this is the only contemporary commentary on de Gaulle's resignation that Roussel provides, the reader is nudged towards believing that this reflects de Gaulle's thinking: 'One can doubt that Malraux would express himself in this way . . . without the agreement, at least tacit, of the General.'[21] Or to take another example, when de Gaulle was promoted general in June 1940 Roussel quotes at length from an article of praise in *Action française* – guilt by association? – and goes on to suggest that the article's dithyrambic tone gives credence to the rumour that de Gaulle had once, under a pseudonym, been the military correspondent of this monarchist newspaper. There is no evidence for this improbable assertion.[22] By subtle insinuations of this kind Roussel subliminally constructs the picture of de Gaulle as an anachronistic right-wing nationalist. So the best biography of de Gaulle is also one that is insidiously hostile to its subject.

THE DE GAULLE BATTLEFIELD

All biographers must guard against the temptation to impose excessive coherence on their subject.[23] The temptation is all the greater in de Gaulle's case because there seems to be a granite-like consistency to his personality and beliefs. The most famous sentence he ever wrote is the opening to his *War Memoirs*: '*All my life* [my italics] I have had a certain idea of France.' One historian has offered an interesting interpretation which views the constitution of 1958 as the embodiment of liberal Catholic ideas de Gaulle had inherited from his family in the late 1890s – the assumption being that de Gaulle's political ideas never changed.[24] But the evidential basis of this intriguing theory is very thin. In the 1960s, foreign diplomats and French politicians, desperate to understand de Gaulle's unpredictable policies, would frequently seek clues in the short book on leadership he had published forty years earlier. But this book offers no doctrine and no explicit views on politics. It is a portrait of what a leader should *be* and it could be read even as a self-portrait in anticipation – but it tells us nothing specific about what the leader should *do*. Indeed one of its key messages is the importance of contingency in politics. This has led one astute (and admiring) commentator on de Gaulle to comment on the 'ideological emptiness of Gaullism: a stance not a doctrine; an attitude not a coherent set of dogmas; a style without much substance'.[25]

De Gaulle's ambiguities made people unsure how to respond to him at different stages of his career and also led to much speculation about what he believed. This was true, for example, of a group of French Socialists who found themselves in London during the war. Like de Gaulle they opposed Marshal Pétain, but many of them were also suspicious of de Gaulle while realizing that, whether they liked it or not, he was becoming a potent symbol of resistance in France. They endlessly debated their position towards him. One of them who decided, not without hesitation, to rally behind him gave his reasons during one of these anguished discussions: 'Even if you do not have confidence in de Gaulle, we need to struggle to transform something that does really exist [that is, de Gaulle], and that does, whether one likes it or not, represent the reality of the resistance of the people of France.'[26] Of course, de Gaulle was not a blank sheet, and those who thought they could 'transform' him were often badly disappointed, but sometimes they were proved right. De Gaulle may have had a certain idea of France 'all his life' but it was not always the same idea.

When de Gaulle came back to power in 1958, no one knew his intentions regarding Algeria, and commentators spilled acres of ink trying to discern what he 'really' thought. Historians and biographers have followed suit. The truth is that, although he had some idea of what he did *not* want to do in Algeria, he was open-minded about the rest. As in 1940, he could be transformed by the context. During the tense months of May 1958 when the French army in Algeria was in revolt against the Paris government and it seemed possible that paratroopers might land at any moment in mainland France, Jean Lacouture, at that time a *Le Monde* journalist, rang Jean-Marie Domenach, a journalist friend who edited the periodical *Esprit*. Domenach was worried about what de Gaulle might do if he took power with the support of the military. Would it be necessary to enter into a new Resistance – this time against de Gaulle? Lacouture was reassuring: 'De Gaulle is not a General, he is a battlefield.'[27] By this he meant that the outcome would be determined not just by the decisions taken by de Gaulle but by political forces over which he had limited control.

Once de Gaulle was in power, and once Algeria had become independent, the new style of Gaullism that emerged during the 1960s was the result not only of the choices made by the President himself but of those imposed by economists, other experts and civil servants, many of whom had opposed his return but now took the view that they could make something of him. As one of them put it: 'Why have the good luck of de Gaulle being there, if the opportunity is not used to solve [certain] . . . problems?'[28] Throughout his political career de Gaulle played with brio the role of charismatic leader whose portrait he had painted in the 1920s, and he harboured certain fixed ideas about the world which he carried with him all his life. But he was also the figure through whom the French fought out their history and politics and they made him as much as he made them.[29]

PART ONE

De Gaulle before 'De Gaulle', 1890–1940

There is no moment of my life when I was not certain that one day I would be at the head of France ... But things worked out in a way that I did not predict. I always thought that I would be Minister of War and that everything would come from that ...

De Gaulle, May 1946, in Claude Mauriac,
Un autre de Gaulle, 99

I

Beginnings, 1890–1908

A VOICE FROM LONDON

De Gaulle was a voice before he was a face. He entered history through a short BBC broadcast from London on the evening of 18 June 1940. Six weeks earlier, the German army had launched its assault on France. The French were overwhelmed with extraordinary rapidity, and on 17 June the head of the French government, Marshal Philippe Pétain, announced on French radio that he would be suing for an armistice with Germany. De Gaulle's speech the next day was a challenge to Pétain's defeatism:

> The leaders who, for many years, have been at the head of the French armies, have formed a government.
>
> This government, alleging that our armies are defeated, has made contact with the enemy to end the fighting.
>
> Certainly we have been overwhelmed by the mechanized forces of the enemy, on the ground and in the air.
>
> Infinitely more than their number, it was the tanks, the aeroplanes, the tactics of the Germans which forced us into retreat. It was the tanks, the aeroplanes, the tactics of the Germans that took our leaders by surprise to the point of bringing them to where they are today.
>
> But has the last word been said? Must hope disappear? Is the defeat definitive? No!
>
> Believe me, I am someone who speaks to you with full knowledge of the facts and I tell you that nothing is lost for France. The same means that conquered us can one day bring us victory.
>
> For France is not alone! She is not alone! She is not alone! She has a vast Empire behind her. She can make common cause with the British Empire which controls the seas and continues the struggle. She can, like England, use without limit the immense industry of the United States.

This war is not limited to the unfortunate territory of our country. This war is not decided by the Battle of France. This war is a world war. Despite all our mistakes, all our failure to catch up, all our sufferings, there are in the world all the means necessary one day to overcome our enemies. Struck down today by mechanized force, we will be able to conquer in the future by a superior mechanical force. The destiny of the world is at stake.

I, General de Gaulle, currently in London, invite the officers and the French soldiers who are located in British territory or who may be in the future, with their weapons or without their weapons; I invite the engineers and the special workers of armament industries who are located in British territory or who may be in future, to contact me.

Whatever happens, the flame of the French resistance must not be extinguished and will not be extinguished.

Tomorrow, as today, I will speak on Radio London.[1]

Few people heard de Gaulle's broadcast. Nor can we hear it today because the BBC did not think it was important enough to keep the recording. De Gaulle spoke many more times over the following weeks, and increasing numbers of people started tuning into his speeches. Later they were vague in their own minds about whether they had actually heard his first broadcast, although they wanted to think they had. One future Gaullist, who was only a boy in 1940, writes in his memoirs: 'On the evening of 18 June in the evening, in an alley bordered by holiday homes surrounded by gardens, I *think I remember* [my italics] having heard the speech of 18 June. The windows of the villa were open and a radio was relaying a speech which seemed unexpected to my ears.'[2] One person who knew he had *not* heard it was the writer Léon Werth who spent the Occupation deep in the French countryside. His diary charts his growing enthusiasm for de Gaulle, but he did not know what de Gaulle had said in that first broadcast until four years later when it was read out again (not by de Gaulle) on the BBC after D-Day. If Werth did not hear de Gaulle's first speech, it was because on that day, like millions of other French people, he was fleeing south as the Germans advanced: 'I was near the River Loire. I only got rumours that I could pick up on the road and incoherent snatches of false information, given out by a poor radio set plugged into a car battery. So on that 18 June I did not hear de Gaulle.'[3] Forty years later, the President of France Valéry Giscard d'Estaing offered a contrasting memory:

As a young boy of 14, I remember hearing in our house in the Auvergne the voice of General de Gaulle. One afternoon, June 18, my uncle came to find us: 'Come along! There is going to be something important. They are announcing a declaration of General de Gaulle.' We sat in a semi-circle around the radio . . . We had the presentiment that the course of events had changed. For each of us, the black band that had come to cover the image of France was on that day wiped away.[4]

Giscard was no Gaullist, and since this 'memory' coincided with a moment when he was desperate for the support of Gaullist politicians, it must be taken with a pinch of salt.

Few contemporary diarists refer to the speech of 18 June. One who did was the Prefect of the Paris Police, Roger Langeron, who wrote in his diary on that day: 'Today is a great day. A voice reaches us from London.' But the famous words he cites from de Gaulle – 'France has lost the battle; she has not lost the war' – were not in the speech of 18 June, even if they convey its essence. Those words are to be found in a proclamation which was produced as a poster by the Free French in London during July. Probably Langeron touched up his diary when it was published immediately after the war to make it seem as if he had heard the broadcast.[5] One rare diarist who did authentically mention the 18 June speech was the art historian and future resister Agnès Humbert, who like Léon Werth had been swept up in the wave of refugees fleeing Paris. On 18 June she landed up in a small village south of Paris. Desperate for news, and luckier than Werth, she found a radio: 'It is tuned to London. By pure fluke I find myself listening to a broadcast in French. They announce a speech by a French General. I don't catch his name. His delivery, jerky and peremptory, is not well suited to the radio. He calls on the French to rally round him, to continue the struggle. I feel I have come back to life. A feeling that I had thought had died for ever stirs again: hope.'[6] Even when Humbert was told the name of the 'French General', it meant nothing to her. A few months later, as a member of one of France's first Resistance groups, she found herself distributing tracts in support of de Gaulle, but she still had little idea who he was:

> How bizarre it all is! Here we are, most of us on the wrong side of forty, careering along like students all fired up with passion and fervour, in the wake of a leader of whom we know absolutely nothing, of whom none of us has even seen a photograph. In the whole course of human history, has there ever been anything quite like it? Thousands upon thousands of people, fired by blind faith, following an unknown figure. Perhaps this strange anonymity is even an asset: the mystery of the unknown![7]

De Gaulle was indeed unknown to the vast majority of the French people. Where did he come from? What did he believe? What did he look like? Few people had any idea. As late as October 1942, Léon Werth, who had become a regular listener to de Gaulle's broadcasts, was still trying to picture him: 'I am trying to find de Gaulle in his voice. It first strikes me as a bit pinched. If I hated him, I would perhaps say that it was a voice wearing a monocle.'[8] When de Gaulle eventually arrived back in France after the Liberation in 1944, people would sometimes rush up to greet one of the more highly ranked generals accompanying him. They assumed mistakenly that de Gaulle must be a five-star general.[9]

As the mysterious name 'de Gaulle' started to circulate more widely through occupied France, it was often taken to be a pseudonym. It seemed too good to be true that the General proclaiming himself France's saviour should be called after Gaul, the ancient name of France.[10] Such was the view of the novelist Romain Gary, if his fanciful autobiography is to be believed. Born Roman Kacew, Gary had arrived in France from Vilnius as a boy in 1928. Since his ambition was to become a 'French' writer, he decided to adopt a more French-sounding name, covering reams of paper with different pseudonyms. None seemed right: 'When in 1940 for the first time I heard on the radio the name of General de Gaulle, my first reaction was one of fury because I had not thought of inventing that splendid name ... Life is full of missed opportunities.'[11] Gary forgave de Gaulle for having beaten him to it, made his way to London and became a pilot with the Free French. In the first months of the Occupation, it is not uncommon to find de Gaulle's name spelt in many different ways: 'Degaule', 'Dugaul' or simply 'Gaul'.[12] Even the successful Parisian lawyer Maurice Garçon, who knew everybody that counted in the French elite, had no clue to the identity of de Gaulle. He noted in his diary on 29 June 1940 that he had heard a speech by 'de Gaule (I have not seen his name written; is that how it is spelt?)'.[13]

FAMILY ORIGINS

The name 'de Gaulle' – and the mystery about what lay behind it – invested the disembodied voice from London with a legendary aura. In fact the name was entirely authentic, although the etymology has nothing to do with Gaul. It possibly originates from an old Flemish word meaning 'the wall' (de walle). If that is so, the 'de' – meaning in this case 'the' – is not in origin an aristocratic particule.

De Gaulles (often spelt 'de Gaule') can be found in thirteenth-century Normandy. A Jean de Gaulle had fought against the English at Agincourt in 1415, and Charles de Gaulle's family tradition claimed him as an ancestor.[14] In truth no direct genealogical line can be traced until the ennoblement of a certain François de Gaulle in Burgundy in 1604. In the eighteenth century, the family moved from Burgundy to Paris where they served the *ancien régime* monarchy as state lawyers and administrators. This gave them the status of minor *nobles de robe* – that is, nobles through office rather than birth. De Gaulle's great-grandfather was arrested during the Revolution and escaped the guillotine only because of the fall of Robespierre in 1794. He kept his head, but the family had lost its position and its wealth.[15]

Charles de Gaulle's grandfather, Julien de Gaulle, was born in Paris in 1801, and died there in 1883, seven years before the birth of his illustrious grandson. After teaching in the northern city of Lille, where he married in 1835, Julien returned to Paris and carved out a career as an antiquarian and scholar. He wrote erudite works celebrating the pre-revolutionary Catholic and monarchist history of France. These included a biography of the French medieval king St Louis and a five-volume history of Paris. Julien de Gaulle's wife, Joséphine Maillot (1806–86), was an even more prolific author than her husband, writing over eighty books. These included uplifting novels, biographies and histories, many of which ran into numerous editions. This frighteningly energetic woman also edited a Catholic newspaper, *Le Correspondant des familles*.

Writing did not make the couple wealthy. Their existence was precarious and they are recorded as having lived at twenty-seven different addresses in Paris. Two of their three children followed Julien de Gaulle's line of antiquarian and slightly eccentric scholarship: one became an expert on Celtic poetry (he was known in Brittany as the 'Celtic bard'), the other an entomologist (he was a specialist in bees). Neither had any children, and it fell to the third child, Henri – Charles de Gaulle's father – to preserve the family name. Henri de Gaulle (1848–1932) had a more conventional career than his brothers or father. He had passed the examinations for the prestigious Ecole Polytechnique but did not take up his place. His elder brother Charles, the Breton poet, had developed a disease which rendered him progressively infirm and unable to support himself financially. Their father was ageing and lacked the financial means to support his son. Henri de Gaulle was therefore obliged to interrupt his studies and take a job to support his family. After some years working as an administrator in the Interior Ministry, he became a teacher of Latin, philosophy and literature at a highly reputed Jesuit school in Paris, the College of the Immaculate Conception, and then at a Catholic private school that he himself set up.

It was Henri de Gaulle who established the family genealogy sketched above.[16] His son Charles knew every detail, and after he became famous he was scrupulous in answering correspondents to correct points of fact.[17] De Gaulle had a strong sense of the values he believed his ancestry had bequeathed him. A British Foreign Office official, finding de Gaulle in an unusually expansive mood at dinner in July 1942, reported on a conversation:

> [De Gaulle said] that there were two sorts of Right in France: the *petite noblesse de campagne* [the country gentry] and the moneyed classes. The former class ('Et j'en suis' [And I am from it]) was inspired with the highest forms of patriotism and was willing to make any sacrifice for the glory of France or for the good of the country; many of the clergy belonged to this group. The latter class, composed of the very rich, was much more self-interested ... He agreed that the Parisian aristocrats, the racing set, those titled ladies who give receptions to their much-loved conquerors were on the same level as the rich industrialists: rotten through riches.[18]

De Gaulle often came back to this idea when looking back over the Occupation in later years. 'For those who had to choose between their material possessions and the soul of France,' he remarked in 1962, 'their material possessions chose for them. Those with possessions are possessed by what they own.'[19]

Despite the provincial origins de Gaulle referred to in his wartime conversation, his father's family had been Parisian for over a century. At other moments of reminiscence, de Gaulle preferred to dwell upon this aspect of his inheritance. He would recall that his grandfather had been born in Paris during the Revolution:

> You can believe an old Parisian: there are no examples of a Paris family that succeeded in lasting three generations without 'succumbing' ... to the infernal round of Paris life: some go mad and others are ruined. Of course if this family allies itself to a family from the provinces, things can last longer: provincial blood brings Parisians stability and money.[20]

De Gaulle presumably had in mind his maternal ancestors, the Maillots, a prosperous bourgeois dynasty from northern France whose wealth came from trade and the manufacture of textiles. De Gaulle's maternal grandmother, Julie Marie Maillot (1835–1912), was partly of Irish ancestry. Her own mother (née MacCartan) descended from one of those Irish families – 'wild geese' – that had served the Jacobite cause fighting English Protestantism in the armies of Louis XIV before settling in Valenciennes (Julie's grandfather, Andronic MacCartan, had been a doctor to Louis XVIII). Another branch of the Maillots had German links. They had married at the start of the nineteenth century into another family of industrialists, the Kolbs of Baden who had arrived in France in the 1760s. The destinies of the Maillots (of Lille) and the de Gaulles (of Paris) had been intertwined for two generations. As we have seen, de Gaulle's paternal grandfather (Julien) had married a Josephine

Maillot; and de Gaulle's father, Henri, married his own cousin, Jeanne Maillot, whose father was a textile manufacturer. Charles de Gaulle was therefore doubly a Maillot.

If on his father's side de Gaulle came from the Parisian *noblesse de robe* fallen on hard times, and on his mother's from the wealthy provincial bourgeoisie, both wings of the family shared similar conservative, Catholic and patriotic values. On the very last day of his life, 9 November 1970, de Gaulle wrote to thank a family friend for sending him a genealogy of the Maillot family: 'It is pleasing to see in all of them – dead and alive – such depths of courage ... and fidelity to religion and to the Fatherland [*patrie*].'[21] Industrialists like the Maillots were imbued with the traditions of Catholic paternalism which were particularly strong in northern France. Employers saw it as their duty to look after the moral and material welfare of their employees. These were the values informing the voluminous writings of de Gaulle's grandmother, Josephine de Gaulle née Maillot. In one of her novels, an industrialist is pilloried as 'fat rich exploiter, an egoist who treats his workers as beasts of burden'; in another the Bourse of Paris is described as a centre of 'immoral speculation'. Although a pious and conservative Catholic, she also wrote sympathetic biographies of the French (pre-Marxist) socialist Proudhon, of the French revolutionary Jules Vallès and of the Irish nationalist leader Daniel O'Connell.[22]

This milieu believed that wealth incurred social responsibilities. The most distinguished member of the family on de Gaulle's mother's side was his great-grand-uncle Charles Kolb-Bernard, a sugar manufacturer who was a major figure in the Catholic bourgeoisie of Lille. Attached in equal measure to the legitimist pretender and the Catholic religion, Kolb-Bernard had set up in Lille a branch of the Societé de Saint-Vincent-de-Paul, a Catholic voluntary organization founded in 1833 to bring succour and morality to the urban poor. He also helped finance the construction of the church of Notre Dame de la Treille (today Lille Cathedral). De Gaulle's maternal grandfather Jules-Emile Maillot (1819–91) was not quite as successful in business but his family was no less pious. De Gaulle's mother, Jeanne, was raised in a household of rigorous and joyless Catholic faith. Two of her sisters were nuns.

FAMILY VALUES

It was in the house of his Lille grandparents, as was the custom among the French middle classes at that time, that Charles de Gaulle was born on 22 November 1890. He was the third of five children, four boys and one girl. The house, at 9 Rue Princesse, which still stands today, was the unostentatious residence of a comfortably off bourgeois family. Two statues of the Virgin stood in niches overlooking the street. One wing of the house was inhabited by de Gaulle's grandparents, Julie and Jules Maillot; the other was inhabited by de Gaulle's aunt, Noémie, who was married to Gustave de Corbie, a professor at Lille's Catholic law faculty. The property next door housed the Maillot family's textile workshop. This was a world of sobriety, religion and work. After three months, his parents took the baby back to Paris, but de Gaulle's links with northern France remained important during his childhood. His Parisian paternal grandparents were no longer alive, and there were no de Gaulle cousins since both his uncles were childless. On the other hand, there was a clan of northern cousins living in and around Lille. Christmas was celebrated, as was customary in the north, on 6 December, the *fête* of St Nicholas. Family holidays were often spent in the region, sometimes in a rented villa at the coastal resort of Wimereux not far from Calais. Although his maternal grandfather, Jules-Emile, died when de Gaulle was only one, his Maillot grandmother, a terrifying Catholic matriarch, continued to preside over the Lille household. When the eighteen-year-old Charles wrote to a Lille cousin that he had been to hear *Carmen* at the Opéra Comique, he warned that 'it goes without saying that not a word of this must reach grandma.'[23]

De Gaulle's son later observed that these Lille roots represented 'not just a birthplace but also an ethic, an education, a way of seeing the world': austere, traditionalist, suspicious of ostentation.[24] De Gaulle's later contempt for politicians as a breed contains something of the northerner's contempt for garrulous and gesticulating southerners who sit all day in cafés drinking *pastis* – a common caricature of the political class when he was growing up. When recuperating from a war wound in 1914 in a hospital at Cognac in south-west France, de Gaulle observed, through his prim northern lenses, that 'contrary to most towns of the south-west [Cognac] is opulent and clean.'[25] The only 'southern' touch to de Gaulle's childhood was a modest house at La Ligerie in the Dordogne bought by his parents in 1900. From Charles's tenth year, part of the summer holidays would be spent there.[26] This offered some relief from the invasive tribe of northern cousins, but de Gaulle later said that his memories of the house were gloomy (*maussade*), unlike recollections of the Wimereux holidays where he appreciated the 'immensity' of the sea.[27] The house was too much of a drain on his parents finances and they sold it in 1924.

But it was in Paris that de Gaulle's parents lived. He concisely describes himself in his memoirs as a *'petit Lillois de Paris'* – a little Lille boy from Paris. At the time of his birth, the family were living on Avenue Breteuil in the seventh *arrondissement*.[28] They moved later to other addresses but

always in the same part of the city. The location was convenient for the
Catholic school where Henri de Gaulle taught, but it was also a *quartier* of
Paris which reflected the family's values and sensibility. It contained two of
the city's grandest *ancien régime* buildings: the military hospital of the
Invalides, built by Louis XIV, and the military academy, the Ecole Militaire,
built by Louis XV. The *quartier* was on the edge of the once fashionable
but slightly faded Faubourg Saint-Germain where Catholic schools, religious institutions, embassies and ministries occupied the premises of former
aristocratic *hôtels*. There was little animation – no theatres, few restaurants
or cafés. De Gaulle was 'an old Parisian' but in spirit his Paris was worlds
away from the revolutionary Paris of the Bastille district, the bohemian
Paris of Montmartre, the plutocratic Paris of the sixteenth *arrondissement*,
the university Paris of the Latin Quarter. In a eulogy he wrote on France's
First World War leader Marshal Foch in the 1920s, de Gaulle articulated
his sense of this historic, noble but slightly soulless *quartier*:

> A large part of Foch's hard-working existence was spent in the context of a
> *quartier* of Paris whose majestic grandeur cannot have failed to exert its
> influence on his soul. The *quartier* of the Invalides and the Ecole Militaire:
> monuments whose architecture, proportions and façade are themselves
> symbols of military order, simplicity and melancholy . . . A *quartier* which
> carries a thousand moving proofs of our triumphs and our tears, where
> famous museums feed the dreams of the conscript, the reflections of the citi-
> zen and the memories of the veteran, where, under a sacred vault, rest the
> flags we have captured, where the bodies of Turenne and Napoleon lie . . .
> A *quartier* where Paris conserves the great military memories of the past and
> nurses the glories of the future.[29]

In two careful sentences of his *War Memoirs*, de Gaulle wrote of his father:
'My father, a man of thought, culture, tradition, was imbued with a sense of
the dignity of France. He made me discover its History.'[30] Later in life, when
asked to name the person who had most influenced him, he would always
unhesitatingly mention his father. Henri de Gaulle was remembered by his
many pupils as charmingly *vieille* France, a gentle survivor from another age:
distinguished and formal, undemonstrative and erudite. In this family, Gaulle
later recalled, 'intellectual work was all that counted.'[31] Henri passed on to
his son a reverence for writers and the life of the mind. In London during the
war de Gaulle ruminated one day on another possible existence:

> The most wonderful job in the world would be as a librarian . . . in a small
> provincial town, perhaps a municipal library in Brittany . . . What calm! What
> a wonderful life! . . . Suddenly, turning sixty, one begins to write an 80-page

monograph entitled: 'Did Madame de Sévigné ever visit Pontivy?' ... One becomes increasingly frenetic, writing stinging letters to the deacon who quibbles about a date.[32]

De Gaulle's hyperactive personality would never have been content with such a life but one could imagine it suiting his father, his bookishly eccentric uncles or the grandfather he had never known.

Of his mother, de Gaulle wrote that 'she had a passion for the fatherland equal to that of her religious piety.' De Gaulle's wife (presumably speaking from bitter experience) put the matter slightly less tactfully, commenting that it was from his mother that de Gaulle inherited 'the aggressive aspect' of his personality: 'She was a domineering woman and formulated judgements about which the least one can say is that they were categorical and passionate.'[33]

Living in the atmosphere of 'military melancholy' – a favourite phrase of de Gaulle's – of the seventh *arrondissement*, the de Gaulle family was out of step with the prevailing political values of the age. In 1871, after the Franco-Prussian War and the fall of the Second Empire of Napoleon III, for a moment it seemed possible if unlikely that France might become a monarchy again for the first time since 1848. This possibility was scuppered when the legitimate Bourbon pretender, the Comte du Chambord, refused in 1873 to accept the throne if it also meant accepting the tricolour flag of the Revolution. From that moment royalism was a lost cause in France. To royalists Chambord was for ever the melancholy symbol of a world they had lost. In 1876, de Gaulle's prolific grandmother dedicated her history of the Marian pilgrimages to the Comtesse de Chambord, his wife. Of Chambord's renunciation, de Gaulle wrote in a letter a few months before his own death in 1970 that it was 'a fundamental and sad event in our history. Fundamental because it wrote an end to everything our country had in terms of institutions. Sad, like everything else signifying that which was and will never be again.'[34]

The more moderate monarchists resigned themselves to the loss of their cause. In 1875, France became officially a republic for the third time. Scarred by the short-lived fate of France's two previous republics (1792-9, 1848-51), the leaders of the Third Republic set about instilling in the French people the idea that the identity of their nation was inseparable from republicanism. In 1879, the revolutionary hymn the 'Marseillaise' became France's national anthem; in 1881 the anniversary of the storming of the Bastille, 14 July, became a national holiday; statues of 'Marianne', the female incarnation of the Republic, were erected all over the country. In Paris, a huge Marianne statue was installed in the Place de la République in 1880, ten years before de Gaulle was born; and another one in the Place de la Nation nine years later. These two squares were in the left-wing Paris of the north-east across the Seine, a world away from the faded grandeur of the seventh. What de Gaulle did not mention in his evocation of the family *quartier* was the presence of the Eiffel Tower built in 1889 by a triumphant Republic to celebrate the centenary of the French Revolution. These were not symbols in which traditionalist families like the de Gaulles recognized *their* France. While not among those royalists who actively plotted against the Republic, the de Gaulles were internal exiles from it.

In the 1900s, French royalism was given a fresh lease of life by the newly founded political organization Action Française (which published the newspaper of the same name). Headed by Charles Maurras, a brilliant young polemicist from Provence, Action Française sought to anchor royalism in a doctrine rather than appealing to sentimental nostalgia for a dynasty. Maurras's theory of 'integral nationalism' deduced the necessity of a monarchy from first principles. He argued that France's survival as a great nation in the face of external enemies – Germany, Britain – required her to abandon republican democracy. He repudiated what he considered to be the disintegrating forces of nineteenth-century romanticism in favour of a return to the classical order of the *ancien régime*. Another part of Maurras's doctrine was the defence of the Catholic Church as a pillar of stability (even though he was personally not a believer), and the exclusion of Jews and Protestants from all positions of influence.

For many conservatives, Maurras offered a bracing reinvigoration of a moribund tradition. Was this true of the de Gaulle family? The question has long exercised biographers of Charles de Gaulle. From the moment de Gaulle became a public figure, he was dogged by persistent insinuations that Maurras's reactionary nationalism had left its imprint upon him. One problem when judging the validity of this claim is establishing what one means by 'Maurrassian'. It was possible to accept Maurras's pessimistic vision of international relations – that France was caught in an existential struggle with her hereditary enemies Britain and Germany – while not subscribing to his belief that the only adequate response to this challenge was a monarchical restoration; it was possible to share Maurras's argument for a monarchical restoration while not accepting his violent anti-Semitism. Henri de Gaulle read *Action française* but so did most intelligent conservatives of the period. As for Charles de Gaulle, although there are no references to Maurras in his writings and letters, his sister confided in 1945 that 'Charles was monarchist, he defended Maurras against his brother Pierre so fiercely that in one conversation he had tears in his eyes.'[35] Unfortunately we have no idea what period of de Gaulle's life she was referring to.

The recent tendency among historians has been to downplay this aspect of de Gaulle's heritage and to argue that the de Gaulle household was more influenced by the newspaper *Le Correspondant*. This represented a royalist tradition different from *Action française*. Its looked back nostalgically to the period 1789–91 when France had experimented with a constitutional monarchy reconciling the principles of the Revolution with the King. Maurras, on the other hand, saw 1789 as the root of all France's problems.[36] It is plausible that the liberal monarchism of the *Correspondant* was more in tune with the values of the de Gaulle family than the diehard and reactionary royalism of Maurras, but the direct evidence is patchy and circumstantial.

Many historians have also noted the importance of social Catholicism in de Gaulle's intellectual heritage. Social Catholics sought to overcome class struggle by finding a middle way between capitalism and socialism. This tradition was strong among the Catholic industrialists of northern France like de Gaulle's maternal ancestors. We shall see later that after 1944 de Gaulle was intermittently obsessed with the idea that it was his mission to promote an 'association' between the working class and their employers. One of the inspirations behind this obsession, which exasperated and puzzled many of his followers, was the doctrine of social Catholicism. This was another political tradition despised by Maurras, who believed in the primacy of *politics* – the return of the absolute monarchy – over utopias of social reconciliation. On the other hand, many social Catholics *were* ultra-conservatives whose vision of politics was quite different from the liberal tradition of the *Correspondant*: their social paternalism often went hand in hand with royalist legitimism.[37]

In short, there is no simple 'key' to de Gaulle – whether Maurrassian nationalism, liberal Catholicism, constitutional monarchism or social Catholicism. De Gaulle was exposed to all these influences through his family. Although we know little about Henri de Gaulle's political views, what is certain is that for families like the de Gaulles royalism was more a sensibility and a culture than a political commitment: it represented loyalty to a family tradition, revulsion at the violence of the Revolution, opposition to the persecution of religion. The de Gaulles were gentle survivors from another age, carrying in their heads a long history of France that went back far beyond 1789. Yet during the Dreyfus Affair, the most violent political conflict of the years when Charles de Gaulle was growing up, there is some suggestion that his father Henri held views that one would not expect from someone from his political milieu.

Alfred Dreyfus was a Jewish army officer accused wrongly of treason in 1894. Supporters of Dreyfus believed he was the innocent victim of a conspiracy fomented by the Church, the army and anti-Semites in order to undermine the Republic; opponents of Dreyfus believed that he was a traitor, and that Jews, republicans and Socialists were inventing a miscarriage of justice to subvert the institutions that bound society together. It was the Dreyfus case that propelled Maurras to fame when he wrote an article in 1898 defending an army officer revealed to have forged documents to convict Dreyfus. While Maurras celebrated the forgery as an act of patriotism, the novelist Emile Zola wrote a violent, blistering attack on the army that opened with the words 'J'accuse'.

It has become an article of faith among biographers of de Gaulle that Henri was convinced of Dreyfus's innocence, a claim rescuing de Gaulle from the insinuation that his family background was 'Maurrassian'. Over the years, from biographer to biographer, Henri de Gaulle's Dreyfusard beliefs become so amplified as almost to transform him into a kind of Emile Zola of the right. One writer alleges that Henri de Gaulle believed in Dreyfus's innocence from the day of his conviction – which is implausible since it was not true of even the most ardent future Dreyfusards. Another suggests that Henri's beliefs caused him to lose his teaching post – which is not true either.[38] If Henri de Gaulle was a Dreyfusard, he was a discreet one. His name does not appear among the supporters of a committee founded by the liberal Catholic Paul Viollet (whom Henri de Gaulle knew) who sought to bridge the chasm between the anti-Semitism of the anti-Dreyfusards and anti-clericalism of the Dreyfusards. The evidence for Henri de Gaulle's beliefs about Dreyfus is anecdotal but it corresponds to what one surmises of his undogmatic and gentle character.[39]

Charles de Gaulle himself referred to the Dreyfus Affair only twice in all his writings. In his history of France's army published in 1938, he deplored the fact that in the wake of the Affair 'under the pressure of pacifist illusions and mistrust of the military' the army had 'lost its cohesion and its force'. He wrote of the Dreyfus Affair:

> In this lamentable trial nothing that could poison the passions was lacking: the probability of a judicial error, which was backed up by forgeries, inconsistencies, abuses committed by the prosecution, but rejected with horror by those who, out of faith or reasons of State, were determined to defend the infallibility of a hierarchy devoted to the service of the fatherland; an exasperating obscurity where a thousand confused incidents, intrigues, confessions, retractions, duels, suicides, trials, enraged and threw two rival packs off the scent; calumnious polemics which were swelled by all the voices of the press, pamphlets and speeches.[40]

In his *War Memoirs* de Gaulle mentions the Dreyfus Affair in passing as one of the many conflicts that 'saddened' him because they weakened

France. These non-committal judgements – 'two rival packs' – suggest that what pained de Gaulle was less the fact of the injustice than its divisive consequences. Perhaps this was also his father's view.

It would be wrong to make the de Gaulle family background more liberal and open-minded than it was. In a biographical note on his family, Henri had written that 'like the Protestant Reformation, the Revolution was, in the words of de Maistre, Satanic in its essence. To like it is to move away from God ... I hope that these sentiments will be perpetuated by my descendants.'[41] A letter from the front by de Gaulle's elder brother Jacques to their father in 1917 reflects similar sentiments. Expressing his 'sense of stupefaction' at the fall of the Tsar and America's entry into the war in the name of liberty, Jacques wrote: 'Is it true then that this war is not only a struggle of appetites but a struggle of democracy against [royal] thrones ... the last and terrible upheaval that will complete the work of the French Revolution? So I am a soldier in this war of so-called liberty of peoples that I consider to be a monstrous inanity?'[42] Jacques was not Charles, of course, but these words offer an insight into the values of this closely knit family.

The de Gaulles will certainly have uncompromisingly opposed the Republic's war on the Catholic Church. The enmity between Catholics and republicans was one of the themes of France's nineteenth-century history. The de Gaulle family experienced this in a direct and personal way. Henri himself had been educated at the Jesuit school where he later taught. One of the teachers to whom he had been especially attached, Père Olivaint, was shot in the revolutionary Paris Commune of 1871. And it was after a decree in 1880 expelling Jesuits from France that Henri had decided himself to become a lay teacher in a Catholic school. It would have been inconceivable for Henri de Gaulle to educate his children in the state schools of the secular and anti-clerical Republic. De Gaulle's primary education between 1896 and 1900 took place at the Ecole Saint Thomas d'Aquin run by the Christian Brothers. He then went on to the Jesuit college where his father taught. After another republican assault on Jesuit teachers in the wake of the Dreyfus Affair, de Gaulle spent a year in exile at another Jesuit school at Antoing in Belgium.

According to the recollections of de Gaulle's elder sister, he 'was not an easy child' – hyperactive and undisciplined – nor a studious schoolboy compared to his brilliant elder brother Jacques. As an adult he reminisced fondly about his huge collection of toy soldiers (as did Churchill) – and also noted that when playing with them with his brothers he always took the role of France.[43] He spent less time studying than reading – and writing – poetry, swapping poems with one of his Lille cousins, Jean de Corbie. What did the young de Gaulle read? He was of course steeped in the classical French literature of the seventeenth century but also avidly read the symbolist poets of the late nineteenth century, especially Verlaine, as well as less well-known figures such as Albert Samain (like de Gaulle from Lille) and the Belgian poet Emile Verhaeven. These two latter names add another 'northern' touch to de Gaulle's sensibility. From de Gaulle's huge reading, one can (somewhat arbitrarily) select two writers who mattered to him. One was Edmond de Rostand (1868–1918), whose poetic drama *Cyrano de Bergerac* he could recite almost in its entirety. At the age of ten, de Gaulle was taken to the theatre to see Rostand's new play *L'aiglon* (The Eaglet) which tells the story of the tragically short life of the son of the Emperor Napoleon and the Austrian Archduchess Marie-Louise. It is set in the Austrian court where the sickly boy was in exile and in effect a prisoner after the fall of Napoleon. Despite his frivolous Austrian mother and the efforts of the scheming Metternich, the young Napoleon continues to dream of France and of the legend of his father until dying of tuberculosis aged twenty-one. De Gaulle all his life had complex feelings about Napoleon, and the royalist traditions of his family did not make them sympathetic to the Bonapartist tradition. But he was as susceptible to the romantic grandeur of the Napoleonic epic as any French adolescent of the nineteenth century.

In a completely different vein from the sonorous romanticism of Rostand, de Gaulle's literary imagination was profoundly marked by his youthful immersion in the works of the seventeenth-century French dramatist Pierre Corneille. Corneille's plays are moral dramas setting personal happiness against heroic duty. Throughout his life de Gaulle could quote from memory long passages from even Corneille's more obscure plays, although in his writings and speeches he cited him only twice. First, in a speech in London in 1942 he bemoaned 'the shame of dying without having fought [*honte de mourir sans avoir combattu*]', a quotation from Corneille's most famous play *Le Cid*. Secondly, in the last volume of his *Memoirs*, referring to the hostility he had constantly encountered from politicians and journalists, de Gaulle quoted from Corneille's *Cinna*: 'What! You want to be spared but you have spared nothing [*Quoi! Tu veux qu'on t'épargne et n'as rien épargné*].' These lines come from the celebrated soliloquy of the Emperor Augustus delivered at the moment when he hears of a plot to kill him by Cinna, a man whom he had trusted. The speech is a long meditation on the melancholy solitude that is the fate of the powerful leader: 'Heavens! To whom can I confide / The secrets of my soul and cares of my life? / Take back the power you have given me / If by giving me subjects it deprives me of friends' (*Ciel! A qui voulez-vous désormais que je fie / Les secrets de mon âme et le soin de ma vie? / Reprenez le*

pouvoir que vous m'avez commis / Si donnant des sujets il ôte les amis).
Although it is not directly quoted, the ascetic stoicism of Corneille's Augustus suffuses the celebrated portrait of the 'leader' depicted by de Gaulle in
his 1920s book the *Le fil de l'épee* (*The Edge of the Sword*) where his ideal
of heroic leadership is quintessentially Cornellian:

> The leader deprives himself of the sweetness that comes from relaxation,
> familiarity and friendship. He dedicates himself to that solitude that is the sad
> fate of superior beings ... That state of satisfaction, of inner peace, of calcu-
> lated joy that people agree to call happiness is incompatible with leadership.[44]

As de Gaulle once remarked to Emmanuel d'Astier de la Vigerie, leader
of one of France's main Resistance movements: 'So you believe in
happiness?'[45]

The unruly adolescent who neglected his school studies in favour of literature is no longer visible in a long letter the seventeen-year-old de Gaulle
sent to his father from the school in Antoing. He expresses mortification that
he had not done better in his algebra exams and all the efforts he is making
to remedy this '*grand malheur*'.[46] What had changed around the time of his
fifteenth birthday was that de Gaulle decided to embark on a military career.
There would be no chance of success without passing the competitive examinations for the military academy of Saint-Cyr. For the first time de Gaulle
applied himself seriously to his studies – not just in history and literature,
where he shone, but also in mathematics and the sciences.

THE GENERATION OF 1905

Although there was no previous military tradition in the de Gaulle family,
many conservative pupils of Catholic schools viewed the army as a way
of serving France while not compromising themselves with the detested
Republic. In that sense, de Gaulle's choice was entirely natural but it was
probably also influenced by the international context.

In March 1905, de Gaulle's fifteenth year – and apparently the year
when he decided to pursue a military career – the German Kaiser Wilhelm II
landed at Tangier to stake a German claim to Morocco. This calculated
provocation inaugurated a new era of international tension. It also triggered a French political crisis culminating three months later in the
resignation of the French Foreign Minister Théophile Delcassé, architect
of the Entente Cordiale with Britain. Delcassé resigned rather than make
concessions to Germany. The impact of that event in France is conveyed
in the reaction of the writer Charles Péguy: 'I knew at 11.30 in the morning

that in the space of these two hours a new period had begun in the history of my own life, in the history of this country, and assuredly in the history of the world. In the space of a morning everyone knew . . . that France was in the shadow of a German invasion.'[47] For Péguy this was an epiphany. Five years earlier, as a passionately committed Socialist, he had been one of Dreyfus's most ardent defenders; the shock of 1905 converted him to patriotism and later to Catholicism.

The first piece of writing we possess from Charles de Gaulle also dates from 1905: a schoolboy essay imagining how in 1930 'Europe declared war on France'. 'Europe' in this case means Germany. In de Gaulle's essay, France is defended by General de Boisdeffre (an interesting choice of hero for someone from an allegedly anti-Dreyfus milieu since the real General de Boisdeffre had been an anti-Dreyfusard) and 'General de Gaulle'. The details of the campaign are given in exhaustive detail. At the end, 'General de Gaulle' saves the situation: 'In a final burst of enthusiasm [*élan*], our plucky little soldiers rush forward with their bayonets ready. Ah! What a beautiful charge it was. How their hearts leapt proudly in their breasts!'[48]

We know nothing about the circumstances of this piece of juvenilia. De Gaulle had certainly experienced no Péguy-style epiphany. Passion for France was the bedrock of the values inherited from his family. The defeat of 1870–71 had generated in France a culture of mourning centred around the 'lost provinces' of Alsace-Lorraine. Generations of schoolboys were brought up on the patriotic verses of the poet Paul Déroulède which kept alive the idea of revenge. In Paris's Place de la Concorde, the statues representing the cities of Metz and Strasbourg were veiled in black crepe. Although with the passing of time the rawness of defeat lost some of its intensity, this was not true in the de Gaulle family. The de Gaulle boys were often taken by their parents to see the war memorial erected at Le Bourget where de Gaulle's father had fought in the campaign of 1870–71. The bas-relief carries the carving of a broken sword with the inscription: 'The sword of France, broken in valiant French hands, will be forged again by their descendants [*L'épée de la France, brisée dans leurs vaillantes mains, sera forgée à nouveau par leurs descendants*].' That phrase haunted de Gaulle. On 13 July 1940 he proclaimed on the BBC: 'Those whose duty it was to wield the sword of France have let it fall from their hands, broken. I have picked up again the pieces of the sword [*le tronçon du glaive*].'

If the sensibility of de Gaulle's patriotism was shaped by his parents, it was also marked by the shadow of 1905, by the experience of his own generation. The values of the '1905 generation' were analysed in a much discussed book *The Young of Today* published in 1913 by two journalists (Henri Massis and Alfred de Tarde) writing under the pseudonym 'Agathon'.

Their book claimed that the young generation was spurning the morbid introspection of the *fin de siècle* and the anti-militarism of the Dreyfusards. The new generation, according to Agathon, displayed a 'taste for action' centred around 'patriotic faith' and a return to religious values. The book was a manifesto rather than a sociological survey; it described what the authors wanted the young to be.[49] But enough books and articles were appearing on the same theme to suggest that something was in the air among young intellectuals. In the same year as the Agathon manifesto, the novelist Roger Martin du Gard published *Jean Barois*; the novel's eponymous hero is a former Dreyfusard activist who finds himself out of sympathy with a younger generation which has returned to Catholicism and nationalism.

One figure emblematic of this *Zeitgeist* was the novelist Ernest Psichari (1883–1914), although he was a little older than the 1905 generation. Through his anti-clerical grandfather Ernest Renan, Psichari was related to one of the most celebrated republican dynasties in France. A committed Dreyfusard, he went through an existential crisis and decided to join the colonial artillery. His autobiographical novel *L'appel aux armes* was the story of a young man who repudiates pacifism and joins the army. In 1913 Psichari converted to Catholicism and considered entering the Dominican Order. After dying in battle in August 1914, he became the subject of a major patriotic cult. In 1936, de Gaulle wrote to a correspondent describing Psichari as the 'spiritual and moral barrage against the upheavals of our times'; when at the front in February 1940, he asked to be sent two of Psichari's books.[50]

Charles Péguy was an even more famous representative of the intellectual evolution described by Agathon. Péguy dedicated one of his books to Psichari and his reaction to the events of 1905 has been quoted. Péguy deserves special attention because he was an author who mattered immensely to de Gaulle, who told one of his ministers in the 1960s: 'No writer more influenced me than Péguy. In the years before the war I read everything he wrote, during my adolescence, then at Saint-Cyr and as a young officer . . . I felt very close to him . . . He experienced things exactly as I experienced them.'[51] It is too simple to describe Péguy as someone who moved from left to right. Even after embracing patriotism and Catholicism, he did not renounce his previous socialism and republicanism or his opposition to anti-Semitism. Péguy's strange incantatory and repetitive prose, which is like nothing else in the French language, aspires to a synthesis of *all* French traditions – as exemplified in his haunting dictum 'The Republic, One and Indivisible, is our Kingdom of France.'[52] His nationalism could not have been more different from that of Maurras, whom he loathed – and who loathed him. Maurras's oeuvre was constructed around exclusions and repudiations – purging France of the impurities that had weakened her since 1789 – Péguy's around accumulations and additions. Péguy did turn violently against those with whom he had worked during the Dreyfus Affair but this was because he believed they had betrayed the nobility of the cause in favour of base partisanship. Hence his most famous axiom: 'All begins as *mystique* and ends as *politique*.' By 1914, Péguy had developed an almost physical revulsion from parliamentary politics – another aspect of his writing that left traces on de Gaulle. So too did Péguy's cult of Joan of Arc about whom he wrote two long plays. There was no moment of France's history which his eucumenical nationalism did not embrace: 'Valmy and Jemappes [two famous battles of the Revolution] are', he wrote, 'in the direct line of Patay [one of Joan of Arc's victories against the English]! . . . They are of the same race, the same spiritual family.'[53] What links the early socialist and republican Péguy and the later nationalist and Catholic Péguy was a sense that throughout history France had had a mystical vocation to bring enlightenment to humanity. The famous opening sentences of de Gaulle's *War Memoirs* comparing France to 'the princess of a fairy story or a Madonna on a fresco wall, preordained to an eminent and exceptional destiny', echo Péguy's statement that he viewed France as 'a queen of nations; a queen, in the old French sense of the world, half serious, half mysterious, half heraldic, half fairy story'.[54]

In his book *France and her Army* published in 1938, de Gaulle referred to the intellectual mentors of his own generation in one densely packed sentence: 'Figures like Boutroux and Bergson who gave new life to the spiritual side of French thought, the secret influence of Péguy . . . in literature the influence of a Barrès'.[55] Each of these three Bs – Barrès, Boutroux, Bergson – exerted an influence on de Gaulle, but none cast a greater spell than Maurice Barrès (1862–1923). Although his style has dated, Barrès was a cult figure for several generations of aspiring French writers. No single writer was mentioned more often in the Agathon study, where he hovers as a tutelary figure over the generation of 1905. He leapt to fame with the publication of a trilogy of novels in 1888–91 under the umbrella title of *Le culte de moi* (The Cult of the Self) which incited their readers to throw off the shackles of convention and assert the principle of individual selfhood. But as he became haunted by France's decline, his focus moved from the individual to the national. His next trilogy was entitled *Le roman de l'énergie nationale* (The Novel of National Energy). It follows the fortunes of a group of six young men from Lorraine whose tragedy is to have lost contact with the traditions of their home region because their schoolteachers have inculcated in them the abstract values of republicanism. Moving to Paris to fulfil their ambitions – another step in their journey of uprootedness (one novel in the trilogy was entitled *Les déracinés* (The Uprooted)) – they all experience different unpleasant fates until one of them is redeemed by rediscovering the importance of regional attachment – what Barrès called the cult of 'the land and the dead'. Barrès, who was from Lorraine, also nurtured a cult of the territories lost to Germany in 1871. De Gaulle's summary of Barrès in *France and her Army* was that he 'gave back to the elite a consciousness of national eternity by revealing the links that attached it to its ancestors'.[56]

Although Barrès was, like Maurras, an ardent anti-Dreyfusard and anti-Semite, his nationalism was different from Maurras's dogmatic reading of France's past. Barrès sought not to turn back the clock to the monarchy but to reinvigorate the Republic with vitalist values. His sensibility was romantic in contrast to Maurras's classicism. This has led some to read Barrès's nationalism as a kind of proto-fascism, but his writing was revered by individuals who followed many different political trajectories. In his day, he was a writer as influential as André Gide and Jean-Paul Sartre in theirs. Among those profoundly marked by Barrès were the novelists André Malraux and François Mauriac (both one day to be passionate Gaullists) but also the Communist novelist and poet Louis Aragon and the fascist novelist Pierre Drieu La Rochelle. It is perhaps the music of Barrès's prose, and the sensibility of his patriotism, that left the greatest trace on de Gaulle. De Gaulle's notebooks are full of quotations from him. Even the famous opening sentence of de Gaulle's *War Memoirs* – 'All my life I have had a certain idea of France' – may be an unconscious echo of Barrès: 'to give a certain idea of France, is to allow us to play a certain role.'[57] Writing in 1954 to thank an author for sending him a book on Barrès, de Gaulle remarked that 'he has never ceased to enchant me.' He responded, he said, to Barrés's 'tortured soul ... what one might even call his sense of despair', even if this was hidden under a 'magnificent off-handedness'.[58] De Gaulle's comment on the first page of his *War Memoirs* that as a young man he felt an 'anxious pride' in France has a quintessentially Barressian ring.

The other two Bs in de Gaulle's list – Emile Boutroux (1845–1921) and Henri Bergson (1859–1941) – were both widely read philosophers who attacked the mid-nineteenth-century positivist view of the world that all phenomena can be explained by scientific determinism and rationalism. Boutroux stressed the importance of contingency and indeterminacy against those who believed in abstract, closed systems and *a priori* reasoning.[59] How directly familiar de Gaulle was with his writings we do not know but they were certainly part of the intellectual *Zeitgeist* when he was growing up, and the notebook he kept while a prisoner of war contains a long quotation from Boutroux on the subject of contingency. In the same notebook he summed up one of Boutroux's works in the following way: 'He is an adversary of mechanistic thinking. He does not accept that scientific laws are everything and that all phenomena are necessarily subject to them. He claims a role for what Pascal called judgement, that is to say the importance of the heart and the soul in thinking about the world.'[60] This approach was to be central to de Gaulle's philosophy of action as it developed in the 1920s.

Boutroux's reputation has been overshadowed by that of Henri Bergson, who became the most celebrated philosopher of his age. Bergson is especially remembered today for his argument that rational intelligence is incapable of conveying the way that consciousness apprehends the passing of time – an important influence on Marcel Proust. But this was only part of Bergson's philosophical quest to assert the importance of intuition over analytical intelligence, *élan vital* against frozen doctrine. De Gaulle often quoted Bergson, and as we shall see his thinking profoundly influenced de Gaulle's conception of leadership. In the 1960s, he expounded the importance to him of Bergson in a conversation with an American journalist:

> I was much influenced by Bergson particularly because he made me understand the philosophy of action. Bergson explains the role of intelligence and analysis. He saw how necessary it is to analyze questions in search of the truth, but intellect alone cannot act. The intelligent man does not automatically become the man of action. Instinct is also important. Instinct plus impulse; but impulse alone is also not sufficient as a basis for action. The two, intellect and impulse, must go together . . . Great men have both intellect and impulse. The brain serves as a brake upon pure emotional impulse. The brain surmounts impulse; but there must also be impulse and the capability for action in order not to be paralyzed by the brake of the brain. I remember this from Bergson who has guided me here through my entire life.[61]

GOD AND FATHERLAND

In the summer of 1907, aged sixteen, de Gaulle volunteered to be a stretcher-bearer at Lourdes. From there he wrote to his mother: 'Yesterday afternoon, I saw a young Italian girl, paralysed and suffering from TB, cured during the procession.'[62] In his year at the Jesuit College of Antoing in Belgium between 1907 and 1908 he was a fervently pious Catholic, one of a minority of pupils to join a religious group known as the Congregation of the Holy Virgin which devoted itself to prayer and religious meditation. In May 1908, he accompanied his brother Jacques to a religious retreat run by the Jesuits. Later that summer, staying in Germany to improve his knowledge of the language, he provided his father with a detailed account of his religious duties: 'I generally attend the curate's Mass at 7.00. On Sunday, High Mass at 8.30; Vespers at 1.30, Benediction at 8.00.'[63]

In this letter the eighteen-year-old boy was possibly reassuring his parents, but throughout his life he remained punctilious in his religious observance.[64] When he became President of France in 1958, he reinstalled a chapel in the Elysée Palace so he could attend Mass privately if he was in Paris over the weekend. But the ostentatious adolescent piety de Gaulle had displayed at Antoing was not characteristic of de Gaulle in adulthood. Beyond his external respect for the rituals of Catholicism, his relationship to religion was mysterious. Those observing him at Mass were struck by how distracted he always seemed to be, peering around to see who was present, looking out of the windows, visibly bored if the ceremony dragged on.[65] The novelist André Malraux commented: 'He talks often of France, never of God.' His aides would sometimes discuss among themselves whether he was really a believer at all and what kind of believer he might be.[66] Some took the view he was a 'Catholic' rather than a 'Christian', meaning that, like the agnostic Charles Maurras, he believed in the Catholic Church as the institution which embodied France and her history. He gave some credence to this idea when remarking one day to one of his nephews: 'I am Christian and Catholic by history and geography.' But others in his presence sensed a profound if discreet Christian faith.[67] All his life he demonstrated remarkable theological confidence. His niece, Geneviève, remembered once that when the Archbishop of Rouen expressed his regret at having broken the host during Communion, de Gaulle replied that Christ was present in all fragments of the host.[68] One day, walking back from Mass in December 1946, he launched into a long monologue to his aide de camp about the importance of Christ's sacrifice to the meaning of Christianity: 'He opened up the horizons of religion beyond the heart of men towards vast regions giving a place to human suffering, to human anguish, to human dignity.'[69] This expression of open religious meditation on de Gaulle's part is remarkable for being unique. Perhaps he was also thinking about himself when he wrote of Marshal Foch in the essay cited above: 'He was profoundly *croyant*. Without ever mixing his religion with his professional activities, it nonetheless remained a vital element of his interior life ... His personality was as it were impregnated by it.'[70]

If de Gaulle ever suffered religious doubts, we have no record of them – although at times he expressed sentiments of almost nihilist pessimism. He often repeated Stalin's comment to him in 1944: 'In the end only death wins.' He also liked to cite an aphorism from Nietzsche: 'Nothing is worth anything, nothing happens and yet everything occurs, but that is a matter of indifference.' A diffuse Nietzscheanism was in vogue among French intellectuals during de Gaulle's youth, but one writer's attempt to enrol de Gaulle as a 'Nietzschean Christian' (whatever that might be) is not convincing.[71]

What is certain is that de Gaulle's Catholicism was inseparable from his patriotism and his sense of France. He would often refer to the 'fifteen hundred years' of the history of France.[72] When asked the significance of that number, he told one biographer:

> For me the history of France begins with Clovis, who was chosen as King of France by the tribe of Franks who gave their name to France. Before Clovis, we have the Gallo-Roman and Gaulish history. The deciding element for me is that Clovis was the first king to be baptised a Christian. Mine is a Christian country and I count the history of France from the accession of a Christian king who bore the name of the Franks.[73]

In the nineteenth century, dating the 'origins' of France was an intensely political issue: conservatives harked back to the baptism of Clovis in AD 496 (1,500 years), the Republicans looked to Vercingetorix who led the Gaulish revolt against the Romans in 52 BC (2,000 years). De Gaulle sometimes used the latter figure[74] – especially during the war when the struggle of the Gauls provided a parallel with the Resistance – but less often than he referred to France's '1,500 years'.[75] In the history of France, the period with which de Gaulle was most out of sympathy was the anti-religious and freethinking Enlightenment when, as he wrote in the 1930s, 'scepticism and corruption . . . dissolved loyalty and paralysed authority.'[76] Voltaire was an author whose corrosive irony he particularly deplored, often citing his verses as proof that 'French intellectuals have always betrayed France.'[77] Of France's nineteenth-century writers, none was more revered by de Gaulle than the romantic René de Chateaubriand whose *Génie du christianisme* played a role in the return to Catholicism of the French bourgeoisie – including families like his own – after the Revolution.

Occasionally de Gaulle's speeches would make explicit references to the Catholic roots of France. At a rally of the RPF, the political movement he founded in 1947, he proclaimed: 'Come to us! You who are animated by the flame of Christianity, that which casts the light of love and fraternity over the valley of human suffering, that which sparks the spiritual and moral values which have inspired France over the centuries.'[78] Once he had returned to power in 1958 as President of a formally secular state, he avoided such overtly religious language. Even so, his quasi-mystical nationalism was saturated by his religious sensibility. For him religion and patriotism, service to Fatherland and God were indistinguishable. As we have seen, the first page of his *War Memoirs* compares France to a Madonna fresco. His war speeches – which he referred to in those *Memoirs* as 'a sort of priestly duty' – often invoked 'Our Lady of France':

> Nothing matters to us and nothing preoccupies us more than to serve her. Our duty to her is as simple and elementary as the duty of a son to an oppressed mother ... We have nothing other to ask from her except perhaps that on the day of victory, she opens maternally her arms to us so that we can cry with joy and that on the day when death comes to claim us she enfolds us gently in her good and holy earth.[79]

In his *War Memoirs* de Gaulle wrote of his mother's death in July 1940 that she had 'offered to God her suffering for the salvation of the fatherland and the mission of her son'.[80]

In the 1900s, de Gaulle's adolescent imagination craved the idea of sacrifice for both France and God as exemplified in Péguy's famous poem *Eve* written in 1913 in the run-up to war: 'Happy those who died for the flesh-warm earth / Provided that it happened in a just war ... / Happy those who died in great battles / Laid out on the soil and facing God ... Happy the ripe grain and the gathered harvest.'

When he was eighteen, de Gaulle composed a poem in the same vein – and wrote it out again from memory (with two mistakes) in his last notebook when he was seventy-seven. It opens:

> *Quand je devais mourir, j'aimerais que ce soit*
> *Sur un champ de bataille; alors qu'on porte en soi*
> *L'âme encor tout enveloppée*
> *Du tumulte enivrant que souffle le combat,*
> *Du rude frisson que donne à qui se bat*
> *Le choc mâle et clair de l'épée ...*

> When I have to die, I would want it to be
> On the field of battle; while
> One's soul is still enveloped
> By the heady tumult of the combat
> By the harsh shudder which is given to those who fight.
> By the virile and clean shock of the sword.

It ends:

> *J'aimerais que ce soit, pour mourir sans regret,*
> *Un soir où je verrais la Gloire à mon chevet*

Me montrer la Patrie en fête
Un soir où je pourrais, écrasé sous l'effort,
Sentir passer avec le frisson de la Mort
Son baiser brûlant sur ma tête.

To die without regret, I would like it to be
An evening when I might see Glory at my bedside
Showing me the fatherland rejoicing
An evening when crushed by my efforts
I might feel under the shudder of Death
Her burning kiss on my forehead.[81]

2

'A Regret That Will Never Leave Me', 1908–1918

THE YOUNG GIANT

Before his final year preparing for Saint-Cyr, de Gaulle spent the summer holidays of 1908 in a village in Baden to improve his knowledge of the language of the 'enemy'. Biographers sometimes observe that he was throughout his life fascinated by Germany. German was certainly the foreign language he knew best; he had some familiarity with German literature; he frequently quoted German authors, especially Goethe.[1] But no 'fascination' with Germany is evident in his letters home during this visit. He seemed largely indifferent to his surroundings – to the countryside, to the architecture, to the culture. His only fascination was with war: the last war and the next one. In one letter, he reported that the newspapers were very anti-French: 'It is clear that something has changed in Europe in the last three years [again note the importance of 1905] and, seeing this, I think of the malaise that precedes great wars, notably that of 1870. I hope that this time the roles will be reversed.' Particularly intrigued by any signs of the 1870–71 war, he observed that every village had a plaque recording the names of soldiers killed in that conflict. The porter carrying his bags to the village had reminisced about the siege of Strasbourg in 1870: 'He spoke about the bombardment of Strasbourg with fanatical enthusiasm. But it is true that on the day I spoke to him he had drunk a bit too much schnapps.' De Gaulle hoped also to talk to an old Bavarian soldier in the village who was said to have served in the wars of 1866 – against Austria – and 1870 – against France.[2]

De Gaulle passed his entry examinations to Saint-Cyr in September 1909. He was ranked only 119 out of 221 entrants but this was creditable since it was rare to be admitted at the first attempt. As a result of the Dreyfus Affair, future officers had to serve a year in the ranks before starting at Saint-Cyr: the intention was to prevent them becoming separated from the lives of ordinary soldiers. De Gaulle chose to serve in the 33rd

Infantry Regiment (33RI). This unit had a prestigious history but his choice was probably inspired by the fact that it was stationed at Arras in north-eastern France, a region he knew well. That the commander of the regiment was Colonel Philippe Pétain was certainly not a factor in de Gaulle's choice. Pétain was not well known at this time. His career had stalled because he opposed the prevailing orthodoxy which prioritized offensive over defensive warfare.

De Gaulle graduated from Saint-Cyr in the summer of 1912, thirteenth in his year. This rise in ranking suggests that he had been an exemplary student. Otherwise we have no evidence that he stood out in any way – except for his height. At 6 foot 4 inches (1.93 metres) he would be considered tall even today, but when the average height in France was 5 foot 3 inches (1.63 metres), he was a giant. There were many other odd features of his physical appearance – his small head, his heavily hooded eyes, his long neck and lack of chin – but his height was what everyone noticed first. When the young diplomat François Coulet, joining the Free French in 1940, tried to find out what de Gaulle was like, the only answer he could get was 'very tall'.[3] Although de Gaulle was not prone to intimate self-revelations, he made occasional – if oblique – comments which hint that the icy reserve he projected was rooted in a certain physical awkwardness about his appearance. To one aide (also tall) he commented in 1943: 'We giants are never at ease with others . . . The armchairs are always too small, the tables too low, the impression one makes too strong.'[4] In the passage of his *War Memoirs* describing the parade down the Champs-Elysées after the liberation of Paris on 26 August 1944, he makes the curious remark, 'I did not have a physique that pleases.'[5] In the newsreels of that event he certainly looks awkward in his movements, as if not quite knowing what to do with his long arms. One journalist wrote: 'He looked like a puppet made of wood . . . intimidated and intimidating. The puppet master looked as if the strings had got mixed up because the General was only moving his lower arms, as if when saluting the crowds, who were all standing anyway, he was saying to them "do get up, my children."'[6] Eventually de Gaulle learnt to exploit his ungainly physique. The stiffness became less evident and he would raise his arms high above his head to symbolize a huge V for victory. In his youth, however, the strange body had not been tamed.

De Gaulle's high marks on graduating from Saint-Cyr gave him the choice of serving in whatever branch of the army he chose. He elected to rejoin the infantry. Biographers used to comment that this was an early sign of de Gaulle's independence of mind since the infantry lacked the glamour of the cavalry. But the most highly ranked graduate of his year,

Alphonse Juin, also joined the infantry – in his case the *zouaves* stationed in the colonies.[7] If anything can be deduced from de Gaulle's choice it is that, in an army where careers tended to be 'colonial' or 'metropolitan', he was firmly in the latter camp. He chose to return to the 33RI where he had already served.

De Gaulle later wrote in his *Memoirs*: 'When I joined the army it was one of the greatest things in the world. Under the criticisms and insults that had been hurled at it, it waited with serenity, and even muted hope, for the days when everything would depend on it.'[8] This may have been true in his imagination but the reality was different – and he knew it. In the early 1920s he scribbled in his notebook:

> For thirty years after 1870 the profession of soldier exercised a fascination for the young bourgeoisie. Officers dreamt of revenge and glory. As a result the mediocrity of their existence did not worry them. And they were treated with respect. But after the Dreyfus Affair, there was a weakening in the military ideal. A so-called social ideal replaced it. The ravages of pacifism were felt.[9]

It was indeed true that the army's reputation was still tarnished by the Dreyfus Affair. The number of applicants to Saint-Cyr had fallen from 2,000 in 1900 to 800 in the year de Gaulle entered. The 'nationalist revival' detected by Agathon affected only the intellectual elite, and anti-militarist sentiment remained strong among the population. The main issue of the 1913 parliamentary elections had been whether to increase military service from two to three years. Supporters of three-year service prevailed, but the passions aroused by the debate made France's leaders so concerned about the reliability of their conscripts that contingency plans were drawn up to arrest pacifist activists in the event of war. It is in this context that one should read the talk de Gaulle delivered to his men in 1913 where he quoted Paul Déroulède, the poet of post-1870 *revanche*: 'He who does not love his mother more than other mothers, and his fatherland more than other fatherlands, loves neither his mother nor his fatherland.' De Gaulle's lecture went on:

> It is impossible to deny, dear comrades, that if really disinterested and generous feelings exist in the world, the main one is patriotism. I do not think that any human love has ever inspired greater and purer devotion . . . And if there is one absolutely necessary obligation whose negation causes also the negation of patriotism, that is military service . . . Certainly war is an evil, I am the first to agree, but it is a necessary evil . . . Nothing more awakens in a people male virtues and noble enthusiasm than the sense that the fatherland

is in danger ... In seeing his fatherland threatened by ambitious enemies, the citizen understands the need to remain manly to defend it better. While prolonged peace provokes the love of gain and the appetite of vice ... war develops in men's hearts much that is good; peace allows what is bad to thrive.[10]

'THE ENTHUSIASM I HAD DREAMED OF'

After a month of tense diplomatic crisis, war between France and Germany broke out on 2 August 1914. De Gaulle later wrote in his *Memoirs*: 'In my youth I imagined without horror and magnified in advance this unknown adventure.'[11] He immediately started to note his impressions in a journal. To rise to the occasion, he adopted a tone of self-conscious solemnity: 'Goodbye to my apartment, to my books, to familiar objects. How much more intense life appears, how the tiniest things take on significance, when perhaps all is soon to end.' His observation that 'the officers now count for something in the town' betrays a grim satisfaction that the politicians of the despised Republic might now realize how much they needed their soldiers.[12]

The general expectation that the declaration of war would spark widespread desertions proved wrong. De Gaulle wrote: 'There are not so many to see us off. But people are resolute and hold back their tears ... This really is the unanimous élan, the kind of restrained enthusiasm I had dreamed of.'[13] Historians no longer agree that the French people went to war in 1914 in a spirit of delirious excitement, but de Gaulle's phrase 'restrained enthusiasm' seems close to the truth. For his entire life, obsessed by France's political divisions, he was haunted by this fragile moment of national unanimity.

As a platoon (*section*) commander, Lieutenant de Gaulle had about sixty-five men under his command.[14] Part of the Fifth Army, whose mission was to block the left wing of the German forces advancing through Belgium, the 33RI was sent to the small Belgian city of Dinant, a key crossing point of the River Meuse. In 1914 most of the city lay on the eastern side of the river in the shadow of a steep cliff surmounted by a citadel. After an exhausting overnight march, de Gaulle's regiment reached Dinant in the early hours of 15 August. His company took up its position in a trench by a level-crossing on the west bank of the Meuse. The men were able to snatch only a few hours' sleep before the German attack. A few weeks later, convalescing in hospital from his wounds, de Gaulle wrote up his impressions of that first morning while they were still fresh in his mind:

At 6 a.m. – boom boom boom; the dance begins, the enemy were furiously attacking Dinant: the first shots of the campaign. What impression did this make on me? Why not admit it? Two seconds of physical emotion: a knotted throat. And that was all. I could even say that a feeling of satisfaction came over me: 'At last we are going to get them' . . . I sat on a bench in the street where the level-crossing was, and remained there out of bravado. In fact there was no merit in this because I didn't feel any emotion. Every quarter of an hour, I went to joke with my men who were safe in the trench.[15]

While de Gaulle's company was in reserve, two others had been sent across the bridge, not knowing that the Germans were already in possession of the citadel. Taken by surprise, the French were fired upon and fell back towards the bridge in disarray. The French artillery seemed not to be responding:

> It was not fear that gripped us but rage. God preserve me from ever being in reserve so close to the line of fire. It was awful! One suffers all the miseries of the fight without actually being able to do anything. One is immobile while one's comrades are dying. We could only witness a sad procession of the wounded!

As the French struggled back across the bridge, de Gaulle's company was ordered to move forward to prevent the Germans crossing the river:

> I screamed out: 'First *section*! Forward with me,' and I rushed forward, realizing that our only chance of success was to move very fast before the enemy, which was now falling back, had time to turn around again. I had the impression at that moment that I had become split in two [*dédoubler*] with one of my selves running forward like an automaton while being watched anxiously by the other. I had hardly covered the twenty metres leading to the entry to the bridge when I felt a kind of whiplash on my knee which caused me to stumble. The four other men with me were also mown down in the same instant. I fell, and Sergeant Debout fell on top of me, killed outright! For the next half-minute there was a terrible hail of bullets around me. I could hear the crack of them on the paving stones and the parapet of the bridge . . . I could also hear them entering with a dull thud into the bodies of the dead and wounded strewn on the ground . . . With my leg completely numb and paralysed, I extracted myself from the bodies around me and crawled along the street underneath the same ceaseless hail of bullets, dragging my sword which was still attached by its strap to my wrist. How I was not pierced like a sieve will forever remain one the great questions of my life.

De Gaulle managed to drag himself back to a house where he took shelter. Here he found himself in the company of an older officer who had been wounded in the head and was in a state of panic: 'He began yelling "Start praying my friends! Start praying . . ." It was a real trial to hear him scream- ing in this way and I told him without much ceremony to keep quiet. Nothing produces a worse effect on the troops than to hear their leaders say that they are going to die.'

To the surprise of the French defenders, the Germans did not storm the bridge immediately, perhaps not realizing how little resistance they would have met. At last the French artillery, silent up to now, moved into action. Another infantry regiment was moved down to the bridge. By the end of the day, the French had succeeded in crossing the Meuse and provisionally taking possession of the citadel again. De Gaulle witnessed none of these events. Along with other wounded soldiers he had been taken to Bouvignes just north of Dinant where the wife of the local mayor had converted part of her chateau into a temporary hospital. The next morning he was driven by the head of the local Red Cross to Charleroi where he briefly saw his sister, Marie-Agnès, who lived in the city, and then he was put on a train to Paris. He was just in time to avoid being taken prisoner because the Germans occupied Charleroi on 20 August. He had been luckier than two of his literary heroes, Ernest Psichari and Charles Péguy: Pischari died seven days after de Gaulle's baptism of fire, at the Battle of Rossignol, and Péguy at the Battle of the Marne on 5 September.

De Gaulle was operated on in Paris. While convalescing in hospital, he penned a short story featuring an officer whose name 'Langel' was almost an anagram of his own. It contained some elements of his own experience and allowed him to fantasize about a battle that he had not experienced: 'How he had dreamt of this war! First in his childhood imagination, then in the adventurous ambition of youth, and finally in the impatience of the professional soldier.' Crouching in the woods waiting for the attack, Langel sees the 'other race' for the first time and feels 'stirring in his blood the hereditary fury of his ancestors'. Once the battle is over, he breaks with his mistress out of respect for her husband who has been killed. As Langel renounces love, he hears that the country has been saved: solidarity between soldiers prevails over love, masculine heroism over sentimental weakness. This is how de Gaulle refought the battle in his imagination even if his own reality had been more prosaic.[16]

In his twenty seconds of combat, de Gaulle had made two discoveries: one about himself, the other about modern warfare. The first was that he was indifferent to physical danger. Throughout his life he would display the same bravado he had shown at the level-crossing at Dinant – to the despair of those in charge of his security. The second lesson was summarized in one sentence of the book on the French army de Gaulle published in 1938: 'In the twinkling of an eye, it became clear that all the virtue in the world is powerless against firepower.'[17] This was sobering for the young officer who had lectured his men in 1913: 'One must have the offensive spirit ... What is one aiming to do in combat? To force the Germans to flee. There is only one way to do this and that is to march on them boldly.'[18] It had not proved so simple.

'THIS IS NOT HOW WE HAD DREAMED OF WAR'

De Gaulle rejoined his regiment on 17 October. He was so desperate to take part in the fighting that he left hospital before his wound was fully healed.[19] He found that the war was already assuming a character very different from his experience on the bridge of Dinant.

The fighting at Dinant had been only a tiny piece in the jigsaw of disastrous tactical and strategic miscalculations committed by the French high command at the start of the war. The tactical mistake was to believe that the offensive élan of the French infantry would overcome all obstacles. This led the high command to pay insufficient attention to the importance of artillery support. De Gaulle clearly diagnosed this in letters to his mother from hospital. The strategic miscalculation was the failure to predict that the main German attack would sweep through Belgium. No one believed that the Germans had enough soldiers to launch such an operation while simultaneously parrying a French offensive further south in Alsace. The Germans had been able to do this only by throwing their reserves into the initial battle in order to deliver a knock-out blow before the French could recover from their surprise.

The German gamble almost succeeded. By the first days of September German forces were within reach of Paris. The situation was saved *in extremis* by a French counter-attack on the River Marne to the east of Paris. The Germans were now forced to retreat northwards with the French in pursuit, each side trying to outflank the other. By the end of the year the two armies had reached the Channel and there was nowhere else to go. They could only dig in opposite each other, soon forming two lines of trenches stretching from the Channel to the Swiss border.

This was the situation confronting de Gaulle when he rejoined his regiment. His sector of the front was relatively quiet while intensive fighting was taking place further north. His journal expressed his frustration about this 'siege war', as he dubbed it: 'Trench warfare has the great disadvantage of exaggerating for everyone a feeling which is difficult to resist in warfare. If I leave the enemy in peace, he will do the same to me. That is deplorable.'[20] In December 1914 he predicted to his mother with clinical lucidity, but seemingly no regret: 'What is this war other than a war of extermination? The loser will the one who first exhausts all his moral and material resources.'[21]

For the French army 1915 was the bleakest year of the war. Today that year is overshadowed in popular memory by the innocent excitement of the offensives of 1914 and the sombre heroism of the defence of Verdun in 1916. Yet more French soldiers died in 1915 than in any other year. The French high command was obsessed by the need to break out of the immobility of trench warfare and penetrate the German lines. This elusive breakthrough was pursued through a series of murderous offensives in the Champagne region to the east and the Artois region further north. The conundrum was that a successful offensive had to be prepared by intensive artillery bombardment, but this had the disadvantage of sacrificing the element of surprise. As a result, any breakthrough quickly ran out of steam because the defenders had prepared a second line of defence. It was never possible to gain more than a few metres of land – and always at a terrible cost in lives. The imperturbable Commander in Chief General Joseph Joffre christened this strategy *grignotage*, 'nibbling away' at the enemy, which the British military historian Basil Liddell Hart compared grimly to 'nibbling' through barbed wire with one's bared teeth.

If the offensives of Artois and Champagne in 1915 left little trace in French memory, no one remembers the hauntingly named village of Mesnil-les-Hurlus, one of the sites of the first Champagne offensive between December 1914 and March 1915. Entirely destroyed in the fighting, the village no longer exists. It was erased from the map and its name later incorporated into that of a neighbouring village. It was to Mesnil-les-Hurlus that de Gaulle was sent in January 1915 to take part in the forthcoming offensive. He had been appointed adjutant to the colonel of his regiment which meant that, rather than viewing events from the perspective of an ordinary company commander, he now had a greater overview of the preparation of the battle, and at the same time his chances of survival were also slightly improved. This increase in responsibility shows that de Gaulle had quickly come to the attention of his superiors. It also reflected the high command's desperation to find able young officers as the death toll mounted. De Gaulle wrote home at the end of 1914: 'The regiment has few officers left because in addition to those we have lost in combat, there are more and more who fall ill, not being able to support this existence which is truly very hard both physically and morally.' For the same reason he was confident that he would soon earn his promotion to captain: 'If I continue to live, the war will necessarily require the promotion of those who are still young because here the old cannot hold out.'[22] The promotion came in the following February.

The first Champagne offensive was launched on 9 January 1915. In two days the 33RI suffered such heavy casualties that it was pulled back from the front line to recuperate while another offensive was prepared. It was then thrown into battle again on 16 February. Again the casualties were horrendous, but this time the orders were to continue 'at any cost'. After three weeks of bloody attacks and counter-attacks the offensive was abandoned. The front had hardly moved and de Gaulle's regiment had suffered over 700 casualties (of which 127 were dead and 220 missing) – an astonishingly high figure for a unit of about 1,550 men.[23] De Gaulle was of course not in a position to express any doubts about a strategy that it was his duty to execute. Four days into the second offensive, he drafted an order which brooked no dissent:

> The considerable efforts asked of the 33RI ... are designed to attract the attention of the enemy whatever the cost, so as to oblige it to use up its reserves in order to contain the élan of our attacks and consequently to allow comrades of other regiments to take possession of important German positions. Everyone must understand that our great and glorious sacrifices are in no way unnecessary.[24]

This is what the young officer said in public. His inner feelings about the offensives which he had witnessed were revealed in what he wrote eighteen months later, once he had been taken prisoner:

> The infantrymen who took part and survive, recall with bitterness and sadness those awful attacks where each day new bodies piled up in the filthy mud; those orders to charge, given on the telephone by a distant high command, after derisory and badly regulated artillery preparation; those attacks without hope carried out against networks of intact and deep barbed wire where the best officers and the best soldiers were sent to be killed like flies in a spider's web.[25]

On 10 March, the day his regiment was pulled back from the front, de Gaulle was wounded in the hand by a bullet. The injury became severely infected and he was hospitalized for a second time. (This injury had permanent consequences: when he later married he wore his wedding ring on his right hand.) When de Gaulle rejoined his unit in June it had been moved to the River Aisne. He was once again a normal company commander, apart from another two-month stint as adjutant in the autumn. Although his unit was in the front line, his sector experienced little fighting at this time. On many days he simply notes in his journal: 'nothing to report'. The enemies were boredom, depression and the weather. As winter approached, the Aisne flooded and submerged the trenches. At the end of the year, de Gaulle reported that his men were 'living in the water like frogs' and wait-ing for the water level to fall 'with the easy stoicism of people who have been at the front for 17 months'.[26] Whatever his private views about the way the war was being fought, nothing dented his belief in victory. He had written in December 1914: 'We *must* conquer. The victor is the one that *wants* victory most energetically.'[27] A year later, his view remained that the French could accept nothing less than 'the absolute and definite Victory of our forces; the peace must be dictated by us: we must harden our hearts and concentrate our energies to repel the multiple temptations that a cun-ning enemy is starting to offer us.'[28]

Throughout 1915, which started out with futile offensives and ended with demoralizing passivity, de Gaulle's letters, like those of many other soldiers, explode with furious indignation. There was the indignation of a right-wing soldier against the incompetence of the civilian parliamentarians: 'Parliament is becoming more and more odious and stupid . . . We will be victorious once we have swept away this rabble [*racaille*].'[29] There was the indignation of the reader of Barrès, fixated on 'our natural frontier on the Rhine', railing against diversionary operations taking place in Salonika in Greece and the Dardanelles in Turkey to break the stalemate in the west.[30] Once the Dar-danelles operation had clearly failed, de Gaulle continued to rail against the 'absurd government's . . . lamentable expedition' to Salonika.[31]

> Today, so as not to admit that they are donkeys, they leave in Salonika 20,000 fine troops and millions of shells that I continue to believe serve no purpose at all and will not kill a single German . . . As no valid strategic reason can be found to throw so many men and so many shells down the drain, they try to console themselves by saying that at least this will cause the enemy some problems!!! I do not believe a word of it!

Finally, there was the indignation of the ardent Catholic shocked by the Pope's refusal to take sides in the conflict despite Germany's alliance with the Ottoman Turks:

> How is it that the Pope can favour the infidel to the detriment of the Cru-saders: or at least hesitate between them? I readily admit that the motives which send our troops to Constantinople are hardly Christian ones; but there is no doubt that our success will be above all a Christian success, and that

the destruction of the Turkish Empire will be a terrible blow to Islam . . . The repercussions will be immense . . . above all in Africa where the doctrine of Mohammed is spreading with frightening rapidity, preventing the success of our missionaries . . . and also the progress of our Civilization.[32]

On 14 February 1916, de Gaulle reported to his mother that his unit was being sent for a few days' rest – much needed relief because his men were 'a little dazed [*un peu abrutis*] by a very prolonged period in the trenches'.[33] This respite was short. One week later the German armies unleashed their offensive at Verdun, and de Gaulle was back at the front for the last time.

The city of Verdun formed a potentially vulnerable salient jutting out into the German lines. Situated on the River Meuse, Verdun, surrounded by a complex system of forts, had long played a crucial strategic defensive role on France's eastern frontier. The German commander Erich von Falkenhayn later claimed that, by forcing the French to defend this symbolically important site, he had set out to bleed the French army to the point of exhaustion. Since there is no contemporary evidence for this claim it might have been a *post hoc* argument. Although the defence of Verdun did test the French armies almost to breaking point, the toll it took on the Germans was hardly less terrible.

On 21 February, the German artillery unleashed against Verdun the most intensive bombardment in the history of warfare so far. Two days later the German infantry attacked, and after three days they had taken the key fort of Douaumont. The French were thrown into panic. De Gaulle's former regimental commander Pétain, now a general, was hastily called in to save the situation. On 25 February, de Gaulle's regiment arrived in the Verdun sector. On 1 March, it was sent to relieve another regiment stationed in the village of Douaumont to the west of the fort, and still in French hands. The apocalyptic intensity of the artillery bombardments meant that units could not be kept in the front line for more than a few days. De Gaulle was sent to reconnoitre the position into which his regiment was being sent. He identified a vulnerable gap between the position earmarked for his regiment and the regiment to its right. Despite this warning, the 33RI was ordered to move forward on the night of 1 March.

At dawn, as the 33RI was settling into its trenches, the Germans attacked from the fort of Douaumont. In front of de Gaulle's company there was a sharp incline which made it difficult to see the enemy opposite. But the Germans also appeared from the side, exploiting the gap de Gaulle had identified. By the end of the day, his company had been almost entirely wiped out. He was believed to have been killed, and Pétain signed a posthumous citation commending him for bravery in the field. A few days later, it became known that he had been taken prisoner. After his return from captivity in 1918, de Gaulle wrote a detailed letter to the colonel of his regiment to explain what had happened. His letter was both matter-of-fact and slightly defensive.

The day had started with an intense artillery bombardment:

> I do not need to describe to you, Colonel, the moral and material effects of this bombardment that you experienced just as we did. In truth the losses it caused us were much less than we believed when in the middle of the hurricane. But each person, unable to move or get the slightest piece of information, has the same feeling: 'It is not possible that anyone else can be left alive except me.'

The moment this demoralizing bombardment abated, it was followed by an assault by grenade-throwing German troops, some of them emerging through the gap on the right: 'There followed a confused and brief combat, in the trench itself, between the *Boches* [Huns] coming from all three sides, with our men stunned by the bombardment, by the assailants who were surrounding them, and by the fact that often their rifles did not work because they were jammed with earth.'

Fearing that his company would soon be wiped out entirely, de Gaulle decided to move down his trench with the few survivors in order to make contact with another company on their right:

> I set off crawling along the trench with my orderly [*fourrier*] and two or three other soldiers. But I had barely gone ten metres when, down a trench perpendicular to mine, I caught sight of some *Boches* crouched down to avoid bullets. They spotted me at the same moment. One of them gave me bayonet thrust that went through my map-case and wounded me in the thigh. Another killed my *fourrier* at point-blank range. Seconds later a grenade exploded literally under my nose, and I lost consciousness.[34]

It was rare to receive a bayonet wound: de Gaulle had clearly been involved in close combat before succumbing.[35] It is also astonishing that he survived the explosion. On 6 March, after less than a week in the hell of Verdun, the 33RI was relieved. One thousand men were out of action, 336 of them dead or missing. The fort of Douaumont was finally retaken by the French in October. By this time de Gaulle had been festering in a prisoner-of-war camp for six months. His active war was over.

Like many former combatants, de Gaulle rarely dwelt on his experience of the front. On one occasion in 1945 he confided to his niece Geneviève de Gaulle, after she had described to him her life in the concentration camp of Ravensbrück. He listened attentively to what she told him, and then remarked of his own experience: 'It crushed [laminé] the soul.'[36] A year after his capture, he reflected on the difference between the war he had expected and the war he had found himself fighting: 'That was not how we once imagined battle, and armies have now become a monstrous mechanism so crushing that there are many who refuse to invest war with the sombre beauty that we used to do.'[37] No pacifist could have excoriated the offensives of 1915 more than de Gaulle when he came to meditate, as a prisoner, on the experience he had lived through eighteen months earlier: 'Imagine what went through the mind of those battalions as they set off to this scaffold, seeing before they left the trenches, their comrades lying on the ground in front of the enemy's intact barbed wire.'[38]

Phrases such as 'that is not how I had imagined it' recur in many other testimonies.[39] A certain innocent vision of heroism had died in the mud and blood of the battles of 1915. The experience did not of course make de Gaulle a pacifist. But much of his inter-war writing is about finding a way to reinvest the soldier's vocation with 'sombre beauty' in a world where industrialized mass warfare seemed to have eliminated any place for heroism and individuality.

PRISONER OF WAR

During his thirty-two months as a prisoner of war, de Gaulle was incarcerated in six different camps.[40] But he spent most time in a fortress near Ingolstadt in Bavaria. This was Fort IX, a high-security prison for recidivist escapees. De Gaulle was interned here from September 1916 to July 1917, and again from December 1917 to May 1918. Since Fort IX concentrated together in one place those most determined to escape, it became notorious as a kind of 'escape academy'. One British prisoner wrote a book on the camp entitled *The Escaping Club*. For this reason the Germans eventually closed it down, and de Gaulle spent the last five months of his imprisonment in the Bavarian camp of Wülzburg.

The main challenge for those wanting to escape was not so much to find a way of slipping out of the camp as to remain undetected until they could reach the safety of the frontier. De Gaulle's first escape attempt took place in November 1916 soon after his arrival at Fort IX. By swallowing picric acid, which gave the symptoms of acute hepatitis, he got himself transferred to the sanatorium, less secure than the main prison. Having managed to escape, he covered 125 kilometres before being apprehended. He was still only halfway to the Swiss border. De Gaulle escaped four other times, but never managed to remain at large for longer than ten days before being discovered. He was not someone who passed easily unnoticed.

Escape attempts were severely punished by a period of solitary confinement. Otherwise the material conditions for officers in prison were not bad. They lived in rooms shared with five others; they received food parcels from home; and they could exercise and play sports. De Gaulle's letters home give little anecdotal information about his life in the camp. Indeed one senses a certain exasperation when his mother tried to prise out details of his daily routine, as if dwelling on such matters was a first step towards accepting one's fate. De Gaulle wrote in March 1917: 'Yet again, I say do not worry in any way about my health which is very good. Anyway, my present fate is of no interest since I am good for nothing.'[41] A month later his exasperation is palpable: 'You never stop asking me for news. Once and for all, I tell you the news is excellent.'[42]

Occasionally de Gaulle succumbed to his mother's pressure: 'You ask me often if I can take a walk. Yes, two hours a day at least inside the fort. The greatest comfort in our situation is the excellent comradeship that rules between us and prevents us from ever feeling morally alone.'[43] This piously bland comment does not reveal much. Most of de Gaulle's fellow inmates in fact remembered him as distant and formal. Officers usually addressed each other as '*tu*' but not de Gaulle. In the Wülzburg camp where conditions were quite basic, one fellow prisoner remembered: 'I got to know the anatomy of all my companions from the most senior ... down to the chaplain, Abbé Michel. All but one: de Gaulle. At what time did he choose to go and wash himself alone? I never thought about it, but the fact is there: I never saw de Gaulle naked.'[44] This may have been the fastidious reserve of a physically awkward and shy young man; it may also have been a kind of self-imposed discipline of the will. In the notebook he kept in prison, de Gaulle sketched what reads like both a self-portrait and a portrait of the leader he was aspiring to be:

> One must become a man of character. The best way to succeed in action is to know how to dominate oneself perpetually ... Dominating oneself ought to become a sort of habit, a moral reflex acquired by a constant gymnastic of the will especially in the tiniest things: dress, conversation, the way one thinks ... One must speak little ... The advantage of being a brilliant conversationalist is not worth anything compared to the capacity to retreat into oneself ... For a man of worth, reflection needs to be concentrated ... In action one must say nothing. The leader is he who does not speak.[45]

These are strange words for a man of twenty-six. In fact many prisoners remembered de Gaulle not as silent but as constantly talking – speculating about the course of the war, analysing the international situation, ruminating on history. But it was in his letters to his mother that de Gaulle confided his intimate feelings even if he ignored her questions about the details of his existence. Endlessly he returned to the 'inexpressible sadness' caused by the humiliation of being a prisoner.[46] After his third abortive escape attempt he wrote: 'At this moment I am gripped by a grief so bitter and so deep that I do not think I will ever again experience anything like it, and it will end only when my life ends.'[47] He tried to refuse his mother's pressing requests to send a photograph since he wished no one to see him as a prisoner. His mother, whose patriotism was no less fierce than her son's, understood his feelings:

> Here the house is empty, the hearth deserted . . . I think of you day and night; of all my children you are the one who has the greatest place in my prayers because you are suffering much the most. When will that blessed moment arrive when we meet again! Let it come soon. But the designs of God are impenetrable. It is true that for Him who sees everything from all his eternity, the few years a man passes on this earth count for little.[48]

De Gaulle's 'odious exile' left him with much time on his hands. Life in the camps may not have been harsh but it was monotonous. He spent hours hunched over German newspapers, pencil in hand, trying to work out through the fog of propaganda what was really happening in the war. He produced his own handwritten communiqués summarizing recent events as he interpreted them, and pinned them up on the wall.[49] He also spent hours reading whatever he could find in the prison library, mostly history and novels. One day, he can be found reading an article about Wagner, on another an article about Rodin (which led him to scribble some reflections on how Bergson's philosophy might help understand developments in the history of art). He noted down aphorisms by philosophers and moralists (Heraclitus, Chamfort, Tocqueville and so on) and made notes on the history of Ancient Greece. His most extensive notes are on the book *Germany and the Coming War* published by the German military writer Friedrich von Bernhardi in 1911.

De Gaulle comes down to us at this time as an earnest and well-read but also rather conventional and priggish young man. On Zola's novel *Pot-Bouille* he comments sententiously: 'this man really has the genius of the dung heap [*le génie de l'ordure*]' (the Zola who was hero of the Dreyfus Affair does not excite his imagination). Writing of Stendhal's *Rouge et le noir* he remarks: 'young seminarist aged between seventeen and twenty-two who spends all his time analysing himself'. Of Flaubert's *Education sentimentale* he notes that it shows us the republicans of 1848 as 'discontented failures of all kinds'. As for his ideas on Germany, de Gaulle told his mother that in the camp he had encountered some Germans 'who have the audacity to come and talk to us from time to time of an alliance between their race and ours after the war!!! There is no answer to this except a simple shrugging of the shoulders.'[50] But the enforced leisure of imprisonment certainly allowed him much time to think, and there are signs of a more thoughtful personality beginning to emerge. We can see this from a series of lectures he gave to his fellow officers probably at the start of 1917.

Organizing lectures and entertainments was one of the main distractions that officers arranged in the camps. De Gaulle's lectures were a kind of instant history of the war drawn from his own experience and whatever German newspapers he could lay his hands on. It was in these lectures that he delivered the scathing verdicts on the errors of the French high command which have already been quoted. For him the root of the problem was the failure to take account of contingency and to escape from *a priori* assumptions about the nature of warfare. This idea owed much to his own experiences of the murderous consequences of the offensives of 1915 but also to his reading of Bergson and Boutroux. His prison notebooks contain a quotation from Boutroux: 'Contingency is the characteristic of what might not have been or could have been different.'[51] This led the young lecturer to reflect on the qualities required for successful military leaders: 'Minds capable of synthesizing, that is to say the ability to generalize, capable of distinguishing the essential from what is accessory.' De Gaulle saw himself as being in that category, remarking in a letter to his mother of his own 'mania for generalization'.[52]

The quality of generalization was in evidence when de Gaulle moved from purely military questions to develop a more holistic analysis of the war, discussing economic planning, diplomacy and politics. He divided the history of the war so far into three periods. In the first, from August 1914 to the middle of 1915, parliamentary government had been suspended and General Joffre exercised a kind of *de facto* dictatorship. De Gaulle argued that this situation, acceptable in the first stages of what was initially expected to be a short war, had rapidly revealed its shortcomings. It was an obstacle to effective coordination between the Allies and to the rational organization of a war economy. In the second period, running from the middle of 1915 to the middle of 1916, parliament had begun to reassert its authority and exercise an 'extremely salutary' degree of surveillance and control which 'prevented a lot of errors'. In the third period, starting in mid-1916, parliament's interference had started to become counter-productive when ministers of war were obliged to waste time defending themselves before parliamentary commissions. But de Gaulle had no doubt that parliament had a role to play: 'To suppress parliamentary life is impossible for a war of such long duration which affects so profoundly the present and future of the country. One cannot allow any government to engage the future of its people without being authorized and monitored.' This measured judgement contrasts with his earlier eruptions of fury against the 'rabble' of politicians.

De Gaulle's lectures offered an analysis of those periods in French history when in his view the relationship between government and army had functioned well. He had particular praise for the organization of the revolutionary armies in 1793 by Lazare Carnot and the Committee of Public Safety; and he commended the efforts of the nineteenth-century republican leaders Léon Gambetta and Charles de Freycinet who had tried to retrieve France's situation after the defeat of 1870. Such personalities are not likely to have been much admired by his family, but de Gaulle seems in this case to have distanced himself from some of the attitudes inherited from his upbringing. While a prisoner, he read Freycinet's memoirs and commented: 'Written by a man many of whose ideas are not my own, but a man whose intellectual distinction and political sense are incontestable.'[53] Similarly when he came to discuss the offensives in Salonika and on the eastern front, de Gaulle, so scathing in 1915 about any distraction from the western front, was prepared to take a broader view: 'One might approve or not approve these measures even if one can recognize that the government had sought to act and was acting.' Selecting the theatre of operations was exactly what governments, with a full knowledge of all the factors in play, should be doing even if 'without being in the secrets of the Gods one might suspect the hostility more or less avowed of our General Staff for the dispersion of efforts'.[54] The one historical exception to de Gaulle's rule about finding the need for an equilibrium between civil and military authority was Napoleon, who had united both in his person. But for de Gaulle Napoleon was the exception that proved the rule:

> The results he obtained were due to his personal Genius and not the organization he synthesized: geniuses of his stature are met only once in 10 centuries. And anyway, is it so clear that, precisely because he did everything himself, France did not lose out overall? . . . He left France smaller than he had found her.[55]

De Gaulle spent much of his life meditating on the example of Napoleon, and his admiration was always hedged by qualifications of this kind.

The ideas which de Gaulle sketched out in these lectures – the nature of leadership, the importance of contingency in war and in politics, the relationship between civil and military power – were developed at greater length in the four books he wrote in the inter-war years. In that sense, de Gaulle's period in prison was extraordinarily important in his intellectual formation. But nothing blunted his obsession with the imperative to escape so that he could return to the fighting. He escaped for the last time in July 1918 by hiding in a laundry basket. After only three days at large he was picked up by the police. In the spring of 1918, a new possibility for release had presented itself when the German and French governments had, through the Swiss government, signed an agreement for a prisoner-of-war exchange. But this was open only to soldiers who promised in return that they would not rejoin the battle. De Gaulle would not accept this condition because he was sure that the war would continue for many more years: 'The prospect of remaining in Switzerland impotent while my brothers and comrades are fighting for victory is odious to me if there is no possibility of returning to the front. And that of returning to France to hide out in some office position totally disgusts me.'[56] Better to remain a prisoner longer and hope that escape might one day succeed.

But de Gaulle's confidence in August 1918 that the war would last 'literally years longer'[57] was proved unfounded. At the start of October, the German Commanders in Chief, Hindenburg and Ludendorff, informed their government that an armistice was inevitable. While being transported back to Wülzburg from a prison where he had been sent as a punishment for insulting a German officer after his most recent escape attempt, de Gaulle witnessed scenes that showed him German morale was crumbling. He wrote to his mother: 'Despite the circumstances which caused this journey I am not unhappy to have made it. Travelling allows a prisoner to see and judge things.'[58] He gave some idea of what he had glimpsed in a short book on the German defeat that he wrote after the war:

> In many places, the population was preventing soldiers leaving for the front. Deserters roamed the streets of big cities, making no attempt to hide themselves and mocking the authorities with impunity ... Large numbers of prisoners of war, no longer under guard, prowled the countryside to try their luck or even went to the cities where they added to the confusion.[59]

De Gaulle's exact movements between his release from the camp and his return to France at the start of December are not known.[60] What we do know is that on 28 November he was at Romanshorn in Switzerland where he was put in a third-class railway carriage on a train to Geneva. Considering that this was beneath his dignity as an officer, he borrowed the sum necessary to upgrade to second class from one of his travelling companions, a Lieutenant Digier. On 1 December Digier was sent a card: 'From the soil of France, in memory and with thanks'. De Gaulle was home.[61]

Two days later he was back with his family in the Dordogne. Three of his cousins had died in the war, including Henri de Corbie, with whom as an adolescent he had swapped poems, but remarkably all four de Gaulle brothers survived. In a photograph of the brothers with their parents in December 1918, de Gaulle stands back slightly as if his two and half years of captivity made him reluctant to push himself forward.[62] Such a reaction was common. Many returning prisoners were greeted with suspicion, and had to fight to get the same recognition as other veterans. It was not until 1922 that those who had died in prison camps were accorded the title of 'dead for France'. In 1927, the government reluctantly agreed to create a medal to reward those prisoners who had fulfilled their duty by trying to escape. To be eligible for this medal extensive documentation had to be provided, and only 16,000 out of a total of 500,000 prisoners were awarded it. De Gaulle was among the recipients.[63] We know all the details of his escape attempts (subsequently corroborated by the German archives) because he had to prepare a detailed report accompanied by sketches and supporting witness statements.[64]

De Gaulle remained in contact with some of his former fellow prisoners. One of them, Rémy Roure, a journalist and future resister, wrote a review of de Gaulle's first book in 1924; another fellow prisoner, the future General Catroux, would join de Gaulle in London in 1940. For the most part, however, de Gaulle's prison experience was not one about which he liked to reminisce. After France's defeat in 1940, huge numbers of prisoners were taken by the Germans. Their heroic suffering was a theme much used by the Vichy regime. Some escaped prisoners formed their own resistance movement, inviting from de Gaulle the dismissive comment: 'A resistance movement of prisoners? Why not a resistance movement of hairdressers?' This caustic *boutade* was typical of his humour, but nothing could have been more alien to him than to claim the experience of being a prisoner of war as a badge of identity. For him, therefore, November 1918 was a bitter-sweet moment. As he wrote to the Colonel of his regiment on returning to France:

> The great joy I share with you is mixed for me, more bitter than ever, with the indescribable regret at not having played a greater role. I think that for the rest of my life – whether it be long or short – that regret will not leave me. Let it at least serve as a spur to think and act better, and to try through many hours of obscure service to compensate for those few decisive and triumphant hours that I will not myself have lived.[65]

3

Rebuilding a Career, 1919–1932

RECOVERING CONFIDENCE

When de Gaulle became famous, his aides would despair at what they called his 'cyclothymic' temperament: his volatile and unpredictable mood swings, his sudden descent into the blackest pessimism. Like Churchill's 'black dog', these moments of despair became incorporated into his myth: the man of destiny surmounting the temptation to give up, bouncing back from adversity to save his country.

The 'cyclothymic' de Gaulle is already in evidence at the end of the war. In September 1918, he wrote to his mother:

> I am one of the living dead. Reading the other day in a newspaper the term 'ghosts' applied to prisoners returned to France, I thought the description horribly apt. You offer to send me books! . . . To work for what? To work one must have an aim. What aim can I have? My career? But if I cannot return to fight before the end of the war, will I stay in the army? And what mediocre future would await me? . . . For officers of my age with some ambition to have a career, the first, the indispensable condition, is to have been in the campaign . . . From the military point of view, I have no illusions, I too am just a ghost.[1]

Four months after penning this despairing letter, de Gaulle was back in France at the infantry school of Saint-Maxient on a refresher course for officers returned from captivity. Rapidly his spirits improved – 'from the point of view of morale I am being reborn' – and he was encouraged to discover that he was less out of touch than he had feared.[2] He had little regard for his fellow officers at Saint-Maxient who seemed only too happy to settle into the routine of peacetime existence. De Gaulle was desperate for action to redeem his wasted years. The best prospect seemed to be the French military mission which was advising the army of the newly independent Polish state. Soon de Gaulle was plunged into despair again, fulminating against the 'ocean of stupidity, laziness and administrative insolence' blocking his efforts to get posted to Poland.[3] Finally he left France in April 1919 as one of 400 officers selected to instruct the officer corps of the new Polish army. Journeying east across a ravaged Europe, he reported to his mother with obvious satisfaction that 'the *Boches* – especially in Prussia – watched us with expressions which were filled with fury and hate, but they were careful not to say anything, so deep are the feelings of defeat and fear into which they have sunk.'[4] Under their 'sneaky servility' he detected 'the hidden resolution one day to seek revenge'.[5]

Arriving in Warsaw, de Gaulle was soon depressed again because there were delays before he could start teaching. His living quarters left much to be desired: 'Everything is very dilapidated and without furniture after the passage before us of the Russians, the *Boches* and the Jews.'[6] He was also pessimistic about his chances of receiving the Legion of Honour in recognition of his service at Verdun. The department in charge of awarding decorations had enquired if his injuries were equivalent to the loss of a limb – to which he had had to reply in the negative. Nor did the signing of the Treaty of Versailles in May 1919 lighten his mood. Although France had recovered the territories of Alsace-Lorraine, lost in 1871, the more ambitious demands of French conservatives, such as detaching the Rhine-land from Germany and creating a buffer state on France's eastern border, had not been achieved. France got no more than the demilitarization of the Rhineland and its occupation by Allied troops for fifteen years. After the signing of the Treaty de Gaulle wrote to his mother: 'Over the course of the years Germany, once she recovers, will become more arrogant, and in the end will not pay us much of what she owes us. One can fear also that our allies will in no time become our rivals and become indifferent to our fate. The left bank of the Rhine must remain with us.'[7] While he kicked his heels in Warsaw before his teaching began, de Gaulle encountered representatives of other nations who had been France's allies in the war and he did not like what he saw:

> While 1,500 French officers prepare to fight with the Polish troops, Americans, British and Italians come running to Warsaw to display their insolence and uselessness. They are part of vague commissions, the main task of which, although not admitted, is to make all kinds of business deals ... Like most of my compatriots, I finish the war overflowing with a general feeling of xenophobia.[8]

Two months later, de Gaulle's mood lifted again. He had started his job and heard also that despite his pessimism he had been awarded the Legion of Honour. After teaching for a few weeks at the officer school of Rembertów near Warsaw, he wrote home: 'At last I am bit by bit getting back to being the kind of person I feel myself to have been before that abominable captivity. I have regained confidence in myself and in my future.'[9] De Gaulle clearly took to lecturing as he had already done in the prisoner-of-war camp. His Polish interpreter testified many years later to the impact of one of de Gaulle's lectures entitled 'Defeat: a question of morale'. The only lecture which survives was his survey of the history of Poland over six centuries delivered to his fellow officers on the French Military Mission. It was a *tour de force* of historical synthesis as well as a warning about why a Polish alliance mattered to France: 'Poland perished in the eighteenth century for lack of necessary allies and the lack of a clear vision by France, of the extreme importance of a strong Poland to balance on her eastern frontiers the Teutonism [*germanisme*] threatening through the ages the old land of the Gauls.'[10]

We know little more about de Gaulle's time in Poland. His interpreter later recalled that he kept aloof from the other French officers and did not join their social outings in Warsaw: 'They found it hard to understand why he never came to their mess, never joked, speaking little and ruminating on thoughts one could only guess at.'[11] By the end of the year, he was ready to return to France. As he put it in a letter to his mother: '[Poland] has done what I intended it to do: allowing me to recover myself militarily . . . After that I will start working on my own account.'[12] He now sought a less demanding position in France to allow him to prepare for the examinations for entry to the Ecole de Guerre, the training academy for senior officers. Any doubts about continuing a military career had been overcome.

Once back in France, de Gaulle landed a stopgap bureaucratic job which proved too boring for his restless temperament. A month later he was back in Poland where events had become more exciting. The country now found itself fighting a full-scale war with Russia. Conflict between the two countries had been simmering for eighteen months while the government of the newly independent Poland, taking advantage of the revolutionary turmoil in Russia, tried to push its frontiers eastwards. In April 1920, the Polish General Józef Piłsudski launched a successful offensive into Ukraine, taking Kiev. But once the Soviet Red Army had finally crushed the internal opponents of the Revolution, it launched a counter-offensive against Poland in July. As the Soviets advanced unstoppably towards Warsaw, the British and French governments sent missions to mediate between the two sides.

Since the Allied missions were technically neutral, de Gaulle found himself reduced to being an impotent bystander: 'We follow the decisive events with passionate interest, our hearts eaten up by the fact we cannot take a direct role . . . I cannot stop thinking about those brave officers who had

attended our lectures at the Rembertów Infantry School, many of whom
have already perished.'[13] On 15 July, as the situation of the Polish armies
became desperate, the French government, more pro-Polish than the British, authorized its military representatives to take a more active role and
offer technical advice to the Polish army. De Gaulle was attached to the
General Staff of the southern Polish army. He witnessed at first hand the
extraordinary reversal of events – the so-called Miracle of the Vistula –
when a bold Polish counter-offensive stemmed the Soviet attack. This plan
was conceived by Piłsudski initially against the advice of General Maxime
Weygand, the head of the French mission (who was later given credit for
the plan). By the end of August, the Red Army was retreating eastwards
as fast as it had advanced westwards a few months earlier. Warsaw was
saved, and the war ended the following year.

By the time de Gaulle left Poland definitively at the end of 1920, he had
served there almost as long as the entire period he had spent fighting on
the western front. What did he take from his Polish experience? On departure, in a report on the Polish army for his superiors, he was scathing about
its lack of organization, its refusal to listen more to the French, and the
disruptions caused by Piłsudski's intervention in military operations.[14] He
was one of those who believed the myth that Weygand had saved the situation.[15] In private he was even more dismissive of the Poles than in his
report: 'Poland is a country very badly governed, not properly administered, with no taste for work . . . It will be hard for us to get anything out
of it.'[16] In Poland, he had witnessed a battle of rapid movement completely
different from the stalemate of the western front. Some writers have speculated that this experience was the seed of de Gaulle's subsequent thinking
about how tanks might be used to reintroduce movement into warfare.
His final report did contain two sentences to the effect that tanks should
be grouped together and 'not dispersed', but he went on to say that they
were there to 'support the infantry and nothing else' – an entirely orthodox
position. On the few subsequent occasions de Gaulle referred to his experience in Poland he never suggested it had influenced his thinking about
tanks. Looking back forty-seven years later, he remembered the Russo-
Polish conflict as a strange battle from which no lesson could be drawn:

> There were bands roaming back and forth, as if they had received no
> orders . . . There was no real front. Those of us who were used to orders
> rigorously transmitted and executed were unable to get used to this. Nor
> were we able to teach method and organization to officers who were going
> into combat. They knew strictly nothing. Luckily for them the Bolsheviks
> knew no more.[17]

What most impressed de Gaulle during his second posting in Poland was the importance of morale and self-belief in warfare confirming views he had already formed about Germany's collapse. On his return to Poland in July 1920, when all seemed lost, he noted: 'What is most worrying is not so much the retreat of the Polish troops as the disarray of public opinion. The politicians, instead of agreeing to support a government, any government, until the end of the crisis, only increase their divisions and intrigues.'[18] In his view, the reversal of the situation a month later was due less to Piłsudski's military skill than to an upsurge of patriotic enthusiasm. The lesson he drew from Poland's victory was that a country is defeated only when it has lost the will to fight – a lesson which influenced his view of France's plight in 1940.

SETTLING DOWN

De Gaulle was keen to return to France at the end of 1920 not only to prepare for his examination for the Ecole de Guerre but because he had recently become engaged. Marriage is a recurring theme of de Gaulle's correspondence with his mother during his first stint in Poland. His elder brother Xavier had married in September 1919, and de Gaulle's mother was pressing him to do the same. He needed no persuading: 'When I have finished the year I have vowed to spend in Poland ... there is nothing that I want more.'[19]

We have a rare and tantalizing glimpse into the social life of the austerely intellectual young officer before the war. When visited at his house in Colombey in January 1947 by two grand ladies – Baronne d'Astier de la Vigerie and the Vicomtesse Salignac-Fénelon (née Viellard) – he joked afterwards to his aide Claude Guy that his heart had beaten faster because 'I met them many times in my youth at balls. Seeing them again I thought to myself: "there are my *danseuses*." '[20] But of his emotional life before marriage, or any sexual adventures normal for a young man of his class and generation, there is no evidence. Scribbled in one of his prison notebooks we find an aphorism: 'Since we consider that at bottom love is more bitter than sweet, let us not ever make it the principal object of our preoccupations but only a seasoning to life.'[21] Were these words based on experience or were they merely a posture of world-weary cynicism? In the short story he wrote while recuperating from his injury at the bridge of Dinant, de Gaulle talks of his hero Langel having 'savoured all the sensual and intellectual delights of love'. Had these also been savoured by Langel's alter ego Charles de Gaulle? We do not know. To one biographer who asked whether the difference in rank between a lieutenant and a colonel meant that he had hardly known Pétain while serving under him in 1913, de Gaulle replied: 'Not at all! At that time I was very keen on women, and so was Pétain; that brought us together!'[22] On another occasion he remarked:

> Pétain liked women as one likes women when one is in one's fifties and I despised them as one despises them when one is twenty. That is to say that we talked about them the whole time. Each week we went to Paris and did the journey together on the train. In short, in Paris, we would from time to time 'bump into each other'.[23]

There have been rumours of a liaison between de Gaulle and a countess in Poland, but since he hardly participated in the social life of Warsaw this seems implausible. Most intriguing is a letter he wrote in London in 1942 to a Frenchman who had asked him to protest against the British bombing of France. De Gaulle sympathized but said that this had to be accepted in the wider interest of liberating France as in the previous war: 'I can even tell you in confidence that this was the cause of one of the greatest personal sorrows of my life because a young girl, who was almost my fiancée, was killed in this way by a British shell in 1917.'[24] Is this 'fiancée' the 'M-L' to whom he refers in a short postcard to his mother in 1917 containing the mysterious words 'are three years not enough to reassure you?' – presumably a reference to some kind of liaison?[25]

That is all we can surmise about de Gaulle's emotional and sexual life before his marriage. It was normal in de Gaulle's milieu for marriages to be closely vetted – if not indeed arranged – by the family. With professional officers there was the further constraint that the spouse had to be approved by the army after a formal inquiry to confirm her moral suitability.[26] De Gaulle's mother had first proposed a Lille cousin, Thérèse Kolb. De Gaulle's response was evasive: 'A while ago she made a strong impression on me. But I have not seen her for years, and I cannot believe that she has anything but the vaguest impression of my modest personage.'[27] His mother wrote to say that she had another idea and de Gaulle assured her that for the moment he had no one else in mind. Once back on leave he was ready 'to see and be seen, judge and be judged. Until then I have no objection in principle to anything nor to anyone.'[28]

Events moved fast. Once de Gaulle was back in Paris on leave, a meeting was arranged with the candidate his mother had had in mind, a young woman known to friends of the de Gaulle family. This was Yvonne Vendroux from a family of prosperous Calais industrialists. Her father owned a biscuit factory and was a figure of standing in the city where he headed the local chamber of commerce. The Vendrouxs did not have the same austere and intellectual high-mindedness as the de Gaulles. Their children had been brought up in a less straitlaced atmosphere, and in greater opulence. But both families shared similar Catholic and conservative values. Yvonne had received the education expected of a well-brought-up bourgeois Catholic girl: not too much learning but sufficient accomplishments to run a household and be a social adornment to her husband. Philippe de Gaulle, their eldest son, later wrote of his mother: 'She played the piano, an absolutely necessary skill, in a mechanical way . . . but with no melody. She knew how to appreciate a piece of furniture or a picture and . . . would never be caught out with an error of taste.'[29] De Gaulle, with no interest in painting himself, was quickly able to witness this for himself. Conversation at the first meeting had turned to a much talked-about painting at the Salon d'Automne by the fashionable painter Van Dongen. It was agreed the pair would meet again for a trip to see the painting, chaperoned of course by Yvonne's parents. A few days later de Gaulle invited Yvonne and her brother to the forthcoming Saint-Cyr ball, and the invitation was accepted. This was an absolutely conventional courtship – except in its rapidity. De Gaulle had returned from leave on 20 October 1920; by 11 November the couple were engaged.

This precipitateness was caused by the fact that de Gaulle was due to return to Poland at the end of the month. He was back for good in February of the following year, and he married Yvonne two months later. Their civil marriage took place in Calais on 6 April 1921, but in this profoundly Catholic milieu it was the religious ceremony on the next day at the Church of Notre Dame that counted. The banquet that followed was concluded by an interminable speech from the Mayor of Calais – a sign of the esteem in which the Vendroux family was held in the city – after which the couple set off for their honeymoon on the Italian lakes. On their return to Paris they moved into an apartment in the Rue de Grenelle in the seventh *arrondissement*. This was a modest dwelling with only three rooms, and a *chambre de bonne* for the maid. The clattering of the *métro aérien* could be heard just outside the window and its passengers were able to see into the small study where de Gaulle often worked at night. But at least he was living in that 'noble' quarter of Paris where he felt at home.[30]

Although Yvonne de Gaulle later acquired a reputation for being a dour, shy and prudish woman, she was at this stage of her life vivacious and outgoing.[31] She and her husband gradually developed close bonds of love and companionship. From the beginning they were united by social compatibility and the reassurance that they understood each other's worlds. The families had overlapping circles of acquaintance among the Catholic bourgeoisie of northern France. Yvonne was delighted to report to her brother: 'Can you imagine it, he spent many family holidays at Wimereux . . .

and happy coincidence he often went to the Chateau of Fouquetone where he met our family friends the Legrands!'[32] In marrying into a family of Catholic industrialists from the north-east of France, de Gaulle was repeating the pattern of his own father. The Vendrouxs were richer than the genteelly impoverished de Gaulles. De Gaulle is said to have told one friend: 'I am marrying into Vendroux biscuits.' In addition to a large family house in Calais, they owned the imposing Château de Sept-Fontaines in the Ardennes. But de Gaulle was also in his way a promising catch. Despite the two years of captivity which had held back his advancement, he had excellent prospects. He had been decorated for his bravery at Verdun and was expected soon to enter the Ecole de Guerre where France's officer elite was trained.

BUILDING A REPUTATION

In February 1921, de Gaulle secured a post lecturing on military history at Saint-Cyr while preparing the entry examinations for the Ecole de Guerre. Having settled down domestically, he set about building a reputation as a writer and military thinker. The first fruit of this was the book *Discorde chez l'ennemi* (*The Enemy's House Divided*) published in March 1924.[33] Of the four books de Gaulle wrote in the inter-war years, this is the least well known, but far from the least interesting. One originality of the book was its subject. Many historical studies of the origins of the war were appearing at this time. Depending on the politics of the author, these books were written to ascribe responsibility for the outbreak of the war to either the French or the Germans. De Gaulle's book addressed a different question: not *who* caused the war but *why* did Germany lose it? The anti-German barbs that peppered his private correspondence were replaced by a respect for the 'valiant enemy'. His preface contrasts the Nietzschean spirit of the Germans – 'a passion to expand their personal power at any cost . . . contempt for the limits marked out by human experience, common sense and the law' – with the French 'sense of balance, of what is possible, of moderation [*mesure*] which alone renders the works of energy durable and fecund'. This led de Gaulle to a celebration of the 'noble melancholy' and 'magnificent harmony' of the classical French garden 'where no tree seeks to stifle the others by overshadowing them and where the plants accommodate themselves to being symmetrically arranged'.[34]

The book's five chapters were framed around an analysis of five turning points in the history of the war. De Gaulle's main source was his intensive study of all the memoirs so far published by Germany's military leaders.

Eschewing superfluous anecdote, he uses each episode to illustrate general principles about leadership, politics and warfare. The 'mania for generalization' he had once mentioned to his mother is visible throughout. Three key themes run through the book. The first is that Germany lost the war because she had not achieved the correct balance between civil and military power. According to de Gaulle, the rot set in when the German government, bowing to pressure from Admiral Tirpitz, took the decision to pursue unrestricted submarine warfare. For de Gaulle, this was a key turning point because it ultimately caused the Americans to enter the war. The abdication of civilian authority culminated in 1917 when Generals Ludendorff and Hindenburg effectively seized total control over the conduct of the war from the civilian Chancellor Bethmann-Hollweg: 'Profiting from the weakness of their sovereign, and abusing their prestige, the military leaders had taken authority and credit from the government. Germany discovered with horror that the logical and necessary balance of the State had been destroyed.'[35]

De Gaulle's second argument is also familiar from his wartime lectures: 'In war – save for some essential principles – there is no universal system, but only circumstance and personalities.'[36] He illustrated this through a chapter on the reasons for the failure of the German offensive in 1914. The German army successfully followed in 1866 and 1870 the principle of allowing a large degree of autonomy to its subordinate commanders. The same general principle proved fatal in September 1914 when General von Kluck disobeyed his orders. Moving his army south across the Marne, he exposed the right flank of the German forces and made possible the successful French defence on the Marne.

De Gaulle's third argument, illustrated by a chapter on the sudden collapse of German resistance in 1918, centred around the importance of self-belief and morale in warfare. He was fascinated by the fact that, although the Germans still had massive military resources, their will to fight had suddenly snapped: 'At a blow, as if by the fatal strike of a magic wand, a sort of moral stupor annihilated the warlike qualities of the German people.'[37] Or as he wrote in a separate unpublished article on morale in warfare: 'German troops were still in enemy territory. [Germany's] factories remained intact and her fields fertile. However, she surrendered ... She refused to make further sacrifices, hoping to end her suffering.'[38]

By the time de Gaulle's book came out, he was a student at the Ecole de Guerre. This proved an unhappy year, the first setback in his strategy to rebuild his career. De Gaulle's cohort cannot have been easy to teach since they all had their own personal experience of warfare to measure against the certainties of their lecturers. One of de Gaulle's fellow students,

Georges Loustaunau-Lacau, with whom he became friendly until their political trajectories diverged in the 1930s, wrote in his memoirs that the students wanted to heckle their lecturers: 'What about the third dimension? What about surprise? What about speed? . . . They presented victories to us as if they were like a cake ready baked behind the lines . . . Listening to them one had the impression that the art of warfare had been frozen for ever.'[39] Loustaunau-Lacau's disaffection did not prevent him ending top in the year. What singled de Gaulle out was less the contempt he felt for his teachers than his refusal to disguise it. His particular *bête noire* (and it was reciprocal) was Colonel Moyrand, in charge of general tactics. In his term report on de Gaulle, Moyrand commented that he was 'intelligent, cultivated and serious; with brilliance and facility' but 'spoils incontestable qualities by his excessive self-assurance, his harshness towards other people's opinions and his attitude of a king in exile'. Another teacher wrote that 'he would get excellent results if he allowed himself with better grace to accept discussion.' All other comments were in the same vein.[40] Quite how bad de Gaulle's relations with his superiors must have been emerges in a letter he wrote to a fellow student at the end of the year. He apologized if his correspondent had encountered problems for being 'too associated with my person during that notorious episode of general tactics where one way of looking at things clashed with another way of looking at things, one solution clashed with another solution and, who knows, perhaps one destiny clashed with another destiny'.[41] This remarkable sense of self-belief from the thirty-four-year-old captain shows why de Gaulle's attitude must have seemed quite insufferable to his superiors. At the end de Gaulle emerged not in the top rank of '*très bien*' but the second tier of those marked '*bien*' (ranked 52 out of 129).

On graduating de Gaulle was posted to the General Staff of the Rhine Army in Mainz. He took his revenge on the Ecole by publishing in March 1925 an article in a military journal systematically refuting the dogmatism – what he called the '*a priori*' doctrine – of official teaching. This article was a rare occasion where he was able to praise Napoleon without qualification: 'There was never a single corpus of doctrine in the army of the First Empire. Seizing the circumstances, adapting to them, exploiting them, that was the basis of Napoleon's conduct.' But, so ran de Gaulle's argument, in the nineteenth century, and especially after 1870, French military thinking 'marched from abstraction to abstraction', elevating the principle of the offensive at all costs into a 'metaphysical principle' – with disastrous consequences in 1914. The moral he drew: 'In every form of action, military, political and industrial . . . the essential role of the leader is to appreciate the nature of the circumstance in each particular case. Action must be constructed on contingency.' In 1914–18, France's situation had been saved by 'minds especially endowed with a sense of realities'. This was a reference to Pétain, who had almost ruined his career before 1914 by his scepticism about the offensive doctrine. De Gaulle's article therefore neatly achieved the double objective of expressing his own ideas and paying homage to Pétain. It was no coincidence that in July 1925, five months after his article had appeared, de Gaulle was rescued from his routine existence in Mainz and seconded into Pétain's *cabinet* (private office).[42]

PÉTAIN'S PROTÉGÉ

When de Gaulle ruminated later on the career of Pétain, he would invari-ably comment that the Marshal was a great man who had 'died' in 1925. What makes this remark curious is that 1925 was the year de Gaulle started working directly for him. The two men remained in close contact until the end of the decade. For a 'dead' man, Pétain was to prove an effective pat-ron when de Gaulle needed one after his disappointment at the Ecole de Guerre. De Gaulle's comment about Pétain related to one specific episode. In 1925 the government had sent the Marshal to the protectorate of Morocco where the French had for several years been fighting a tribal uprising against their rule. Pétain's appointment was seen as a snub to the French Governor, the legendary Marshal Lyautey, who resigned in pro-test. De Gaulle believed, like many others, that by allowing himself to be used by politicians in their vendetta against Lyautey Pétain, who had little experience of North Africa, had not behaved honourably. He took it as a sign that Pétain was becoming a prisoner of his own legend.

There were two military legends in 1920s France: Pétain and Foch. Each represented a different approach to the war. Ferdinand Foch was the arch-exponent of the offensive and the believer in the importance of will as a key to victory; Pétain was known for his emphasis on the need for meticu-lous preparation. Pétain had become a national icon for his tenacious defence of Verdun in 1916 and for his role in stemming the mutinies which broke out in the army in 1917. Some believed that his caution bordered on defeatism, and in 1917 it was Foch who was appointed inter-Allied commander and directed the successful offensives of the summer of 1918. After 1918, the two men, who loathed each other, headed a competing system of patronage. To secure advancement, it helped to be in either the *maison* Foch or the *maison* Pétain. De Gaulle's voluntarist temperament might suggest a more obvious affinity with Foch, whom he did indeed admire. But as someone who had lived through the consequences of the reckless offensives of 1914–15, he was also aware of the salutary influence of Pétain in 1916–17. His view was that the qualities of both men were complementary: Pétain the cautious tactician, Foch the bold strategist.

If de Gaulle's article attacking *a priori* doctrine was pitched partly to attract Pétain's attention – the Marshal was the only First World War commander he singled out for praise – it also carried the implicit caveat that Pétain's lessons from the previous war must not become a general rule for the next. Presumably Pétain was more alive to the compliments than to the warning. As Colonel commanding the 33RI, he had known de Gaulle since 1913. But if Pétain chose to bring de Gaulle into his *cabinet* in 1925 it was above all because the younger man had revealed himself to be a stylish writer. With an eye on the Académie Française, Pétain was planning to write a history of the French army. Since he had no literary gifts, de Gaulle was an ideal candidate to act as his ghostwriter. Pétain's choice of de Gaulle was possibly also a snub to the Ecole de Guerre, whose teaching before 1914 had been diametrically opposed to his own views. It seems indeed that, if Pétain had not intervened, de Gaulle's marks on graduating from the Ecole would have been even worse than they were. Pétain also secured an invitation for de Gaulle to give three lectures at the Ecole in 1927. He turned this into a major occasion by attending the first lecture himself. This is a classic moment in most biographies of de Gaulle: the young nonconformist at the rostrum of the main lecture hall of the Ecole taking his revenge on the institution which had snubbed him. In fact it hardly seems likely that many of the pupils present had any knowledge of this past history, and a number of de Gaulle's former teachers had left. Only in the most coded and oblique way can de Gaulle's three highly abstract lectures on leadership be considered as an attack on the teaching of the Ecole. Whatever the truth, de Gaulle certainly wanted to read the events in this way. He wrote to his father: 'My partisans were jubilant, those who were neutral just smiled and the sharks who circled round the ship waiting for me to fall in the water kept a good distance.'[43]

The closeness of the relationship between de Gaulle and Pétain must not be exaggerated. It is a myth that de Gaulle named his eldest son Philippe after Pétain: the name Philippe was a reference to the family ancestor Jean-Baptiste Philippe de Gaulle. It is also a myth that Pétain was the godfather of Philippe de Gaulle. Philippe de Gaulle's godfather was his uncle Xavier. From time to time, the de Gaulles were invited to dinner by Pétain at the Grande Café in the Place de l'Opéra in the company of Pétain's wife, a divorcee whom he had finally married in 1920. Her divorce would in itself have precluded Pétain being the godfather to Philippe. Yvonne de Gaulle's disapproval of Pétain's irregular private life did not facilitate relations between the two couples. Pétain's wife, the *Maréchale*, commented cattily of Yvonne de Gaulle: 'She was as reluctant to come as I was to receive her. We had nothing to say to each other. The conversation dragged. She was an excellent woman, self-effacing and discreet. She liked to make jam.'[44]

While working for Pétain, de Gaulle also started to frequent the circle of Colonel Emile Mayer, forty years his senior.[45] Mayer was a nonconformist military thinker whose promising military career ended in 1898 when he became the target of right-wing attacks for publishing articles in defence of Dreyfus. Forced out of the army, he became a prolific writer on military affairs, expressing heterodox, original (and often prescient) ideas on the nature of the next war. He had helped the Socialist leader Jean Jaurès develop his military thinking in the 1900s. Through his son-in-law, a friend of the Socialist politician Léon Blum, Mayer was connected to a milieu of left-wing republican intellectuals and politicians. Every Sunday morning at his apartment in Paris he hosted a salon attended by an eclectic range of figures from the worlds of journalism, literature, publishing and politics. Mayer had noticed de Gaulle's article on '*a priori* doctrine'. He wrote to congratulate him on it, and de Gaulle gradually became a habitué of the Sunday gatherings. De Gaulle started sending his articles to Mayer before publication. They did not agree on everything, but the Mayer salon, where ideas were debated freely and openly, must have been a bracing contrast to the hushed reverence of Pétain's *cabinet*. The atmosphere of the Mayer circle is nicely conveyed by the lawyer and journalist Jean Auburtin who attended regularly: 'It was not quite a political circle nor a literary one . . . [Mayer] gathered every Sunday, in an oval salon thick with cigarette smoke, a faithful group where students . . . rubbed shoulders with French and foreign personalities, and with ministers . . . in an atmosphere of fraternal animation.'[46] Those who came to know de Gaulle after 1945 noted that Mayer was one of the few people from his pre-war life about whom he talked with emotion and respect. The Mayer salon opened new intellectual horizons, introduced de Gaulle to a world outside the army and extended his range of contacts to include journalists and intellectuals like the distinguished author Daniel Halévy, whose salon he also attended on at least one occasion.[47] But the two individuals from Mayer's circles to whom he became closest were Auburtin, who had good political connections, and Lucien Nachin, editor of a series of military classics for the publisher Berger-Levrault. They formed part of a tiny coterie of admirers that began to form around de Gaulle himself.

In 1927, de Gaulle's secondment to the Pétain *cabinet* came to an end. His relations with Pétain began to sour. Having worked on the Marshal's history of the army for two years, he was beginning to worry either that

Pétain had lost interest in publication or that there would be no acknow-ledgement of his contribution. His letters to Mayer at this time refer to Pétain irreverently as 'the great personage' and 'the Imperator'. Then came a bombshell from another member of Pétain's *cabinet*, Colonel Audet, who wrote to inform de Gaulle that he had been asked by Pétain to draft the sections of the book relating to the Great War. De Gaulle's outraged response displays a remarkable degree of self-belief:

> A book is a man . . . That man, up to now, was me. If anyone else, whether it be Montesquieu – or whether it be you, Colonel – becomes involved in it, only two things can ensue: either he will write another book or he will demolish mine . . . If the Marshal wants you to do another book, I have no objections. I will simply take my book back. But if it is a matter of mauling my philosophy and my style, I oppose it . . . Even if I were dealing with Paul Bourget and André Gide I would use the same terms.[48]

A few days later de Gaulle compounded his insolence by writing to Pétain himself in a tone quite extraordinary for a mere captain addressing the most venerated military figure in France. With 'respectful insistence' he 'warned' Pétain against any change in their agreement: he could not allow others to be involved in the writing of the book. He expressed the hope that Pétain was still planning to publish and asked for the inclusion of a preface acknowledging his own role. Knowing Pétain's 'repugnance' for writing, people would recognize that he could not have written the book alone.[49] That anyone could write to Pétain like this scandalized Audet: 'As long as we are serving a great leader, what we are worth is only through him and by him.' Pétain himself took de Gaulle's 'respectful' insolence more equably. He reassured him that no one else would be involved and that once the book had been published de Gaulle's contribution would be rec-ognized.[50] This put an end to the quarrel for the moment – but also seemingly to the book.

De Gaulle attributed the problem to the influence of Pétain's sycophantic entourage, jealous of the favour bestowed on him. But perhaps the problem was also the book that de Gaulle had written. Since Pétain's view of 'style' was to eliminate all adjectives – his motto was that a sentence needed only a subject, verb, object – he may have realized belatedly that de Gaulle's highly wrought prose could never pass as his own. From time to time, de Gaulle tried unsuccessfully to revive Pétain's interest in publishing the book. He had no interest in breaking completely with Pétain, and still tried to make himself useful from a distance. In 1929, Pétain's *cabinet* was much absorbed by working on the speech the Marshal would deliver on his reception at the Académie Française (to which he had just been elected).

Pétain was obliged to deliver the customary eulogy to the previous holder of the chair to which he had been elected – who happened to be his enemy Foch who had died earlier that year. De Gaulle drafted a speech but commented to Nachin that it was a delicate task because 'one of them could not stand the other and it was reciprocal.'[51] None of de Gaulle's suggestions ended up in the eulogy Pétain finally delivered in 1931. They were insufficiently critical of Foch to pass muster.

GOD'S GRACE

There were strict rules about how long an officer could remain in a staff position, and in 1927 de Gaulle was back on regimental duty commanding a battalion stationed in Trier as part of the French occupying force in the Rhineland. His subordinates found him as disconcerting as he was exacting. The elevated intellectual tone of his lectures to his junior officers was not what they were used to. One lecture, in which de Gaulle quoted Ibsen, led to his being mocked for filling his lectures with 'Ibsenities'. The text of that lecture has not survived, but a phrase from another lecture, where de Gaulle declared, slightly misquoting Shakespeare, that 'like Hamlet we will be great by waging in silence our great quarrel' (*Etre grand, c'est soutenir une grande querelle*) gives a sense of what might have perplexed his listeners.[52] From Trier, de Gaulle wrote to Mayer nostalgically: 'I often regret the interesting discussions and the Socratic methods you excel in practising. Here in the Army of the Rhine intelligence is in short supply. Perhaps that is for the better, for what can one "do" with intelligence ... Mars was beautiful, brave and strong but not a great mind.'[53]

More serious than his 'Ibsenities' was an incident that blew up when a soldier complained about the way he had been treated by de Gaulle. In de Gaulle's view, serving with the Rhine army was an honour, but many conscript soldiers disliked being away from France and angled for a posting back to the fatherland. De Gaulle highhandedly decreed that any soldier who made such a request would be imprisoned. He carried out the threat when a soldier obtained a transfer thanks to the intervention of his *député* (member of parliament). De Gaulle was then himself threatened with sanctions by the Ministry of War, but Pétain intervened on his behalf and the matter was closed.[54]

The real drama of this period occurred in de Gaulle's personal life. The first years of his marriage could not have proceeded more smoothly. A first child, Philippe, was born in December 1922. The family moved to a larger apartment in the Square Desaix close to the Ecole de Guerre. Here they lived for five years, a long time in de Gaulle's nomadic military existence. A second child, Elisabeth, was born in 1924. The de Gaulle couple would dine most Sunday evenings with Yvonne's parents at their apartment in the Boulevard Victor in the fifteenth *arrondissement*. In August the two families would hire villas close to each other on the beach at Wissant on the north coast. Part of the month was usually spent at the Vendroux domaine of Sept-Fontaines.

De Gaulle, who had never hunted before, would often join the family for the annual autumn hunting parties at Sept-Fontaines, although according to his brother-in-law he was usually too distracted by his thoughts to bag much game.[55] He could also be persuaded sometimes to join the family playing bridge where his extraordinary visual memory made him a dangerous opponent. The Vendrouxs lived on a grander scale than the de Gaulles, who were not rich. Their new flat in Paris did not have a *chambre de bonne*, and Yvonne de Gaulle never seemed able to keep a maid for long. Service abroad brought a pay supplement and while they were in Trier de Gaulle bought their first car, a Citroen B14, which they sold on returning to France. In every way Yvonne and Charles lived the perfectly regulated existence of a bourgeois French family of the period.[56] The only clouds were two moments of family sadness: in 1925 de Gaulle's brother Xavier lost his wife in childbirth, and the following year de Gaulle's younger brother Jacques was afflicted by encephalitis which progressively paralysed him.

In the summer of 1927, the entire de Gaulle family – his parents and all five children – set off on a pilgrimage to Lourdes in fulfilment of a vow his mother had made if all four sons returned alive from the war. Yvonne de Gaulle did not accompany the family since she was pregnant for the third time. Her third child was born on the first day of 1928. De Gaulle wrote to Lucien Nachin to announce the birth:

> We will call her Anne. Perhaps she will see the year 2000 and the great fear that will doubtless be unleashed on the world in that year. She will see the new rich become poor and the former rich rediscover their fortunes as a result of political upheavals. She will see the Socialists quietly turned into reactionaries. She will see France, once again victorious, miss the chance of taking the left bank of the Rhine.[57]

In retrospect, the light-hearted tone of the proud young father takes on a tragic hue. Anne lived to see none of these things. Within a matter of months, it became apparent that something was wrong. When the baby was one year old, Yvonne de Gaulle wrote to a friend: 'We would give up everything, ambition, fortune, etc. if that could improve the health of our little Anne.'[58] It turned out that Anne had been born with Down's Syndrome or, as it was commonly called at the time, Mongolism. Although we now know that the handicap is caused by a chromosomal aberration, in the 1920s it was a mystery shrouded in lurid fantasies about degeneration, inherited defects in the bloodline or even the morality of the mother. The de Gaulle parents grieved over their daughter's handicap but also desperately tried to understand its causes, dreading that they might be responsible. Yvonne de Gaulle thought the cause might have been the shock of witnessing a street brawl in Trier between some of her husband's troops and a group of German war veterans while she was pregnant.

Children with irreversible mental handicaps were usually sent to asylums or hospitals. But Yvonne and Charles decided to keep the small girl in the family. She remained constantly with them until her early death in 1948. We know nothing about the discussions between the mother and father that led them to take a decision that was presumably rooted in their deep Catholic faith. De Gaulle rarely talked outside his family about 'poor little Anne', as he called her. In 1940 he unburdened himself to the chaplain of his regiment: 'Her birth was a trial for my wife and myself. But believe me, Anne is my joy and my strength. She is the grace of God in my life . . . She has kept me in the security of obedience to the sovereign will of God.'[59] After Anne's premature death he wrote to her elder sister: 'Her soul has been liberated.'[60]

It was not for another two years that the girl's handicap became obvious to outsiders. At the age of three she could still neither walk nor feed herself and was subject to fits of uncontrollable anxiety. Anne's handicap caused this already private couple to turn in on themselves even more than before. In the summer of 1928, instead of joining the Vendrouxs at Wissant, the de Gaulles took a villa in Brittany where, says his son Philippe, they wanted to recapture a 'bit of family autonomy'.[61] The difficulties of 'poor little Anne' can occasionally be glimpsed in letters – for example Yvonne accepting an invitation from her brother 'providing all is well with Anne between now and then'.[62] Never was Anne able to utter more than a few inarticulate sounds; her sight was bad but she could not be made to wear glasses. It was only at the age of ten that she was able to take her first faltering steps. At this time de Gaulle was stationed in Metz. The Director of the botanical gardens would open up the gates for de Gaulle at the end of the day to allow father and daughter to walk together hand in hand along the deserted paths.[63] The tenderness of the relationship between de Gaulle and his little daughter – the one person perhaps who was not in awe of him – shines out of a photograph of de Gaulle in dark formal suit, sitting in his deck-chair on a beach in Brittany with the little girl on his knees, her fingers entwined in his. This strangely austere man who found it so hard to express affection would spend hours playing with his child, singing her songs, telling her stories she could not understand, encouraging her to play with small toys or to clap her hands – almost as if, in the words of his son Philippe, he was 'obstinately trying to deny the reality of the tragedy that was torturing him'.[64]

The birth of Anne also explains why the de Gaulle couple had no more children. Theirs was a world in which bearing children was a patriotic and religious duty. On hearing the news that his sister had given birth, de Gaulle had written to his mother in 1916 that 'beautiful little French babies are going to be necessary to replace those who have died for the Fatherland'.[65] When the somewhat colourless politician Paul Deschanel was elected President of the Republic instead of the hero of the war Georges Clemenceau, de Gaulle wrote to his mother that he was surprised but not too unhappy: 'I think he has all the necessary aptitude for the role. And above all he is married with children.'[66] De Gaulle's brothers Pierre and Xavier each had five children, and his sister Marie-Agnès had seven. But Charles and Yvonne de Gaulle had no more after Anne – another source of private grief.

The birth of Anne tested and deepened the ties of the couple. Two years after Anne's birth, de Gaulle was posted to Beirut. The entire family moved with him. Soon after his arrival, de Gaulle was sent on a mission out of the city. While he was away this undemonstrative man wrote to his wife: 'I love you with all my heart. Everyone is asking me here: "And has Madame de Gaulle found this change too difficult?" I answer the truth, that is to say "no", but I think to myself that perhaps she did but that she is so brave and so courageous that she has pretended to be happy.'[67]

IMPERIAL INTERLUDE

De Gaulle's two years in the Levant were the only 'imperial' moment in his pre-war career.[68] The Levant had entered France's colonial orbit after the collapse of the Ottoman Empire in 1918 when the victorious Allies carved up the Middle East, the British taking Iraq and Palestine, the French taking Syria and Lebanon. All these territories were held 'in mandate' while supposedly preparing them for independence. De Gaulle's former prisoner-of-war companion General Georges Catroux, who served as Governor of the Levant for four years, had shown great diplomatic skill negotiating between the different ethnic and religious communities whom the French played off against each other. The French had suppressed various risings against them in the 1920s. When de Gaulle arrived the situation was peaceful and there were no major military operations during his two years in the region.

Because so much of de Gaulle's future career was bound up with decolonization, biographers have sought clues to his future policies during his eighteen months in Beirut. In these years, the Empire had a strong hold on the French popular imagination. In literature and films, it was the backdrop for adventures where heroes either succumbed to the decadent temptations of the exotic or proved their masculinity through heroic sacrifice. As an adolescent de Gaulle had penned two short stories in this vein. One, set in New Caledonia, tells the story of an officer attracted by the 'savage beauty' of a Polynesian girl. She tries to kill them both with a bouquet of poisoned flowers so that they can be united for ever in death. The second story, which the fifteen-year-old de Gaulle (using the pseudonym Lugal) had managed to get published in a magazine, is about an army officer in Algeria who falls in love with the daughter of a tribal chief. She kills him to avenge her father.

Apart from these adolescent orientalist fantasies, de Gaulle had never previously shown much interest in the Empire. Soon after arriving in Beirut he wrote to Mayer: 'How can one not believe in the army when one sees it completing the Empire? Is it a good thing to become an Empire? That is another story.'[69] It is not clear why de Gaulle chose the Levant in 1929. Most officers served a stint in the Empire and perhaps he felt this was an obligatory rite of passage. He wrote to his mother-in-law: 'it is an effort that must be made once, and made now or never.'[70] Yvonne de Gaulle's biographer suggests that the choice might have been related to the recent birth of Anne. But one might think, on the contrary, that de Gaulle would have thought twice about uprooting his family thousands of kilometres with a severely handicapped girl. The decision seems to have been sudden, and he did not initially plan to stay long since within two months of arriving he was in contact with Pétain about the possibility of securing a professorship at the Ecole de Guerre. We can assume that for de Gaulle the Levant was an interlude before he could return to the centre of things in Paris.

The family arrived in Beirut in December 1929. The city was not yet the elegant metropolis it was to become in the 1930s. De Gaulle's first impressions were negative. His letters home show that oriental exoticism had little allure for this man of the rainy north:

> Arriving here the first impression is one of disorientation [dépaysement] for people like us who have always lived in countries that are clean and ordered. In the streets, the houses, the shops there is an incredible swarming mass of

humanity ... Their only preoccupation is to scrabble together as quickly as they can, and by whatever means, the few sous necessary to buy a *galette*, some olives and a cup of coffee. After that there is nothing more to do other than lounge around until the next day ... In the end, I see here, especially clearly, that nowhere is one better off than in France.[71]

A year later his opinion was no higher:

The Levant is still calm if one can use such a word given the state of perpetual agitation of the oriental mind ... There are populations here who are never satisfied by anything or anyone but who submit to the law of the strongest if it is ready to express itself and to a mandatory power which has not yet really worked out how to go about exercising its mandatory power.[72]

Nothing about his posting excited de Gaulle's imagination except that he was in the land of the Crusades. One expedition took him to the River Tigris and he wrote to his father that 'it was not without emotion that we dipped our hand in this river' – the first French soldiers to do so since the Crusades.[73]

The de Gaulles lived in a modern and comfortable apartment block in the city's newly constructed residential district. He wrote to his mother-in-law: 'I think one can live here in a sufficiently agreeable and comfortable manner providing it does not last too long.'[74] Their two elder children attended the best Catholic schools, while Madame de Gaulle was absorbed with looking after Anne. She was usually only seen at Mass with her husband on Sundays. De Gaulle worked in the army's Deuxième and Troisième Bureaux responsible for intelligence and operations respectively. The Deuxième Bureau analysed the reports of the sixty or so intelligence agents posted in the region. These concerned a multiplicity of problems: the situation of the Christian minorities, the activities of the Kurds, the stirrings of Arab nationalism, British policies in the region. In his leisure time de Gaulle was not to be seen at the racecourse, the clubs or the bridge parties that formed the daily routine of the French community. He spent his leisure time reading, writing and thinking.

It is a sign of how little can be gleaned from de Gaulle's time in the Lebanon that the episode which has most excited his biographers is the speech he gave at a prize-giving ceremony at the St Joseph University of Beirut. In his speech de Gaulle invited the youth of Lebanon to prepare themselves to build the future of their country. It was a piece of uplifting rhetoric, perfect for a school prize-giving, and delivered with the panache which de Gaulle had already demonstrated as a lecturer. But to see it as a prophetic vision of an independent Lebanon – as some writers have done – stretches credulity. We have little idea what de Gaulle finally concluded about the future of the mandate. His most sustained reflections are contained in a letter to Mayer:

> The Levant is a crossroads where everything passes through . . . while nothing changes. We have now been here ten years. My impression is that we have hardly penetrated and that the people are as foreign to us, and vice-versa, as they have ever been. It is true we have adopted the worst system for such a country, that is to say we have invited the population to get up and do something on their own with our encouragement, while in fact nothing has ever been constructed here, neither the canals of the Nile nor the aqueduct of Palmyra, nor even an olive grove, except under constraint. In my view, our destiny will be either to do that or leave. The cynical would add a third solution: to continue our current practice of feeling our way in the dark, since here time does not count and the systems which exist, like the bridges and the houses, will somehow remain standing in their rickety way. The only man who understood Syria properly and knew what to do was General Catroux. That is why he left.[75]

This letter can be read as an argument for a more active imperial policy and as an argument for leaving. If the Lebanese experience left any imprint on de Gaulle it was possibly to sharpen a suspicion of Britain which was never far under the surface among Frenchmen of his generation. Although the British and French had signed an entente in 1904, and fought the war of 1914–18 as allies, they had been enemies more often than they had been friends. In the late nineteenth century, they had clashed while carving out their respective empires in Africa. One famous incident occurred at Fashoda on the upper Nile in 1898 when a small military force despatched by the French government to secure French control over Sudan was forced to turn back by a British force under General Kitchener. This caused outrage in France. In the first pages of his *War Memoirs* de Gaulle remembers Fashoda as one of the moments of national humiliation that formed the backdrop to his childhood.

In the inter-war years the Levant was the only region where Anglo-French imperial rivalry remained acute as the two powers struggled for influence over the spoils of the Ottoman Empire. This was the theme of one of the best-selling novels of the inter-war period, Pierre Benoit's *La Châtelaine du Liban*, published in 1924 five years before de Gaulle set off for Beirut. The book depicts the British as a malevolent presence manoeuvring to oust the French from the region and fulfil T. E. Lawrence's dream of a unified Arab kingdom under British patronage. Its hero is a French intelligence officer who falls fatally in love with a mysterious countess of

Russian origin. Seeing herself as a reincarnation of the nineteenth-century British adventuress Hester Stanhope, the Countess has many lovers including a scheming British intelligence officer who is the opposite number to the novel's French hero. De Gaulle succumbed to the lures of no countess, but his work for the Deuxième Bureau will have alerted him to the activities of British intelligence officers of the kind described in the book. The seeds of de Gaulle's violent clashes with the British over the Levant in 1940 were sown in these years. Behind every British officer in the region he was programmed to suspect the baleful shadow of Lawrence.

'MILITARY MELANCHOLY'

De Gaulle's two years in the Lebanon gave him the leisure to write up as a book the lectures he had given at the Ecole de Guerre in 1927. It was published in 1932, under the title *Le fil de l'épée* (*The Edge of the Sword*). Pitched at a high level of abstraction, the book's five densely argued chapters allow de Gaulle to parade his erudition. In this short text he contrives to cite a remarkable range of writers, including Goethe, Bergson, Francis Bacon, Flaubert, Socrates, Tolstoy, Anatole France, Jarry, Shakespeare, Cicero, Villiers de l'Isle-Adam, Barrès, Maeterlinck, Heine, Musset. This list is far from exhaustive, although curiously two writers whom the book often brings to mind – Thomas Carlyle and Machiavelli – are not mentioned.

In essence, the book is a tract on leadership. De Gaulle returns to his obsession about the perils of *a priori* thinking. In his view the successful leader had to combine, to use de Gaulle's Bergsonian phrase, a 'creative spark' with a capacity for abstraction and critical intelligence. The leader also has to cultivate mystery and keep his distance while exercising a 'large dose of egoism, of pride, of hardness and of ruse'. Leadership is a solitary exercise of the will, a semi-ascetic vocation: 'An intimate struggle, more or less intense according to the individual, but which at every moment lacerates his soul as the flint tears the feet of the penitent sinner'.[76]

The Edge of the Sword was not just a timeless meditation on leadership. It also had contemporary purpose, articulating de Gaulle's disillusionment with the trend of French politics and diplomacy since the mid-1920s. In the first half of the decade, French governments had done all they could to exact the reparations owing to them under the Treaty of Versailles. In 1923, the premier Raymond Poincaré had even sent troops into the Ruhr to enforce German compliance. But this policy foundered because the British were moving to the view that Germany had been too harshly treated at Versailles. As a result French governments were forced to downscale their ambitions. During the second half of the decade, France embarked on a policy of reconciliation with Germany, whose architect was the almost immovable Foreign Minister Aristide Briand. The backdrop to this policy was a public mood of pacifism reflected in films and novels. In 1928, the length of military service was reduced from eighteen months to one year.

De Gaulle, like many conservatives, was appalled by all these developments. On the ship taking him to the Levant in 1929, he had heard the news that the government had fallen. This was hardly a novel event in the Third Republic, but the new premier was André Tardieu, who had been close to Georges Clemenceau. De Gaulle for once saw a reason for optimism: 'Let him try his hand! ... Let him reverse inside and outside the policies that Briand and his cowardly admirers have so shamefully denationalized.'[77] If de Gaulle was out of sympathy with 'Briandism' it was because he believed it to be a fantasy contrary to the laws of history. As he had put it in one of his prison-camp lectures in 1917:

> This war is not the last. Whatever the horrors, sacrifices, grief, tears that it has brought in its wake, men have not been changed by it. For some years there will be a sense of shame and fear; then the smell of blood will fade; and everyone will sing its glories; the century-old hatreds will revive in more extreme form and one day peoples will hurl themselves at each other again, determined to destroy each other but swearing before God and mankind that they had been attacked by the other.[78]

In another lecture he delivered in 1918, he was no less pessimistic: 'The peoples of old Europe will end up signing a peace that their statesmen will call a peace of reconciliation! But everyone knows that it will in reality be a peace of exhaustion. Everyone knows that this peace will only be a cover for unsatisfied ambitions, ever more acute hatreds.'[79] This was his view in 1916; it was his view in 1918; and it remained his view ten years later. Writing in 1928 to thank Mayer for having sent him his latest book, he commented: 'We disagree on whether there will be war again; the army of the Rhine is not for much longer; *Anschluss* is close and then Germany will want back what she has lost of Poland and then Alsace ... This seems to me to be written in the stars.'[80]

In *The Edge of the Sword*, de Gaulle was writing against the current, against a world which was spurning military values in favour of pacifist ones, patriotism in favour of internationalism, against politicians who wished to dwell only on the horrors of the last war and not on what was, in de Gaulle's words, 'effective and grandiose' in warfare. His son Philippe remembered being taken by his father as a young boy in 1928 to see the film *Verdun, visions d'histoire* which used a mixture of newsreel and dramatic reconstruction (with real veterans acting the main roles). After twenty minutes de Gaulle stormed out in fury because of the film's pacifist message.[81] *The Edge of the Sword* was written to remind the French that war had always been a motor of history – 'How can one conceive of life without force?' – that war was as integral to human existence as birth and death, and part of the endless cycle of decline and renewal. De Gaulle viewed this not as a glorification of war but as a statement of fact: 'How can one conceive of Greece without Salamis, Rome without her legions, Christianity without the sword, Islam without the scimitar, the Revolution without Valmy?'[82]

In this mood de Gaulle wrote to his friend Nachin in 1929 a letter that has been much quoted: 'Ah what bitterness there is nowadays in wearing the harness! But we have no choice. In a few years they will attach themselves to our coat-tails to save the *patrie* . . . and the rabble [*canaille*] into the bargain.'[83] De Gaulle's handwriting is often hard to decipher and the 'our' of this letter used to be read as 'my' – as the symptom of a personal ambition. In truth it was the bitterness of a man who had chosen to be a soldier in a society which did not value its army. *The Edge of the Sword* is suffused with what de Gaulle calls his sense of the 'melancholy of the *corps militaire*', with a sort of morose delectation of the soldier's fate – unloved, unappreciated, sacrificing personal happiness to patriotic duty.

To de Gaulle's sense of 'military melancholy' was added a more personal sadness when his beloved father died in May 1932. Two weeks later, he wrote an unusually emotional letter to his brother Xavier.

I found yesterday by chance while sorting out papers a letter from our father. The joy of coming upon his words again was not diminished by this sadness that has not left me for two weeks. Yes, my brother, I use the word joy. The word does not frighten me and I am not ashamed to use it. Joy at having been able to share with you the happiness [*bonheur*] at having been raised by such a man. That is the cause of my joy. How strange it is that, at the moment I bury my father, being now myself over 40 years old, my childhood floods back into my memory and the nostalgia for happy times allows me to measure the loss of the person whom we five used to call with fear and affection 'papa' . . . What a man, what a father, what a figure in our lives. I do not know what the future is going to bring me but if my destiny offers me honour of any kind, it will have been to live in the image of Henri de Gaulle, my father.[84]

4

Making a Mark, 1932–1939

MILITARY BUREAUCRAT

In December 1927, de Gaulle wrote to Mayer who had congratulated him on a recent promotion to battalion commander: 'It is indeed pleasant to "advance up the ranks" but the real issue is to "make a mark"[1] – not an easy ambition for soldiers to achieve during peacetime.

De Gaulle's expectation before setting off for Beirut had been that he would either return to Pétain's *cabinet* or secure a professorship at the Ecole de Guerre.[2] Neither materialized. Pétain no longer wanted de Gaulle in his *cabinet* but he did promise to intervene on his behalf at the Ecole. Perhaps because de Gaulle had remained *persona non grata* with the Ecole since his lectures there in 1927, perhaps because Pétain was less inclined to put himself out for this unruly protégé, no post at the Ecole was forthcoming either. Pétain suggested de Gaulle apply instead for a position on the Secretariat of the Conseil Supérieur de la Défense National (CSDN).[3] This turned out to be good advice. However much de Gaulle mocked him in private, Pétain remained a useful patron.

The CSDN was the interface between the military and the government, the forum where defence planning was discussed at the highest level. The role of its Secretariat, which de Gaulle joined, was to prepare policy documents for discussion by full sessions of the Conseil. Much of the work was highly technical. For example, it fell to de Gaulle to draft the minutes of the committee preparing the government's instructions to the French delegation at the Geneva disarmament conference – not a job he is likely to have enjoyed.[4] Despite the arid nature of his duties, de Gaulle's new post gave him a ringside seat that enabled him to observe the strained, often dysfunctional relationship between the military and civil authorities at a time when budgetary difficulties were pushing the government to impose cuts in military spending. It also provided insights into the arcane bureaucracy of defence planning, and the problems of developing a coherent defence policy given the rapid turnover of governments. He later wrote with no exaggeration: 'From 1932 to 1937, under fourteen ministries, I found myself involved . . . in all the political, technical and administrative activity concerning the defence of the country.'[5]

One of de Gaulle's major responsibilities was to prepare the law on the 'Organization of the Nation for War'. The endless redrafting of this 'veil of Penelope' (as de Gaulle put it) had been going on for a decade until the law was finally adopted in 1938. It covered every aspect of military planning from the mobilization of the armies to the organization of a war economy.[6] De Gaulle's drafts for this document allowed him to refine his ideas about the relationship between civil and military authority in wartime:

> We are concerned not with the legislative role of the two parliamentary chambers which is regulated by the constitution, but with the exercise of their right to control. The last war showed how this control tended to become more and more exigent as the war went on. It showed also that the investigations and the pressure of parliament were not without value despite their often confused and passionate nature. It has thus seemed desirable . . . to take the bull by the horns and determine precisely in the *projet de loi* the conditions and limits of parliamentary control in time of war.[7]

Since de Gaulle's work at the CSDN was part of a collective effort it is not easy to pinpoint his own specific contributions. But we have a revealing annotation in his own hand on an internal document resisting the creation of a single General Staff for all three services. This document had suggested that the structures already in place were adequate to respond to military and political requirements. This led to a sarcastic explosion from de Gaulle in the margin: 'Ah politics! So we *do* need the Foreign Ministry and the Interior, but does not the economy also matter? And the financial situation? Etc. etc. in short the government as a whole and not just three erratic blocs.'[8]

MILITARY CRUSADER

De Gaulle's experience as a military bureaucrat broadened his horizons and deepened his knowledge of defence policy but it was not going to help him 'make a mark'. His strategy for doing this in the 1920s had been through his writing, but his publications had so far won him only a *succès d'estime* among a tiny band of admirers. It was through the publication of his third book *Vers l'armée de métier* (*Towards a Professional Army*) in 1934, written while working at the CSDN, that de Gaulle finally reached a wider audience. He had been working on the book since the end of 1932,[9] and just before publication he described it to a correspondent as his 'proclamation-book'.[10] Instead of rarefied intellectual musings on leadership, he was now offering a manifesto for the modernization of the French army.

The book had two central arguments.[11] The first was that mechanization, especially the invention of tanks, had revolutionized warfare and rendered obsolete the central lesson that the French high command had taken from the experience of 1914–18: that firepower gave supremacy to the defender over the attacker. In this official view the role of tanks was to accompany and support the infantry. But de Gaulle argued that if tanks were deployed autonomously, their combination of speed and firepower would make it possible to wage offensive warfare without risking the terrible massacres of 1914–17. To achieve this he proposed the establishment of six divisions of heavy tanks grouped together into a single army corps. The book's second argument was that operating these tanks was beyond the capacity of conscripts – especially after army service had been reduced to one year in 1928 – and required highly trained and specialized soldiers. De Gaulle's solution was the creation of a professional army of 100,000 men operating alongside the conscript army. Not only would these professional soldiers have technical expertise, they would be imbued with a sense of purpose, *esprit de corps* and pride. This was de Gaulle's solution to the 'military melancholy' of the 1920s. In that sense the book can be seen as the continuation – or the second part – of *The Edge of the Sword*. In the earlier book he had analysed the qualities needed to be a leader; in this one he described the nature of the army the leader would command. The spirit of the new army would be 'analogous to that of our old cavalry'; its soldiers would offer 'spiritual and moral ballast' to a society that had lost its bearings.[12] These two strands of argument give de Gaulle's book a curiously hybrid tone. Technical recommendations about the organization of tank divisions accompany elevated reflections about the nobility of the military vocation. Indeed it is not entirely clear what de Gaulle's starting point had been. When he first trailed the ideas of his book in an article in May 1933, tanks were hardly mentioned.[13] In the book itself, whose title was after all *Towards a Professional Army*, tanks are mentioned only twenty-nine times in 211 pages. De Gaulle was supposedly advocating the creation of a 'modern' army but he was also proposing a way to recreate the heroic virtues which had once been seen as the essence of the military vocation.

This tension in the book's arguments would prove a handicap in winning converts. But the combination of de Gaulle's literary panache – he peppered his text with showy epigraphs from authors including Hegel, Epictetus, La Rochefoucauld, Maeterlinck – with an effective publicity campaign ensured that the book received a great deal of attention. De

Gaulle mobilized all the press contacts he had built up in the previous years, and in the year before publication he published four articles to popularize his ideas in non-specialized periodicals.[14] The book sold about 1,500 copies and within a year it had been translated into Russian and German. When de Gaulle arrived in London after France's defeat in 1940 the book was rapidly translated into English under the title *The Army of the Future*. Emblazoned on the cover were the words: 'A 1934 prophecy! France disregarded it! Germany worked on it.' The first biography of de Gaulle in 1942 (by the son of his great literary hero Barrès) portrayed him as a prophet who had foreseen the nature of modern warfare but whose misfortune was that it was the Germans not the French who had adopted his ideas. A copy of the German translation with some approving annotations by Hitler himself was found by French troops in Berchtesgaden in 1945. Although the influence of the book on military thinking in Germany should not be exaggerated, it was certainly read by the German General Guderian who published his own manifesto for tank warfare in 1937.[15]

Historians have demolished the more extravagant claims made for de Gaulle's book. They point out that he was no prophet regarding the crucial role of airpower in modern warfare (underlined when a reprint of the book in 1943 interpolated a new sentence on airpower that had not been in the original); that most of his ideas on tank warfare had been anticipated by other writers; that he is frustratingly vague in technical detail. All these criticisms are correct but they judge the book as something it was not intended to be. In the inter-war years there was an extensive technical literature by military writers in many countries speculating about how advances in military technology might change the future of warfare. Among titles published around the same time as de Gaulle's, one could mention two British publications – Basil Liddell Hart's *The Future of Infantry* (1933), J. F. C. Fuller's *On Future Warfare* (1933) – the French translation from Polish of Władysław Sikorski's *Modern Warfare* (*La guerre moderne*) (1935), and the French theorist Emile Alléhaut's *Motorisation and the Army of Tomorrow* (1929). Although de Gaulle's book was considered important enough for the American Military Attaché in Paris to mail a copy to Washington with the comment that it had 'attracted considerable attention in France', de Gaulle was never considered to be one of the authorities on the subject of tank warfare comparable to figures like Liddell Hart and Fuller.[16]

De Gaulle drew on this specialized literature – and wrote to Alléhaut acknowledging his influence on him[17] – but the aim of his book was different. Rather than offering a technical study targeted at other military specialists, he sought to link the issue of army modernization to wider geographical, political and diplomatic issues. His starting point was the geographical vulnerability of France's north-eastern frontier with Belgium and Luxembourg: 'Just as a portrait suggests to an observer the impression of a destiny, so the map of France reveals our fate.' The 'century-old weakness' of France's frontiers was rendered more acute by the speed of modern warfare: Paris was now only one hour by plane from the frontier. French military planners were of course well aware of this. In 1928 French governments had begun the construction of what came to be called the Maginot Line, a defensive network of fortifications covering France's eastern frontier up to Luxembourg. For a variety of technical and financial reasons, the Maginot Line stopped at the Belgian border, but its existence freed up forces to protect that part of the frontier which remained exposed. De Gaulle had himself in 1925 published a short article on the importance of fortifications in French history.[18] In no sense did he oppose the Maginot Line, although he believed it was complacent to think that it guaranteed France's security: 'Fortresses have their value but are not a panacea.'[19]

But de Gaulle was not only addressing France's military vulnerability. The point of his book was to argue that without the capacity for offensive action France would have to downscale her international ambitions. This was the subtext of the book: he was arguing not just for tanks but for a certain idea of the role that France should be aspiring to play in the world. While not singling out any one task for the newly reorganized army, he suggested that it might be employed in all kinds of ways: to protect the Empire, to give teeth to the collective security ambitions of the League of Nations, to intervene pre-emptively against Germany. Another possibility was to align France's military capacities with her diplomatic obligations. To compensate for the disappearance of her former Tsarist ally, French governments had formed a number of preventive alliances with the successor states that emerged in 1919 (Czechoslovakia, Poland, Yugoslavia). Without an army capable of intervening rapidly to defend these states against Germany, France would have to abandon any hope of containing German expansionism.

What especially irritated his superiors about de Gaulle's book was the implication that no one else in France was aware of the need to modernize the army. In reality, modernization was the subject of intensive policy debates; no military planner believed that the Maginot line had solved all France's problems. The new Chief of the General Staff in 1930, General Weygand, had embarked upon a programme to modernize the cavalry by equipping it with tanks. As a result, by 1933 France had her first armoured division employing light tanks. But units of this kind were not suitable for the kind of operations advocated by the proponents of a heavy armoured corps able to act autonomously. Opponents of this solution pointed out the technical difficulties of producing tanks with the right balance of speed, firepower and armoured protection. De Gaulle soared above such details.

De Gaulle's book appeared just when the international situation might have won him converts. Hitler had come to power in January 1933. In October Germany left the World Disarmament Conference that had opened in Geneva in the previous year. In response, on 17 April 1934, the French Foreign Minister announced that France would take the necessary measures to ensure her security: rearmament and an attempt to reinvigorate France's alliance system in eastern Europe. De Gaulle's book was published at exactly this moment. But what caused problems for his superiors was his argument that the creation of tank divisions required a professional army. The commitment to the idea of the 'nation in arms' was sacred in France as a way of linking the nation to its army. Although de Gaulle was not arguing for the abolition of conscription, the creation of a professional army alongside an army composed of conscripts would have involved a massive reorganization. In fact the army leaders were not opposed to professionalism as a necessary complement to the shortening of military service. But it was not clear that it would be possible to recruit enough professional soldiers for both the professional corps and the rest of the tasks that had to be done. All these points were seized upon by de Gaulle's opponents in the army. Some of the most distinguished military figures in France – Marshal Pétain (anonymously), Generals Weygand and Gamelin – published articles attacking de Gaulle's ideas in widely read non-specialist reviews. 'No to two armies' was one theme of their opposition. De Gaulle's book may have helped him to make his mark, but it did not advance the cause in the army of those who shared his ideas about the need for tank divisions.

Since de Gaulle had addressed his book to a general public, the opposition of the military hierarchy might not have mattered if his ideas had been calibrated to appeal to France's politicians. Although the concept of the professional army raised all the historical demons of the French left about military adventurers, the left was not entirely opposed ideologically to the idea of professionalization, especially if this facilitated shorter military service for conscripts. But this idea needed to be sold more effectively than in de Gaulle's provocative celebration of the *esprit militaire*. When he wrote that 'a successful soldier is one who is accustomed to living outside society' or that it was necessary to 'break the links that attached the soldiers to a peaceable society and create in their souls reflexes of discipline, cohesion and courage' he was not speaking a language that would win him many supporters on the left.[20] The leader of the Socialist Party Léon Blum devoted a long series of articles in the Socialist daily newspaper to rebutting de Gaulle's book. So although de Gaulle had won a degree of relative notoriety it was not of the kind that would help to advance his ideas. Reading the concluding pages of his book, one can see why some politicians might have been alarmed:

> If the professional army is to come to birth in future with the fresh resources and spirit that it must possess in order to be more than just a vague hope then a master must appear . . . A man strong enough to impose himself, skilful enough to seduce, great enough to carry out great things . . . There is no group, no party, no political figure who does not talk of recovery, of a new order, of authority [this inflammatory sentence not in the British 1940 translation] . . . If the remaking of the nation has to start with the army, that is altogether in conformity with the natural order of things. The military is the most complete expression of the spirit of a society. In the task of remaking France the new army will be both an essential solution [*recours*] and a leaven of change.[21]

At any time such words might have raised alarm bells; in the tense political crisis of the 1930s they sounded almost insurrectionary.

DE GAULLE AND THE POLITICAL CRISIS OF THE 1930S

In de Gaulle's career, 1934 was important for the publication of *Towards a Professional Army*; in French history, it was important as the year politics exploded. The catalyst for this explosion was a demonstration in Paris on 6 February. War veterans' associations and anti-parliamentary right-wing organizations had gathered in the Place de la Concorde to demonstrate against the centre-left government of Edouard Daladier. The pretext was a financial corruption case involving a swindler, Alexandre Stavisky, alleged to have enjoyed the protection of crooked politicians. But the deeper cause of public discontent was the inability of governments to deal with the economic depression. France had been hit by the world economic slump in 1931, somewhat later than the rest of the world. Falling tax revenues and increased spending on unemployment benefit caused severe budget difficulties. In the two years between 1932 and 1934, no fewer than nine governments had come and gone with different plans to eliminate the budget deficit by more expenditure cuts, but the only result had been to push the economy further into depression. An ugly anti-parliamentary mood developed among the population at a time when liberal democracy throughout Europe seemed to be in crisis.

The demonstration of 6 February 1934 turned violent. When it seemed as if the demonstrators were planning to cross the bridge separating the Place de la Concorde from the parliament building across the Seine, troops guarding the bridge opened fire. Fifteen demonstrators were killed. The left believed that the forces of order had thwarted a fascist plot to seize parliament; the right believed that honest patriots had been gunned down to defend corrupt politicians. The centre-left government resigned and the conservative politician Gaston Doumergue came out of retirement to form a government of 'national unity' which was in reality a government of the right. This did not resolve the crisis of confidence in French institutions. Conservatives talked of a need to reform the state and strengthen the executive. One of these was the brilliant right-wing politician André Tardieu, who resigned from the government and launched a crusade to reform the Republic, strengthen the powers of the Presidency and weaken the power of parliament. Tardieu's ideas were moderate compared to some of the right-wing anti-parliamentary 'Leagues' which had been boosted by the events of 6 February. These Leagues included the monarchist Action Française which had been around since the start of the century, but there were other new ones like Croix de Feu whose military-style demonstrations aped the fascist movements which had emerged throughout Europe in the 1920s.

Hitler had taken power in January 1933, and it is understandable that the French left felt that there was a fascist danger in France also. The previously disunited parties of the left, from the Communists on the extreme left to the Radicals on the centre-left via the Socialists in the middle, reacted by forming an alliance called the Popular Front. At the elections of June 1936 the Popular Front triumphed. The Communists, who had previously had only a handful of *députés*, were now a major player in French politics. The Socialist leader Léon Blum became premier of the first Socialist-led government in French history. Soon afterwards in Spain, where a Popular Front government had also been elected, there was a military uprising, prelude to a three-year civil war. All this only further radicalized French conservatives. Politics in France reached unprecedented levels of verbal and physical violence. Although the French army had traditionally kept out of politics, some army officers so feared the threat of Communism that they set up clandestine networks ready to intervene in politics in case of revolution. Members of Pétain's entourage were involved in these conspiracies.

What was de Gaulle's attitude to this crisis? Despite his belief that French society needed to value its soldiers, the idea that the army should intervene in politics was anathema to his conviction that it must be the servant of civil power. As the political crisis in France became more acute he conceded to one correspondent in private that a professional army might be more reliable than conscripts or colonial troops in keeping public order – but, significantly, he envisaged the enemy of order as coming from either the extreme left or the Leagues on the extreme right.[22] 'Spain not France', he wrote to another correspondent, 'is the land of *pronunciamentos*.' But revealingly he went on: 'The day when general opinion has moved in favour of an overthrowing of the established order, the existing form of military organization cannot prevent its fall . . . Regimes fall by their faults, not at all through their soldiers.'[23] Did he believe that this moment of collapse was close in France?

One way of approaching de Gaulle's political beliefs at this time is through an exchange with his father who before his death had been reading the manuscript of the history of the French army de Gaulle was writing for Pétain. At one point in his text, de Gaulle had made some appreciative remarks about Hoche, one of the most brilliant generals of the French Revolution, who had carried out massacres of royalists during the Vendée uprising of 1793. This led to de Gaulle's father to comment: 'Hoche does not seem to me to merit this unreserved praise.' He regretted that his son had shown 'so much sympathy for those who guarded the doors of the abattoirs while the victims were having their throats cut'. At another point, de Gaulle mentioned Dumouriez, a general who had helped the republican armies win the Battle of Jemappes in 1792 before going over to the side of the counter-revolutionaries. De Gaulle wrote of Dumouriez's 'treason'; his father amended this to 'defection' (which de Gaulle retained) – suggesting that he had some sympathy with Dumouriez's action. These might seem flimsy foundations upon which to erect an interpretation of de Gaulle's politics, but in France the way people viewed the past was central to political identities. His father's rebuke that he was showing excessive indulgence to the Revolution is another sign of de Gaulle distancing himself from the conservatism of his parents.[24]

Given de Gaulle's admiration for Péguy, his inclusive view of France's past, so different from the more doctrinaire position of Maurras, is not so surprising. On the other hand, this had not prevented de Gaulle sending his first book to Maurras personally dedicated with his 'respectful homage'. He also sent Maurras a copy of *Towards a Professional Army*, following it up a few weeks later with a letter to the military correspondent of *Action française*, expressing his hope that 'M. Maurras will bring his powerful support to the professional army. In truth he has been doing so for a long time already, at least through his body of doctrines.'[25] At the same time, however, de Gaulle was a member of the free-thinking Mayer circle

presided over by someone who, as a Jew and former Dreyfusard, represented everything Action Française execrated.

In the Mayer circle, de Gaulle had encountered some of those young
intellectuals, mostly born around 1905, whom historians have dubbed, for
want of a better label, the 'nonconformists' of the 1930s.[26] They were an
eclectic group who had little in common except the conviction that existing
political labels had no purchase on contemporary problems. They were
united by a haunting a sense of disenchantment with contemporary politics, a diffuse *Inquiétude* to quote the title of a 1926 book by one of them,
the Catholic intellectual Daniel-Rops (Henri Petiot) whom de Gaulle
encountered in the Mayer circle. He also met the young intellectual Robert
Aron, who with his friend Arnaud Dandieu had founded a small review
called *Ordre nouveau* (*New Order*) whose main theme was that politics,
whether of right or left, was caught in the same trap of materialism: liberal
capitalism and Marxist socialism were merely mirror images of each
other.[27] This brought *Ordre nouveau* close to the ideas of the Catholic
'personalist' philosopher Emmanuel Mounier, whose solution to the crisis
of civilization was to advocate communitarian forms of social organization
to escape from the dead-end of liberal individualism. One of Mounier's
mottos was that liberal democracy, at least as practised in France, was a
kind of 'institutionalized disorder'. The aspiration towards 'order' – though
not necessarily in an authoritarian sense – was much in vogue in these
circles. The future trajectories of the so-called nonconformists would later
take them in markedly different political directions but they all shared the
sense, as de Gaulle wrote to a correspondent in 1935, that 'the world is
trembling on the bases that we have known up to now.'[28]

If de Gaulle was, through his parents, linked to the generation of the
1870s, and by his birth to the generation of 1905, the 1930s generation
also marked his thinking durably. We shall see this later in regard to de
Gaulle's social ideas about finding a middle way – a third way – between
capitalism and socialism. But because the nonconformists had such varied
future political trajectories, we are no further advanced in answering concrete questions about de Gaulle's political beliefs in the mid-1930s. What
did he think about Mussolini, the Popular Front, the French 'fascist'
Leagues, the Spanish Civil War? His letters are silent on all these topics.
Up to a point, this silence is itself revealing. His letters contain none of the
standard obsessions of the extreme right – that there was a Jewish conspiracy to undermine France (he never mentions the Jews), that the Popular
Front was leading France to revolution, that the Republicans in Spain were
raping nuns – but nor do they contain any condemnation of the Leagues

or express concerns about the threat to democracy posed by the riots of 6 February 1934. Indeed de Gaulle's response to those riots seemed entirely positive:

> Today the ground under us is giving way. Since February, when the volcano erupted, all is upheaval. In truth, this is nothing less than the start of a revolution. Where will it lead? In my humble opinion to a reinforcing or even better a restoration of order but not without many more upheavals. In any case, the old Republic of committees, elections and personal favours is in its death throes [à l'agonie]. It is giving way to altogether different ideas. We are entering a kind of 1848 in reverse. In my view the issue is this: whether the change occurs without there being too many victims and without leading to an invasion.[29]

This excitable language puts de Gaulle squarely in the camp of those on the right who saw the events of 6 February as a salutary challenge to parliamentary democracy – but it is not clear what positive alternative he favoured.

If one tries to place de Gaulle's view of politics in a longer perspective, two themes stand out. The first was a preoccupation with a 'rational' – the word recurs often in his writings – organization of society. The need for a more rationally organized state was an idea shared widely across the political spectrum in the pre-war years by those dissatisfied with the inadequacies of the working of the parliamentary Republic. It was the critique underlying Robert de Jouvenel's classic text *La République des camarades* or the writings of the centre-right political theorist Charles Benoist. Both these authors are cited in de Gaulle's notebooks.[30] De Jouvenel's book, published in 1914, had lambasted the politicians of the parliamentary Republic as an isolated caste cut off from the realities of the nation: its most famous observation was that two *députés* of different parties always had more in common with each other than with their electors. Benoist was a conservative republican whose disillusion with democracy had led him to move progressively towards Action Française.

During the war, a new strand was added to this concern with rational organization. This was the idea that the organization of the state could be improved by adopting the methods of modern industry. Two names often cited in this respect were those of Henri Fayol and the American F. W. Taylor, both popularizers of the theory of management science.[31] Mayer was a great admirer of Fayol, and although there is no direct mention of Fayol in de Gaulle's writings, he does display a fascination with what he dubbed the 'Taylorization' of society – mass production, mass spectator sport, modern advertising – both because of the threat it posed and because of the lessons it offered. 'Play and our desires are haunted by machines,' he wrote in *Towards a Professional Army*:

> The gap between the expectations of society and the sclerosis of the social system has become so flagrant that it will soon need to be overcome. Our generation which is so obsessed with efficiency: with horsepower, records, series (mass production), specialists, cost prices; our era which is so eager for clarity: for naked lights, clean lines, hygiene, women in bathing costumes; our century which sets such store on displays of strength: competition, cartels, elites, propaganda, nationalism – will no longer put up with the slowness, the confusion and weakness which earlier periods were ready to accept.[32]

One historical figure who exemplified de Gaulle's ideal of a rational organizer was Louis XIV's War Minister, the Marquis de Louvois, the man responsible for the modernization of the *ancien régime* army. To his mother, de Gaulle wrote in 1919: 'We have great need of a Louvois or a Richelieu.'[33] It is worth quoting de Gaulle's portrait of Louvois in the history of the French army he had been writing for Pétain:

> Disdaining theories, he was careful not to disrupt or destroy; but as a realist he never ceased in his efforts to reform and improve. Though obstinate in pursuing his ends, he was capable of being flexible. An enthusiastic planner, he knew also how to bide his time. Unencumbered by scruples, he used whatever means seemed simplest and most expedient. He was severe in his judgements of men while not despising them. Clear-sighted without being sceptical, devoid of illusions while not lacking faith, he was implacable regarding incompetence . . . He was distant but also approachable, ready to read reports while in the end making his own judgements, welcoming advice but jealously keeping the final decision for himself. He had enemies and allies, but no friends.[34]

Louvois operated in the structured and hierarchical society of the *ancien régime* that was forever lost – except in the mind of a Maurras. But while de Gaulle's view of the organization of society was, like Maurras's, unashamedly elitist – words like freedom and democracy do not figure in his writing in this period – he knew he was living in a world where 'the antique deference' to authority no longer existed.

A second strand of de Gaulle's thinking was the need for leadership in a society of mass politics, a society fashioned by industrialization and standardization, and suspicious of individuality – the 'civilization of the termite heap' as he called it.[35] De Gaulle was also influenced by the writings of the social theorist Gustave Le Bon (1841–1931) whose analysis of crowd psychology influenced figures as various as Theodore Roosevelt, Mussolini, Sigmund Freud and Hitler.[36] For Le Bon, crowds in modern urban society were irrational and malleable; their emotions needed to be harnessed and manipulated by leaders who knew how to exploit their irrationality. De Gaulle quoted Le Bon in his notebooks, and in 1916, after reading an article by him on the Revolution, he wrote: '[Le Bon] refutes the legend of the divine people, always sacrosanct in its follies, its crimes, and notes that the people during the Revolution were effectively and continuously "led".'[37] De Gaulle's thoughts on 'prestige' (which we might translate as 'charismatic leadership') in *The Edge of the Sword* read like direct citations from Le Bon (with a dose of Bergson): 'One does not stir up the crowds other than by elementary sentiments, violent images, brutal invocations'; 'Men cannot do without being led, any more than they can do without eating, drinking and sleeping'; leaders had to be able to stir the imagination and excite the 'latent faith of the masses'; the leader's authority is not susceptible to rational analysis any more than 'love which is explicable only as the action of an inexpressible charm'. In short, the leader was a 'master towards whom people's faith and dreams are directed'.[38]

In a note he penned in 1927 on the memoirs of the French statesman Raymond Poincaré, de Gaulle sketched his impressions of what a political leader should *not* be. Poincaré, a sober and hardworking conservative who had served as France's President during the war, had been overshadowed from 1917 by the more charismatic Georges Clemenceau who had acted as his Prime Minister. Of Poincaré's memoirs de Gaulle wrote:[39]

A very good exercise from a statesman who is not too sure of himself, confusing History with Politics . . . There is intelligence and savoir-faire but one looks for the grandeur, the elevation, the summits of courage which Clemenceau several times attained . . . Poincaré is a man of texts, a mechanically organized intelligence . . . One nowhere sees in his book that he had any intuitive perception of the France of 1914 [all this is pure Bergson]. He speaks to us only of ministers, diplomats, Senate and Chamber, when these insignificant entities played just walk-on parts. He believes in telegrams, messages, proclamations . . . while there was only a ferocious law of the species, an implacable fatality that pushed the world to war. He passes over the essential, that is to say what any peasant felt clearly from 20 July and even before. Indeed he had – he says it himself candidly – no contact with the people . . . Poincaré was an executant [*commis*] of the first rank. If there had been a great Frenchman to harness his talents: think what he might have given under Louis XIV! But left to himself, he was half great, half honest, half understanding. In short, a statesman tailored to the requirements of the Republic.

If we assemble all these pieces, de Gaulle's political ideal in the mid-1930s seems to combine elitist and managerial authoritarianism with charismatic leadership. In practical terms this could have led him in directions which had little in common with parliamentary democracy. But the path he did take was determined by two other factors: his discovery of a new patron who happened to be a key player in the existing political system, and his disgust at the stance taken by many conservatives in the face of a resurgent Germany.

A NEW PATRON

In December 1934, Jean Auburtin set up a meeting between de Gaulle and Paul Reynaud, a leading centre-right politician. Reynaud who had held several important ministerial posts, was one of the most able politicians of his generation, but when he met de Gaulle his career had stalled. In 1934 he had broken with the political establishment by arguing that France would not recover from the depression without a devaluation of the franc. After the dollar and sterling had been forced off the gold standard in 1931 and 1933, France's exports were being priced out of world markets. But for most politicians of the period the strong franc was viewed as a symbol of national pride and devaluation as immoral. By challenging this consensus, Reynaud put himself beyond the political pale, although he was gambling that his moment would come. He did not always help his cause by insufferable self-righteousness and never hiding his justifiable conviction that he was cleverer than most people around him.

Of his first meeting with Reynaud, de Gaulle commented in his *Memoirs*: 'I saw him, I convinced him, and from that moment, I worked with him.'[40] Whether or not it was actually quite so simple, Reynaud had nothing to lose by taking up another challenge to prevailing orthodoxies. He was by far the most important politician to show serious interest in de Gaulle's ideas on army reform. From this point, whatever his intimate thoughts about the working of the parliamentary Republic, de Gaulle, through Reynaud, was gambling that the best way to see his ideas accepted was to play the system from inside. Loustaunau-Lacau, to whom de Gaulle had been close in the 1920s, later remembered a conversation with him around this time. De Gaulle had told him 'one cannot remake the present State. It is what it is.'[41] Loustaunau-Lacau made a different choice, became involved in subversive army plots against the Republic and ended up supporting the Vichy regime.

Reynaud's first public intervention in favour of de Gaulle's proposals occurred during a parliamentary debate in March 1935 over a government bill to extend military service to two years. Reynaud made a speech explaining the need for a professional army, and tabled a bill that de Gaulle had drafted for him. De Gaulle was in the public galleries to hear his speech, whose key point was that the current organization of the French army prevented it taking offensive action. Reynaud did not say much about tanks.[42] Although he did not refer to de Gaulle in the speech, his name was explicitly raised twice in the subsequent debate by two left-wing opponents of Reynaud's bill: Léon Blum and the Communist leader Maurice Thorez. They deplored any return to the theories of the offensive that had been so costly in 1914: 'all that is missing are the red trousers,' declared Thorez in reference to the red trousers worn by French soldiers as they marched to their deaths in 1914.[43] De Gaulle, who presented himself as a modernizer of the army, was depicted as a throwback to the past.

Although Reynaud's bill was defeated, de Gaulle had now hitched himself firmly to Reynaud's star. He wrote to him two months after the debate declaring that Reynaud had a 'great national task to accomplish' and that he was 'ready to be "your man"' in such an eventuality'.[44] In letter after letter, de Gaulle shamelessly flattered his new patron – 'in the current void in which we live you are the statesman who has ideas, a programme and courage'[45] – but he genuinely believed, as he told Mayer, that Reynaud was a 'real statesman'.[46] On the face of it Reynaud's prospects seemed to have dimmed after the electoral victory of the left-wing Popular Front in May 1936. The new Minister of National Defence was the left-of-centre Radical Edouard Daladier, a close supporter of the army Chief of Staff, General Gamelin. Both men firmly opposed the professional army. But de Gaulle clearly believed that the new political coalition would not last. He told Reynaud that 'perhaps soon' there would be 'a national regrouping' as politicians became alive to the threat from Germany.[47] So confident had de Gaulle the soldier become in his relationship with Reynaud the politician that he started offering his patron tactical advice on political matters. In 1935, he drew Reynaud's attention to other politicians coming round to their views. After the elections of 1936, he arranged to meet the Radical politician Camille Chautemps. Although Chautemps was one of the most notorious wheeler-dealers of French politics, de Gaulle told Reynaud that he might prove an ally because he was known to be a rival of Daladier.[48] For someone who affected to despise the grubby world of Third Republic politics de Gaulle was remarkably attuned to the uses that could be made of it. This love–hate relationship with politics persisted through his entire career.

If de Gaulle remained optimistic about Reynaud's chances, it was because the conditions that had caused the Popular Front victory in May

1936 changed rapidly after the election. The left won because of the economic crisis and because people feared that the anti-parliamentary Leagues represented a threat to democracy. Foreign policy had hardly figured in the election. To the extent that the Popular Front had any position on foreign affairs, it was a mixture of hopeful internationalism and idealistic pacifism. During the 1936 election campaign, the pieties underpinning such a policy had already been challenged when in March Hitler sent troops into the Rhineland. The threat from Germany could not be ignored, and some on the left embarked upon an anguished reappraisal of their internationalist and pacifist position on foreign affairs.

While the left had suddenly woken up to the threat of Nazism, de Gaulle merely viewed it as a new version of the eternal combat between France and Germany. He saw nothing especially significant about Nazism, which is never mentioned in *Towards a Professional Army*. 'Hitler', de Gaulle told one correspondent in 1938, 'is not Napoleon. He has never won a battle. His force comes above all from the cowardice of others.'[49] For de Gaulle the arrival of Hitler was in some sense a positive development since it served to dissipate illusions regarding Germany which he had never shared.

When the government had consulted Gamelin in March 1936 on the possible responses that France could offer to the reoccupation of the Rhineland, he had nothing to offer except an unwieldy general mobilization. Hitler's bold action in occupying the Rhineland had been a bluff since he was not yet ready to fight, but this was a bluff that the French government had been unable to call because its army was not organized in a way that would allow it to take rapid offensive action. All this made de Gaulle's arguments seem less far-fetched than they had in 1934. The lesson was not lost on Léon Blum, who had forcefully opposed de Gaulle's ideas two years earlier. In October 1936 Blum granted de Gaulle an audience. De Gaulle's account of the meeting (we do not have Blum's) was written many years after the event to make a point about the workings of parliamentary government – but it rings true:

> During our conversation, the telephone rang ten times, diverting Léon Blum's attention to minor parliamentary or administrative questions. As I was taking my leave and the phone rang again, he made a weary gesture: 'You see if it is easy for a head of government to keep his mind on the plan you have outlined when he cannot remain five minutes thinking about the same idea.'[50]

Although nothing came from this meeting, Blum's new government, elected to implement social reforms, announced in September 1936 an ambitious programme of rearmament, including the production of tanks. At the same, time the government decided on the creation of two heavy armoured divisions (DCRs) of the kind de Gaulle had been advocating. All this was encouraging to de Gaulle even if he worried that Germany was moving faster: 'It is true that if there was an international competition for organizing defensive fortresses we would certainly win it.'[51] De Gaulle continued to bombard Reynaud with information for his speeches and public interventions.

The fact that Socialists like Blum were now converting to the need for rearmament suggests that de Gaulle was right to have predicted to Reynaud that there would be a regrouping of French politics in the face of the German threat. Such a regrouping was indeed about to occur but not in the way that de Gaulle had hoped. Some on the left now seemed ready to abandon pacifism and internationalism, which might have offered common ground with conservative nationalists (like de Gaulle) who believed that France's security was best guaranteed by rearmament and the strengthening of her alliances. It was in this spirit that in 1934 the conservative government of Doumergue had started the process of building up ties with France's eastern allies including the Soviet Union, resulting a year later in the signing of a security pact with Moscow. But when the pact came up for ratification in parliament in February 1936, some 150 conservative *députés* voted against because of their concern about the rising influence of Communism in France. This was a sign of new political alignments to come.

After the election of the Popular Front, as hysteria about Communism in France intensified, some conservatives began to view Hitler's Germany as the lesser evil. If Hitler wished to expand eastwards against the Soviet Union, why should France worry? Appeasement of this kind was anathema to de Gaulle. He wrote to his mother in December 1936:

> You ask me, dear *maman*, what I think of the 'Franco-Russian pact'. My answer is very simple. We are heading rapidly towards war with Germany and, if things turn out badly for us, Italy will not fail to profit from the fact and kick us when we are down. All that matters is to survive. The rest is just words. So I ask you, on whom can we count to aid us militarily? Poland is nothing, and anyway she is playing a double game. England has her fleet, but no army and her air force is very behind. We do not have the means to refuse the help of the Russians, whatever horror we have for their regime. It is the same story as Francis I allying with the Muslims against Charles V. I know that the relentless and very cunning propaganda of Hitler has succeeded in making many honest people in France believe that he has nothing against us and that it is enough, to buy peace, to allow him to conquer Central Europe and the Ukraine. But personally I am convinced that this is hypocrisy and that his principal aim is to crush France after having isolated her.[52]

Where others saw the 'Soviet Union' de Gaulle saw 'Russia', where others read the world through the lenses of ideology, de Gaulle read it through the lens of geography. As he had written already in 1919: 'Bolshevism will not last eternally in Russia. A day will come, it is inevitable, when order will be restored and Russia, reconstituting her forces, will start to look around her again.'[53]

Over the next two years de Gaulle's worst fears about Germany's expansionism were confirmed first by the *Anschluss* with Austria in March 1938, and then in September 1938 when Hitler's demand to take over the German-speaking parts of Czechoslovakia – the Sudetenland – took France and Britain to the brink of war with Germany. This was averted at the last minute by the Munich Agreement, which gave Hitler most of what he wanted. De Gaulle was plunged into despair and indignation:

> The French, like startled chickens, utter cries of joy while German troops enter triumphantly into the territory of a State that we ourselves helped to construct, whose frontiers we guaranteed and which was our ally. Step by step we accept the habit of humiliation and retreat so that it becomes a second nature. We are drinking the cup to the dregs.[54]

De Gaulle was especially shocked by what he described as the 'terrifying collapse' of Munich, signifying that 'France has ceased to be a great power,'[55] by the 'aberration of a part of French opinion – that which usually is the best part'. This comment was directed against the conservative right which was his natural home. While on the left of the political spectrum Léon Blum confessed to feeling what he called a 'cowardly relief' that war had been averted, many conservatives welcomed Munich without even that qualifying adjective, among them Action Française. On those issues where de Gaulle had shared some ground with Maurras – his bleakly pessimistic view of international relations and his Germanophobia – this was the moment of rupture. But one might say that in this case it was Maurras who had ceased to be Maurrassian not de Gaulle. For Maurras, internal enemies like the Jewish Socialist Blum had replaced the external enemy Germany as the greatest threat to France. De Gaulle's priorities were the opposite. Although he had failed to persuade Blum of his ideas, his letters reveal a frustrated respect for him which would not have been shared by many others from his background. 'How can a man of Blum's stature', he wrote to Mayer, 'not see that one of the principal causes of our reverses is the military impotence in which we are placed by an absurd military organization?'[56] De Gaulle made an interesting remark to his brother-in-law in the 1950s when they were discussing Maurras, whose descent into collaboration after 1940 had put him beyond the pale of respectable politics. De

Gaulle commented: 'It is true that I appreciated the fact that he was attached to the defence of order in life and in the State, and to classicism in art.' But he went on that he could not accept 'certain exaggerations in his political views' which led him in 1940 to 'sordid exaltation' of dictatorial regimes: 'He created for himself a world into which his deafness had imprisoned him. Perhaps that is an explanation for the final aberrations of this solitary individual, who was cut off from the world and because of this became unhinged.'[57] This is similar to the apocryphal remark de Gaulle is alleged to have made: 'Maurras was so right that it drove him mad.'

Maurras had always been as Anglophobic as he was Germanophobic. And the rare comments de Gaulle had previously made about Britain were usually negative too. In the Levant, he had experienced Britain as the hereditary enemy. Now the threat from Germany was causing him to revise his views. He told Reynaud that preparing France for the coming war would require not only a reorganization of the French army but also a real coordination with the British – an 'entente of the democracies' in his words.[58] In 1938, de Gaulle became a subscriber to the recently founded Christian Democratic newspaper *Temps présent*. Christian Democracy, which had sought since the nineteenth century to reconcile the values of democracy and Catholicism, was not part of his ideological inheritance – unlike the social Catholic traditions of the Nord. What presumably attracted him to the Christian Democrats at this time was the fact that their anti-Nazism was leading them to oppose appeasement of Germany. For de Gaulle this was *the* issue of the day, leading him in potentially new political directions.

DE GAULLE'S HISTORY OF FRANCE

By the time of the Munich Agreement, de Gaulle was no longer working at the CSDN. In September 1937, he had been posted to Metz to command a tank regiment following his promotion to colonel. His boldness in publicly promoting his ideas did not harm his advance up the ranks. He had always sedulously cultivated political patrons who could be useful to him. In 1925, when working for Pétain, he was in touch with the centrist politician Joseph Paul-Boncour who had shown interest in one of his early articles.[59] Ten years later he lobbied both Paul-Boncour and Reynaud to get himself promoted to colonel.[60] In this case de Gaulle was unsuccessful but he was manoeuvring a year later, telling Reynaud that he was being blocked because of his heterodox views: 'some would find it very attractive to stifle the ideas by strangling their advocate.'[61]

In truth, de Gaulle was not being 'strangled' at all. The army high command was remarkably tolerant of its unruly subordinate. De Gaulle advanced no less quickly up the ranks than his two distinguished near contemporaries Alphonse Juin and Jean de Lattre de Tassigny, who were in no way iconoclasts. Juin and de Lattre each became captains at twenty-eight (de Gaulle at twenty-five), majors at thirty-eight (de Gaulle at thirty-seven), lieutenant colonels at forty-four (de Gaulle at forty-three), colonels at forty-seven (exactly as de Gaulle) and brigadier generals at fifty (also exactly the same as de Gaulle). Given the handicap of having spent half of the First War as a prisoner, de Gaulle had managed his career remarkably successfully.[62]

Promotion mattered for financial reasons as well as status. Soldiers' pay had declined in real terms after the war. Although the de Gaulles did not live lavishly, a married officer was expected to maintain a certain style of life. The de Gaulles also bore the added financial burden of looking after Anne. In 1932 they took on a full-time carer, Mlle Potel, who would remain with them continuously for the next twelve years, living as a member of the family. This required them to move to a larger flat in the Boulevard Raspail after de Gaulle's return from Lebanon. That de Gaulle's finances were straitened is suggested by a letter he wrote to his brother-in-law Alfred Caillau after the death of Henri de Gaulle: 'That announcement in the newspapers cost 950 francs (!) that I have paid and for which I send you the receipt. As you have agreed to coordinate these sad expenses, and as I find myself personally a bit under pressure with expenses of all kinds, I am giving you these figures now.'[63]

Yvonne de Gaulle's father also died in 1932 and her mother in 1933. The small inheritance she received as one of four siblings, plus the small inheritance de Gaulle had received on the death of his father, allowed them to contemplate buying a house in the country. After searching for two years, they alighted upon La Boisserie, a property in a remote part of eastern France at the tiny village of Colombey-les-deux-Eglises (320 inhabitants) in the Champagne region. Since this was not a fashionable region for second homes, unlike Brittany or Normandy, the house was affordable. Its price of 45,000 francs was about the equivalent of the annual salary of a lieutenant colonel (51,000). The vendor was a widow who had had difficulties in finding a buyer. So the de Gaulles were able to purchase the property under the *viager* system: a down-payment of 17,000 on purchase and then 6,000 per year during the life of the vendor. This turned out to be a good deal because she drowned in her bath two years later. Another advantage of the house was that it was equidistant between Paris and the eastern frontiers of France where military garrisons were situated. Since the de Gaulles could no longer afford a car, they made the five-hour journey by train from Paris to the nearest station at Bar-le-Duc. From there they were driven by the *garagiste* of Colombey, the only person in the village to own a motor vehicle.

The house was modest with minimal comfort: no running water for the first two years, no central heating, and electricity only in some rooms. There were two hectares of garden in which Anne could be taken for walks away from the gaze of strangers. The de Gaulles took possession of it in July 1934, but initially the house was habitable only in the summer. De Gaulle wrote in August 1936 to Mayer before the holidays: 'I hope you have better weather than the weather that is keeping me confined for the moment in my shack [*bicoque*] in the Haute Marne face to face with the last (and most difficult) chapter of my next book.'[64]

The book in question had been commissioned by Daniel-Rops, whom de Gaulle had got to know through Mayer. Having no time to start anything new, de Gaulle decided to resuscitate the history of the French army that had been gathering dust ever since Pétain decided to shelve it a decade earlier. The 'most difficult chapter' he needed to write was on the Great War, which involved treating the delicate subject of the relationship between Foch and Pétain.

Once the proofs of the book were ready in August 1938, de Gaulle informed Pétain that he was publishing it. He asked if he might include a preface to let readers know that Pétain had originally inspired the book. Not unreasonably taken aback by this cavalier behaviour regarding a manuscript he regarded as belonging to him, Pétain forbade de Gaulle to publish. This produced a long self-justificatory reply from de Gaulle assuring the Marshal that he had eliminated all his corrections – 'not without the book being the worse for it', he added with flattering insincerity – which meant it contained nothing of which one could not say 'with absolute certainty it is de Gaulle'. He went on:

> I was thirty-seven; now I am forty-eight. Morally I have suffered blows – even from you M. le Maréchal – lost illusions, given up ambitions. At the time, my style and my ideas were not known, as they are now beginning to be. In short, I no longer have the plasticity and the 'incognito' that would be necessary for me to ascribe to the credit of others whatever talent I have in the fields of letters and history.[65]

Pétain agreed to discuss the matter in person. The two men met one Sunday afternoon in August at Pétain's Paris apartment. The meeting went badly, although there are different versions of what was actually said. Many years later de Gaulle told a journalist that Pétain had angrily asked for the proofs to be handed over to him and de Gaulle had refused with the words: 'You can give me orders in military matters but not in literary ones.' De Gaulle would certainly have been capable of this impertinence. In the end, since Pétain had no means of preventing publication, he agreed to draft a dedication to himself to be inserted on the title page. De Gaulle's final provocation was to ditch Pétain's pedestrian draft – 'To M. le Maréchal, who readily helped me with his advice' – with one of his own: 'To M. le Maréchal who wished this book to be written.' Pétain was justifiably aggrieved, reminding de Gaulle in an angry letter that he had *not* wished the book to be written. When the publishers became alarmed, de Gaulle told them to reply 'ingratiatingly in form but evasively in content'.[66]

De Gaulle had no qualms about burning his bridges with Pétain because in Reynaud he had a powerful new patron committed to his ideas. The literary spat between Pétain and de Gaulle has significance in the light of later events. De Gaulle was almost unique in 1940 in sharing none of that reverence for Pétain which affected most of the French political class. Whether Pétain had really 'died' for him in 1925 as he later claimed, he certainly was 'dead' for him by 1939. This was intellectually liberating. As for the book, published in September 1938, it sold relatively well – over 6,000 copies by the end of the year – but de Gaulle's hopes for wider critical success were blighted by the fact that General Weygand published his own history of the French army at almost exactly the same time. De Gaulle's book was a more accomplished literary achievement but Weygand, as one of the army's most senior generals, received all the publicity.

The style of *France and her Army* is so unmistakably de Gaulle's that one can see why in the late 1920s Pétain had decided to abandon the project of publishing under his name. The book is a distillation of the themes of all de Gaulle's inter-war writings – on leadership, on the relationship between state and army, on the pitfalls of (*a priori*) doctrinaire thinking and so on – as illustrated in the history of France from the Gaulish warriors Brennus and Vercingétorix through to those heroes of the Great War Pétain and Foch. It opens: 'France was made by the sword [*épée*]. Our fathers entered into History with the two-edged sword [*glaive*] of Brennus.' This densely written work is not constructed as a continuous narrative. Each of the seven chronologically arranged chapters selects an epoch in French history to draw out lessons. Thus of the battles of the Hundred Years War, de Gaulle writes: 'At Crécy, then at Poitiers and later at Agincourt, we can see the beginning of an era in which neither ardour [*fougue*] nor numbers counted any longer without the art of warfare ... Thus because France had not adapted her army to the new requirements of the era, she was plunged into the worst crisis of her History.' De Gaulle's book is not military history but rather a study of the way in which over different periods governments were – or were not – able to forge an army worthy of the role that France was destined to play in the world. In his emphasis on the importance of the state to counter and discipline the tendencies of the French people to fragmentation and individualism, de Gaulle writes in the spirit of the Action Française royalist historical school, especially the best-selling inter-war history of France by the popular historian Jacques Bainville. Also in the spirit of Action Française is de Gaulle's observation that the logic of French history 'always brings the Teutons into a struggle against the Gauls'. But where de Gaulle differed from the Action Française vision of the world was in his readiness to judge different periods of French history pragmatically and unideologically. He was ready to find virtues in any regime, or any individual, that had successfully defended French grandeur. For this reason he writes warmly of Lazare Carnot, the revolutionary leader and member of the notorious Committee of Public Safety, who reorganized the French armies in 1793–4. Thanks to Carnot, writes de Gaulle, the revolutionary Republic 'renouncing the illusions which on two occasions came close to throwing her into the abyss, understood that order and discipline are the necessary conditions of strength'. De Gaulle also has warm words for the republican Léon Gambetta who tried in vain to organize the French army in 1870–71 and reverse the defeats of the Franco-Prussian War.

But the regime for which de Gaulle displays the most instinctive sympathy is the *ancien régime* of the seventeenth and eighteenth centuries. His chapter on this period opens: 'The policy of the *ancien régime* was one of circumstances, avoiding abstractions but holding on to realities, preferring the useful to the sublime, the opportune to the spectacular [*retentissant*], seeking for each particular problem not the ideal solution but the practical one, showing few scruples about the means of achieving this, but showing greatness in its careful balance between the aims pursued and the forces available to the State.' This is the context of de Gaulle's admiring portrait of Louvois that has already been quoted. For these reasons, de Gaulle cannot unreservedly admire Napoleon, to whom he devotes a full chapter: 'In the presence of such a prodigious career, our judgement is torn between blame and admiration.' In his view admiration was appropriate until 1807 when 'his policy, however ambitious and exigent, was marked by a relative moderation', but after that point he started to 'ignore all limits [*mesure*]'. Of Napoleon's end he writes: 'His fall was gigantic, in proportion to his glory ... It was the tragic revenge of *mesure*, the just fury of reason ... but the superhuman prestige of genius and the marvellous *vertu* of combat.' The 'but' is important. For all his admiration for realism and order, de Gaulle believed no less in the importance of national sentiment and élan. The word 'ardour' appears in the book hardly less often than the word 'order'. Thus de Gaulle's Cartesianism was always balanced by his Berg-sonianism, his classicism by his romanticism. In his analysis, organization, method and order are impotent if they are not harnessed to national energy; but national energy and élan without order can lead only to chaos.[67] Thus although de Gaulle's book singles out a few individual heroes (Louvois, Carnot, Napoleon) most of the chapters are constructed around pairings of individuals whose qualities complement each other since the perfect balance is rarely encountered in one person: Turenne and Condé in the *ancien régime*, Dumouriez and Hoche in the Revolution, Poincaré and Clemenceau during the war. 'Poincaré embodied France's reason; Clem-enceau her fury.' Finally, the book closes with the coupling of Pétain who had a sense of 'the art of the real and the possible' and Foch who embodied energy and ardour – 'it is hard to see what Foch's plans and his élan would have achieved without the instrument modelled by Pétain.'[68]

'UP TO MY NECK IN TANKS'

De Gaulle took up his new position at the head of the 507th Tank Regiment at Metz in September 1937.[69] The other candidate for this position was Lieutenant Colonel Jean-Paul Perré, three years younger than de Gaulle and considered to be one of the army's tank experts. He had published more widely on the subject than de Gaulle but was a defender of the traditional role of tanks as an accompaniment of infantry. That the post was given to de Gaulle is another sign not only that he had not harmed his career by his public advocacy of his ideas but also that the debate was moving in his direction. Even so things moved slowly. Although in 1936 Gamelin had ordered the creation of two heavy tank divisions, these were not due to be operational before September 1939 at the earliest. De Gaulle's new regiment was one of eleven infantry tank regiments equipped with light and medium tanks. This was not what de Gaulle had been arguing for during the last three years, but at least he now had the chance to learn how tanks worked in practice rather than writing about them in theory. Before taking up his post he was sent on a short training course. The observations of his su-periors followed a familiar pattern: 'Natural gifts of rare quality and especially a fine talent for exposition ... But this is too often hidden by a cold and haughty attitude which seems like a camouflage. He displays a lot of suspicion, rarely puts himself forward and does not often open up.'[70]

De Gaulle threw himself completely into his new post. For the first time since 1919, he had no spare time for writing or even for family life. Although he was usually punctilious about family obligations, only a few weeks after their arrival in Metz his wife had to write to apologize to her brother because her husband would not be attending the annual autumn hunt at Sept-Fontaines: 'Charles is so occupied that he has asked me to respond to your invitation . . . Charles sleeps standing up, he is just back from manoeuvres and heads off again at 4.30 tomorrow morning.'[71] De Gaulle was, as he wrote to his friend Nachin, 'up to my neck in tanks'.[72] Although 'infinitely saddened' by the news of the death of Emile Mayer in November 1938, he was not able to attend the funeral. To his wife he apologized for being at Colombey so little over the summer; to his friend Auburtin because he had found so few occasions to get to Paris.[73]

De Gaulle's excitement about his new post is palpable in a letter he wrote to Reynaud six weeks after arriving in Metz:

> Seeing things now from below, I can already draw this conclusion: the modern tank is a huge fact. *Whether on foot, on horseback or in vehicles one has to see it moving, firing, crushing all in its path to understand that its appearance is a revolution in the form and the art of war.* All tactics, all strategy, all arms from now revolve around it.

His own observations 'from below' confirmed what he had been writing for the last three years except that he now emphasized less insistently the idea that tank divisions required a professional army. There needed to be a 'solid and substantial backbone of professional specialists', but otherwise the idea of using conscripts was not ruled out.[74] It might have helped his cause if de Gaulle had reached this conclusion earlier.

Two months after arriving in Metz de Gaulle organized for Armistice Day a spectacular parade of over sixty tanks through the streets of Metz. Two weeks later he repeated the operation on the occasion of a visit by the Minister of Defence, Daladier. With an innate sense of showmanship de Gaulle used these occasions to publicize tanks and counter the prevailing consensus which endlessly celebrated the defensive qualities of the Maginot Line. Tanks needed to be 'sold' to the population and to visiting politicians – and even to his own superiors. During his two years in Metz de Gaulle clashed on numerous occasions with his superior General Henri Giraud, commanding the military region where Metz was situated. During an exercise on how to respond to a possible breach of the Maginot Line, de Gaulle planned to reach the town of Pont-à-Mousson in a day. Giraud responded: 'as long as I am in command of the region, your tanks will move at the speed of the infantry.' There were several incidents of this kind. De Gaulle was not without allies, however, and he got on well with General Charles Delestraint who commanded the 3rd Tank Brigade. Both Giraud and Delestraint were to cross de Gaulle's path again during the war – the latter as an ally, the former as an enemy. De Gaulle gave ammunition to his critics by working his tanks so relentlessly that on two occasions there were complaints about the rate of deterioration of the equipment at a time when French industry was working flat out to increase tank production and the supply of spare parts was lagging behind.[75]

Even if he was not able to visit Paris as much as he wanted, de Gaulle kept in regular contact with Reynaud. He did not want to be forgotten just at the point when Reynaud's moment seemed about to arrive at last. In April 1938, the Popular Front had finally collapsed. A 'national unity' government was formed under Daladier. Reynaud returned to office for the first time since 1932 – although his portfolio as Minister of Justice, and then Finance Minister, did not give him any influence over defence policy. Like de Gaulle, Reynaud deplored the Munich Agreement but decided not to resign from the government on the grounds that this would leave the coast clear for the appeasers. In many people's eyes – not least his own – he was the coming man.

De Gaulle had now moved beyond the ideas expressed in his *Towards a Professional Army*. Or rather he had come to believe – partly through his own experience of French military bureaucracy – that his plans for the modernization of the army required root-and-branch political solutions. He had told Reynaud soon after they met: 'Do not expect the military corps – any more than any other – to transform itself alone. The technicians are too occupied by their current tasks and also – it is inevitable – too taken up by their theories, their activities and their rivalries.'[76] Two years later, his solution to this problem was to draft for Reynaud a project for the setting up of a reorganized Ministry of Defence properly integrating all three services. Clearly he knew who should head it.[77]

There had been two de Gaulles in the 1930s: the public crusader and the anonymous military bureaucrat; the de Gaulle who celebrated in mystical terms the nobility of the soldier's vocation and the de Gaulle who grappled with technical questions of military organization; the de Gaulle who mused on charismatic leadership and the de Gaulle who aspired to a rationalization of the machinery of the state. By the end of the decade these strands converged as his ideas about his own future took shape in his mind. 'Who will give a Louvois to the Republic?' he asked Mayer in 1927.[78] Now he had an answer. That would be Reynaud's mission once he became head of government; and Reynaud's Louvois would of course be de Gaulle. He wrote to Reynaud after Munich: 'Your destiny as a Statesman is to restore France to her rank in all areas. The difficulties are proportionate to the grandeur of the task. Whatever happens, please do not forget that I remain entirely at your disposal.'[79]

5

The Battle of France,
September 1939–June 1940

WAITING FOR THE CALL

When the Munich Agreement was signed in September 1938, de Gaulle wrote to his wife:

> As usual, we capitulate without fighting faced with the insolent demands of the Germans and hand over our Czech allies to the common enemy. German and Italian money has flooded the so-called 'national' press . . . The series of humiliations will go on. It will continue with the abandonment of our colonies, then with that of Alsace, etc., unless a sudden recovery of honour wakes the nation up . . . Today's capitulation will give us a short respite, like the aged Madame du Barry on the revolutionary scaffold begging '*Encore un petit moment, M. le bourreau* (Just a moment longer, Mr Executioner).'[1]

The respite was not long. In March 1939, Hitler sent troops into Prague, breaching the promises he had made at Munich. To show that they were willing to go no further down the road of concessions, the British and French governments agreed jointly to guarantee the security of Poland, Greece and Rumania. Over the summer, to give teeth to these commitments the two governments for the first time started seriously to explore the possibility of a full alliance with the Soviet Union, and go beyond the limited Franco-Soviet Pact of 1936. But since Russia had no common border with Germany, any military assistance to France would involve crossing Poland. The Poles, as suspicious of the Russians as of the Germans, were unlikely to agree; squaring this circle would probably have been impossible. Meanwhile Stalin was being secretly approached by the German government about signing their own agreement. On 23 August, while French and British negotiators were still negotiating in Moscow, the German and Soviet governments announced to almost universal astonishment that they had concluded a non-aggression pact. Although this announcement was a terrible shock to the west, if the French high command had been forced to choose between the Soviet Union and Poland it would probably have chosen the latter. Trust in the Red Army had been shaken by Stalin's purges, while the Polish army, the fourth largest in Europe, inspired surprising confidence. These prejudices were bolstered by political suspicion of Communism.

De Gaulle's response to the German–Soviet Pact is not known. Since he had strongly supported the Franco-Soviet Pact in 1936, and since he had not been favourably impressed by the Polish army in the 1920s, one can suspect that he harboured few illusions about the capacity of the Poles to hold out. And he lost no opportunity to point out to correspondents that, if he had been listened to, France would not have found herself about to enter war in such unpromising conditions. It would have been possible to call Hitler's bluff when he reoccupied the Rhineland in March 1936.[2] But for de Gaulle the most important fact was that the Allies had abandoned their illusions about Hitler. In his view, France's continued existence as a great power depended on preventing further German expansion into eastern Europe or the Balkans.

On 1 September, German troops invaded Poland; two days later, France and Britain declared war on Germany. The Allies were planning for a long war. Their strategy was to impose a blockade. The intention was to asphyxiate the German economy, spark a revolt against Hitler and bring to power more moderate forces ready to make peace. If this did not work, the Allies would at least have won the time necessary to exploit their superior economic resources and prepare for a military victory within three years. The pressure was on Germany to win a short war before the Allies were ready to win the long one. Here Poland proved a terrible disappointment. Gamelin had expected the Poles to hold out for about six months, but within a week it was clear that this was wildly optimistic.

The French were not in a position to offer the Poles any immediate help. On 7 September French forces advanced into German territory a few kilometres beyond the Maginot Line, 'taking' a few abandoned villages. But this was merely a symbolic demonstration, not the prelude for a general offensive. On 4 October, after Poland's defeat, the French fell back behind the Maginot Line. Although the essence of the Allied plan was to sit tight and continue rearming, this did not rule out the possibility of military operations on the peripheries while avoiding any frontal attack on Germany. There was much discussion of an operation to cut off German supplies of iron ore from Scandinavia. But since no agreement could be reached on the details of such a plan, for the moment nothing was done.

No one found this phoney war – or *drôle de guerre* as it came to be called in France – more frustrating than de Gaulle. At the outbreak of war he had been promoted to command the tanks of the Fifth Army stationed in Alsace. Since these were only light tanks, dispersed in five battalions, this was a far cry from the armoured divisions he had been advocating since 1934.[3]

In a prophetic letter to Reynaud six weeks after the outbreak of the war, de Gaulle pinpointed the pitfalls of the Allied waiting strategy:

Our military system has been exclusively built around defence. If the enemy attacks us tomorrow I am sure we will hold out. But if he does not attack, we are reduced to almost compete impotence. In my opinion the enemy will not attack for a long while. His interest is to let us stew in our own juice . . . Then when he judges that we are weary with waiting, disoriented and unhappy about our own inertia, he will launch an offensive with, from a psychological and material point of view, much better cards than he holds today . . . In my humble opinion there is nothing more urgent and necessary than to galvanize the French people instead of comforting them with absurd illusions of defensive security.[4]

While hoping for a change of strategy de Gaulle had little to distract him at his command post at the village of Wangenbourg apart from receiving dignitaries who were visiting his sector of the front: the President of the Republic, Albert Lebrun, on 23 October, the Duke of Windsor a week later, Paul Reynaud on 3 January 1940, Gamelin and the British General Ironside on 9 January. He had enough time on his hands to write to a friend asking to be sent copies of two books by Ernest Psichari and various books by Guy de Pourtalès on the lives of composers ('Wagner? Beethoven? Mozart? Schubert? Etc.').[5] Meanwhile he worried about his wife isolated in Colombey with their little girl. He asked his sister to write to her often: 'She is very much alone, full of worries, all the more so because, as you know, she does not show her feelings.'[6]

Chafing under his enforced inactivity, de Gaulle spent these months meditating on what could be learnt from the defeat of Poland. He drafted several notes for his superiors arguing that the rapid defeat of Poland vindicated his views on tank divisions.[7] One change was that he now stressed the role of aviation more than he had before: 'the qualities of strength and speed of the German divisions have been multiplied by the cooperation with an air force which disposed of crushing numerical superiority and benefited from exceptional atmospheric conditions.'[8] One of de Gaulle's papers was discussed by the General Staff a month later and the response was not entirely negative. Some like General Duffieux rejected the idea that the conditions in Poland were comparable to those in France; others like General Billotte supported de Gaulle's line. The first two heavy armoured divisions were about to enter service, and it was decided that two more should be formed over the coming months.[9] The proponents of an armoured corps were gaining ground but only gradually. For that reason de Gaulle took the bold step in January 1940 of sending a long 'Memorandum' setting out his ideas to eighty important political and military figures:

> So many wars have been at their outset a surprise for at least one of the belligerents . . . The striking successes that the enemy has achieved in Poland thanks to motorized warfare will only encourage him to go further down this new road . . . To break this mechanical force, only mechanical force is certain to be effective . . . Even if we restrict our military action within our frontiers, the creation of an instrument of shock, manoeuvre and speed is absolutely imperative for us . . .
>
> The conflict which has just begun could well be the most widespread, complex and violent ever . . . The political, social and moral crisis which gave rise to it is so profound and widespread that it will inevitably lead to a complete upheaval of peoples and states. The mysterious harmony which rules great events has produced in the mechanized army a military instrument exactly in proportion to this colossal revolution. It is high time that the French drew the necessary conclusions.[10]

In sending this document de Gaulle was appealing again to the political class above the heads of the military. As in the past, this extraordinary step got him nowhere.

De Gaulle's real chance of influencing military policy lay in his relationship with Reynaud. In January, he was in Paris for two days when he dined with Reynaud in the company of Léon Blum. It was an open secret that the days of Daladier's government were numbered. Like Neville Chamberlain in Britain, Daladier was seen as a man of Munich who lacked the qualities of a war leader. So he was opposed both by those committed to a more vigorous approach to the war – the *bellicistes* who thought he was not acting with sufficient energy – and by former appeasers who still hoped the war could be stopped. Reynaud, waiting in the wings, was the candidate of the *bellicistes*. Sensing that Reynaud's moment was close, de Gaulle sent him another plan for the establishment of a War Cabinet, with himself running its secretariat. As he wrote: 'In total war a national strategy passes to the realm of politics.'[11] A month later he tried again:

> One could say that the war is lost. But there is still time to win another. This other war could undo what the enemy has accomplished in the first. The necessary condition for this is, by a massive effort, to substitute . . . an active policy . . . for our policy of passivity. If we fail to do this, the world, starting

with our country, will habituate itself bit by bit to the new order Hitler is in the process of setting up in most of Europe.[12]

Seeing Daniel-Rops around this time, de Gaulle told him, 'we need to prepare for victory in 1945.'[13]

On 21 March, Daladier's government fell. The President of the Republic, Albert Lebrun, called upon Reynaud to succeed him. De Gaulle hurried to Paris where he helped Reynaud draft his investiture speech to parliament. He was in the public gallery for the 'lamentable' debate, as he described it in his *Memoirs*. Pacifists of the left and anti-Communist pro-Germans of the right combined against Reynaud whose government scraped through with the slenderest of majorities. Reynaud's arrival in power turned out to be frustrating for de Gaulle, who had been gambling on him for five years. But he proved less resolute in government than he had been in opposition. Stymied by his weak parliamentary position, Reynaud was forced to give posts to his political enemies. Daladier, who opposed de Gaulle's ideas on tanks, remained Minister of Defence. Reynaud did set up the War Cabinet de Gaulle had proposed a few months earlier, but as its secretary he appointed a banker, Paul Baudouin, who was lukewarm about the war. As his key military adviser, Reynaud chose Colonel Paul de Villelume, who had performed the same role for Daladier. Villelume was a proponent of the waiting strategy of asphyxiating the German economy. But like Baudouin he was not convinced the war could be won. Such choices were counterbalanced by other figures like Reynaud's *directeur de cabinet*, the diplomat Roland de Margerie, who had been an anti-appeaser in the 1930s. But de Gaulle was too divisive a figure to be given major responsibility and Reynaud failed to form a united team committed to the war. In this climate de Gaulle, before returning to post, paid a visit to General Gamelin at his headquarters in Vincennes.

With his hopes disappointed, de Gaulle returned to the front. He wrote to his mother that the atmosphere in Paris was 'too bad', and relations between Reynaud and Daladier too tense, for him to be capable of serving any purpose. But since Reynaud promised to call him back soon, 'I am waiting without impatience' – an improbable claim from this extraordinarily impatient man.[14] He told his friend Nachin: 'I am provisionally back at my post; in agreement with P[aul] R[eynaud] until the political situation is settled, his position is stronger and he can govern. It will become clear this week. If he prevails, I must work at the *présidence du conseil*.'[15] But that moment did not come. De Gaulle was in Paris for two days in late April but again nothing came of it.[16] Back with his tanks, he appealed once more to Reynaud: 'In France the great figure of this war will be a Carnot or no one.' He urged Reynaud to seize the opportunity to wrest the control of defence policy from Daladier, and offered his services again.[17]

Although he was not quite the determined war leader that some had hoped for, Reynaud's style of government was more activist than Daladier's. One of his first decisions was to go to London and sign an agreement with the British government on 28 March promising, as a symbol of France's commitment to the war, that France would not sign a peace treaty without British consent. Otherwise Reynaud continued his predecessor's strategy, albeit in a slightly more vigorous way. The Daladier government had spent three months discussing a Scandinavian operation to cut off German iron imports. But this led nowhere because the government had been divided on the issue. There were similar hesitations in London where Churchill, who had entered the government as First Lord of the Admiralty, was the keenest proponent of the idea. At the start of April, Reynaud persuaded the British to accept a plan to mine the waters off the Norwegian port of Narvik. But on 9 April, five days after the laying of mines had commenced, German forces surprised everyone by invading Norway and Denmark. The French and British responded by hastily despatching troops to Narvik and another Norwegian port, Trondheim. Although Reynaud bombastically announced to parliament on 12 April that Germany's iron supplies had been 'permanently cut', the Allied operation, largely the responsibility of the British, was poorly planned and disastrously executed.

It is not clear that de Gaulle really had for the moment any realistic alternative. The offensive action he craved was impossible without a military reorganization that could not be effected overnight. The heavy tank divisions (DCRs) were only coming on stream slowly. The first mention of de Gaulle in the British archives appears on 4 April 1940 from a British liaison officer (whose information came from Margerie) reporting that de Gaulle was 'a determined advocate of *attaque*. In the first days of the war he was very keen to attack the Siegfried line [the fortifications built by the Germans to protect their western border].'[18] But on his visit to Paris in April de Gaulle helped Reynaud draft a strong letter to Daladier on the need to pursue the Scandinavian operation more effectively.[19] The truth was that, though an operation against Germany in the west might have been possible – although risky – in 1939, it was not feasible in 1940 without the attacking force for which de Gaulle had been arguing for years. There was no immediate alternative to the strategy the government was pursuing.

Although disappointed by Reynaud's arrival in power, de Gaulle received a consolation. With three DCRs about to go into operation, the high command was preparing a fourth. De Gaulle was informed unofficially at the start of May that he would command it. He wrote to his wife on 8 May:

> I am spending what I think will be the last days in my current post . . . I am hoping to pass through Colombey on 13 May. The result of the Norwegian business is without doubt going to cause Paul Reynaud some problems although it is not his fault, quite the contrary. We had counted on the British fleet which in the end did not do much because the old men of London (like Chamberlain) prevented Churchill from taking risks. I do think, however, that Reynaud will survive.[20]

This is the first mention of Churchill from the pen of de Gaulle. His optimism regarding Reynaud was vindicated, and it was in fact Chamberlain who suffered the consequences of the Norway failure. On 9 May he was replaced as Prime Minister by Churchill. De Gaulle's planned visit to Colombey never materialized. At dawn on 10 May, just as he received official confirmation of his new position, German forces invaded Belgium, Holland and Luxembourg. The war in the west had begun.

MISSION IMPOSSIBLE

General Gamelin had been expecting this attack through Belgium and Holland. French troops, accompanied by ten divisions of the British Expeditionary Force, were sent into Belgium. Although a cautious man, Gamelin was so certain he knew what the Germans were intending that he also rashly despatched his best reserve troops, the Seventh Army under General Giraud, across the Belgian frontier and deep into Holland to link up with Dutch forces. This was a disastrous decision. What Gamelin did not realize was that the main thrust of the German offensive was coming further south, through the Ardennes. The French high command believed that the hilly terrain of the Ardennes forest, plus the natural barrier of the Meuse river, would make any rapid advance by tanks impossible. For this reason the area was guarded only by reservist troops who were traumatized when ten German Panzer divisions crashed through the Ardennes between 10 and 13 May supported by intense air bombardment. By the time Gamelin had realized what was happening, the first German tanks had crossed the Meuse. With much of the French reserve trapped in Belgium, the response of the high command was to assemble a new Sixth Army out of troops from the Maginot Line and to cut the German advance westwards.

On 14 May, de Gaulle was summoned to Gamelin's HQ to receive his orders. His tank division, the 4th DCR, was given the task of attacking the flank of the German Panzers to slow their advance and provide a breathing space for the Sixth Army to move into place.[21] De Gaulle wrote to his wife on 15 May: 'Called upon yesterday in extreme urgency to form a division ... I have been given all they could give me. We will see what happens. The events are very *serious*.' Although he insisted that Colombey was not in immediate danger, he advised her to 'assure yourself *very discreetly* about an eventual means of transport. But I assure you, *in conscience*, that I don't think things will come to that.'[22] His letter is torn between a desire not to alarm his wife unduly while alerting her to the danger of the situation.

Originally it had been planned to assemble de Gaulle's DCR over several weeks, but the sudden German attack upset this timetable. On taking up his command on 15 May, de Gaulle wrote to one of his former staff officers: 'Given that this large division is being formed in a rush, I hope I will not have to commit it for a few days. But one never knows.'[23] In the end even 'a few days' would have been too late. Of his first sight of the chaos of the French forces retreating from the Meuse, de Gaulle later wrote in his *Memoirs*: 'The spectacle of this frantic population and this military disaster, the stories I heard about the contemptuous insolence of our enemy, filled me with a fury without limits. What a stupid waste [*Ah! C'est trop bête*] ... Whatever I was able to achieve afterwards, it was then that my resolution was made.'[24]

At 4.15 a.m. on 17 May de Gaulle's division went into action well under full strength at the village of Montcornet, 20 kilometres west of Laon. The first tanks of the first Panzer division had arrived there during the night.[25] The Germans were taken by surprise by the French counter-attack, which was initially successful. But it soon lost momentum because of the technical deficiencies of the French heavy tanks. These had not been conceived for warfare at this speed and needed refuelling every 20 kilometres; they also lacked adequate radio equipment (a problem identified by de Gaulle during the Phoney War). Another problem was that because de Gaulle's division was not up to its full infantry strength, he lacked the ground troops to hold the positions he had taken. Stuka bombers attacked, and de Gaulle's men were thrown back. German casualties were high – about 200 men killed or taken prisoner – and French ones lower, but the French had lost a third of their eighty-five tanks. Two days later (19 May), at the village of Crécy-sur-Serre, 30 kilometres west of Montcornet, de Gaulle's division attacked again. The Germans were now at greater strength, de Gaulle's infantry reinforcements had still not arrived, and his attack was repulsed more easily than the first one. After these two battles de Gaulle wrote to his wife:

I am writing to you after a long tough battle which went *very well* for me. My division is developing as it fights and I am not being denied what I need because, if the general atmosphere is bad, it is excellent for your husband. I do not know where events are leading. But I have the slightly better impression of our high command which is beginning to recover itself. But do be ready to leave if necessary.[26]

De Gaulle's division was now out of action until it could be brought back to strength. By the time he wrote to his wife again on 24 May in surprisingly optimistic mood she had almost certainly already left Colombey: 'I have the impression that the surprise has been overcome and we are reestablishing ourselves. But we have lost a lot of feathers and will lose many more.'[27] It is unclear what motivated de Gaulle's brief flurry of optimism except perhaps that he had heard the day before of his promotion to the rank of brigadier general – the youngest general in the French army. On 27 May, he was writing to his wife less optimistically: 'I think for the moment that it is better you do not remain at La Boisserie. But you should try to take the silver because uninhabited houses – I see it here – are liable to be pillaged not so much by soldiers as by refugees.'[28]

After a week's lull, de Gaulle's division was back in action at the city of Abbeville on the mouth of the Somme river.[29] Despite Gamelin's original fears, the Germans had not moved towards Paris after breaking through on the Meuse. Instead they wheeled north-east towards the Channel, reaching Abbeville on 20 May and forming a bridgehead to the south of the Somme. The next stage of the German plan was to move north to cut off and destroy the British and French troops retreating from Belgium. Dislodging the Germans from Abbeville before they were ready to turn south again was a major strategic objective of the Allied high command. A British attack at Abbeville on 27 May had been repulsed. On the following day, de Gaulle's division was ordered into the battle. On 28 and 29 May, his tanks succeeded in pushing the Germans back, overrunning half the Abbeville bridgehead and inflicting severe casualties on the Germans. De Gaulle's poor radio contact with his tanks meant that he did not know how close he had been to succeeding if he had pressed his advantage harder. But during the afternoon of 29 May the attack ran out steam because of the fatigue of the troops, the loss of about 100 tanks, and – once again – the lack of sufficient infantry.

By 30 May the German defenders in Abbeville had recovered, and that evening de Gaulle was ordered to end his attack. Although he had not succeeded, the operation at Abbeville won him the plaudits of the high command when there was little other good news to report. He wrote to his wife that the battle had been 'a great success . . . You must have seen the communiqué about it (400 prisoners, a lot of material taken).' But he offered no comfort regarding the future. Yvonne had, as he suggested, left Colombey and was now staying 260 kilometres west of the village with her sister in the Loiret. De Gaulle advised her to go further south or west, to the Dordogne or Brittany.[30] As for de Gaulle himself, he was summoned to Paris and his three weeks as an active tank commander were about to end.

One must not inflate the importance of the three attacks undertaken by de Gaulle's division. He had after all suffered three defeats. But they did show what a commander as offensive minded as de Gaulle might have achieved with a tank division at full strength, and equipped with tanks more suitable for mobile warfare. All witnesses were unanimous about his resourcefulness, energy and complete indifference to physical danger. He wrote to his wife on 2 June that since 15 May he had slept only three nights. The chaplain of the division noted in his diary soon after meeting him:

> Does he take the time to eat? No one knows, except his chief of staff, Major Chaumel, who shares his hasty and sparse meals. Does he sleep? The cigarette butts one finds in his room in the morning allow one to calculate the extremely short time between the last and first cigarette. The mess, relaxation ... all that counts little for de Gaulle. A map, a map properly set up and properly lit, a map constantly and exactly updated ... that is the essence of his command post.[31]

The only signs of the tension under the mask of imperturbability were the endless cigarettes. He pushed himself to the limits and he expected the same from his men. The chaplain continued:

> De Gaulle is very often alone, alone when he eats, alone when he has his coffee, alone when he takes a stroll around the command post, alone when he visits the front. He leaves his car and his chauffeur protected by a hedge or a wood, and heads off, very visible, too visible, but with a complete indifference to any danger, on to a bit of high ground, to study with his binoculars the positions of the enemy and the possibilities of an offensive. I ask: 'Why are you always alone, Colonel? One would like to meet you and talk with you.' The answer comes immediately and chokes off any desire to ask more questions. 'To say what, M. l'Aumonier?' Then to soften the roughness of the response behind which one senses he means 'Can't you just leave me in peace' ... de Gaulle adds with a certain deference for my clerical status and a certain benevolence towards me: 'One does not speak in an operating theatre or piloting a ship ... What I have to say, as leader, putting my men and my tanks into battle, requires calm and reflection. As you know better than me, what would even the word of God be ... without solitude, silence and

reflection? All those who have done something valuable and durable have done so alone and in silence.'[32]

One member of his staff, Captain (eventually General) Paul Huard, wrote a detailed history of the two battles around Laon. His impressions of de Gaulle as commander coincide with those of the chaplain:

He exercised a command that was independent, exclusive, authoritarian and egocentric, based on the conviction that his judgement was, in every case, the best ... Insisting in all circumstances on the signs of respect that the regulations required, he kept his officers at six paces, creating around him a void where he stood out in the centre unless he preferred to be visible from far away, standing on a mound, even waiting on a heap of stones for an officer less tall whom he wanted to impress; he received a report without saying a word; disconcerted people by his ironic sallies ... In the very brief dialogues, where no rejoinder was permitted, he practised intimidation, raising his slow voice which suddenly would become peremptory, while his chestnut eyes without flame seemed to look through his interlocutor, or beyond him.

Huard seemed divided in his view as to how the men under his command responded to this treatment: 'The authoritarianism of Colonel de Gaulle was systematic and not necessary towards experienced corps commanders who had a high conception of their duty.' On the positive side, his constant presence on the battlefield among his men 'created and propagated a feeling of confidence which was the main reason for the rapid cohesion of this forces on the battlefield cobbled together out of various element thrown together'.[33]

It has often been remarked that none of the men under de Gaulle's command were to join him in London. This hardly seems significant since it was difficult for anyone to escape from France except with the most extraordinary resourcefulness. Even so, de Gaulle's three weeks in command of the division do not suggest that he had all the human qualities to be an inspirational military leader on the battlefield. We will never know because politics was now to absorb the rest of his life.

'ON THE EDGE OF THE ABYSS'

De Gaulle arrived in Paris on 1 June where the situation was dramatically different from when he had last seen Reynaud six weeks earlier. After the initial French reverses, Reynaud had made major changes to the government and the high command. Two decisions were especially fateful. On 16 May, he replaced the Commander in Chief Gamelin with the seventy-two-year-old General Maxime Weygand, who flew hastily back from Beirut where he had been in charge of French forces in the Middle East. Despite his age Weygand was energetic and carried the prestige of having been Foch's Chief of Staff in the previous war, but he soon realized that he had been asked to redress an impossible situation. Although doing his best to save the army's honour, he rapidly came to the conclusion that an armistice would soon be unavoidable. There was a hidden agenda behind this conviction. Weygand was a man of reactionary views who blamed the politicians for dragging France into a war that could not be won. He wanted, after a last-ditch battle, to force the politicians to assume responsibility for the debacle (as General Ludendorff had done in Germany in 1918). Since the Battle of France was clearly lost, the issue was essentially political: would the government sign an armistice ending hostilities or would it leave French soil and continue the struggle from North Africa or elsewhere?

Reynaud's second fateful decision was to offer an honorary post in his government to the venerable Marshal Pétain. His hope was that Pétain's presence would bolster morale, but Pétain's innate pessimism was leading him, like Weygand, to the view that an armistice was inevitable. He and Weygand both blamed the British for not having done enough to help France. One of Weygand's constant laments was that the British refused to throw their entire air force into the battle. The British unsurprisingly wanted to retain aircraft for the defence of Britain, should it come to that. As scapegoats needed to be found for France's catastrophe, the poison of Anglophobia spread among French leaders. This situation was not helped by General Louis Spears, the man whom Churchill had sent over as his liaison with the French government. On the face of it Spears, who would play a crucial role in de Gaulle's career, might have been ideally suited to act as intermediary between Britain and France. Although born of British parents, Spears had been brought up in Paris and was perfectly bilingual. He had acted as a liaison between the French and British armies in the First War. After it, he resigned his commission and went into politics. He was devoted to Churchill and like him opposed appeasement in the 1930s. In Britain, Spears was seen as a Francophile – he was jokingly called the Member of Parliament for Paris – but many Frenchmen distrusted him as the kind of Francophile who loved France only for its aristocratic country houses and *foie gras*. In 1940, Spears found himself in the difficult position of countering Weygand's accusations and defending the British while preventing a breach between the Allies. Since Spears had a temper as short as Weygand's, he was not the ideal candidate for this delicate task despite his fluent French.

Reynaud was an instinctive Anglophile and genuinely wanted to go on fighting and stay in the war. But quite apart from the mistake in appointing Weygand and Pétain, he was stymied by his continued failure to form a united government dedicated to prosecuting the war – if necessary from abroad. There might have been a political rationale for this at the start – on the principle that it was better to have defeatists in government than leaving them to snipe outside it – but it meant that many members of his entourage, like Villelume and Baudouin, profited from their proximity to Reynaud to undermine his will to fight on. They found an ally in Reynaud's mistress Madame de Portes, who was passionately convinced of the need to sue for an armistice. Madame de Portes hovers in the background of almost every memoir of 1940. She is a baleful and ubiquitous presence in Spears's narrative. Even if her influence has been exaggerated, she certainly helped to sap Reynaud's resolution.[34] This was the snake pit de Gaulle encountered when arriving in Paris on 1 June.

He went first to his tailor and emerged fifteen minutes later kitted out as a brigadier general, the rank to which he had been promoted ten days earlier. Although he had been called to Paris by Weygand, de Gaulle's priorities are clear from the fact that his first visit was to Reynaud. After that he went to see Weygand. The two men did not know each other well. De Gaulle had admired Weygand's role in Poland in 1920, and also the way that Weygand, as Commander in Chief in the early 1930s, had tried to defend the army from budget cuts. Weygand had opposed de Gaulle's writings on tanks in the 1930s, but this did not single him out. The loathing that the two men would come to feel for each other was still in the future. Weygand had awarded de Gaulle a generous citation for his action at Abbeville, and now asked his advice on the future deployment of tanks. Although he had already begun to think about an armistice, he did not breathe a word of this to his subordinate.

On returning to his headquarters de Gaulle sent Weygand a note proposing that what remained of France's heavy tank divisions should be regrouped into one single tank corps: 'This would serve as the hammer in the next great defensive or offensive battle. Without modesty but with the sense of being capable of it, I propose myself to command this corps.'[35] De Gaulle drafted a note to Reynaud on the same lines. But his real ambitions now lay elsewhere. At best a new tank corps would only have delayed an inevitable defeat. The real question was how the government managed the consequences of that defeat – a political not a military question. De Gaulle and Reynaud had clearly talked about another government reshuffle and a possible entry of de Gaulle into the government. This is what de Gaulle wanted – but on his own terms. Following their meeting he wrote to

Reynaud in 3 June in a tone he had never used before. No longer an impatient if deferential soldier, he was setting out his terms uncompromisingly:

> We are on the edge of the abyss and you bear France on your shoulders. I ask you to meditate on this:

1. Our initial defeat comes from the application by the enemy of ideas that are mine and from the refusal of our commanders to apply those same conceptions.
2. After this terrible lesson, you who were alone in supporting me, you are in charge, in part because you supported me and people knew it.
3. But, having achieved power, you have abandoned us to the men of the past. I do not deny their past glory, nor the merits they once had. But I tell you that the men of the past – if they are left to themselves – will lose this new war.
4. These men fear me because they know I have the necessary dynamism to force their hand. They will therefore do all they can, today as yesterday – and perhaps in good faith – to prevent me obtaining the post where I could act with you.
5. The country senses the need for renewal as a matter of urgency. It would salute with hope the appearance of a new man, the man of the new war.
6. Shake off conformism, established positions, the influences of vested interests. Be Carnot or we will perish. Carnot created Hoche, Marceau, Moreau.
7. To join you without having real responsibility as *chef de cabinet* or policy adviser? No! I want to act with you but to act properly. Otherwise there is no point! And I prefer to return to my command.[36]

While waiting to hear his fate, he wrote to his wife on 5 June: 'A new effort from the enemy is imminent. Although I nurse the hope that it will be less unlucky [for France] than the first, one can predict that things will go badly again.' He advised her to look for somewhere to stay in Brittany 'for the summer' – suggesting that even he had not realized how disastrous the situation had become.[37]

De Gaulle's ultimatum to Reynaud paid off. On 5 June he was appointed Under Secretary of State for Defence. For the next eleven days, until the resignation of Reynaud on 16 June, de Gaulle was closer to the centre of power than he had ever been – and yet at the same time on the sidelines. As a junior minister he was not entitled to attend full Cabinet meetings, and at several critical moments he was absent on various missions to London, to Brittany and elsewhere. In his memoirs Spears describes one day 'wishing to catch the elusive de Gaulle who had a remarkable knack of disappearing without trace in spite of his size'.[38] Thus de Gaulle was more a horrified witness than a central actor in the final stages of France's defeat. But these days were pivotal for his future. On three occasions he met Churchill. As a result he was not entirely unknown to the British when he decided to leave France for London. It meant also that he arrived in London not merely as a recently promoted French general but as someone who had been a member – albeit a junior one – of the last regularly constituted government of the Third Republic.

Although other aspects of Reynaud's reshuffle, such as the sacking of Daladier, attracted more attention than de Gaulle's appointment, it was noticed by the press. *The Times* commented that he was 'rather aggressively "right wing", intensely theoretical, an almost fanatical apostle of the mass employment of armoured vehicles, he is also clear-minded, lucid and a man of action as well as a man of dreams and abstract ideas'. His ideas and 'his manner of expressing them' seemed to some to be incompatible with democracy. In the Socialist newspaper *Le Populaire* Blum was in favour and called de Gaulle's appointment a 'quasi-revolutionary' act. Also in favour was *Action française*, which recalled that Henri de Gaulle had been a 'very remarkable and highly cultured man'.[39]

On 6 June de Gaulle installed himself at the Ministry of War, in the Rue Saint-Dominique, where Reynaud was based. Finding a spare office was not easy, but de Gaulle was not prepared to work anywhere else. Proximity to Reynaud was his only hope of enjoying any influence. Villelume, who saw the appointment as a 'catastrophe', wrote in his diary: 'De Gaulle comes into my office. His first words are to say how happy he is to have me under his orders. I reply forcefully that I am in no way dependent on him.'[40] Villelume and Baudouin drafted a decree trying to limit de Gaulle's authority, but Reynaud was less receptive than they would have liked. Pétain told Baudouin that de Gaulle was 'vain, ungrateful and embittered', and should not be invited to participate in the morning meetings where senior figures discussed policy.[41] One of de Gaulle's few allies was Roland de Margerie, who deplored the influence of the defeatists around Reynaud. Someone who shared similar views was the young diplomat Geoffroy de Courcel who had been drafted into de Gaulle's *cabinet*. He was to become one of de Gaulle's closest aides over the next few years.

By the time de Gaulle joined the government, the Battle of France was entering its final stages. Over the previous two weeks, the Allies had averted complete disaster by evacuating many of the troops encircled in Belgium and north-eastern France. Between 26 May and 4 June some 330,000 troops were shipped to Britain from the French port of Dunkirk. This great success also caused acrimony because the French high command suspected the British of choosing to evacuate their troops before French ones. In fact over 100,000 French troops were saved from capture.

Now the Germans were ready to move south again. Weygand had organized what he intended to be a last-ditch French defence on the rivers Somme and Aisne. In this final stage of the battle, French forces resisted much more tenaciously than had been expected, but the numbers were now stacked against them. On 6 June the Germans broke through at Abbeville, where de Gaulle had been fighting a week earlier. It was only a matter of days before the Somme–Aisne line gave way entirely, leaving the route open to the Seine – and to Paris.

On his first day in office de Gaulle had immediately drafted a note for Reynaud on what to do once the Germans crossed the Seine. He identified a number of zones of defence from which eventually the government, and army, could withdraw to continue the struggle from abroad. One of these was Brittany.[42] The idea of a 'Breton redoubt' had been floating around for a few days and was not de Gaulle's invention. Later he underplayed the extent to which he had supported it, as opposed to moving to North Africa, but it was his preferred option at this time. When the idea was discussed on 8 June, Villelume, addressing himself to Reynaud because he refused to acknowledge de Gaulle's presence, poured scorn on the idea as impracticable – which was probably right.[43]

Later that day, de Gaulle paid a visit to Weygand at his HQ in Montry, about 45 kilometres east of Paris. The meeting was a disaster. Weygand now wanted an armistice immediately although he had not yet formally proposed the idea to Reynaud. Not only was Weygand's view of the future diametrically opposed to de Gaulle's, but it must have rankled that he was required to explain himself to this arrogantly confident young General who only three days earlier had been his subordinate. De Gaulle returned to Paris convinced that Weygand had to be replaced, but Reynaud held back from such a drastic step.

On the next morning (9 June), accompanied by Margerie and Courcel, de Gaulle flew to London. After meeting French and British officials, he went to see Churchill at Downing Street. The main purpose of his visit was to reassure the British of the French government's resolve. Most of the discussion was about the air force. Churchill reiterated that he could not commit all British planes to France. De Gaulle defended the official French line that they should all be thrown into the Battle of France but the British record reports that 'speaking for himself' de Gaulle admitted that he 'agreed with our policy'.[44] Curiously nothing seems to have been said about arranging transport of troops to North Africa – further evidence that this was not de Gaulle's primary concern at this stage. Although the meeting solved nothing, de Gaulle made an excellent impression on Churchill, who was only too aware of the defeatism affecting many of France's leaders. He described de Gaulle to the Cabinet afterwards as a 'young and energetic general' who had given a 'more favourable impression of French morale and determination'. In a telegram to Roosevelt he referred to him as 'young General de Gaulle full of vigour'.[45]

Returning to France in the evening, de Gaulle's plane landed with difficulty at the airport of Le Bourget, which had been destroyed by bombs. Back in Paris de Gaulle was woken in the small hours by the news that the Germans had crossed the Seine and would soon reach the capital. Much of the day (10 June) was spent debating the appropriate course of action. De Gaulle argued that, although the government had to leave Paris to retain its freedom of action, the city should be defended. Reynaud accepted Weygand's view that to save lives and buildings Paris should be declared an open city. Weygand and de Gaulle had another acrimonious exchange. When de Gaulle tried to counter Weygand's pessimism by saying that there were alternatives to an armistice, Weygand asked what he was proposing. De Gaulle snapped: 'The government does not propose, it gives orders.'[46] Reynaud agreed that de Gaulle should sound out General Huntziger as a replacement for Weygand. The first priority, however, was to evacuate Paris before the Germans arrived.

De Gaulle left Paris that evening in the same car as Reynaud. Their progress south was slow because the roads were encumbered by endless streams of civilian refugees. They arrived at Orléans at 1.30 a.m. where the Prefect was woken up and found them two rooms for the night. Over the next four days, the chaos was compounded by the fact that ministers and officials were dispersed in chateaux scattered around the Loire region. Reynaud was in the Château de Chissay near Tours, de Gaulle in the Château de Beauvais a few kilometres away. Many of these residences lacked telephones, and driving from one to another was slow because the roads were clogged with refugees.

In the morning (11 June), de Gaulle set off to see General Huntziger at Arcis-sur-Aube, about 160 kilometres to the east. The choice of Huntziger as a replacement for Weygand was curious since he was anything but dynamic. He had been in command of the Second Army, whose performance in May 1940 had been particularly disastrous. Later he would be a loyal servant of the Vichy regime. But de Gaulle was convinced that anyone would be better than Weygand, and perhaps the attraction of Huntziger was that he would at least obey orders and not defy the government. According to de Gaulle's account of their meeting, Huntziger agreed that he would be willing to take command of the armies with a view to continuing the struggle from North Africa. Huntziger later claimed that de Gaulle had mentioned only the idea of resisting from Brittany, and that he had told him the idea was absurd. Since de Gaulle confided to Courcel that Huntziger was not 'not the man I expected', perhaps Huntziger's account is closer to the truth.[47] In the end the matter was irrelevant because Reynaud could still not bring himself to dismiss Weygand.

While de Gaulle was on his mission to Huntziger, Reynaud had urgently summoned Churchill to come over to France so he could update him on the situation. Communication was difficult. One call that Churchill tried to make to Reynaud from Downing Street ended up being taken by a local innkeeper whose telephone was immediately commandeered by the authorities. De Gaulle arrived back in time to attend the meeting with Churchill that took place at the Château de Muguet near Briare. At this meeting Weygand gave a catastrophic account of the plight of the armies punctuated by occasional grunts of acquiescence from Pétain. Reynaud was hardly more encouraging. De Gaulle was mainly a mute and appalled observer. Spears writes:

> A strange looking man, enormously tall; sitting at the table he dominated everyone by his height, as he had done when walking into the room. No chin, a long drooping, elephantine nose over a closely cut moustache, a shadow over a small mouth whose thick lips tended to protrude as if in a pout before speaking, a high, receding forehead and pointed head surmounted by sparse back hair parted in the middle. His heavily hooded eyes were very shrewd. When about to speak he oscillated his head slightly like a pendulum, while searching for words . . . I had noted that he had ceaselessly been smoking cigarettes, lighting one from another, his lips pursed and rounded in a characteristic movement I had already observed. Not a muscle of his face had moved. Nothing had been said that had caused his expression to move.[48]

De Gaulle intervened only once with a practical suggestion – the only one to be made by anyone at this meeting – to amalgamate British and French tank divisions. Churchill leapt on this as something to be 'examined at once', but Weygand immediately poured scorn on any idea of forming further defensive positions.[49] At the dinner which followed, de Gaulle made no attempt to disguise his contempt for Weygand. Anthony Eden, the Secretary of State for War, reports that when this 'tall and somewhat angular figure walked by on my side of the table . . . Weygand invited him pleasantly to take a place on his left. De Gaulle replied, curtly as I thought, that he had instructions to sit next to the British Prime Minister. Weygand flushed up, but made no comment, and so the meal began.'[50] This was de Gaulle's second meeting with Churchill.

On the next morning (12 June), the discussions resumed, going over the same ground as the night before. Churchill and his party left at midday, realizing that the French were close to giving up. The only substantive outcome of this two-day conference was the decision that Churchill would send a telegram to Roosevelt appealing for help. This was a measure of desperation and a delaying tactic. De Gaulle had not been present at the morning meeting because he had driven to Brittany to investigate with General Altmayer the possibility of preparing the Breton redoubt. Since he fails to mention this meeting in his *Memoirs*, and writes instead that he spent the day working at the Château de Beauvais on the transport of troops to North Africa, one must assume that he was in retrospect somewhat embarrassed by his support for the chimerical Breton plan.

Once the British party had left, Reynaud convened a meeting of the French government at the Château de Cangé at Saint-Avertin where the President of the Republic was housed. At this meeting, in de Gaulle's absence, Weygand for the first time formally told the government that he wanted an armistice. Pétain supported him. This was no surprise for Reynaud but other members of the government, not previously aware of the seriousness of the situation, were horrified. It was agreed that no decision would be taken before consulting Churchill. Driving back to Chissay with Reynaud, Baudouin tried to talk him out of the idea of further resistance. De Gaulle arrived at Chissay late that evening to hear the news of the day's events. As Baudouin recounts the scene: 'In the great vaulted dining hall of the Château de Chissay, the two of us [he and Reynaud] dined under the anguished gaze of Mme de Portes while de Gaulle strode up and down with huge steps defending his conception of resistance in Brittany.'[51]

The next morning (13 June) de Gaulle was back at Chissay. He persuaded Reynaud to draft a firm letter to Weygand ordering him to hold out as long as possible in Brittany and the Massif Central while the government prepared to move to North Africa. Madame de Portes constantly burst in during de Gaulle and Reynaud's discussions. At one point de Gaulle lost his temper, exploding to Reynaud that it was impossible to work in a henhouse – though he did not include this jibe in his *Memoirs*.[52] Madame de Portes did succeed in delaying the despatch of the letter to Weygand. Reynaud spent the rest of the morning closeted with the presidents of the two parliamentary assemblies. From time to time de Gaulle was called in. The President of the Senate, Jules Jeanneney, seeing de Gaulle for the first time, noted: 'Pale with short answers sparing no one, a man of cold passion who undoubtedly holds back in front of civilians.'[53] Oliver Harvey, a British diplomat, described the events in similar terms: 'De G[aulle] the only calm and intelligent soldier left . . . Scene at the Chateau completely chaotic. Everyone . . . talking and telephoning in the same room. Margerie dictating a telegram to Roosevelt in one corner; [British] Ambassador and Spears and me talking in another; Madame de Portes rushing about with untidy hair.'[54]

That afternoon, having returned to his lodgings at Beauvais, de Gaulle suddenly heard from Margerie that Reynaud had invited Churchill, who had left only the previous morning, back for another meeting at Tours a few kilometres away. De Gaulle subsequently believed that Reynaud had purposefully failed to inform him of this meeting.[55] This may be true, but Reynaud for mysterious reasons had kept the news from all his ministers – to their subsequent annoyance. On the British side, there were eight participants at this meeting; on the French side, only Baudouin and Reynaud. Reynaud asked how the British would react if the French were forced to sue for a separate peace. The British party requested a break to consider their position. De Gaulle arrived just as the meeting was reconvening, making him the third Frenchman present. In the cramped room he took the armchair which Sir Alexander Cadogan, Permanent Under Secretary of the Foreign Office, had been had been using before the break. Cadogan perched on the arm of another chair. Churchill's response was that he could not approve any separate peace, and he urged Reynaud to do nothing before a final appeal to Roosevelt.[56] But Baudouin, twisting Churchill's use of the words 'je comprends' – which were meant in the sense of 'I understand what you are saying' not in the sense of 'I agree with what you are saying' – began putting it about immediately after the meeting that Churchill had said he would 'understand' if France concluded a separate peace.

The events at Tours on 13 June crystallized de Gaulle's conviction that it served no purpose for him to remain in the government. Late that night he drafted a letter of resignation.[57] A member of de Gaulle's *cabinet* communicated this news to the Minister of the Interior, Georges Mandel, who summoned de Gaulle to see him. Mandel had been the right-hand man of Clemenceau in the previous war; in Reynaud's government, he was the Minister most firmly opposed to the armistice. According to de Gaulle's account, Mandel, as if passing on the baton of History, exhorted de Gaulle not to give up, telling him that as someone who was still 'intact' he had important duties to fulfil. The resignation letter was never sent.

On the morning of 14 June, as German troops approached the Loire, French ministers were on the road again, heading to Bordeaux. On arrival, de Gaulle made his way to Reynaud's residence, and found the ever fluctuating Prime Minister in a more determined mood, ready to move the government to North Africa. De Gaulle offered to go to London again to discuss the transport of French troops across the Mediterranean. Since no plane was available, de Gaulle decided to drive through the night to Brittany and take a boat across the Channel. Before leaving, he dined rapidly at the Hôtel Splendide where Pétain was sitting at another table: 'I went over in silence to greet him. He shook my hand without saying a word. I was never to see him again.'[58] Before reaching Brest, de Gaulle made a short detour to visit his wife and children, who had left Colombey about three weeks earlier and ended up joining other members of her family in the village of Carantec in north-west Brittany. He warned them that Brittany might soon become a fighting zone and advised them to head further south.[59]

Crossing to Plymouth in the small hours, de Gaulle arrived in London at dawn on 16 June. While he was installing himself at the Hyde Park Hotel, two Frenchmen presented themselves: Charles Corbin, the French Ambassador, and Jean Monnet. Monnet, whose career was to intersect with de Gaulle's on many occasions over the next thirty years, was an international civil servant and financier with extensive contacts in Britain. In 1939 he was appointed head of the French Purchasing Committee in London whose role was to coordinate the organization of the French and British war economies. Monnet and Corbin arrived at de Gaulle's hotel with bad news. During de Gaulle's long journey to London, Reynaud, bowing to pressure from Pétain and Weygand, had formally asked the British government how it would respond if France approached Germany about signing an armistice. The British government was meeting that morning to decide its answer. Monnet's fear was that the British might reply positively in return for assurances that France's fleet would be kept out of German hands. He believed that a dramatic gesture was necessary to persuade Reynaud to stay the war.

In the previous few days, some British and French officials had been floating the idea of a complete union between the two nations of Britain and France in order to consolidate the alliance. Monnet latched on to this idea as way of bolstering Reynaud's resolve. De Gaulle, although sceptical, allowed himself to be convinced that the proposal might offer Reynaud the ammunition he needed to resist the armistice faction. In consultation with de Gaulle and Monnet, British officials prepared a draft. When de Gaulle, Monnet and Corbin met Churchill at lunch, they heard that the British had, as Monnet feared, sent a telegram releasing the French from their undertaking not to sign a separate peace as long as the French fleet was sent to British waters. The three Frenchmen put the case for the Union as a last-ditch attempt to keep France in the war. Churchill, initially as sceptical as de Gaulle, agreed that there was nothing to lose, and the British Ambassador in France was instructed to withdraw the telegrams permitting the French to seek an armistice. De Gaulle rang Reynaud to give him the news. Reynaud replied that he needed a concrete proposal fast because the government was meeting again in a few hours. Time was running out.

The British War Cabinet began discussing the Union at 3.00 p.m. while de Gaulle and Corbin waited outside the Cabinet room. A final draft was taken to de Gaulle who read it, according to Churchill, 'with an air of unwonted enthusiasm'.[60] Its key sentence ran: 'At this most fateful moment in the history of the modern world the governments of the United Kingdom and the French Republic desire to make a declaration of indissoluble union.' Churchill now returned to the Cabinet room with de Gaulle. As Churchill's Private Secretary Jock Colville recorded the scene slightly implausibly in his diary: 'everybody has been slapping de Gaulle on the back and telling him he shall be Commander in Chief . . . Is he to be a new Napoleon? . . . He treats Reynaud (whom he calls *ce poisson gelé*) like dirt and discourses familiarly on what he will do in France . . .'[61] De Gaulle rang Reynaud again to dictate the text down the phone. It was agreed that Churchill would go to France the next day to meet Reynaud in Brittany. Churchill provided de Gaulle with a British plane for his return to Bordeaux.

The planned meeting between Reynaud and Churchill never took place. While de Gaulle was flying back to Bordeaux, the French government had rejected the Union idea, Pétain commenting that it would be like 'fusion with a corpse'. Reynaud resigned and the President of the Republic, Albert Lebrun, called on Pétain to form a government. At 9.30 p.m. on 16 June, de Gaulle arrived back at the airport where members of his *cabinet* were waiting to break the news to him. He rushed to see Reynaud, who seemed to him like a man 'relieved of an unbearable burden' but also someone who had 'come to the end of any hope'. Spears describes Reynaud's mood that evening in similar terms.[62] De Gaulle next called on the British Ambassador, Ronald Campbell, and told him that he planned to return to London in the British plane in which he had just arrived. A member of de Gaulle's *cabinet*, Jean Laurent, offered him the keys of his pied-à-terre in London. The next morning, before leaving, de Gaulle called on Reynaud again and was provided with 100,000 francs out of government funds. At 9.00 a.m. the small plane took off with de Gaulle, Courcel and Spears on board.

De Gaulle comments in his *Memoirs*: 'The departure took place without romanticism and without difficulty.'[63] He insisted on this point because Spears's own memoirs (published before de Gaulle's) gave a more colourful version of events. Spears recalls that when he went to see Reynaud on the evening of his resignation, he stumbled upon de Gaulle hiding in the shadows behind a pillar 'very white' and 'overwrought', whispering that

Weygand wanted to have him arrested. He asked Spears if he could return to England in the plane which was (says Spears) at Spears's disposal. They worked out a subterfuge by which de Gaulle would pretend he had come to see Spears off, and at the last moment Spears would haul him on board.[64] Since Spears had quarrelled irreparably with de Gaulle when he wrote this account, it needs to be treated with caution. Spears's unpublished diary, on which his memoirs were based, contains few of these picturesque details and seems to accept that the plane was not 'his' but de Gaulle's (as lent by Churchill). It was not so much Spears taking de Gaulle to London as de Gaulle taking Spears. The portrait of the 'white' and 'overwrought' de Gaulle does not ring true. But even Spears's undoctored diary does report that de Gaulle 'was very afraid of either being arrested or being sent to some distant part by Weygand'.[65] Given that Mandel, the other resolute opponent of an armistice, had been arrested (although quickly released) when Pétain's government was formed, it was not unreasonable for de Gaulle to be worried.

According to Spears, as he and de Gaulle drove to the airport in the morning they made two stops, allowing de Gaulle to fix appointments for the afternoon to put people off the scent. The chauffeur was given instructions to keep the engine running 'so as to make a quick get-away if necessary'.[66] Courcel, the only other witness of these events, remembered that at the airport they came upon two officers who seemed in no way surprised that de Gaulle should be taking a plane. According to Courcel the main problem of the departure was that the airport was so chaotic that they could not initially find their plane. Because the plane was so small they needed to obtain a rope to lash their four suitcases – two for Courcel and two for de Gaulle – to the outside – 'excruciating for de Gaulle who expected to be stopped at any moment', says Spears.[67] The truth about the departure probably lies somewhere between Spears's cloak-and-dagger account and de Gaulle and Courcel's more prosaic one. One can however permit Spears the last word on one other detail of the journey when the plane touched down in Jersey to refuel:

> I asked de Gaulle if he wanted anything, and he said he would like a cup of coffee. I handed it to him, whereupon, taking a sip, he said, in a voice which indicated that without implying criticism he must nevertheless proclaim the truth, that this was tea and he had asked for coffee. It was his first introduction to the tepid liquid which, in England, passes for either one or the other. His martyrdom had begun.[68]

Se non è vero . . .

THE DECISION

In his *War Memoirs* de Gaulle writes of this moment in his life:

> I appeared to myself, alone and deprived of everything, like a man on the edge of an ocean that he was hoping to swim across ... I felt that a life was ending, a life that I had lived in the framework of a solid France and an indivisible army. At the age of forty-nine I was entering into an adventure.[69]

It is indeed hard to exaggerate the extraordinary nature of the step that de Gaulle was taking. Equipped with two suitcases and a small stock of francs, he was heading for a country in which he had set foot for the first time ten days earlier, whose language he spoke badly and where he knew almost no one. He was going into exile.

Since the French Revolution, exile has had only negative connotations in French political culture. In the notebook he kept while a prisoner of war, de Gaulle referred to a phrase from Tocqueville: 'The malady of exile which teaches nothing and immobilizes the intelligence'.[70] As the French revolutionary leader Georges Danton proclaimed in March 1794: 'One does not carry the fatherland on the soles of one's shoes.' The philosopher Raymond Aron, who spent the war in London, remarked: 'The idea of defending France from the outside remained abstract, because there was no memory, no tradition to support it.' Exile in French memory is associated with those émigré aristocrats who had cut themselves off from the national community by fleeing abroad to Germany or Britain. In French republican demonology, the term 'émigrés of Coblentz' summons up an image of squabbling exiles, cut off from the *patrie*. The monarchist tradition of de Gaulle's family did not view exile so negatively. De Gaulle himself had spent a year in 'exile' when sent to complete his schooling in Antoing in Belgium. That experience offered a model of exile not as treason but as fidelity to one's conscience. Nevertheless this was at odds with the dominant French tradition. One of the most prominent members of the Free French in London opened his memoirs: 'We were never émigrés. Never for us was London a kind of Coblentz, even a republican Coblentz ... There certainly were émigrés in London ... but they were not with us: their intrigues, their plotting in grand hotels never affected us.'[71]

The core of Pétain's appeal to the French people in 1940 was his decision to remain on French *soil* to defend his compatriots, to defend French lives, while de Gaulle left France to defend what he later called his '*idea* of France'. The conflict between these conceptions of patriotic duty was remarkably anticipated in the 1920s in an exchange between the two men over the wording of a passage in the manuscript of the book that would become *France and her Army*. De Gaulle had written that the Revolution had made France's generals the victims of political upheavals which had 'deprived them of prestige, often of life, sometimes of honour'. Pétain amended this to 'deprived them of prestige, sometimes of honour, often of life'. De Gaulle annotated Pétain's correction: 'It is an ascending hierarchy: prestige, life, honour.' 'Honour' or 'life' – protecting an 'idea' of France or protecting (or believing that one was protecting) the French – that was the nub of the conflict between Pétain and de Gaulle in 1940.[72]

When did de Gaulle come to the decision that to 'save' France he would have to leave France? In 1942 he told a British diplomat that it was on 13 June – the night he wrote his letter of resignation – that 'he had felt treachery in the air for the first time, and thereupon made his decision.'[73] But when de Gaulle left for England on 15 June the ultimate destination he had in mind was French North Africa, not London. The purpose of going to London had been to prepare for a move by Reynaud's government to North Africa. Seeing his wife briefly before setting off, he made no mention of a move to London.[74] The decision to leave for London came once Reynaud's government had fallen.

De Gaulle's decision was a combination of reflection and instinct similar to what he had analysed (following Bergson) in *The Edge of the Sword*. He is often credited with prophetic lucidity for predicting that the Battle of France was only the first stage in the world war that the Allies could win. But that analysis had also underpinned Reynaud's attempt to oppose the armistice. What is remarkable about de Gaulle in 1940 is not so much his intellectual analysis of the future of the war as his readiness to *act*. De Gaulle was always torn in his judgement of Reynaud and would defend him from detractors: 'Never in these tragic days did Paul Reynaud cease to be master of himself . . . It was a tragic spectacle to see this man of great worth unjustly crushed by excessive events . . . Everything had been swept away . . . In such conditions the intelligence of Monsieur Reynaud, his courage, the authority of his office acted in a kind of void.'[75] One can read this judgement in conjunction with his diagnosis of leadership in *The Edge of the Sword*:

> The intervention of human will in the chain of events has something irrevocable about it . . . Responsibility presses down with such weight that few men are capable of bearing it alone. That is why the greatest qualities of intelligence do not suffice. Undoubtedly intelligence helps, and instinct pushes one but in the last resort a decision has a moral element.[76]

De Gaulle, who spent much of the inter-war years reflecting on the nature of leadership, had written the script. Now he was ready to act it out even if this meant disobeying France's most revered military leader. In *The Edge of the Sword* he had also quoted a judgement by the First Lord of the Admiralty on the British Admiral Lord Jellicoe after the Battle of Jutland: 'He has all the qualities of Nelson bar one: he does not know how to disobey!'[77]

This was the moment for which de Gaulle had been living in his mind for many years. As he wrote in the 1920s: 'When events become grave, the peril pressing . . . a sort of tidal wave pushes men of character into the front rank.'[78] Or to quote from one of his prisoner-of-war lectures in 1917:

> Without the Peloponnesian War, Demosthenes would have remained an obscure politician; without the English invasion, Joan of Arc would have died peaceably at Domrémy; without the Revolution, Carnot and Napoleon would have finished their existence in lowly rank; without the present war General Pétain would have finished his career at the head of a brigade.[79]

Without the Fall of France, de Gaulle would undoubtedly have become a leading general in the French army, probably a minister of defence, perhaps even head of the government – but he would not have become 'de Gaulle'.

PART TWO

Exile, 1940–1944

*They make me laugh with their Appel of 18 June ... What every-
one seems to ignore is the incredible mixture of patience ... of
obstinate creativity ... the dizzying succession of calculations,
negotiations, conflicts ... that we had to undertake in order to
accomplish our enterprise.*

Claude Guy, *En écoutant de Gaulle,* 85–6

6

Rebellion, 1940

TWO DAYS IN JUNE: THE SPEECH

De Gaulle and Spears arrived in London in the early afternoon of 17 June. De Gaulle deposited his belongings at the small flat in Seamore Grove (today Curzon Place) overlooking Hyde Park, whose keys he had been lent, lunched at the RAC Club with Spears and then went with him to 10 Downing Street. De Gaulle records the meeting laconically in his *Memoirs*:

> Churchill immediately gave me his support and as a start put the BBC at my disposal. We agreed that I would use it when the French government had asked for an armistice. That evening the news arrived that this had happened. On the next day, at 6 p.m., I read out on the microphone that speech that everyone knows.[1]

This account glides over many details. De Gaulle knew that not one of those four sentences was entirely true. But even he was not aware of all the twists and turns of the next twenty-four hours before the British unenthusiastically allowed him to broadcast.

The first inaccuracy in de Gaulle's version of events regards the timing of Pétain's speech announcing that he would seek an armistice. The speech had been broadcast at 11.30 a.m. British time while Spears and de Gaulle were flying back to England.[2] When de Gaulle saw Churchill, both men must have known that the speech had taken place. If Churchill asked de Gaulle to wait before broadcasting, he was either fobbing him off until the situation was clearer or delaying until he could consult his Cabinet. We cannot be sure since Churchill never mentioned the meeting with de Gaulle in his own memoirs – and even misdated de Gaulle's broadcast as taking place that evening. De Gaulle was far from his main preoccupation on that day. The only other witness to the meeting was Spears, whose relations with de Gaulle later deteriorated so badly that nothing he says can be entirely trusted. In one version he remembered Churchill as greeting de Gaulle with great warmth; in another he remembered that he gave a 'polite welcome, glad to see anybody joining us, but he dismissed General de Gaulle after couple of polite sentences ... It was quite obvious from his manner that he was displeased.'[3] Since Churchill had formed a positive impression of de Gaulle at their three previous meetings, he had no reason to be displeased, but he probably assented somewhat distractedly to de Gaulle's request to broadcast, having little idea what he intended to say.

Whatever Churchill did promise de Gaulle, the British government was hoping to work through the Pétain government, not against it. Its nightmare scenario was that France's fleet could fall into German hands. Telegrams left London for Bordeaux almost hourly urging the French government to send French ships to British ports before signing any armistice. De Gaulle also held back from breaking openly with the French government. On 17 June, he wrote to the French War Office that he was in London continuing the mission that had been interrupted two days earlier. He asked: 'Must I continue the negotiations? I hold myself at your orders.'[4] This was strange behaviour from someone planning to defy the French government on the radio. The likeliest explanation is that he was covering himself. If he really had any illusions about the French government, these were not in evidence when he dined with Jean Monnet that evening. Monnet, who had not witnessed events in France at close hand, was startled by the violence of de Gaulle's hostility to Pétain. When de Gaulle shouted that the Marshal was 'on the road to treason', Monnet tried to calm the atmosphere, advising him to keep his voice down because the waiter was a Verdun veteran. When Monnet's wife asked de Gaulle about the nature of his mission, he snapped back: 'I am not here on a mission, I am here to save the honour of France.'[5] By the end of the evening Monnet was convinced that de Gaulle was either a mystical lunatic or an ambitious adventurer. This would weigh heavily in the future relations between the two men.

De Gaulle spent the next morning (18 June) finalizing his speech. Once ready, it was typed up by Elisabeth de Miribel, an acquaintance of Courcel working for the French economic mission in London. Meanwhile Churchill had decided to despatch two separate missions to Bordeaux. One, headed by A. V. Alexander, First Lord of the Admiralty, and Dudley Pound, First Sea Lord, was sent to appeal to the head of the French Fleet Admiral François Darlan; the other, headed by Monnet, was sent to sound out leading French politicians and offer them transport out of France. Since it made no sense to provoke the French government while simultaneously trying to win it over, this put a question mark over the idea of allowing de Gaulle to broadcast. The British War Cabinet met at 12.30 p.m. Chaired by Neville Chamberlain because Churchill was preparing a speech for the Commons that afternoon, the Cabinet agreed that it was 'not desirable that de Gaulle, persona non grata in France', should deliver any speech as long as there was anything to hope for from the Bordeaux government.

Spears lunched with de Gaulle at 2 p.m. but seemingly did not inform him of this setback. De Gaulle returned to his flat to add last-minute touches to his speech. Spears meanwhile decided to try and reverse the Cabinet's decision. Going round to Downing Street at 5.00 p.m. he found Churchill taking a siesta after his Commons speech. He pressed de Gaulle's case, and Churchill agreed that he could speak providing that the rest of the Cabinet were won round. 'Looking hot and miserable,' according to Colville, 'Spears set forth on his tour of conversion.'[6] He was successful in winning over enough members of the Cabinet but meanwhile another hitch interfered with de Gaulle's plans. Churchill's special adviser Desmond Morton, and Robert Vansittart, former head of the Foreign Office, who still had influence in Whitehall because he now had an official role as Chief Diplomatic Adviser to the government, arrived at Number 10 to persuade Churchill to send yet another envoy to Bordeaux in the person of Lord Lloyd, Secretary of State for the Colonies. There were now three missions to Bordeaux! Vansittart argued that this made it necessary to revert to the Cabinet's orginal decision to keep de Gaulle off the radio. In the end, with the surprising support of the cautious Foreign Secretary, Lord Halifax, Churchill agreed that de Gaulle should be allowed to speak. Halifax's view was that 'we should pull all strings at once: they might get crossed e.g. Lord Lloyd might get a cool reception if de G[aulle] spoke; but there was already such confusion in France that a little more would scarcely do any harm.'[7] When de Gaulle turned up at the BBC at 6 p.m. to record his speech, he was blissfully ignorant of these behind-the-scenes negotiations. Having recorded his four-minute broadcast, he dined at the Langham Hotel opposite the BBC. Not until two hours later did the BBC receive authorization to broadcast the speech. It went out at 10.00 p.m. BST (8.00 in France) and was repeated four times over the next day.[8]

Not only was it touch and go whether de Gaulle would be allowed to broadcast but the speech he delivered was different from the text which has come down to us – as we know because his words were picked up by the radio-listening services of the Swiss and French governments. The 'official' printed version opens: 'The leaders who, for several years, have been at the head of France's armies have formed a government. This government, alleging the defeat of our armies, has contacted the enemy to end the fighting.' What de Gaulle actually said was: 'The French government has asked the enemy under what conditions the fighting could cease. It has declared that if these conditions are dishonourable, the struggle should go on.' Since this spoken version was marginally less insulting to the Pétain government, one must assume that de Gaulle had watered his version down in deference to – or under pressure from – the British government.[9]

Despite this variation, the essential thrust of the speech had not changed. It offered a diagnosis, a prediction, an appeal and a message. The diagnosis: the defeat was a purely military affair caused by the superiority of German armaments and tactics. The prediction: the defeat of French forces was not definitive since France still had an Empire, she had an ally in the form of Britain, and behind both was the United States. In short, this was a 'world war' which would not be 'decided by the battle of France alone'. The appeal: 'I, General de Gaulle, currently in London, invite the officers and the French soldiers who are located in British territory or who may be in the future, with their weapons or without their weapons; I invite the engineers and the special workers of armament industries who are located in British territory or who may be in future, to contact me.' The message: 'The flame of French resistance must not be extinguished and will not be extinguished.'

It is common to talk of the 'myth' of 18 June because so few people heard the speech and even fewer acted upon it. But the speech was no myth, and what matters is that it was made. All de Gaulle's future action – what he would later call his 'legitimacy' – derived from that moment. His was the first public voice to oppose the idea of an armistice in France, and he offered not merely a moral appeal but an argument explaining why all was not lost.

IN LIMBO

De Gaulle had ended his speech by saying that he would broadcast again on the next day. His collected speeches contain the speech he supposedly delivered. In fact he did not speak, because the British would not let him.[10] When the speech he wanted to make was sent over to the Foreign Office, the Permanent Under Secretary Alexander Cadogan buttonholed Halifax: '[I] told him this can't go on. No 10 is like behind the scenes at the circus and every crank in the world is getting hold of the PM and making half-baked decisions. It must stop.'[11] The reason for the change of heart was expressed by the Foreign Office official William Strang, who minuted: 'It seems to me that we ought to be careful not to ride two horses at the same time. So long as we are gingering up the present French Government, and with some success, it would be disastrous if we should appear at the same time to be coquetting with a possible successor in London.'[12]

The results of 'gingering up the French government' through the three missions to Bordeaux were inconclusive but not entirely negative. Monnet had been unable to persuade any politician to come back to London with him; Pound reported Darlan's assurance that in no circumstances would the fleet be surrendered; Lloyd returned with the impression that the Pétain government might still go to North Africa if the armistice terms were unacceptable. Since de Gaulle seemed not to have harmed the British government's attempts to win the goodwill of the French government, for the moment the British strategy was to wait for the result of the armistice negotiations – and avoid any further provocation of the French government. A Whitehall committee, chaired by Vansittart, which had been set up to formulate policy towards France, resolved at its meeting on 22 June that 'no further manifestation of General de Gaulle should be permitted' despite Spears's lobbying on his behalf.[13]

Encouraging rumours reached London that various French imperial proconsuls were inclined to oppose an armistice. The most important of these was General Charles Noguès in French North Africa. On 19 June, de Gaulle sent Noguès a telegram offering to serve under him if he would come out against the armistice. On the following day, de Gaulle saw Cadogan who, in his own words, 'explained to de Gaulle why he should keep quiet until the situation clears. He accepted that and said that, if he was convinced that Weygand was organising resistance overseas, he would be the first to offer his services.'[14] Given de Gaulle's private view of Weygand he cannot have taken this prospect too seriously. Nonetheless on the same day he wrote to both Weygand and the French Military Attaché in London assuring them that he was ready to obey orders to return to France.[15] It seems inconceivable that de Gaulle would really have contemplated returning to Bordeaux. Presumably he was still covering his tracks to avoid being accused of outright dissidence before an armistice had been signed – and while he had no official status with the British.

In these days while everyone was waiting to hear the German armistice terms, various Frenchmen in London who had heard de Gaulle's 18 June speech answered his appeal and came to offer their services. The French Embassy did not make it easy by releasing no information about his whereabouts, but some people managed to track him down to the apartment in Seamore Grove. Those who arrived at night were received by de Gaulle in his cabin-sized bedroom, every surface strewn with papers, because the sitting-room windows overlooking Hyde Park were too big to be blacked out. De Gaulle had nothing to offer his visitors. One of them on 19 June was a left-wing lawyer, André Weil-Curiel, who urged de Gaulle to rally the French community in London. De Gaulle brought him back to earth:

> The English are in no hurry to commit themselves. They are waiting for the French politicians who have, it seems, left Bordeaux ... For the moment I don't even have premises where I can set up my desk. I have neither money nor men. I don't know where my family is. We are starting from zero. You could begin by holding the fort. That way de Courcel and I can go and have lunch and at least there will be someone to answer the telephone or open the door when we are not there.[16]

In these uncertain days between the 18 June speech and the signing of the armistice on 22 June, the only good news was the unexpected arrival of de Gaulle's family, whom he had last seen briefly at Carantec in Brittany on the 15th. Since then they had had no news of his whereabouts – unsure whether he was in London, Bordeaux or North Africa. Churchill had sent a plane over on the 18th to collect them before they fell into enemy hands, but the plane crashed, killing the entire crew. Yvonne de Gaulle, knowing nothing of this, had decided on her own initiative to cross over to England. With little more than the clothes they were wearing, she managed, with her three children and Anne's nurse, to squeeze on to a boat from Brest crammed with French refugees. Arriving in Falmouth, they checked into the first hotel they could find. In crumpled clothes, with no luggage and a severely handicapped child, they did not inspire confidence and were forced to pay for their room in advance. Buying a newspaper, Philippe found a tiny article on an inside page about a 'certain General de Gaulle' in London. Despite his almost non-existent English, he persuaded a policeman that he was the son of this 'de Gaulle', although given the initial scepticism he wondered if the policeman was under the impression that de Gaulle was as common a name as Smith. On the evening of 20 June, the family arrived at the Hotel Rubens, close to Buckingham Palace, where de Gaulle was now sleeping. Philippe remembered the reunion between his parents as 'one of the very rare times when the two of them kissed in the presence of anyone else'.[17]

On 21 June, the French government received the armistice terms. To maximize French humiliation Hitler had chosen as the site of the negotiations the forest of Compiègne where the 1918 armistice ending the Great War had been signed. In truth there were no negotiations because the French delegation, headed by General Huntziger – whom a few weeks earlier de Gaulle had envisaged as a replacement for Weygand – was presented with terms it could only accept or reject. Although the conditions were tough there were enough incentives for the French to sign: Paris would be occupied but half of French territory would remain 'free', and there were no claims on the French Empire. One clause especially worried the British: all French warships were to be 'disarmed under German control' while remaining in French waters. The French government signed the armistice on the evening of 22 June. That evening, Churchill broadcast to France. He fiercely attacked Pétain's government and condemned an armistice that placed France in servitude. Spears had been pressing him for days to allow de Gaulle to speak again.[18] There was no longer any reason to refuse. De Gaulle's proposed text was submitted to the Cabinet and he was finally allowed to broadcast that evening. This second speech – after four days in London – was the first of de Gaulle's to be preserved by the BBC. Its thrust was identical to the 18 June speech but its form was more elaborate. De Gaulle argued that the armistice was contrary to 'good sense, to honour and to the higher interests of the Fatherland'. Weygand immediately responded by revoking de Gaulle's promotion to general. From now on he was referred to in France as 'the ex-General de Gaulle'. There was no turning back.

De Gaulle seized upon Churchill's fury against the armistice to push his advantage further. He wrote to him on 23 June to say that given 'my name has a certain notoriety . . . [and] that I was a member of the last independent French government' he was setting up 'with some notable French personalities a National Committee to pursue the war in common with the allies'. De Gaulle asked the British government to recognize this committee as 'qualified to represent the French nation'.[19] Meeting that morning, the War Cabinet astonishingly decided to support this idea. After the Cabinet meeting, de Gaulle saw Churchill – for the only second time since his arrival in London – and assured him that he had the backing of figures like the famous novelist André Maurois, who was in London, and the French Ambassador Corbin. De Gaulle hesitated over how best to present his case. He suggested that the task of organizing this committee 'could explicitly be associated with my own name' but said that he 'did not wish to appear to be pushing himself forward'. The best solution would be to find a political figure to 'appear at the head of it'.[20] It was agreed that he would broadcast for a third time that evening to make the announcement.

Having got wind of this initiative, three leading French personalities in London started to lobby the British in the hope of undoing this decision. These were Monnet, Corbin and Alexis Leger, the former head of the French Foreign Office who had arrived a few days earlier. Their objection was that de Gaulle was an unknown personality with no credibility. Negotiations went on all day. Cadogan noted:

Spears and de G[aulle] arrived about 7.00 when H[alifax] had gone to the
King. After a tussle, got de G[aulle] to alter his declaration, taking out names,
in particular his. H[alifax] back at 8.00 and got him to agree declarations
by 8.30 ... Monnet called to urge de G[aulle] idea all wrong. 9.15.
Van[nsittart] rang up ... to say he had Corbin and Leger with him and that
'De G[aulle] must change his broadcast!' ... I said [to Halifax] we couldn't
change our minds every 5 minutes. There were only two alternatives: Deny
BBC to de G[aulle], or let it rip. He favoured latter.[21]

De Gaulle broadcast that evening. This was followed by a communiqué
from the British government declaring that it could 'no longer regard the
Bordeaux government as the government of an independent country'. The
British would recognize the 'Provisional National Committee ... so long
as that Committee continues to represent all French elements resolved to
fight the enemy'.[22]

Churchill and de Gaulle had different ideas about what exactly the
British were committing themselves to. De Gaulle was bidding for recognition as a kind of counter-government; Churchill saw the committee only
as a sort of 'underground railway as in the olden days of slavery ... a
Scarlet Pimpernel organisation'.[23] On the next day, the government backtracked when it became clear that de Gaulle's 'Committee' contained no
important French names – no Maurois, no Corbin, no Monnet, no Leger –
and Halifax, who had been ready for de Gaulle to 'let rip', now instructed
the press not to publish the British government's communiqué.[24] De Gaulle
had overplayed his hand by failing to establish in advance that anyone was
ready to join him and no more was heard about the committee. But this
abortive episode did de Gaulle considerable harm. It revealed the extent
of his ambitions – he was pitching to head a dissident government – and
aroused the suspicion of those Frenchmen who were wary of soldiers
involving themselves in politics.

The British government now explored two other possibilities. The first
was to contact a number of important French parliamentarians, including
Mandel and Daladier, who had set off on a ship – the *Massilia* – from
Bordeaux to North Africa before the armistice terms had been received.
The Pétain government had agreed to this in order to ensure that some key
political figures were out of German reach if the armistice terms proved
unacceptable. But by the time the *Massilia* arrived in Casablanca the armistice had been signed, and its passengers found themselves depicted by the
French government as 'deserters' whereas in truth they were the ones most
committed to continuing the struggle against Germany. The British hoped
that in these conditions they might agree to set up a dissident French

government in North Africa. The British Minister of Information, Duff Cooper, was sent to Casablanca to make contact with them. At the same time, British officials in the colonies were in touch with French colonial governors in the Middle East and North Africa who might be ready to reject the armistice. There were still great hopes of General Noguès, who had at his disposal forces dwarfing anything de Gaulle might offer. De Gaulle himself wrote to Noguès again on 24 June. There was a subtle shift in his position. In his telegram to Noguès on 19 June de Gaulle had offered to serve him; his telegram of 24 June invited Noguès to join *his* committee – which did not in fact any longer exist.[25]

The British were no longer sure what to do with de Gaulle. The irascible Cadogan noted on 25 June:

> Having washed my hands of de G[aulle] – Van[sittart] having butted in and I having handed de Gaulle over to him – I now find that Van is getting into difficulties with him and wants me to take him back. Not on your life! So like him to want to shuffle it off directly it begins to get difficult! And he is boxing the compass – one day for de G and the next against. I'll have nothing more to do with it.[26]

But de Gaulle was allowed to continue broadcasting. What ensued was an extraordinary oratorical duel on the airwaves between himself and Pétain. On 23 June, Pétain had broadcast, ostensibly replying to Churchill's condemnation of the armistice on the previous day. But his speech was also a reply to de Gaulle (without mentioning his name) and argued that the armistice was not contrary to France's 'honour'. On 24 June, de Gaulle broadcast again to express his 'shame . . . and revulsion' at the armistice, and declared that there were 'powerful forces of resistance rising up to save France's honour'. The next day (25 June) Pétain, again without mentioning de Gaulle, reiterated the reasons why the war was over for France and why he refused to 'shed the blood of the French to prolong the dream of some Frenchmen badly informed about the conditions of the struggle'. He would share the trials of the French and 'not place my hopes and my person outside the soil of France'. Finally he invited the French to work together with him for a 'moral and intellectual recovery'. De Gaulle prepared his reply. Gladwyn Jebb, later British Ambassador in Paris and at this time a junior Foreign Office diplomat, had the disagreeable task of communicating the British view that his draft was too hostile to Pétain to be broadcast:

> I rushed round to the Hotel Rubens where de Gaulle was still having his dinner: he emerged clearly in a bad temper, and gazing down on me said:

'*Qui êtes vous?*' I explained that I was a mere subordinate; that Sir Alec Cadogan himself had been eagerly looking forward to discussing with the general the draft broadcast, but owing to its late arrival it had fallen to me to propose certain 'slight modifications'. He looked. Awful pause, '*je les trouve ridicules, parfaitement ri-di-cules.*'[27]

We do not have the original draft, but the final version with the 'ridiculous' amendments was fierce enough. It opened: 'M. le Maréchal, across the airwaves above the sea, a French soldier is going to speak to you . . . In these hours of shame and anger for the *Patrie*, a voice must answer you. This evening that voice will be mine.' Repeating that France's defeat was caused not by moral deficiencies but by military ones, he asked accusingly: 'Whose fault is that, M. le Maréchal?' Reiterating that the armistice would reduce France to a state of servitude, he plunged the knife in: 'To accept such an act of enslavement we did not need you, M. le Maréchal, we did not need the victor of Verdun. Anyone else would have done.' This was the first time that de Gaulle had directly addressed Pétain. For the most junior General – ex-General – in the French army to address as an equal France's most revered soldier was blasphemy. It was de Gaulle's public *adieu* to Pétain – but not the way to win the support of those imperial proconsuls imbued with reverence towards the victor of Verdun.

De Gaulle no longer expected these to rally. He was preparing to assume the role of saviour himself. His chance came because all British attempts to find another solution had failed. On 27 June, Noguès refused even to receive Duff Cooper in Casablanca or to allow him to meet the passengers on the *Massilia*, who had fallen into a trap. On the previous day, de Gaulle drafted a memorandum for the British proposing that although he had failed to form a 'National Committee' he should at least be granted the opportunity to form a 'French Committee' to organize a 'force of volunteers'.[28] He followed this up on the next day with a letter to Churchill proposing instead a 'French Legion'. As he noted bitterly: 'Time is passing and time is precious.'[29] This time he was successful. Noguès in North Africa had declared his allegiance to Pétain; no politician had arrived from France; no one else had proposed themselves. Churchill said to de Gaulle in private: 'You are alone – well, I will recognize you alone.'[30] On 28 June he agreed officially to recognize 'General de Gaulle as leader of all the Free French wherever they might be'.

The next day de Gaulle announced that in the light of this step 'of the most profound significance' he was 'taking under my authority all the French on British soil'. This was a somewhat tendentious interpretation of what Churchill thought had been agreed. Corbin was immediately assured that the French in Britain were at liberty *not* to join de Gaulle. He was merely the organizer of a military movement against Germany and this did not affect Britain's desire to maintain regular relations with the French government.[31] The British had not completely given up on Pétain. On 27 June, de Gaulle was summoned by the French government in Bordeaux to appear before a military tribunal for refusing to obey orders.

In these ten days de Gaulle had achieved less than he had initially hoped. Permitted *in extremis* to broadcast on 18 June, he had had to bide his time between 19 and 22 June; he had gained ground between 22 and 24 June before being forced to retreat again between 25 and 27 June. His ambitions had been scaled down from a 'National Committee' to a 'French Committee' to a 'French Legion'. These ten days were a condensation of de Gaulle's relationship with the British over the next two years: whether to gamble on him or on the legal French government. The British remained unsure, in Strang's metaphor, which horse to ride. De Gaulle's strength during these ten days was that he was the only political figure in London who knew exactly what he wanted to do.

It remained to translate Churchill's recognition of de Gaulle into a formal relationship. This was ratified in an exchange of letters on 7 August after tough negotiations. On the British side the letters were described as a 'Memorandum' which had been submitted to the French; de Gaulle preferred to describe them as an 'Agreement' between him and the British. The British government agreed to meet the costs of equipping de Gaulle's followers against a promise of ultimate repayment. They would preserve 'to the greatest extent possible the character of a French force' commanded by de Gaulle, who would accept the 'general directives of the British high command'. Finally it was stipulated that de Gaulle's force would 'never bear arms against France' – to avoid eventual accusations that the Free French were British mercenaries. De Gaulle was also allowed to set up a 'civil organism comprising administrative services necessary for the organization of his force' – a seemingly anodyne clause which de Gaulle would interpret liberally. In an accompanying letter, Churchill committed himself after the war to the 'complete restoration of the independence and greatness [*grandeur*] of France'. But another letter made it clear that this phrase had 'no precise relation to territorial frontiers' although 'of course we shall do our best'. De Gaulle replied that he hoped that 'one day circumstances will allow the British government to consider these issues with less reserve'.[32] All in all this was a pretty good result, as one of de Gaulle's biographers remarks, for a 'penniless Brigadier exiled in a land whose language he did not know'.[33] But the ever vigilant de Gaulle was worried by Churchill's caveat about frontiers. As he wrote in his *War Memoirs*, how could the French be sure that 'on one hand, the hazards of war might not lead Britain to make a compromise peace; that on the other hand she might not be tempted to take one of our overseas possessions'?[34]

RECRUITING

In the six weeks between Churchill's recognition of de Gaulle on 28 June and the signing of the Memorandum on 7 August, events in France had moved rapidly. Bordeaux, like Paris, fell into the zone occupied by the Germans. For this reason Pétain's government moved to the small town of Vichy in the 'Free Zone'. On 9–10 July, members of the French parliament gathered in Vichy's casino to vote Pétain full power to draft a new constitution. The circumstances of the vote were dubious since many members of parliament had been unable to attend the meeting – including those on the *Massilia* who would certainly have voted 'no'. In the end only eighty voted against: the parliament of the Republic had committed suicide. On the next day, Pétain used his new powers to prorogue parliament indefinitely, grant himself full executive powers and proclaim himself Head of State. As Prime Minister Pétain took the wheeler-dealer Third Republic politician Pierre Laval.

Many of those who voted for Pétain were only expressing the veneration they felt for France's most distinguished military leader. He was not known as someone of markedly right-wing views and this was not necessarily a vote of approval for what became known as the 'Vichy regime'. But the authoritarian, repressive and anti-Semitic nature of the new government rapidly became apparent. Pétain announced that he was carrying out a 'National Revolution' to regenerate France and purge internal enemies. The new regime's attitude to Germany was not initially clear. Some of its key figures, like Weygand, were hostile to Germany – even if they had considered the armistice inevitable. Weygand favoured strict observance of the armistice while keeping a certain distance from Germany. But other Vichy insiders, like Laval, made no secret of their view that France's future lay in seeking good relations with Germany – what was later dubbed 'collaboration'. No one really knew what Pétain himself believed.

In theory, Vichy was neutral, but Laval made no secret of his Anglophobia. Relations with Britain nearly tipped into war when on 4 July the British, still terrified that France's navy would fall into German hands, bombed part of the French fleet at Mers-el-Kébir in North Africa after first offering it the chance to sail under British escort to the West Indies. Thirteen hundred French sailors were killed at Mers-el-Kébir. The Vichy government retaliated by bombing Gibraltar but drew back from declaring war. From now on there were no official diplomatic links between the French and British governments; contact took place through informal emissaries. The British instituted an economic blockade of France.

It was against this background that the French in Britain had to decide how to respond to de Gaulle. From 23 June, he had been provided with premises at St Stephen's House, a shabby building on the Victoria Embankment belonging to Scotland Yard. His dingy rooms on the fourth floor were a step up from the exiguous flat in Seamore Grove but they were hardly a prepossessing venue to impress those who might rally to him. A month later, de Gaulle moved to more imposing premises at 4 Carlton Gardens, a grand town house overlooking the Mall. This gave the Free French the use of about seventy offices over seven floors (at a rent of £850 per month). As the Free French numbers expanded over the next few years, annexes were set up at other addresses (Hill Street, Duke Street), but Carlton Gardens, where de Gaulle had his offices, remained the centre of operations.

De Gaulle's efforts to recruit among the thousands of French servicemen who had ended up in Britain after the Fall of France were largely unsuccessful. These men were assembled in makeshift camps around the country: the Aintree racecourse outside Liverpool, Trentham Park outside Newcastle, the White City stadium in London and so on. Trentham Park held some 7,000 soldiers from the French Expeditionary Force to Narvik in Norway who had been evacuated to England. Their commanding officer, General Antoine Béthouart, had been a contemporary of de Gaulle at Saint-Cyr. Béthouart told de Gaulle that he understood his desire to go on fighting but felt that his responsibility was to his men. He offered them the choice of joining de Gaulle or being repatriated to France. De Gaulle went to Trentham Park on 30 June, but most of the men chose repatriation – along with Béthouart. De Gaulle's visit to White City was equally disappointing. Of the 1,600 or so troops that passed through the stadium in the next two months, only 152 signed up with de Gaulle.[35]

Naturally the Mers-el-Kébir attack did not help de Gaulle's cause. French servicemen were not well disposed to a country that had killed over a thousand of their comrades. That evening de Gaulle confided to Spears that he wondered whether he should not retire to Canada as a private citizen. All would depend on whether the French government declared war on Britain. This did not happen, and after four days of embarrassed silence de Gaulle broadcast to France on 8 July to give his response to the attack. His line was that although the British act was 'detestable and deplorable' it was preferable to the risk of French ships falling into German hands. Spears (not usually a generous commentator) wrote later: 'This decision went beyond heroism, it was that of a man prepared to face martyrdom for the sake of his country.'[36] De Gaulle had little choice, but this must have been one of the hardest speeches of his life. Many years later he said in private that he completely understood why the British had acted in this way.[37] He would hold many grudges against the British – some of them dating back hundreds of years – but Mers-el-Kébir was not one of them.

Simultaneously with the Mers-el-Kébir operation, French navy personnel in British ports were forcibly taken off their ships and interned. Most ended up at Aintree. Spears, who visited the camp to bolster de Gaulle's efforts, found a copy of a pro-de Gaulle propaganda sheet where the word 'ex' had been inserted before every mention of 'General' de Gaulle, and the words 'bought by England' scribbled after his name. Where the British blockade of France was mentioned, the defacer of the document wrote: 'That is how the English treat your women and children in France. It is true that M. de Gaulle risks nothing since his family is safe and sound in England.'[38]

By the end of August de Gaulle had recruited only about 7,000 troops in total. The odds were certainly stacked against him, but his personality did not help. Spears remarks of de Gaulle's visit to one camp: 'He showed himself utterly unable to make contact with his audience. His speech was received in cold silence. Nor did he succeed in conveying a human touch when he reviewed the men.'[39] Although Spears's testimony is suspect, it corresponds to what one young twenty-year-old recruit, Daniel Cordier, wrote in his diary when de Gaulle – the first 'real' General he had ever seen – visited his camp:

> Under his leggings his excessively long legs seem too fragile to support such a massive body. He makes me think of a heron . . . His strange appearance is accentuated by the strange intonation of his voice: 'I will not congratulate you for coming: you have done your duty.' His visit lasted hardly more than a few minutes . . . I remain in my place stunned. So this is my leader: this cold, distant, impenetrable, rather antipathetic individual.[40]

Cordier was more impressed when hearing de Gaulle speak on the radio on 8 July. He seemed more attractive as a voice than in the flesh.

De Gaulle was hardly more successful when trying to win over individuals as distinct from groups. One wrote to Churchill recounting his experience of Carlton Gardens: 'Many Frenchmen who have offered themselves to the general were received and interviewed in such a way that they came out with their confidence shattered.'[41] Very typical was the experience of the young captain André Dewavrin, evacuated from Norway, who came to offer his services to de Gaulle:

He made me repeat my name . . . then posed a series of brief questions in a sharp, incisive almost brutal way . . .

After these de Gaulle asked: 'Any other qualifications? Do you speak English?'

'I have a degree in law and speak English fluently.'

'Where were you during the war?'

'In the Norwegian expeditionary corps.'

'So you know Tissier [another recruit from the Narvik force]? Are you senior to him?'

'No, mon Général.'

'All right. You will be head of the 2nd and 3rd Bureaux [intelligence services] of my General Staff. Goodbye. See you soon.'

The conversation was over. I saluted and went out. His welcome had been glacial . . . Perhaps there was a degree of pride or contempt, or perhaps also a kind of shyness.[42]

De Gaulle made no attempt to seduce. For him it was self-evident where patriotic duty lay. Sometimes, in more expansive mood, he would treat his visitors to a kind of long geopolitical disquisition explaining why the war would be won. At his first meeting with de Gaulle in June the journalist Maurice Schumann was given a lecture on why the Nazi–Soviet Pact would not last and why the Russians would join the Allied side.[43] Another journalist, the Socialist Georges Boris, among the first visitors to Seamore Grove on 19 June, remembered: 'Through the bay window under the implacable azure sky of June 1940, one could see the green of Hyde Park right over to Kensington. The noise of the street rose up muffled. I listened to this slow voice, with its gentle inflexions, giving me this clear lesson, composed of logic, sangfroid, firmness and honour.'[44] In cases like this de Gaulle was not so much persuading as ruminating aloud – almost as if his interlocutor was not there.

Two other journalists working in London, Robert Mengin and his friend Pierre Maillaud, went to see de Gaulle on the same day as Boris, and emerged less impressed. Mengin remembered:

> While he spoke to Pierre Maillaud, I could see only three-quarters of him from the side. I saw only one eye. The idea came to me that it was like the eye of an elephant . . . The absence of chin, which made me wonder if he had had a war injury, gave the impression not of softness but rather of self-importance, as did the lips above which was a minuscule moustache . . . Once in the street Maillaud asked me my impression . . . I told him that the General seemed full of himself.[45]

Mengin would become an implacable anti-Gaullist. Maillaud, who reported this conversation, was also uncertain about de Gaulle. But he painted a more nuanced portrait:

> His slightly reticent handshake which seemed to hold something back, the extraordinary reserve . . . that gaze which managed to be both lacking curiosity and coldly inquisitorial, with a suspicion of irony, all that gave to the distant and irreducible determination of his eyes something more than, as Mengin had said, just a soldier who was 'full of himself' . . . I saw a man of another age. Very tall, wearing a uniform and leather leggings, he held himself rigidly upright . . . But it was the way he carried his head, indefinably distant, and in the expression of the face that one saw the stiffness. His features reminded one, at first sight, of a medieval drawing. One could imagine them encased by a helmet and chain mail . . . What characterized the eyes was that they seemed not to register the outside world; their expression did not seem to vary depending on whom he had in front of him . . . It was as if they were in some sense predetermined . . . I thought of the awkwardness of a scholar in the presence of human contact . . . It was absolutely impossible to detect not just an emotion other than the emotions that came from within, but any reaction at all to his interlocutor . . . There was in these eyes a kind of abstract fire, capable of suddenly lighting up, but more to express an idea than to communicate . . . There was something of a pedagogue and a crusader.[46]

Throughout that summer, the French in London debated what to do. Their decision was motivated not only by personal impressions of de Gaulle, if they had met him, but also by their view of the course of action he was proposing. Although de Gaulle had had to abandon the idea of setting up a committee, which would have been the embryo of a government in exile, it was clear that his ambition was not just to form a 'French Legion'. He had witnessed at close hand the attitudes of the armistice faction in Reynaud's government, knew Pétain well and harboured no illusions about him. This lucidity put him at odds with the prevailing consensus that Pétain was an honest patriot without political ambitions. Spears received a report from someone who had visited many French soldiers in British military hospitals. They refused to believe that Pétain was a traitor, wanted only to return to their families and were 'deeply suspicious' of de Gaulle: 'The main reason for this suspicion is the alleged existence by his side of a political committee containing men towards whom they feel as some of us feel towards the Chamberlain gang . . . I know de Gaulle would get thousands of recruits if he came out with a declaration that he was a purely military leader with a purely military job and not concerned with politicians of any colour.'[47] As Maillaud put it in his diary: 'If I continue the war, it will not be against our own government but against Germany in the British army.'[48] He ended up joining a team of French journalists working at the BBC but always kept his distance from de Gaulle.

It is difficult to generalize about the early recruits to the Free French except that they were mostly young and had less to lose than individuals with established careers or family obligations.[49] The Narvik force had included a half-brigade of the Foreign Legion containing many Spanish Republicans and some Jewish refugees from central Europe. Unsurprisingly they mostly decided to stay, but this had less to do with de Gaulle than with the reception they would be liable to receive in Pétain's France. Outsiders of a different kind were a surprising number of individuals of aristocratic origin. One of the earliest to present himself was Claude Hettier de Boislambert (b. 1906), from a family of Normandy gentry. Called up in 1940 he had found himself fighting with the 4th Armoured Division commanded by de Gaulle. But when he managed to escape to London by boat on 18 June he had had no idea that de Gaulle was there. Hearing on arrival about de Gaulle's speech, he went to the French Embassy to find out how he could contact him. The Embassy officials had refused to give any information, but the concierge took him aside and whispered into his ear the whereabouts of this dissident General.[50] A slightly later arrival was Philippe de Hauteclocque (b. 1902), from an aristocratic family from Picardy, who had once been a pupil of de Gaulle's father Henri. A career officer who had been taken prisoner in the Battle of France, Hauteclocque had escaped and made his way to London through Spain. With his head still bandaged from a wound he had received in the fighting a few weeks earlier, he was received by de Gaulle in mid-July. Another colourful early recruit was Georges Thierry d'Argenlieu (b. 1889), a former career naval officer who had left the navy after the First War to join a monastic order but returned to active service in 1940. Completely different in social background from these three men – but also in their way outsiders – were the 130 fishermen from the tiny Ile de Sein off the coast of Brittany who having heard de Gaulle speak on the radio on 24 June left for England in five boats.

Among those who joined de Gaulle at the start there were, however, no senior diplomats, no prefects or senior civil servants, no well-known writers or intellectuals, and only two obscure parliamentarians. Almost the entire French Embassy staff chose to return home. Among diplomats, one disappointment for de Gaulle was Roland de Margerie, with whom he had worked closely during his time in the Reynaud government. Margerie, whose reputation in the 1930s had been as an anti-appeaser, was sidelined by the Pétain government by being appointed French Consul in Shanghai. Passing through London in July before taking up his appointment, he saw de Gaulle, and dithered for two weeks about what to do. In the end, he decided to accept the posting. He later offered many reasons to explain a decision whose consequences haunted him until the end of his life. These included a sense of duty ('It seemed to me that having served France abroad for 20 years while she was victorious, powerful and envied, it would be indecent to give up serving her in her misfortune, after her defeat') and his repugnance for civil war ('civil war has always appalled me; in defeat it appeared to me more abominable than ever').[51]

Less surprising was Jean Monnet's decision. Although he had worked with de Gaulle on the Franco-British Union proposal of 16 June, he quickly became wary of de Gaulle's political ambitions and did everything possible to sabotage his abortive committee. He argued in a long letter to de Gaulle that 'it is not from London that this effort of resurrection' can come: a movement based in London would seem 'protected by England, inspired by her interests'. This was an ironic comment from the internationalist Monnet and in view of the stormy relations de Gaulle would have with the British over the coming years.[52] Monnet instead decided to offer his services to the American government.

Monnet's closest aide, René Pleven, hesitated over what course to follow. Pleven, thirty-nine years old, was director of the European branch of an American electrical company until Monnet drafted him into the London purchasing committee. He had been involved in the Franco-British Union proposal, translating into French the amendments made by the British War Cabinet on 16 June. Given his extensive contacts in the United States and his friendship with Monnet, it would have made perfect sense for Pleven to accompany him to America. We can follow his hesitation in the letters he wrote to his wife who was already in America:

> 1 July 1940: Today I drafted Monnet's letter of resignation [from the purchasing committee] to Churchill . . . Denis [another close associate of Monnet] has joined the de Gaulle organization. Motive: we must be united, not fall into the French fault of always scattering our efforts. Monnet remains very opposed and I oscillate.
>
> 3 July: I am still wondering what to do. De Gaulle asked me to come and see him yesterday. His little phalanx is reduced to a few thousand people, young and enthusiastic. There is no longer any question of a national Committee or other such phantasmagorias, but he wants me to take over relations with the Foreign Office and the Empire . . . I admit to being tempted but Monnet is pressuring me not to.

8 July: I have still not taken a decision. Everyone more or less close to the Embassy tries to stop me joining de Gaulle who does however seem to me to be the only point around which one can rally despite his initial errors.

9 July: The news of the suppression of the Constitution, the arrival of Laval in power, convinces me. I am going to join de Gaulle.

28 July: I am sad that you don't approve my decision to join de Gaulle. But I assure you that when one sees all those who have *run away* [in English] one feels proud at facing the danger.[53]

Maurice Schumann and René Pleven, who rallied to de Gaulle, and Pierre Maillaud and Jean Monnet, who did not, were on good terms with each other; all opposed the armistice; all shared broadly similar values. The fact that they made different choices in 1940 shows how the decision to join de Gaulle was more about instinct than about calculation. It was rarely based – as emerges from Pleven's ten days of hesitation – on any immediate *coup de foudre* for this disconcerting, strange, shy, antipathetic individual.

Faced with a dearth of recruits, de Gaulle allocated jobs as best he could. René Cassin, a distinguished professor of law, who was at fifty-three one of the oldest recruits, arrived just in time to assist de Gaulle in negotiating the juridical details of his 7 August agreement with the British.[54] The journalist Maurice Schumann, whom de Gaulle heard one night speaking on the radio, was given responsibility for Free French radio broadcasts. Captain Dewavrin, whose frosty reception by de Gaulle has been quoted already, was put in charge of setting up an intelligence service. He had no experience in this area – but nor did anyone else among those who had presented themselves to de Gaulle. Jules Antoine, who had before the war been manager of a French electrical company, was placed in charge of the civil administration of Carlton Gardens. Some choices proved less inspired than others, as we shall see, but de Gaulle had few people to choose from.

The few French naval vessels that had rallied to de Gaulle were put under the command of Admiral Emile Muselier, who had arrived in London at the end of June. Muselier, the most senior officer to rally, had a dubious reputation in the French admiralty partly because he made no secret of his leftist opinions. Forced into retirement at the end of 1939, he was a volatile and unstable character – and also an opium addict – who looked more like a pirate than an admiral. Almost at once the British found him impossible to deal with. De Gaulle was warned that he must stop the Admiral threatening to shoot as a deserter every French sailor who wanted to serve with the British navy. In the end, however, the British reluctantly agreed that they had no choice but to work with him since, as one official put it wearily, 'he was the only Admiral available' – just as de Gaulle was the only general.[55]

Since de Gaulle was an almost unknown figure, the British needed to sell him to the public. Cadogan commented disparagingly in June: 'I can't tell you anything about de Gaulle except that he's got a head like a banana and hips like a woman.'[56] For the purposes of propaganda, Spears produced a short note on de Gaulle with a few career details. It stated that he was 'extremely reticent' about his private life, had three children and was 'fond of sport, particularly of horse riding, plays tennis and is a keen bridge player'. Where this mixture of truth and fantasy came from is not clear.[57] A British journalist, Richmond Temple, was commissioned to write a book on de Gaulle under the title *De Gaulle's France and the Key to the Coming Invasion of Germany*. It presented de Gaulle as a visionary soldier who had predicted the character of the future war. This was published in September to the accompaniment of dithyrambic articles in the press.[58]

Selling de Gaulle to the British public. This 1941 English translation of de Gaulle's book *Vers l'armée de métier* (1934) presented him as a military visionary.

De Gaulle had a chance to present himself to the British public when on 17 July Denis Saurat, the Director of the French Institute in London, organized a meeting at the Queen's Hall to present him to the British public. But on this occasion the guest of honour refused to speak, despite the audience crying out his name. The *Evening Standard* the next day headlined its report of the event 'the Silent General'. De Gaulle was presumably handicapped by his lack of English. He had told Saurat that he was reading his book *The Spirit of France* but was slowed down by his poor level of English (a rare admission of weakness on de Gaulle's part). Saurat and de Gaulle saw each other almost daily in the General's first summer in London – Saurat was one of the few members of the French London community to rally to him – and the French Institute was for a few months almost a kind of second home for the Free French. As well as directing the French Institute, Saurat was a professor of French at King's College with wide intellectual interests ranging from Milton to the occult. He was a long-time fixture in London, a member of the Athenaeum and well connected within the British establishment. This made his support especially valuable, but de Gaulle, who appreciated the company of intellectuals, may also have enjoyed their conversations. Some of these, noted by Saurat in his diary, have a somewhat fantastical quality. On one occasion he reports de Gaulle telling him: 'it is not too soon to prepare a philosophy for us; do it for me. What is the name of the person who did it for Hitler?' This may well have been de Gaulle's way of finding this rather self-important busybody something to do without giving him any real responsibility. It did not take long for the relationship to sour once Saurat realized this. But in these early days de Gaulle sought supporters wherever he could find them.[59]

RALLYING AFRICA

A central argument of de Gaulle's 18 June speech was that the French Empire offered France the resources to continue the war. Because of Noguès's loyalty to Pétain, de Gaulle's hope of rallying North Africa had been disappointed, but there was still much to play for in other parts of the Empire. The first French possessions to come over to him were the small Pacific islands of the New Hebrides, minute territories literally on the far side of the world, whose governor Henri Sautot declared for de Gaulle on 22 July. There were also encouraging signs in French Equatorial Africa, a vast swathe of territories stretching from the Atlantic coast through the Sahara to the southern border of Libya. It comprised the territories of Chad, French Congo and Gabon, and adjoined the Cameroons, a former German colony that the French had held in mandate since 1919. The governor of Chad, Félix Eboué, had been in contact with the British authorities in Nigeria about joining them. It was vital to act before the Vichy government replaced him and put a reliable loyalist in place. De Gaulle despatched three emissaries to seize the opportunity: Philippe de Hauteclocque (who took the name Leclerc to protect his family back in France), Claude Hettier de Boislambert and René Pleven. Only Boislambert had any prior knowledge of Africa since he had been a passionate big-game hunter in the inter-war years. Under the codenames 'Sullivan', 'Douglas' and 'Charles', the three men flew to Lagos on 8 August. There they made contact with Colonel de Larminat, previously chief of staff to the French high command in the Middle East, who was on his way to join de Gaulle in London having failed to persuade the French military authorities in Damascus to break with Vichy. The four conspirators proceeded to divide up their tasks.

On 26 August, Pleven flew to Fort Lamy, the capital of Chad, where a much relieved Eboué greeted him. The rallying of Chad to de Gaulle was formally announced the next day. This was the signal for Boislambert and Leclerc, accompanied by twenty-two men, to cross that night in three motorized canoes from the British Cameroons to the French port of Duala in French Cameroon. Arriving at Duala in the early morning, they contacted a band of local sympathizers, proceeded to the main administrative buildings and announced on 27 August that they had taken over the colony in the name of General de Gaulle. Captain Leclerc tore the braid off one sleeve of his uniform and added it to the other, instantly promoting himself to colonel. Meanwhile, Larminat had been sending pro-de Gaulle tracts from Léopoldville in Belgian Congo across the river to Brazzaville in French Congo. With Chad and the Cameroons secured, on 28 August Larminat crossed to Brazzaville, and with the complicity of some local colonial officials arrested the Governor and declared that the Congo was in the hands of de Gaulle. In three days, the Cameroons and most of Equatorial Africa had rallied to de Gaulle without a shot being fired.

This spectacularly encouraging news arrived just as de Gaulle was setting off in person on an Anglo-French flotilla to rally the French colonies of West Africa. The British and Free French had been discussing an expedition to Dakar, the capital of French Senegal, since early July. As the most westerly port in Africa, Dakar was strategically important: in German hands it would pose a real threat to British shipping in the Atlantic. For the Free French, winning Dakar would be the key to controlling the French Empire in West Africa and providing a possible base for future operations into North Africa. After the Dakar operation had failed, everyone tried to pin the blame on someone else. De Gaulle claimed in his *Memoirs* that the idea had been Churchill's.[60] In fact the two men worked each other up into an enthusiasm that swept aside the more cautious views of British military planners. Little account was taken of the elaborate port defences of Dakar because the premise of the expedition was that a show of force would lead the French authorities to rally peacefully to de Gaulle as in Equatorial Africa. On 19 August, de Gaulle wrote to the British Admiral Andrew Cunningham, who was put in command of the operation: 'The situation in the city is confused. It is certain that many people continue to disapprove of the armistice and consider the English as allies.'[61] This is certainly what de Gaulle wanted to believe. Evidence about the state of opinion in Dakar was patchy but not entirely discouraging.[62] The news from Equatorial Africa can have only bolstered de Gaulle's optimism.

The Anglo-French convoy set off from Liverpool on 31 August.[63] The destination was top secret. When it was necessary to find scapegoats for the failure of the operation, it was alleged that leaks had occurred, even that de Gaulle, buying himself a tropical outfit at Simpsons, had announced that he was heading to West Africa. Nothing could be less plausible given de Gaulle's obsessive secrecy. But it is true that while the ships were being loaded at Liverpool a crate burst open and scattered all over the port leaflets intended for the population of Dakar. None of this played the slightest role in the failure of the expedition. The Vichy government did not get wind of it until the last moment. What mattered more was that Vichy had appointed Pierre Boisson as a new, ultra-loyal governor who was not going to give up without a fight, unlike his colleagues in Equatorial Africa.

Of course none of this was known when the flotilla set off from Liverpool. Since the Free French did not have sufficient ships, de Gaulle was on board the Dutch ship *Westernland* with 2,400 French troops. The British forces were commanded by Admiral Cunningham and General Irwin on the battleship *Barham*. De Gaulle was accompanied by Courcel and the inevitable Spears. During the journey more good news arrived. In early September, the governors of Tahiti and of the five tiny French possessions in India (Pondichéry, Chandenagore, Karaike, Mahé, Yaman) announced that they were rallying to de Gaulle. The diary Spears kept on the trip, unsullied by his later animus against de Gaulle, offers a running commentary on the General's mood. After the nervous tension of the last three months, these were de Gaulle's first days of relaxation. Spears found him 'light-hearted' and they spent hours talking together: 'When told a good story he lifts his head, turns it aside, laughs and invariably lifts one hand and clasps it on the other.' De Gaulle laughing is not something that many other memorialists describe. But Spears also detected warning signs that de Gaulle would be prickly if he suspected that anyone wanted to infringe on his independence. One night they were sitting on deck after dinner 'talking on every imaginable subject as we do by the hour' and Spears suggested de Gaulle might speak to the men:

> He said something to the effect: 'Don't tell me what to do; this is my business.' I was very taken aback and said 'So you do not want suggestions' to which he replied: 'No, for these personal matters, I like to hunt in my own way.' This is odd because I have made many suggestions to him which he had listened to.[64]

On 13 September, about 480 kilometres north-west of Dakar, they heard the news that a force of six Vichy warships from Toulon had sailed through the Straits of Gibraltar, unopposed by the local British commander who had received no orders to the contrary. These ships had been sent to recover Equatorial Africa but when alerted to the presence of a British fleet in the vicinity, they headed instead for Dakar. This was a terrible blow. Spears, de Gaulle, Irwin and Cunningham held a council of war, Spears recalled, 'in that dark and hideously hot and airless cabin, where the participants with shining, streaky, yellow faces clutched long glasses containing warm whisky as they discussed the situation, the Englishmen at great pains to ensure that de Gaulle understood all that was said'.[65]

  Arriving at the British port of Freetown in Sierra Leone on 17 September, they received the news that the War Cabinet had decided to suspend the operation. Spears was no less appalled than de Gaulle: 'Frightful and the worst example of pusillanimity encountered yet. Terrible blow to de Gaulle, who went ... right into his shell.' Spears protested vigorously to London: 'De Gaulle's presence here must inevitably be known, and it is quite clear that if he fails to seize the opportunity so obviously within his grasp of rallying West Africa ... his power to rally any other part of the Empire is lost for ever.'[66] Cunningham, who had initially been sceptical about the operation, supported this position. Churchill himself wanted to call the operation off but was persuaded to let it continue. Eden, the War Secretary, took the view that otherwise de Gaulle 'had no political future'.[67] De Gaulle received the green light to continue.

  When the Franco-British force appeared in front of Dakar harbour on 23 September, nothing went according to plan. It had been hoped that the population of Dakar would wake up to the view of the impressive naval flotilla in the sunlight across the bay. Instead they woke up to dense sea fog (very unusual for the time of year) through which they could see nothing. They could only hear de Gaulle's voice eerily broadcasting throughout the day, calling upon them to rally to him. Two emissaries of de Gaulle, trying to land in Dakar harbour with a letter to Governor Boisson, were fired upon. One of them,

Thierry d'Argenlieu, was badly wounded. A group of French soldiers was landed at the end of the day, under the cover of fog, at the port of Rusfique 8 kilometres south-east of Dakar. They too were fired upon and had to retreat. For the first time since de Gaulle had arrived in London, Frenchmen had fired upon Frenchmen. Hostilities recommenced the next day with the fog only slightly less bad. The British ships fired on the port. That afternoon de Gaulle and Spears boarded Cunningham's ship to decide what to do next. De Gaulle's view, supported by Spears, was that, however disastrous the consequences, it was preferable to call off the operation than risk a full-scale battle between the French.[68] Irwin and Cunningham seemed to agree but were overruled from London. On the next morning, when the fog had at last lifted, they resumed the operation. The British battleship *Resolution* was hit by a torpedo, and at that point Cunningham decided to stop.

De Gaulle put on the bravest possible face. The next day he gathered round him the French officers and briefed them on the line to be given to the men. One of the officers noted his words:

> 'We had reason to hope that our friends in Dakar would have been able to assist our operation. Unfortunately Vichy was there before us ... These things happen in a war ... Fortune cannot always be favourable to us ... And I did not want a battle between Frenchmen.' Evidently this explanation does not by magic transform our bitterness into enthusiasm ... But was there anything 'better' to say? The soberness in the expression, the calmness of the tone worked on us.[69]

De Gaulle's calm was also noted by Irwin, who recorded that his bearing was 'remarkable for its brave acceptance of a great disappointment and immediate readiness to offer constructive proposals'.[70]

Underneath this surface calm, which reassured his followers, de Gaulle was badly shaken. Cooped up in his sweltering cabin as his boat docked again at Freetown, he started to read the telegrams flowing in with head-lines from all over the world reporting the 'Fiasco at Dakar'. There was no doubting the magnitude of the setback and the possibly fatal blow to his prestige. De Gaulle hinted later on one or two occasions that he had con-templated suicide. Talking with one of his ministers in the 1960s about Pierre Corneille, he suddenly came out with the startling comment: 'You know, once at Dakar, when I was sitting on the deckchair, the sky was blue, the sea was blue, the heat was unbearable, reflected by the awning over the bridge, and all was lost. I can tell you that at the moment, I thought about suicide.'[71] As a Catholic for whom suicide was a mortal sin, just to mention the idea was possibly de Gaulle's way of conveying the depths of his despair. D'Argenlieu (another profoundly believing Catholic), still recovering from his wounds, remembered de Gaulle visiting him in his cabin: 'In my bunk, above the thousand sounds of the engine of the ship, I heard this plaintive cry: "If you knew, Major, how alone I feel."'[72]

Spears was alarmed by de Gaulle's mental state: 'He is considerably shaken and this worries me . . . He is brave, but is more of a resolute gambler than a resolute man it turns out. For the moment he cannot see his way.' Traumatized by the fact that Frenchmen had fired upon Frenchmen, de Gaulle talked 'endlessly' to Spears about going to Egypt with some of his men. There it would be possible to fight the Italians in East Africa and show the world that his enemy was the Axis not the French. Spears thought that on the contrary de Gaulle should instead consolidate his position in that part of the Empire that had rallied to him: 'The problem is that [in Egypt] he can't get any more recruits . . . Here he can easily increase and consolidate his position . . . threatening the Vichy position in Senegal. To go to Egypt means he is like Boulanger, throwing up the sponge.'[73] The comparison with the nineteenth-century French adventurer General Boulanger, who never went to Egypt but did 'throw up the sponge' by committing suicide on his mistress's grave in Brussels, seems slightly odd. But Spears does convey the intensity of de Gaulle's depression in the aftermath of Dakar.

However intense de Gaulle's despair, it was brief. The letter he wrote to his wife on 28 September is not that of a man about to give up: 'For the moment the entire roof has fallen on my head. But the faithful remain faithful and I am hopeful for the next stage . . . How much I thought of you and think always of you and the *babies* [in English] during the bombings.' Soon after his departure the Germans had started their intensive bombing campaign on London. De Gaulle also reassured his wife that the Germans had lost the Battle of Britain, that the Axis powers would now turn their attention to Africa and that the Americans would soon intervene in the war: 'This is the greatest drama of History and your poor husband is thrown into the forefront facing all the inevitable assaults directed against those who are on the stage. Let us hold firm. No storm lasts indefinitely.'[74] At the same time he cabled his team in London to announce that despite the Dakar fiasco he had 'taken the decision to continue' – which suggests that he had at least considered giving up. His intention was to 'establish himself' in Equatorial Africa and set up a central organization to link the colonies together.[75]

BREAKING FREE

De Gaulle's mood lifted when he left Freetown and took a flying boat to Lagos in Nigeria. There he was greeted by the Governor and put up in

Government House. After lonely days brooding in his cabin, his confidence was boosted by the evidence that the British were still treating him as a person with a future. But although he had decided to continue, he must have been apprehensive about the reception he would receive in French Equatorial Africa so soon after the Dakar debacle. He knew perfectly well that the territories had rallied only as the result of a series of palace revolutions thanks to the panache of Leclerc and his fellow conspirators. There had been no popular movement in de Gaulle's favour. The colonial planters of Chad were motivated less by patriotism, or allegiance to a man about whom they knew nothing, than by the fact that through British Nigeria they could export their produce to the British Empire. Likewise the tiny French possessions in India and the Pacific had 'rallied' because of their close economic dependence on Britain – not because of de Gaulle.[76]

For de Gaulle's arrival by boat at Duala in Cameroon on 7 October, Leclerc had organized a guard of honour on the quayside. There was a spectacular parade. Crowds were cheering, flags were flying and there were cries of 'Vive la France, Vive de Gaulle'. De Gaulle reported to London that twelve million inhabitants of the Empire had rallied to him; two days later, in a telegram to Churchill, he upped the number to fourteen million.[77] Both figures were entirely fictitious. An internal Free French note some months later suggested the total population of these territories was closer to six million.[78] The truth was that Equatorial Africa (AEF) had always been considered the poor relation of France's African empire. One member of the Free French remembered Fort Lamy, capital of Chad, as 'a collection of huts and shacks with corrugated iron roofs, dirt roads, a smell of latrines competing with the smell of rotting meat . . . a miserable little place with about 20,000 inhabitants and no electricity'.[79] There were some positive points. Equatorial Africa was to prove unexpectedly useful to the Allied effort since it allowed the British to transport planes and equipment across Africa by air rather than using the longer Cape route. It gave de Gaulle territories stretching north through the Sahara to the southern border of Libya, which offered the opportunity of entering the war against Italy. And it was also a source of manpower: most of the soldiers of France Libre at this time were black troops recruited in these territories. But the real importance of the AEF, as Jean Lacouture comments, was that 'Charles sans terre' – previously just a squatter on the banks of the Thames – now nominally controlled a huge swathe of French imperial territory.[80] The first street in the world to be named after de Gaulle was at Yaoundé in the Cameroons in August 1940 – although the writer of the sign missed out an 'l' and another had to be clumsily inserted. Brazzaville, the capital of French Congo, with a population of about 40,000 (1,500 Europeans), became the capital of the Free France. It harboured a radio transmitter which eventually allowed de Gaulle some independence from the BBC, although until the end of 1942 it was too weak to be heard in most of France.

Before he arrived in his new capital of Brazzaville on 24 October, de Gaulle's regal progress from Duala took him to Fort Lamy. Here, on 18 October, he was met at the airport by General Catroux, who had arrived the day before. This was another boost after the rapturous reception at Duala. Catroux, who had had a distinguished colonial career, was considerably senior to de Gaulle. Although the two men had shared a room as prisoners of war at Ingolstadt we know little of their relationship at that time. While de Gaulle was meditating on leadership and delivering his lectures, Catroux was translating Goethe's *Faust* to keep himself intellectually agile. De Gaulle much admired Catroux's work at the head of the French mandates of Lebanon and Syria. As Governor General of Indo-China in 1940, he had been sacked by Vichy and made his way to London on 17 September. De Gaulle had already departed for Africa but left a letter inviting Catroux to take responsibility for rallying North Africa, which was the next objective after Dakar.[81] Catroux's arrival in London was a major event. He was immediately granted an interview with Churchill. 'Much the greatest "name" de Gaulle has to dispose of,' noted Colville. Cadogan was also impressed: 'Long talk with Catroux . . . just arrived. He is more impressive than de Gaulle, and seems very nice.'[82] A dapper man with a touch of the dandy, slightly precious with a curiously high-pitched voice, the 'very nice' Catroux could not have been more different from the prickly and austere de Gaulle. Delighting in the trappings that came with being an imperial proconsul – with a formidable wife who enjoyed them even more and was notoriously ambitious for her husband – Catroux turned up in London with endless trunks of luggage and a suite of Indo-Chinese servants. Despite his *faiblesse* for the grand life, Catroux was charming, urbane and easy-going – everything the British might have wished de Gaulle to be. Catroux claims in his memoirs that at their first meeting Churchill proposed he take over the leadership of the Free French. Whether or not this is strictly true, Catroux's intentions certainly worried the Free French in London at a moment when morale was low. Catroux was not impressed by the amateurishness of the set-up at Carlton Gardens.[83] De Gaulle, instinctively on his guard against everyone, wrote to Catroux warning him about Muselier ('he has been criticized, he has faults, but also qualities'), but at the same time wrote to Muselier sounding him out about Catroux ('what is Catroux's attitude in London?').[84] De Gaulle, on his way to Dakar, was alarmed to hear that Churchill had taken it upon himself to send Catroux on a mission to Cairo. He protested to the Prime Minister sharply about this breach of

1. De Gaulle's father, Henri, in 1886.

2. De Gaulle's mother, Jeanne, in 1900.

3. De Gaulle (*centre*) in 1900, aged ten, with his four siblings (*left to right*): Xavier (b. 1887), Marie-Agnes (b. 1889), Jacques (b. 1893), Pierre (b. 1897).

4. De Gaulle (*middle row, third from left*) in 1904, aged fourteen, at the College of the Immaculate Conception. His father (*front row, centre*) was the class teacher.

5. (*above*) Aged seventeen, at the Lycée Stanislas, preparing the entrance exams to Saint-Cyr.

6. (*right*) The twenty-year-old's first publication, *La Fille de l'Agha* in *Journal des Voyages* 6 February 1910 (*see* p. 65).

7. Le Bourget Memorial to the war of 1870–71, where de Gaulle used to be taken by his parents as a small boy (*see* p. 19).

8. (*right*) Convalescing from his second war injury in 1915.

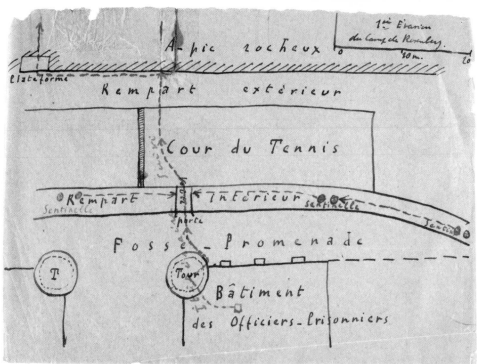

9. De Gaulle's map of his escape attempt in July 1917 from the Fort of Rosenberg in Bavaria, one of the four camps in which he was imprisoned.

10. The marriage of Charles de Gaulle and Yvonne Vendroux in Calais, 6 April 1921.

11. Lecturing at Saint-Cyr, 1921 – and already making an impression on his colleagues.

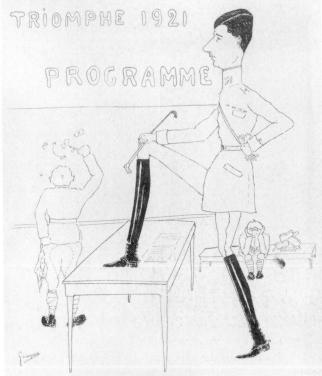

12. With his daughter Anne (b.1928) on a Brittany beach in 1933.

13. 'Poor little Anne' ten years later with her governess, Marguerite Potel, in Algiers.

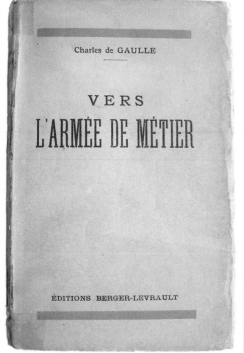

Charles de GAULLE

VERS

L'ARMÉE DE MÉTIER

ÉDITIONS BERGER-LEVRAULT

14. De Gaulle's 1934 'proclamation book' (*see* p. 73) advocating the modernization of the army.

15. De Gaulle's mentor Colonel Emile Mayer (1851–1938) in 1935.

16. Colonel de Gaulle showing off his tanks to the President of the Republic Albert Lebrun on 23 October 1939.

17. In the margin of power: members of the newly formed government of Paul Reynaud on 5 June 1940 with the Under Secretary of State for War, General de Gaulle, standing at the back.

18. The voice of France: de Gaulle broadcasting at the BBC.

19. (*left*) 'France has lost a battle! But France has not lost the war!' Free French poster on the walls of London, July 1940.

20. (*above*) Stepping out of 4 Carlton Gardens, 1941.

21. Lunching with Spears at the Coq d'Or, summer 1940.

22. Reviewing Free French troops in Whitehall, 14 July 1940.

etiquette – though Spears persuaded him to tone down the telegram – while
reassuring Catroux that his reaction was 'in no way about your own person
in which I have total confidence'.[85]

All this meant that, before their meeting at Fort Lamy, de Gaulle had
reason to be wary.[86] As de Gaulle alighted from the plane, Catroux saluted
and declared himself to be 'at your command, General'. As they were heading to their car, de Gaulle motioned for Catroux to go first; Catroux held
back, pointing to the stars on his sleeves, and signalled to de Gaulle to go
ahead – a gesture which was noticed by everyone present. This allegiance
of a five-star general to a two-star brigadier general was of incalculable
symbolic important – and became one of the foundational myths of the
Free French. Catroux later explained: 'He was my leader because he was
France and I was at the service of France.' De Gaulle comments pricelessly
in his *War Memoirs*: 'No one was unaware of the importance of this
example . . . I felt that he was departing a greater man than when he had
arrived.'[87] The truth is that Catroux probably realized he did not have the
personality for the kind of enterprise on which de Gaulle was embarked.
But their relationship over the next three years was often tense since de
Gaulle's propensity to pick fights was completely at odds with Catroux's
propensity for conciliation and diplomacy. Another factor was the anti-
Gaullism of Madame Catroux – described by one British official as a kind
of French Lady Astor – whose ambitions for her husband were a running
theme of British reports over the next four years: 'We should all find
Catroux of greater assistance if it should please the good God to strike
Madame Catroux dumb,' remarked one of Churchill's advisers at the start
of 1941.[88] Catroux must sometimes have wondered if he had been right
to bow before de Gaulle's authority.

De Gaulle had little other good news. The conclusion the Foreign Office
drew from the Dakar fiasco was that it might be necessary to explore the
possibility of a *modus vivendi* with Vichy while not breaking with de
Gaulle. This was not done behind de Gaulle's back, but it nonetheless
alarmed him.[89] For the British, the signals from Vichy remained confusing.
On 22 October a French academic, Louis Rougier, arrived in London
claiming to be an unofficial emissary from Pétain. This seemingly encouraging sign was contradicted by the fact that in the same week Hitler and
Pétain had met at the small town of Montoire in central France as Hitler
was returning from a visit to General Franco. Pétain followed this encounter with a speech announcing that he was ready to 'go down the road of
collaboration' with Germany. In a way, the Montoire meeting might have
served de Gaulle's purposes since it suggested that nothing could be hoped
for from Vichy. But it raised the prospect that anti-German elements in the

Vichy government might break with Pétain. Hopes centred on General Weygand, who had recently been appointed Vichy's representative in North Africa. If Weygand could be induced to break with Vichy, taking North Africa with him, he could offer the British much more than de Gaulle.

To pre-empt this, de Gaulle sent Churchill a telegram warning that, if Weygand made any overtures, the British should tell him that he would need to rally to the Free French. He offered magnanimously to welcome figures like Weygand into his movement 'without any rancour or recrimination'.[90] The British, knowing Weygand's 'intense personal dislike of de Gaulle', realized he was unlikely to submit to any conditions from de Gaulle.[91] Cadogan sniffed at the 'ridiculous telegram from Brazzaville, showing that that ass de Gaulle is contemplating "summoning" Weygand to declare himself. Just exactly what de Gaulle should not do at the moment.'[92] De Gaulle was only an 'ass' if his objective was to win Vichy leaders over to the British side but not if he was seeking to ensure that he – and no one else – was recognized as the leader of the French who were continuing the fight. If Weygand had rallied, the Allies would have gained; de Gaulle would have lost.

De Gaulle raised the stakes further on 27 October by issuing a manifesto from Brazzaville, announcing that there was 'no longer any proper French government' because the 'organism situated at Vichy' was 'unconstitutional and subject to the control of the enemy'. Consequently he had a 'sacred duty' to take control of the French effort in the war. To this end he announced that he was setting up an Empire Defence Council (Conseil de Défense de l'Empire – EDC) and exercising his powers 'in the name of France'. He undertook to 'render account of his acts to the representatives of the French people' once they were able to choose them freely. A few days later he also announced that he was creating a new decoration, the Order of the Liberation, for those who had served the cause of French patriotism. In the absence of real power this was a way for the Free French to assume symbolically one of the regalian functions of a state. Holders of the Order were to be designated 'Companions of the Liberation' and the decoration consisted of bronze shield with a two-barred cross. This cross, historically associated with Lorraine, had been adopted as a fitting symbol of the Free French because Lorraine was after all the birthplace of that universal symbol of French patriotism, Joan of Arc.[93]

The British, seeing de Gaulle's actions over the these weeks as a declaration of war on Vichy, instructed the press not to publish the Brazzaville manifesto.[94] But de Gaulle now started to sign his telegrams in the name of the EDC. He threatened that any attempt to make an agreement with anti-German elements at Vichy would cause 'grave divisions'.[95] De Gaulle now seemed out of control. The Foreign Office, which had always been sceptical about Churchill's impulsive decision to back him, hoped this would offer a chance to reassess British policy. Churchill did indeed tell Eden that 'There is no doubt that men like Weygand and Noguès when searching their souls about their own misdeeds harden themselves against us by dwelling on the insubordination of de Gaulle.' But his faith in de Gaulle remained intact. Hoping that it would be 'easier to point all these things out to him at close quarters than when he is a distant potentate', Churchill pressingly 'invited' de Gaulle to return to London.[96] De Gaulle hesitated. The temptation to stay on 'French' soil was great, but London was the centre of things. He agreed to return in order to clarify matters, after which he planned to go back to Africa.

There was a final piece of unfinished business in Gabon, the one territory of Equatorial Africa that had not rallied to de Gaulle. A military operation was launched against Gabon at the end of October. The commander of the Vichy forces surrendered to Leclerc on 10 November and committed suicide four days later. The total losses were small – about thirty-five dead on the Vichy side and eight on the Free French side – but this was exactly the fratricidal combat between Vichy and the Free French that de Gaulle had tried to avoid at Dakar. De Gaulle asked the BBC to portray it as a small 'police operation', but when he arrived three weeks later at Libreville, the capital of Gabon, his welcome was muted. There was no repetition of the Duala apotheosis.

'DE GAULLE' IS BORN

The six weeks de Gaulle had spent in Africa were an epiphany. Years later he recalled the impact of the cheering crowds that had greeted him in Duala:

> There were thousands of people and they began to shout out 'de Gaulle, de Gaulle'. I was taken aback. Until then, in London, my contacts had all been personal and individual, with ministers, soldiers and so on. But here was the people, the voice of the crowds. And suddenly I realized for the first time what a heavy burden I bore, what a reponsibility I had to all these people who were counting upon a man named de Gaulle to liberate them . . . I realized then that General de Gaulle had become a living legend, that they had formed a certain image of him. There was a person named de Gaulle who existed in other people's minds and was really a separate personality from myself. From that day on I would have to reckon with this man, this General de Gaulle . . . I became almost his prisoner.[97]

This was not just a retrospective reconstruction of his feelings. A letter written to his wife at the time expressed the same idea in language reminiscent of Le Bon: 'My task is materially and morally a heavy one. One must accept – and I do accept – all the consequences of this drama whose events have made of me one of the principal actors. It is the person with the strongest willpower who will finally prevail not just in fact but in the minds of the sheeplike crowds.'[98] It is from this moment in his *War Memoirs* that de Gaulle starts to talk of himself in the third person. 'De Gaulle' appears as a figure whom the narrator – 'I' – of the *Memoirs* watches.

What de Gaulle did not say was that another 'de Gaulle' was emerging at the same time in metropolitan France. In his first broadcasts, de Gaulle had been primarily addressing those Frenchmen who were already on British soil rather than the population of France itself. One speech on 23 July did call on the French people to 'resist passively by all means'; and from Africa he sent a telegram to London stressing the need to 'inject more dynamism' into BBC broadcasts and incite the French to resistance.[99] This was hardly specific, and de Gaulle had no notion of 'the Resistance' as it would develop over the next three years. Nor did anyone else. De Gaulle's objective was to develop a force *outside* France that could play its role alongside the Allies. But what is remarkable is how quickly his name began to circulate *within* France.

From mid-July, the BBC started broadcasting a half-hour nightly programme called *Les Français parlent aux Français*. This was run by a group of French journalists working directly for the British. They aimed to combat Vichy propaganda rather than specifically support de Gaulle. Some of them (like Pierre Maillaud) were quite suspicious of him. In addition to *Les Français parlent aux Français*, a five-minute slot was allocated to the Free French. At first no one in London had any idea if anyone in France was listening. These broadcasts were a bottle thrown desperately into the sea. But gradually letters started to reach London from France addressed sometimes just to 'BBC London'.[100] These were smuggled out across the Spanish or Swiss borders, usually anonymous, sometimes written in capitals to disguise the author's identity. One letter dated 4 August started: 'At 8.15 the whole family falls silent and drinks in the voice of the English radio, of our Free French . . . An invisible thread ties us to you.'[101]

Few listeners will have picked up on the nuances between the two French teams of broadcasters. The mysterious name 'de Gaulle' was the only one that most listeners knew. For this reason, de Gaulle became the name to which early resisters attached themselves as they penned their first tracts against the occupier. The first act of open defiance of the Germans in Paris occurred on 11 November when about 3,000 students demonstrated at the

Arc de Triomphe. There were shouts of '*Vive de Gaulle*' and '*Vive la France*'; some of the demonstrators carried two fishing rods (*deux gaules*).[102] A widely circulated tract in December offered a version of the Lord's Prayer beginning: 'Our de Gaulle who art in heaven . . . Let your will be done.'

De Gaulle was not a natural orator, but the oddity of his delivery and diction gave an extra aura to his speeches. His voice would rise up and down unexpectedly, chopping up his phrases in curious ways.[103] The Paris lawyer Maurice Garçon, although ferociously anti-Pétain, criticized the speeches in his diary as showing exactly how not to speak according to the normal rules of rhetoric: 'The poor man has a deplorable voice. He always manages to stress the wrong syllable.'[104] The effectiveness of the speeches lay above all in the intellectual clarity of the message and the emotional force of the rhetoric rather than in the style of delivery.

De Gaulle was not the most frequent speaker in the Free French slot. That was Maurice Schumann, who spoke over a thousand times in the course of the war. De Gaulle himself spoke only sixty-seven times on the radio, the greatest concentration of broadcasts occurring in the twenty speeches he made before leaving for Africa. When he returned to London in November he spoke five more times before the end of the year. Thus in the six months between June and December 1940 he had spoken twenty-five times. From then on his broadcasts became less frequent and were reserved for major occasions. He spoke fifteen times in 1941, eighteen in 1942. But once his name had established itself, the relative rarity of his interventions gave them an extra weight. It was in this period before any organized resistance emerged in France that de Gaulle imposed himself as seemingly the only public voice to offer an alternative view of the future from that of Pétain. If almost no one heard the 18 June speech, soon almost no one had not heard *of* it.

The propaganda of Vichy and the collaborationist press in Paris also helped to build up the de Gaulle myth.[105] In August 1940 de Gaulle was condemned to death for desertion; in December, he was stripped of his nationality. In other respects, Vichy was not sure how to best deal with him. In order not to build him up, Pétain never once mentioned his name in any speech, but everyone knew what the Marshal meant when referring to 'dissidents'. The Vichy police started to call those arrested for subversive activity 'Gaullists'. In that sense 'Gaullism' was partly the creation of de Gaulle's enemies. The more extreme French ultra-collaborators in Paris, who found Vichy too lukewarm in its attitude to Germany, showed less restraint than Vichy in their treatment of de Gaulle. He was attacked with direct insults. The general line of this propaganda was that he was a British mercenary out to destroy the French Empire. One poster showed a French

sailor at Dakar firing on a small rowing boat in which Churchill, with a
sinister Jewish figure looking over his shoulder, is fishing with de Gaulle
hanging at the end of his fishing rod as bait.

In propaganda posters de Gaulle's face was often blocked out by a radio
microphone – a common soubriquet was 'The Microphone General' – and
for cartoonists this surmounted the problem of depicting someone whose
features were unknown. Some cartoonists made him tall, others made him
small, some gave him a big nose and others a small one, some gave him
the three stars of a divisional general (which was to promote him), some
the two stars of a brigadier general (which was correct). One feature of
this anti-Gaullist propaganda was to invent an entirely fanciful visual
imagery of de Gaulle, portraying him as a precious and old-fashioned cavalry officer with a monocle and sword at his side, thus suggesting a
reactionary and blimpish figure out of touch with the real concerns of the
French people. Since listening to the BBC was a punishable offence in
France, tuning in to de Gaulle had to be done in secret. This gave a deeper,
almost religious intensity to the relationship de Gaulle built up with the
French population over the airwaves.

Churchill fishing. The text reads: 'With that
"Gaulle" you will get nowhere, *Messieurs*.'
Gaule is the French word for fishing rod.

De Gaulle depicted here by Vichy
propaganda as the microphone General
surrounded by sinister Jews.

On his return to London in December, de Gaulle decided to test his reputation in France by calling on the population to remain at home for one hour on New Year's Day between two and three in the afternoon. This was the first time he had issued a formal appeal for action to the French population. It is hard to judge the success of this initiative. Since 1 January was a holiday – and a cold day – one cannot know why people had stayed at home if they had.[106] But de Gaulle had intuitively grasped that a myth was developing around his name in France – and that he could exploit it to his advantage.

By the end of 1940, de Gaulle's successes were uneven. He had acquired a French colonial base, but most of the Empire remained loyal to Vichy; he had secured the backing of the British government but had not persuaded it to make a complete break with Vichy; he had gathered a group of followers but fewer than he had hoped. It was the emergence of the mythical 'de Gaulle' in France that was to prove his most powerful weapon. The British would soon find, like Frankenstein, that they had created a monster they could not control.

7

Survival, 1941

LONDON WINTER

On 17 November 1940, de Gaulle returned to his first winter in London – a deflating experience after being acclaimed as a hero in Africa. He had seriously considered staying permanently in Brazzaville, to the alarm of the British who wanted him where he could be watched. The prospect also worried his team in London who desperately needed him back. Jokes circulated in Carlton Gardens that de Gaulle was starting to behave like an African potentate, especially when news arrived from Brazzaville of the setting up of the Order of the Liberation.[1]

In de Gaulle's absence, the embryonic Free French organization in London was in disarray. Suspicious of threats to his own authority, de Gaulle had delegated the running of the Free French to an informal triumvirate of Antoine, Muselier and Passy. Antoine seemed on paper to have the necessary administrative experience but turned out to be abrasive, tactless and unashamed at flaunting his extreme right-wing opinions. He quarrelled badly with the no less abrasive André Labarthe whom de Gaulle had put in charge of arms procurement. Since Labarthe had a scientific background and had acted as technical adviser to the Popular Front on rearmament issues this seemed a natural choice. But Labarthe, a dazzlingly clever and irreverent conversationalist, was also a fantasist – it was not clear if he really had all the scientific qualifications he claimed to have – and probably a Soviet spy. It was inevitable that he would quarrel badly with Antoine. So too did Muselier who resented the fact that, as the first senior officer to have joined de Gaulle, he was not in sole charge. Dewavrin (who had taken the pseudonym Passy by which he was always to be known in the future) tried to mediate between the two men, but being only a thirty-year-old captain he lacked the authority to do so. After the failure of the Dakar expedition, Muselier started throwing his weight around even more. De Gaulle received letters from Antoine complaining about Muselier, from

Muselier complaining about Antoine and from Passy complaining about both of them.[2] De Gaulle sent Muselier a sharp reprimand: 'Your behaviour causes me considerable dissatisfaction . . . I order you to concern yourself only with military questions.'[3]

These squabbles fuelled the doubts of those at the Foreign Office who wondered if it had been right to back de Gaulle. It was reported that the 'de Gaulle HQ is appalling' and would reflect badly on Churchill if things were not sorted out.[4] This was ammunition for the anti-de Gaulle mutterings of the many French people in London who had kept aloof from de Gaulle. One of these was the former French Ambassador Roger Cambon, almost an institution in London, and much respected by the British. Cambon's flat became a meeting point for French exiles in London who dripped anti-Gaullist poison into the ears of the British.

Two important French publications were founded in London in the months after the defeat: a daily newspaper entitled *France* and a periodical entitled *La France libre*. The editor of *France*, the journalist Charles Gombault, came away from his first meeting with de Gaulle believing he had met a new incarnation of General Boulanger. Although the first issue of *France* in August 1940 published a message by de Gaulle, it otherwise kept its distance from him while never attacking him openly. *La France libre*, founded in November 1940, was a monthly review with heavyweight articles of great intellectual seriousness. It was set up by André Labarthe, who had ceased any formal collaboration with de Gaulle while not actually breaking with him. One of its regular contributors was the young philosopher Raymond Aron who would after the war become one of France's most distinguished public intellectuals. Despite its name, *La France libre* was not officially linked to the Free French, and kept a certain distance from de Gaulle. Only the initiated would have picked up the subtle differences between these publications and the Free French – just as only the initiated would have picked up the nuances that distinguished the two French teams at the BBC – but new French arrivals in London were sucked into this bitter émigré milieu of mutual suspicion and malicious gossip.

This atmosphere had unfavourably impressed Catroux when he arrived in September. It had a similar effect on Gaston Palewski, who appeared in London at the same time. Palewski was the rare example of someone who already knew and esteemed de Gaulle from before the war in his role as political aide to Paul Reynaud. He had been present at Reynaud's first meeting with de Gaulle in 1934. After the defeat, Palewski made his way to London to put himself at the service of de Gaulle. Unlike most of de Gaulle's recruits, he knew England well already, having spent a year of his education at Oxford. This experience gave him many British contacts and a taste for the lifestyle of the British upper classes. Palewski was sociable, snobbish, charming and, despite his unprepossessing pockmarked countenance, an irrepressibly successful womanizer. But he was also fiercely patriotic. Like de Gaulle, he had been disappointed by his patron Reynaud in 1940 and had also suffered at the hands of Madame de Portes. For his British contacts alone, he was just the kind of recruit de Gaulle needed. But he was appalled by the 'lack of organization and backbiting' at Carlton Gardens, and wondered if he had made the right choice. While awaiting the General's return, and keeping aloof from Carlton Gardens, Palewski did the rounds of his British contacts. Orme Sargent of the Foreign Office was relieved at last to meet 'someone who knows de Gaulle'.[5] To another British official, Palewski confided his view that de Gaulle's EDC was 'ridiculous' and that he should 'get away from the idea of a nigger kingdom and repair his damaged military prestige'.[6] Once de Gaulle had returned, Palewski surmounted his doubts and became a ferociously loyal supporter. But that someone so favourably predisposed to de Gaulle should have hesitated before committing himself casts a revealing light on the reputation of the Free French in London during these first months.[7] None of this helped de Gaulle to win the confidence of the British, who found him so different from the more pliable Frenchmen they had known in the past. In September 1941, a French civil servant, Hervé Alphand, arrived from Washington to join de Gaulle. He was immediately told by a worried Treasury official that 'de Gaulle was not "*sage*" and there needed to be someone to interpret him to the British.'[8] In fact he needed also to be 'interpreted' to the French.

Part of de Gaulle's problem was that he had so few experienced people around him. A phrase he often used about the early days of the Free French was 'I have had to build all this up with matchsticks.'[9] One person he trusted completely was Pleven, and on returning to London he summoned him back from Africa. In the early days of the Free French, whenever a problem arose, the refrain was 'Go and see Pleven.'[10] But Pleven could not be everywhere at once.

De Gaulle himself was never much interested in details of organization. Dealing with these was not the role of the leader as he had conceived it in *The Edge of the Sword*: 'To aim high, see the big picture ... To personify the contempt for contingencies while the masses work out the details.'[11] Hettier de Boislambert remarked of working for de Gaulle that he was essentially a '*machine à penser* ... Once his orders had been given he assumed they had been executed.' Another adviser noted in the same period that 'administrative issues bore him to death.' His reflex response on being informed about a quarrel in his team was to say 'let them sort it out among themselves [*qu'ils s'entendent*].'[12] Passy, who was a formidable organizer but no intellectual, noted ruefully in his memoirs that de Gaulle especially appreciated people with 'the capacity to juggle general ideas with panache'. This explains why he remained surprisingly indulgent towards Labarthe for as long as he did.[13]

But however much de Gaulle might have wished to soar into the intellectual stratosphere, he could not avoid the nagging contingencies of personality clashes and organizational details. This made him even more impossible to work with than usual. Such was the experience of Jacques Bingen, a young engineer who had worked in the shipping industry before the war.[14] Bingen's background made him the obvious person to liaise between the British government and that part of the French merchant navy which happened to be in Britain at the time of the armistice. Attached to the British Ministry of Shipping, he decided not to enrol formally in the Free French. His experience of de Gaulle was not likely to change his mind: 'I am completely disillusioned with our great leader (he could do with a strong dose of psychoanalysis) and he acts like a dictator but a rather incompetent one . . . A genuine collaboration with him seems to me impossible.'[15] Passy was also disappointed by how long it took de Gaulle to impose order on Carlton Gardens: 'No sensible decisions about the running of the organization. Meanwhile impossible to talk to.' Everyone, Passy included, was treated as a 'cretin' and an 'idiot'.[16]

It was not only in London that de Gaulle's leadership style caused problems, and not only with people unused to a military style of command. Larminat wrote from Africa to complain: 'Your authority is not in question, it is your way of exercising it that we contest.'[17] Catroux became so exasperated by de Gaulle's imperiousness that he tendered his resignation in February 1941. This worried the British, who saw the loss of Catroux as 'disastrous' but dared not intervene.[18] De Gaulle managed to persuade Catroux to retract while not really apologizing: 'If you persist in refusing your services to the Free French this would be an abandonment . . . Your greatness consists precisely in offering your assistance without conditions or susceptibilities.'[19]

De Gaulle's mood was not helped by the fact that he was at this time completely alone, far from his wife. In their first months in London, before de Gaulle's departure for Africa, the couple had rented a property in Petts Wood in south-east London (in the borough of Bromley). This rather hideous mock-Tudor villa – de Gaulle was entirely indifferent to his physical surroundings – had the advantage of being relatively cheap, fully furnished and not too inaccessible. De Gaulle would travel to Carlton Gardens every day either by train or in a car that had been put at his disposal by

Alfred-Etienne Bellanger, the London director of Cartier's, and (along with Saurat) a rare supporter among the French community in London. But because Petts Wood was close to an important railway junction, once the Blitz had started the area was subject to regular bombing raids and it was also on the flight path of German planes heading further north. The constant air-raid warnings and explosions terrified Anne de Gaulle. While her husband was away in Africa, Yvonne de Gaulle managed to find a house far away from the bombing at Ellesmere in Shropshire, which was also conveniently situated near to the convent school in Shrewsbury where de Gaulle's other daughter Elisabeth was a pupil. The disadvantage of the new location was that it was so far from London that de Gaulle could visit only about once a month and he lived at this time in a flat in Grosvenor Square. For Yvonne de Gaulle these were months of isolation, material hardship and loneliness far from anyone she knew and with only intermittent contact with her husband. A remark that this most private of women made to Admiral Muselier (of all people) suggests how hard this period was for her: 'The absence of letters is painful and yet I would not want my husband to be unoccupied.'[20] De Gaulle would never have made a confidence of this kind to anyone – and certainly not to Muselier – but the absence of his wife may have weighed upon him.

De Gaulle was on one of his irregular trips to Ellesmere in the New Year when he was rung up to be told the stunning news that Muselier had been arrested by the British. Their intelligence services had received documents claiming that Muselier was a traitor who had alerted Vichy to the attack on Dakar. The entire affair turned out to be a hoax manufactured by some rogue elements working for the Free French intelligence service. Nothing incriminating was found in Muselier's possession except some drugs.[21] Once back in London, de Gaulle launched into a passionate defence of the Admiral despite having private reservations about him. The British, extremely embarrassed, quickly released Muselier. De Gaulle's main complaint was that the British had interfered in French affairs without consulting him in advance.

The mini-crisis over Muselier was quickly resolved and left no traces except to stoke de Gaulle's suspicions about the British secret services. There were many other causes of friction. At the start of 1941 the Home Office had set up a Patriotic School where foreign nationals arriving from enemy territory were debriefed. De Gaulle believed, correctly, that the British were seizing the opportunity to win French recruits for themselves. In July 1940 Churchill had set up the Special Operations Executive (SOE) to organize sabotage against the Germans in occupied Europe. Its Section F was in charge of operations to France. In March 1941, SOE also set up

Section RF to work with the Free French. Passy, who had no other way of getting agents to France, needed to establish good working relations with SOE. De Gaulle was convinced that Passy was too trusting of the British. He was right to be suspicious. In December 1940, an internal SOE directive stated that F Section should know everything the Free French were doing but the Free French should know nothing about SOE operations in France. As the head of SOE, Major General Gubbins, observed two months later: 'If the British provided the violins they should also choose the music.'[22] Passy gradually came round to de Gaulle's point of view, but he was still obliged to work with the British.

These tensions with British intelligence did not yet cloud de Gaulle's harmonious relations with Churchill. But it was risky to be so dependent on the whim of one man – even if he was Prime Minister – and de Gaulle tried to cultivate his own contacts with other British policy makers. He even started to take English lessons. The unenviable task of teaching de Gaulle English was taken on by a M. de Valence, a Mauritian working for the BBC.[23] In fact at that time most members of the British elite spoke good French, and de Gaulle did not need to practise his shaky English too often. (De Gaulle occasionally liked to quote what he claimed Charles V had said on the subject of English: 'One speaks French to men, Italian to women, German to horses, Spanish to God but who ever heard of one speaking English?')[24]

Although de Gaulle rarely patronized the eating establishments – the Escargot, the Ecu de France, Prunier, Le Coq d'Or, Chez Rose, Le Petit Club Français in St James's Place, Chez Rose and the York Minster in Soho (today the French House) – where the Free French congregated to recreate a miniature version of the world they had left behind in France, he regularly lunched with British politicians, civil servants and journalists at the grand hotels and restaurants in which the British elite liked to transact business during the war: the Hyde Park Hotel, the Savoy, the Ritz, the Waldorf, the Connaught. For de Gaulle these were not social encounters – he resisted invitations from the socially well-connected Boislambert to join him for country weekends with his grand English friends[25] – but opportunities to promote the Free French cause by cultivating supporters in Westminster, Whitehall and the press. In the same spirit, in January 1941 he addressed a Foyle's literary luncheon. Although his lunch companions were reported often to find him 'sticky', de Gaulle could be, when relaxed, a charming lunch or dinner companion.[26]

Leo Amery, the Secretary of State for India, who dined with him on 16 January, wrote: 'He is rather unimpressive at first sight, very large with a small head and rather young looking, but he seems very well balanced and shrewd in his judgment.' About three weeks later they met again: 'Pleasant evening. Increasingly struck by de Gaulle's modesty and good sense.'[27] Not many people commented on de Gaulle's modesty. On one occasion the Director of the National Gallery, Kenneth Clark, was invited to lunch. De Gaulle (ever vigilant about anything touching French interests) had written to complain that he had not been invited to an exhibition of French painting organized at the National Gallery. To his agreeable surprise Clark found himself in the presence of an intellectual keener to talk about Bergson than about politics.[28] The Labour politician Hugh Dalton, Minister for Economic Warfare, lunched with de Gaulle on various occasions. On the first in July 1940 he found him 'not an inspiring or romantic figure, rather stiff and a Staff Officer more than a Commander in Chief'; at the next lunch four months later de Gaulle (who was possibly tailoring his remarks to his interlocutor) talked 'left-wing stuff' and seemed 'pretty sensible and subject to good influences'; the third lunch, at the Connaught, was 'a bit sticky ... de Gaulle wishing, I suppose, to seem very English, had ordered some very desiccated beef cooked in the English manner'.[29]

Harold Nicolson, who worked at the Ministry of Information, also fluctuated in his opinions:

> 20 January 1941: lunch with de Gaulle. First meeting. Accuses my Ministry of being Petainist. I say we are working for 'la France entière'. 'La France entière' he shouted, 'c'est la France libre, c'est moi' [The whole of France ... is France Libre, it is me]. Tired and not wholly benevolent look in his eyes. I do not like him.
>
> 27 February 1941: Attend lunch for de Gaulle and Muselier. Lots of talk with de Gaulle. Dislike him less ... He has tired, ruminating but not unkindly eyes. Curiously effeminate hands: not feminine but without arteries or muscle.[30]

Nicolson was not the only person to remark on de Gaulle's hands.

De Gaulle rarely had a chance to see Churchill in person, but his relations with him at this stage were harmonious and he was a weekend guest at Chequers in early March. He had two regular interlocutors on the British side. One was Churchill's special adviser Colonel Desmond Morton. In the 1930s, while working for the Secret Intelligence Service, Morton had leaked intelligence information about Germany to Churchill (he lived very close to Churchill's home Chartwell), and on becoming Prime Minister Churchill took him into his private office. His responsibilities included the handling of relations with governments in exile and with the Free French. Morton had been one of the first to encounter de Gaulle because he had been involved in drafting the Franco-British Union plan. On that occasion he had curiously described him as 'a magnificent crook ... another Max Beaverbrook' – which seems to have been meant as a compliment. Morton's personal links to Churchill caused irritation in Whitehall and his influence diminished when more conventional bureaucratic procedures supplanted Churchill's predilection for working through his own cronies. This impacted on Morton's opinion of de Gaulle. When the General's stock started to fall with Churchill, Morton seems to have felt that the best way to win Churchill's favour was to stoke his suspicions of de Gaulle.[31]

De Gaulle's other regular interlocutor was Spears, who was still head of the official mission to the Free French, the so-called Spears Mission. But Spears's relationship with de Gaulle began to fray after Dakar. This was inevitable because Spears saw himself as the man who had invented de Gaulle, which even someone less touchy and proud than de Gaulle would soon have started to resent – as he had also quickly come to resent similar pretensions on the part of Denis Saurat, Director of the French Institute. Once back in London, de Gaulle wrote to Churchill that since France Libre was no longer 'merely a "movement"' but also a 'territorial, military and economic unit' it would be desirable to have direct relations with relevant British ministries rather than through the Spears Mission.[32] Despite his understandable efforts to emancipate himself from Spears's tutelage, Spears was still de Gaulle's firmest supporter in Whitehall. Spears wrote in a memorandum in January 1940 that the British were wrong to 'blow hot and cold' in relation to de Gaulle:

> The obscure personality of last June, whom so many considered a hopeless figure to back because he was so little known, is a world figure today. That position he could not have obtained without British support, but it has been achieved primarily by his own efforts. He has made his mistakes and I for one have deplored them, but he is nevertheless a very great man.[33]

Spears denounced any attempt to work through Vichy as the equivalent of 'feeding lettuce to a rabbit that is being chased by a stoat – a waste of lettuce, at best, since if the rabbit were grateful, which would be unlikely, it will remain at the mercy of the stoat'.[34] His support for de Gaulle was not entirely disinterested. Spears was a maverick in Whitehall, one whose influence derived from his friendship with Churchill. The Free French were his *raison d'être*. De Gaulle, who had a shrewd sense of where power lay, may have sensed that Spears's support was a questionable asset.

If the British government blew 'hot and cold', it was because de Gaulle had brought so little. The British continued to hope that Weygand, or another personality of the Vichy regime, would switch camps. In anticipation of this, in January 1941 de Gaulle organized a consultation of the members of the Empire Defence Council. Since its members were scattered, this had to be done by telegram. Three questions were posed: what attitude should the Free French take to Pétain if (1) his government continued on its existing course of technical neutrality; (2) it transferred to North Africa but remained neutral; (3) it decided to join the Allies?

To the first question, there was unanimity: unofficial contacts need not be ruled out (Catroux was the most emollient, Eboué and Leclerc the most intransigent) but there could be no compromise on the principle that the armistice had made Vichy illegitimate. To the second question, the answers were similar: no compromise unless Vichy re-entered the war. The third question was the most difficult: all agreed that in such an eventuality it would be necessary to rally to Vichy but also that de Gaulle must be given a role ranging from 'important' (Muselier) to 'predominant' (Leclerc) or quite simply Head of State (Eboué).[35] These were more or less the answers de Gaulle wanted to hear. But had the third eventuality come to pass, he would have been in no position to dictate terms. His intimate conviction, knowing Pétain well, and having closely observed Weygand in 1940, was that no important Vichy leaders were going to rally – 'Weygand has never had the taste for taking risks,' he wrote – but his own future depended on this being right.[36] To show the British he had left no avenue unexplored, he allowed Catroux to make some informal approaches to Weygand and Noguès. These produced from Weygand the satisfactory (from de Gaulle's point of view) answer that if de Gaulle fell into his hands he would have him shot.[37] De Gaulle himself wrote curtly to Weygand on 24 February for the last time proposing they unite to bring the Empire into the war. He ended: 'If your reply is yes, I assure you of my respects.' This almost insulting curtness was guaranteed to produce a negative reply or no reply at all. The British regretted he had not found it possible to be a 'little more friendly and cordial'.[38] Cordiality did not come naturally to de Gaulle, but in this case it would not have served his purposes.

If de Gaulle went to the trouble of consulting the EDC, it was not because he wanted to hear its views but because he needed it to shore up his legitimacy. Otherwise the members of EDC were too dispersed – Leclerc in the Libyan Desert, Eboué in Chad, Catroux in Cairo – to play any role in the day-to-day running of the Free French. To avoid a return to the chaos of the autumn, de Gaulle carried out a reorganization of Carlton Gardens. Passy remained in charge of intelligence and Muselier in charge of the navy. The heads of the different services met twice weekly under de Gaulle's chairmanship. When de Gaulle left London again, that coordinating role was handed over to Pleven or Cassin. This embryonic structure provided what Casssin called later an 'apprenticeship of government'.[39] But the numbers were exiguous. The entire staff working at Carlton Gardens in February 1941 was about ninety.[40] The Free French remained very much a one-man band. De Gaulle always had someone acting as a kind of mixture between a *chef de cabinet*, an aide de camp and a general factotum. Initially this had been Courcel until he went off to join the Free French fighting in Africa. The position was then held by a young diplomat, Claude Bouchinet-Serreulles, whose admiration for de Gaulle was tinged by frustration at the asperities of de Gaulle's personality.

One aspect of the civil organization of Carlton Gardens that did not function well was the Department of Political Affairs, which de Gaulle had entrusted to Palewski. De Gaulle intended it to create a kind of clandestine organization of the Free French in France by making secret contacts with influential French personalities.[41] The plan was ultimately to set up secret Free French committees in every locality of France. This would have been ridiculously ambitious in any circumstances, but it was impossible given the way de Gaulle conceived the relationship between Palewski's department and Passy's intelligence service, which had now been named the Central Bureau for Intelligence and Military Action in France (Bureau Central de Renseignements et d'Action Militaire – BCRAM). Following the tradition of the army's Deuxième Bureau, de Gaulle conceived of Passy's role as collecting military intelligence, a task distinct from the political objectives ascribed to Palewski. By the end of 1940, Passy had succeeded in sending his first agents to France with the help of the British. The mission of these agents was ill defined. They collected 'military' intelligence but also sought out signs of opposition to Vichy and the Germans. This meant that the lines between 'political' and 'military' objectives were blurred, but de Gaulle wanted to keep them distinct.

Passy tried to persuade de Gaulle in February 1941 that it would be more logical to channel all activity in France through him. This would make it easier to coordinate with the British rather than presenting them with two entirely separate organizations which needed to get people to France. De Gaulle refused. Passy felt de Gaulle was 'dividing to rule'. There may have been truth in this, but de Gaulle – in so many respects a rebel – was respecting a traditional division between political and military activity even if it made little sense in these unprecedented circumstances. The result was that Palewski had a political mission but no agents to carry it out; and Passy had a few agents who were forbidden to stray into what de Gaulle viewed as politics. Palewski, frustrated by this impossible situation, soon asked to be posted abroad to serve with Free French troops. His successor was the diplomat Maurice Dejean, who had arrived in London in January 1941. Dejean had no more success than Palewski for exactly the same reason.[42]

De Gaulle's stubbornness on this issue also reflected the fact that he was not really convinced of the importance of *action* in France – apart from propaganda or procuring intelligence. This was a source of considerable frustration for Passy, who moved out of Carlton Gardens to premises in St James's Square and later in Duke Street. Bouchinet-Serreulles tried to interest de Gaulle in Passy's activities but with limited success: 'He received him for half an hour from time to time . . . or would just say something like "fine, fine, just continue the good work".'[43] In the long run this benefited Passy. Left to his own devices, he turned the BCRAM into the sinews of the Free French – a mini-state within the mini-state that the Free French would one day become. The BCRAM eventually became the link between the Free French in London and the Resistance in France. But de Gaulle, for all his imagination, was slow to grasp the importance of this. Saving France, in his eyes, would be done on the world stage – through the military forces he could build up and the territories he could bring into the war.

'IN OUR POSITION, WHOEVER STANDS STILL FALLS BEHIND'

Just before leaving Africa in November, de Gaulle had presented Larminat with a whole series of ambitious military directives which included attacking Vichy-held West Africa and moving north into the Libyan Desert. He ended with the words: 'No question of discussion. We must go forward.' Since most of these plans were completely impracticable without British help, Larminat ignored them. But for de Gaulle the details were less important than the principle that inspired them: 'In our position, whoever stands still falls behind.'[44]

This was in tune with de Gaulle's restless temperament – and with his Bergsonian view of the world – but he was right that if the Free French were to survive they had to show that they 'existed' beyond the squabbles of Carlton Gardens. This was not easy given the meagre forces at his disposal. Since the conquest of Gabon in November, the Free French had made little military impact. One Free French battalion was sent to join up with the British who were fighting the Italians in East Africa. In February 1941, it took the fort of Kub-Kub in Eritrea at the cost of sixteen dead and thirty-nine wounded. This was the first time Free French forces had fought against the Axis powers – as opposed to fighting the French in Dakar and Gabon. Leclerc had taken a column of about 400 men some 2,000 kilometres across the desert from Chad, with minimal motor transport, into southern

Libya – one of the objectives de Gaulle had set out to Larminat three months earlier. The result of Leclerc's operation was the capture on 1 March of the oasis town of Kufra. This event was given greater publicity than the capture of Kub-Kub because it had involved the Free French alone. One of the founding legends of the Free French was Leclerc's 'oath' at Kufra on 3 March 1941 that he would not lay down his arms until Strasbourg had been captured from the Germans. Larminat, who was coming to know how his leader's mind worked, advised de Gaulle not to make any difficulties with the British about the garrisoning of Kufra. It was just 'a heap of pebbles without interest' except as a 'symbol of our will to fight'.[45]

De Gaulle was acutely sensitive to the importance of symbols, but when he left London again on 14 March for his African territories, once more accompanied by Spears, his sights were set on more than heaps of pebbles. He had two objectives. The first was France's East African port of Djibouti, whose position at the entrance of the Red Sea gave it great strategic importance. The Governor was a Vichy loyalist. Since the British were fighting the Italians in East Africa, de Gaulle saw an opportunity to interest them in an operation to take Djibouti. He proposed that the British blockade the port, force the French Governor to capitulate and allow the Free French to take possession. General Wavell, commander of the British forces in the Middle East, preferred to cut a deal with the Vichy Governor, agreeing to leave him alone providing he remained neutral. De Gaulle was incensed by what he saw as appeasement. He telegraphed menacingly to Catroux in Cairo, declaring that Djibouti would be a test case of the British attitude to Vichy: 'We will draw the consequences one way or another.'[46] In fact Djibouti remained in Vichy hands until the end of 1942.

Even more important potential prizes were the French mandates of Syria and Lebanon.[47] Catroux's original mission in Cairo had been to win over General Dentz, the Vichy commander in the Middle East. Once it was clear this would not happen, another idea was hatched at Carlton Gardens. The Free French would foment an internal anti-French revolt by promising the local population independence. Having undermined Dentz's authority a small Anglo-French operation would topple him and bring Syria and Lebanon into the Allied camp.[48] Catroux poured cold water over this. He realized that the British did not care whether Vichy held on to its territories in the Middle East providing they did not fall under German influence. Otherwise the British would prefer the status quo. He concluded: 'The Free French must bend to this policy. Taking back the Levant for the Free French would encounter obstacles which cannot for the moment be overcome.'[49] It would be hard to imagine a course of action – or rather inaction – less likely to appeal to de Gaulle.

As in the case of Djibouti, the man de Gaulle needed to persuade was
Wavell. Responsible for a vast area of territory stretching from Egypt into
Palestine and Iraq, round the Persian Gulf and into the Sudan, Wavell was
massively overstretched. He had had some success against Italian forces in
Libya, but in April 1941 Hitler had sent two divisions to North Africa to
help Mussolini. Wavell was also fighting the Italians in East Africa, and in
May he was ordered by London to send troops to Greece where a German
attack was believed to be imminent. In these circumstances, the last thing
he wanted was to open up yet another front in the Middle East.

Arriving in Cairo from Fort Lamy on 1 April, de Gaulle immediately
went to see Wavell, 'irrupting', as he put it, 'inconvenient and pressing . . .
into his small and stifling-hot office'.[50] His aim was to persuade the British
of the risks of allowing Syria and Lebanon to remain in Vichy's hands.
Wavell would have none of it. He was helped by the fact that the Free
French were themselves divided about how best to proceed. De Gaulle's
preference was for a Free French operation with minimal British support.
Catroux, who had reluctantly come round to the need to act in Syria,
believed that any operation would require considerable British support.[51]
This worried Spears and de Gaulle, who took the view that to insist on
British participation was the likeliest way of ensuring that nothing would
ever happen. But did the Free French have sufficient forces to go it alone?
At one key meeting with Wavell, the British Ambassador in Cairo, Miles
Lampson, noted 'how jealous de Gaulle is of any suggestion that Free
France is being run in any way with British assistance'.[52] De Gaulle's most
compelling argument was the threat to British interests if Germany obtained
a foothold in the Middle East. Although Vichy was supposedly neutral,
there was a danger that Pétain's government might not be able to resist
German pressure. Given how overstretched he was, Wavell preferred to
take this risk.

Having failed to make Wavell budge, de Gaulle left for Brazzaville with
Spears on 16 April, leaving Catroux behind to press the case for action.
From Brazzaville de Gaulle wrote ominously to Catroux that, if the British
were not ready to help, the Free French would die: 'If they die, the French
nation will not pardon England and out of anger and despair give itself up
to collaboration with Germany.'[53] De Gaulle lashed out against the British,
announcing that he would not allow British planes to land at Fort Lamy
in Chad whose small aerodrome was a useful stopping point for British
planes flying from Nigeria to the Sudan, thereby avoiding a long detour
round the Cape. Spears forced de Gaulle to back down from this act of
gratuitous vindictiveness, but it was another of those moments of revelation which would eventually lead to a complete estrangement between the

two men.[54] In Brazzaville the British Consul General, Robert Parr, found de Gaulle 'extremely tired . . . and exceedingly depressed'. Since the British seemed to attach so 'little value to the moral side of his movement' he was not sure where his duty lay: 'He said he was the one man alone on whom this responsibility fell and that the burden was becoming more than he could bear.' Despite his 'profound discouragement' he did not want to go back to London where he would be 'caught in a web of problems'.[55] All his life de Gaulle, who thrived on movement and action, was subject to these bouts of despair.

'COMPLICATED ORIENT'

De Gaulle was rescued from his impasse by developments at Vichy. When pressing the case for action in Syria, it was obviously in de Gaulle's interest to put the worst possible complexion on Vichy's intentions. But it was difficult for the British government to decide whether he was right because the Vichy regime was so hard to read. The worst fears of the British, that the Montoire meeting between Hitler and Pétain in October 1940 was the prelude to an intensification of Franco-German collaboration, had proved groundless. This was not because Vichy did not want collaboration but because the Germans were not willing to offer enough concessions to make it worthwhile. In December 1940 Laval was suddenly sacked by Pétain. It was not clear initially if this was a sign that Pétain was distancing himself from collaboration or if the move was prompted only by internal rivalries. After a short interlude during which Pétain took as his Prime Minister the conservative French politician Pierre-Etienne Flandin, Laval's successor as the dominant figure in Vichy for the next eighteen months was Admiral François Darlan.

Where Laval had never made any secret of his pro-German proclivities, Darlan was harder to interpret. Like most French naval officers he was instinctively anti-British but he had not initially been among the most ardent proponents of an armistice in June 1940. The truth is that Darlan was above all an opportunist. Convinced that Germany would win the war, his aim was to secure, through collaboration, the best possible deal for France in a German-dominated Europe. His chance to relaunch col-laboration occurred when an anti-British nationalist rising erupted in British-controlled Iraq at the end of April. The Germans, seeing an oppor-tunity to weaken the British in the Middle East, offered to provide the Iraqi rebels with aircraft to support their ground forces. Meeting Hitler at Berchtesgaden on 15 May, Darlan agreed to allow German troops to use

French airfields in Syria in return for German concessions on the application of the armistice in occupied France. The British soon got wind that German planes were landing in Syria. This vindicated de Gaulle's warnings that Vichy 'neutrality' could not be relied upon. Wavell, although still unconvinced, was now overruled by Churchill. De Gaulle took the step of sending Churchill a telegram in English, which he never had before and would never do again – 'Thank you ... You will win the war'[56] – and set off for Cairo again.

Churchill had changed his mind about an operation to Syria because he assumed that Darlan's open collaboration with Germany would make Dentz unlikely to resist the Free French. This is what Catroux and de Gaulle had been assuring the British in order to lure them into the operation: an 'armed political inroad' by the Free French requiring minimal British support would bring Syria and Lebanon over to the Allied camp. But Catroux's secret contacts with Dentz's forces soon showed him that this was optimistic. Darlan's rapprochement with Hitler had not, in Catroux's words, 'sparked in the ranks of the Levant Army the reactions of honour that one might have desired'.[57] So Wavell, as he had feared, was forced to develop plans for a full-scale military operation by joint Free French and British forces. De Gaulle had succeeded in dragging the British into something much bigger than they had intended. The operation also turned out to be unnecessary for British strategic interests because German help had arrived too late to prevent the anti-British rising in Iraq from being successfully crushed. But it was too late for either the British or the French to turn back.

Once the Syrian operation had been agreed, it still remained to be decided how it would be presented. In the end the Free French retained the original idea of offering the populations of Syria and Lebanon a promise of independence. Since Dentz himself had made some statements on these lines, Catroux advised de Gaulle that it would be 'regrettable to be outflanked' on this by Vichy.[58] The British, in agreement with Catroux, proposed a joint proclamation guaranteeing independence since they wanted to demonstrate to Arab opinion that they had no designs on the French Empire. De Gaulle immediately suspected the worst since it was in his view not for the British to make promises to the population of a French colonial possession. As he wrote in his *Memoirs*: 'Hardly had the decision been taken than the British let their intentions be seen.'[59]

On 8 June the joint operation was launched. Australian and British troops marched into Lebanon, and 5,400 Free French troops commanded by General Legentilhomme entered Syria. The Vichy forces resisted strongly and seemingly with more vigour against the Gaullist troops than against the British ones. Legentilhomme himself was wounded, and the Free French suffered over 600 casualties. De Gaulle writes in his *Memoirs* of his profound sadness at the 'horrible waste' of this fratricidal conflict – even though he had written previously to Catroux on the subject of Djibouti that it was impossible to 'make the omelette of liberation without breaking a few eggs'.[60] But the violence of de Gaulle's behaviour over the next months was partly driven by his obsession with countering Vichy accusations that he had supported a British enterprise to dismember the French Empire.

On 21 June de Gaulle arrived in Damascus, where he installed Catroux as his 'High Commissioner in the Levant' – a title which worried the British who wondered where that left the promise of future independence. The commanders of the British forces fighting Dentz had been embarrassed to be greeted by the local population as liberators from the French. One of them, General Slim, could not bring himself to reveal to a Syrian who 'welcomed us as deliverers . . . and trusted the French would never return' that he thought 'General de Gaulle might have different views.'[61] He was of course right, and the issue of independence was to fester for the next three years. But the immediate quarrel between de Gaulle and the British occurred over the terms of the armistice to be offered to the defending Vichy forces. De Gaulle had anticipated that Dentz would try to get the British to allow him to repatriate his forces to France, and that the British, anxious to bring Dentz to the negotiating table as fast as possible, would be tempted to agree. De Gaulle, on the other hand, was eager to have a chance to recruit for the Free French among Dentz's troops after their surrender. After some tetchy exchanges, the British government had agreed to this. De Gaulle was therefore understandably incensed when he heard that the initial British response to Dentz's request for an armistice had omitted any reference to the Free French.

De Gaulle's next move was very odd. Just before the negotiations over the armistice were due to start, he suddenly flew back to Brazzaville, leaving Catroux in charge but with few instructions. Perhaps he had not realized what would happen next; perhaps he knew perfectly well and wanted to avoid responsibility for an armistice that he expected to be unacceptable; perhaps he was trying to create a situation of maximum drama. Perhaps the truth is to be found in his *Memoirs*: 'I had no other means of limiting the damage than to keep my distance, to ascend to a cloud and swoop down from it against an agreement that did not commit me, and that I would tear up to the extent that that was possible. That cloud was Brazzaville.'[62]

The British General in charge of the armistice negotiations, Henry Maitland Wilson, was out of his depth in these political waters. Anxious for an armistice to be signed as soon as possible, and feeling more affinity with the regular French soldiers of Dentz than with the Free French rebel soldiers, he signed a document which made no mention of the Free French. Since the surrendering Vichy forces refused to recognize the Free French as having any official status, Wilson included Catroux in his delegation only as an observer. Dentz's negotiators would not even acknowledge his presence except to salute perfunctorily while loudly proclaiming their loyalty to Pétain.[63] Wilson also signed a secret protocol (not seen by Catroux) which did not allow the Free French any contact with the surrendering troops. Since the Free French had been entirely excluded at every stage of the discussions, de Gaulle was not dramatizing when he wrote in his *Memoirs* that this agreement represented 'a pure and simple transmission of Syria and Lebanon to the British'.[64]

The armistice was signed at Acre on 14 July. Catroux's account in his memoirs is rather defensive. 'Lacking instructions' and 'closer to the realities of the situation than General de Gaulle', he felt his only alternative would have been to leave the room, declare the armistice unacceptable and risk a public break with the Allies in the presence of the Vichy representatives: 'Wisdom required more circumspection' – not a quality in de Gaulle's repertoire.[65] The armistice terms also worried the British authorities in Cairo who rightly feared the worst from de Gaulle. Anthony Eden, who had replaced Halifax as Foreign Secretary, recognized that it 'differed in important respects' from what had been agreed and 'I fear will be a shock.'[66] This was an understatement.

With exquisite bad faith, de Gaulle wrote to Catroux that he assumed he had not signed this armistice 'contrary to my intentions and my instructions'.[67] He then set off for Cairo. Meanwhile Carlton Gardens produced a closely argued refutation for the Foreign Office, asking politely 'to what degree it might be possible to alleviate the modalities of the application of the armistice'.[68] De Gaulle's own methods were more brutal. He arrived in Cairo on 20 July and on the next morning stormed into the office of Oliver Lyttelton, British Minister of State for the Middle East. Lyttelton was apprehensive, as Spears put it, 'at the prospect of facing de Gaulle on so bad a wicket'.[69] But nothing prepared him for what happened next. In his description of this encounter in his *Memoirs* de Gaulle claims that 'I tried to avoid an explosion . . . enveloping myself in ice'; he reported to his team in London that he had been 'quite calm in tone, very categorical on the substance'.[70] Lyttelton experienced the meeting differently. He reported that de Gaulle had burst into his office 'white with suppressed passion' and delivered a 'violent tirade' lasting over two hours. At the end he handed over a document formally withdrawing all Free French troops in Libya from British command within three days. Spears, who had seen many sides of de Gaulle, had never witnessed anything like this: 'In the worst mood I have ever known him in. He looked frightful . . . as if he had not slept for a week. He was extremely intransigent and very rude.'[71] Lyttelton refused to accept de Gaulle's document on the grounds that it could 'only be read as terminating the alliance'. He proposed reconvening after lunch and a siesta.

Far from taking a siesta, Lyttelton and Spears prepared their response. They were alarmed enough to consider putting de Gaulle in prison and replacing him with Catroux. At the afternoon meeting, however, de Gaulle seemed to have calmed down and was, said Spears, 'comparatively speaking, amenable'. The reaction of the British Ambassador in Cairo, Miles Lampson, revealed both the embarrassment and the dilemma of the British: 'De Gaulle is evidently behaving very badly, indeed it almost sounds as if he is slightly cracked; and I dare say it would be on balance a relief if he could be got to fade out of the local picture but I suspect if he went in a huff it might upset bigger things.'[72]

Negotiations to amend the armistice began. Lyttelton reported to London: 'We are by no means out of the wood . . . After our first conversation yesterday both Spears and I felt a complete breach was inevitable and that our minimum military requirement could not be safeguarded so long as General de Gaulle remained leader of the Free French.'[73] The negotiations finally resulted in the so-called Lyttelton–de Gaulle accords which offered an 'interpretation' of the armistice – effectively a repudiation of it. The Free French were to be offered full opportunity to recruit from among Dentz's troops. As de Gaulle reported to London, the new version gave reasons for 'serious satisfaction' and recognized 'our entire sovereignty over the states of the Levant'.[74]

The problems were not yet over. Arriving in Beirut de Gaulle saw that local British officials were doing all they could to obstruct the implementation of the new agreement. When the Vichy French General de Verdilhac departed Beirut for France he was given full military honours; and the band of Australian soldiers whom he had been fighting a few weeks earlier played the 'Marseillaise'. Spears, seeing de Gaulle in Beirut, reported to Lyttelton that 'The tone of the conversation took on the tone of your first meeting with the General. He showed every sign of having lost control.'[75] In the end only about 5,500 soldiers rallied to the Free French and 30,000 preferred to return to France. Most of Dentz's troops viewed the Gaullists as rebels.

The quarrel over Syria was the first major flare-up between de Gaulle and the British. De Gaulle opened the chapter of his *Memoirs* on this crisis with the famous sentence: 'To the complicated Orient, I set off with simple ideas' (in French this line is a perfect Alexandrine). He did not mean this in a spirit of self-criticism. In reality, having served in the Levant between 1929 and 1931, he was perfectly aware of the complexities of local politics. But as far as the British were concerned, his views certainly did display all the simplicities of a character out of *La Châtelaine du Liban*. He summed up his views of the British in one sentence: 'A team lacking scruples but not means . . . supported by the Prime Minister . . . aimed to install British leadership. English policy thus sought, sometimes underhandedly and sometimes brutally, to replace France in Damascus and Beirut.' Catroux, owing to his 'desire to seduce and his penchant for conciliation', had failed 'to discern the full depth of the malevolence of the British plan'.[76]

The truth was more complicated. It was de Gaulle who had bullied and cajoled the reluctant British into the operation in the first place. The Acre armistice had been a disaster for the Free French, but this was attributable more to the naivety of Wilson than to any anti-Gaullist conspiracy. There certainly were British army officers in the region who had no liking for the Free French and also some British Arabists only too happy to terminate the French mandate. But this was not the official policy of the British government. Churchill's own policy was an improvised, and slightly incoherent, response to the quagmire into which de Gaulle had dragged him. On one hand, he instructed Lyttelton that, as far as the future of the mandate was concerned, 'the Arabs bulk far more largely in our minds than the Free French, and there can be no question of any delay in negotiating treaties which satisfy them and convince them that they have not merely exchanged one set of Frenchmen for another'; on the other hand, he stated that there was 'no desire to supplant France in her privileged and favoured position in Syria'.[77] There was a tension, if not a contradiction, between these two objectives.

Overall de Gaulle was satisfied by the results of his intervention. He reported to his team in London that the crisis had been 'salutary' since the British despite their 'irritation' will have learnt that 'to count on us they must take account of us'.[78] The moral he drew for Legentilhomme was that 'with the English you need to bang the table, they will flatten themselves before you'.[79] Unwisely he said much the same to Spears, who reported to London that he doubted de Gaulle's mental balance. It is not clear how much of de Gaulle's performance with Lyttelton was put on, but if it was performance it was entirely in the grain of his character. Diego Brosset, a Free French officer who witnessed the affair at close hand, wrote that, playing for 'high stakes', de Gaulle was displaying that 'seed of recklessness, whether it be folly or genius, without which one cannot achieve great things'.[80] Certainly Catroux did not have that 'seed of reckleness'. One of Spears's team had commented of him a few weeks earlier:

Catroux is wise but weak ... He is generally liked because he is pliable and diplomatic. He never attempts to force an issue. A quiet life is all that matters ... He tries very hard to be loyal to de Gaulle ... but is fundamentally opposed to him, comprehensibly enough perhaps given the way he has been treated ... As for Mme Catroux, her anti-Gaullism amounts to a phobia ... Catroux would be a very good peacetime ambassador here ... But the cause of the Free French will never thrive and prosper under his guidance.[81]

De Gaulle's reversal of the armistice was certainly a success but his method carried serious costs. The affair caused a complete breach with Spears, who reports something de Gaulle said to him at this time as a kind of epiphany: 'I don't think I shall ever get on with *les Anglais*. You are all the same, exclusively centred upon your own interests and business ... You think I am interested in England winning the war? I am not. I am only interested in France's victory.' When Spears commented that these were the same, de Gaulle snapped back 'Not at all.'[82] In the negotiations over the Acre armistice Spears was reported by Lampson to be 'more violently disposed' against de Gaulle than anyone else.[83] Once de Gaulle's greatest supporter, he had become his most determined enemy almost overnight – all the more bitter because he knew how much de Gaulle owed him.

Since Spears had always been on the margins of power in London, losing his support was not so serious. More damaging was the effect of the crisis on Churchill, who was appalled by the reports of de Gaulle's behaviour. His initial decision to support de Gaulle in June had been a slightly impulsive gamble which had not entirely paid off since de Gaulle failed to attract as many supporters as either of them had hoped. But Churchill had stuck with him because the romantic and sentimental side of his nature was seduced by the quixotic nobility of the General's solitary struggle. And he never imagined that, from a position of complete dependence, de Gaulle would cause him any serious problems. What he had not understood, any more than Spears had, was that de Gaulle's ambition was much more than just to lead a group of Frenchmen to fight for the interests of the Allied cause. Given the treason, as he saw it, of the Vichy government, de Gaulle believed that it was his mission to embody and represent the interests of the French nation. It meant showing vigilance whenever France's interests seemed to be threatened – even by her allies. And to show that France still had teeth, he was ready to bite the hand that fed him. Churchill's attitude to de Gaulle never fully recovered from the shock caused by the General's behaviour in the summer of 1941 – with greater consequences for the life of the Free French than de Gaulle's short-term 'victory' in overturning the

Acre armistice. This was certainly the view of the Free French team in London, who were alarmed by the tone of de Gaulle's telegrams to Churchill. Twice they wrote to warn him about the 'essential importance' of the British alliance.[84] Unrepentant, de Gaulle was confirmed in his view that no one else could be trusted with the interests of France: 'I invite you to be more firm and not give the impression that those who represent me do not follow my policies exactly. Our force and our grandeur reside only in our intransigence regarding the interests of France.'[85] De Gaulle had turned his own personality into a philosophy of action.

De Gaulle returned from Beirut to Brazzaville in an anti-British frenzy. The British received a report of a conversation he had had with a French Canadian on the plane: 'At heart the English no more like the French than the French the English. In fact there is no people that likes any other. Their character and habits are too different.'[86] It was one thing to make such remarks in private but quite another to do so in public – as de Gaulle now did. In an interview with an American journalist on the *Chicago Daily News* on 25 August, he speculated that Britain had formed a kind of implicit deal with Hitler over Vichy: Vichy served Hitler by keeping the French submissive, but it also served Britain by keeping the French fleet neutral. The analysis was not without some truth, but it was folly to attack in public the government that was bankrolling and supporting him. Whether de Gaulle got carried away, or whether he had not realized his words would be published, he immediately saw that he had gone too far. But it was too late to block publication of the interview.

'IT MAY WELL BE THAT WE SHALL FIND THAT DE GAULLE IS CRAZY'

This interview caused consternation in London both among de Gaulle's own team and among the British. One member of the Spears Mission wrote that he hoped Spears would be coming back with de Gaulle because 'people are reluctant to see the lion let loose without its *dompteur* [trainer]'.[87] This was out of date: the beast had long escaped the *dompteur*. Carlton Gardens also awaited de Gaulle's return with apprehension. Bingen wrote in his diary: '*Le Grand Charles* is about to arrive. What new wind of madness is about to blow through the Household … He is going to wreak havoc everywhere. Everyone will present him with their plan and he will listen to no one.'[88] That was indeed what happened. Bouchinet-Serreulles found him in 'the foulest of moods … hurling anathema at everyone and especially the English. He sees almost no one and there is a kind of void around him. He spends entire days sounding off against the English in general and Spears in particular. This situation is very difficult for his entourage to put up with.'[89]

De Gaulle wrote to Churchill on 3 September but more in a spirit of self-justification than apology. For the moment Churchill's instructions were that de Gaulle should 'stew in his own juice' and not be allowed to broadcast. Even Eden, who was better disposed towards de Gaulle than his predecessor Halifax, wrote to Churchill, 'it may be that we shall find that de Gaulle is crazy; if so he will have to be dealt with accordingly.'[90] From Brazzaville, the British Consul General, also well disposed towards de Gaulle, reported: 'I am inclined to think de Gaulle is on the edge of a nervous breakdown.'[91] The only British official allowed to see de Gaulle in these days was Morton. He reported to Cadogan:

> In my opinion de Gaulle is a very clever man ... He is not a diplomat, but there lies a calculating brain behind the curious countenance, and though absolutely sincere and honest, he is undoubtedly swayed by deep prejudices. He is also a sentimentalist ... I do not think he is penitent ... He is not mad. If he raves like a lunatic at one moment and attempts to charm at another by quiet reasonableness, it is because he thinks that such an attitude is the more likely to gain his ends with the person in question.[92]

The only good news for de Gaulle during the tense days 'stewing in his juice' and waiting to be allowed to see Churchill was the arrival in London on 10 September of 185 escaped French prisoners of war. Theirs had been an extraordinary adventure. Each had individually escaped from German captivity and made their way east to the Soviet Union – only to find themselves in prison again because Russia and Germany had signed a non-aggression pact. Only when Hitler invaded the Soviet Union in June 1941 were they released and allowed to join de Gaulle in London. One of them, Captain Pierre Billotte, was the son of a general killed in the Fall of France, and he was quickly given a place in de Gaulle's military *cabinet*. Most of them were young and unknown, but the arrival of so many recruits on one day was a propaganda coup at a moment when de Gaulle desperately needed good news.[93]

Perhaps even more liable to impress the British was the arrival over the summer of two senior French civil servants, both *inspecteurs des finances*: Hervé Alphand, who had defected from the French Embassy in Washington, and André Diethelm, a former *chef de cabinet* of Mandel. Alphand was astonished by the hostility to de Gaulle shown by every British official he encountered and also by many of the French in London. His own first meeting with de Gaulle was not a success: 'I do not think that we really established a "contact" ... The man seems animated by one single aim, that of his mission to bring France back into the war. He shows no sign of any desire to please, no care for nuance, no spirit of negotiation.'[94]

This evidence of de Gaulle's growing reputation meant that the British had to think carefully about the consequences of breaking with him. Eden had continued his speculation to Churchill about whether de Gaulle might be mad by saying that if the General showed signs of repentance he should be forgiven since 'if he is of little importance outside France, he is of considerable importance inside it today as a rallying point against Vichy.' One member of the Spears Mission was torn in the same way: 'No HQ in this country is more unkempt. No word of appreciation of brilliant service ever escapes his lips' – but it had to be admitted also that he was 'a broadcasting genius' and his disappearance would be 'disastrous'.[95]

De Gaulle finally met Churchill on 12 September. He gave little ground, saying that if 'between two rapid plane trips' he had made disobliging remarks, he was ready to apologize. But his defence was that if the Free French were not exigent about the interests of their country they would not be who they were. Despite some possible embellishments Colville's account conveys the strangely passionate relationship that had developed between the two men. Churchill normally liked to take every opportunity to try out his approximate French, but on this occasion Colville was told to act as interpreter:

> Punctually at 3.00pm the General arrived. Churchill rose from his chair in the middle of the long Cabinet table, inclined his head slightly and gestured to the selected chair opposite him. De Gaulle seemed quite unabashed. He walked to his chair, sat down, gazed at the Prime Minister and said nothing. 'General de Gaulle, I have asked you to come here this afternoon.' Churchill stopped and looked fiercely at me. 'Mon Général,' I said, 'je vous ai invité de venir cet après-midi.' 'I didn't say "Mon Général",' interrupted the Prime Minister, 'and I did not say I had *invited* him.'

After stumbling on a little longer, Colville was thrown out of the room, and another interpreter was summoned. Quickly he 'emerged, red in the face, and protesting that they must be mad'. The two men remained closeted alone:

> An hour slipped away and I began to fear violence. I tried to eavesdrop ... but I could hear nothing. I walked out into the hall and tried on General de Gaulle's cap, registering surprise at the remarkable smallness of his head. I did my best to concentrate on the papers on my desk. I had decided it was my duty to burst in, perhaps with a bogus message, in case some dire act had

been committed. Perhaps they had strangled each other? Just then the bell rang and I went to find the two of them sitting side by side with amiable expressions on their faces. De Gaulle, no doubt for tactical purposes, was smoking one of the Prime Minister's cigars. They were talking French, an exercise Churchill could never resist.[96]

Although the meeting ended amicably on the surface, the two sides could not even produce jointly agreed minutes. De Gaulle commented on the British minutes that they were 'tendentious and inexact', and Morton on the French ones that they bore 'not the slightest resemblance to what was actually said', according at least to what Churchill had reported to him.[97] There were wildly divergent interpretations of the only substantive agreement to emerge from the meeting. Churchill had proposed (said the British record) that de Gaulle consider setting up a formal committee which would have an 'effective voice in shaping the policy of the Movement'; de Gaulle accepted the idea with alacrity as a sign (said the French record) that the British government attached such importance to the Free French that they 'desired to favour its development to the point of considering Free France as France itself'. What Churchill proposed as a way of controlling de Gaulle, de Gaulle accepted as a way of further legitimizing himself. The next two weeks would reveal which interpretation would prevail.

The idea of a committee had emerged when the British got wind of the anxiety in Carlton Gardens about de Gaulle's erratic behaviour over Syria. The most vocal critic was Muselier, who had contrived not to be among the welcoming party to meet de Gaulle on his return to London. But even less volatile individuals like the former diplomat Maurice Dejean were ready to share their doubts about de Gaulle with the British. In Dejean's view 'residence at Brazzaville, surrounded only by negroes and a handful of a poor type of French officials whose point of view was coloured by the bad climate and libations of whisky, always has an unfortunate effect on the General.' For this reason Dejean thought he should stay in London where his 'lack of political sense should be supplemented by a Council which would lessen the General's importance as the sole repository of the lost soul of France and put that arduous responsibility as it were in commission'.[98] The British plan to put de Gaulle 'in commission' (Churchill's phrase) meant diluting his power by dividing it among the membership of a committee.

Muselier saw his opportunity to strike. A week after de Gaulle had seen Churchill, the Admiral presented de Gaulle with his own nominees for an Executive Committee. The list included André Labarthe who had now completely broken with de Gaulle and joined Muselier in opposition to him. Muselier proposed himself as the chairman of his committee while confining de Gaulle to a largely honorary position. What de Gaulle did not know was that on the next day Muselier dined at the Savoy (over a lot of brandy) with Morton and Lord Bessborough (head of a Foreign Office department in charge of helping French refugees) who encouraged and supported his initiative. The idea of setting up a committee had turned into an anti-de Gaulle conspiracy. At this point Muselier overplayed his hand, threatening that he would secede from the Free French, taking the navy with him. The British had not intended to create a complete schism among the Free French, which is what Muselier was presenting them with. While suspicious of de Gaulle, even Morton, who had been involved in the plot, told Churchill that Muselier was an adventurer who could not be fully trusted.[99]

Churchill summoned de Gaulle to see him on 23 September. De Gaulle quickly realized he was not going to back a Muselier secession and this emboldened him to hold firm.[100] He wrote to Muselier on the same day accepting some of his names for the Committee but not all of them, rejected the idea that anyone besides himself should chair it and threatened to denounce Muselier publicly if he did not accept the conditions he had been offered. On the same day, he gave a press conference announcing the formation of a National Council.[101] On 24 September Muselier and de Gaulle were both at the Foreign Office. Since Muselier refused to address de Gaulle directly, they were put in different rooms while British officials scurried between them to work out a compromise.[102] De Gaulle agreed to allow Muselier on the Committee with responsibility for the navy, but de Gaulle himself would be its president with the power to choose the other members. Muselier gave in.

Apart from Muselier, the eight members of the Committee were firmly behind de Gaulle: Pleven was in charge of economic matters and the colonies, Cassin justice and education, Dejean foreign affairs, the recently arrived Diethelm interior and information, and so on. Although the members were called commissioners rather than ministers, the Committee was clearly another step towards the formation of a government in exile with de Gaulle at its head. As the historian François Kersaudy comments: 'It required a great deal of imagination to see the creation of the committee as weakening de Gaulle's power.'[103]

The British had not intended this outcome. Bessborough, who had been supporting Muselier, told Churchill that it was a committee of 'Yes Men and de Gaulle in the Chair . . . simply a dictatorship, under Democratic guise'. Churchill agreed that it was 'very unpleasant' and that 'our weight in the immediate future must be thrown more heavily against de Gaulle than I had hoped would be necessary.' Eden was more sanguine. He accepted that the Free French were not easy 'and run round with their quarrels to anyone they can find who will listen to them', but he took the view that the British 'could not out of the material available in this country have materially improved the Council even if we had chosen every member ourselves'. Churchill's retaliation was an instruction that de Gaulle should not be allowed to leave the country without permission. But the embargo on broadcasting was lifted. De Gaulle had already been allowed back on the airwaves on 18 September, and he spoke another nine times before the end of the year. Every time he did so, it became a little harder for the British to remove him.

8

Inventing Gaullism

APOLITICAL GENERAL

While de Gaulle was causing havoc in the Middle East, Desmond Morton, that far from consistent friend of the Free French, wrote to René Cassin:

It will not have escaped your notice that many important people . . . accuse General de Gaulle of being a 'political' General . . . When however you come to examine the contention that General de Gaulle is a 'political general' I doubt if the accusation sticks. You and a few of the General's close associates – even I myself – may think we have had some indication of the General's political views in private. In point of fact, have we? Anyway, when has he made any political speech or political declaration in the usually accepted meaning of that term? Surely a political policy requires a complete platform, and in the case of the Free French Movement would entail a statement of how the Movement proposed that France and the French Empire be governed . . . Nor can I see that General de Gaulle is justly accused of being a politician because he condemns Vichy root and branch. He and his move-ment are pledged to fight the Germans. Vichy is pledged to collaborate with them. That is not politics but common sense. Pursuing what seems to me to be logic, I ask if it is not desirable either for the Free French Movement to strike a strong line of counterpropaganda refusing to accept the implication of being a 'political' movement, or else for the Free French Movement to state publicly their political aims admitting that they are a political movement.[1]

At exactly the same moment, the same question – what did de Gaulle think about politics? – was being asked in private by Jacques Bingen, whose reservations about the General we have already noted: 'Left or right? Demagogy or dictatorial fascism? Return to the past or construction of a new utopia?'[2] Many people wanted answers but de Gaulle refused to pro-vide them.

When asked about his political views by a British journalist in August

1940 de Gaulle declared: 'I am a free Frenchman. I believe in God and the future of my homeland . . . I declare solemnly that I am attached to no political party, nor linked to any politician of any kind whether of the right, centre or left. I have only one aim: to deliver France.'³ For a year he did not deviate from this position. Aware of the negative effects of the Free French squabbling during his first absence from London, when leaving again in March 1941 he issued an order that was posted throughout Carlton Gardens: 'All the Free French must implacably reject any suspicions or prejudices in their relations with each other. Whatever anyone's beliefs and origins, they must be a brother for all the others from the moment they begin serving France.'⁴

De Gaulle strictly respected this principle. The only person whose support he refused in the first months of the Free French was the left-wing politician Pierre Cot, who had been Minister of Air during the Popular Front. Cot's nationalization of the aircraft industry had made him hated by conservatives who blamed him for the problems experienced by the French air force in 1940. His presence at de Gaulle's side would have alienated officers of the air force whom the General needed to attract. When Cot presented himself to de Gaulle in June 1940, de Gaulle suggested that he go to the United States instead. He explained in his *Memoirs* that Cot was 'too visible' for his membership of the Free French to be 'desirable'.⁵ He was not alone in holding this view. When the possibility of using Cot was floated again a year later, even a figure of unimpeachably democratic credentials like René Cassin, who was always trying to push de Gaulle to make public commitments to democracy, advised that Cot was too divisive.⁶

Otherwise de Gaulle excluded no one. He was unusual in his seeming immunity to the anti-Semitism that was such a feature of French society at this time, so much a fact of life that Cassin felt it necessary to inform him when arriving in London that he was a Jew. De Gaulle's only comment was: 'I know.'⁷ Two of the first people to visit de Gaulle on 19 June, Georges Boris and André Weil-Curiel, were Jews. Once de Gaulle had been recognized by Churchill, they both presented themselves again. Boris arrived on a day when de Gaulle was away on one of his recruitment efforts among French soldiers in British camps. The officer on duty made it clear to Boris that he was not welcome. As soon as this came to de Gaulle's attention, he overruled the decision. He is reported as saying: 'Whether he is a Jew, a partisan of Léon Blum or all manner of other things, I see only one thing: that he is a Frenchman who at the age of 52 enrolled in order to fight . . . I do not know difference of race or political opinion among us. I know only two kinds of Frenchmen: those who do their duty and those who do not.'⁸ Whether or not these were his exact words, they represent the position he adopted. When one of his representatives in Africa wrote to complain that he could not make use of all the 'stateless Jews' who seemed to want to offer themselves, he was sharply rebuked by de Gaulle for the content and tone of his message.[9]

In the entire corpus of de Gaulle's correspondence, there is hardly a trace of anti-Semitism. One exception was a letter from Poland in 1919 where he wrote: 'In the middle of all this, there are innumerable XXXX hated to death by all classes of society, all enriched by the war ... and disposed to foment social revolution where they would stand to make lots of money in exchange for some shady deals.'[10] Since his son who edited the edition felt it necessary tactfully to erase the word used, one assumes that 'XXXX' must be more pejorative than simply 'Jews'. In this case de Gaulle was reflecting the widespread anti-Semitism of most sectors of Polish society at this time.[11] In another comment he remarks of Warsaw in 1920 with a certain disdain that 'the theatres were full, it is true, but with people of very Israelite elegance.'[12] These two comments suggest that de Gaulle certainly shared some of the anti-Semitic prejudices of his class – it would have been remarkable if he had not – but more remarkable is that it never affected his attitude to individuals. Nevertheless there was a persistent undercurrent of anti-Semitism at Carlton Gardens, and figures like Boris and Cassin were wary of pushing themselves forward too much. Cassin wrote in his journal in July 1940: 'Because I am Jewish and because I don't know English, I have made the *sacrifice* not to interfere in matters relating to foreign affairs.'[13] Weil-Curiel was advised by Cassin that he would be best advised to keep a low profile.[14]

A low profile was also advisable for individuals too identified with the left. The first people to rally to de Gaulle included many figures of unimpeachable democratic credentials like Cassin, Boris, Schumann and Pleven, but they had the sense of being an embattled minority. Bingen wrote about Maurice Dejean in July 1941: 'At least he is not a fascist, which is rare in the household.'[15] The term 'fascist' was loose but it was true that many military figures who had joined de Gaulle, like Leclerc and Larminat, made no secret of their ultra-conservative, often royalist, opinions, and their delight that the hated Third Republic had fallen.[16] It was not only military figures who held such views. At Carlton Gardens, Antoine made no secret of his rightist views, nor did the jurist Pierre Tissier, who was the person who had sent Boris packing. Many of the recruits to Passy's intelligence services were markedly conservative. Gilbert Renault (alias Rémy), one of his most intrepid agents, wrote from Spain in 1940 that he approved Vichy's domestic reforms and rejected 'the slime of Jews and half-castes who had scuttled abroad like rats'.[17] Passy himself never shook off unfounded gossip that he had been a member of the ultra-right-wing 1930s conspiratorial organization the Cagoule, a rumour started by the mischievous Labarthe. This was not true, but Passy unwittingly gave an insight into his conservative view of the world in a lapse he made in a BBC broadcast in April 1941: 'People say the Free French is made up of Jews and Freemasons and will bring back all the errors of the past. That is false . . . The huge majority of Free French are honest individuals.'[18] One sign which worried people on the left was that while the first broadcasts of the Free French had been introduced by the words 'Liberty, Equality, Fraternity', de Gaulle dropped this after a few weeks in favour of the motto of the French army, 'Honour and Fatherland'.

The first official declaration of the Free French was the Brazzaville Manifesto of 27 October 1940 arguing that the Vichy regime was illegitimate and illegal. This was followed by an 'Organic Declaration' of 16 November 1940 which put the case even more explicitly. If Vichy was illegal, the implication by default was that de Gaulle's movement represented the continuity of the Third Republic abolished by Vichy. But de Gaulle did not adopt Cassin's suggestion that he include a commitment to 'democracy' in these two documents.[19] Indeed neither of the words 'democracy' and 'Republic' appeared in any speech of de Gaulle for the first eighteen months of the Free French. The Organic Declaration was accompanied by de Gaulle's first official 'Ordonnances' as leader of the Free French which were couched in almost monarchical language: 'Through the Empire and the French People, We, Charles de Gaulle General de Gaulle, leader of the Free French, declare . . .'. This led one British official to comment that the whole declaration sounded 'quite fascist'.[20] This was another loose use of the word 'fascist', but it suggests that, if there was a republican side to de Gaulle's movement, it was not one that struck contemporary observers.

Cassin was not the only figure trying to nudge de Gaulle in a more democratic direction. Another was Henry Hauck, a trade unionist who had been working as Labour Attaché to the French Embassy before the defeat. Hauck stayed in London with de Gaulle rather than returning to France with other Embassy staff. In a long paper to de Gaulle in October 1940 he argued that there were signs the French working class was turning against the Pétain regime. The moral he drew was that the Free French should 'proclaim that our movement is Republican, that it is anti-capitalist, and that it intends to establish in France a new regime founded on democratic liberties'. He worried that otherwise the mass of the French working class would be driven towards Communism.[21] Passy's first agents to France returned with a different line: 'The vast majority of the French people are

Gaullist (regarding external matters) [that is, against collaboration with Germany] and Pétainist (on internal ones) [that is, hostile to democracy and the Republic].'[22] The truth was that no one, neither Passy nor Hauck, had any idea what the French were thinking. Each read the situation according to their own personal predilections. De Gaulle took no account of Hauck's advice, although before leaving London in March 1941 he did support his proposal to send an envoy to make contact with underground labour organizations in France.

De Gaulle continued his tightrope act of avoiding any political commitments. When in February 1941 Larminat wrote to complain that the newly founded journal La France libre contained the motto 'Liberty, Equality, Fraternity' on its masthead, de Gaulle replied that the review was entirely independent, and that 'whatever one's personal opinions might be, one cannot pretend to forbid the printing of a slogan that has been engraved on all our public monuments for 150 years.'[23] On the other hand, when six months later Cassin tried again to push de Gaulle into making a public commitment to democracy, he was rebuffed:

> If we proclaim simply that we are fighting for democracy, we will perhaps win provisional approval from the Americans but we would lose a lot with the French which is the principal issue. The French masses for the moment link the word democracy with the parliamentary regime as it operated before the war . . . That regime is condemned by the facts and by public opinion.[24]

None of this tells us much about de Gaulle's private convictions about politics at this time – if he had any. At lunch with Churchill at the end of 1940, when the two men were still on good terms, de Gaulle expressed scepticism about the Prime Minister's idea that they should stress that the enemy was Nazism rather than Germany: 'We fought the last war against the Hohenzollerns and German militarism; we crushed them both; and then came Hitler – et toujours le militarisme allemand [always German militarism].'[25] The root of de Gaulle's opposition to Vichy lay not in the regime's internal policies but in the signing of an armistice which had subjected France to German domination. De Gaulle's speeches gradually started to include attacks on Vichy's suppression of political liberties, but this was never for him the central issue: that issue was the armistice.

Although from the mid-1930s de Gaulle – thanks to his association with Reynaud – had been trying to work through the existing parliamentary regime, everything was changed in his eyes by the debacle of 1940. What appalled him was that at France's greatest moment of peril the Republic had let the country down. In a speech on 1 March 1941, he denounced the 'intolerable abuses of the parliamentary system', responsible for a 'grave

weakening of the authority of the State'.[26] He told a British official after
his return to London in September that year that the two main French
newspapers in London were speaking the language of 'outdated politicians
of 1935'. At the same time he refused to be drawn on details of the future
while agreeing 'that the French people had not repudiated the principles
of 1789'.[27] This left a lot to the imagination.

De Gaulle's refusal to commit himself publicly to democracy or the
Republic was one factor fuelling the hostility of many French exiles in
London and America. In September 1941, Cot, who had by now convinced
himself de Gaulle was a fascist, sent Pleven a long document from the
United States offering political suggestions for the Free French. This was
passed on to de Gaulle, whose scribbled annotations give a flavour of his
views at this juncture. Had Cot seen these comments, they would have
confirmed his worst suspicions:

> Cot: De Gaulle should bring over some politicians from France. De Gaulle:
> 'at no price'.
>
> Cot: De Gaulle should have an advisory council of men with 'political
> competence' and 'not only those whose competence is purely technical'. De
> Gaulle: 'I do not agree. There is no such thing as being "purely technical" in
> a total war.'
>
> Cot: This advisory council should prevent de Gaulle acting just on a 'mili-
> tary level and make contact with the popular masses who are the real national
> resistance'. De Gaulle: 'what a joke! Who is the person who has the ear of
> the national resistance?'
>
> Cot: Why had the Free French avoided reference to the Republic and
> abandoned any reference to 'Liberty, Equality, Fraternity'? De Gaulle: 'The
> Republic abdicated! Not all the Free French have the same views as M. Pierre
> Cot.'
>
> Cot: The Vichy regime was trying to establish in France a 'fascist' regime.
> De Gaulle: 'I think that is a somewhat simplistic conception.'
>
> Cot: De Gaulle should form a government in exile which respected the
> sovereignty of the people or the power of parliament. De Gaulle: 'No: that
> might have been true in 1936 or 1939 but no longer today. Parliament abdi-
> cated.'
>
> Cot: De Gaulle should surround himself with representatives of France's
> political majority. De Gaulle: 'I am surrounded by men representative of the
> national majority that is fighting the invader. At no price will we take back
> the parliament of 1939.'
>
> Cot: 'Democrats need to know where they are being led.' De Gaulle: 'The
> phraseology of a parliamentarian.'

Cot: 'The Free French should draw on the revolutionary action of the democratic and popular masses': De Gaulle: 'on the action of the *national* masses'.[28]

'LIBERTY, EQUALITY, FRATERNITY'

Just as he was penning these outbursts of sarcastic contempt against the defunct regime, de Gaulle's views had started to evolve. During his stormy encounter with Churchill in September 1941, when the latter had suggested that de Gaulle set up an advisory committee, the idea was presented as a way of scotching accusations that the General had 'moved towards certain Fascist views'. De Gaulle countered that such insinuations would not stand up in the light of 'further statements that he planned to make'. He proceeded to give two speeches that offer some clues to what he might have meant. In the first, at a meeting in the Albert Hall on 11 November 1941, he announced that although it would be for the French to choose their political system at the end of the war, the principles underlying France's future institutions would be inspired by the two mottos '"Honour and Fatherland" *and* "Liberty, Equality, Fraternity"' (the first time he had uttered these words) so as to be 'faithful to the democratic [the first time he had uttered this word] traditions of our ancestors'.[29] Ten days later in a long speech in Oxford, de Gaulle affirmed that Britain and France were jointly engaged in a 'battle for liberty and the development of the individual' and that both opposed regimes which 'only recognized the right to a national or racial collectivity'.[30]

What caused this evolution in de Gaulle's rhetoric? Although we have no internal evidence to answer the question, there are two likely explanations. First, political ambiguity was turning out to have more disadvantages than advantages. De Gaulle's refusal to make political statements so as not to alienate potential supporters carried the risk of satisfying no one. As Bingen put it (with a degree of exaggeration) the Free French enjoyed 'a doubly unfortunate image of being a Judaeo-Masonic Popular Front movement to people in France, and a fascistic and anti-Semitic movement to the Anglo-Saxon democracies'.[31] In London many French exiles persisted in spreading the idea that de Gaulle had dictatorial aspirations. A group of French Socialists in London had organized themselves into the so-called Jean Jaurès Group where they frequently aired their concerns about this disconcertingly 'political' General. Numerically this group was insignificant, but its members had contacts with left-wing British journalists. None of this helped de Gaulle's reputation with British politicians – as shown by Churchill's comment on de Gaulle's 'Fascist views'.

This negative image of de Gaulle was even more prevalent in America, and de Gaulle's representative there, Jacques de Sieyès, was ineffective at counteracting it. Sieyès, a contemporary of de Gaulle's from Saint-Cyr, was working for a perfume company in New York at the time of the defeat. Knowing almost no one in America, de Gaulle enthusiastically embraced Sieyès's offer to represent him. Things got off to a bad start when he wrote to Sieyès in July 1940 that, although he had been unable to set up a committee in London because no politicians were willing to join him, there was 'no reason to regret' the absence of 'the most disreputable politicians of the regime'. Sieyès naively made this letter public; and since several of the 'disreputable' politicians in question had ended up in the United States, this did de Gaulle's cause no good.[32] It was in his interest to set the record straight.

A second reason pushing de Gaulle to make some kind of political statement was the entry of the French Communist Party into resistance. Until June 1941, those Communists who opposed the German Occupation were stymied by the non-aggression pact between Hitler and Stalin. Officially the Party refused to take sides in a war depicted as an imperialist conflict between two capitalist powers, Germany and Britain. This changed when Hitler invaded the Soviet Union. The Communists started organizing direct attacks on German soldiers in France – something no other Resistance organization had yet done. On 22 August 1941, a German naval officer was shot on a Paris metro station by a young Communist. Other attacks followed. In retaliation Hitler ordered fifty French hostages to be shot for every German killed. This played into the hands of the Communists, whose aim was to radicalize the French population and turn it against Vichy. De Gaulle was initially unsure how to react. When Schumann remarked to him that such acts of violence were futile, his immediate reaction was the opposite: 'This river of blood is necessary, collaboration will be drowned in it.'[33] But after reflection he took a different line in a broadcast on 23 October. He warned his listeners that, while it was 'absolutely normal and justified that Germans are killed by Frenchmen', nothing would be served by provoking the Germans into indiscriminate reprisals: 'There are tactics in warfare. The war of the French must be conducted by those who are in charge of it, that is by me and the National Committee . . . The order I give for the moment in occupied territory is not openly to kill Germans.'[34]

In reality de Gaulle was in no position to give 'orders' to anyone in France. But the prospect of the Communists becoming a major player in the struggle against the Occupation lent weight to Hauck's argument that the Free French should reach out to the French working class. Hauck returned to this theme after de Gaulle's return from the Middle East in

September 1941. Although de Gaulle had authorized him to contact trade unions in France, the envoy Hauck had lined up for this mission was still waiting to be parachuted into France. Attributing this delay (correctly) to Passy, who controlled all departures to France, Hauck denounced 'the extreme right political sympathies' of Passy's entourage for cutting de Gaulle off from the French people. 'The "Gaullist" spirit', he wrote to de Gaulle, 'is not a conservative or totalitarian one, or monarchist, it is Republican and democratic.'[35]

If this was the 'Gaullist spirit', it not clear that de Gaulle was yet a 'Gaullist'. The inflection in his political position in the autumn of 1941 was tentative. He had been testing the water, but he resisted those urging him to embrace democracy and the idea of the Republic more explicitly. This emerged in a revealing exchange at the start of 1942 between de Gaulle and the Catholic philosopher Jacques Maritain, living in exile in the United States. Maritain was the most internationally respected voice of liberal Catholicism; his book *A travers le désastre* (1940), the most famous post-mortem published on the defeat, argued that France was engaged in a spiritual struggle against Nazi totalitarianism. His book had had little to say about de Gaulle except that 'it is not in a man but in the people of our country that our best hope lies.' In November 1941, however, Maritain wrote directly to de Gaulle at the prompting of Hauck. His line was that, since the bourgeoisie had betrayed France, the country required a new regime 'reconciling Christianity and Liberty . . . the tradition of St Louis and the tradition of the Declaration of the Rights of Man'. It is hard to imagine a language more liable to resonate with the syncretic vision of French history de Gaulle so admired in Péguy. Delighted to receive a long letter from a figure of Maritain's stature, de Gaulle wrote back expressing his agreement while also being non-committal: 'I am not worried for the future of democracy. Its enemies are only ciphers. I don't fear for the future of religion. The bishops have behaved badly but there are good curés, simple priests, who are saving us.' This evasive reply did not satisfy Maritain who wrote again in March 1942 expressing his worry that if 'Gaullism' had not rallied more people it was because they worried that de Gaulle might just want to continue the 'policy of the Marshal without the Marshal'. This time de Gaulle did not reply except in a telegram urging Maritain to join him.[36]

When Bouchinet-Serreulles tried to elicit a more positive response to Maritain, de Gaulle dug his heels in, saying that he had made himself clear at the Albert Hall five months earlier: 'If people want to block up their ears and not listen, I can do nothing about it.'[37] By this point Hauck was becoming so disillusioned that he wrote to de Gaulle in March 1942 threatening to make his worries public.[38] At the same moment, Alphand was screwing up his courage to persuade de Gaulle to make a formal commitment to the Republic. He was pessimistic about his chances of success: 'De Gaulle's rigidity in the tiniest issues is part of his personality.'[39] Alphand was right about de Gaulle's rigidity when people tried to push him – and between Hauck, Maritain, Bouchinet-Serreulles and Alphand there clearly was a concerted campaign – but he underestimated de Gaulle's pragmatic adaptability. Within a few weeks, de Gaulle's public commitment in favour of democracy had gone further than anyone could have imagined. To understand why, we need to appreciate the importance that the Resistance was beginning to assume in his thinking.

DISCOVERING THE RESISTANCE

For the first year of the Occupation Resistance movements hardly counted in France – and little was known about them. Passy's agents had stumbled upon some embryonic groups and he was beginning to wonder if some military use might be made of them. De Gaulle, fixated on his relations with the Allies as the key to France's liberation, was sceptical. While not opposed to the idea of propaganda in France he did not think there was anything to be hoped for from military *action* there. He also continued to insist on a strict division between the gathering of military intelligence – Passy's role – and political action in France. The latter, which had been entrusted unsuccessfully first to Palewski and then to Dejean, was given to the Commission of the Interior headed by André Diethelm. But like his predecessors Diethelm came up against the problem that de Gaulle's ambitions in this respect were hazy and unrealizable. In October 1941, de Gaulle wrote to Hugh Dalton, the political head of SOE, asking if the British would be ready to lend support to his idea of undertaking political action in France by setting up a 'secret network of propaganda'. After some weeks Eden brushed him off with the reply that the British could not 'associate themselves with political propaganda designed to secure the post-war establishment in France of any . . . particular persons as a government' – by which he meant that the British would not do anything to help de Gaulle's own personal ambitions.[40] The only hope would have been to work through Passy, but this breached de Gaulle's separation between military action and propaganda. De Gaulle remained at a loss how to deal with whatever might be happening in France.

All this changed with the arrival in London of Jean Moulin, the most senior French civil servant to have made the journey from France. In June

1940 Moulin had been Prefect of Chartres near Paris. When the Germans tried to force him to sign a document blaming French Senegalese troops for atrocities that had been committed by German soldiers, Moulin attempted suicide by cutting his throat with a piece of broken glass. The Germans, who in these early stages of the Occupation were trying to win French goodwill, abandoned the attempt to make him sign the compromising document. Moulin continued as Prefect for the next few months. Sacked by Vichy in December 1940, he spent months travelling incognito around the Unoccupied Zone collecting information about the embryonic Resistance movements. He arrived in London, via Lisbon, on 21 October 1941.

Moulin's arrival was a major event. Whatever information Passy's agents had gleaned about the Resistance was patchy. They were never sure whether resisters were bluffing about their importance. Moulin brought information about the three main Resistance movements that had emerged in the Unoccupied Zone, but not being a member of any of them, he offered a degree of objectivity. He also came with a strategy for how to use the Resistance. In a long report drafted in Lisbon, he argued, on the one hand, that the Resistance movements were in desperate need of money, arms and radio contact with London, and, on the other, that if properly coordinated they could act like 'an army of parachutists already in place, knowing the terrain'.[41]

Moulin had not decided before reaching London whether to offer his services to the British or to de Gaulle. He drafted his report with both audiences in mind. His first meeting with de Gaulle took place on 25 October. Since Moulin died tragically before the Liberation, we do not really know what impression de Gaulle made on him. Many others left vivid sketches of their first encounter with the General; Moulin did not have the chance. He was a man of the left from a family that had been fiercely republican since the middle of the nineteenth century. During the Popular Front government he had been a member of Pierre Cot's *cabinet* where he organized secret arms shipments to Republican Spain. This had also brought him into contact with de Gaulle's future London enemy André Labarthe, an important figure in Cot's entourage. After the defeat of 1940 Moulin remained in close touch with Cot in America and was presumably aware of his view that de Gaulle was a fascist 'without knowing it'. He must also have known of Labarthe's hostility to de Gaulle. None of this would have predisposed Moulin favourably towards de Gaulle. But second-hand if unauthenticated comments attributed to him suggest he was impressed enough by de Gaulle's force of character, lucidity about the war and total rejection of Vichy to see his political views as a secondary issue for the moment. He is said to have told one resister on his return to France:

'What does he think really of the Republic? I can't tell you. I know his official position but is he really a democrat?' He apparently also wrote to Cot: 'For the moment one has to be with de Gaulle. Afterwards we can see.'[42] These fragmentary comments conform with what Moulin told the SOE officer who debriefed him two weeks after his meeting with de Gaulle: 'Any considerations as to whether to allow him . . . to form a provisional government would not worry those people who had actively contributed to resistance. The matter of whether de Gaulle stayed or went could be settled afterwards. He was very emphatic on this point and on the supplementary point that de Gaulle's prestige, at any rate as a vague idea, was already "formidable".'[43] On 30 October, Moulin also met Morton and asked to be remembered to Churchill, whom he had met in 1939 when he was Prefect of Chartres and Churchill was visiting France. The message was the same:

> Whereas until a few months ago General de Gaulle's name was largely only a symbol of Resistance in France, General de Gaulle's person has now become real to a large majority of Frenchmen owing to the great decline in the prestige of Pétain . . . If the enthusiasm for the organization of Resistance on the part of hundreds of young men in France were not to meet a response, there is the gravest danger that they will turn from General de Gaulle to the Communists.[44]

Within days of meeting de Gaulle, Moulin had clearly made his choice. So it seems had de Gaulle. Quite apart from Moulin's heroism in June 1940, his official status – he was the first Prefect to arrive in London – made him a major recruit. De Gaulle was probably struck, like everyone else, by Moulin's intelligence, natural authority, strong sense of the state and patriotic conviction. The official who debriefed him noted: 'He is the first person I have met or heard of having not only authority to negotiate on behalf of the three [Resistance] organisations in question, but also having the sort of natural authority which his past history gives him.'[45] Moulin arrived at a time when de Gaulle needed to find a strategy for action in France. Their meeting occurred only two days after he had sought to prevent indiscriminate Communist attacks on Germans – knowing that he actually had no means of stopping them. Moulin's report argued that, if left to its own devices, the Resistance would either fragment into anarchy or end up falling under Communist influence.

During several meetings with de Gaulle in the autumn of 1941, Moulin's exact role was worked out. He was designated de Gaulle's 'Delegate' for the Unoccupied Zone with a mission to 'realize in this zone the unity of action of all elements resisting the enemy'. He was delegated both to support the propaganda efforts of the Resistance movements and to organize their military action. The original draft of Moulin's mission contains some revealing handwritten corrections by de Gaulle specifying that 'the centralization and coordination [of the Resistance] will take place in London' and that 'all operations will be activated on the personal order of General de Gaulle.' These documents were microfilmed so that that Moulin could show them to the Resistance leaders once back in France. He was also provided with funds to persuade the Resistance to accept what was in effect a subordination of their activities to the overall leadership of de Gaulle.[46] Moulin was finally parachuted into France on 1 January 1942. De Gaulle still clung to the idea that political action (the responsibility of the Commission of the Interior – CNI) and military action (the responsibility of Passy's BCRAM) must remain separate. This meant that for the different parts of his mission Moulin reported separately to the CNI and to Passy's BCRAM – a source of confusion to London and annoyance to Moulin.

GAULLISM IS BORN

Since Moulin's key task was the *military* organization of the Resistance it did not necessarily have any direct impact on de Gaulle's political thinking. But it did mean that the Resistance started to figure more centrally in his mind than it had previously. This made de Gaulle more receptive than he might otherwise been to the arguments of the first Resistance leader to arrive in London in March 1942 two months after Moulin had left. This was Christian Pineau, one of the leaders of the Resistance group Libération-Nord, which had emerged in the Occupied Zone. Libération-Nord recruited primarily in trade union and Socialist circles, giving it a left-wing identity that was not shared by all the early Resistance movements. Pineau had made the journey to London to secure assurances for his members about de Gaulle's political beliefs. His description of his first meeting with de Gaulle is one of the classics of the genre:

> Immense in his brigadier general's uniform, he moved towards me while his hand moved up to reach mine at the very moment I arrived in front of him. His gestures were both unctuous and firm, those of an authoritarian prelate. Without saying a word, he led me to an armchair, sat me down, pushed a box full of cigarettes towards me, sat down himself in his armchair, then looking me in the eyes, uttered his first words: 'Now tell me about France' ... Imagine yourself before an examiner who asks you to cover the largest

subject imaginable without your knowing if your words are those he expects. When I came to mention the message that the Resistance wanted him to send them, there was a slight frown . . . but he did not interrupt.

Once Pineau had finished de Gaulle spoke in his turn:

> His words were not a response to mine . . . No question on the Resistance, no personal questions. Asking me if I had had a good journey might have been banal but this was hardly a journey like any other, at least for me. It might have deserved a mention . . . He reacted in no way to my descriptions of the dangers that we were facing, the anguish of the occupation and the repression. It was clear that for him every fighter was doing his duty in risking his life, that there was no difference between the danger faced by someone fighting in a tank in the African desert and someone carrying clandestine tracts in Occupied France . . . We were interpreting our actions through the prism of Liberty; he interpreted them through the prism of History.[47]

During his month in London Pineau saw much of the other French Socialists in the city – those who warned him that de Gaulle was a 'fascist', but also those like Hauck who had rallied to de Gaulle despite reservations. Pineau met de Gaulle on three more occasions, with Hauck present to hammer out the wording of the 'message' he was due to take back. They pored over every word. Pineau was not happy about one phrase implying that the defunct Republic and the Vichy regime were as bad as each other: 'A moral, social and political regime abdicated in defeat. Another has been born out of capitulation. The French people condemn both of them.' De Gaulle would not give way. Pineau asked at their last meeting if the General had a more personal message he wanted to convey: 'He said with a smile that froze my blood: "Just tell these good folk [*braves gens*] that I will not betray them."' Of de Gaulle's farewell, Pineau noted that it was 'about as warm as de Gaulle could manage . . . one might think he was ashamed of showing humanity'.[48] But at the aerodrome, as Pineau was about to board his plane, a motorcyclist suddenly arrived with an envelope containing a revised text of the declaration which reinforced the criticism of Vichy ('a regime born out of *criminal* capitulation and exalting personal power').

While inching reluctantly towards the wording preferred by Pineau, de Gaulle had delivered two incendiary speeches whose political radicalism contrasted with anything he had said so far. It was as if a psychological dam had burst and de Gaulle was ready to give full vent to his contempt for the elites who had betrayed France in 1940. On 1 April 1942 he announced:

Betrayed by her elites and privileged classes we are living the greatest revolution of France's History ... Her secret agony is creating an entirely new
France whose leaders will be new men. Those who are surprised not to find
among us used-up politicians, somnolent academicians, businessmen ... or
generals exhausted by their decorations make one think of those backward-
looking denizens of the courts of Europe who during the great French
Revolution were offended not to find Turgot, Necker etc. sitting in the
Committee of Public Safety. That is how it is. A France in revolution always
prefers to win a war with General Hoche than lose it with Marshal Soubise
[one of the generals of the *ancien régime*]. To proclaim and impose the
Declaration of the Rights of Man, a France in revolution always prefers to
listen to a Danton than to the soothing reassurances of outdated ideas.[49]

The word 'revolution' appeared four times in the course of this one speech.
Then in another speech on 18 April de Gaulle declared: 'National liberation
cannot be separated from national insurrection.'

This rhetoric was alarming to those conservative soldiers like Leclerc
and Larminat who had been among de Gaulle's first supporters. Leclerc
wrote to de Gaulle in May 1942 warning him that these developments
were 'worrying the great majority of Free French'. In his view, the victory
of the Free French had to be followed by 'national revolution' – the term
used by Pétain for his own anti-democratic, reactionary and anti-Semitic
policies.[50] When Leclerc went further and told de Gaulle he was repeating
the errors of the 1930s, he was sharply reprimanded.[51] Larminat was also
worried. He wrote to de Gaulle: 'France is gathering behind you because
you are fighting the *Boche* not because you are defending one or other
political ideal.'[52] But in the end Larminat consoled Leclerc with the fact
that at least the left was rallying to de Gaulle: 'A precious guarantee for
the future. It is better that things are run by him than by ... by whom else?
I cannot see anyone.'[53] These conservative officers may have been the military heroes of the Free French, but they were no longer part of the argument
about the political future of Gaullism.

9

On the World Stage,
September 1941–June 1942

PLAYING THE RUSSIAN CARD

For his first eighteen months as leader of the Free French, de Gaulle had dealt almost exclusively with the British. As the war became global – first with Hitler's invasion of the Soviet Union in June 1941 and then with the entry of the United States after the Japanese bombing of Pearl Harbor in December 1941 – he was presented with a larger canvas on which to operate. In one sense, the globalization of the war was a threat because it diminished the relative importance of France; in another sense, it presented opportunities. The entry of Japan into the conflict gave new strategic importance to the Free French possessions in the Pacific; the entry of Russia and the United States offered the chance to leverage influence for the Free French by probing tensions in the relations between the Allies. De Gaulle threw himself into the great game of international diplomacy with undisguised relish. He started with the Soviet Union.

When Germany attacked the Soviet Union on 21 June 1941, de Gaulle was in Jerusalem. From London, his foreign affairs spokesman Maurice Dejean issued an immediate declaration of support for the Soviet Union. De Gaulle approved but wanted to go further. His instructed his representatives to approach the Russian Ambassador in London, Ivan Maisky, to explore whether the Soviets would be willing to establish direct relations with the Free French. If so, might they be ready to guarantee the 'integrity' of France's pre-war borders where Churchill had restricted himself to a cautious commitment to the post-war 'independence and grandeur' of France.[1] De Gaulle also asked his delegate in Ankara, Gérard Jouve, to approach the Soviet government but (revealingly) 'not through the intermediary of the English'.[2]

On 26 September, the Soviet government recognized the Free French in exactly the same terms as the British. De Gaulle immediately called on Maisky, who was astonished by the 'flood of virulent remarks' the General poured out against the British.[3] This particular tirade was not just the fall-out from de Gaulle's recent tensions with Churchill. For de Gaulle, who had supported the Franco-Soviet pact in 1936, the Russian alliance was an underlying geopolitical reality of France's national interest. He would usually refer to 'Russia' and rarely to the Soviet Union. As he wrote later in his *Memoirs*: 'Before philosophizing it was necessary to live, that is to say conquer. Russia offered the possibility. Also her presence in the Allied camp offered the Free French, in relation to the Anglo-Saxons, a counter-weight that I certainly intended to use.'[4] This was not just a retrospective analysis, coloured by later conflicts with Roosevelt and Churchill. It is remarkably similar to what he instructed Jouve to tell the Soviet government in September 1941:

> The Soviet Union and France, being continental powers, have other objectives and other preoccupations from the Anglo-Saxon states, primarily maritime powers; in addition, a victorious outcome to the war would inevitably pose to the two continental powers issues that the Anglo-Saxon powers would not always be able to understand or take into account.[5]

A chance to play the Soviets off against the British presented itself in the autumn as de Gaulle sought new openings for his troops to play a role in the war against the Axis. There had been no opportunities since Leclerc's skirmishes in the Libyan Desert in March 1941; in the Levant, Frenchmen had been fighting Frenchmen. The recruitment of some of Dentz's troops – although disappointingly few – increased de Gaulle's total forces sufficiently to allow him to organize them into two so-called 'divisions' although they were closer in size to brigades. Knowing that the British were planning an offensive in Libya, in October 1941 de Gaulle asked whether his troops could be included in the fighting. The response of Churchill's chief military adviser General Ismay was evasive. To accept de Gaulle's request would have obliged the British to arm the French troops and incorporate them at a late stage into their battle plans. De Gaulle retaliated with a threat: if the British did not want his forces, he would send a division to assist the Soviet Union on the eastern front.[6] The tactic paid off. After protracted negotiations, the British agreed to equip and utilize two Free French brigades.[7]

At the same time de Gaulle continued his attempts to persuade the Soviet Union to look favourably on the Free French. In January 1942, he made a speech paying homage to the 'Russians' after they had halted the German advance: 'France which suffers is with Russia which suffers. France which fights is with Russia which fights. France sunk into despair is with Russia which has started to climb from the shadows of the abyss to the light of greatness.' Despite his efforts, de Gaulle hardly figured in the calculations of the Soviet government at this time. Maisky told the British in March 1942 that de Gaulle was 'sedulously cultivating him'. He was scathing about 'the nonentities' on the Free French National Council (apart from Pleven) and thought its prospects were 'not very bright'.[8]

'A STONE IN A POND'

De Gaulle was lunching at home with his wife on Sunday 7 December 1941 when they heard the news of the Japanese attack on Pearl Harbor. Passy, who was with them, remembered de Gaulle remarking immediately: 'The war is now definitely won! And there will be two future phases: the first will be that the Allies will save Germany; the second will be a war between the Russians and the Americans.'[9] A few days later he apparently offered another prediction to his military aide Pierre Billotte: 'From now the English will do nothing without the agreement of Roosevelt.'[10] If de Gaulle really did make this second remark, it was certainly prophetic, but a few weeks after Pearl Harbor he was also mooting to Palewski the entirely different – but also plausible – scenario that tensions between the British and Americans over the British Empire might be exploited to French advantage.[11]

A key argument of de Gaulle's 18 June speech was that American industrial power would be a crucial element in an Allied victory even if America was not (yet) in the war. Although de Gaulle had no first-hand knowledge of the United States, during his work for the CSDN in the 1930s he had studied plans for economic mobilization abroad – in Germany, Italy and the United States – and had published an article on the subject. The frequent and lengthy telegrams he sent his representative in America, Jacques de Sieyès, during the summer of 1940 show the supreme importance he accorded to America from the start.[12]

There were scattered French possessions in the western hemisphere – Martinique, Guadeloupe, Saint-Pierre-et-Miquelon – which de Gaulle hoped to win from Vichy. His first official act of diplomacy after the founding of the Empire Defence Council in October 1940 was to send a note to the State Department via the American Consul in the Belgian Congo. In return for help in taking over these territories, de Gaulle offered to provide the Americans with bases.[13] In his inflammatory 1941 interview with the *Chicago Daily News* which had so horrified the British de Gaulle had repeated his offer, this time publicly, and added that he had not 'asked for any destroyers in return'. This was a sly dig at the British who had a year earlier signed an agreement granting America permission to use their possessions in the western Atlantic and Caribbean as bases in return for providing the British navy with badly needed destroyers. It was also a pitch for American support in the hope of emancipating himself from exclusive dependence on the British – a good example of how quickly de Gaulle was attempting to project himself on the world stage.[14]

The Americans made no reply. The truth was that Roosevelt, who had been deeply shocked by France's defeat, took the view that the country had lost any claim to be treated as a great power. On the other hand, he was pragmatically ready to deal with Vichy if this could serve American interests, and he sent an ambassador to Pétain in the form of the Catholic and very conservative Admiral William Leahy. Roosevelt's policy did not in principle rule out contacts with the Free French, but he concluded from the Dakar fiasco that de Gaulle enjoyed little support and was just a creature of the British. He viewed the Free French with a mixture of suspicion and derision, and was confirmed in his suspicion by Leahy who reported that the Vichy regime was so opposed to de Gaulle that any move in his direction would push Vichy towards the Germans, exactly the opposite of Roosevelt's policy of gambling on Vichy.[15]

Roosevelt's negative view of de Gaulle was reinforced by the numerous French exiles in the United States, many of whom were well connected in elite American circles. These included Jean Monnet and Alexis Leger who had both while in London tried to warn Churchill against making an agreement with de Gaulle in June 1940. Other prominent French exiles suspicious of de Gaulle included writers like André Maurois and Antoine de Saint-Exupéry (author of *The Little Prince*), the filmmaker Jean Renoir and former Third Republic politicians like Camille Chautemps. Many of the brightest talents of pre-war France were in America – and few of them were pro-de Gaulle. De Gaulle's letter of July 1940 expressing his contempt for Third Republic politicians had fed suspicions of his political ambitions. The French politician Henri de Kérillis, a close friend of Reynaud and the only French parliamentarian to vote against the Munich Agreement in 1938, sent de Gaulle a devastating account of the situation in the United States:

> It is hardly necessary to describe to you the divisions and heartbreak to be observed in the French circles here . . . Wherever there are twenty Frenchmen they start fighting with each other. There are those who are for de Gaulle, those against him; those who are for him and against the English; those who are for Pétain; those who are for Weygand . . . There are the imbeciles, the cowards and the fearful . . . The terrible tragedy has taught them nothing and changed nothing.[16]

Even the supposed Gaullists were fighting among themselves. Independently of de Gaulle's official representative, Sieyès, who proved disappointingly ineffectual, another group of French exiles had set up a pro-Gaullist news-paper entitled *France for Ever*, but they did not get on with Sieyès. By the spring of 1941 de Gaulle saw it as an 'urgent necessity' to remedy this dis-astrous cacophony.[17] His inevitable choice to lead the mission was René Pleven, who had the advantage of speaking perfect English and knowing America well. Pleven set off in May and spent the next four months in the United States. He arrived to a 'glacial' reception. Roosevelt never found the time to meet him, but Pleven did see several leading members of the administration.

By the end of his five months in the United States Pleven had established a functioning Free French Delegation in Washington to replace the ama-teurish efforts of Sieyès, although he had not been able to persuade Jacques Maritain to come on board. The Delegation included Etienne Boegner, a businessman who was son of the head of the French Protestant churches, and Raoul de Roussy de Sales, a French journalist who had worked in America for many years. To head the Delegation de Gaulle chose Adrien Tixier, a French representative at the International Labour Organization in America. Although this step corresponded to de Gaulle's tentative moves to the political left in the autumn of 1941, Tixier was not an ideal choice. He lacked any diplomatic qualities and had a ferociously bad temper exacerbated by the terrible injuries he had suffered in the Great War when he had lost an arm. According to another member of the Delegation, he managed the feat of being anti-Gaullist when talking to the Americans and anti-American when communicating with de Gaulle.

On 11 November, soon after Pleven's departure, Roosevelt announced that equipment under the Lend-Lease programme would be made available to the Free French without needing to pass through the British. This hope-ful sign, which de Gaulle over-optimistically interpreted as a 'decision of principle in our favour',[18] was due less to the good work of Pleven than to the fact that Roosevelt wished to have as many irons in the fire as possible where France was concerned. At the same time Vichy's stock seemed to be falling. In November 1941, as a sop to the Germans, Darlan had sacked Weygand from his post in North Africa. Since Weygand was the Vichy leader considered least favourable to working with Germany, this seemed to suggest that the regime was shifting towards an even more collabora-tionist position.

But if after Pearl Harbor de Gaulle might have expected America to move further in his direction, he was to be rapidly disappointed. The immediate test would be Roosevelt's attitude to France's possessions in the western hemisphere. Roosevelt informed Pétain on 13 December that he would not challenge the status quo in the region provided that Vichy continued its formal policy of neutrality. De Gaulle immediately grasped the implications of the decision: instead of encouraging France's Empire to enter the war on the Allied side, the Americans were pursuing a 'policy of neutralization, bit by bit, of the French empire'.[19] To challenge this policy, de Gaulle took the extraordinarily provocative decision to occupy the tiny French islands of Saint-Pierre-et-Miquelon off the coast of Newfoundland.[20]

The 5,000 inhabitants of Saint-Pierre were believed to be favourable to de Gaulle but the Vichy administrator had prevented the holding of a plebiscite. What made the islands more than just symbolic was the presence of a radio transmitter which could be used to provide German submarines with information about Allied convoys. De Gaulle had twice approached the British during 1941 about sending a small force to take over the islands. The Admiralty, worried about the radio transmitter, was in favour but the Foreign Office hesitated for political reasons. Matters were precipitated when a telegram reached Carlton Gardens from a group of 'Patriots' in Saint-Pierre. In November 1941 de Gaulle decided to act and sent Muselier to inspect some ships based in Newfoundland. This mission was only a pretext. In reality Muselier was being sent to take over the islands. But before Muselier arrived the situation was transformed by America's entry into the war. The Admiral contacted de Gaulle to ask if the operation could still go ahead, and de Gaulle now felt obliged to ask Churchill if there was any British objection to what he disingenuously called this 'petit coup de main'.[21]

De Gaulle was asked to wait until the Americans had been consulted. When he was told on 17 December that the Americans opposed the operation, he seemed initially ready to abandon it. But almost immediately afterwards he changed his mind, perhaps because he had heard that the Canadians were about to take control of the radio station themselves, which he saw as foreign interference in French territory. Without consulting other members of the National Committee, on 18 December de Gaulle ordered a reluctant Muselier to go ahead. The landing took place on the night of 23 December to popular enthusiasm on the islands. Initially neither Roosevelt nor Churchill was inclined to take the matter too seriously, but the American Secretary of State Cordell Hull felt personally affronted. He issued an unfortunate communiqué denouncing this 'arbitrary action' by 'three so-called Free French ships'. Churchill, who had just arrived in Washington for his first meeting with Roosevelt, found himself in the middle of an international crisis.

In de Gaulle's career it is often hard to disentangle recklessness from calculation. In this case the calculation – if that is what it was – may have been that he had nothing to lose since the Americans seemed set on neutralizing the Empire. At least he could put down a marker to ensure that the policy did not go uncontested. He told Muselier that he wanted to stir things up – 'throw a stone in a pond of frogs'.[22] Even so it is hard to believe he had predicted the fury of the American government. In his relations with the United States this was a moment of truth similar to the crisis with the British over Syria in 1941. It showed what de Gaulle on a subsequent occasion called his capacity to 'create an event' – his showman's instinct to force himself on the attention of those who wanted to ignore him.[23] The Saint-Pierre-et-Miquelon affair was hardly a pinprick in the wider history of the war, and yet it made de Gaulle headline news for a few days. This was certainly not diplomacy of a normal kind. Like de Gaulle's 'intransigence' over Syria, it was a weapon of the weak. But whether by intuition or luck, the effect of his provocations was often so to enrage his opponents that he ended up regaining the moral high ground he ought to have lost. Hull's reference to the 'so-called' Free French shocked American public opinion; in retaliation newspapers mocked the 'so-called' Secretary of State.

Churchill, aware that British opinion and his own Cabinet sympathized with de Gaulle over this affair, made a speech in Ottawa paying vibrant homage to the Free French. For Hull this was more proof that de Gaulle was merely a British puppet. De Gaulle incorrectly concluded that he might be able to play the British off against the Americans; more correctly he had his first insight into the role public opinion could play in his battle for recognition over the heads of Allied governments. He may have been an admirer of the measured statecraft of the *ancien régime* but, as shown by his democratic turn at the end of 1941, he was developing a shrewd understanding that the ideological dimension of the war could be exploited to his advantage. He wrote to Tixier once the crisis had died down: 'If war was just a game of chess, where the pieces are objects without soul, we might be able to understand the position of the State Department regarding France. But war is a moral phenomenon. For men to wage war it is necessary that they feel morally obliged to do it.'[24]

Although Churchill publicly defended de Gaulle, he was privately furious that his crucial first meeting with Roosevelt had been hijacked by this insignificant crisis. This was another black mark against de Gaulle. Once back in London, Churchill had a meeting with him even more strained than the one after the General's return from Syria. When de Gaulle suggested that Churchill seemed to be casting doubt on the agreement of August 1940, Churchill's answer was a veiled threat to review the agreement 'because of the ill success which had attended the de Gaulle movement'.[25] Eden was left to pick up the pieces and find a face-saving compromise. This was not easy because de Gaulle, who found it 'troublesome that His Majesty's Government attached so much importance to giving satisfaction to the United States', told him that 'it was for Mr Hull to find a means of saving his face . . . [and] he was not prepared to make any gesture merely to please the United States.'[26] Behaving like a great power was Gaulle's way of becoming one.

Eden's role in this crisis revealed a shift in Whitehall attitudes to de Gaulle over the past year. Initially the Foreign Office had been sceptical about Churchill's indulgence of the General. A year later, just as Churchill's patience with him was wearing thin, it had come to realize that de Gaulle was there to stay. As Eden put it after the Saint-Pierre-et-Miquelon affair:

> The trouble with de Gaulle is that he sees himself in the role of Joan of Arc liberating his country from Vichy. His war is a private war against Vichy and co-operation with the Allies is secondary in his mind . . . He knows he is on strong ground here and that the great majority of people in this country, and no doubt a considerable section of American opinion, support him.[27]

FREE FRENCH CRISIS

The Saint-Pierre-et-Miquelon crisis sparked another internal crisis among the Free French only six months after Muselier had challenged de Gaulle in September 1941. Muselier returned to London from Saint-Pierre embittered by the awkward situation de Gaulle had put him in but emboldened by the American reaction. At the meeting of the National Committee on 3 March, he startled everyone by announcing his resignation. Several members of the Committee felt that de Gaulle had treated the Admiral in a very cavalier fashion, but his open challenge forced them to rally behind de Gaulle. De Gaulle, delighted at this opportunity to eliminate his opponent, retaliated by announcing that if Muselier left the Committee he would also lose his command of the Free French navy.

What might have been a purely internal Free French conflict escalated into a major crisis when the British government intervened. Although the British had initially found Muselier hardly any easier to deal with than de Gaulle, over the past eighteen months he had successfully created a naval force in exceptionally difficult circumstances given the poisonous legacy of the British attack on the French fleet at Mers-el-Kébir. Using mainly ships and material supplied by the British, the Free French navy had provided precious support to the British in the Battle of the Atlantic. So under pressure from the Admiralty the Cabinet on 5 March insisted that de Gaulle reinstate Muselier. De Gaulle refused. In a stormy interview with Eden he denounced Muselier as a 'tired man who indulged in drugs'. He followed this on 8 March by a more reasoned letter explaining that French sovereignty was at stake. The British government held firm. Charles Peake, the Foreign Office official who had inherited the unenviable position of acting as British liaison with the Free French, was sent to mediate. He found members of the Free French, including Pleven, in 'an atmosphere of considerable excitement' addressing him 'in terms which suggested a farewell speech from the scaffold'.[28]

Over the next week, de Gaulle stealthily goaded Muselier into increasingly erratic behaviour. When on 11 March the General went to address officers of the Free French navy at Westminster House, Muselier started heckling from the front row. The meeting was abandoned to shouts of '*Vive Muselier, Vive de Gaulle*'. De Gaulle now informed the British that he wanted Muselier sentenced to thirty days' detention for insubordination. When they refused, he raised the stakes further by announcing that he was withdrawing to his current home in Berkhamsted north of London and would take no further part in the affairs of the National Committee. He communicated a sealed testament to his immediate colleagues. It ended melodramatically: 'Men pass, France continues.'[29] De Gaulle wrote to Pleven on the following day: 'The worst thing about this affair is that people think we are playing a poker game.'[30] Obviously his theatrical withdrawal contained a strong element of bluff, but he had worked himself into a genuine frenzy about Muselier. Hour after hour he ranted against the perfidy of the British: 'It is not enough for them to have burnt Joan of Arc once. They want to start again . . . They think perhaps that I am not someone easy to work with. But if I were, I would today be in Pétain's General Staff.'[31] Bouchinet-Serreulles, the recipient of these tirades, regretted that de Gaulle seemed incapable of negotiating. But if the General found it hard to control his temper, he could also use it as a weapon. He knew that, however much they might deplore his tactics, the members of his Committee were behind him. Muselier's only card was the fleet, but it soon became clear that most Free French sailors were not going to rally to him either. By the end Muselier's only support on the British side came from the Admiralty.

The War Cabinet backed down. On 23 March, three weeks since the crisis had exploded, Peake was despatched to Berkhamsted with a face-saving agreement that Muselier be sent on sick leave. De Gaulle had summoned the members of the National Committee for the occasion. After a tirade against Muselier, de Gaulle accepted the agreement. Peake described the scene with humour:

> He accepted providing that the National Committee – of which he reminded me he was but a member although its head – concurred in this view. I said

that I felt his influence with this latter body was so great that they would allow themselves to be persuaded by his arguments, about which he had the grace to smile ... I subsequently took tea with the General and Madame de Gaulle who received me most kindly, and with the National Committee who, cowed and anxious, sat in a semi-circle at the other end of the table and did not venture to institute any conversation unless I or my hosts gave the lead.[32]

Muselier was offered a junior post, which he refused. His participation in the Free French was over.

In the long term, Muselier's elimination increased the cohesion of the Free French. His was the last open challenge to de Gaulle from within the movement. But in the short term the crisis convinced many British, American and Soviet observers that de Gaulle would not survive much longer without major changes in his team. Rumours circulated about dissent in the ranks of the Free French. This mood was picked up by Adrien Tixier, who arrived in London for his first meeting with the man who had appointed him to head the Free French Delegation in Washington a few months earlier. Tixier took the temperature of many conversations and reported to Peake:

The General was getting so free a run that unless something could be done to check him he would become unmanageable ... With a really strong Committee to challenge the General's arguments and force him to think out what he wanted to do, the General's value to France and to the Allies would be enormously improved. He had a powerful and original mind, but it suffered from lack of other minds on which it would, so to speak, sharpen itself.[33]

This was from the head of de Gaulle's American Delegation. There was talk on the British side of persuading Leger and Maritain to join de Gaulle as a way of reining him in. Churchill himself wrote to Leger personally on these lines. But Leger was deaf to any solicitations.[34] Maurice Dejean, who had his own reservations about de Gaulle, commented bitterly to Peake about those Frenchmen who claimed to fear the General's 'fascist' tendencies but who 'were quite unwilling, when it came to the point, to take an active part in putting right what they thought was wrong'.[35]

In April 1942 the British became interested in a possible alternative to de Gaulle in the person of another general who had suddenly emerged into the spotlight. This was General Henri Giraud, former commander of the Seventh French Army, who had been taken prisoner in 1940. In April 1942 the sixty-three-year-old General had managed to escape from the Fortress of Königstein in spectacular circumstances, descending by rope down the 45-metre cliff which protected the castle, and then making his way in disguise by train to the French frontier. The exploit made Giraud a hero and was celebrated on the London radio by Schumann. Giraud was received by Pétain on 29 April. This affair was a major embarrassment to the Vichy regime since Giraud, while showing respect to Pétain, refused his pleas to give himself up to the Germans. For the Vichy regime to hand him over, or for the Germans to seize him, would have destroyed any illusions that Vichy enjoyed genuine sovereignty. Giraud seemed poised to play the role of anti-German patriot without being tarnished by the opposition to Pétain which discredited de Gaulle in the eyes of some of the French. Indeed Giraud was an admirer of the internal policies of the Vichy regime while being opposed to collaboration.

Eden, usually a supporter of de Gaulle, wrote to Churchill on 24 April that if Giraud could be induced to come to Britain 'we should then have a real leader of the Free French movement, a man whose name and record inspires devotion among all sections of the French army and people. Many possibilities would be open to us which are now closed.'[36] Churchill wrote in a similar vein to Roosevelt five days later: 'I am highly interested in the escape of General Giraud and his arrival at Vichy. This man might play a decisive part in bringing about things of which you had hopes' – which presumably meant finding a plausible Vichyite alternative to de Gaulle.[37] But Giraud showed no interest in coming to London.

All these dreams of replacing de Gaulle – with Leger or Muselier or Giraud or anyone else – were wishful thinking. The Muselier affair had shown the strength of de Gaulle's position among the Free French. But the stress of these months possibly contributed to de Gaulle's severe physical collapse with a temperature of 40 in the second half of April. The illness turned out to be malaria, which he must have picked up on one of his two trips to Africa. On one trip he had batted away the advice to protect himself against mosquitoes with a joke: 'Mosquitoes do not bite General de Gaulle.' But it seems that they did. The news of his illness was kept from all but his closest advisers, but he had to cancel all appointments.[38]

CRISES WITH THE ALLIES

As soon as de Gaulle had recovered, he found himself confronted with two simultaneous crises in his relations with the British and the Americans. For once neither was of his own making, except inasmuch as his previous behaviour had exhausted any capital of goodwill on which he might draw. Following in close succession, these two crises intensified de Gaulle's sense of embattled isolation and suspicion regarding the motives of his allies.

The American crisis concerned the islands of New Caledonia.[39] This Pacific territory had rallied to de Gaulle in September 1940 thanks to the intervention of the Governor of the New Hebrides, Henri Sautot. Since the islands were vulnerable to attack from Japan, Sautot had secured an agreement from the Australian government to contribute to their defence. De Gaulle accepted this but, ever suspicious, he wondered if Sautot would be sufficiently vigilant in protecting France's interests in the region from the covetousness of her allies. Sautot seemed in his eyes to have an unhealthily good relationship with his British and Australian counterparts. De Gaulle therefore decided in 1941 – at a time when he was locked in conflict with the British over Syria – to despatch a High Commissioner of the Pacific Territories to keep a watchful eye over Sautot. This task was entrusted to one of the more colourful members of the Free French, the sailor-monk Thierry d'Argenlieu, whose loyalty to de Gaulle was almost religious in its intensity.

New Caledonia acquired major strategic importance for the Americans after their entry into the war against Japan. De Gaulle, knowing that without American help the islands would be defenceless against Japan, agreed to allow the Americans to install a base there. In return he obtained public recognition from the State Department of Free French authority over the territory.[40] Since the Americans could easily have taken over without de Gaulle's permission, and since de Gaulle knew he could not protect the islands without American help, this was an example of his skill at leveraging everything he could from a weak position. He excitedly telegraphed d'Argenlieu that this marked 'a turning point in the policy of Washington' but warned him to 'watch jealously over the maintenance of our sovereignty'.[41] In March 1942, American troops, under the commander of General Alexander Patch, started arriving on the islands. The Free French authorities were startled by the size of this force, which eventually totalled 40,000 men. D'Argenlieu thought he was witnessing an American takeover and warned de Gaulle that Sautot was being too accommodating to these American 'occupiers'. In April, de Gaulle recalled Sautot to London. When Sautot appealed against the decision, d'Argenlieu had him forcibly expelled. Since Sautot was popular with the local population, riots broke out. D'Argenlieu was convinced these had been fomented by the Americans, who were exploiting local rivalries to undermine the Free French. This was a total fantasy even if General Patch had underestimated how alarming the irruption of his troops would seem to the French. D'Argenlieu's reactions – more Gaullist than de Gaulle – were an example of the hypersensitivity of the Free French. De Gaulle of course believed d'Argenlieu's version. Although the New Caledonia crisis had blown over by the end of May, it left bitterness on both sides – and began to insinuate into Roosevelt's mind doubts about whether the French should be allowed to hold on to their Empire after the war.

De Gaulle, who had once hoped for so much from America, now worked himself up in a paroxysm of fury against the United States. He started referring regularly in conversation to the threat of American 'imperialism'. When Etienne Boegner, one of the Free French American delegates, arrived in London in May to meet de Gaulle for the first time, he was subjected to a tirade when he tried to defend American policy. Boegner reported back to one of his colleagues in America:

> My first contact with de Gaulle was one of rare violence. I was insulted as I have never been before in my life ... In this storm the man appeared to me not as a soldier, or a politician, or an administrator, but as a kind of phenomenon who, once one touches on anything French, immediately electrocutes you with a violent shock.[42]

Boegner was more specific in his account to the anti-Gaullist Alexis Leger. He told Leger that de Gaulle had screamed at him: 'You tell that old fool Hull from me that he is an arsehole, a moron, an idiot [*un con, une ganache, un idiot*]. To hell with them. The war will sweep them away and I, France, I will remain and I will judge them.'[43]

On 5 May, while the New Caledonia crisis was reaching its zenith, de Gaulle heard the news that the British had landed a force in Madagascar – a French colony loyal to Vichy.[44] Like New Caledonia, the island, which commanded key British communication routes with India, had acquired strategic importance once the Japanese entered the war. No one realized this faster than de Gaulle who wrote to Churchill a week after Pearl Harbor proposing that the Free French take over the island, backed by British air support. His argument, as always, was that Vichy France could not be relied upon to prevent any eventual Japanese incursion. Despite several more letters de Gaulle received no reply, and assumed he was being snubbed because of Saint-Pierre-et-Miquelon.[45] Even his suspicious nature had not spotted the true reason: Churchill had decided to launch a purely British operation, about which he was adamant that 'de Gaulle's people should be misled.' He was convinced, after the Syrian experience, that a joint operation with the Free French was likelier to increase the intensity of Vichy's resistance. The British, landing at Diego Suarez in the north of Madagascar, overcame tough resistance from the Vichy forces within three days. But fighting on the rest of the island went on for several more months since the Vichy Governor Annet refused to give in. The French held out longer against the British in Madagascar in 1942 than they had against the Germans in 1940.

De Gaulle heard about the British invasion of Madagascar when telephoned by a press agency. The news caused consternation at Carlton Gardens where even the General's most level-headed supporters wondered if their movement had any future.[46] Never before had the British carried out an operation on French territory independently of de Gaulle and behind his back. It suggested that the British had lost faith in de Gaulle and were aligning themselves with the American policy of working with whatever local French authorities were in place. The National Committee issued a solemn declaration of protest on 6 May, stating that if the Free French were to be excluded in this way the movement 'has lost its *raison d'être*'.[47] To Tixier in the United States, de Gaulle wrote that the Free French organization risked extinction:

> If we liquidate the organization, the opinion of the French who come from France and elsewhere is that this would be the equivalent of liquidating France … Vichy will be swept away. And what will be left is a France given up to anarchy, divided and lacking anything to believe in. As for Gaullism without de Gaulle, I am quite ready to try that. But I am convinced unfortunately that it would be the end of everything.[48]

De Gaulle waited six days before accepting a meeting with Eden on 11 May. He was calmer than might have been expected. For once he did not need to dramatize the situation. Eden was embarrassed and felt that de Gaulle had justifiable grievance. In his diary Oliver Harvey, Eden's Private Secretary, expressed the Foreign Office view that the problem was caused by the military 'who cannot get out of their stupid heads that de Gaulle is a "rebel" whereas Vichyites are "loyalists"' – but also by the fact that Churchill 'now so loathes de Gaulle, he almost prefers Vichy'.[49] This was an exaggeration, although Churchill certainly did write to Eden on 30 May that 'there is nothing hostile to England this man may not do once he gets off the chain.'[50] De Gaulle's meeting with Eden produced an agreement that the Free French would be invited to play their 'due part' in the future administration of the island. Despite this, there was no immediate invitation to include any Free French representative in the British negotiations with the Vichy Governor of Madagascar.

One of de Gaulle's favourite negotiating tactics was to intimidate his opponents by threatening to resign – in the confidence that his bluff would not be called. This had worked in the Muselier crisis. So when in mid-May he sent a telegram to his representatives abroad to assure them that things were *not* as bad as they seemed, one can assume he was genuinely worried. His line was that although New Caledonia and Madagascar might give 'a certain impression of malaise' the influence of the Free French was progressing daily in France, and the Soviet Union was becoming more supportive.[51] Both statements were true. Stalin was coming to see that he could make use of the Free French. His current obsession was the need for a second front in western Europe to relieve the pressure on the Soviet armies, but the British believed that this was for the moment risky and premature. If a second front were not possible, it was in Stalin's interest to have the maximum of German troops pinned down in the west. This was the logic underlying the Communist Party's strategy of violent resistance in France. De Gaulle had originally opposed this strategy, but his speech of 18 April 1942 declaring that French liberation must be accompanied by 'national insurrection' signalled an inflection in his position. The speech was designed for Soviet consumption. De Gaulle also made it clear to Maisky that he was missing no opportunity to urge the necessity of a second front on the British and Americans. This objective convergence between de Gaulle's interests and those of the Soviets did not go unnoticed in Moscow. The Soviet Foreign Minister Molotov told Maisky: 'De Gaulle has become in some sense the symbol of that France which refuses to submit to the invaders.' He suggested that the Soviets might go as far as to recognize the National Committee as a provisional government. When Molotov paid a visit to London he accorded de Gaulle an interview on 24 May. De Gaulle poured out his bile against the Allies and hoped the Russians might be able to help him over Madagascar; Molotov hoped in return that de Gaulle might be able to help on the issue of the second front.[52]

This forms the background to one of de Gaulle's most extraordinary initiatives of the war. On 6 June, he called on Alexander Bogomolov, the Soviet representative to the Free French. After some routine outbursts against 'American imperialism', he asked whether the Soviets would welcome him on their soil in the event of rupture with the British: 'It is my last card! I cannot wait any longer.' A startled Bogomolov warned against any precipitate decision but did not refuse.[53] On the same day, de Gaulle sent a telegram to his representatives around the Empire warning that the next move of the 'Anglo-Saxons' was likely to be an operation against Dakar or Niger (part of Vichy-held French West Africa) or both – from which the Free French would be excluded. In that case, continued cooperation with Britain would become impossible. The only way to 'fight imperialism' of this kind would be to fall back on the territories which the Free French possessed, hold on to them 'against everyone' and inform the world by radio.[54] Since these operations against Dakar and Niger were a figment of de Gaulle's imagination, where did the idea come from?

Ever since his return to London in September 1941, from Syria, the British had found reasons not to allow him to leave again. Churchill was so worried that 'the General might slip away to Brazzaville' that he ordered a 'special watch to be kept on his telephone to keep abreast of his intentions'.[55] Eden's view was that preventing de Gaulle from leaving was calculated to fuel his resentments even more, but Churchill was adamant. In April, Eden used the pretext that the British needed de Gaulle in London to discuss recent internal developments in the Vichy government. Whether or not he saw through the ruse, de Gaulle accepted with surprisingly good grace.[56] On 5 June he again raised the idea of going abroad, and Eden invented another pretext to dissuade him without formally forbidding him to leave. De Gaulle accepted with relative equanimity, but after returning to Carlton Gardens he began to mull over the matter. By the end of the day he had convinced himself of the worst: the British were planning another Madagascar-style operation and wanted him in London where he could not cause trouble.[57] This was the origin of the extraordinary telegram and of the *démarche* towards Bogomolov.

De Gaulle's representatives abroad were all amazed by his telegram. As he had intended, they called on the local British diplomatic representative to express their entire support for the General in this matter (even if Catroux characteristically assured the British Minister of State in Cairo that 'he in no way shared de Gaulle's anxiety').[58] As de Gaulle had also intended, his initiative caused alarm in London. Eden set about trying to smooth his feathers. He wrote to the Chiefs of Staff asking them to consider inviting de Gaulle to discuss issues of grand strategy so as to allay this 'very suspicious General's suspicions'. As he said, 'a little attention goes a long way with this difficult man.'[59]

After a few days, de Gaulle's mind seemed to be set at rest. All talk of moving from London to Moscow was abandoned. The Soviets were told that de Gaulle had 'involuntarily' exaggerated the problem. He received an invitation to meet Churchill, whom he had not seen since January. In fact Eden had been trying to persuade a reluctant Prime Minister to agree to this for ages, and Churchill had already conceded before de Gaulle's extraordinary proposal to Bogomolov. But since the General did not know this, he was reinforced in his belief in the virtues of brinkmanship. Everyone waited nervously for his meeting with Churchill, which was fixed for 10 June.

LONDON LIFE

De Gaulle's violent mood swings in this period were exacerbated by his sense of being a prisoner in London. The eleven months following his return from the Middle East in September 1941 were the longest continuous period he spent in the city. Every day provided a reminder of his humiliatingly total dependence. His telegrams had to go via the British; he needed British aircraft to travel abroad and British permission to leave; the British ferried his agents in and out of France; the British provided his funds. To anyone this would have been frustrating; to a man like de Gaulle it was almost physically unbearable. Bouchinet-Serreulles compared him to a caged beast lashing out indiscriminately to vent his fury.[60] One recurring source of irritation was the requirement to submit his speeches to the BBC for approval twelve hours before they went on air. Sometimes de Gaulle ignored this rule and had to be called to order. He would retaliate by threatening to stop Free French broadcasts. But as one British official noted, the prospect could 'be faced with equanimity' since this would harm no one more than de Gaulle himself.[61] Schumann, who spoke on the radio more often than de Gaulle, circumvented the censorship issue by becoming friendly with the two censors he had to work with – but this was not de Gaulle's style.[62]

De Gaulle's London life followed a strict routine. In September 1941, when he returned from the Middle East, his wife had moved back from Shropshire, and they rented a house in Berkhamsted 55 kilometres north of London. De Gaulle could now return home every weekend while living at the Connaught Hotel during the week. After September 1942, the couple moved for a third time, to Frognal Lane in Hampstead, which meant that now de Gaulle lived permanently at home. Although close Free French colleagues like Passy, Pleven and Billotte would sometimes be invited to his home, de Gaulle jealously guarded the privacy of his family – especially from the British. There were occasional exceptions. On one occasion Leo Amery dined with the General and his wife, commenting that she was 'a rather sad, quiet attractive little lady'.[63] The only time Yvonne de Gaulle was seen by the public was when de Gaulle allowed photographs of their domestic life at Berkhamsted to be published. This was done at the urging of Churchill, who thought (despite his periodic eruptions of irritation against him) that de Gaulle should be better known. The photographs showed husband and wife in various domestic poses. Madame de Gaulle is seen washing up, dusting, playing the piano (with a portrait of the General visible), holding a flower up adoringly to her startled husband. Both of them detested these photographs. Although staged, the impression conveyed was not far from the truth. De Gaulle looks stiff, awkward and ill at ease; Yvonne de Gaulle's plain dress conveys her simple tastes.[64] Meeting Yvonne de Gaulle during the war, one member of the French community in London was struck by her dowdy appearance – a contrast with the ostentatiously elegant Madame Catroux.[65] Encountering de Gaulle for the first time in the summer of 1942, Pleven's wife, on a visit to London from the United States, observed with amazement the monastic austerity of his surroundings:

> There are no *gadgets* [in English], no exterior signs of anything, no showcase of cabinets with objects 'presented by ...' This is more than simplicity ... It shows a man who belongs to a task ... I have never seen that before. There is no caricature of him, no souvenir, no object with a cross of Lorraine – nothing ... and no one could guess visiting him whose house one was in. I have never seen that before with any man in a prominent position. He
> • *belongs to the job* [in English] with a noble tranquillity.[66]

During his days at the Connaught, de Gaulle dined in a private room with one or two aides, and saw little of other guests. The National Committee met at Carlton Gardens every Wednesday. Although the Free French organization was no longer the one-man band it had been at the start, de Gaulle's style remained authoritarian. Meetings were brief, and important decisions were taken by him alone. Bouchinet-Serreulles noted: 'The General lives alone in an Olympian solitude. He thinks alone, he decides alone ... But he does think, he does decide.'[67] One member of the Free French wrote to de Gaulle with unusual frankness in November 1942:

> Your way of treating people ... arouses in us a painful preoccupation, I would even say a real anxiety. There are subjects where you tolerate no contradiction, not even any debate. Moreover these are issues where your position is especially emotional, that is to say precisely those where you have the greatest interest in testing the reactions of other people. In such cases your tone makes your interlocutors think that in your eyes their disagreement reveals infirmity in their mind or their patriotism.[68]

The truth was more complicated. De Gaulle could be a good listener, and one observer noted how he would fix his 'cobra-like gaze' on his interlocutor, watching warily out of the side of his eyes, ready to pounce. De Gaulle's default reaction to advice was to reject it, but those with strong enough nerves to hold their ground were often surprised to find subsequently that he had adopted their ideas. When Pineau arrived in London, Hauck, who had acquired experience of dealing with de Gaulle, told him: 'Do not hesitate to speak out to him. He will give the impression he is not listening, that his mind is on other matters. But you will see he has listened.'[69] It was, however, almost physically impossible for de Gaulle to admit he was wrong. He told one resister at the end of the war: 'I only esteem those who stand up to me but unfortunately I cannot stand them.'[70] A case in point was the sending of a motorcyclist with the amended text of the declaration to the Resistance only a few minutes before Pineau's plane was about to take off.

It saved de Gaulle having to admit in person that he had conceded that Pineau was right. Alphand had a stormy interview with the General before a press conference in July 1942 when de Gaulle proposed to outline all his grievances against the Americans. De Gaulle lost his temper, but the next day Alphand noticed that all his ideas had been accepted.[71] When de Gaulle was not in a rage he could be a polite and attentive listener. Annette Pleven noted:

> He gives the impression of listening to you with such attention and so rapid an intelligence, served by such a remarkable memory, that you have the feeling that not a single inexactitude or stupidity would pass unnoticed. And yet he is excessively courteous and not in any way officious [pas du tout pion] . . . He also asks you lots of questions and makes you speak.[72]

This side of de Gaulle was rarely witnessed by the British because he was always wary in their presence. He explained one day to Charles Peake his fear of becoming an 'émigré':

> Emigrés ended up by taking on the complexion of their hosts, and so becoming an embarrassment to them as well as an object of contempt to their own people . . . He was only too aware that if he could become like a good Englishman, his popularity here would at once increase . . . But he had his duty to do . . . He was convinced that his attitude was, in a long view, in our own interests, so far as France was concerned, for the French would not love us the more if they thought he was a mere instrument of our policy.[73]

There was surely no danger of de Gaulle becoming 'like a good Englishman', but he was constantly on his guard. After lunching at the Ritz with de Gaulle and various Frenchmen, including Palewski, Harold Nicolson noted that although Palewski was one of the 'most conversational men I know . . . in the presence of de Gaulle a great hush falls on the French'.[74] But this was because the British were present. In other circumstances, de Gaulle thrived on talk. His 'conversation' was often an unstoppable monologue whose recipients felt they were witnessing the eruption to the surface of an interminable conversation taking place in his head between himself and France. Sometimes these monologues took the form of philosophical and historical meditations; sometimes tirades against the enemy of the moment – there was always an enemy – and in this case they operated as a safety valve preventing de Gaulle from some action he might otherwise regret. Very characteristic is the account by François Coulet of his first meeting with de Gaulle. Coulet was a young diplomat stationed in the Middle East who had rallied to de Gaulle in the summer of 1940. Their first meeting did not take place until April of the following year when de

Gaulle was in Cairo. The occasion was a formal dinner organized by a British colonial official:

> The atmosphere was heavy despite the conversational ease of the perfectly bilingual Spears [this was before their falling out] and the urbanity of Catroux ... It was an awkward dinner during which de Gaulle whom I so wanted to hear and from whom I could not take my eyes remained silent and withdrawn; and even for someone who had never seen him before and could not make any comparison with his usual behaviour, he was clearly in the worst of moods ... He features remained totally rigid, not the slightest expression on his face, the only movement an imperceptible movement of the head.

It probably did not help de Gaulle's mood that one of the other guests was a Frenchman in RAF uniform. At the end of the evening, the hitherto smoulderingly silent de Gaulle invited Coulet up to his room. For the next two hours, as he paced up and down, hardly pausing to draw breath, all the thoughts he had been silently ruminating upon during the dinner rushed to the surface: the reasons for the defeat and armistice (Pétain was a traitor, who had 'died' in 1925 and was eaten up by ambition), the current mood of France, the failure of Dakar, the future ambitions of the Free French ('after the war we will have our own interests to defend which are not those of the English') and so on: 'He did not speak to convince, but almost for himself ... as if drawing up a balance sheet of where things stood.'[75] Coulet was won over for the rest of his life not least by the fact that de Gaulle should have bothered to spend so much time with such a relatively unimportant footsoldier of his movement. In reality de Gaulle was talking to himself.

Whether in listening mode, ranting mode or philosophical mode, de Gaulle never ceased to emanate a chilly reserve which repelled intimacy. He found it impossible to express affection or gratitude and was incapable of apologizing. One journalist who managed to get to London at the end of 1941 remembered that at her first meeting with de Gaulle she 'expressed to him in a phrase which might have seemed melodramatic and sentimental all the fervour people felt for him in France'; he replied 'perfectly nicely but not with the right kind of words, not the words he would have used if he had any heart'. Seeing him again the next day she mentioned the case of someone planning to come to London but waiting for his daughter to be released from prison first: 'He replied with cutting brutality: "the family does not count when the destiny of France is at stake."'[76] When Bingen remarked to Bouchinet-Serreulles that he wished de Gaulle might occasionally show a more human face, the reply was 'it is impossible to make someone who is tone deaf appreciate music any more than it is possible to ask de Gaulle suddenly to develop human contact.'[77] Passy once suggested to de Gaulle that he might show a bit more warmth towards his subordinates. The next day, he witnessed de Gaulle stopping on the stairs of Carlton Gardens to address a supposedly friendly question to one of the sentries. But his tone and manner so petrified the tongue-tied man that the General could only continue on his way with a shrug.[78]

Where de Gaulle did show emotion was in his terrifying and unpredictable rages, which were usually sparked off by an imagined (or genuine) slight. The long-suffering Charles Peake was always apprehensive about de Gaulle's moods. After one gruelling encounter, he wrote that he would be 'strongly tempted to plead that my weak state of health forbids me to visit again soon'.[79] On another occasion: 'I saw the unpropitious signs with which I have been only too familiar in the past. His pallor increased and his eyes began to blaze.'[80] But Peake also wondered whether de Gaulle in a good mood was preferable – such as the occasion he found him 'in high fettle and [he] greeted me with a superior smile which I have rather learnt to dread'.[81] Those around de Gaulle saw their role as acting like shock absorbers between him and the outside world. Frequently he would decree to his aides that no British person was ever to be invited to his table again. When the rage had subsided a day later, the order was quietly forgotten. Mary Borden, who like her husband Spears was latterly no friend of de Gaulle, wrote perceptively of him:

> He felt the dishonour of his country as few men can feel anything, as Christ according to the Christian faith took on himself the sins of the world. I think he was like a man, during these days, who had been skinned alive and that the slightest contact with friendly well-meaning people got him on the raw to such an extent that he wanted to bite . . . The discomfort that I felt in his presence was due, I am certain, to the boiling misery and hatred inside him.[82]

Harold Macmillan, who had much to do with de Gaulle in the following year, made the same point in a slightly different way:

> The arrogance that makes him from time to time almost impossible to deal with is the reverse side of an extreme sensibility. I have never known a man at once so ungracious and so sentimental. He has a considerable sense of wit and a certain mordant humour, but really carefree and gay laughter I think he has never experienced . . . He belongs to the race of unhappy and tortured souls to whom life will never be a pleasure to be enjoyed but an arid desert through which the pilgrim must struggle.[83]

That phrase 'skinned alive' (*écorché vif*), employed by Borden about de Gaulle, was used by de Gaulle himself once to describe the psychology of the Free French in general. Pleven put the same point in slightly different words: 'They are all extremely sensitive ... because all of them suffer through their love of their country, because their ideals have been trampled upon, and because they are cut off from those they love.' Another referred to a 'constant feeling of humiliation'.[84] For this reason, although many Free French were exasperated by de Gaulle's intransigence, terrified by his rages and wounded by his icy aloofness, they shared an extraordinary communion with him. De Gaulle's idea of himself as the true incarnation of France seemed not to be mystical hyperbole but an evidential truth. As Bouchinet-Serreulles wrote to Maritain when trying to overcome his scepticism towards de Gaulle:

> I would not be a soldier of the Free French if I did not believe that de Gaulle was the only faithful interpreter of the wishes and hopes of our people ... It is from this close communion with the soul of France that de Gaulle draws his most authentic strength; he is the provisional depository of the Grail. Please do not suspect despite the tone I am employing that I feel any fanaticism for the person of de Gaulle; all my fervour goes to the ideas which he is defending.[85]

The Free French were on average young, and many of them after the war would recall the almost filial relationship they felt with de Gaulle.[86] One young recruit, Roger Barberot (aged twenty-five in 1940), wrote later: '1940 broke all the links that attached us to our previous world ... We felt ourselves lightened of all our past. De Gaulle filled this void with his exclusive passion for, and obsession with, France.'[87] Jean-Louis Crémieux-Brilhac (twenty-three in 1940), one of that group of escaped POWs who had arrived in London in September 1941, wrote soon afterwards to express what Gaullism meant to him:

> We want it to be known that our blood is boiling in our veins and what we ask is to offer it up ... For us, our engagement with de Gaulle is not a kind of slavery. We have rallied to de Gaulle: we did not know him. More cut off from the world [in the POW camp] than the French of France, none of us had even heard his voice. Often we would ask each other: 'Who is he? What is he like?' ... We never imagined that our silent plebiscite could be anything other than unanimous: de Gaulle was he in whom we hoped and we gave him our recognition and our fidelity because he had taken his responsibilities, because he acted, because he was fighting ... One morning, in September 1941, under a clear sky we found ourselves with new names and wearing new clothes from head to toe: this had something of a baptism or a marriage. We threw ourselves into the Free French as if into a storm of passion.[88]

The one thing that did worry some members of the Free French were de Gaulle's bouts of Anglophobia. Larminat and Eboué wrote in September 1941 to warn him against those who 'in order to pay court to you or just out of stupidity feel it necessary constantly to denigrate the English. One ends up asking oneself who we are fighting the war against.'[89] But this gradually ceased to be to be an issue partly because the force of de Gaulle's personality succeeded in imposing his way of seeing the world on his followers and partly because objective circumstances had given some credence to de Gaulle's suspicions. Passy, who had started out with few of these prejudices, found himself battling constantly against the British secret services; and even the most Anglophile Free French were shocked by the Madagascar landings. Through proximity to de Gaulle, Palewski developed a passionate loyalty to the cause of the Free French which sat oddly with his urbane and sociable Anglophilia. But as François Coulet, an intense French Protestant quite different in personality from Palewski, remarked when the latter accused him of being a fanatic: 'explain to me how one can be Gaullist and not fanatical.'[90] René Pleven, as moderate, level-headed and Anglophile a Frenchman as it would be possible to imagine, who had joined de Gaulle in July 1940 with considerable reservations, was sure two years later that his 'necessary act of faith' had been vindicated:

In my eyes, the crucial fact of these last two years is that in the General France has a genuinely great man ... I have seen him operate in the most difficult circumstances and each time he comes out of it bigger in my eyes. He has learnt a lot from his responsibilities over the last two years. He continues to see what is essential. He needs around him men who administer ... who look after the details, who sometimes need to soothe wounds, but he is in the great line of heroes who have saved France from the perils that have faced her.[91]

10

Fighting France, July–October 1942

MEETING THE RESISTANCE

The long-anticipated meeting between de Gaulle and Churchill took place on 10 June 1942. They talked over a bottle of whisky with no one else present. Seemingly nothing of substance was discussed, but the mood was cordial. De Gaulle accepted Churchill's assurances that the British had no designs on France's Empire. After the meeting there was a palpable sense of relief in Carlton Gardens that peace had broken out even if, as it turned out, only briefly.[1] The atmosphere of continuous guerrilla warfare against the British was exhausting for those who lacked de Gaulle's combative temperament – what one Free Frenchman described wryly as de Gaulle's 'delectation for quarrelling conceived as a kind of sport'.[2]

De Gaulle and Churchill had met against the background of the heroic fighting by the Free French in the Western Desert. In May, the German commander General Rommel had launched a new offensive in Libya to push the British back to the Suez Canal. Rather than attacking the Allied line frontally, Rommel planned to outflank it from the south and fall on the British Eighth Army from behind. The oasis fort of Bir Hakeim, at the southern extremity of the line, was held by a Free French brigade commanded by Pierre Koenig. This was one of those two units de Gaulle had with difficulty persuaded the British to arm six months earlier. The 3,600 Free French troops held out against Rommel's 37,000 troops for a week from 6 June. The French casualties were heavy – 980 killed or captured – but Koenig's force was not destroyed. After the fall of the fort, his surviving troops managed to join the British. Bir Hakeim was a battle of symbolic importance at a time when there was little good news for the Allies on any front. It was the first time that the Free French had fought the Germans rather than Italians (or French). The heroism of Koenig's troops made headlines all over the world; the British press compared the exploit to Verdun. When de Gaulle and Churchill met, the battle was in its final stages. Bir Hakeim gave Churchill something to be charming about, and de Gaulle's euphoria at the heroism of his troops made him more relaxed than usual.

This was the start of a short-lived honeymoon in de Gaulle's relations with the British, bolstered by evidence of his growing support in France. On 14 July, Bastille Day, the British recognized his movement as the 'Fighting French' – a term de Gaulle had been using for several weeks. This meant that he was recognized as leader not only of the Free French outside France but of those fighting the Germans *in* France. In August 1942, the two most important Resistance movements in the Unoccupied Zone published a communiqué recognizing de Gaulle as 'the first resister in France'.

The rallying of the Resistance to de Gaulle was helped by the declaration which Pineau had taken over from London in June and also by the patient work of Jean Moulin. Since returning to France as de Gaulle's delegate in January 1942, Moulin had cajoled and bullied the Resistance movements of the Unoccupied Zone to coordinate their activities more closely. Although balking at a formal merger, they agreed in the autumn of 1942 to set up a coordinating committee and to pool their exiguous military forces into a single organization dubbed the Secret Army. Moulin also pushed them to declare their support for de Gaulle.

This was not a foregone conclusion. The first Resistance movements had emerged in France independently of de Gaulle. Even once aware of his existence, many resisters felt that it was they not he who were running the real risks. One later remembered: 'We took our initiatives without him, and we would have taken them whether or not he had spoken on 18 June. He was not on national territory and so he did not share our dangers.'[3] When the history of the Resistance later became intertwined with people's memories of de Gaulle, there was something ritualistic – even desperate – about the assertion of Resistance leaders that they had *not* acted because of de Gaulle's 18 June speech.[4] Resisters in general were not immune to the prejudice against 'émigrés'; left-wing resisters were suspicious of political generals; conservative resisters were alienated by the ferocity of de Gaulle's attacks on Pétain. The belief that Pétain was doing his best behind the scenes to resist Germany was widely shared. Many resisters hoped to win the secret support of Vichy insiders, especially the cadres of the Armistice Army – the force of 100,000 men that the French were permitted to keep under arms by the terms of the armistice. This was the position of Henri Frenay, a former army officer whose movement Combat was the most important Resistance organization of the southern zone. The other important movement, Libération-Sud, founded by the journalist Emmanuel d'Astier de la Vigerie, had never harboured any illusions about Vichy but it was unsure about de Gaulle's political beliefs. Gradually it became increasingly difficult for Resistance leaders to ignore de Gaulle since his name was the only one that the public knew. A journalist who spent time in both zones during the first two years of Occupation before reaching London wrote: 'When a worker writes on the wall with chalk the words "Long Live de Gaulle" it is just a way of saying "Long live the Resistance"; he does not know who de Gaulle is, does not know what he expects of him and has not yet started to pose questions about him.'⁵

The degree to which resisters had to take de Gaulle into their calculations was revealed at the end of 1941 when an alternative figure presented himself. This was General de La Laurencie, one of the few French officers to have distinguished himself in the 1940 campaign. Once the battle was over de La Laurencie had believed that the armistice was inevitable, and the Vichy regime had appointed him as its delegate to the Occupied Zone. During 1941 he increasingly distanced himself from the regime and made contact with Resistance leaders who were attracted by the idea that he might bring elements of Vichy's Armistice Army over to them. But when de La Laurencie met Frenay and other resisters in December 1941, the prospect of agreement foundered because they insisted he had to reach an agreement with de Gaulle. De La Laurencie, a member of the tribunal that had condemned de Gaulle to death, magnanimously (as he saw it) agreed to amnesty him and even find him a subaltern post – possibly as Military Governor of Madagascar. Talk of using de La Laurencie was still in the air when Moulin arrived back in France in January 1942, but he assured London that he would have no problem in 'definitively sinking' him. In short, whether they liked it or not, Resistance leaders had already incorporated de Gaulle into their view of the world.⁶ Libération-Sud was the first movement to rally to de Gaulle in its underground newspaper on 20 January 1942, recognizing him as the 'symbol of French unity and will to resist'. Frenay was slower to abandon his illusions about Vichy.

For at least the first eighteen months of the Occupation, the French public had been divided and confused about its response to Vichy. Although de Gaulle's popularity had been rising steadily, many people simultaneously held in their minds the idea that Pétain was doing his best to protect them from the impact of the Occupation. It was even widely believed that there was some kind of secret deal between Pétain and de Gaulle. But from the first months of 1942 this became increasingly hard to believe. As the German advance on the eastern front ran into the ground the Nazi regime started to turn the screws more tightly on all the occupied territories. The Vichy government came under mounting pressure to provide workers for German factories, and as Communist attacks on their soldiers multiplied, the Germans insisted that Vichy repress 'terrorism' more vigilantly. To implement these policies the Germans bullied Pétain into taking Laval back as his Prime Minister. Darlan had hardly been a lukewarm collaborator but his motivations had been opportunist; Laval was ideologically committed to the policy.

On 18 April 1942, Laval returned to office and the ageing Pétain lost any real power. Two months later Laval made a notorious speech announcing that he wished for the victory of Nazi Germany because the alternative would be the victory of Bolshevism. This shocked even those who were far from pro-Communist. Laval's return to power destroyed Frenay's last illusions about Pétain. It was the signal for him formally to condemn Pétain in his underground newspaper *Combat*.

Did this mean that Frenay, like d'Astier, was now ready to rally to de Gaulle? The answer became clear in Frenay's reaction to the emergence of another symbol of Resistance in the form of General Giraud. We have seen already that Giraud had caught the attention of the British in the spring of 1942. Because of the dramatic circumstances of his escape from his imprisonment in Germany, he was a more potent symbol of opposition to collaboration than de La Laurencie, but like him he did not reject all the political values of Vichy. In short, Giraud might have been a possible bridge between repentant Pétainists and de Gaulle – or even an alternative to de Gaulle. It was not clear which way he would jump. Over the summer, the BCRAM put feelers out to Giraud on de Gaulle's behalf without getting any response.[7] The Resistance leaders were also hoping to attract Giraud, but Frenay wrote to him in mid-August 1942 insisting that an agreement with de Gaulle was a necessary precondition:

> The people have the need to fix their hope and faith in a man. Marshal Pétain who has disappointed us can no longer play this role. The star of General de Gaulle has grown on the horizon at the same time as that of Marshal Pétain has diminished. The population, beginning with that of the occupied zone, has become Gaullist . . . He is the truly national and definitive symbol of the French desire for liberation.[8]

That Frenay, so suspicious of de Gaulle in 1940, could write in this way two years later shows how far the Resistance had moved. As resisters started to rally to the 'symbol' of de Gaulle, they also wanted to meet him in person. During the second half of 1942, Resistance leaders in London were no longer the exotic creatures they had been when Pineau arrived in March. They were ferried over to London by the British in Lysanders, small aircraft capable of landing at night on improvised airstrips. The first arrival, on 28 April, was Pierre Brossolette. As a journalist who had strongly opposed the Munich Agreement in 1938, Brossolette had been one of the rising stars of the Socialist Party. After the defeat, he had been involved in Resistance groups in the Occupied Zone. His information complemented that which Moulin had brought from the Unoccupied Zone. He was a charismatic, forceful and often abrasive personality to whom no one was indifferent. One of those seduced by him was Passy because Brossolette shared views about the role of BCRAM that Passy had been urging unsuccessfully on de Gaulle for eighteen months: that it made no sense to divide responsibility for political and military action in France between the BCRAM and the Commissariat of the Interior. The report that Brossolette drafted on his arrival in London will have been music to de Gaulle's ears:

> General de Gaulle symbolizes that France which did not despair, which did not give in. He alone acted. At a moment when people feel that force of character is the essential quality for a leader, the name of General de Gaulle exerts on the French a political attraction which perhaps London is not aware of . . . France needs a myth, and for the moment France has fallen so low that this myth cannot be found in a formula or an idea: it needs to be incarnated in a man. Whatever the person of de Gaulle may be . . . if France is to remake herself again it can only be around the 'de Gaulle myth'.[9]

Brossolette put himself at the service of the Free French and returned to France as an agent of the BCRAM. The next arrival was d'Astier on 12 May. As leader of his own Resistance movement, Libération-Sud, d'Astier certainly had no intention of putting himself completely at de Gaulle's service. Even stripped of its ironic and literary tone, his later account of his first meeting with de Gaulle at the Connaught is remarkably similar to that of Pineau:

> The Symbol entered. He was even bigger than one expected. His movements were slow and heavy, like his nose. His small head and waxen face are supported by a body which seems to have no shape. His most frequent gesture is to lift his forearms while keeping his elbows close to his side. At the end of his arms, his inert, very white, rather feminine, hands with their palms turned downwards attached to very slender wrists, seem to lift a world of abstract burdens. He asked me no questions. We dined. He does not like his fellow men. He likes their history, above all that of France, of which he was acting out a chapter which he seemed to be writing in his head as he went on, as if he were Michelet . . . He spoke as if he were bearing a thousand years of history or as if he watched himself in that history a hundred years in the future. He painted a bleak picture of his Calvary – that of the person that was France.[10]

In fact, d'Astier and de Gaulle hit it off remarkably well. With the demeanour of a nonchalant aristocratic adventurer, d'Astier was one of those intellectually flamboyant personalities with whom de Gaulle often got on well. Before his return to France the General sent d'Astier to the United States to drum up support for the Free French. To add to the drama, during his public appearances he wore a mask and took the assumed name of Durand so as not to reveal his identity back home. D'Astier was back in London in September, this time with his rival Frenay who was annoyed that d'Astier had got to London before him. Frenay, a former army captain, was a stiffer, more prickly, less charming personality than d'Astier, and was wary of anyone whom he suspected of wanting to infringe the independence of his movement, Combat. But his letter to Giraud shows that he too understood (if reluctantly) that the future of the Resistance was inextricably bound up with de Gaulle.

THE POLITICIANS RALLY

Although the support of the Resistance was a boost to de Gaulle, it did not necessarily impress the Allies. The Resistance leaders had emerged from nowhere, and it was not clear how representative they were. In terms of speaking for 'France', did they count more than respected figures like Paul Cambon in London or Alexis Leger in Washington who were deeply suspicious of de Gaulle? But de Gaulle was also beginning to win support from some leading political figures of the defunct Third Republic whose opinions certainly did carry weight with the British.

In June 1942 Philippe Roques, who had been the *chef de cabinet* of the respected conservative Georges Mandel, arrived in London with messages of verbal support for de Gaulle from both Reynaud and Mandel. As the member of Reynaud's government most firmly opposed to the armistice, Mandel had been imprisoned by the Vichy regime along with Reynaud. Based on his conversation with Roques, Eden reported to the Cabinet that 'the number of people who await his [de Gaulle's] return is estimated at approximately 85 or 90 per cent. In the free zone the number is slightly less, on account of the absence of the enemy and intense propaganda in favour of the Marshal. It is nonetheless estimated at 70 or 75 per cent.'[11] Morton, who met Roques twice during his time in London, offered one of his feline commentaries after the second meeting:

Monsieur R was a good deal more insistent on this occasion than he was when I first met him on the importance of the person of General de Gaulle, who seems to have exercised over Monsieur R that uncanny influence that I have noticed before in the case of Frenchmen, and which is the opposite to the effect which continued contact with General de Gaulle produces upon most Englishmen.[12]

Roques returned to France with letters from de Gaulle soliciting the support of other politicians like the former presidents of the Chamber and Senate Edouard Herriot and Jules Jeanneney.[13] Two months later a warm personal letter of support from Mandel arrived in London.[14]

If Mandel represented one end of the political spectrum, the other was represented by Léon Blum, one of the iconic figures of the European left, admired by many in the British Labour Party and by American New Dealers. Blum, as a Jew, a Socialist and a former Popular Front Premier, incarnated everything that the Vichy regime hated. Imprisoned along with Reynaud and others, he was put on trial at the start of 1942. But his brilliant defence turned the tables on his accusers and Vichy suspended the trial in March 1942, further enhancing his reputation. He remained in jail but was allowed to receive visitors. In May, he sent London a message of unconditional support for de Gaulle.[15] He had already met de Gaulle before the war but his choice was reinforced by the view of his close friend Georges Boris who had been one of the first people to join the Free French. Boris's letter to Blum about de Gaulle in June 1942 deserves to be quoted at length because it offers a nuanced judgement from an astute observer who had observed de Gaulle at close quarters from June 1940:

When I learnt the news of the armistice ... de Gaulle gave me back honour, the possibility of being able to look people in the face again, my sense of being a Frenchman. It is thanks to him that I am not purely and simply an émigré ... He has the most profound, far reaching, and often prophetic views on events ... There is no doubt that he has a very high sense of his duties and his mission, and it is in this way that one can talk of pride.

In my view he would be a great man, even a very great man, if his understanding of men equalled his understanding of events and ideas, and if he could more easily make contact with people. Undoubtedly it is because he despises them that he does not understand them ... This leads me to think that in politics he is better as a strategist than as a tactician ... To a large degree, his unwillingness to bend, his intransigence are willed. He likes to say that, being as weak as he is, intransigence is his only weapon. Moreover, I must say that in those cases where this has been most held against him, he has been right on the substance if not the form ... De Gaulle would become

suppler if he were accorded some degree of recognition which would safeguard the dignity of France whose repository he believes himself to be ...
His intransigence also manifests itself towards his own entourage. It is also
the case that this entourage is, given the circumstances, mediocre. There is
no really forceful personality who could, with authority and right, stand up
to the solitary man ... It has been said, and this is true, that he does not
incline naturally to democratic ideas. He has come to them through reason
and through experience, and because he despises the old elites, because he
has come to recognize that all that is healthiest in France is to be found in
the people ... In such a case, when there is no long-standing democratic
inclination, there is the danger of jumping from one extreme to another, I
mean towards Communism. As a military man he has a great admiration for
what the Russians have achieved, and compares these to those of France and
Britain. I would add that the Russians have been very skilful, and at a time
when the Anglo-Saxons, especially the Americans, kept the Free French at a
distance, they have vigorously supported him.[16]

An important Socialist arrival in London over the summer was André
Philip. A professor of economics and Socialist parliamentarian before the
war, Philip was the most high-profile politician to arrive in London so far,
and he had also been closely involved in the Resistance movement
Libération-Sud. De Gaulle used Philip to try again to overcome the reservations of Jacques Maritain in America. While inching closer towards de
Gaulle, Maritain had written suggesting he would be better advised to
confine himself to a symbolic role rather than aspiring to form a government in exile: 'Can one imagine Joan of Arc worrying about exercising
political power and preparing a government?' Philip confronted this challenge directly:

> You cite Joan as not creating a government. It seems to me on the contrary
> that this was the essential point of her mission. What her voices called on
> her to do was to have the Dauphin crowned in Reims so as to give him back
> his lost sovereignty ... General de Gaulle represents not only Joan of Arc ...
> but the legitimate government of France ... a moral base uniting all citizens
> in the same sense of solidarity.[17]

Philip was no mystical French Catholic but a Protestant and a Socialist
academic who had spent much time in the United States. That someone of
his intellectual background could use such language is testimony to the
potency of the de Gaulle myth.

SUMMER HONEYMOON

De Gaulle appointed Philip to head the CNI. This choice was not an entire success since Philip's chronic disorganization made him a disastrous administrator: papers were always being mislaid and possibly even used to light his pipe. De Gaulle, who had initially enjoyed their intellectual exchanges – he was another of those intellectuals by whom the General was seduced – eventually became frustrated by this side of Philip. But quite apart from these deficiencies, which only gradually became evident, Philip's appointment signalled an important change in the organization of the Free French. De Gaulle had finally capitulated to the arguments of Passy, strongly supported by Brossolette, that the division between the CNI and the BCRAM – one responsible for political action in France and the other for military action – was unsustainable. Wires were constantly crossed; agents would be sent out on different missions without knowing of each other's existence; they would be required to report separately to the BCRAM and the CNI for different parts of their mission. This situation had deeply frustrated Moulin. In the reorganization, the CNI was still responsible for 'political' matters but BCRAM was now designated the single agent of execution. It dropped the final 'M' (Militaire) to signify this. At the same time de Gaulle made a new appointment to his London National Committee. This was Jacques Soustelle, a young anthropologist who had had a stellar pre-war academic career. Appointed at the age of twenty-six in 1938 to be Deputy Director of Paris's ethnographic museum, the Musée de l'Homme, Soustelle was one of those intellectuals who had been passionately involved in the Popular Front. Since his academic expertise in pre-Columbian civilization gave him numerous contacts in Central America, de Gaulle had sent him in 1940 to organize Free French committees in Latin and Central America, a task at which he proved brilliantly successful. Now he returned to London, as Commissioner for Information. His brief was to streamline Free French propaganda. One of Soustelle's achievements was to create a Gaullist newspaper in London, *La Marseillaise*, whose first issue appeared on the symbolic date of 14 July 1942. Oddly enough, the Free French had previously had no newspaper of their own in London, and the two existing French publications in London were far from Gaullist.

The presence of figures like Brossolette, Philip and Soustelle – and of other Socialists arriving in London during the summer of 1942 – reinforced Gaulle's move to the left over the previous few months. In Carlton Gardens there were now fewer uniforms and more suits, fewer conservatives and more Socialists. Fighting France was becoming a more professional and substantial enterprise than it had been only a few months earlier when some observers seriously wondered if it would survive the crises of the spring. In the autumn, de Gaulle summoned Gaston Palewski back to London from Africa to run his *cabinet*. Palewski now deepened his knowledge of British high society by embarking on a passionate (at least on her side) affair with Nancy Mitford, but this did not get in the way of his fanatical loyalty to de Gaulle.

The main cause of tension in this period between de Gaulle and the British related to the Resistance. As it emerged as a serious force in France, the SOE and British intelligence were keen to establish their own independent contacts with it. This could lead to costly mistakes. SOE had discovered the existence of Carte, a Resistance organization, whose leader was a painter called André Girard, living on the Côte d'Azur. He claimed to have tens of thousands of people working with him and also to enjoy privileged contacts with Vichy insiders seeking an opportunity to switch sides. He requested 50,000 guns to arm his men, a bluff audacious even by the standards of the Resistance. Since Girard was strongly anti-Gaullist, his appearance on the scene encouraged SOE to believe that it might be in Britain's interest to build relations with the Resistance independently of de Gaulle. An SOE agent sent to Antibes in August 1942 returned to London so convinced of Girard's credibility that it was even agreed to put a transmitter at his disposal which would broadcast as if it were based in France under the name of Radio Patrie. Not until the end of the year did it emerge that Girard was a total fantasist, and the embarrassed SOE put an end to its support for him. De Gaulle knew nothing about the Carte hoax in the summer of 1942, but it showed that his suspicions of the British were not unfounded.[18] He and Passy were annoyed, for example, that d'Astier's first visit to London had been organized by the British without telling the Free French at all. De Gaulle had a major 'fit of vapours', in the words of one SOE official, and wrote several times over the summer to Eden pointing out that 'Resistance is an indivisible whole' (in reality this assertion was far from true) and that it was the role of the Fighting French (not the British) to organize it (not all resisters would have agreed).[19]

Despite these spats, the evidence arriving from France about de Gaulle's popularity was becoming so unequivocal that it offered Eden ammunition to counter Churchill's sporadic bouts of Gaullophobia. Eden presented a paper to the Cabinet in early August which went so far as to suggest that, since de Gaulle would probably be the 'predominant French authority in Metropolitan France liberated by the action of Allied forces', there was a case for bringing him into the discussions about the future of liberated

France.[20] De Gaulle seemed to be on the crest of a wave and this made him less prickly towards the British. On occasion he revealed aspects of his personality the British had been rarely privileged to witness. At a dinner with Charles Peake on 3 July de Gaulle was in 'very friendly mood and impressed everybody'. Another guest had the same impression: 'Asked about the prospects for Anglo-French friendship, the General said that at present French sympathy was divided equally between England, America and Russia but he thought we should eventually again become the favourite ally "*car les Américains deviendront trop fatigants et les Russes trop inquiétants* [the Americans will become too tiring and the Russians too worrying].""[21] On 14 July, he addressed about 300 MPs at the Houses of Parliament and so charmed his audience that when he finished they spontaneously burst into the 'Marseillaise'. At the dinner which followed, Morton, whose usual tendency, according to Harvey, was to 'hot up the PM' against de Gaulle,[22] could not conceal his enthusiasm for de Gaulle's performance:

> Although he was clearly very tired after his exertions of the afternoon . . . he obviously put himself at great pains, not only to be friendly and courteous, but to answer sincerely and intelligently the many military questions . . . He answered, with equal profundity and skill, very difficult questions put to him by certain members of parliament who were also present. He dealt with the 'second Front' and the military situation in Russia and Egypt. I lay no claim to military knowledge myself, but have naturally heard a great deal recently from our high military experts and others . . . Seeing that de Gaulle cannot have access to this mass of fact, his handling of the questions betrayed a military brain of the very highest order.
>
> I was particularly interested to see that for a great part of the time de Gaulle discussed these questions in quite understandable English. He has evidently been studying our language privately and has made considerable progress.[23]

Relations improved also with the United States government which agreed for the first time on 9 July to recognize the Free French as a military partner in the war. It appointed two military representatives to the French National Committee. On 14 July, one of these, Admiral Stark, was present at a parade of the Fighting French in London – a marked contrast to the situation only a few weeks earlier, at the celebrations for Memorial Day in Washington, when representatives from the Vichy Embassy had been invited to attend but not the Free French.[24] In the summer of 1942 Warner Brothers in Hollywood even conceived the idea of a film about de Gaulle, seemingly at the suggestion of Roosevelt himself. The novelist William

Faulkner was commissioned to write the screenplay. He spent several months on the project and produced 1,200 pages of script portraying de Gaulle as an almost Christ-like figure. Faulkner's problem was that de Gaulle's representatives in the United States, consulted on the script, were continuously raising nitpicking points of detail. Faulkner became so exasperated that the project was ultimately abandoned. By this time the Roosevelt administration had turned firmly against de Gaulle and was certainly not pushing Faulkner to continue. The film was never made.[25]

STORM CLOUDS AGAIN

One reason for the fleeting American honeymoon with de Gaulle was that the American military were keen to open a second front in western Europe despite the scepticism of the British. If there was to be an imminent landing in France, the Resistance – and therefore de Gaulle – might have a role to play. Pushing his luck somewhat, de Gaulle wrote to Churchill and Stark on 27 July suggesting that he should be brought into any discussions regarding any landing in France.[26] He asked Tixier to make the same point in Washington: 'You can add without ambiguity that I am all the more determined to get satisfaction ... since my confidence in the perspicacity and strategic skill of the allies is not unlimited. Without causing unnecessary wounds, you need not hide this.' Presumably even the famously tactless Tixier did not feel it necessary to pass on every detail of this message.[27]

In July, General George Marshall, the American Chief of Staff, arrived in London to discuss the next stage of the war with the British. The American proposal for a landing in France in 1942 or 1943 was overruled by the British who believed this was dangerously premature. Instead the Americans accepted the British plan for a Mediterranean strategy beginning with an invasion of French North Africa. Since North Africa was strongly Vichyist, and had little Resistance presence, de Gaulle no longer figured in America's calculations. De Gaulle knew nothing of this when he was invited to meet General George Marshall and a galaxy of other American generals at Claridge's on 23 July. De Gaulle wanted to find out whether a second front was being planned, but his interlocutors, sworn to secrecy about the planned operation in North Africa, told him even less, as General Mark Clark commented, 'than he would have learned by reading the morning newspapers'. The meeting was a disaster. The Americans had ordered a bottle of champagne to break the ice; de Gaulle refused to touch a drop. Since the Americans could say nothing and de Gaulle was not there for small talk, the meeting was punctuated by ever more embarrassing silences. Suddenly de Gaulle got up and announced curtly that he would not 'take up any more of your time'.[28] Two Gaullist aides who were present both assumed that the Americans had been intimidated by de Gaulle – which reveals more about the effect de Gaulle had on his collaborators than about their perspicacity.[29] De Gaulle himself assumed wrongly that the Americans had been unforthcoming because they had not decided what to do next.[30] To Peake, however, he pretended that the 'conversation had been long and interesting' and that 'they had expressed great interest in what he had to say.'[31]

Despite this disappointment, de Gaulle seemed in good spirits when he set off for Africa at the end of August – his first trip abroad since his return from the Middle East in September 1941. The fact that he was allowed to go at all showed the improvement in his relations with the British. Meeting Eden before his departure, the General assured him that 'he need have no fears' of any 'unfriendly statements' while he was abroad. Relations, he said, were 'now good' apart some friction over Syria.[32] If de Gaulle meant this, his assurances turned out to be hollow.

Having been tantalized over the summer by the prospect of a second front, de Gaulle quickly sensed that events were conspiring against him again. In the flight taking him to Cairo, he found himself travelling in the same plane as the American diplomat Averell Harriman. Harriman was on his way to Moscow for a meeting with Stalin where he and Churchill were to break the news that there would be no second front in western Europe that year while consoling him with news of the planned Allied attack on North Africa. The plane, a bomber adapted for transport, was cramped and de Gaulle and Harriman, two extremely tall men, found themselves opposite each other, their knees locked together for twenty hours. Harriman wrote afterwards: 'de Gaulle is a dull companion, he never loosened up. I confess I did not try much.' His own account of the 'conversation' certainly portrays his own contribution as even more laconic than de Gaulle's. De Gaulle remembered the flight similarly: 'This ordinarily frank and fluent diplomat seemed this time to be constrained by a heavy secret.' That was indeed the case and the fact that Harriman could not share his secret with de Gaulle fuelled the latter's rancour at his exclusion from Allied decision making. There was a stopover at Gibraltar where de Gaulle could see that preparations were under way for some massive and imminent military operation: 'I noted the sybilline manner of the governor of Gibraltar, usually so relaxed on other occasions. All this showed me that a big operation would soon be taking place in the Mediterranean, without us.'[33]

All this put de Gaulle in a mood to pick a fight with the British despite his promises to Eden. The pretext was presented by the Middle East, where tensions had been exacerbated by Spears's appointment in March 1942 as

British Minister to Syria and Lebanon. After his break with de Gaulle in 1941, the Middle East became the new passion of Spears's life. He saw his mission as ousting the French from the region and creating a grateful Arab clientele for the British.[34] This was not, however, official British policy, which remained as confused as it had been in 1941. As Churchill put it to Spears: 'What people might learn to do against the French in the Levant might be turned to account against us later. We should discourage the throwing of stones since we had greenhouses of our own – acres of them.'[35] At the same time the British were keen to win Arab support by holding the French to their promise to grant independence to the mandates of Syria and Lebanon. Over the spring, Spears had clashed with Catroux, de Gaulle's representative in the region, by insisting that elections should be held in the mandates as a preliminary to preparing for independence. Catroux took the Free French line that this would be dangerously destabilizing while the war was going on. De Gaulle left Catroux to defend the French position but took some delight in pointing out that the British were hardly hurrying to hold elections in India or their own mandate of Palestine. He pointed out threateningly that Catroux might remind the British that they had an interest in being more supportive of the French who were being solicited by the Zionists in their own struggle against the British in Palestine.[36]

Arriving in Cairo on 8 August, de Gaulle saw the British Minister of State Lord Casey, who raised the issue of elections. In Casey's words, the meeting started with long silences and 'degenerated into an undignified shouting match'. Two days later – familiar Gaullist tactics – they had a 'calmer and less disagreeable discussion'.[37] Nothing was resolved when de Gaulle set off for the Levant. He spent the next few weeks on a kind of royal progress to the main cities of the region – Beirut, Damascus, Aleppo and so on. Large crowds turned out to cheer, and this confirmed de Gaulle in his view that the mass of the population was animated by no anti-French feelings and that the only problem was the 'sabotage' of the British. Looking in a mirror rather than trying to understand the true reason the crowds were cheering – they believed the promises that had been made regarding independence – de Gaulle wrote that they saw in the Free French 'something courageous, remarkable and chivalric which seemed in their eyes to correspond to the ideal image of France'. Passing through the Lebanon he told the Free French soldier Diego Brosset that he had come to 'shake up the English'. Brosset commented: 'Amiable and authoritarian with as always this element of excessiveness that make him like a mystic [illuminé], he soars above the reality of the moment with a curious mixture of realism and prophetic vision.'[38]

Buoyed up by the adulation of the crowds, de Gaulle became wilder in his actions. He sent messages to Churchill, Casey and others insisting that if Spears were not recalled he would withdraw his troops from British command. In Beirut he poured out his resentment against the British to Roosevelt's representative in the region Wendell Willkie; and he cabled his own representatives in London instructing them to approach the Soviet and American embassies to convince them of British perfidy. All this culminated in a forty-page memorandum presented to the British denouncing their policy and their supposed designs on the French Empire.[39] During the four-week tornado of his trip round the Middle East de Gaulle's mood became worse and worse. Bouchinet-Serreulles, travelling with him, was the recipient of violent tirades:

> France tomorrow will be in a state of collapse, exhausted ... That is why after the war it will be necessary to give Europe a sense of herself; if not, American political administrators will come to colonize Europe with their primitive methods and their overweening pride. They will treat us all as if we were negroes in Senegal! To rebuild Europe, we will need Germany, but a Germany that has been first defeated unlike the situation in 1918.[40]

There was much more in this vein. De Gaulle's spirits improved on leaving Damascus to fly to Fort Lamy on 14 September. He was almost childishly excited to be travelling not on a British aircraft but on a Lockheed plane recently obtained from America. One of the major frustrations for the Free French, and one of the major humiliations for de Gaulle, was that the few planes at his disposal were in a pitiful state, rendering it difficult to travel round his 'Empire'. (One of them transporting him to Fort Lamy in 1940 had been forced to make an emergency landing in a swamp.) But when the Americans entered the war they were keen to exploit the French airbase of Pointe Porte in French Congo. De Gaulle would agree only if in return he was provided with seven Lockheed planes – somewhat ironic, not to say hypocritical, given his implied criticism six months earlier of the British destroyers-for-bases deal in 1940.[41] De Gaulle was also delighted to be able to fly from Damascus in French Syria to Fort Lamy in French Africa without needing to land on British soil. The moment he saw that they were flying over 'French' territory he grabbed Bouchinet-Serreulles's sleeve excitedly, saying 'look the vegetation is beginning ... what wonderful country' as he indicated a few scrawny bushes below them.[42]

De Gaulle in an euphoric mood was even more alarming to the British than de Gaulle on the warpath. His volatile behaviour during his Middle East trip also worried the National Committee in London, especially the Commissioner for External Affairs, Maurice Dejean, who believed that the General's tactics were counterproductive. In his view, trying to play the

Americans against the British when it came to defending the French Empire was doomed to failure. De Gaulle wired back unrepentantly: 'Twenty-four years of French pusillanimity have produced the results we see. I will not allow this to continue. Only one thing stands in the path of the stupid voracity of our allies here, and that is their fear of pushing us too far.'[43] In a repetition of the situation a year earlier, the British were desperate to get de Gaulle back to London. They tried a mixture of carrot and stick. Since it looked as if Vichy resistance in Madagascar would soon be over, de Gaulle was told that before he could be allowed to take over the administration of the island, as had been promised, an agreement was first needed over the Levant.

Away from the influence of the National Committee, which had to deal with the British on a daily basis, de Gaulle was subject to fewer voices urging him to show restraint. He also felt he had little to lose. He gave his reading of the situation in a telegram to London at the end of August. The Allies, in his view, had turned cold because they had decided they no longer needed him. They were planning an operation in North Africa from which he would be excluded but, contrary to Allied hopes, this would not stop the Vichy forces in North Africa from firing on them. Finally, the Germans would use the Allied operation as a pretext to send troops to North Africa.[44] Every one of these predictions came to pass two months later exactly as de Gaulle had said. De Gaulle's intuitions could be eerily prescient.

In these circumstances de Gaulle was loath to return to London, where the Allies wanted 'less to consult me than to control me'.[45] But, as on previous occasions in 1940 and 1941, he withdrew from the brink, recognizing reluctantly that London was the centre of things. He returned on 25 September, recording in his *Memoirs* the sense of deflation he always felt on leaving French territory:

> Suddenly everything had changed. How distant were the loyal territories, the ardent troops, the enthusiastic crowds which only yesterday surrounded me with the assurance of their devotion. Here, once again, was what is known as power stripped of the contacts and the recognition that sometimes manage to sweeten it. Here were nothing but tough problems, bitter negotiations, painful choices.[46]

De Gaulle's tactics during his Middle East journey backfired dramatically. The Foreign Office, exasperated by Spears's personal diplomacy in the Middle East, had itself been angling to have him removed. One official commented: 'If only de Gaulle had controlled himself, we could have got Spears out by now thanks to the complaints we have received from all sides. But de Gaulle has played into his hands.'[47] Churchill made the defence of Spears a personal matter, telling de Gaulle before he left for the Middle East: 'Spears has many enemies but he has a friend: the Prime Minister.' It was against his better judgement that Churchill had allowed de Gaulle to leave. Now he was furious that the General had again used his trip to whip up anti-British feeling in the Middle East. His meeting with de Gaulle on 30 September reached new levels of acrimony. De Gaulle smashed a chair in his fury. The minutes of the meeting concluded with 'registration of complete disagreement'. The two men went over familiar ground as to whether de Gaulle genuinely represented France:

> De Gaulle: this very serious situation called into question the collaboration between France and England.
>
> PM: corrected General de Gaulle, and said between General de Gaulle and England.
>
> G de G: asked why we were discussing matters with him if he were not France.
>
> PM: De Gaulle was not France but fighting France.
>
> De G: why then were we discussing French questions with him . . . ?
>
> PM: The difficulty was to decide what was France. He was always trying to derive a just impression of what was France. He recognized General de Gaulle as a very honourable part of France but not as France. There were other parts and aspects of France which might become more prominent.[48]

In the light of the Allied plans to launch an operation in North Africa, this was a menacing comment. After the meeting, the British implemented the usual retaliation against de Gaulle. He was forbidden to broadcast. Meanwhile behind the scenes, officials on both sides set about picking up the pieces. Consistent with his usual tactic of wrongfooting his opponents, alternating outbreaks of more or less simulated fury with moments of disconcerting charm, de Gaulle received Peake on 6 October in the best of moods. 'Kindly, putting his arm through mine and seating me in an armchair . . . saying that he wished to speak to me as a friend', de Gaulle said he 'was at a loss to understand' why anyone should have 'taken exception to anything he had said since he had been calm and correct throughout the interview' with Churchill.[49] This was de Gaulle's reading of a meeting about which Eden – usually an ally of de Gaulle – remarked that 'he had never seen anything like it in the way of rudeness since Ribbentrop'.[50]

Two days later de Gaulle was in such a mischievously friendly mood that, dwelling on his excellent relations with Maisky and Bogomolov, he offered himself to Peake as intermediary between the British and the Soviets since he said the latter 'were apt to be rather spiteful about us'.[51] De Gaulle enjoyed stirring things up in this way but he was possibly also worried that he had gone too far in his meeting with Churchill. He wrote to Catroux that faced with the 'cold and passionate anger of Churchill and Eden' he had offered a 'tough and justified response' while warning that there might be a backlash with the British attempting to 'manoeuvre against us from the inside by affecting to identify difficulties with my personality'.[52] He was clearly pre-empting any attempt by the British to play the 'conciliatory' Catroux off against him. In this case de Gaulle need not have worried. Catroux was as exasperated by Spears as was everyone else. When it looked as if Dejean in London had reached a compromise with the British over a date for elections in Syria and Lebanon, it was Catroux who intervened from Beirut to protest. De Gaulle seized the opportunity to sack Dejean on 18 October. Dejean complained bitterly to de Gaulle that he was no less a patriot than him. De Gaulle replied: 'Perhaps – but you are no longer Commissioner for External Affairs.'

Although the dismissal of Dejean was a purely internal matter which never threatened to become a repeat of the Muselier affair, de Gaulle was faced simultaneously with a worrying political row which was not of his making. During the General's absence overseas, Brossolette had organized the transport to London of a repentant Pétainist, Charles Vallin, who had been a leader of the extreme-right Croix de Feu before the war. The event was given much publicity, and Vallin broadcast on the BBC on 17 September. Brossolette's idea was that Vallin in London would complement André Philip, demonstrating that support for de Gaulle went across the political spectrum – from the Socialists to the extreme right. But for many anti-Gaullists of the left in London the arrival of a 'fascist' stoked all their suspicions of de Gaulle. Brossolette fuelled the controversy by publishing an article in *La Marseillaise* arguing that former divisions between left and right no longer had any meaning: there were only Gaullists and traitors. He advocated a 'profound renewal' of French politics which would see the best elements of right and left united under the banner of Gaullism but excluding 'all the old political foxes who are today hiding in their holes'.[53]

The Vallin affair was discussed in an acrimonious meeting of the Jean Jaurès group of Socialists. Philip, Brossolette, Boris and others defended the position that former political labels had been made redundant by the Occupation. Philip raged against Socialist colleagues whom he accused of living in a time-warp: 'You fill me with disgust. You are supporting treason. You are behaving like émigrés. You no longer have any sense of the nation.' On the other side Gombault and others refused to have anything to do with 'fascists' and argued that Brossolette had moved closer to Vallin than Vallin had to the Socialists.[54]

De Gaulle, who had strongly supported the idea of bringing Vallin to London, kept aloof from the quarrel.[55] French trade unionists in London who wrote expressing their concerns were referred by him to Philip and Brossolette for 'all the necessary reassurances'.[56] But seeing that the plan had backfired, de Gaulle quietly shelved his intention of bringing Vallin on to the National Committee, and sent him off on a mission to Africa. The Vallin affair showed that the future evolution of 'Gaullism' remained a matter of debate and had not been resolved by de Gaulle's adoption of democratic rhetoric. It might seem alarmist to suspect Brossolette's advocacy of a single political Gaullist movement transcending left and right as a kind of proto-fascism, but it is understandable that it might have worried supporters of traditional parliamentary democracy.

If de Gaulle wanted to put the matter behind him, it was because Brossolette's critics had good contacts in the British press; the affair had been widely reported by the *Observer*. The last thing de Gaulle wanted was to offer ammunition to those in Britain ready to seize upon evidence of allegedly undemocratic tendencies just as his officials were patching things up with the British over Syria. Eventually a compromise over Syria was reached fixing a timetable for elections. But de Gaulle was back in a gloomily anti-British mood. After one conversation in October, Alphand noted: 'I am struck again . . . by his Anglophobia. For him England is perfidious, egoistical, and only thinks of stripping us of our Empire. She is incapable of conducting the war and is not even aware of the collapse of her power. He places his hopes in the United States and the Soviet Union.'[57] Although de Gaulle later developed a reputation for anti-Americanism, what is striking about this period of de Gaulle's career, despite his occasional tirades against American 'imperialism', is how often the Free French in London worried about de Gaulle's idea that he could play off the Americans – or the Russians – against the British.

Realizing that a major Allied operation was imminent in North Africa, de Gaulle wrote a twenty-page defence of his position addressed to Roosevelt. He had never before written directly to him, but all the efforts of his representatives in the United States had failed to move the President from his deluded view that Vichy could be brought over to the Allied camp.[58] To explain why the Free French were so prickly in their defence of French interests, de Gaulle opened with an extended history lesson whose theme was that France, having emerged from the previous war exhausted and uncertain of herself, had been deeply humiliated by the defeat of 1940. Finally he came to his own personal situation, challenging the idea that he harboured dictatorial ambitions in France after the war. He envisaged himself as exercising an 'essentially provisional authority, responsible before the future national electorate and applying the laws of the Third Republic'. But he insisted that he had not sought such a role. It had been forced upon him in 1940 because no one else had been willing to assume it:

> I have been told that we should not be playing politics. If by that is meant that it is not our role to take a position in the partisan struggles of the past, or one day to dictate to France the institutions of the future, there is no need of such warnings because it is our principle to abstain from such pretensions. But we do not refuse the word 'political' if it is about gathering together not only various troops but the French nation in the war or if it is a matter of discussing with our allies the interests of France at the same time as we defend them for France, against the enemy.

When this movingly eloquent plea was received in Washington, one official commented: 'It is two years too late and takes some ten pages of introduction to get down into the very little meat there is in it.'[59] Nothing could be more revealing of American suspicion of de Gaulle than this curt dismissal of a document of such sustained argument. The war was about to change dramatically with the American-led Allied landings in North Africa; but de Gaulle had not succeeded in changing the attitude of the American government towards him.

II

Power Struggles, November 1942–
November 1943

FRENCH TRAGEDY

On 11 November 1942, the Free French assembled in the Albert Hall to hear their leader. These occasions had become a ritual for them. It was in the Albert Hall that a year earlier de Gaulle had for the first time invoked 'Liberty, Equality, Fraternity'. At another meeting in the Albert Hall on 18 June 1942, for the second anniversary of the 1940 *Appel*, he had delivered one of his most brilliant speeches, opening with a quotation from the eighteenth-century moralist Chamfort:

> Chamfort wrote: 'The reasonable have survived. The passionate have lived.' It is now two years since France, delivered to the enemy and betrayed at Bordeaux, has nonetheless continued in the war through her armies, through her territories, through the spirit of the Fighting French. During these two years we have lived a lot because we are passionate. But we have survived as well. Ah yes, how reasonable we are!

The rest of the speech embroidered on these two themes of reason and passion. It ended:

> Once our task is finished, our role complete, following on from all those who have served France since the dawn of her History, preceding all those who will serve her for the eternity of her future, we will say to France, simply, like Péguy: 'Mother, look upon your sons who have fought for you.'[1]

The mood at the Albert Hall on 11 November 1942 was more sombre. It was one of the foggiest London days for years and those heading for the meeting had literally to feel their way along the pavements. Proceedings opened with messages from recent arrivals from France. A fourteen-year-old boy read out a short speech ending '*Vive de Gaulle*'. After he had finished, a somewhat awkward de Gaulle took the boy into his arms to embrace him. Then de Gaulle's opening words were interrupted by shouts from a senile anti-Gaullist general in the audience who had to be forcibly removed. But the real drama was occurring in France. Four days earlier, American troops had landed in Algeria and Morocco in Operation Torch. In retaliation, and to secure France's southern coast, on 11 November the Germans moved troops into the previously non-occupied zone. All of France was now occupied and many of de Gaulle's listeners must have been worrying about the fate of family members back home. The gleam of hope in the fog – that the liberation of French North Africa portended the start of the Allied fightback against Germany in western Europe – was clouded by the fear that the Americans, once established in North Africa, would exclude de Gaulle from the next stages of the war. Their plan was to use General Giraud to front their operation in the hope that his presence would reduce the likelihood of resistance from the defending Vichy forces.

De Gaulle had been woken early in the morning, on 8 November, to be informed of the American landing. Furious that he had been given no advance warning, he screamed: 'I hope the Vichy people throw them back into the sea.'[2] For the whole morning Carlton Gardens was in a state of agitation more about what enormity de Gaulle might perpetrate next than about the military operation itself. But when an apprehensive Charles Peake arrived to see if he intended to keep a planned lunch appointment with Churchill, he found the General 'not as bad' as he had feared.[3] At lunch, an embarrassed Churchill explained truthfully that it was Roosevelt who had insisted the Free French be kept in the dark about the operation. He reiterated that for the British de Gaulle remained 'the only authority recognised' to organize the French.[4] These soothing reassurances worked. Eden, who was present, reported to Oliver Harvey that 'the General was at his best. He said that it was necessary to think of France and we were right to choose General Giraud for this.'[5]

De Gaulle left lunch almost 'euphoric' according to several witnesses.[6] His broadcast that evening was perfect from the Allied perspective. He urged the French of North Africa not to fight against the Americans: 'Reject the claims of the traitors who want to persuade you that our allies want to take over our Empire for themselves.' His reaction was so sanguine not only because of Churchill's reassurances but also because, despite his initial shock, this operation had not surprised him (unlike the British attack on Madagascar). And it presented him with great opportunities. North Africa contained a French army that could massively boost his potential military forces once the territory was in Allied hands. But events moved in a worrying and unexpected direction – and de Gaulle's euphoria was short-lived.

As an anti-German French officer who had never openly broken with Pétain, Giraud had seemed the perfect candidate to persuade the Vichy army in North Africa to rally to the Allies. On the eve of the landings, however, Giraud was still in Gibraltar negotiating with the Americans. Insisting that he be appointed commander in chief of the entire operation, he was already revealing that mixture of obstinacy, stupidity and bad judgement that would ultimately be his downfall. By the time he arrived in Algiers on the afternoon of 9 November, American hopes of a painless operation had foundered. The defending Vichy forces were resisting hard. Unexpectedly the Vichy leader Admiral Darlan, who happened to be in Algiers visiting his sick son, emerged as the man on the spot who might broker a solution. Confusion reigned for several days while the American commanders negotiated with Darlan. If Darlan rallied to the Allies opportunistically, he would be seizing the opportunity that Weygand had rejected in 1940 when the British had such high hopes of him. If that latter eventuality had transpired de Gaulle would probably not have survived because in 1940 he represented nothing and his only asset was Churchill's recent and impulsive backing. By November 1942, however, he had acquired a level of support in France, and an international reputation, that made him a force to be reckoned with. He could not be so easily cast aside. On the other hand, there was a factor that had not existed in 1940: the Americans were calling the shots and they had made no commitments to de Gaulle. Roosevelt had persistently gambled on Vichy, and in an unexpected way the gamble seemed to be paying off.

This was the danger facing de Gaulle when he addressed his supporters in the Albert Hall on 11 November. In another stirring rhetorical performance, he reaffirmed the moral purity of his crusade: 'The cement of French unity is the blood of those Frenchmen who never accepted the armistice, those who have been dying for France since Rethondes [where the armistice had been signed], those who did not accept, in the words of Corneille, "the shame of dying without having fought".' The whole speech, while avoiding any direct criticism of the Allies, was a celebration of French unity and a coded warning to the Allies against pitting one group of French (in Algiers) against another (in London): 'The nation no longer accepts leaders except those of her liberation just as in the great Revolution, she only accepted those committed to the cause of Public Safety.'

DE GAULLE V. DARLAN: 'TODAY DARLAN GIVES ME ALGIERS, AND I CRY *VIVE DARLAN!*' (ROOSEVELT)

De Gaulle's revolutionary eloquence counted for little against Roosevelt's pragmatic cynicism. His priority was to end hostilities in North Africa as fast as possible because for the Americans every day counted. While Darlan was negotiating with the American military commanders in Morocco, the Vichy authorities were allowing German forces to land in Tunisia – as de Gaulle had predicted would happen two months earlier. During these two confused weeks, de Gaulle was an impotent and appalled observer of events over which he had no purchase. Peake, a regular visitor, came upon him one day with piles of newspapers 'heavily scored in red and blue, and interspersed with telegram flimsies and cuttings from the tape machines spread out in front of him. Having no other occupation, he had spent the whole day poring over the contents, and between times listening to the radio.'[7] De Gaulle raged to his aides: 'It is not Hitler that the Allies are fighting but me.'[8]

The American military finally reached a deal with Darlan on 22 November. In return for ordering a truce, Darlan was installed as High Commissioner in North Africa. The next day General Boisson, de Gaulle's nemesis at Dakar, also rallied to the Allies and joined the governing council set up by Darlan.[9] Hearing this news, Leclerc commented: 'Judas Iscariot in every sense of the term – except that he will never commit suicide.'[10] Other members of Darlan's governing council included General Noguès, who had refused to rally to de Gaulle in 1940, and Marcel Peyrouton, who had been Pétain's Minister of the Interior.

Once his worst nightmare had materialized, de Gaulle fought back in four ways. First, he tried to win over public opinion by occupying the moral high ground – as in his speech of 11 November. His rhetoric touched a chord with Allied public opinion, forcing Roosevelt to backtrack. On 17 November he announced that Darlan was only a 'temporary expedient'. His embarrassment was palpable in the fact that he contrived to use the word 'temporary' five times in this one short communiqué. But how temporary? The danger for de Gaulle was that the longer Darlan remained in place, the more the memory of his collaboration with Germany in the past would be erased by the services he was providing the Allies in the present. De Gaulle's further efforts to publicize his views were smothered by the Allies. On two occasions (21 November, 3 December) he was forbidden to broadcast on the BBC. His speeches went out on Radio Brazzaville but its radius was limited. The offending passage in the second speech was a phrase attacking the new authorities in Algiers as representatives of 'capitulation, collaboration and usurpation'. The Free French circumvented this censorship by printing the banned speeches in *La Marseillaise*, which also published a blistering article by Brossolette drawing the logical conclusion about American policy: 'If Algiers is worth a Darlan, might not Paris be worth a Laval?' Although these articles were disseminated in the British press, the radio ban was an emasculation for de Gaulle. As Oliver Harvey put it: 'The poor General is in a frenzy and is anxious now to broadcast what he thinks of Darlan. He has been prevented. We cannot obviously have a direct conflict with America over this; we have bigger fish to fry together, but it is unfair to de Gaulle, our only French friend in our darkest hour.'[11]

De Gaulle's second tactic was to lobby the British and American governments. He saw Churchill four times in November. Embracing wholeheartedly his new role as a revolutionary leader, this admirer of *ancien régime* Realpolitik warned Churchill that the world had moved beyond eighteenth-century wars fought by mercenaries: 'Today war is made with blood and soul of peoples ... You will perhaps win the war militarily; you will lose it morally and there will be only one victor: Stalin.'[12] De Gaulle reported to Tixier in America that each time Churchill was 'warm on the surface but evasive underneath'.[13] This was perceptive. Although Churchill had told Roosevelt on 17 November that because of Darlan's 'odious record' an agreement with him 'would not be understood by the great masses of ordinary people whose simple loyalties are our strength', a month later he made a secret speech in parliament so hostile to de Gaulle that sections of it were omitted from the version published after the war. After detailing all de Gaulle's misdeeds, he ended:

> I continue to maintain friendly personal relations with General de Gaulle and I help him as much as I possibly can. I feel bound to do this because he stood up against the men of Bordeaux and their base surrender at a time when all resisting will-power had quitted France. All the same I could not recommend you to base all your hopes and confidence upon him, and still less to assume that it is our duty to place, so far as we have power, the destiny of France in his hands.[14]

To work on Roosevelt, de Gaulle sent André Philip to the United States. As a moderate Socialist admirer of the New Deal, who spoke English perfectly, Philip seemed the ideal emissary. In fact the meeting was an unmitigated disaster. The notoriously disorganized Philip arrived late and then, accompanied by the outspoken Tixier, he harangued Roosevelt on the iniquity and immorality of his policy. Roosevelt responded in kind by losing his cool: 'Today Darlan gives me Algiers, and I cry *Vive Darlan!* If Quisling gives me Oslo, I will cry *Vive Quisling!* Let Laval give me Paris tomorrow and I will cry *Vive Laval!*' The American minutes of the meeting recorded:

> It would be quite impossible to attempt to report the latter part of the conversation ... They [Philip and Tixier] both of them howled at the top of their lungs and spoke at the same time, and paid not the slightest attention to what the President was saying to them ... neither one of them expressed the slightest gratitude or recognition of the liberation of North Africa by American forces ... [15]

In public, Roosevelt produced an old Balkan proverb to justify his position: 'It is permitted in time of grave danger to walk with the devil until you have crossed the bridge.'[16] The only positive result of the meeting was a vague invitation to de Gaulle to meet Roosevelt in Washington, but that visit kept being postponed.

De Gaulle's third tactic was to stir up mistrust between the Allies. He told Eden on 9 December that only three forces counted in France: Vichy, the Communists and the Gaullists. Of these three, only Gaullism had consistently supported the British alliance. If America allowed Gaullism to disappear, Communism would triumph in France after the war, but if Britain supported the Gaullists she would have the opportunity to take the moral leadership of Europe from America.[17] Two days later, de Gaulle dangled a different scenario in front of Maisky. He warned him that, after their deal with Darlan in North Africa, the Allies might try the same with fascists in Italy and even 'acceptable' Nazis like Göring. Taking his leave of Maisky, de Gaulle looked him in the eye and said: 'I hope the Russians will arrive in Berlin before the Americans.'[18] This tactic was unsuccessful. Although the North African operation was not the second front Stalin wanted, he would not quarrel with his allies for de Gaulle's sake. He told Churchill on 27 November that he understood Roosevelt's position. Using an allegedly Russian proverb – the habit of covering the betrayal of de Gaulle by old folk proverbs was infectious – he said that military necessity might require the use not only of Darlan but 'even [of] the Devil himself and his grandma'.[19]

De Gaulle's fourth tactic was to forge his own contacts in Algiers to put pressure on Darlan from below. With an intuitive sense of political power worthy of the Communist Party, he told Tixier that if the Allies could not be won over, it would be necessary to 'force union with us to come from the bottom upwards' – on the ground in Algiers.[20] The problem was that public opinion in North Africa was pro-Pétainist. The only Resistance presence was the tiny group Combat led by René Capitant, a university lawyer completely devoted to de Gaulle's cause. After several requests, the Americans grudgingly allowed de Gaulle to send a representative to North Africa. For this role he selected General François d'Astier, brother of the Resistance leader. After three days in Algeria, d'Astier was expelled by Darlan. Nonetheless he was able to hand over some funds to Combat, meet Eisenhower and see Giraud, who seemed unhappy that Darlan had side-lined him. This opened up the possibility of a Giraud–de Gaulle axis against Darlan.[21]

For the moment, however, Darlan enjoyed the full backing of the United States. And every day he was entrenching himself further. Churchill, embarrassed at the outset, told Eden at the end of November that Darlan 'has done more for us than de Gaulle'.[22] At the end of the year de Gaulle was in despair. He poured out his woes to Peake: 'No ally however well-meaning could give France back her soul, and indeed the greater the efforts made on her behalf, if she did not fully share in them, the greater would be her own sense of impotence and inferiority when the war was won.' Insisting that he was speaking 'after much thought', he said that if the Allies had decided that Darlan was to be a 'method of winning the war', there could be no future for the Free French.[23] De Gaulle certainly had no intention of giving up, but for the moment there seemed no way forward.

ANFA: DE GAULLE V. ROOSEVELT

Dining with de Gaulle on 8 December, Alexander Cadogan noted: 'De Gaulle's one remedy is "Get rid of Darlan." My answer is: "Yes but how?" No answer.'[24] The answer came on Christmas Eve 1942, when a young royalist, Fernand Bonnier de la Chapelle, ambled into Darlan's study and shot him dead. The assassin was executed two days later with suspicious haste. Algiers was so thick with plots that we will never know for sure who organized the assassination. Everyone had a motive: the Americans to be rid of an embarrassment; the Gaullists to be rid of an obstacle; Giraud to be rid of a rival. What makes it unlikely that de Gaulle was responsible is that the BCRA had no agents in Algiers.[25] De Gaulle might have wanted to eliminate Darlan but lacked the means to do so. If the prime suspect of a crime were necessarily its immediate beneficiary, the finger would point at Giraud, whom the Americans now installed in power as they had origi-nally intended.[26]

Despite de Gaulle's remark to Cadogan about getting rid of Darlan, after the assassination he commented jocularly that he now regretted Darlan's death because he had been making 'numberless converts' for the Free French.[27] This was not just a joke. Unlike Darlan, Giraud was untarnished by collaboration. Upright, honest, dim and reactionary, he presented himself as a simple soldier who only wanted to fight the Germans. Although opposed to collaboration, he entirely approved of the domestic policies of the Vichy regime – a point in his favour with the army cadres in Algiers – and he retained all the former Vichyites (Peyrouton, Noguès) who had been appointed by Darlan: Vichy's anti-Semitic laws were kept in place and Communists were interned. Under the patronage of the American army, the Vichy regime, headed by Giraud, had in effect reconstituted itself in Algeria. People meeting Giraud for the first time were regaled with a blow-by-blow account of his escape from imprisonment in 1942. This party piece always went down well, but the effect wore off when it turned out he had no more to say because there was little more in his head. None of this worried the Americans, who wanted someone apolitical and capable of galvanizing the Pétainist French army in North Africa. Giraud's weakness was that he had no understanding of the anti-Vichy France that was being forged out of the Resistance.

Having served under him in Metz, de Gaulle had a shrewd sense of Giraud's political inadequacies and was confident of swallowing him up fast. His plan was to establish a single committee merging the Giraudist administration in Algiers with his London National Committee. Giraud would be Commander in Chief; de Gaulle would exercise political power. A few days after Darlan's assassination, he confided his plans to Hervé Alphand:

> De Gaulle: There is only one alternative: Pétain–Vichy or the Republic . . . that is to say the Free French who are continuing the Republic . . . Giraud does not represent the Republic and has not brought the masses into Resistance . . . Within fifteen days the Americans will come round.
>
> Alphand: Do you realize they see you as a man so intransigent that you are impossible to negotiate with?
>
> De G: I cannot compromise on the fundamental interests of France.
>
> A: Could there not be a transitional stage, which would be a kind of duumvirate?
>
> De G: A lame solution.
>
> A: On occasion it is necessary to limp along a little before being able to walk straight. There were sometimes two consuls in Rome.
>
> De G: But in France there was a First Consul [that is, Napoleon].[28]

Alphand's caution was well founded. Although de Gaulle was right that Giraud was politically naive, he underestimated his obstinacy and vanity, and the lengths to which the Americans would go in backing him. Five months elapsed between this conversation and de Gaulle's arrival in Algiers on 31 May – and not as 'first' consul but one of two.

Immediately after Darlan's assassination, de Gaulle sent Giraud a message suggesting they meet. After Giraud's evasive reply, de Gaulle increased the pressure by going public with a communiqué announcing that he had offered to meet Giraud in order to establish a 'central political power' respecting the 'laws of the Republic'. The Foreign Office allowed this to be published but thought de Gaulle was overplaying his hand. De Gaulle's confidence that he was in a position to 'dictate our conditions'[29] was boosted by the arrival in London on 11 January 1943 of Fernand Grenier, a representative of the French Communist Party. A few days later, Grenier made a speech on the BBC praising de Gaulle as the man 'who had the merit not to despair while all was crumbling'. This was a massive fillip to de Gaulle's prestige just as the heroism of the Red Army at Stalingrad was wiping away the stain of the Ribbentrop–Molotov Pact of 1939 and giving Communism a new aura. It is not surprising he felt confident.

At this point, the initiative was taken out of de Gaulle's hands. Churchill, who was attending a conference in Morocco with Roosevelt, invited de Gaulle over to meet Giraud. De Gaulle's immediate instinct was to refuse. He saw no reason for the Allies to interfere in a purely French matter. This resulted in a four-day psychodrama during which the British tried to break down the resistance of what one official called this 'species of mule'.[30] On one occasion de Gaulle excused himself from a meeting with the Foreign Office because 'he couldn't trust himself not to burst out with remarks he would afterwards regret' – to which Cadogan responded 'What a baby.'[31] Churchill sent another telegram so violent that Eden toned it down before daring to show de Gaulle. De Gaulle was in a genuine dilemma. Refusing Churchill's invitation ran the risk that key decisions about the future of French North Africa would be made without him; accepting the invitation ran the risk of being forced to ratify an unfavourable agreement. In the end he decided that the risk of refusal was too great.

The Anglo-American summit was meeting in Anfa, a plush suburb of Casablanca where the Americans had commandeered several villas. The main purpose of the meeting was to plan the next stage of the war. Roosevelt and Churchill agreed again to postpone a second front in France and instead to launch an attack on Italy once the Germans were cleared from Tunisia. Despite all that was at stake, the mood at Anfa was, in the words of one participant, 'a mixture between a cruise, a summer school and a conference' with Roosevelt behaving like a 'schoolboy on vacation'.[32] This accounts for the playful mood in which Roosevelt approached the problem of French North Africa, hardly his most pressing concern. He told Churchill: 'We'll call Giraud the bridegroom, and I'll produce him from Algiers, and you get the bride, de Gaulle, down from London, and we'll have a shotgun wedding.' When it looked as if de Gaulle would refuse to attend, Roosevelt cabled to Washington: 'our friends could not produce the bride, the temperamental lady de Gaulle who has got quite snooty about the whole idea ... and is showing no intention of getting into bed with Giraud.'[33]

De Gaulle was mercifully unaware of this levity or he would certainly not have agreed to attend. Arriving in Anfa on 22 January, accompanied by Palewski, Catroux and others, he was shocked to see only American flags as if he were on American not French soil. At their first lunch together, Giraud opened insultingly with the words 'Bonjour, Gaulle' as if de Gaulle were still his subordinate at Metz. This was not a promising start. Before lunch, de Gaulle refused to sit down until French soldiers had replaced American sentries. When Giraud had regaled the company with yet another account of his escape from captivity, de Gaulle commented acidly: 'And now, General, perhaps you could recount to us the circumstances in which you were taken prisoner.'[34]

De Gaulle had a preliminary meeting with Churchill in the afternoon. Nothing was resolved but the tone was relatively cordial. At de Gaulle's first ever meeting with Roosevelt in the evening, heavily armed secret service men were hidden behind a curtain. Roosevelt's adviser Harry L. Hopkins commented later: 'None of this hocus-pocus had gone on when Giraud saw the President, and it was simply an indication of the atmosphere in which de Gaulle found himself at Casablanca.'[35] Roosevelt turned on his fabled charm, even talking in French. His message, however, was not welcome:

> The sovereignty of France, as in our country, rested with the people, but ... unfortunately the people of France were not now in a position to exercise that sovereignty ... The Allied Nations fighting in French territory at the moment were fighting for the liberation of France and they should hold the political situation in 'trusteeship' for the French people ... France was in the position of a little child unable to look out and fend for itself.[36]

Despite Roosevelt's discouraging words, de Gaulle, normally suspicious and wary, claimed to his entourage that the conversation had gone well and that Roosevelt had shown himself to be impressed by what the Free French represented.[37] If he really believed this, de Gaulle had been

hoodwinked. Seeing de Gaulle in the flesh confirmed all Roosevelt's prejudices. The General's startling intensity was anathema to his smooth
patrician urbanity. He told Churchill that he was 'concerned at the spiritual
look' in de Gaulle's eyes.[38] He afterwards recounted, with many embellishments in the retelling, that de Gaulle had compared himself to Joan of Arc.
The truth was more complicated. When Roosevelt told de Gaulle he
could not recognize him because he had not been elected, de Gaulle replied
that Joan of Arc had not been elected either but that her legitimacy had
come from taking arms against the invader. The two men were talking an
entirely different language: de Gaulle was making an historical argument,
Roosevelt a constitutional one, de Gaulle invoking 'legitimacy', Roosevelt
legality.

There was no further progress the next day (23 January). At a second
meeting with Giraud, when the latter suggested a kind of triumvirate of
himself, de Gaulle and another general, de Gaulle's caustic reply was: 'You
want to be First Consul? So where are your victories? Where is your plebiscite?' De Gaulle insisted that the precondition of any agreement must be
a formal condemnation of the armistice. Throughout the day advisers and
officials scurried anxiously from villa to villa trying to broker a deal. Feeling like a prisoner in the fenced compound of Anfa, de Gaulle smuggled
out an alarmist letter to a former Saint-Cyr student of his living in Casablanca. He warned him that the Americans were planning to 'establish in
North Africa and, if possible throughout the French Empire, and then in
France itself, a French authority that is completely beholden to them'. If
he found himself prevented from communicating with the outside world,
he wanted it known that he had not 'betrayed' the French. He ended by
comparing the atmosphere in Anfa to that of Berchtesgaden. He was presumably referring either to the occasion at Berchtesgaden in February 1938
when Hitler had bullied the Chancellor of Austria, Schuschnigg, into
accepting the *Anschluss,* or the one in September 1938 when he had bullied
Chamberlain into accepting the Munich Agreement. In both these analogies Roosevelt was Hitler.[39] The comparison might seem an example of de
Gaulle's paranoia except that even Oliver Harvey, de Gaulle's Foreign
Office admirer, had predicted that de Gaulle might be 'Muniched' at Anfa,
that is forced to accept an American diktat and subordinate himself to
Giraud.[40] But de Gaulle was made of sterner stuff than Schuschnigg or
Chamberlain.

Sunday 24 January was the last day of the conference. There was still
no agreement. On the previous evening British and American officials had
concocted a joint agreement for the two generals. De Gaulle refused to
sign. This led to a furious meeting between him and Churchill where the

latter said subsequently that he had been 'pretty rough' with the General, and the former that it was a meeting of 'extreme bitterness . . . the toughest of all our encounters'. Churchill threatened to denounce de Gaulle publicly; de Gaulle refused to budge an inch. But when arriving to take his leave of Roosevelt at noon, de Gaulle at the last minute agreed to shake Giraud's hand. As if by magic, photographers emerged out of the bushes to capture the moment for posterity – 'the long stiff-necked de Gaulle gingerly proffering his hand, though without the flicker of a smile'.[41] In the photographs the seated Roosevelt beams contentedly as the 'Bride' and 'Bridegroom' shake hands while looking past each other. The handshake saved the face of the Allied leaders. It was followed by the publication of a terse communiqué registering the fact that the two men had met and were both committed to liberation and the 'triumph of human liberties' (the phrase Giraud preferred to de Gaulle's 'democratic principles').[42]

Rarely had de Gaulle's force of personality been more tested than during these three days at Anfa. He had resisted the combined assault of Churchill, Roosevelt and their many advisers. Churchill told his doctor Charles Wilson, who accompanied him on the trip:

> 'His country has given up fighting, he himself is a refugee, and if we turn him down he is finished. Well, just look at him . . . He might be Stalin with 200 divisions behind him. I was pretty rough with him. I made it quite plain that if he could not be more helpful we were done with him.'
>
> 'How', I asked, 'did he like that?'
>
> 'Oh,' the PM replied, 'he hardly seemed interested. My advances and my threats met with no response.'
>
> Harry Hopkins had told me of the President's quip that de Gaulle claimed to be the lineal descendant of Joan of Arc. I repeated this to the PM. He was not amused. It did not seem at all absurd to him.[43]

Churchill's attitude to de Gaulle was always shot through with this mixture of exasperation and grudging admiration. Only his intervention prevented the conference being even more unfavourable to de Gaulle. Without informing Churchill, Roosevelt had signed a memorandum committing the Allied governments to the position that 'all the French fighting against Germany [should] be reunited under one authority' and recognizing Giraud as that authority – a total contradiction of his own policy that no *one* authority had the legitimacy to speak for France. When Churchill discovered this after the conference, he had the document amended, adding de Gaulle's name. For all his bouts of fury against de Gaulle, he felt an obligation to him. Or at least, if de Gaulle was to be dropped, he did not want the decision foisted upon him unknowingly.[44]

Returning to London de Gaulle called a press conference on 9 February putting his case uncompromisingly. His combative tone worried even the few committed supporters he had in Algiers like René Capitant.[45] Although de Gaulle now realized that Giraud was not going to give way gracefully, he returned from Anfa convinced that his rival was 'a ghost from 1939' with no understanding of how the war had changed the world – by which he meant that the Resistance in France would never accept this attempt to impose a pseudo-Vichyite government on the French.[46]

CHANNELLING GAULLISM

The political future of France was now being fought out in North Africa because what remained of the Vichy regime in mainland France had become a fiction. In the beginning a defender of Vichy could claim that the regime had salvaged three things from the shipwreck of defeat: an unoccupied zone in France, the Empire and the fleet. But these three successes had evaporated in the autumn of 1942. First, once the Germans had occupied all French territory in response to the American landings in North Africa, there was no longer a 'Free Zone'. Secondly, Vichy no longer controlled any of the French Empire: Equatorial Africa and the Levant had been lost to the Gaullists in 1940–41, Algeria and Morocco had been taken over by the Allies in November 1942, and a month later the Governor of French West Africa, Pierre Boisson, who had fired on de Gaulle at Dakar, switched sides and rallied to the Allies. Thirdly, the French fleet scuttled itself on 27 November when the Germans took over the port of Toulon. Vichy had no cards left to play. On the other hand, de Gaulle now had an unprecedented opportunity in North Africa to assemble a serious military force.

The conflict between Giraud and de Gaulle for control over that military force was not merely a clash of ambitions between two primadonna generals, as Roosevelt wanted to believe. There were fundamental principles at stake. Giraud was interested above all in bringing the French army back into the war. Providing the Americans were ready to arm it, he was not interested in making difficulties about politics. This suited Roosevelt perfectly. American policy was to deal on a case-by-case basis with whatever local French authorities were in place – without recognizing any of them as having the authority to speak for the French nation as a whole. For Roosevelt, France's defeat in 1940 meant that no one could rightfully claim to represent France. For de Gaulle the political question was central because accepting this provisional political void meant there would be no recognized authority to defend French national interests at the Liberation:

France would have the status of a defeated nation. For him, French troops of course had to play a role in victory at the side of the Allies, as Giraud wanted, but the key question was to set up a political French authority to which those troops would be answerable.

As he pondered his next move in London, de Gaulle was no longer virtually alone as in 1940. This was a strength but also meant that he had to take account of other opinions, of different factions trying to influence him. There was an intense debate among the Free French about how best to deal with Giraud. Among the most uncompromising was Billotte, head of de Gaulle's military *cabinet*. Knowing Giraud from before the war, Billotte argued that his vanity made him an easy prey for the Americans, who planned to set him up in France after the war so as to reduce France's influence in any post-war settlement: 'The healthy and active part of French opinion would never accept this Anglo-Saxon combination.'[47] Billotte had opposed de Gaulle going to Anfa, which he saw as an 'American Montoire'; Roosevelt in his view was a 'gangster with the smile of an angel'.[48] In the same uncompromising camp were Soustelle and Palewski. In the camp of conciliation were Catroux and Jacques Bingen, who argued that instead of alienating Giraud by pushing him to accept the political views of the Free French it would be preferable to reach a military agreement first and then win him over gradually.[49]

These more compromising voices were reinforced by the recent arrival in London of René Massigli, the highest-ranking diplomat to have rallied to de Gaulle. Number two at the Quai d'Orsay (the French Foreign Office) in the 1930s, he had fallen out of favour owing to his opposition to the appeasement of Germany. Not surprisingly in view of his past, he was dismissed by Vichy at the end of 1940. Initially he hoped Pétain might be brought back into the Allied camp and considered that de Gaulle's attacks on him were counter-productive. But by the end of 1942 Massigli had despaired of Pétain and was ready to take the plunge. He arrived in London in January 1943 where de Gaulle immediately offered him the post of Commissioner for External Affairs. Massigli hesitated for some days before accepting. The intransigence and Anglophobia of what he called the '*pur et dur*' Gaullists was contrary to all his instincts as a diplomat. In the end he accepted the offer, writing to his former chief, the violently anti-Gaullist Leger in Washington, that 'Gaullism properly channelled and reformed' represented France's only chance of survival.[50] But could Gaullism be 'channelled'?

Other new arrivals in London also felt out of place among the original Gaullists. This was true of the veteran Third Republic politician Henri Queuille, who reached London in April. Queuille was impressed by his first meeting with de Gaulle but alarmed by what he called the 'super-gaullists'.[51] Another arrival at the same moment was the high-ranking civil servant Pierre Laroque, who was shocked by how the 'original faithful hang on to their *chef* ... like vassals to a *seigneur*, a clan chief'. One of them told him that after Liberation the Gaullist movement would have to become a party: 'Perhaps de Gaulle does not want to go further but it is his duty. In any case the duty of the Gaullists is to be more Gaullist than de Gaulle.'[52]

Ultra-Gaullism was embodied in the editorials of the *La Marseillaise*. One theme since the events of November 1942 was extreme anti-Americanism – an editorial even compared the American 'occupation' of North Africa to France's occupation by Germany – accompanied by a revolutionary rhetoric of purity and revenge. As one article put it:

> Gaullism is a revolution of the young made by the young against the senile regime of the Marshal ... We were once alone, but this was the solitude which preserves religions at their genesis. We were alone like Robespierre ... There is behind Gaullism a force which outstrips it, and which impels it forward, and with which those who think it is just a burst of national pride are going to have to deal.[53]

Another feature of this intransigent Gaullism was suspicion of the political parties accused of having betrayed France in 1940. This was the theme launched by Brossolette's controversial article in *La Marseillaise* in September 1942. De Gaulle's 'Republican' turn in 1942 left open many questions regarding his views on France's political future. One Socialist resister arriving in France was startled to be told by de Gaulle that the disappearance of the political parties in post-war France was inevitable.[54] It was in this context that Raymond Aron published an article in the London-based periodical *France libre* in August 1943 invoking the 'shadow of the Bonapartes', which was headed by a cautionary epigraph from Napoleon III: 'the nature of democracy is to be personified in a man'.[55] The article did not mention de Gaulle by name but there was no doubt that de Gaulle was its target.

DE GAULLE V. THE RESISTANCE

How would de Gaulle choose between those like Massigli, Catroux and others hoping to make him less 'Gaullist' and those like Billotte, Soustelle and the team at *La Marseillaise* hoping to make him more 'Gaullist'? De Gaulle himself rarely used the word 'Gaullism' and his choices were guided by that pragmatism – his doctrine of 'circumstances' – which always mitigated his intransigence.

In the battle to prove his legitimacy to the Allies, de Gaulle came to see that the old political parties so despised by the 'super-Gaullists' could be a useful weapon. He had been happy to solicit the support of respected politicians like Mandel and Blum but the parties had not previously counted in his eyes. This now began to change, especially in regard to the Socialist Party. Unlike the Communist Party, which had its own specific Resistance organizations, the Socialists, although they had reorganized their party underground from 1941, had no distinct Resistance movement of their own. Increasingly the Socialists who joined Resistance organizations as individuals worried that their contribution as Socialists was unrecognized. They risked being squeezed between the non-Communist Resistance movements on one hand and the Communists on the other. For this reason, Socialist resisters began to lobby for some recognition of their collective contribution to the Resistance through the creation of an institution including representatives of political parties as well as Resistance movements.[56] Three Socialist resisters arrived in London in January to lobby de Gaulle in person. The document they presented to him stated the case clearly:

> Can Fighting France ignore the existence of parties or must it accept them as a fact? . . . De Gaulle necessarily needs an intermediary between himself and the French masses . . . The Resistance cannot play this role alone . . . De Gaulle, if one can use such a brutal expression, is looking for France. France is looking for de Gaulle. The geometrical point of that encounter can only be in an association of the movements and the political parties.[57]

De Gaulle quickly took the point. Three weeks later – on the same day as sending a warm message to the Central Committee of the Communist Party – he wrote to Daniel Mayer, leader of the underground Socialist Party, that he accepted his party's 'legitimate ambitions' and that the Resistance should accommodate 'diverse and traditional political tendencies'.[58]

What this meant in practice was worked out when Moulin, whom de Gaulle had not seen for over a year, returned to London on 14 February. Moulin had independently reached the conclusion that concessions needed to be made to the Socialists and that the old political parties could be used to reinforce de Gaulle's legitimacy in the face of the Allies.[59] He proposed the creation of a body – eventually to be dubbed the National Council of the Resistance (Conseil National de la Résistance – CNR) – to include representatives of both the Resistance movements and political parties, even those which had played no role in the Resistance. After a month in London, Moulin was sent back to France on 19 March with 'new instructions' which he had played a key role in drafting. He was now de Gaulle's sole delegate to the whole of France – both the former 'Free Zone', as previously, and the former Occupied Zone – with a mission to set up the Resistance council he had proposed. De Gaulle would never see him again.

Moulin's task was complicated by the fact that Resistance leaders despised the old political parties for having let France down in 1940. Although rallying to de Gaulle as a 'symbol', they were wary of any encroachment on their autonomy. Frenay was among the most reticent. He had arrived in London for the first time in September 1942, and was there when the Americans landed in North Africa. His three months in London showed him that de Gaulle needed the movements almost as much as they needed him. Before returning to France, he lunched with de Gaulle, Passy and Soustelle at the Savoy. They discussed the future relationship between de Gaulle and the Resistance movements. 'What will happen', asked Frenay, 'if we cannot agree with Rex [the pseudonym of Moulin]?' De Gaulle replied: 'You will come back here and we will try to find a solution.' 'If that proves to be impossible?' 'In that case, France will have to decide between you and me.'[60]

When this conversation took place, the bone of contention was not yet the CNR but the control and deployment of the single Secret Army into which Moulin had persuaded the Resistance movements to merge their military forces. Frenay hoped to be appointed its commander, but this was not acceptable to the leaders of the other movements. Instead they settled on a compromise candidate from outside the Resistance, the retired senior General Charles Delestraint. He had supported de Gaulle's ideas on tanks in the 1930s but had no direct experience of the Resistance. This set Frenay's mind at rest. He assumed Delestraint would just be a figurehead while the Resistance organizations retained control. De Gaulle's instructions to Delestraint were that the Secret Army must remain in reserve until he gave the order to act. He feared that premature action might result in a blood-bath or anarchy, or both.

This *attentiste* position became harder to sustain in March 1943 when a major crisis blew up in France. The Vichy government, under pressure to provide labour for German factories, had instituted a compulsory labour draft (Service du Travail Obligatoire – STO). Thousands of young men fled their homes to avoid being called up. Many of these *réfractaires* who refused the labour draft service took refuge in the countryside where they formed the first bands of rural *maquisard* resisters, named after the *maquis* scrubland of the hills of southern France. This offered the existing Resistance organizations a massive reservoir of potential recruits impatient to act. But Resistance leaders also feared that de Gaulle's veto against premature action might demoralize these men and drive them into the hands of the Communists who were in favour of immediate action. De Gaulle used the STO crisis to ask Churchill to arm up to 50,000 resisters. Churchill refused because he did not have the means – nor the desire – to encourage premature action of this kind.[61] This is certainly the reply de Gaulle had expected, and probably wanted, but in France the Resistance leaders suspected they were being deliberately starved of funds by de Gaulle, acting through Moulin, to tighten the Free French grip upon them.

   None of this simplified Moulin's task of persuading Resistance leaders to join a body with representatives of political parties. His relations with the Resistance leaders became increasingly tense, sometimes violently acrimonious; nerves frayed as the Germans intensified their repression of the Resistance and every meeting was overshadowed by the fear of arrest or betrayal. To achieve his ends, Moulin was able to play upon the rivalries between the Resistance leaders. Frenay and d'Astier, very dissimilar personalities – the one rigid and self-righteous, the other concealing his ambition under annoyingly languid charm – were locked in competition with each other to be acknowledged as the most important Resistance leader. Jean-Pierre Lévy, leader of Franc-Tireur, the other important movement of the former Unoccupied Zone, while sharing the general suspicion of the political parties, was more emollient, had less *amour-propre* and occasionally acted as honest broker. An additional problem for Moulin was the fact that Pierre Brossolette was pursuing a different policy from him – also supposedly in de Gaulle's name. Brossolette had been sent from London on a mission, with Passy, to coordinate the military activities of the Resistance movements in the north (the former Occupied Zone) where Resistance unity was less advanced than in the south. He saw himself as the boss of the north, the counterpart to Moulin in the south. But Moulin's 'new instructions', drafted after Brossolette's departure from London, had promoted him to being de Gaulle's delegate for all of France. Before Moulin arrived back in France with his increased authority and new instructions, Brossolette set about putting his own stamp on the organization of the Resistance in the north. He entirely shared the suspicion of the Resistance leaders regarding the old political parties. When Moulin returned to France, he had violent arguments in Paris with Brossolette, whom he accused of sabotaging his mission.

   The ingredients were in place for a major crisis in the relations between de Gaulle and the Resistance just when the General needed to rally maximum support behind his name. In April, Lévy and d'Astier arrived in London to launch a concerted campaign against the 'bureaucratization' of the Resistance.[62] 'Bureaucratization' was a coded attack on Moulin's attempt to bring the Resistance under Gaullist authority. In early May, Moulin fought back with a long report defending himself. The atmosphere was so poisonous that Moulin took the precaution of having this report delivered personally to de Gaulle rather than through the BCRA (since Passy was a close ally of Brossolette). Having discovered that Frenay was in touch with the American secret services in Switzerland about finding extra sources of funding for the Resistance, Moulin put the worst possible complexion on this, suggesting that Frenay was preparing to ditch de Gaulle in favour of Giraud. It was in Moulin's interest to present things in this way, but it was probably not true. Frenay was certainly trying to claw back some financial autonomy from de Gaulle, and he may have blinded himself to the risks of these contacts with the Americans, but he was certainly not intending to defect to Giraud.[63]

We do not know what de Gaulle thought about these quarrels. His *Memoirs* rarely descend from the 'summits' where he gazed upon the destiny of France to the contingent squabbles of personalities, and the archives tell us little more. Carlton Gardens was riven with conflict in relation to this crisis, but we rarely find evidence of de Gaulle intervening directly. Moulin's insinuations about Frenay's American contacts are likely to have touched a chord with de Gaulle, as they were intended to do. On the other hand, there are indications that de Gaulle was wondering if Moulin was being too tough on the Resistance. Bingen wrote to André Philip some months later recalling that, faced by the onslaught of complaints from the Resistance leaders, Philip and de Gaulle had been 'inclining to arbitrate between Rex and the movements' rather than defending Moulin outright.[64] If de Gaulle did briefly wobble in his support for Moulin, it was because he so desperately needed the support of the Resistance at this time. Presumably with the General's approval, Philip wrote to Moulin on 10 May suggesting he might have gone a 'bit too fast down the road of centralization'.[65] De Gaulle was even ready to concede ground on the control of the Secret Army. On 21 May he sent a 'personal and secret instruction' to Delestraint accepting the principle of immediate action to be decided by the Resistance movements themselves – a tactical retreat in the wider cause of bringing the Resistance leaders to accept the CNR.[66]

LONDON V. ALGIERS

If de Gaulle was ready to make these tactical concessions it was because his negotiations with Giraud were proving more difficult than he had originally anticipated. On 23 February, two days after de Gaulle had signed his 'new instructions' to Moulin, the National Committee in London published a memorandum setting out its conditions for unity with Giraud. Its starting point was the need for a single committee uniting all the forces fighting for French liberation while excluding anyone with 'large personal responsibility' in defending the armistice. This targeted figures like Noguès, Peyrouton and Boisson, who were all part of Giraud's team. De Gaulle was pitching for unity in Algiers on his terms.[67]

Catroux had managed to have himself appointed as de Gaulle's negotiator in Algiers despite the hesitation of the ultra-Gaullists.[68] De Gaulle accepted because at this stage he remained confident that Giraud would concede. His 'mood of brooding and righteousness' reminded Peake 'of nothing so much as a tiger who, having feasted, has the taste of raw meat in his mouth and knows exactly where the next meal is coming from. I confess I do not like him like this.'[69] While awaiting the result of Catroux's negotiations, de Gaulle hoped that he might be allowed to visit his African territories, but Churchill refused him permission to leave the country. When Peake formally conveyed this news, de Gaulle replied icily: 'So I am a prisoner.' He announced that he would take no further part in the activities of the National Committee and retired to Hampstead. This tactic, successful against Muselier a year earlier, cut no ice this time. Churchill, delighted to have de Gaulle out of the way, phoned Peake to hold him responsible for ensuring that the 'Monster of Hampstead' did not escape. Realizing that his 'strike' had backfired, de Gaulle returned to Carlton Gardens after a week. He saved face by claiming that the STO crisis in France required his attention. Even de Gaulle knew when to give ground.

For the moment, he was condemned to watch events in Algiers from the sidelines. His interventions were erratic. At some moments, he was desperate to go to Algiers, especially when Giraud wanted to keep him away; at others, when it looked as if Giraud would allow him to come, he worried about walking into a trap. He was perpetually worried that Catroux could not be trusted to stand firm. The situation in Algiers was complicated by the fact that both Churchill and Roosevelt had also sent representatives to Algiers. The British emissary was the Conservative MP Harold Macmillan. De Gaulle, with no idea of Macmillan's brief, was initially suspicious. In fact Macmillan quickly got the measure of Giraud's inadequacies, viewing him as 'an old-fashioned, but charming colonel, who would grace the Turf Club'.[70] On the American side was Robert Murphy, a conservative diplomat who detested de Gaulle – another Admiral Leahy. Less easy to pin down was another American envoy, Jean Monnet. Since leaving London in June 1940, Monnet had become a remarkably influential player on the

American scene. He knew every major figure in the Roosevelt administration and had played a role in elaborating the Lend-Lease programme. Roosevelt, aware of the difficulties in 'selling' the reactionary Giraud to American public opinion, sent Monnet on a mission to Algiers to instil some political sense into Giraud. Monnet remained as suspicious of de Gaulle as he had been in 1940. If someone of his democratic and liberal convictions was ready to support Giraud over de Gaulle, it was because Giraud claimed that his only objective was to bring the French army back into the war. De Gaulle, despite his democratic rhetoric, clearly had political ambitions even if he had promised that once France was liberated the people would be consulted over their political future.[71] But did he mean it? Not knowing the answer to this question Monnet was ready to accept that the 'apolitical', although conservative, Giraud might be less of a threat to democracy than the clearly 'political', if supposedly democratic, de Gaulle.

Under Monnet's influence, on 14 March Giraud delivered what he later called the 'first democratic speech of my life'.[72] He paid homage to the Resistance and declared his respect for the Republic. He drew the line, however, at Monnet's recommendation that he promise to re-establish the French citizenship of the Jews of Algeria which had been revoked by the Vichy regime. Even so Giraud's speech was a sensational event, and he followed it up by inviting de Gaulle to come to Algiers. De Gaulle and Catroux could not have reacted to Giraud's speech more differently. For Catroux, it was a positive sign that Giraud had made 'a great step in our direction'; for de Gaulle it was an attempt by Giraud to 'paint himself in democratic colours and drive us into a corner'.[73] He insisted Giraud provide a formal response to the National Committee's memorandum, not just a speech.

In the meantime, de Gaulle tried to gauge the mood of public opinion in North Africa. He wrote to a member of Catroux's negotiating team to find out if his arrival in Algeria would unleash a popular movement of enthusiasm. He wanted an open-top car prepared for him since 'the shock of public demonstrations' would be crucial.[74] The austere and cerebral soldier was every day honing his new role as a democratic tribune. The answer from Algiers was not encouraging. It warned de Gaulle against thinking he could force union on Giraud through the pressure of Algerian public opinion, which was far from Gaullist.[75] This only whetted de Gaulle's desire to leave immediately and show himself. For this he needed the consent of the British.

On 2 April, after weeks of heroic diplomacy by Massigli, de Gaulle and Churchill had their first meeting since Anfa.[76] It went off surprisingly well. The main point of conflict was de Gaulle's insistence that he could not join any committee which included individuals compromised at a high level with Vichy. When Churchill said that he had invited former political opponents like Chamberlain and Halifax into a coalition government, de Gaulle reasonably responded that the situations were hardly analogous. Neither Halifax nor Chamberlain had fired on Churchill, as Boisson had done on de Gaulle at Dakar, or been members of a government that had put him on trial, as was true of Peyrouton. To Churchill's remark that Boisson had been helpful to the Allies, de Gaulle responded: 'The only question is whether or not Governor Boisson has served France.'[77] Nonetheless, Churchill agreed that de Gaulle could go to Algiers. But two days later, as he was about to leave, de Gaulle was informed that General Eisenhower, the American commander in North Africa, wanted his departure delayed. American forces were engaged in fierce fighting with the German troops that had been sent to Tunisia soon after the American landings in Algeria and Morocco. Eisenhower's pretext for delaying de Gaulle's arrival was that he wanted no political distractions until the Germans had been definitively driven out of North Africa. This threw de Gaulle into a rage since he assumed that Churchill was behind the decision to keep him trapped in London. Even his suspicious nature had not enabled him to guess the truth: Eisenhower's intervention had been prompted by Catroux, who felt de Gaulle's presence would be counter-productive for his negotiations with Giraud.[78]

Catroux arrived in London on 9 April with Giraud's response to the National Committee's memorandum of 23 February. This document, drafted by Monnet, conceded some ground. It accepted the idea of a unified committee to administer liberated French territories under the chairmanship of a 'Civil and Military Commander in Chief' (obviously Giraud). Quite apart from the pre-eminent role this gave to Giraud, the proposal failed to meet de Gaulle's central point that there needed to be a *political* authority – a government in all but name – to defend French national interests, not just a body to administer territories as they were liberated. Catroux was struck in London by the fact that everyone around de Gaulle was 'completely fixated on France, that is the Resistance', while he was having to deal with the realities of Algiers where 'the opinion of France is not necessarily sovereign'.[79] During his stay in London he unburdened himself to Eden, who found him more openly critical of de Gaulle than ever before. He bemoaned the fact that the only people who had influence with de Gaulle were 'those who encouraged him down the path which he wished to tread' – especially Palewski. Since the only way to deal with de Gaulle was by threats, Catroux said he had been offering his resignation on a regular basis. If de Gaulle did not moderate his position, he was tempted to throw in his lot with Giraud. Eden could only agree that it was a pity de Gaulle ignored the truth that he and Churchill had 'throughout our political lives based our policies on friendship with France and seemed instead to suspect that we had no desire in life but to trick and weaken Frenchmen'.[80]

Before returning to Algiers, Catroux had persuaded de Gaulle to accept the idea of a single committee run as a duumvirate under the alternating presidency of himself and Giraud. He returned to Algiers to sell this idea to Giraud. Meanwhile de Gaulle reverted to threats when he received General Bouscat, an emissary of Giraud. He gave Bouscat a message to take back to Algiers: 'If no agreement is reached, too bad! All France is with me ... Giraud should look out! ... Even if he eventually goes to France victorious but without me they will fire on him ... France is Gaullist, fiercely Gaullist.'[81] A week later he intensified the pressure, telling Bouscat: 'Who is Giraud? What does he represent? He has no one behind him. It could all be simple ... I arrive by plane. I head for the Palais d'Eté [seat of the Governor]. On the journey the crowds cheer me ... The two of us go on to the balcony. Union is sealed. It is all over.'[82] De Gaulle also tried to stir up Gaullist opinion in North Africa through André Peladon, an envoy sent by the BCRA. This annoyed Catroux, who believed that since Gaullists were 'only a small fraction of opinion' in Algeria this would only make Giraud dig his heels in more.[83] Catroux was close to breaking point when told of de Gaulle's fantasy about the open-top car, which also alarmed Monnet.[84] He was so hostile to de Gaulle at this time that the British thought he was planning to double-cross him, proposing himself as a compromise between the two generals. Catroux's ambitious wife, who much obsessed the British, was rumoured to be pushing him in this direction.[85]

In truth the conflict between de Gaulle and Catroux was essentially about tactics: those of a populist tribune against those of a French Whig – as Macmillan aptly described Catroux.[86] Catroux was certainly more attuned to Giraud's psychology than de Gaulle was, and Macmillan also helped him to whittle down Giraud's resistance. When urging Giraud to accept Catroux's idea of a duumvirate he found him in 'stubborn, egotistical and even defiant mood ... He is so naive but also so stately and stupid.'[87] But at the end of April Giraud finally cracked. He accepted the duumvirate and proposed that other outstanding issues be settled directly between himself and de Gaulle in person. It seemed that de Gaulle could now head for Algiers.

One detail remained to be settled: where would the two generals meet? Giraud proposed the remote town of Biskra in the Sahara because he feared that in Algiers de Gaulle would be buoyed up by the crowds. This was exactly what de Gaulle wanted. Still dreaming of his open-top car, de Gaulle worried that in a remote locality like Biskra he would be vulnerable to pressure from Giraud's American backers. He expressed the problem in his inimitable style, telling one of his aides: 'We are living a revolution and in such periods half-measures are not possible ... Can you imagine Clovis, Joan of Arc, Danton or Clemenceau going to Biskra? If I went, America's conditions would be forced upon me.'[88] Catroux argued that de Gaulle should not risk everything on such a trivial issue. Macmillan felt the same: 'the trouble is, that even if you stack the cards and give de Gaulle four aces and a joker, he still throws in his hand and will not make a bet.'[89]

De Gaulle raised the stakes in a speech at Grosvenor House on 4 May. Massigli pleaded with him to be conciliatory: 'Do not say anything that could make Giraud fear that we want unity to absorb him first and then eliminate him. You should even flatter him. Do not risk compromising everything by making too much of this issue of the meeting place.'[90] De Gaulle did the opposite. His speech painted a sarcastic picture of Algiers in thrall to Pétainism and refused an invitation to discuss the future of France in a remote oasis.[91] The 'pur et dur' Gaullists in London were delighted. Soustelle recalled with relish in his memoirs 'Massigli's shattered expression ... his complexion more bilious than ever'.[92] The appalled Catroux was yet again on the verge of resigning, but Massigli pleaded with him to stay, although there was little help he could offer: 'I have become suspect here ... But as long as there is a chance of avoiding a rupture I will struggle on however bitter the pill I have to swallow.'[93] No one was more outraged than Monnet: 'The perfect example of a Hitlerian speech and methods ... The conclusion must be that an agreement with him is impossible; that he is an enemy of the French people and its liberties ... That in consequence he must be destroyed in the interest of the French, the Allies and peace.'[94] But two days later de Gaulle, following his favourite tactic of blowing hot and cold, or possibly fearing he had gone too far, sent a conciliatory message to Giraud assuring him that he would not allow any 'inappropriate demonstrations' in Algiers – an assurance Giraud would have been foolish to believe.[95]

Two factors encouraged de Gaulle to hold his ground. The first was that troops from the regular French army in North Africa had starting defecting to the Free French forces of Leclerc. In November 1942, de Gaulle had ordered Leclerc to move north from Chad through the Fezzan Desert in southern Libya and join up with the British Seventh Army at Tripoli on the North African coast. With 4,700 men and 780 vehicles Leclerc crossed the 5,000 kilometres of desert and arrived in Tripoli in late January. The British government had not been keen because it did not think it could make much use of Leclerc's force. But it agreed to the operation providing that on his march north Leclerc did not attempt to take over the Fezzan region on behalf of the French. De Gaulle graciously conceded and then ignored his promise. Each oasis that Leclerc passed was put under French administration. De Gaulle was anticipating that once the war was over he could absorb the Fezzan, part of Italian Libya, into French Chad – a remarkably bold stroke of imperial expansion from someone with barely a division at his disposal. Although annoyed, the British decided not to make an issue of it. Quarrelling with de Gaulle was an exhausting business and they comforted themselves with the idea that the Touareg population of the region was ethnically closer to the population of Chad than to the Arabs of Libya. As one official minuted: 'As General de Gaulle is so tiresome, I should be inclined not to treat with him but to let the position remain as it is, de facto French occupation, and leave the final settlement to the Peace Settlement.'[96]

Whatever his long-term objectives, for de Gaulle the main purpose in sending Leclerc through Libya was to ensure that the Free French – and not only the regular French army under Giraud – played a role in what was proving to be a tough battle against the Germans in Tunisia. Although the 13,000 Free French troops were greatly outnumbered by 'Giraud's' regular French troops, they had acquired a glorious reputation thanks to Leclerc's heroic exploits. Once the battle was over Leclerc refused to allow his men to march alongside the regular French forces in the victory parade in Tunis on 20 May. He joined the British troops instead. It was against this background that troops from the regular army started defecting to the Free French. De Gaulle formally instructed Leclerc to accept these 'deserters' (as the Giraudists called them), overruling Catroux who feared another unnecessary provocation of Giraud. The defections – euphemistically described as 'voluntary change of assignment' (changement volontaire d'affectation) by the Gaullists – were not enormous in number (about 2,750 at most), but they received much publicity and added to the impression that Giraud's prestige was crumbling.

The second factor encouraging de Gaulle to hold out was the imminence of an agreement over the CNR in France. On 14 May, a telegram arrived from Moulin announcing that he had at last secured an agreement from the Resistance on the CNR. Soustelle immediately published a communiqué falsely alleging that the CNR had already met and declared its allegiance to de Gaulle. In his Memoirs de Gaulle presents this as the decisive event in overcoming Giraud's resistance. The coincidence of dates might suggest he was right: on 17 May, Giraud finally agreed to meet de Gaulle in Algiers – not Biskra. In reality Giraud's final concession owed more to the persuasive powers of Catroux and Macmillan. If anything, the news about the CNR was calculated to increase Giraud's resistance by making it seem as if he was succumbing to external pressure; Macmillan did not think it worth mentioning the CNR in his diary; Catroux and Massigli both found the announcement unhelpful.[97] There is little evidence that it made any difference except in encouraging de Gaulle to hold firm.

De Gaulle formally accepted Giraud's conditions on 21 May. What de Gaulle did not know was that, just as he seemed to have achieved his goal, Churchill was closer to breaking with him than ever before. Since 11 May, the Prime Minister had been in Washington where Roosevelt dripped his anti-de Gaulle poison into him. He reported back to London: 'Hardly a day passes that the President does not mention him to me.' Churchill also met Leger, who warned him that 'while affecting Communist sympathies [de Gaulle] had Fascist tendencies'. Churchill asked if Leger might be ready to head a French Committee in London: 'We need you. All the men in London are too frightened of de Gaulle. Massigli is feeble and frightened of him.' Leger's response was that it was necessary to 'depersonalize Gaullism without making de Gaulle a martyr'.[98] After these exceedingly implausible speculations Churchill wired the Cabinet that it was time to break with de Gaulle but not the French National Committee (an impossible aspiration).[99] At a special meeting on the evening of Sunday 23 May the Cabinet overruled Churchill on the grounds that 'it is the name of de Gaulle alone that counts for the *résistants*' even if 'the de Gaulle they are following is obviously a semi-mystical figure who is very different from the de Gaulle we know'.[100]

There was no further impediment to de Gaulle leaving. As for the CNR, it met in conditions of ultra-secrecy on 27 May in a flat in the Rue du Four on the Paris Left Bank. Under the chairmanship of Jean Moulin, eight Resistance leaders and the representatives of eight political parties supported a motion calling for a provisional government to be established under the leadership of de Gaulle. By the time the news reached London on 4 June, de Gaulle was already in Algiers.

'BETWEEN A MADMAN AND AN ASS'

Accompanied by Philip, Massigli, Palewski and Billotte, de Gaulle landed near Algiers at midday on 30 May. Catroux and Giraud were present to greet him, with the British and American representatives standing behind them. Although the 'Marseillaise' was played and French flags were in evidence – unlike at Anfa six months earlier – the occasion was low key.

In the car driving them to the Palais d'Eté where an official lunch had been laid on, de Gaulle and Giraud had a frosty exchange:

'Who are your people on the Committee,' asked de Gaulle; 'mine are Philip and Massigli.'
'Jean Monnet.'
'That little financier in the pay of the British . . .'
'And General Georges.'
'. . . He was not much good [*assez moche*] in the war . . . I want to eliminate Noguès, Peyrouton, Boisson.'
'We will see. But one must say "we" and not "I". I presume you are going to see Eisenhower tomorrow.'
'Not on your life! I am in France here. I will go to see him if he first comes to see me.'[101]

At lunch, Giraud and de Gaulle sat opposite each other with their teams around them. The protagonists eyed each other up warily. De Gaulle writes of this moment: 'Thus were reunited all those Frenchmen, so different, and yet so much alike, whom the tide of events had swept to such different shores and who now seemed just as restless and sure of themselves as they had been before the drama began!'[102] Among those present was the aged General Georges, whom Churchill had plucked out of retirement. Georges had been an enemy of de Gaulle in the 1930s and Churchill hoped he might be a counterweight to him now.

Although de Gaulle complained in his *Memoirs* that his arrival was hidden from the population – no open-top car! – and although Catroux had advised discretion, Capitant's Combat movement had organized a demonstration in his honour at the Algiers war memorial in the afternoon. De Gaulle appeared and raised his arms in a V – a gesture that would become a trademark of his crowd appearances. Arriving at his villa, he found it stuffed with microphones – whether by the Giraudists, the Americans or the British – and had them removed.[103] That evening de Gaulle met Monnet for the first time since June 1940. Monnet told Macmillan that de Gaulle's mood veered from 'comparative calm to extreme excitability', denouncing the 'Anglo-Saxons' and shouting that after the war France would have to lean towards Germany and Russia. Monnet could not decide if de Gaulle was 'a dangerous demagogue or mad or both'.[104] This may have stirred memories of their dinner on 17 June 1940 when de Gaulle had railed against Pétain. Mad or not, on that previous occasion de Gaulle's judgement of Pétain had been far more perceptive than Monnet's turned out to be.

The next morning (31 May) was the first meeting of the bicephalous

French Committee of National Liberation (CFLN). Each co-President had been allowed to select two members. Giraud chose Georges and Monnet, de Gaulle Philip and Massigli. Since Catroux was also a member in his own right, de Gaulle had a built-in majority. He could have bided his time and gradually imposed his authority, but this was not his style. He opened the meeting by demanding that the Committee immediately accept two principles: the military commander must be subordinate to civil authority – in other words Giraud to de Gaulle – and all high-ranking officials tarnished by association with Vichy must be dismissed. Monnet, Catroux and Massigli tried to mediate by proposing that the Committee delay discussing substantive issues until it had established its working procedures. Thereupon de Gaulle stood up, snapped his briefcase shut and left the room, slamming the door behind him.[105]

The next day, de Gaulle gave his version of events to Macmillan. This was Macmillan's first exposure to him. He found that de Gaulle 'spoke of himself as a separate power'; his villa was like 'the court of a visiting monarch'. The General told Macmillan that Georges was 'old gentleman' completely out of touch and Monnet 'a good man, but more of an internationalist than a Frenchman'. He then launched into his theme of the moment that France was experiencing a revolution: 'Just as the Royalist Army after 1789 was torn in conflict and divided loyalties, so had the French Army been. It must be renewed by the spirit of the revolution. It must be officered by the young and untried men. All these old generals must be got rid of.' Macmillan's overall impression was that, whether demagogue or madman, de Gaulle was a 'more powerful character than any other Frenchman' he had yet met.[106]

That evening, knowingly or not, de Gaulle sparked a mini-crisis. The former Vichy Minister Marcel Peyrouton, realizing that his time was up (or hoping to cause mischief), wrote to de Gaulle resigning from his post as Governor General of Algeria. De Gaulle, without consulting Giraud, issued a communiqué accepting this resignation. Giraud responded with an unhinged letter accusing de Gaulle of wanting to 'establish in France a regime copied from Nazism, backed up by the SS'.[107] This had been drafted by André Labarthe, the London anti-Gaullist who had fetched up in Algiers to offer his services to Giraud. Over the past five months Giraud had become a kind of magnet for de Gaulle's trail of embittered and defeated enemies. Another was Admiral Muselier, whom Giraud had appointed chief of police. The atmosphere was thick with rumours: Giraud believed the Gaullists were planning a putsch; de Gaulle feared that Giraud's men might arrive at any moment to seize him in his villa.[108]

On 2 June, Catroux, Macmillan and Massigli worked feverishly behind

the scenes to defuse the crisis. Catroux told Macmillan that he found himself 'between a madman and an ass'. Macmillan dissuaded him from
resigning.[109] By the end of the day, de Gaulle was ready to lower the temperature, a familiar tactic in his overall strategy of intimidation. He wrote
to Giraud proposing that the Committee reconvene the next morning. On
this occasion (3 June), de Gaulle was all smiles. The meeting adopted the
same anodyne draft that had been ready on the first day. The controversial
issues that de Gaulle had raised at the start were left for another occasion.
At the end, de Gaulle went around the table shaking everyone's hand and
embraced Giraud. Churchill reported to Roosevelt that the outcome was
satisfactory. If de Gaulle 'proves violent or unreasonable' he would find
himself isolated in a minority of five to two.[110] It is not clear how Churchill
reached this calculation, which was the opposite of the truth. Or perhaps
he had knowingly massaged the truth to keep Roosevelt happy. Despite
his intermittent bouts of rage against de Gaulle, which were entirely genuine, Churchill's attitude to him was more complicated than it seemed. The
only occasion when he had formally suggested to his ministers breaking
with de Gaulle was sparked off by his desire to curry favour with Roosevelt
and was made in the certain knowledge that he would be overruled. Equally
it is striking that after Anfa, when Roosevelt had tried behind his back to
omit de Gaulle's name from the memorandum he planned to sign with
Giraud, Churchill had intervened to prevent this. At some level Churchill,
instinctively Francophile in a way that Roosevelt was not, probably
accepted that France's interests were in some way embodied in de Gaulle –
the man he had impulsively backed in 1940.

On 7 June, it was agreed to increase the membership of the Committee
to fourteen. Day by day, de Gaulle was nibbling away at Giraud's power.
While his new nominees – Diethelm, Tixier and Pleven – were loyal to him,
Giraud's were pragmatic figures whose allegiance to him was not unconditional. This was true, for example, of the brilliant civil servant Maurice
Couve de Murville. Couve was an official in the Ministry of Finance who
had served Vichy as long as he believed the regime could be used to defend
French interests from Germany. Having lost faith in Pétain he had arrived
in Algiers to put himself at Giraud's service but had no special loyalty to
him. Even Monnet, who had been so hostile to de Gaulle a few weeks
earlier, and certainly remained suspicious of his future political ambitions,
was coming to realize that he was of an altogether different stature from
Giraud. So de Gaulle could have bided his time while waiting for his nominees on the Committee to arrive from London. Instead he went on the
offensive again. On 9 June, he sent the Committee a letter criticizing the
anomaly by which one co-President (Giraud) was also Commander in

Chief. Until the matter was resolved, he announced that he was withdrawing from the Committee. He claimed implausibly that he would happily renounce politics and take command of a tank division.[111] The work of the Committee was suspended.

These were standard tactics in de Gaulle's repertoire of intimidation. Macmillan was not taken in: 'My impression is that he was rather enjoying the commotion he had raised ... there is a certain element of mischief in him which makes him enjoy scenes. He was quite friendly and even amusing.'[112] On the fourth day of this new crisis (14 June), Macmillan and de Gaulle spent the afternoon at the small seaside town of Tipasa where Macmillan liked to swim. Macmillan plunged into the water naked while de Gaulle sat on a rock draped in his uniform and his dignity. Macmillan wrote of their afternoon:

> Spent three-and-a-half hours of driving, walking in the ruins, and continuous talk with this strange – attractive and yet impossible – character. We talked on every conceivable subject – politics, religion, philosophy, the classics, history (ancient and modern) and so on. All was more or less related to the things which fill his mind ... The only trouble was that while we were walking in the ruins we were recognised. The word went round and a little crowd collected in the village, which cheered him wildly and demanded a speech. This is very bad for him![113]

The letter de Gaulle wrote to his wife that evening does not show a man who was about to give up politics. He told her that 'we are advancing' despite the 'atmosphere of lies and false news', and that she would be able to join him shortly.[114]

The next day, as if nothing had happened, de Gaulle announced that he was ready to rejoin the Committee since all members had arrived from London. Now Roosevelt, informed by Murphy, suddenly realized that, after only ten days, de Gaulle was close to assuming full control of the Committee. In what one Foreign Office diplomat described as a 'hysterical diatribe', Roosevelt wrote to Churchill on 17 June suggesting – again – that the time had come to break with de Gaulle entirely.[115] Eisenhower was instructed to tell de Gaulle that French North Africa was occupied territory and the Americans would permit no weakening of Giraud's authority. This was exactly the wrong tactic. Not for the first time, de Gaulle had goaded his adversaries into such an extreme reaction that even those who deplored his methods felt obliged to rally around him. Overt foreign intervention was guaranteed to cement French unity.

Eisenhower, with no desire to become mixed up in politics, reluctantly summoned Giraud and de Gaulle to see him on 19 June. De Gaulle refused to give ground and threatened to announce on the radio that he was being pressurized by 'foreign interference'. Macmillan, who was in the next room, observed: 'De Gaulle left first, evidently in a great rage – I think partly simulated . . . Giraud left a few minutes later, dignified but flushed. Eisenhower seemed rather taken aback by de Gaulle's powerful personality (he had never seen him "in action" before) . . .'[116] Behind the scenes British officials were working – against Churchill – in de Gaulle's interest. Churchill had instructed on 19 June that he would continue to fund the Resistance only providing it did not fall under the 'control of de Gaulle and his satellites'. But Lord Selbourne of SOE got the decision reversed: 'Giraud counts for very little indeed in France. The name of Georges is mud. The name of anyone else in power in 1940 is manure.' If de Gaulle left the CFLN 'it is very likely the Resistance Movements . . . would disintegrate.'[117]

On 22 June, the Committee accepted a compromise negotiated by Monnet. Giraud remained Commander in Chief of the North African Army and joint head of the Committee. De Gaulle was granted theoretically equal status as commander of the rest of the French forces (that is, the Free French). Each force would have a separate General Staff. This hybrid solution retained the existing duumvirate between Giraud and de Gaulle and embedded it in the two armies. But the crucial point was that the overall organization of the armed forces was entrusted to a single military committee chaired by de Gaulle. As de Gaulle reported to Carlton Gardens, this 'provisional compromise' offered the prospect of 'precipitating the internal dislocation' of Giraud's forces as the first step to creating a unified army.[118]

De Gaulle was now sure enough of his own position to invite his wife on 24 June to come and join him: 'I am alone against America and only America . . . All the reptiles in hock to the State Department and poor old Churchill are screaming and frothing at the mouth.'[119] The next day, de Gaulle gave an audience to André Gide, one of France's most famous writers, who was living in North Africa. Gide was not one of his preferred authors but receiving great writers was the act of a head of state – the role which de Gaulle was rehearsing. With writers he was always deferential. Gide wrote afterwards: 'I had been told of his charm; and this was no exaggeration. But one did not feel with him an excessive desire or care to please . . . The General remained very dignified and even a little reserved, somehow distant.' They spent most time discussing the Académie Française, about which de Gaulle proved astonishingly well informed. The only tense moment occurred when Gide tried to defend the writer André Maurois who, from the United States, remained faithful to Pétain: 'The General's features contracted a bit and I am not sure if my vehement plea had not irritated him.'[120]

ENDGAME

De Gaulle had not yet finished with Giraud. As Alexis Leger once observed: 'De Gaulle needs not just to defeat his enemies but to crush them as well.'[121] This took another few months. In *The Edge of the Sword* de Gaulle had compared the self-control of the leader to that of the gambler whose 'elegance consists in reinforcing his outward appearance of sangfroid at the moment that he takes the winnings'.[122] It took three more throws of the dice to eliminate Giraud. Throughout he was helped by Giraud's unerringly bad judgement. As Macmillan commented at one moment: 'The old boy . . . is really out of his depth.'[123]

De Gaulle's first throw of the dice occurred in mid-July after Giraud had returned from a three-week tour of North America at the invitation of Roosevelt, who hoped it would boost Giraud's reputation. In fact, it had the opposite effect, as Churchill had suspected when he warned Roosevelt that it would be 'dangerous to leave the field to de Gaulle . . . When the cat's away the mouse will play.'[124] Seeing Leger in Washington, the supposedly apolitical Giraud was only too aware of the danger. He told him:

> I have no illusion about de Gaulle . . . An entourage of gangsters, ready to resort to anything by any means . . . Their propaganda is extremely skilful . . . I do not underestimate the danger . . . I prefer to have recourse to a progressive method which will take six months. I will get de Gaulle to reveal his position and unmask him . . . and use him up in the eyes of public opinion. I count on his inevitable clumsiness in view of his character and temperament.[125]

Giraud's tactics for 'unmasking' de Gaulle could hardly have been more maladroit. At a press conference in Ottawa, he made remarks praising some achievements of National Socialism. The next day's headlines read: 'Giraud sings the praises of the Nazis.' Meanwhile back in Algiers, the Committee became used to working under de Gaulle's sole leadership. De Gaulle visited Rabat and Tunis where large crowds were for the first time exposed to the power of his rhetoric. His speech in Algiers on Bastille Day (14 July) was rapturously received by a huge crowd: 'Our people is unified to fight the war. And also for national renewal . . . France is not a sleeping princess who will be suddenly awakened by the genie of Liberation. France is a tortured captive who, under the blows she receives, has once and for all taken the measure of the cause of her misfortunes and the infamy of the tyrants.'[126] This was more in tune with the times than Giraud extolling the benefits of National Socialism.

On Giraud's return, de Gaulle struck again. He told the Committee that the existence of two separate army structures was an obstacle to the development of a single French army. After acrimonious debate, a new compromise was reached. Instead of a committee with two rotating presidents, each would now have a specific area of responsibility: Giraud for military affairs and de Gaulle for the rest. But in reality Giraud's power was further constrained since there was to be a new Defence Committee to oversee the merger of the armed forces – with de Gaulle as its chairman. De Gaulle's private gloss on this arrangement was that he now had 'political preponderance' and a 'sort of military preponderance'.[127] Curiously the obtuse Giraud, after five days of wrangling, also seemed happy. He told Murphy that his military position had been strengthened.[128]

Giraud presented de Gaulle with his next opportunity five weeks later after the liberation of Corsica. From November 1942, Corsica had been occupied by the Italians. After Mussolini had fallen from power in July 1943 and the Italian government had signed an armistice with the Allies at the start of September, the Resistance movements in Corsica seized the opportunity to launch an uprising. At almost the same moment German troops landed on the island, and the Corsican Resistance contacted Algiers to ask for military help. Giraud immediately sought the permission of the Allies to send two destroyers to Corsica – but without informing the CFLN. He then paid a visit to liberated Corsica. All this annoyed de Gaulle, who believed that Giraud had gone behind his back so that he could take personal credit for the first liberation of a French *département*. De Gaulle need not have worried. The loyal Gaullist François Coulet, sent to take the Corsican situation in hand, reported back on 22 September on what he had seen: 'Undisputed, exclusive Gaullism, almost embarrassing when one accompanies General Giraud, as I did yesterday. It is true that he behaved very correctly throughout and seems no longer to be surprised when he finds himself acclaimed with cries of "Long Live de Gaulle."'[129]

This humiliation for Giraud was not enough for de Gaulle. He presented the issue as a matter of principle: the Commander in Chief had no right to act independently of the CFLN. His solution was that there should be one single President and clear subordination of military to civil power. On 21 September, the CFLN met to discuss de Gaulle's proposals, while Giraud was in Corsica inspecting French troops. Eliminating Giraud from the co-presidency in his absence was a step too ruthless for all but the most committed Gaullists. De Gaulle found himself in the unusual position of being outvoted.[130] He describes this in his *Memoirs* with sublimely disingenuous mendacity. He claimed that while 'ministers were pressing me to effect the change of structure' that would prevent any repetition of the

Corsican affair, he on the other hand preferred to 'proceed with due respect for the great soldier who had rendered such brilliant service'.[131] The truth was exactly the opposite.

De Gaulle spent the next few days preparing the ground. On 26 September Macmillan, finding de Gaulle in 'very cheerful and rather mischievous mood', avoided falling into a trap that was being set for him: 'He was anxiously seeking an intervention by the Allies as an excuse for patriotic rallying.'[132] Even without such an intervention, de Gaulle got his way at the next meeting of the Committee. He proposed setting up a new Commissariat for National Defence to which the Commander in Chief (Giraud) would be answerable. Giraud would remain a formal co-signatory to decisions taken by the CFLN until he took up command in the field. At this point he would cease to sit on the Committee.[133] On the CFLN only General Georges opposed this proposal.

The last round in Giraud's elimination took place in early November when de Gaulle moved to broaden the base of the CFLN by bringing in elements from the metropolitan Resistance. All members of the Committee signed a letter resigning their portfolios to allow a reshuffle. Giraud, who often signed papers without reading them, realized only too late the implications. He wrote plaintively to de Gaulle: 'Journalists have asked me if it was true that I was no longer on the Committee. I had to tell them I had no idea that this was the case.'[134] Neither Giraud nor Georges was appointed to the reconstituted Committee. Giraud had no allies left. Seeing Georges during this crisis, Macmillan found that even 'he was losing patience with Giraud much as he distrusted de Gaulle.'[135] And whatever future weapons Roosevelt had in his armoury against de Gaulle, Giraud was no longer one of them. It was clear to American military leaders in North Africa not only that Giraud was politically incompetent but that his military ideas were hopelessly outdated as well. The 'great soldier' remained Commander in Chief for another few months but politically he was finished.

Looking back at the end of 1944, Macmillan wrote of Giraud:

> I would suppose that never in the whole history of politics has any man frittered away so large a capital in so short a space of time . . . Of his decline and fall he has been himself the sole author . . . He sat down to play cards with every ace, every king and almost every queen in the pack . . . but succeeded by some extraordinary sleight of hand in cheating himself out of his own stake.[136]

The contest had been unequal from the start. Hervé Alphand, visiting Algiers in May 1943 before de Gaulle's arrival, came away with no doubt about the ultimate outcome: 'Giraud gives the impression of being a man completely out of date, very much a man of 1912, knowing nothing about great modern economic problems, about social issues (he said to me: civil unrest can be crushed with machine guns) . . . No comparison with that unchained force – brutal and furious – that figure who breaks with all the past, that explosion against errors, mistakes and treason that is de Gaulle.'[137] Giraud's only asset was the support of the American government, but this was ultimately a liability. Faced with de Gaulle's political ruthlessness, brilliance as a popular tribune and total clarity about what he wanted to achieve, Giraud never stood a chance.

12

Building a State in Exile,
July 1943–May 1944

On 26 August 1943, when the conflict between de Gaulle and Giraud had several weeks to run, the three Allied powers simultaneously recognized the French Committee of National Liberation (CFLN). Under pressure from his Cabinet, Churchill had been urging Roosevelt to do this for weeks: 'I am no more enamoured than you of de Gaulle but I would rather have him on the Committee than strutting about as a combination of Joan of Arc and Clemenceau.'[1] The matter had been discussed between Churchill and Roosevelt at a meeting in Quebec where, according to Cordell Hull, the 'President said he did not want to give de Gaulle a white horse on which he could ride into France and make himself master of a government there'.[2] Once Roosevelt had agreed, it remained to find an appropriate form of words. Numerous drafts shuttled across the Atlantic. Again Churchill wrote to Roosevelt: 'What does recognition mean? One can recognize a man as an Emperor or as a Grocer.'[3] In the end, each Allied government chose a different formula, somewhere between these extremes. The Soviet one was the most expansive (recognizing the CFLN as 'representative of the governmental interest of the French Republic') and the American the most restrictive (recognizing the CFLN as 'administering those territories which acknowledge its authority'). The British wording lay in between.[4]

Only two weeks later, the French had proof of how little this 'recognition' meant. In July, Allied troops landed in Sicily and later that month Mussolini was ousted from power by an internal coup. On 3 September, Allied troops landed on the Italian mainland and signed an armistice with the new Italian leader, General Badoglio, after days of secret negotiations about which the French had not been informed. When Macmillan arrived with Murphy to brief de Gaulle and reassure him that secrecy had been imposed by military security, the reaction was not encouraging:

with a certain sardonic humour he congratulated us that the war between our countries and Italy was at an end. He considered that France was still

at war with Italy as he was not party to the armistice. When I observed that
military secrecy and necessity should appeal to him as a soldier, he said, 'I
am not a soldier.' I was tempted to ask why he dressed himself up in those
peculiar clothes which surely no one would choose to wear unless military
necessity imposed them upon him. As we left de Gaulle, we saw Massigli
coming in, looking very frightened.[5]

In fact Massigli was no less annoyed than de Gaulle. Both feared that if
the Allies were ready to cut such a rapid deal with Badoglio, as previously
with Darlan, they might one day do the same with Laval or Pétain. Other
snubs followed. Meeting in Moscow at the end of October, Roosevelt,
Stalin and Churchill set up a European Advisory Commission to plan post-
war policy. The French were not on it. Nor was de Gaulle invited to a
summit at Tehran at the end of November where the decision for D-Day
was taken. De Gaulle drew the moral in his memoirs: 'There was no doubt!
Our allies were in agreement to exclude us, as much as possible, from
decisions concerning Italy. It was to be predicted that in the future they
would agree the destiny of Europe without France. But they needed to be
shown that France could not permit such an exclusion.'[6]

    For de Gaulle the only way of fighting back was to present the Allies
with a fait accompli by building the CFLN into a kind of state in exile with
which they would be forced to deal at the Liberation. To do this, it would
be necessary to amalgamate the Gaullist London-based National Committee with the existing – and largely Pétainist – administration in Algiers. What
worried some Gaullists was how this would affect the nature of 'Gaullism'.
Would it be absorbed by 'Algiers' or would 'Algiers' be transformed by
'Gaullism'? The future of Gaullism remained an open question.

ALGIERS LIFE

Since 1940, those who claimed to represent France had squatted in faded
hotels at Vichy, in colonial villas in Brazzaville and in grand mansions in
central London. Now a fourth 'France' was housed in the premises of the
Lycée Fromentin, a large girls' school set in a park overlooking the bay of
Algiers. Here the CFLN's commissariats (as ministries were still designated) were installed in pavilions that had once housed the school's
dormitories, refectories and classrooms. These were not the best conditions
in which to organize a government. Most ministerial archives were in Paris;
telephones were so unreliable that it was quicker to send a messenger on
foot across the city; paper was of poor quality and in short supply; cactus

thorns served as paperclips.[7] Another problem was that all communication with the Resistance went via London. For this reason – and also because Britain was likely to be the place from which the eventual landings in France would depart – all the CFLN commissariats continued to have representatives in London. Massigli, who was in charge of foreign affairs, was represented in London by the moderate Socialist Pierre Viénot, who had joined de Gaulle in April 1943. The BCRA also had both a London and an Algiers section. This created ample opportunity for crossed wires. Those who disapproved of policy decided in one city could find ways of sabotaging it in the other.

After arriving in Algiers on 30 May, de Gaulle had occupied a small and uncomfortable villa near the Lycée. But with his wife's arrival he moved into the Villa des Oliviers, an imposing Moorish-style construction about 3 kilometres from the centre of the city with spectacular views over the Bay of Algiers. Although indifferent to his personal surroundings, he wanted a residence grand enough to mark his position as a head of state – and to match Giraud who, having arrived first, occupied the grander Palais d'Eté where governor generals had previously lived. Yvonne de Gaulle joined her husband at the end of July. We have a glimpse into how much de Gaulle had missed his wife from a short but poignant note he scribbled to her one night soon after arriving in Algiers:

> He is there writing at his desk. He has in front of him the portrait of his dear little wife whom he so admires and so loves! And suddenly all the love flows into his heart and he hurries to tell Yvonne. The two of us, physically and morally supporting each other, will go far on the sea, and in life, for the better and for the worse.[8]

Yvonne de Gaulle's journey from London to Algiers was risky. The plane had to fly low because Anne could not be made to wear an oxygen mask. In Algiers, Yvonne was obliged occasionally to assume the duties of the wife of a head of state, to become a kind of 'first lady'. This was an ordeal for this shy woman absorbed in the problems of looking after her handicapped daughter. After one official dinner, Macmillan's successor as representative to the CFLN, the British politician Duff Cooper, commented with the hauteur of someone married to the glamorous Diana Cooper: 'I sat between Mme de Gaulle and Mme Catroux . . . Mme de Gaulle is a rather pathetic little woman who I think has a hard life. She is obviously forbidden to put on makeup.'[9] Diana Cooper dreaded dinners where she might find herself sitting next to the 'Mr and Mrs Wormwoods', as she dubbed the de Gaulle couple, whereas she enjoyed chatting to the gossipy Madame Catroux. Most of the time, Yvonne kept out of the public eye. Those invited to dine privately at the de Gaulles' villa were startled by the austere simplicity of their lifestyle.[10] This was a contrast with Catroux who, having preceded de Gaulle in Algiers, had characteristically grabbed the most splendid villa available where he installed his grand furniture. The de Gaulle couple lived modestly, as their son Philippe remembered many years later:

> The house was uncomfortable and lacking most facilities . . . As my mother recalled: 'we ate on clay plates which were produced locally and drank out of glasses which were sawn-off bottles. To get an electric light was like pulling teeth [*la croix et la bannière*]. And one had to be constantly vigilant because everyone was stealing – even taking the locks off the doors. Every day was a struggle for the simplest things.' For example Anne could not eat solids, only boiled foods – she only had very poor *dents de lait* and my mother had to go to the most extraordinary lengths to find powdered milk. She had brought over some sheets, blanket and clothes since my father did not really care providing he was correctly turned out. 'You know him, once he has two uniforms and a few shirts he has all he needs.'[11]

Few people caught glimpses of the intimacy of the de Gaulles' domestic life. The resister Pierre Guillain de Bénouville, who one day returned unannounced to the villa because he had forgotten his briefcase after a meeting, stumbled upon de Gaulle with 'in his arms his sick little girl to whom he was singing a little love song'.[12]

De Gaulle's key aide in this period was Gaston Palewski, who remained *directeur de cabinet*. Palewski remained a curious combination of charming conversationalist, socialite and uncompromising Gaullist. In Duff Cooper's diary he is described as the 'inevitable Palewski', and Cooper came to dislike him intensely both because of the intransigence of his Gaullism and because he was an even more inveterate womanizer than he was. Palewski jealously guarded his position as gatekeeper to de Gaulle but had to contend with a new figure in the Gaullist constellation. This was Louis Joxe, a former teacher of history, who had been a member of Combat, that small Resistance group of Gaullists formed in Algiers before the Allied landings. De Gaulle needed someone loyal with local knowledge of the treacherous and unfamiliar Algerian scene. Joxe fitted the bill perfectly and was appointed Secretary General to the government which gave him responsibility for preparing meetings of the CFLN. The post of Secretary General was an administrative innovation of the 1930s, but Joxe upgraded its status by persuading de Gaulle that he could not function effectively if not actually present at the CFLN meetings – like the British Cabinet Secretary at meetings of the Cabinet. De Gaulle came to rely closely on Joxe, who proved to be the perfect mandarin administrator, for the smooth running of the Committee. Inevitably this caused tensions with Palewski, who resented any dilution of his exclusive access to de Gaulle.[13]

However bucolic the surroundings of the Lycée Fromentin, the political atmosphere of Algiers was rank with hatreds. Free French from London, resisters from France, former Third Republic politicians, repentant Pétainists, disappointed Giraudists and *attentiste* civil servants (those who were hedging their bets to join the winner) all cohabited uneasily, eyeing each other suspiciously and jockeying for de Gaulle's favour. Resisters and Free French were wary of each other but united in their contempt for everyone else. Civil servants and politicians who had neither compromised themselves with Vichy nor rallied to de Gaulle in 1940 felt looked down upon. As Joxe put it: 'For some Free French, chronology played an important part. To have been the first to rally to de Gaulle was a badge of honour.' One former diplomat referred sardonically to the '18 June Club'.[14]

The need to establish a functioning administration made it impossible to be too purist. This was certainly the view of the career diplomat Massigli whose delicate task was to rebuild France's diplomacy abroad. By the end of 1943, thirty-seven governments had recognized the CFLN. Diplomatic representatives had to be accredited to each of them. Since the French diplomatic corps had been largely faithful to Vichy until the end of 1942, compromises were unavoidable. Despite some raised eyebrows from the *purs*, Massigli persuaded de Gaulle to appoint the experienced career diplomat Henri Hoppenot as Ambassador to Washington. Having been Vichy's Ambassador to Uruguay, Hoppenot had initially rallied to Giraud. He now displayed all the eagerness of someone keen to work his passage back to favour despite one notorious faux pas when he ended a speech in praise of de Gaulle '*Vive le Maréchal*'.[15]

If traditional diplomats were rehabilitated, what role was left for the Free French committees that had sprung up all over the world in 1940 in opposition to Vichy's official representatives? These 'Resisters of Fifth Avenue, Buenos Aires and Montevideo', as one diplomat contemptuously described them, hoped their moment had arrived. But Massigli believed they had no place in serious diplomacy. He quarrelled violently with Soustelle, who had played a major role in setting up the committees in 1940. In the end, de Gaulle imposed a compromise that recognized the past role of the committees but gave them no official status as representatives of the CFLN. Soustelle's honour was intact, but Massigli had seen off what he described as an attempt to turn the Free French committees into a version of the Nazi Brown Houses. The use of such an analogy says much about how people like Massigli viewed the *pur et dur* Gaullists. Massigli and Soustelle never spoke to each other again.[16]

De Gaulle could be pragmatic because he had nothing to prove. He told Georges Boris who worried about the compromises de Gaulle seemed ready to make with former Vichy officials: 'One can only govern with the French ... and they were Pétainist.'[17] But at the same time de Gaulle had forgotten nothing. New recruits arriving in Algiers were required to sweat a little before being admitted to favour. Joxe witnessed one excruciating encounter when a certain General X (he does not give the name), arriving for an appointment with de Gaulle, was made to kick his heels for some minutes before being admitted. De Gaulle told Joxe: 'I have been waiting for him for two years. He can wait a little longer.' When the unfortunate individual was ushered in, smiling and with his hand stretched out, de Gaulle remained seated, motionless and impassive. The General, after a moment's hesitation, put his *képi* back on and saluted. Immediately de Gaulle stood up and held out his hand: 'Bonjour X ... How are you? Delighted to see you.'[18] Jean Chauvel, a senior Quai d'Orsay official, encouraged to come to Algiers by Massigli, found himself frozen out by de Gaulle for several weeks. His memoirs recall bitterly the distinctions in Algiers between the 'chosen, the catechumens, the outcasts'. Only after several weeks was he, in his own words, admitted into the 'Presence'. Chauvel's career did not suffer but he never forgave de Gaulle.[19]

Nowhere was de Gaulle more willing to be pragmatic than in the reorganization of the army. His priority was to create an effective fighting force to allow the French to participate in the Allied victory. This meant amalgamating the original Free French forces, which numbered 50,000 by the summer of 1943, with the regular army in North Africa, which numbered 700,000. There were deep hatreds on both sides. For the officers of the regular army, Free French 'generals' like Leclerc, Koenig and Larminat were jumped-up captains, and de Gaulle was a traitor. One of these regular officers, General de Monsabert, wrote in his diary on 7 May: 'The army cannot bear de Gaulle! Because of Syria, because of Dakar and above all because he represents the politics of yesterday. The army does not forgive the regime for having led us to defeat. It accepted the Marshal but it loved him because he crystallized all the resentment against the regime which consummated France's defeat.' Or six months later: 'How sad to see a man like de Gaulle who might really have incarnated the salvation of France if he were not playing the little political game of the Third Republic ... The émigrés of the Republic and the defeated Regime who have "learnt nothing and forgotten nothing" and who cannot even claim the great honesty of the émigrés of the revolution.'[20] On the other hand, soldiers like Larminat who had been with de Gaulle since 1940 talked continuously of the need for 'revolution', by which they meant a thorough purge of those officers who had compromised themselves with Vichy. De

Monsabert and Larminat had shared much the same values in 1940 and both were equally committed to fighting the Germans – but now they were divided by the abyss of France's civil war and the personality of de Gaulle.

To command the French Expeditionary Force that was being assembled to fight in Italy, de Gaulle chose not a Free French soldier but General Alphonse Juin, who had served Vichy loyally until November 1942. Even after the American landings in North Africa, Juin had hesitated for days before deciding where duty lay. He had been an exact contemporary of de Gaulle at Saint-Cyr – making him one of the few people whom de Gaulle addressed as 'tu' – but de Gaulle's reasons for using him were unsentimental. Juin was a man of great leadership qualities acceptable to the cadres of the regular army. The day after arriving in Algiers, de Gaulle wrote to him in the warmest terms. Juin, who declared himself 'infinitely touched', must also have been infinitely relieved by this olive branch of absolution.[21] A group of resisters who went in delegation to de Gaulle to complain about Juin's promotion were treated with typical contempt: 'So you know about the value of Generals do you? ... All that you have said is right. But Juin will command in Italy and he will be decorated before you.'[22]

Although Giraud went round repeating to everyone who would listen that de Gaulle had told him that once back in France he would erect a guillotine in every village,[23] it was de Gaulle's pragmatic moderation which made it possible for figures like Couve de Murville, originally a Giraudist, to rally to him. Desmond Morton, visiting Algiers in July, reported on a conversation with Couve whom he described as 'a most detached personality for a Frenchman':

> There is no doubt in Couve de Murville's mind that, whether he, we or anyone like it or not, de Gaulle is now bound to play a most important part in post-war France as a politician and not as a soldier ... The danger of the American attitude, which he fully understands, is that it enhances the danger of a sort of post-war communism in France, against which Couve de Murville by no means gladly regards de Gaulle as the sole visible barrier.[24]

For the same pragmatic reasons Monnet had now reluctantly accepted the inevitability of de Gaulle.

THE MAKING OF A POLITICIAN: 'FEEDING THE DUCKS'

In Algiers, de Gaulle learnt to adapt his style of leadership from the early days of the Free French. Although one of the most committed Gaullists since arriving in London in June 1942, André Philip was shocked by the manner of de Gaulle's brutal elimination of Giraud after his return to Algiers. He wrote to him:

> Since your arrival in Algiers you have committed a number of errors by acting too fast, and consulting no one except yourself . . . No one however much of a genius can decide alone . . . Your profound contempt for human nature . . . tends to distance you from the spirit of democracy . . . Then there is your pride. I always said to myself that I would reserve my view on your character until the day when, marching at the head of your troops down the Champs-Elysées . . . one would judge if you were capable of surmounting the pride in victory. Alas, victory is not there yet but the pride already is and that is what makes you lack charity or psychology in your relations with individuals, making you sometimes needlessly harsh and wounding as you have been recently towards some of our colleagues during our recent discussions . . . So if you do not *now* adopt the habit of consulting your colleagues and winning a majority by skilful persuasion, you will never acquire it and, whatever your intentions, you will end up, once back in France, taking an authoritarian attitude and I guarantee that the working-class and Republican mass of the people who have confidence in you today will at once abandon you.[25]

We have no idea what de Gaulle thought of this letter, which he does not seem to have answered. During one of the many crises with Giraud, he had been heard to remark: 'I have smashed so many doors when leaving rooms that soon there will be no doors left for me to come back through.'[26] But as the CFLN acquired greater authority and widened its membership, door-smashing became less effective. De Gaulle needed to woo politicians and win votes. We have seen already how he was outvoted at his first attempt to exclude Giraud from the CFLN in September 1943. But paradoxically, once Giraud had been removed, thanks to the introduction on to the Committee of resisters and Third Republic politicians, de Gaulle found his hands tied even more. There was a striking example of this in November when yet another crisis exploded in the Middle East.

The elections that the French had promised to the populations of Syria and Lebanon ever since June 1941 finally took place in September 1943. They resulted in the victory of nationalist candidates. Encouraged by Spears, the new Lebanese 'government' announced its intention to abolish the mandate unilaterally. The French Governor, Jean Helleu, lacking the tact of his predecessor Catroux who was now in Algiers, dissolved parliament and arrested the ministers. Although believing privately that Helleu's reaction had been 'a little too vigorous', de Gaulle was certainly not prepared to disavow him.[27] The British threatened to intervene unless Helleu released the arrested ministers. De Gaulle, convinced that the British were retaliating for his ousting of Giraud, sent Catroux to find a solution. Even Catroux, not prone to rhetorical outbursts, described the British ultimatum as a new Fashoda affair; and the Anglophile Massigli thought the French were faced with a concerted 'intrigue' fomented by the British.[28] But although de Gaulle was not alone in being shocked by the British reaction, where his instinct was to give no ground, Catroux's was as usual to seek a solution. He reinstated the imprisoned ministers and negotiated a vague timetable to end the mandate. This deal was yet another fudge which delayed a final decision over independence, but even so it was too much for de Gaulle. From Algiers, he overruled Catroux; from London, Pierre Viénot threatened to resign rather than pass on de Gaulle's wilder threats to the British government. He wrote to Massigli: 'I see only too well the harm that has been done in the past by these ways of proceeding ... To embark on war against England, you will have to find someone else besides me.'[29] Viénot did not need to resign because, contrary to the previous two Levant crises, de Gaulle was no longer a free agent. On 23 November, Catroux received the support of a majority of the CFLN. De Gaulle stormed out of the meeting, slamming yet another door. Massigli reported delightedly to Macmillan that there was a complete change from de Gaulle's 'almost dictatorial authority a few months ago' since he could no longer ignore the new members of the Committee.[30]

Massigli was too optimistic, and it was rare for de Gaulle to be overruled. But he did need to achieve his objectives more subtly than in the past. This was noted with amused admiration by the old Third Republic insider Henri Queuille, who had joined the CFLN in November 1943. Queuille's journal charts the gradual changes in de Gaulle's leadership style:

> 6 October 1943: He is really a curious man, with his sudden impulses, his explosions, then after reflection a moment of retreat, the appearance that he has changed his mind but as soon as the moment is propitious, he resumes the path he has set himself.
>
> 23 November 1943: We discuss the measures to be taken on arrival in France ... The General discusses, proposes, with a moderation, wisdom, political sense which surprise us agreeably.
>
> 20 December 1943: [After de Gaulle had seemed to accept an idea Queuille had proposed two days earlier] This is not the first time that I observe that although he seems not to take any account of observations made to him, after reflection, they come back into his mind, he mulls them over, and his opinion evolves.

10 March 1944: [After a debate in the CFLN on whether to grant citizenship to Muslim Algerians] De Gaulle has certainly changed his policy . . . but he explains that change with a finesse, flexibility and artistry that show we are witnessing the creation of a politician. We are a long way from the explosions that used to occur.[31]

Despite observing the proprieties of collective government de Gaulle could not resist the occasional sarcastic barb. Philip, turning up one day in shorts, was greeted with the words 'You forgot your hoop, Philip.' On another occasion, after worries had been expressed about the kind of reception the CFLN representative would receive when arriving in Guadeloupe, which had previously been under Vichy authority, de Gaulle declared: 'People will shout Long Live—'; then sensing the intake of breath around the table at what he would say next, he checked himself: 'Long live the collective and depersonalized authority of the French National Committee of Liberation.'[32] The dutiful and highly strung Massigli was the most frequent butt of de Gaulle's sallies. De Gaulle was by nature suspicious of diplomats whose *déformation professionelle* was compromise over confrontation. He remarked of Massigli, 'He is a doormat . . . on which the Allies wipe their shoes,' while doing exactly the same to him himself.[33]

Although de Gaulle had to tread more carefully to achieve his objectives, his sense of superiority remained intact. To a visiting Canadian diplomat who asked about collective responsibility on the CFLN, de Gaulle replied:

In the final analysis the responsibility (and he pointed a finger at himself with an impressive gesture) 'c'est de Gaulle'. It is not, he said, Massigli, Pleven, Monnet to whom the French people look or who will be held responsible by the French people for the acts of the Committee; it is de Gaulle. Throughout he referred to himself always in the third person . . . He did not give the impression of a mystic hypnotised by any visions of grandeur but rather of a practical man stating fact without emotion.[34]

As well as observing the conventions of collective government, de Gaulle honed some of the skills of a parliamentary politician in dealing with the newly created Consultative Assembly. This body had been created in Algiers to act as a mouthpiece for different currents of French opinion in the absence of a proper parliament. Since it was obviously impossible to hold elections in France, the members of the Assembly were nominated by Resistance movements from their members and also included pre-war parliamentarians who had not voted for Pétain in July 1940. De Gaulle conceived the Assembly as another way of broadening his political legitimacy in the eyes of the Allies. Its first meeting in November served his

purposes perfectly. Speakers attacked Giraud and demanded that the
CFLN include more representatives of the Resistance. De Gaulle seized
this as his pretext to reshuffle the CFLN and exclude Giraud.

Otherwise de Gaulle did not conceive of the Assembly playing an independent role. He wanted it to support not contest him. But the Assembly,
containing wily Third Republic politicians and ambitious resisters, grew
in confidence and started to act more like a proper parliament. It set up
committees to discuss policy and established its right to summon ministers
to account for their actions. No one in the Assembly dared criticize de
Gaulle personally, but other members of the CFLN found themselves in
the firing line – especially André Philip, whom de Gaulle had put in charge
of relations between the Assembly and the CFLN. Once again Philip tried
to offer de Gaulle some home truths:

> In an admirable chapter of the *The Edge of the Sword* you drew the portrait
> of the leader, cold, reserved, accepting the need to be alone and repressing
> his feelings . . . You need to establish a human contact; the tragedy with you
> is that you do not feel this: your intelligence is Republican, your instincts
> are not. This Assembly is consultative; it must be consulted if only to give it
> a feeling of fulfilling a useful role.[35]

De Gaulle took the point. He appeared before the Assembly twenty times
and delivered some important policy speeches to it. Jean Chauvel (a hostile
witness) gives an amusing account of de Gaulle receiving members of the
Assembly's Foreign Affairs Commission.

> I arrived with my notes. The General took them and laid them out on his
> desk saying almost under breath: 'Yes bread for the ducks.' Then the ducks
> came in. They were visibly intimidated. De Gaulle sat them round a table,
> gave them some explanations, answered a few questions . . . Then drawing
> himself to his full height, he unfolded a map of Italy and gave in a semi-
> religious silence some 'confidential' indications on the operations under way;
> then shaking each hand in turn, he sent them back to their own business.
> The performance, very skilfully conducted, had interested me. I said to him
> that things seemed to have gone well. To which he replied: 'Yes, yes; bread
> for the ducks.'[36]

One major point of tension with the Assembly arose because its members
felt the CFLN was too lukewarm about the reforms to be carried out in
France after Liberation. Despite the rivalries and different political origins
of its leaders, the non-Communist Resistance shared the conviction that
France had been betrayed by her elites in 1940, and that it was the role of
the Resistance not only to expel the Germans but also to spearhead a social

and political regeneration of post-war France. The ideology of the Resistance was summed up in the title of a book by André Hauriou, a lawyer who had been a member of Combat before joining the Algiers Consultative Assembly: *Towards a Doctrine of the Resistance: Humanist Socialism.* This humanist socialism, conceived within the framework of a reinvigorated Republic, was imbued also with the liberal Catholic values of figures like Jacques Maritain.

Although many Resistance leaders resented de Gaulle's attempt to emasculate their independence, they simultaneously hoped that he might be ready to put himself at the head of a new movement to carry their ideals into the post-war world. He had used them; now they would find a way of using him. One Resistance leader arrived in Algiers with an entire scheme on these lines which he presented to de Gaulle: 'Just as your appeal of June 1940 was the catalyst of the Resistance, now your programme of 1943 could be the catalyst of Renovation.'[37] Diego Brosset, one of the first soldiers to rally to de Gaulle in 1940, also passed through Algiers with his own manifesto for de Gaulle, warning against the dangers of allowing the old political parties to recover influence.[38] This remained a constant theme of the editorials of the ultra-Gaullist *La Marseillaise.* For former parliamentarians like Queuille this had the ring of 'social-fascism', and the Socialist Félix Gouin wrote to de Gaulle protesting about the violence of these broadsides against Third Republic politicians. In reply de Gaulle quoted Talleyrand – 'all that is exaggerated does not count'[39] – as a way of evading specific commitments about the future.

The most striking feature of de Gaulle's rhetoric after he arrived in Algiers is that the word 'revolution' disappeared. Instead he started talking about 'order'. The moment of transition was his speech of 14 July 1943 delivered while Giraud was in the United States. Since de Gaulle still sought to present himself as a populist tribune against the 'reactionary' Giraud, the speech promised a new republic to overthrow vested interests: 'In a struggle between the people and the Bastille, it is always the Bastille which ends up on the wrong side.' But the next sentence warned that this process must be 'orderly' so that the French did not plunge into 'internal struggles'. So the Bastille would be taken . . . but in an orderly fashion.[40] Never again did the word 'revolution' appear in de Gaulle's Algiers speeches.

For those who had read de Gaulle's book *France and her Army* – built around the tension between order and élan – this should not have been a surprise, but Georges Boris, looking back after the war, believed that in Algiers de Gaulle had reverted to the values of his 'caste' and allowed himself to be annexed by the forces of 'reaction'.[41] The truth was more complicated. De Gaulle's obsession with 'order' in this period was counterbalanced by constant reiteration of the need for 'renovation' (which replaced 'revolution' in his rhetorical lexicon). The word 'renovation' appeared three times in just one short speech on 10 January 1944. Occasionally de Gaulle tried to flesh out what this might mean. In November 1943 he proclaimed that 'the sources of national wealth' should in the future be in the hands of the nation and 'profit all the people of France'; or in March 1944 that there must be 'structural economic and social reforms' to create a 'social democracy'.[42] This was in tune with the diffuse anti-capitalism of the Resistance. De Gaulle told Macmillan that he had been reading the Beveridge Report which he found 'very striking'. He believed there needed to be changes in French social structure between 'the extreme of Communism and capitalism in the old sense'. Macmillan was surprised how much this seemed to interest de Gaulle.[43]

One theme about which the Consultative Assembly was especially vociferous was the need to purge collaborators after Liberation. Here also de Gaulle was more cautious than he had been in the past. When asked about the purge at a press conference on 7 August 1943, he replied that any measures should be carried out in an orderly manner by the state. In this short declaration, the word 'state' appeared five times.[44] The CFLN set up a Purge Commission in the following month to prepare the ground. It resolved that those who had collaborated with Germany or participated in the 'pseudo-governments' of Pétain would be formally judged 'as soon as the circumstances permit'. There were many questions to be answered: would collaborators be judged by special tribunals or regular courts? What would be done about those who had committed minor offences and could not be punished under Article 75 of the Penal Code which applied to 'collusion [*intelligence*] with the enemy'?

In December 1943 de Gaulle ordered the internment of Boisson, who had fired on the Free French at Dakar, and of Pierre-Etienne Flandin, who had been Pétain's premier for three weeks at the end of 1940. The decision to intern these individuals outraged Churchill and Roosevelt. Roosevelt remained grateful to Boisson for having rallied West Africa to the Americans at the end of 1942; Flandin was an old friend of Churchill from before the war (despite having supported the Munich Agreement). According to Macmillan, Churchill was in a state of 'apoplexy' about the matter; Roosevelt told Churchill that it presented an opportunity to 'eliminate' de Gaulle.[45] Such interference in internal French matters was hardly calculated to change de Gaulle's mind. He took pleasure in pointing out that it was illogical of the Allies to accuse him at one moment of being authoritarian and at the next to blame him for taking measures advocated by the nearest that France had to a democratic assembly. In the end, de Gaulle defused the situation with assurances that the internees would be well treated and that they would be tried only once France had been liberated. For him these internments were primarily symbolic.

More problematic was the case of Pierre Pucheu, who had been Pétain's Minister of the Interior. Pucheu had been closely associated with Vichy's repressive policies after the first Communist attacks on Germans in the summer of 1941. When the Germans started to select French hostages to shoot in reprisal, Pucheu was alleged to have supplied them with the names of Communists who were in French prisons – although the fact they had been in prison at the time of the attacks meant they could have played no role in them. For this reason Pucheu was execrated by the Resistance in general and the Communist Party in particular. After November 1942, Pucheu jumped ship and put himself at the service of Giraud, arriving in Algiers the following May. But although Giraud offered him guarantees of safe conduct, he was immediately imprisoned. Pucheu was so controversial a figure that it was felt his trial could not wait till the Liberation. He was sentenced to death by a military court and shot on 22 March 1944 after de Gaulle had chosen not to commute the sentence. The summary nature of the trial shocked even those who harboured few regrets about Pucheu's fate. Although his responsibility for Vichy repression was incontrovertible, the prosecution found no evidence that he had provided the Germans with the names of hostages. Duff Cooper observed to Eden: 'The most pertinent comment on this lamentable and badly conducted trial is perhaps the comment made by my Soviet colleague ... "You should have consulted Vishinsky [the notorious prosecutor of the Soviet show trials]." '[46] For French conservatives, Pucheu's execution was an act of ruthlessly arbitrary violence perpetrated to appease the Communists. In fact reports received from France suggested that the execution was desired by the entire Resistance.[47]

Even so, the decision not to pardon Pucheu does seem to have caused de Gaulle a crisis of conscience. He was implacable, not sanguinary. He explained his reasoning to the Commissioner for Justice, the Catholic resister François de Menthon:

It is a grave decision. It is one I take in my soul and my conscience for reasons of State ... This is someone who was in the government. One is in a government or not. No one forces you to do it. Civil servants are different. They are agents who execute orders ... France would not understand that one forgives those who collaborated with the enemy, who made Frenchmen wear German uniforms. I am not interested in the rantings [*élucubrations*] of the Communists in this affair. I am not interested in the intentions of the individual ... I cannot judge intentions. Only the facts count and their results.[48]

Although de Gaulle rejected the imputation that Pucheu's execution was a sop to the Communists, he was certainly aware of the Communist threat. Only a few days after arriving in Algiers he told Macmillan that he had no intention of becoming a Kerensky.[49] This was another reason why he began to talk of 'order' not 'revolution'.

Ever since Fernand Grenier had arrived in London in January 1943 to announce the Central Committee's support for de Gaulle, the Communists had played a devious game. During the conflict with Giraud, the Party avoided choosing between the two generals. At the first meeting of the CNR, Moulin had had to quash an attempt by the Communist representative to table a motion supporting both generals. When Giraud was finally excluded from the CFLN, the Communist Party rustled up some demonstrators to protest in the streets of Algiers. Although it seems on the face of it paradoxical that the Communists should have supported someone ideologically more conservative than de Gaulle, it was in their interest to keep the CFLN divided while building up their influence over the Resistance in France.

De Gaulle tried to neutralize the Communists by offering them two posts in the CFLN during the November 1943 reshuffle. But he was ready to do this only on his terms. He chose two Communists who had played an incontrovertible role in the Resistance, and offered them relatively minor portfolios.[50] The Communists, apart from coveting more important posts, wanted to use the opportunity to rehabilitate Party members who had in 1939 enthusiastically accepted the Nazi–Soviet Pact like the Party's leader Maurice Thorez, who had deserted and spent the war in the Soviet Union. There had even been a murky episode in 1940 when some Communists in Paris entered into negotiations with the Germans about allowing the Party newspaper L'Humanité to reappear. This never came to anything, but it was a reminder of the Communists' awkward position until Hitler's invasion of the Soviet Union in June 1941.

During the negotiations with de Gaulle in November 1943, the Communist Central Committee asked why he would not allow Thorez to come to Algiers from Moscow. If it was held against Thorez that he had deserted in 1939 how was this different from de Gaulle who had 'deserted' in 1940? De Gaulle refused to give ground on any of these points and in the end the Communists did not join the CFLN. This did not cause them undue concern. Freed from any obligation to show collective responsibility, they kept up a barrage of attacks on de Gaulle for his leniency towards former servants of the Vichy regime. The Communist Party's strategy was to build up its influence in France for the moment of reckoning at the Liberation; de Gaulle's was to prepare the administrative structures that would allow the CFLN to counter any threat to its authority after Liberation.

'ORDER AND RENOVATION':
PLANNING FOR POWER

The CFLN spent much time planning for power after Liberation, behaving as if it were already France's government. One ordinance in February 1944 laid down arrangements for the baccalaureate examinations right down to specifying what texts would be tested for the English literature exam. In the spring of that year, students at the French lycée in Madrid could choose which of the two rival baccalaureate exams – Vichy's or Algiers' – they wished to sit.[51] De Gaulle was not of course involved in such details, but he did chair the committee responsible for overseeing the transition arrangements between the Allied landings and the CFLN's arrival in France from Algiers. It created a new echelon of super-prefects – *commissaires de la République* – who would represent de Gaulle's government in the regions, keep order once the Vichy regime had collapsed and avoid a power void at the Liberation which might be exploited either by the Allies or by the Communists. In choosing the names of the *commissaires* there was a tension between Resistance movements which hoped to bring in new blood and de Gaulle who inclined towards individuals with administrative experience. De Gaulle's annotation to an ordinance setting out how the *commissaires* would be chosen is revealing. Where the original draft specified that nominations would be made 'with the agreement' of the Resistance, de Gaulle changed this to 'after consultation'.[52]

Nonetheless de Gaulle's authority over the Resistance had suffered a major blow soon after his arrival in Algiers. For some months Moulin had been complaining that he was dangerously overstretched. His last letter to de Gaulle on 15 June 1943 was the *cri de coeur* of a man who sensed that his days were numbered. When first acting as de Gaulle's delegate in France from January 1942, he had been based mostly in Lyons where the Resistance movements of the former Unoccupied Zone had their headquarters. But after being put in charge of both the northern and southern zones following his second visit to London in February 1943, Moulin spent much time travelling between Paris and Lyons. Each train journey, involving frequent checks of identity papers, carried the risk of discovery and arrest. Moulin's last letter to de Gaulle reported the devastating news that General Delestraint, the man appointed to command the Secret Army of the Resistance, had been arrested in Paris on 9 June. The letter singled out Frenay as one of the involuntary culprits because his 'violent campaign' in Resistance circles against Delestraint had 'drawn attention to us'. He ended with a desperate appeal for help: 'We must now save the Secret Army. I entreat you, General, do what I have the honour to ask of you.'

Before Moulin's letter reached de Gaulle in Algiers, Moulin had himself been arrested on 21 June in the Lyons suburb of Caluire at a meeting of Resistance leaders to choose Delestraint's successor. He died some days later after atrocious torture at the hands of the Gestapo chief Klaus Barbie. When de Gaulle received the news of Moulin's arrest from Passy on 28 June, he hid his deepest feelings as always. His only comment was a sort of melancholy resignation: 'Ah! . . . Well, we have to go on [Ah . . . Continuons].' But there is no other figure about whom he later wrote more effusively in his Memoirs, using words that have something also of a self-portrait as well:

> This man, still young, but with an experience already formed by his career, was cast from the same mould as the best of my companions. Filled to the brim of his soul with a passion for France, convinced that 'Gaullism' should be not just about struggle for liberation but also the spur to a complete renovation, penetrated by the idea that the State was embodied in the Free French, he aspired to great feats. But being also a man of judgement and seeing people and things as they were, he watched each step that he took along a road encumbered by the traps set by his enemies and the obstacles erected by his friends. Being a man of faith and calculation, not doubting but sharing a general mistrust, an apostle but at the same time a minister, in eighteen months Moulin accomplished a great task.

A few days before Moulin's arrest, de Gaulle's former aide Bouchinet-Serreulles had been sent over to France to help him, and he now held the fort until a permanent successor was found. The most obvious choice might have been Pierre Brossolette, who certainly had the stature and experience to replace Moulin, but whose powerful personality had won him many enemies in London. After three months, a compromise candidate was found in the person of Emile Bollaert, a former prefect who had been sacked by Vichy. The choice suited de Gaulle because it fitted his sense of hierarchy that the representative of the state – of him – in France should, like Moulin, be a prefect. The choice suited Brossolette because Bollaert's lack of previous involvement in the Resistance gave him reason to expect he might become the power behind the throne. But in February 1944 Brossolette and Bollaert were both arrested. Brossolette committed suicide; Bolleart was deported to Germany. As a result, six months after Moulin's death, de Gaulle still had no permanent replacement for him.

This allowed the Resistance movements to claw back some of the autonomy lost to Moulin. To replace him as chairman of the CNR, they selected an internal resister, Georges Bidault. Since Bidault had worked closely with Moulin, this was not a choice necessarily alarming to Algiers. But where Moulin had been both head of the CNR *and* de Gaulle's delegate, these two posts were now separated. The CNR, originally imposed by Moulin on the Resistance to support de Gaulle, was now emancipating itself from him. In a further assertion of independence, the CNR conceived the idea of setting up departmental liberation committees (CDLs) throughout France. The danger for de Gaulle was that these might conceive their role as competing with, rather than supporting, the *commissaires* appointed by the CFLN.

This danger was exacerbated by the void left by Moulin's death. The CFLN and BCRA did have several representatives acting in France – for example, Francis-Louis Closon, who had been sent out to guide the Resistance movements in selecting *commissaires*. But these representatives were sent out on specific missions and lacked clear instructions from Algiers or London on other matters. Presented with the CNR's plan to set up departmental liberation committees, Closon had to improvise a response. He wrote to Algiers in despair in January 1944 that, not having received a single communication for weeks, he had no idea if his policies met with de Gaulle's approval and wondered whether his existence in France had been forgotten.[53]

De Gaulle seemed much less focused on what was happening in France than three months earlier when he had been fixated on the Resistance as the solution to his conflict with Giraud. It may be that he was uncertain about the course to follow. There was no individual in whom he had the same confidence as Moulin and, with so many other matters crowding in upon him, it was difficult to form a view.[54] One BCRA operative reported to Passy in November 1943:

> General de Gaulle is unhappy about the current functioning of mail from France. He thinks he is personally ill-informed about important issues. On these questions he either receives nothing at all or voluminous documents that he does not have the time to read as he did before; I repeat that he does not have the time to read.[55]

De Gaulle was also distracted by his power struggle with Giraud. Brossolette, passing through Algiers in September 1943, found him 'preoccupied 90 per cent by governmental problems here ... and thinking only intermittently about France'. Brossolette judged that the intrigues of Carlton Gardens faded into insignificance compared to the 'frenetic agitation' and 'permanent crisis' in Algiers.[56] Finally it may be that de Gaulle believed he had neutralized the two most vocal Resistance 'barons', Frenay and d'Astier. Frenay had arrived

in London in May 1943 to pursue his campaign against Moulin. After Moulin's death made this redundant, Frenay moved his attack from the person
of Moulin to the entire relationship between de Gaulle and the Resistance.
He spent the summer writing de Gaulle long recriminatory reports. His idea
was that the Resistance should establish its own representation in London
or Algiers to match de Gaulle's in France.[57] De Gaulle would have none of
this. He wrote at the start of October in terms revealing of his contemptuously instrumental view of the Resistance: 'I will not allow Charvet's [Frenay's
pseudonym] intrigues . . . If he causes me problems I will reveal his game
publicly. Then we will see what is left of it.'[58] De Gaulle's way of dealing
with 'Charvet' and d'Astier was to invite them to sit on the CFLN in November 1943. With some misgivings both accepted. They realized that de Gaulle
wanted to keep a close watch over them but felt that the opportunity could
not be missed. De Gaulle may now have felt confident that he had sufficiently
domesticated the Resistance. If so, he had not fully grasped how rapidly the
Communists were extending their influence over it.

Although de Gaulle never missed an opportunity to alert the Allies to
the Communist threat, he did not take it as seriously as he pretended.
Corsica had offered a test case of what might happen at the Liberation. As
we have seen, the local Resistance had launched its insurrection without
the prior knowledge of Algiers and before the arrival of CFLN representatives. In many localities power was seized by local liberation committees,
often dominated by the Front National, the Communist Party's front
organization. Self-proclaimed Resistance leaders had themselves 'elected'
at open assemblies in town squares. This might have been an alarming
precedent for what might happen in France, but Algiers quickly despatched
representatives to take control. One of them, François Coulet, reported
back to de Gaulle reassuringly:

> Corsica is Gaullist, resistant, homogeneous, and open to the idea of sacri-
> fice . . . I really think the Front National is made up of decent people who
> belonged not so long ago to all kinds of Resistance organizations, all perfectly
> Gaullist, until they were recently absorbed into the Front National. These
> are honest types who risk having the wool pulled over their eyes by a tiny
> band of Communists (who do not dare to say who they really are). The
> solution is first to speak of 'Gaullism' and 'authority' (the authority of the
> Prefect over the little soviet that set itself up) then to extol Republicans and
> take back without violence the machine guns that have been liberally handed
> out to twelve-year-old children.[59]

Although it turned out not to be quite so easy,[60] the lesson de Gaulle might
reasonably have drawn was that the Communists could be contained as

long as the CFLN had structures in place for the moment of Liberation. But this gave rise to another question: were the Allies prepared to accept the *de facto* authority of the CFLN in France after Liberation?

TROUBLE WITH THE ALLIES

On 7 September 1943, the CFLN had presented the Allied governments with a memorandum proposing how it could work with Allied military commanders during the period of liberation.[61] After the German defeat at Stalingrad in the winter of 1943, it was clear that the war had turned decisively in favour of the Allies and that at some point a landing in France would be attempted. De Gaulle sent two representatives to London to start training liaison officers to be ready to work with the Allied forces in the event of a military operation in France. The CFLN memorandum sought to pre-empt any attempt by the Allies to treat liberated France as a defeated power on the model of Italy, which was run by an Allied Military Government of Occupied Territories (AMGOT). Given the kind of comments Roosevelt was making in private at this time, the French fear of AMGOT was not absurd, even if the French were blissfully ignorant of his more fantastical ideas. In November 1943 he mused to his Chiefs of Staff that after the war the United States might need permanently to station two divisions in France and create a new buffer state between France and Germany running from the Channel to the Swiss border.[62] This was not the first time that he had speculated about carving a new state of Wallonia out of French territory. Even if such an idea was not official American policy, it revealed Roosevelt's assumption that France would be treated after the war as a defeated nation, not as a partner in victory. One worrying sign was that the Americans had made it clear they intended to provide their troops with banknotes issued officially by the 'Allied military command' – as had been done in Italy.

It was said that every time the CFLN memorandum reached the top of the pile of papers on Roosevelt's desk, he shuffled it back to the bottom. He always managed to find new pretexts for his anti-Gaullism. In some moods he viewed de Gaulle as a proto-Communist, in others as a proto-fascist. His attitude to de Gaulle, once explicable on grounds of pragmatism, becomes increasingly hard to understand in rational terms. The administrative and territorial resources of the CFLN were superior to those of any other government in exile – and yet only the CFLN was not recognized as a government. Most of the President's advisers (even Cordell Hull) now accepted that it was necessary to deal with de Gaulle, but Roosevelt would not be moved. The only logic behind his anti-Gaullist obsession lay in his vision of the world order after the war. From 1942, he had come to the view that parts of the French Empire should be held in trusteeship in preparation for decolonization. Having a properly constituted government in France after Liberation – especially one headed by de Gaulle – was an obstacle to such a plan.

French representatives in Washington and London had the thankless task of putting the CFLN case. In Washington, this fell to the Washington Ambassador Hoppenot and to Jean Monnet, who had left Algiers in September 1943 to negotiate a French relief programme after Liberation. Monnet hoped by this means to obtain by stealth a *de facto* recognition of the CFLN. He deployed his unparalleled network of American contacts to argue the need to work with the CFLN – although a few months earlier he had been portraying de Gaulle as a proto-fascist.[63] Monnet wrote repeatedly to de Gaulle in the first months of 1944 assuring him that an agreement was imminent – but still Roosevelt would not budge.[64] Meanwhile in London, Massigli's representative Viénot was working on the British. Eden would regularly tell him how frustrated they were with the 'political ignorance' of the Americans, but this never translated into any results because Churchill was not ready to cross Roosevelt.[65]

By the end of October Massigli was in despair. The situation was frustrating enough to cause even this convinced Anglophile to worry that the Americans were secretly nursing the idea of using Vichy for a compromise peace with Germany. He was perpetually worried that in retaliation de Gaulle would be tempted to turn to the Soviet Union. He confided to Viénot his 'nausea' at 'constantly battling with a "gang" of young Turks who are trying to bring me down because I am not in favour of going headlong into a kind of war against Washington, and eyes closed into a Russian alliance exclusive of any other'.[66] He was incensed and alarmed in late September to hear that de Gaulle had sent a personal letter to Stalin behind his back.[67]

It is true that some people around de Gaulle, among them Maurice Dejean, were arguing for a more pro-Soviet policy.[68] It is true also that de Gaulle did on occasion give some credence to Massigli's fears. Eden, passing through Algiers on his way to Moscow on 11 October, reported that de Gaulle had made him an 'emphatic statement that France must be with Russia in the future'. In his view the Soviets would have 'a great work of reconstruction to do after the war and would seek for strategical and political security' involving 'the incorporation of the Baltic States, satisfaction of territorial claims in Poland, Rumania and Finland, and the establishment of States on her Western frontiers' that could be 'counted upon not to be hostile'. But they would be 'satisfied if truly popular Governments were established; it would not be necessary for these countries to have Communist governments'. Eden, with Massigli nodding vigorous approval, could only reply that he hoped that 'France would always first look to us' and not think of 'playing Russians and ourselves one against the other'.[69] A Dutch envoy was told ten days later that de Gaulle 'did not believe there was anything to fear from the Soviet Union. That country would be too busy with its own reconstruction and internal affairs to start a revolution in other countries. Indeed, the Russian red wine had already become *très rosé*.'[70] The American diplomat Averell Harriman reported similar views: 'He spoke of France and Russia as the only two powerful countries in Europe, after the collapse of Germany. The British, after all, would retire to their islands and the Americans would go home across the Atlantic ... Therefore French policy should be tied to the Soviet Union.'[71]

These remarks, uttered when de Gaulle was still smarting from his exclusion from the discussions relating to the Italian armistice, were obviously designed to frighten the British and Americans into showing greater consideration to the CFLN. He stopped talking in this way in November after the Communists had made it clear that they were not ready to join the CFLN except on their terms. Since the Communists did nothing without Moscow's approval it was obvious that the Soviet Union was not interested for the moment in any closer relationship with de Gaulle. Despite these rather blatant attempts to use the Soviet Union as a way of exerting pressure on the British and Americans – the kind of game of great-power politics that de Gaulle enjoyed playing – in general his line to the British and Americans at this time was that he was their most reliable bulwark against Communism in France: as he had told Macmillan, he had no intention of becoming a French Kerensky.

De Gaulle's attempt to reassure the Allies that he could be trusted did win him some credit with Eisenhower, who had previously viewed him suspiciously as someone interested only in playing politics. The two men met at the end of 1943 to sort out a serious difficulty that had blown up over the deployment of French forces in Italy. In November, a French Expeditionary Force (CEF) of two French divisions, under the command of Juin, had been sent to Italy to join American Fifth Army.[72] This French force, formed out of the regular French army in North Africa, had been armed by the Americans. It gave the French their first opportunity to play a serious role in the war. The CFLN proposed that the next division to go to Italy should be one of the original Free French divisions commanded by Diego Brosset, but since his unit had been equipped by the British it was difficult to integrate into an American army. Giraud had done nothing to re-equip it with American matériel because he did not want to divert resources from what he saw as 'his' divisions. When the American high command refused to accept the 'Brosset division', Giraud offered another division of the regular army. De Gaulle overruled this decision. This was not merely a skirmish against Giraud: it would have been a terrible blow to the morale of the Free French officers to be excluded from the fighting in Italy.[73] Since this was not a consideration that weighed with Eisenhower, he in turn overruled de Gaulle and threatened to suspend the entire French rearmament programme. All the ingredients of a major crisis were in place.

De Gaulle proposed a top-level meeting to resolve the matter. His aim was to seize the opportunity to discuss the deployment of French forces in the next stages of the war in all theatres. His worry was that, if all French forces were committed to Italy, the French would not be able to play any role in the eventual Liberation of France. Meeting Eisenhower's Chief of Staff, General Bedell Smith, on 27 December de Gaulle received satisfaction regarding the deployment of the Brosset division, but also reassurance that he would be consulted about the future deployment of French forces on other fronts. On 30 December, before heading to Britain to take up his command of the Allied forces in preparation for the cross-Channel invasion now planned for 1944, Eisenhower paid a farewell visit to de Gaulle. The meeting was exceptionally cordial. Eisenhower admitted to de Gaulle that he had misjudged him in the past; de Gaulle replied – in English – 'you are a man' (using the words Napoleon had addressed to Goethe when they met in 1808). Eisenhower went on: 'If I find the occasion, I am ready to make a declaration expressing the confidence that I take away from our contacts, recognizing the injustice I have committed towards you and adding that you are ready, on your side, to offer us your full cooperation.' De Gaulle gave a long account of this meeting in his *Memoirs* while Eisenhower did not think it important enough to mention in his. But de Gaulle was not exaggerating the cordial tone, and one of Eisenhower's aides described the meeting as a 'love fest'.[74]

De Gaulle had less success with Churchill, who arrived in Marrakesh in July 1944 to recuperate from an illness and invited de Gaulle to meet him. De Gaulle was insulted that Churchill should presume to issue an invitation to a French leader on French soil; Churchill was insulted that de Gaulle did not leap at the chance to see him. Their respective advisers were on tenterhooks for a week about whether the meeting would go ahead. Events followed a familiar script. De Gaulle found a formula that allowed him to see Churchill without losing face, but the meeting solved nothing. On the British side Cooper reported that de Gaulle had been 'very difficult and unhelpful', behaving 'as if he were Stalin and Roosevelt combined'; on the French side, Massigli, 'trembling until the last moment', felt that there had been a 'good atmosphere'.[75] 'Good atmosphere' meant that the two men had not actually screamed at each other. To Roosevelt, Churchill reported that their talk had 'consisted mainly of a prolonged complaint and lecture by me, in good manners and bad French, upon his many follies'. He told some MPs in London two weeks later what he had said to de Gaulle:

> Look here! I am the leader of a strong and unbeaten nation. Yet every morning when I wake my first thought is how I can please President Roosevelt, and my second is how I can conciliate Marshal Stalin. Your situation is very different. Why then should your first waking thought be how can you snap your fingers at the British and the Americans?[76]

Despite this tetchy encounter, during these months of anticipation de Gaulle, for whom conflict was the oxygen of politics, remained remarkably equable, apart from his explosion over Syria in November. In late October, Macmillan found him 'calmer' than usual 'with a greater sense of responsibility and less sense of inferiority'; Alphand reported that he was affecting 'complete indifference' to the question of recognition; and from London Cadogan admitted in May 1944 that for 'for months he displays – we must admit it – great patience under our rather odd trend of policy dictated from the White House.'[77] De Gaulle's assumption was that the realities of power would ultimately resolve the issue of CFLN recognition in his favour. He told Queuille that it might even be better if the Allies did not recognize the CFLN: 'We will be able to say to them later: you were wrong, and we owe you nothing.'[78]

De Gaulle's surface calm required a powerful effort of will. Underneath he was continuously churning with fury. We have an exceptionally vivid portrait of him at this time from Jacques Lecompte-Boinet, a Resistance leader who had arrived in Algiers in November. Lecompte-Boinet's movement was one of the most important in the Occupied Zone, but he was personally a modest individual lacking the touchy *amour propre* of leaders like Frenay or d'Astier. Invited to dine with de Gaulle one evening, he wrote up his impressions immediately afterwards. Before dinner, Lecompte-Boinet offered de Gaulle a Gauloise to be told that he now smoked only English cigarettes. Over dinner, in the presence of Yvonne de Gaulle, there was no discussion of politics. After she had retired to bed, de Gaulle let rip:

> For three hours he spoke to me without drawing breath or posing a single question . . . He is not someone to put you at your ease. He does not seem to listen, poses no personal questions, his interlocutor is just a kind of inanimate object . . . Yet he was perfectly relaxed, seemed happy that I was there,

and happy to talk ... While he was talking I thought about how different he was from the idea that my Resistance comrades and I had developed about him. What force of will! What intelligence! What contempt for humanity! ... He says that France will have to recover alone. She can only count on herself ... England is governed by a doubtful individual, not very intelligent, who despises and fears intelligence ... The only problem now and after Liberation is the Communists: certainly they will be the loudest to shout 'long live de Gaulle' but they will do their best to sabotage all his projects from the wings. The war is over and there is nothing to worry about in arming the Resistance. Its role is to ensure order to prevent the Anglo-Americans interfering in our affairs ... The British will arm the Giraudists and the Communists to sink de Gaulle (he calls himself de Gaulle) ... Nothing about us resisters. Not a word of thanks. Our problem is in the past. He affects not to have any need of us. Not a word about what is going on in France. He talks and talks, passionate, and riveting to listen to, using violent epithets when he talks about the men of Algiers. But what he was saying to me he might have been saying to anyone. I do not exist ... One has the impression he does not listen but it does seem that he registers what is said to him. The problem is that anyone timid and polite would not have a chance of being heard by him; you need to make your point at once ... He cuts himself off from most people and his immense contempt for humanity in general risks distorting his judgement on individuals ... He is a man alone, too immense, who does not have access to our world ... Twice I said I should be leaving; it was long after midnight; twice he kept me, then he accompanied me to the door ... He smiled at the moment he shook my hand. 'I am tired,' he said, and when I replied that he must look after himself for France whose leader he was, he replied: 'Poor leader' ... a sudden flash of humanity which moved me to the depths of my soul.[79]

TOWARDS D-DAY

In February 1944 de Gaulle suffered a second severe bout of malaria. He was completely out of action for about ten days and remained weak until the middle of March. Once he had recovered, the next three months were a period of intense activity as the CFLN prepared feverishly for the planned Allied landings – while still unsure what role it would be allowed to play.

To increase its control over the military activity of the Resistance, at the end of 1943 the BCRA had divided France into twelve regions to each of which it sent a military delegate (Délégué Militaire Régional – DMR) to coordinate Resistance action with the Allied military operations. A national military delegate was appointed to crown this structure in Paris. At the same time, the military forces of the Resistance – the Secret Army (AS) which Moulin had worked painstakingly to create – merged with the Communist Francs-Tireurs et Partisans (FTP) to form the so-called French Forces of the Interior (Forces Françaises de l'Intérieur – FFI). Remaining separate from the FFI were the not inconsiderable forces of Vichy's former Armistice Army which had now gone underground, taking the name Organisation de Résistance de l'Armée (ORA). Since many of the ORA cadres retained Giraudist sympathies, de Gaulle moved to prevent any dissident action on their part by consolidating his control over the French intelligence services. Traditionally in France the secret services – counterintelligence, espionage and so on – had been a specialized branch of the army. But the role that the BCRA had come to play was more extensive. It was the sinews of the Gaullist state in exile, aiming to ensure the triumph of the CFLN in France, and run by a man completely devoted to de Gaulle. But after his arrival in Algiers, Giraud was in control of the regular army's traditional secret services. These were staffed by professional soldiers suspicious not only of the unconventional methods and – as they saw it – amateurism of the BCRA but also of its political allegiance to de Gaulle. The danger of two parallel and competing secret services had emerged during the liberation of Corsica where Giraud had used his own networks to circumvent de Gaulle. De Gaulle had to avoid any replication of this situation on the mainland. ORA, supported by the army intelligences services, was the last possible bastion of Giraudism.

De Gaulle's first solution was a compromise. The secret services would be headed from London by General Cochet, who had opposed Pétain from 1940 while never rallying fully to de Gaulle. But de Gaulle was warned in ever more alarmist terms by Passy, Boris, Philip and others that Cochet had surrounded himself with unrepentant Vichyites and was creating a separate Giraudist secret service operation.[80] De Gaulle therefore decided to order the full amalgamation of the two intelligence services under the authority of the ultra-loyalist Soustelle. When Giraud objected to such a post being held by a civilian de Gaulle replied sardonically: 'If that worries you I will dress him up as a General.'[81] In April 1944 de Gaulle made his final move against Giraud. He removed him from the position of army Commander in Chief and offered him instead an honorary position – *inspecteur général des armées* – which Giraud refused. Giraudism was dead.

The real threat to de Gaulle's authority at the Liberation lay not in Giraudism but in the possibility of dual power shared between the

Resistance – especially the Communist Resistance – and the CFLN. In February 1944 the CNR set up a military committee (Comité d'Action Militaire – COMAC), dominated by the Communists, which claimed authority over the FFI. The CFLN in Algiers retaliated with an order (10 March) denying the COMAC operational control over the FFI. De Gaulle followed this by appointing General Koenig to be his military delegate in London and commander of the FFI. Koenig was a shrewd choice because, as the hero of Bir Hakeim, he was respected by the Allies. But whether Koenig or COMAC or the DMRs or the BCRA or anyone else would be able to control the disparate forces of the Resistance was another matter.

Having theoretically asserted its authority over the military forces of the Resistance, the CFLN turned its attention to what would occur in France after the Allied landings. This was the subject of an ordinance of 14 March stipulating that in the fighting zone the local military delegates of the CFLN would have responsibility for liaising with the Allied armies. Elsewhere authority would be exercised by the CFLN's *commissaires de la République* – with the departmental liberation committees (CDLs) enjoying a purely advisory role. The Communists denounced this ordinance as setting up a 'French AMGOT' to prevail over the Resistance, and the CNR fought back on 23 March by reasserting the role of the CDLs. It also voted to install local liberation committees in every locality – exactly the dispersal of power de Gaulle sought to avoid. More encouraging for de Gaulle was the Communists' decision that it served their purposes better to be in the CFLN than outside it. When he renewed his invitation to them to join his government, they were ready to scale down their conditions. Two Communists entered the CFLN on 4 April on de Gaulle's terms. This imposed a minimum of governmental solidarity on the Communists even if it did not prevent them pursuing their own objectives in mainland France by trying to infiltrate themselves into the CDLs and turn them into a counterweight to the central power that de Gaulle was planning to exercise through the CFLN.

To consolidate his authority further in France, de Gaulle now moved fast to appoint a new delegate to fill the void left by the death of Moulin and then the arrest of Bollaert. His choice was Alexandre Parodi, an experienced civil servant in his forties who had been active in the Resistance. Having seemed curiously indifferent to France for several months, de Gaulle was now fully focused. The order appointing Parodi was taken to France directly by a BCRA agent as part of a mission designated by de Gaulle as having 'priority over all others'.[82] In a speech to the Consultative Assembly on 18 March de Gaulle again hammered home the message he had been repeating for the last six months: 'Nothing can be done except in an orderly manner . . . There cannot be, I repeat with force, there cannot be any other authority except that which emanates from the central power [that is, the CFLN].'[83] This was a message to the Communists – but also to the Allies, warning them against the temptation of last-minute deals with Vichy.

   Another worry for de Gaulle was that the Allies would renege on Eisenhower's promise to include the French among the armies preparing to liberate France. In fact Eisenhower did not have the authority to give such an assurance. As de Gaulle's military representative in Washington reported in February: 'Eisenhower has no power to decide if we will participate in a landing in northern France; the decision lies entirely with Washington.'[84] As the fighting in Italy continued to be tough, it was not impossible that the Allied high command would decide that the French armies were more useful there than in liberating France. It was alarming when the British General Maitland Wilson, Supreme Allied Commander in the Mediterranean, summoned de Gaulle and Giraud to a meeting 'to disclose' – the term seemed sinister – his latest thinking about the use of French forces. De Gaulle sent Giraud to represent him with vague instructions: 'Do not commit yourself to anything. We will see what the whole thing is about. Actually I have a good idea . . . The government [that is, the CFLN] will have to take a decision and it is preferable that for the moment I keep myself in reserve.'[85] This seems reminiscent of de Gaulle sending Catroux to negotiate the Syrian armistice in 1941 while preparing himself to descend in fury from the clouds if necessary. In the end the CFLN was satisfied that French troops would participate in the liberation of France while not being reassured of its right to be consulted on such issues. The problem was that, while among the other Allies decisions of this kind were taken at governmental level, the CFLN was only able to communicate officially with Allied chiefs of staff because it was not recognized as having the attributes of a government.[86]

   There seemed to be no progress on the issue of recognition. The currency issue also rumbled on. The American Treasury Secretary Henry Morgenthau had proposed as a compromise that the notes issued by the Americans would be labelled 'French Republic', but Roosevelt refused to accept even this, taking to a level of absurdity the principle that no one had the right to prejudge the kind of regime the French would adopt after the war. Nonetheless Roosevelt finally agreed on 15 March that Eisenhower, once in France, might 'consult the CFLN', but that he could also deal with any *de facto* French authority although 'not the Vichy government as such'. The Free French, understandably paranoid by this stage, were not reassured. Viénot in London, not usually prone to de Gaulle's mistrust, worried that the Americans had a dangerously elastic view of what they meant by Vichy: 'The recourse to Admiral Darlan was presented as a way of destroying the powers of a Vichy incarnated at that time by Laval. Against a Vichy incarnated tomorrow by Doriot [an ultra-collaborationist] the recourse to the same Laval could be justified as a new step towards the destruction of Vichy.'[87] Even Cadogan wondered in May if Roosevelt was not still 'hankering after Vichy'.[88]

No one was more frustrated than Eisenhower, who took it upon himself to start talks with Koenig at the end of April. He was sharply reminded by Roosevelt that any discussions must be 'tentative' and that he should feel at liberty to consult others besides the CFLN.[89] British officials and ministers were desperate to see Roosevelt's policy overruled, but Churchill was still unwilling to do anything to jeopardize his relations with the American President. Seeing Viénot on 4 April, Churchill advised him to tell de Gaulle not to 'rub Roosevelt up the wrong way', while giving no indications of what the right way might be. He took the opportunity to rehearse all his grievances about de Gaulle: 'All his life he had been a friend of France. He was still looking for the France he used to know. He did not find it in General de Gaulle.' Massigli found this so alarming that he kept it to himself.[90] This was not the only information Massigli held back from de Gaulle for fear that it would cause an explosion. As the tempers of the French negotiators in Washington became increasingly frayed, Hoppenot wrote to Algiers blaming Monnet's informal diplomacy for the lack of progress. On the grounds that it was not 'elegant' for one former Giraudist to try to win favour with de Gaulle by blaming another, Massigli refused to pass the letter on.[91] When starting his mission Hoppenot had been ready to show a 'lot of patience . . . and swallow many affronts with smiling dignity'; now he had reached such a level of frustration that he no longer worried about '*outbursts* [in English] from the General'.[92]

An 'outburst' occurred, and de Gaulle's eerie calm finally cracked, when on 17 April, with D-Day approaching, the British announced a cipher ban on all communication with Britain for security reasons. This decision cut the CFLN in Algiers off from its representatives in London. Massigli formally protested, but de Gaulle went a step further. He refused forthwith to receive any Allied representatives in Algiers, and instructed Koenig and Viénot in London to break off their unofficial negotiations with Eisenhower and the British. He also decided to play the Russian card more overtly than in the past. On 9 May, he made a speech in Tunis condemning the Allied refusal to talk to the CFLN and paid warm homage to 'dear and powerful Russia' which he hoped would become a 'permanent ally'. Two weeks later he saw Bogomolov and poured out bile against Churchill for an hour: 'We have no confidence in the English even when they talk of an alliance with France . . . Churchill has understood nothing of my mission . . . He does not see in Gaullism that there is a new France. France for him is finished . . . He wants to turn me into an instrument of his policy.' As for America it wanted a 'docile France to make it a base for their European policy'.[93] This was the kind of talk that terrified Massigli, although Bogomolov did not take it too seriously.

In London, Koenig simply ignored de Gaulle's instructions about ending contacts with Eisenhower, and Eisenhower, desperate to invite de Gaulle to London, pushed to the limits what was permitted by Roosevelt. Roosevelt seemed on the verge of conceding that de Gaulle could be brought into technical military discussions about the Liberation as long as the discussions avoided 'politics': he told Eisenhower that the French were 'shell-shocked' (his way of explaining away the irrefutable evidence of de Gaulle's popularity). Eisenhower replied that there seemed to be only two factions in France: the 'Vichy gang, and the other characterized by unreasoning admiration for de Gaulle' (the 'unreasoning' presumably added for Roosevelt's benefit).[94] In the same vein, even Churchill cabled Roosevelt arguing that 'it is very difficult to cut the French out of the liberation of France.'[95] He was under increasing pressure from British public opinion, parliament and his own government to bring de Gaulle into the discussions about the Liberation.

On 25 May, Duff Cooper presented de Gaulle with an invitation from the British government to come to Britain. There was a week of suspense before the General decided to accept. Since he was not told whether any representative of the American government would be present, he was wary of being lured into assurances that CFLN representatives would assist Allied forces to establish their authority in French liberated territory while not obtaining in return recognition of the political authority of the CFLN. If no American were present at the discussion, how would it be possible to grant cooperation in exchange for recognition? Massigli threatened to resign if de Gaulle refused to go. Churchill sent another pressing message: 'Come please now with your colleagues at the earliest possible moment and in the deepest secrecy. I give you my personal assurance that this is in the interests of France.'[96] On the evening of 2 June the CFLN met for five hours to discuss whether de Gaulle should go to London despite having no guarantee of American participation in the talks. Only four members, including Philip and Pleven, were opposed. At the same meeting, the CFLN proclaimed itself the 'Provisional Government of the French Republic' (Gouvernement Provisoire de la République Française – GPRF).

On the morning of 3 June, de Gaulle took his leave of the Committee in his most statesmanlike mode: 'We need to look far into the future, that of Franco-British relations ... It must not be said that France was absent from the Allied Headquarters at the moment of the assault on Europe.'[97] Until the last moment Duff Cooper was on tenterhooks, as de Gaulle had intended:

> I felt extremely anxious this morning and was most relieved when Palewski turned up with a letter from de Gaulle agreeing to go ... We then had to make the necessary arrangements as soon as possible ... We arrived at the airfield about 3 p.m ... most of the party had assembled. De Gaulle himself was the last to arrive and I was relieved when I saw him inside the plane.[98]

On the same day Eisenhower wrote to Washington:

> We have our own direct means of communication with the Resistance Groups in France but all our information leads us to believe that the only authority these Resistance Groups desire to recognize is that of de Gaulle and his Committee ... De Gaulle is now controlling the only French military forces that can take part in this operation. Consequently, from the purely military viewpoint we must ... deal with him alone. He, however, takes the attitude that the military and political matters go hand in hand and will not cooperate militarily unless political recognition of some kind is accorded him.[99]

It was clear what conclusion Eisenhower wished to draw. As he set off for England, de Gaulle sensed that his position was strong.

13

Liberation, June–August 1944

THE LONGEST DAYS, 4–9 JUNE

De Gaulle landed at Northolt near London on the morning of 4 June. Everything was done to flatter him. A military band was on hand to play the 'Marseillaise', and he was handed an effusive message from Churchill which opened: 'Welcome to our shores.'[1] A car was waiting to take him to Churchill, who had eccentrically installed himself in a railway carriage at a small siding station near Portsmouth in order to be closer to events. Eden remembered: 'The Prime Minister, moved by his sense of history, was on the track to greet the General with arms outstretched. Unfortunately de Gaulle did not respond easily to such a mood.'[2] Just before de Gaulle arrived in Britain, Churchill had cabled Roosevelt declaring that he was sure 'de Gaulle can be persuaded to say the right thing.'[3] This confidence must have been based on hope rather than experience.

De Gaulle was tense and wary, Churchill warm on the surface but apprehensive underneath. Rather tactlessly Churchill had also included among others on the British side the South African premier, Jan Smuts. Smuts was a member of the War Cabinet but had caused much offence to the French in a speech in December 1943 announcing that France was finished as a great power. The first difficulties arose when Churchill said it might be desirable to discuss 'political matters'. De Gaulle replied that there was no point unless the Americans were also involved. Eden interjected that there was reason to believe that, if de Gaulle agreed to go the United States, preliminary discussions might start at once with the American Ambassador. The Minister of Labour, Ernest Bevin, chipped in to express the view that it would be 'regrettable' if de Gaulle failed to grasp this opportunity. At this point de Gaulle exploded:

> Why do you seem to think that I need to submit my candidacy for the leadership of France to Roosevelt? The French government exists. I have nothing

to ask, in this respect, of the Americans or the British. That being said, it is important for all the allies that we organise relations between the French administration and the military command. We proposed this nine months ago. As your armies are about to land, I understand your haste to see the question settled. We are ready to do so. But where is the American representative? Without him nothing can be concluded. Go ahead, fight the war alone with your false money!

Churchill exploded in his turn: 'You must know that when we have to choose between Europe and the open seas, we will always be with the open seas. Each time I have to choose between you and Roosevelt, I will choose Roosevelt.' This was de Gaulle's rendering of Churchill's words. They rankled for the rest of his life and he would often recall them. The British minute of the meeting reports what Churchill said slightly differently, but the sense is similar.[4]

None of this put de Gaulle in a good frame of mind for his visit to Eisenhower's HQ later in the afternoon. Eisenhower wanted nothing more than to reach an agreement with de Gaulle, but his hands remained tied by Roosevelt. Eisenhower flattered de Gaulle by asking his opinion whether, if the weather continued to be bad, he should run the risk of delaying the D-Day operation until the tides were favourable again. De Gaulle advised not to wait. As he was leaving, Eisenhower, 'with obvious embarrassment' in de Gaulle's words, handed over the speech he planned to deliver when Allied troops landed.[5] De Gaulle found it unacceptable since it called on the French population to obey the American military authorities and made no mention of the CFLN. Bedell Smith, Eisenhower's Chief of Staff, calmed de Gaulle by suggesting that he could propose amendments. The meeting ended on a note of ambiguity as to whether changes were possible at such a late stage. De Gaulle returned to London and installed himself in the Connaught; nothing had been resolved.

On the next day (5 June), Eisenhower decided to launch the operation in the early hours of 6 June. Peake was sent to ask de Gaulle if he would broadcast after Eisenhower. Since it had become clear that Eisenhower's message could not be changed because copies were ready to be dropped over France, de Gaulle replied that he would not speak immediately after Eisenhower. Otherwise he would seem to be approving what Eisenhower had said. He also refused to allow French liaison officers to accompany the Allied troops. De Gaulle's exact words to Peake got lost in translation. Over the next few hours, contradictory messages sped across the Atlantic: 'The General will not speak,' 'the General will speak,' 'the General has changed his mind.'[6]

Churchill, wrongly believing that Gaulle had refused to speak at all, flew into a rage. Cadogan reported that the Cabinet that evening 'endured the usual passionate anti-de Gaulle harangue from PM ... It's a girls' school. R[oosevelt], P[rime]M[inister] – and it must be admitted de G[aulle] – all behave like girls approaching the age of puberty.'⁷ At 10.30 p.m. on 5 June, as the landing craft were leaving for France, Viénot arrived at the Foreign Office to clear up the misunderstanding over de Gaulle's speech. He agreed to try to persuade the General to relent over the liaison officers. Returning to the Connaught, Viénot was screamed at by de Gaulle for an hour. As the first parachutists were landing in France in the early hours of 6 June, Viénot was back at the Foreign Office to be screamed at this time by Churchill. When Viénot left, Churchill sent for Morton to order him to send de Gaulle forcibly back to Algiers – 'in chains if necessary'. Harvey commented: 'PM is almost insane at times in his hatred of de Gaulle, only less insane than the President.'⁸

It fell to Eden to pick up the pieces. Ignoring Churchill's instruction to have de Gaulle deported, he sent Peake to urge de Gaulle to broadcast as soon as possible. A prolonged silence by de Gaulle after Eisenhower had broadcast would become embarrassing. De Gaulle agreed to speak around noon on 6 June. Since Viénot was 'too frightened' to ask for a copy, all the British could do, in Cadogan's words, was to 'check de Gaulle from the disc and stop it if it was too bad'.⁹ But would they get an opportunity to hear a recording in advance? One British official, who was there to receive de Gaulle at the BBC, described the scene:

> Five minutes before his appointed time the giant figure of General blocked the entrance door. His face was set. One glance told me that he was in his grimmest mood. His greeting . . . was restrained but friendly. I introduced him to the three Americans. He stiffened into complete frigidity, made three half turns as he gave the limpest of hands to each, then, drawing himself to the full stretch of his immense height, strode forward along the stone corridor.

The real problem was that de Gaulle had no text and only a few scribbled notes, while insisting that the broadcast go out live. If told to submit an advance recording of his speech for approval it was likely he would refuse to go ahead. One of the BBC staff present suddenly had a brainwave. He flattered de Gaulle by telling him that the broadcast was so important that the BBC wanted to arrange for it to be translated into twenty-four other languages for the rest of the world. For that reason they needed a recording.¹⁰ Whether or not he saw through the ruse, de Gaulle agreed. A recording was made and the speech went out at 6.00 p.m. It was one of de Gaulle's great rhetorical performances:

The supreme battle has begun . . . It is of course the Battle of France, and the battle for France! . . . For the sons of France, wherever they may be, whoever they may be, the simple and sacred duty is to fight the enemy by all the means available. The directives given by the French government . . . must be followed to the letter . . . Behind the heavy clouds of our blood and our tears, the sunshine of our grandeur is re-emerging.[11]

As Churchill wrote to Roosevelt the next day, the speech 'is remarkable, as he has not a single soldier in the great battle now developing'.[12] This was true since although de Gaulle had secured agreement that French troops would participate in the Liberation of France none had yet been deployed on French territory. Most provocative from the British point of view was the reference to the 'French government' – no longer even designated as 'provisional' (one wonders if the French people to whom the speech was addressed had the remotest clue what 'government' was being referred to). Eden decided to let this pass and deal with Churchill afterwards.

The issue of the liaison officers remained outstanding. Cooper and Eden went to work on de Gaulle in the afternoon of 7 June. With bad grace, he agreed to send twenty liaison officers of the 120 planned for the first batch. Later in the evening Eden saw de Gaulle again to discuss the organization of civil administration in liberated areas: 'He was personally trying, I think, to make himself pleasant, but politically stiff. He is convinced that this is the only way to get anything out of the Americans and ourselves, whereas so far as Churchill is concerned the tactics could not be worse.' De Gaulle launched into a 'long lament' about how badly he was being treated: 'I retorted that it was a fatal mistake in national policy to have too much pride. "She stoops to conquer" was an action which we could each of us find useful to observe at times.' It took some moments to find an adequate translation for a phrase that was quite outside de Gaulle's range of reference, not only linguistically.[13] In the end, de Gaulle conceded that he would not object to Viénot talking to the British about liaison arrangements.

Two days later (9 June), there was another flare-up when Eisenhower announced that he was issuing the currency prepared by the Americans. De Gaulle issued a stinging press release to denounce this – the first time these quarrels had been made public.[14] Roosevelt wrote to Churchill: 'It seems that prima-donnas do not change their spots.'[15] Back in Algiers, Massigli was far from happy with what he was hearing about de Gaulle's behaviour in London. He indicated where his sympathies lay by showing the British Chargé d'Affaires the content of the telegrams he was receiving from de Gaulle in London.[16] But everyone on the CFLN was united behind de Gaulle on the currency issue. Most important was the fact that de Gaulle had conceded that Viénot could talk informally to the British about liaison arrangements with the Allied forces. He confirmed this in a slightly less angry telegram back to Algiers on 9 June. While he refused any official agreement until the Americans were brought in, this 'naturally does not signify that we should refuse to talk with the English'.[17] By any other name, this was a retreat – perhaps stooping to conquer.

Had it been worthwhile? Everything de Gaulle refused on 6 June, he had conceded three days later. At the height of the conflict, Cadogan commented: 'We always start by putting ourselves in the wrong, and then de Gaulle puts himself *more* in the wrong. He deserves to lose the rubber.'[18] It depended on the game being played. After the war, Billotte reported what de Gaulle had once confided to him about negotiating tactics:

> Begin by saying 'no'! Two things will follow: either your 'no' is destined to remain a 'no' and you have shown yourself to be someone of character. Or finally you end up saying 'yes'. But then (a) you have given yourself time to reflect; (b) people will be all the more grateful for your final 'yes'.[19]

Both these elements were in play during these six days. For the first four days, saying 'no', de Gaulle had put himself at the centre of things, proving that 'France' existed and could not be taken for granted. He had added some epic pages to his future *Memoirs* while knowing that he was not taking any significant risks since the British were soliciting him rather than the other way around. On the other hand, having played the 'man of character', a few days' reflection had revealed that the situation was different from what he had believed it to be on arrival. As Viénot reported to Massigli:

> The position taken by the CFLN has the gross disadvantage, by its simplistic intransigence, that it did not allow us to exploit the divisions within the British cabinet: the anti-Gaullist and pro-American current is diminishing by the day ... It took a few days for the General to realise this situation ... Through contact with reality the General has progressively evolved.[20]

14 JUNE, BAYEUX

De Gaulle's more accommodating position was reinforced by his successful visit to Normandy on 14 June. Although the Allies had not achieved all their initial objectives for D-Day – the city of Caen, a target for early capture, remained in German hands until 21 July – within a week they had established a bridgehead about 100 kilometres long and 25 kilometres deep. De Gaulle was understandably desperate to visit this fragment of liberated territory as soon as possible. Churchill unenthusiastically agreed. He warned the local British commander General Montgomery that he had to 'inflict on you a visit from General de Gaulle', whom he should not take the trouble to receive at the beach. His instructions were that de Gaulle should be allowed to visit the town of Bayeux but not hold any meeting: 'If however the people are anxious to welcome him on his way through, it is not for us to deny this.' Churchill's ideal was that de Gaulle should 'drive slowly through the town, shake hands with a few people, and then return'.[21] De Gaulle had other ideas.

In de Gaulle's battle to be recognized by the Allies, the ultimate test would be the reactions of the French population. On the day de Gaulle visited French soil Roosevelt, ever deluded where the General was concerned, confided to the American Secretary for War, Henry L. Stimson, that 'de Gaulle will crumble and that the British support of de Gaulle will be confounded by the progress of events . . . Other parties will spring up as the liberation goes on and de Gaulle will become a very little figure.'[22] It was certainly true that the reception de Gaulle would receive was no foregone conclusion. Although the Vichy regime had long forfeited any credibility with the French population, Pétain still retained some prestige. In April 1944, he had paid his only visit to Paris during the entire Occupation. Substantial crowds turned out to greet him. On this tour Pétain visited cities which had been destroyed by Allied bombing and he was able to pose for a last time as protector of the French people against the ravages of war. And few parts of the country had been more hit by bombing than Normandy. It had not been a region of major Resistance activity and the Normans had a reputation for being conservative and cautious. So there were many reasons why de Gaulle could not count on receiving a deliriously enthusiastic welcome.

Bayeux, with a population of 15,000, was the largest city so far liberated. It had been remarkably unscathed by fighting or bombing.[23] Life continued relatively normally while the war raged a few kilometres away. The city was run by a group of Allied civil affairs officers who kept out of politics and did not interfere with the Vichy authorities they found in place, a Vichy *sous-préfet* eager to win favour and a Pétainist bishop who helped organize those made homeless by the fighting. But there was also a local Resistance liberation committee that had put up posters calling for a purge. Bayeux therefore existed in a strange administrative limbo where the Vichy authorities, the Resistance and the Allies cohabited. There was no CFLN presence because the *Commissaire* appointed to take over the region was trapped behind enemy lines and unable to reach this pocket of liberated territory. Two days before leaving for France, de Gaulle informed François Coulet, who had proved his effectiveness in Corsica, that he would accompany him to Bayeux and remain behind as provisional *Commissaire*. Churchill was told nothing about this.

The night before his departure, de Gaulle dined with some Foreign Office officials. Harvey, who was among the guests, wrote: 'Dinner was grim. I have never seen de Gaulle look so worn, *"martyrisé"*.'[24] De Gaulle, accompanied by his large party, set off from Portsmouth in the morning. The sea was very rough and everyone was heavily sedated with Nautamine. According to Boislambert, who was one of the party, this induced slightly euphoric effects. Not it seems on de Gaulle. He was tense and silent throughout. When Viénot tried to break the ice by remarking that it was four years to the day since the Germans had arrived in Paris, he received the curt reply: 'That was a mistake.'[25] Landing on the coast, some of the party were sent ahead to Bayeux to prepare de Gaulle's arrival, while de Gaulle was driven in a jeep with General Béthouart to Montgomery's HQ.

After paying his respects briefly to Montgomery, de Gaulle set off for Bayeux with Béthouart. The few people they passed on the largely deserted roads seemed surprised to see French uniforms. At one moment when the jeep stooped, it was surrounded by an excited group who, seeing Béthouart's four stars, took him to be General de Gaulle about whose appearance they had no idea.[26] The jeep also encountered two gendarmes. When told they were in the presence of de Gaulle, the two men saluted and pedalled off to announce his imminent arrival in Bayeux. De Gaulle turned to his companions and said 'recognition has taken place', meaning that he had been accepted implicitly as head of the government.

In Bayeux, loudspeakers informed the population that de Gaulle was arriving. Coulet had preceded him at the prefecture where he was welcomed by the Vichy *sous-préfet* who clambered on to a chair to remove the portrait of Pétain before greeting de Gaulle respectfully. De Gaulle refused a glass of champagne and met local dignitaries, including the bishop. The transition from one regime to another was effected in a matter of minutes. De Gaulle now proceeded on foot to the central square where he made a speech. Whether bemused or flattered, the peaceable Norman peasants who had not suffered terribly under the Occupation until the recent Allied bombing were enjoined by him to 'continue the combat today as you have never ceased to do since the start of this war and since June 1940'.[27]

To one of de Gaulle's party the population seemed 'egoistical, reserved and in reality not very Gaullist', displaying 'great enthusiasm without in my view real emotion'.[28] Viénot's opinion was that they seemed to have little idea what this new government was. Coulet's impressions were not quite so negative: 'Warm and sympathetic enthusiasm, but in no way delirious and curiously natural – men in their bourgeois clothes, women in their summer dresses, a few gendarmes, no soldiers – it was rather as if a very esteemed and popular Republican dignitary had come one Sunday in peacetime to inaugurate a local fair.'[29] If this was an accurate description, it could hardly have suited de Gaulle better since it implied the absolute normality of the transfer of power to him. Nonetheless in his *Memoirs* de Gaulle later transmuted the reality of this rather under-powered occasion in his inimitable style:

> At the sight of General de Gaulle the inhabitants were overcome by a kind of stupor which exploded into cheers and tears ... Women were smiling. Men held their hands out to me. We went our way together, overwhelmed and fraternal, feeling our patriotic joy, pride and hope surging up from the abyss.[30]

After visiting two other small localities, de Gaulle returned to the beach. The propaganda services of the CFLN rapidly produced a short film of the visit. We see de Gaulle arriving at the coast, shaking a few hands while his eyes dart around with a look of extraordinary suspicion as if he were thinking that at any moment some British officer might appear to spoil his visit; his jeep sets off and on the deserted road a cassock-wearing priest raises his hat in joyful salute; the jeep passes through a small village where people are waving and cheering from windows; walking through the crowded streets of Bayeux the General stops from time to time for a stiff handshake; at one moment the flicker of a smile even seems to cross his lips; a girl hands him a posy of flowers which miraculously disappears from his hands a second later (perhaps it is handed to Maurice Schumann who is at his side); in the Place du Château, he addresses quite a large and enthusiastic crowd in front of a tricolour with the Cross of Lorraine; finally he is seen confidently shaking the hand of Montgomery and looking almost as if he is giving him orders.[31]

Whatever the intimate feelings of the population about de Gaulle's brief appearance, the British and American press described it as a triumph. Montgomery reported to Churchill slightly differently that the reception 'was definitely lukewarm and there was no real enthusiasm'. But he failed to note the most important result of the visit. Taking his leave of Montgomery, de Gaulle had casually remarked to him that Coulet and three other people would be staying behind in Bayeux. Montgomery, who did not grasp the significance of this information – 'I have no idea what is their function' – raised no objection.[32] Their function was to assume power on de Gaulle's behalf. Just before leaving, de Gaulle told Coulet, 'Don't give them any politics; that is not what they want.' Coulet followed this advice. He found himself dealing with citizens who mostly harboured no negative feelings towards Pétain. Even the leader of the local liberation committee had a portrait of Pétain in his house. The bishop was ardently Pétainist and what worried him most was that Coulet was Protestant. When Coulet wanted to organize an event to mark the speech of 18 June he discovered that the date meant little to anyone. Although he did replace the Vichy *sous-préfet*, his main concern was to ensure that order was maintained and the population fed.[33] This is exactly what the Allied civil affairs officers wanted. In the absence of any orders to the contrary, they accepted this stealthy Gaullist *coup d'état*, and were ready to accept the authority of the CFLN. All this offered yet more ammunition to those trying to push Roosevelt into abandoning a policy that was being rendered redundant by events on the ground.

INTERLUDE

De Gaulle returned to Algiers in the best of moods. On 26 June his speech to the Consultative Assembly was so statesmanlike that one Foreign Office official commented that it might 'almost have been delivered by the Secretary of State in the House of Commons so closely does it coincide with our own view of the situation'.[34] Between 27 June and 30 June, de Gaulle was in Italy to pay homage to the role of the French armies in the Italian campaign. The Italian theatre of the war has been overshadowed by the Normandy campaign, but it involved some of the toughest fighting on the western front. It was generally agreed that the four French divisions had played a decisive role, at the cost of 32,000 casualties. Juin's slow progress up the Italian peninsula in the face of tenacious German opposition did not have the epic quality of Leclerc's marches across the desert or of Koenig's David against Rommel's Goliath at Bir Hakeim, but it was the first time that de Gaulle could justifiably claim that his armies were playing a part in the Allied victory. This campaign heralded the return of France as a serious military force. While de Gaulle was engaged in his furious exchanges with Churchill on the eve of D-Day, Juin's troops were entering Rome.

Having congratulated French troops, de Gaulle was received by Pope Pius XII whose attitude to fascism had hardly been glorious. De Gaulle's description of this encounter in his *Memoirs* is, as one early biographer noted, 'a little masterpiece of *vacherie*'. The General observed that the Pope judged matters 'from a point of view which goes beyond men, their enterprises and their quarrels'. Although the 'Holy See, in conformity with its eternal prudence, had hitherto ignored Fighting France' and maintained relations with Vichy, the 'Holy Father desired the defeat of Hitler but was worried about the future of Germany'. De Gaulle concluded that Pius showed 'piety, pity and political sense in the highest sense of the word'. What he does not say was that the Pope, who expressed his fear of the power of Communism in the post-war world, was worried about possible reprisals against a Catholic hierarchy in France that had supported Vichy to the end.[35]

Between 5 and 12 July, de Gaulle paid his endlessly discussed but endlessly delayed visit to the United States. He had several meetings with Roosevelt. The story that at one lunch, where Admiral Leahy was present, Roosevelt turned to his former Ambassador to Pétain and said he should be drinking Vichy water, is probably apocryphal. And another story recounted by an American observer that, to break the ice after one dinner, the Chair of the House Committee on Foreign Affairs, who was also a professional entertainer, offered a mystified de Gaulle a trick cigar, seems improbable.[36] De Gaulle's account of the visit in his *Memoirs* does not dwell on such trivialities but drips with irony. He remembers Cordell Hull as displaying an 'elevation of soul' that was 'handicapped by his limited knowledge of everything that was not America'. He tells us that before leaving he presented Roosevelt with the gift of a small mechanical submarine made by the workers of the arsenal of Bizerta and that in return Roosevelt gave him a photograph dedicated to 'General de Gaulle who is my friend'.[37] (What de Gaulle did not know was that Roosevelt passed on the submarine at Christmas to his youngest grandchild Curtis. When his wife pointed out that it was not proper to dispose in this way of a present from a head of state, Roosevelt replied that de Gaulle was only head of 'some French committee'.)[38]

De Gaulle met a wide range of political figures and even paid a visit to General Pershing, the eighty-four-year-old leader of the American forces in the Great War. Pershing, living in a military hospital, asked to be remembered to his old friend Pétain. As a public relations exercise, de Gaulle's American trip could not have gone better. Before leaving Washington, he gave a press conference where his masterly performance impressed reporters for whom he had been built up into a kind of bogeyman. He seemed, one reporter noted, 'surprisingly gentle in manner'.[39]

After four days in Washington, de Gaulle paid a short visit to New York. Mayor La Guardia had laid on a popular reception. De Gaulle remarked of the cheering crowds, so different from the stuffier atmosphere of Washington, that he was being cheered by 'the Jews, the negroes, the crippled and the cuckolds'.[40] He received the French community at the Hotel Waldorf Astoria. He had asked in advance that the invitations be as 'liberal as possible' and exclude only 'the most violent and public adversaries'. These

included Leger, who would never have accepted an invitation from someone he could bring himself to refer to only as 'that man'. In New York, de
Gaulle was awed by the palpable sense of American power and wealth.
Gazing out of his hotel window at the stream of cars going down Park
Avenue, he mused: 'This is huge . . . this country has built no cars for three
years and yet look at them all . . . what capital they represent . . . what
powerful industry.'[41]

That power was impressive but also worrying – as had been de Gaulle's
conversations with Roosevelt. Curiously there is no American record of
their meetings and we have only de Gaulle's account: 'By small touches
Roosevelt sketched his vision, so well that it was impossible categorically
to contradict this artist and seducer.' That vision was a post-war world run
by a directory of four powers – America, Russia, China and Britain – with
America taking the predominant role. There is no reason to disbelieve this
account, which squares with what is known of Roosevelt's views, but it
may explain why Roosevelt told Churchill nothing more about the visit
than that it had 'gone off very well'. De Gaulle, savouring any opportunity
to insert grit in the relations between the Americans and British, gave a full
account to Cooper once back in Algiers. He told him that Roosevelt
planned military bases in French and British colonies in Asia and Africa.
Churchill was so annoyed by this that he proposed sending a copy of what
de Gaulle had told Cooper so as to allow Roosevelt 'an opportunity of
denying it'. But Eden dissuaded him from threatening the fragile improvement in relations that had been achieved with de Gaulle. In a reversal of
the normal state of affairs, Churchill wanted to stop the President's 'honeymoon with de Gaulle' and remind him of 'the way that de Gaulle interprets
friendliness'.[42] All this would have delighted the subject of these exchanges.

The most positive result of the visit was that Roosevelt finally recognized
de Gaulle's Committee as the *de facto* authority for the civil administration
of France. The British wanted to go a step further and recognize it as the
French provisional government, but Roosevelt blocked this. Back in Algiers
the Canadian Ambassador Georges Vanier found de Gaulle more relaxed
than he had ever seen him before: 'With stunning bad faith the General
assured me that the recognition of the Committee by M. Roosevelt had
massively irritated the British government.' All de Gaulle's resentments
about the days of June poured out:

> I experienced the contrast between the warm personal welcome of President
> Roosevelt and the deplorable treatment inflicted upon me by the Prime
> Minister . . . I saw M. Churchill only on one occasion the day of my arrival
> [4 June]. General Smuts was there and that is something I will not forget.[43]

This was partly Gaullist mischief-making, partly a reflection of de Gaulle's true fury over how he had been treated on 4 June.

PARIS

At the end of July, events started to move fast in France. Since the D-Day landings, Allied troops had been hemmed into their Normandy bridgehead unable to break through the German defences. Coulet continued to administer the small pocket of liberated territory, working harmoniously with the Allies. From time to time, the Communists in Algiers would write to de Gaulle criticizing Coulet for not having carried out a proper purge of the Vichy administration and not making use of the local 'Patriots' – by which they meant Communists. On 19 July, the Communist François Billoux wrote to de Gaulle: 'Yes or no, is the government for a National Insurrection? . . . As Liberation proceeds the GPRF must base itself above all on the People and the organizations representing it' – by which he meant the Communists.[44]

The Communists never let de Gaulle forget his famous declaration of 18 April 1942 that 'national liberation' was inseparable from 'national insurrection' – words which he had uttered when he was anxious to win Soviet support. De Gaulle repeated the idea on other occasions, but after July 1943 the word 'insurrection' disappeared from his speeches (along with the word 'revolution'). In the run-up to D-Day, the BCRA spent much time developing a strategy for the military forces of the Resistance. By March 1944, detailed instructions were ready for the CFLN's military delegates in France. The importance de Gaulle attached to this document was shown by the fact that he personally received the agent, Lazare Rachline, who was sent to take it over to France. De Gaulle impressed on Rachline that 'There must be no national insurrection except on my orders.' Rachline had not paid especial attention to this aspect of his instructions until, once in France, he found himself being constantly reminded by resisters of the speech that de Gaulle had delivered two years earlier on the need for a national insurrection.[45] In another set of instructions for the Resistance drawn up on 16 May, only weeks before D-Day, de Gaulle scored out the word 'insurrection' and replaced it with the somewhat vaguer term 'generalized actions of force'.[46]

The BCRA plans for the Resistance had included a number of coordinated plans for sabotage to be launched in conjunction with the Allied landings: *plan vert* for the railways, *plan violet* for telecommunications, *plan tortue* to slow down German communications, and so on. On D-Day, these plans were activated. The CFLN and BCRA later claimed that they had contributed importantly to the success of the Allied landings, demonstrating the perfect control that the BCRA exercised over the Resistance. According to the analysis carried out subsequently by the British, *plan vert* was the most successful but it was not clear if the sabotage actions had been the result of planning or of spontaneous local initiatives. Whatever the truth, the sabotage operations were also accompanied by sporadic and spontaneous local risings which the Germans repressed with brutal ferocity. For example, resisters 'liberated' the small town of Tulle in the Corrèze on 7 June; two days later the Germans returned and hanged 100 men in the town square. With the Allies holed up in Normandy, more actions of this kind would have been suicidal. But this did not stop the Communists pressing their strategy of insurrection.

Historians have long since scotched the idea that there was any Communist plan to 'seize' power at the Liberation. The only person with such a plan was de Gaulle. But it was true that the Communists were aiming to fragment power by encouraging localized uprisings under the aegis of departmental and local liberation committees which might offer an opportunity to challenge the authority of de Gaulle's government once it was installed in France. It was because he feared such an outcome that de Gaulle had cooled towards the idea of national insurrection. But would he be able to stop it? Nowhere was this question more acute than in Paris, where the CNR and its Communist-dominated military committee were based. There was also a Parisian Liberation Committee (CPL) chaired by a Communist, André Tollet; and the commander of the FFI in the Paris region, Rol-Tanguy, was also a Communist. If the Communists had wanted to seize power, they were nowhere better poised to do so than in Paris.

On 31 July, American troops finally broke through the German lines at Avranches; two weeks later, they had advanced halfway to Paris. De Gaulle's efforts to ensure that French troops would be allowed to participate in the Liberation were now about to bear fruit. A French army of six divisions – dubbed the French First Army – was designated to land on the south coast of France with the Americans. The privilege of commanding this force went not to General Juin, who had performed so effectively in Italy, but to General de Lattre de Tassigny, who had initially served Vichy loyally but had then tried to resist the German occupation of the Free Zone in November 1942. Thus he was judged to have acquitted himself marginally more honourably in November 1942 than Juin, who had been slow to rally to the Americans in North Africa. Thus de Lattre, although insufferably boastful and vain, was deemed more acceptable to the internal

Resistance. It is through such careful discriminations that one can read the tortured history of France since 1940.[47] The Allies had also agreed to allow a French division to participate in the liberation of Paris. The privilege was accorded to the 2nd Armoured Division of General Leclerc, which had been transported from North Africa to Britain in March. Leclerc's division disembarked in Normandy on 1 August. Two weeks later, on 15 August, Allied forces, de Lattre's First French Army among them, landed on the southern coast of France and made remarkably rapid progress against crumbling German resistance.

This news raised the political temperature in Paris, where sporadic strikes had been breaking out since mid-July. The dangers of a premature insurrection were dramatically illustrated by an uprising that broke out in Warsaw on 1 August. Although initially successful, it turned into a blood-bath massacre when Soviet troops remained stationary spectators on the other side of the River Vistula. The extent of this horror was not immediately apparent, and de Gaulle's real fear was that premature action in Paris might either benefit the Communists or offer the Allies a pretext to take control themselves.

De Gaulle's two most important representatives in the city were his delegate Alexandre Parodi – playing the role that might otherwise have fallen to Moulin – and the CFLN's military delegate, Jacques Chaban-Delmas, a resister in his twenties. On 31 July, de Gaulle sent Parodi a message: 'Always speak loud and clear in the name of the State. The numerous acts of our glorious Resistance are the means by which the nation fights for its salvation. The State is above all these manifestations and actions.'[48] Since it was difficult to send any communication out of Paris in these days of chaos, Parodi never received this message. If would have made no difference if he had because events in the capital were skidding out of his control.[49] As the Communist-dominated CPL pressed ever more insistently for immediate action, Parodi negotiated an agreement according it the right to 'lead the national insurrection'. Miraculously this was one message that did get through to Algiers. It led to an immediate rebuke, communicating de Gaulle's 'surprise' and reiterating that 'there can be no question of divesting ourselves of any power'.[50] That message never reached Paris. In making his agreement with the CPL, Parodi may have been confused by a speech of de Gaulle on 7 August from Algiers: 'Everyone can fight. Everyone must fight ... In the countryside, in the factory, in the workshop, in the office, in the street ... you can always weaken the enemy.' This speech, which seemingly contradicted other signals de Gaulle had been giving, showed the tightrope he was walking. While wanting to avoid premature action, he feared being outflanked by the Communists and opening himself to accusations of *attentisme*. De Gaulle also wanted the French to play a part in their own Liberation, providing the process was controlled. As he had said in July 1943, the Bastille should be taken . . . but in an orderly fashion.

On 10 August, Paris railway workers went on strike; five days later the police followed suit. On the 19th Parodi, succumbing to the pressure of the CPL and CNR, gave his seal of approval to the call for an insurrection. This was his only hope of keeping some control over events. Sporadic skirmishes broke out between resisters and German troops; the Resistance took over the Prefecture of Police. Parodi sent a message to London urging that Allied troops arrive in Paris as soon as possible to avoid a bloodbath.

De Gaulle decided the time had come to return to France. For this he needed the permission of the Allies. Only a few days previously he had refused to meet Churchill, who was passing through Algiers. This snub was all the more gratuitous since on 3 August Churchill had paid an unusually warm public tribute to him and had included France among the four great powers who would settle European affairs after the war. Massigli was so exasperated by de Gaulle's behaviour that he told Cooper hopefully that he was sure de Gaulle would not last a year in power once back in France. Nonetheless the British did not object to de Gaulle's return to France, but, as Cooper noted, he then started 'giving trouble about this as he does about everything'. He insisted on flying in a French plane and would accept an American one only if it bore French cockades.[51]

On the morning of 20 August, de Gaulle landed near Saint-Lô in Normandy and immediately made his way to Eisenhower's HQ at Rennes. His objective was to urge Eisenhower to allow Leclerc, whose troops had reached Argentan about 150 kilometres west of Paris, to head straight for the capital. What he did not realize was that Eisenhower had decided to skirt the capital, fearing that an assault on the city would slow his advance east. Thus he gave de Gaulle an evasive reply to the effect that Leclerc's division would be sent to Paris 'soon'.

De Gaulle's characteristically suspicious interpretation in his *Memoirs* was that the Americans were gambling on a last-ditch attempt to exclude him from power by sponsoring a government of transition organized by Laval.[52] Laval had certainly been plotting such an outcome. On 13 August, the German Ambassador Otto Abetz had allowed Laval to fetch from house arrest in Nancy the respected Third Republic politician Edouard Herriot, who had been President of the National Assembly in June 1940. Herriot had pledged his support to de Gaulle in 1942, but Laval hoped he might lend his name to some kind of transitional regime between Vichy and the defunct Republic, thus sidelining de Gaulle. Probably even Herriot was not vain enough to be tempted by this implausible scheme, but we will never know because the Germans refused to back it and reinterned Herriot. Along with Pétain, Laval was forcibly relocated to the castle of Sigmaringen in southern Germany. Here they were joined by hard-core ultra-collaborators accompanied by mistresses, wives, fanatics, crooks and hangers-on. In this Ruritanian setting Vichy lived out its last eight months as a futile and impotent government in exile under complete German control. All that remained in Paris were the Germans on one side and various Resistance groups, including the Communists, on the other. The Americans were not implicated in the abortive plot to sideline de Gaulle. A Darlan/ Badoglio solution was no longer an option for them.

Eisenhower's motives for circumventing Paris were entirely military; it was de Gaulle whose motivations were political: to take control of Paris before anyone else. On 21 August, he wrote again in even more pressing terms to Eisenhower arguing that Allied intervention was necessary to avoid 'serious trouble' and a 'situation of disorder'.[53] Events in Paris had escalated. After a day of street skirmishes, a truce was negotiated on 20 August by the Swedish Consul Raoul Nordling: the Germans agreed to allow Resistance forces to remain safely in buildings they had already occupied; the Resistance agreed not to attack the German troops retreating from the capital. The truce, denounced by the Communists, lasted only a day. On 21 August, fighting resumed. De Gaulle heard of the truce on 23 August, and later commented in his *Memoirs* that it had made an 'unpleasant impression' on him – although it conformed entirely to the logic of his strategy of avoiding premature action – perhaps because by the time he heard of it Eisenhower had finally given Leclerc the order to move on Paris. De Gaulle certainly wanted Paris to be seen to liberate itself – but only at the moment the Allies arrived.

Eisenhower had received de Gaulle's letter on 22 August, by which time he had already taken the decision to move on Paris. De Gaulle was beating at an open door. Eisenhower had received a lot of convergent information that Paris was on the verge of explosion but also that the German forces were severely demoralized. He had also been worried that if the Germans remained in Paris they would remain a threat to the Allied flank. At 6 a.m. on 23 August, the 400 vehicles of Leclerc's armoured division rolled towards Paris. Their first tanks arrived at the Hôtel de Ville on the evening of the next day. On the 25th, Leclerc himself reached Paris with the bulk of his troops. He installed his headquarters in the Gare Montparnasse, where the German military commander was taken to sign the surrender. De Gaulle himself arrived at the station at 5.00 p.m. Every step that he took during the remainder of that day was meticulously calculated.

At the Gare Montparnasse, de Gaulle reprimanded Leclerc for having allowed Rol-Tanguy, the Communist leader of the FFI, to sign the surrender document. After being introduced for the first time to his military delegate Chaban-Delmas – he was amazed how young he was – he was driven to the Ministry of War in the Rue Saint-Dominique where he had been Under Secretary of State for Defence for five days in 1940. It was here that de Gaulle chose to install himself. This was not an act of modesty but a deliberate political statement to demonstrate symbolically that the four years of Vichy had been a parenthesis during which he had embodied the continuity of the French state in London. To give weight to this fiction he wrote in his *Memoirs* of his arrival at the Rue Saint-Dominique: 'Not a piece of furniture, not a rug, not a curtain had been disturbed. Nothing was missing except the State. It was my duty to restore it: I installed my staff and got down to work.'[54]

De Gaulle was then visited by Parodi, who advised him go to the Hôtel de Ville to meet the CNR waiting there to greet him. With bad grace, he accepted. At 7.00 p.m., he headed in an open-top car across the river to the Prefecture of Police to meet Charles Luizet, the Prefect who had been appointed by the CFLN. Having visited two institutions of the state – the Ministry of War and the Prefecture of Police – he walked the short distance to the Hôtel de Ville to meet the representatives of the Resistance (CNR). It was at the Hôtel de Ville that in 1848 and 1870 the Second and Third Republics had been proclaimed. Would de Gaulle now proclaim the Fourth? The hall on the first floor was crowded. Most of those present had never seen de Gaulle before. He was greeted by emotional speeches from the Communist Georges Maranne, Vice-President of the CPL, and by Georges Bidault, President of the CNR. De Gaulle then launched into a speech which he claimed in his *Memoirs* was improvised but which he had carefully prepared in advance. Its opening is one of the great passages of French twentieth-century political oratory still hard to hear today without being moved:

> How can one hide the emotion that grips all of us, who are here, *chez nous*, in Paris which has risen up to defend itself and which has done so by itself. No! We will not hide this sacred and profound emotion. There are moments which go beyond each of our poor lives.
>
> Paris! Paris outraged! Paris broken! Paris martyred! [Long pause] – but Paris liberated! Liberated by itself, liberated by its people with the help of the armies of France, with the help and assistance of the whole of France, of that France which fights, of the only France, of the true France, of eternal France.[55]

What is striking about the rest of the speech, after this stirring opening, was the deliberate absence of any reference either to the Allies or to those resisters (some of them present) who had risked their lives so that they could live this moment. After the speech, Bidault asked de Gaulle if he would now declare that the Republic was restored. De Gaulle's curt reply expressed the thought behind every action he had taken since arriving in Paris: 'The Republic has never ceased to exist ... Vichy was always, and remains, null and void. I am President of the Republic. Why should I proclaim it?' He then appeared briefly at the open window on the first floor. As the crowds below cheered, he jumped on to the windowsill to wave to them. A few minutes later he strode off to his car and returned to the Ministry of War, leaving everyone dumbstruck.

One witness of these events was the resister Lecompte-Boinet, a member of the CNR but in no way hostile to de Gaulle. He observed how even the Communists had seemed momentarily seduced, 'drinking in the General's words as if they were listening to the gospel being read. It is the first time I have seen these Communists moved.' But their mood quickly changed when de Gaulle refused to declare the Republic. Lecompte-Boinet himself was 'shocked' by this.[56] The CNR rapidly convened and agreed that Bidault should ask de Gaulle to reconsider his decision. Another observer, also not ill-disposed to de Gaulle, noted:

> That first contact was a bit disappointing ... That speech at the Hôtel de Ville – brief, authoritarian ... Very good, perfect, but even so he could have said a word of thanks to the CNR and to Alexander Parodi who had made such efforts for him ... Physically tall, morally dominant, impassive face ... None of the smiling seduction of Leclerc, rather a man anxious to produce a certain effect. One would have liked him to show a bit of emotion. Instead of: 'M. le Préfet, would you please present me your principal collaborators.'[57]

Before leaving the Ministry of War to meet the CNR, de Gaulle had instructed that on the next day he would stage a procession down the Champs-Elysées. His plan was not for a military parade but to walk slowly down the Champs-Elysées and show himself to the population, to 'his' people. There was no precedent for a 'walkabout' of this kind, risky in a city swarming with snipers, but the idea was a supreme example of de Gaulle's instinctive showmanship.[58] Even so, no one could have predicted the extraordinary success of the parade. The size of the crowds is impossible to estimate. It was probably the largest gathering of its kind in the history of France. Tricolour banners with the words '*Vive la République*' and '*Vive de Gaulle*' had been distributed in advance to the crowds.[59] This led the Communist head of COMAC, Maurice Kriegel-Valrimont, to concede bitterly: 'The Free French Delegation had done its work well.' This

25 AOÛT 1944

— Mon grand !

25 August: De Gaulle returns to Paris.

was true, but there was nothing manufactured about the delirious enthusiasm of the crowds. As de Gaulle would write in his *Memoirs*:

> Ahead stretched the Champs-Elysées. It looked more like the sea. A huge crowd was massed either side of the street. Perhaps two million souls. The roofs were also black with people ... People were hanging from ladders, flagpoles and lamp posts. As far as the eye could see, there was only this living tide of humanity, in the sunshine, beneath the tricolour.[60]

On de Gaulle's left was Bidault, on his right Parodi, both ordered to keep slightly behind him. Behind them were Leclerc, Koenig, members of the CNR and other dignitaries. Bidault waved from time to time, but no one knew who he was. Lecompte-Boinet, also in the procession, noted that people were taking photos of him and others, but he thought it would be more interesting to photograph the crowd: 'The extraordinary intensity of those strained faces who are seeing HIM for the first time.' It was indeed de Gaulle, towering over everyone else, whom the crowds had turned out to see and to cheer. The voice from London was made flesh at last.

Arriving at the Place de la Concorde, and no longer able to move forward because of the crowds, de Gaulle clambered into an open-top car and headed to his next destination, the Cathedral of Notre-Dame, for a celebratory Mass. As he arrived, Parisians were brutally reminded that the war was not over when bursts of gunfire broke out. It was unclear where they were coming from. Once in the Cathedral, more shooting was heard. De Gaulle, always impervious to physical danger – and certainly feeling he must be seen to be – remained upright and impassive. The shooting stopped, but the Mass was cut short. Perhaps as almost exactly thirty years earlier, at the bridge of Dinant, de Gaulle experienced a kind *dédoublement* in Notre-Dame. In his *Memoirs*, de Gaulle claimed that the firing was the work of Communists. There is no evidence for this and he certainly did not believe it at the time. He wrote to his wife that it had just been a bit of 'showing off': 'There are people here with arms who, excited by the days of fighting, shoot towards the rooftops on any pretext . . . It will not last.' Signing off 'your poor husband', he requested that Juin bring him over some fresh clothes and shoes from Algiers.[61]

THE MORNING AFTER

On the next morning, de Gaulle received the 'secretary generals' who had been running the ministries in the short interregnum between the outbreak of the insurrection and his arrival. These men were not Communist fire-brands but distinguished civil servants or technicians designated by the CFLN. Nonetheless de Gaulle subjected them to the terrifyingly icy formality which came easily to him. The economist René Courtin wrote:

> I presented myself: 'René Courtin. Secretary General for the Economy.' The same completely impassive face . . . A single question again: 'Who are you?' Under the illusion that the General might accord me at least some sympathy, I continued rapidly so as not to waste his time: 'I am a former Resistance activist, friend of François de Menthon [a resister who was on the CFLN] and André Philip.' The face remained impassive. It was clear that these details did not interest him in the slightest . . . He simply repeated: 'But who are you?' I thought that perhaps what he wanted to hear was: 'Professor at the University of Montpellier'. That was indeed the answer he wanted, the only one that interested him, and I moved aside.[62]

Another one present remembered the occasion in a similar way: 'Each of us was interrogated. We were like school children. Trembling we each answered . . . Not a word of congratulation was uttered.'[63] The same question was asked of everyone. The point of the exercise was to let them know that they would be expected to resume their former occupations and leave the task of governing to de Gaulle.

That evening de Gaulle received the members of the CNR at the Rue Saint-Dominique. Ill at ease, they were searched on entry. Lecompte-Boinet wrote the encounter up in his diary immediately afterwards:

> 'Algiers' was receiving 'France' with obvious suspicion . . . We were in a fortress, the fortress of external Gaullism; this was a Troy in which there was no question of letting our horse enter . . . We went up to the first floor where de Gaulle was waiting . . . His features were strained but his face seemed to express lassitude rather than tiredness, that of a Head of Government overwhelmed by the irritations of the politics he detests . . . But he tried to be friendly. He made us a little speech where it was less a matter of his thanking us than giving us advice to show moderation and calm, advice which was more like an order than it was like advice. My God how tall he is! His eyes seemed to be looking at the horizon from his great height, making an effort to get down to our level . . .
>
> Our spokesman Bidault, very intimidated, explained with some difficulty that we were really happy to be received but that we would be even happier if the General would be willing to participate in our work.
>
> A silence from de Gaulle. His cigarette, whose curling smoke made him half close his eyes, replied politely that he did not quite see what utility our 'work' now had.
>
> He asked if there were any questions, and Gillot [a Communist member of the CNR], eventually daring to speak, asked if de Gaulle had approved of the 'truce'. De Gaulle's face, smiling politely at the start, no longer hid his real feelings after 20 minutes of Gillot's monologue. We wondered if he was not going to throw us all out of the room. The General profited from a pause to speak in his turn and, with a tense smile, he said: 'Do you really think, M. Gillot, that what you call the "truce" has such a great importance in the history of France?'

Lecompte-Boinet worried that his colleagues were not giving the best impression of the CNR. This was also true of the next intervention by the Communist Pierre Villon, who asked when Maurice Thorez would be allowed back into France: 'At that point the General, manifestly exasperated, got up: "I hope to see you again soon. *Au revoir Messieurs.*"'[64] That was the first – and last – meeting between de Gaulle and the CNR. On the next day, de Gaulle meted out similar treatment to a number of Resistance leaders, including leaders of COMAC and the FFI. After it was over one declared: 'I have known human ingratitude but I never imagined it could rise to such levels.' On the same day (28 August) de Gaulle announced that the FFI General Staff would be disbanded and all members of the FFI incorporated into the regular army.[65]

On 1 September, Lecompte-Boinet went to see de Gaulle alone. On this occasion he was there not in his capacity as a member of the CNR but as Secretary General of the Ministry of Public Works. He started to tell de Gaulle what he had been doing for the last two weeks:

> From the first phrase I could see that I was not at the level he wanted and he could not care a damn about all this. I tried a new tack: 'The Resistance . . .' He interrupted me: 'We have moved beyond the Resistance. The Resistance is finished. The Resistance must now be integrated into the Nation. Because you must understand, there was the Resistance – but now there is the Nation.'[66]

PART THREE

In and Out of Power, 1944–1958

Of course I would not redo the Second Empire because I am not the nephew of Napoleon and one does not become Emperor at my age. Only the Republic is possible. But we need to finish with the regime of parties.

De Gaulle, 19 September 1949, in Georges Pompidou,
Pour rétablir une verité, 89–90

14

In Power, August 1944–May 1945

ORDER

The day after his procession down the Champs-Elysées, de Gaulle asked Eisenhower for the loan of two American divisions as a show of force to impress the Parisian population. Eisenhower was not able to oblige, but on 29 August 1944, in the company of the American General Omar Bradley, de Gaulle reviewed two American divisions passing through Paris on their way east to fight the Germans. De Gaulle did not mention this event in his *Memoirs*, nor did he mention his request to Eisenhower two days before. But they both demonstrate how obsessed he was by the need to restore order and assert his authority even at the price of soliciting American help.

By 9 September, de Gaulle had formed his new government. It was a careful balance of Free French, resisters, former politicians (providing they had not blotted their copybook under Vichy) and civil servants or experts. Georges Bidault accepted de Gaulle's invitation to become Minister of Foreign Affairs, although only a few days earlier the CNR had agreed that none of its members would accept government positions. Bidault assured his colleagues that this was not an 'individual kidnapping'. But depriving the CNR of its President was bound to weaken it, and this is certainly what de Gaulle intended. For the same reason he also offered a post to the most prominent Communist member of the CNR, Pierre Villon, who refused it. Two other Communists were given Cabinet posts but not key ones: Charles Tillon as Minister of Air and François Billoux as Minister of Public Health. The only leader of a major Resistance movement to be given a post was Henri Frenay – but it was the relatively innocuous portfolio of dealing with returning prisoners of war. Among early members of the Free French, positions were found for Pleven (in charge of the Empire), Tixier (Minister of the Interior) and Catroux (in charge of North Africa).

The first meeting of France's new provisional government in Paris took place on 9 September at the Hôtel Matignon. This might have been considered an historic occasion, but de Gaulle gave no effusive speech to open the proceedings. He entered the room and announced: 'The government of the Republic, modified in its composition, continues.' This was another moment in the narrative de Gaulle was striving to create: history would pick up where it had left off in 1940, and Vichy had never existed. The former resister Pierre-Henri Teitgen, Minister of Information, was so startled by de Gaulle's impregnable sense of natural authority that he scribbled a note to his neighbour Bidault: 'He is extraordinary.' Bidault scribbled back: 'Lucifer was the most beautiful of the angels.'[1]

Although there was now in theory a government in Paris it had little possibility of communicating with the rest of the country – let alone administering it. Most bridges over the Loire and Rhône had been destroyed; not a port was usable (and the Germans still held pockets on the Atlantic coast); most telephone lines were down; Paris had electricity for only forty-five minutes a day. It was a moment of high emotion for Louis Joxe in Paris when he received his first telephone call from Toulouse at the end of September.

De Gaulle's immediate priority was to stamp his authority on the country through a series of regional visits, starting with Lyons, Marseilles, Toulouse and Bordeaux between 14 and 18 September. Each visit was a local re-enactment of de Gaulle's consecration on the Champs-Elysées. As one newspaper in Lyons put it after his visit, the population had been able to 'engrave for ever in their memory the living image at the same time as the voice of the Liberator'. In Nancy on 26 September de Gaulle announced: 'You have seen me, you have heard me.' These visits were also seen by the entire population of France through carefully edited newsreels.[2]

The main purpose of this grand tour was to bring the Resistance to heel by establishing de Gaulle's own direct relationship with the population. Everywhere he assumed what he called in his *Memoirs* an appearance of 'calculated solemnity'. In Marseilles, as a motley group of resisters paraded in front of him, he growled under his breath, 'What a masquerade.' Nowhere was his icy contempt more in evidence than in Toulouse, which had acquired the reputation of being a miniature 'Red Republic' where bands of resisters and Spanish *guerrilleros* roamed the streets challenging the tenuous authority of the government *Commissaire*, Pierre Bertaux.[3] De Gaulle arrived in Toulouse by plane from Marseilles on 16 September. On the drive from the airport, he rebuked Bertaux because for security reasons the *Commissaire* had ignored his instruction to lay on an open-top car. Once they arrived in the city, de Gaulle walked through the streets and presented himself to a cheering crowd from the balcony of the town hall. Having established his own direct contact with the population, he received what he condescendingly called in his *Memoirs* the 'picturesque processions' of the local FFI Resistance fighters. Each was asked the ritualistic question 'When did you join the Resistance?' – to which the correct answer was 18 June 1940. The twenty-four-year-old resister Serge Ravanel remembered:

> I can still see us all, lined up in a salon of the Prefecture, so proud to be presented to the Head of State . . . What did de Gaulle do? He passed in front of each person, stony-faced, with just one question: 'What is your rank in the army?' As if that was what really mattered. This did not worry the career officers. It was humiliating for the FFI officers.

To Ravanel in person, de Gaulle's opening shot was: 'Who authorized you to wear the ribbon of the order of the Liberation?' Ravanel replied that he believed he had been awarded it; de Gaulle snapped: 'That is not true.' Ravanel, for whom this encounter was one of the saddest moments of his life, recalled many years later: 'I had discovered that what mattered above all to him was to bring us to heel. And to draw a line under all that we had learnt and all that made the originality of the Resistance.'[4] He and other Resistance leaders were so upset by this reception that there were murmurings about kidnapping de Gaulle and taking him to meet a group of real *maquisards*. Bertaux tried to persuade de Gaulle to receive the Resistance leaders again and smooth their bruised egos. De Gaulle refused: 'Why? They were only doing their duty.' Bertaux tried to defend the FFI by invoking the glorious example of the revolutionary volunteers of Jemappes and Valmy. De Gaulle answered: 'You cannot teach me the history of the French army. There is only one French army and that is the army of France.' As Lacouture comments aptly, de Gaulle was now sounding more like Giraud than like the de Gaulle of 1942.[5] This was consistent with his obsession with restoring the authority of the state and allowing no challenges to its – to his – authority.

On the same visit, de Gaulle also sought to establish the *French* character of the Liberation. Bertaux was reprimanded for having invited to lunch a British SOE representative George Starr (Colonel Hilaire) who had organized an FFI group in the region. Meeting Starr, de Gaulle fumed that as a foreigner he had no right to do this: 'Take them away with you . . . they are traitors and mercenaries.' Starr left the country ten days later. When a group of Spanish Republicans marched past (some wearing German helmets painted blue because they had no uniforms of their own), de Gaulle asked Ravanel: 'What are all these Spaniards doing here bothering us?'[6] (Starr was in fact later decorated by the government, and Ravanel got his Croix de la Libération.)

During his next stop in Bordeaux, de Gaulle was in better humour because the city had a less turbulent reputation. He purred contentedly in his *Memoirs* that the *Commissaire*, Gaston Cusin, had presented 'the usual procession of functionaries, officers and delegations' with the Archbishop at their head.[7] De Gaulle, the rebel of 1940, felt more at home in this company of former Vichyites than with the ragged troupe of resisters encountered in Toulouse and Marseilles. Present among the dignitaries in Bordeaux was a certain Maurice Papon who had been *sous-préfet* under Vichy and, it later emerged, assiduous in overseeing the deportation of Jews. Whether or not de Gaulle was aware of this, the issue was not one that loomed much in anyone's mind at the time. What de Gaulle will have known was that Papon was an ultra-efficient administrator who could be relied upon to obey him as he had obeyed Vichy. Papon was confirmed as deputy to the *Commissaire*.

There were visits to other regions of France over the next few weeks – including de Gaulle's birthplace of Lille on 30 October – but otherwise the government in Paris now got down to work. There was no chance of holding parliamentary elections while French territory was not fully liberated and over one million Frenchmen remained prisoners in Germany. Instead the Consultative Assembly was transported from Algiers and its membership was widened further. It was hardly an effective check on de Gaulle's authority. De Gaulle was in his most imperious mode and this government was, in the words of one minister, more like a school class – with de Gaulle as headmaster – than a forum of discussion. When on one occasion the Socialist Vincent Auriol tried to intervene by remarking that a particular issue had already been discussed by the Popular Front government of 1936 of which he had been a member, de Gaulle looked at him glacially and then continued as if nothing had been said. Not taking the hint, Auriol tried again. This time de Gaulle interrupted: 'You are raising for the second time the coming to power of the Popular Front; you should next expound to us how it ended.'[8]

In de Gaulle's immediate entourage Palewski remained a key figure as his *directeur de cabinet*. As always his closeness to de Gaulle excited jealousy, especially from Louis Joxe, who continued to exercise the same role as Secretary General of the government that he had held in Algiers. Joxe installed himself at the Hôtel Matignon where the head of government was usually located, but de Gaulle continued running the government from the Ministry of Defence in the Rue Saint-Dominique. When his wife arrived in Paris from Algiers de Gaulle moved to live in a villa (which during the war had been commandeered by Göring) in Neuilly just outside Paris. After arriving at this grand mansion Yvonne de Gaulle remarked characteristically, 'It is a degree above what I would have liked.'[9]

As during the war de Gaulle relied heavily on his aides de camp. There was Claude Guy, a dashingly handsome young lieutenant who had served, and been wounded, in the Free French air force. He also had the advantage of speaking perfect English since his mother was American. He was joined in 1945 by Gaston de Bonneval, an army officer who had joined the Resistance, been deported to Mauthausen and returned to France more dead than alive after the liberation of the camp. Both men were devoted to de Gaulle. Another important figure in his entourage was the diplomat Etienne Burin des Roziers, who had arrived in London in 1942 where he served as de Gaulle's ordinance officer and now joined his *cabinet* to advise on foreign affairs.[10]

By the end of October, de Gaulle felt strong enough to make a final move to bring the Resistance to heel by dissolving the unruly Patriotic Militia. These were armed groups of resisters whose numbers had paradoxically swelled after Liberation. They attracted former FFI fighters who resented the order to join the regular army and also included many so-called 'September Resisters', opportunists who had done nothing under the Occupation but who seized this opportunity to rehabilitate themselves once the danger was past. The Patriotic Militia carried out arbitrary attacks on alleged collaborators. Although not controlled exclusively by the Communist Party (PCF) – or by anyone else – it saw them as another opportunity to extend its influence.

On 28 October, the government announced the dissolution of the Patriotic Militia. The CNR was divided about how to respond and its criticism was muted apart from some ritual muttering from the Communist Party. De Gaulle commented to an aide on the next day:

> If they resist we will shoot . . . in the air. But they will not resist . . . And if some poor policeman is killed I will regret it for him but it will at least have the advantage once and for all of putting the police on the right side and making the others seem hateful . . . At the Conseil des Ministres [Council of Ministers – what in Britain would be called the Cabinet] I said to them: 'Billoux, Tillon . . . That is what the government has to do . . . That is what it will do' . . . But they did not react, *they stayed in their place*, and from that moment, from the moment two Communists assumed responsibility for the decision, the battle was won . . . The Communists are reeds painted as iron. You cannot have a revolution without revolutionaries. And there is only one revolutionary in France: that is me.[11]

'YOU SPEAK OF . . . PURIFICATION . . . WHAT I SEE, ABOVE ALL, IS VICTORIOUS FRANCE'

The price of Gaullist 'order' was a creeping sense of disillusion among many former resisters. The symbol on which they had projected their hopes during the dark nights of Occupation seemed so different from what they had imagined. Books appeared with titles like *The Resistance Betrayed* or *We are the Rebels* (as opposed to de Gaulle was the implication of that title).[12] Since de Gaulle was still the object of a massive popular cult, these books did not attack him directly. Their theme was that the forces of conservatism and reaction had captured 'our de Gaulle'. As one Resistance newspaper wrote as early as September 1944: 'All the supporters of the old regime, all the repentant Vichyists, all the scared rich, are prowling around the Head of the Resistance [that is, de Gaulle]. They speak to him of Order with a big "O", bourgeois capitalist order . . . We too want order, but with a small "o", democratic order.'[13]

None of this seriously threatened de Gaulle because the concrete objectives of the Resistance were so vague – apart from a pervasive sense that the purge of collaborators was not being pursued with sufficient vigour.

De Gaulle had no illusions about the conduct of his compatriots under Occupation but his priority was national unity. Cynicism towards humanity in general inured him against being vengeful towards individuals in particular. As he had already shown in Algiers, he believed that France could not be reconstructed without drawing on individuals whose record had not been unblemished. When setting up courts to try collaborators, it would have been impossible to avoid using magistrates who had compromised themselves with Vichy since only one had refused to take the oath of allegiance to Pétain. De Gaulle also deplored the sectarianism and boastfulness of many resisters – an attitude that later came to be dubbed 'resistentialism'. When the venerable politician Jules Jeanneney, President of the Senate in 1940, found himself criticized at the end of 1944 for having made flattering remarks (like so many others) about Pétain four years earlier, de Gaulle defended him to the Assembly: 'I take you as witness that one could conceive different ways of serving the Fatherland and the Republic at that moment.'[14]

On the other hand, de Gaulle accepted that a purge was unavoidable. As he wrote later, 'to wipe the slate clean over so many crimes and abuses' would have permitted a 'monstrous abscess to infect the country for ever'.[15] What he wanted was to end manifestations of 'popular justice' and bring the purges under the jurisdiction of the courts. His pretext for dissolving the Patriotic Militia had been their role in a number of summary executions. When it looked as if Charles Maurras in Lyons risked the lynch mob for his support of the Vichy regime, de Gaulle had him transferred to Paris for a proper trial at which he was sentenced to life imprisonment in January 1945.[16]

The CFLN in Algiers had spent months discussing the legal mechanisms for trying collaborators. The key text was an ordinance of June 1944 setting up special Courts of Justice. These were modelled on the traditional French assize courts except that the jury had to be selected from among a pool of candidates whose patriotic credentials ('proof of national sentiments') had been approved by departmental liberation committees. The crimes of alleged collaborators were covered by article 75 of the Penal Code: 'Collusion [intelligence] with the enemy.' More minor misdemeanours were to be covered by a new offence of 'national indignity', which was criticized by many jurists as an example of that retroactive jurisdiction which had sullied the Vichy regime. But while Vichy's retroactive laws had led to people being executed, the penalties for national indignity were largely symbolic.

The early trials were unsatisfactory because most hard-core collaborators were still at large in Germany where they had fled in August 1944. The first prominent trials were of journalists against whom it was easy to construct a case because their writings were available to convict them. De Gaulle's only direct involvement arose when the accused were sentenced to death. As provisional head of state he had the right to commute death sentences to life imprisonment. This soon became a matter of intense controversy. While the Communists pushed for the harshest retribution, the respected novelist François Mauriac emerged as a powerful voice for clemency. Since Mauriac had impeccable Resistance credentials, his arguments could not be seen as special pleading.

The first case to come before the Paris court was that of the journalist Georges Suarez who had written articles in the collaborationist press denouncing resisters and calling for Jews and Communists to be executed. Since he had also received money from the Germans, the case was uncomplicated. Tried in October, Suarez was executed on 9 November 1944. Another open-and-shut case was that of Paul Chack, an anti-Semitic polemicist who had incited his readers to fight with the Germans against Bolshevism on the eastern front. He was sentenced in December 1944 and executed on 9 January. The case of the journalist Henri Béraud was less clear-cut. He was sentenced to death on 29 December 1944 despite no evidence of any contacts with Germans. If he was a 'collaborator', it was only because he had continued to express during the Occupation the same violently Anglophobic views he had expressed before it. This spurred Mauriac, increasingly uneasy with the idea of executing writers because of their opinions rather than their actions, to write a number of articles appealing for 'mercy'. He became dubbed 'St Francis of the Assizes'. The rising literary star Albert Camus replied by advancing the claims of 'justice' over mercy.

Mauriac's voice counted for de Gaulle for many reasons. He was France's most famous 'Catholic' novelist – Catholic in the sense that all his novels treated the themes of sin, guilt, betrayal and (sometimes) redemption among the Catholic bourgeoisie of the Bordeaux region in which Mauriac had been raised. Talking about literature on the plane taking him to Algiers in 1943, de Gaulle had remarked that Mauriac was the living novelist he admired most 'for the totality of his oeuvre'. Mauriac had in the 1930s become estranged from his own conservative and Catholic milieu when he denounced atrocities committed by the Nationalists in the Spanish Civil War. During the Occupation, he was almost the only member of the ultra-Pétainist Académie Française to support the Resistance. On 25 August 1944, with the Paris press free for the first time in four years, he celebrated de Gaulle in quasi-religious terms in an article entitled 'The First among Us'. De Gaulle, he said, had granted to France the 'gift of his person' (a phrase Pétain had famously used about himself), and the French had collectively 'shared his suffering' through the blood of their martyrs 'which has baptized us all with the same baptism of which de Gaulle is the living symbol'.[17]

Mauriac was the first writer to be received officially by de Gaulle on 1 September, only a week after his return to Paris, just as he had received André Gide in Algiers only ten days after arriving there. Mauriac's visit was followed in quick succession by those of three other literary giants: Paul Valéry, Georges Duhamel and Paul Claudel. This was a ritual where de Gaulle demonstrated the reverence he felt for writers while basking in the reflected glory of their admiration for him. But it was consecration he sought, not advice. Recollecting his first meeting with de Gaulle many years later, Mauriac could not hide his sense of disappointment that the General had wanted only to talk about the Académie Française and seemed uninterested in his views on politics:

What I wanted to know, that morning, was what the General thought about the problems of amalgamating the FFI with the regular army, the difficulties of keeping order in the provinces while all our forces were thrown into the battle against the Germans; would France be present on the final day of reckoning? I was part of the National Front [Resistance movement] where I was struggling in the traps laid by the Communist Party. I would have had my advice to offer on tactics . . . But no: de Gaulle was interested in André Gide and the Académie Française.[18]

Mauriac settled into the role of 'master of ceremonies of triumphant Gaullism'.[19] At the Comédie-Française on 30 October he organized in de Gaulle's presence an evening devoted to the poetry of the Resistance. Another thread in the relationship between de Gaulle and Mauriac was that Mauriac's son Claude, also a budding writer and journalist, had joined de Gaulle's staff immediately after the Liberation. He was assigned the task of managing his correspondence. Claude Mauriac was a long-standing friend of de Gaulle's aide Claude Guy but being the son of François Mauriac also helped.

Whether or not Mauriac's advocacy of clemency played any role, de Gaulle commuted Béraud's sentence after receiving his defence counsel on 6 January 1945. When Claude Mauriac commented that his father would be pleased that de Gaulle had judged the matter not only politically but also sentimentally, de Gaulle snapped back: 'For me it is neither a question of sentiment nor politics but justice . . . Collusion with the enemy? I have studied the file closely and while Chack ordered the French to enrol in the Germany army . . . for Béraud I look in vain for any sign of collusion with the enemy.'[20]

The next high-profile case to come to the court was that of Robert Brasillach, one of the most prominent intellectuals to have supported collaboration. Brasillach was sentenced to death on 19 January 1945. Although Brasillach had often insulted him in the press, Mauriac took up his case in the name of Christian charity and of the right of writers to express opinions however obnoxious. Mauriac was one of the most important signatories of a petition signed by fifty-seven writers and artists requesting that de Gaulle grant a pardon. Those who signed included Claudel, Valéry, Colette and Camus (despite his previous disagreement with Mauriac); those who refused to sign included Jean-Paul Sartre, Simone de Beauvoir, Gide and Picasso. Mauriac went to see de Gaulle in person, and found the experience as disconcerting as his first meeting. Although de Gaulle was 'courteous . . . and polite' he was struck above all by 'his prodigious force of contempt . . . pride and the sense of his own superiority'. He told his son he had the disagreeable experience of 'being confined for half an hour with a cormorant who spoke only cormorant'.[21]

Perhaps because Mauriac did not speak 'cormorant', he came away with the impression that de Gaulle was inclining towards a pardon. It may be that de Gaulle had not yet consulted the file on the case, as he did later that evening when receiving Brasillach's defence lawyer, Jacques Isorni. For years afterwards, Isorni liked to dwell on the story of his evening visit to de Gaulle to deliver the clemency petition and plead for mercy. According to his account, de Gaulle remained implacably silent. His only interruption was to ask at one point if the writer Abel Hermant had signed the petition. Since Hermant was himself in prison for collaboration, Isorni assumed this was a joke in bad taste:

> He picked up the cigar that he had started to smoke and blew the smoke towards me. I asked myself if this was really the moment to be smoking cigars. There was perhaps a metre between us – perhaps a bit more. His eyes set closely together seemed to be fixed on something in the distance – and I never succeeded in catching his gaze . . . In a meeting between two men where the life of someone is at stake, it takes great strength of will to continue when one only meets silence.[22]

Having spoken for fifteen minutes, Isorni asked if de Gaulle needed any more information, and was told 'there is no need to bother.'

Isorni, so emotionally invested in the case, constructs his narrative to paint the portrait of de Gaulle as heartless and sanguinary. The encounter was the beginning of a career of anti-Gaullist militancy. Isorni's loathing of de Gaulle remained intact until his dying day. If one strips away his own personal feelings, however, his narrative has a ring of authenticity and sounds like many other encounters with de Gaulle. But if de Gaulle was certainly implacable, he was not sanguinary. According to Claude Guy, he used to dread his meetings with Maurice Patin, the President of the committee that dealt with pardons (Commission des Graces). De Gaulle's Minister of Justice, the resister Pierre-Henri Teitgen, who later had little good to say about de Gaulle, remembered that he had been deeply troubled by the execution of Chack.[23] De Gaulle systematically pardoned all minors and all women; in total, he commuted 998 out of 1,554 death sentences. He was in fact more clement than his successor, the mild Socialist Félix Gouin, despite the fact that he was making his decisions in the period when passions were at their highest.

In the case of Brasillach, there was no pardon. De Gaulle signed the decree to carry out the death sentence on the evening he had seen Isorni. What made him pardon Béraud and not Brasillach? One tenacious myth holds that the file contained a photograph of a visit to the German army on the eastern front by various French collaborationists including Jacques Doriot wearing German uniform. Since, like Doriot, Brasillach wore glasses, it has been suggested that de Gaulle mistook the one for the other. But such

23–4. Posing with his wife for the press at their home in Berkhamsted, autumn 1941 (*see* p. 217).

25. False identity papers of Jean Moulin on his arrival in London, October 1941.

26. The Battle of Bir Hakeim, in which the Free French fought off the German troops in the Libyan Desert, between 26 May and 21 June 1942. De Gaulle later wrote of his reaction to the news: 'Heart beating with emotion, sobs of pride, tears of joy'.

27. General de Gaulle ('the bride') and General Giraud ('the bridegroom') about to shake hands at Anfa on 25 January 1943 with Roosevelt and Churchill watchful and relieved.

28. Members of the French National Committee at Carlton Gardens, May 1943. *Left to right*: General Vallin, André Diethelm, René Cassin, General Catroux, de Gaulle, René Pleven, André Philip, René Massigli, Admiral d'Argenlieu.

29. (*above*) On the Normandy coast, setting off for Bayeux.

30. (*right*) Testing his popularity in the streets of liberated Bayeux.

31. Speaking in Bayeux at the end of the afternoon, Allied flags and the Cross of Lorraine flying, Maurice Schumann, directly in front of de Gaulle, wearing a beret and glasses.

32. Setting off down the Champs-Elysées: to the left of him is Georges Bidault and to the right Alexandre Parodi. On the very right of the picture, half visible, is Claude Guy.

33. Learning to use his hands on the Champs-Elysées (*see* p. 29).

34–5. Sometimes they looked in the same direction, and sometimes they didn't: de Gaulle and Churchill in Paris on Armistice Day, Anthony Eden to de Gaulle's left (*above*).

36. Arriving at Kursky train station, Moscow, 2 December 1944.

37. Molotov signing the Franco-Soviet Treaty on 11 December 1944, with de Gaulle and Stalin looking on.

38. De Gaulle in Antibes, January 1946, pondering his future (*see* p. 381).

a photograph is not in the file – unless it has been removed. De Gaulle's only comment on the affair was that 'In literature as in everything talent confers responsibility.' If this really was his view, it meant that one of the arguments used by Isorni and Mauriac to save Brasillach – his distinction as a writer – was actually what condemned him in de Gaulle's eyes.[24]

For the most important servants of the regime – ministers and top officials – the government had set up a special High Court which convened at the start of 1945. One of the first to be tried was General Dentz, who had fought against the Free French in Syria. He was sentenced to death in April, but de Gaulle immediately commuted this to life imprisonment. The moment everyone was waiting for, however, was the trial of Pétain. De Gaulle had wanted the trial to be conducted *in absentia* without the presence of the eighty-nine-year-old Marshal since he knew only too well that for many Frenchmen Pétain remained a figure of 'respect or pity'. The actors of the final tragicomic days of Vichy at Sigmaringen had fled to various destinations in the early days of April as Allied troops advanced into Bavaria. Some went into hiding successfully; Laval got to Spain from where he would be extradited; Pétain was escorted by the Germans to the Swiss frontier. Although de Gaulle would have preferred him to remain in Switzerland, Pétain presented himself at the French frontier on 25 April. A trial was unavoidable.

It lasted from 23 July to 15 August 1945. Isorni was one of his defence team. Pétain refused to recognize the authority of the court, remaining silent throughout and often seemingly unaware of what was going on around him. After two weeks of courtroom wrangling, Pétain was condemned to death with a recommendation that this be commuted to life imprisonment. This is what de Gaulle had always intended.

As was inevitable with passions so high, and the events so recent, the trial cast little light. For de Gaulle, however, the problem was that the prosecution concentrated on what he saw as the secondary question of the internal policies and crimes of the Vichy regime rather than on what he considered the central issue: the signing of the armistice from which, in his view, all the rest followed. This is what separated his reading of the Occupation from that of the Resistance. He expressed this with astonishing frankness – not to say cynicism – in a passage which he ultimately decided not to include in his *Memoirs*:

What had immediately determined me to pursue the struggle against the enemy and condemn Vichy was the refusal to admit that France was defeated, occupied and enslaved while she still had the means to fight. For me, it was essentially about safeguarding independence, participating in the victory so that she reappeared, if not bigger than before, at least with her grandeur. It is certainly not that I wanted to neglect that flood of ideas and feelings that had surrounded the conflict and, for my part, I did not fail to make use of these currents of opinion. Nor did I misunderstand the existence and importance of destinies and passions, which existed before the war and were further stirred up by it. On the contrary, I used them all and appealed in turn to the cult of tradition, national pride, the mystique of Christianity, liberal ideas, Jacobin fury, social revolution ... The political elements that had emerged or reappeared through the resistance had not, I must say, exactly the same way of looking at things. In the defeat of 1940 and installation of Vichy they were aware, and felt with grief, the humiliation of France. But whatever their patriotism, it was the unfortunate fate of their ideologies, the persecutions inflicted on their groups, the triumph of their political adversaries that many of them felt most acutely.[25]

De Gaulle put the same idea more pithily to Claude Mauriac, who was drafting a letter for him and had included the words 'France purified and restored to honour and liberty'. Crossing out the word 'purified' de Gaulle exploded: 'You speak of liberty, honour and purification ... And what about victory? What I see, above all, is victorious France.'[26]

JOURNEY TO MOSCOW

What place would there be for a 'victorious France' in the post-war world? In de Gaulle's narrative, the answer was simple. The war was a thirty-year conflict where some battles were won and others lost: France had won the Battle of the Marne in September 1914, had lost the Battle of France in May 1940 and would win the final battle in 1945. In this perspective, once the war was over, France could resume her role as one of the great powers. De Gaulle knew perfectly well, however, that France's partners did not accept this narrative. For most of the world, France's collapse in 1940 had been more than just an incident. Whatever de Gaulle hoped, one man could not substitute himself for an entire nation. The reality facing him in 1944, as sketched out by Roosevelt at their meeting in July, was a world dominated by two superpowers, with Britain probably in the orbit of America, and France irremediably weakened. To counter this vision and find ways of leveraging new influence for France, de Gaulle began to talk more and more about 'Europe'. In the adolescent fantasy he had penned in 1905 imagining himself as General de Gaulle, it was 'Europe' that had declared war on France; now 'Europe' might be France's salvation.[27]

The CFLN had begun discussing the post-war international order in the autumn of 1943. At a dinner in October, there was a fascinating conversation between de Gaulle and Monnet on post-war Europe. Monnet outlined his vision of a unified European entity including France and Germany. De Gaulle was sceptical: 'You need to take account of traditions. Never after this war will you put the Germans and the French together in the same grouping.' Instead he envisaged some kind of economic bloc which could include the Rhineland (which he no longer saw as part of Germany) and perhaps also Italy. It would have close ties to Russia and Britain, although Britain would not participate in it because she was 'torn between . . . Europe and her Empire'.[28] In March 1944 in a speech in Algiers, de Gaulle floated publicly a different plan for a 'sort of Western grouping'. This would be a 'strategic and economic federation' including Belgium, Luxembourg and Holland, and also the Ruhr and Rhineland, with Britain associated if she wished to be. The Channel, the Rhine and the Mediterranean would be the 'arteries' of this grouping. Massigli was instructed to study the idea.[29] This was different in two ways from de Gaulle's suggestion to Monnet, because it seemed to envisage British participation, and because the adjective 'western' implied that the grouping would stand in opposition to the Soviet Union. For this reason, the speech was denounced by the Communist Party and the Soviet Union. Four months later, de Gaulle penned a note outlining yet another possible future: 'Progressively act on the small States and the neutral ones, even on Italy and Spain, to try and establish on these future questions a European doctrine around us.'[30]

Each of these configurations represented a different way in which de Gaulle's restless intelligence sought to find a role for France as a world power. But they all had one thing in common: the destruction of what he called 'the frenetic power of Prussianized Germany'.[31] As well as discussing the future of 'Europe', in the autumn of 1943 the CFLN began, under de Gaulle's prodding, to develop its ideas about the future of Germany.[32] No detailed proposals could be drafted without some idea of what the Allies were thinking, but already it was clear that de Gaulle's preference was to eliminate any central German authority – breaking Germany up into some form of pre-1870 confederation – to incorporate the Rhineland and the Saar into France, and to find a way of neutralizing the industrial might of the Ruhr. When Massigli produced a note in October 1943 expressing scepticism about the idea of breaking Germany up, de Gaulle annotated it with the comment 'All that weakens Germany reinforces us'; when in another note in August 1944 on the future of the Rhineland Massigli observed that Clemenceau had wanted permanent occupation of the region in 1919, de Gaulle annotated it with 'Events proved he was right.'[33]

Massigli, to his relief, was no longer in charge of French foreign policy. He now became Ambassador in London where he hoped to blunt the edge of de Gaulle's hostility to Britain. The new Foreign Minister, Georges Bidault, found his task even more thankless than Massigli before him. It was said mischievously that, to control his government, de Gaulle had chosen as Interior Minister someone who had not been in France for years (Adrien Tixier had been in Washington) and as Foreign Minister someone who had hardly ever been abroad (Bidault). This was probably too Machiavellian an interpretation. Bidault was in many ways a comprehensible choice. As a journalist before the war, he had written on international affairs and won much respect for his opposition to the Munich Agreement. During the Occupation, he had worked closely with Moulin in the Resistance before himself heading the CNR, which was a point in his favour. He lacked experience of diplomacy, but since de Gaulle had a dim view of the propensity of career diplomats to seek compromise this may not have counted against him. What may have annoyed the General, since he valued professionalism and orderly working habits, was that Bidault's were erratic and his lifestyle bohemian. He often received journalists in his dressing gown and it was soon common knowledge in Paris that he was often the worse for drink.

Bidault's main problem lay elsewhere. Having started out ready to idolize de Gaulle, he rapidly discovered that the General intended to keep foreign policy entirely in his hands. When in September 1945 the Soviet Foreign Minister Molotov remarked to Bidault, 'All is not very clear to me in French policy,' Bidault could only reply, 'Nor to me.'[34] On another occasion, a member of de Gaulle's government sent a deputy to the British Embassy to see if it could throw any light on French policy since 'apart from the Minister of Foreign Affairs, who was himself sometimes not very clearly informed, members of the Cabinet had only the French press as guidance.'[35] The British Ambassador Duff Cooper reported to London that there was little contact between the Rue Saint-Dominique, where de Gaulle was installed, and the Quai d'Orsay: 'The General is a law unto himself, and so far as he trusts anyone, it is Palewski, "mon cher ami Gaston", as I call him, whom I distrust and dislike the more I know him.'[36] Bidault became increasingly frustrated by the contempt with which de Gaulle treated him; to the head of the Quai, Chauvel, de Gaulle would refer to him often as 'your poor minister'. Like Massigli before him, Bidault was frequently on the verge of resigning.

For the first weeks after his return to France, de Gaulle's priority was to consolidate his domestic position. Until the Allies had formally recognized his provisional government he was not in a position to embark on a foreign policy. Recognition was finally accorded on 23 October 1944. As usual the American government procrastinated until the last moment, and then sprang on the British a policy which London had been advocating for weeks. The next day, when asked for his view at a press conference, de Gaulle answered sardonically: 'The government is satisfied that it is now being called by its name.' Duff Cooper went to dinner that night at de Gaulle's residence:

> They sent a guide to lead us to the villa somewhere in the Bois where he is living; and which is obviously very difficult to find since all the other guests were late . . . It was an extremely frigid and dreary party – worse even than his entertainments usually are. He made no reference at all when I arrived to the fact that his government had been recognised by the three great powers that afternoon, and when I said that I hoped he was glad it was finished, he shrugged his shoulders and said it would never finish . . . Beatrice Eden [wife of Anthony] said that the things one dreaded were usually not as bad as one expected but this had been worse.[37]

On 11 November, the French were also admitted to sit on the European Consultative Commission, whose role was to discuss the future of Germany. France was inching back towards 'normal' status.

Churchill had decided he would like to visit France on Armistice Day. De Gaulle grumbled beforehand that 'he wants to steal my 11 November', but the visit went well. De Gaulle, better as host than as guest, was eager to demonstrate how much he dominated the French political scene. Only four months earlier he had needed Churchill's permission just to spend an afternoon in the city of Bayeux. Massive crowds turned out to cheer the two leaders. Churchill visited the Hôtel de Ville to meet Resistance leaders. He was presented with a swastika flag that had been captured during the fighting. De Gaulle comments in his *Memoirs* with a cynicism and lack of generosity startling even from him that Churchill had met the 'men behind the insurrection' in the possible hope of 'finding opponents of de Gaulle among them'.[38] Churchill remarked that they seemed more like members of the Labour Party than revolutionaries: 'All the better for public order. A pity for the picturesque.' In fact he had been deeply affected and was in tears for most of the day. The resisters found him more moved by their exploits than de Gaulle had ever been.

The talks between de Gaulle and Churchill over these three days were cordial enough but resolved no outstanding issues: the slowness with which the Allies were rearming the French army, friction over Syria, the future of Germany, and so on. In his *Memoirs* de Gaulle reports that he proposed a kind of privileged partnership between their countries so that they could stand up to both the Soviet Union and United States. Not only was this as grandiose as it was vague, but since de Gaulle knew perfectly well that Churchill prioritized his close relationship with Roosevelt, one can assume that these comments, if they were made at all – and they are not registered in the British record – were made with his *Memoirs* in mind rather than intended as a serious proposition. But de Gaulle did not miss the opportunity again to put some grit in the relations between Roosevelt and Churchill. He asked Churchill if the President had talked to him about his idea of America establishing bases abroad. 'Dakar?' asked Churchill. 'Yes. And Singapore,' replied de Gaulle.[39]

Shortly before Churchill's visit, de Gaulle had asked Bogomolov for an invitation to visit the Soviet Union. For de Gaulle, this was the chance for a spectacular entry into the world of international diplomacy. There were also more practical objectives. De Gaulle wanted to probe whether the Soviet Union might be more ready to back French objectives in the Rhineland than the British and Americans. He set off for the Soviet Union on 24 November. Because of the intense fighting on the eastern front, the Soviet government had proposed that he travel to Moscow by train from Baku. He therefore had to fly first to Tehran via Cairo, and then board the train from Baku. He was away from France for just over three weeks. That he was prepared to risk being absent for so long when the internal situation was still so uncertain and parts of French territory had still not been liberated shows the huge importance he attached to this trip. 'Let us hope there is no revolution,' he remarked drily as he was setting off.[40] Just after the dissolution of the Patriotic Militia de Gaulle had finally announced an amnesty for Thorez, who had deserted in 1939 and spent the war in Moscow. This paved the way for his own visit to Moscow, and probably he had a shrewd idea that Thorez would be a moderating force in French politics. On the eve of his departure Thorez was received by Stalin, who gave him strict instructions: 'Communists had not yet understood that the situation in France had changed. The situation is different, new, and favourable to de Gaulle. The Communist Party is not strong enough to strike at the head of the government.'[41]

The slow train journey from Baku to Moscow took five days, passing through the endless tracts of devastation around Stalingrad. At one stop where they were shown the terrible scars of the war, de Gaulle exclaimed to the diplomat Jean Laloy, who had accompanied him as interpreter: 'What a great people' – by which he meant the Germans. The party arrived in Moscow on the morning of 2 December. During his stay in the city he was disconcerted to find that the Russian public took no interest in him and barely knew who he was. His first meeting with Stalin took place that evening. Stalin doodled impassively, hardly looking up, while de Gaulle tested his reactions to his ideas on the future of Germany. Stalin refused to make any commitments without having talked to his allies.

The next evening there was an official reception at which Stalin and de Gaulle exchanged some sinister banter. When Stalin remarked that an unruly country like France must be hard to govern, de Gaulle replied: 'Yes, and to do it I cannot use you as an example because you are inimitable.' When Thorez was mentioned, Stalin observed jocularly that he seemed to be a genuine French patriot and that in de Gaulle's place he would not put him in prison – 'at least not immediately'.[42]

After this sparring, Bidault and his opposite number Molotov began negotiations for a Franco-Soviet Treaty. At this point, the Soviets revealed their hand. They would sign a treaty only if the French agreed in return to recognize the Polish 'Lublin Committee'. This Committee, stuffed with Communist stooges, was Moscow's candidate for the future government of Poland against the official Polish government in exile based in London. At his second set of talks with Stalin on the evening of 6 December, de Gaulle made a strong plea for a genuinely independent Poland, and refused to give ground on the Lublin Committee. Then another hitch occurred. The Soviets, who had kept Churchill informed of the discussions, reported London's suggestion that instead of a bilateral treaty with France there might be a tripartite pact between the three countries. De Gaulle was furious. As Oliver Harvey reported, he saw Britain's 'cloven hoof' attempting to sabotage French policy.[43] In fact the British had no strong views on the matter, and it was Stalin who kept the idea bubbling as a bargaining counter which he planned to give up later.

To signal his displeasure, de Gaulle refused on 8 December to leave the Embassy and participate in the tedious tourist visits that the Soviets inflicted on their visitors. That evening he had a third tête-á-tête with Stalin who had now dropped the idea of a tripartite pact, as he had always intended. In return, de Gaulle, while not agreeing to recognize the Lublin Committee, at least agreed to meet its representatives on the next day. He was not impressed, commenting to one of his aides, in a rare flash of anti-Semitism, that they were just a 'bunch of rabbis, a bunch of yids [*youpins*] with no popular support'.[44]

Negotiations were still going on when the French party was invited to a final banquet on the night of 9 December – the last round in this protracted poker game. As the interminable banquet dragged on – with de Gaulle sitting glumly at Stalin's side – Stalin began proposing menacing toasts to his generals and ministers. Each was summoned to leave his seat and chink glasses with him. After dinner, while the diplomats continued their discussions, Stalin shouted out merrily that if they did not reach an agreement soon they would be shot. In the meantime he proposed a series of threatening toasts to some of his ministers and officials: 'Here's to the Minister of Railroads. His trains run on time and help our armies. If they didn't, he knows he would pay for it with his head.' When coffee and brandy were served in another room while the diplomats resumed their negotiations, Stalin continued his sinister playacting. Pointing to Bulganin, one of the Soviet negotiators, he shouted, 'Bring the machine guns; let's liquidate the diplomats.' De Gaulle joined in this game of psychological warfare. Finding himself seated next to the American diplomat Averell Harriman he pointed at Bulganin and remarked loudly enough for the Russian interpreter to hear: 'Is that the man who arrested so many Russian generals?'[45]

After the meal the guests trooped off to a private cinema where they were forced to watch a tedious anti-German propaganda film. Once it was over, Stalin proposed screening something more cheerful, including a film about Donald Duck in Hitler's Germany. At this point, de Gaulle abruptly decided to end this comedy whose purpose, as he observed in his *Memoirs*, was to 'impress the French by demonstrating Soviet power and the dominance of the man who was in charge of it'. He rose suddenly from his seat, curtly said his goodbyes and announced that he would be taking the train home the next morning. He left behind two French negotiators to continue the discussions – but not Bidault, who had already drunk a lot. Although it would have been a major loss of face to return from a week in Moscow with no agreement, de Gaulle gambled that, having pushed him to the wire, the Soviets would finally make an offer. This is what occurred. At 2 a.m., Maurice Dejean arrived with a new draft which de Gaulle accepted after some final adjustments. It was signed at 4 a.m. in Molotov's office while Stalin joked to a visibly nervous Molotov that the French had outwitted him. After yet another meal and more toasts, de Gaulle's party left later in the morning.

In the famous pages de Gaulle devoted to this visit in his *Memoirs*, accompanied by some marginally doctored documents,[46] he portrayed himself as having for a week resisted Stalin's pressure to recognize the Lublin Committee and contrasted this with what happened two months later at the Yalta Conference where Roosevelt and Churchill effectively abandoned eastern Europe to Stalin. Since de Gaulle was not present at Yalta – he was not invited to attend – he was able to claim that his hands were clean in this. Time and again, he would return to his idea that Yalta had revealed to the world 'that there was a correlation between France's absence and Europe's new laceration'. The truth is that Yalta was a recognition of the realities of power on the ground – the presence of the Red Army – and despite his presentation of events, de Gaulle had bent to the same realities during his visit to Moscow. He had certainly resisted on the form – he did not recognize the Lublin Committee – but he conceded the substance of what Stalin wanted by agreeing to an exchange of representatives between the Lublin Committee and the French provisional government. At Yalta, when Churchill complained to Stalin that he was not properly informed about Poland, Stalin told him: 'De Gaulle has a representative at Lublin. Could you not do the same?'[47] France was to be the first western government to recognize the Polish government officially in June 1945. It is quite possible also that de Gaulle would have gone further during his talks in Moscow if Stalin had been willing to offer him more on Germany. This is certainly what he implied to Claude Guy two years later:

> My intention in going to Moscow was not simply to exchange signatures with Stalin on a piece of paper . . . I wanted to see what he was really think-ing about the Rhine. And I was ready, deep down, to engage myself to support him in Poland, Rumania, etc. in exchange for categorical support from him in our combat for the Rhine.[48]

Overall de Gaulle had failed to secure any support from Stalin on the western frontiers of Germany. The treaty obliged the signatories to assist each other not only in the case of German aggression but even if one of them was 'implicated' in hostilities against Germany after taking 'all neces-sary measures to eliminate any new threat from Germany'. In plain language this meant that France could find herself dragged into a war to defend Soviet interests in eastern Europe. This was somewhat hypothetical given that Germany was hardly likely to be a threat for many years, but that someone so punctilious about details was ready make this commit-ment shows de Gaulle's desperation to secure a treaty to mark France's re-entry into great-power diplomacy.

De Gaulle had few illusions about his Moscow visit. As the train was leaving the city, he remarked gloomily to Laloy: 'This is not the domination of a party, nor of a class, but that of a single man. It is not a regime of the people. It is against the nature of man. We will have them on our hands for a hundred years.'[49] Yet however horrified he was by what he saw in Russia, de Gaulle's carefully chiselled portrait of Stalin is suffused with a certain fascination for the 'saturnine charm' of this 'humanly solitary leader' who 'loved [Russia] in his own way'. Stalin was a 'man for whom everything was manoeuvring, mistrust and obstinacy'.[50] This sounds almost like a self-portrait.

Although the Quai was unhappy about the pact, it was well received in France as evidence of France's re-entry into world politics. But how little Stalin cared about France was demonstrated at Yalta only six weeks later when he was the leader least favourable to French interests. While pushing Churchill and Roosevelt to recognize the Lublin Committee, he remarked mischievously that de Gaulle's democratic base of support in France was no greater. At Yalta, France was in fact granted a zone of occupation in Germany, a permanent seat on the Security Council of the newly created United Nations and a seat on the Inter-Allied Control Commission in Berlin – although this last concession was resisted by both Stalin and Roosevelt until the last day of the conference. These French successes were won by the arguments of Churchill with some support from Roosevelt's special adviser Harry Hopkins. In this case, Churchill's Gaullophobia was trumped by his Francophilia: the need for a strong France to restore a normal balance of power in Europe and act as a counterweight to Germany and the Soviet Union. De Gaulle himself admitted in his *Memoirs* that Yalta had offered France 'important satisfactions', but he made this observation only in passing. In his eyes this did not make up for the fact he had not been invited to attend.[51] He never lost an opportunity in later years to fulminate against this humiliation while knowing perfectly well that France had done remarkably well out of the conference. Perhaps over the years he even came to believe the Yalta myth he had constructed.

De Gaulle took out his irritation at not having been invited to Yalta by refusing Roosevelt's invitation to meet him at Algiers on his way home – a gratuitous snub which achieved nothing. More serious was de Gaulle's refusal to agree to be one of the four inviting powers to a conference to be held in San Francisco in April to discuss the founding of the United Nations. He was not willing to put his name to a document in whose drafting he had played no part. He was anyway circumspect about an organization that he suspected might be a tool for American anti-colonialism. Bidault was allowed to participate in the debates at San Francisco but was kept on such a tight leash by de Gaulle that France's impact was minuscule. De Gaulle's instruction to Bidault contained one revealing idea which provides another indication of how his mind was working in regard to finding a new great-power role for France. He told Bidault that he should try to support the potential influence of smaller powers in the structure of the organization. These 'small and medium powers which in previous times formed [our] clients' could be 'useful again in the future'.[52]

TENSIONS WITH THE ALLIES

De Gaulle's exclusion from Yalta – and some months later from the next meeting of the Big Three at Potsdam – reinforced his conviction that to defend her interests France could rely only on herself. In his view France's main bargaining counter would lie in whatever military contribution she might be able to make to the end of the war. Stalin's famous comment to Laval 'How many divisions has the Pope?' expressed a philosophy of power that de Gaulle shared. Where the majority of the French population believed that Liberation signalled the end of the war, de Gaulle hoped exactly the opposite, as he wrote with startling frankness in his *Memoirs*:

> That the war was still going on was undoubtedly painful with regard to the losses, damages and expenditure that we the French would still have to bear. But when considering the superior interest of France – which is quite different from the immediate advantages of the French – I did not regret it.[53]

The greater the contribution France could make to the final months of fighting, the greater the influence she might play in the final peace settlement.

At the start of September France had about 560,000 men under arms. But there were difficulties about increasing that number. One major source of tension with the Allies was that France was entirely dependent on America for her rearmament. De Gaulle constantly complained about how slowly his forces were being armed. There was also the problem of integrating the Resistance fighters of the FFI into the regular army. Leclerc told him that more than three-quarters of these men were probably 'useless or even detrimental'.[54] Difficulties also arose in persuading officers who had been with de Gaulle from the start to work with – or under – those who had not. Leclerc, after his successes in Paris, found that his unit was to be incorporated into de Lattre's First Army which had landed in Provence in August 1944 and marched rapidly north up the Rhône corridor. The meeting between the two forces had occurred on 12 September in Burgundy. Leclerc would have preferred to remain with the American army. He told de Gaulle that his own division was more like a 'crusade than a regular unit' behind a leader who raised the 'standard of holy war' rather than a general who, although superior in rank, had served Vichy. De Gaulle, who hated dealing with the quarrels of subordinates, replied with a phrase he often used in such circumstances – 'all that is exaggerated is pointless' – to which Leclerc countered that 'all we have done that is useful and great following you over the last four years was "exaggerated"'.[55] But Leclerc had to give in.

Despite these tensions French armies fought hard in Lorraine and Alsace during the winter of 1944. De Lattre's troops took Mulhouse on 21 November and Leclerc liberated Strasbourg on 23 November (despite the order that de Lattre should have this honour so as to have a victory to match Juin's in Rome and Leclerc's in Paris). The liberation of Strasbourg was a hugely symbolic moment, allowing Leclerc to respect the famous oath he had taken at Kufra four years earlier.

A few weeks later this triumph was thrown into doubt. On 16 December, Hitler caught the Allies off guard with a last desperate gamble by launching an offensive through the Ardennes. Through tactical surprise this succeeded in punching a hole of about 50 kilometres in the American line. To regroup his forces and prepare a counter-attack, Eisenhower decided that de Lattre must concede the territory he had taken in Alsace and fall back on the Vosges mountains. This meant evacuating Strasbourg. Quite apart from the blow to French morale, the evacuation of Strasbourg would have exposed the population of the city to German reprisals. While de Latttre tried to win time before implementing the order, Juin, now Chief of the French General Staff, was sent to Eisenhower's HQ to put the French position. On 2 January 1945 Juin reported back to de Gaulle that the Americans would not budge and it would be necessary to give ground. De Gaulle refused and their ensuing dialogue was very characteristic:

> Juin: I completely understand; you are right a thousand times over, but this is not possible. The Americans will not allow de Lattre to go against the order he has been given. If you try to override them, they will cut off our supplies, arms, petrol.
>
> De Gaulle: It is true that we are dependent on them but conversely they are dependent on us. If they do that I will cut off their access to our railways and ports . . . We will defend Strasbourg . . . if necessary house by house. We will make it a French Stalingrad.[56]

De Gaulle wrote sharply to de Lattre forbidding him to abandon Strasbourg whatever his orders. De Lattre pleaded with him on 3 January to get the evacuation order changed by the Allies so that he could reconcile his 'duty to you, my political and military commander' and his 'duty of discipline' towards the Allied high command – which did not please de Gaulle.[57] De Gaulle did, however, appeal at the same time to Eisenhower, Roosevelt and Churchill to reconsider. On the afternoon of 3 January, he went in person with Juin to Eisenhower's HQ at Versailles where, to his surprise, Churchill was present. As de Gaulle recounts the events in his *Memoirs*, Eisenhower was won over by his argument that an evacuation of Strasbourg was probably militarily avoidable but certainly politically disastrous.[58] In fact by the time de Gaulle arrived, Eisenhower had already been persuaded to abandon the evacuation by Churchill.[59]

De Gaulle, who never liked being in anyone's debt, simply recorded that

Churchill had backed up his arguments. Duff Cooper was startled when Palewski drafted a communiqué to the effect that 'de Gaulle had summoned a military conference which the PM and Eisenhower had been allowed to attend'.[60] After the meeting was over, Churchill and de Gaulle had a conversation in which the former tried to be genial and the latter was obstinately silent. Juin afterwards remarked that de Gaulle might at least have thanked Churchill: '"Bah!" he answered with a gloomy expression and went back to his thoughts.'[61] Two years later, discussing the Strasbourg crisis with an American historian, de Gaulle said: 'I still ask myself what Churchill was doing there that day' – although he had in fact appealed for his help.[62]

De Gaulle's opposition to the evacuation of Strasbourg was vindicated militarily when the German offensive petered out. Although his account of the denouement of the crisis is distorted, it is hard to imagine anyone else displaying the same nerve as he did over these three days. Less successful were his other conflicts with his allies in the last months of the fighting. His view was that the more territory the French occupied at the moment of the German surrender, the better their future bargaining position. On 21 April, French forces under de Lattre took Stuttgart. It had been agreed beforehand that for operational reasons the city would be occupied by the Americans. De Gaulle ordered de Lattre to stay put and this caused an immediate conflict with the new American President Harry Truman, who had taken over after Roosevelt's sudden death on 12 April.

Truman sent a sharp telegram threatening to retaliate with 'an entire rearrangement of command'. De Gaulle held his ground and tried some characteristic blackmail in a meeting on 4 May with the American Ambassador, Jefferson Caffery. Expressing his fear that 'Russia will take over the entire continent in due course,' he insisted that he wished to establish good relations with United States: 'I would much rather work with the United States than any other country. The British Empire will not be strong enough after this war to count for much. If I cannot work with you, I must work with the Soviets in order to survive even if it is only for a while, and even if in the long run they gobble us up too.' The tone of the meeting was relatively cordial. De Gaulle turned on the charm he could exert if he took the trouble, wrongfooting interlocutors more used to his iciness or rudeness. Caffery cabled Washington: 'Although this may sound a silly thing to say, when I left, instead of saying goodbye to me at the door as he had always done before, he accompanied me through several rooms to the place where I had left my hat and coat.'[63] De Gaulle could make people pathetically grateful for the smallest gestures. But neither threats nor charm worked in this case, and the French had to leave Stuttgart. One result of the mini-crisis

over the city was to poison his relations with a new President who harboured none of the anti-Gaullist animus of his predecessor.

The only possible benefit of the crisis over Stuttgart was that it had
forced the British and Americans to reopen negotiations over the contours
of the future French zone of occupation. Perhaps this had been the real
purpose of de Gaulle's brinkmanship.[64] There were, however, no visible
benefits of any kind from the crisis that erupted a few weeks later, over the
small Alpine region of Val d'Aosta on the Italian frontier. French troops
under General Doyen had occupied the area contrary to the orders of the
Allied high command. The Americans suspected the French of annexation-
ist ambitions. De Gaulle's denials seemed undercut by his threatening
reminder that the population of many of the villages was Francophone and
that he had in mind only some 'very minor territorial adjustments which
he hoped to take up amicably' with the Italian government at a later date.[65]
The situation reached crisis point when on 2 June de Gaulle instructed
Doyen to hold on to the region 'by all the necessary means'.[66] A furious
Truman wrote back that it would be extraordinary if, almost one year after
D-Day, 'French soldiers bearing American arms' were to find themselves
fighting the Americans who had liberated France a year before. He threatened to cut off all military supplies to the French.[67] Juin was despatched
to broker a deal with the Allied commanders at Caserta near Naples on 8
June. He conveyed his private opinion that de Gaulle's behaviour had been
'unreasonable and impetuous' and had been opposed by almost his entire
government.[68] De Gaulle was forced to withdraw his troops.

In his *Memoirs* de Gaulle described this tiny affair as proof of the American 'taste for hegemony' egged on by the British.[69] He was confirmed in
this view by the simultaneous eruption of the gravest Anglo-French crisis
of the period. As usual the spark was Syria. De Gaulle had seemingly won
a victory when Spears was finally recalled to London at the start of 1944.
But Spears's departure did not solve the underlying problem that, having
promised independence in 1941, the French had ever since been doing all
in their power to delay it. There was also the question of what 'independence' meant. French policy, as stated once again by de Gaulle in the autumn
of 1944, was that the 'traditional position' of France in the region had to
be maintained. This was certainly not independence as the Syrians and
Lebanese conceived it.[70] De Gaulle warned Bidault in October 1944 against
'the reality and duplicity of London's policy'.[71] As usual, London's policy
in the Middle East was more confused than duplicitous; and, as usual, the
British were torn between their desire to remain on good terms with France
and their wish not to alienate Arab goodwill. In a conversation with the

Syrian President in February 1945 Churchill had insisted that it was Britain's view that France should be allowed to keep a 'privileged position' in the region.[72]

Tension between the French authorities and the population had been growing since the end of 1944. In January 1945 violent anti-French demonstrations broke out in Damascus. The French responded by sending in tanks, which only made matters worse. Against the advice of the Quai, in April de Gaulle despatched troop reinforcements to the Levant. Throughout May, anti-French strikes and violent demonstrations spread through all major cities. On 29 May, the French General Oliva-Roget ordered the shelling of public buildings in Damascus. His troops fired on the crowds, causing about 1,000 casualties. Although desperate not to be sucked into the conflict, Churchill felt constrained on 31 May to issue an ultimatum, warning that unless French troops returned to their barracks the British commander in the Middle East, General Paget, would intervene to restore order. By an unfortunate error of timing this was announced in parliament one hour before de Gaulle was informed. On 4 June de Gaulle, receiving Duff Cooper, 'could not have been more stiff if he had been declaring war'. A French naval cruiser, the Jeanne d'Arc, was ordered to sail for Beirut and de Gaulle instructed French soldiers to fire on the British if necessary.[73]

In the end, de Gaulle was forced to back down. As he told Cooper: 'We are not, I recognize, in a position to wage war on you at the moment. But you have outraged France and betrayed the West. That cannot be forgotten.'[74] In the fifteen pages he devoted to this affair in his Memoirs over ten years later, de Gaulle showed he had certainly not 'forgotten'. The pages burn with rage again the 'insolence' and 'insults' of the British, and the 'public humiliation' their 'brutal intervention' had inflicted on the French. An earlier draft was even more violent: 'The events proved that for England, when she is the stronger, there is no alliance which holds, no treaty which is respected, no truth which matters.'[75] De Gaulle's supremely tendentious account, passing over the heavy civilian casualties, argued that the British had chosen to intervene at the moment when the French had succeeded in getting the situation under control – while the truth was that fighting was still taking place on the evening of 31 May. De Gaulle also claimed that he had ordered a ceasefire on the evening of 30 May and that the British knew this perfectly well – but his own Ambassador in London, Massigli, cabled Bidault four days later to say he had never heard of such an order.[76]

DREAMS OF EMPIRE

The Syrian conflict was part of a more general crisis of the French Empire. Although blinded in the Middle East by his suspicion of the British, de Gaulle was otherwise aware that the Empire could not survive without reform. For this reason, in January 1944 the CFLN had organized a major conference at Brazzaville to discuss the future of Black Africa. This event later won de Gaulle the reputation of a prophet of decolonization, but the truth is more complicated than the 'myth of Brazzaville'.

The conference was a pre-emptive strike against the anti-colonial views of Roosevelt, a propaganda exercise to prove that the French were aware of the need for change.[77] But one of its organizers, Henri Laurentie, certainly intended it as more than a cosmetic exercise. Laurentie was a colonial civil servant who had been an adviser to Eboué in August 1940 when Chad rallied to de Gaulle. Laurentie, who prided himself on being one of the first Gaullists, was a maverick in the staid world of colonial officialdom. He was a surrealist poet in his spare time and unique among colonial officials in not addressing black servants by the familiar 'tu' form. In preparation for the Brazzaville conference he developed bold proposals to transform the Empire into a federal structure with mainland France at the apex of a hierarchy of states whose evolution would depend on their readiness for administrative autonomy, an arrangement not dissimilar to the British Commonwealth. In the end, however, the conference, dominated by the colonial governors, rejected such radical ideas. It declared unequivocally: 'The civilizing mission accomplished in the colonies excludes any idea of autonomy, all possibility of evolution outside the French bloc; also excluded is the eventual establishment of *self-government* [in English] in the colonies, even in a distant future.'[78]

It is hard to know whether de Gaulle inclined more towards the reforming ambitions of Laurentie or towards the timid official conclusions of the conference. His only direct contribution was an opening speech as grandiose as it was evasive. He praised France's 'civilizing mission' while also recognizing the need for renewal. But his conclusion was that that no definitive decisions about Empire could be taken until France had been liberated. Ten months later, at a press conference in October 1944, he made remarks which seemingly inclined in a reformist direction, going beyond what he had said at Brazzaville, but whenever it came to implementing concrete policies, de Gaulle's decisions bore no relation to the generous rhetoric.[79]

The greatest immediate challenge was in North Africa, where French authority had suffered an irremediable blow in 1940. This was one reason why the organizers of the Brazzaville conference decided to confine its remit to Black Africa. In February 1943, the moderate Algerian nationalist leader Ferhat Abbas drafted a manifesto demanding that the Muslim population of Algeria be accorded the same rights as the Europeans. It sought full autonomy in some kind of federal union with France. De Gaulle's response was a speech at Constantine in Algeria in December 1943, generous in spirit but vague on details. Like the Brazzaville speech a month later, it was his way of recognizing the need for change without conceding any substance. When the CLFN began to discuss the details of reform, de Gaulle came down in favour of the more conservative option (to the regret of Catroux and Philip).[80]

The result was an ordinance in March 1944 according full citizenship to only 65,000 Muslims. This reform was not enough for Abbas, whose disappointment pushed him towards the more radical position of advocating full independence. On the other hand, it was too much for the European population. On VE Day 1945, demonstrations by Algerians at Sétif and Guelma in the country's Constantine region were violently repressed. Possibly 20,000 people were massacred. Algerian nationalists would later choose this event as the beginning of the Algerian War of Independence. In his *Memoirs* written in the mid-1950s de Gaulle dismissed the Sétif massacre in one sentence in terms suggesting that he neither understood the significance of the event nor especially regretted it: 'In Algeria, the beginning of an insurrection, in the Constantine region, and synchronized with the Syrian riots of May, was repressed by the governor.' De Gaulle's suspicion that these events were linked to the machinations of the British in Syria was entirely imaginary, although revealing of how he was reading the world at this time. The demonstrations had in reality been sparked by his own government's decision a few weeks earlier to arrest another nationalist leader, Messali Hadj.[81]

Simultaneously, France was faced with a crisis in French Indo-China. In 1940 the Vichy Governor of Indo-China, Admiral Decoux, had been presented with an ultimatum by the Japanese government. He was given a choice between providing military and economic facilities and facing an invasion. Decoux had little option but to give in and for the next four years Indo-China lived in a strange peaceable bubble, with the French authorities collaborating with the Japanese while escaping formal occupation.

Suddenly this fragile equilibrium was shattered on 9 March 1945 when, confronted with imminent defeat by America, the Japanese decided to occupy Indo-China. Almost at a stroke, what remained of French power in Indo-China was eliminated. De Gaulle made a speech celebrating acts of French resistance against this Japanese coup, although these had been almost non-existent. It was on this occasion that he used the phrase quoted earlier about 'creating' events: 'Were there only two Frenchmen fighting in the north of the country it would be necessary, in the face of the eventual pretensions of the Americans, to create the event.'[82] A few weeks later the Minister of Information was reprimanded for not giving enough publicity to these tiny acts of the resistance: 'I attach much importance to this matter. The country must be constantly kept interested in Indo-China along with the future of our power and influence throughout the Far East.'[83]

De Gaulle's government responded to the Japanese invasion with a solemn declaration on 24 March 1945 proposing that the territories of Indo-China – Vietnam, Cambodia, Laos – should become part of a French 'Community'. The Community would elect a Federal Assembly but power would rest with the Governor General. The problem with this document, France's opening gambit to seize back the initiative, was that it looked like a hastily improvised response to the Japanese coup rather than a genuine attempt to rethink the nature of the Empire. It was too little, too late. The Japanese surrender a few months later left a power vacuum which offered an opportunity for Ho Chi Minh, leader of the Vietnamese nationalists (Vietminh), to proclaim his country an independent republic. Ho did not have real power but nor did anyone else. The Gaullist declaration of 24 March had been rapidly overtaken by events.

This was immediately understood by Laurentie, who had already written to de Gaulle in June 1945 that France was in the throes of a 'full colonial crisis' and had to develop more imaginative solutions.[84] His views were shared by Catroux but not by most officials of the Colonial Ministry or the Quai – or by de Gaulle. De Gaulle's first objective was to re-establish French power in the region – before the Allies arrived. At the Potsdam conference, it had been agreed that for the purposes of receiving the Japanese surrender Indo-China should be divided into two zones along the 16th parallel: the British in the south and the Chinese in the north. To safeguard French interests de Gaulle sent out a French expeditionary force under Leclerc and appointed Thierry d'Argenlieu as Governor of Indo-China. This was an odd choice because, although both men were fanatically loyal to de Gaulle, it was no secret that they loathed each other. The former cavalry officer Leclerc was on the surface direct and blunt but in practice pragmatic and flexible; d'Argenlieu displayed on the surface the unctuous slipperiness of the cleric he had once been but in reality he was rigid and uncompromising (as he had shown to disastrous effect in New Caledonia). We have no idea why de Gaulle hitched together these two dissimilar personalities except in the spirit of a divide-and-rule policy he had used in the past, and in the knowledge that they would be competing assiduously to win his favour.[85] His instructions to d'Argenlieu were unequivocal: no promises of any kind to the Vietminh until the French were in a position of strength; and 'no confidence' to be shown in the English given their 'hypocritical attitude' and the likelihood that they would repeat in the Far East the 'ignoble game' they had played in Syria.[86] Leclerc was told to make no contact with the rebel forces 'until we are in a position of strength'.[87]

Leclerc arrived in the third week of August. By the end of the year he had succeeded in re-establishing French authority south of the 16th parallel. Most of the north remained under the influence of Ho. Unless the French were prepared to countenance prolonged military conflict a political solution would have to be found. But de Gaulle's instructions were that there was to be no retreat from the conservative position outlined in the declaration of 24 March.[88] On 14 December, de Gaulle had a meeting with Vĩnh San, the legitimate representative of the Vietnamese imperial dynasty who had been deposed by the French in 1916 aged sixteen and had lived in exile ever since. Nothing came of this encounter because Vĩnh San died in an air crash two weeks later. Some Gaullists later saw this as a tragic lost opportunity. It is hard to agree. Reinstating a figure who had not set foot in the country for several decades, and who, however liberal his intentions, could only have been perceived as a French stooge, would certainly not have satisfied the Vietminh. On receiving d'Argenlieu's report on the situation in Indo-China at the end of the year, de Gaulle observed: 'We are returning to Indochina because we are the strongest.'[89] De Gaulle the decolonizer was far in the future where Indo-China and the Levant were concerned.

ISOLATION

While de Gaulle was struggling to hold on to France's leaking Empire, in Europe he could celebrate the fact that French armies had participated in the final victory against Germany. The German surrender was signed at Reims near Eisenhower's Headquarters on 7 May, to take effect the following day. The Soviet government insisted also on a ceremony in Berlin, which took place on 8 May. De Gaulle noted with satisfaction in his *Memoirs*: 'Of course I did not fail to fix in advance with the Allies France's participation at these two cermonies.'[90] The truth was slightly different. For the ceremony at Reims the French signatory, General Sevez (deputy to Juin, who was away in the United States), was informed only at the very last moment; his name was clumsily inserted on the surrender document by a different typewriter; and he was there only as a witness. De Lattre de Tassigny was present at the signing of the German surrender in Berlin on 8 May, but this was such a surprise that the Soviet hosts had to improvise a French flag stitched together from pieces of Nazi banners and some worker overalls. Even so, after the humiliation of 1940, any French presence on these two occasions was a remarkable achievement, inconceivable without de Gaulle's tenacity, obstinacy and political skill.[91]

But France's symbolic presence among the victors did not mean that she been fully readmitted to the rank of great power. De Gaulle was not invited to the Potsdam conference in July where the Big Three met to discuss the immediate post-war settlement. One of the major decisions of that conference was to agree the principle of the restoration of a central authority in Germany, which was exactly contrary to de Gaulle's intentions – 'inadmissible' for France as he put it.[92] One positive outcome from France's point of view was the setting up of a Council of Foreign Ministers, including France, to discuss the future of Germany. At the first meeting in London when Bidault put forward France's maximalist position on Germany – the detachment of the Rhineland, the internationalization of the Ruhr, and so on – he found himself completely isolated. In a note for the Quai d'Orsay in September, de Gaulle gave no ground:

> In the current situation, what would be best is to organize the administration of central Germany by creating and making a reality of a State of Bavaria, a State of Baden, a State of Württemberg, a State of Hesse-Darmstadt, a State of Hesse-Cassel, a State of Hanover ... When this has been done we can see if there is a case for allowing these different states to federate and in what conditions.[93]

Although, as de Gaulle's biographer Eric Roussel suggests, this seems like de Gaulle at his most 'Maurrassian', his views were in reality more nuanced. At the first meeting of a committee chaired by de Gaulle to discuss the future of Germany in July, the conclusions were more open-ended: 'The reconstitution of Germany does certainly not represent an immediate danger ... The policy of "zones", even with a view to the dislocation of Germany, seems to offer at the present moment more disadvantages than advantages ... We need to follow a supple policy giving no hostages to fortune for the future [ménager l'avenir].'[94] At the start of October de Gaulle made a three-day visit to the the left bank of the Rhine and to Baden, and the theme of his speeches, which caused some amazement, was reconstruction and the need for the French and Germans to work together.[95] The speeches emboldened one of the French administrators in the French zone to draft a directive on the need to work towards a rapprochement with the German population. When Claude Hettier de Boislambert, one of de Gaulle's oldest 'companions', was sent to take over as Governor of part of the French zone in October he was told by de Gaulle: 'Do not forget that one will not make Europe again without Germany.'[96]

Despite these signs that de Gaulle's ideas were not fixed, for the moment French foreign policy seemed to have reached an impasse. De Gaulle, over Stuttgart, Val d'Aosta, Syria, Indo-China, had antagonized almost everyone. Oliver Harvey, the most consistently pro-Gaullist Foreign Office official, commented after the Syrian crisis: 'De Gaulle has shown himself to be impossible. We can never have normal relations with such a man.'[97] The French Embassy in Washington cabled in July 1945 that France had in a few months squandered 'an enormous capital of sympathy' and the Americans now 'accorded us little attention'.[98] Summing up the situation, Burin des Roziers, an unconditional de Gaulle loyalist, had to admit that France was suffering 'persistent diplomatic isolation'.[99] As Lacouture nicely puts it: 'Too weak to bend in 1940, de Gaulle was not strong enough to impose his views in 1945.' In the transition to peacetime government de Gaulle seemed incapable of adapting the methods he had successfully developed in exile and in war when his primary objective had to been to show that 'France' existed through the force of his personality. He had offered Bidault his philosophy of diplomacy: 'You will see, if you say "no", they will crawl to you and offer you the moon.'[100] Now that he was a head of government, these tactics backfired.

In reality de Gaulle's intransigence had always been tempered by a strong dose of pragmatism. On several occasions he pushed the Free French to the brink of rupture with the Allies and then drew back. Few leaders have reflected more cerebrally and self-consciously on the nature of leadership than de Gaulle had done in his writings before 1940. His portrait of the charismatic leader, drawing heavily on Gustave Le Bon, was balanced by his respect for contingency and the 'force of circumstances'. In this respect it is worth quoting again what he had once written admiringly about the *ancien régime*: 'Avoiding abstractions but holding on to realities, preferring the useful to the sublime, the opportune to the spectacular [*retentissant*], seeking for each particular problem not the ideal solution but the practical one'. His criticism of Napoleon was in the same vein: 'Once the balance between the ends and means is snapped, the manoeuvres of a genius are in vain.'[101] But in power after the Liberation de Gaulle seemed to find it hard to achieve that balance. He has been rightly credited for his remarkable intuitions in 1940 about the future course of the war. His diagnosis in the summer of 1942 about what would happen in North Africa during the autumn was uncannily accurate. He had also rapidly understood the ideological dimension of the conflict and made brilliant use of in his struggle against Giraud and his American backers. But if de Gaulle had frequently said of the war that it was a great revolution he seems not to have grasped the full dimensions of that revolution for the international position of France, the future of her Empire or of her relationship with Germany. It is of course possible – even plausible – that he would have evolved. The Brazzaville speech suggests that he had at some level understood that the Empire would need to change; the tone of some of his speeches on Germany suggests that he might have abandoned his proclaimed ambition of destroying a united Germany. But for the moment it was not his pragmatic and realistic side but his theatrical, romantic and intransigent one that seemed most in evidence.

Speaking to the Assembly de Gaulle declared in March 1945 that France needed to chose between the 'sweet shadow of decline or the harsh light of renewal'. But was his foreign policy really offering renewal? And were these Manichean antinomies a helpful reading of the situation faced by France after Liberation? The living conditions of the French at the end of 1945 remained parlous. There were shortages of the most basic commodities, the black market was thriving, bread rationing had been reintroduced, coal was scarce. How, in these circumstances, should France's limited financial resources be best deployed? The question came to a head at the end of the year in a conflict between de Gaulle and the Assembly over the military budget for 1946 when the Socialists proposed a reduction of 20 per cent in order to devote scarce resources to reconstruction and modernization. As Christian Pineau, former resister and now a Socialist député, put it in December: 'The policy of grandeur need not be a policy of puffing oneself up like a frog.'[102]

Until the end of 1944, de Gaulle's foreign policy positions had been broadly supported at home – the Russian treaty was seen as a great success – but this consensus did not last. His snub to Roosevelt after Yalta was not well received by French public opinion. Nor was there enthusiasm for his actions in Syria in May 1945. What especially enraged de Gaulle during that crisis was the lack of support from the Consultative Assembly. As he wrote in his *Memoirs*:

> To hear the way they spoke ... what had happened in Syria was the result of the abuses of our policy since the start ... Not a word to salute the civilizing work that France had carried out in Syria and Lebanon ... The

Assembly listened to me with attention. It applauded me as usual when I left the tribune. And then it voted for a motion lacking any force which expressed in reality a policy of renunciation.[103]

This developing breach between de Gaulle and France's politicians did not bode well for his great objective in domestic politics: to transform the nature of France's political institutions.

15
From Liberator to Saviour, May 1945–December 1946

'FRANCE IS A COUNTRY THAT IS CONTINUING'

At the start of 1942, in letters written within a few weeks of each other to two Frenchmen living in America, de Gaulle offered diametrically opposed readings of the significance of what had occurred in 1940. To Jacques Maritain in January 1942, he wrote:

> Like you I believe that our people are suffering from a kind of moral collapse. I thought that to climb out of the abyss the first thing was to prevent people resigning themselves to infamy and slavery . . . I think that we will then have to profit from the national *rassemblement* around pride in ourselves and resistance to lead the nation towards a new domestic ideal.[1]

To the journalist Philippe Barrès (son of his great literary idol Maurice Barrès and author of the first propagandist biography of de Gaulle in 1942), he wrote in February:

> Put simply, our country has been stunned by a brutal defeat, like a man who slips on an orange peel. But it understands in its depths that this 'accident' does not correspond to its real worth. Vichy is only an unfortunate episode. Vichy has no roots and France will soon have buried it.[2]

These contrasting diagnoses – the defeat as profound 'moral collapse' or as 'accident' – were written with different interlocutors in mind but they reflected genuinely conflicted feelings: what de Gaulle feared to be true and what he wanted to believe. They were also symptomatic of that oscillation between pessimism and optimism that was a constant feature of his personality.

Two and a half years later, back in France, and faced with the daunting task of rebuilding the country, pessimism prevailed again. Replying to a note from a member of his *cabinet* in October 1944 on the need to mobilize the French around clearly defined policies, de Gaulle wrote:

> What the French of good faith are waiting for is, in sum, that France today is something else than what she is, that is to say a nation gravely sick for a long time, without institutions, without administration, without diplomacy, without hierarchy . . . and totally empty of men of government. That is something neither I nor anyone else will be able to remedy in two months. It is an enterprise requiring long and hard effort and at least a generation.[3]

How to set about this task? De Gaulle's approach offers another illustration of the way in which his outlook differed from that of the Resistance leaders. They believed that the new elites thrown up by the Resistance would carry out a moral regeneration of French society. The spirit of the Resistance would be continued into post-Liberation France by a new movement transcending the former political parties with possibly de Gaulle at its head. De Gaulle's scepticism was encapsulated in a conversation on 24 August 1944, the day before he entered Paris, with Philippe Viannay, leader of one of the Resistance movements of the Occupied Zone. The young and idealistic Viannay excitedly poured out his ideas for the future, expressing his conviction that if de Gaulle harnessed the energies of the Resistance, anything was possible.

> He did not interrupt me . . . The smoke from the cigarette stuck in the corner of his mouth rose up towards his half-closed eyes; his arms were folded. Only his head moved a little as if to signify that he was there. When I had finished, he simply said as if stating the obvious: 'France is not a country that is beginning; it is a country that is continuing.'[4]

In truth the rhetoric of the Resistance about moral and social 'revolution' was vague when it came to details. In March 1944, the CNR had produced a programme centred on the idea of universal welfare and extensive nationalizations. Although inspired by the Communists, this programme drew broadly on the socialist humanism which was the nearest that the Resistance had to an ideology. De Gaulle's speeches in Algiers before the Liberation had recognized the need for social and economic change after Liberation, but he too had avoided details. In this respect Gaullism was doctrinally a blank sheet upon which some of the Free French and some resisters hoped to write their own script.

One member of the Free French with a clear agenda was Georges Boris. An economic adviser to Léon Blum before the war, Boris was one of the first people in France to read Keynes's *General Theory*. As he became more confident of his position within the Free French, he saw an opportunity to influence the economic policy of de Gaulle's future provisional government. In a memorandum of July 1944, he observed that de Gaulle's ideas about the future seemed limited to the reassertion of French national sovereignty and grandeur. Given 'the excessively vague character of the idea of Grandeur', he saw an opportunity to 'work out what it might contain'. Boris's aspiration was to harness Keynesian economics to democratic socialism: the state, taking over banks and heavy industry, would plan the economy through a new National Economics Ministry. To work on de Gaulle, Boris astutely translated this vision into the idiom of Gaullism: 'A Plan (plan of reconstruction first, over 3, 4 or 5 years, then a plan for development) is the necessary instrument of a "Gaullist" policy aiming at the re-establishment of the grandeur of France, and a necessary condition for the success of any Gaullist experiment.'[5]

Boris had the support of the Socialist André Philip[6] and also of the talented young politician Pierre Mendès France. In 1932, Mendès France, on the left wing of the centrist Radical Party, had been the youngest *député* in parliament. Unusual among French politicians for his interest in economics, Mendès France first met Boris while serving in a junior capacity in Blum's short-lived second government in 1938. The two of them drafted a programme inspired by their reading of Keynes. In 1940 Mendès France was among that group of *députés* who boarded the *Massilia* bound for North Africa because he wanted to carry on fighting – only to find himself arrested and imprisoned as a deserter. Escaping from prison, he arrived in London in February 1942. Initially he avoided taking a political role in the Free French because as a Jew he had been deeply wounded by the accusation of desertion. He felt the need to prove his patriotic credentials by signing up for the Free French air force. In November 1943, de Gaulle persuaded him to join the CFLN with an economics portfolio.[7]

Mendès feared that the Liberation would unleash inflation. The most basic commodities were likely to be very scarce and the French money supply had increased during the occupation. His solution was a deflationary policy of austerity to curb demand. On the face of it, this might seem to be a 'conservative' policy, but Mendès France's inspiration was Keynesian and socialist: a strategy of state-sponsored economic planning to direct investment towards reconstruction and modernization. Although he had reached these views independently of Boris, the two men quickly came to see each other as allies.

Feeling that his ideas were not supported by most members of the CFLN, Mendès France wrote de Gaulle a letter of resignation on 15 March 1944. Since a political conflict of this kind was the last thing de Gaulle needed in the lead-up to the Liberation, he defused the situation by making a speech to the Consultative Assembly reiterating the need after Liberation for 'rigorous measures regarding rationing, prices, money and credit'.[8] This reassured Mendès France and gave de Gaulle a breathing space before he was forced to commit himself. Mendès France wrote to Boris: 'I think in the long run we will win out. I am sure in his heart of hearts the General is now convinced. Unfortunately he is distracted by a thousand secondary reasons concerning day-to-day policy rather than long-term perspectives.'[9] It might still be possible to turn the General into a proto-socialist.

In de Gaulle's post-Liberation government, Mendès France was given the Economics Ministry that he had advocated, with Boris as key adviser. They conceived an ambitious programme involving the nationalization of credit and of heavy industry. But they were stymied by the fact that real power lay with the conservative Ministry of Finance. De Gaulle's provisional government did carry out some nationalizations in the months after Liberation – of the Renault car factory and some coal-mining companies – but these were motivated more by the urge to punish their owners for collaboration than by any coherent strategy for structural reform of the economy. In January 1945, Mendès France proposed a radical anti-inflationary plan of monetary reform centred around an exchange of banknotes and an inventory of wartime profits, as had occurred in Belgium. The idea was that the huge sums of money that were accumulating in the hands of black-market profiteers could be flushed out if they had to be exchanged against new notes. The Minister of Finance, René Pleven, opposed such a radical plan because it would be electorally dangerous, and Mendès France offered his resignation again. Their quarrel occurred during the crisis over the evacuation of Strasbourg, and again de Gaulle prevailed upon Mendès France to postpone any decision.

In March 1945, Mendès and Pleven were invited to present their cases to de Gaulle in person. De Gaulle sided with Pleven, and Mendès resigned. One problem was that Mendés's ideas crystallized opposition from all sides – on the left from Communists and Socialists who opposed wage restrictions and curbs on demand, on the right from liberals and conservatives who distrusted planning and structural reforms. The debate between the two men subsequently became mythologized as a lost opportunity to strangle inflation before it took hold on the French economy. But there were reasonable arguments to support Pleven's view that the economic medicine proposed by Mendès was too strong – especially given the presence of a powerful Communist Party ready to exploit social discontent.

After Mendès France's resignation, the National Economy Ministry was attached – in reality subordinated – to the Ministry of Finance. Boris continued to push for the idea of a plan in the kind of language he hoped might resonate with de Gaulle: 'The Plan is a doctrine but also a faith. The spirit or mystique of the Plan is the spirit of war – in what is most disinterested and efficient – applied to the world of peace.'[10] In reality, the argument was tilting further away from such views even if the government embarked on another round of nationalizations in the second half of 1945. At the end of that year de Gaulle approved an altogether different policy presented by Jean Monnet, whose only resemblance to that of Boris and Mendès France was that it included the word 'plan'.[11]

Since the autumn of 1943, Monnet had been in the United States negotiating a relief programme for liberated France. This tided the French over the first months after Liberation but it was not clear what would happen once the war was over and American Lend-Lease ceased. Monnet hoped to persuade the American government to continue its aid to France by providing guarantees that funds would be channelled into reconstruction, preparing France to play a role in a liberalized world economy. He wrote a memorandum, which de Gaulle presented to Truman in August 1945, promising to submit a French modernization programme for approval to the American government – at the very moment that the General was creating conflicts with America over all manner of other subjects. Monnet also realized that American aid would ultimately force the French to scale down their ambitions in relation to Germany.[12]

To secure American financial backing, Monnet conceived the idea of setting up a so-called Planning Commissariat (Commissariat du Plan) to allocate resources during reconstruction. He presented this idea to de Gaulle in a memorandum on 4 December 1945. Like Boris, he portrayed the choice facing France in terms liable to attract de Gaulle's attention: 'modernization' or 'decadence'. He was successful, and the setting up of the Planning Commissariat was adopted by the government three weeks later. Since this institution came to play a key role in French economic policy over the next three decades, the decision took on mythical proportions – both for the far-sightedness of Monnet in conceiving the idea and for the boldness of de Gaulle in accepting it. That is not how it seemed at the time. Monnet had presented the idea as a provisional solution to the immediate problem of obtaining further funding from the United States. One of de Gaulle's more socialistically inclined advisers, Louis Vallon, warned him that Monnet's idea was dependent on purchasing from America; it was more a 'rationalization of production' than 'a permanent planification of our economy'. Boris was also unenthusiastic.[13] De Gaulle's acceptance of the Monnet memorandum was a minimalist and cautious choice – a 'plan' not a 'Plan'.

The attempt to transform de Gaulle into a kind of proto-socialist had failed. But given how much his political rhetoric had evolved between 1940 and 1942, the idea had not been as far-fetched as it might seem. In the end, his economic choices in 1945 were pragmatic not ideological, faithful to his doctrine of 'circumstances'. For him the fundamental problems of France were political and institutional. Economic choices might change according to context, but for him the precondition of success for any policy was to establish effective political institutions.

THE 'FRENCH CRISIS'

In November 1943, as the conflict with Giraud was moving to its resolution, Harold Macmillan reported on a remarkable conversation with de Gaulle. De Gaulle told him that in historical perspective the conflict was of little significance:

> In reality the French crisis had begun in 1789 and had lasted until the outbreak of war with varying temporary systems but no permanent solution. It was his duty to bring about such a degree of national unity as would make possible a solution of the social and economic problems of France, without disorder on the one hand or extreme policies on the other.[14]

To present oneself as solving the history of France since 1789 was a bold ambition. Since de Gaulle was obviously not proposing to turn the clock back to 1789, what did he mean by this? What was the 'French crisis' and what was his solution to it?

The most important legacy of the Revolution of 1789 for French political culture was a suspicion of executive authority.[15] In the worldview of French republicans the executive was always suspected of working to thwart the sovereign will of the people expressed in the single National Assembly. In the nineteenth century, this suspicion was reinforced by the experience of the Second Republic (1848–51) which had ended when the directly elected President, Louis Napoleon, seized power and proclaimed himself Emperor. The assumptions of the republican generation of the 1860s was formed in reaction to this experience. 'Personal power' was the enemy. The republicans were viscerally hostile to the idea of a directly elected president, and even to the existence of a second Upper Chamber, either of which might impede the sovereign will of the people.

The Third Republic, founded after the fall of the Empire in 1870, did not fully reflect these ideas since its constitution was not drafted by 'pure' republicans. The Assembly elected in 1871 comprised a majority of monarchists. But their dream of a monarchical restoration was scuppered when the Bourbon pretender, the Duc de Chambord, refused any flag other than that of France's *ancien régime*. Moderate monarchists, converted to the inevitability of a republic, managed to introduce elements to dilute the principles of republicanism in what became the Republic of 1875. This included an indirectly elected second chamber – the Senate – to curb the unrestricted sovereignty of the lower Chamber, and a president elected for seven years – in the hope that he might become a monarch. The fact that the President was elected by the two chambers and not by universal suffrage reduced his independent legitimacy, but he had the right to dissolve parliament. On paper the constitution, with its checks and balances, looked more like the ideal of the liberal monarchists than that of the pure republicans. In practice things worked out differently. In 1877, the first President Marshal MacMahon exercised his right to dissolve parliament because he disapproved of the political complexion of the Assembly that had won the elections. This was seen by republicans as a coup against the expression of popular sovereignty. Never again did any Third Republic president dare to dissolve parliament, and the president became an increasingly ceremonial figure. Executive authority, such as it was, lay in the hands of the so-called *Président du Conseil* – Chairman of the Council of Ministers – who was the nearest that France had to a prime minister. But governments were always liable to be overthrown by parliament.

Despite this 'republican' victory over 'personal power', the politicians of the Third Republic became progressively aware that they lacked the tools of effective government. This was starkly revealed in the initial stages of the First World War when the government found itself unable to exercise sufficient control over the military. The repeated economic crises of the inter-war years also posed new challenges to government. In the 1930s some conservative politicians like André Tardieu proposed a more 'presidential' system: re-establishing the president's right to dissolve parliament, allowing him to use referenda over the heads of the politicians, and so on. These ideas were too much for the republican establishment, but many other politicians with unimpeachable republican credentials, unwilling to go as far as Tardieu, began to reflect upon ways of improving the efficiency of government while respecting the 'republican' model. This rationalizing impulse led to a number of technical innovations such as the setting up in 1935 of a Secretariat to offer administrative support to the Présidence du Conseil which was also given its own home at the Hôtel Matignon. Governments also resorted increasingly to the use of emergency decree powers voted by parliament for a limited period to address specific crises.

What did de Gaulle think about these issues? First, we have already seen

that he was intellectually in sympathy with the calls for the 'rational' organization of government that were so widespread in the inter-war years. One
subtext of his first book, *The Enemy's House Divided*, had been the need
for governments to control their military. After 1940, de Gaulle found
himself having to invent his own style of government from scratch. As the
Free French moved from being the one-man band of the first months, it
drew on some of the precedents of the Third Republic. For example, when
de Gaulle started to issue 'ordinances' in 1940, it was specified – despite
the monarchical resonance of the term – that they be considered juridically
as the continuation of 'the decree powers as defined by the legislative dispositions existing in France before 23 June 1940'.[16] Once in Algiers, de
Gaulle reinstated the relatively new institution of a government Secretariat.
As we have seen, Louis Joxe, who was appointed to head this Secretariat,
persuaded him that the role would be more effectively carried out if the
Secretary General was also present at the meetings of the CFLN like the
Cabinet Secretary in Britain. The CFLN thus became a laboratory for a
more streamlined and 'rational' government. Joxe writes of the CFLN
period when he acted as Secretary General: 'A meeting of the CFLN had
nothing in common with the Conseil des Ministres of the pre-war period
which was like a picnic where everyone brought along their own
contribution.'[17]

Secondly, in de Gaulle's vision of French history – as articulated in his
inter-war writings – the key distinction was not between republicans and
anti-republicans, but between those who defended the state – the embodiment of the general interest – and those who sought to weaken it – defenders
of particular interests. Thus in de Gaulle's mind there was a continuity
between the feudal barons who weakened the French medieval monarchy,
the *frondeurs* who weakened Louis XIV in 1648 and defenders of interest
groups in the modern world – political parties, trade unions, etc. It is hard
to exaggerate the intensity of de Gaulle's almost religious reverence for the
state. When he finally resigned in January 1946, Joxe wanted to join him
in solidarity but de Gaulle dissuaded him because he was serving the state
not an individual. In a speech in 1959, the General described the 'service
of the State as the most noble and important action that exists in the temporal order'.[18]

De Gaulle had been shocked by the 'abdication' of the Third Republic
in 1940, which he viewed as a crisis of leadership and of institutions. Hence
his lapidary comment on the role of President Lebrun in 1944: 'What he
lacked as Head of State was that he was no Head and there was no State.'[19]
An American diplomat reported on a conversation with de Gaulle in
November 1943: 'It is his belief that France cannot return to the same

system of weak corrupt government which it had before the war . . . France will have a republic and a democratic form of government, but the government will be stronger. These, he said, were his ideas, but the people of France will decide.' As for whether he planned to be dictator, 'he smiled and asked whether anyone who knew the French people believed they would accept a dictator.'[20] This left a lot to the imagination.

For the moment de Gaulle was reluctant to be pinned down. This was observed by the Commissaire de la République of Angers, Michel Debré, when de Gaulle visited his region in January 1945. Debré tried to impress upon de Gaulle his belief that deciding France's political insitutions was a priority, but the General did not seem interested.[21] Despite this disappointment, Debré was later to play a crucial role in the gestation of de Gaulle's constitutional ideas. Debré was from one of those elite French Jewish families – his father was a distinguished doctor – viscerally attached to the ideals of the Republic to which they historically owed their emancipation (though Michel himself converted to Catholicism). As a promising young civil servant in the 1930s, he was recruited by Paul Reynaud into the brains trust he had formed on becoming Minister of Finance in 1938. From this experience at the centre of power, and from his shock at the defeat, Debré developed what was to be a lifelong obsession with the need to reform the French state – both its administrative machinery and its political institutions – while also respecting the principles of liberal democracy which he had inherited from his family. He was a perfect mandarin, but a mandarin possessed by a missionary zeal to reform. He came to view the British system – or at least the system as he interpreted it – as a model in balancing the requirements of liberalism and efficiency, liberty and authority. During the Occupation he had been one of a group of resisters working on constitutional-reform projects for the Liberation.

Debré's Gaullist epiphany occurred at his first meeting with de Gaulle in Angers on 22 August 1944, a few days before the liberation of Paris. As he later described the moment: 'Here I was on 22 August, faced with General de Gaulle, during these amazing days . . . At the age of 32 it seemed that my life had found its reward and also its completion.'[22] Although at their second meeting five months later he had failed to convince de Gaulle of the urgency of tackling constitutional issues, Debré was invited in March 1945 to join the General's cabinet. This might have been prompted by Palewski, who had known Debré since working with him under Reynaud. Debré's official brief in the cabinet was administrative reform and resulted in the setting up of the Ecole Nationale d'Administration (ENA), designed to offer training to France's administrative elite. Such an ambition was in line with the ideas for administrative rationalization which had been so widespread in the inter-war years. De Gaulle writes in his *Memoirs* that ENA 'came all prepared from the brain and the work of Michel Debré'.[23] But being a man of inexhaustible energy and strong convictions, Debré also became a key player in shaping de Gaulle's constitutional ideas.

For someone who had so boldly announced to Macmillan that he planned to solve 150 years of French history de Gaulle was remarkably uncertain how to do it. His archives for this period contain a plethora of constitutional drafts submitted by jurists and politicians of all stripes. Most carry the words 'Vu par le Général' while giving no indication what the General thought.[24] To one aide at this time de Gaulle commented: 'We are in an unprecedented situation. In previous revolutions, there was also a regime ready to emerge . . . Here there is not just one regime that has collapsed but two. What is the best way to proceed?'[25]

The issue at stake was not only France's future constitution but the procedure for drafting and approving it. On 2 June 1945, at the end of a long press conference mostly devoted to denouncing British policy in Syria, de Gaulle outlined three possibilities: first, a simple return to the constitution of 1875; secondly, the election of a sovereign constituent assembly to draft a new constitution; thirdly, a draft constitution submitted by the government directly to the people (presumably by referendum). On other occasions when de Gaulle set out three possibilities in this way, he often seemed to be preparing opinion for the third one.[26] In this case he seemed genuinely unsure. Indeed over the next three months he seemed to be inclining to the first solution – an extraordinary outcome for someone who had spent four years denouncing the impotence of the previous regime.

If de Gaulle even countenanced the possibility of returning to the Third Republic, it was not because he had abandoned the idea of change. The rules of the Third Republic allowed for the two houses of parliament to meet jointly as a single National Assembly and amend the constitution. This would have been a minimalist approach to the problem of constitutional reform, allowing the Assembly to eliminate the worst features of the old constitution. De Gaulle's fear of the second solution was that a sovereign constituent assembly, probably dominated by the Communist Party, would be completely uncontrollable. He was also obsessed by the memory of the Revolution, complaining to one adviser, 'your Assembly will become another Convention.'[27] But Debré warned de Gaulle that a parliament elected under the old constitution also risked being dominated by the Communists. He argued that the government must retain control over the drafting of the constitution – as in de Gaulle's third solution.

For a month after the press conference of 2 June, the situation was extraordinarily confused. Many of those around de Gaulle argued that going back to the constitution of 1875 was breaking the commitment he had made under the Occupation to allow the French to choose a new constitution. Socialist and Resistance members of his own government were also up in arms against such a solution. In mid-June, de Gaulle seemed to be ready to resign if he did not get his way – although, as one of his advisers pointed out, blackmail by de Gaulle in the cause of saving the Third Republic would have been an extraordinary turn of events. On 8 July Claude Mauriac, who was not privy to secrets but in frequent contact with the circle around de Gaulle, noted in his diary: 'De Gaulle's obstinacy about the principle of electing two Chambers [that is, the Third Republic solution] seems to have been a feint . . . I admit I do not understand the ins and outs despite Palewski's explanation.'[28] Mauriac was not the only one to be confused. If the plan was a 'feint' it seems unclear what its objective was. The likeliest explanation is that de Gaulle was feeling his way.

By the time Mauriac wrote that diary entry, de Gaulle had been persuaded to abandon his first plan to revert to the Third Republic. Debré was instructed to draft a text to curb the untrammelled power of a Constituent Assembly.[29] The solution finally adopted was complicated – and a breach with precedent. Elections would be held for a single Assembly. At the same time, the electorate would be asked two questions by referendum. The first question was whether the Assembly should have constituent powers: that is, the power to draft a constitution. The answer 'no' would signify that the French people wanted a return to the Third Republic. In that case, electors would return to the polls to elect a Senate, and the two houses could then meet together to propose some amendments to the constitution. The answer 'yes' would mean that the elected Assembly would have constituent powers. In that case, electors would be asked a second question: should the constitution drafted by the Assembly be submitted to the population in a referendum? On the left, this idea summoned up all the demons associated with the plebiscites of Louis Napoleon. For de Gaulle it was a way of limiting the sovereign power of an Assembly that might have a Communist majority.

In a number of speeches over the summer, de Gaulle made it clear that his preference was for a double 'yes' – 'yes' to the need for a new republic, 'yes' to the limitation of the sovereign power of the Constituent Assembly. The Communists called for a 'yes' to the first question and 'no' to the second. In the elections on 21 October, a return to the Third Republic was massively rejected by 96 per cent of the electorate who voted 'yes' to the first question; and a less resounding majority of 66 per cent voted 'yes' to the second, ensuring that de Gaulle had prevailed in his desire to limit the sovereignty of the Assembly.

The elections provided the first accurate picture of the balance of political forces in post-Liberation France. The Communists emerged as the largest party with 5 million votes (26 per cent and 158 seats). Not far behind, with 4.5 million votes, came the Christian Democrat Party, the MRP (23 per cent and 152 seats). This was a new party founded to give a voice to the many Catholics who had played a role in the Resistance. It included resisters like Bidault and members of the Free French like Maurice Schumann. Just in third place came the Socialists with 4 million votes (22 per cent and 142 seats). These three parties were overwhelmingly the dominant force in French politics. Since the MRP presented itself as the party of 'fidelity' to de Gaulle, its emergence as a major political player was encouraging for him. The new assembly could have resulted in a purely Socialist–Communist government, as the Communists wanted. But the Socialists feared that, as the junior partner, they would be swallowed up by the Communists. The Socialists instead advocated a tripartite coalition including the MRP. The Communists had to accept this since they were not strong enough to form a government on their own.

RESIGNATION

This was the first time de Gaulle had been faced with a properly elected parliament. On 13 November, the Assembly met to deliberate on whether or not to vote for de Gaulle as head of government. That day Churchill, visiting Paris as a private citizen – he had been ejected from power by the British general election in July – was invited to lunch by de Gaulle. Duff Cooper, who had been dreading the event, was pleasantly surprised:

> De Gaulle was wearing a dark blue suit in which he looks so much better than in uniform. I never liked him or admired him so much. He was smiling, courteous, almost charming, and on this day and almost at the hour when his whole future was at stake not only was he perfectly calm but one might have thought he was a country gentleman living far away from Paris. There were no interruptions, no telephone calls or message, no secretaries hurrying in and out, no sign that anything was happening, although Winston insisted on staying till 3.30 talking about the past and the Assembly was meeting at 3.00.[30]

It was not difficult for de Gaulle to be relaxed because the result was hardly in doubt. The Assembly voted almost unanimously to elect him as the next head of government. But as de Gaulle observed sardonically in his *Memoirs*: 'I knew that this vote was a homage addressed to my past actions not a promise which engaged the future.'[31] The real conflict came next. As de

Gaulle prepared to form his government, Thorez demanded that, as the largest party, the Communists should be granted the three key ministries of the Interior, Foreign Affairs and Defence. This was a replay of the conflict between de Gaulle and the Communists in Algiers, but this time the Communists, as the largest party in parliament, were in a stronger position.

De Gaulle refused. The Communists went publicly on the offensive against him. On 17 November, de Gaulle broadcast to the nation to put his case: that, while wanting to form a government of 'national unity', he could not allow the Communists – whom he did not mention by name – to be in control of France's foreign or defence policy. Appealing to the people over parliament was a breach with 'republican' tradition which shocked even some of his advisers. Duff Cooper was expressing the general view of the political class when he observed: 'Everyone agrees de Gaulle made a great mistake in broadcasting. Obstinacy, tactlessness and lack of political experience have always been his drawbacks.'[32] In fact de Gaulle was at the same time negotiating behind the scenes with the party leaders, including Thorez. He had many times in the past used the blackmail of resignation to bring his opponents to heel. In this case he meant it. His staff started to prepare the removal of his archives. On 19 November, he summoned the Canadian Ambassador in the middle of the night to explore the possibility of going to Canada as a private citizen for a period if he proved unable to form a government.[33]

In the end, a compromise was reached. The Communists withdrew from the brink. They received three economic portfolios – National Economy, Industrial Production, Labour – and the Defence Ministry was split to allow a Communist to become Armaments Minister without however having control over defence policy. Thorez was made a minister of state. But this was only the first round. Over the next month de Gaulle found himself increasingly at odds with the Assembly against a deteriorating economic background. At the end of December, as we have seen, he clashed with the Assembly over the defence budget. Most worryingly for him, the deliberations of the commission drafting the constitution, dominated by the Socialists, were heading in a direction which seemed to weaken executive power even more than in the Third Republic. Debré bombarded de Gaulle with alarmist notes on this subject.[34] In taking this path, the Assembly was reacting against the recent experience of authoritarian power during the Occupation.

Realizing he had lost control over the shaping of the constitution, de Gaulle turned increasingly to thoughts of resignation. Appearing in the Assembly on 1 January 1946 to make the case for the defence budget, his

speech contained a passage which no one seemed to notice (or believe) at
the time:

> I am speaking for the future. We have begun the process of rebuilding the Repub-
> lic. You will continue it. However you set about it, I would like to say to you in
> conscience, and this is without doubt the last time that I will speak in this
> hemicycle . . . that if you do it without taking account of the lessons of our polit-
> ical history over the last fifty years and especially what occurred in 1940, if you
> do not take account of the need for the authority, dignity and responsibility of
> the government, you will head for a situation where, one day or other, I predict,
> you will bitterly regret having taken the road you have taken.[35]

On 6 January, de Gaulle left Paris for an eight-day break at a villa in
Antibes with his immediate family – Yvonne his wife, Jacques Vendroux
his brother-in-law and Pierre his brother. De Gaulle was not a natural
tourist, and this curiously shy man who adored the acclaim of crowds
hated being the object of curiosity for individual passers-by. As he remarked
on one occasion to his aide Claude Guy when a girl came up to ask for his
autograph: 'Crowds are not disagreeable when they are grouped together.
What I don't like is the crowds one by one, in tiny groups [petits paquets].
Looking at you and asking for autographs.'[36] There is a photograph of de
Gaulle clambering on the rocks at Antibes, looking startled and displeased
at having been caught unawares by a photographer.

   Most of the time was spent in the villa in endless discussions about what
he should do next. Pierre argued that, if he resigned, the public would turn
against him for having 'deserted'; Vendroux, who sat in the Assembly as a
member of the MRP, favoured resignation to teach the politicians a lesson
and show them that they were incapable of governing without him. These
discussions continued, 'sometimes heatedly' according to Vendroux, all
through the night on the train back to Paris on 14 January. By the time de
Gaulle was met at the station, as protocol demanded, by the Socialist Minister of the Interior, Jules Moch, his mind was made up. As they were
driving back to the Rue Saint-Dominique, he told Moch in the strictest
confidence that he had decided to resign:

> The debate over the reduction of credits has convinced me that it is – he
> articulated each syllable – im-poss-sible to gov-ern with the par-ties . . . I do
> not feel I am made for this kind of fight. I do not want to be attacked, criti-
> cized, contested every day by men whose only claim is to have had themselves
> elected in some small corner of France.

Moch launched into a long plea that de Gaulle should reconsider his decision. His argument was that the General could reasonably have taken the

decision to abandon power after Liberation on the grounds that his mission was over, but that having chosen to stay on he had assumed responsibilities that he must accept:

> De Gaulle listened to this diatribe with rare patience and even, I thought, a certain indulgence. At the end he put his hand on mine, and as the car was entering the Rue Saint-Dominique, he said to me in a low voice, slowly and as if lost in his thought, a phrase which left me amazed: 'Perhaps you are right: one can't indeed imagine Joan of Arc married, a mother, and who knows, deceived by her husband.'[37]

By this enigmatic phrase he presumably meant that Moch was right: he should have gone sooner. Over the next few days de Gaulle confided his decision to a few close aides and performed his duties as head of government. One of his last interventions was a missive to the Minister of Defence warning against the English tendency to want to 'entrench' themselves in French territory in North Africa. Another was an instruction to Koenig, now in command of French occupying forces in Germany, which opened with the characteristic words 'I do not agree,' and making it clear that he conceived the future of Germany as a collection of separate states.[38]

On 17 January he chaired the Council of Ministers, giving no indication that this was the last time he would be performing the role. A report by Bidault on the terms of the French evacuation from the Levant was the signal for a characteristic outburst:

> Every time the British commit a *saloperie* the Foreign Office declares: it is not our fault but that of individuals in place. But these individuals are never moved or replaced by others who are better.
>
> They want to be in the Middle East because that is their old policy of rivalry with us and then because they want to be anywhere they can keep an eye on the Russians . . . For these two reasons we must not go . . . We must stick to the agreements signed or if not tell them to go and screw themselves [*allez vous faire foutre*].[39]

On 18 January he annotated a telegram from Massigli on the Levant with the word 'idiotic', and railed against the British Foreign Office for being 'faithful to the policy of Lawrence'.[40]

On Saturday the 19th there was a meeting of the Defence Committee at which the Communist Minister Charles Tillon made a remark about army logistics and received an hour-long lecture from de Gaulle about the history of logistics in the French army from the *ancien régime* until the present. He closed the meeting at 8 p.m., and almost no one present had any inkling that he was going to resign on the next day.[41]

When de Gaulle suddenly convened a special meeting of the government for midday on Sunday 20 January, most ministers had no idea why. He entered the room, invited his ministers not to sit around the table but to gather around the fireplace and delivered a short declaration announcing his 'irrevocable' decision to resign. He shook hands, left the room, got into the car that was waiting for him outside and drove away, leaving his speechless ministers wondering what to do next.[42] The inoffensive Socialist politician Félix Gouin was chosen to replace him.

De Gaulle's resignation cannot be called an impulse since he had been thinking about it for weeks. But the timing was curious. Since the underlying reason was his difficulty in working with the parties and his disapproval of the constitution that was being drafted, it would have made more sense to leave either earlier – after the elections of October 1945 when he could have announced that he had fulfilled his mission to restore democracy in France and was temporarily taking a back seat – or later – when the draft constitution was ready and he could have announced that he did not approve of its terms. The timing suggests that his decision was more emotional than rational.

De Gaulle was exhausted and seething with bitterness against politicians unworthy of their liberator. If his resolution had wobbled after returning from Antibes, it would certainly have been reinforced by an incident in parliament on 16 January. The government had decided to confirm Vichy's decision to award the Legion of Honour to French soldiers killed while fighting against the Americans in North Africa in November 1942. This decision was criticized by Edouard Herriot – the veteran politician who had been contacted by Laval in July 1944 about the possibility of setting up a transitional government. De Gaulle, appearing in parliament for the last time, defended the government decision:

> M. Herriot will excuse me for answering him with all the more clarity and simplicity given that after 1940 my dealings with Vichy were not confined to exchanges of letters and messages with Vichy but also included gunfire . . . The government of the Republic does not want to snatch from the coffins of the dead soldiers or the breasts of wounded ones, decorations that were obtained in atrocious conditions for which they were not responsible.[43]

If the timing of de Gaulle's resignation was curious, the manner of it was even more so. The next day, he wrote to his successor Gouin explaining his decision. His justification was that he had successfully restored order after

Liberation and the economy was recovering even if 'many problems remain'.[44] Given that only a few weeks earlier, the franc had been devalued and bread rationing reintroduced, this optimism was not widely shared. It risked conveying the impression of unjustified complacency or an evasion of responsibility. As Cooper reported back to London: 'General de Gaulle has not retired because all was well but on the contrary because all was going wrong.'[45] Some of de Gaulle's entourage urged him to speak out on the grounds that 'the man who had entered History by the *Appel du 18 juin*' could not take his leave of History with 'a letter to Monsieur Gouin'.[46] It seems de Gaulle originally intended to follow his resignation with a radio broadcast but thought better of it after a worried letter from the Socialist Vincent Auriol urging him not to deepen France's divisions, and warning that it would be improper to broadcast once he was no longer in office. De Gaulle assured Auriol that he had never had any intention of doing so, though a broadcast by him had in fact been advertised in the newspapers for 21 January. Auriol was terrified that de Gaulle might be planning a coup or a Boulangist appeal to the people over the heads of the politicians.[47]

Even if de Gaulle had played his hand badly, he knew he possessed none of the cards that would have made a coup possible. The amount of time he spent justifying his resignation to visitors over the next few weeks suggests that he wondered if he had not made an error of judgement. To Claude Guy and others who reproached him with not offering a convincing public explanation of his resignation, he answered that nothing was more effective than silence: 'One's acts have to be picturesque ... What is picturesque is not forgotten. I take my mystery away with me.'[48]

Drama was always a key weapon in de Gaulle's repertoire but this time it fell flat. He probably hoped that the shock of his departure would create an upsurge of protest, forcing the politicians to accept his return on his own terms. He wrote to the novelist André Malraux on the evening of 20 January that he would move out of his villa in Neuilly because he wanted to 'avoid possible demonstrations around my person'.[49] This was wishful thinking: there were no demonstrations. The prefects whose role it was to monitor public opinion reported that de Gaulle's departure had been met with surprise but no particular concern, less indeed than had been aroused by the conflict between de Gaulle and Thorez in November.[50] The situation was perfectly encapsulated by the Communist Marcel Cachin on the day of the resignation: 'Historic day. We got rid of de Gaulle without frightening the population.'[51]

De Gaulle's worry was that soon he might be marginalized. For this reason he resisted any attempts by the government to 'normalize' his 'status'. When in April the government proposed a retrospective promotion to the rank of five-star general and also to the highest rank of the Legion of Honour, de Gaulle politely refused. In private he fulminated against this attempt to 'put me in a frame, to "hold" me down ... diminishing me by making me, if I accepted, a man like others ... I recreated France from nothing, from being a man alone in a foreign city ... I am not a victorious general. One does not decorate France.'[52]

In the weeks following his resignation de Gaulle remained silent, refraining from public appearances of any kind. He did not even attend the funeral in Grenoble of his brother Jacques who had died at the age of fifty-three after his twenty-year illness. On the day of his resignation, de Gaulle immediately moved out of his villa in Neuilly. But he was not yet able to move back to Colombey. His house La Boisserie had been seized by the government in 1940 and put on sale. No buyer had been found and it had been used as a barracks by German troops. By 1944, it was in a state of ruin and empty of furniture. While repairs were being carried out, de Gaulle rented a seventeenth-century hunting lodge situated in the park of Marly about 25 kilometres from Paris. This property, belonging to the state, was all that remained of a chateau and park built by Louis XIV. Despite these grand origins, the house was small, badly heated, damp and ill-equipped. On the day de Gaulle moved in, Claude Guy found Madame de Gaulle scurrying around to find crockery. What attracted de Gaulle to Marly was its isolation and separation from the world of Paris politics. In this self-imposed exile, he continued to be served by his two aides de camp Claude Guy and Gaston de Bonneval. Claude Mauriac continued to deal with his correspondence. He was told when answering letters not 'to give the impression I am going for ever. Give neutral responses.'[53]

The diaries of Mauriac and Guy are a precious source for understanding de Gaulle's volatile state of mind over the next few months. On his first night of 'freedom' at Marly, he plunged into a biography of Disraeli by André Maurois. At one point he triumphantly read out a passage where Bismarck told Gladstone: 'Never defend yourself in front of a popular assembly except by attacking; in the pleasure that your opponents get from the new attack they forget their attack on you.'[54] After dinner, he returned to his reading with continuous interruptions of rage: 'When one can crush someone it should be done at once. After Muselier and other such small fry, it was necessary to crush Giraud.' A few minutes later there was a rant against French politicians: 'The parties and the current regime will every day lose more credit with public opinion. The fruit will ripen and fall ... They are committing the same psychological error in regard to me as Churchill and then Roosevelt. Those two were always wrong about me! They saw me only as a military man.'[55] There was much more in this vein.

Whether writing or reading, de Gaulle was endlessly ruminating, conducting this interior monologue which would burst to the surface when he received visitors or when some item in the newspapers sparked a tirade. His themes never varied: the turpitude of the pygmy politicians ('poor old father Gouin', 'poor little Bidault', etc.), visions of apocalyptic disaster if they governed France for much longer, the likelihood of war with Russia, the perfidy of the British, the stupidity of the Americans. He would often launch into a long riff on how his life had been an endless series of failures: the failure to convert the army to his ideas before 1940, the failure to persuade the French government to move to North Africa, the failure of Dakar, and so on.

Hervé Alphand, who visited on 17 March, was subjected to a long monologue on international affairs ending with the prediction: 'When the Russians are in Paris, the English and Americans will see what a big mistake they committed in raising up Germany and not France.' After this 'cataclysmic conversation', Alphand left somewhat groggy: 'In the car taking me back to Paris, I looked at passers-by in the street . . . as if they were people condemned to death but blissfully unaware that their fate was fixed.'[56] François Mauriac was equally shell-shocked after his visit on 16 February: 'In front of him you feel yourself to have become a total idiot . . . He does not see you. You hardly exist in his mind as a distinct person.'[57]

At the end of April, the Constituent Assembly finished its deliberations. Under the influence of the Communists and Socialists, it drafted a constitution with institutions that could not have been more different from de Gaulle's preferences. All power would reside in a single Chamber; the President of the Republic was even more of a cipher than before 1940. De Gaulle continued to remain silent. His hope was that the MRP's opposition to this draft would ensure that the electorate rejected it. De Gaulle's attitude to the MRP was conflicted. Its support was necessary if he was to succeed in blocking the constitution in parliament, but he resented the fact that its ministers had not resigned with him in January. In March he wrote to Maurice Schumann, who was trying to hold out an olive branch: 'Compared to the great drama from which we have recently emerged and which, sooner or later, we are going to enter again, I attach to the contortions of the parties, yours included – please excuse me – too little importance to remain a prisoner of them.'[58]

On 5 May, 59 per cent of voters rejected the constitution in the referendum – a setback for the Communists. This was confirmed at the elections for a new constituent assembly on 2 June. The MRP now emerged as the largest party with 28 per cent of the vote; the Socialists fell back to 24 per cent and the PCF to 26 per cent. During the election campaign de

Gaulle continued to remain silent. Having moved back to Colombey on 26 May, he was ready to speak out.

RETURN TO THE FRAY: BAYEUX TO EPINAL

De Gaulle chose to make his political comeback on 16 June in a speech at Bayeux where almost exactly two years earlier he had first spoken on French soil as liberator of France. His speech reminded his listeners that in just two lifespans France had been invaded seven times and had lived under thirteen constitutions (the two facts of course being linked in his mind). Then he came to the moral of his story, that France needed political institutions based on a clear separation of powers between legislature and executive:

> It is from the Head of State, placed above parties, elected by an electoral college encompassing parliament but much wider than parliament ... that executive powers must proceed ... His mission is to name ministers and first of all the Premier, who must direct the policy and work of the government. It is the Head of State's function to promulgate laws and decrees ... to preside over the Government Councils and exercise in them a continuity which a nation cannot do without. He serves as arbiter above political contingencies, either normally through the Council of Ministers, or, in moments of grave confusion, by inviting the country to express through elections its sovereign decision. If it should happen that the fatherland is in danger, his duty is to be the guarantor of national independence.[59]

Of this speech, Lacouture relates that de Gaulle 'wrote it over two months, delivered it in twenty-seven minutes, repeated its ideas over ten years, and put it into practice after twelve'.[60] The speech has been seen as a prophecy of the 1958 Fifth Republic, as the Brazzaville speech was a prophecy of decolonization. In fact only in the most general way can this somewhat obscure speech be seen as the model for anything.[61] In many respects the Fifth Republic would turn out very differently. But given that the Bayeux speech has acquired such legendary status, it is extraordinary how little we know about its drafting. Claude Guy, pious chronicler of almost every word uttered by the General at this time, notes simply on 4 June 1946: 'He worked all morning on his speech. Only the final touches since the bulk of it was ready before he left Marly.'[62] This leaves many questions unanswered.

Who did de Gaulle consult and what did he read before making the speech? The only authority he cites is Solon: 'The Greeks once asked the sage Solon: "What is the best Constitution?" He replied: "Tell me first for what people and in what period?"' De Gaulle had had many discussions with Debré and with the jurist René Capitant, who had been one of his passionate supporters since the Algiers days. But one must not overplay their influence. Debré considered the electoral system to be the most crucial issue for ensuring that any government had a stable majority, and de Gaulle did not mention this at Bayeux; Capitant, an advocate of direct democracy, considered referenda to be the key instrument for giving the President power over the head of the parliament, but de Gaulle did not mention this either.[63] The General had shown some interest in the American constitution during the war but had been astonished to discover that the President did not have the power to dissolve Congress.[64] What he proposed at Bayeux was not a Presidential constitution on the American model since he conceived the President not as executive but as 'arbiter'. De Gaulle had also followed the intense debates about constitutional reform in the mid-1930s. In 1946 he was re-reading the speeches of André Tardieu, who had advocated ideas similar to those in the Bayeux speech.[65]

There is no single key to de Gaulle's constitutional ideas. He was no more a jurist in 1946 than he was a tank expert in 1934. He was as imprecise on constitutional details in 1946 as he had been on technical details when discussing tanks in 1934. Before writing his speech he had read widely – as before writing *Towards a Professional Army*. The synthesis he produced was the distillation of his reading as filtered through his overarching view of French history. His use of the notion of separation of powers, one of his key themes, would not have been recognized by Montesquieu or Locke, for whom the concept was a way of balancing the power of absolutism. He sounds at times more like James Madison in the *Federalist Papers* denouncing the power of faction (though it seems unlikely he had read Madison). The phrase in the speech claiming that executive power 'proceeds' from the head of state is considered meaningless by jurists. The French word '*procéder*' is a theological term meaning 'engendered' – as in the Father and Son engender the Holy Spirit. No less obscure was de Gaulle's suggestion that the head of state could 'invite the country to express through elections its sovereign decision'. Did this mean a referendum or the right to dissolve parliament and call elections – or both? These are classic examples of de Gaulle's genius for suggestive obscurity.[66]

Ultimately the obscurity matters less than the fact that the speech challenged the entire political culture of French republicanism. In that tradition, the Republic was not just a set of institutions but the embodiment of principles established by the French Revolution and representing the march of humanity towards democratic progress. De Gaulle was never an 'anti-republican' in the style of Maurras, but he was never 'republican' in the way that republicans were 'republican'. Coming from a monarchist family, he carried in his head a longer history of France where the Republic was only one of the forms assumed by the state. In the Bayeux speech the word 'state' appears eleven times and the word 'republic' is never mentioned except to recall the failed precedents of the First, Second and Third French Republics, and those of Weimar and Spain. But de Gaulle's speech was no mere abstract philosophizing on France's constitutional future. It was a bid for power: he was presenting the kind of constitution that would allow him to govern as wished to govern. What he offered as his solution to 150 years of French history was also his solution to the problem of General de Gaulle.

This did not help him win support for his ideas. The devoted Maurice Schumann wrote to him a few days before the Bayeux speech imploring him not to go public with his constitutional proposals but instead to find a way of communicating them to the MRP so that they could work on his behalf. The problem with France, Schumann said, was how to 'graft Gaullist thinking on to a Republican sensibility'. The implication was that de Gaulle was not the best person to do this.[67] The negative reaction of the Communist Party was predictable. One Communist wrote: 'We know where General de Gaulle's sympathies lie. Like Marshal Pétain he does not talk of the Republic ... he talks only of the State ... This is a plebiscitary dictatorship ... The candidate of the powers of reaction for the post of First Consul.' The reaction of Léon Blum was hardly more favourable, although more moderate. Blum demonstrated presciently that the logic of de Gaulle's ideas was the election of a president by universal suffrage – with all the ghosts of Bonapartism that such an idea aroused.[68]

De Gaulle's only hope of seeing the ideas of his speech translated into reality was if they were adopted in the Constituent Assembly by the MRP. But the MRP did not have a majority and some of its leaders were hardly less suspicious of de Gaulle than the Socialists were; others, like Schumann, who were devoted Gaullists, took the view that France could not remain in constitutional limbo for ever and that an imperfect solution was better than none. The debates in the Assembly suggested that the new draft would be better than the previous one from de Gaulle's point of view – the President would have the right to dissolve parliament – but not enough to meet his requirements. De Gaulle received numerous visitors over the summer urging him to accept a compromise. No one was more pressing than Debré, who visited Colombey twice. De Gaulle remained implacable:

Look, Debré, I have been rained on many times before. There is not a single
example, not one, of a man or a group of men who have not suffered as a
result of betraying me ... Whether Muselier ... or Giraud, those who
betrayed me have rapidly become wrecks. It will be the same for the MRP ...
After a few months, give it even two years, there will no longer be in parliament more than a skeletal group. A group of 30 wrecks.[69]

The prediction was not false, but its timing was optimistic.

De Gaulle equally gave no encouragement to Capitant, who had set up
after the Bayeux speech a movement calling itself the Union Gaulliste to
campaign for de Gaulle's ideas. On the other hand de Gaulle did not publicly disavow Capitant, despite being urged to do so by some of his
followers.[70] When Capitant visited him at Colombey, he came away no
wiser about whether the General supported his initiative or not.[71] De
Gaulle was presumably waiting to see what would happen: reap the benefits of the Union Gaulliste if there were any, and make sure he was not
associated with it if there were none.

On 18 September 1946, the Assembly approved another draft constitution with the support of the MRP. The MRP leaders took the view that
even after it had been implemented the constitution could still be revised
and they hoped not to burn their bridges with de Gaulle. This hope was
scuppered when de Gaulle delivered his verdict in a speech at Epinal on 29
September. The constitution was better than the previous draft but still
unacceptable. Although this speech contained the word 'republic' twelve
times, as a possible concession to those who had been alarmed by its absence
from the Bayeux speech, it was also an open declaration of war on the MRP
(rather than, as previously, private rants against them). This was the parting
of the ways and the end of the MRP's boast of being the 'party of fidelity'.
For some, like Bidault, this was no matter for regret since their experience
of working for de Gaulle had left a bitter taste. For others, like Schumann,
it was agonizing to have to choose between de Gaulle and the need to follow his party's line that a constitution, even if imperfect, had to be accepted.
Schumann, declaring himself de Gaulle's 'oldest and most faithful companion', wrote him some tortured letters over the autumn. He reproached the
General for being the architect of his own difficulties. Speaking out against
the first draft constitution before the first referendum would have increased
the number of 'noes' and helped the position of the MRP in the subsequent
elections: 'The imperfection of the present text is the consequence of your
silence and your abstention.' There was much truth in this analysis, but de
Gaulle did not take kindly to such criticism.[72]

De Gaulle's only remaining hope was that his opposition would persuade enough voters to reject the constitution. But he had few illusions on this score. For someone so contemptuous of party politics – and someone who had played such a disastrous political game in 1946 – de Gaulle had good political antennae. In the week before the referendum he predicted that the results would be eight million 'yes', seven million 'no', nine million 'abstentions'.[73] This was more or less correct. De Gaulle's condemnation of the draft constitution at Epinal had been enough to ensure that the new Republic was accepted by the electorate with a mixture of indifference and hostility – but not enough to block it entirely.

Now the electorate were called upon to vote for the third time in a year: this time to elect the first parliament of the Fourth Republic which they had just unenthusiastically approved. The same three parties – the PCF, the Socialists, the MRP – still dominated the scene, although the PCF was now back in first place. Capitant's Union Gaulliste obtained only about 600,000 votes (3 per cent): Gaullism without de Gaulle clearly had no future.

Over the summer and autumn Colombey had been a busy place as politicians and advisers – Palewski, Debré, Schumann, Capitant and so on – traipsed down from Paris to batter down de Gaulle's implacable hostility to the constitution. Now the house was eerily silent. Guy wrote on 18 December:

> The General is hibernating. For the first time since his return to Colombey [from Epinal on 29 September] he went out the front gate of the garden to visit for a few moments, yesterday afternoon, the bedside of one of the local farmers who has been paralysed for seven years. Apart from a turn around the garden in the daytime, he retires to his study where he has started to work again on his Memoirs ... Yesterday he asked Madame de Gaulle to buy a notebook where he can minutely write down a few 'thoughts', and also quotations picked out of his reading ... He writes no letters. He never telephones. Palewski has not been to see him for several days. The only political contact is the radio at 19.45 and the morning papers which arrive with a 24-hour delay.[74]

During the autumn, de Gaulle at Colombey desultorily and half-heartedly resumed the writing of his *Memoirs*. His frustrating sense of confinement was punctuated by short-lived flurries of optimism, as in mid-December when it seemed that the parties in parliament would be unable to agree on the formation of a government: '*they* will come to me like whipped dogs. And they will get a welcome they will not forget.'[75] But *they* did not come, and the political deadlock in Paris was temporarily solved when the veteran Socialist Léon Blum agreed to form an all-Socialist caretaker government. This paved the way for parliament in January to elect as the first President of the Fourth Republic Vincent Auriol, another veteran Socialist. Now that Blum had fulfilled his role of setting the regime on its way, a new tripartite government of Socialists, MRP and Communists was formed under the leadership of another Socialist, Paul Ramadier. De Gaulle watched all this from Colombey with gloomy delectation.

Guy had left to join his own family for Christmas and returned in the New Year to hear an account of the melancholy holiday de Gaulle and his wife had spent alone at Colombey with Anne:

> He had been counting on his son to be there to act as aide de camp . . . But like an old couple the General and Madame de Gaulle waited in vain for their son who did not arrive till 27 December. Elisabeth, having fallen ill, could not come at all. Madame de Gaulle described to me the unforgettable sadness of this Christmas that the General – for the first time since 1940 – had wanted to be gay: he had ordered a copious Christmas lunch.
>
> Then there was the sadness of the midnight mass spoilt by a photographer who blinded them with his flash . . . The sadness of this scene: Marie the servant lighting the way to the Church with a storm lamp . . . Then the return, just the two of them for the *reveillon*, whose infinite melancholy she described to me.[76]

During the weeks since September, de Gaulle had been plunged into one of his periodic moods of apocalyptic pessimism – about the politicians who had betrayed him, the abandonment of any French ambitions in Germany, the dislocation of the Empire. On one day he mused: 'It is perhaps the end of France . . . Oh of course there will always be a few Frenchmen left even after an atomic war . . . A few cooks and hairdressers.' On another day, there was a rant about the position of France in the world:

> All the socialists and demagogues make me laugh when they talk about the position of France in the world . . . To hear them talk you would think France began to count in the eyes of humanity in 1789! . . . On the contrary since 1789 we have not ceased to decline! 1789? Bah! What about the intellectual and spiritual prestige of France in the seventeenth and eighteenth centuries . . . Since Athens and Rome there has not been a power to match.[77]

In the end, however, these lugubrious meditations should not be taken seriously. Just as de Gaulle was predicting the end of France, he was planning his next move. He realized that he had played his cards badly in 1946. As he remarked on various occasions during these days, 'we are going to have to begin again from zero.'[78]

16

The New Messiah, 1947–1955

'A NEW 18 JUNE'

On 5 February 1947, de Gaulle gathered some close followers – Palewski, Guy, Soustelle, Debré – for a secret meeting at his brother-in-law's flat in the Avenue Mozart in Paris. It was his first visit to the capital for five months, and he was in high spirits, not only because he had escaped the monotonous inactivity at Colombey but because he had a plan. For a quarter of an hour he outlined what he had in mind. Since the constitution that the French people had unenthusiastically chosen would lead to decadence, inflation and the end of the Empire, he would create a movement of his own to defend his constitutional ideas. His listeners were mostly unenthusiastic.[1] Most of those present worried that, by descending into the political arena, he would tarnish the legendary aura of 18 June. De Gaulle was not put off. In his current mood, he was ready to accept the comparison with 18 June: 'The country is accepting the occupation by the parties with the same apathy as it accepted the German occupation. It is the same thing.'[2] No one was more sceptical than his wife. When de Gaulle mused about a new 18 June, she proffered a rare political opinion: '*Pauvre ami.* Nobody will follow you.' De Gaulle's reply was: 'Shut up, Yvonne, I am old enough to know what I want to do [*Fichez-moi la paix Yvonne! Je suis assez grand pour savoir ce que j'ai à faire!*].'[3] He would have done well to listen.

De Gaulle launched his movement in a number of carefully calibrated public interventions over the next two months. At the first, on 30 March, he appeared at a ceremony in the village of Bruneval in Normandy to commemorate an Allied commando raid during the war. This was ostensibly a non-political ceremony, but de Gaulle's speech hinted at a day when the 'immense mass of the French people will gather around the name of France' – that is to say, de Gaulle.[4] On 7 April, at a huge meeting at Strasbourg, de Gaulle announced he was forming a new *rassemblement* (gathering) to save the country from catastrophe. Claude Mauriac, although sceptical about the idea, was carried away despite himself: 'Never shall I forget this huge crowd ... drunk with enthusiasm each time the General was called back to the balcony.'⁵ Finally, on 24 April, de Gaulle, attired reassuringly in a suit rather than a uniform, gave his first press conference since October 1945. He batted away suggestions that he was aiming at a dictatorship. The 'Gathering of the French People' (Rassemblement du Peuple Français – RPF) was launched.

The government was rattled. Rumours of de Gaulle's intentions had started to leak even before he spoke at Bruneval. On the same day, Prime Minister Ramadier delivered a speech warning against the temptation of 'Boulangism'. He was sufficiently alarmed to make the long drive to Colombey on 2 April, announcing himself to a startled de Gaulle late in the night. The purpose of the visit was to warn him that, unless he desisted from political interventions, the government could no longer accord him official honours during public appearances. De Gaulle refused to provide any such assurances. Having given Ramadier a glass of cognac (or a cup of weak coffee in other accounts), he sent him on his way, sarcastically offering him 'all my compliments for your government'.⁶ Once the RPF had been formally launched, de Gaulle was banned from the airwaves.

The RPF was a new departure for de Gaulle. In 1943, he had adopted Moulin's policy of rehabilitating political parties over Brossolette's vision of a new political force uniting around 'Gaullism'; in 1943–4, he had rejected the idea of lending his name to a new Resistance party; in 1945, when Pleven, Debré, Schumann and others had sought his advice about their political future, he recommended they join one of the existing parties. De Gaulle was banking on his charisma to oblige the parties to swallow their differences and accept his leadership. His model was something like the 'Sacred Union' of the Great War or the Free French when politicians had agreed to subsume their political differences in the higher cause of saving France. These had of course both been exceptional war situations, but for de Gaulle 'saving' France was a never ending struggle. He also had a visceral distaste for being associated with 'faction'. In the autumn of 1946, when hesitating over what to do next, de Gaulle had resisted the temptation to form his own political movement. Claude Guy had been witness to a tetchy exchange on this subject at Colombey one afternoon over tea between de Gaulle, his wife and their son. When Philippe de Gaulle launched into a vehement plea that his father should create his own party, Madame de Gaulle was provoked to look up from her letter writing and interrupt him with a rare political opinion: 'Why get mixed up in all that? Perhaps events will force *them* [the politicians] to give in to events; they will seem to surrender to you because opinion has forced them to ... You will bring things back to order, and then *pauvre ami* they will betray you at the first opportunity . . . As for forming your own party, it would betray you in fifteen days.' De Gaulle rounded on both his wife and son: 'You are talking like a child, Yvonne! Both of you make me laugh with your advice. Neither of you understands anything.'[7] De Gaulle's irritation reflected his own genuine uncertainty about what to do, but he certainly did not want to set up a normal political party. He prophesied to Guy a month before this conversation: 'Sooner or later, an organization of that kind would become a political party. You cannot gather a majority just by talking of the Empire or the position of France in the world . . . Sooner or later there are interests to satisfy.'[8]

Although de Gaulle changed his mind because everything else had failed, he still hoped initially that the RPF would remain above party. Its members were not required to leave whatever party they belonged to. But the other political parties rapidly squashed any idea of 'dual membership'. The Communists and Socialists were obviously never going to allow it, and the MRP quickly moved to forbid it as well. Two prominent MRP members, Edmond Michelet and Louis Terrenoire, both of whom had been in the Resistance, were expelled from their party when they chose to join the RPF.

Despite refusing to call itself a party, the RPF quickly started behaving like one. At the end of May, de Gaulle announced that it would be presenting candidates at the municipal elections in the autumn. He embarked on a speaking tour of France, addressing massive crowds in Bordeaux (15 May), Lille (29 June), Rennes (27 July), Lyons (20 September), Vincennes (5 October). All his speeches were variations on a theme of catastrophe. Without new institutions (and by implication his return to power to preside over them), he predicted that the young Fourth Republic would lead France to economic ruin, jeopardize her national security by allowing the re-emergence of a powerful Germany and compromise her international standing by abandoning the Empire. Defence of the Empire was one of de Gaulle's key themes: by the end of 1946, any attempt to reach an accommodation with Ho Chi Minh in Indo-China had failed (partly because of the intransigence of d'Argenlieu, whom de Gaulle himself had put in place) and France was sucked into a full-scale colonial war.

What gave the imperial argument new urgency was the beginning of the Cold War, which transformed the conflict in Indo-China into a battleground of the international struggle against Communism. When de Gaulle initially conceived the RPF, the Communists were hardly seen by him as more threatening than the parties in general. This quickly changed as the Cold War started to impact on domestic French politics. In May 1947, just after de Gaulle had launched the RPF, the Communists, who refused to back the Ramadier government's economic policies, were summarily sacked. The Communist Party now entered into increasingly strident opposition. Just as the wartime unity between the Allies was now degenerating into open conflict between the United States and the Soviet Union, so in France the unity of the Resistance, embodied in the uneasy tripartite coalition of Communists, Socialists and MRP, was definitively over. In his speech at Rennes on 27 July, de Gaulle launched a violent diatribe against the Communists, whom he dubbed 'separatists' – implying that they no longer formed part of the national community. He warned menacingly that Russia's western border was only distant by two laps of the Tour de France. Anti-Communism became one of the most important themes of the RPF.

ENDING THE CLASS STRUGGLE

As well as attacking the Communists as an internal enemy, the RPF also offered a positive alternative to Marxist class struggle by developing a distinctive social doctrine. This was encapsulated in the idea of an 'association' between employers and workers, capital and labour. This idea was entirely de Gaulle's. He had first raised it at the meeting in February 1947 where he unveiled his intentions to his immediate followers. A few weeks later, he expressed frustration that whenever he mentioned 'association' he encountered only a 'lack of curiosity, complete ignorance, indifference, if not indeed resistance'. What he really encountered was incomprehension because no one had a clue what the term meant. This was true even of Palewski, who had known de Gaulle longer than anyone and worried that what he seemed to be suggesting had a 'connotation of paternalism'. De Gaulle offered no enlightenment but enjoined the small group to turn the idea into a practical policy.[9] To those present at these first meetings where the RPF was being set up, association seemed like some cranky notion of de Gaulle's that might soon pass. They were wrong. In de Gaulle's mind this idea was more than just an opportunistic response to the Communist Party; it was one to which he was to return intermittently for the rest of his career.

Before 1940, one finds only one fleeting reference in his writings and letters to social issues (about which he admitted 'I have no expertise'), in a letter de Gaulle wrote to his friend Auburtin in 1937:

> Money questions (wages, profits, holidays etc.) would be very quickly settled
> if there was something that could bring the protagonists together morally.
> That something, one has to admit, has been found by fascism, and also

Hitlerism, and yet how can we accept that social harmony has to be paid for by the death of liberty? What is the solution? Christianity, one can agree, had its solution. But who will discover the one that is valid for our times?[10]

De Gaulle's inter-war writings do contain many warnings about the challenge posed to human civilization by mechanization and industrial civilization. There are eloquent passages on these lines in both *The Edge of the Sword* and *Towards a Professional Army*. De Gaulle returned to this theme in his speech at Oxford in November 1941. The ostensible purpose of the speech was to patch up his relations with the British after his first quarrel with Churchill two months earlier. Where previously he had portrayed the war as a struggle against the 'eternal appetite of Germany', he now argued that the 'life and death of western civilization' was also in the balance because of the nature of Nazism. For the first time he offered an interpretation of Nazism, which he viewed as a consequence of 'the transformation of the conditions of life by machines, the growing concentration of the masses and the resulting gigantic collective conformism' threatening the freedom of the individual:

> From the moment that humans find themselves subjected, by their work, their pleasures, their interests, their thoughts, perpetually joined together, in their thoughts, from the moment that their houses, their clothes, their food become progressively identical, from the moment that they read the same things at the same time in the same newspapers, see everywhere in the world the same films . . . from the moment that the same means of transport lead men and women to the same offices and workshops, the same restaurants and canteens, the same sports fields and the same theatres . . . the result is a sort of general mechanization of existence in which the individual is sure to be crushed.

Such fears were shared by many cultural commentators and intellectuals in inter-war Europe. They are reflected in films like Chaplin's *Modern Times*, René Clair's *À nous la liberté* and Fritz Lang's *Metropolis*. The Belgian symbolist playwright Maurice Maeterlinck expressed these ideas in best-selling books of what might be described as 'cultural entomology' in which he compared the social habits of insects to those of humans. His *Life of Termites* in 1926 was a cautionary tale warning that the crushing of individual freedom under Bolshevism was reducing humans to the level of termites. De Gaulle had read Maeterlinck, and the comparison between modern civilization and the 'termite heap' was one he frequently used. Few of his listeners presumably realized that the analogy had been coined by Maeterlinck. This was also a theme of the Catholic novelist and polemicist

Georges Bernanos (1888–1948), who published in 1947 a book entitled *France against the Robots*, denouncing the way that the 'civilization of machines' (*machinisme*) was destroying the human spirit. The affinities between Bernanos and de Gaulle are worth underlining even if de Gaulle never succeeded, as he put it a bit regretfully, in 'harnessing' him fully to his cause. A former pupil of de Gaulle's father at the College of the Immaculate Conception, Bernanos had started out as a fervent monarchist and supporter of Action Française. His famous novel of 1936, *Journal of a Country Priest* (*Journal d'un curé de campagne*), described the anguish of a Catholic priest in a small village of northern France wracked by physical ailments and disgusted by the indifference of his parishioners to Christianity. Those who thought they knew where to situate Bernanos politically were startled when he published a violent polemic in 1938 denouncing the conduct of the Catholic Church during the Spanish Civil War. In 1940, living in self-imposed exile in Brazil, he pushed his heterodoxy a stage further by instantaneously denouncing Vichy. He became a passionate supporter from afar of the Free French, writing regularly in its newspaper *La Marseillaise*, while never allowing himself to be enrolled formally into the organization. He viewed the Free French as a crusade for the purity of France's soul against dishonour but also against the totalitarianism which he saw as the most terrifying manifestation of modernity, even more than liberal democracy or socialism, for which he had little liking either. A kind of romantic Christian anarchist, Bernanos was a man out of his time, dreaming of a lost civilization of saints and heroes. There is no way in which one can say that he 'influenced' de Gaulle. And as a passionate advocate in the 1930s of army modernization and the rationalization of the state, de Gaulle might seem in some sense his antithesis. But the rage that animated Bernanos's attacks on modernity drew on the same Catholic heritage and intellectual influences (they were both admirers of Péguy) that inspired de Gaulle's own musings on industrial civilization. *France against the Robots* can be found in de Gaulle's library at Colombey, and on more than one occasion he remarked that the *Journal of a Country Priest* was the work of fiction published in the inter-war years that he most admired.[11] The idea that socialism and capitalism were two sides of the same coin – rooted in the materialism of industrial civilization – was also a theme of those 1930s 'nonconformist' thinkers whom de Gaulle had encountered in the salon of Emile Mayer.

How de Gaulle alighted upon association as his answer to the problem of modern civilization is less clear. One influence was surely social Catholicism. The search for 'social harmony' (that elusive ideal referred to in de Gaulle's 1937 letter quoted above) had started to preoccupy the Catholic

Church in the late nineteenth century as socialist parties emerged to organize the new industrial working class. To meet this challenge Pope Leo XIII had in 1891 issued his encyclical *Rerum Novarum* which enjoined industrialists to show social responsibility to their workers. *Rerum Novarum* was the foundational text of social Catholicism, a strand of Catholicism influential among the industrial bourgeoisie of northern France – the milieu of de Gaulle's maternal grandparents.[12] Social Catholics also drew inspiration from the Catholic social theorist Frédéric Le Play (1806–82), who preached the social responsibility of industrialists and engineers – an idea that was taken up in a different form by the French colonial soldier Marshal Lyautey, whose famous 1891 article on the 'social role of the officer' inspired generations of French army officers. Social Catholic thinking drew upon the idea of 'corporatism' – bringing together workers and employers into single 'corporations' where their interests could be reconciled. Corporatism was taken up by inter-war fascist movements, although once in power they used the ideology to justify their suppression of trades unions. The doctrine also influenced some members of the Vichy regime, as did social Catholicism in general. It is interesting in this context to note that in his *Memoirs*, which he started writing at this time, de Gaulle was to pay a curious tribute (the only one he ever paid) to Vichy's corporatist legislation which he says was 'not without attractions' but was vitiated by the fact that it was linked to a regime born out of defeat: the result was to 'push the masses towards an entirely different mystique'.[13]

This gave de Gaulle's social doctrines a highly conservative – even some said 'fascist' – tinge. But another possible source of the association idea were the writings of French pre-Marxist socialists like Fourier and Proudhon whose social thinking revolved around the idea of 'cooperation' and social harmony, not class struggle. On one occasion, de Gaulle himself referred to association as 'an old French idea' defended by 'those figures, generous if not always practical, of goodwill and personal worth, who in the years 1835, 1840, 1848 had developed what was then called French socialism'.[14] It seems unlikely de Gaulle had any personal acquaintance with these texts – although his maternal grandmother had written a biography of Proudhon – but they were perhaps suggested to him by Louis Vallon, one of those RPF members who became an enthusiast for the idea of association. Vallon, among those several Socalists who had joined de Gaulle in London in 1942, had in the 1930s been an economic adviser to the trades unions as well as being linked to the 'nonconformists'. He provides a direct link between them and de Gaulle's social ideas. Vallon would have rejected the idea that the social doctrines of the RPF were reactionary or 'fascist'. He wrote in 1957: 'Thanks to de Gaulle in 1940 the French could again have hope in their history ... So I became "Gaullist". Since my youth I have been socialist and socialist I remain.'[15] The most committed supporters of the doctrine of association would come to call themselves 'left Gaullists'.

As far as de Gaulle was concerned personally, his social ideas were also inspired by the pursuit of unity, which was one of his obsessions: in relation to his constitutional ideas, bridging the conflict opened up by the Revolution – or, as he once put it, 'reconciling the left to the State and the right to the Nation' – and in relation to his social ideas, bridging the conflict between capital and labour. It was also his way of giving greater intellectual weight to his movement, answering critics who alleged that the aims of 'Gaullism' as it developed after 1945 – apart from bringing de Gaulle back to power and reforming France's institutions – were no more than an anachronistic obsession with national 'grandeur'. Boris and Mendès France may have failed to turn de Gaulle into a socialist in 1944–5; the Resistance leaders may have come away frustrated that he did not share their belief that a social regeneration of France was possible. The doctrine of association was de Gaulle's response.

MANOEUVRES, 1948–1949

It was less the lure of association than the fear of Communism that swelled the ranks of the RPF. In the second half of 1947, France entered a period of acute social conflict fuelled by sharp rises in the cost of living. Now that the Communists had left the government, nothing held them back from fanning the flames of social unrest. Communist-inspired strikes broke out in coalfields and on the railways, with pitched battles between police and strikers. There were riots in several cities and in December sixteen people died after sabotage caused the derailment of a train on the Paris–Tourcoing railway line. The right accused the Communists of pursuing a strategy of political insurrection. In short, the Cold War had irrupted into French politics. The strange mood of panic was revealed by Claude Guy's suggestion to Yvonne de Gaulle in October to hide a machine gun in the cellar at Colombey in case of an attack. In her no-nonsense way, she rejected the idea on the grounds that de Gaulle would have no idea how to use such a weapon, adding philosophically that 'if the Communists want to kill him ... they will kill him.'[16]

This background explains the triumph of the RPF at the municipal elections of October 1947. Obtaining 40 per cent of the vote – a stunning result for a movement that had not existed six months earlier – it won control of thirteen of the largest cities in France including Paris (where de Gaulle's brother Pierre became the chair of the municipal council), Bordeaux (where Jacques Chaban-Delmas, who had been de Gaulle's military delegate to Paris in 1944, became mayor), Marseilles, Lille and Strasbourg. The American Ambassador in Paris, Jerome Caffery, convinced that de Gaulle would be swept to power, kept in close contact with Palewski and others.[17] The Americans now viewed de Gaulle as the most reliable bulwark against Communism, although Caffery was worried by the 'fascist' resonances of the General's social ideas.

De Gaulle too was convinced his moment had arrived. Listening to the results of the first round of the elections at Colombey he exulted to Claude Guy: 'It is the death of the regime.' He spent the week before the second round preparing the declaration he would issue once the definitive results were known: 'I will grab the microphone to declare that on arriving in Paris I have taken note of the disintegration of the existing political authorities, that on arriving in Paris I see that there is nothing left in Paris . . . and that in the absence of any government I will temporarily head the government to accomplish the necessary task of national salvation.' And if the situation were to become more 'complicated', he mused that he might be compelled to speak from Brazzaville or Algiers – as during the war. There was much more in the same vein over the rest of the week, with his wife occasionally sounding a note of caution and trying to calm him down. She told Guy: 'It will all end badly . . . The General is always "laying into" the bourgeois ["*taper" sur les bourgeois*]: but he should stop because it is the bourgeois who have made him what he is. And for all his denials, he is one himself.'[18] Once the second round of the elections, on 26 October, had confirmed the results of the first, de Gaulle published his declaration calling for the dissolution of parliament. This would pave the way for new legislative elections and a total overhaul of the constitution.[19] A week later he set off for Paris to give a press conference. All this time he remained in alarmingly high spirits, reminiscing nostalgically one evening about some of his more violent quarrels with the British and Americans during the war. On 17 November, he gave a press conference where he described the RPF as an unstoppable torrent: 'The wave will swell and surge. I pity those who do not understand this. If they want to fight against this force . . . they too will be swept away. If they want to remain on the banks pointlessly speechifying, their curses will have no more importance than spitting in the sea.'[20] Afterwards he was extremely pleased with himself, especially with his phrase about spitting in the sea which he repeated delightedly to Guy several times more.[21]

In reality de Gaulle had disastrously overplayed his hand. He certainly would have been swept to power in the event of parliamentary elections. But his problem was that there was no constitutional reason for these to take place just because the RPF had won municipal elections. All would depend on whether France's politicians held their nerve. No one was more worried, but also no one was more determined, than Vincent Auriol, the President of the Republic. Auriol was a moderate Socialist elder statesman, close to Léon Blum. He had rallied to de Gaulle in the war. After being elected to the Presidency at the start of 1947, he had tried to keep on good terms with de Gaulle, hoping he might gradually reconcile him to the new Republic. Immediately after his election, he invited de Gaulle to a 'house-warming' at the Elysée *en famille*, expressing the hope that he might be willing from time to time to give him advice. De Gaulle turned down the idea with icy politeness. The idea of the General taking tea decorously at the Elysée while offering the President disinterested counsel somewhat stretches credulity. Auriol began to wonder about de Gaulle's sanity on receiving a letter from him in February 1947 turning down the Médaille Militaire which the French government had simultaneously awarded to Stalin, Churchill and Roosevelt (posthumously). De Gaulle replied that he could not accept the decoration because in the war he had acted as France's head of state, and the 'State does not decorate itself'.[22] He was rather pleased with this letter and remarked privately: 'One has got to amuse oneself as best one can.'[23]

Auriol was not amused as de Gaulle's ambitions became clearer. He was increasingly alarmed by the incendiary tone of de Gaulle's speeches with their calls for existing political institutions to be swept away. He wrote in his diary: 'He is really off his head; he speaks in the first person plural.'[24] Auriol took his responsibility as President of the Republic seriously. The constitution was perhaps imperfect, but it was the only one there was. Although it granted him only limited powers, Auriol was determined to be as active a President behind the scenes as the rules permitted. After the municipal elections in October 1947, he urged the politicians to hold firm against de Gaulle. With his encouragement, one of the leaders of the Socialist Party, Guy Mollet, called for all true 'republicans' to rally in defence of democracy. This was an appeal for the parties of the centre (essentially the MRP) and moderate left (Socialists) to swallow their differences against the two extremes of the PCF and the RPF. Mollet's appeal touched a chord and revived a kind of Third Republic mystique around the idea that democracy was in danger – an idea which was given some plausibility by de Gaulle's provocative rhetoric. Out of this was born the so-called 'Third Force' coalition that would govern France for the next three years.

Although the MRP and the Socialists were the ballast of the Third

Force, a vital role was also played by a number of small centrist parliamentary groups whose political importance was out of all proportion to their actual numbers, as often happens in coalition politics. These included the Radical Party, a shadow of its former self under the Third Republic but still mustering a few *députés*, and a new group called the UDSR (Union Democratique et Socialiste de la Résistance), which was all that survived of the hopes of creating a great new Resistance Party after the Liberation. Over the three and a half years after November 1947, there were no fewer than nine governments. But the same faces – Robert Schuman (MRP), René Pleven (UDSR), Georges Bidault (MRP), Henri Queuille (Radical) and so on – would reappear again and again, giving a kind of reassuring stability to the bewildering political merry-go-round. This was of course the antithesis of the charismatic politics preached and practised by de Gaulle.

Caffery, the American Ambassador, felt that by playing for the highest stakes – a dissolution of parliament and nothing else – de Gaulle had missed his opportunity to take power at the end of 1947. But even if de Gaulle had misjudged the situation immediately after the elections, it was not absurd for him to hope that events would move in his direction if he held his ground. He was banking on two potentially favourable scenarios. The first would arise if the threat from Communism came to seem so irresistible that the Third Force politicians felt they had to reach an agreement with him – even on his terms. The second would arise if the Communist threat receded and exposed the ideological divisions between the Third Force parties. In other words, de Gaulle's future depended on the degree to which the politicians' opposition to him prevailed over either their fear of Communism or their mistrust of each other. Any shift in these variables offered de Gaulle an opportunity.

For six months following the municipal elections, the first scenario seemed plausible. It was widely feared that Communists throughout Europe were set on a revolutionary path. In February 1948, Communists had taken power in Prague through a bloodless *coup d'état*, and all eyes were now on Italy where the Communists stood a good chance of winning the elections due in April. Against this menacing international background, de Gaulle made a speech at Compiègne on 7 March warning that the international Communist threat made it vital to 'join together on the road to salvation'. Was this an olive branch to the other parties? That is how René Pleven chose to interpret the speech. Pleven was one of those Free French who had not followed de Gaulle into the RPF but had instead joined UDSR. De Gaulle did not easily forgive betrayals of this kind, but he retained respect for Pleven and agreed to see him at Colombey on 10

March. Although he gave little ground, he allowed Pleven to make a public statement on the need for the parties to reach an agreement with de Gaulle.[25] Other party leaders did not respond positively, but Pleven continued behind the scenes to try to broker a deal between the General and the Third Force. He persuaded de Gaulle to meet the current Prime Minister, Robert Schuman, one of the leaders of the MRP.[26] A special itinerary was worked out so that Schuman could drive to Colombey on 4 April without the public knowing. Again the meeting got nowhere. Another secret meeting took place in August between the General and Maurice Schumann (no relation of Robert), who had never entirely recovered psychologically from his breach with de Gaulle in the previous year. The news that de Gaulle would receive him produced on his part tears of joy, but the encounter was inconclusive.[27] Making these politicians trek to Colombey to see *him* was de Gaulle's way of demonstrating his indispensability.

By the time Maurice Schumann saw de Gaulle, the Communist threat was receding. At the Italian elections in April 1948, the Communists failed to win an overall majority – the first serious setback to international Communism since the start of the Cold War. This opened up the second possible scenario for de Gaulle's return to power: the breakup of the Third Force, which there were good reasons to expect. The two main parties of the Third Force, the Socialists and the MRP, had opposite views on economic policy and religious schools – a traditionally divisive issue in French politics – and it was primarily fear of Communism that bound them together. In July 1948, their divisions erupted into a crisis and the Socialists brought down the government of Robert Schuman. Over the summer there were hectic political negotiations as attempts were made to stitch together another coalition government. These culminated in the formation of another Third Force government in September 1948 cobbled together by the centrist politician Henri Queuille, whom de Gaulle had known in Algiers. De Gaulle should have remembered that Queuille was a shrewd political operator who had served effectively on the CFLN. Instead, with his tendency to despise his opponents, he declared: 'He is past it [Queuille was only six years older than de Gaulle himself]; already in Algiers he used to trip over the carpet.'[28] How long could this inoffensive former country doctor possibly hold a government together?

In November 1948, the RPF did well at the elections to the indirectly elected Senate. The main casualty was the MRP. This led its leaders to wonder if association with the Socialists in the Third Force was becoming an electoral liability and causing its voters to defect to the RPF. De Gaulle saw a chance to exploit this chink in Third Force unity. The Gaullist Edmond Michelet, who had remained on good terms with his former MRP colleagues, organized a secret meeting between de Gaulle and Bidault at the Hôtel La Pérouse in Paris on 12 November. Bidault nervously fortified himself in advance with a large brandy which, as things turned out, was not necessary. Since de Gaulle wanted to wean the MRP from the Third Force, he was in a mood to be charming. He assured Bidault that he held no grudge against him for not leaving the government in January 1946 – 'the real problem came when you ratified the constitution' – and appealed to his heart by reminding him they were both social Catholics: 'You must help me . . . Only together will we be able to free the working class.' He urged Bidault to persuade his *députés* to support a dissolution of parliament and new elections.[29] Nothing came of this encounter. Bidault could not forget the way he had been treated by de Gaulle when acting as his Foreign Minister in 1945. In any case, even if he had wanted to reach out to the RPF he would probably have been unable to carry his own *députés* who were annoyed when news of the meeting with de Gaulle leaked out.

Despite these wobbles on the part of the MRP, Queuille proved adept at holding his coalition together. His principle of government was to postpone the solution of problems until they no longer mattered. His government survived for a year – a record in the Fourth Republic so far. It surmounted the challenge of another serious wave of Communist strikes in the autumn of 1948, when the Socialist Minister of the Interior Jules Moch did not hesitate to deploy riot police to restore order. Who needed de Gaulle if Queuille's government was able to see off the Communist threat? At the same time, the French economy started to show signs of recovery thanks to the arrival of American Marshall Aid. Jerome Caffery, who had been in frequent touch with de Gaulle's entourage in the early months of 1948,[30] had come to the view by the end of the year that, since the Third Force was proving such an effective barrier against Communism, de Gaulle was more of a problem than a solution. As a sign of de Gaulle's falling stock one Embassy official said of him at this time: 'He talks about economics as a woman talks about carburetors. His advisers are ill-assorted, incompetent, self-seeking and unstable.'[31]

When Queuille's government fell in October 1949 after losing the support of the Socialists, de Gaulle made one last attempt to prise the MRP away from the Third Force. Through Michelet he sent a message to its leaders urging them to prevent the formation of a new government and assuring them he was ready to 'pick up the broken chains' of the past (*renouer les chaînes du temps*). Robert Schuman replied non-committally that de Gaulle was 'the solid block on which France could rely if the need presented itself' – which in his view was not yet.[32] Queuille's fall had not so much exposed the fragility of the Fourth Republic as demonstrated that de Gaulle – and the Communists – now seemed so much less threatening that the parties could risk a political crisis with impunity.

For a man outside 'the system', hurling anathema against France's pygmy politicians, de Gaulle had done a lot of manoeuvring in these two years. He had had secret meetings with Pleven, Maurice Schumann, Robert Schuman and Bidault – and had allowed other overtures to be made on his behalf. This went against the grain of his temperament, and after each meeting he would rage against his entourage for having lured him into these abortive encounters. In the end, all these contacts were doomed to failure because de Gaulle was not seeking an accommodation with the parties. He wanted to force elections so that the RPF could form a government whose first act would be to impose a new constitution. For the moment, he could only rail against the system:

> The regime hangs on desperately. It floats on the surface of the country like a cork on the ocean. Nobody believes in it. It goes on precisely because of this contemptuous indifference. In fact, at the first serious event it will disappear without any resistance and leaving no trace. But until then it can vegetate in its own nullity.[33]

De Gaulle made regular predictions of this kind over the next three years. In private he had a register of a largely untranslatable – and sometimes unprintable – epithets for the politicians of the Fourth Republic: the 'vinegar pissers', the *polis-petits-chiens* (well-bred little puppy-dogs), *politichiens* – for the politicians of the Fourth Republic. But all this was born of frustration. As the sense of impending catastrophe that had hovered over French politics for two years began to dissipate, so did the prospect of de Gaulle's return to power. The 'system' had held out. De Gaulle could only bide his time, wait for the parliamentary elections due in 1951 and keep his followers believing they could still win.

THE 'COMPANIONS'

The RPF was not just a one-man show. It was run by a small Executive Committee that met every week; a National Committee of about 150 members that met once a month; a network of regional delegates who gathered in Paris regularly under de Gaulle's chairmanship; and an annual congress (dubbed 'Assizes' to make it sound as if the RPF were not really a political party). In addition, there was a policy think-tank called the Comité d'Etudes, a newspaper and specialized organizational groups (with their own newpapers) representing different professional categories.

The key institution was the Executive Committee, which had its weekly meeting at the RPF's headquarters in the Rue de Solférino in Paris. There was a preponderance of figures who had been in the Free French and to a lesser extent in the Resistance. Although René Pleven, Maurice Schumann and André Philip had refused to follow de Gaulle into this new adventure, many veterans of the Free French viewed the RPF as a continuation of their wartime struggle. Members of the RPF were referred to as 'Companions' – as the Communists called each other 'comrade' – to emphasize this link to the Free French (as in the Companions of the Order of Liberation).

Apart from de Gaulle, the two key figures of the RPF were its Secretary General, Jacques Soustelle, in charge of organization, and André Malraux, in charge of propaganda. Soustelle had proved indispensable to de Gaulle during the war – first in setting up Free French committees in Latin America, then in streamlining Free French propaganda in London in 1942, and finally in taking over the secret services in Algiers. In agreeing to run the

The propaganda of the RPF played on the parallels with the Free French: de Gaulle's 'appel' of 1940 is here put alongside his new 'call' in 1947 – with the Cross of Lorraine linking the two.

RPF, Soustelle sacrificed a brilliant university career as an anthropologist. Although a supremely efficient organizer he never won the hearts of the RPF activists. He found it impossible to hide his sense of intellectual superiority and, when looking back on the period, RPF activists would refer ritualistically to his 'glacial' exterior. Those few people who knew Soustelle well realized that his intimidating mask concealed a sensitive and tormented personality, desperate for de Gaulle's approval. De Gaulle ruthlessly exploited Soustelle's devotion, often treating him with savage cruelty. If he made Soustelle his number two, it was not only for his organizational skills but because his lack of charisma meant he would never be a threat.

Unlike Soustelle, André Malraux was a relative latecomer to Gaullism. He had leapt to literary stardom in the 1920s, becoming one of the most famous writers in Europe. In the 1930s, no French intellectual was more prominently involved in the struggle against fascism. During the Spanish Civil War he organized an air squadron to support the Spanish Republicans and then immediately fictionalized this experience in a book and a film. In 1943, he joined the Resistance, taking as his pseudonym the name of a character from one of his novels, Colonel Berger. With Malraux art and life, fantasy and truth, were impossible to disentangle. He was not among the first batch of writers invited to meet de Gaulle in Paris at the Liberation, possibly because of his 1930s reputation as a Communist fellow-traveller.

Malraux's Gaullist epiphany dated to the day in August 1945 when a car drew up at his door with a message from de Gaulle: 'The General asks you in the name of France if you would be willing to come to his aid.' This encounter had been set up by members of de Gaulle's entourage who had reason to think Malraux might be susceptible to such an appeal. A few months earlier, he had made a passionate speech at the congress of the Movement of National Liberation (MLN), an organization made up of former Resistance movements. Malraux warned the MLN against any temptation to amalgamate with the Communist Resistance organization, the Front National. This revealed to the world that Malraux had repented of his former admiration for Communism and was ready to strike out in a new direction. De Gaulle's summons could not have been more timely.

Of the first meeting between Malraux and de Gaulle, we have only Malraux's embroidered recollections. If he is to be believed, the two men managed in their first conversation to discuss Nietzsche, Stalin, Marx, Victor Hugo, Voltaire, the French Revolution, the decline of the Roman Empire and much else. De Gaulle seems hardly to have got a word in edgeways.[34] This rings true since Malraux was famous for the pyrotechnics of his conversation which left his interlocutors dizzy and never sure they had

understood anything he had said – especially since his delivery was punctuated with furious nervous tics caused possibly by Tourette's syndrome.[35]
Raymond Aron once suggested that Malraux was 'one-third genius, one-
third charlatan and one-third incomprehensible'.[36] Perhaps in Malraux de
Gaulle had for the first time encountered someone who intellectually
intimidated him; perhaps he was flattered to be treated as an intellectual
equal by such a dazzling interlocutor. But what he must have sensed immediately is that he had a potential disciple. Malraux nurtured a cult of heroic
historical figures. His personal pantheon had previously included Napoleon, T. E. Lawrence and Saint-Just. Now de Gaulle replaced them all. For
his part, de Gaulle revered writers, but wanted them to know their place –
hence François Mauriac's disappointment that the General wanted to
discuss only literature, not politics. Malraux, however, was different. He
was not offering opinions: he was offering himself body and soul.

Within days of the meeting in August 1945, Malraux had been co-opted
into de Gaulle's *cabinet* to look after propaganda. He was among the tiny
group to whom the General unveiled his plan to set up the RPF. De Gaulle
may have hoped that Malraux would rally leftist intellectuals to the RPF.
This never happened because the leftist Malraux of the 1930s had been
eclipsed by the Gaullist one of the 1940s.[37] Instead his role in the RPF was
to use the magic of his rhetoric to transfigure the banality of day-to-day
politics into Legend and History. As he had once said of his previous hero
T. E. Lawrence: 'It is not the man who makes the legend but the legend
that makes the man.'

Malraux and Soustelle were the heart and head of the RPF, jockeying
for de Gaulle's favour. Tellingly de Gaulle had made Malraux a Companion
of the Liberation, despite his late entry into the Resistance, while Soustelle,
who had been in the Free French from the start, was never accorded this
coveted honour. It is true that de Gaulle usually reserved the distinction
for those who had actually fought with the Free French army or put their
lives at risk in occupied France, but it had been awarded to Pleven and
Cassin who fitted neither category. That de Gaulle passed over Soustelle
reflects his personal estimation of each man: Soustelle he used, Malraux
he admired.

The third key figure of the RPF was Gaston Palewski (also a Companion
of the Liberation) who, given his historical relationship to de Gaulle, might
have been expected to have Soustelle's job. De Gaulle favoured Soustelle
because Palewski's easy charm and familiarity with the world of parliamentary politics did not suit him to running a movement whose *raison d'être*
was suspicion of party politics. De Gaulle noted of Palewski at this time:
'Nothing harms him more in my mind than this obsession he has through

vanity to be mixed up in everything and to be everywhere.'[38] Instead Palewski was put in charge of the Comité d'Etudes which drafted policy documents on subjects ranging from constitutional reform to economic policy. Other members included Michel Debré, who worked on constitutional reform, and Raymond Aron, who provided expertise on economics. Although during the war Aron had been among those in London suspicious of de Gaulle's authoritarian tendencies, he was now drawn to him by anti-Communism, while never being a fully paid-up anti-Gaullist.

In addition to the inner circle of Malraux, Soustelle and Palewski, de Gaulle had his personal *cabinet*. The role of *directeur de cabinet*, once held by Palewski, now fell to Georges Pompidou, another latecomer to Gaullism who had played no part in either the Resistance or the Free French. The son of a schoolteacher from a village in the Auvergne, Pompidou was a brilliant product of the meritocratic French education system. He had spent the war unremarkably as a teacher of literature at one of France's most prestigious lycées while working on an anthology of French poetry. He might have gone on to a distinguished academic career had he not been recruited into de Gaulle's *cabinet* at the Liberation by a former university colleague. Pompidou quickly made his mark thanks to his agile intelligence and unflappability. When Yvonne de Gaulle decided after the war to set up a foundation for children with learning difficulties, de Gaulle asked Pompidou to handle the details. Nothing better demonstrated de Gaulle's complete trust in him.

Pompidou viewed the human comedy with a wry detachment. Of the Comité d'Etudes, he remarked that Debré 'drew up constitutions in their hundreds' while Aron 'described with lucidity the economic and monetary situation, and formulated with supreme confidence predictions that were never borne out by the facts'.[39] Although he had no formal position in the RPF apparatus – he was not even a paid-up member of the movement – he made himself indispensable to de Gaulle. But even Pompidou sometimes found his direct access to the General filtered by de Gaulle's two fiercely loyal aides de camp, Claude Guy and Gaston de Bonneval.

Inevitably there were poisonous rivalries within the inner circles of the RPF. Soustelle, to whom fell the unglamorous tasks of administration and organization, was irritated by the grand airs of Malraux, who had set himself up in luxurious offices near the Opera rather than in the more cramped RPF headquarters across the river in the Rue de Solférino. Palewski resented the fact that he had been slightly sidelined by both men despite having served de Gaulle for longer than either. Pompidou, who owed his position entirely to de Gaulle's confidence in him and had no Free French past, never fully lost the sense of being a privileged outsider in the inner circle of Gaullism. And others were always there to remind him of the fact if he should forget. Writing on one occasion to express his appreciation of Pompidou's contributions, Palewski ended with a slightly backhanded comment: 'Our small group, so tiny in the first days, squeezed together to welcome and make a place for you.'[40]

At least Pompidou had never been embroiled in Vichy, unlike another important RPF figure, the former diplomat Léon Noël, who had briefly served the regime in 1940 as its delegate to the Occupied Zone. He quickly repented, became slavishly devoted to de Gaulle after the war and was given a senior position in the RPF. De Gaulle was pleased to be able to welcome into the ranks of the movement such a grand establishment figure while knowing that the absolution he had bestowed for past errors guaranteed complete loyalty. When invited to join the RPF's National Council, Noël wrote to thank de Gaulle but put in a plea that he should not be required to enter 'by the back door, head lowered, like a guilty man forced not to attract attention to his faults'. This was a dig at the 'perfidious manoeuvres' of Palewski who, according to Noël, never lost an opportunity to remind people of his brief Vichy flirtation. For good measure he added that the fact this 'singular individual has not the slightest drop of French blood in his veins might incite him to greater modesty' (a comment which suggests that Noël's brush with Vichy had left its traces).[41]

As always de Gaulle affected to despise and soar above these squabbles. On one occasion he exploded to Guy:

> In London it was the same . . . In fact that is what it is always like . . . The most annoying was Cassin! And then there were Pleven and Dejean . . . All of them! Always the same story of telegrams between them; one would complain the other was keeping telegrams to himself. If there was one tiny piece of paper that one of them had not seen, they were immediately in my office complaining, in a state of agitation.[42]

But de Gaulle was not entirely innocent. When leaving London for Dakar in 1940 he had divided power between Muselier, Antoine and Passy; in Indo-China in 1945 he had set Leclerc and d'Argenlieu against each other; the same was true of the RPF period. Pompidou, who was a shrewd judge, observed: 'Around a man like de Gaulle there are necessarily intrigues, clans, struggles to win favour. And the General helps a bit by stoking the rivalries.'[43]

De Gaulle had never been easy to work for, but his frustration made him more impatient and cutting than ever. Debré, who was new to this side of de Gaulle, wrote to him in December 1948: 'Is it quite necessary to spend so much time attacking other people? Has anyone ever told you how much the form of some of your words wounds people? I do not believe that General de Gaulle need be so systematically sarcastic.'⁴⁴ This plea for de Gaulle to be less like himself had as little effect as similar pleas by Brossolette in 1942 or Philip in 1943. De Gaulle commented to Pompidou on receiving this letter: 'Poor Debré is always standing at the Wailing Wall.'⁴⁵ But even Pompidou could find de Gaulle's severity trying: 'He is maladroit with people, humiliating them, wounding their sense of self-esteem.'⁴⁶

The RPF spent much time discussing policies, but de Gaulle rarely involved himself in details. Faithful to his doctrine of circumstances, he did not want to be tied down in advance. He wrote to Soustelle in November 1947: 'I repeat yet again that no one must make any declaration to anyone regarding anything that concerns me personally. What I think, what I do, what I plan, is my business. It is for me only to say or not to say.'⁴⁷ De Gaulle's speeches hammered repeatedly at the same ideas: constitutional reform, the Communist threat and the association between capital and labour. He remained obsessed too by the threats to the Empire: even at the end of 1950 when the war in Indo-China was beginning to look unwinnable, he warned Pompidou against an 'Asian Munich'.⁴⁸

Although the themes of the RPF mostly remained in 1951 the same as in 1947, de Gaulle's thinking on foreign policy evolved. In 1949, France had signed the Atlantic Alliance setting up NATO despite a strong neutralist current in French opinion which argued that France should remain free of both the western and the Soviet blocs. This argument might have appealed to de Gaulle, but he was persuaded by Aron that the Communist threat made such a position untenable. De Gaulle was not entirely happy with the way NATO was structured, but his position was that an imperfect pact was better than none. He was at this time a committed Atlanticist. But as Cold War tensions subsided, he began to warn against the danger of French military dependence on America.⁴⁹ By 1952, he was putting the existence of an 'American protectorate' almost on the same level as 'Soviet servitude'.⁵⁰

At the same time de Gaulle's view of Germany evolved. France's hopes of preventing the re-emergence of a central German authority had failed once it became clear that America would not back such a policy. From 1949, Germany was divided by the Cold War into a Soviet puppet state in the east – which the non-Soviet bloc did not recognize – and the German Federal Republic in the west. De Gaulle realized that this development was irreversible, and his speeches from 1949 started to float the possibility of, as he put it, an accord between 'Gauls and Teutons' and alluded to the need to rebuild the Franco-German entente that had been shattered by the death of Charlemagne.⁵¹ In 1948 he told Pompidou:

Supporting America at any price is not a cause! If only there was something in Europe! Europe has always been the entente between the Gauls and the Teutons. We will need at some point to place our hopes in Germany, hope that she can create a European mystique . . . I don't mean that one needs to build a Europe against America, nor against Britain, nor against Russia, but one does need to create a Europe.[52]

De Gaulle's policies in the Fifth Republic ten years later are already contained in these lines.

TOURS OF FRANCE

For the rank-and-file Companions of the RPF, these shifts of policy were not important. The essence of the movement for them lay in the mass meetings where they experienced their collective communion with de Gaulle. In the first two years of the RPF's existence, these meticulously choreographed rallies attracted crowds on a scale matched by no other political party – except occasionally the Communists. On two occasions in 1947, the RPF filled the giant Vél d'Hiver sports stadium in Paris; in April 1948 de Gaulle seemed to be addressing the entire population of Marseilles when he spoke at the city's Vieux Port. No rally equalled that at the Vincennes racecourse outside Paris on 5 October 1947. The doors opened at midday, and the buzz of anticipation had reached fever pitch when de Gaulle arrived in the late afternoon to the accompaniment of military music. Alone he mounted the steps to a podium decorated by an immense tricolour and the Cross of Lorraine. As he raised his arms in a V above his head, the crowd went wild. After his first words – 'We are half a million here' – there were more roars from the crowd and cries of 'De Gaulle to power'.[53] De Gaulle followed his speeches by plunging into the crowds. After a meeting at the Vél d'Hiver in 1950, even the reporter for Le Monde, not a pro-Gaullist newspaper, was carried away by the atmosphere: 'By the end, the Vél d'Hiver was peopled by a huge army ready to march to victory behind a man who spoke to them only in the language of destiny.'[54]

When de Gaulle could not attend a meeting, Malraux was the most popular substitute. His lyrically mystical orations transformed the General into a combination of the medieval crusader St Bernard and the revolutionary Saint-Just. But, even when not there in person, de Gaulle was always 'present'. At one meeting in the Vél d'Hiver, a message from him was read out, and after the singing of the 'Marseillaise', Louis Vallon announced:

'Companions of de Gaulle, you have all felt his presence among us; he is there by each of us . . . I am sure that in Colombey, in the solitude where he watches over France, he will hear you.'[55]

The Communists compared these gatherings to the fascist rallies of the 1930s. Auriol on several occasions wrote in his diary that he did not want to open the way to 'fascism'.[56] Sometimes the PCF tried to break up RPF meetings, and scuffles occurred between the activists of the two parties. At a meeting in Grenoble in December 1948 an anti-RPF demonstrator was killed. But violence on this scale was exceptional and was usually provoked by the Communists. The cult of violence was not a feature of the RPF, and militarist symbolism was absent from its meetings – although de Gaulle usually appeared in his uniform. Whatever the fantasies of the more excitable activists, the General was not tempted by popular insurrection. After the municipal elections of 1947, Malraux declared: 'De Gaulle marched us to the Rubicon and then told us to take out our fishing rods.' In his more apocalyptic moments Malraux dreamt of a kind of popular insurrection that would sweep away parliament, but he observed a bit regretfully to Claude Mauriac, 'the General is not a man of violence.'[57]

A Communist poster for the elections of 1951:
de Gaulle as 'fascist threat'.

But the RPF certainly had similarities with those movements of populist anti-liberal nationalism that have periodically surfaced in French politics since the nineteenth century, whether in the form of Bonapartism, Boulangism or the 'Leagues' of the 1930s.[58] De Gaulle had many reservations about Napoleon I, he felt contempt for Napoleon III and for Boulanger, and he had never been involved in the Leagues, but he too offered himself as a saviour standing above parties with a promise of social reconciliation and national unity. The style of the RPF made some supporters uneasy. On one occasion Claude Mauriac commented: 'The Croix du Feu side of the ceremony troubles me and excites the enthusiasm of the crowd but not mine.'[59] In December 1948, Debré wrote to de Gaulle to warn against 'sectarianism at the base' of the RPF:

> I have been Gaullist from the moment that de Gaulle came into existence . . . [But] I have 'Republican reflexes'. It is second nature with me. I shudder, in the middle of the Touraine countryside, to see the propagandists of the RPF in bomber jackets, wearing berets . . . and I feel ill at ease in the Rue de Solférino where it seems to me there is no possibility of speaking freely . . . I am not afraid of wise and strong leadership, but I do fear dictatorship. You offer wise and strong leadership but, behind you, there are so many partisans of empty dictatorship.[60]

In the end Debré and Mauriac swallowed their reservations. Mauriac averred: 'I will go to the end with de Gaulle. Fidelity is the only faith I have left.'[61]

Ultimately it was 'fidelity' to Gaulle that bound the RPF together. The movement was a community of believers around a charismatic leader and saviour. Rank-and-file RPF activists saw themselves as a new order of chivalry continuing the epic of the Free French. Many of them were too young to have been in the Free French but through it they felt they were living a surrogate Resistance.[62] The memoirs of three activists convey the intensity of this relationship to de Gaulle. The youngest was Bernard Marin (aged nine in 1940), who had been 'converted' by watching de Gaulle on the Champs-Elysées on 25 August 1944:

> I found him magnificent. One just had to look at him to be sure that everyone would submit to his authority, and that the unity of the country would be guaranteed. I do not think enthusiasm for any man will ever equal, in France, that which de Gaulle unleashed walking down the Champs-Elysées on foot . . . I felt that that day had marked me indelibly and that I would never cease to seek the chance to live that atmosphere again.

Claude Guiblin (eleven in 1940), who believed that he had heard the *Appel* of 18 June on his parents' radio but was not sure, joined the RPF after the war 'as one enters a religion . . . Our sole ambition was to devote ourselves entirely to the cause of de Gaulle and his companions.' The third activist was Jacques Dauer (fourteen in 1940), who wrote: 'The "companion" phenomenon is an exclusively Gaullist notion, a notion of fidelity, of filiation . . . My relationship to the General was one of a vassal to his sovereign. Obedient for the essentials, free for the rest.'[63]

The massive RPF rallies became less frequent after 1949. They were expensive to organize and it became harder to attract such enormous crowds once the sense of crisis had subsided. But in anticipation of the 1951 elections de Gaulle continued to tour the country. In 1950, he visited seventy *départements* and was on the road for fifty-three days. The pretext for his visits was often the unveiling of a monument commemorating some event of the war. This caused problems of protocol. The government had ruled that de Gaulle could be accorded official honours at commemorative events but not political ones. This meant that the Prefect would greet de Gaulle for the unveiling but would vanish when he made his speech. De Gaulle played on this blurring of genres. At the commemorative events he would appear in uniform, reminding the public of an historic 'legitimacy' transcending the 'so-called governments' (as he liked to put it) that happened to be in power.

Many of these regional visits were on a small scale, de Gaulle travelling alone by car with his wife and one Companion. Sometimes they would stop for a picnic. One member of the RPF's National Executive who accompanied him on a provincial tour remembered sitting by the roadside with the General and his wife, eating a picnic and hearing de Gaulle's booming voice call out 'Another hard-boiled egg, Baumel?'[64] This was a world away from the heady atmosphere of the first two years when it seemed as if de Gaulle might be swept to power. The point of these visits was to keep up the spirits of the local RPF delegates for whom a personal encounter with the General was a moment to treasure for the rest of their lives, although the reality was often excruciating for both sides. As we have seen, de Gaulle was more ill at ease with individuals than with crowds: 'Overcoming his timidity the local delegate would begin a tentative conversation. The General – doubtless reciting silently to himself the speech he was about to deliver – would remain silent, gazing into the distance.'[65]

QUIET DAYS IN COLOMBEY

If de Gaulle subjected himself to the tedium of these regional tours, it was partly to escape the routine of Colombey. Before 1940, Colombey had played only an intermittent part in his life; now it was his only home. On his weekly visits to the RPF headquarters in the Rue de Solférino in Paris, he always stayed at the Hôtel La Pérouse near the Place de l'Etoile, once remarking drily that this reminded him of his previous 'exile' at the Connaught.[66]

During the repair works in 1946, de Gaulle had extended his property by adding a round tower in which he established his study. Even so, La Boisserie remained a comparatively modest dwelling. There is a poignant passage in Claude Guy's journal describing the occasion when he and de Gaulle stayed up through the night to listen to the results of the first 1946 referendum, pen and paper to hand. Initially they seated themselves in the dining room, but the radio did not work:

> So we went up to the first floor. We put Anne in a guest bedroom and settled down in hers next to a radio with an anti-interference shield. Sitting in front of pink furniture and an assortment of dolls and childish drawings, we installed ourselves. From the next room we took in a table, recently painted, too large for us to carry without tilting it over. The drawers all fell out at our feet with a terrible din.[67]

At Colombey, de Gaulle lived the life of a modest country squire. He attended Mass every week, and the curé was regularly invited to lunch. This unassuming country priest, who might have strayed out of a nineteenth-century novel of French provincial life, was treated with the deference that de Gaulle extended to any representative of the Church.[68] All visits to La Boisserie followed an immutable ritual. Before lunch, the guest would be taken into the study for a 'conversation' about the state of the world. Lunch was served at precisely 12.30 and rarely lasted more than thirty-five minutes. It was followed by coffee and desultory conversation in the sitting room, with Madame de Gaulle knitting in the background. De Gaulle was a courteously old-fashioned host, personally filling his guest's glass and refusing to allow anyone else even to put a log on the fire. This offered the pretext for a piece of melancholy play-acting: 'Leave that to me, it is about the only thing I have left to do.'[69]

The visitor would then be taken on a long walk round the grounds. De Gaulle would delight in pointing out in the distance the bleak panorama of endless forests with no human habitation to be seen. If he felt in the mood, he would launch into a tirade on the theme of how wrong it was to talk of 'la douce France'. For him, France was a country of grand landscapes appropriate to the grandeur of her history. To Claude Mauriac on one visit, de Gaulle became ever more carried away: 'He made the climate ever harsher, raised the mountains, swelled the rivers with a kind of ferocity as if there could be no grandeur in moderation.' He compared this to Britain 'with her little cottages alongside little lanes in the little countryside with the gentle [*petite*] rain'.[70] Louis Joxe was told 'life is not gay here . . . One does not come here for fun [*pour rigoler*].'[71] After their walk, the visitor would be offered a cup of tea before returning to Paris, leaving de Gaulle to his melancholy and apocalyptic meditations.

Descriptions of a visit to Colombey became a literary genre. Many visitors were subjugated and entered fully into de Gaulle's imaginative construction. One wrote that he felt himself immediately 'under the influence of the site, so in accord with the personality' of de Gaulle; it seemed like a 'sort of austere "Wuthering Heights" with a horizon grandiose in its monotony'.[72] Another noted: 'This place, elevated, isolated and windy, was in tune with his personality. Solitude is his lot.'[73] In no report of a visit to Colombey does the sun ever seem to shine or the wind not blow.

Not everyone was seduced. The five-hour journey from Paris to Colombey did not facilitate the smooth running of the RPF. Soustelle developed a phobia about 'this inconvenient and distant residence in a lugubrious countryside to which one gives excessive honour by baptizing it "forest of the Gauls"'. He came to loathe the 'atmosphere dripping with ennui . . . and the sound of Madame de Gaulle's knitting needles as the rain lashed the windowpanes . . . I am convinced that so many things would have been different if the journey between the General's house and Paris had, like Cleopatra's nose, been shorter.'[74] Soustelle penned these words after he had broken with de Gaulle, but others felt the same. Even the equable Pompidou on one occasion deplored the 'bad "mental hygiene"' of Colombey where de Gaulle was in touch with the outside world only through the radio and occasional visitors. Louis Terrenoire, who later took over from Soustelle as Secretary General of the RPF, observed that de Gaulle's 'solitary furies, behind the closed shutters of his residence, are often the result of what he hears on the radio'.[75] The General was cut off in Colombey because he disliked using the telephone, and the line from Colombey was unreliable, like most of the French telephone network at this time.

Whatever the effect of Colombey on de Gaulle's volatile moods, it added a new strand to his myth, especially after the RPF's stamp campaign in 1948.[76] Members of the public were invited to buy a sticker bearing the General's portrait and send it to his address at Colombey. This was conceived as a kind of popular plebiscite around the name of de Gaulle, circumventing the machinations of the politicians. It was also designed to raise money for the RPF, which was chronically short of funds. The campaign was extraordinarily successful. By the time it closed, after a month, about 2.3 million letters had been received. The campaign did not overturn the regime or solve the RPF's financial problems, but it anchored in the public mind the idea of de Gaulle as an austere Cincinnatus who had retired to his country estates ready to come out of exile to save the nation. De Gaulle played on this idea in a famous passage of his *Memoirs* describing how he had walked round the garden 15,000 times watching the 'wild depths where the forest invades the site like the sea beating at the promontory ... In the tumult of men and events, solitude was my temptation. Now she is my friend.'[77]

This was the myth. The truth, as it emerges from Claude Guy's journal, the most detailed day-by-day account of life at Colombey between 1946 and 1949, seems different – even if Guy's views were jaundiced by his tense relations with Yvonne de Gaulle, who resented the presence of anyone trying to lure de Gaulle back to politics. She had never got over her scepticism about the entire RPF venture. She told Guy a few days after de Gaulle had launched the idea: 'We are too old now. At our age it is best to stay at home.' Recalling the precedent of Pétain not knowing when to stop, she told Guy that a fortune teller in Poland had told de Gaulle that he would die hanged. The only way to disprove the prophecy was to keep out of politics.[78] Guy paints a picture of claustrophobic monotony, punctuated by occasionally tetchy conversations between the General and his wife, and by de Gaulle's explosions of rage against the politicians. The emotional centre of de Gaulle's life at Colombey was his daughter Anne. After any absence, his first act was to rush up to her room.

On 6 February 1948, Anne died at the age of twenty after catching bronchitis. The family had lived with the knowledge that the weak immune systems of children with Down's Syndrome made them vulnerable to infection. But Anne's death was a terrible blow. The curé noted in his diary: 'I found the General collapsed in awful grief. He said to me: "I am a man annihilated. You decide everything: the time and the day. I want a funeral as they are done at Colombey."'[79] De Gaulle wrote to his other daughter Elisabeth, who was at that time living in Africa:

Anne died in my arms with her mother and Madame Michigau [the nurse since the retirement of Mlle Potel] by her side while the doctor administered an injection *in extremis*. M. le Curé came over to bless her ... The disappearance of our poor suffering child, our little girl without hope, has caused us immense grief. I know you will feel the same. From heaven let little Anne protect us and first of all protect you, my dearest Elisabeth.[80]

De Gaulle told Guy:

She was a prisoner. There was something very special and very touching about this little human being and I have always had the feeling that if she

had not been as she was, she would have been a rather remarkable person . . .
If there is a God, he has liberated her soul and called her to him.[81]

Three months later de Gaulle wrote again to Elisabeth: 'Your mother and
I are very alone. Little Anne, whatever her state, played such a role through
her presence, as a subject of interest and affection.'[82] Yvonne de Gaulle
plunged herself even more into the running of the foundation she had set
up for mentally handicapped girls. On the anniversary of Anne's death,
every year the curé would come to the house to say a Mass in her memory.
For both parents, Colombey was now a place of sadness from which they
were happy to escape.

WAITING FOR THE ELECTIONS, 1950–1951

'There are only two motors to human action, fear and vanity,' de Gaulle
told Pompidou in one of his Le Bon moments: 'Either there is a state of
catastrophe and then fear dominates. Or there is calm and then it is vanity.'[83] As the mood of catastrophe in which the RPF had been born receded,
so too did the fear which had led so many electors to vote for de Gaulle.
De Gaulle had to hope that enough memory of that mood remained to win
a parliamentary majority in 1951.

  Although de Gaulle conceived the RPF as standing above the left–right
divide, it had assumed a markedly conservative identity in the anti-
Communist conjuncture of its birth. Its electors included many former
Pétainists who would have execrated de Gaulle at the Liberation. De Gaulle
was ready to make some gestures to these voters by making public his
unease at the fate of Pétain who, since his conviction in 1945, had been
imprisoned in a fortress on the Ile d'Yeu off the coast of Britanny. Now in
his nineties Pétain was often described in the press as the 'oldest prisoner
in the world'. De Gaulle declared on various occasions that it was wrong
that this old man, now harmless and senile, who had once 'rendered great
service to France' should die alone in prison without ever again seeing
'trees, flowers, friends'.[84] De Gaulle was walking a delicate tightrope since
he had probably not said enough to satisfy most former Pétainists while
shocking former resisters. One former *maquisard*, who described himself
as 'a Gaullist of 1940', wrote to express his indignation: 'So the blood shed
for France, the terrible tortures suffered by so many of us, the total sacrifice
that we freely made, everything that was done to liberate France and bring
you to power no longer counts.'[85]

De Gaulle was in fact not willing to go too far down this road of national reconciliation – as Colonel Rémy discovered to his cost in 1950. Rémy was the Resistance pseudonym of the film producer Gilbert Renault, who had founded an important Resistance network that worked closely with the Gaullists. Rémy had opposed the armistice from the beginning, but this did not cause him ever to modify his ultra-conservative views. After the war, he started publishing his best-selling multi-volume memoirs which made him to the public the epitome of the cloak-and-dagger secret agent. Rémy joined the RPF, and the notoriety of his Resistance exploits, and his facility as a writer, made him the ideal candidate to write a popular biography entitled *The Unknown de Gaulle* – an exercise in shameless hagiography. Rémy opened by remembering how he had noticed the 'deep kindness' of de Gaulle's eyes at their first meeting (many people noticed the General's suspicious hooded eyes but not their kindness) and ended with de Gaulle in the 'restful family atmosphere' of Colombey reluctantly re-entering the fray to save France again (though in reality he was bursting with impatience in his enforced retirement).

The book also contained a short passage in which Rémy remembered de Gaulle once telling him that France had needed two strings to her bow – that of Pétain and that of de Gaulle. De Gaulle had amended Rémy's original typescript by adding the words 'providing that both were used in the service of France'.[86] Perhaps because few people noticed this exercise in saccharine propaganda, these words, even after de Gaulle's emendation, passed almost entirely unnoticed.[87] In April 1950, encouraged by de Gaulle's public remarks about Pétain, Rémy repeated de Gaulle's alleged remark in the Gaullist newspaper *Carrefour* without de Gaulle's qualification. He ended by appealing for Gaullists to offer the hand of reconciliation to former Pétainists. While not repudiating his opposition to the armistice, he now seemed more exercised by the excesses of the Liberation which 'fill my heart with shame and disgust'. The next day, de Gaulle issued a terse statement denying he had made the statement attributed to him – although he almost certainly had. Rémy resigned from the executive of the RPF. The incident ended Rémy's attempt to create a kind of Pétaino-Gaullism with de Gaulle's benediction.

The Rémy affair reflects de Gaulle's complicated relationship to Pétain. Musing in 1950, he returned to his old idea:

Marshal Pétain was a very great man who died in 1925. I was there for his death throes. That said, the history of France did not begin on 18 June 1940. There was Verdun. People say that it was not Pétain who won Verdun, but it was Pétain who introduced the tactics thanks to which the French army held out . . . Foch was incapable of introducing tactics. Pétain was a tactician. That is why in 1939 he predicted the defeat but did not see the world conjuncture.[88]

Pétain finally died in July 1951. When Pompidou announced, 'Pétain is dead,' de Gaulle corrected him: 'Yes, the Marshal is dead.' And when Pompidou remarked, 'The affair is now over once and for all,' de Gaulle disagreed: 'No, it was a great historical drama, and an historical drama is never over.' This was to be a better prediction than Pompidou's, as the latter would find to his cost when he was President many years later.[89] Yet nothing changed de Gaulle's overall judgement of the armistice. When in 1953 André François-Poncet, Pétain's successor at the Académie Française, made a speech reiterating the thesis that Pétain had been the shield to de Gaulle's sword, de Gaulle retorted that the shield had not prevented 'France being pillaged, the French held in servitude, the fleet lost'. Yet he understood that the 'speech . . . reflects the profound opinion of a great part of the "notables"'[90] – whose support the RPF needed.

The electoral prospects of the RPF were compromised when in 1951 the parties of the Third Force concocted an electoral law whose purpose was to crush the two parties of the extremes – the PCF and RPF. The law allowed parties to form joint lists (*apparentements*), and ruled that any list obtaining a majority of the vote would automatically be allocated all seats. Most of de Gaulle's advisers shared his instinct not to compromise the integrity of the RPF, although he did in the end allow eleven *apparentements* out of ninety-five constituencies – too few to affect the overall result but enough to annoy purists.[91] Another issue was whether de Gaulle himself would stand in the elections. He had never had any intention of doing so. As he told Soustelle: 'Can you see me hanging up my hat in a little locker of the cloakroom of the Palais Bourbon [the parliament building]?'[92]

During the election campaign, de Gaulle toured the country making speeches in which he resuscitated the language of catastrophe which now seemed disconnected from reality and the current experience of the French. In Nîmes in January 1951 his speech painted an apocalyptic picture of Notre-Dame in Paris and the Colosseum in Rome destroyed by bombs at the end of the next world war. In another speech, on 1 May, he announced that 'when the people have spoken I will be there for them. Where? On the Champs-Elysées.'[93] Such comments were designed to keep up the spirits of the more activist members of the RPF, but they allowed de Gaulle's opponents to revive the accusation that he was an insurrectionist, even a 'neo-fascist'.

'BETRAYAL'

The RPF emerged from the elections as the largest group in parliament with 119 seats but short of the 200 seats needed for an absolute majority. The *apparentements* system had worked: with 22 per cent of the vote the RPF obtained only 19 per cent of the seats. But even without the law the RPF would have got only 143 seats.

The new parliament contained six groups roughly equal in size. From left to right these were the PCF, the Socialists, the MRP, the Radicals, the *modérés* (conservatives) and the RPF (which resented being required to sit on the extreme right). Given that the Communists were beyond the pale, this 'hexagonal' chamber offered two possible majorities: a continuation of the centrist Third Force (extended to take in the conservatives) or a right-wing one (the conservatives, the centre and the RPF without the Socialists). The former solution required the Socialists and conservatives to surmount their many policy differences; the latter solution required the RPF to play the parliamentary game. Immediately after the results were announced de Gaulle stated his terms: his parliamentary representatives would only be ready to lead a coalition government whose other members were committed to constitutional reform (making it possible for de Gaulle to return to power). Since this was not on the cards, he had little to offer his *députés*, who found themselves the largest group but with no prospect of power.

De Gaulle had reached an impasse. In 1947, having won the wrong election he had to wait for the right one; in 1951, he had lost the right election and there was nothing to wait for. His position in January 1952, as expressed to his regional delegates, was that the only purpose of the RPF in parliament was as a force of obstruction: 'It is possible that, under the pressure of events, a majority could be formed . . . I admit that I do not believe at all in the value of any government I would not have the honour of presiding over.'[94] De Gaulle realized this would put a great strain on the loyalty of the *députés*, many of whom had jumped on to the RPF band-wagon without being deeply committed to the cause. He commented cynically to Pompidou before the election: 'Out of the 200 I am going to get elected [it turned out to be fewer of course] . . . 180 will arrive with the intention of sharing out titles and baubles.'[95] President Auriol was shrewdly calculating the same. Still believing that de Gaulle represented a threat to democracy, he was determined not to be, as he put it, the Hindenburg of France's Fourth Republic – a reference to the German President who had invited Hitler into power in 1933.[96]

In January 1952, Auriol summoned for consultations the leaders of all the parliamentary groups, including Soustelle for the RPF.[97] Although Soustelle did not accept this invitation without de Gaulle's approval, de Gaulle immediately became suspicious. On 9 January, while Soustelle was at the Elysée, the Executive Committee of the RPF met at the Rue de Solférino. De Gaulle opened proceedings in a ferocious temper: 'Can we begin while the new President du Conseil is forming his government? I wonder where he will put me? . . . Ministry of Sport perhaps or Education?' This was only the start. When Soustelle arrived, de Gaulle kept up the barrage of sarcasm while those present squirmed at this public humiliation: 'Ah, here is the head of the government! Well, Mr Prime Minister, how are your consultations going?' There was more in this vein until Soustelle was on the verge of tears.[98]

In fact Soustelle had politely rebuffed Auriol's overtures. The government that emerged from the President's consultations lasted only two months. At the start of March, he again summoned parliamentary leaders for discussions. Soustelle, having learnt his lesson, was non-committal and this time he took the precaution of suggesting that Auriol invite de Gaulle directly for talks, something he had omitted to do on the previous occasion.[99] But he also knew that members of the RPF parliamentary group were frustrated that de Gaulle's tactic of non-cooperation was reducing them to impotence. Soustelle could not win. When he telephoned Colombey to report on his talks, de Gaulle shrieked down the line so violently that Soustelle hung up, and announced he was sick and would not attend the scheduled meeting of the parliamentary group.

Pompidou and Louis Terrenoire (who had taken over as Secretary General since Soustelle had begun chairing the parliamentary group) were so alarmed that they persuaded the reluctant Soustelle to drive with them to Colombey on 3 March. Soustelle was like a contrite schoolboy – although he had done nothing wrong – terrified in front of the headmaster. He offered his resignation if de Gaulle felt he had acted inappropriately. De Gaulle refused it and explained: 'Your role consists in being torn and receiving blows from both sides. That is your way of participating in the great national ordeal that affects each of us.' Although when his visitors left, de Gaulle seemed mollified, on the next day it was as if the visit had never occurred. At the Rue de Solférino, he launched into another public humiliation of Soustelle. Debré and Palewski intervened to defend him, but to little avail.[100]

On 6 March 1952, twenty-seven members of the RPF parliamentary group broke ranks and voted for a government headed by the conservative politician Antoine Pinay. Auriol's plan to split the RPF had succeeded. To everyone's surprise Pinay turned out to be a popular figure in the country at large – one of the few Fourth Republic politicians to achieve a certain following based on his reassuring reputation as the defender of the rentier. For the next few months de Gaulle could not decide what to do. If he allowed his *députés* some leeway he might be able to preserve the formal unity of the movement; if he insisted on strict discipline and expelled the rebels, there was a danger that his movement would never recover. At a press conference on 10 March, he was less extreme than some had feared. Asked if he would accept being a member of a government of which he was not the head, he replied: 'Doubting that the other ministers would find this situation comfortable, I will spare them the ordeal.'[101] Pompidou, who could read de Gaulle's fluctuating moods, found him in June to be 'tormented . . . completely destabilized' and genuinely unsure whether he should go on with the RPF.[102]

De Gaulle called a meeting of the National Council of the RPF in July to debate what to do next. Having opened the meeting, he took his place on the floor among the delegates. Soustelle spoke first and tried to curry favour by announcing that there could be no 'Gaullism without de Gaulle'. Malraux was no less intransigent: 'If you abandon a certain number of *députés* or if they abandon you, that is . . . an incident. If you abandon an idea, that is not an incident, it is a suicide.' The debates were heated and three speakers who took a different line were booed. De Gaulle summed up the debates by declaring: 'Duty does not consist in abandoning General de Gaulle under the pretext of putting him in power.'[103] The meeting ruled that *députés* must in future respect party discipline or leave. Twenty-seven *députés* resigned, and were immediately excluded from the RPF. Others joined them over the next few months.

This might have been the end of the RPF, but de Gaulle found it impossible to make the break. Pompidou, writing to de Gaulle during his summer holidays in 1952, urged him not to give up: 'No one would like it more than me to "go back home" and live far from politics. And yet my instinct tells me that you do not have the right to abandon France to her decadence.' But he also urged de Gaulle to have more confidence in those who wanted to serve him: 'If you tell them clearly what they can do, they will succeed, or at least try their best with resolution and loyalty.'[104] Pompidou was thinking here of the unfortunate Soustelle, who had written to de Gaulle pleading to be allowed to resign from chairing the RPF parliamentary group. De Gaulle, having treated him with such brutality, now did everything to talk him out of it.[105]

In December 1952, Pinay's government fell. Auriol set about the usual round of consultations. He called once again on Soustelle. On the night of

25 December, Soustelle took the 'all too familiar' route to Colombey, where de Gaulle was recuperating from a cataract operation. Soustelle thought he had obtained the General's approval for his cautious response to Auriol. Terrenoire and others judged that he had handled the situation in an exemplary fashion and used the opportunity to raise the parliamentary profile of the RPF without giving anything away. But they were worried, with some justification, about 'what the boss will think'.[106] In an exact repetition of his reaction a year earlier, de Gaulle was incensed that he had been betrayed. As he put it to Pompidou a few months later: 'From the moment that Soustelle goes to the Elysée and discusses the formation of a government, he is still with me sentimentally but he is against me politically.'[107] In the end, Pinay was replaced in January 1953 by a government headed by the conservative René Mayer, who succeeded in winning the support of an even larger number of RPF *députés* than his predecessor.

It was increasingly difficult to discern the *raison d'être* of the RPF. De Gaulle's intention when founding it had certainly not been to find himself managing – even at one remove – a parliamentary group. He had a shrewd sense of political power but not the skills or inclination to play this kind of game. Soustelle was not alone in finding him increasingly intolerable to work for. The same was true of the treasurer of the RPF, Alain Bozel, who had been one of de Gaulle's most devoted followers ever since September 1941 when he was among those 185 prisoners of war whose arrival in London was such a boost to the Free French at a moment when relations with Churchill were at a low point. But by the end of 1951 Bozel could take no more. His letter of resignation contained some home truths:

> The more you go on the less you attract men to you although you are the only solution to the problem of France ... This terrifying mistrust that constantly haunts you, alarms and worries the best among your supporters. Soustelle asked me if I knew why you were going around telling everyone that you had no confidence in him ... At the same time your universal contempt is getting worse and you put people off you with your ferocity.[108]

Some months later another old Free French loyalist, Raymond Dronne (famous for having been in the first of Leclerc's tanks to reach Paris on 24 August 1944), who was among the RPF MPs elected in 1951, wrote to warn de Gaulle about his behaviour in similar terms: 'More and more you are frightening people, even those faithful to you, in keeping too aloof from them, placing yourself too high ... It is more essential than ever that you receive a few parliamentarians one by one, that you speak to them, listen to them and establish relations of human contact and confidence ... If not the RPF will head towards shipwreck.' For once de Gaulle listened, invited

Dronne to a personal meeting and temporarily set his mind at rest.[109] But soothing susceptibilities went too much against the grain of his character for him to sustain it for long. He soon lapsed into one of his regular moods of self-pitying hubris. He told Pompidou: 'There is nothing more to do . . . I will write my memoirs . . . I held out singlehandedly. Without me there would have been a few French airmen in the RAF and a few conspirators in France, a few would-be ministers . . . It is the collapse of the elites.'[110]

The municipal elections of April 1953, six years after the triumph of 1947, were a disaster for the RPF. The movement lost about half the seats it had gained at its peak in 1947. De Gaulle could take no more. He issued a statement on 6 May 1953 announcing that any *députés* elected under his banner in 1951 would be free to enjoy the 'poisons and delights of the system' but they would no longer be doing it in the name of the RPF.[111] A few months later, he offered his diagnosis of the situation to the RPF regional delegates:

> As long as de Gaulle is in a state to govern, to exercise public affairs, chang-ing the regime . . . means de Gaulle taking power. It means that or nothing at all. One can enumerate all the possible combinations. Everyone knows that the very fact of putting de Gaulle into it will change the regime. It is possible that he will never be put in. In that case the regime will not change. If de Gaulle had not entered Paris, there would not have been the victory of the Resistance. That is how it is . . . I can do nothing about it; we are obliged to take things as they are.[112]

It was precisely because he knew that calling upon de Gaulle to form a government was tantamount to a change of regime that Auriol had never taken that step. De Gaulle's rages against Soustelle made him the scapegoat for the tactical dead-end into which he had cornered himself. The RPF had failed.

17

In the 'Desert', 1955–1958

LAST HOPES

'De Gaulle is like a rabbit released from a trap,' remarked Louis Terrenoire after de Gaullle's communiqué giving his *députés* their 'liberty'.[1] For several months de Gaulle had been detaching himself psychologically from the RPF. On a visit to Africa in 1953, he exploded to an aide who wanted him to receive some local RPF activists: 'You are beginning to piss me off [*vous commencez à m'emmerder*] . . . with *your* RPF.'[2] On his return from that visit, Terrenoire observed that 'less and less can he bear anything relating to the RPF.' De Gaulle proved this on the next day by cancelling a meeting for the following week: 'It bores me, and I would not know what to say . . . I do not want to be tied down. In 1946 I refused to be tied down by the parties, and I do not want today to be tied down by the RPF.'[3] Yet he could not bring himself to wind up the experiment entirely. The final stages were like a painful divorce as he kept drawing back from the brink.

Although de Gaulle eventually devoted only twelve lines of his *Memoirs* to the RPF, it had occupied seven years of his life – more than the Free French. Why this refusal to wind up the organization when it had obviously failed? Perhaps he could not admit to himself that he had made a mistake; perhaps he felt a residual sense of obligation towards the thousands of people who had given up their lives to serve him in this enterprise. One reason for hanging on was his hope that the RPF might have a role to play in what he considered the most pressing political issue of the mid-1950s: the European Defence Community (EDC). The origins of the EDC went back to the outbreak of the Korean War in 1950 when the Americans found themselves engaged in yet another front of the Cold War. This led the US government to urge west European states to assume a larger part in their own defence. One solution was to allow West Germany to re-establish a military force, but so soon after the war this was obviously political dynamite in France. Instead the French government came up with the idea (originally hatched by the fertile brain of Jean Monnet) of absorbing German rearmament into a 'European' army – the EDC. The treaty approving the EDC was signed in May 1952, but it still had to be ratified by the French parliament. Although the EDC had been initially a French proposal, for two years the issue aroused a passion which one observer compared to the intensity of the emotions of the Dreyfus Affair fifty years earlier.[4]

The idea of a supranational 'European' army sponsored by the Americans, and supported from the sidelines by the British, was anathema to de Gaulle. On this issue the RPF found itself objectively on the same side as the Communists, who opposed the EDC for different reasons. For some leftist members of the RPF like René Capitant, de Gaulle had the chance to become a kind of French Tito, neutral between the two blocs, or a western Gandhi, preaching disobedience to the soldiers of a European army.[5] Even though he had no intention of going so far, he could not accept the idea that France might surrender an iota of her military independence. If the RPF in parliament could block the ratification of the EDC, then he was not yet ready to pull down the final curtain. In a press conference in November 1953 he gave full vent to his sarcasm:

> Nothing is more curious than the public and private interventions of the United States to compel our country to ratify a treaty that would condemn her to decay. Curious indeed! For the United States are not part of this treaty. And if they find that it is so good for the French and Germans to merge, why do they not merge themselves with Mexico, Brazil, Argentina? . . . For other reasons Great Britain is also demanding that we join the so-called 'European' army though nothing in the world would induce her to join herself. Sacrificing one's sovereignty, abandoning one's soldiers to the discretion of others, losing one's dominions, that is good for Paris, not for London![6]

At a press conference on 7 April 1954, de Gaulle returned to the theme in even more brutal terms. He also announced mysteriously – and menacingly – that on 8 May, the anniversary of the end of the war, he would pay his respects to the Unknown Soldier at the Arc de Triomphe. This curious announcement suggests that he still nursed the fantasy that a popular movement might sweep him back to power. He knew that there was increasing malaise in the army about Indo-China, where the French were bogged down in a conflict impossible to win. Army leaders felt that civilian governments were starving them of the means to win the war. At a ceremony at the Arc de Triomphe on 4 April, army officers had insulted the current Prime Minister and his Minister of Defence.

A week before he was due to go to the Arc, de Gaulle wrote to his son:

'The situation is tense in military circles. Things seem to be moving . . . The ambience of the ceremony will be interesting.'[7] Then on 7 May the French army in Indo-China suffered a devastating defeat at Dien Bien Phu after a siege that had lasted several weeks. This was the worst French military humiliation since 1940. The ingredients were in place for a major political crisis. De Gaulle was in an excitable mood. He told Terrenoire: 'I will come back to power. I want to . . . We will see what happens tomorrow. But I think a lot of people will be there. In a few days, I will make a statement about Dien Bien Phu; then if there is a ministerial crisis, I will intervene.'[8] The next morning, he received the Chief of the General Staff, General Paul Ely. Immediately after the meeting, Ely noted what de Gaulle had said to him: 'The French had gathered around him when there was a certain tension but then they abandoned him. In the end, only the army could save the situation.' Somewhat taken aback, Ely asked whether this meant a *coup de force*: ' "No," replied General de Gaulle. But what he said did not seem so different; the leaders of the army had to move in his direction and all would be fine.'[9]

The government was alarmed by the potential impact of de Gaulle's public appearance and sent in police reinforcements. It need not have worried. At 4.00 p.m. de Gaulle arrived at the Arc de Triomphe, standing in an open-top car. He bowed silently in front of the tomb, but the crowd of 15,000 was smaller than the one that had turned out to see the President of the Republic in the morning. Although there were some shouts of 'De Gaulle to power,' this was no popular movement. 'The people are not really there,' de Gaulle remarked ruefully. He shook a few hands and left after fifteen minutes.[10]

Dien Bien Phu did spark a major governmental crisis, but its beneficiary turned out to be not de Gaulle but Pierre Mendès France, his old collaborator. Mendès France had not been a minister since his resignation from de Gaulle's government in 1945. But he retained the aura of a man of integrity who had been prescient about the dangers of inflation. In the politics of the Fourth Republic, he was a maverick figure: as a left-wing member of the tiny centrist Radical Party he was part of the 'system', but his denunciation of the policies pursued by all governments made him an outsider. Over the Indo-China War, he assumed the role of a Cassandra, condemning the pursuit of an unwinnable war that swallowed up resources better spent on economic modernization. The disaster of Dien Bien Phu vindicated him. The government was forced out of office and Mendès became premier, vowing to negotiate an honourable withdrawal from Indo-China within 100 days. He also sought de Gaulle's public benediction. On the day he formed his government, which happened to be 18 June, he sent de Gaulle a message: 'On this anniversary day, which is the day I assume heavy responsibilities, I live again the great lessons of patriotism and devotion to the public good which your confidence allowed me to receive from you.'

Mendès's sense of purpose presented a contrast to all his predecessors. Many Gaullist *députés* were seduced. Fifty-nine of them voted for him, fourteen abstained and several took key positions in the government. De Gaulle himself was thrown off balance by the advent of *mendésisme*. Pierre Koenig, former hero of Bir Hakeim and now an RPF *député*, who tried to discover whether or not de Gaulle approved of his joining the government, could not get a clear answer: 'Koenig, I don't ask you to be a minister but I don't ask you not to be.'[11] Koenig took this as a kind of green light, which de Gaulle had not intended it to be. On 22 June, the General issued a statement making it clear he would not offer Mendès France his benediction:

> Whatever the intentions of any individual, the current regime can only produce illusions and actions which lead nowhere . . . I will take no part in any of its combinations. National recovery is possible. It will begin after the end of this system without head, without soul, without grandeur, built against me after victory and which has since squandered the last opportunity for France and the men who could serve her.[12]

During his first months in power, Mendès was a whirlwind of energy. Having negotiated an end to France's presence in Indo-China, he turned his attention to extricating France from Tunisia, where anti-French nationalist discontent had been simmering for several years. In private, de Gaulle could not but admit reluctantly that Mendès was doing well.[13] He and Mendès met at the Hôtel La Pérouse on 13 October 1954. This was supposed to be secret but the news leaked out. De Gaulle reported on their conversation to Terrenoire:

> I told him: the regime might permit you to settle Indochina, the EDC, Tunisia and so on, that is to say relieve it of its burdens, but the regime will not allow you to carry out a constructive policy, a French policy . . . From time to time passers-by will wave their hats when you pass because you are new and likeable, but when you have got rid of the problems that are causing trouble to the regime, the regime will get rid of you.[14]

Mendès emerged from the meeting disappointed. He had found de Gaulle aged and judged that he was 'finished'.[15] The truth is that de Gaulle could not hide his dismay that it was Mendès, someone he genuinely respected, to whom it had fallen to save France. De Gaulle wanted France to be 'saved' – but by himself.

In the end, de Gaulle's analysis of Mendès France's political predicament turned out to be accurate. As Prime Minister he lacked a broad party base of his own, his government was defeated in parliament in February 1955. But although it lasted only eight months, the Mendès France 'moment' was hugely important. Mendès France had infused a new style of government into French politics. One novelty was the way he used the radio each week to speak directly to the population over the heads of other politicians. His personal charisma created a cult around him, especially among intellectuals and civil servants who responded to his call for economic modernization.[16] His style had made him in some sense a kind of left-wing de Gaulle; his fall seemed further proof that the 'system' was dysfunctional; and many disappointed 'Mendésistes' would later rally to de Gaulle in the same way as some disappointed Gaullists had rallied to Mendès in 1954.

During Mendès France's brief premiership, parliament finally refused to ratify the EDC, about which Mendès himself was lukewarm. For de Gaulle, the burial of the EDC meant that the RPF had lost its last remaining *raison d'être*. In December 1954, he announced that the movement was over. The members of the former RPF group in parliament renamed themselves the Social Republicans. To ensure that there could be no confusion, de Gaulle called a press conference on 30 June 1955 announcing that he no longer intended to speak about politics and would play no part in the next elections. His tone was valedictory: 'Everything leads one to predict that we will not meet again for a long time.'[17]

CREATING THE LEGEND

For several years already de Gaulle had been living more in the exhilarating past of the war than in the disappointing present of the Fourth Republic. He had started writing his *Memoirs* a few days after resigning in 1946 – and had probably been writing them in his mind long before. He told Duff Cooper in January 1944 that he tried 'every day for a short time, to imagine himself looking down on events without prejudice, and from the point of view of the future historian'.[18] The early years of the RPF had left him little leisure for writing. As he began to lose faith in the RPF, the *Memoirs* began to take over his life. Already in October 1951 Pompidou noted: 'He is more and more a man who is writing his memoirs.'[19] Two years later, usually punctilious about family obligations, de Gaulle did not join the Vendroux family for the annual shoot because he was absorbed in writing. A reading aloud from the work in progress became a new ritual for visitors to Colombey.

Writing the *Memoirs* was a major effort because de Gaulle's literary ambitions were high and because he did not as he said have '*la plume facile*'. His manuscripts are in places almost illegible as he endlessly crossed out and rewrote, seeking (not successfully) to eliminate certain verbal tics of the French classical style such as the triads of the so-called *style ternaire* (*Russia 'observe, calcule, se méfie'; with peace came the end of 'l'union, de l'élan, du sacrifice'* and the emergence of '*les intérêts, les préjugés, les antagonismes*', and so on).[20] Unlike Churchill, whose own memoirs of the war were a collective team effort, stamped of course by Churchill's own style, de Gaulle worked alone in the solitude of his study at La Boisserie apart from an assistant who would come down every so often to provide documentation. 'I want to write a *work*,' he declared, 'unlike Churchill who has never written a properly composed book, just interesting observations and lots of documents . . . one thing after another.'[21] As a model and inspiration, he had in 1946 started to re-read the *Mémoires d'outre-tombe* of René de Chateaubriand – as he was to do again when starting his second set of *Memoirs* in 1969.

De Gaulle's *War Memoirs* certainly are a 'work', not only because of their highly wrought prose, their formal structure (three volumes each covering two years), and their deployment of all the arts of classical French rhetoric, but also because, in addition to offering de Gaulle's narrative of 'his' war, they are a distillation of his vision of the world and his philosophy of history. As far as the narrative of the war is concerned, the thread running through all three volumes is de Gaulle's ceaseless struggle to defend French independence from all sides – from allies as much as enemies. Every detail of every quarrel with the British and Americans is recounted in meticulously unforgiving detail. Unsurprisingly the reader is given a minute account of the conflicts with the British over the Levant but remarkable space is also accorded to the most insignificant spats. One example was the so-called Dufour affair to which de Gaulle devotes fully three pages. In 1943, Dufour, a Frenchman living in London, claimed to have been tortured by the BCRA. The case was seized upon by de Gaulle's left-wing enemies, delighted to find evidence of the BCRA's 'Gestapo' methods. Dufour took legal action against Passy. The affair rumbled on for some months until the British government realized that Dufour was a fantasist or a blackmailer – or both. But the fact that it had originally been ready to believe Dufour was for de Gaulle a black mark that could not be forgiven. An objective reader of de Gaulle's *Memoirs* might be tempted to adapt his own comment to the Communist Gillot who tried to berate him over the truce signed during the liberation of Paris: 'Do you really think, M. Gillot, that what you call the "truce" has such a great importance in the history of France?' But for de Gaulle no instance of British perfidy was too insignificant to pass over.[22]

Despite picking over the scabs of every conflict with his allies, de Gaulle's *Memoirs* simultaneously aspire to an Olympian and atemporal detachment: each actor in the epic is ascribed their rightful place and memorialized appropriately. There are carefully chiselled and admiring portraits of Roosevelt and Churchill – 'great artists of a great history' as de Gaulle calls them. His account of his rivalry with them is in some sense depersonalized because in his view it conformed to laws of history which transcended their personalities. Of one of his quarrels with Churchill he remarks: 'He naturally felt in his soul the breath of the soul of Pitt.'[23] Describing the meeting where in 1944 Roosevelt sketched out his vision of the future of the world, de Gaulle writes: 'As is only human, the desire to dominate was dressed up in idealism.'[24] He goes on: 'In affairs between States, logic and sentiment do not weigh much compared to the realities of power: that what matters is what one can take and what one can hold on to; that France, to recover her place, could count only on herself.'[25]

Viewing the struggles of nations as written into the nature of the human species, de Gaulle has little to say about either fascism or Nazism. For this reason, he even permits himself when coming to Hitler's final defeat to linger for a moment on the 'sombre grandeur of his combat' which ended in suicide: 'Not to be chained Prometheus threw himself into the chasm.' One even senses on his part a certain fascination with Hitler and a regret about his own situation: 'He knew how to entice, and how to caress. Germany, profoundly seduced, followed her Führer ecstatically. Until the very end she was to serve him slavishly, with greater exertions than any people has ever furnished any leader.'[26]

France's history between 1940 and 1945 was for de Gaulle only part of an eternal cycle, endlessly repeated, of 'summits' and 'abysses', glories and defeats. The first sentences of the *War Memoirs* (1954), which describe how 'Providence created her [France] for complete successes or exemplary misfortunes', take up exactly where *France and her Army* (1938) had left off: 'Poor people, which from century to century carries without flinching ... the heaviest burden of woes, made to be an example ...'; and the last sentence of the *War Memoirs* (1959) shows that the struggle goes on: 'Poor France, weighed down by History, bruised by wars and revolutions, coming and going ceaselessly from grandeur to decline.'[27]

If this vision of France forms the overarching architecture to the work, each volume has its particular thread. The theme of the first volume, which covers the period up to 1942, is the emergence of 'de Gaulle' as a legendary historical actor who becomes the instrument of a history transcending his

own person. It is de Gaulle's role to 'assume' France. The title of the first
volume, *The Call*, has a double meaning: de Gaulle's 'call' to the nation in
his speech of 18 June and de Gaulle's answer to a 'call coming from the
depths of history'.[28] The third-person 'de Gaulle' who appears for the first
time at Duala in October 1940 is present fifty times in the first volume, a
hundred in the second. De Gaulle did not, like Caesar in his history of the
Gallic Wars or Trotsky in his history of the Russian Revolution, write
entirely in the third person. There is a first-person narrator – '*le pauvre moi*'
as he sometimes puts it – observing the historical 'de Gaulle'. On one occasion he describes watching 'those who did not join me but whose gaze
followed General de Gaulle'.[29] As he wrote to the Colonel who had been
his commanding officer in 1916: '18 June is an affair in which I watch
myself as all others do, for it is France that did everything.'[30] The last lines
of the first volume, although ostensibly referring to the end of 1941, are a
reminder to the readers of 1954 that de Gaulle is still there:

> Looking into the chasm into which the fatherland has fallen, I am its son,
> who calls it, shows it the light, shows it the road of salvation. Many have
> already joined me. Others will come, I know it. Now I hear France answer-
> ing me. From the depths of the abyss, she raises herself, she marches on, she
> climbs the slope. Ah! Mother, such as we are, we are here to serve you.[31]

The theme of the second volume, *Unity* (1942–4), is how the shattered
unity of France is gradually reconstructed around the legendary 'de Gaulle'.
In telling this story, de Gaulle gives remarkably little place to the internal
French Resistance and much more to every feat of French arms from the
first engagements of the Free French in the Libyan desert to the role of the
French armies in Italy and Germany in 1944–5. Leclerc is mentioned on
sixty-seven pages, and even Juin, who had remained loyal to Vichy until
the end of 1942, appears on forty-one, while leading resisters like Frenay
and d'Astier merit only ten mentions each. One reviewer observed, with
permissible exaggeration, that there was more about the various Free
French committees scattered around the world than there was about the
entire Resistance. This second volume culminates in the apotheosis of de
Gaulle's triumphal walk down the Champs-Elysées:

> One of these miracles of national consciousness, one of these gestures of
> France, which sometimes, over the course of the centuries, comes to illuminate
> our history. In this community, with one thought, one élan, one cry, differences
> are effaced, individuals disappear ... Ah how you resemble each other![32]

The third volume, *Salvation* (1944–6), covers the period between the Liberation of Paris and de Gaulle's resignation. Despite the upbeat title, the

tone of this volume is sombre. It describes how, thanks to de Gaulle, the French found themselves among the victorious nations in May 1945 – but also dwells increasingly on the failure of the 'parties' to ascend the 'summits' of 'grandeur' to which de Gaulle invited the people of France. One constantly repeated theme of this volume is how that 'communion', the 'shared emotion', the 'frisson of unanimity' characterizing de Gaulle's encounters with the French is increasingly poisoned by the 'academies', 'elites', 'assemblies' and 'parties' who interpose themselves between the Saviour-Guide and his People. This sense of disillusion culminates in de Gaulle's resignation in 1946. The theme of this volume is one of salvation offered but snatched away as the nation slips back into a new cycle of decadence. By the time this third volume appeared in 1959 – and before the last pages were written – de Gaulle had returned to power. When he ends with himself as an 'old man, never weary of watching out in the shadows for the glimmer of hope', the reader already knows the good news that the 'old man' has been 'called' again.[33]

The moral of this redemptive drama of fall and salvation, with de Gaulle as both prophet and saviour, was that France required a strong state to counter the 'ferments of dispersion' mentioned on the first page. The tension between unity and fragmentation, order and disintegration, summits and abysses, grandeur and decadence, is a leitmotiv of the book. Even when France seems most united, the danger of fragmentation is never far away. In the long passage describing de Gaulle's triumphal descent down the Champs-Elysées in August 1944, a paragraph is devoted to the monuments on which he gazed and the glorious memories these evoked: Joan of Arc, St Louis, Henry IV. He writes: 'The History condensed in these stones and these squares seemed to smile on us.' But the following paragraph evokes sadder and more tragic memories inspired by the same monuments: the revolt of the barricades, the massacres of St Bartholomew in 1572, the Fronde, the execution of Louis XVI.

Since de Gaulle's *Memoirs* were intended to have an exemplary value, they eliminate the anecdotal apart from a few memorable setpieces like the meeting with Stalin in December 1944. De Gaulle's family is hardly mentioned. This led Malraux to remark famously that there is no 'Charles' in the *Memoirs*. This may be superficially true, but on the other hand the sensibility of the narrator 'I' ('Charles') saturates the entire work from the first three pages where he describes his 'enthusiasm', 'sadness', 'joy', 'despair', 'anxious pride' in the varying fortunes of France.[34] It is in the literary sensibility of the *Memoirs* that the mark of Chateaubriand is most evident. If de Gaulle started to re-read Chateaubriand when embarking on his *Memoirs*, it was because, as he wrote in 1949 to the Comtesse de Durfort,

Chateaubriand's great-grand-niece, the work of her illustrious ancestor had 'haunted me for forty-eight' years – which would mean that de Gaulle first read him when he was eleven.[35] He remarked to Claude Guy of Chateaubriand: 'I feel things as he does.'[36]

It is easy to see why de Gaulle so identified with Chateaubriand, who had like him been born into a legitimist family and had adapted to the modern world, describing himself as 'between two centuries as at the confluence of two rivers'. As a young man, Chateaubriand had been presented at the court of Louis XVI and he had died during the Revolution of 1848. De Gaulle commented: 'To have as an adolescent been present at the Estates of Brittany [in 1789] and in the evening of one's life to have meditated on the future of Communism in Europe, what a destiny!'[37] One theme of Chateaubriand's writing, after he abandoned political activity in 1830, was how to reconcile his aristocratic values, and commitment to the legitimist monarchy, with the world created by the French Revolution: 'In my interior and theoretical existence, I am the man of dreams; in my external and practical existence I am the man of realities.' 'What', de Gaulle once wrote, 'have I tried to do except to lead the French by dreams?' As a man of action who half yearned to be a writer, he was in some sense the mirror image of Chateaubriand, a writer who dreamt of being a man of action. What de Gaulle responded to above all in Chateaubriand was what he called his 'despairing lucidity'. He said to Claude Mauriac: 'He is a man in despair . . . but his despair is full of . . . [he starts again] even in his despair he confronts it . . . In his despair he straightens himself up to his full height.'[38] At the end of the third volume, de Gaulle describes himself in his retreat at Colombey in language reminiscent of Chateaubriand: 'Looking up at the stars, I allow myself to be penetrated by the insignificance of things.'[39]

The comparison must not be overplayed. If Chateaubriand retired to his estates in 1830 to devote himself to his memoirs, de Gaulle conceived *his* memoirs not as a political testament but as a new form of action after the failure of the RPF. François Mauriac had rightly predicted that the RPF would tarnish the legend of 18 June. Through his *Memoirs* de Gaulle sought to distance himself from the failure of the RPF and recapture the purity of his role as Saviour. Just before the first volume was published, at the end of October 1954, he wrote to his son: 'We will see what this gives. I mean of course what effect it has on opinion.'[40]

For a man who had allegedly renounced the world, de Gaulle was assiduous in ensuring that his *Memoirs* received the maximum publicity. He interviewed three possible publishers – Gallimard, Laffont and Plon – and ended up selecting Plon. This was a safe choice. Plon was the most venerable and respectable, and since the late nineteenth century it had carved out a reputation for publishing the books of French *académiciens* and marshals – including those of Pétain. In 1948 it had also secured the translation of Churchill's war memoirs. De Gaulle's royalties went to the Fondation Anne de Gaulle which he and his wife had set up after the war. Extracts were published in *Paris Match* in October 1954, which devoted the whole issue to this 'historic event' with de Gaulle on the cover. De Gaulle even allowed photographers into the house. The accompanying article adopted a suitably Gaullist tone (right down to the metaphor of storms beloved by de Gaulle): 'He knows that the lightning of events might bring the pilot back to the helm. So he keeps vigil. This temporal priest of the fatherland waits for the annunciation that will arrive.'[41]

The first four copies were dedicated by de Gaulle in person to the Pope, the royalist pretender the Comte de Paris, the President of the French Republic and Queen Elizabeth II of Great Britain. 'All de Gaulle is contained in that logical order,' noted Louis Terrenoire.[42] The success of the *Memoirs* exceeded any expectations. The first volume was an instant bestseller with 100,000 copies sold in a month. The critical reception was dithyrambic. Mauriac wrote: 'Like Caesar, like Napoleon, de Gaulle has a style that corresponds to his destiny.' He was compared variously to Bossuet, Tacitus and Corneille. Only the Communist newspaper *L'Humanité* ignored the publication. The sole carping note was sounded by embittered anti-Gaullist conservatives nostalgic for Vichy. General Weygand, whose rancour against de Gaulle had not diminished with age, produced a book detailing alleged inaccuracies about the events of 1940.[43] The reception of the second volume two years later in 1956 – on 18 June – was no less enthusiastic, apart from some former resisters resentful about the degree to which de Gaulle had downplayed their role. In a critical review, Frenay wrote: 'Our refusal of a pure and simple subordination to him ... was in his eyes a felony.'[44]

GLOBETROTTER

De Gaulle's other main activity from 1953 was a series of foreign tours around the French Empire. In March 1953 he was in West and Equatorial Africa for twenty-five days, in October 1954 in East Africa (Djibouti, Madagascar) and the Indian Ocean (Réunion). In July and August 1955 he flew to the Caribbean from where, after visiting the French islands, he took a long boat trip to the Pacific (Tahiti, the New Hebrides, New Caledonia). Finally, in March 1957, he made an eight-day tour of the Sahara. Like the writing of his *Memoirs*, this was a return to the past – in this case the African and Pacific origins of the Free French. He wanted to bathe again in the atmosphere of the Free French and purge himself of the memory of the RPF. It must have been a tonic to receive the adulation of the crowds in the Empire – recalling that first *bain de foule* of Duala in 1940 – when at home the French seemed to have turned their backs on him. In parts of Gabon and Congo there had even developed after 1945 a kind of sect who practised a syncretic cult, 'Ngol', inspired by the name of de Gaulle.

In his visits to Africa de Gaulle was also subliminally reminding the world of another strand of the de Gaulle myth built around the ambiguous Brazzaville declaration of 1944. Another purpose of his trips was to inform himself about the situation in the Empire. He planned his itineraries carefully. When one aide expressed surprise that while in Chad de Gaulle should want to visit Abache in the far north-east of the country, hundreds of kilometres from the capital Fort Lamy, the General replied that he was interested in this area because it was in the forefront of the Islamic penetration of Africa. As he told Terrenoire on his return from one trip, 'I did not go to see nature but to see humanity.'[45] The only journalist to accompany him on the Pacific voyage, Jean Mauriac, younger son of François, discovered this to his cost when one night he excitedly tried to get de Gaulle on deck to see a spectacular full moon. 'To hell with your full moon' was de Gaulle's response.[46] Yvonne de Gaulle had no better luck during a plane journey over Africa when she grabbed her husband's sleeve to point out a herd of elephants below them. De Gaulle looked up irritated for a minute, muttered gently, 'Leave me be, Yvonne,' and plunged back into his reading of Conrad's *Lord Jim*.[47] De Gaulle was not a natural tourist.

Between stops on the long Pacific sea trip, de Gaulle spent hours reading Balzac, Flaubert and Mauriac. He would hold court every evening at dinner, often reminiscing about the war. His extraordinary physical constitution was much in evidence. He seemed indifferent to heat or rain, he seemed never to sweat, and on the long night journeys on the plane everyone wondered when – if ever – he slept. De Gaulle was accompanied by only a few aides, who handled the complicated issues of protocol. He was travelling as a private citizen but of course he was not a private citizen like any other. Technically he could not be accorded the honours of a head of state, but ingenious ways were found to circumvent these difficulties and treat him with the respect due to the man who had once been 'France'. The fact that the government was ready to turn a blind eye to these irregularities was perhaps a bad sign for de Gaulle. It was evidence that he was a figure from the past who no longer frightened France's politicians.

THE 'DESERT'

With de Gaulle in 'retirement', the Gaullists dispersed. Pompidou joined the Rothschild bank; Malraux returned to writing his interminable book on the history of art; Palewski became Ambassador to Rome. Since there was no longer any official movement linked to de Gaulle, Gaullism fragmented into a diaspora of networks and groups, each working in its own way for the cause. Some Gaullist *députés* – now calling themselves Social Republicans – accepted posts in government.[48] They were viewed with suspicion by rank-and-file RPF activists who tried to keep the flame burning. One of these, Jacques Dauer, a Paris-based printer, founded a newspaper *Télegramme de Paris* devoted to bringing de Gaulle back to power, and held himself in reserve to organize pro-de Gaulle poster campaigns if the day should come. Free French veteran associations offered another form of Gaullist sociability, as did being a Companion of the Liberation. Many Companions held important posts throughout French society and politics. With the end of the RPF, there were no longer 'Gaullists' anywhere, but 'gaullists' were everywhere, poised to serve when the time came.

Some members of this gaullist diaspora operated with de Gaulle's discreet encouragement; others desperately sought signals from him as to what they should do. In this period, the two key figures of the inner circle – the 'entourage' as it was known – were Olivier Guichard and Jacques Foccart. Guichard (b. 1920) had taken over from Pompidou as de Gaulle's *directeur de cabinet* in 1951. Descended from a baron of the Napoleonic Empire, Guichard came from a conservative bourgeois family that had supported Vichy at the beginning. His father was indeed a close aide to Darlan. He joined the Resistance in 1943 when he was twenty-three. 'Not really Gaullist' in his own words at the Liberation, the RPF met his ideal of a movement transcending boundaries between left and right. Then came his first meeting with de Gaulle. He wrote later that he had been born three times: first in 1920, a second time in 1940 at the moment of defeat, and finally in 1947: 'Having discovered the source of a new life in my encounter with the General. Three births, two fathers.'[49] Starting out as a regional organizer for the RPF, he came to the attention of Pompidou who recruited him as his successor.

The other key Gaullist aide in this period, Jacques Foccart (b. 1913), had run an import-export business before 1940. During the Occupation he joined a Resistance network attached to the BCRA. After the Liberation, he was flown to Britain to train as a parachutist for a mission into Germany, but the war ended first. The Resistance was the formative experience of Foccart's life. He retained a passion for parachuting which he continued to practise well into his fifties. He remained in touch with many former members of his Resistance network, some of whom had entered the French secret services. Foccart was a fixer, a man of contacts and undercover networks. He joined the RPF at the beginning and first met de Gaulle in December 1946. Because his business activities gave him contacts in Africa and the French Empire, he was put in charge of organizing the overseas section of the RPF, especially Africa. Although de Gaulle terminated his association with the RPF in 1954, the organization was never formally dissolved, and Foccart became its Secretary General after Terrenoire. His role was to keep up the spirits of the former local activists in case they should be needed again. Foccart differed from other members of de Gaulle's immediate entourage in that he was neither an intellectual – he had never even obtained his baccalaureate – nor a public servant. But what both he and Guichard offered was unquestioning devotion, a lack of personal ambition and a capacity to read de Gaulle's shifting moods and interpret his wishes.[50]

On the margins of this inner circle was Michel Debré, who had become closer to de Gaulle than in the early days of the RPF. Although he was an elected Gaullist senator – which did not endear him to de Gaulle – he refused to participate in any Fourth Republic government – which did. But it was Debré's opposition to the EDC which created a new bond with de Gaulle. He opposed the plan with extraordinary violence, comparing Monnet's proposal for a European army to Laval's collaboration with Germany. Otherwise de Gaulle kept his distance from Gaullists who had been elected to parliament, especially if they held ministerial office. De Gaulle had nothing to offer those Gaullists who wanted guidance whether they should stand in the elections of 1956. When Terrenoire tried to get a ruling, he was told that Jacques Vendroux had asked the same question and been told that de Gaulle would not dissuade him – but that he would refuse to see anyone who was elected. This at least had the virtue of being more explicit than his message to Koenig the year before.

In Gaullist mythology this period is called the 'desert', although it is not known who invented this term with its biblical resonances. De Gaulle's refuge in the 'desert' was Colombey. His routine followed an almost immutable ritual. Never an early riser, he would come down from his room at about 10.00 after reading the Paris newspapers. Then he would embark on the first of his many walks round the grounds of La Boisserie. From 10.30 to 12.00 he would work in his study with its plunging views over the surrounding forest. At 12.00 he would install himself at the bridge table in the library, listening to the radio news while playing endless games of patience. On a sheet of paper he kept a meticulous statistical tally of the number of times he won or lost. Lunch, at 12.30, was followed by coffee in the library. Then after another long walk, often in the surrounding forests of Dhuits or Clairvaux, de Gaulle would return to his study at 3 p.m. and remain there until 7.00 p.m. after which he rounded off the day with another long walk around the grounds before dinner at 8.00 p.m. (Whether or not he kept as careful a tally of his tours round the garden as he did of his games of patience, his claim in his *Memoirs* that he had made 15,000 circuits of the grounds of La Boisserie seems entirely plausible.) On Sundays he and his wife would attend Mass in the tiny church of Colombey, arriving about five minutes before the service. If there was reason to anticipate crowds, they often decided at the last moment to go instead to one of the other churches in the area: Rizaucourt, Juzencourt, Argentolles.[51]

There were few visitors to Colombey in this period. The de Gaulles were mainly alone except for the cook and housekeeper, who were very much part of the household.[52] One of their housekeepers after the war, Augustine Bastide, could be sharp-tongued with her famous employer. De Gaulle recounted with amusement an exchange he had had with her one day in 1946. Bumping into her in the hallway, he declared dramatically: 'Ah my poor Augustine! Politics, what a terrible business!' Her reply was: 'Bah! Politics! Don't give me that. You could not do without it!' 'So you think I am getting some personal advantage from it?' 'If you didn't get something from it you would have given it up a long time ago.'[53]

Claude Guy, to whom the General told this story, left de Gaulle's employment in 1949 after a painful incident. It came to de Gaulle's attention that Guy had once casually remarked in a moment of bitterness that he had often had to dip into his own pocket during his period serving the General without ever asking for extra remuneration. When de Gaulle heard of this complaint made behind his back, Guy was sacked after being told he should first claim for any unpaid expenses. In matters regarding loyalty to his person, de Gaulle was always implacable. In this case he softened the blow by writing to Guy that 'you have reached an age and you have a personality which excludes this extreme dependence.'[54] Yvonne de Gaulle was certainly pleased with the removal of an aide whom she blamed for encouraging de Gaulle's political ambitions. Guy, whose devotion to de Gaulle was filial and almost religious in its intensity, lived in the shadow of this estrangement for the rest of his life.

Of his life at Colombey in these years de Gaulle wrote in his last volume of *Memoirs*: 'I was, at that time, completely retired, living at La Boisserie whose door was open only to my family or to people from the village, and going only from time to time to Paris where I only agreed to see very occasional visitors.'⁵⁵ This needs to be taken with a pinch of salt. For a hermit, de Gaulle managed to see a lot of people. He usually visited Paris every Wednesday, giving 'audiences' at the RPF headquarters in the Rue de Solférino. He would leave Colombey at 7 a.m. and the meetings started at 11.00. After a night at the Hôtel La Pérouse, he would have another day of meetings before returning to Colombey in the late afternoon.

It was Guichard's role to organize de Gaulle's 'audiences' in this period. In 1955 and 1956, when the General's political stock was at its lowest, Guichard struggled to fill the diary.⁵⁶ Rue de Solférino was not the hive of activity it had once been. To one visitor it seemed like the 'waiting room of a dentist with a poor and Gaullist clientele'; to another 'the waiting room of a doctor's surgery in a spa town out of season'.⁵⁷ Even so de Gaulle's appointment diaries show that he managed officially to see at least 550 people in this period at the Rue de Solférino – many of them several times – and there were other more discreet evening meetings at the Hôtel La Pérouse.⁵⁸ He received diplomats, civil servants, ambassadors, intellectuals, foreign and French journalists, as well as some of the faithful who had gone their own way but remained available for future service. These included Geoffroy de Courcel (thirteen audiences) and Pompidou (twenty). Soustelle, however, was seen only twice in 1956, and three times in 1957. These audiences were partly de Gaulle's way of keeping in touch. Up to 1951, he knew personally most ministers in Fourth Republic governments, who had invariably served in his post-war government or emerged out of the Resistance or Free French. From 1952, there was a changing of the guard.

De Gaulle could be an excellent listener, but his audiences were also a performance. They allowed him to float ideas, distil confidences and keep his name in people's minds. He would be by turns gnomic, provocative, teasing, apocalyptic, self-deprecating. His interlocutors would emerge perplexed or seduced, impressed or depressed. As one visitor reported: 'He does listen ... or seems to listen ... From time to time he growls what seems like approval which encourages you to go on and then, when you are flailing around, he suddenly destabilizes you with a disillusioned reflection; sometimes he goes off at length with his memories.'⁵⁹ Jean-Marie Domenach, a former Catholic resister, and editor of the influential left-of-centre Catholic periodical Esprit, had his first ever meeting with de Gaulle in July 1955: 'Never was I more intimidated. I tried to tell him this, and I was wrong. The idol does not give a flicker of reaction when one praises him.' Domenach attempted another tack and asked de Gaulle why he had left politics: '"I have tried to save France three times ... I do not want to become importunate." I found I was addressing a statue. But he was funny, almost a clown at times.' After a long disquisition on history and politics, de Gaulle ended the conversation with a melancholy comment from Barrès about the futility of human existence.[60] The historian and journalist Robert Aron, who had just published a relatively indulgent history of Vichy, was received one day in 1955. De Gaulle's opening shot was: 'Monsieur, I have read the book you neglected to send me.' His second was: 'Your book is very objective but so much so that it sometime ends up not being objective.' The conversation moved on to politics. Aron, who had been a leading member of the generation of 'nonconformists' in the 1930s, hoped de Gaulle might agree with him that France's problems went back to the failure to reform French politics in the 1930s. This had no more success than any of his conversational gambits. De Gaulle responded that the problems went back to the sixteenth century if not before.[61]

De Gaulle's mixture of melancholy and hubris was never more evident than in an extraordinary conversation in August 1956 with Hervé Alphand, who was about to leave for Washington where he had been appointed French Ambassador, while de Gaulle was about to leave on his Pacific tour. The fact that Alphand supported the process of European integration in the 1950s and was close to Jean Monnet did not endear him to de Gaulle, but on the other hand he had been an important figure in the Free French and de Gaulle was presumably flattered that he still counted enough for this senior diplomat to wish to pay his respects and seek advice before taking up his new posting. The two men had not met since 1951 and Alphand was struck by the changes and the similarities he detected in de Gaulle:

> Dressed entirely in black like a Spanish King. He now wears huge thick glasses. His voice is curiously altered and no longer has the strength and depth it had before; it is almost the voice of an old man; he sounds slightly more feeble whatever the force of the words and the ideas. His scepticism has reached the most gigantic proportions. I find myself facing a man who has given up the struggle, disgusted not only by the institutions that he has not ceased to condemn, and the 'foreigners' who want to do us harm, but also by the French in general who have not responded to what he expected of them.

Their conversation opened against the background of the crisis that had broken out a few days earlier when President Nasser of Egypt suddenly nationalized the Suez Canal. Alphand referred to the seriousness of the situation as they were both about to leave Europe:

> Serious! Serious! Don't make me laugh. All decided. It is over (huge operatic laugh). The English will accept a compromise which will allow them to save

face in the Suez affair . . . The Americans will not act and you will see that once again it is us the French who will carry the cost of the operation . . . In this situation if one does not act in 48 hours all is lost. But, what can one do, de Gaulle was not there.[62]

This led to some comments by both men on how they had been disappointed by the reactions of the French people after 1945. Then de Gaulle checked himself:

> But I do not despair of France. You probably remember a 'chap' [type] called Clovis. Well when he arrived the outfit [baraque] had to be defended against everyone. We were at rock bottom. But Clovis began to take us back up again. He beat the Barbarians at Tolbiac, and two hundred years later that permitted France to be great again and to have Charlemagne. Perhaps in two hundred years it will be judged that we started to climb up again thanks to de Gaulle.

When the Franco-British response to the Suez crisis did indeed end in failure, de Gaulle took the opportunity, while talking to another visitor, to direct some barbs against the British and the French Socialist politicians who had launched the operation: 'You need to be a Socialist to believe in the military virtues of the English. Yes, of course there was Waterloo, but they were dealing with a Napoleon who was exhausted and had been running around Europe for fifteen years.'[63]

Nowhere was de Gaulle more playfully elusive than in his intermittent meetings with the pretender to the French throne, the Comte de Paris, who credulously recorded each encounter for posterity. The two men first met privately in 1954. De Gaulle talked as if they were both exiles from their own kingdom: 'If France is to die, it is the Republic that will finish it off . . . If France is to live, then the monarchy will have a role . . . In adapting it, and giving it a meaning, it can be useful.' He followed this up with a message to the Comte saying that 'he must count on me in everything, and for everything.' At another meeting a year later, de Gaulle 'seized the occasion to tell me that he was monarchist'; as he was about to leave he remarked that 'great men are made by their abilities and by events.' Moments later, he stopped his car and returned to correct himself: 'By great men I mean to say great princes; you are eternal: I am just a man who passes.'[64] De Gaulle also had three audiences with Prince Napoleon, great-grandson of Jérôme Bonaparte, but we have no record of what was said.

Did de Gaulle still believe that he might return to power? As always, his mood fluctuated violently; his conversation is no guide to what he was really thinking. He was increasingly haunted by the fear that time was running out. Visitors in the mid-1950s noticed that he had aged markedly. In the first volume of his *Memoirs*, he had written his memorable portrait of Pétain, destroyed by 'the shipwreck of old age'. When Pétain took power in 1940, he was eighty-four years old, and de Gaulle when he wrote those words was still only in his sixties. But he had often said of Pétain that he had 'died' in 1925 – at the age of sixty-nine. De Gaulle dwelt frequently on the ravages of old age. In a conversation in 1948 he lamented: 'Old age is an even greater drama than death! . . . The loss of memory: in everything that is forgotten on earth there is a little bit of death. Death continuously irrigates life . . . That is only fair since life continuously irrigates death.'[65] In 1953 de Gaulle wrote in the notebook where he scribbled down occasional thoughts: 'I am sixty-three years old. From now everything that happens to me occurs in relation to my death.'[66] A little before his sixty-fifth birthday, he told Bonneval: 'I am only too aware of the disadvantages of an old man governing France to want to play that role myself after a certain age.'[67]

De Gaulle's brother Xavier, only two years older than him, had died in 1955. On the whole de Gaulle's own health and physical resilience remained remarkable. In 1947, he stopped smoking after a doctor warned him that it had inflamed his throat with a risk of cancer. Since he had been almost a chain-smoker, it was painful to stop. He told Claude Guy: 'I will begin again only if there is a war.' Even so he was convinced he would die of cancer. Predictably, after he gave up smoking he started to put on weight, making him seem more like a benevolent paterfamilias than the angry soldier of the 1940s. His eyesight began to cause problems. In December 1952, he had a first cataract operation and a second one in March 1955. After the second he wrote to a niece that he was not sufficiently presentable to attend her wedding: 'I am an old man who is losing his sight.'[68] The operation was followed by an alarming post-operative reaction with dangerously high pulse and blood pressure. A doctor was summoned urgently in the middle of the night to the clinic where de Gaulle was recovering. De Gaulle told the doctor he was vomiting uncontrollably and was sure he was going to die.[69] This incident was kept entirely secret. Despite his two eye operations, de Gaulle was now extremely short-sighted. He needed to wear glasses in public which, out of vanity, he hated doing.

WAITING FOR CATASTROPHE

In his declaration of May 1953 'releasing' his parliamentarians, de Gaulle had said that the RPF would exist 'as a kind of moral force ready to play its role if the occasion presented itself – that occasion risks, alas, arriving in the form of a grave upheaval'.[70] De Gaulle added the 'alas' on the prompting of Pompidou, but he certainly needed a 'grave upheaval' if there were any chance of returning to power.[71] He was constantly on the lookout for 'ripples'. In March 1956 he wrote to his son: 'In Paris, the atmosphere is sombre. One has the feeling that things are germinating. But I fear this will only come to fruition on the occasion of a catastrophe (general revolt in Africa).'[72] For years de Gaulle had been predicting 'catastrophe', but from 1956 there were signs that Africa – specifically Algeria – might at last provide it.

In November 1954, a series of coordinated armed attacks took place throughout Algeria. Responsibility was claimed by an organization calling itself the National Liberation Front (FLN). Impatient with the moderate tactics of previous Algerian nationalist movements, the FLN had been formed a few days before Mendès France signed the accords that sealed France's defeat in Indo-China. Mendès France made it clear at once that Algeria was different from Indo-China: Algeria, he declared, is 'France'. His Interior Minister, François Mitterrand, said the same: 'Algeria is France and the only negotiation is war.' War it was to be. What made the case of Algeria so complicated was that administratively it was not a colony but part of France, as it had been ever since the French arrived there in 1830. In reality, however, the population of nine million Muslims did not enjoy equal rights with other French citizens. All attempts to introduce democratic reforms were subverted by the European population, popularly known as *pieds noirs*. The *pieds noirs* formed a sizeable minority – one million out of a total population of ten million – and many of them had lived in Algeria for generations. Feeling themselves to be in equal measure Algerian *and* French, they formed a powerful lobby in parliament.

Violence in Algeria escalated throughout 1955 without becoming full-scale war. Mendès France appointed Jacques Soustelle as Governor General in the hope that he would implement liberal reforms to defuse the crisis. When he arrived Soustelle was viewed with wary suspicion by the *pieds noirs*. But Soustelle's Algerian experience converted him into a passionate advocate of 'French Algeria'. He left a year later as a hero of the Europeans. Algeria became the new passion of Soustelle's life, psychologically filling the emotional void left by de Gaulle's increasing distance from him. He remained as committed to de Gaulle's return to power as ever, but for him the point of de Gaulle was now to save *Algérie française*. If he was ever faced with a choice between the two, it was not clear where his loyalties would lie.

By 1956 Algeria was becoming the central issue of French politics. Few people at this stage supported Algerian independence. Some advocated a liberal policy of reforms to win the Muslim population over; others feared that any concession to the FLN was a slippery slope to independence. Responses to the Algerian crisis cut across normal party lines and began to destabilize the political system. Most parties contained both liberals and diehard supporters of *Algérie française*. Parliamentary elections took place in France in January 1956, but no clear majority emerged. The Communists were the largest party but no one would consider allying with them. The second largest party were the Socialists, and their leader Guy Mollet became premier with the support of centrist parties. Mollet's plan for Algeria was summed up in the slogan: 'Ceasefire, elections, negotiations'. He decided to replace Soustelle with the venerable and experienced General Catroux, who had a reputation for being liberal. This alarmed the *pieds noirs*. When Mollet visited Algiers on 6 February 1956, hostile *pied noir* crowds pelted him with tomatoes. These demonstrators were not rich *colons* but ordinary poor Europeans hardly different from the electors of Mollet's Socialist Party in France. Mollet experienced a kind of epiphany, abandoned the idea of appointing Catroux and chose instead the Socialist Robert Lacoste with a mission to restore order in Algeria at any price.

The 6th of February 1956 was as much a turning point in the history of the Fourth Republic as 6 February 1934 in that of the Third Republic. On both occasions, the street had imposed its will on the government. The demonstration of 1956 encouraged radical *pied noir* activists to believe they could bend the government in Paris to their will. Mollet and Lacoste took the view that the war had to be won before any negotiations. When the French government enthusiastically sponsored the Suez operation with Britain against Egypt in October 1956, its motive was to cripple a regime that was helping the FLN. The French army in Algeria was given carte blanche to restore order by any means, and it began to act independently of the government in Paris. Army officers viewed Algeria as an opportunity to restore the honour lost at Dien Bien Phu. In October 1956, the army illegally grounded a Moroccan plane carrying a number of FLN leaders, all of whom were arrested. The government in Paris, which had not ordered this breach of international law, had no choice but to assume responsibility. In 1957, the army began systematically using torture to destroy the FLN. The tactic worked in the short term to weaken the FLN in the city of Algiers, but in France liberal opinion started to question the moral legitimacy of the policy. Algeria was seeping into every crevice of French politics.

Guy Mollet's government fell in May 1957. The next government, led by Maurice Bourgès-Maunoury, fell after only four months, and it took almost a month before another government was formed at the end of

October 1957, headed by a young centrist politician, Félix Gaillard. There was a growing sense of political crisis in France; talk of constitutional reform was in the air. It was also becoming harder for French governments to pretend that Algeria was a purely internal conflict as France found herself increasingly criticized at the United Nations. Gaillard, in his investiture speech, was the first politician to employ the words 'Algerian War'.

SPHINX

De Gaulle watched all this closely but refused to speak out. When Terrenoire suggested in October 1956 that he might say something, de Gaulle refused because his words could have no effect: 'But if the inhabitants of Algiers seized the Palais d'Eté [residence of the Governor] and refused to give in, that would be different.'[73] De Gaulle picked up on the simmering discontent in the army after the abandonment of the Suez operation.[74] It was the convergence of these two elements – pied noir anger and army discontent – that would eventually cause the fall of the Republic in 1958. But it was not obvious that this would serve de Gaulle's cause. Algeria had been strongly Giraudist in 1943 and the most radical pied noir activists had no love for the man who had introduced some moderate democratic reform in March 1944 in Algeria. Army attitudes to de Gaulle depended often on whether soldiers had been in the Free French or had remained loyal to Pétain and Giraud. Jacques Massu, the General in command of the paratroopers in the city of Algiers, was fervently devoted to de Gaulle; the overall army commander in Algeria, General Salan, was more reserved about him.[75]

At the start of 1956, de Gaulle had written gloomily to one of the former regional delegates of the RPF: 'I simply don't see how to get any hold on things.'[76] A year later, writing to the same correspondent, he was more optimistic: 'The coming year will be hard for France. But it seems to me that the French are beginning to join France again' – which in 'de Gaullespeak' meant that he sensed he was being noticed again.[77] An opinion poll of December 1955 showed that only 1 per cent of French voters viewed him as a possible head of government; and it was said that many young people believed, despite the success of his Memoirs, that he was dead. From this low point, his popularity rose gradually, if hardly dramatically, in opinions polls: 5 per cent of the population wanted him back in April 1956, then 9 per cent in July, 11 per cent in September. In June 1956, the left-wing periodical Express, which had been founded essentially to support Mendès France in 1954, made de Gaulle its man of the week.

De Gaulle's greatest strength was his silence. His *Memoirs* reminded the population, at two-year intervals, that they had a saviour in the wings; his silence allowed everyone to read the saviour as they wished. No one knew what he thought about the most pressing issue of the day: he was a blank sheet on to which the French could project their hopes and aspirations. This is how he intended it to be. 'If I have a plan,' he told Terrenoire, 'I will be careful not to let people know what it is.'[78] His only public intervention in the eighteen months between June 1955 and February 1958 was a communiqué stating that 'remarks sometimes attributed to General de Gaulle in the press commit only those who make them.'[79] It is not clear who was being rebuked by this mysterious communication, but its purpose was to allow de Gaulle to keep his hands entirely free. As he was to say in the press conference of May 1958 which brought him back to power: 'I am a man . . . who belongs to no one and to everyone.'

Anyone trying to persuade de Gaulle to break his vow of silence was told the same as General Juin in May 1956: 'For the moment silence is the most impressive attitude that I can take . . . If I speak out one day it will be to act.'[80] To various visitors, de Gaulle distilled gnomic confidences about his views of Algeria but gave little away. This was the experience of General Pâris de la Bollardière, a hero of the Free French and a Companion of the Liberation. Serving in Algeria from July 1956, he had asked to be relieved of his post rather than find himself complicit in torture. De Gaulle agreed to receive him at the Rue de Solférino:

> I felt the need, given what de Gaulle represented for me, to know his views on the human drama I had lived in Algeria. He received me at length with perfect courtesy. He said little and assured me that he did not hold my attitude against me. But whether out of discretion or indifference, he did not give any sense of how he situated himself personally in regard to the army's unacknowledged acceptance of torture.[81]

If de Gaulle himself refused to pronounce, he did not discourage the activities of the various members of the gaullist diaspora. In November 1957, Michel Debré founded a newspaper entitled *Le Courrier de la colère* whose theme was that the situation was as grave as that of 1788: France was on the verge of the abyss and would lose Algeria unless the regime was swept away and de Gaulle returned to power. Simultaneously another Gaullist, Jacques Chaban-Delmas, became Minister of Defence in the Gaillard government that Debré was denouncing every week in ever more violent terms. De Gaulle once remarked sardonically of Chaban-Delmas, who had held several other ministerial portfolios, that 'his period in the desert was marked by stops at many oases', but in fact these were extremely useful to him.[82]

Among RPF footsoldiers, Jacques Dauer joined up with former members of the Free French to launch a petition and a campaign of letters to the President of the Republic, René Coty, urging him to call de Gaulle to power. Coty was deluged by letters whose tone is revealing of the providential expectations that de Gaulle's name was capable of arousing. One read: 'If Joan of Arc came back to earth, she would say this to you: have pity on the kingdom of France, you must kick all the scoundrels out of parliament and call to power General de Gaulle, the only man capable of saving the country.'[83] Coty, who been elected to succeed Auriol at the start of 1953 after a protracted series of ballots, did not need these letters to be persuaded of the merits of de Gaulle. He was a self-effacing conservative politician with a strong sense of duty. In his first message to parliament after his election, he had gone out of his way to pay homage to the 'First resister' of France, to whom the 'Fatherland owes a recognition that no divergence of opinion could erase'. He dropped many hints that he believed de Gaulle's return to power to be desirable. In January 1956, he told Debré in private that 'I see my *raison d'être* as being to prepare the return of General de Gaulle.'[84]

Jacques Foccart, who had the thankless task during the years in the 'desert' of reassuring ex-RPF activists that all was not lost, was more genuinely upbeat at the start of 1958 than he had been for a long time. He wrote to one local organizer: 'As you notice in the press, people are again starting to talk a lot about the General.'[85] De Gaulle still refused to speak but he did not discourage those working on his behalf. In January 1958, he wrote to one correspondent: 'I do not despair of our country. I only doubt if, in the current context, any message would be able to reverse the course of events. If the ambience changes, then yes, it will be necessary to act. As for that ambience, let those who are in a position to do so start preparing it now.'[86] But there had been many other false dawns over the last twelve years.

In October 1957 de Gaulle and his wife had spent a holiday with Jacques Vendroux in Brittany. Holidays were rare because the private de Gaulle so hated being in the public gaze. Trips needed to be planned carefully to ensure complete anonymity. During this holiday they often picnicked by the road, as in the days of the RPF, to avoid being spotted in restaurants. One day looking out over the granite peak of the Roc'h Trevezel in the Finistère, de Gaulle, who adored such bleak landscapes, mused on how its solidity symbolized the eternity of France and contrasted this with the current state of French politics: 'Our country will not put up much longer with the weakness of those who are in charge of it. The will of the people will once again lead us out of the abyss ... Without doubt the Algerian drama will be the cause of the wake-up call [*sursaut*] for thousands of French people.' Whether or not he really believed this would happen – or when – we do not know. At Christmas the Vendrouxs and the de Gaulles were planning another holiday to another wild region of France – the Ardèche region in the Cevennes mountains.

Meanwhile the Algerian crisis did seem to be reaching a new stage. On 8 February 1958, French planes bombed the Tunisian village of Sakhiet, on the Algerian border. Seventy people were killed. Claiming that FLN fighters were hiding in the village, the French army had again presented Paris with a fait accompli. The bombing caused international outrage and the American government forced France to accept a 'good offices' mission headed by the diplomat Robert Murphy (who had backed Giraud in North Africa over de Gaulle in 1943) to broker a solution to the resulting Franco-Tunisian crisis. The Tunisian government withdrew its Ambassador from Paris. Before leaving, he asked to be received by de Gaulle at Colombey. Immediately afterwards, on 10 February, de Gaulle issued a short states-manlike but non-committal communiqué to announce that the meeting had taken place.[87] This was his first public intervention for two and a half years. Its purpose was to remind the world that he existed.

Meanwhile the holiday planning continued. In March 1958, Vendroux was at Colombey to finalize the details. The two families swotted up on guidebooks, and Vendroux was asked to start booking hotels anonymously. The trip was planned for ... May 1958.[88]

18

The 18 Brumaire of Charles de Gaulle, February–June 1958

De Gaulle's library at Colombey contains a novel, *Kaputt,* by the Italian writer Curzio Malaparte published in 1947. It does not however contain Malaparte's most famous book, published in French in 1931. At that time Malaparte, a disillusioned former supporter of Mussolini, was in exile in Paris. His book, *Technique of a Coup d'Etat,* examined the mechanics of a *coup d'état* by studying examples like those of Lenin and Mussolini, as well as Primo de Rivera's in Spain and Piłsudski's in Poland. As a counter-example, he took the failed Kapp Putsch in Germany in 1920. For Malaparte the exemplar of the modern coup was the '18 Brumaire' of 1799 when Napoleon seized power as First Consul.[1] He saw Brumaire as the perfect 'grafting of revolutionary violence on constitutional legality'. The absence of Malaparte's *Technique of a Coup d'Etat* from de Gaulle's library tells us nothing because his pre-war books were dispersed when the house was ransacked during the war. Given the book's celebrity it is unlikely he had not read it.

De Gaulle had certainly meditated on the precedent of 18 Brumaire. In the weeks after resigning in 1946, he often came back to that event: 'When Napoleon I carried out the coup of 18 Brumaire, it was because all France was pushing for it . . . I was dealing with a public opinion that was pushing in quite the opposite direction, which was collapsing under my feet.'[2] When he finally gave up the RPF in 1953, de Gaulle ruminated on the circumstances of his 1946 resignation in a speech to his regional delegates:

Other possibilities presented themselves to me, for example a *coup d'état.* That would have led to nothing except dictatorship. Dictatorship is a thing that the Romans invented and which, at certain moments in History, imposed itself in the name of public safety . . . But that was not the issue at the Liberation, the issue was about making the economy work again, things going back to what they were, feeding as many people as possible . . . Founding a dictatorship would have been pointless. The idea of public safety did not impose itself, which meant that establishing a dictatorship would have been artificial. Perhaps people would have put up with it for a time, although even that is not certain. It would not have been accepted internationally by the English, the Americans and especially by the Soviet Union.[3]

De Gaulle's objections to a coup were, then, entirely pragmatic. He had certainly been tempted to 'push' history in the right direction when he appeared at the Arc de Triomphe in May 1954. But he quickly realized he had misjudged the mood. As he wrote in the 1930s, the action of soldiers was never enough to change a regime unless 'general opinion has moved in favour of an overthrowing of the established order'.[4] In 1958, however, there was reason to believe such a moment was close.

Political instability was no novelty in the Fourth Republic, but the creeping sense of malaise had reached unprecedented levels. From the fateful day in February 1956 when the Socialist Premier Guy Mollet had reversed his Algerian policy after being pelted with tomatoes by angry *pieds noirs*, the poison of the Algerian crisis was beginning to infect the entire French body politic. Politicians in Paris had less and less control over the army in Algeria; the military were more and more suspicious that the politicians were ready to cut a deal with the Algerian nationalists. Politicians of the Resistance generation who had taken power after 1945 with such high hopes of moralizing French politics found themselves implementing and condoning methods of repression they had condemned during the Occupation. Claude Bourdet, one of the former leaders of the Combat movement, wrote a famous article in February 1955 denouncing the French 'Gestapo of Algeria'. François Mauriac, the conscience of liberal French Catholicism, was another vocal intellectual critic of torture in Algeria while Pierre Mendès France resigned from Mollet's government in May 1956 in protest against the repressive Algerian policy. After Mollet's government finally fell in June 1957 his successor, Maurice Bourgès-Maunoury, heading the eighteenth government in the ten years of the Republic, lasted only five months. His successor Gaillard had been in power for only three months when the Sakhiet crisis exploded. In the left-centre periodical *Esprit*, one writer at the end of 1957 described himself as feeling like an exile in his own country, comparing the situation to 1940: 'For the first time since 1940 everyone is asking under their breath the question: does France still exist?' That same issue of *Esprit* reviewed a flurry of books with titles like *Crisis of Regime* and *Crisis of the Nation*. The review ended, however, with the warning that the solution to the crisis should not be the 'pure and simple recourse to a Great Man'.[5]

DECODING THE GENERAL,
FEBRUARY–MARCH

Against the background of the Sakhiet crisis, de Gaulle pursued his weekly ritual of Paris visits. Over two months, he gave at least forty 'audiences'. One senses that he felt power was within his grasp. Receiving Louis Terrenoire on 3 March, he told him that he had almost finished his *Memoirs* and would soon be a 'free man'. Detecting a 'surge of Gaullism' in the country, he wondered if people fully understood that his return to power would not be just another government but 'a new universe'. He ended with a flurry of indignation against Murphy, and some remarks about the United States being a power in decline.[6]

De Gaulle's visitors the next day included Léon Delbecque, a Free France veteran who had become RPF regional organizer in the Nord. He was one of those gaullist activists who favoured direct and if necessary illegal action to bring the General back as head of state. Delbecque's business interests took him regularly to Algeria where he had served as a reserve officer. For this reason, when Jacques Chaban-Delmas became Minister of Defence in the Gaillard government, he appointed Delbecque as a semi-official representative in Algeria to keep him informed of developments while bypassing official channels. This was a good example of de Gaulle's interests being discreetly served by Gaullists in government even if he affected to disapprove of their collaboration with the 'system'.[7] Delbecque interpreted his Algerian brief with considerable latitude and began developing a network of *pied noir* activists and army officers poised to support de Gaulle.

Delbecque had never been in the inner circles of the RPF, but what he had to say on 4 March 1958 clearly sparked de Gaulle's interest. Normally each visitor was accorded strictly half an hour. Not on this occasion. As Delbecque later recalled: 'Three times Bonneval poked his head round the door, and three times, with a wave of his hand, the General conveyed to him that we were to be left alone.' Delbecque was there to persuade de Gaulle that, despite Algeria's Giraudist past, he had supporters there who were only waiting for a signal. Having opened the meeting in his most apocalyptically pessimistic vein, de Gaulle became increasingly intrigued by what Delbecque had to say. Delbecque sought assurances that de Gaulle was committed to *Algérie française*. De Gaulle replied gnomically: 'Come on, Delbecque, have you ever known de Gaulle to give up?' As Delbecque was leaving, de Gaulle said to him: 'Keep Foccart informed ... *Bon courage*. But be careful, be very careful. If you go too far, you risk ending up in the clink [*gnouf*].' Delbecque took this as if not a green light at least an amber one. Under the suspicious eyes of the authorities – and despite being in Algeria on behalf of a minister in the government – he started organizing a 'Vigilance Committee' poised to act on de Gaulle's behalf in the event of a crisis.[8]

De Gaulle was especially gnomic when on the next day he received Albert Camus, who was increasingly anguished by the situation in Algeria, torn between his own *pied noir* background and his liberal politics. The two men had never met before and Camus was left perplexed by de Gaulle's affectation of phlegmatic cynicism. If Camus's note of the encounter is to be believed, the General brushed off Camus's fears that the situation in Algeria might degenerate into a bloodbath by remarking: 'I am 67 and apart from myself I have never known Frenchmen kill other Frenchmen.'[9] Two weeks later, on 19 March, de Gaulle received General Petit, an aide to the Chief of the General Staff, General Ely. Petit was a key insider but also robustly loyal to de Gaulle. De Gaulle opened the interview with a characteristic gambit: 'In the choice between de Gaulle and giving up, France will always choose to give up.' Petit, unused to decoding de Gaulle's signals, seemed to take this too seriously: 'So you have given up the idea of coming back to power?' De Gaulle quickly corrected himself: 'I will come back if I am called or if there is a revolutionary situation.' Petit replied: 'That is easy to organize.' As soon as Petit had uttered these words, de Gaulle abruptly ended the meeting, leaving Petit worried if he had gone too far. To throw some light on the situation, on the next day Petit went to see Guichard who could only tell him that, although de Gaulle never revealed the content of his conversations, he had specifically commented, 'I am always pleased to see General Petit.' The perplexed General, looking for firm ground in these shifting sands, took this to mean that although de Gaulle had not given a green light – or even an amber one – he had not given a red one either.[10]

The next day, de Gaulle saw Raymond Triboulet, leader of the rump of Gaullist *députés* in parliament. Triboulet's information was that President Coty would approach de Gaulle to form a government if Gaillard failed to resolve the Sakhiet crisis. De Gaulle poured cold water on this notion: 'Do you see me being called to the Elysée, sounded out, subjected to a debate in the Assembly, and then failing to get a majority? Do you see de Gaulle playing this comedy?' When Triboulet sketched out a possible scenario de Gaulle answered with 'not a yes, but a "perhaps" or a "pah!" followed at once by a "but you will see, they won't make a step towards me"'. Triboulet interpreted this as a step in the right direction and relayed the information to Coty.[11]

The next visitor after Triboulet was Gladwyn Jebb, the British Ambassador. Jebb's only other meeting with de Gaulle since the Liberation had been in January 1957, when the General received him in his bedroom at the Hôtel La Pérouse. This time it was at the Rue de Solférino – 'if anything dingier', noted Jebb. De Gaulle, 'affable enough but considerably older and greyer that a year ago', was in elegiac mood and read out the passage from the last volume (not yet published) of his *War Memoirs* describing Churchill's electoral defeat in 1945:

> This led him to compare his own character and career with that of Sir Winston and to reflect on their respective destinies. The British leader had probably been wrong to wish to return to power ... He for his own part would, when the time came, prefer to abandon power of his own accord rather than be turned out by his political opponents.

But he did not expect to have the chance: 'I tell you, M. l'Ambassadeur, that all the chances are that before this regime collapses de Gaulle will be dead!' Just as Jebb was leaving, the General stood up and made a speech about the greatness of England, and 'his eyes filled with tears.' Jebb concluded:

> Either the General is a great actor, or his interests are more concerned with the past and future than the present. I did not discern any particular desire to return to power at the present time ... I continue to believe that, while he will not of course refuse power if it is offered, he will do little or nothing to achieve this end, still less will he take part in any conscious effort to overthrow the regime.

Jebb was certain of only one thing: 'the General is not like anyone else, either physically or psychologically.'[12] The General was indeed a great actor.

Back in Paris a week later (27 March), de Gaulle was blowing hot and cold to the Gaullist Alexandre Sanguinetti, spokesman of a group of war veterans: 'Parliament will never recall me before a final catastrophe ... This situation could go on for 30 or 40 years ... Yet there seem to be signs of a slight revival over the last two years ... If it is confirmed I will face my responsibilities.'[13]

PRESSURIZING THE GENERAL, APRIL–14 MAY

In March, Roger Barberot, a former soldier in the Free French, and Companion of the Liberation, took the initiative of writing to all other Companions, sounding them out on whether they might support a campaign calling for de Gaulle's return to power. Many respondents were enthusiastic, but one of them replied: 'The problem is that de Gaulle having been Joan of Arc has become Charles VII [the former Dauphin whom Joan of Arc helped make king]! It is now he who needs to be convinced that he should be crowned.'[14] How to convince him? The former RPF activist Jacques Dauer organized a poster campaign in support of de Gaulle. On one night in March, 175,000 pro-de Gaulle posters went up all over France.

In early April, Murphy's American 'good offices' mission delivered its report recommending that France make a number of concessions to the Tunisian government. The French government had recently negotiated a large loan from the American government, and there were rumours that future loans would depend on accepting the Murphy proposals. This caused outrage in the French parliament, toppling the short-lived Gaillard government. The international crisis sparked by the Sakhiet bombing had now become an internal French political crisis.

President Coty started the usual round of consultations to form the next government. The mood of the Europeans of Algiers was increasingly febrile. They feared that any new government might be ready to compromise on the future of French Algeria. Delbecque's Vigilance Committee prepared a pro-*Algérie française* demonstration for 26 April. The demonstration passed off peacefully, but the situation was beginning to worry Robert Lacoste, Governor of Algeria. He decided to expel Delbecque and send him back to France. Lacoste was himself a supporter of *Algérie française*, but he did not want to be accused of endorsing subversive activities or street violence. Back in Paris, Delbecque sought out someone to take his place. He alighted upon Lucien Neuwirth, another former RPF activist whose devotion to de Gaulle dated back to the Occupation. Before leaving for Algiers, Neuwirth went to see de Gaulle on 30 April. When de Gaulle asked what he was going to do in Algiers, Neuwirth replied: 'We will make an appeal to you.' De Gaulle answered: 'I will answer you.' Neuwirth saw this as a 'trigger' and excitedly reported the news to Delbecque.[15] Delbecque, who had become exasperated by de Gaulle's elusiveness, was not so sure. He wrote to him on 4 May that the success of the demonstration of 26 April showed that he did have support in Algeria: 'The proof is there that these men and women (God knows they have not always thought like you) are waiting for you with impatience.' De Gaulle annotated this letter 'interesting', while noting his doubts about the '"Gaullism" of Algiers'.[16]

On 5 May, General Ganeval, head of the military household of the Elysée, secretly contacted de Gaulle's aide de camp Bonneval to say that President Coty was going to sound out the MRP politician Pierre Pflimlin about forming a government. Coty did not expect that Pflimlin would be able to muster sufficient support in parliament. In that event he had resolved to call on de Gaulle to form a government and was ready to resign if parliament refused to accept this solution. What Coty wanted to know was whether de Gaulle would agree to visit the Elysée secretly to discuss the terms. This message seemed important enough for Guichard and Bonneval to trek to Colombey on 7 May and sound out de Gaulle's reaction. De Gaulle's oral answer, conveyed to the Elysée on 9 May, was that if invited to form a government according to the normal procedures, he would provide a formal response. His condition of acceptance would be a reform of the constitution and he would not agree to appear before parliament and present his government in the normal way.[17] Sensing that events were moving in his favour, de Gaulle felt he could dictate his terms. We do not know what Coty thought of this answer, and for the moment he continued to pursue the Pflimlin option.

Pflimlin started his round of consultations with party leaders. His chances of getting a parliamentary majority were slim since parliament was so divided on Algeria. Supporters of *Algérie française* viewed him as a 'liberal' who favoured negotiations with the FLN. The Governor, Lacoste, threw oil on the flames by declaring publicly that the army would not accept a 'diplomatic Dien Bien Phu'. Delbecque, who had been banned from Algiers a few days earlier, now flew back to work on Lacoste and the army. Lacoste, despite his provocative declaration, refused to be dragged into open defiance of Paris and announced that he was giving up his post and retiring to France. Delbecque had more luck with the army. He saw five senior generals including General Salan, the overall Commander in Chief in Algeria. This resulted in a telegram from Salan to Ely, the Chief of the General Staff in Paris, warning that the army would not tolerate an abandonment of Algeria. Delbecque also succeeded in winning over Alain de Sérigny, editor of the most influential Algiers newspaper. As a former Pétainist, Sérigny had no love for de Gaulle but he was now persuaded that only de Gaulle could save *Algérie française*. On 11 May, he published an editorial entitled 'Speak out General'. He also announced that another big demonstration would take place in Algiers at the city's main war memorial on 13 May, an idea concocted with Delbecque. The intention was ostensibly to pay homage to three French soldiers who had been killed by the FLN. It was also a warning to Pflimlin that the *pieds noirs* would not tolerate a government that could contemplate 'abandoning' Algeria. Still de Gaulle kept silent.

So many plots were brewing in Algiers that Delbecque began to worry that the situation might slip out of his control. The most radical *pied noir* activists did not trust de Gaulle and wanted to sweep away parliamentary democracy entirely. One of them, Robert Martel, believed that de Gaulle was really a Jew working for an international conspiracy masterminded by the Rothschilds.[18] Delbecque needed to channel the anger of the street away from these activists towards de Gaulle. The obvious candidate to do this was Soustelle, who was both a loyal Gaullist and idolized by the *pieds noirs*. Soustelle was torn between staying in Paris to vote in parliament against Pflimlin or heading to Algiers to stir things up. But he did not want to go to Algiers without a signal from de Gaulle. On 12 May, Guichard drove to Colombey for the second time in a week to get a ruling from de Gaulle. He found the General in a black mood, irritated that people were trying to force his hand. De Gaulle provided a grudgingly non-committal reply for Soustelle variously reported as 'I have nothing to say' or 'let him do what he wants'. Guichard took it upon himself to convey the least negative version of what the General had said. In this game of Chinese whispers, Soustelle allowed himself to believe that de Gaulle had given his benediction to his leaving for Algiers.[19]

Delbecque envisaged the 13 May demonstration as peaceful show of force: a shot across the bows of the French parliament and a way of increasing the pressure on de Gaulle to declare his hand. Crowds started to gather in Algiers during the afternoon as Pflimlin appeared before the National Assembly in Paris. In the late afternoon, a thousand or so demonstrators mounted the stairs leading from the war memorial up to the Forum where the Government House was located. A tiny group of radical *pieds noirs*, led by the student Pierre Lagaillarde (wearing his reserve paratrooper uniform), tore down the metal fences around Government House, broke into the building and started to sack the premises. Shortly afterwards General Massu arrived to get the measure of the situation. To appease the angry crowds assembled in the Forum, Massu appeared on the balcony to announce that he was setting up a Committee of Public Safety. Immediately afterwards, a telegram was sent to President Coty: 'Due to the seriousness of the situation and absolute necessity of maintaining order to avoid any bloodshed, we demand creation of a government of public safety in Paris, the only thing capable of retaining the whole of Algeria as an integral part of mainland France.'

At this point, Delbecque, who had been wrongfooted by these events, arrived on the scene and managed to have himself appointed vice-president of the Committee. This gave the Gaullists a foot in the door, and Delbecque now worked to win the Committee over to the idea of calling on de Gaulle. Another telegram was sent to Paris announcing that 'the military authorities believe in the imperative necessity of appealing to a national arbiter, in order to set up a government of public safety capable of reassuring Algerian opinion.'[20] Although de Gaulle's name was not explicitly mentioned, the identity of this arbiter was not in doubt. The news of these events reached Paris in the early hours of the morning while parliament was still debating whether to accord Pflimlin's government a vote of confidence. There was a surge of unity on the floor of parliament to defend democracy against this seeming insurrection. Pflimlin, who might well not otherwise have secured a majority, found himself confirmed as Prime Minister by a substantial margin, 280 votes to 126. Massu and Delbecque appeared on the balcony again to denounce this 'government of abandonment'.

In reality, the government in Paris had no control over events in Algiers even if Pflimlin's political position was further strengthened when the leader of the Socialist Party, Guy Mollet, joined his government to defend the Republic against the Algerian insurgency. Pflimlin tried to win time by granting General Salan, the army Commander in Chief in Algiers, emergency powers to deal with the situation. Thus the army commander who had not intervened to prevent the insurrection was appointed to represent the government against which it was directed. This was not as flawed a tactic as it seemed. Salan was no firebrand and had not yet shown his hand. By not sacking him, the government was gambling that he might remain loyal. On the morning of 15 May, Salan addressed the crowds from the balcony of the Government General in the Forum. He assured them that Algeria would remain French and ended with a rousing cry of '*Vive la France! Vive l'Algérie!*' After a short pause, he added the words: '*Vive le Général de Gaulle!*' It was Delbecque standing at his side who prompted him to utter these fateful words (though he did not have a pistol pointed at Salan's back as some accounts claimed). This did not yet mean that the inscrutable Salan had broken with the government or chosen de Gaulle. He was using de Gaulle's name both to sideline the *pied noir* radicals and to give himself a bargaining counter with the government. Salan's priorities were to preserve the unity of the army and to keep Algeria French.[21]

THE GENERAL SPEAKS, 15–27 MAY

On 14 May, de Gaulle was in Paris for his usual Wednesday meetings which included one with his publisher to discuss the final volume of his memoirs. Although Salan had not yet uttered the magic words, this must have been a slightly surreal meeting as the two men presumably avoided the only issue that was on everyone's mind. In the afternoon, de Gaulle met with his inner circle, including Foccart and Guichard – but still held back from breaking his silence. It seems that he had arrived from Colombey with a declaration in his pocket but decided not to use it yet.[22] The next day, a few hours after Salan had called out de Gaulle's name, de Gaulle finally broke his silence with a brief communiqué: 'In the past, our country from the bottom of its heart [*dans ses profondeurs*] showed its confidence in me to lead it to salvation. Today, in the face of the ordeals that are once again confronting us, I let it be known that I am ready to assume the powers of the Republic.'[23] Pflimlin remarked in private: 'It could have been worse.'[24]

The next day (Friday 16 May), Pflimlin asked parliament to grant him emergency powers to resolve the crisis in Algiers. These were granted by an even larger majority than he had obtained when forming his government. But the key event of the day was less the size of Pflimlin's majority than the intervention of Guy Mollet, who threw out three questions for de Gaulle: did he recognize the legality of the Pflimlin government? Would he condemn the events in Algeria? If called upon to form a government, would he respect the normal parliamentary procedures? That a member of the government, and leader of the Socialist Party, was ready publicly to envisage the possibility of de Gaulle's return to power was a remarkable development. Mollet's intervention was a double-edged sword: it could be read as an invitation to de Gaulle to establish his democratic and legalistic credentials or as a way of flushing out his insurrectionary ambitions.[25] On Saturday 17 May, de Gaulle announced that he would give a press conference on Monday 19 May.

Over the weekend of 17–18 May, the breach between Algiers and Paris widened. The government had forbidden Soustelle to leave Paris and his apartment was watched by the police. He managed to evade this surveillance by escaping concealed under a rug on the back seat of a car driven by the Gaullist Guillain de Bénouville. Having reached Brussels, Soustelle boarded a plane to Algiers where he arrived on the afternoon of 17 May. Salan was far from happy about this development, which threatened his delicate balancing act between the government, the insurgents and de Gaulle. He tried to keep Soustelle's arrival secret but it was immediately made public by Neuwirth and Delbecque.[26] Salan had no choice but to allow the darling of the *pieds noirs* to appear with him on the balcony of the Government General to shouts of '*Vive Algérie française, Vive de Gaulle*'. Salan's hand had been forced. From now on he too was playing the de Gaulle card. The next day (18 May), two officers, Major Robert Vitasse and Captain Jean-Marie Lamouliatte, set off from Algeria to France with a dual mission: to test whether the army on the mainland would be willing to take action to support de Gaulle and to sound out how de Gaulle would react to this.

At 3 p.m. on 19 May, de Gaulle gave his press conference in a large conference room at the Palais d'Orsay, packed with hundreds of journalists and photographers. The official French television network was not allowed to report the event, and the footage we can see of the event today was filmed by foreign television crews. Hundreds of police lined the streets outside; helicopters buzzed overhead. This was de Gaulle's first official public appearance for almost three years. People were struck by how much older he looked, and how much weight he had put on, but this also made him seem more reassuring. It was quickly clear that his mind was as sharp as ever, as was his sense of drama, repartee and showmanship. He opened with an explanation of why he had decided to break his silence: 'the extremely grave national crisis' might be 'the beginning of a kind of resurrection' offering him the chance to be 'useful' to his country again. He was studiously non-committal about the future of Algeria except to say that he was prisoner of no faction. Asked to answer Mollet's three questions, he launched into a piece of flattery of Mollet, remembering fondly how they had stood side by side in 1944 at the balcony of the town hall of Arras. In fact the two men had never met. De Gaulle was evasive about the means by which he might return to power except that it would have to be an 'exceptional procedure'. Asked to condemn the army, he sidestepped the question by pointing out that the government itself had given Salan full powers. He agreed that it was the normal role of the army to be an 'instrument of the State' but on condition 'that there is a state'. Asked whether he would be a threat to freedom, he parried by recalling that he was the man who had restored democracy in 1944. He ended: 'I have said what I have to say. Now I am going to return to my village and hold myself at the disposition of the country.' He left to applause.[27] Two members of the British Embassy staff who attended the press conference reported that, although de Gaulle's 'voice seemed rather feeble and he looked pale', he was in 'extremely good form and indeed master of the situation'. Their interpretation was that he did not seem to have associated himself with the rebels but that there was a danger they might try to install him by military means. As a result France 'might well be on the way to becoming a sort of South American Republic or at best a kind of Franco-Spain'.[28]

De Gaulle had already left for Colombey when Foccart had his first meeting with Captain Lamouliatte, one of the two military envoys who had arrived in France from Algiers. The other one, Vitasse, had flown to Toulouse to see General Miquel, the senior army figure in the south-west region of France where most parachute regiments were based and without whose support no military operation could have succeeded. Meanwhile, on the evening of 19 May, Lamouliatte met Foccart at the Rue de Solférino.

Before returning to Algiers, he was back at the Rue de Solférino again, this time accompanied by Vitasse.[29] These were only exploratory soundings, but the two army envoys came away reassured that de Gaulle had not ruled out calling on the army if all else failed. Vitasse, in the report he wrote a few weeks later, noted that there had been 'complete agreement' with de Gaulle's representatives at the Rue de Solférino.[30] Since the government knew about these meetings through wiretaps, the threat of military action weighed on the situation before any serious plans had yet been drawn up.[31]

Over the next week, de Gaulle remained silent at Colombey to allow the situation to mature. He did not come to Paris for his usual Wednesday meetings. Although his press conference had been impressive, it had not entirely worked in convincing the politicians that he could be trusted. He raised a laugh when he joked, 'do you think that at sixty-seven I am going to begin a career as a dictator?' – but many people remembered that Pétain had begun such a career at the age of eighty-four. The left was not reassured. The immediate result of the press conference was to increase the size of Pflimlin's parliamentary majority even further. Pierre Mendès France spoke in parliament of the sadness of those 'who will never forget 18 June 1940' when the same voice now 'provides the insurrection in Algiers with a respondent on the mainland'. With tears in his eyes he told a friend: 'This is a chapter of almost 20 years of my life that has come to an end ... De Gaulle remained de Gaulle. Now he has chosen the rebels against the Republic; it is finished.'[32] The government started preparing a constitutional reform bill to take some of the wind out of de Gaulle's sails. Pflimlin had few illusions about this, but continued to go through the motions of being Prime Minister despite having no control over events in Algeria.

Although staying put at Colombey, de Gaulle pursued his exercise of seduction by receiving visitors at his home. On 22 May, he was visited by Pinay, France's most respected conservative politician. Nothing concrete emerged, but Pinay came away charmed. He reported to Pflimlin the next day that de Gaulle was 'a real gentleman, a great Frenchman'. The next day's visitor (23 May) was Georges Boris, who had been among the first to rally to de Gaulle in 1940. As Mendès France's closest friend, Boris could have been an important convert. On his return to Paris, Boris noted their conversation in detail:

> Immediately the General took me into his study. Friendly and informal, his first words were: 'So Boris, you are not happy?' ... Throughout his manner was one of serenity: no sarcasm or irony on this occasion. He downplayed any implication in the events in Algeria: 'I can't prevent them shouting 'Vive de Gaulle.'

Boris was struck by the way that de Gaulle uttered Salan's name 'with a sort of contempt'. On the other hand, although he sensed a certain 'awkwardness' when Soustelle's name was mentioned, de Gaulle would not disavow him. The name of Mendès was mentioned: '"I understand he is emotional," said the General in substance, "but why is he attacking me in this way?" I protested that it was not an attack but the expression of a profound heartbreak that was felt by others, myself included.'[33]

Nothing said at this meeting was liable to change Mendès France's mind. But Mendès was a political loner without an important party behind him. The person whose support de Gaulle most needed was Mollet, leader of the largest party in parliament. De Gaulle knew through Guichard that Mollet was willing to meet him privately; he therefore had reason to believe that he was close to his goal. He wrote to his brother-in-law the next day (24 May) that 'things are now on course for the best.'[34] Another sign of his confidence was the presence of Georges Pompidou at Colombey for lunch the same day. Since the end of the RPF, Pompidou had kept out of politics. But he remained one of the people de Gaulle trusted most. Now he was instructed to start preparing a team for government and drafting documents for de Gaulle's legal return to power.[35]

At this moment, the situation took a dramatic turn. On 24 May, news arrived in Paris that yet another Committee of Public Safety had taken power in Corsica with the support of the army. The insurrection had now spread beyond Algeria. The original responsibility for the Corsican operation is difficult to establish, but Gaullist activists in Algiers certainly played a role. On 25 May the ubiquitous Delbecque arrived on the island. Up to a point, the Corsican events served de Gaulle's purposes by increasing the pressure on the government. But they also complicated his position by increasing the pressure on him to condemn the army which had moved another step down the road of sedition. Meanwhile in Algiers, army plans for a landing in France were reaching fruition. The operation was christened 'Resurrection' – following de Gaulle's use of the term in his press conference – and was provisionally fixed for 30 May. Ominously for the government, Committees of Public Safety were set up in several cities in south-west France.

Since de Gaulle had not condemned the events in Corsica, Mollet changed his mind about a secret meeting. Instead he wrote him a long letter which was halfway between a rupture and an appeal: 'Madmen have launched an attempt at a *pronunciamento* and up to this moment you have not disavowed them. France risks being the only country in Europe to experience a putsch; its authors claim to act in your name and you say nothing! I do not understand and I express to you my anguish.' Guichard carried the letter to de Gaulle in Colombey on the morning of 26 May. De Gaulle drafted an emollient reply suggesting that they should meet.[36] The same day, he also received a letter from Salan appealing to him to act before the army did.

All this incited de Gaulle, as he put it in his *Memoirs*, to 'accelerate the progress of good sense'. He sent Pflimlin a message suggesting a secret meeting. The two men agreed to meet secretly at midnight on 26 May in the Parc de Saint-Cloud outside Paris. It was here that Napoleon's coup of 18 Brumaire had taken place. De Gaulle chose the venue not for these associations but because it offered a discreet and neutral terrain, and because he knew the guardian of the park, who had been in the Resistance. Pflimlin slipped out of the Hôtel Matignon by a back door away from the gaze of journalists and was driven to Saint-Cloud Park in a private car. On the way, the car broke down. A policeman who appeared to help out did not even recognize the passenger as the Prime Minister – a fact that seems perfectly to symbolize the insignificance of the legal government of France. Pflimlin, who had never met de Gaulle before, was struck by his contempt for the Algiers putschists ('not very interesting people'). Even so, he refused to denounce the army publicly: if he did, how could he be sure that Pflimlin would then cede power to him? Pflimlin wrote later: 'This time I felt we were at the heart of the matter. He was observing me, weighing me up, mistrustful, a little disdainful, and doubtless coldly calculating.' Pflimlin replied that, if de Gaulle condemned the army, the government would resign and smooth his return to power. De Gaulle was not convinced: 'When one has power, it is generally because one wants to keep it.' The truth was that Pflimlin was desperate to divest himself of the non-existent power he was exercising but he wanted to respect proprieties.[37]

The meeting resolved nothing, but de Gaulle offered a way forward by suggesting a further secret meeting with the leaders of the main political parties. This was what Pflimlin believed had been agreed when he left de Gaulle at 2 a.m. He was therefore flabbergasted later that morning (27 May) to be handed a communiqué in which de Gaulle announced that he had 'started the regular process necessary for the establishment of a government'. This was de Gaulle's third public intervention since the beginning of the crisis.

Pflimlin decided not to contradict Gaulle's tendentious interpretation of their meeting, because he assumed the General had acted in this way to pre-empt an imminent move by the army. The last words of de Gaulle's communiqué, warning against 'all action, from whatever side, which threatens public order', seemed to suggest this. That morning, Vitasse was back at the Rue de Solférino to tell Guichard, Foccart, Debré and others that Operation Resurrection was ready to be launched. Assuming that de

Gaulle had been informed of this meeting – and one cannot be sure since he was back at Colombey – his decision to precipitate matters could be explained by the need to prevent an operation that was about to go ahead. Even if he had not been informed, he might have calculated that the government would assume that he had his reasons for precipitating events. Whether his communiqué was a bluff or a double bluff, it worked. In the early hours of the morning of 28 May, Pflimlin resigned.

But Pflimlin's resignation did not necessarily mean that de Gaulle had succeeded. A few hours earlier, the Socialist parliamentary group had voted almost unanimously 'in no circumstances' to accept de Gaulle's return to power. Without Socialist support, de Gaulle would not have been able to form a regular government.

ENDGAME, 28 MAY–2 JUNE

On the morning of 28 May, de Gaulle received General Dulac, an emissary of Salan. De Gaulle deployed all his arts of ambiguity. He opened with a typical gambit: 'They don't want de Gaulle, what are you going to do?' Dulac gave de Gaulle the details of Operation Resurrection. The conversation ended with de Gaulle saying: 'It would have been immensely preferable that my return to power take place by means of the regular process [processus] . . . It is necessary to save the show [sauver la baraque]! Tell General Salan that what he has done and what he will do is for the good of France.' This was characteristically gnomic but not a fully green light.[38]

In the afternoon, Guichard at the Rue de Solférino received yet another military envoy, this time from General Miquel in Toulouse. Guichard told him: 'There are some difficulties in the elaboration of the processus to permit the General's coming to power legally. But the General has the firm intention not to draw back [aller jusqu'au bout] and in the case of events going beyond the legal framework, he will take the situation as it presents itself.'[39] This was also gnomic but not so different from what de Gaulle had said to Dulac.

While keeping the army in play, de Gaulle wrote on the same day to the Socialist elder statesman and former President Vincent Auriol in an attempt to win over the Socialists. Auriol, who had once vowed he would not be Hindenburg to de Gaulle's Hitler, had now reached the conclusion that only de Gaulle stood between the Republic and a military putsch. He had written to him seeking reassurances, and de Gaulle now provided them. He told Auriol that he would 'consent to receive power from no other source than the people or its representatives'. If this proved not to be possible the consequences would be anarchy or civil war: 'As for me I could do no more, until my death, than remain in my sorrow.'[40] On the same afternoon, the parties of the left and trade unions demonstrated against de Gaulle in the Place de la République. The demonstrators included revered figures of the left like Mendès France and the Socialist André Philip, both of whom had been with de Gaulle during the war. Although the numbers were large, the demonstration was a melancholy affair, more funereal than combative, because few participants had any illusions that they could stop de Gaulle. While they were on the streets proclaiming their opposition, they knew that behind the scenes the leaders of the Socialist Party were easing de Gaulle's return.[41]

While the left was on the streets on the afternoon of 28 May, de Gaulle was at another secret meeting at Saint-Cloud – this time with the top official of the Elysée, the Secretary General of the Presidency, Francis de Baecque – to discuss the conditions of his return to power. Baecque, who had never met de Gaulle before, reported back to Coty immediately: 'Cold but courteous, he sat me down and said to me "I am listening." I surprised myself by speaking to him in the third person.' One stumbling block was whether or not de Gaulle would appear before parliament to submit his government to a regular vote. De Gaulle refused. Baecque suggested de Gaulle might appear before parliament, make his ministerial declaration and then leave: 'The General's irritation was visible but he said nothing.' At various points in the meeting, Pompidou was seen poking his head round the door. The meeting resolved nothing, but it did not shut off the possibility of de Gaulle's legal return to power.[42] The next step was another meeting at Saint-Cloud that evening, between de Gaulle and the presidents of the two parliamentary chambers, Gaston Monnerville and André Le Troquer. With no government in place they were constitutionally the two highest authorities in the state. The meeting was a disaster. Monnerville, President of the Senate, was conciliatory but his colleague Le Troquer, President of the Assembly, adopted a truculent tone perfectly calibrated to exasperate de Gaulle, who needed to be coaxed not bullied into concessions. Instead of offering these de Gaulle felt in a strong enough position to declare not only that he would not appear before parliament but also that he wanted full powers for a year to draft a new constitution. Le Troquer shouted: 'You have the mentality of a dictator.' It is possible that Le Troquer purposefully sabotaged the encounter in the hope that this might drive Coty to resign. In that event, it would fall *ex officio* to him as President of the Chamber to take over as President. At 1 a.m. Monnerville and Le Troquer reported back to Coty on the failure of their discussions.

Once again there was an impasse. That morning (29 May), Vitasse was back at the Rue de Solférino with another soldier, General Nicot, to meet Guichard, Foccart and another Gaullist aide, Pierre Lefranc. Those present at this meeting later remembered it completely differently. The two officers claimed they received formal approval for Operation Resurrection to go ahead. Nicot said that de Gaulle was rung while he was there; Foccart denied he himself was even present at the meeting; Lefranc and Guichard did not deny their presence but formally contested that they had obtained any approval from de Gaulle. The story of the telephone call seems implausible since no important communications with Colombey took place by telephone during this month.[43] In another sign that the Gaullists of the Rue de Solférino were being less cautious than previously, Salan claimed that Guichard had rung him that morning to say, 'things are not looking good. It is for you to play now.'[44] Guichard denied this later.

In retrospect, all these military protagonists had an interest in playing up the encouragement they had received, and de Gaulle's entourage in playing it down. The truth probably lies in between. Since de Gaulle's legal return to power seemed to have stalled, his entourage was giving the military more overt encouragement than previously, but the ambiguities enveloping that encouragement were ignored by army officers straining at the leash to launch their operation. The same day, de Gaulle wrote from Colombey to his son in terms suggesting that he too had despaired of a legal solution: 'According to my information an operation is imminent from the south to the north ... It is infinitely likely that nothing will be possible with the current regime which is no longer capable of taking decisions of any kind [*vouloir quoi que ce soit*].'[45]

During the rest of the day (29 May), orders and counter-orders about Operation Resurrection flew across the Mediterranean. According to the plan, 50,000 parachutists flown from south-west France and Algiers would seize key strategic political sites in Paris.[46] After Dulac had returned to Algiers from meeting de Gaulle at Colombey, Salan sent a telegram to Vitasse in the early hours of 29 May: '*Le Grand Charles* asks us firmly to avoid for the moment any intervention.'[47] But Vitasse after his meeting at the Rue de Solférino later that morning sent a telegram to Algiers announcing that '*Grand Charles* is totally in agreement' for the operation to go ahead.[48] With Salan's approval the code message to trigger the operation – 'the carrots are cooked' – was sent by Delbecque; and Salan himself sent a message to Miquel saying that 'after personal contact with *Grand Charles*', he would soon be giving instructions for the operation to go ahead.[49] That afternoon, six Dakotas set off from Le Bourget towards Perpignan where a regiment of parachutists was ready to be taken to Paris.

In the late morning, Gaston Bonneval was rung by the Elysée to be told that Coty planned to issue a public declaration that evening. Bonneval replied: 'If this declaration is not public by 15h, I fear it will be too late, for the dice are thrown.'[50] At 3 p.m. Coty's message was read out to parliament: 'With the country on the verge of civil war . . . I have turned to the most illustrious of Frenchmen, towards him who, in the darkest years of our history, was our Leader for the reconquest of liberty.' He called on de Gaulle to discuss the immediate formation of a government. If such a government could not be formed, Coty announced he would resign. Once again Salan ordered Resurrection to be put on hold; the planes on their way to Perpignan turned back. After Coty's message, de Gaulle headed back from Colombey, arriving at the Elysée at 7.30 p.m., where crowds of photographers were massed at the entrance. He now slightly scaled down his demands, agreeing to appear before parliament and to accept full powers for six months rather than a year.

Resurrection was not completely abandoned because it was still possible that de Gaulle would not receive a majority in parliament. Only the previous day, after all, the Socialists had voted almost unanimously against him. The question was whether Mollet would be able to change them. Mollet visited La Boisserie on 30 May. This was the first time that he had ever met de Gaulle, who deployed all the charm he could exercise when he needed to. Even before Mollet reported back to the Socialist group, there were signs that his party was inching closer towards de Gaulle. The publication of de Gaulle's response to Auriol during that day had a very positive impact. Mollet addressed the Socialist group in the evening after returning from Colombey. He told them: 'I consider that meeting, whatever happens, as one of the great moments of my life: de Gaulle is a great gentleman. Our interview was not a monologue but a dialogue.' No decision was reached but it was agreed that two Socialists – Paul Ramadier and Mollet – could attend a meeting the next morning at the Hôtel La Pérouse where de Gaulle had invited the leaders of all the parliamentary groups except the Communists. At that meeting de Gaulle kept up his offensive of reassurance and charm, promising the party leaders that he could be trusted to exercise power democratically. But there was also a threat: 'I need a large majority tomorrow in parliament. If I do not have it, I will return to Colombey and then I cannot answer for anything.'[51] In the afternoon Mollet appeared before the Socialist parliamentary group again to beg them to understand that de Gaulle was all that stood between parliament and a coup. The group took the almost unprecedented step of allowing its members a free vote – the first time since July 1940 when the same decision had been taken about whether to approve the vote of full powers to Pétain.

On 1 June, de Gaulle appeared before parliament – the first time he had entered the Chamber since January 1946. He read his speech in a monotone to complete silence, asking for full powers to govern by decree for six months, the suspension of parliament during that period and authorization for the government to draft a new constitution to be submitted to a referendum for approval. De Gaulle gave not the slightest indication of how he intended to use these powers and left as soon as he had finished. In the debate that followed nine speakers intervened for de Gaulle and nine against. Among the opponents was the right-wing anti-Gaullist Jacques Isorni who had been Pétain's defence lawyer in 1945. As another right-wing anti-Gaullist *député* remarked the next day, it was like the Assembly listening to the defence lawyer of Louis XVI. The most powerful speech was from Pierre Mendès France, who declared he could not accept 'blackmail by civil war'. But he held out an olive branch for the future:

> If History can one day say that de Gaulle eliminated the fascist menace, that he restored and maintained liberties, that he re-established discipline in the administration and in the army, that he extirpated the torture that dishonours the state [*Protests from the right*], in a word that he consolidated and cleansed the Republic. Then, but only then, will General de Gaulle incarnate legitimacy. I am not speaking of the formal legitimacy of votes and procedures; I am speaking of profound legitimacy, precisely what he invoked in 1940.[52]

The debate had started at 3.00 p.m. and six hours later the Chamber voted: de Gaulle was invested by 329 to 224 votes. The Socialists were almost evenly split with forty-nine voting against de Gaulle and forty-two for him. Even after this vote some final hitches emerged on the next day regarding the procedure for the drafting of the constitution. No one had forgotten July 1940 when parliament had granted full powers to Pétain to produce a new constitution. The result had been the Vichy regime. One *député* who took some delight in recalling this unhappy memory was the right-winger Jean-Louis Tixier-Vignancour who had himself voted for Pétain in 1940 – and reluctantly did the same for de Gaulle in 1958. Many in parliament were unhappy that they would not be consulted over the constitution. It looked as if a sweetener would be necessary. This was found in the idea of creating a Consultative Constitutional Committee made up of a number of *députés* and senators which offered parliament the illusion of being included in the process.

To general surprise, de Gaulle himself appeared in parliament again on 2 June to defend his proposed bill. Where on 1 June he had been stiff and ill at ease, now he was relaxed and reassuring, but he would not give way on his refusal to allow the draft text of the constitution to be discussed in parliament. As for his assurance that the constitution would recognize the 'necessary existence of an assembly elected by universal suffrage' he offered as 'past proof' his own restoration of democracy after the war – and 'the pleasure and honour I have in finding myself among you today'. This was in fact the last time that de Gaulle would ever find himself in a parliamentary assembly. 'Operation sedition followed by operation seduction', as one Communist *député* put it.[53]

While the votes were being counted at the end of the debate, de Gaulle remained in his seat. *Députés* sidled up to the government benches for the chance to shake his hand. De Gaulle remained in his seat and got up only to shake the hand of the veteran Paul Reynaud, who had given him his first ministerial post in 1940. When Georges Bonnet, a proponent of appeasement in the 1930s, came over to shake his hand, it was, according to one observer, 'as though de Gaulle had touched a slug, so quick was he in withdrawing his hand'.[54] At the end of the day, the government's bill passed; de Gaulle left the Chamber and never set foot in it again.

That evening Léon Delbecque, who had not seen de Gaulle since their fateful interview three months earlier, was smuggled into the Hôtel La Pérouse by a side entrance. He had flown to Paris on the evening of 29 May ready to play his role in Operation Resurrection. On arrival he was informed that the operation was on hold, and Foccart told him to keep out of sight until de Gaulle had been officially invested – 'otherwise it will be for Algiers to play'. At the hotel on 2 June, de Gaulle greeted Delbecque with a double-edged compliment: 'Bravo. You played well, but you must admit that I did as well.' De Gaulle was scathing about the Committees of Public Safety and said that they must be wound up. As Delbecque was leaving, he saw de Gaulle's cases being prepared for the move to the Hôtel Matignon. Delbecque, who had played a key role in preparing the coup, already sensed that there might not be a place for him in its aftermath.[55]

ANATOMY OF A COUP D'ETAT

'I want 18 Brumaire without the methods of Brumaire,' de Gaulle had once remarked. In 1799, as in 1958, French political elites had lost faith in the political system. They sensed that things had to change but wanted to avoid either a monarchist restoration, from the right, or a return to the Terror, from the left. Napoleon was the providential figure who offered a middle way. But Napoleon had not taken power as smoothly as he had hoped. One of the two houses of parliament supported him on 18 Brumaire but the other refused to do so on the next day. Soldiers were sent in to expel the *députés*. In 1958 the threat of soldiers had been enough.

In 1958, the choice was between a military coup on the right or a Popular Front alliance with the Communists on the left. It was partly because he so mistrusted the Communists that Mollet had rallied to de Gaulle as a lesser evil. Although the politicians were not sure de Gaulle could be trusted to save them from the army, and the army was not sure de Gaulle could be trusted to save it from the politicians, any other option seemed riskier to both parties. Most successful coups contain an element of legality. Mussolini came to power in 1922 less because of the 'march on Rome', which could easily have been stopped, than because the King chose to appoint him Prime Minister. The Italian elites no longer believed in their own system. The threat from the street in Italy in 1922 was probably less real than the threat from the military in Algeria in 1958. Another precedent hovering over the events of 1958 was the 'legal' vote of full powers to Pétain in July 1940. Although some who voted for Pétain later claimed that they had felt intimidated, the army in Algiers in 1958 was certainly no less threatening than the army in 1940. Whether or not it is true that de Gaulle had said to Monnerville and Le Troquer that he would leave them to 'have it out with the parachutists', that fear was at the back of everyone's mind.

De Gaulle was able to 'legalize' his coup because France's elites had lost confidence in the existing regime to resolve the Algerian crisis. This was true of Mollet – leader of the largest party in parliament – and of Coty – President of the Republic. It was also true of the Chief of the Defence Staff, General Ely, who resigned during the crisis; and of the Prefect of Police Papon, who had said that he could not answer for the loyalty of the police. De Gaulle was pushing at an open door. Coty and Mollet did all they could to facilitate his return to power, but de Gaulle did not make it easy for them. It is possible to imagine a different scenario in which de Gaulle, publicly condemning the army's dissidence, would have rallied a larger number of politicians (including Mendès France). Had he come to power in this way, it is hard to see how an army coup could have succeeded since the army had no other plausible candidate to front its operation. The conditions of de Gaulle's return to power complicated his own position for the next four years. He had not created the overmighty army but he had created a dangerous precedent, reinforcing the army's conviction that it could bend Paris to its will. If he was ready to take this risk, it was because he was playing for high stakes. He wanted to come back on his terms: to break the system, not to enter it. As he had told Terrenoire in March, those who wanted him back had to understand that this would not just be just another government but a 'new universe'. De Gaulle's skill was to have kept the Algerian rebellion simmering – so that he could force the politicians to accept his terms – but not exploding – to enable him to return to power legally.

The question remains: how deep was de Gaulle's complicity in the Algerian insurrection? He was not directly implicated but that is not quite the point. As François Mitterrand, who opposed de Gaulle in 1958, put it: 'He was no more involved directly in the plot than God in the creation.'[56] De Gaulle's presence at Colombey certainly allowed him to keep an Olympian distance. At the height of the crisis on 28 May, one supporter of de Gaulle commented to Gladwyn Jebb that the General's isolation in Colombey was a problem: 'De Gaulle insisted on conducting all these important political manoeuvres from a country house four hours by car from Paris; would not talk on the telephone; and had no staff except for a couple of quite unimportant secretaries, who were in no way in his confidence. It almost seemed as if he did not really want political power.'[57] This was how de Gaulle wanted things to appear, but in fact he was extremely well informed while also being adept at keeping his hands clean. Never had Colombey served him better. It allowed him to impose his own rhythm on events while also keeping his distance. The government had a police car tailing de Gaulle's comings and goings from Colombey to Paris, but since his Citroën 15CV was faster than the police Peugeot 203 this attempt to monitor his movements was rather ineffective.[58]

Away from the febrile agitation of Algiers and Paris, Colombey was a surreal oasis of calm. During his visit there on 23 May, Georges Boris had a few minutes on his own with Madame de Gaulle while Guichard, who was accompanying him back to Paris, conferred alone with de Gaulle: 'She made conversation as best she could, spoke about the garden, the cold winter and at length about the birds in the park: "they are the only ones making a noise here. The house is silent, no coming and going, no telephone ringing." '[59] De Gaulle disliked the telephone, and since the lines were tapped it could not be used safely – unless de Gaulle wanted information to leak. Thanks to wiretaps Pflimlin was well informed about the various plots brewing in Algiers. De Gaulle was in Paris on only five occasions between 14 and 31 May. Otherwise he communicated through Guichard and Foccart. Guichard was in Colombey five times during the crisis, carrying messages to and from the General. Driving back to Paris on 26 May with de Gaulle's letter to Mollet, he met Foccart's car heading for Colombey with a letter from Salan.

Dulac's visit to Colombey was the only *direct* encounter between de Gaulle and the military during May. De Gaulle's previous signals in March and April – to Delbecque, Neuwirth and Petit – had been as evasive as they were encouraging. Since few people in this month had direct access to de Gaulle, Foccart and Guichard acted as filters and conduits. Delbecque, such a key player in the Algerian events, saw de Gaulle only twice (on 4 March and 2 June) but met Foccart many times. Foccart encouraged him to continue his good work but with a strong warning: be careful: 'The main thing is not to "implicate" [*mouiller*] the General and not to go around saying: "the General said to me."'[60] The government telephone taps picked up a conversation between Salan and one of his contacts in Paris on 15 May. When asked what he should do, Salan was told 'shout *Vive de Gaulle*'. 'Is that what he wants?' Salan asked. When told 'It is what his collaborators say,' Salan replied: 'That is not the same thing.'[61] But there was nothing else to go on.

Foccart reports de Gaulle's words to him just before leaving Paris in the wake of his press conference of 19 May: ' "I am going back immediately to Colombey. I think that this time the process is under way. But listen to me carefully." Emphasizing his words, and in his most solemn voice he said: "I want you to occupy yourself with nothing. To see no one." '

Foccart knew de Gaulle well enough to decode this:

> If I had obeyed to the letter, I would have gone back home to Luzarches, unplugged the telephone, and done some crosswords. I know the General well enough to know how to interpret his instructions. He rarely gave me such precise instructions but even in this case I considered that I had to act in the direction of the objective he had defined or led me to understand he wanted, even if this meant disobeying him formally.[62]

De Gaulle's aides allowed themselves considerable latitude in interpreting his wishes knowing they would be disavowed if they were caught out. On 12 May, Delbecque in Paris was told by Foccart that he had the green light to continue his activities in Algiers. Later Foccart admitted to Delbecque that he had had no authority to give this assurance. As the crisis reached its paroxysm on 29–30 May, no one knew exactly what had been said or how it should be interpreted. Vitasse remembered of his first meeting with members of de Gaulle's entourage: 'They were rather shifty types [*pas des gars francs*].'[63] The military wanted simple directives; de Gaulle's entourage sought to maximize ambiguity. To add to the confusion, those acting on behalf of de Gaulle were sometimes operating independently of each other. On 17 May, an envoy sent by Debré to sound out General Petit's views was surprised to stumble upon Bonneval doing the same.[64] Debré, who was immobilized throughout the crisis by an attack of sciatica, was less ambiguous in his signals than Guichard and Foccart, who were in closer personal contact with de Gaulle.

If a parliamentary majority had proved impossible and Operation Resurrection had done ahead, de Gaulle, in Guichard's words to Miquel, would probably have 'taken the situation as he found it'. The date of 13 May was certainly not one de Gaulle wanted to remember. Four years later, in a speech on 8 June 1962, he referred to it dismissively as an 'enterprise of usurpation from Algiers'.[65] When his Minister of Information, Alain Peyrefitte, expressed surprise at this description of the event that had triggered his return to power, de Gaulle replied with superb disdain for the facts:

> The phrase was chosen on purpose. I had nothing to do with the insurrection of Algiers. I knew nothing of what was being prepared before 13 May; I was informed of what was going on like everyone else through the radio . . . I did not raise a little finger to encourage the movement. I even blocked it when it took the shape of a military operation in France.

As Guichard remarked to Peyrefitte on hearing this: 'He played superbly on the excitement of Algiers, the panic in Paris and desire of the French to finish with the Fourth Republic. It was done with great art; and today he denounces us into the bargain.'[66]

19
Président du Conseil,
June–December 1958

'IT WAS VERY DARK YESTERDAY! BUT
THIS EVENING THERE IS LIGHT!'

On 27 June 1958, a month after returning to power, de Gaulle gave a televised address to the nation: 'I call for Unity! That means I call on everybody. It was very dark yesterday! But this evening there is light! *Françaises, Français*, I need your help.'[1]

The idea that overnight the French people had moved from darkness to light, from division to unity, from the 'abyss' to the 'summit', was a recurrent theme of de Gaulle's speeches for the next ten years. When visiting the regions of France early in his Presidency, he sometimes affected surprise at their rapid recovery from the war – as if the years between 1946 and 1958 had not existed. One effective propaganda weapon in the referendum campaign for de Gaulle's constitution in 1958 was a film depicting a procession of indistinguishable politicians on the steps of the Elysée Palace in the endless merry-go-round of Fourth Republic politics. The message was simple: this was the past from which de Gaulle had (again) saved the French.

The 'light' of Gaullist rhetoric has cast the Fourth Republic into a 'darkness' from which it has never fully recovered. In reality, the governments of the Fourth Republic achieved a great deal in exceptionally difficult conditions. De Gaulle often built on what they had done, even if he never acknowledged it. The achievements of the Fourth Republic appear in a more positive light today than when viewed in the 1950s through the rainy windows of Colombey.

The Economy: Looking back over the period between 1949 and 1979, the economist Jean Fourastié described them as the 'Thirty Glorious Years' of the French economy ended abruptly by the oil crises of the 1970s. The 'glorious' years were marked by rapid economic growth, full employment and rising wages. Growth was kick-started by Marshall Aid and sustained by increases in productivity and the rebuilding of infrastructure after the war. Between 1949 and 1959, French GDP grew by 4.5 per cent per annum.

It took time for people to realize what was happening. To those living through them, these years did not initially seem so 'glorious'. About 25 per cent of electors regularly voted for the Communist Party, which was still propagating the ludicrous theory that the working class was becoming 'pauperized'. Whether or not any Communist voter really believed this, it was true that economic growth had not immediately translated into higher living standards. Since governments had prioritized investment in heavy industry and infrastructure, housing was in short supply. In the winter of 1954, the housing crisis was the headline issue of French politics. The underlying economic improvement was also masked by France's high inflation, fuelled by the crippling burden of paying for colonial wars. There were endemic crises in the balance of payments and public finances. Fourth Republic governments lurched from one financial stabilization plan to another. Nonetheless de Gaulle had the good fortune to return to power at a moment of underlying economic growth whose benefits soon became apparent.

The Constitution: The instability of politics during the Fourth Republic was its most obvious weakness. But its presidents were not entirely ciphers: Auriol had manoeuvred skilfully to keep de Gaulle out of power; and his successor Coty manoeuvred no less skilfully to do the opposite. Although 1958 seems like a radical break in France's constitutional history, from the mid-1950s many politicians had come to accept that some modification of the constitution was necessary to reduce ministerial instability and limit parliament's capacity to impede executive authority. The Gaillard government had a constitution-reform project ready in March 1958 but fell before it could be discussed; the Pflimlin government had another one ready in May before it too fell. Several of the ideas contained in these projects to streamline the parliamentary system reappeared in de Gaulle's constitution of 1958. That is one reason why the political class was ready to accept his reforms. Whether or not he had come back to power, France's political system would have changed.[2]

The Empire: On the face of it, the Fourth Republic had failed miserably to deal with decolonization. For eight years it had fought an unwinnable and financially crippling war in Indo-China ending in the debacle of Dien Bien Phu – although that conflict was a poisonous legacy of de Gaulle's 1944–5 provisional government. But once Mendès France had successfully extricated France from Indo-China in 1954, Fourth Republic governments started to pursue more imaginative colonial policies. Mendès France paved the way for Tunisia to claim independence in 1955, and his successor Edgar

Faure did the same for Morocco. Fourth Republic governments had also tried to accommodate the demands of Black African nationalist leaders pushing for greater autonomy if not indeed independence. In 1956, Mollet's government passed the so-called Loi Cadre which devolved considerable autonomy to elected assemblies in the territories of Equatorial and West Africa while leaving key areas of sovereignty like defence, foreign and monetary policy in French hands. Although the Loi Cadre had been conceived as a way of preserving the Empire, it also offered a possible route to a post-imperial future for Black Africa. This was a stark contrast to the failure to find a solution for Algeria. But Algeria was viewed more as an internal French problem than as a colonial one – and the drama of Algeria should not obscure the Fourth Republic's other successes in the field of decolonization. Here again de Gaulle had precedents to build on.

France in the World: In the twelve years after 1946, the governments of the Fourth Republic had implemented three important measures to protect France's security and restore her international position. The first was to sign the NATO Treaty in 1949; the second to launch the process of reconciliation with Germany and European unity from 1951; the third to begin building a French nuclear military capability from 1954. There were ups and downs in the implementation of these policies, but taken together they represented a substantial achievement.

The organization of NATO was not ideal from the French point of view. The French resented being junior partners to Britain and America, and they intermittently lobbied to change this situation by proposing some kind of three-power directorate to run NATO and institutionalize France's claims to be a world power.[3]

The first step towards reconciliation with Germany had been the Iron, Coal and Steel Community (ECSC) of 1951, signed by Robert Schuman but conceived by Jean Monnet. Since one condition of Marshall Aid had been that the French should abandon their attempts to weaken Germany, Monnet's stroke of genius was to make a virtue of necessity in devising the ECSC as a supranational organization to manage in common the coal and steel resources of France, Germany, Benelux and Italy. The path towards reconciliation with Germany hit a stumbling block over the European Defence Community which finally collapsed, as we have seen in Chapter 17, when the French parliament refused to ratify it in 1954 – although the proposal had originated with France as a way of selling German rearmament to the French public. The idea of European unity – and Franco-German reconciliation – was relaunched by the Treaty of Rome in March 1957. The long-term aim of the Treaty was to 'lay the foundations of an ever closer union among the peoples of Europe'. The first stages of that process were to be the creation of the Common Market – or European Economic Community (EEC), to give it its formal title – establishing a customs union between its six signatories. The first stages of that customs union were due to come into operation from January 1958. French commitment to 'Europe' was reinforced by the Suez crisis in 1956 when the French and British had been forced by the Americans to abandon their operation against Nasser. The French and British drew different conclusions from the disaster. The British government decided to consolidate ties with the United States, the French government to strengthen ties with Europe. On the day that the Suez crisis reached its culmination the German Chancellor Konrad Adenauer was meeting Mollet in Paris to clear the final obstacles towards the signing of the Treaty of Rome in the following year. He told Mollet: 'There remains only one way of playing a decisive role in the world; that is to unite to make Europe . . . We have no time to waste: Europe will be your revenge.'[4]

European unity also had implications for French defence. Increasingly there were reasons to question whether a transatlantic alliance signed in 1949 was still appropriate in the same form ten years later. America no longer had a nuclear monopoly once the Soviets had tested their first atomic bomb in August 1949; and in 1957 the Soviet Union was the first country to send a satellite – the Sputnik – into space. This raised fears that the Soviets were pulling ahead of America technologically and also led Europeans to worry whether America would be willing to risk nuclear annihilation for Europe. In 1957, the American government had agreed to modify in Britain's favour the terms of the 1946 US Atomic Energy Act (McMahon Act) which forbade the sharing of nuclear technology. This was a victory for Britain's policy of increasing ties to the United States, but it had the longer-term consequence that the British, for whom the costs of their own nuclear deterrent were an increasing strain, would become more dependent on the United States. To allay the concerns of Europeans about their own defence, the Americans proposed to locate missiles (ICBMs) in Europe.

Although de Gaulle's provisional government had set up an atomic energy authority (Commissariat à l'Energie Atomique – CEA) in 1945, this organism had initially only studied the civil applications of nuclear energy. It was the Mendès France government, after the humiliation of Dien Bien Phu, which decided in December 1954 to extend the CEA's brief to include the military uses of nuclear power. Finally, in April 1958, the Gaillard government took the decision to test France's first atomic bomb within two years.[5] How an eventual French nuclear programme might dovetail with France's overall defence policy, and with the deepening of her commitment to Europe, had yet to be worked out. In November 1957 and April 1958, the French, German and Italian governments had signed secret accords to discuss the possibility of sharing nuclear technology for both military and non-military purposes. This was a tentative beginning to what might have become a common European nuclear policy.[6]

Thus de Gaulle came to power at a critical juncture in the relationship between France, Europe and America. Gaillard's government had fallen in May 1958 because the French parliament would not stomach the American plan to resolve the Franco-Tunisian dispute after the bombing of Sakhiet. Its terms were judged humiliating to France. The Franco-American crisis of 1958 was the fall-out of a wider French reappraisal of the relationship with America in the wake of Suez.[7] De Gaulle is famous for having called into question France's Atlantic Alliance, but we should be aware that his return to power was as much a *consequence* of a crisis in that Alliance as a cause of it.

All the issues raised by de Gaulle would have come up even if he had not returned to power. The American President Eisenhower observed in November 1957 that the French government was threatening 'the most dire things such as a complete breakup of the Atlantic Alliance'.[8] Harold Macmillan noted in his diary a month later: 'All kinds of usual accusations about *perfide Albion*. We and the Americans are accused of (a) trying to dominate NATO . . . (c) preventing France becoming a nuclear power etc.'[9] Such Anglo-American concerns about France would become ever more familiar over the next few years. At the end of 1957, however, the French premier was Félix Gaillard – and de Gaulle was still festering in inactivity at Colombey.

THE NEW TEAM

What line de Gaulle would take on these issues was unknown. He had been out of power for twelve years, and silent for three. He had always denounced moves to European supranationalism, most famously in the case of the European Defence Community – but would he tear up the Treaty of Rome? Like Fourth Republic leaders he had resented France's junior status in NATO – but how far would he go to redress the situation? He had certainly abandoned the policy of breaking up Germany – but how far would he go down the road of reconciliation?

During the 'desert' years de Gaulle kept in touch through his weekly 'audiences', and through those members of the Gaullist diaspora who had taken posts in government. But the transition from opposition to power was abrupt. Only a month before returning to power, de Gaulle had been brooding at Colombey and planning a holiday in the Cévennes. The French

Ambassador in London told the British, who were fretting to ascertain de Gaulle's views, that the General 'had not seen a file for twelve years and that briefing him was a major operation' – but that 'his officials found him very much more debonair than the de Gaulle of ten years ago'.[10] There was much improvisation at the beginning. The *conseiller d'état* Raymond Janot, who was to play an important role in drafting the constitution, had been hastily recruited only a few days before de Gaulle took over. The way this occurred was revealing of the frenetic speed with which events had moved. On 28 May, Janot was working in his office when he received a call from Pompidou:

> 'Remind me what it was you were saying to me the other day about constitutional revision.' I told him, and he said: 'Good, the simplest thing is that you explain it to the General; he is en route [from Colombey] at the moment; he has been summoned by the President of the Republic.' And we set off. The two cars met, headlights were flashed, the cars stopped, and Pompidou went to see the General; he presented him to me; the General took me into his car ... 'What have you to tell me?' ... I found him receptive. The interview finished and the General said on taking his leave of me: 'Good; if things go all right, you will look after constitutional matters in my *cabinet*.'[11]

There was so little space in de Gaulle's suite at the Hôtel La Pérouse that Janot found himself working in the bathroom. Meanwhile on 2 June, one of de Gaulle's entourage, Pierre Lefranc, set off on a reconnaissance mission to the Hôtel Matignon:

> Complete silence, everything completely still. I had the impression there were ears behind each door, people looking through every keyhole. I was the invader. Did I eat children and steal clocks? One of Pflimlin's collaborators came to find me ... He received me in the office that was about to become mine. Not a file; not a bit of paper to be seen.[12]

In de Gaulle's six months as the last Prime Minister of the Fourth Republic, his *directeur de cabinet* was the trusted Georges Pompidou. Given that de Gaulle was away from Paris for almost a month (one long visit to Africa, five to Algeria), Pompidou's role was crucial in the smooth running of the government.[13] He was assisted by other members of the Gaullist team from the years at the Rue de Solférino – Guichard, Bonneval, Foccart, Pierre Lefranc. But although this group had formed close bonds based around personal loyalty to de Gaulle, it would be wrong to see what happened in May 1958 as a group of Gaullist 'outsiders' investing and taking over the state. There was no purge: all ambassadors and prefects remained in place; so did the Paris Prefect of Police, Maurice Papon. Nor were the new

Gaullist 'insiders' in any real sense outsiders (except certain indidivuals like Guichard and Foccart). A perfect exemplar of this hybrid insider–outsider status, showing how in some sense Gaullism was consubstantial with the idea of service to the state, was René Brouillet, whom de Gaulle brought into his *cabinet* in 1958. As a young civil servant during the Occupation, Brouillet had played a key role in the Resistance as an aide to Bidault in his role at the head of the CNR after Moulin's death. Brouillet, a man of strong Catholic convictions, had first met Bidault in Christian Democratic circles before the war. At the Liberation he was taken on by Palewski as his deputy in running de Gaulle's *cabinet*. He was also, as it happens, the person who brought his close friend Georges Pompidou into the Gaullist inner circle. After de Gaulle's resignation in 1946, Brouillet opted for a diplomatic career rather than joining the RPF, but this did not make him in his eyes – or de Gaulle's – any less of a 'Gaullist'. Back in power in 1958, de Gaulle summoned Brouillet back from a diplomatic posting to the Vatican to take responsibility in his *cabinet* for the most sensitive portfolio: Algeria. Then when de Gaule moved to the Elysée in 1959 he took Brouillet with him into his *cabinet* there.[14]

There was considerable continuity in the composition of the government – to the disappointment of the Algiers activists. De Gaulle's first government was a mixture of former Fourth Republic politicians, 'experts' and Gaullists. In the first group were Pflimlin, Mollet and Pinay; in the second group was the new Minister of Foreign Affairs, Maurice Couve de Murville (whom de Gaulle knew well from Algiers in 1943), who was plucked from his post as Ambassador to Bonn, and the new Minister of Defence, Pierre Guillaumat, who had been head of the French Atomic Energy Commission; in the third group were Debré, the Minister of Justice, and Malraux, with no specific portfolio.

Although it was no secret that de Gaulle's new constitution would involve a stronger Presidency, as long as he remained premier in the Fourth Republic it was with the premier that power now lay. The formal meetings of the Council of Ministers (Conseil des Ministres), chaired by President Coty at the Elysée, were perfunctory. Little information was conveyed under the courtesies. Previously the President and Prime Minister had sat opposite each other; now they sat side by side. De Gaulle had a box of matches always ready to light Coty's cigarette, but only grudgingly agreed to allow the Council to hear even short reports on foreign affairs from Couve de Murville.[15] The real decisions were taken by de Gaulle's team at the Hôtel Matignon.

These six months when de Gaulle found himself serving as the last Prime Minister of the Fourth Republic had the same sense of purpose and energy as the first months of the Consulate of Napoleon. They resulted not only in the drafting of a new constitution, the implementation of a major financial plan and several new initiatives in foreign policy but also a legislative frenzy resulting in the promulgation of over 300 ordinances covering the most eclectic range of subjects: penal reform, hospital reform, change to the social security system, new regulations for the film industry. There were measures on hunting permits, wheat prices, the status of prison officers, flood relief, juvenile delinquency, the highway code. Some reforms, like the extension of the school-leaving age from fourteen to sixteen, had a major influence on the life of the French. In many cases, these measures had been mouldering for years in the offices of civil servants (as with many of the measures introduced by Napoleon after 1799) and what made their rapid implementation possible were the unique conditions under which de Gaulle had six months of untrammelled power to govern without parliament. The reforms mostly had little to do with de Gaulle directly, but he involved himself in the detail to a surprising extent, especially those relating to scientific research.

'I HAVE UNDERSTOOD YOU'

On 4 June, de Gaulle flew to Algiers, where the population awaited him in a febrile mood of expectation. They wanted to hear directly from his mouth the magic words *Algérie française*. *Pied noir* activists and army officers in the Committees of Public Safety were disappointed that de Gaulle's government included so many Fourth Republic politicians (including Pflimlin, against whom their insurrection had been directed) but not their hero Soustelle (who had played a key role in the insurrection). On this first visit, de Gaulle was accompanied by two junior ministers, who were treated with scant respect by the military authorities. A car whisked de Gaulle from the airport but his two ministers had to find their own transport to the centre of Algiers. At the end of the day, as de Gaulle was about to address the Algiers crowd, they were seized by members of the Committee of Public Safety and locked in a cupboard.

De Gaulle arrived at the seat of the Government General in the late afternoon. A huge crowd had gathered in front of the building. Salan and Soustelle appeared briefly on the balcony to announce de Gaulle. As the crowd's anticipation reached a hysterical climax, de Gaulle walked out on to the balcony and raised his arms in a V. Once the roars of the crowd had temporarily subsided he opened: 'I have understood you.' The crowd erupted into cheers. What did he mean by these four words? A government official observing the scene from another balcony at the side offered one reading:

> De Gaulle found himself in front of an expectant baying and uncontrolled crowd that was difficult to calm. Listening to them, he quickly realized that they were not applauding him. They were calling for Soustelle ... He advanced right to the edge of the balcony. I will remember this all my life: he lifted his arms in a V as he often used to do, but the crowd did not stop shouting. He couldn't get to speak ... On a terrace at the side, I could see him very clearly. And I had the impression that he was getting very irritated by this crowd that would not let him speak ... And then, as always in crowds, there was a moment of calm which lasted a few seconds. And he seized the moment to bellow into the microphone that phrase which has been so commented upon: 'I have understood you.' In my mind what it meant was this: 'All right. I have heard your shouting. I have heard you shouting for Soustelle. I understand. Now shut up and let me speak.'[16]

This is an unusual interpretation but not entirely implausible. Most people, however, believe that the four words were intended to win the hearts of the crowd with a statement so ambiguous that every listener could read into them what they wished. De Gaulle's next words were no less seductively opaque:

> I know what has happened here. I see what you have wanted to do. I see that the road you have opened in Algeria is that of renewal and fraternity [Applause]. I say renewal in every way. But because quite rightly you have wanted to begin at the beginning, that is to say our institutions, that is why I am here [Long ovation].

Once his listeners had been 'lassoed', as one observer put it, what followed was not necessarily what they wanted to hear.[17] De Gaulle saluted the 'courage' of the fighters who had taken up arms against France and offered them reconciliation; he announced that Muslims and Europeans would now be fully French and their votes would count equally in elections. He ended: 'Never more than here and never more than this evening, have I understood how beautiful, how great, how generous France is.' One English journalist present wrote of the speech: 'It was a superb performance ... Admirable in length, perfect in composition, noble in style and delivery, magnificent in ending. They cheered him to the echo and far beyond – and had quite obviously not understood one word.'[18] This was not quite true. Although offering Muslims full equality with Europeans could be read as the beginning of the implementation of that idea of total 'integration' between Algeria and France which the *pied noir* activists desired, they were alarmed that de Gaulle had not uttered the magic words *Algérie française*. On the next day, at an angry meeting of the Algiers Committee of Public Safety Delbecque declared: 'We did not cross the Rubicon to go fishing. We will continue to the end what we began on 13 May.'

Over the next two days, de Gaulle toured the country making more speeches – but always avoiding the two fateful words everyone was waiting for – until his last speech at Mostaganem on 6 June. He ended as usual, '*Vive Mostaganem, Vive l'Algérie, Vive la République, Vive la France,*' and started to move away from the microphone. The crowd started screaming '*Algérie française, Algérie française*'. At this point, de Gaulle turned back, raised his arms and shouted, '*Vive l'Algérie*' – and then after a pause he added, '*française*'. Immediately the propaganda services of the army got working to doctor the tape so as to smooth out any hesitancy. Their version was broadcast as: '*Vive Mostaganem, Vive l'Algérie française, Vive la République, Vive la France.*'[19]

This subsequently became an embarrassment to de Gaulle. He did not include it in his collected speeches. When the speech was published after his death by his son, the offending words were omitted – but no one denies they were uttered. Some years later, when Algeria was independent, de Gaulle tried to explain it away disingenuously: 'Today still, I hope that Algeria remains France as Gaul remained Roman! I want it to be nourished and irrigated by our culture and our language.'[20] But in the context of 1958, as de Gaulle knew, his words were charged with a specific meaning. Perhaps he had been carried away by the emotion of the moment; perhaps he had momentarily succumbed to the intense psychological pressure to utter the words; perhaps he had decided to offer a scrap of reassurance to an army whose loyalty he needed.

De Gaulle was back in Algeria for five days at the start of July. This time he was accompanied by an apprehensive Guy Mollet, who had not set foot there since being pelted by tomatoes some two years earlier. De Gaulle visited areas where support for the FLN was strong. In Batna, in the Aurès region, he amazed everyone by plunging into a dense crowd of Muslims regardless of security. In Algiers, he refused to receive the Committee of Public Safety. Although again he never mentioned 'integration', he did announce that in future there would be a single common stamp for mail between Algeria and France. Was this 'integration' by stealth or just lip-service to the idea? On his return to Paris, as a concession to the army and the *pied noir* activists, de Gaulle made Soustelle Minister of Information. To a journalist travelling on the plane back to France, de Gaulle poured out his bile against the army:

The Generals hate me. And I feel the same about them. All idiots . . . Cretins preoccupied only by their promotions, their decorations, their comfort who have never understood anything and never will. Salan is a drug addict . . . [General] Jouhaud a total idiot [*un gros ahuri*] . . . And Massu! A good sort but hardly a rocket scientist [*n'a pas inventé l'eau chaude*].[21]

Over these months de Gaulle sent ever more tetchy letters to Salan about the political activities of the Committees of Public Safety and the need to restore normal authority.[22] Massu, whose brief moment as kingmaker and continuing activities as President of the Algiers Public Safety Committee had gone to his head, was sent a not so coded warning: 'You are a soldier. And what a soldier! That is what you must remain. That is how you will remain my companion and my friend. But my task is not yours.'[23] For the moment, however, de Gaulle did not feel secure enough to push matters further. First he needed to consolidate his position in France by drafting a new constitution and securing popular approval for it.

DRAFTING THE CONSTITUTION

Pierre Pflimlin wrote of the first meeting of the committee to draft the new constitution: 'I expected the General to produce from his pocket an already elaborated constitution. That was not the case at all.'[24] De Gaulle merely outlined some ideas in line with the Bayeux speech, but since that speech was too vague to offer much guidance a lot was left to the imagination.[25] Despite the years that the RPF had spent discussing constitutional reform, the drafting of the 1958 text was marked by improvisation and compromise.

The constitution was drafted in secrecy over six weeks. Even the President of the Republic, Coty, was kept in the dark. The key role was played by Michel Debré. On de Gaulle's instructions, he set up a group of 'experts' to draft preliminary proposals. Debré was an obvious choice since he had been writing about constitutional reform for years. A passionate admirer of the British parliamentary system, his ideal was a rationalized parliamentary system on the Westminster model (as he interpreted it). The government would be responsible to parliament (unlike the American system of separation of powers) but procedural changes would restrict parliament's ability to bring down the governments as easily as in the Third and Fourth Republics.

As Debré's group produced its proposals, they were submitted to a small ministerial committee chaired by de Gaulle. Among its members were key Fourth Republic politicians like Mollet and Pflimlin. The constitution of the Fifth Republic, at least in its original form, was a collective document drafted with the full cooperation of the leading politicians of the previous regime. We only have the minutes of the first meeting of the committee because de Gaulle, irritated when Mollet quibbled about inaccuracies in the record, ruled that no more minutes would be taken. Our only knowledge of the debates therefore comes from the subsequent recollections of the committee's members. De Gaulle played an active role, but his views did not always prevail. For example, to respect the separation of powers, he wanted ministers to be obliged to relinquish their parliamentary seats in order to be free of any electoral pressure. This was accepted, but de Gaulle also wanted to forbid them holding office as mayors, a common practice for national politicians in France. Mollet, who was proud to be Mayor of Arras, protested against this idea, while de Gaulle listened in quiet fury. After the meeting he launched into a tirade of abuse against the 'politicians', threatening to 'leave them to stew in their own juice . . . and deal by themselves with Algeria'.[26] Of course he had no intention of doing this, and he conceded the point with bad grace.

De Gaulle would not, however, accept any compromise on the clause of the constitution (ultimately Article 16) that authorized the President to assume full powers in a national emergency. He batted away worries that this would open the road to dictatorship by pointing out that the authorization to assume full powers had to be countersigned by the President of the Senate. De Gaulle's argument was that if such a clause had existed in 1940 the President of the Republic, Albert Lebrun, could have overruled Pétain and taken the government abroad. One minister pointed out mischievously that this would have made de Gaulle unnecessary; another that there was no guarantee, even with such a clause, that a weak man like Lebrun would have used his powers. De Gaulle answered: 'A text cannot cover every eventuality, but if the man in place did not act there would be a General de Gaulle to go to London.'[27]

After six weeks, the text was ready to be submitted to the full Council of Ministers. At a meeting lasting two days, de Gaulle read out each of the seventy-seven articles and Debré offered a commentary: 'A prophet interpreting the Tables of the Law under the majestic and vigilant gaze of the Creator.'[28] Although the overall thrust of the proposals was to strengthen executive power, defenders of a parliamentary system were reassured by the article stating that it was for the government, under the leadership of the Prime Minister, 'to determine the policy of the nation' and that the government was responsible to parliament. Parliament's ability to impede the work of the government was curbed, but after the experience of the Fourth Republic there was a general consensus that this was desirable. Although the constitution did not set up a presidential system, the President of the Republic was given greater democratic legitimacy, and therefore potentially greater power, by being elected not just by two houses of parliament but by a wider electoral college including representatives of local government – a key proposal of de Gaulle's Bayeux speech. The President also had the right to dissolve parliament, and consult the people directly by referenda.

Even so, the exact role of the President remained ambiguous. At the first meeting of the drafting committee de Gaulle said that he envisaged the President as an *arbitre* (referee/arbitrator) – as also adumbrated in the Bayeux speech – but Mollet pointed out that it was beyond the role of a referee to dissolve parliament and in effect dismiss the government. Janot had already highlighted this contradiction to de Gaulle and suggested the need to be more 'transparent' (*lumineuse*) on this point.[29] Transparency was exactly what de Gaulle did not want. He told Janot that the constitution should be short, and obscure enough to allow it to be adapted to different circumstances.[30] He later commented that the referee in a football match can confiscate the ball and do what he wants with it.[31] These ambiguities led René Capitant, one of the main Gaullist constitutional experts, to call the document the 'worst-drafted constitution in our history'.[32] Capitant, an ardent believer in direct democracy, would have liked a greater role for referenda in the constitution. But he was abroad teaching in Japan during 1958 and was not involved in the drafting. De Gaulle, happy to keep matters vague, did not summon him back.

The final step in the drafting process required the constitution to be submitted to the Consultative Committee of worthies chaired by Paul Reynaud. This had been de Gaulle's reluctant concession to those who wanted some public debate. The Consultative Committee introduced one important modification to that part of the constitution covering relations between France and her African territories. Although this soon turned out to be academic because the territories became independent, the issue aroused much passion at the time. The question was how the constitution would dovetail with the structures established by the Loi Cadre of 1956. Some African leaders hoped it would offer a transition to a federal relationship between France and her African possessions; others that it might be the first step to a looser confederation that could eventually allow independence. Both options were discussed in the drafting of the constitution. The problem with a genuinely federal system was that it might allow the population of the overseas territories to participate fully in decisions affecting France: France could end up being colonized by its colonies, as one participant in the debate put it.[33]

This debate became so technical that most people got lost in the thickets. At a meeting on 23 July, one official described de Gaulle as intervening with such forceful eloquence that 'all appeared simple and luminous'. The official in question was despatched to draft a text on the lines of de Gaulle's 'luminous' remarks but immediately ran into problems: 'We quickly realized that translating the General's thoughts into articles of law would not be an easy task because the extraordinary talent with which he had expressed himself glided over the complexity of the subject and masked a certain ambiguity.'[34] De Gaulle had a gift for suggestive obscurity. The conundrum whether to opt for a 'federation' or a 'confederation' was solved by inventing the term 'Community', a word used by de Gaulle himself in a speech on 13 July. It had the advantage of sounding generous while having no precise juridical meaning – indeed no meaning at all. In reality, the new constitution offered the African states no more than the Loi Cadre of the Fourth Republic. All key areas of sovereignty – foreign policy, defence, finance – remained with France; and the states retained the French flag and national anthems. The result was less than many African leaders wanted.

SELLING THE CONSTITUTION

The constitution, making the French President head of the 'Community', gave the population of France's African territories a vote in the referendum to ratify it. To ensure a favourable result, de Gaulle set off on a five-day imperial odyssey round Africa where he hoped to capitalize on his prestige dating back to the Free French and on the Brazzaville Declaration of 1944. In Tananarive in Madagascar, Abidjan on the Ivory Coast and Brazzaville in Equatorial Africa he was greeted by ecstatic crowds. The Africans were offered the choice between accepting the terms of the Community – a 'yes' vote – and independence. The implication of choosing independence was that France would cut all links. This implicit blackmail was not to the taste of Ahmed Sékou Touré, the young nationalist leader of Guinea in West Africa. To his cost, he would discover that de Gaulle was not bluffing. Guinea's capital Conakry was the fourth lap on de Gaulle's tour. Sharing the podium with de Gaulle, Sékou Touré declared to cheers from the crowd that his people would 'prefer poverty in freedom to wealth in slavery'. Up to now, de Gaulle had been used only to cheering African crowds. Visibly irritated, he extemporized a reply which made it clear that France would 'of course draw the necessary consequences'. Refusing to attend an official dinner with 'that individual', he had his meal sent up to his room. He rescinded a previous offer to give Sékou Touré a ride on his plane to the next stop of his tour in Dakar, and at the airport shook his hand with the words 'Adieu, Guinea.' In the end, Guinea was the only black African territory to vote against the constitution. As he had threatened, de Gaulle drew the consequences and all French aid to Guinea ceased immediately.

The population of metropolitan France was more compliant than the Guineans. In the weeks before the referendum on 28 September, the country was bombarded with propaganda. Hundreds of thousands of posters lined the road calling on the population to vote 'yes for France' – a difficult poster to deface since opponents could hardly amend it to read 'no to France'. The most spectacular moment of the election campaign was a huge rally organized by André Malraux in the Place de la République in Paris. As symbolic as the place was the date, 4 September, anniversary of the declaration of the Third Republic in 1870. Malraux deployed all his skills as choreographer of Gaullism. Behind the statue of the Republic in the centre of the square rose an immense V 40 metres high – representing V for Victory and V for Fifth. Opening with a traditional Republican greeting – not 'Français, Françaises' but 'Citoyens, citoyennes' – Malraux went on to invoke the First Republic, Saint-Just, the soldiers of Year II who made 'Europe dance to the name of liberty'. He ended, 'Ici Paris! Honneur et Patrie! You are now going to hear General de Gaulle' – a not so subliminal reminder of the years of the Occupation when the Free French broadcasts would begin with exactly those words but beginning 'Ici Londres'. At that moment, a curtain parted, a Citroën appeared, de Gaulle stepped out, mounted the steps to the podium and lifted his arms above his head – in a giant V. At the end of his speech he called for the singing of the 'Marseillaise', and then dived into the crowd. The 100,000 people present had received personal invitations, and the official film of the occasion showed nothing of the violent scuffles between police and anti-Gaullist demonstrators in the streets around the square.

The most vociferous opponents of the constitution were unsurprisingly the Communist Party. Mendès France also denounced the whole process: he claimed that the electorate were being bullied into a plebiscite to support an individual – in the style of Napoleon III – rather than being genuinely consulted on an issue. But one of the heavyweights of the Socialist Party, Gaston Defferre, Mayor of Marseilles, who had opposed de Gaulle's return to power, decided to rally to the constitution. The Socialist Party officially voted to support it, and this led to a faction splitting off and forming a new dissident Autonomous Socialist Party (PSA). Le Monde, barometer of progressive liberal opinion, advocated a qualified 'yes'.

The result surpassed the most optimistic expectations of the Gaullists.

In mainland France the level of participation was a massive 85 per cent, 79 per cent of whom voted 'yes'. This meant that several million traditionally Communist voters must have ignored the recommendation of their Party to vote against. In the overseas territories, only Guinea voted no. One should not assume that most voters had much idea about the constitution they were approving. A poll on the eve of the referendum found that 49 per cent of respondents had not read a word of it; 56 per cent had never discussed it with family, friends or colleagues.[35] The electorate realized that they were being asked to vote not so much for or against a constitution as for or against a man. One astute analyst of the situation was the political philosopher Raymond Aron who had had a complex relationship to Gaullism. In 1943 he had written a famous article in London on the 'shadow of Bonaparte' (everyone knew whom he had in mind); after 1947 he had rallied to the RPF out of anti-Communism; in 1958, he was a reluctant supporter of de Gaulle's return to power despite the conditions in which it had occurred – although he was soon to move against de Gaulle again. He characterized the referendum as a classic 'bonapartist' conjuncture: 'Its three principal characteristics are: a climate of national crisis, the discredit of parliament and politicians, the popularity of a man . . . Whether Bonaparte, Boulanger, Pétain or de Gaulle, whether an adventurer, a ditherer, an old man or an authentically great man.'[36]

The new constitution was formally promulgated on 4 October. Parliamentary elections were set for the following month. These elections were another success for de Gaulle but not entirely as he had intended. Although there had been no official 'Gaullist' Party since the winding up of the RPF, Guichard, Soustelle and Chaban-Delmas set about rapidly creating one. Dubbed the Union pour la Nouvelle République (UNR), it fielded candidates in 341 constituencies, although de Gaulle ensured that none stood against any minister in his government (so Pflimlin, Mollet, Pinay and four others had no UNR candidates against them). Most UNR candidates had backgrounds as activists in the RPF or other para-Gaullist organizations; many of them had held some kind of elective office before. De Gaulle's aim in the elections was to avoid an excessively fragmented parliament which would make it impossible to form a stable majority – hence the formation of the UNR served his purposes – but equally he wanted to avoid a parliament dominated by any one party which might restrict his freedom of manoeuvre – even if that party, like the UNR, was supposedly acting in his name. To avoid the first danger, he opted against proportional representation in favour of a first-past-the-post system over two rounds; to avoid the second he opted against multi-member constituencies (*scrutin de liste*) where the victorious list receives all the seats in a *département*. Instead he went for two-round elections in single-member constituencies as had been the practice in the Third Republic. Electoral wisdom held that in the first round electors voted for the candidate they wanted and in the second for the one they least disliked. In theory, the second round acted as a shock absorber, preventing any landslide by any extremist party.

Although de Gaulle was kept abreast of the setting up of the UNR, he remained aloof from it. Before the elections he announced:

> Everyone will understand that I do not want, that I cannot get involved directly in this election. The mission that the country has entrusted me with precludes me from offering my support to anyone. I will speak in favour of nobody, even those who have always showed me friendly devotion through all vicissitudes . . . That impartiality obliged me to insist that my name, even in the form of an adjective, should not be used by any group or any candidate.[37]

This did not stop UNR candidates finding ways of suggesting that they were the 'true' supporters of de Gaulle. But so too did candidates from all other parties except the PCF. The Socialists reminded electors of Mollet's role in helping to draft de Gaulle's new constitution. The subliminal message was that a vote for the Socialists was a vote for de Gaulle. This ambiguous situation suited everyone. The Socialists hoped to benefit from de Gaulle's popularity, de Gaulle wanted the Socialists to perform respectably so that he would not be the prisoner of any one party – especially one organized by someone whose ideas about Algeria were as fixed as Soustelle's. This gave the election a slightly unreal atmosphere: officially 'Gaullists' were nowhere but de Gaulle was everywhere.

After the excitement generated by the referendum, the election campaign aroused little public interest. Electors clearly believed that in voting 'yes' to the constitution in September, they had already expressed their support for de Gaulle. At 23 per cent, the rate of abstention was higher than in any election during the Fourth Republic. The defection of many Communist voters from their Party's line in the referendum was confirmed in the first round of these elections in which the PCF lost 1.6 million votes. Its share of the vote, which had never dropped below 25 per cent since 1945, fell to 19 per cent. The second surprise was that the UNR which had been created only two months earlier secured 17.6 per cent of the vote, making it the second-largest party after the Communists. The Socialists and MRP, who had been the centrist linchpins of the Fourth Republic, held up reasonably well with 15.7 per cent and 10 per cent respectively.

The results of the second round were an even bigger surprise than those of the first. The UNR increased its share of the vote to 28 per cent and ended up with 189 out of 482 seats in parliament. This made the 'Gaullists' the largest party, although not with an overall majority. The Socialists ended up with only forty seats. This was a political earthquake which confounded everyone: of the 465 elected *députés* 131 had not sat in the previous parliament. France's leading expert on political parties Maurice Duverger expressed himself 'flabbergasted' that, contrary to the rules he himself had laid down in his book on political parties, the second round had amplified rather than blunted the effect of the first.[38] Electors who wanted to support de Gaulle had taken the view that the most logical choice was to support the party most credibly claiming to speak in his name. To choose the UNR had been in some sense to choose the centre ground, not the extremes.

Commenting on the results at the Council of Ministers, de Gaulle said he would have preferred more Socialists to have been elected. This was partly said to please Guy Mollet and the Socialists in his government, but it was probably also true. Several political commentators noted that the result of the elections had been to elect a *chambre introuvable* crammed with deputies possibly more Gaullist than de Gaulle – or at least thinking that they were.[39]

'RAISING THE FLAG'

During these five intense months of Algerian and African visits and constitutional reform, de Gaulle also rapidly imposed his mark on foreign policy. Within three weeks of returning to power, he took two hugely important decisions which were not immediately made public. One broke with the policies of his predecessors; the other confirmed them. The former occurred at the first meeting of the Defence Committee on 17 June when he put an end to the sharing of nuclear information with Germany and Italy which had been initiated at the end of 1957. The second occurred two days later, at the first meeting of an inter-ministerial committee on foreign policy, when he decided, despite his hostility to European integration, that France would respect the rules of the Treaty of Rome and begin reducing import tariffs on 1 January 1959.

France's allies viewed de Gaulle's return to power with a mixture of surprise, relief and apprehension.[40] Until the last moment, few foreign observers believed it would happen. Once the surprise had passed, there was relief at the prospect of France having a period of political stability, after the upheavals of the last few months. But there was also apprehension about de Gaulle's unpredictability, his reputation for anti-Americanism, and his hostility to European integration. Jebb, who saw him on 25 June, wrote that there was 'much less melancholy ... but less charm and less desire to please'. His views on NATO seemed 'less disastrous' than he had feared: 'I think it is not at all necessary to assume that the sombre thoughts which in a mood of frustration occur to a great statesman in opposition are necessarily those which will occur to him when he is once more on the top.'[41] This turned out to be as misguided as most of Jebb's predictions about de Gaulle.

As it happened, both the current American President, Eisenhower, and the current British Prime Minister, Harold Macmillan, had had close dealings with de Gaulle during the war. Their respect for him was mixed with wariness. Eisenhower, recalling various wartime spats, told the American Secretary of State, John Foster Dulles, 'to watch out for' de Gaulle because he was 'capable of the most extraordinary actions', such as his threat in 1944 to remove his forces from Allied command. Eisenhower told Dulles he had replied that de Gaulle could do what he wanted but at the risk of excluding France from a victory that the Allies would enjoy with or without France. He warned however: 'This attitude is not recommended, of course, for adoption by the State Department in present circumstance, particularly in light of de Gaulle's present position of power. It is offered only as an illustration of the type of action that de Gaulle is capable of.'[42] It was a sign of the importance of de Gaulle's return to power that both Dulles and Macmillan quickly made the journey to Paris to assess the intentions of their adversary – if adversary he was. Each was treated to a lecture on de Gaulle's philosophy of history. Macmillan was told that 'old Russia will bury the current regime' and that Soviet expansionism had more to do with the tradition of the tsars than with Communism.[43] Dulles, launching into a lecture on the dangers of international Communism, was startled to be told that when the Soviets talked about 'the Party' to justify their policies it was 'a bit like you talking of "the Congress"'.[44]

Apart from these generalities, de Gaulle had specific issues to discuss with each interlocutor. At their meeting on 29 June, Macmillan wanted to discover de Gaulle's attitude to the Treaty of Rome. The British had kept aloof from the negotiations leading up to the Treaty of Rome in the hope that they would come to nothing. But once the Six had taken the decision to set up the EEC the British wanted to protect their interests by negotiating a free trade agreement with it. Negotiations had been proceeding for months with no resolution. Since de Gaulle had previously opposed moves towards European unity, Macmillan hoped he might be more accommodating on this issue than his predecessors. Here he was disappointed since, as we have seen, one of de Gaulle's first decisions was to accept the Treaty. De Gaulle stuck to the cautious line of previous French negotiators regarding a free trade agreement with Britain just as the new Common Market was getting under way. Unwisely Macmillan tried to twist his arm by suggesting that if the French were not more conciliatory the British might need to reconsider their entire commitment to the defence of the continent and 'seek our friends elsewhere'. De Gaulle dramatized this encounter in his *Memoirs* by claiming that the British had threatened him with a continental blockade. This was not what Macmillan had said, but his attitude had been threatening enough to reinforce de Gaulle's decision to accept the Treaty of Rome, which was all the more attractive to him if the British were so keen to sabotage it.[45] Nothing was resolved. Even so Macmillan came away from the meeting surprisingly reassured about de Gaulle in his new incarnation:

> He displayed a modesty and simplicity of approach which was quite new to me. All the old conceits and prejudices seemed to have gone. One felt the same kind of confidence in him as one might feel in speaking to a priest. He is clearly in a very *éxalté* state about his duty ... He spoke of his affection for Britain. He said that the reason he had been so tiresome during the war was that he was representing a country that was ruined and dishonoured.[46]

With Dulles, the main bone of contention related to nuclear weapons. De Gaulle made it clear that France hoped for American assistance in the development of her atomic programme. Dulles responded that since the Americans were going to put their intercontinental missiles at the disposal of NATO the Europeans did not need their own nuclear weapons. These missiles would be controlled through a so-called 'double key' system operated by both the Europeans and the Americans. Since the Americans had the ultimate veto this did not allay European – and even more French – fears as to whether America would risk war for her allies – especially since Dulles said that the doctrine of 'massive retaliation' needed rethinking. Although cordial on the surface, the meeting served only to highlight disagreements.

Over the summer two international crises occurred to confirm de Gaulle's suspicion of his allies. The first took place in the Middle East, which had been the source of such bitter conflicts with the British during the war. In July there was a coup in Baghdad against the pro-western King Faisal. To prevent any kind of domino effect in the region the British and Americans sent troops to Jordan without consulting the French. Soon after this another mini-crisis flared up in August in the Far East when the Chinese navy bombarded the two islands of Quemoy and Matsu. To protect the non-Communist Chinese regime based in Formosa the American government despatched naval and air forces to the region. Since this was an area that lay outside the zone covered by the NATO alliance the Americans had not consulted their European allies. These incidents were part of the background to the famous Memorandum de Gaulle despatched to Eisenhower and Macmillan on 17 September. The time for sparring was over.

This Memorandum had been several weeks in the drafting and the final version was extensively rewritten by de Gaulle in person.[47] It was secret and only published many years later, although its broad contents soon became widely known. It highlighted two problems. First, France, Britain and the United States had global interests which the geographical remit of NATO, covering Europe and America, did not take account of. Secondly, the NATO alliance had originally been predicated on atomic weapons being 'a monopoly of the United States', which made it logical that defence issues were 'practically delegated' to the United States. This was also no longer 'justified in reality'. In short: 'France could, therefore, no longer consider that NATO in its present form meets the conditions of security of the free world and notably its own.' Instead de Gaulle proposed to supplement and reinforce the Alliance by a tripartite organization consisting of the United States, Great Britain and France.

Although the Memorandum ran to little over 500 words, it was both highly explosive and somewhat vague. The British and Americans were not sure how seriously to take it. After seeing de Gaulle at a NATO meeting at the end of the year, the British Foreign Secretary, Selwyn Lloyd, got the impression that the General felt 'the present NATO might as well be scrapped and a fresh start be made under triumvirate auspices'. But at the same meeting Dulles saw the French Foreign Minister, Couve de Murville, and was more reassured: 'None of De Gaulle's advisers share his rather extreme views about the triumvirate and NATO.'[48] De Gaulle had in his words 'raised the colours' – but no one knew yet how far he intended to go.

TWO OLD MEN AT COLOMBEY

De Gaulle's other major foreign policy initiative was directed towards Konrad Adenauer, the Chancellor of West Germany. Adenauer had dominated German politics since the foundation of the Federal Republic in 1949. Having lost his position as Mayor of Cologne when Hitler took power, he had in no way compromised himself with Nazism. As the leader of the Christian Democrats after the war, he worked stealthily to bring Germany back into the community of nations, seizing every opportunity to form a good working relationship with French Fourth Republic foreign ministers, many of whom were also Christian Democrats. Viscerally anti-Communist, and fearful of the Soviet Union with its puppet regime in East Germany, Adenauer had been disappointed by the failure of the EDC which he saw as an opportunity to build up Western German military strength. But he had received a consolation prize in the form of German entry into NATO. The two keystones of his foreign policy were the American alliance and European unity.

Although reliant on America, Adenauer was perpetually anxious about the depth of America's commitment to German security. Now de Gaulle's arrival in power was another worrying development. Throughout the events of May 1958, Adenauer had not taken the prospect of de Gaulle's return seriously. He commented in his diary during the crisis: 'Herr de Gaulle is supposed to be in very poor health; he is almost blind in one eye, and he has really grown fat.'[49] When this complacency turned out to be misplaced, Adenauer had to rethink his position. He had never met de Gaulle but viewed him as a traditional French nationalist, with worryingly pro-Soviet proclivities. He told the American Ambassador in July 1958 that everything that had happened in the world over the last ten years 'has passed de Gaulle by without leaving any traces'.[50]

After de Gaulle had seen Macmillan and Dulles in Paris, his master-stroke was to invite Adenauer to spend the night at Colombey. No other foreign leader was ever granted this privilege. Arriving at Colombey on 14 September – a little late because his car first ended up in another village called Colombey-les-Belles – Adenauer, expecting the worst, was pleasantly surprised to be greeted by a courteous and dignified host who seemed keen to build a strong personal relationship. These two old men were both Catholic traditionalists who shared many values. After an introductory lunch, de Gaulle suggested that they send their advisers away so that they could talk alone. An interpreter remained on hand but his services were only intermittently required. Another surprise for Adenauer was that de Gaulle expressed himself reasonably well in German. De Gaulle's charm offensive was shameless. 'You are the younger of us,' he told the Chancellor who was six years older than him, 'I do not have your psychological and physical force.'

Their conversation ranged widely. De Gaulle declared that only a close Franco-German relationship could 'save Western Europe'. He also played on Adenauer's insecurities by planting a few barbs against the British 'who were not proper Europeans' and the Americans who 'were not reliable, not very solid and understand nothing about History or Europe'. What struck Adenauer most was de Gaulle's comment about how he saw his role:

My most difficult task is to bring down to earth and to a sense of realities those nationalist Frenchmen who float in their nationalist clouds ... The French people have been suffering from a long illness. They were a very great people. Above all, they believed themselves to be very great. They saw themselves as the stars of the world stage. It is true they have often been that. But they have not adapted to the real situation.

Adenauer spent the night at the house as a guest and was seduced by the old-fashioned hospitality and family atmosphere. De Gaulle wrote to his daughter afterwards: 'Maman arranged everything perfectly. Perhaps at dinner (14 people) we could have done with more help. But maman insisted that the house would be just as it always is.'[51] De Gaulle had also borrowed his brother-in-law's ferociously anti-German femme de ménage to help out. She returned to Calais with her anti-German feelings attenuated by Adenauer's old-fashioned good manners.[52] Adenauer returned to Bonn in a trance. He reported back to the German President: 'De Gaulle lives in a very barren part of the country, with a poor population, in a very simple house, that has only a few well-furnished rooms on the ground floor but otherwise it is very primitive ... Everything appeared to be very solitary surrounded by forest and no village.' Adenauer concluded that he had had to 'throw away all the prejudices that he had formed from German reports and conversations with Americans'.[53]

Adenauer fell back to earth two weeks later when he heard about de Gaulle's Memorandum to Macmillan and Eisenhower – sent three days after the historic Colombey meeting. He was upset not only by the content – that de Gaulle was bidding for a privileged partnership with Britain and America – but also that he had not breathed a word of his intentions. Macmillan, who happened to be meeting Adenauer at that moment, warned him, as someone who had known de Gaulle since 1943, that 'he was apt to treat his friends with this curious ineptness and rudeness. It was because of his mysticism and egotism.' Macmillan was delighted to twist the knife in the wound, seeing an opportunity to play on Adenauer's annoyance and win support for British attempts to obtain a free trade agreement with the European Community. After their meeting, he purred contentedly: 'Adenauer very hurt and angry. I do not think he will ever trust de Gaulle again.'[54] Perhaps de Gaulle had genuinely not predicted Adenauer's annoyance; perhaps he had gambled that it would not last. If that was the case, he proved correct. Although, as Adenauer's biographer writes, the honeymoon of Colombey lasted 'exactly twenty-seven days',[55] its magic never entirely wore off.

De Gaulle seized an opportunity to rebuild Adenauer's confidence a few weeks later when a major international crisis exploded over Berlin. On

10 November, the Soviet leader Nikita Khrushchev suddenly announced that he no longer recognized the Potsdam agreement according to which Berlin was divided into four zones. He demanded that the city become a demilitarized free city and that all Allied troops should leave. His reasons for sparking this crisis are not entirely clear. It was possibly a way of forcing the west to recognize the German Democratic Republic, which it had always refused to do. Although categorically rejecting the Soviet demand in public, the British and Americans did not privately rule out the idea of exploring a compromise solution. De Gaulle, however, adopted a position of intransigence. He genuinely believed that Khrushchev was bluffing, but the crisis also gave him the opportunity of insinuating into Adenauer's mind, at their second meeting in Germany on 26 November, that the Americans and British could never be trusted. At the same meeting, de Gaulle not only reaffirmed his commitment to the Treaty of Rome but formally committed France to respecting the 1 January 1959 deadline for the first tariff reductions. Previously everyone had assumed that the French would request a delay until their balance of payments situation improved.[56] This made it easier for de Gaulle to force his partners to accept France's veto of a free trade agreement with Britain. That veto was announced publicly on 15 November, ten days before de Gaulle's second meeting with Adenauer. Although the announcement was not a complete surprise, the brutal suddenness with which it was announced marked a break in the style of France's foreign policy. Jebb wrote later: 'Up to that moment we had often taken France for granted. Now it became clear that she might no longer be a difficult, though essentially subservient, partner. On the contrary a quite formidable adversary was about to emerge.'[57]

THE RUEFF PLAN

The undertaking to respect the deadline for implementing France's obligations under the Rome Treaty without invoking an opt-out clause was the most important decision made by de Gaulle in his first six months in power. It was a bold move given that the French economy had been traditionally protected by high tariff barriers and was suffering from high inflation, budget deficits and massive balance of payments deficits. Without severe economic medicine, the decision could have been disastrous for the stability of the French currency and public finances.[58]

De Gaulle's Finance Minister, the conservative Antoine Pinay, had staved off an immediate financial crisis by floating a loan that was quickly subscribed. But this was only a stopgap, and over the summer de Gaulle harried Pinay to produce a more durable financial plan. After procrastinating, Pinay's response in September was to set up a small advisory committee under the chairmanship of Jacques Rueff, a brilliant but maverick economist whose lifetime obsession was the eradication of inflation and the pursuit of monetary stability. He had clashed with Keynes on the subject in the 1930s. The Rueff Committee took evidence from economists, civil servants and bankers, but Rueff already knew what he wanted to do. He had a radical plan which included a restructuring of the French credit system – in effect limiting the Bank of France's ability to print money – increasing taxes and cutting expenditure. Quite apart from the political fallout of such drastic measures, many of those consulted by the Rueff Committee were convinced that the deflationary impact of such measures risked asphyxiating the economy.

The Rueff Committee met thirty-nine times, working against the clock because the government's authority to govern by ordinance ran out on 1 January. That was also the date when France was supposed to impose the first tariff cuts required by the Treaty of Rome. Rueff's report was ready by the start of November and ignored the reservations which others had expressed. He presented his proposals directly to de Gaulle, Pompidou, Pinay and the Governor of the Bank of France on 18 November. When the Governor of the Bank of France, Wilfrid Baumgartner, an old enemy of Rueff, who saw the Governor as too lax on monetary policy, was asked for his opinion by de Gaulle, he replied that 'there would be a lot to say.' To which de Gaulle snapped in reply: 'Then say it.'[59] It was clear to those present that de Gaulle backed the plan. On 25 November he received Rueff in private to interrogate him further. The eloquence with which Rueff presented his ideas could not have been better calibrated to resonate with him. Rueff's original report to Pinay had opened with the words: 'This programme cannot be that of a group or a party but only that of all the French who want their country to continue to exist.'[60] De Gaulle was no economist but this was the kind of language he understood.

On the evening of Christmas Day, the day before the government met to discuss the Rueff Plan, de Gaulle summoned Roger Goetze, one of the financial officials attached to his *cabinet*, and asked him point blank for his view:

> Everyone is against the plan. I am going to ask you a question and you will only reply tomorrow morning: do you guarantee that the plan has a two-thirds chance of success? I consider that in politics there is always a third of uncertainty and risk. That is the part that concerns me. But you are the expert. You will tell me tomorrow morning if you consider whether the plan has a two-thirds chance of success. If yes, I will adopt it.[61]

Goetze was a representative of the post-1945 generation of Ministry of Finance officials whose gospel was Keynes. For people like him Rueff was a neo-liberal relic from another age. In this case, however, the issue was more technical than ideological. On the next day, Goetze assured de Gaulle that the French economy was robust enough to take the medicine.

The meeting of the government to discuss the plan started in the afternoon and finished at midnight. Rueff, who was in attendance, remembered the 'tragic atmosphere' and 'profound hostility' he could read in the eyes of most ministers.[62] His measures included a reduction in a wide range of tariffs accompanied by an immediate devaluation of 17.5 per cent in order to allow France to recover her competitiveness. The psychological impact of devaluation was mitigated by a currency reform: 100 old francs would now be worth 1 franc. Taxes were to be increased and there were to be extensive cuts in a range of state subsidies. Especially controversial was the cut in the pensions of war veterans and ending the indexation of agricultural prices. Alienating two of the most powerful lobbies in France – veterans and farmers – was a high-risk strategy. But, despite a few tweaks, the plan was adopted in its entirety. After the meeting, the Socialist leader Mollet submitted his resignation. Although this would not have prevented the implementation of the plan by ordinance, it would have represented a blow to the unity government de Gaulle had presided over since June. In the end, Mollet was prevailed upon to suspend his resignation until the transition to the new Republic on 8 January. With the façade of political unity preserved, de Gaulle announced the economic measures in a televised speech on 28 December. He translated the dismal language of economics into the golden rhetoric of Gaullism: 'Without these efforts and these sacrifices, we would remain a country that lags behind, oscillating perpetually between drama and mediocrity. On the other hand if we succeed, what a step this will be on the road that leads us to the summits.'

Although usually called the Pinay–Rueff Plan, de Gaulle's close personal involvement in it makes it more appropriate to talk of the Rueff–de Gaulle Plan. Pinay had been far from enthusiastic. This was the second time in his career that de Gaulle had intervened decisively in a major issue of economic policy. The first was in 1945 when he rejected the equally radical measures proposed by Mendès France. De Gaulle had few fixed views on economics, although he responded instinctively to Rueff's defence of 'sound' money. Goetze remarked that de Gaulle had economic ideas of 'simple good sense, a bit peasant-like'.[63] What made it possible to be so bold in 1958 – unlike 1945 – was an unprecedentedly favourable political context unlikely ever to be replicated. Almost any single measure in the Rueff Plan would have been enough in normal circumstances to bring down a Fourth Republic government. But three months earlier de Gaulle had won a massive referendum victory followed by successful parliamentary elections, and for a few days more he had also the power to legislate by ordinance. He could do what he wanted. When Goetze warned de Gaulle that the measures risked being massively unpopular, the reply was: 'So the French will squeal . . . and then what?'[64] De Gaulle could act in the confidence that the Algerian crisis made him for the moment indispensable in the eyes of the political class. Six years later, when the Algerian War was over and de Gaulle was facing a miners' strike and much opposition from trade unions, his then Prime Minister Pompidou remarked wryly: 'Ah 1958, those were the good old days! All one had to say was Algeria, Algeria, and one had no problems with the unions.'[65]

BACK TO ALGERIA

Behind the smokescreen of his ambiguous rhetoric – no one really knew what he was thinking about Algeria – immediately on returning to power de Gaulle had initiated secret contacts with the FLN through the intermediary of the moderate Algerian nationalist Abderrahmane Farès. In total, de Gaulle had six meetings with Farès between June and September. Farès paid four visits to the FLN leader Ferhat Abbas in Switzerland, and conveyed de Gaulle's message that he was ready personally to meet FLN representatives on French soil to discuss the terms of a ceasefire. The FLN answer was always the same: negotiations must take place not on French soil but on neutral ground, and the FLN must be recognized as the only accredited representative of the Algerian nation. Since neither condition was acceptable to de Gaulle it is surprising that the contacts stayed open as long as they did.[66] They remained at the level of informal conversations, but de Gaulle even went as far as to authorize Pompidou to confirm in writing his willingness to meet FLN emissaries to discuss a ceasefire.[67] This was not entirely new. Guy Mollet's government had tried the same in 1956 before reverting to a more hardline position.

If de Gaulle hoped that his reputation would allow him to succeed where Mollet had failed, he could not have been more wrong. To regain the initiative after de Gaulle's return to power, in August 1958 the FLN unleashed for the first time a wave of terrorist attacks on French territory, including an attempt to assassinate Soustelle. On 19 September, the FLN leaders in Cairo announced that they were forming a provisional government (Gouvernement Provisoire de la République Algérienne – GPRA) under the presidency of Abbas.

After the referendum de Gaulle paid a third visit to Algeria in October. At the city of Constantine he announced on 3 October a massive five-year investment plan for the Algerian economy. This included measures for the redistribution of land and to facilitate the recruitment of Muslims into the administration. The Constantine Plan had in fact been prepared before de Gaulle's return to power, but the fact that he had embraced it signified that in some form he envisaged Algeria as part of France – although he continued studiously to avoid any reference to Algeria's political future.[68] In his first press conference since coming back to power, on 23 October, de Gaulle made what seemed like a spectacular gesture. In one of those striking phrases for which he had a gift, he proposed to the FLN a 'peace of the brave' while again paying homage to their courage. He offered full security to any leader of the rebellion ready to come to France to negotiate an end to the fighting – though the effect of his words was undermined by an unfortunate reference to the 'white flag' raised by emissaries of peace when shooting stopped. This sounded as if he was calling for surrender. As one member of the FLN said in private: 'De Gaulle has thrown us some flowers but we would have preferred that he insulted us if at the same time he spoke of independence.'[69]

Despite this spectacular initiative de Gaulle must have known that his offer had no chance of success. He was offering in public what the FLN had already rejected in private. The point was to score easy points with the French public, and in this he succeeded. Even *L'Humanité* praised the tone of the speech. Its curt rejection by the GPRA was widely condemned. In publicity terms de Gaulle had won that round. And a letter he wrote to Salan immediately afterwards reveals how restricted his intentions really were:

> One might one day foresee the Ferhat Abbas organization asking to send 'delegates' to the mainland. In such an eventuality these 'delegates' will not be taken to Paris. They will only see – in some corner of the provinces – representatives of the military command. They will only be allowed to discuss the issue of a 'ceasefire' and this 'ceasefire' will necessarily include the handing over of their arms to the military authorities.[70]

Although the referendum on the constitution had seemingly been a success for de Gaulle in Algeria as well as in mainland France, it had also demonstrated how little he controlled the army. His instructions to Salan had been clear that the vote was not to be presented as a preference for any one Algerian solution over any other but only as a vote of confidence in himself.[71] The army ignored this and presented the referendum as a vote for integration. Great pressure was exerted on the electors to give the 'right'

39. (*above*) Addressing a massive RPF rally in Vincennes, in 1947.

40. (*left*) Visiting Lille, the city of his birth, in 1949.

41. Madame de Gaulle shopping at Morgat in Brittany, an RPF poster in the bakery window, June 1949.

42. La Boisserie, Colombey, bought in 1934 and from 1946 his only home.

43. The first page of de Gaulle's *War Memoirs* bears out his comment '*Je n'a pas la plume facile* [I do not find writing easy].'

44. 4 June 1958: de Gaulle tells the crowd in Algiers that he has 'understood' them.

45. (*above*) The four
putschist generals in Algiers,
April 1961. From left to
right: André Zeller, Edmond
Jouhaud, Raoul Salan,
Maurice Challe.

46. (*left*) 23 April 1961:
de Gaulle in uniform
denounces on television the
putsch by the '*quarteron*'
of generals.

47. (*left*) Michel Debré (1958–62): ultra-loyalist torn between his devotion to de Gaulle and his commitment to French Algeria.

48. (*above*) Georges Pompidou (1962–8): a steely operator behind his façade of genility.

49. Maurice Couve de Murville (1968–9): an icily efficient administrator who never revealed his intimate view of de Gaulle's more extravagant initiatives.

50. André Malraux, Minister of Culture, showing de Gaulle round an exhibition of Mexican art at the Petit Palais in 1962. 'How does Malraux know so many things?' de Gaulle asked.

51. (*below*) President Ahidjo of Cameroon and de Gaulle at the Elysée Palace on 21 June 1967, with Jacques Foccart inevitably in the background.

52. Visiting the monument to the Free French at Mont-Valérien on 18 June 1964.

53. The 'Pantheonization' of Jean Moulin, December 1964. De Gaulle, in uniform, visible on the extreme right.

answer. This was not what de Gaulle had wanted, but at least the referendum now gave him the confidence to issue formal instructions, on 9 October, that the military cease any participation in the Committees of Public Safety.[72] This was comparable to his decision in 1944 to abolish the Patriotic Militia. The army obeyed reluctantly, but this was not enough to ensure that it would faithfully carry out his instructions, as emerged in the run-up to the parliamentary elections of November 1958. For the first time Muslims in Algeria would enjoy equal voting rights. De Gaulle was explicit in his instructions to Salan that the elections must occur in 'absolute conditions of liberty and sincerity' with the possibility of competing lists: 'The worst pitfall would be single lists favoured by the authorities.'[73] De Gaulle was seeking a moderate Muslim middle ground to undercut the FLN. In this regard the elections in Algeria – entirely manipulated by the army to ensure that only hardline proponents of full 'integration' could stand – were a disaster.

All this confirmed de Gaulle's view that he needed to replace Salan, who was moved from Algiers and appointed to a new honorary role in France (Inspector General of Defence). Informing Salan of this decision on 25 November, de Gaulle wrote that he esteemed him not only as a 'loyal servant [féal] of very great quality but as my companion and my friend'. Not to be outdone in hypocrisy, Salan replied that the letter 'is the greatest pledge of confidence that I could receive from him who is in the eyes of the People, of France, of the Army, the salvation of the Fatherland'.[74] What de Gaulle really thought of Salan can be seen from his marginal annotations – 'verbiage' occurs on several occasions – to Salan's final report on leaving Algeria. Where Salan talked of the need for 'absolute justice' to reign in Algeria, de Gaulle scribbled, 'about time that he takes note of that'; where Salan commented on the economic development of Algeria, de Gaulle scribbled, 'for the profit of a few and the misery of the majority'; where Salan complained that he had not had sufficient military forces to fulfil his task, de Gaulle scribbled, 'Alexander conquered the world, Caesar Gaul, Napoleon Europe with less.'[75]

On 21 December de Gaulle was elected President of the Republic – for a seven-year term as had already been the case for the previous two Republics – by the electoral college of about 80,000 electors created by the new constitution. This included the members of both houses of parliament and representatives of elected departmental and municipal councils. There were other candidates but de Gaulle's election by 78 per cent of the electors was a foregone conclusion. The transfer of powers between President Coty and President de Gaulle, between one Republic and another, took place at the Elysée on 8 January 1959. After the short official ceremony, followed by a lunch, the two men were driven together to the Arc to lay a wreath on the tomb of the Unknown Soldier. De Gaulle, who was supposed to have accompanied Coty back to his car, took his leave somewhat abruptly with a curt '*Au revoir*, Monsieur Coty' and threw himself into the crowds, leaving his somewhat disconsolate predecessor to make his way alone to the car that drove him back to obscurity in his home town of Le Havre. De Gaulle got into his car and was driven down the Champs-Elysées, scene of his triumphal parade fourteen years earlier. At his side was Georges Pompidou. Probably few people watching had any idea who Pompidou was, but it was de Gaulle's way of thanking him for the role he had played in the momentous six months since May 1958.

PART FOUR

Republican Monarch,
1959–1965

If what has been done, in answer to my call and through my actions, over the last thirty years, to give back to our country, in accordance with the thousand-year lessons of the royal house of France [les leçons millénaires de la maison de France], her purpose, her rank and her universal vocation, becomes the starting point of a new upward path in our history, I will be able to thank God, from the other world, for the Destiny he has accorded to me.

De Gaulle to the Comte de Paris,
5 May 1969, in LNCIII 1053

20

'This Affair Which Absorbs and Paralyses Us', 1959–1962

On 9 January 1959, the first government of the Fifth Republic was pro-claimed. De Gaulle immediately named Michel Debré as his Prime Minister. With an ultra-loyal Gaullist Prime Minister, a near-majority in parliament and the support of public opinion, de Gaulle was in an unprecedentedly strong position to carry out the 'resurrection' he had announced in his press conference of 19 May 1958. He had in mind not only the reform of France's political institutions but also a reassertion of France's position in the world. Over the next four years, much of his time was indeed taken up by foreign affairs. Just in the first three months of 1960, he hosted a long state visit to France by Nikita Khrushchev, paid state visits to London and North America and hosted a big international summit in Paris. His obses-sion was to reorient France's defence policy away from the Atlantic Alliance and towards the creation of an independent nuclear deterrent.

But for the first four years the gnawing problem of Algeria was always in the background, sucking up the energy he hoped to devote to other matters. Seeing de Gaulle in November 1960, Pierson Dixon, who had replaced Jebb as British Ambassador two months before, observed:

> He gave the impression of a man who was having to make an effort to switch his mind from Algeria, which to judge from the comings and goings at the Elysée, must occupy his working day ... Until he can make headway with Algeria I expect we must reckon with him as more or less of a passenger on the wider issues.[1]

Given the dizzying number of Gaullist initiatives on foreign affairs, de Gaulle as 'passenger' was a curious suggestion, but Algeria was certainly never far from his mind. A year later, the French Ambassador in London, Jean Chauvel, was in Paris to prepare an Anglo-French summit, but he hardly got to see de Gaulle because of another flare-up in Algeria.[2] For this reason, although a separate chapter devoted to Algeria does not entirely convey the way that events crowded in upon de Gaulle in his first four years in power, it is not too serious a distortion. As de Gaulle himself wrote to his son in January 1961, Algeria was 'this affair which absorbs and paralyses us'.[3] It did so for four years.

'PRINCE OF EQUIVOCATION'

A few weeks after de Gaulle's return to power, Robert Buron, an MRP minister with liberal views on Algeria, wrote in his diary: 'What does de Gaulle think of the Algerian business? I defy any of the ministers present to give a definite answer to this question.' Fourteen months later, he was no wiser: 'Where is this prince of equivocation leading us?' A year later, the mystery remained: 'If I am still hoping, I understand less and less.'[4] Fifty years later historians remain no less perplexed. In his book *The Edge of the Sword*, de Gaulle had propounded the idea that leaders should employ mystery and ruse to achieve their objectives. Nowhere does he seem to have followed these precepts more faithfully than in his approach to Algeria after 1958. Or is the truth that he had no control over events – that what seemed like duplicity and calculation were in fact hesitation and improvisation?

In his *Memoirs* de Gaulle claimed to have been totally consistent:

> There was in my view no solution but that Algeria should have the right to dispose of her own destiny ... That was my strategy. As for the tactics, I had to move by stages, and carefully ... Without ever changing objective, I had to manoeuvre, until the moment when finally good sense shone through the fog.[5]

In reality, no one did more to create the 'fog' than de Gaulle himself. Before 1958, he had said nothing publicly about Algeria for four years. His private comments were studiedly ambiguous, tailored to what his interlocutors wanted to hear. Liberals were told one thing, hardliners another.

In the fog, only two certainties stand out. First, de Gaulle never believed in the 'integration' favoured by the most uncompromising advocates of *Algérie française*.[6] That idea had been launched by Soustelle in 1955.[7] Previously France's policy had been one of 'assimilation': making the Muslims 'French' so that one day – far off – they might become full citizens. 'Integration' was different because in theory it respected the cultural differences between Muslims and Europeans while simultaneously proposing the integration of Algerian institutions into those of France and making Muslims full citizens. Although for decades the *pieds noirs* had refused to extend any rights to Muslims, they now accepted 'integration' as a new way of hanging on to their power: the nine million Muslims, who were a majority in Algeria, would be a controllable minority once 'integrated' into a wider electorate of forty-five million French voters.

To prove that de Gaulle had betrayed the *pieds noirs*, Soustelle later cited a letter of December 1956 that seemed favourable to integration. In fact, the letter was characteristically evasive. It seemed to support Soustelle's ideas for Algeria – nevertheless avoiding the word 'integration' – while implying that they could not be implemented without a change of regime. It was reasonable for Soustelle to have concluded that de Gaulle was in his camp.[8] But when lobbying Alain de Sérigny on de Gaulle's behalf in 1958, the best Soustelle could find to say was that 'de Gaulle was not won over to integration' but might be if convinced that the Muslims wanted it.[9] Supporters of *Algérie française* drew comfort from the 'fraternization' that had allegedly occurred between Europeans and Muslims during the pro-de Gaulle demonstrations of May 1958. One Gaullist described this 'miracle of reconciliation' as 'one of the most astonishing in our history', proof that the Muslims did genuinely want integration.[10] Immediately after arriving in Algiers on 17 May 1958 to push for de Gaulle's return to power, Soustelle sent him an excited telegram: 'there is a new fact of capital importance; the "thawing" of the Muslims. They are demonstrating in tens of thousands with the Europeans. This evening I have seen Muslim women burn their veils in front of the governor's palace and embrace the Europeans.'[11] In reality, 'fraternization' was orchestrated by the army, but supporters of integration were convinced that the magic of de Gaulle's name had converted the Muslims of Algeria to France.

De Gaulle never believed in 'integration' nor did he welcome it. When the recently elected Gaullist *député* Alain Peyrefitte met de Gaulle for the first time in March 1959, he was startled to be told that those who supported integration were 'asses' (*jean-foutre*):

> Have you seen the Muslims with their turbans and their djellabas? You can see that they are not French. Try and integrate oil and vinegar. Shake the bottle. After a moment they separate again. The Arabs are Arabs, the French are French. Do you think that the French can absorb ten million Muslims who will tomorrow be twenty million and after tomorrow forty? If we carry out integration, if all the Berbers and Arabs of Algeria were regarded as French, how would one stop them coming to settle on the mainland where the standard of living is so much higher? My village would no longer be called Colombey-les-deux-Eglises but Colombey-the-two-Mosques.[12]

De Gaulle made other private comments in the same vein. He was sceptical about integration because his beliefs were not grounded in that progressive tradition according to which the universal values of French republicanism had created a community of equal citizens superseding racial or ethnic identities. In Algeria, that ideal had always been more honoured in the breach than in the observance, but it gave Soustelle's commitment to integration an ideological coherence rooted in the progressive left. For that reason Soustelle was not wrong to dub de Gaulle's opposition to integration 'racist'.[13] Although de Gaulle kept his religion separate from his politics, historically he conceived of France as part of a European Christian civilization. In 1945, his provisional government had drawn up policies to promote immigration as a way of overcoming France's demographic weakness. In these discussions, he came down on the side of controlled immigration to limit the 'influx of Mediterraneans and Orientals' and to encourage those from northern Europe.[14] Many politicians who supposedly subscribed to race-blind republicanism subconsciously shared the same views. What distinguished de Gaulle was his clear-headedness about what 'integration' would really mean if it were taken seriously. The irony was that the logic of Soustelle's progressive republicanism led him to defend any means – including torture – to keep Algeria French while de Gaulle's pragmatic conservatism led him ultimately to accept Algerian independence.

Independence, however, was far down the road when de Gaulle returned to power. The second certainty about de Gaulle in 1958 is that he believed that Algeria should remain 'French' in some form. Those who argue the opposite can find evidence for their views – as one can find evidence for most things where de Gaulle is concerned – starting with a comment the General made to André Philip in 1944: 'You know that autonomy will end in independence.' But that comment was made precisely at a moment when de Gaulle had opted *against* autonomy: it was a marker of his commitment to keeping Algeria French. The frequent private comments he made in the 1950s about the inevitability of Algerian independence were quips in his catastrophist vein – predictions about all the disasters facing France if the Fourth Republic continued. The implication was that, if he returned to power, things might be different. In 1958, only a tiny minority supported Algerian independence. They included intellectuals of the extreme left, such as Jean-Paul Sartre, and lucid conservatives, of whom the most notable was Raymond Aron, who believed that the economic costs of holding on to Algeria were unsustainable. Since de Gaulle had unveiled a costly plan of economic investment at Constantine in October 1958, this was clearly not his view.

If de Gaulle believed neither in integration nor in independence, what did he believe? In 1958, these two extreme positions did not seem to be the only options. Since the outbreak of the Algerian War, French officials had been elaborating innumerable federalist or multi-communitarian schemes for an Algeria linked to France. De Gaulle's archives contain a document, drafted soon after his return to power, outlining future scenarios for Algeria. At the two ends of the spectrum were independence and integration, but the document considered no fewer than fifteen other possibilities in between.[15] Most of these schemes presupposed the emergence of interlocutors in Algeria between the FLN and the *Algérie française* hardliners. It was for this reason that de Gaulle had genuinely wanted fair elections in Algeria in November 1958. Before those elections, he had a conversation with Soustelle in which he outlined his idea of 'drowning the rebels in democracy'. The next day, Soustelle wrote to de Gaulle that he was sceptical about this tactic. He talked of the Muslim majority's attachment to France but in reality he knew that it no longer existed:

And what if they drowned us in our democracy? In other words I worry that cunning and violent men . . . use their elective positions . . . to work on the masses and detach them from us . . . Is there not a risk that the mass of Muslims will become disaffected if they see elected candidates preaching freely against France? It seems to me that to avoid this danger . . . it is necessary to reaffirm the mission of the army in Algeria to take charge of the mass of Muslims and give them confidence in the presence of France.

This elicited an ironic comment in the margin by de Gaulle: 'so that is what he really means!'[16] It was Soustelle's method that the army employed. The election was entirely fixed. But de Gaulle had not abandoned hope of finding a genuine independent Muslim middle ground to cut the ground from under the FLN. This remained a key thread of his policy for the next two years.[17] The other was to win the war against the FLN as the necessary precondition of a political solution.

To achieve these twin objectives, de Gaulle ended the anomaly, dating from the crisis of May 1958, by which the army commander in Algeria, Salan, was also the government's political representative. Salan's replacement, the loyal Gaullist General Maurice Challe, was told he would be provided with the resources needed to win the war, but that he must leave politics to de Gaulle's newly appointed civil representative, Paul Delouvrier. The appointment of Delouvrier, a brilliant young left-wing economist with no experience of politics, showed the importance de Gaulle attached to the economic development of Algeria. It was another sign that he was not planning to give Algeria up.

'A PROBLEM WITH NO SOLUTION'

Before appointing Delouvrier, de Gaulle sent him on a fact-finding mission to Algeria in the autumn of 1958. Briefing de Gaulle on the content of his report, Delouvrier decided not to mince his words:

> Immediately I said to him: 'General, my conclusion is that Algeria will be independent.' The General barely reacted except to say almost offhandedly: 'Perhaps ... but in 20 years.' I replied: 'I know you cannot say that it will be independent tomorrow even if that is what you think, but it is enough for me that you imagine this to be possible in 20 years for me to continue with my report. Otherwise there would be no point.'[18]

He accepted the appointment on the understanding that, although de Gaulle did not see any solution in the immediate term, 'the doors were left open.'[19] De Gaulle's official instructions to Delouvrier were sonorously vague: 'You are France in Algeria ... The government's desire is that Algeria, through her trials, and despite lost time, reveals herself more and more in her profound reality thanks to the action undertaken by France as a whole.'[20] When Delouvrier tried to ascertain what these words actually meant, de Gaulle's only unhelpful advice was: 'Never say *Algérie française*.'[21]

To complicate matters, de Gaulle's Prime Minister, Michel Debré, was strongly committed to *Algérie française*, if not to the most radical version of integration.[22] When Delouvrier, otherwise an admirer of Debré, commented to de Gaulle that this would put the two of them in an impossible position, de Gaulle snapped back: 'That is my business.'[23] These were not the only complications. Debré's *directeur de cabinet* Pierre Racine made no secret of his belief that Algeria should be granted significantly greater autonomy. The head of de Gaulle's military *cabinet*, General Beaufort, was firmly committed to *Algérie française* but de Gaulle took as one of his main advisers on Algeria Bernard Tricot, a career civil servant with considerable North African experience and liberal views on Algeria. Before agreeing to take on the post, Tricot expressed his concern that de Gaulle's first decisions seemed to point towards integration. De Gaulle replied: 'No decision has for the moment been taken concerning integration.'[24] This was enough for Tricot to accept.

All these conflicting views meant that Delouvrier was often in the dark about what he was supposed to be doing:

> Every time I went to the Elysée I was pulled between the military and the civil advisers ... The latter composed of Courcel [Secretary General of the Elysée]

(sometimes assisted by Tricot) said to me: 'Don't listen to what the military *cabinet* tell you. We are the sole repositories of the deepest beliefs of de Gaulle on Algeria' ... But on his side General Beaufort would say to me: 'I am the sole repository of the thinking of General de Gaulle on Algeria. Don't listen to Courcel (who is for independence).'[25]

These contradictions reflected the divisions of France's elites over Algeria – but they also served de Gaulle's purposes by maximizing his freedom of manoeuvre. He wrote to General Ely at the start of 1959:

> Whatever policy is to be carried out regarding Algeria, it is completely my affair and I expect of subordinates nothing other than this: that they execute it honestly. It is possible that a day will come when integration is possible. But that day has not come since we are having to kill 1000 enemy fighters each month ... One must recognize that integration is at present just an empty word.[26]

For the moment de Gaulle's policy was to wait. As he remarked to one politician in 1958: 'The most common error of all statesmen is to believe firmly that there exists at any one moment a solution to every problem. There are in some periods problems to which no solution exists.'[27] A few months later, he said the same in a meeting of the Council of Ministers: 'There is at present no political solution: Algeria needs to be transformed and the solutions will appear then.'[28] In public, de Gaulle's preferred phrase of the moment was that Algeria should be allowed to develop her 'courageous personality' (13 October 1958), her 'living personality' (23 October 1958), her 'new personality'. In April 1959, he tested the water by remarking off the record to a journalist that the 'Algeria of granddad [*l'Algérie de Papa*]' was dead. Immediately afterwards the Elysée contacted the press to qualify the words. But saying that the future Algeria would be different from the past Algeria was a statement with which even Soustelle would have agreed – although he would have meant something different from de Gaulle.

To win over moderate Muslim opinion, de Gaulle amnestied 7,000 internees in Algeria at the start of 1959. He also tried to rein in the abuses of the army. After hearing the case of a girl who had been killed by the army while allegedly trying to escape capture, he wrote to Debré drily: 'I cannot conceive, *a priori*, that our forces have no other remedies to prevent a young girl from fleeing except to fire on her.'[29] Municipal elections in April 1959 resulted in the election of about 12,000 Muslim local councillors. Even if many of these were 'official' government candidates, this was a first step towards creating a middle ground. Although de Gaulle's liberal gestures alarmed the army, he fully supported Challe's military operations,

PART FOUR: REPUBLICAN MONARCH, 1959-1965

which were proving remarkably successful. Previously the army's strategy had been to respond to each FLN attack as it occurred. The problem was that this dispersed French forces. Challe instead concentrated on one sector at a time, pinning down his opponents and then sending in heavy firepower and helicopters to destroy them. He also tried to cut the FLN off from its support by 'regrouping' the civilian population into camps. This policy had short-term military benefits, but in the longer term it destroyed the structures of civil society in the Algerian countryside, undermining the chances of developing a credible Muslim middle ground.

'ONE MUST MOVE OR DIE'

The signs of military success on the ground decided de Gaulle that the time had come to act. On 12 August 1959, at the start of the summer break, he informed his startled ministers that the Council of Ministers would meet in two weeks, despite the holidays, and everyone would be invited to offer their views on the future of Algeria. Since ministers were rarely given the opportunity to discuss Algeria – or indeed anything – this suggested that something was brewing. De Gaulle now left for his own 'holidays' in Colombey during which he found the mental energy to complete the final volume of his *War Memoirs* for which his publishers were clamouring.

In anticipation of the meeting of the government, Bernard Tricot had prepared a plan to undercut the FLN by offering the Algerian people a chance to vote on their future once peace had been restored.[30] Meanwhile Debré went to see de Gaulle at Colombey with his own plan to offer Algeria strictly limited autonomy for a period of twenty-five years.[31] He was alarmed when de Gaulle showed him some heavily corrected pages of a speech that he was drafting on the lines of Tricot's plan. Debré worried that this was 'ambiguous' and did not offer anything immediate. When the ministers reconvened on 26 August to give their views, Malraux and the Justice Minister Edmond Michelet were the most 'liberal' while Soustelle was predictably the least willing to concede any ground. De Gaulle, offering no insights into his own views, ended gnomically: 'In matters like this one must move or die. I have chosen to move; that does not exclude the possibility of also dying.'[32]

Apart from Challe's military successes in the field, there are two reasons why de Gaulle felt the time had come to act. The first was his concern about the impact the Algerian War was having on the army. Not only had it been sucked into politics (to de Gaulle's benefit in May 1958) but it was also developing a tunnel vision of the world, seeing everything through the lenses of Algeria. Massu later wrote: 'I knew little of the France of 1960 having not served there for a decade.'[33] De Gaulle expressed his concerns to Debré in the autumn of 1959:

> If the war goes on in Algeria, we will have an army that is diverted from modern technology, and, what is more, politicized. Only my intervention prevented the army, *nolens volens*, from taking over a governmental power that it would have been incapable of exercising. Our national interest and international standing would not have recovered . . . We can only remake the army in depth once the Algerian war is over. Until then we must 'command' the army, forbid it to play a role in politics . . . and from time to time call to order one or other of its leaders.[34]

By 'modern technology' de Gaulle was referring to his ambition to develop an independent nuclear deterrent and reduce French dependence on the Atlantic Alliance. While it would be wrong to say that the senior ranks of the army were entirely opposed to the nuclear deterrent, there was concern that this policy would lead to a shift of resources away from other military spending. As General Jouhaud, Chief of the Air Staff, wrote in December 1958: 'What would the atomic bomb bring us in the pacification of Algeria?'[35] De Gaulle also knew that many army leaders were totally committed to the American alliance and viewed the struggle in Algeria as part of an international crusade against Communism.[36] In their view, any moves towards anti-Atlanticism would jeopardize any prospect of America supporting France in Algeria in the spirit of anti-Communism. This only reveals how the army leaders were living in a fantasy world: the truth was that the American government, keen to increase its support in the Arab world, was coming under increasing international pressure to support the cause of Algerian independence.

This international context was the second reason for de Gaulle to act.[37] Although militarily weakened in Algeria, the FLN was scoring successes on the international stage. The Arab states, which had all recognized the GPRA, began to lobby on its behalf through the General Assembly of the United Nations. In the autumn of 1958, the Assembly had debated for the first time a motion supporting the 'right of the Algerian peoples to independence'. Over the next three years, the autumn debates of the General Assembly became a key battlefront for the future of Algeria. De Gaulle affected to ignore what he saw as interference in internal French affairs. He told the Australian Foreign Minister in August 1959: 'I will not accept that Ghana dictates France's policy to her.'[38] Despite this bravado, he was only too aware of the importance of the United Nations. It is striking that all his policy initiatives on Algeria – starting with the 'peace of the brave' declaration in October 1958 – were launched in the autumn.

The American government had abstained at the United Nations debate in December 1958, a decision that satisfied neither the French government nor the Arab states. In September 1959, President Eisenhower paid a state visit to France. De Gaulle gave him advance notice of the initiative he was planning to take over Algeria. He also tried to explain the complexity of the situation, asking Eisenhower to imagine the presence of forty million Red Indians in California seeking independence. Algeria had been French for 130 years, and there had been no pre-existing state – only a 'scattering of inhabitants' – when the French arrived. Nonetheless he said that he had taken the decision to allow Algeria to decide its future – once the FLN had been defeated. But never would he recognize the right of the FLN to speak for Algeria since it was a 'group that existed only by machine guns'. If it was ever in power, it would govern by 'totalitarian means'.[39] De Gaulle's reassurances helped to keep the American government on side, although it abstained again in the vote on Algeria at the United Nations in December 1959.

De Gaulle announced his new policy towards Algeria in a televised address on 16 September 1959. He declared that the people of Algeria would be offered the chance to decide their own future. In a referendum on self-determination, they would be invited to choose between three possible solutions. The first was independence or 'secession' (*scission*), as de Gaulle dubbed it. He painted this in the darkest possible colours as a disaster for Algeria and for France. A second option was what he described by the neologism of 'francisation', which was his way of describing what advocates of *Algerie française* called 'integration': the chance to become an 'integrated part of the people of France who would stretch from Dunkirk to Tamanrasset'. The third option was 'the government of Algeria by the Algerians, supported by the aid of France and in close union with her', with a federal system internally in Algeria where the different communities would cohabit peacefully.[40]

Many historians have seen this speech as the turning point in de Gaulle's Algerian policy.[41] The press was also unanimous that using the term 'self-determination' had broken a taboo.[42] But Raymond Aron, a perceptive contemporary analyst of de Gaulle's Algerian policy, correctly downplayed the novelty of the speech.[43] De Gaulle still insisted that nothing would happen until peace had been restored, he still ruled out negotiating with the FLN and he did not envisage the referendum on self-determination occurring for 'several years'.[44] As for the eventuality of 'secession', it was hedged about with dire warnings. It would oblige the French government to take the necessary measures to protect those who wanted to remain French, which seemed to imply partition, and to protect French oil interests, which seemed to imply some permanent French presence in the Sahara. De Gaulle was offering the Algerians a way forward – but on his terms and at his own speed. In private he told his brother-in-law that he favoured the third solution of 'association' but wondered if it was not too late to avoid 'secession'.[45] Although he had taken the risk of setting in motion a process he might not ultimately be able to control, his preferred vision of Algeria's future had not changed.

Two weeks after de Gaulle's speech, the GPRA announced its willingness to discuss the 'military and political conditions of a ceasefire'. De Gaulle forbade any official response because this would accept the FLN/GPRA as a valid interlocutor.[46] Feeling that he had now regained the initiative, at a press conference on 10 November to discuss 'the conditions for the end of hostilities', he reeled off a list of statistics to prove that the French were winning the battle on the ground. The GPRA riposted by designating its imprisoned leaders as its negotiating team in any future talks. Since this was unacceptable to de Gaulle the situation seemed blocked.

WEEK OF MADNESS

A few weeks after the speech on self-determination, Challe and Delouvrier found themselves travelling with de Gaulle. Delouvrier's report of the conversation is a revealing example of the impossibility of pinning de Gaulle down:

> 'Challe and I have had a discussion regarding the words you have used. Challe claims that you are for "francisation"; I think that you are for "association". Naturally you are not for "secession".'
> De Gaulle: 'There will be a referendum. We will see then.' Silence. He spoke about the beauty of the countryside . . . I tried again: 'General, this is vitally important. If there is a referendum, the army will consider it its duty not to remain neutral . . . Now, if they are for "francisation", how could I remain at my post? . . . In the presence of the commander in chief that you have placed under my authority, I ask you: "francisation" or "association"? You must resolve our disagreement.' Silence again.[47]

Whether or not Challe really believed that de Gaulle favoured 'francisation', the *pieds noirs* were becoming increasingly suspicious of his intentions.[48]

In January 1960, in an interview with a German newspaper, General

Massu expressed his worries about de Gaulle's Algerian policy. 'The greatest disappointment for us', he lamented, 'is that General de Gaulle has
become a man of the left.' De Gaulle summoned Massu to Paris and
relieved him of his command in Algiers. This was the signal that the *pied
noir* activists had been waiting for. Joseph Ortiz, a café owner who had
organized the demonstration against Mollet in 1956, and Pierre Lagaillarde, the student agitator who had played a leading role during the events
of May 1958, seized the opportunity to whip up the population. They
called a demonstration of solidarity with Massu on Sunday 24 January. At
the end of the day, the demonstrators refused to disperse and started to
build barricades. When the police tried to demolish these barricades, shots
were fired and fourteen policemen were killed.

Hearing the news, de Gaulle cut short his weekend in Colombey. In
the early hours of the Monday morning (25 January), he recorded a short
radio declaration ordering the insurgents to disperse. His words were
ignored and only revealed the impotence of the government in Paris. At
the Cabinet meeting later that morning, the government was divided on
how to respond. De Gaulle fulminated against Challe and Delouvrier
for not acting more firmly to restore order. Soustelle, who sympathized
with the rioters, remarked sarcastically that the solution was to drop a
nuclear bomb on Algiers.[49] De Gaulle reluctantly allowed Debré to pay a
flying visit to Algiers to assess the situation. Alarmed by the mood of some
army officers, Debré reported back to the government on 27 January that
force would only make the situation worse. Over the phone, de Gaulle
urged Delouvrier to act more vigorously: 'There are moments when French
blood needs to be shed. If you think that I enjoyed doing this at Dakar or
in Syria! But sometimes blood has to flow.' Debré, in receipt of similar
instructions, later wrote in a rare criticism of de Gaulle: 'This is the only
time in my life that I burnt a few lines rapidly drafted by the General. I did
not want his image to be sullied by a repression that it seemed to me possible to avoid.'[50]

Also ignoring de Gaulle's instructions, Delouvrier tried to negotiate a
bloodless end to the crisis. Pressed by politicized young army colonels to
support the rising, and by Delouvrier to remain loyal to the government,
General Challe developed a psychosomatic foot disease and spent the week
prostrate with his feet bandaged. The army did not join the insurgents but
nor did it do anything to dismantle the barricades. After four days of
unsuccessful parleying, Delouvrier decided that he and Challe must leave
Algiers so that the insurgents could not claim they enjoyed his tacit support. He announced this in a long rambling speech on Thursday evening
(28 January):

People of Algiers! ... If I have to leave Algiers, I leave with you the most sacred things a man can give: my wife and children. Look after Mathieu my youngest son: I want him to grow up as a symbol of the unbreakable attachment of Algeria to France ... Bring down these barricades, on which we dream of embracing each other, while fearing we might kill each other.[51]

Away from the highly charged atmosphere of Algiers, listeners in Paris thought Delouvrier had taken leave of his senses. In fact, his words touched a chord with the population in Algiers just as heavy rain began to douse the resolution of the insurgents.

This was the situation when de Gaulle intervened a second time in a televised speech on Friday 29 January, five days after the outbreak of the events. Having been shown an advance draft of the speech, Debré urged de Gaulle to show a bit more heart to the *pieds noirs* who have 'the feeling they are neither understood nor loved'.[52] De Gaulle took no notice. He also showed the speech to General Ely, who wanted a passage to affirm that the defence of Algeria was the defence of the west. De Gaulle ignored this too, and commented only: 'I cannot pronounce the word integration.'[53] In his speech he adopted a tone of command not persuasion. In no other speech during the Fifth Republic did he use the first person more imperiously and more frequently: '*I* order ...', '*I* must be obeyed ...', etc.[54] Heightening the sense of drama, he appeared in uniform, opening with the words: 'If I have put on a uniform to speak today on the television, it is in order to show that it is General de Gaulle who is speaking as much as the Head of State.' After reiterating his determination to allow the people of Algeria to decide their future, he addressed himself first to the Europeans of Algeria. He assured them that France would never 'leave Algeria and hand it over to the rebels'. Then he addressed the army, praising its successes against the FLN but reminding it that its duty was to serve the state: 'I am the person responsible for the destiny of the nation. I must be obeyed by all French soldiers.' Finally, shifting his tone from the imperious to the paternal, he addressed France herself: 'So my dear old country, here we are together again facing a great ordeal.'[55]

De Gaulle's eighteen-minute speech was a rhetorical *tour de force* perfectly timed. The barricades were rapidly taken down; Lagaillarde gave himself up and Ortiz fled to Spain. This was the most serious crisis de Gaulle had faced since returning to power. He wrote to his son soon afterwards:

There was a moment, before my speech ... when I felt positively that everyone around me was giving up and prostrating themselves on the pretext ...
'One must not shed blood', 'one will not be obeyed'. In fact it was enough

for willpower to be demonstrated on the radio for everyone to recover themselves and everything return to order.[56]

Whether or not the vigorous repression de Gaulle wanted would have ended the crisis earlier or made it worse by tipping the army fully into rebellion, the events of Barricades Week had revealed that the authority of the state hung by a thread despite de Gaulle's new constitution. As Raymond Aron wrote immediately afterwards: 'During these five days, nothing existed any more, neither the regime, nor the Constitution, even less the hesitant and divided Republic; there remained only one man – and a man alone.'[57]

After Barricades Week, de Gaulle decided to take tighter control of Algerian policy by creating a new committee on Algerian affairs which he chaired personally. Debré was a member, but the agenda was drafted at the Elyseé by Tricot. Challe was removed from his command in Algiers and given a position back in France. De Gaulle also wanted to sack Delouvrier but was talked out of this by Debré, who persuaded him that Delouvrier could not have acted more honourably. Instead de Gaulle sent one of his old Free French followers, François Coulet, to assist Delouvrier but really to watch over him. A few weeks after the crisis, Soustelle was summoned to the Elysée to be told by de Gaulle that he had been sacked. Soustelle's later description of the meeting is inflected by the hatred he had come to feel for de Gaulle, a hatred no less intense than that of historical anti-Gaullists like Jacques Isorni: 'I said to him: "I regret that you did not at least wait until 18 June; that would have made 20 years exactly to the day I responded to your appeal." He made a tiny gesture with his hand as if flicking away an annoying insect.'[58]

HIATUS

In France de Gaulle's popularity ratings soared to unprecedented levels after Barricades Week. But feeling he must heal the bruised morale of the army, he made a three-day trip to Algeria in March giving impromptu talks to groups of officers. This so-called 'tour of the messes' came to haunt him later. The soldiers certainly heard what they wanted to hear, but de Gaulle gave many hostages to fortune. One group of officers was told: 'Never will I treat with the FLN ... Never will the flag of the FLN fly over Algiers ... The French army will remain in Algeria.' To another group he declared that there would be 'no diplomatic Dien Bien Phu' in Algeria'.[59] Although these comments were off the record, de Gaulle certainly did make them.

They did not technically contradict his existing policy since he had always said the FLN had to be defeated. But the army propaganda machine produced its own version of de Gaulle's words for the press. Back in Paris, de Gaulle was alarmed by how his comments had been reported.[60] He issued a corrective communiqué reiterating that Algeria would be allowed to decide her future – and introduced subtle changes in the presentation of the three choices he had outlined six months earlier. 'Francisation', now described as 'direct domination' by France, was ruled out as 'impossible'. 'Secession' was still described apocalyptically. The third solution of 'association', now described as 'probable', was enveloped in a new phrase which no one remarked upon at the time: 'An Algerian Algeria, linked to France, and uniting the diverse communities'.[61]

For the next two months, while de Gaulle's time was taken up by intensive diplomatic activity – a state visit to France by Nikita Khrushchev (23 March–3 April), state visits to London (5–8 April) and North America (8 April–4 May) and so on – the French authorities in Algeria were picking up some interesting signals that the internal unity of the FLN was under strain. The FLN had divided its operations in Algeria into military regions known as Wilayas. In March 1960, a leader of Wilaya IV, Si Salah, got a secret message through to the French authorities in Algeria that he was ready to discuss a ceasefire. Bernard Tricot at the Elysée was informed and brought into the preliminary discussions. These seemed promising enough for the three leaders of Wilaya IV, including Si Salah, to find themselves suddenly flown to Paris in great secrecy. To their astonishment, on the night of 9 June, they were driven to a side entrance of the Elyseé Palace and ushered into the presence of de Gaulle himself. This extraordinary encounter was the only occasion during the entire conflict when de Gaulle met face to face with any members of the FLN. Bernard Tricot, who was present, left the only existing account of what transpired. The meeting was short. Refusing their request to be allowed to meet the imprisoned nationalist leader Ben Bella, de Gaulle informed the three men that he was planning to make another public appeal to the FLN in the next few days. When the meeting was over he said it would be inappropriate to shake their hands but expressed the hope that they would meet again.[62]

On 14 June, de Gaulle spoke on television again. More solemnly than ever, he appealed to the rebel leaders to enter into negotiations for a ceasefire. This would be followed in due course by a referendum on the future of Algeria which de Gaulle now envisaged as 'an Algerian Algeria' in union with France. Four days later, the GPRA formally accepted the offer. On 25 June, three Algerian representatives arrived at the small town of Melun outside Paris to begin discussions. They were held incommunicado, almost like prisoners, and their interlocutor on the French side was a relatively junior official who was instructed not to discuss political questions but only the conditions of a ceasefire. De Gaulle's handwritten annotations to the report on the first day of talks show that the inflexibility on the French side was a direct result of his orders:

> To the request of the Algerians that they be allowed to contact 'Ministers of the GPRA' held in detention in France, he wrote: 'There are no "Ministers" but men who are fighting us and committing attacks.'
>
> To their request to be allowed to have contacts with the Tunisian Ambassador, he wrote: 'No contact is to be permitted with any Embassy.'
>
> To their complaint about tracts in Algeria suggesting the FLN had given in, he wrote: 'As long as the FLN continues fighting the army will use the means to combat it which it considers necessary.'[63]

After three days the talks were broken off. This was a public relations disaster for de Gaulle partly because the press had excessively raised expectations.[64] The only beneficiary was the FLN, which had proved to the world that de Gaulle seemed not to be serious in offering to talk. Some people blamed Debré for the failure, but the intransigence had been de Gaulle's.[65] The loyal Gaullist Louis Terrenoire, who had replaced Soustelle as Minister of Information, was perplexed by the General's attitude: 'De Gaulle is like a fisherman who has landed a big fish and lets it tire itself before pulling in the line. But it can happen that the fish, with a twist of its body, breaks the line.'[66] In his attitude to the FLN de Gaulle seemed hardly to have moved beyond his 'peace of the brave' offer two years earlier. It may be that the dissent in Wilaya IV (which de Gaulle never mentioned in his *Memoirs*) led him to overestimate the divisions within the FLN. His extraordinary step of meeting three rebel leaders in person at the Elysée suggests he had taken the matter seriously. It is possible that he hoped that at Melun the FLN as a whole would give him what he had been offered by the leaders of one Wilaya. Perhaps he also assumed that he could reactivate the Wilaya IV option if the Melun talks failed. If this was the case, he was to be disappointed. Soon after the abortive Melun talks, the FLN leadership purged the dissident leaders of Wilaya IV. De Gaulle was left with no fall-back position.

When in the following year rumours of de Gaulle's secret meeting with Si Salah started to leak, France's army leaders in Algeria saw this as proof of his perfidy. In their view, he had spurned the chance of negotiating with a group ready to seek peace and break with the FLN leadership. This was wishful thinking. The leaders of Wilaya IV had not abandoned the idea of independence and their dissidence concerned only tactics. If the mysterious affair of Wilaya IV had any importance at all, it was that it led de Gaulle to overestimate France's negotiating strength at Melun.[67]

IMPASSE

At the same time as the failure at Melun, another possible solution for Algeria was closed off by the demise of the post-imperial French Community de Gaulle had set up in 1958 along with the new constitution. De Gaulle was so adept at covering his tracks, and laying false scents about shifts of policy, that it is difficult to be sure what he thought about the Community. The journalist Jean Mauriac later quoted a conversation with him on the subject in August 1958. When de Gaulle had asked Mauriac for his views, Mauriac replied enthusiastically that de Gaulle was creating an edifice to last for generations. De Gaulle shot back at once: 'You think so! The Community is nonsense [foutaise]! As soon as these people enter it, they will only have one idea in their heads: to get out of it.'[68] This sally should not be taken at face value. The amount of time de Gaulle invested personally in the Community belies the pessimism he affected to Mauriac.

The executive council of the Community met no fewer than six times in 1959. These must have been tedious and trying occasions which allowed African leaders to vent their grievances, but de Gaulle chaired them with remarkable forbearance.[69] When in October 1959, he refused attempts by the Quai d'Orsay to build bridges with Sékou Touré of Guinea, his reason for refusing was that this would 'be an encouragement for the dissolution of the Community'.[70] Everything suggests that he hoped the Community would last. But at the end of 1959 Sudan, Senegal and Madagascar formally demanded their independence. At the last meeting of the council of the Community in March 1960, de Gaulle still brandished the threat that if France could not achieve a satisfactory relationship with her former African colonies, she would need to rethink her entire relationship with them. This was a last-ditch attempt to ward off independence.[71] In the end de Gaulle bowed to the inevitable. The French government revised the statutes of the Community to allow membership to be compatible with independence. All France's sub-Saharan African possessions had acquired independence by the end of July 1960. The Community, as originally conceived by de Gaulle, had failed to withstand what a few months earlier Harold Macmillan had called the 'wind of change in Africa'.

If de Gaulle struggled to keep the Community together, it was because he envisaged it as a possible model for France's relationship with Algeria or a structure into which Algeria might eventually be inserted without becoming fully independent.[72] From the summer of 1960 that pathway was closed, and de Gaulle had run out of ideas.

To the extent that there was any policy towards Algeria at this time, it was by default Debré's. Debré had reconciled himself to de Gaulle's promise of Algerian self-determination but interpreted it in an even more restrictive way. He envisaged a transition period of twenty-five years during which the French government would encourage the emergence of other Muslim interlocutors besides the FLN while preparing the ground for a permanent association between Algeria and France. De Gaulle did not forbid such a policy but his annotation of Debré's proposal to sponsor a rival political organization to the FLN betrays his scepticism: 'On condition that it is Muslim and not created by us.'[73] The search for the elusive middle ground received a new lease of life in the summer of 1960 with the setting up of four so-called *commissions d'élus*, joint bodies of Muslim and European representatives elected to discuss issues like the economic development of Algeria or the future relations between the communities. As these *commissions* started their surreal deliberations about a future that seemed increasingly improbable, clarification was sought from de Gaulle as to whether any one of the three possibilities outlined by his speech of September 1959 should be privileged over the others.[74] He does not seem to have answered – and it is revealing of the obscurity of his intentions that the question needed to be asked.

At the same time, de Gaulle was warned that France was likely to be attacked even more vigorously at the forthcoming session of the United Nations than in previous years.[75] At a press conference on 5 September, he listed all the improvements that had taken place for the Muslims of Algeria over the last two years and blamed the FLN for blocking a solution. But he had nothing new to say except to slip in yet another gnomic phrase to describe the palette of possible futures envisaged for Algeria. Once he had talked of an 'Algerian personality', then of 'Algerian Algeria'; now he threw out the idea of an 'Algerian entity'. This was reminiscent of the way that he had gradually moved the Free French, or the Free French had moved him, to embrace the Republic between 1941 and 1943, but it is not clear in either case if he knew the end point of his journey – or wanted to end up where he did.[76] To Challe's successor General Crépin, de Gaulle wrote in October 1960 that he needed military victory as a prelude to a political settlement. That was no different from what he had said in 1958.[77]

De Gaulle's press conference of September 1960 aroused universal disappointment. Since he failed to offer any convincing sense of direction, the field was left open to the extremes. Supporters of *Algérie française* in France, like Soustelle, organized themselves to lobby opinion. They received a publicity boost when the retired General Salan gave a press conference denouncing de Gaulle's policies before heading into exile in Spain. In November, de Gaulle's old comrade in arms Marshal Juin announced that he was breaking with de Gaulle after a 'fifty-year friendship'. On the other side of the Algerian divide, Raymond Aron, who had so far cautiously given de Gaulle the benefit of the doubt, was plunged into 'despairing anger' by the September press conference. In an angry diatribe, he accused de Gaulle, despite an appearance of liberalism on Algeria, of being no different from the 'ultras' in his refusal to negotiate with the FLN, which, like it or not, was the 'incarnation of Algerian nationalism'. He concluded: 'The mental mechanisms of General de Gaulle are, I fear, typically French . . . France grants favours but does not let others snatch them from her.'[78] The editor of Le Monde Hubert Beuve-Méry was no less critical: 'To arbitrate is finally to choose . . . The most prestigious leader in the world cannot isolate himself indefinitely in his ivory tower . . . fobbing off doubters who are worried with sibylline phrases.'[79]

In September, 121 prominent intellectuals, including Jean-Paul Sartre, signed a manifesto supporting conscripts ready to desert from the army rather than fight in Algeria. The government seized issues of leftist periodicals like Esprit and Temps modernes which printed the manifesto. It also banned a demonstration by the student union UNEF in October in support of Algerian self-determination. When the demonstration went ahead anyway, there were violent clashes with the police. Left-wing observers suggested that there was something strange about a government banning demonstrations in favour of a policy it was allegedly pursuing.[80] In fact the government was divided as to how to respond. Debré, who wanted tough sanctions against these protesters, bombarded the liberal Justice Minister, Edmond Michelet, with criticism about the laxity of the judiciary. In one letter he wrote: 'You told me yesterday: "it is not my fault if Sartre is not being prosecuted" . . . When I see yesterday how sad the General is, I am annoyed that you cannot seem to understand.'[81] Michelet and Debré were each fanatically loyal to de Gaulle, but apart from his famous (and possibly apocryphal) quip about Sartre – 'One does not arrest Voltaire' – de Gaulle did not intervene, allowing Michelet and Debré each to believe that they were the true Gaullists.

In the autumn of 1960, de Gaulle was close to despair. Debré was so alarmed by his state of mind that he drafted endless versions of a letter imploring him not to resign.[82] Even the more phlegmatic Pompidou was worried. Although having no official position at this time, Pompidou remained in close contact with de Gaulle. After seeing him in October, he wrote to him in terms calculated to appeal to his sense of providential destiny: 'If Pericles had been abandoned or imprisoned, it is the Athenians one would blame: if Pericles had abandoned Athens in the thick of the Peloponnesian War, it is them that history would blame.' Pompidou took the opportunity for a few barbs against Debré. He advised de Gaulle to be less repressive towards the signatories of the various manifestos and resist 'the natural tendencies of Debré . . . who is in other respects an exemplary prime minister'. He recommended that de Gaulle speak to the nation again: 'I am sure that the French who have admired you and moved towards you for their salvation, are only wanting to love you again. If you show them that you are conscious of the difficulties but ready to overcome them, tired but resolute, indulgent rather than mocking, you will rally them around you again.'[83]

Though Debré and Pompidou, as seasoned observers of the General, were convinced that he was in a state of depression, they should also have remembered that these moods of despair were a recurring feature of his personality, sometimes genuine, sometimes performative – but always the prelude to a sudden recovery of will.

'THE ALGERIAN REPUBLIC THAT WILL EXIST ONE DAY'

In one draft of his letter imploring de Gaulle not to give up, Debré wrote: 'You need to go on the offensive. The success of "Gaullism" has always come from a correct analysis of the ills of the nation and a spirit of attack to try to overcome them.'[84] Debré was soon to be taken at his word – but not in the way he had intended. On 4 November, de Gaulle delivered another television address on Algeria. As usual he celebrated the army's successes and the emergence of Muslim elites in local government. He went on to expand on his vision of the future: 'An emancipated Algeria, an Algeria in which the Algerians themselves decide on their own destiny, an Algeria which, if the Algerians want it – as I think is the case – will have its government, its institutions and its laws.' Then came the bombshell: de Gaulle invoked 'the government of the Algerian Republic, which will exist one day, but has never yet existed'.[85]

The speech had been shown to Debré in advance without the words about the 'Algerian Republic'. Debré was so appalled that he took the unusual step of ringing the Elyseé; even more unusually, a clearly embarrassed de Gaulle agreed to take the call, claiming disingenuously that the phrase had entered his mind at the last minute. Debré, who had a month earlier begged de Gaulle not to resign, now wanted to resign himself. He poured out his 'profound unease' in a long letter to de Gaulle. 'A Gaullist', he wrote, 'has not the right to be more Gaullist than de Gaulle.' But for him Gaullism was a 'will to dominate events with the objective of main-taining the influence and authority of France' and a rejection of the idea of a 'movement of history against which we can do nothing'.[86] This was one interpretation of Gaullism, but de Gaulle had always emphasized the need to adapt to circumstances, and the need for a policy that respected realities. He replied: 'We have to accomplish decolonization. I have the responsibility to do this . . . Never is it more evident that "wishful thinking" [in English] would be the worst of policies.'[87] In the end, Debré stayed on, as de Gaulle had gambled he would. A year earlier, the General had taken aside Debré's *directeur de cabinet* Pierre Racine and sounded him out obliquely as to whether Debré would follow him to the end of the road on Algeria. Racine replied: 'I think yes, and in any case I see my role as helping him to.'[88]

Someone who did resign was Delouvrier – not because he disapproved of the new policy but because he resented the way it had been sprung upon him. This provided de Gaulle with the opportunity to take ever tighter control of Algerian policy. He created a new Ministry of Algerian Affairs which was entrusted to the loyal Louis Joxe. A few days after his speech of 4 November on the Algerian Republic, de Gaulle announced a referendum to seek the approval of the French population for his Algerian policy. At the same time, he drafted instructions for what would follow the referendum. The govern-ment would establish a provisional executive for Algeria to act as a transitional authority pending negotiations over a definitive solution. To ensure that the FLN agreed to negotiate, de Gaulle was also ready to announce a unilat-eral military truce. Having decided on a course of action, he was now ready to move with startling rapidity and single-mindedness.[89]

In December 1960, de Gaulle paid his last ever visit to Algeria – his eighth since returning to power. This could hardly have been more different from the triumphal tour of June 1958. Violent clashes erupted between Europeans and Muslims; *pied noir* activists fought street battles with the French police; Muslims descended on the streets waving Algerian flags. In Algiers, sixty people were killed. De Gaulle continued to plunge imperturb-ably into the crowds, but his visit to Constantine had to be cancelled when the security forces uncovered a plot to assassinate him by *pied noir* radicals. In the end his visit was cut short by twenty-four hours. 'Fraternal' Algeria was dead.

In the referendum on 8 January 1961, some 75 per cent of voters approved de Gaulle's Algerian policy. The result was no surprise, but it gave him the authority he needed to move forward. Before the referendum, he had already authorized feelers to the FLN through the intermediary of a Swiss diplomat. These paved the way for two secret meetings in Switzerland in February and March, between Georges Pompidou and two FLN representatives. De Gaulle briefed Pompidou carefully: 'The term independence is indifferent to us because in the present world it does not mean much except for propaganda. No state is independent because it is always in reality more or less linked to others' (an ironic admission from a leader whose entire foreign policy was built around the idea of French independence). Pompidou was told that only two areas were out of bounds. First, the Sahara, with its important petrol reserves, was not to be considered part of Algeria. Secondly, if Algerian self-determination resulted in a complete break with France, the French would seek guarantees about the future of the *pieds noirs*.[90]

Pompidou reported back that he had 'at no moment gone even to the slightest degree beyond the directives you gave me'. He found his FLN interlocutors wary and suspicious, 'haunted by the memory of Melun' and prone to propaganda tirades.[91] Nonetheless the two sides cleared enough ground to be able to announce that formal negotiations would commence in April at Evian near the Swiss border. The French team would be led by Louis Joxe. There was a final hitch when Joxe announced that the French were also ready to talk to other possible representatives of the Algerian people such as the more moderate nationalist movement, the MNA. The FLN took this as a pretext to call off the Evian meeting until receiving assurances that the French would not be talking to 'lackeys of colonialism'. To signal to the FLN how far he had moved, at his next press conference on 11 April de Gaulle's tone about Algeria was one of dismissive indifference:

> In today's world and in the epoch we are living in, France has no interest in keeping Algeria under her laws or dependent on her . . . Indeed the least one can say is that Algeria costs us more than it brings us . . . That is why today France would contemplate with the greatest sangfroid a solution by which Algeria would cease to belong to her.[92]

It is hard to overestimate the shock caused by the tone of these remarks. One listener who declared himself 'ill and heartbroken' by them was the novelist Jules Roy, a committed supporter of Algerian independence and passionate admirer of de Gaulle. But as someone who had been born in Algeria, Roy could not but also be sensitive to the plight of the Europeans. He wrote in his journal: 'For me General de Gaulle died on 11 April. His place has been taken by a cynical accountant.'[93] If this was the reaction of an almost religious admirer of de Gaulle, it is not difficult to imagine the response of the army leaders in Algeria.

'LOST SOLDIERS'

We do not need to imagine it. In the early hours of Saturday 22 April, elite paratrooper and Foreign Legion regiments seized key buildings in Algiers.[94] The population of the city woke to hear a message from General Challe: 'The army has taken control of Algeria and the Sahara . . . *Algérie française* is not dead . . . There is not, and will never be, an independent Algeria.' The operation was headed by three generals, including Challe. On the next day Salan joined them from Spain.

De Gaulle was woken at 2.30 a.m. to be told the news. He immediately ordered Joxe and General Olié to fly to Algeria and report back. In the course of the morning the police in Paris had arrested a number of officers who were preparing to extend the coup to the mainland. When the Cabinet met in emergency session in the afternoon, there was unanimity that the situation was serious enough to justify recourse to emergency powers under Article 16 of the constitution. Even so de Gaulle did not, on the surface, seem unduly perturbed. He remarked to one aide that morning: 'What shocks me is that an intelligent man like Challe can perpetrate such stupidity.'[95]

Meanwhile Joxe and Olié were in Algeria. Avoiding Algiers itself, which was in putschist hands, they flew to Oran where the commander, General Pouilly, had remained loyal to de Gaulle. Next they went to Constantine where the General in charge refused telephone orders from Challe to arrest them. But as soon as they had left for France he changed his mind and joined the putschists. Back in France on Sunday afternoon, Joxe reported in person to de Gaulle that the situation was still fluid.[96] At 8 p.m., de Gaulle appeared on television to announce that he was taking emergency powers. As during Barricades Week, he was in full uniform. His tone was one of imperious command and barely suppressed fury:

An insurrectional power has established itself in Algeria by a military pronunciamento . . . This power has an appearance: a handful [*quarteron*] of retired generals; it has a reality: a group of fanatical, ambitious and partisan officers. This group has a basic and limited understanding, but they only see the world and the nation through their frenzy. Their enterprise can result only in a national disaster . . . Here we see the State flouted, the nation defied, our power degraded, our international prestige struck down, our role and our place in Africa compromised – by whom? Alas! Alas! Alas! By men whose duty, honour and *raison d'être* it was to serve and obey. In the name of France, I order that all means, I repeat all means, be employed everywhere to bar the road to these men until they have been defeated. I forbid any Frenchman, and in the first place any soldier, to execute any of their orders . . . *Françaises, Français!* See what France risks, compared to what she is in the process of becoming. *Françaises, Français! Aidez-moi!*

The full flavour of this remarkable piece of Gaullist oratory – the pathetic appeal at the end, the triple 'Alas' – is difficult to convey in translation. The word 'handful' does not render the withering contempt of '*quarteron*'. This dismissive epithet, which de Gaulle had used in 1942 in a speech denouncing Darlan which the BBC refused to allow him to broadcast, is an archaic word meaning a quarter of something or twenty-five – perhaps a 'pint pot of generals' would convey the sense.

That night rumours spread in Paris that soldiers from Algiers were going to land in France. A few hours after de Gaulle's speech, a distraught and unshaven Debré appeared on television calling for the people of Paris to occupy the airports around the city: 'When the sirens sound, head off on foot or by car to convince the soldiers they have made this grave mistake.' De Gaulle's future biographer, Jean Lacouture, recalls that he headed to Orly airport with another journalist to see what was happening but found no one else there. Although Debré's speech aroused some derision – commentators joked that to his words 'on foot or by car' he should have added 'or on horseback' – it did galvanize opinion. The unions called a one-hour general strike on Monday afternoon in which ten million workers participated. The panic caused by Debré also served de Gaulle's purposes in making his recourse to Article 16 seem justified.

After de Gaulle's speech, volunteers including many left-wing intellectuals gathered at the Ministry of the Interior, ready to defend the Republic. Some of them dusted down weapons last used in the Resistance. In the courtyard they were harangued by Malraux, reliving his experience of the Spanish Civil War. The Prefect of Police commented drily: 'Paris is peaceful but I could not say the same of the Ministry of the Interior.'[97] Later de Gaulle dressed down the Minister of the Interior, Roger Frey: 'Can you explain to me the reasons for this grotesque tumult you organized outside my window.'[98] It was easy to mock after the event, but the sense of panic was genuine. Foccart spent four nights sleeping at the Elysée to be close at hand for de Gaulle. He had a plane ready at an aerodrome outside Paris to whisk him away if the Elysée were attacked.[99] That night de Gaulle handed his will to Foccart in a sealed envelope.

The night of Sunday to Monday (23–24 April) was the key moment if the coup was to have any chance of success – but it was already running out of steam. The effect of de Gaulle's speech had been electrifying. The thousands of conscript soldiers who comprised the bulk of the army in Algeria listened on their transistor radios. Once it was clear that they would not support the insurrection, Challe, who did not have the temperament of a putschist, turned himself in on Tuesday 25 April. General Zeller was captured a few days later. The other two generals, Jouhaud and Salan, went into hiding. The attempted coup was over.

Although de Gaulle had assumed emergency powers, he affected in private not to have taken the putsch too seriously. Robert Buron, a minister who had found himself in Algeria at the moment of the coup and been arrested, found it hard to interest him in the details when he arrived back in France eager to recount his adventures. Instead de Gaulle preferred to philosophize in his inimitable style: 'There is a factor they did not take account of, an essential factor however, and one that ruined all their calculations; that factor is de Gaulle. I don't understand it always myself . . . but I am a prisoner of it.'[100] To another visitor he remarked at the height of the events that successful revolutions required a Mirabeau, Danton, Bonaparte, Atatürk, Lenin – not a Challe who lacked the character, despite being intelligent.[101]

The planning of the putsch had indeed been amateurish. Challe, who disliked Salan, had agreed to join only at the last moment after the shock of hearing de Gaulle's 11 April press conference. The conspirators had no coherent political strategy. The more exalted among them dreamt of landing in Paris but did nothing to plan this. Challe himself wanted not a political seizure of power in Paris but a kind of provisional secession from France during which the army would win the war against the FLN and present de Gaulle with a military victory. He seemed to believe he would win in three months a war that the army had been fighting for six years. As a further example of the fantasy world in which the putschists were living, Challe even told the population of Algiers on the radio that he counted on 'our American friends' – despite the fact that America supported Algerian independence. The conspirators presumably hoped to repeat the scenario of 13 May 1958 when de Gaulle had returned to power. But the conditions were different. They faced not Pflimlin but de Gaulle himself; there was no de Gaulle figure in the wings to whom they could appeal; and whereas in 1958 the previous regime had lost credibility, only a few weeks before the attempted coup of April 1961 the French population had massively expressed its support for de Gaulle's Algerian policy.

On 23 November 1961, in a speech to officers in Strasbourg commemorating the seventeenth anniversary of the liberation of the city by Leclerc, de Gaulle developed his interpretation of the putsch: 'From the moment that the State and the nation chose their path, military duty was once and for all settled. Outside these rules, there are not, there cannot be, anything but lost soldiers.'[102] Some of the military later wondered if de Gaulle, the supreme Machiavellian, had had advance notice of the plans for a putsch and allowed it to go ahead as a means of finally breaking the resistance of the army.[103] There is no evidence for this, but it is true that the coup had served de Gaulle's purposes, up to a point. He wrote to his son immediately afterwards that 'It lanced a boil which, in any case needed to be cleaned ... The event will, in that respect, allow me to do many things.'[104]

NEGOTIATIONS

The Evian talks opened on 20 May. De Gaulle announced that the French would unilaterally observe a one-month military truce. This was a sign of how far he had come since 1958 when his condition for any discussion was that the FLN accept a ceasefire. The discussions were secret, although each day a communiqué was issued. Four points of contention quickly emerged:[105]

1. Who would sit on the provisional executive responsible for organizing the referendum on Algerian self-determination, and what period would elapse before the referendum occurred?
2. How long would the French be allowed to maintain military bases in Algeria after independence?
3 What rights would the European population enjoy in independent Algeria?
4. Would the boundaries of Algeria include the Sahara?

The last two issues were the most difficult. The French wanted to protect the rights of the *pieds noirs*; the FLN negotiators were wary of giving them any special privileges like double nationality. The Sahara was of major economic importance since the discovery of oil in 1956, and it was also where the French tested their atomic weapons.

De Gaulle kept closely in touch with Joxe. With extraordinary optimism he seemed to think that everything could be settled in two weeks.[106] But his refusal to concede on the Sahara, as Joxe wanted, made this impossible. After twelve long sessions, the discussions started going round in circles. On 13 June, de Gaulle, to the surprise of the FLN, suspended the negotiations to allow 'time for reflection'. They resumed for another week in July, but because de Gaulle still rejected any shift in the French position, this time the FLN broke them off. A standoff was reached, and de Gaulle ended the military truce.

Debré, who had been almost totally sidelined in the making of policy to Algeria, saw a final chance to reactivate his idea of a middle way. De Gaulle authorized secret negotiations to set up a provisional executive in Algiers composed of representatives from the *commissions d'élus* which had been set up in the previous year.[107] The ostensible purpose was to prepare an Algerian vote on self-determination bypassing the FLN. Debré may still have believed this was possible, but for de Gaulle it was only a tactic to bring the FLN back to the negotiating table. He told Alain Peyrefitte: 'The FLN is afraid of making peace. It is afraid of assuming its responsibilities. It only knows how to do two things: train troops in Tunisia and Morocco and, for its propaganda, line up as many countries as possible against us ... A negotiated solution will work only if we have another one ready. One must always have two irons in the fire.'[108] De Gaulle was also experimenting with a third 'iron'. In two speeches during the summer, he floated the idea of a partition of Algeria by regrouping the European population. In July, he suggested that Peyrefitte publish something on these lines. Peyrefitte took this as an order, spent the summer researching the subject and published four articles in *Le Monde* in September. These articles caused a stir and he received a message from the Elysée that he might turn his ideas into a book.

Meanwhile Tricot and Joxe had been arguing through August for concessions on the Sahara. Debré, who scented the danger, spent August trying to keep de Gaulle firm.[109] To no avail. At the end of the month, de Gaulle decided to concede more ground. His new mantra was that France had to 'disengage' from Algeria come what may. He announced to the Cabinet on the last day of August:

> If these people are ready to agree something acceptable with us, they can still do it. If not we will find other people. If they don't agree either, we will disengage anyway ... They make me think of those paintings of primitives where one sees the devils pulling the condemned down towards hell. The damned do not seem to mind and shake their fists at the angels. Well, let the devil take them.[110]

This was a prelude to de Gaulle's press conference on 5 September, acknowledging publicly that 'there is not a single Algerian who does not think that the Sahara must be part of Algeria and there would not be a single Algerian government, whatever its relationship to France, which would not claim sovereignty over the Sahara.'[111] Although the decision to drop the Sahara was enveloped in rhetorical reassurances that there were other ways to preserve French interests besides formal sovereignty, this was as dramatic an announcement as de Gaulle's phrase about the 'Algerian Republic' a year earlier. Once again Debré had not been told in advance.

He was especially appalled that de Gaulle had announced this change publicly. As he wrote in his *Memoirs*, in a rare criticism of de Gaulle: 'What is given is no longer an object of negotiation.' Pompidou was also shocked: 'Abandon the Sahara! If he had said it earlier I could have concluded with [the FLN negotiator] Boumendjel. But he forbade me to concede.'[112]

Debré drafted endless versions of yet another tormented letter of resignation; again de Gaulle would not release him from the rack.[113] The resignation of the Prime Minister at such a delicate moment would have been a serious problem, but Debré had other uses. Originally he had covered de Gaulle's political flank on the right against those Gaullists in parliament supporting *Algérie française*. He no longer served this purpose because he had swallowed too much to have any credibility with these diehards. But he was now usefully covering de Gaulle's political flank on the left. As the Algerian crisis seemed to drag on without any resolution, de Gaulle's admirers found the man to blame. In November, Mauriac wrote an article speculating about why his hero de Gaulle had still not extricated France from Algeria. His answer was to suggest that the President had been 'betrayed by one of his own men' – by which he meant Debré.[114]

De Gaulle's press conference on the Sahara allowed secret contacts to resume in Switzerland between Joxe and representatives of the GPRA. When Debré seemed again to want to slow things down, de Gaulle slapped him down: 'We must not endlessly accumulate objections.'[115] This also meant that the 'iron in the fire' of partition no longer served any purpose. When Peyrefitte went to the Elysée in early December because his book on the subject was ready to appear, de Gaulle opened the conversation with a piece of bad faith spectacular even by his standards: 'So they tell me you are campaigning for the partition of Algeria.' He had now changed his tune:

> You want to create a French Israel ... Your maps only leave the FLN the poor part ... Look at Israel. The entire Arab world is against it. But at least the Israelis fought for their independence after having conquered it. The *pieds noirs* do not want their independence: they want us to be their dependants as in the past ... We can absorb the *pieds noirs* who come here ... We are not going to suspend our national destiny according to the mood of the *pieds noirs*! If we follow your solution we will put the entire world against us.[116]

CIVIL WAR

In retrospect we know that France was entering the countdown to final disengagement from Algeria, but to contemporaries it felt as if the country was sliding into civil war.[117] The defeated putschists had formed a terrorist organization, the Organisation d'Action Secrète (OAS), ready to defend French Algeria to the bitter end. Their enemy was not so much the FLN as French 'liberals' and the French police. Having started in Algeria, the OAS spread to the mainland. On the opening of the Evian talks, the city's Mayor was murdered. Despite its violence, the OAS benefited from the complicity of journalists and politicians who were still not resigned to the loss of Algeria. Its ultimate target was de Gaulle himself. On 8 September 1961, as the President's car was heading to Colombey, a bomb suddenly exploded on the road at Pont-sur-Seine outside Paris. The driver accelerated through the sheet of flame and miraculously there were no casualties. In Paris the sinister backdrop to the winter of 1961 was the sound of car horns, three short and two long: *Al-gé-rie fran-çaise.*

The OAS violence was mirrored from the start of September by a new wave of FLN attacks in Paris. Over the five weeks, thirteen policemen in Paris were killed. The reasons for this FLN campaign are not clear. Perhaps the Paris branch of the organization was acting on its own account; perhaps the operation had been ordered as a means of keeping up the pressure on de Gaulle. In response, the police authorities in Paris resorted to more radical repression. In August, Debré had secured de Gaulle's agreement to replace the liberal Justice Minister Michelet. The new minister was a more pliable figure, and this was a signal to the Paris Prefect of Police, Maurice Papon, that he could resort to any methods he wished to fight the FLN. Having served previously as a prefect in Algeria, Papon transplanted the methods used against the FLN there to the streets of Paris. One of his innovations was a new quasi-military brigade of Arab 'native' police. Torture began to be used systematically in Paris.

This provided the context for the two most violent episodes of police brutality to have occurred in France since the war. The first took place on 17 October in response to Papon's decision to impose a curfew on the Algerian population of Paris. The Paris branch of the FLN called for Algerians to demonstrate peacefully in protest. The police repressed the demonstration with unrestrained savagery. Many Algerians were brutally beaten and drowned in the Seine. The official government line was that the police had intervened against a violent and illegal demonstration, and that three demonstrators had been killed. In reality the demonstration had been entirely peaceful, the violence had been only on the police side and the true number of dead was between 50 and 300. Even the lower estimate would be extraordinary for a demonstration in a western democratic state in peacetime. On the night of the massacre, the television news led with a different story and then followed with an item about FLN violence.

In the following days, the press tried to uncover what had really happened. Papon with the help of the Minister of the Interior, Roger Frey, was successful in sabotaging parliamentary efforts to set up a commission of inquiry. De Gaulle's only recorded reaction when two ministers raised their concerns at the next Cabinet meeting was that the press was exaggerating the affair as a means of attacking him: 'The Minister of the Interior must avoid excesses but it is astonishing that there were not more deaths.'[118] Afterwards he remarked in private to the Minister of Information, Terrenoire, that the root of the problem was the presence of 400,000 Algerians in France: 'When the situation in Algeria has been settled in one way or another, this question also needs to be settled. It is a fiction to consider these people as French like any other. They are in truth a foreign mass and we will have to look into the conditions of their presence on our soil.'[119]

The government was successful in suppressing the truth. Only decades later did the full horror of the events come to light. This was not the case with the second incident of police violence – perhaps because here the casualties were French rather than Algerian. Trade unions and student organizations had been orchestrating demonstrations since the autumn to protest against the police's failure to act more firmly against the OAS. Although ostensibly in support of de Gaulle's Algerian policy, these demonstrations were banned by the authorities. On 7 February, OAS violence in Paris reached a climax with bomb attacks targeting journalists and political personalities. One of these was Malraux, who was absent when a bomb exploded in his apartment building, but a four-year-old girl living in the building lost her right eye. Outraged by photos of the child's disfigured face, a number of left-wing organizations called for a demonstration of protest on 8 February. Although forbidden by the government, the march went ahead anyway. Nine demonstrators were killed. The official line was that this was a tragic accident when demonstrators trying to flee the police were crushed against the closed gates of the metro in the Rue de Charonne. The truth was that some of the victims had their heads smashed by police beatings.[120] Once again Papon's police had acted with unrestrained violence. On 13 February, the day of the funeral of the victims, the trade unions called a general strike. The coffins of the victims were accompanied by the largest gathering seen in France since the 1930s.

The affair left de Gaulle as cold as the deaths in October. When the government discussed the matter on 17 February, he remarked that although the 'accident' was 'deplorable', the culprit was the Communist Party for organizing the demonstration.[121] His annoyance was directed at the media and he instructed that the press be given low figures for the number of participants in the protest strike otherwise the 'good "progressives" of our TV news will go round saying everywhere that the strike was massively followed'.[122] Alain Dewerpe, the historian of the Charonne demonstration (in which his mother was killed when he was ten years old), notes: 'The only trace of the massacre from de Gaulle's pen was an order to play down the size of the protest strike which accompanied the funeral of the victims.'[123]

De Gaulle's unsentimentality was entirely in character. What does need some explanation is why he created the situation in the first place by allowing the curious even-handedness of repressing demonstrators who supported his policy of independence for Algeria – why, to quote a speech of November 1960, he seemed to put on an equal footing the two 'rival packs' (a term he had once used about the two sides in the Dreyfus Affair), supporting, on the one hand, 'sterile immobility' and, on the other, 'vulgar abandonment'. One explanation popular at the time was that this represented an implicit deal with a police force which contained many sympathizers with *Algérie française*. Allowing the police free rein against 'subversion' on the streets of Paris reassured the police that the government was not soft on 'Communism'. Or as one author puts it pithily: in return for their support in the putsch the police were offered a massacre.[124] This may be true – although there is no proof – but de Gaulle's attitude to the two 'packs' is also revealing of his conception of democracy, and how power should be exercised. In his view, once the people had offered him their support in referenda, they should allow him to govern without interference. In a speech on 5 February 1962, just before the OAS attack which sparked the Charonne demonstration, he had compared himself to the captain of the ship: 'This transformation [in Algeria] implies inevitable upheavals. These can shake the ship and cause those with weak hearts to get seasick. But as long as the rudder is held firmly, the crew are at work, and the passengers remain confident and in their place, there is no risk of shipwreck.'[125] This perfectly encapsulated de Gaulle's elitist and charismatic view of political leadership. If some heads got broken as the captain steered the ship, the fault lay with the unruly passngers.

COUNTDOWN

By this time, de Gaulle knew that the end was near. The secret negotiations Joxe had been conducting since the autumn had cleared the ground. For the last stage he was joined by the centrist politician Jean de Broglie and the MRP Minister Robert Buron. Before Buron set off, de Gaulle gave him firm instructions: 'Succeed or fail but do not let the negotiations go on indefinitely . . . Do not fixate on details. There is the possible and the impossible . . . For the Sahara do not complicate matters.'[126]

The negotiations took place in complete secrecy in a lodge in the skiing resort of Les Rousses. On the first day, the three French negotiators, who were housed in another chalet, arrived in the morning equipped with skis pretending to be tourists. This subterfuge was soon dropped and they decided it would be easier to sleep on site. By the end, they were almost dropping with exhaustion in the increasingly fetid and smoky atmosphere of the overheated lodge. Each day, de Gaulle and Debré followed the events closely by telephone.

After a week, an agreement seemed imminent. What had started almost four years earlier with de Gaulle addressing cheering crowds in the Forum of Algiers on 4 June 1958 drew to a close on the morning of 19 February 1962 as the three French negotiators huddled round the phone to receive their final instructions from de Gaulle. Buron wrote in his diary:

> Extraordinary contrast at the moment of the most important decisions for the Fifth Republic; at the other end of the line the President in front of his table, presumably in the large room of the Elyseé with its gilded panelling, silence and solemnity; at the other end, three men in crumpled clothes in a bedroom of 8m² with an unmade bed.[127]

De Gaulle spoke to each of the three Frenchmen in turn, insisting each time on the fact that Debré was at his side and in full agreement. The transcript of the telephone conversation reveals de Gaulle's desperate haste to obtain an agreement at any cost:

> De G: You tell me that for military questions things are still up in the air [en cause].
> Joxe: You gave me instructions yesterday and I am applying them.
> De G: But all is still up in the air?
> J: Up in the air how? They are going to reply this afternoon.
> De G: They are going to reply, but if they don't agree with you?
> J: I would be astonished if they did not agree . . .
> De G: Good! I suppose that this afternoon – because we are talking about this afternoon – you will reach agreement, a complete agreement?

Then Buron took the receiver:

> De G: What are your views?
> Buron: Well, their intellectual categories are very different from ours.
> De G: Yes.
> B: The discussion always goes off on the usual 'oriental' track.

De G: Good [One has the impression de Gaulle was not interested in any of this] . . . So what is your impression about a conclusion?

B: They will agree on everything except perhaps the military delays . . .

De G: Good . . . After having heard all three of you I will dictate Joxe a final instruction especially about the military issues.

The phone was passed to Broglie:

De G: So?

Broglie: Concerning the Sahara the essential elements of an agreement are reached . . .

De G: Good. The rest?

B: The other problems are almost resolved . . .

De G: So can it be swallowed overall?[128]

After further brief conversation with Broglie, de Gaulle dictated his final instructions to Joxe:

The essential is to reach agreement which includes a ceasefire followed by self-determination, as long as this agreement does not cause sudden upheavals in the present condition relating to the material and political interests of the Europeans, the French military presence in Algeria, the practical conditions of the exploitation of oil and gas . . . This is the result, I repeat, this is the result that you must reach today.[129]

Having read out these instructions de Gaulle asked:

De G: Is that clear, *cher ami*?

J: Entirely General. But there is one thing. One of the most difficult points is the duration and amount of the aid programme we are granting; does it remain at the same level as now?

De G: Yes, for the trial period . . . After that if there is nothing to be done with them of course we will take our money [*billes*] back . . . If there is something to be done with them, it is very likely our aid to Algeria will remain what it is at the moment . . . but all will depend on what happens . . . So whatever principles we enunciate now have no great importance; they are just intentions . . . It is the same for Mers-el-Kébir and the Sahara.

J: I totally understand and you can be assured that these are the principles we have been applying . . . You have explained very well that we need to distinguish between a trial period and the rest. Should we insist on that difference by making commitments on the four coming years . . . ?

De G: It is best not to accumulate too many precise details.

After some more discussion de Gaulle came back to his obsession:

De G: You must finish tonight.

J: Yes, *mon Général,* that is my most devout wish. We have been locked up here for five days. We never go out. We have only one idea: to be 'let out' . . .

De G: So if you succeed tonight you will be back tomorrow?

J: We will come back tonight . . .

De G: And if you don't succeed in concluding tonight?

J: We will.

De G: If you don't?

J: If not we will say: 'This is our last shot. Give us a reply in 48 hours.'

De G: Yes. Good . . . But are they willing right now to publish a communiqué . . . ?

J: I have never spoken about a communiqué but we could do one . . .

De G: We can't leave people in uncertainty, you understand.

J: I prefer not to publish a joint communiqué.

De G: Of course, I agree, and so does M. Debré.

J: I will telephone you this evening . . . Can I do it after dinner?

De G: You mean about 9.30?

J: Yes. But do not worry if I do not ring . . . If all progresses smoothly I will not call.[130]

Joxe did not need to call. Two days later the French team were back in Paris, and on 21 February they reported back to the government. As on special occasions, de Gaulle allowed each minister to express a view. Malraux made a lyrical speech celebrating this as a victory comparable to the Liberation of France; Debré, who complained afterwards that Malraux's words had made him feel physically sick,[131] refused to hide his sense of disappointment: 'Algeria existed through France. Will she be able to exist really without France? It is the end of a painful ordeal. Alas, it is above all a victory over ourselves.' De Gaulle summed up briskly: 'We are human beings and perhaps we have made mistakes, as our predecessors made mistakes; but we had to extricate France from a crisis that brought her only misfortunes. The agreements are unpredictable . . . As for France, she has to move on to other things.'[132] Speaking privately to Debré and Terrenoire afterwards, de Gaulle declared: 'In truth it is miraculous that we have reached this agreement. Think of it: for 130 years "they" have never ceased to be dominated, lied to, despoiled, humiliated. It is a miracle that they are still willing to live with the Europeans.' Debré pointed out that France had done a lot for the country; de Gaulle grudgingly conceded that this was true.[133]

All that remained was a final round of talks at Evian to ratify the agreements that had been reached. This was expected to be a formality, but the FLN negotiators, sensing French desperation, knew that time was on their side. It took another twelve days to sign an agreement. By the end, the French had abandoned almost every negotiating position they had started with nine months earlier. The transitional provisional authority, which Debré had once optimistically hoped might last for twenty-five years, had been whittled down to three months. The French starting position over the lease of Mers-el-Kébir had been that it should last for ninety-nine years; by the end this had been reduced to fifteen years with a possibility of renewal. On the thorny issue of the rights of Europeans, the compromise reached was that for three years the *pieds noirs* could hold double citizenship before deciding whether to become full Algerian citizens.

AFTERMATH

On 18 March de Gaulle announced the signature of the Evian accords on French television. In April they were approved in a referendum by 91 per cent of those voting. France remained theoretically the sovereign power in Algeria, with a French high commissioner presiding over an executive of three Frenchmen and eight Algerians to prepare the referendum in Algeria on independence. This took place on 1 July, at which point Algeria became officially independent. In these three months before the Algerian referendum, Algeria descended into chaos as the OAS embarked on a scorched-earth strategy. When reprisal attacks on Europeans took place, de Gaulle was implacably opposed at the Council of Ministers on 4 May to the suggestion that, until independence was formally declared, it was the duty of the French army to protect them. He was quite clear: 'France's interest has ceased to be confused with that of the *pieds noirs* ... Independence is independence ... It will not be established without terrible upheavals ... Napoleon said that in love the only victory was flight. Where decolonization is concerned also, the only victory is to leave.'[134]

There was much discussion in the government between March and June regarding the 'repatriation' of the *pieds noirs*. By mid-May 100,000 had left; by the end of the year 680,000. They arrived in France destitute, uprooted from a country in which many of their families had lived for generations. When Peyrefitte tried to alert de Gaulle to the difficult conditions in which these refugees, many of whom had never set foot in France before, were living in makeshift camps in the south of France, de Gaulle was not interested:

None of this would have happened to them if the OAS had not been able to operate among them like a fish in water ... They unleashed violence and they are surprised that it comes back to hit them in the face. So they rushed like sheep on to their boats and planes. Do not try to make me feel sorry for them! I have found this page of our history as painful as anyone. But we have turned it.[135]

Coulet once told de Gaulle that he should treat the *pieds noirs* not as 'delinquent children' but as 'retarded children'.[136] He found this impossible and the best he could manage, in a speech of 8 May 1961 specifically addressed to 'Algerians of French origins', was: 'With all my heart I ask them, on the very day that we commemorate a victory to which they have contributed so much, to give up their outdated myths and their absurd agitations.' Many would have agreed with Pierre Racine, favourable to de Gaulle's policy, who commented: 'One of my profound regrets is that General de Gaulle ... never said a word to touch the hearts of the French Algerians ... Every time he made a speech, the Prime Minister said to him, "General, say something a little kind for the French of Algeria! Say that whatever happens we will look after them" ... But no, the words never came, as he knew how to do, when he wanted to.'[137]

But if the 'words' never came, at least the French government did its minimal duty to the *pieds noirs* by allowing them to come to France. This was not the case for the Harkis, those Algerian Muslims who had been drafted or volunteered as auxiliaries to serve with the French army. Most of them faced reprisals and almost certain death in Algeria. Of some 300,000 who had fought for France, fewer than one in ten found asylum in France. Here de Gaulle's attitude was even less sympathetic than to the *pieds noirs*: 'Obviously the term "repatriated" does not apply to the Muslims: they are not returning to the land of their fathers.'[138] This statement, made to the Council of Ministers, was followed by an explicit policy instruction the next day from de Gaulle in person:

> We need to finish with the affair of the Harkis. No Harki must be allowed to embark for the Metropole without the express and formal approval of the Minister of the Armies. Any Harki who within 8 days has not accepted the job offered to him must be sent back to Algeria. The actual number of Harkis in the Metropole must not increase ... The Harkis were recruited in the past from among down-and-outs, and they want it to continue at the expense of the French. This is a bad joke that has gone on long enough.[139]

Or as de Gaulle put it crisply a year later: 'I would like there to be more French babies and fewer immigrants.'[140] This takes us back to the reasons for his scepticism about integration from the start. In this, at least, he had been consistent.

De Gaulle's 'granting' of Algerian independence, while avoiding civil war in France, is often counted as one of his greatest achievements. This judgement needs to be qualified. He did not 'grant' independence: it was wrested from him. And he only partially avoided civil war. The truth is that the FLN had won independence by fighting and by mobilizing international support. Although de Gaulle gradually resigned himself to this outcome, he did so reluctantly – and by the end he had salvaged nothing of his original expectations. By the standards of Debré, he was a model of lucidity, but not by the standards of, for example, Bernard Tricot or Raymond Aron. By moving slowly in the hope of granting limited independence on his terms, he was cornered into a series of abrupt tactical retreats which left him nothing to negotiate by the end. A year was wasted between the abortive Melun talks in June 1960 and the first round of Evian talks in May 1961; and another three months between May and September 1961 before he dropped his insistence on retaining the Sahara. By this point the French had no cards left. De Gaulle's caution could be explained by the need gradually to 'sell' the policy to the army and the French population, but if anything the steady retreat, and the twists and turns of policy, exacerbated the army's sense of betrayal. The result was something close to the civil war he had supposedly avoided. De Gaulle had inherited an overmighty army – and perhaps no one could have done any better, but it is hard to see that anyone could have done much worse. The Fourth Republic had struggled with Algeria for four years; de Gaulle, with all his prestige and all the powers at his disposal, struggled on for another four.

De Gaulle's achievement, then, was less to have 'granted' independence than to have persuaded people that that is what he had done; to make them believe that he had controlled the process; and to create a compelling narrative that explained France's disengagement from Algeria and turned it into a victory rather than a defeat. Now France had to look forward, 'marry her century' and embrace the future.[141] Or as he put it at the meeting of the Council of Ministers which approved the Evian accords on 18 March: 'Now we must turn to Europe. The era of organized continents has succeeded the colonial era.'[142]

21

Turning Point, 1962

In his annual report on the state of France at the end of 1961, the recently appointed British Ambassador, Sir Pierson Dixon, predicted: 'Future historians will I think point to 1961 as the year in which General de Gaulle's fortunes and his authority began to decline.' Dixon's judgement was that, with Algeria almost out of the way, 'the regime might crumble quickly' and de Gaulle would 'be ungratefully thrown aside'.[1] Such views were widely shared. The Ambassador was only reporting what he had picked up in the press and from his Parisian political contacts.

De Gaulle's political position since returning to power had been anomalous. As the Gaullist Party (UNR) did not have an overall parliamentary majority, the government relied on the support of other groups. Most of the leading politicians who had facilitated de Gaulle's return to power progressively moved into semi-opposition. Guy Mollet's Socialists had left the government at the end of 1958 because they opposed the Rueff Plan. The conservative Antoine Pinay, de Gaulle's Finance Minister, had resigned in January 1960 because he disapproved of de Gaulle's foreign policy. Since Pinay was, with Mendès France, the only survivor of the Fourth Republic with a major political reputation, his resignation might have been a threat. But its impact was rapidly blunted by Barricades Week.

There was much sniping in parliament against many of de Gaulle's policies during these years, but the new constitution made it hard to obstruct a determined government. The key provision was Article 49 clause 3 which allowed the government to transform any vote into a question of confidence. A law was regarded as adopted unless the opposition tabled a motion of censure, which required an absolute majority of all votes – with abstentions treated as votes in favour. During the debates in the autumn of 1960 on the five-year defence programme, committing France to an independent nuclear deterrent, the opposition presented three motions of censure but all of them fell short of the necessary majority. The truth was that de Gaulle's parliamentary opponents balked at a complete rupture as long as the Algerian crisis continued. After the approval of the Evian accords in April 1962, it seemed that 'normal' politics might resume.

In May 1962, Guy Mollet, who had been so instrumental in de Gaulle's return to power in May 1958, published a book entitled *13 May 1958–13 May 1962*. It defended his decision to support de Gaulle in May 1958 but also demonstrated why he was ready to oppose him now.[2] Meeting Pierre Pflimlin around this time, Mollet predicted that the regime would fall within six months: 'The problem will be to watch out that de Gaulle is treated with dignity because, despite everything, I do feel a certain attachment to him.'[3] De Gaulle may not have been aware of this condescending solicitude, but he knew that the politicians were sharpening their knives – and he was preparing to take them on. Briefing the newly appointed Minister of Information Alain Peyrefitte in April 1962, he told him that the coming year would witness a 'great turning point'. When Peyrefitte took his leave he was none the wiser because de Gaulle had not told him what 'turning point' he had in mind.[4]

EXIT DEBRÉ

The most immediate turning point after the ratification of the Evian Accords was the change of Prime Minister. On 14 April, Michel Debré resigned. This had been agreed with de Gaulle several months earlier. Debré's four years as Prime Minister had allowed the new constitution to be tested out in a sometimes fractious relationship between the man who had mainly written it and the man for whom it had been written. From the beginning, de Gaulle established certain ground rules that were not fixed by the constitution. For example, in the Fourth Republic the government regularly met in what were known as *conseils de cabinet* chaired by the premier, distinct from the Council of Ministers, chaired by the President: de Gaulle himself held *conseils de cabinet* in his six months as the last premier of the Fourth Republic. On becoming de Gaulle's Prime Minister, Debré had assumed he would do the same until it was made clear to him by de Gaulle that the practice must cease: ministers would not meet collectively except under *his* chairmanship. From time to time, de Gaulle would rebuke Debré when he felt his Presidential prerogatives were being infringed.[5] Debré retaliated by trying to assert his Prime-Ministerial prerogatives. When a minister was due to be replaced in 1959, Debré reminded de Gaulle: 'The constitution is very precise: it is the Prime Minister who submits to the President of the Republic his proposals for the composition of the government'; on another occasion, he expressed 'surprise' at not being consulted sufficiently on the 1960 defence bill.[6]

These tensions were exacerbated by Debré's restlessly interfering personality. As a workaholic, he wanted to be involved in everything, constantly bombarding his ministers with hectoring notes and directives. Although he had to tread more carefully with de Gaulle, he did not hold back from offering his views on every subject from the future of Africa to the management of the economy, from the reorganization of the Paris region to foreign policy. He would often pour out his soul to de Gaulle in long missives written in the small hours. These would be waiting on the President's desk in the morning. Despite his religious devotion to de Gaulle, Debré could be quite frank with him. Sometimes he would lecture him on how to be a 'true' Gaullist; sometimes he would be confessional; sometimes he sought reassurance. He had enough self-awareness to sense how wearing these outpourings must have been to their recipient, but he could not help himself. One of them ended: 'I ask you to forgive me for this long letter. It probably makes you regret the fact that I have taken a few days' holiday! As you know, sometimes I feel weary and wonder if I am the best person to be in this role – or if someone else would not do better.'[7] A month later he was at it again: 'I don't want to write you a new "letter". But I want you to know that I need to talk to you.'[8]

The fundamental cause of Debré's despair was Algeria. What worried him was not only the content of de Gaulle's policies but the way the crisis was altering the balance of power between President and Prime Minister. A shift of power from Prime Minister to President was inevitable given the force of de Gaulle's personality, but the Algerian crisis accentuated and accelerated the process. In the autumn of 1959, at a congress of the UNR, Jacques Chaban-Delmas had invoked the concept of a 'reserved presidential sector' of policy, comprising foreign policy and Algeria, where de Gaulle should be allowed to decide for himself.[9] This concept had no constitutional authority and was invented to deal with a possible mutiny among the UNR rank and file dissatisfied with de Gaulle's Algerian policy. As de Gaulle himself once remarked: 'We know what Constitutions are worth; we have had seventeen in 150 years, and the nature of things is stronger than texts drawn up by politicians.'[10] The most direct victim was Debré, who found it harder and harder to preserve the prerogatives the constitution in theory granted him. After Barricades Week de Gaulle decided to sack his Defence Minister and replace him with the loyal Gaullist Pierre Messmer, who some years later recalled how this had happened: 'General de Gaulle did not even ask Michel Debré's opinion before naming me minister ... he called me back from Algeria and said, "you are minister, return to your house and don't answer the telephone until one in the afternoon. I need to begin by informing the prime minister.""[11] De Gaulle was prepared to observe constitutional proprieties – but only perfunctorily.

Every escalation in the Algerian crisis was a pretext for de Gaulle to extend his personal power by deploying the panoply of options available to him under the new constitution. After Barricades Week, he got parliament to allow him to govern by ordinances for a year; after the attempted putsch of April 1961, he applied the controversial Article 16 giving him full emergency powers – as he had already wanted to do after Barricades Week. In practice, he used the powers that Article 16 allowed him with moderation. But even Debré felt uneasy that de Gaulle kept Article 16 in play long after the emergency had passed. He wrote to him in September 1961:

> We are in neither a parliamentary democracy nor a dictatorship. We are not completely in a democracy since decisions which are not submitted to discussion can affect individual liberties . . . Yet we are not in a dictatorship since the press is free, as is the radio and parliamentary activity . . . and everyone is against the government since no one is associated in a sustained way with the way it is exercised.[12]

From the man who hoped the new constitution he had helped to draft would create for France a rationalized parliamentary democracy, this was a damning verdict. De Gaulle grudgingly accepted in September 1961 that the emergency was over, and that Article 16 need no longer apply.

A few months later, in January 1962, de Gaulle had a conversation with Debré which revealed that they profoundly disagreed on the nature of the constitution they had created. Debré believed that, once the Algerian crisis was over, there should logically be a change of government – with the replacement of the Prime Minister – and possibly parliamentary elections. De Gaulle agreed that the Prime Minister should be replaced but saw no need for elections since this implied that the government was an emanation of parliament. He told Debré that he did 'not like the term "change the government" which suggested that the government existed independently of the President whereas in his view they were one and the same'. Debré replied that this was 'only partially exact' – a polite way of saying that it was entirely contrary to the constitution. In this same conversation, Debré and de Gaulle agreed that it would soon be necessary to change the Prime Minister. De Gaulle twisted the knife in the wound until the end saying that 'I am sure you will resent me for this.' Debré replied that never would he resent anything that de Gaulle did, but at the same time he took the opportunity to reel off a list of some of the humiliations he had suffered:

de Gaulle summoning ministers without consulting him, notes sent to ministers by de Gaulle's advisers over the head of the Prime Minister, hearing de Gaulle announce in public policies quite different to those he had outlined previously to Debré (as in the case of the Sahara).[13]

ENTER POMPIDOU

In his first Prime Minister, de Gaulle had found someone ready to immolate himself, and sacrifice his convictions regarding Algeria, on the altar of his personal loyalty. He had exhausted his usefulness; it was time to move on. As Debré's successor, de Gaulle chose Georges Pompidou, who had served him so well behind the scenes on many occasions. Pompidou, who had nothing of the zealot about him, could not have been more different from his anxiously earnest predecessor with his habit of working into the small hours every night. He enjoyed the good life, had an elegant flat on the Ile Saint-Louis in Paris where he and his wife enjoyed entertaining artists and people from the world of entertainment and fashion. In January 1960, he wrote to a close friend in de Gaulle's entourage that things would be better if Debré 'toned down his reforming temperament. He should not try to interfere in everything and transform everything at the same time . . . I know that Debré is temperamentally in a hurry. I know that the General is no longer young and that he wants to do as much as possible in the minimum of time. But believe me, sometimes one needs to take a breath, especially if one wants to build something durable.'[14] This was Pompidou's philosophy of government.[15]

Pompidou's admiration for de Gaulle was always tinged with a certain detached irony. He was almost the only person who sometimes permitted himself to talk of 'de Gaulle' and not 'the General'. He told an American diplomat in 1962: 'I did not want to be Prime Minister but we are living under a dictatorship and each person must do what he is ordered.'[16] Debré would never have made a joke of this kind. Jokes were not in his repertoire, especially if they concerned de Gaulle. Beneath his languid façade, Pompidou was a shrewd operator with a finely tuned intuition about de Gaulle. He knew the role required of him and was happy to play it (or so he thought). He remarked privately after his appointment that he would not allow the slightest divergence of view between himself and the President: 'That is the spirit of the regime. And it is my role. I am not like Debré: I have no existence of my own. I am only the reflection of de Gaulle. I have no policy of my own, no electors, no clientele. I have only the ideas of the General.'[17] In saying this, he presumably expected that, while de Gaulle occupied himself with defence and foreign policy, he would not wish to interfere in the day-to-day management of the economy where Pompidou believed he was the expert.

Briefing Alain Peyrefitte on how Pompidou's appointment was to be presented to the press, de Gaulle delivered his own extraordinary (mis) reading of the constitution. He told him not to use the phrase 'change of government' because the government had been renewed, not changed: 'I am the head of the government. The Prime Minister is the first among ministers.' Peyrefitte was also instructed that communiqués after the meetings of the Council of Ministers should never say 'General de Gaulle concluded' but rather 'the government concluded'. The reason: 'When I draw the conclusion of a deliberation – not a discussion because the Council deliberates, it does not discuss – it is the government that speaks through my mouth. The government has no existence outside me. It exists through me. It can only meet if I summon it, and in my presence, on an agenda decided by me.'[18]

Appointing a Prime Minister who had never held elective office and was unknown to the public was in itself a political statement, not to say a provocation. Pompidou was visibly ill at ease on his first appearance before parliament. On going up to the podium to make his first speech, he took the wrong staircase because he had never set foot in the Chamber before. Nonetheless Pompidou was a shrewd choice. He may have lacked parliamentary experience but he was a quick learner. And his affable steeliness made him a plausible candidate to build a broadly based government in the post-Algerian context. This was shown when he succeeded in persuading members of the centrist MRP, including Pflimlin, to join his government. He seemed to have started well.

Pompidou's first problems, only a month after his appointment, were caused not by his own inexperience but by de Gaulle's unpredictability. Expatiating on his conception of Europe at a press conference on 15 May 1962, de Gaulle launched into a diatribe against 'hybrid' supranational Europe: 'Dante, Goethe, Chateaubriand all belong to Europe to the extent that they were respectively and eminently Italian, German and French. They would not have been much use to Europe if they had been stateless and if they had thought, written in some kind of "Esperanto" or "Volapük".' He went on to deride those who believed that Europe could be created magically by some kind of Aladdin's lamp: 'Let us begin with realities at the base of the edifice and when we have done the work we can comfort ourselves with the fairy stories of the One Thousand and One Nights.'[19] Since commitment to Europe was the MRP's most fundamental conviction, Pflimlin took de Gaulle's words as a personal insult and was determined to resign. De Gaulle, who could not resist a rhetorical sally, had genuinely not predicted its impact. Although he rarely used the telephone, and hated to be a supplicant, he rang Pflimlin at midnight. For thirty minutes he pleaded, cajoled and bullied him to stay in the government. Pflimlin would not be swayed.[20]

Pompidou tried to take the matter philosophically but was upset that within a month de Gaulle had sabotaged his attempt to form a broadly based government. He told Peyrefitte that because de Gaulle was 'cyclothymic' his ministers needed to restrain his impulses: 'If not, he would set the whole world against us ... We must be the velvet glove on this fist of iron ... Unlike Debré who was a horsehair glove.'[21] As he got into his stride, Pompidou elevated this into an art of government: 'One serves the General best in hiding certain things from him. He needs not stimulants but tranquillizers.'[22] In this instance, it was too late. The damage was done.

DE GAULLE ON TRIAL

Pompidou's hopes of calming the political atmosphere received another blow only a few days later with the unexpected outcome of the trial of General Salan. De Gaulle had used his powers under Article 16 to set up a Special Tribunal to judge the four putschist generals. Juridically this was problematic since it breached the principle that a person could not be tried by a court that did not exist at the moment of their alleged crime. No one worried too much about this nicety. Two of the generals, Challe and Zeller, had been apprehended immediately after the putsch. Their trials took place in May 1961. Since Zeller was the most minor figure among the four, and since Challe had been a reluctant conspirator, they were each given relatively light sentences of fifteen years in prison.

In March 1962 the other two generals, who had been hiding in Algiers, were both arrested. The context of their trial was more dramatic than those of Challe and Zeller since the year in between had seen the emergence of the OAS. The semi-farcical putsch was now overshadowed by the terrifying violence of the OAS. Tried in April 1962, Jouhaud was sentenced to death. Since Jouhaud was generally seen as an honest soldier who, being of *pied noir* origin, had deep personal involvement in the fate of French Algeria, most people expected de Gaulle to commute the sentence. This was indeed his intention once a verdict on Salan had been delivered.

Salan, whose trial opened on 15 May, was the most prominent of the four rebels, and the nearest they had to a ringleader. After making his opening statement, he refused to utter another word – like Pétain in 1945. The defence summoned a roster of distinguished witnesses, including even the widows of Marshals Leclerc and de Lattre, to explain Salan's motives. The theme that ran through all defence testimonies was betrayal: France's betrayal of the French citizens of Algeria (the *pieds noirs*) and de Gaulle's betrayal of the promises he had made to the army. Recalling that de Gaulle had told him in March 1959 'you can tell your men that we will never negotiate,' one general expressed his bitterness about what had actually transpired: 'the sum of abnegation, sacrifice, devotion ... which was asked of us for the honour of France and the flag of France, and the hecatomb of our men, of our officers, of our comrades, all counted for nothing.'[23] At the end of the trial, defence counsel produced a previously unknown letter from de Gaulle to Salan in October 1958 assuring him that whatever happened France would 'not give up Algeria'.[24] Also telling was the testimony of General Pouilly, who had not joined the putschists: 'I took an altogether different route from that of General Salan; I chose the route of obedience. But in choosing obedience I also chose to share with my fellow citizens the shame of abandonment ... History will perhaps say that their crime was perhaps less grave than ours.'[25]

To those who claimed it was the duty of soldiers to obey the government whatever their personal convictions, the trial was an opportunity to return to the circumstances of de Gaulle's own return to power in 1958. In his opening statement, Salan pointed out that the first time he had acted illegally was in 1958 – on behalf of de Gaulle. Léon Delbecque, Guillain de Bénouville and General Miquel, all actors in the events of 1958, went over the circumstances of de Gaulle's return to power. Bénouville (who had smuggled Soustelle out of his apartment in May 1958) stated that his actions in that year were the 'culmination of the efforts we had been pursuing since 1946 when de Gaulle had left power'.[26] As the trial raked further over the past, nothing was more embarrassing than defence counsel's exhumation of Michel Debré's incendiary articles before 1958 justifying insurrection against the regime (that is, the Fourth Republic) if it proved incapable of defending French Algeria. He had written to Sérigny in 1957: 'The struggle for *Algérie française* is a legal struggle; insurrection for *Algérie française* is legitimate insurrection.'[27] There were indeed suspicions that Debré's defence of insurrection had gone beyond words. It was rumoured he had been involved in (or had at least known in advance about) a bazooka attack against General Salan who was then viewed as lukewarm about *Algérie française*. Salan had escaped unhurt but one of his officers had been killed. Among the witnesses called by the defence was François Mitterrand, who had been Minister of Justice at the time of the bazooka affair. Although he studiously avoided mentioning Debré's name, everyone knew what he meant when he declared: 'Today Salan is a rebel, and a defeated rebel. These are two faults that will never be forgiven him by the man who defeated him, and who never respects the State more than when he incarnates it himself.' For Mitterrand, the civil war of the OAS against the French state had begun with the civil war against the 'institutions of the Republic by a clan in 1957' – by the Gaullists.[28] As Talleyrand remarked, treason is a matter of timing.

By moving beyond *Algérie française* to ask when – and if – it was ever justifiable to rebel against a legal government, the trial opened up issues that had been at the heart of de Gaulle's entire career since 1940. De Gaulle remarked privately after the putsch that the problem went back to Vichy.[29] There were indeed haunting echoes of that past. Salan's lawyer, Tixier-Vignancour, was an extreme-right-wing activist who had been in Pétain's government in 1940. At a trial in the following year of the OAS conspirator Captain Bastien-Thiry, one of the defence lawyers was the same Jacques Isorni who had defended Brasillach and Pétain in 1945. Isorni's line was that the thread running throughout de Gaulle's career from Vichy to Algeria was an abstract 'idea' of France indifferent to the sufferings of the French people – whether the population of metropolitan France in 1940–44 or the *pieds noirs* in 1960–62.[30]

Pétainist nostalgia was not the only argument against de Gaulle in 1962. Defenders of *Algérie française* included many who had been in the Resistance or Free French. They invoked de Gaulle's own career to justify acts of disobedience to a government perceived as betraying France's interests. Asked at the trial to comment on the issue of 'legitimate insubordination' one former resister replied: 'I think that in 1940 we had an illustrious example.'[31] Many defenders of *Algérie française* used the idea that de Gaulle in 1962 had betrayed the values he incarnated in 1940. One group declared in December 1960 (inverting de Gaulle's own phrase in 1940): 'France has not lost the battle but she will lose the war.'[32] Bidault, who had been the second head of the CNR in 1943, set up in 1962 a new CNR to defend a new 'resistance'. In one OAS trial, one of the defendants opened with a summary of his career: 'The Resistance, Gestapo, Buchenwald, three stints in Indo-China, Algeria, Suez, Algeria again ... One can ask a lot of a soldier. One cannot ask him to contradict himself, to lie, to cheat, to break his oath.'[33]

Salan's trial ended on Wednesday 23 May. After deliberating for three hours the judges found Salan guilty on all counts but with extenuating circumstances. He was sentenced to imprisonment not death. Hearing the news that evening, de Gaulle summoned the Minister of Justice, Jean Foyer, to the Elysée. Foyer found him in a state of uncontrolled fury that the

defence should have succeeded in turning the Salan trial into the trial of
de Gaulle. The clemency of the judges was a public humiliation and also
a negative judgement on much of de Gaulle's career since 1940. It was in
this context that he made his speech (quoted on p. 543) distancing himself
from any implication in the insurrection of 1958.

After meeting with Foyer on the Wednesday evening, de Gaulle decided
to dissolve the Special Tribunal and implement the sentence to shoot Jouhaud. The execution was fixed to take place at dawn on Saturday. Foyer
was appalled by this act of sheer vindictiveness, which sacrificed a subordinate for the crimes of his superior. On Thursday he went to plead with
de Gaulle to change his mind. De Gaulle was implacable. He wrote to
Pompidou the next day: 'Foyer seems to have lost his head over Jouhaud . . .
We will have to replace him.'[34] Pompidou was of the same mind as Foyer.
He went to see de Gaulle the day after the verdict: 'I found de Gaulle in
one of his bad days, grey, eyes blazing. His prey had escaped. He needed
a substitute victim.'[35] Pompidou drafted a resignation letter and, in a further letter, he put the case against Jouhaud's execution:

> I have nothing to add to what I have said to you about the human side of
> the issue.
>
> But it is my duty to draw your attention to its political aspect in the most
> elevated meaning of the term.
>
> Shooting J[ouhaud] is not the same as shooting Pucheu [in 1944]. It would
> be the equivalent at the Liberation, if Pierre Laval had escaped the death
> penalty, of shooting instead Bichelonne [a collaborating Minister of Econom-
> ics] as a scapegoat.
>
> To shoot J at the moment that Algeria is evolving and accepts Evian would
> be to allow certain leaders of the OAS who want to rekindle terror and
> violence to make you the person responsible for it. This violence might sweep
> everything away with it.
>
> To shoot J despite the documents in your possession would be to mete
> out the most rigorous treatment to someone who is a *pied noir*, and a man
> of the people, and certainly the most moderate of them all.
>
> You have based your actions on a dynamic of peace. If you shoot J that
> will work against you.
>
> The 'Shoot Jouhaud' placards do not emanate from the people. They are
> the work of Communist Party cadres who are not thinking of your interests
> nor of your historical reputation.
>
> In all conscience, and setting aside all other considerations, it is my view
> that once the effects of the Salan verdict have faded, you would destroy
> everything at a stroke and commit a decisive error.[36]

On Friday, the day before the execution, Foyer found a way of winning time after Salan's defence counsel had presented him with an appeal for judicial review. Foyer seized upon this to argue that as Minister of Justice he was legally bound to transmit this request to the appeal court, the Cour de Cassation, while not himself pronouncing on its admissibility. It was inevitable that the Cour would rule it inadmissible, but a few days would be gained. Foyer returned to see de Gaulle on Friday afternoon with Pompidou and Joxe as reinforcements. Although suffering 'one of the most disagreeable hours I have had in my life', Foyer was able to win de Gaulle over.[37] In the end, the Cour de Cassation rejected the appeal, but by this time things had moved on. Salan and Jouhaud had made a public appeal to the OAS on 29 May to cease its violence in Algeria. Jouhaud's life was saved, although de Gaulle did not officially commute the sentence for another six months – and did so with bad grace. When Guillain de Bénouville wrote to thank de Gaulle for this gesture of mercy the reply was '*qu'il aille se faire foutre*'.[38]

Whether or not he was convinced by the arguments of Foyer, Pompidou and others, de Gaulle had accepted the way out they offered him to avert a serious political crisis. At least eight other ministers were prepared to resign if the execution took place.[39] After the crisis was over de Gaulle told Pompidou: 'Between two evils, your resignation and a pardon for Jouhaud, I chose the lesser one.'[40] Pompidou believed that he had saved de Gaulle from an act that would have stained his reputation as durably as Napoleon's execution of the Duc d'Enghien in 1804.

De Gaulle could not, however, be stopped from disbanding the Special Tribunal that had defied him. Instead he set up a new a Military Court of Justice to try any remaining OAS activists. To preside over the court he appointed General Larminat, one of the first soldiers to join him in 1940. Larminat supported de Gaulle's Algerian policy but he found this responsibility too much for him. He was hospitalized soon after being appointed and wrote to de Gaulle explaining that 'my nerves have cracked and I am suffering a crisis of depression' and could not 'physically and mentally carry out the duty that has been assigned to me'.[41] A few days later he shot himself in the head. His appointment was not the only cause of Larminat's suicide but it was a contributory factor – another poignant illustration of the tragic conflict of conscience that the Algerian affair had inflicted even upon army officers completely devoted to de Gaulle.[42]

This was not the end of the OAS frenzy. On Wednesday 22 August, towards the end of the summer holidays, de Gaulle was in Paris to chair the Council of Ministers. He decided to return to Colombey the same evening. Since the failed assassination attempt at Pont-sur-Seine in September

1961, his usual routine was to drive to the aerodrome of Villacoublay in the south-west suburb of Paris and then take a plane to Saint-Dizier, about an hour's drive from Colombey. At 20.15, thirty minutes after leaving the Elysée, his car reached the roundabout of Petit-Clamart in the southern suburbs of Paris. Lying in wait were eleven conspirators in two vehicles, one of which was stuffed with explosives. Two gunmen opened fire on de Gaulle's car, piercing its body and puncturing two tyres. A second vehicle waiting in a side road accelerated towards de Gaulle's car and more shots were fired. A bullet went through the back window, narrowly missing de Gaulle and his wife who had obeyed when their son-in-law Alain de Bois-sieu, sitting in the front seat, bellowed to them to bend down. Astonishingly no one was wounded. Many stories circulated in the press immediately afterwards about the unflappability of the de Gaulles. These were not invented if one is to believe the letter de Boissieu sent Debré a week later:

> My mother-in-law is an extraordinarily courageous woman . . . She was impassive . . . and only agreed to lower her head when I cried out a second time after the General did the same . . . He told me . . . that I had when necessary a 'voice of authority'! That voice also made my mother-in-law obey!!! The General remained impassive, only grumbling that there had been no riposte from our side . . . Alas the defence measures in the third car [of the Presidential escort] were completely inadequate . . . It is hardly believable that we escaped unscathed when one thinks that as well as the two groups which the press talked about I saw a third one at the corner of the N306 . . . which could have done a lot of harm since we were going at only 60kph given that two tyres were punctured. In the end Providence was watching over the General.[43]

The conspirators were quickly arrested and in January 1963 tried by the new military tribunal. Four were condemned to death but only one, the French air force officer Jean-Marc Bastien-Thiry, was executed. Bastien-Thiry's trial was the last great setpiece trial of the Algerian War. He had revealingly called the conspiracy to kill de Gaulle Operation Charlotte Corday – a reference to the royalist who had assassinated the revolutionary Marat in his bath in 1793. Bastien-Thiry, unrepentant, compared himself to Claus von Stauffenberg, who had tried to assassinate Hitler in 1944, and claimed that in the case of de Gaulle assassination was even more legitimate because at least Hitler had not sullied the honour of the army. The extreme-right anti-Gaullists elevated Bastien-Thiry to the status of a sacrificial martyr, joining Brasillach and Pucheu among the victims of de Gaulle's bloodlust.

This was not the last attempt to assassinate de Gaulle. Among more fantastical operations was one which involved wrapping two dogs in explosives. The last serious attempt occurred in August 1964 when a bomb was planted in a vase containing a pot plant at the memorial in Mont Faron where de Gaulle had arrived to commemorate the 1944 landings in Provence. The bomb did not go off, though this was probably not because, as myth soon had it, a conscientious gardener had innocently watered the vase.[44]

'PERMANENT COUP D'ETAT'

A week after the Petit-Clamart attack, de Gaulle remarked that it 'could not have been more timely'.[45] He saw an opportunity to capitalize on the emotion aroused by the event to carry out a constitutional change he had been planning for some months. This was the 'turning point' he had in mind when talking to Peyrefitte a few months earlier. As we have seen, under the constitution of 1958 the President was elected by an electoral college of about 80,000 members. De Gaulle's own personal authority and historical reputation meant that this restricted franchise was no impediment to his power. The same would not necessarily be true for his successors. For this reason, de Gaulle wanted the President in future to be elected by universal suffrage, although this was contrary to France's republican tradition as it had developed since the nineteenth century. Republicans had been obsessed by the fear of 'personal power' and remembered the example of the last President elected by universal suffrage, Louis Napoleon in 1848.

In a private conversation with Pflimlin in February 1961, de Gaulle wondered whether a monarchy might not be the best system for France. After this piece of characteristic provocation, he went on to suggest that the next best solution might be to elect the President by universal suffrage. He dropped a public hint to the same effect in a press conference in April 1961.[46] After testing the water in this way, he said no more for a year. When asked at his press conference in May 1962, he batted the question away by saying that such a measure was 'not for the moment', but in a radio speech in June he said that the reform would come at the 'required moment'.[47]

The question was not only 'when' but 'how'. In theory Article 89 of the constitution laid down clear procedures for constitutional revision. Any proposal had first to be discussed and approved by the two houses of parliament before being submitted to referendum. This cumbersome procedure was not necessarily guaranteed to succeed or to give de Gaulle the result he sought. Over the summer of 1962, he began to nurse the idea of using instead Article 11 of the constitution, which allowed him to consult the electorate directly by referendum without going via parliament. His own legal adviser at the Elysée offered the view that amending the constitution by this route would be both unconstitutional and provocative.[48] De Gaulle had probably not yet made up his mind. He told Pompidou in June that he would not choose this procedure.[49] The Petit-Clamart attack offered him the chance to go on the attack and use Article 11.

Three weeks later, de Gaulle announced his intentions to the Council of Ministers. Ministers were told that they would be invited to express a view at the next meeting a week later – with the clear implication that if they did not agree they would have to resign. At that meeting on 19 September, Jean Foyer expressed his strong reservations about the procedure de Gaulle was proposing to use but did not formally oppose the policy. Another minister who announced that he had similar 'scruples' was interrupted by de Gaulle with the words: 'The Justice Minister has scruples but he overcomes them.' Almost everyone else, including Pompidou, felt uneasy about the procedure but in the end only one minister, Pierre Sudreau, Minister of Education, resigned.

How seriously this procedural matter was considered can be illustrated by tracing the 'scruples' of one of the most ultra-loyalist Gaullists, the former diplomat Léon Noël, whose veneration for de Gaulle dated back to the RPF. In this case, his opinion mattered since he was President of the Constitutional Council, a new independent body created under the constitution of the Fifth Republic to advise on whether proposed laws were in accordance with the constitution. Its rulings were not binding. Received by de Gaulle before the Council of Ministers on 19 September, Noël told him that using Article 11 to revise the constitution would be unconstitutional. When de Gaulle announced on television the next day that this was what he intended to do, Noël noted in his diary that this would 'in the long term destroy' the constitution since it seemed to establish the precedent that the President could do anything provided he could secure support for it in a referendum: 'To admit this is very close to the Hitlerian conception of the law.'[50] Before the Constitutional Council met to discuss the referendum proposal, several of its members were received individually by Pompidou. Noël asked Pompidou afterwards: 'What would one say if in the United States, before an important decision of the Supreme Court, the President received each of its members in succession?'[51] On 2 October, the Constitutional Council voted almost unanimously that the government was acting unconstitutionally. A real crisis would have arisen if the Council had decided to flex its muscles further and refuse to ratify the official result of the referendum vote, one of its constitutional roles. Noël pleaded with his colleagues not to cross this Rubicon since it might 'push de Gaulle into a kind of coup d'état'.[52]

If a devoted Gaullist like Noël could make private comparisons to 'Hitlerian law' and 'a kind of coup d'état', it is not surprising that those not bound by personal fidelity to de Gaulle should have openly expressed their outrage. The most spectacular example was Gaston Monnerville, President of the Senate. Monnerville was a principled believer in the traditions of French republican democracy, but he was not animated by any visceral anti-Gaullism. In May 1958, he had been more emollient than his colleague Le Troquer, President of the Chamber of Deputies, at the secret meeting at Saint-Cloud to discuss the conditions of de Gaulle's return to power; he had voted for the new Republic in September 1958; in his capacity as President of the Senate he had authorized de Gaulle's use of Article 16 in 1961; he had voted 'yes' in both referenda on Algeria. But he started to have increasing qualms about the liberties that de Gaulle was taking with the constitution and the law. The referendum of April 1962 on the Evian Accords had required one single answer to two quite different questions: whether to approve the Accords and whether to allow the government to carry out by decree any additional measures it considered necessary to implement them. This seemed reminiscent of the plebiscites of Louis Napoleon: less a vote to approve a specific question than a blank cheque of support for an individual. (As one journalist pointed out, it was like asking the population to give only one answer to the two questions 'are you hungry and would you like a leg of lamb?')[53] Monnerville swallowed his doubts in the cause of Algerian independence, but he was not ready to go further down this road.

On 1 October, at the Congress of the Radical Party, Monnerville made a speech denouncing de Gaulle's decision to use Article 11 to amend the constitution as a *forfaiture*. According to France's Penal Code this term describes a 'crime committed by a public servant in the exercise of his functions'. Coming from the second highest officer of state after the President this sensational accusation enraged de Gaulle. A few days later, in the Senate, Monnerville repeated his criticisms (without this time using the offending word *forfaiture*). The Senate voted by a large majority to have his speech printed and posted up in every town hall under the banner heading 'The Constitution is being violated, the People are being abused'. War had broken out between de Gaulle and the political class.

On 3 October, parliament met to discuss the proposed referendum bill. For the first time in the short history of the Republic, a motion of censure was passed against the government. Pompidou resigned. On 10 October, de Gaulle dissolved parliament and called new elections to follow the referendum. The leaders of all the main political parties formed themselves into the so-called 'Cartel of the Noes' to urge the electorate to vote against de Gaulle's constitutional proposal. The problem with this Cartel was that most of its leaders were figures from the past like Mollet, Pflimlin and even the venerable Paul Reynaud. They were easily depicted as wanting a return to the bad old days of the Fourth – even the Third! – Republic. Another problem was that its members were united only in their opposition to de Gaulle's proposal. Some of them completely opposed the proposed reform; others opposed only the procedure by which de Gaulle had chosen to implement it.

Of the referendum campaign of 1958, a *Le Monde* journalist had written that 'never since the Second Empire, except perhaps in the elections of 1877, has there been in France such a deployment of official propaganda.'[54] This was no less true of the short referendum campaign of October 1962. The opposition was given little access to television. The television broadcast of the parliamentary debate devoted only two minutes to extracts from speeches by Mollet and Reynaud while Pompidou's defence of the project was fully covered in twenty minutes. De Gaulle made four television speeches calling for a 'yes' vote. His last one on 26 October, two days before the vote, made it clear that this was a vote of confidence in him personally: 'If the French nation ... decides to repudiate de Gaulle, or even to accord him only a vague and doubtful confidence, his historical task would become impossible and consequently it would be over.'[55] De Gaulle's threats of apocalypse in the event of defeat were fortuitously helped by the fact that the last stages of the campaign were overshadowed by the Cuban missile crisis when for a few days the world seemed poised on the edge of a nuclear precipice.

In the end de Gaulle's constitutional reform was approved on 28 October 1962 by 62.25 per cent of those voting. But the 23 per cent abstention rate meant that he had obtained only 47 per cent of the registered voters, among whom for the first time he had not obtained a majority. After the referendum Monnerville petitioned the Constitutional Council to rule on whether the result was in accordance with the constitution. By six votes to four the Council declared itself incompetent to rule. De Gaulle commented menacingly to Peyrefitte that it was lucky the Council had not opposed the will of the nation: 'It did not commit that folly. We would have drawn the necessary consequences.' As for Monnerville, he was treated with extraordinary vindictiveness. Although in terms of protocol second only to the President of the Republic, he was never again invited to any official events at the Elysée. On the occasions when he rather than one of his deputies was presiding at the Senate, de Gaulle would allow the government to be represented only by an under secretary, never a full minister.[56] When de Gaulle had a prostate operation in 1964, Monnerville wrote to wish him well. De Gaulle, usually so punctilious in such matters, sent no reply. In his eyes, Monnerville no longer existed.

Although the referendum result was less decisive than de Gaulle had hoped, the Fifth Republic had entered into a new era. Two years later, in January 1964, de Gaulle at a press conference underlined this in an extraordinary exegesis of the Fifth Republic constitution:

> A constitution is a spirit, institutions and a practice ... But it must also be understood that the indivisible authority of the State is entrusted entirely to the President by the people who elected him, that there exists no other, neither ministerial, civil, military, judicial, which is not conferred and maintained by him.[57]

As one commentator remarked about this speech, it was as if over the six years since 1958 three successive constitutions had appeared one out of the other like Russian dolls: 'At the hard wooden centre: the compromise of 1958; the Constitution of 1962; the Constitution that appeared out of the press conference of 31 January 1964'.[58]

A few months later, François Mitterrand published a fiercely polemical book entitled *The Permanent Coup d'Etat*, attacking de Gaulle's regime as a 'dictatorship because, in the end, that is what it most resembles, because it tends ineluctably towards the continuous reinforcing of personal power'. Having gone through all the liberties de Gaulle had taken with his own constitution, Mitterrand also noted that the General had finally 'killed his constitution' in a few phrases thrown out 'in passing during a press conference'.[59] Like any polemic Mitterrand's pamphlet was excessive – a 'dictatorship' would never have allowed such a philippic to appear – but it contained more than a grain of truth.

What fewer people observed, however, was that in reality the constitution was operating differently from the way de Gaulle described it. He aspired to be a charismatic leader transcending political divisions, but the results of the parliamentary elections following the referendum had created a different configuration. After returning to power, de Gaulle had done everything he could to distance himself from the UNR, the party that had been set up to defend his ideas in 1958. This was a cause of tension with Debré, who felt de Gaulle was always passing over loyal Gaullists. In the parliamentary election of 1958 de Gaulle had not allowed any candidate to use his name. But he displayed no such scruples four years later. In a speech on 7 November, he launched a violent diatribe against the old parties arrayed against him and called explicitly for a vote for the Gaullist party.[60]

This polarization was accentuated by Mollet, one of the leaders of the

No Cartel. Asked what he would recommend voters to do in the second round, Mollet recalled the old adage: 'In the first round one chooses and in the second one eliminates.' Faced in the second round with the choice between a Communist and a Gaullist, he proposed that voters choose the Communist. This was a bombshell. Since the breakup of the Resistance tripartite coalition in 1947, the Communists and Socialists had been bitter enemies. One of the reasons Mollet rallied to de Gaulle in 1958 was that the alternative might have been a government of the left that included Communists. Mollet's comment in 1962 brought the Communists back into the fold of respectable politics, embarrassing the centrists and conservatives in the No Cartel. It guaranteed that the second round of the elections would effectively be a contest between the Gaullists and the left, and that the centre would be squeezed out. In the elections in November, the Communists and Socialists increased their tally of seats but the Gaullists triumphed. For the first time in the history of French democratic politics one party came within a few votes of an overall majority in parliament. The shortfall was easily made up by a few independent conservatives on the centre right.

The referendum and election put de Gaulle in a position of complete political dominance – but as leader of a party rather than as leader standing above party as he aspired to be. This result satisfied Pompidou, who was pleased that de Gaulle had had to give up 'his utopia of unanimity'.[61] In fact de Gaulle had not given it up, and the tension between his dream of being a charismatic leader above party and his actual role as an undeclared party leader was to persist for the rest of his career. For the moment, however, his dominance was not in doubt. A year after his pessimistic predictions about the General's future, Ambassador Dixon could not but conclude that de Gaulle was 'the master of France'; he was 'apparently prospering and his authority visibly consolidated'. The 'apparently' was a way of salvaging something from his original prediction a year earlier. Dixon was still convinced that if one viewed de Gaulle's career 'in terms of a parabola' it was now on the 'downward curve'.[62] This was another hostage to fortune. A few weeks later, on 14 January 1963, de Gaulle, in the most spectacular press conference of his entire career, delivered a devastating broadside against Britain which plunged the British government, and Dixon, into despair. There was no 'downward curve' yet.

22

The Pursuit of Grandeur, 1959–1963

A 'CERTAIN IDEA' OF THE WORLD

At the start of 1960, Harold Macmillan wrote to Eisenhower: 'I do not know if you have read the third volume of his [de Gaulle's] Memoirs; it is wonderfully written and gives a picture of his rather mystical thinking on these great matters.'[1] Macmillan's comment captures only half the truth. The *Memoirs* reveal de Gaulle to be as much 'realist' as 'mystic'. The tension between the 'mystical' and the 'realistic' runs through all three volumes – from the second sentence where de Gaulle himself observes that in his vision of France 'sentiment inspires me as much as reason.'

As far as 'reason' was concerned, de Gaulle's starting point was the nation state, which he viewed as the fundamental reality governing human existence. One could fill pages with quotations on this theme, from de Gaulle's talk to conscripts when he was a young lieutenant in 1913 to pronouncements uttered right up to the end of his career:

> 1913: National feeling is natural to all nations and all countries. It is as natural as filial love or family feeling . . . Nationalism is a form of egotism.[2]
>
> 1962: Peoples do not change. They do not die except if there is some terrible accident. They remain what they are with their own characteristics, with their collective temperaments, with their soul. They last as long as the olive tree . . . A people needs to be proud of itself. It needs to have the pride to be able to keep saying: 'I am the fruit of a history which is that one and no other.'[3]

For de Gaulle, history and geography always prevailed over ideology. In 1958, when John Foster Dulles was expatiating on the international Communist threat from the Soviet Union and China, de Gaulle replied that Russia and China would inevitably enter into conflict. Russia, he said on many occasions, will 'soak up Communism as blotting paper absorbs ink'.[4] During the Vietnam War, he told an American visitor that Vietnam would become Communist but 'this will be an Asian Communism, as there is already

Chinese Communism ... Each to their own Communism.'[5] For de Gaulle, the conflict between nations was the eternal law of history. 'Like all life,' he told the French people in a televised address in 1960, 'the life of nations is a struggle.'[6] Or as he said on another occasion: 'It is what Antiquity called "destiny", Bossuet called "Providence", Darwin called "the law of the species".'[7] Since conflict was an eternal phenomenon, there was no point in regretting it. But de Gaulle did not view it as negative: 'One needs adversaries to exist.'[8] One of his favourite quotations – he quoted it in a lecture to officers in 1927 – was from *Hamlet*: 'To be great is to sustain a great quarrel.' (Shakespeare's words were slightly different: 'Rightly to be great is not to stir without great argument, but greatly to find quarrel in a straw when honour's at the stake.') Since life was a struggle, harmony in human affairs was not natural and was forged out of the balance of competing interests:

> Man, 'limited in his nature', is 'infinite in his desires'. The world is full of opposing forces. Certainly human wisdom sometimes prevents these rivalries from degenerating into bloody conflicts. But the competition between these efforts is the condition of life ... In the last analysis, as always, it is only in balance of forces that the world will find peace.[9]

All this made de Gaulle sceptical about idealist internationalists or European supranationalists. They were in his view either deluding themselves about the nature of history or cloaking national ambitions in the language of internationalism. This was as true of Aristide Briand in the 1920s as of Robert Schuman in the 1950s. Nations were the repositories of historical legitimacy, binding a people together by their 'own soul, their own history, their own language, their own misfortunes, glories and ambitions'. Artificially created communities, lacking that legitimacy, could not call on the loyalty of their citizens. As a result, they left people vulnerable to the ambitions of stateless technocrats or foreign powers: 'Supranational organizations have their technical value, but they do not have, they cannot have, political authority, and consequently political efficacy.'[10] For de Gaulle, the precondition of the existence of a nation state was its ability to wage war. This is why he had attacked no supranational organization more ferociously than the abortive European Defence Community.

If we leave 'reason' behind and move to 'sentiment', where did France fit into the Gaullist view of international relations? France was of course involved in the struggle for existence like any other country but the 'sentimental' de Gaulle seemed to exempt her from the national egotism he believed to be the motor of history. As he said in a speech in 1959: 'French power and grandeur ... are directed to the well-being and fraternity of mankind.'[11] Or as he put it eight years later: 'Our action is aimed at reaching goals . . . that because they are French are in the interest of mankind.'[12] This was not just public rhetoric. De Gaulle said the same in private:

France's vocation is to work for the general interest. It is while being fully French that one is the most European, that one is the most universal . . . While other countries, when they develop their interests, try to subject others to their interests, France, when she succeeds in developing her interests, does it in the interest of all . . . Everyone feels it obscurely in the world; France is the light of the world, her genius is to light up the universe.[13]

No sentence of de Gaulle's is more famous than the last line of the opening paragraph of his *War Memoirs*: 'France cannot be France without grandeur.' The term 'grandeur', over which a lot of ink has been spilled, is an elusive concept which de Gaulle never really defined. On the first page of his *War Memoirs* he illustrated it through imagery rather than argument: the Arc de Triomphe in the sunshine, Notre-Dame at dusk, the Princess in the fairytale. Grandeur was as much a state of mind and a sense of ambition as a concrete objective: 'it is the road one takes to surpass oneself,' as he put it elliptically on one occasion.[14] The effort was no less important than the result. The imperative for 'grandeur' was also intrinsically linked to de Gaulle's obsession with the idea of France as continuously threatened by 'demons' of disunity, 'germs' of division, the old 'Gaulish propensity to divisions and quarrels'. To overcome the threat of fragmentation, France needed a strong state which could realize the national 'ambition' which allowed the French to transcend their divisions.

As often as he talked of 'grandeur', de Gaulle used the words 'rank' – 'France must be in the front rank' – and 'independence'. His obsession with independence is explicable in the context of his own experience of the war when he was utterly dependent on the British or of the 1930s when French foreign policy was so closely aligned with that of Britain. But the concept of 'independence', like 'grandeur', is more slippery than it initially seems. It did not mean that he believed France could achieve her aims by going it alone. It was after all de Gaulle who had in 1940 rejected the 'France alone' stance of Vichy and clung to the alliance with Britain. For him, alliances were necessary as long as one remembered that allies were also pursuing national ambitions. This takes us back to 'reason'. All ambitions for 'grandeur' needed to take account of 'realities'. What de Gaulle admired in the diplomacy of the *ancien régime* was that it exhibited the 'just proportion between the ends pursued and the forces of the State'. The failure to do this was his most fundamental criticism of Napoleon; and the same idea lies behind his defence of the French garden as a model of classical *mesure* in his first book on the reasons for Germany's defeat in 1918. For him, the pursuit of 'grandeur', whatever that meant, needed at least in theory to be counterbalanced by realism and restraint – even if in practice he was not always successful himself at keeping the two in equilibrium.

None of de Gaulle's ideas about France and the world were unusual for a conservative nationalist of his generation. His conception of the nation is similar to that articulated in 1882 by Ernest Renan in his celebrated lecture 'What is a Nation?' His idea of a special 'vocation' for France was similar to that of the nineteenth-century French republican historian Jules Michelet. His idea of the French as a uniquely quarrelsome people was a trope that could be found in any history book of the nineteenth century (its latest avatar can be found in the disputatious Gauls of the *Astérix* series). His idea that only a strong state and national ambition could neutralize the 'ferments of dispersion' was the stock in trade of the Action Française historical school – as was his 'realist' conception of international relations. What is remarkable about de Gaulle is less the originality of the ideas than the imagination, single-mindedness and willpower with which he set about applying them.

For de Gaulle, the implementation of ideas always needed to be adapted to the circumstances of the moment. Bergson had taught him that life was about endless movement; nothing was fixed. As he mused in 1962:

> Any day the most extraordinary events could happen, incredible reversals of situation, as there have always been in history. America could explode because of terrorism or racism, or something else, and become a threat to peace. The Soviet Union could explode, because Communism could collapse, because its people might start quarrelling among themselves. She could become threatening again. No one can ever say in advance where threats will come from.[15]

How in the particular circumstances of the early 1960s did de Gaulle set out to restore France's 'grandeur' and independence?

There were two central axes to his foreign policy in his first four years in power.[16] One was to increase France's influence in the Atlantic Alliance, the other to push for European political union. The first was embodied in the memorandum that de Gaulle submitted to Macmillan and Eisenhower in September 1958. The second was encapsulated almost simultaneously in a note communicated to France's five European partners (Germany, Italy and Benelux): 'While avoiding integration . . . France intends to promote European cooperation and organize a sort of European concert.'[17] At a meeting of the Council of Defence in January 1959, he explained that France had to 'play on two registers: one with the two other western world powers, the other with the smaller powers'.[18] His aim was simultaneously to break into the Anglo-American club of the 'Two' and become leader of the European club of the 'Six'. He conceived these objectives as complementary: being the first of the Six reinforced France's case to join the Two; joining the Two vindicated France's claims to lead the Six. He told Peyrefitte in August 1962:

> What is the point of Europe? The point is that one is not dominated by either the Russians or the Americans. As Six, we ought to be able to do as well as either of the superpowers. And if France organizes things so as to become the first of the Six, which is within our reach, she could use this as a lever of Archimedes. She could take the others with her. Europe is the means by which France can become again what she has ceased to be since Waterloo. First in the world.[19]

Even if the bravado of that final rhetorical flourish should not be taken too seriously, de Gaulle's challenge to the existing structure of the Atlantic Alliance was bound to lead to conflict with the United States. As a result, he has frequently been seen as 'anti-American'. But what kind of anti-American? At some level, de Gaulle felt that the divergent histories of Europe and America made it impossible for either completely to understand the other. In July 1967, he had a conversation with the Soviet leader Kosygin, who was returning from a meeting of the United Nations in New York. Kosygin remarked that he found New York 'vile and horrible'. De Gaulle replied:

> You must never forget that America has not existed very long. It is composed of people who have come from everywhere . . . It has not always existed like Russia or France . . . It has no depth nor roots . . . It has never suffered, never been invaded . . . Its reactions are always those of a country that does not know what it is to suffer.[20]

Even so, there was never any doubt in de Gaulle's mind that France must be part of the western alliance. But to him it was necessary to be as vigilant against allies as against enemies. He was certainly 'anti-American' in the sense that America threatened to be a dangerously invasive ally. He had been stunned by the sheer energy and power of America when he visited for the first time in 1944. As he said to Peyrefitte in 1963:

> We are witnessing today an almost physical phenomenon, like a tidal wave or the eruption of a volcano, which to some extent is out of the control of the American leaders themselves. American power is so crushing, they are so in advance in cutting-edge technologies, they are so rich . . . Their expansion has something elemental about it.[21]

He put the same thought slightly differently on another occasion when comparing his attitude to Britain and to America:

> England is instinctively against France, everywhere, but within certain limits. America is neither for nor against France. She pursues her own policy. For

her there are no limits. I once said to Roosevelt: 'America is becoming aware of her role as a great power. France is no longer one but knows what it is to be one. When one is a great power one does not accept resistance.'[22]

There is another kind of French anti-Americanism which opposes America on cultural or ideological grounds – America as the embodiment of laissez-faire capitalism or soulless materialism. This idea had roots in France among the Socialist left and the Catholic right. It was prevalent in the thinking of those 'nonconformist' circles de Gaulle had encountered during the 1930s. De Gaulle, the reader of Bernanos and Péguy, harboured intellectually a conception of Europe – of France – as a civilization rooted in Catholic humanism, representing a kind of third way between Communism and liberal capitalism. But it was also the case that his wariness of industrial civilization was tempered by his obsession with French modernization. In the end he was probably more jealous of American power – the 'elemental expansionism' he mentioned to Peyrefitte – than he was uneasy about the values that fuelled it. In that sense his 'anti-Americanism' was more existential than cultural. At other times France's main rival had been Britain or Germany; now it was the United States: 'It is an eternal history. Each Empire in its turn aspires to hegemony. This will go on until the end of the world.'[23]

DE GAULLE IN ACTION

De Gaulle's view of the world was not shared by most of the Quai d'Orsay diplomats and officials whose responsibility it would be to turn it into policy. In the 1950s, many of them had been seduced by the European federalist vision of Jean Monnet; many of them were instinctively Anglophile. During the 1960s, the British Ambassador Pierson Dixon often referred in his despatches to 'our friends in the Quai', as if to reassure himself that in Gaullist France Britain did have friends. When de Gaulle returned to power, France's Ambassador in London was the Anglophile Jean Chauvel, who had no love for the General; and France's Ambassador in Washington was Hervé Alphand, who had been in the Free French, but managed the rare feat of combining admiration for de Gaulle with friendship for Monnet. In the 1950s he had strongly supported the EDC. One Quai official was so opposed to de Gaulle's anti-Atlanticism that when France left NATO in 1966 he secretly wrote a speech for Pleven who denounced the decision in parliament.[24] But over time the Quai became more 'Gaullist' as the diehard opponents were marginalized.[25]

Whatever their reservations about de Gaulle, all the ambassadors in post recognized, even if reluctantly, that he was a global superstar. On his foreign visits, they were awestruck by his physical and intellectual resilience – especially his capacity to deliver entirely from memory long speeches which he had written himself. His historical stature as the last survivor of the Second World War 'Greats' guaranteed that wherever he went massive crowds thronged the streets to cheer him. His instinctive showmanship was always in evidence. One of his favourite tricks was always to deliver a speech – or part of a speech – in the language of the country he was visiting (unless that language was English). To the terror of his security guards, he would unexpectedly dive into the crowds, to shake hands and experience physically the electricity of popular acclamation. During his state visit to America in 1960, it was said that his reception could only be compared to that which had greeted the returning hero General MacArthur in 1951. Hervé Alphand may have been one of France's most seasoned diplomats, but he was so overcome by the enthusiasm of the crowds during the visit that reading his diary entry a few days later he felt it contained the outpourings of 'a star-struck shopgirl'.[26] After witnessing de Gaulle's state visit to Italy in 1959, Jean-Marie Soutou, a Quai d'Orsay official profoundly hostile to every aspect of de Gaulle's foreign policy, could not but admit a grudging admiration: 'His speeches were remarkable. How could someone like me not feel a breath of fresh air, a sense of intellectual invigoration? Not that I am an unconditional admirer of de Gaulle's style which is for me a kind of pastiche lying between Cicero and Chateaubriand, but there was a mastery, an underlying philosophy, ideas, facts.'[27] Nowhere was the enthusiasm of the crowds greater than during de Gaulle's visit to Germany in September 1962. Le Monde, a newspaper usually critical of him, opened its coverage of the tour by reporting soberly that the population of Bonn had accorded him a 'good-natured welcome'. Two days later, it was talking of an 'unleashing of popular enthusiasm which has taken the organizers by surprise as the crowds burst through the barriers'. At the end, it reported that the visit had assumed 'enormous proportions which even taking account of the force of attraction emanating from the personality of General de Gaulle, has something fabled [fabuleux] about it'.[28]

De Gaulle conducted no purge of ambassadors on returning to power. The only new appointment was in Bonn because the incumbent Ambassador Maurice Couve de Murville had been appointed Foreign Minister. One diplomat who dreaded his first encounter with de Gaulle was Roland de Margerie, who had so disappointed de Gaulle in 1940 when he accepted his appointment by Vichy to serve as Consul in China. De Gaulle had again appealed to Margerie to join him in 1941 but received no reply. When de Gaulle returned to power in May 1958, Margerie was serving as Ambassador to the Vatican. Three months later, he had his first meeting with de

Gaulle since that day in the summer of 1940 when he had left London. His account of the meeting reveals his own bad conscience and de Gaulle's implacability: '"Since those days, I owe you an explanation that I would like to give you today." From the other side of the desk came the glacial response with the emphasis on the last word: "I have not asked you to justify anything."' Nonetheless Margerie launched into a long explanation which he had been ruminating over for a decade. At the end of it, de Gaulle had mellowed slightly: 'M. l'Ambassadeur . . . No, I mean Roland de Margerie, I did indeed send a message to you in 1941 . . . You replied by speaking to me about your conception of duty. It was not for you to judge your duty, it was for me to judge . . . I counted on you, you failed me, you were wrong.'[29] The air was cleared. Having made Margerie squirm, de Gaulle absolved him. The matter was never discussed again and their conversation moved on to the Vatican, with de Gaulle displaying an encyclopaedic knowledge of the politics of the Papal Curia. Margerie was later promoted to the important post of Ambassador to Bonn.

Although suspicious of diplomats as a breed, de Gaulle respected the professionalism of the Quai. His view was that if they were given firm guidance, ambassadors would do their duty. The man to provide that guidance was de Gaulle's Foreign Minister, Couve de Murville. Couve had known de Gaulle since 1943 when he arrived in Algiers as a Giraudist. A formidable negotiator with an unparalleled mastery of technical detail, he was unflappable, discreet and chilly – the epitome of a French Protestant. No one knew what he thought intimately about de Gaulle's more extravagant ideas. 'The General is impulsive' was the most critical comment he could be induced to make. Master of the art of understatement, Couve muffled the impact of some of de Gaulle's more dramatic gestures. His soporific reports on foreign affairs in the Council of Ministers made his colleagues feel they were listening to the platitudes of Proust's M. de Norpois. Underneath this imperturbable surface Couve embodied the French administrative mind at its most terrifyingly effective.

Couve's ten years in post made him the longest-serving Foreign Minister since the Comte de Vergennes under Louis XVI. He was the loyal servant of policies whose shape was entirely determined by de Gaulle. But de Gaulle also carried out much diplomacy personally. He regularly received his ambassadors, giving them instructions which often took the form of a history lecture. His opening gambit would often be 'So what are your Italians/your Germans/etc. up to now?' – as if the natural *déformation professionnelle* of any ambassador would be to go native. He also regularly received foreign ambassadors and carried on an extensive correspondence with foreign leaders.

On the surface, de Gaulle was different now from the intense and prickly personality of the war years. His visitors in the 1960s encountered a paternal figure of exquisitely old-fashioned courtesy. This was all part of the display of confidence and grandeur which he sought to present. Foreign leaders were often put up in the magnificent surroundings of the Château de Rambouillet: here, as de Gaulle put it in his *Memoirs*, 'housed in the medieval towers where so many of our kings had stayed, passing through apartments once occupied by our Valois and our Bourbons . . . our guests were made to feel the nobility behind the geniality [*bonhomie*] and the permanence behind the vicissitudes of the nation which was their host.'[30] What better place for this republican monarch to receive visitors? One ritual to which foreign ambassadors and foreign leaders were invited were the autumn shoots at Rambouillet which Harold Macmillan described as an 'extraordinary and strangely old-fashioned ceremony', a bit like 'Edwardian shoots in England'. De Gaulle would never participate, but he invariably emerged for the last round, positioning himself behind the nearest shooter – a disconcerting experience for whoever this victim happened to be. They were usually put off their stride and de Gaulle would comment consolingly, 'I don't think you hit.'[31] Receptions for foreign leaders were held at Versailles, and de Gaulle also embarked on an expensive refurbishment of Louis XIV's Grand Trianon in the grounds of Versailles so that foreign leaders could be put up there in the style appropriate to French grandeur. He was punctilious about who could be invited to Versailles.[32] When asked why the honour had been accorded to the Grand Duchess of Luxembourg and not to the King of Morocco, de Gaulle explained: 'I receive in Versailles only sovereigns of ancient dynasties.'[33] This was a sign of his obsessive attention to the minutiae of protocol, and his respect for the monarchical principle.

Under his stately and benign exterior, de Gaulle remained a suspicious and vigilant guardian of French interests. Pierson Dixon, who had often been wrong about him, became a seasoned de Gaulle watcher. Having learnt his lessons the hard way, he wrote to the British Foreign Secretary in November 1962:

He is the French Government. My staff and I have to spend our time picking up and analysing such information as we may acquire about his state of mind. The public at large, journalists, officials and ministers offer us various interpretations. They and we have intuitively to divine what he will do or think. He is the subject of endless stories, jokes and conversations. That is what he wishes. He believes in mystery. Even some of the quotations may be apocryphal . . . He possesses neither of the Christian virtues of compassion and humility. He is intolerant, unscrupulous, revengeful, ungenerous, ungrateful yet served with great loyalty by able and honest men. He exerts an extraordinary fascination and charm when he chooses. Part of his charm is a quaintness of manner and appearance which he knows how to exploit in a beguiling way. He has an unerring sense of style . . . He is merciless in his judgments.[34]

On the arrival of a new Foreign Secretary, Patrick Gordon Walker, two years later, Dixon updated his diagnosis:

He has to be approached with some care and in the knowledge that he is always trying to exploit everyone else to his own advantage, and often doing so with great skill . . . There is no doubt of the brilliance of the General's intelligence or the range of his comprehension of world problems . . . It is no use trying to argue General de Gaulle into doing something he does not want to do or into not doing something he has decided to do. The most that can be done is to leave him with the impression that it would be in his interest to change his mind. For this reason alone discussion with him is difficult unless one is merely interested in his views. But it is still further complicated by the fact that he frequently says not what he thinks but what it suits him for the other person to believe or what he wishes him to repeat. (He assumes that everything he says to anyone is going to be repeated. The inmost secrets he keeps for himself.) He is not in the least worried by saying different things to different people . . . To put it bluntly he often does not tell the truth . . . But in his presence it is almost impossible to remember that he may be trying to deceive one. Especially when he is trying, his charm, if a little quaint and old fashioned, is enormous. Conversation with him, providing one does not have to argue too much, is extremely agreeable . . . He often mixes startling frankness with his calculated deceptions . . . For him international relations are a game on the grandest scale of which he is a player of genius.[35]

What made de Gaulle's style of diplomacy so disconcerting was the mixture of transparency and secrecy. In his twice-yearly setpiece press conferences, he would offer dazzling lectures on international politics and history, throwing in a few provocations for dramatic effect (for example, the mocking references to a Europe of Volapük and Esperanto in 1962). But the implementation of policy was often shrouded in mystery. No world leader spent more time explaining publicly how he saw the world, but none was harder to read. At a particularly low point in relations with America, one White House staff member observed that 'our working situation in Gaullist France is not unlike that in the Soviet Union where we have to look to the small, symbolic actions to identify significant policy trends.' The CIA even supposedly had an informant among de Gaulle's close advisers, but since his closest advisers themselves often had no idea of his plans, a mole served little purpose.[36] Dixon's predecessor, Gladwyn Jebb, who had known de Gaulle in several incarnations, summed up the problem neatly in September 1958: 'In the old days the General seemed to be rude and very precise whereas nowadays he is polite, indeed cordial, and thoroughly vague.'[37]

'INCREASINGLY TROUBLESOME'

The more one reads the Memorandum of September 1958 in which, as he later put it, de Gaulle had 'raised the colours', the more 'thoroughly vague' it seems. As often with de Gaulle, what seemed limpid became muddier the more it was scrutinized.[38] This meant that he was the only judge of whether his demands were being met. In this short document, he referred variously to 'NATO' and to the 'Atlantic alliance', but these were not identical. It is often said that his Memorandum had proposed setting up an Atlantic 'directory', but the word 'directory' never appears in the text which mentions 'organized consultations'. Were these intended to take place separately from existing NATO structures or were they intended to dovetail with them so as to create a two-tier organization? Whatever de Gaulle really wanted, by the end of 1958 nothing substantive had been done to satisfy him. Dulles commented that he was becoming 'increasingly troublesome'.[39]

'Increasingly troublesome' could serve as a description of de Gaulle's attitude for the next three years – but 'troublesome' was as far as it went. Franco-American relations were strained but never close to breaking down. Even so, Alphand's task as Ambassador cannot have been enviable since he was 'constantly at the State Department, whether to pass on our complaints or to receive theirs'.[40] In two long letters in May and October 1959 de Gaulle reminded Eisenhower that the issues raised in the Memorandum – NATO's restricted remit and the inequality of treatment between France, on the one hand, and the British and Americans on the other – were still outstanding.[41] The US government's response was what it called a 'middle of the road policy': trying to satisfy de Gaulle where this was possible and evading the issue where it was not.[42] The Americans offered regular tripartite meetings at ambassadorial level and the setting up of a special telephone line between Paris and Washington, as existed between London and Washington. This was a start but de Gaulle remained prickly whenever he believed he was not being consulted, as during the civil war that broke out in the Congo in August 1960.[43]

Meeting Macmillan in September 1960, Eisenhower declared himself 'baffled' by what de Gaulle really wanted since he 'simply clams up' when specific issues were mentioned. He wondered if de Gaulle's advisers were counselling him not to put his thoughts down on paper: 'This would make the situation irretrievable since de Gaulle would find it hard to back down.'[44] If Eisenhower declared himself 'baffled', it was because the nub of the problem was not in the 'directorate' nor in 'consultations'. De Gaulle's real concern was the integrated military command of NATO and France's ambition to have her own nuclear deterrent. Before his first meeting with de Gaulle in 1958 Dulles was advised: 'What will be particularly difficult to explain is why we will not provide France with the same nuclear information we intend to supply the British.'[45] This was the elephant in the room.

In April 1960, France exploded her first atomic bomb. Other tests followed. These were only the first steps to the development of a fully functional nuclear deterrent. During the autumn, the government pushed through parliament a five-year plan for the development of nuclear weapons and the means to deliver them. France could certainly have benefited from American assistance over such matters as missile delivery systems or warhead technology and, although de Gaulle's official position was never to appear as a supplicant for aid, he did not prevent overtures being made. But the American government hid behind the 1946 McMahon Act which restricted nuclear cooperation – although an exception had been made for Britain from 1957. At one meeting with Eisenhower, de Gaulle could not contain himself: 'McMahon Act indeed! . . . You tell me it is dangerous for me to know something that a thousand Soviet corporals already know.'[46]

Three years after the Memorandum, nothing much had changed. For the moment de Gaulle did not push matters further. His hands were still tied by the Algerian crisis and by major Cold War tensions over the status of Berlin. He also ran the risk that too overt a challenge to America might upset his European allies just as he was trying to win them over to his plan for French leadership of a politically organized Europe.

POLITICAL EUROPE

De Gaulle's attitude to Europe was more complicated than it seemed on the surface. Although he opposed supranationalism, once he had accepted the Treaty of Rome he was determined to make it work for France. The Treaty had envisaged the organization of a Common Agricultural Policy to complement the relaxation of tariff barriers for industry. The prospect of securing a protected agricultural export market in Europe for her farmers was of special interest to France with her large but inefficient agricultural sector. This was a point of conflict with Germany, a food-importing nation which preferred low agricultural prices. The Treaty of Rome had assumed that the transition to a Common Agricultural Policy would not occur before 1970. De Gaulle decided to accelerate the pace. A clause of the Treaty stipulated that implementing the second stage of the reduction of industrial tariff barriers could proceed only with unanimous agreement. De Gaulle threatened to withhold his approval unless agreement was also reached on a common agricultural policy. In the intensive negotiations in Brussels to develop a Common Agricultural Policy (CAP), France was objectively on the same side as the European Commission, which was the epitome of that supranationalism which de Gaulle supposedly deplored. The Commission was keen on any measures that would further the European project; the French were ready to accept a policy that might increase the powers of the Commission provided these enhanced French interests.[47]

While squeezing what he could out of Europe economically, de Gaulle simultaneously launched his vision of a political Europe. He first raised the issue during a visit to Italy in 1959.[48] In the following year, he decided to play on his close relationship with Adenauer. Ever since his masterstroke of inviting Adenauer to Colombey in 1958, de Gaulle had continued to court the German Chancellor assiduously. He was helped by the continuing Berlin crisis. His line was that the Soviets were bluffing, that they had no intention of going to war over Berlin and that the west should not be intimidated.[49] This was a contrast to the attitude of both the Americans and the British, who sought to defuse the tension. Macmillan even took it upon himself in March 1959 to pay a visit to Moscow. Although he claimed that this was a mission of 'reconnaissance' rather than 'negotiation', it alarmed Adenauer. De Gaulle turned out to be right that Khrushchev would back down and his firm position won him credit with Adenauer. The tough line cost him nothing since in the event of conflict America would have been in the front line. There were dark mutterings on the French and German side about the British being ready to do a 'Munich' over Berlin. De Gaulle played on this skilfully.

De Gaulle's relationship with Adenauer was not always smooth. Suspicion of the French leader simmered under the surface. Adenauer was pleased that in a press conference on 25 March 1959 de Gaulle announced his support for eventual German reunification. This cost de Gaulle little since the prospect was remote, and he told Eisenhower privately a few months later that he was 'not too much in a hurry' to see it.[50] Adenauer was less happy that in the same breath de Gaulle said that reunification would need to respect the 'present' frontiers of Germany, that is to say the Oder–Neisse Line which had fixed Germany's frontier with Poland after 1945 (but which the Germans had never formally accepted). He was also aggrieved, as were other European leaders, by the assumption of de Gaulle's famous (if supposedly secret) 1958 Memorandum that France had the right to a privileged global status which was not on offer to his own country. After the French had exploded their first bomb, Adenauer asked Seydoux, the French Ambassador: 'I would like to know whom this bomb is directed against.'[51] The German Chancellor was also upset at comments by Michel Debré in parliament in the spring of 1960 that only countries with nuclear weapons could expect to have a say in global affairs, the others being in effect satellites. It was clear which category Germany was in. By the eve of a summit with de Gaulle at Rambouillet in July 1960, Adenauer had whipped himself up into a frenzy of mistrust.

De Gaulle did all he could to recreate the cordial atmosphere of Colombey, even throwing out the idea at Rambouillet that one day Germany might have access to nuclear weapons. Some historians have taken these comments seriously. More plausibly this was a bauble de Gaulle could offer orally without committing himself to anything: one of his first acts after coming to power had been to suspend talks on nuclear cooperation with Germany and Italy.[52] Having eased some of Adenauer's worries at Rambouillet, de Gaulle presented him with a nine-point memorandum for the organization of Europe. It proposed regular meetings of European governments, prepared by joint commissions of experts from each country. In the longer term, it envisaged a consultative parliament of representatives from each national assembly. This was de Gaulle's most ambitious attempt to circumvent the supranational institutions at Brussels by building a 'political' Europe. Most controversial was the fourth point:

> To bring an end to that American 'integration' in which the Atlantic Alliance currently consists and which contradicts the existence of a Europe having at an international level its own personality and point of view. The Atlantic Alliance must be founded on new bases. It is for Europe to propose them.[53]

The term 'personality' was one of those elusively suggestive Gaullist terms which could mean anything. But in a speech two months earlier de Gaulle had also mentioned the idea of building European defence. This was his real ambition.[54]

Since the Rambouillet meeting had gone well de Gaulle encouraged Couve the day after to 'strike while the iron is hot.'[55] Back in Bonn,

Adenauer, who had seemed receptive to de Gaulle's ideas about the future development of 'political' Europe, immediately had second thoughts.[56] One problem was that the German Foreign Ministry, and German public opinion, were warier of de Gaulle than he was. Under these other influences the troubling magic of de Gaulle's presence lost its potency. One must also remember that if de Gaulle was using Adenauer to wean Europe from America, the wily Adenauer was also partly using the threat of de Gaulle to extort greater commitments from the United States regarding the defence of Europe against the Soviet Union.[57]

Having wanted to 'strike while the iron was hot', de Gaulle told Debré a few weeks later that it would be necessary to 'temporize' and not 'throw oil on the flames':

> For the moment let us keep things simmering, rather than attempting to light a fire ... I regret that I spoke so frankly to Chancellor Adenauer. I thought him more European than he is in reality. Also tone down our opposition to Community organizations ... If we succeed in giving birth to a Europe of cooperating States, the supranational Communities will *ipso facto* be put in their place.[58]

To keep Adenauer's support, de Gaulle was ready to backtrack. He offered the Chancellor reassurances that there was no question of 'distancing America from the defence of Europe'.[59] Meeting him again in February 1961, he teased away at Adenauer's doubts about the United States, insinuating that although the Americans seemed to care about Europe at the moment, it might one day 'appear more foreign to them' because of their obligations in other parts of the world.[60]

There seemed enough common ground for the representatives of the Six in February 1961 to agree to set up a Commission chaired by the Gaullist Christian Fouchet to develop concrete proposals to move towards political union. What de Gaulle had in mind was an institutionalized 'concert' of nations meeting regularly to discuss foreign policy and defence.[61] Despite the suspicion of the smaller nations – especially the Netherlands – of anything resembling Franco-German domination or a threat to the Atlantic Alliance, an agreement seemed in reach by the end of 1961. On 13 January 1962, the Quai produced a plan for the Fouchet Commission on the lines of the discussions that had taken place over the last year. It proposed institutionalized cooperation on culture, foreign policy and defence with reassurances that this would not threaten the predominant role of the Atlantic Alliance. When this draft reached de Gaulle on 17 January, he made several last-minute amendments, removing any reference to the

Atlantic Alliance and any reassurances about NATO. Since the Quai document represented the limit of what de Gaulle's partners could accept, de Gaulle's amendments caused consternation. Fouchet suspended the talks to avoid a formal rejection.

One can only speculate about why de Gaulle had seemingly sabotaged the political union which he claimed to want. Perhaps the Quai draft conceded more than he could swallow. Perhaps the fact that only three days earlier an agreement had been reached on a Common Agricultural Policy meant that de Gaulle felt he no longer had to treat his partners with kid gloves.[62] Perhaps French success over the CAP made him over-confident about what he could extract from them. Another possibility is that the whole affair was the result of crossed wires on the French side: Quai officials did not believed they could challenge de Gaulle's corrections, while Couve de Murville, who realized that the corrections would sink the negotiation, had expected the Quai to make its objections known to the Elysée.[63] When one (anti-Gaullist) French diplomat involved in the negotiations warned Fouchet that the amended text would not pass, he claims to have been brushed off with the remark that these were only 'minor corrections ... inspired directly by the hand of the General out of concern for the purity of the French language, of which he is one of the most brilliant masters'.[64]

That de Gaulle miscalculated rather than intentionally sabotaged his plan is suggested by the fact that over the next two months, at meetings with both Adenauer and the Italian premier Fanfani, he desperately tried to undo the disastrous result of his intervention. He told Adenauer that he was ready for the text to refer to 'supranationality' and to the Atlantic Alliance.[65] The French finally agreed a draft not so different from the one de Gaulle had amended. It was too late. De Gaulle had lost the trust of his partners. His original amendments had revealed too much of his (never very hidden) anti-Atlanticist agenda. On 17 April 1962, the newly revised Fouchet plan was vetoed by the Dutch and Belgian governments. From this point, de Gaulle seemed to lose interest. In the following month he made his provocative remarks denouncing a Europe of Volapük or Esperanto. And when in July the Italian government showed signs of wanting to revive the idea of a political Europe de Gaulle was unenthusiastic: 'it would be bad, tactically speaking, to appear too keen to want this. We must moderate the inclinations of M. Bérard [French Ambassador in Rome] in favour of negotiation and agreement at any cost, inclinations which he learnt in another school from that which is in command today' – a typical Gaullist swipe at the Quai d'Orsay.[66]

GRAND DESIGNS

De Gaulle had not so far succeeded in his attempts to join the Club of the Two or to organize the Club of the Six. But he was forcing his partners to rethink their strategies and assumptions. Although self-interested, the questions he posed about the applicability of an alliance formed in 1949 were legitimate. At that date America had enjoyed a predominance in world affairs almost unique in history. But by the time de Gaulle returned to power that hegemony was becoming less absolute: the Soviets now had nuclear weapons, the Europeans were recovering power and confidence after the devastation of the war, the Americans were suffering acute balance of payments difficulties caused partly by imperial overreach. Since the late 1940s the Americans had envisioned international relations as a 'partnership' where one partner was in fact supremely dominant. De Gaulle drew on a different model of international relations based around the idea of balance and equilibrium. In the words of Henry Kissinger, at that time a Harvard professor whose first book had studied European diplomacy in the age of Metternich, de Gaulle's challenge to America 'raised the philosophical issue of the nature of Atlantic cooperation in a way which turned into a contest for the leadership of Europe and, for America, into a reacquaintance with the historic style of European diplomacy'.[67]

In response to these problems – and to the problem of de Gaulle – the British and American administrations developed their 'Grand Designs' to match de Gaulle's. 'Grand Design' was the title of a remarkable document Macmillan drafted in January 1961. He had come to the view that the British, having failed to dilute the European Community from outside, would need to join it. To achieve de Gaulle's support, he was ready to intercede with the American government to offer France nuclear cooperation. Once in Europe, his plan was that the British would work to counter the anti-American tendencies of the French. In July 1961, the British announced their intention to seek entry to the European Community.

In the United States, the arrival of the new President John F. Kennedy in January 1961 led the State Department to draft a 'New Approach to France'. Underlying this document was a fear of nuclear proliferation: allowing a French deterrent would make it difficult in the future to prevent other European powers, most notably Germany, obtaining a deterrent of their own. To counter this threat, the American administration moved towards the idea (already floated under Eisenhower) of creating a NATO Multilateral Nuclear Force (MLF). The MLF did not however give Europe equality since the United States would retain the ultimate veto on the use of the weapons. The second pillar of the Kennedy plan was to abandon the policy of so-called 'massive retaliation' – a Soviet attack on Europe triggering an American one on the Soviet Union – in favour of a 'graduated' or 'flexible' response involving in the first instance conventional forces. Its third pillar was to encourage the move to further European unity by supporting the British application. The idea was that a more coordinated Europe could become an equal partner in the new 'Atlantic partnership', and assume a larger burden in defence.

The American and British 'Grand Designs' were not entirely complementary. Macmillan saw entry into Europe as a way of allowing Britain to become the privileged partner – the bridge – between Europe and the United States; the Americans saw partnership with Europe replacing a privileged one with Britain. The logic of the MLF was that Britain would eventually have to trade its nuclear independence for membership of the pooled MLF. This was not acceptable to the British and also sabotaged Macmillan's idea of offering a nuclear deal to France. As for the American rhetoric about a new 'Atlantic partnership' with Europe, this hardly disguised the fact that this would remain an unequal partnership because the United States retained the ultimate veto on the use of the nuclear weapons. These contradictions offered de Gaulle ample opportunities to manoeuvre.

De Gaulle ensured that the incoming Kennedy administration was made aware of his Memorandum of September 1958.[68] Given the more dynamic thrust of American policy under Kennedy, it was inevitable that Franco-American relations would be more tense than they had been under Eisenhower. Eisenhower was always slightly in awe of de Gaulle – he would often return in conversation to that dramatic moment in 1944 when de Gaulle had refused to evacuate Strasbourg – and also had a sneaking sympathy for his nuclear ambitions. As he told Lauris Norstad, the general in command of American forces in Europe, in 1959: 'In fairness to de Gaulle, we would react very much like him if the shoe were on the other foot.' Or as he said on another occasion: 'It was as if we had been fighting wars with bows and arrows and then acquired pistols. Then we refused to give pistols to the people who were our allies even though the common enemy already had them.'[69]

Kennedy, prone to hero worship, was fascinated by de Gaulle as one of the towering statesmen of the century – and after the General's election victory in 1962 even enquired of the American Embassy in Paris if there were campaign lessons he might learn for himself[70] – but essentially he admired him as a figure of the past. His team of clever idealistic young advisers believed they were making the world a better and brighter place. Especially antagonistic to de Gaulle was Kennedy's adviser on Europe, George Ball, a great admirer of Monnet. As he later put it in his memoirs, Ball saw de Gaulle as a 'superb actor' leaving 'only legends and transient playbills', a 'twentieth-century Don Quixote, seeking to preserve old forms and restore old patterns'.[71] Ball was extreme in his anti-Gaullism, but in general the Kennedy administration displayed a brisk impatience with de Gaulle that contrasted with Eisenhower's baffled weariness.

Before Kennedy's first visit to Europe, de Gaulle and Adenauer discussed what he might be like. They agreed that there seemed to be 'many masculine prima donnas in his administration'.[72] In advance, Macmillan gave Kennedy fatherly advice about de Gaulle: 'Conversations with General de Gaulle are quite difficult to conduct. He has a remarkable command of language but naturally does not like being rebuffed directly and so sometimes puts his thoughts in a rather elliptical form. But he is extremely quick to take a point.'[73] As an exercise in public relations, Kennedy's visit in June 1961 was a huge success, helped by the glamour of his French-speaking wife Jacqueline – 'a couple of great charm' de Gaulle allowed in his *Memoirs*. His more considered – and slightly condescending – judgement of Kennedy was that his 'idealism impelled him to interventions that calculation did not justify. But the experience of the Statesman would undoubtedly have progressively curbed the impulsions of the idealist.'[74] It was the 'idealist' de Gaulle encountered in Paris in June 1961. The main points of contention were predictably the MLF and the idea of 'flexible response'. De Gaulle told Kennedy that the logic of the latter policy was that 'Western and Central Europe would be laid waste by Soviet and American tactical nuclear weapons respectively, while both Russia and the United States remained unscathed.' When Kennedy observed that the American security guarantee remained credible because the security of western Europe and North America were indivisible, de Gaulle answered:

> Since you say so, Mr. President, I believe you, but still can one be certain? At what moment will the United States consider that the situation calls for the use of atomic weapons? One hears that the United States intends to raise the threshold for the use of atomic weapons. This must mean that the United States has decided that such weapons will not be used in all cases. When are they going to be used?

To Kennedy's observation that the same could be said of a French nuclear force, de Gaulle answered that 'the Rhine is much narrower than the Atlantic and, therefore, France might feel more intimately tied to German defence than the United States might feel tied to French defence.'[75] The tone became more tetchy in subsequent correspondence after Kennedy wrote that one of his reasons for opposing a French nuclear deterrent was that 'we would have no ground on which to resist certain and heavy pressure from the Germans for parallel treatment. Yet it is imperative that the Germans have no nuclear weapons of their own; memory is too strong, and fear too real, for that.'[76] De Gaulle's reply was acerbic:

I find it entirely natural that a power like you, which disposes of such means, prefers not to share the secrets with a foreign state, even one that is an ally. However, without discussing the reasons that you give me for this refusal – that is to say that fact that it would be impossible for you to refuse to Germany the aid you would give to France in this area – I do not think, after what has occurred over the last fifty years, that you could have, on the French side, the same 'strong memories' and the same 'fears' which determine you to refuse eventual help to the Germans.[77]

The new American approach to Europe offered de Gaulle leverage in his relationship with Adenauer. The idea of the MLF was attractive to Germany since it offered a foot in the nuclear door, but the doctrine of flexible response seemed a step in the other direction – away from a guaranteed American commitment to European defence. Adenauer was also concerned by America's reaction to a new escalation of the Berlin crisis in August 1961 when the Soviets built a wall to stem the exodus of refugees to the west. The Kennedy administration showed worrying signs of wanting to negotiate an agreement over Berlin – giving de Gaulle another opportunity to play on Adenauer's insecurities.

If de Gaulle had so easily reconciled himself to the failure of the Fouchet plan it was because he had always had in mind a fall-back position of intensifying bilateral cooperation with Germany.[78] In April 1962, Adenauer paid a six-day official visit to France. No foreign visitor to de Gaulle's France was ever treated with greater pomp. De Gaulle met him personally at Orly airport, an honour generally accorded only to heads of state. Grand receptions were laid on at Versailles and the Hôtel de Ville, a gala at the Opera. The most symbolic event was the attendance by the two leaders at a Mass at the Cathedral of Reims which had suffered so badly in the First War. After the private wooing of Colombey, this was more like a public engagement. The only cloud over the visit was that the streets were largely deserted and the French population seemingly indifferent. During their talks, the two men agreed that if political union of the Six seemed for the moment impossible, France and Germany would start the ball rolling with a bilateral agreement.

Adenauer's visit was followed by an extraordinarily successful visit by de Gaulle to the Federal Republic in September. *Der Spiegel* commented: 'De Gaulle came to Germany as President of the French and he returned as Emperor of Europe.'[79] De Gaulle was not exaggerating when he wrote to his sister after returning to France: 'incredible from the point of view of popular support and enthusiasm. People will talk for a long time about this kind of explosion.'[80] He delighted crowds by delivering many of his speeches in German. In Bonn he declared, '*Sie sind ein grosses Volk*' (You are a great people), and his homage to German military prowess in his address to the Military Academy of Hamburg had special resonance given de Gaulle's own past history. It was as if de Gaulle was granting the Germans his absolution. Adenauer's biographer observes that no one had addressed the Germans like this since Hitler; Adenauer himself wondered if de Gaulle had not been a bit 'Führer-like'.[81] When a British journalist made the same point to Couve, he saw no problem: 'It was a good thing the German people should be fascinated by someone like de Gaulle, just as it was bad that they should have been fascinated by Hitler. If the Germans were fascinated by de Gaulle, France could channel that fascination in the right direction.'[82]

'THE ENGLAND OF KIPLING IS DEAD'

While de Gaulle was sedulously courting Adenauer, negotiations had started on Britain's application to join the Common Market. The technical side of the negotiations took place in Brussels over eighteen months with representatives of all member states. But during the same period de Gaulle and Macmillan also had four long meetings where Britain's application was the central item of discussion. These two ageing statesmen who had known each other since Algiers in 1943 had much in common. Both had fought and been wounded in the trenches of the Great War; both liked to dress up their policies in grand historical speculations.

Macmillan seemed to believe that during his six months in Algiers in 1943 he had both won de Gaulle's friendship and acquired special insights into his psyche. In 1959 he responded to an outburst of frustration by Eisenhower in the resignedly condescending manner of one seasoned de Gaulle watcher to another: 'You and I know, from old experience, how difficult he can be in one mood and yet how accommodating in another.'[83] After a long meeting with de Gaulle at Rambouillet in March 1960, he wrote in his diary that their talks, which had been 'intimate, and as far as I can judge, friendly', had 'revitalised our old friendship'. He would have been wise to keep the 'as far as I can judge' at the forefront of his mind. Macmillan was right that no one on the British side had done more to help de Gaulle in 1943; wrong to think that in de Gaulle's eyes this made any difference. Gratitude, especially concerning relations between states, was not in de Gaulle's repertoire. He probably enjoyed the reversal of roles that had occurred since their first encounter: Macmillan the patron had become Macmillan the supplicant. Despite his general optimism, Macmillan also picked up some warning signs in their conversation at Rambouillet in March:

I had fortunately read the last volume of memoirs, and I asked de G why he continuously harped on the theme of the Anglo-Saxons. Apart from a general feeling that he is left out of Anglo-Saxon talks, and of jealousy of my close association with this particular President, it clearly all stems from the war . . . he goes back too – in his retentive mind – to all the rows about Syria; about D-Day; about the position of the French army in the last stages of the war; about Yalta and the betrayal of Europe and all the rest.[84]

Macmillan was right that for all de Gaulle's affectation of *Realpolitik* in international affairs, the tiniest slight could spark off his resentment of the humiliations he had suffered during the war. His reasonable side believed that that is how states behave; his emotional side still smarted from the memory. He once said, in jest, that the British had placed him in Carlton Gardens because it is 'a dead end, with the only way out through Waterloo Place'.[85] De Gaulle's prickliness in relation to Great Britain was observed by his London Ambassador Chauvel (never a friendly witness). Chauvel's suggestion to the General in 1958, soon after his return to power, that he make a courtesy call on Macmillan in Britain (as Macmillan had done to him in France) was rejected: de Gaulle would go to London 'in majesty' once he was President. To another idea that he might invite Macmillan to Colombey, de Gaulle replied, with a smile, that the house was too uncomfortable to receive guests – although it had seemingly been comfortable enough for Adenauer. In the preparations for the state visit in March 1960 (the first time de Gaulle had set foot in England since June 1944), he was even more of a stickler than usual about the tiniest details of protocol. He rejected the British suggestion that, owing to the uncertainties of the weather, he travel by sea rather than air. He felt it would give too much importance to the trip and the British were assured there would be no weather problems, leading one official to comment: 'I can only assume that among the special powers he has now assumed he assumes control of the weather.'[86] Chauvel's suggestion that de Gaulle pay a visit to the ailing Churchill was initially rebuffed until it was presented to him in the form of 'General de Gaulle visiting Winston Churchill' as one might visit the Arc de Triomphe. Chauvel managed with difficulty to persuade de Gaulle to pay a visit to Carlton Gardens as a mark of his gratitude for what the British had done for him in the war, but he drew the line at going to Hampstead where he had lived in 1942. None of these memories of exile were happy ones.

As usual, the visit was a popular triumph. Huge crowds turned out to cheer the returning General. Accorded the rare honour of addressing the joint Houses of Parliament, his homage to the traditions of Westminster democracy was a *tour de force* of Gaullist eloquence which excited universal admiration – and amazement at his ability to deliver such a long, intricate speech from memory while never deviating from the distributed text:

> Although since 1940 you have gone through the hardest vicissitudes in your history, only four statesmen, my friends Sir Winston Churchill, Lord Attlee [had they ever met?], Sir Anthony Eden and Mr Harold Macmillan, have guided your affairs over these extraordinary years. Thus, lacking meticulously worked-out constitutional texts, but by virtue of an unchallengeable general consent, you find the means on each occasion to ensure the efficient functioning of democracy without incurring the excessive criticism of the ambitious, or the punctilious blame of the purists.[87]

He paid an eighteen-minute visit to an almost completely comatose Churchill whose parting words, according to de Gaulle, were '*Vive la France*'. Since in an earlier draft of the *Memoirs* he had remembered the words as '*Vive l'amitié*' one cannot be sure that either version was true.[88] One name absent from the invitation lists to meet de Gaulle during the visit was his old patron and antagonist Spears. Once de Gaulle was back in France, Spears wrote 'from that same desk where you began the career which brings you back here' to say how 'saddened' he had been not to receive an invitation. De Gaulle's secretariat drafted a friendly reply which de Gaulle massacred so as to remove every pleasantry ('*Mon cher Général*' became the curt '*Général*'). He ended: 'As for you and Madame Spears I wrote in my memoirs what I considered appropriate and equitable to mention.'[89]

The royal family was much in evidence throughout the visit. De Gaulle recounts that in his private audience with the Queen, when she asked for his advice on dealing with the problems facing the world, he replied: 'In the place where God has placed you, be who you are, Madam. I mean be that person around whom, thanks to your legitimacy, everything in your kingdom is organized, around whom your people see their *patrie* and whose presence and dignity contribute to national unity.'[90] Whether or not he said exactly these words, the sentiments express that mixture of admiration, regret and envy that he felt for the continuity of Britain's monarchical tradition. In the long history he carried in his head, England was France's hereditary enemy and historic rival, but that memory was overlaid by a more recent one: a bewilderment that Britain had allowed herself to lose a sense of national ambition and become, in his eyes, an American satellite. As he remarked to Peyrefitte around this time: 'Churchill was magnificent until 1942. Then, as if exhausted by the excess of effort, he passed the flame on to the Americans and abased himself before them.' De Gaulle endlessly returned in conversation to that primal scene of an incandescent Churchill shouting on 4 June 1944 that in a choice between 'Europe and the open sea' he would always choose the latter.[91] This was the mental baggage de Gaulle took to his series of talks with Macmillan.

Although Macmillan had in his 'Grand Design' envisaged nuclear sharing as a possible bait for de Gaulle, the issue in the end played little part in their bilateral talks.[92] The nuclear issue had first been raised at the meeting at Rambouillet in March 1960 before Macmillan penned his 'Grand Design'. According to the British record de Gaulle had asked if, in the light of the American refusal to provide any help with nuclear weapons, the United Kingdom might 'assist even with the means of delivery only'. Macmillan had replied that there would be 'complications' since the British success in getting the United States to bend the McMahon agreement in their favour did not allow them to extend this to other countries. The British minute reported: 'General de Gaulle understood this.'[93] De Gaulle may have understood but he certainly did not approve, and curiously there is no mention of this exchange in the French record of the same meeting.[94] What might have changed the situation in Macmillan's mind was that Britain's exemption from the McMahon Act had been allowed because of her 'substantial progress' in developing nuclear technology; Macmillan perhaps hoped to persuade Kennedy that since the same would soon be true of France there was a case for offering another exemption. But this idea was scuppered by Kennedy, who wrote to Macmillan in May 1961 that no nuclear aid could be granted to France. Since he had nothing to offer in this area, Macmillan's tactic during his four encounters with de Gaulle was to play up Britain's conversion to the idea of European political unity and emphasize British support for de Gaulle's objection to supranationalism; de Gaulle's response was to deflect the conversation from political question towards the economic obstacles to British entry. The two men talked past each other with perfect courtesy, Macmillan's tone becoming increasingly desperate as the prize seemed to be slipping away.

This pattern was set when they met again at Rambouillet in January 1961.[95] Macmillan sketched out the common ground between their visions of Europe and de Gaulle politely doused his enthusiasm: 'If we include British agriculture and all the products of the Commonwealth the Common Market will explode.' Macmillan managed somehow to come away from the talks persuading himself that they had gone well: 'I think we made good progress, De G was relaxed, friendly and seemed genuinely attracted by my themes.'[96] But it is hard to see what glimmers of encouragement Macmillan had read into de Gaulle's final summing up:

The United Kingdom had decided to come nearer to Europe. They were prepared to open a new chapter ... He recognized that Great Britain had played a major part in securing victory in the Second World War and that the American intervention had been decisive. At that time power had passed to the United States and Britain had very reasonably decided to align herself with the Americans in the belief that this was the best way she could influence United States policy. He quite saw that the United Kingdom had not entirely abandoned hope that this policy might still be successful ... As regards the economic arrangements in Europe the United Kingdom was not in a hurry ... He would advise the United Kingdom to take her time and move little by little.

Since Macmillan *was* in a hurry, this was not what he wanted to hear.

The next meeting took place in November 1961 at Macmillan's private country house, Birch Grove in Sussex. De Gaulle's visit caused some upheaval in the household. Since he was under constant threat of assassination, de Gaulle travelled with blood plasma for which a special fridge had to be found; police swarmed round the garden and Macmillan noted with satisfaction that one of their dogs 'happily bit a Daily Mail man in the behind'. There was little else to be pleased about in the meeting. Although de Gaulle declared himself 'very impressed' by Macmillan's declaration of Europeanism, he dwelt again on all the technical difficulties – especially the Commonwealth. He worried that Britain would bring her 'great escort' with her.[97] This time Macmillan was more discouraged than on the previous encounter. He noted that Couve, a 'cold Protestant fish', was just a 'functionary' who did what he was told, and Debré sensible but 'loyalty personified'. Everything depended on de Gaulle:

> The Emperor of the French ... is older, more sententious and far more *royal* than when I last saw him ... While he has extraordinary dignity and charm, is nice to servants and children and so forth ... he does not apparently listen to argument ... He merely repeats over and over again what he has said before ... He talks of Europe but means France ... The tragedy is that we agree with de Gaulle on almost everything. We like the political Europe ... that de Gaulle likes. We are anti-federalists; so is he. We fear a German revival and have no desire to see a revived Germany. These are de Gaulle's thoughts too ... We agree; but his pride, his inherited hatred of England ... his bitter memories of the last war; above all his immense vanity for France ... make him half welcome, half repel us, with a strange 'love-hatred' complex. Sometimes when I am with him, I feel I have overcome it. But he goes back to his disgust and his dislike, like a dog to his vomit.[98]

To Adenauer a few days later, de Gaulle merely commented that Macmillan had made a 'great sentimental scene' about his desire to join Europe.[99] Macmillan would not have found this coldly dismissive tone encouraging. More significant than anything said at Birch Grove was the fact that de Gaulle was simultaneously pushing his partners for an agreement on CAP. After the meeting, he wrote to Macmillan that he hoped Britain might join 'one day' on the 'same conditions' as the other members – just as he was endeavouring, through the CAP, to make those conditions less easy for Britain.[100]

The fourth meeting between Macmillan and de Gaulle took place in June 1962 at the Château de Champs, a residence outside Paris that had once belonged to Madame de Pompadour and had been owned by the French state since 1935.[101] The Quai's advance briefing was to 'win time and allow a worrying uncertainty about our real intentions'.[102] The phrase 'worrying uncertainty' has a very Gaullist ring even if de Gaulle was not the author of the note. Macmillan, who described de Gaulle as playing the 'role of a stately monarch unbending a little to the representatives of a once hostile but now friendly country',[103] made his most sustained attempt to convince de Gaulle that Britain had changed: that the young felt 'more European than the older people who had been brought up in the days of Kipling' (which the French record translated as 'the England of Kipling is dead') and that Britain did not 'want to be a satellite of the Americans'. These remarks do seem to have made some impression on de Gaulle, and certainly succeeded in wrongfooting him slightly, but he gave no ground:

> The sense of being an island [*sentiment insulaire*] remains very strong with you. England looks to the sea, towards wider horizons. She remains very linked to the United States by language, by habits and by certain agreements. The natural course of your policy leads you to seek the agreement of the Americans because you are '*mondiaux*' . . . Your entry will change everything.

Macmillan's remaining hope was that if the negotiations in Brussels on the technical aspects of British entry were successful de Gaulle would not be able to stand out against his European partners. He would have been less optimistic about this tactic had he known about a small meeting de Gaulle had chaired after the Champs encounter. Its purpose was to discuss what stance the French should take in Brussels. Pompidou's line was that 'It is in our interest that the English affair does not succeed . . . It is not desirable that we take responsibility for the rupture of the negotiations. It would be best for them to run into the sands.' De Gaulle agreed but worried that the British might end up accepting the conditions demanded of them: 'That would be very annoying for us.'[104] In fact, the British were constrained in the concessions they could make by their domestic agricultural lobby and by the Commonwealth. By the autumn the negotiations in Brussels were moving into the sands as the French hoped.[105]

DENOUEMENTS

Although the nuclear issue had played almost no part in the talks between Macmillan and de Gaulle, it did overshadow their final meeting at Rambouillet in December 1962. Six weeks earlier, the world had come to the brink of nuclear catastrophe when American intelligence discovered the existence of Soviet missiles on Cuban soil. On 22 October, Kennedy announced a naval blockade of Cuban waters as Soviet ships were sailing towards them. Just before his announcement, he went through the motions of consulting his allies. The elder statesman Dean Acheson arrived at the Elysée for an ultra-secret meeting six hours before Kennedy's broadcast. Acheson admitted to de Gaulle that he was there to inform rather than consult. But he said that the decision 'opens the way for a lot of advice from the Allies'. De Gaulle played to perfection the part of the exemplary ally. When Acheson offered to show photographs of the missile sites, de Gaulle at first refused to see them: 'A great nation like yours would not act if there were any doubt about the evidence.' Having seen the proof, he graciously offered full support. When Acheson was told afterwards that he had made a good impression, he remarked that this 'was Louis XIV saying a nice word to an Ambassador from the Sultan of Turkey'. In no way could the Americans fault de Gaulle's response.[106]

Once the crisis was over, many Europeans were uncomfortable with the idea that their security – and the security of the world – had hung on the presence of Soviet missiles on a Caribbean island. Could they be sure that the Americans would have behaved as firmly over Berlin as they had over Cuba? Macmillan was genuinely upset at having been informed but not consulted about the American decision; de Gaulle pretended to be upset but was secretly satisfied that he had been vindicated in his view that the Alliance was one-sided. He wrote menacingly to Adenauer that the crisis should have 'consequences for the current workings of the political and strategic policy of Europe'.[107]

It was not only because of Cuba that nuclear issues came up during the fourth and last of the de Gaulle–Macmillan meetings at Rambouillet in mid-December 1962.[108] Immediately after it Macmillan was due to fly to the Bahamas to discuss with Kennedy the future of the British nuclear deterrent. The current British deterrent was reaching the end of its life. The British had originally signed up to buy a new American missile, Skybolt. In November 1962, it was suddenly cancelled for reasons of expense. This was a shock to the British, even threatening the survival of the government. Macmillan was due to see Kennedy to discuss as a fall-back position the British purchase of American Polaris missiles. Macmillan briefed de Gaulle on this at Rambouillet. He agreed with de Gaulle that each should have weapons under their control but he admitted that Polaris might make Britain more dependent on America. De Gaulle must have felt a certain satisfaction about Britain's difficulties. He was blunter than he had ever been before: 'I think England has become more European than she was in the past. But I note that she is not yet ready to accept the Common Market as it stands.' And he recalled – once again – that encounter with Churchill in June 1944. Macmillan declared himself 'astonished and profoundly wounded' by de Gaulle's words. In his diary he noted that it was a 'very depressing experience, the brutal truth, of course, cleverly concealed by all the courtesy and good manners which surrounded the visit in all its details'.[109] Macmillan was allegedly on the verge of tears when he briefed the British Embassy on the talks. Whether or not de Gaulle knew this, at the next meeting of the Council of Ministers, he made some patronizing comments about Macmillan which he allowed Peyrefitte to communicate to the press: 'What could I do except quote to him Edith Piaf's song "*ne pleurez pas, Milord*"?' It is hard to imagine a more calculatedly contemptuous leak. At the same time, de Gaulle told Peyrefitte to announce a press conference for 14 January. Peyrefitte asked if he knew what he was going to say:

> Of course I know . . . First I am going to settle once and for all [*vider*] the entry of Britain into the Common Market. *Vider!* You see what I mean? . . . This has dragged on long enough. If at some point one does not have the courage to say 'no' one ends up being ensnared . . . We are going to have some fun.[110]

De Gaulle had resolved to bring matters to a head for several reasons. First, having won the constitutional referendum and obtained a parliamentary majority, he was politically unassailable at home. Secondly, relations with Adenauer were better than ever. It was therefore unlikely he would object to a veto on British entry. But time was pressing because Adenauer had made it clear he would soon be retiring. Thirdly, de Gaulle worried that if the British made enough concessions in the ongoing talks at Brussels an agreement might be more difficult to veto. He was always suspicious of the tendency of negotiators to seek compromises. In this case he need not

have worried. After hearing from Edward Heath, the chief British negotiator in Brussels, Macmillan noted in his diary in early December: 'The
French are opposing us by every means, fair and foul. They are absolutely
ruthless. For some reason they *terrify* the six . . . The crunch will come in
Jan or Feb. It will be a trial of nerve and will.'[111] He was right – and no
one had nerve and will in greater supply than de Gaulle.

Between the Rambouillet meeting in December 1962 and de Gaulle's
press conference in January 1963, Macmillan met Kennedy in Nassau. This
was a fraught encounter. Although Kennedy offered to supply Polaris as
part of a multinational NATO force, Macmillan feared this was a ruse to
eliminate the British independent deterrent and subsume it in a multilateral
force, the MLF, under American control. Macmillan's only bargaining
counter was to threaten a public breakdown in the Anglo-American relationship. Kennedy finally agreed that, while the Polaris missiles would be
ascribed to NATO, the British would receive an opt-out provision if
'supreme national interests' were at stake. The two leaders agreed to make
an identical proposal to de Gaulle.

Kennedy's offer was communicated to de Gaulle by the American and
British ambassadors. Historians remain unsure what was being offered.
Was it a multi*national* force or a multi*lateral* one? The confusion arose
partly because the American administration was itself divided. George Ball,
in Paris on 10 January 1963, put a more multilateral spin on the offer than
had originally seemed the case. Some historians believe that a proposal de
Gaulle might have been able to accept was sabotaged by Ball; others that
de Gaulle missed the opportunity to probe these ambiguities; still others
that no interpretation of the deal could have been acceptable to de Gaulle.[112]
This last judgement is the most plausible. Quite apart from the improbabil-
ity of de Gaulle accepting any offer negotiated behind his back, the type
of nuclear warheads which the French had been developing would, unlike
the British ones, have been initially incompatible with Polaris. Since even
Macmillan was unsure on his return from Nassau if he had been 'out-
smarted' by Kennedy into accepting an MLF,[113] it is hardly surprising that
de Gaulle was even more suspicious. He told his Council of Ministers on
3 January:

> We do not have the choice, like the English, between something and nothing.
> We are going to have something of our own . . . Britain imagines she has kept
> her autonomy since the text contains the words 'if her supreme interests are
> involved'. These are just words. It is throwing dust in the eyes . . . A system
> of defence is a complex, concentrated, interconnected mechanism that one
> cannot just undo even if one wants to.[114]

De Gaulle could have kept the discussions over the Polaris offer simmering, but it presented him with perfect extra ammunition as he was preparing his press conference on Britain's application to the EEC. Even by de Gaulle's standards that press conference on 14 January 1963 was a spectacular piece of theatre. Part of the effect was surprise. A few days before, de Gaulle had falsely assured Dixon that he would be 'prudent' in what he said. Dixon was all the more devastated by the 'irrevocably negative' tone of de Gaulle's remarks. He reported to London later that it had been like living 'in a Kafka world . . . where even our good friends lie to us'.[115] De Gaulle's own ministers were no less startled. In blissful ignorance of what was about to happen in Paris, de Gaulle's Minister of Agriculture Edgard Pisani was settling down that afternoon in Brussels to discuss 'New Zealand butter, frozen meat and Australian rabbits' when he heard to his incredulity from one of his foreign colleagues what de Gaulle was saying at that moment in Paris.[116]

De Gaulle's press conference was a double 'no': to British entry into Europe and to Kennedy's offer at Nassau. As well as rehearsing all the economic reasons rendering British entry into Europe impossible for the moment – the structure of her economy, her links with the Commonwealth and so on – the Nassau deal gave him the perfect pretext to portray Britain in Europe as an American Trojan Horse:

> The entry of Britain would completely alter the entire set of arrangements understandings, compensations, rules that have been agreed between the Six because all those states, like England, have very important peculiarities. So it would be a different Common Market that we would have to think of building and one that would be presented with problems in its economic relations with a host of other states, above all with the United States . . . It is predictable that the cohesion of all its members . . . would not last for very long, and that it would take on the appearance of a colossal Atlantic community under American dependence and direction. That is not at all what France aims to achieve, and is working to achieve, which is a strictly European construction.[117]

As he had predicted to Peyrefitte, de Gaulle had a lot of 'fun'. At the Council of Ministers two days later he did not even mention the press conference except in a passing remark: 'Curious epoch, *messieurs*, when one can provoke such a racket [*hourvari*] just by saying that England is an Island and that America is not Europe.'[118]

De Gaulle drew a final rabbit out of his hat with the signing of a formal Franco-German Treaty when Adenauer visited Paris a week later. This was the culmination of the rapprochement that had been taking place with

Adenauer since the summer. The prospect of a formal treaty had been so last minute – it was not even mentioned at the preparatory discussions a month earlier[119] – that the Germans did not have ready the special blue paper or the leather folder that was required for treaties. (A member of the German delegation had to find something at the Hermès store in Paris.) The Treaty took on a potentially anti-American complexion in the light of the press conference about which Adenauer had known nothing in advance. When he arrived in Paris, Jean Monnet rushed to the German Embassy to urge him to make the signing of the Treaty contingent on continued negotiations with the British in Brussels. Adenauer refused.

The terms of the Treaty were more symbolic than substantial. They provided for regular meetings between political leaders and civil servants from the two countries to discuss cultural and educational cooperation. In their discussions Adenauer and de Gaulle also agreed to continue exploring a common defence policy – but nothing concrete was decided.

AFTERMATH

After de Gaulle's press conference on 14 January, Macmillan noted despairingly in his diary: 'All our policies . . . are in ruins.' The Permanent Under Secretary of the Foreign Office was more acerbic: 'The cross of Lorraine we can bear without too much difficulty, the double cross I find less tolerable.'[120] Alphand reported from Washington: 'The Americans have the impression that the edifice of their foreign policy is collapsing.'[121] This was to speak too soon. The next round was won by America.

De Gaulle and Adenauer had signed the Treaty with different aims in mind. For de Gaulle, it was a step towards a joint defence strategy; for Adenauer a symbolic recognition of Germany's return to the concert of nations and a means of putting pressure on the United States.[122] On 14 January, the day of de Gaulle's press conference, Adenauer had told George Ball that Germany would participate in the MLF. He confirmed this two days later in a letter to Kennedy. This may have been a way of neutralizing his opponents at home but it suggests that he did not feel bound by de Gaulle's ideas on European defence if he could squeeze more out of America. Jean Monnet actively lobbied his German contacts to undercut the Treaty, as did the Americans. As a result, when the Bundestag came to ratify the Treaty in May, it inserted a preamble reaffirming a commitment to 'close cooperation' with America and to 'common defence in the framework of the Atlantic Alliance'. It was not in de Gaulle's style to admit defeat. Visiting Bonn on 2 July, he affected not to care: 'Treaties are like young girls or roses: they last as long as they last. If the Franco-German treaty is not applied it will not be the first time in history.'

In the end, de Gaulle had achieved neither a reorganization of the Atlantic Alliance nor a political organization of Europe around a common defence policy. He had kept the British out of Europe but the Americans had emptied the Franco-German alliance of substance. All the different 'Grand Designs' had cancelled each other out. The 'sentimental' de Gaulle seemed blind to the fact that France's partners, following the same principles of national egotism in which the 'realist' de Gaulle believed, might not see France as working disinterestedly for the benefit of humanity – or even of Europe. If France resented the domination of America, Holland, Belgium or Italy might reasonably feel the same about France. De Gaulle had tried to play on two stages – the great power one and the European one – but France was not big enough for the first, too big for the second.

This should not lead us to conclude that by the middle of 1963 de Gaulle had 'failed'. Naturally he was disappointed that he had not yet laid the foundations of a European defence policy weaning Europe away from dependence on America. But in his view of international relations as a process of endless flux, where nothing was fixed, where movement was life and immobility was death, the aim was not necessarily to achieve specific objectives but rather to have a 'great national ambition' to 'sustain a great quarrel' – to be noticed. In this he had certainly succeeded. After the Nassau meeting, a study commissioned by Kennedy observed that 'de Gaulle stood at the centre of all questions'.[123] Dean Rusk commented: 'Talking with de Gaulle was like crawling up a mountain on your knees, opening a little portal at the top, and waiting for the oracle to speak.'[124] This would have been music to de Gaulle's ears. In the summer of 1963, Kennedy made a tour of Europe, leaving out France. The highpoint of his trip was his visit to Berlin where he delivered his famous speech declaring '*Ich bin ein Berliner.*' This was his answer to de Gaulle's triumphal tour of Germany a year earlier. After Kennedy had returned, one adviser told him that a public opinion survey of the results of the tour showed that 'you beat de Gaulle in a close election in Germany.'[125] Had he known that the Americans were using him as a marker to test their success, de Gaulle would have legitimately regarded it as a kind of victory. For the first time in decades France could not be taken for granted.

In December 1966, de Gaulle gave an audience to the pro-Gaullist journalist Cyrus Sulzberger of the *New York Times* whom he usually saw once a year. After Sulzberger had exhausted his prepared questions, de Gaulle seemed in a mood to go on talking. Sulzberger rapidly improvised some more questions. He asked which person had most influenced the General.

The answer was shot back without hesitation: 'My father . . . He was a modest professor but a very eminent man.' Sulzberger was forced to dream up another question: what had been de Gaulle's greatest failures and successes? Momentarily caught off guard, de Gaulle reflected for a few moments:

> How do you define success or failure? Only history itself can define these terms. In reality, life and action are always made up of a series of successes and failures. Life is a combat and therefore each one of its phases includes both successes and failures. And you cannot really say which event was a success and which event was a failure. Success contains within it the germs of failure and the reverse is true.[126]

This was de Gaulle's philosophy of life. The struggle went on.

23
Going Global, 1963–1964

IMPASSE IN EUROPE

Wondering what de Gaulle would do next, Macmillan mused that it was 'terribly reminiscent of the 1930s – waiting on Hitler'.[1] This curious comment tells us more about the impact of five years of Gaullist power on the British Prime Minister than it does about de Gaulle himself. Talk of madness was often in the air. Speaking on the telephone after the de Gaulle veto, Kennedy and Macmillan had agreed that the French President 'had gone crazy . . . Absolutely crazy'.[2] Dixon, after a meeting in July 1963, found de Gaulle 'amiable' although 'crazier than ever in his basic approach to world politics' – but the tone of Dixon's 'strange' despatch led the Foreign Office to wonder if 'the Ambassador is going mad too'.[3] After another meeting Dixon commented: 'Despite the virtuosity of the performance, I could not help being reminded of the eccentric philosopher in the Aristophanes play loftily treading on air and thinking about the sun.'[4] One Foreign Office official even reported in February 1963 that it was being 'seriously canvassed' in London medical circles that the General was suffering from the advanced stages of syphilis contracted in London during the war. Nietzsche and Maupassant were cited as having displayed similar symptoms.[5]

The British consoled themselves with the thought that de Gaulle would not be there for ever. The Foreign Secretary Alec Douglas-Home took the line that it was necessary 'to weather a storm which should gradually subside after de Gaulle disappears'.[6] The same position was adopted by the Americans, who tried to avoid open conflict: 'There is no point in reviling a tornado,' suggested Kennedy's adviser Arthur Schlesinger soon after de Gaulle's press conference.[7] He went on:

> The prevailing Anglo-American impression of de Gaulle is of an unyielding, imperious, messianic figure, oblivious to tactics and prepared to wait until the rest of the world comes round to his view. Nothing could be more wrong.

The record shows de Gaulle to be one of the most consummate, flexible and skilled politicians of the 20th century. Only a man with de Gaulle's exquisite sense of timing and initiative could have dealt with Roosevelt and Churchill during the war and emerged unscathed: he always knew how far he could press the interests of France without provoking the Anglo-Saxons to the final act of stripping him of his power and putting him under arrest.

And commenting on de Gaulle's more recent handling of the Algerian crisis, he observed:

> De Gaulle the politician concealed his purposes for a time behind a smoke-screen of cryptic phrases, delphic pronouncements and technical formulas. And in both cases he worked coldly, intelligently and perseveringly for his chosen goal. As someone once said of Martin Van Buren, 'He rows to his destination with muffled oars.'[8]

De Gaulle's oars were never that muffled but this was a more sophisticated analysis than anything offered by those inclined to write the General off as a madman. On the other hand, it did not offer much concrete guidance on how to deal with him. The American Ambassador to Paris, Charles Bohlen, remarked ruefully in 1964:

> It is always easier to say what should *not* be done in regard to De Gaulle than what should be done. It should always be borne in mind that De Gaulle cannot have very many more years of being in power, and the present indications are that a very large portion of the objectionable features of current French policy would disappear with his departure from power.[9]

This waiting strategy was embraced, after Kennedy's assassination in November 1963, by his successor Lyndon Johnson. Kennedy had been exasperated by Gaulle but intellectually fascinated by him. His administration was constantly commissioning studies of the 'de Gaulle problem'. The less cerebral Johnson shared the exasperation but not the fascination. It has been said that he saw de Gaulle as 'a recalcitrant Senate Committee baron on whom he did not, for the moment, have a handle and therefore had no reason to bother his head about'.[10] Discouraging public attacks on de Gaulle by the administration, Johnson encapsulated his method for dealing with him in various baseball analogies – 'when the pitcher throws a fast bowl let it go into the catcher's mitts' – which the new French Ambassador, Charles Lucet, never fully understood while getting the general idea.[11] De Gaulle and Johnson were only ever in each other's presence for thirty minutes. They met at Kennedy's funeral where de Gaulle's towering physical presence, and the history he carried with him, made him the dominating personality. He was the first foreign leader to be received personally by a somewhat apprehensive Johnson, who thought the meeting had gone well. But they never met again except for a handshake at Adenauer's funeral in 1967.

After the Kennedy funeral, Johnson made an inadvertent faux pas by announcing in good faith that a scheduled visit by de Gaulle to the United States would still go ahead. But the General's view was that this plan had lapsed with Kennedy's death and that it was for Johnson to visit him first. One telling, if minor, symbol of de Gaulle's rancour against the 'Anglo-Saxons' was his refusal to attend the ceremonies planned for June 1964 to celebrate the twentieth anniversary of D-Day. When quizzed in private about the wisdom of this snub, de Gaulle launched into a tirade against the humiliation he had suffered on 4 June when France was 'treated like a doormat'.[12] In any matter touching the war, de Gaulle's precarious balance between sentiment and reason tipped towards the former.

Behind these symbolic spats, the real issue remained the nuclear one. Although the foundations of the French atomic programme had been laid discreetly by the governments of the Fourth Republic, the decisive impulse to push for an entirely independent deterrent came from de Gaulle. The government's five-year defence programme, which incorporated the spending plans for the deterrent, had faced three opposition censure motions before being finally approved in the autumn of 1960. Discretion about the nuclear programme was also a thing of the past. When the first bomb was exploded in February 1960, de Gaulle publicly proclaimed 'hurrah for France'. But testing a bomb was only the first stage to having an operational deterrent. When in August 1963 the Americans, Russians and British signed a nuclear test ban treaty, de Gaulle refused to sign on the grounds that this was a club of those who already had weapons designed to keep out those who did not. Although de Gaulle's commitment to an independent nuclear deterrent was widely attacked in France, even the pro-Atlanticist Raymond Aron, who deplored many of de Gaulle's foreign policy positions, counselled the Americans that any French citizen would resent the idea that bombs became a problem only once they crossed the Channel. He warned that American attitudes on this matter 'would be enough to irritate a man less prone to irritation than General de Gaulle'.[13] There was a strong emotional investment on de Gaulle's part in the possession of atomic weapons as a symbol of France's 'rank'. In 1967 when he witnessed in Murao the explosion of a French nuclear bomb, Peyrefitte, who was accompanying him, found him in a state of exalted excitement that he had never witnessed before. He claimed this was a 'resurrection' – the 'culmination of all that we have tried to do'.[14]

But what was the bomb for? French military strategists had been grap-
pling for years to come up with an answer to the question how small
atomic/nuclear weapons could ever offer a credible deterrent.[15] One of the
most vocal experts was General Pierre Gallois, who had managed to secure
an interview with de Gaulle at the Hôtel La Pérouse one evening in April
1956 when he was still in opposition. De Gaulle had not shown much
interest in the subject before and Gallois was there to convert him. Gallois
arrived laden with files and gave his hour-long briefing; de Gaulle then
spoke at great length 'as if he needed to embed in his memory my commentary and the ideas they suggested to him'.[16] Gallois's theory was based
on 'proportional deterrence': that even small nuclear weapons could be
dissuasive if their destructive effect was sufficient to make the potential
cost of aggression unacceptable. This was an argument de Gaulle put to
Kennedy on one occasion: 'How can one appreciate the degree of destructive power where dissuasion begins? Even if the adversary is armed so as
to be able to kill ten times over the person he wants to attack, the fact that
the person has what it needs to kill him once, or even just tear off an arm,
could after all make him reflect.'[17] Another French theorist, General André
Beaufre, developed a different defence of nuclear weapons for a country
like France: that a small French deterrent could, if necessary, operate as a
kind of tripwire, forcing allies to step in. Another concept, associated with
the French General Charles Ailleret, and strongly supported by de Gaulle,
was the notorious *tous azimuts* policy. This was an artillery term to express
the idea that, since nuclear systems were designed to have a long life, it was
impossible to be sure who the adversary might be in twenty years' time:
the nuclear force should potentially be able to strike anywhere in the world.
The *tous azimuts* strategy was formally unveiled in an article by Ailleret
in 1967, but it was no different to what de Gaulle had already said in a
speech at Saint-Cyr in 1959: 'since it is theoretically possible for France to
be destroyed from any point of the world, our force must be made to act
anywhere on Earth.'[18] De Gaulle was not ultimately wedded to any particular position. When Beaufre sent one of his books to de Gaulle, he
received a non-committal reply.[19] On the same day as replying to Beaufre,
de Gaulle wrote to Aron, who had him sent his own book on the subject:
'I read the *Great Debate* as I often read you, here and there, on the same
subject . . . All comes down to one single issue, "yes or no, is France to be
France?" That was the issue during the time of the Resistance. You know
the choice I made but I also know there is no rest for theologians.'[20]

De Gaulle was not ultimately interested in questions of nuclear
'theology'. His ambition for a French deterrent was anchored in his fundamental pessimism about the unpredictability of history, and in his belief

that a great power needed to have the means to act independently. In this sense Lacouture is correct to write that the independent deterrent was 'consubstantial with the State Gaullism' of the 1960s.[21] As in his defence of a striking force in the 1930s, de Gaulle worried less about the details than about the principle. But in the medium term the French bomb was for him the necessary precondition to emancipating Europe from dependence on American protection by offering France's partners the eventual alternative of a French nuclear umbrella. For this reason, the MLF was his biggest bone of contention with the Americans in 1963-4. His suspicions of American motives were amply justified by what Kennedy told his security advisers in January 1963: 'It is through the multilateral concept that we increase the dependence of the European nations on the United States and tie these nations closer to us.'[22] That is exactly why de Gaulle opposed it. The Americans also hoped that the MLF would drive a wedge between France and Germany. Even Adenauer, when signing the Franco-German Treaty, had told the Americans that he supported MLF. Ludwig Erhard, who succeeded Adenauer as German Chancellor in 1963, was even keener on the idea. As an instinctively Atlanticist liberal economist, Erhard was one of those German politicians who believed Adenauer had been bewitched by de Gaulle. Erhard was never accorded the honour of a stay at Colombey, but he did spend two days in December 1964 on Johnson's ranch in Texas complete with cowboy hat – a revealing symbol of the changing of the guard in Germany.

In the MLF debate, de Gaulle had some cards to play. The British were not enamoured of a scheme that threatened their own independent deterrent. And the Germans were worried by the fact that, while tempting them with the MLF, the American government was rethinking its policy on nuclear weapons – raising the threshold that would trigger a nuclear intervention so as to encourage the Europeans to increase their conventional forces. This allowed de Gaulle to argue that the Americans would prefer Europe to become a battlefield if the alternative was Soviet nuclear retaliation on their own territory: 'There is therefore an essential divergence at the strategic level between America and Europe. This need not prevent their "Alliance". But it makes "integration" unjustifiable.'[23] Or as he put it more pithily in private: 'MLF is a device to make the Europeans believe they have access to the atomic trigger. Except that the Americans control the other trigger without which no one can shoot; so nothing has changed.'[24]

At a meeting with Erhard in July 1964, de Gaulle played on German anxieties by making an off-the-cuff comment that the Germans might one day be associated with the French deterrent. Exactly what he said was lost in translation and seems to have been over-interpreted.[25] When the

Germans tried to test the water by asking if they could be permitted to observe a French nuclear test, de Gaulle's answer was unequivocal:

> As long as the application of the Franco-German Treaty is as empty as it is ... we are not to open to the Germans the slightest door on what we are doing in the domain of atomic weapons. Since they place their confidence in the United States, it is to Washington that they should address themselves to be informed about what they want to know.[26]

Relations between the two countries sank to their lowest ebb since de Gaulle's return to power. As his frustrations with Germany increased, the ambiguities of his German policy became more evident: he seemed to be offering partnership but not equality. What was the benefit to Germany, while the Cold War lasted, of exchanging American protection (perhaps not totally reliable but certainly effective) for French protection (worryingly close and incomparably weaker)?

At the end of 1964, de Gaulle made it clear to the German government that the MLF was incompatible with the Franco-German Treaty. This was the final nail in the coffin of the MLF, whose passing no one regretted. Killing it off was a success for de Gaulle, but in other respects his European policy was still at a dead end. As he put it at the Council of Ministers some months earlier: 'Italy is not serious; so she does not exist. The English console themselves with the decline by claiming that they share in American hegemony; Germany is broken.'[27] For the moment, there was nothing to be hoped for from Europe, America or Britain. Instead de Gaulle now fixed his gaze on wider horizons. His televised address to the French at the end of 1963 announced that France would now need to pursue 'a global policy'.[28] He never made statements of this kind without having something in mind.

'RETURN TO ASIA'

On 27 January 1964, brief communiqués issued simultaneously in Paris and Peking announced that France had recognized the People's Republic of China, the Communist regime that had taken power in 1949. China had already been recognized by several other countries – including Great Britain – but France went further by announcing an exchange of ambassadors. At a press conference three days later, de Gaulle launched into one of those geopolitical *tours d'horizon* he so enjoyed, taking his listeners through a thousand years of Chinese history as if he were lecturing in the classroom at Saint-Cyr.[29]

De Gaulle had been thinking about the recognition of China for some years. In June 1962 he had mused to Peyrefitte:

> The interest of the world will be, one day or another, to speak to them, to get on with them ... to allow them to come out from behind their wall. A *cordon sanitaire* policy only ever has one result: to make the country on the other side more dangerous; its leaders look for diversions from their difficulties, denouncing the capitalist, imperialist plot ... We should not leave the Chinese to stew in their own juice. Otherwise they will become venomous.[30]

Once he was ready to act, de Gaulle sidestepped the Quai. In the autumn of 1963 he sent the former Fourth Republic politician Edgar Faure on a secret exploratory mission to China. Faure was chosen because he had visited China on several occasions and published a book on it. After his visit events moved fast.[31]

De Gaulle's ministers were taken entirely by surprise when he informed them on 8 January 1964 that recognition of China was imminent. This was one of those occasions when he permitted a 'discussion' – purely for form – after which he summed up his position: 'The fact of China is there. One day, perhaps sooner than people imagine, China will be a great political, economic and even military reality.'[32] The main argument against recognizing China was that it would annoy the United States, never a reason to hold back in de Gaulle's eyes. The predictable remonstrations of the American government rather pleased him.[33] In Washington, Ambassador Alphand, 'astonished and worried by such audacity', asked for a 'personal message that I might be able to hand over to the unfortunate Johnson, perfectly well disposed towards us, and personally wounded'. He was given nothing.[34]

For the American government, France's recognition of China was especially inopportune in the light of the situation in Vietnam. The agreement which Mendès France had negotiated at Geneva in 1954, ending France's presence in Indo-China, had divided Vietnam at the 17th parallel. Elections were scheduled north and south of the line to decide Vietnam's future, but these never occurred. Tensions between South Vietnam and the Communist North gradually escalated into open conflict. The Americans started sending 'advisers' to help the South defend itself. Advisers were followed by soldiers, and gradually the Americans were sucked into a conflict they viewed as a key battleground of the Cold War.

In his *Memoirs* written eight years later, with the advantage of hindsight, de Gaulle recalled telling Kennedy in June 1961: 'I predict that you will sink step by step into a bottomless military and political quagmire, however much you spend in men and money.' The contemporary French and American records of what de Gaulle said are less forceful but not much different.[35] De Gaulle also told Kennedy that he would not stand in the way if America felt obliged to intervene. But in August 1963, as American involvement escalated, de Gaulle decided to go public in a solemn communiqué announcing the need for a unified, independent and neutralized Vietnam. It was no coincidence that he simultaneously set in motion the process that would lead six months later to the recognition of China. As he remarked afterwards to Peyrefitte: 'This is the return of France to Asia . . . We are going to turn the colonial page.'[36]

Over the next two years, de Gaulle's criticisms of American involvement in Vietnam became more strident.[37] His solution for Vietnam was characteristically vague. His favourite term was 'neutralization' without it being clear if this would apply to both the North and the South. The details were less important than the fact that de Gaulle saw France's historic links to the region as an opportunity to leverage a mediating role in a conflict he was sure the Americans could not win. From time to time Johnson despatched envoys to Paris to put the American case that in Vietnam they were fighting a necessary war against international Communism. But they were all brushed off with the same message. In June 1964, George Ball was told: 'I do not believe that you can win in this situation even though you have more aircraft, cannons, and arms of various kinds . . . I do not mean that all of the Vietnamese are against you but they regard the United States as a foreign power and a very powerful foreign power.'[38] The American Senator Arthur Goldberg was told a year later: 'Ho Chi Minh is a Communist but he is also a national figure, the one who expelled the French and will do the same to the Americans. This is what he is using his Communism for. He did it in the past against us, he is doing it now against you, he will do it perhaps in the future against China.'[39]

De Gaulle's private comments were even more brutal. He told Peyrefitte in 1965 that for the moment the United States could bear the strain of the conflict but 'when they start sending thousands of boys, people will start to notice. When the coffins start coming back that will make people think. And once that combines with their problems with the Blacks and with the dollar, it will create a context of discontent which will get worse with their dirty war.'[40] De Gaulle's prescience was mixed with a strong dose of *Schadenfreude* and self-interest as he prepared the French 'return to Asia'.

'AN EXCELLENT TENOR'

De Gaulle's other major 'global' initiative in 1964 was a long tour of South America.[41] Before leaving he told Debré: 'I am going to Latin America without any very precise diplomatic programme, but in a sort of way instinctively. Perhaps it is important. Perhaps this is the moment.'[42] He may not have had a programme but his motivation was simple: 'Latin America is a magnificent card to play . . . Latin America detests the Americans, she ardently desires to escape their hegemony but nor does she want Russia or China.'[43] De Gaulle hoped to play on the popularity of the Free French in Latin America during the Second World War. Of the 400 or so world-wide Free French committees 300 had been in Latin America.

De Gaulle preceded his South American tour with a visit in March to America's backyard – Mexico. In advance of his arrival, France returned three flags that had been seized during the ill-fated expedition of 1862–4 to install a French puppet Emperor (Maximilian) in Mexico. When the flags arrived in Mexico on 5 March, the country's President knelt down to kiss them as they were taken off the plane. This set the tone for de Gaulle's visit between 16 and 19 March when he deployed all his arts of showman-ship. On the first day, in uniform, de Gaulle was driven through the streets in an open-top car. Later that day he spoke in Spanish (from memory as always) to a massive crowd from the balcony of the National Palace (the only foreign leader ever accorded such a privilege). On day two, this time dressed in a suit, he addressed the Mexican parliament. On day three, he visited the university. The crowds were so vast that his car could not con-tinue, and he did the final stages of the journey on foot. A cartoon in an American newspaper showed President Mateos with a bubble above his head watching de Gaulle and thinking 'Maximilian'. Perhaps he was – but this did not prevent the visit being an extraordinary popular success.

De Gaulle's South American tour in the autumn was a remarkable feat of resilience. In April 1964, the seemingly indestructible septuagenarian had been hospitalized for an operation on his prostate. Four months later, in the space of three weeks, he visited ten countries and fourteen cities (some at high altitudes), and made almost 100 speeches all from memory, some in Spanish. Even in Montevideo, where it rained torrentially throughout the visit, enormous crowds turned out to cheer. The adrenalin of adulation worked its magic. On his return, Pierson Dixon noted a touch disconsolately that de Gaulle looked healthier than he had ever done and was 'clearly feeling far better at the end of the tour than at the beginning'.[44]

The tour may have bucked de Gaulle up but its real achievements were less evident. Two themes ran through all his speeches in Latin America.[45] First, he denounced what he called the 'rival hegemonies'. Everyone knew what this meant, but he avoided being more explicit out of respect for the susceptibilities of his hosts, who all had close relations with the United States. The second theme was the idea of 'Latinness' – the shared Latin and

Catholic roots of France and South America. This was another not so sub-liminal anti-American message. It did not always go down well even when the crowds cheered. In countries like Bolivia and Peru, with large Indian populations, the emphasis on Latinity was problematic. In Colombia President Guillermo Valencia seemed responsive to de Gaulle's message, but not President Alessandri of Chile, if his subsequent report to a friend is to be believed:

> When the General arrived in Chile I went to meet him at Valparaíso and we drove back together alone to Santiago . . . I was shocked and surprised that de Gaulle delivered a violent attack against the United States throughout the two hours of the journey. He described the United States as an octopus exploiting the countries of Latin America . . . He urged me to liberate Chile from the American grasp . . . Although embarrassed and shocked I replied to him that our relations with the United States were not bad at all.[46]

There were some unintended consequences of the tour. In Argentina, from where the former populist leader Juan Perón had been exiled since 1955, de Gaulle's visit was an opportunity for Peronist supporters to manifest themselves publicly and disrupt some of the official ceremonies. De Gaulle's idea of rejecting the two blocs was taken as a version of Perón's slogan of a 'tercera posición'. On de Gaulle's next stop, Paraguay, the situation was reversed. Here he found himself appropriated not by the opposition but by the regime. The repressive military dictator General Stroessner, an inter-national pariah, hoped to use his visit to burnish his reputation. De Gaulle was presented as one General-President visiting another. The authorities issued a stamp with the two generals side by side in uniform. De Gaulle seemed quite happy to play the Caudillo. In this case, despite his rhetoric of liberty and anti-Americanism, he unwittingly helped rehabilitate a virulently anti-Communist regime which was closely reliant on the United States.[47]

The Johnson administration affected indifference to the tour. American ambassadors reported that, despite the large crowds, de Gaulle had not mobilized the same enthusiasm as Kennedy during his tour in 1961. Their overall conclusion was that, while the trip had demonstrated de Gaulle's 'remarkable physical constitution', it would matter only if the French were able to follow it up with concrete aid: 'one can ask if the results of the trip are matched by the immense expense of time and energy.' This was a shrewd assessment. The results were indeed minimal. The French won the contract for the Mexican metro; there were some cultural projects like the founding of a French lycée in Buenos Aires – but little else. In the years after de Gaulle's tour, most of the countries he had visited became more not less economically dependent on the United States, less not more democratic. Jean-Marie Soutou, de Gaulle's main critic in the Quai d'Orsay, who visited the continent four years later, was told by people he met that it had all been 'very moving, very beautiful, in a country where opera is popular, and de Gaulle was an excellent tenor, but it changed nothing'.[48]

NEW SCRAMBLE FOR AFRICA

De Gaulle's chances of making a durable impact in the world outside Europe seemed more promising in France's former African Empire. Although the role of the African Empire in the war gave rise to the notion that he harboured a sentimental relationship with the continent, his attitude was clinically utilitarian. His initial disappointment about the breakup of the Community led him briefly to wonder in 1961 if there was any future in pursuing 'some chimera of "loyalty" from the Africans'.[49] This temptation to give up on Africa was countered by Debré, who argued that the continent offered France 'difficult, changeable and uncertain clients but above all clients that other powers envy us'.[50] This line was given credence by Kennedy's decision to appoint a high-profile Democratic politician, Mennen Williams, as Under Secretary of State for African Affairs, suggesting that America was making it a priority to build up relations with newly independent African states. Williams became a *bête noire* of de Gaulle. His attitude to him was encapsulated in a note of July 1962: 'I am very much on guard against the "negotiations" that the Quai d'Orsay is embarking upon with the Americans (Williams) on the subject of Africa. Why these negotiations? It is as if we were ourselves bringing the Americans . . . into *our* African affairs.'[51] That 'our' is very revealing.

De Gaulle was not only interested in 'our' African affairs. Any Frenchman with so long a memory remembered that, during the carve-up of Africa in the late nineteenth century, Belgium had won out over France by securing the huge colony of Congo. French Congo was tiny by comparison. When in 1960 the future of Belgian Congo began to look precarious, de Gaulle wanted the Belgian government to be reminded 'in a friendly way' that a treaty of 1908 had given France pre-emptive rights over Congo if the King of the Belgians should renounce his sovereignty. If there was to be a 'general carving up [*remembrement*]' of African territory France wanted her rights respected.[52] This startling instruction from someone soon to invent a persona as a visionary decolonizer was never followed up because a few months later it was the Congolese themselves – not the French – who took their country over. The newly independent Congo was immediately ravaged by a bloody civil war when the mineral-rich province of Katanga tried to secede under the leadership of Moïse Tshombe. While the Americans, acting through the United Nations, worked to protect the unity of the new state, French mercenaries fought to support Tshombe. De Gaulle was not directly implicated but was certainly kept informed.[53] For him the tragedy of the Congo was not a ruinous civil war but the danger that the country might become an American bridgehead in Africa. In the end Congolese unity was preserved, and the French abandoned Tshombe.

It was former French Africa that offered the best opportunities. Once it was clear that the Community was over, de Gaulle announced in December 1960 that 'France is changing from the outdated colonial system to a system of fruitful but friendly cooperation.'[54] 'Cooperation' became his new mantra. Its showcase was to be Algeria. Presenting the Evian Accords that ended the Algerian War as an example of France 'lighting up the universe', de Gaulle envisaged Algeria as the 'model of relations between the west and the under-developed world'.[55] He revealed what lay behind these grandiose words in an informal briefing that he gave to France's first Ambassador to independent Algeria, the economist Jean-Marcel Jeanneney:[56]

> At various moments people have hung on to myths, but now the deeper realities have made themselves apparent: the incompatibility of the French and Algerians is what explains and justifies what I have called withdrawal [dégagement]. This incompatibility was masked as long as the French had force on their side and the Algerians were their slaves, workers and cleaned their shoes ... When we stopped crushing [écrabouiller] them, we said to them 'now cope by yourselves' ... What we can most usefully do for them is to educate and instruct them ... Thus we can establish between French and Algerians close contacts but in a form completely different from in the past ... As for Algerian immigration, 'enough of that' ... As for economic aid, we must continue it but cut it off each time they let us down.

The problem with making Algeria a showcase of cooperation was that, almost immediately after the signing of the Evian Accords, the FLN leadership had moved to a more radical position which denounced 'cooperation' as the maintenance of 'colonialism in the form of neo-colonialism'.[57] Ben Bella, who took power in Algeria almost immediately after independence, had not been one of the Evian negotiators. In 1963, the Algerian government seized most remaining French assets in Algeria. A meeting between Ben Bella and de Gaulle at the Château de Champs in March 1964 – a remarkable event only two years after the end of the war – patched up relations. But Ben Bella was in turn ousted by the more radical Houari Boumédiène in the following year.

Nonetheless there was no rupture between France and Algeria

despite 'cooperation' being entirely one way. If de Gaulle showed such uncharacteristic forbearance it was because he had staked so much on the relationship. As Jean de Broglie, the Minister in Charge of Algerian Affairs, put it in 1964: 'Algeria is the door through which we penetrate into the Third World. A quarrel between France and any other state of North Africa is only a matter of simple bilateral tension. A quarrel with Algeria would go beyond the confines of Franco-Algerian relations and risk undermining the efforts of our diplomacy in the entire world.'[58] In this case, de Gaulle was prepared to play a long game. As he remarked in 1963 when Boumédiène started his ascent: 'The course of revolutions has three stages . . . first Danton, then Robespierre, who in his turn is replaced by the Thermidorians. Ben Bella is Danton. Boumédiène is Robespierre. There is a period of terror. The time of the Thermidorians will come.'[59]

De Gaulle's patience with Algeria contrasted starkly with his implacable refusal to forgive Sékou Touré of Guinea. In the case of Algeria, having created the fiction that he had granted independence, de Gaulle found it easy to be generous. Not in the case of Guinea, where he had been publicly defied by Sékou Touré in August 1958 and where independence had been seized. Immediately after Guinea's 'no' to the Community, France ended all cooperation, froze financial aid, ceased paying the pension of 20,000 war veterans and tried to block Guinea's entry to the United Nations. The French were involved in a campaign of dirty tricks against the regime: they secretly supported mercenaries trying to bring down the government and flooded the country with fake banknotes to undermine its currency. There was even a plot to put holes in Sékou's socks to make him look ridiculous while at prayer.[60]

The logic behind this policy was to prevent the contagion of independence infecting the Community. Once the Community had disintegrated, the policy lost its *raison d'être*. Only vindictiveness was left. This counterproductive policy turned Sékou Touré into a Third World hero. After the Evian Accords, Sékou Touré sent a warm message to de Gaulle in the hope of establishing normal relations. He received the curtest of replies. De Gaulle resisted all pressure from his advisers to rethink his position. In 1965 diplomatic relations between the two countries were broken off.[61] When it was suggested in 1967 that it might be in France's commercial interest to change the policy, de Gaulle fulminated against this 'unfortunate tendency to run after the Guineans' which he blamed on the Quai d'Orsay.[62] He never forgave Sékou Touré for the slight he had endured at Conakry in August 1958.

The relationship between France and her other former sub-Saharan colonies was in theory the responsibility of a new Ministry of Cooperation. This Ministry was often at odds with the Quai d'Orsay, which had its own

African Department. But both the Quai and the Ministry of Cooperation had to contend with de Gaulle's chief adviser on African affairs, Jacques Foccart. Thanks to his network of African contacts, dating back to RPF days, Foccart had been appointed Secretary General of the Community. After the Community's collapse, Foccart was made Secretary General for African and Madagascan Affairs, directly answerable to de Gaulle. Although his name hardly appears in de Gaulle's *Memoirs*, few figures in the Fifth Republic were as influential. He acquired a reputation as a sinister *éminence grise* lurking in the shadows – an impression accentuated by his nondescript appearance, somewhere between a provincial bank manager and Alfred Hitchcock. When photographed with de Gaulle Foccart is invariably at the side of the picture or in the background as if wanting to avoid the limelight.

Once a week, Foccart chaired a meeting between representatives of the Ministry of Cooperation and the Quai's African Department. His trump card when conflicts arose between them was his closeness to de Gaulle. One of his diary entries shows how his influence operated:

> The structure of the government concerning relations with Africa is so complicated . . . that I had to ring Couve that evening to communicate to him what the General had said on the subject of Central Africa and how I thought it should be interpreted, then telephoned Broglie, Charbonnel and Journiac.[63]

To the magic words 'what the General had said . . .' there was no answer. And Foccart knew what the General had said because every evening – unless he or de Gaulle were absent from Paris – they had a private meeting. Foccart's African Secretariat was housed in an *hôtel particulier* on the other side of the Seine from the Elysée, but he also had an office in the Elysée. His tête-à-tête with de Gaulle, starting at 7.10 p.m., was usually the General's last formal engagement of the day. It lasted half an hour, sometimes longer if de Gaulle was in the mood.

Foccart saw his mission as maintaining France's influence over her former African colonies by building up a network of reliable African client states whose leaders would defend French interests against any rival – the Soviet Union, the United States or Third World ideologues. Foccart viewed sub-Saharan Africa as France's backyard, which he controlled by a skilful mixture of carrot and stick. The independence of the former French colonies had usually been accompanied by secret agreements granting France privileged access to raw materials in return for providing financial aid, and if necessary military protection. Foccart, who relished the cloak-and-dagger world of the secret services, had good contacts in the French intelligence services as well as his own network of agents, many of them individuals he knew from his days in the Resistance. Foccart's other asset was his close personal relationship with African leaders – in some cases he was even godfather to their children. African leaders were free to ring him up at any time of the day or night. In France, they would be put up lavishly at the Château de Champs, and there was a special suite for them at the Hôtel Crillon in Paris. These visits would be topped off by an invitation to Foccart's own country house at Luzarches.[64] The highlight was an audience with the General himself.

The most ardently Francophile African leaders needed little persuasion to rally to Foccart's view of the world. President Fulbert Youlou of Congo had wanted to keep the 'Marseillaise' as the national anthem until told that this would be impolitic; President M'ba of Gabon had hoped that even after independence his country would remain a French *département*. The threat to French interests did not come from the leaders of the newly independent states but arose when these leaders were challenged by internal political opponents – as when a coup toppled Youlou in August 1963. Foccart viewed this as an alarming precedent because if African leaders lost confidence in French protection they might seek out patrons elsewhere. Thus when in February 1964 there was a coup against M'ba of Gabon – whose mineral reserves made it, in the words of one diplomat, one of the 'richest pieces of real estate of its size in the world' – Foccart with de Gaulle's approval acted fast.[65] French troops based in Senegal and the Central African Republic intervened at the cost of fifteen Gabonese and two French lives. M'ba was reinstated. Since it had been impossible to contact the Vice-President to ensure that he formally requested French intervention, an antedated letter was produced after the event. In the future, Foccart made sure that undated letters were always ready for such eventualities.

The French intervened militarily only as a last resort since Foccart wanted to avoid accusations of neo-colonialism. Usually he preferred to find ways of working pragmatically with the new authorities. When General Bokassa seized power in the Central African Republic in January 1966, Foccart quickly realized that he was no threat to France. The French Military Attaché reported that it was in France's interest to keep Bokassa in power 'as long as he remains reasonable'.[66] As for Youlou's successor in Gabon, the French indulged him for several years until de Gaulle decided his policies were becoming too anti-French: 'Let's put an end to this comedy and turn off the tap,' he told Foccart in 1966. A coup followed two years later.[67]

In Foccart's opinion, Quai d'Orsay diplomats did not have the appropriate frame of mind for the role he required of them. He preferred to work through former colonial administrators or loyal Gaullists. This was often the preference of the African leaders themselves. After he had been reinstated, M'ba himself was not happy with the new Ambassador, whom he saw as an excessively smooth Quai diplomat. He asked Foccart to 'send me a colonial administrator'. In M'ba's presence, Foccart explained to the new appointee that he was to 'respect the forms of independence' but not hesitate to act in the manner of a 'dynamic [colonial] commissioner'.[68]

Foccart kept a detailed journal of his daily meetings with de Gaulle, which he dictated every Sunday. Most memorialists of de Gaulle record his monologues and visionary disquisitions on history. But Foccart's journal is a more down-to-earth document in which he is as much a protagonist as the General. He arrived every evening armed with his voluminous dossiers and a clear sense of what he wanted to achieve. His assets were his unparalleled knowledge of the African scene, his elephantine memory and his extensive personal contacts. He would brief de Gaulle on which leader should be invited to Paris and what level of reception should be arranged; which leader should receive a letter of congratulations and which should receive a dedicated photograph; which French ambassador was doing a good job and which was not. Their discussions descended to the minutest details. One evening in October 1967 they debated what play President Soglo of Benin, who would shortly be arriving, should be taken to see at the Comédie-Française. Foccart thought that Feydeau was too trivial but de Gaulle for some reason vetoed Molière's *Malade imaginaire*. They compromised on *Cyrano*.[69]

Foccart had an intuitive sense of de Gaulle's tiniest shifts of mood – when he was tired, when he was relaxed, when he was preoccupied by other matters, when it was appropriate to raise a particular issue, when it might be better to wait. Sometimes, reading the situation wrongly, he would be treated to a tirade of abuse and beat a retreat. Usually the next day, de Gaulle, although never apologizing (something he found almost physically impossible), would be uncharacteristically warm to make up for his previous evening's temper. Foccart would press his case again, often successfully. He also knew how to play on de Gaulle's habitual suspicion of the Quai. If this did not work, he brought out his heavy artillery: the threat that the Americans were trying to get their hands on African mineral resources.[70] In relation to America, the tiniest incident could set de Gaulle off. Hearing that some American scientists had asked to be allowed into Polynesia to view an eclipse, he was immediately suspicious of their real motives: 'You must not give anything to the Americans on the spot; refuse them everything, even if they ask us for a box of matches.'[71] These sudden squalls would pass quickly, like de Gaulle's explosions against the British during the war, but they lasted long enough for Foccart to achieve his immediate aim. Threats from America were pure fantasy except when French reactions sometimes inadvertently created them. In Gabon the naive but well-meaning American Ambassador Charles Darlington, animated by no feelings of hostility towards France, found himself contacted by opponents of the regime who opposed the corruption, authoritarianism and megalomania of the President supported by France. This led to his being suspected of involvement in the coup against M'ba, about which he had known nothing. In his memoirs Darlington bitterly entitled his chapter on these events 'The Seamy Side of Grandeur'.[72]

De Gaulle did not wish to know every detail of Foccart's activities. He realized that Foccart's methods were unorthodox and it was implicit between them that, if things went wrong, Foccart would bear the consequences. After the Gabon intervention, Foccart told Peyrefitte: 'De Gaulle must never be in the front line for this kind of tough action. We must deal with them without telling him. We speak in his name and inform him when it is over. He can always disavow us when it is over.'[73] Sometimes there would be a raised eyebrow, as on the occasion when Foccart communicated the election results in the Cameroons. He noted: 'The General finds the 99.8 per cent a bit too much.'[74] After hearing of a failed dirty-tricks operation against Sékou Touré, de Gaulle pretended to be annoyed and then said: 'Pity you did not succeed.'[75] In March 1965, the deposed President Youlou escaped from prison thanks to a secret operation mounted by Foccart. After the event, Foccart briefed de Gaulle: 'He ought to have been surprised that I knew so many details ... but did not even bother to pretend that he was. His only comment was: "Good."'[76]

On some occasions de Gaulle had to be consulted in advance. In January 1965, Foccart informed him that M'ba was ill: '"Extraordinary, you seem to know everything." I told him that in this case luck had served me: M'ba's doctor had got in touch with my doctor ... The General smiled; I hope he believed me because it was true.'[77] The problem was to locate a successor for M'ba. Foccart had the constitution of Gabon rewritten so that the eventual transition would in formal terms be legal. He alighted upon M'ba's young *directeur de cabinet* Albert Bongo whom he thought could be groomed appropriately. Bongo was summoned to Paris for a kind of tutorial with de Gaulle to test if he was up to the job.[78] When M'ba died, the transition took place smoothly. For better or worse – usually worse – Bongo ruled Gabon for the next forty years (and his son still rules today).

Foccart organized numerous meetings between de Gaulle and visiting African leaders, with whom the General had a somewhat paternalistic relationship, dispensing advice and offering benediction. After de Gaulle had met President Apithy of Benin in September 1965, Foccart observed: 'The General treats these problems with the African Heads of State in a very direct way. Almost brutally. His prestige is so great ... that they come out of his office sometime a bit stiff but accepting from him what they would accept from no one else.'[79] After meeting President Tombalbaye of Chad in March 1965, de Gaulle told Foccart that he had 'made a lot of progress, he was doing his job well and he should be supported'.[80] President Ahidjo of Cameroon was always tongue-tied when meeting de Gaulle, who was therefore surprised when Foccart told him that he was normally loquacious.

Foccart's influence caused much annoyance at the Quai d'Orsay. Jean-Marie Soutou, Director of the African Department until being removed by Foccart, told the British Ambassador in 1968:

> In the all too frequent crises in francophone African countries, French Ambassadors would urge intervention to support the existing Government. De Gaulle would have to be consulted and often woken up. He would make some sibylline remark and then there would be fierce argument about what he meant while action suffered.[81]

This was not too far from the truth except that if de Gaulle was woken up and Foccart was not around, no one knew what to do – as during the coup against Youlou in 1963. Riots in the capital had broken out in mid-August, the depths of the French summer holidays. When Youlou, holed up in his palace, rang Paris, Pompidou was away on holiday and Foccart could not be contacted because he was on a fishing trip. Exceptionally the duty officer at the Elysée put the call through to Colombey where a startled de Gaulle (watching his two grandchildren play tennis) was called to the phone. He hated to be disturbed at Colombey. The transcript of the conversation reads:

> Youlou: My Palace is encircled . . . I think that in a few minutes I am going to have to shoot. I don't know. I would like you to give precise orders to the French army so as not to allow international Communism to take over.
>   De Gaulle: Could you repeat that please?

Taken completely unawares, and clearly not having a clue what to say, de Gaulle asked to be passed to the French Ambassador standing at Youlou's side. The Ambassador's advice was that it would be impossible for the French to intervene without significant loss of life and with no guarantee of success. De Gaulle told Youlou there was nothing he could do.

> De G: There is nothing more for you to do than give yourself over to our military forces for your personal security.
>   F: I am remaining in my Palace, *mon Général.*
>   De G: I do not see how this will help you.
>   F: I have asked for armoured vehicles not to shoot but just disperse the crowd.

De G: Yes, but from what I am told one cannot disperse without shooting, and politically France cannot take responsibility for that.[82]

Youlou was forced from power. On his return from fishing, Foccart was furious about the advice de Gaulle had been given – a typical example in his view of Quai d'Orsay pusillanimity – and was convinced Youlou could have been saved.

Officials at the Quai were wrong to see Foccart as de Gaulle's evil genius, 'dripping his poison drop by drop' and guilty of 'manipulation of an old man' (in Soutou's words) in pursuit of a reactionary policy at odds with the noble aims of cooperation proclaimed by de Gaulle.[83] De Gaulle had few illusions about decolonization. As he remarked privately in 1962:

> I know that decolonization is disastrous. That most of the Africans are hardly at the stage of our Middle Ages. That they are attracted by cities like mosquitoes by lamps while the bush will return to its savagery. That they are again going to experience tribal wars, witchcraft, cannibalism. That fifteen years more of control by us would have allowed them to modernize their agriculture, give them better infrastructures, completely eradicated leprosy ... But what can I do about it? The Americans and Russians think they have a vocation to free the colonized populations and are outbidding each other to do so. That is the only thing they have in common. The two superpowers claim to be two anti-imperialists while in fact they are the last two imperialisms.[84]

De Gaulle's 'Fashoda complex', as for many other Frenchmen of his generation, was never far below the surface. As he said to Jean Charbonnel, who took over the Cooperation post in 1966: 'If France is not just an annexe of the Foreign Office it is thanks to Africa.'[85] Foccart was the instrument of that policy; he was serving de Gaulle, not manipulating him. Foccart worshipped de Gaulle; de Gaulle trusted Foccart. The relationship worked because in the end they were pursuing the same objectives. De Gaulle translated the base metal of Foccart's dirty tricks into rhetorical gold, but like the cynically conservative hero of Lampedusa's novel *The Leopard*, they agreed on the essential: in Africa everything had to change so that everything could stay the same.

24
Modernizing Monarch, 1959–1964

'A KIND OF POPULAR MONARCHY'

A month after his election as President of the Republic, de Gaulle embarked on a four-day visit to the south-west of France (14–17 February 1959); two months later, he was in Burgundy for four days (16–19 April), and a month after that he toured four *départements* in the centre of France (7–15 May). This gruelling schedule of regional visits, renewing a tradition he had started after the Liberation, became a ritual of his Presidency. Presidents of the Third and Fourth Republic had also carried out such tours – they had little else to keep them occupied – but not with such intensity. De Gaulle's two immediate predecessors, Coty and Auriol, usually scheduled about seven stops on each visit; de Gaulle's average was nearer forty. By June 1962, he had carried out nineteen tours and visited sixty-seven *départements*; by the time he left office in 1969 he had visited every *département* and made thirty-one regional tours.[1]

The ritual was invariable. In each town, after a greeting from the Mayor, de Gaulle would reply with a few gracious words paying homage to the virtues of the locality he found himself in. He usually ended with a stock formula: 'I want to say to X [Insert name of the place] what a comforting memory, what confidence in the unity and the destiny of the country I take away from my too short visit to X. Long live X! Long live the Republic, Long live France!' The more banal the speech, the more frenetic the applause.[2] De Gaulle was a master of these exercises in empty rhetoric. Some of them became legendary: 'I salute Fécamp, a seaport which wants to remain a seaport and will remain one.' Often de Gaulle added a personal touch. In Dunkirk: 'When I was a boy, I used to go to the Mass here at the Church of St Eloi near by. To pay for the chair I would give a sou and I was given back 2 centimes.' In Vichy: 'I cannot but think that my presence here has a rather special character given past events that you will know about.' In larger cities, his speech would be longer and offered the chance to float an idea for a forthcoming policy announcement.[3]

The style of de Gaulle's regional visits was different from that of his predecessors. In the Third and Fourth Republics, the President would usually meet local dignitaries before being presented formally to some representative figures – a worker, a pensioner, a farmer and so on. But the public would be kept at a distance. De Gaulle, on the other hand, would throw himself into the crowd shaking hands, kissing, embracing – and allowing himself to be touched, kissed, embraced. A *Le Monde* journalist who spent years studying de Gaulle wrote an amusing account of these *bains de foule*:

> To say that he mixes with the crowd is an understatement: he plunges into it, wallows in it. One can keep track of him not so much because of his height, but because he is the virtual centre of a whirlwind. Disappearing in one spot, he pops up in another for a moment, then is lost to sight again for a long, underwater stretch, only to surface like a diver at the other side of the street . . . He has been seen to emerge with three buttons missing, uniform torn, hands scratched . . . but eyes sparkling with pleasure, looking delighted to be alive.[4]

De Gaulle saw this as the embodiment of his communion with France and an opportunity for the 'people' to gather around their 'guide'. The motivations of those who turned out to cheer were of course mixed, ranging from veneration to simple curiosity. But the visits were an important moment in the history of each local community. After his resignation in 1969, one of the tens of thousands of letters received by the Elysée was from an inhabitant of Douai who remembered the man 'who shook my hand when I was ten years old during his visit to the city'.[5] The Prefect of the Haut-Rhin wrote to the Elysée after de Gaulle's visit in November 1959 that the 'almost delirious enthusiasm' of the crowds had been 'exceptional' and 'much greater than initially predicted'.[6] This was what the government wanted to hear, but even the Communist press, always inciting its readers to boycott these occasions, paid a kind of involuntary homage to their success:

> What is most striking about the demonstrations organized on these occasions is the personal and quasi-mystical character of the ceremonies in towns and villages. General de Gaulle does not travel round France as a President of the Republic. He is the king meeting his subjects, receiving their homage and preaching the good word . . . An exercise of mass infantilization.[7]

The monarchical comparison was made by others who were not hostile to de Gaulle. A minister accompanying him on one trip could never get out of his mind the 'image of this woman who held her baby above the heads of the crowd, begging the General to touch it; perhaps she was rediscovering that tradition which accorded to the kings of France the power to cure cripples.'[8] Peyrefitte, who often accompanied de Gaulle in his capacity as Minister of Information, was struck by the number of times he would hear someone in the crowd cry out with a kind of awe 'he touched me' or 'he saw me'. Peyrefitte also saw echoes of monarchy: 'Perhaps the success of his visits comes from the fact that de Gaulle, incarnating lost legitimacy, has removed from the French the obscure feeling of guilt at having destroyed the legitimacy of the *ancien régime*.'[9]

France's monarchical past was often in de Gaulle's mind. After returning to power, he continued occasionally to receive the Comte de Paris. At a

The satirical weekly magazine *Le Canard enchaîné* ran a regular column in the style of St Simon depicting de Gaulle as a reincarnation of the Sun King.

meeting in February 1961, he told him: 'I think that France is gently returning to its old and traditional monarchy, and if she does not reach the goal,
it will be communism and the end.' A year later, he was saying that since
he was too 'old' and 'tired' to stand for re-election, the Count should prepare to succeed him. Four years later, in January 1966, having surmounted
his 'tiredness' and been re-elected, de Gaulle was less encouraging: 'Personally I would have liked the monarchy, you know my views about this.
You are the king ... But I don't think it is possible.'[10] Although he enjoyed
flattering and teasing his credulous interlocutor, this little comedy contained a grain of genuine romantic nostalgia, and a tinge of regret. Peyrefitte,
who tried to find out what de Gaulle really thought about the pretender,
was told 'he encapsulates in his person the forty kings who made France',
even if de Gaulle also recognized that 'he no longer corresponds to this
century.'[11] De Gaulle wrote to his son Philippe in 1961 that he himself had
created a 'kind of popular monarchy which is the only system compatible
with the character and perils of our epoch'.[12]

De Gaulle believed that the 'popular monarchy' had 'instituted a new
legitimacy which makes a link to the legitimacy interrupted by the Revolution'.[13] In that way he had achieved the ambition outlined to Macmillan in
1943. 'Legitimacy' was a key notion for de Gaulle. Although he saw it as
deriving from the 'sovereign people', in his own case there was also his historical role. In the speech he made during Barricades Week he invoked the
'legitimacy I have incarnated for 20 years'. The extraordinary implication
of this remark was not just that Pétain had never been legitimate but nor
had any government between 1946 and 1958. In power or out of power,
elected or unelected, de Gaulle was France's only 'legitimate' leader.[14]

In his 'desert' years, de Gaulle wrote up that fiction in his *Memoirs*; once
in power, he set out to embody it in the official calendar of his new Republic. One way of doing this was to make the anniversary of 18 June a major
event. After de Gaulle's resignation in 1946, the government had invited
him to attend a ceremony that year to commemorate 18 June at the Arc
de Triomphe. But de Gaulle refused to attend. Instead he paid his respects
alone at the fortress of Mont-Valérien a few kilometres to the west of Paris
where during the occupation over a thousand resisters had been shot by
the Germans. It was at Mont-Valérien that on 11 November 1945 – the
anniversary of Armistice Day – de Gaulle's provisional government had
chosen to organize a ceremony to commemorate the war. The bodies of
fifteen French fighters were solemnly transferred to Mont-Valérien in a
conscious echo of the burial of the Unknown Soldier at the Arc de Triomphe in 1920. They included soldiers who had fought in 1940, members of
the Free French who had fought in the colonies and in the armies of the

Liberation, and also two resisters. This gave a distinctly Gaullist identity to a site that during the Occupation had essentially been associated with the internal Resistance. It downgraded the specificity of the Resistance to support de Gaulle's argument that what had happened between 1940 and 1944 should be read as the last stage of a thirty-year war against Germany. De Gaulle's decision to boycott the official 18 June ceremony at the Arc de Triomphe in 1946 and instead attend his own private ceremony at Mont-Valérien was another stage in the appropriation of that space by Gaullism. In future years, celebrating 18 June at the Arc de Triomphe without the presence of de Gaulle seemed increasingly problematic and the date lost its aura. Instead 18 June became almost an intimate family ceremony of Free French loyalists, organized by the Order of the Liberation at Mont-Valérien. For Gaullist loyalists this was a mute reproach to the governments in power, but no one else really noticed.[15]

All this changed after de Gaulle's return to power. In 1959, the ceremony at Mont-Valérien was broadcast live on television. Prefects were instructed that the government wished to give the event 'the maximum impact and solemnity'. De Gaulle also ordered the construction at Mont-Valérien of a memorial to the Free French to replace the temporary crypt that had been installed there after the Liberation. This completed the confiscation of this space of Resistance martyrdom to the benefit of the memory of the Free French. The new monument – a huge Cross of Lorraine at the entry to the crypt – was unveiled for the twentieth anniversary of 18 June in 1960. This was now an important date in France's ceremonial calendar, although de Gaulle would not go as far as to adopt Malraux's suggestion that it should be a national holiday. Even so the 18 June ceremony continued to have a slightly hybrid character: it was organized not by the government but by the Order of the Liberation. It was always kept short. De Gaulle would visit the crypt alone, review the veterans who were present and then leave in silence. This sobriety conferred an almost sacred character on the occasion.[16]

The culmination of this mythologization of de Gaulle's role in the war was a solemn ceremony in January 1964 to transfer the ashes of Jean Moulin to the Panthéon. Despite his major role in the Resistance, Moulin was a surprisingly forgotten figure after 1945, partly because many Resistance leaders still remained bitter about his actions on de Gaulle's behalf. Moulin was no longer around to put his side of the story. In his *Memoirs* de Gaulle had downplayed the role of the Resistance and given Moulin a starring role. By now choosing to celebrate Moulin, he harnessed the Resistance to his purposes for a second time. Choosing the route of 'Panthéonization' also carried a contemporary political message. The Panthéon, originally a church, had been transformed into a secular mausoleum during the Revolution. Associated with France's republican history, it had become a bit of a memorial backwater and no one had been 'Panthéonized' since Louis Braille in 1952. At a time when the left accused de Gaulle of not being a proper republican, it did his reputation no harm to bring the Panthéon back to the centre of French consciousness and link himself to it.

The ceremony was presided over by André Malraux, Minister of Culture. Malraux had been disappointed not to receive any important ministerial portfolio after 1958. The newly created Ministry of Culture, which he headed during de Gaulle's ten years in power, was his consolation prize. At meetings of the Council of Ministers he enjoyed the privilege of sitting directly on the General's right. He was incandescent with joy when in 1970 he read the careful phrase that de Gaulle devoted to him in his *Memoirs*: 'On my right, I had and would always have André Malraux. Owing to the presence at my side of this friend of genius ... I knew that in any debate, when the subject was serious, his dazzling talent would help to dissipate the shadows.'[17] Given the famed obscurity of many of Malraux's pronouncements, this may have been a sly joke. On the other hand, Malraux was a surprisingly effective minister. He cleaned up many historical monuments in Paris, organized the elaborate restoration of the Grand Trianon and established regional 'Maisons de Culture' to bring French high culture to the provinces. De Gaulle also used Malraux as a roving cultural ambassador – a sort of cultural *force de frappe* – across the globe where he hypnotized and baffled his interlocutors without committing de Gaulle to anything.

Another of Malraux's roles was to be the Bossuet of the Fifth Republic, the regime's public orator, celebrating historical figures like Joan of Arc and delivering funeral orations for personalities like Georges Braque and Le Corbusier. No performance achieved the fame of his oration for Jean Moulin. On a freezing winter's day, in the presence of de Gaulle and his entire government, the remains of Moulin were transported to the Panthéon. The highlight of the ceremony was Malraux's speech, delivered in a trembling voice at the foot of an enormous catafalque. His final incantation, to the accompaniment of the rhythmic drums of the Garde Républicaine, was especially haunting:

> Enter here Jean Moulin with your terrible cortège of shadows ... Here is the funeral march of ashes. Alongside those of Carnot with the soldiers of Year II, those of Victor Hugo with *Les Misérables*, those of Jaurès watched over by justice, let them rest with their long cortège of disfigured shadows. Today, youth of France, think of this man as you would have reached out your hand

to his poor battered face on its last day, the lips that did not speak; on that day it was the face of France.

Malraux's rhetoric also contained a history lesson. The speech argued that Moulin had forged an army out of the dispersed forces of the Resistance. Hence the reference to Carnot, who had created the armies of the Revolution in 1793 (it was also a rebuke to those attacking de Gaulle as a Bonapartist). Moulin's crowning achievement for Malraux was 'perhaps to affirm what has since become known as Gaullism. It was certainly to proclaim the survival of France.' This was a simple syllogism: without de Gaulle, acting through Moulin, there would have been no Resistance; and since the Resistance equalled Gaullism, and Gaullism equalled France, there would have been no France. Few resisters would have agreed – but they did not have the floor.[18]

TELEVISION STAR

The 'Panthéonization' of Moulin was broadcast live on television – a striking example of television's role in consolidating de Gaulle's power.[19] Before 1958, television had played little part in French politics. The first televised event to receive public attention in France – even if few people yet owned a television – was the coronation of Elizabeth II in June 1953. This aroused almost as much interest in France as in Britain since the French did not yet have their King. But there were so few transmitters in France that the broadcast reached only Paris and Lille. And some Alsatians bought German sets to receive the broadcasts from Germany where there were more transmitters. The first French political event to be televised was the election of President Coty in December of the same year. This proved such a protracted shambles that it was decided to suspend broadcasting after six days because it was giving such a bad impression of French politics.

De Gaulle came to power at the moment when the ownership of televisions in France was set to increase significantly. In 1958, only 7 per cent of households possessed a television set. By 1964 the figure had risen to 39 per cent; by 1968, to 62 per cent. De Gaulle was remarkably quick to grasp the potential of television. Created by the radio between 1940 and 1944, he ruled through television after 1958. He remarked that, once the Algerian crisis was over, the politicians would try to eliminate him as they had done after the Liberation – but 'in 1946 I did not have television'. He was, in the words of one historian, the first politician in the world 'totally to integrate television into his communication strategy'.[20]

De Gaulle's first televised speech on 13 June 1958 was not a success. He refused to wear make-up, and every wrinkle and blemish was visible. Reading through thick glasses, he looked down at his script rather than at the camera. This performance was watched with appalled incredulity by the publicity magnate Marcel Bleustein-Blanchet, a former member of the Free French. Contacting the Elysée to express his concern, he was startled to receive a summons from de Gaulle in person. De Gaulle went straight to the point: 'It seems I was bad on television.' 'Very bad, General' was the response.[21] De Gaulle quickly learnt his lesson. For his second appearance, on 27 June, he had learnt his text. No longer wearing glasses, he looked directly at the camera. He also started taking lessons from an actor at the Comédie-Française and hired the services of France's leading make-up artist Charles Koubesserian (who also worked for Brigitte Bardot).[22]

De Gaulle became a brilliant performer. During the Algerian War, between 1958 and 1962, he addressed the nation thirty-one times on television. In one sense the French lived the conflict through de Gaulle on television. His two most spectacular interventions were those masterpieces of performative rhetoric during Barricades Week and the abortive putsch in April 1961. One of his most effective rhetorical tricks was to turn each speech into a personal encounter between the French and himself: '*Françaises, Français, aidez-moi*,' 'you can see the importance of the "yes" that I ask from each and every one of you,' 'So here we are together once again . . .' He ended his short speech calling for a 'yes' vote in the referendum on Algeria in January 1961: 'I need, yes I need, to know what is in your minds and hearts. That is why I turn to you over and above all intermediaries. In truth – and who does not know this? – this is an affair between every one of you and me.'[23]

De Gaulle was also a master at expressing ideas in a simple way. Before a speech on 14 June 1960, his advisers prepared for him a mass of complex data on the economy.[24] De Gaulle turned these into a speech beginning: 'Once upon a time there was an old country weighed down by habits and caution. Having been in the past the most populous, the richest, the most powerful of the countries on the world stage, after suffering many misfortunes, it turned in on itself.' De Gaulle had a clear idea of what he was trying to do in these speeches: 'You need to speak to them like children and yet at the same time you must get to the bottom of things.'[25] Both these elements were in evidence: he had a genius for simplification (when he was not deploying his equal genius for obscurity), but at the same time he always had something to say. As during his wartime speeches, de Gaulle's rhetoric invariably contained an argument and an appeal to reason.

After the Algerian War, de Gaulle's television interventions became less frequent – twenty-two between 1963 and 1969 – and the context was less dramatic. But de Gaulle was always ready to warn the French that the 'abyss' was never far away if they did not follow him to the 'summits'. Another favourite metaphor was the stormy sea where the French needed a 'guide' and 'captain' to steer them to safer waters. In its more rhetorical flights the style lent itself to parody, and one anti-Gaullist journalist wrote a brilliant pamphlet in 1959 mocking the 'Style of the General'.[26] Not everyone could have carried off the following lines but de Gaulle just about managed it: 'The road is hard but beautiful! The objective is difficult but how great it is! Let us start the journey! The departure has sounded.'[27] De Gaulle was not just a great rhetorician but also a brilliant visual showman. He would bang the table, point at the camera, stretch out his arms, shrug his shoulders, as well as deploying a mesmerizing repertoire of facial expressions. But he had thought carefully about the art of performance and the need not to overdo the histrionics: 'For this seventy-year-old, seated alone, behind a table under the implacable lights, the aim was to appear animated and spontaneous enough to catch people's attention, without excessive gestures or pulling faces inappropriately.'[28]

De Gaulle was fascinated by the possibilities of television, not just as a performer but as a viewer. His evening meetings with Foccart always ended before 8 p.m. so that he could hurry back to his private apartment to catch

De Gaulle the television performer through the eys of the *Le Canard enchaîné*.

the evening news. He watched other programmes as well and would bombard Peyrefitte with suggestions as to how television programmes could be made more lively (he thought there should be fewer programmes about fashion). This interest in television made de Gaulle a politician in advance of his time. Debré hardly watched television and was too hectoring to be effective on the small screen; Pompidou did not even own a television when he became premier and listened to de Gaulle on the radio.[29]

De Gaulle's mastery of television was helped by the absence of competition. French television was tightly controlled – there was only one channel until 1964 – and opposition politicians rarely appeared on it. For de Gaulle this was sweet revenge as he had been banned from the radio after 1946. Since these were the early days of the new medium, it fell to de Gaulle's government to organize the relationship between broadcasters and the government. In 1963, Peyrefitte established a daily meeting between government representatives and television news programmers who would receive 'guidance'. All de Gaulle's provincial tours were covered at length, with cameras managing to show large crowds even when numbers were sparse. A visit to Toulouse in February 1959 took up twenty of the twenty-five minutes of the next day's news bulletin, with close-ups of the spectators' exultant faces.[30] The opposition press mocked this kind of coverage, but de Gaulle was not perturbed. He translated the impact of his visits into his idiom: 'The desired effect is attained since the people have lifted up their heads and looked to the summits.'[31] One should not exaggerate the degree of state control. France was not the Soviet Union, and the television extensively covered a prolonged miners' strike in 1963.[32]

When Peyrefitte argued that a more liberal approach would be more effective, de Gaulle gave no quarter: 'Liberal, liberal, you call liberal someone who gives up their power to others to exercise it in their place . . . Your role is not to relax your hold on power but to hold on to it.'[33] De Gaulle was also obsessed by the idea that the press, especially Le Monde – which he liked to dub L'Immonde (The Filth) – was consistently hostile to him, one of the 'feudalities' against which he was in perpetual struggle. For this reason, he considered it fair game that he had his own means of communication. While neutral observers saw television as a sycophantic tool of government, de Gaulle inundated Peyrefitte with furious notes criticizing 'your radio and your television' for negative reporting. In his view, the television always showed too much rain, too many strikes, too many reports of people complaining.[34] To one of his press advisers he wrote: 'I will not accept that the Radio-Television is put at the disposal of a critic, or an author, or a politician, who takes de Gaulle as their subject without having given my consent.'[35] Occasionally television journalists tried to mutiny against the tight leash on which they were kept. Two days before the referendum of October 1962, one television journalist's report was doctored by his superiors. His colleagues went on strike in protest, and that night the television news was replaced by pictures of a lily pond with musical accompaniment. This does not seem to have affected the result of the vote.

As well as broadcasting de Gaulle's addresses to the nation, and covering his provincial tours, television also broadcast in their entirety his biannual press conferences that could last up to two hours. De Gaulle had honed the art of the press conference during the war, and then continued to deliver them regularly during the RPF years. In 1947 he outlined his philosophy of these occasions to Claude Guy:

> If journalists come each time it is because they know what to expect [à quoi s'en tenir]. They know that there will be 'sport' ... The immense 'fun' [drôlerie] of it all ... One can guess what questions are going to be asked in advance. The important thing is to work out a text synthesizing the answers I want to make. Then either I am asked the questions I want and I reply; or they do not and I deviate the conversation on to the ground that I have chosen in advance. Or they ask a question I do not want to answer and in that case I sidetrack to another answer ... What matters above all is to prepare some devastating answer to knock out the assailant and cool off any desire they have to attack again.[36]

Once de Gaulle was President he was able to control these occasions even more tightly with a much larger captive audience. It was Eisenhower who first introduced cameras into a press conference in January 1958. But de Gaulle's press conferences – dubbed by some 'conférences [the French word for "lecture"] to the press' – could not have been more different from Eisenhower's informal style. They were held in the grand Salle des Fêtes of the Elysée Palace. Stifling in the heat of the bright television lights, some 800 journalists and many foreign diplomats crammed into rows of seats facing a stage.[37] On the stage was a single table at which de Gaulle would sit. A few minutes before his arrival, his ministers trooped in and took their places dutifully to the left of the stage; the other side was reserved for de Gaulle's Elysée advisers. At precisely 3.00 p.m. de Gaulle would walk on to the stage from behind a curtain and everyone would stand up. He always began with an introduction and then took questions, which he grouped into themes before answering any of them. This was a purely formal exercise since he knew in advance exactly what he was planning to say. The entire event was fully scripted. Jacques Fauvet of Le Monde commented in 1966 that the journalists present were witnesses to the questions de

16 *mai* 1961

— Il me semble avoir entendu, au fond de la salle, quelqu'un
ne pas me poser la question à laquelle je vais répondre
maintenant.

Gaulle was asking himself.[38] A cartoon in *Le Figaro* made the point effectively: de Gaulle, looking into the distance, says, 'I think I heard at the back
someone not ask me the question to which I am now going to reply.'

De Gaulle spent several days locked away preparing these conferences.
He delivered his text from memory over two hours. Since he was not reading, he was able to act out his performance with great panache, raising and
lowering the pitch of his voice, banging the table, stretching out his arms,
shrugging his shoulders and so on. His comedic talents were inexhaustible.
Sometimes his own ministers would hear about a policy for the first time
but usually these were not occasions for policy announcements but rather
opportunities for de Gaulle to deliver a lecture conveying his thoughts on
the world: a long disquisition on Chinese history in January 1964, a long
lecture on the international monetary system in February 1965. Raymond
Aron described them as a 'politico-historical high-wire act . . . a work of
art where the orator, flying up above the planet, recalls the past and throws
a few rays of light into the future'.[39] Although the events were scripted,
occasionally a questioner would get in under the net. This allowed de
Gaulle to deploy his impressive powers of repartee: one journalist who
managed to slip in a question asking why de Gaulle had been slow to deal

with a political scandal that was attracting much press attention (see p. 694 below) was crushed with the words: 'Put it down to my inexperience.'

De Gaulle's different forms of public interventions – the speeches during his regional visits, his television addresses and his press conferences – were each different in style but they were all a one-way conversation with the French, operating on his terms. He explained what he wanted to explain, left mysterious what he wanted to be mysterious. Secrecy was as much part of de Gaulle's style of government as loquacity. As Raymond Aron observed after one press conference: 'Some readers have asked me for my views of General de Gaulle's last press conference . . . I will endeavour to respond to their curiosity but must first remind them of the rules by which the remarks of the Head of State must be interpreted, rules as subtle as those needed to interpret ancient manuscripts.'[40] After attending his first Cabinet meeting in his capacity as Minister of Information, Peyrefitte prepared a communiqué for the press. Thereupon de Gaulle massacred this document, telling him that 'the idea is that as little as possible is known'. For Peyrefitte's text he substituted one beginning: 'The Minister of Foreign Affairs spoke on the international situation; the Minister of Algeria spoke on Algeria, and so on.'[41] After other occasions of this kind, Peyrefitte managed to persuade de Gaulle that obsessive secrecy was counter-productive and that it would be more useful to offer the press some morsels of information. De Gaulle would not give too much ground. His view of the relationship between 'leader' and people remained, as it had always been, unashamedly elitist. As he once remarked in the RPF period to Mauriac, in the purest style of Gustave Le Bon: 'The people are difficult to know, and difficult to manage . . . They want to be led, but do not want to give their consent to whoever wants to lead them. They want to be taken but refuse to give themselves.'[42]

It was the style of de Gaulle's rule as much as the substance of his policies that offended the left. This is conveyed by the ferociously anti-Gaullist editorials of Jean-Jacques Servan-Schreiber, editor of the influential centre-left magazine L'Express:

> 26 March 1959: We are reduced to interpreting a sphinx. One feels ashamed at being reduced, politically, to the status of object, a kind of larvae.
>
> 29 October 1959: For each of us this man is an enigma. There is not a discussion, a conversation, an analysis, a prediction which does not turn finally around this sole and unique subject of French politics: what does de Gaulle think? What is de Gaulle going to do?
>
> 2 June 1960: We are all Gaullists. That is to say spectators. Our compass points are de Gaulle's speeches, our themes of discussion or reflections are

his *bons mots* ... We are, whether or not we admit it, determined by this fundamental image: de Gaulle is France ... We are forced to watch this unsurpassed
actor and then to comment upon his performance endlessly among ourselves.

27 September 1962: 'If Bonaparte was the inventor of the first modern
coup d'état, de Gaulle is the first artisan of the electronic *coup d'état* ...
Through the television de Gaulle and his decisions penetrate at a stroke into
households and minds, destroy our convictions, crush our café discussions.[43]

Servan-Schreiber's anti-Gaullism was extreme but this makes his comments
all the more telling. They were an inverted tribute to de Gaulle's hypnotic
powers and his success in occupying the entire space of French politics.
Another left-wing intellectual, less viscerally hostile to de Gaulle than
Servan-Schreiber, the young historian Michel Winock, expressed the same
dilemma when pondering how to vote in the referendum of October 1962:

To vote 'no' is to vote for the departure of the Magician; to prefer the
unknown, to opt for difficulties, perhaps for the worst – but can we be sure?
The worst seems to me this apathy of the masses who have abdicated everything into the hands of this anachronistic General. My 'no' is anarchic, I fully
realize it ... but I can't resign myself to the rule of this grandiose illusionist.[44]

What made de Gaulle's dominance possible was not just his brilliance as
communicator, and his control over television, but also the discrediting of
the political elites of the Fourth Republic and the implosion of the parties
that had dominated French politics since 1945. The only survivor of this
shipwreck was the Communist Party, but many of its members nonetheless
voted 'yes' in de Gaulle's referenda. These developments led to much commentary in the early 1960s about the 'depoliticization' of French society.[45]
Political scientists and journalists saw this as a worrying development – but
not the Gaullists. Michel Debré – whose conception of politics was in many
respects different from de Gaulle's – embraced the notion of depoliticization in his first appearance before parliament as Prime Minister:

Individuals want to lead their daily life; they are absorbed by their personal
problems and those of their families ... It is good that this is the case ...
The ordinary citizen, a real democrat, constructs for himself in silence a
judgement on the government of his country, and when consulted, at regular
intervals, for the election of a deputy, for example, expresses his agreement
or disagreement. After which, as is normal and healthy, he returns to his
preoccupations.[46]

The term 'depoliticization' might seem curious for a period of such intense
conflict over Algeria. But apart from the highly mobilized minorities on

each side, there was a palpable lassitude about politics at this time. What is striking about an event even as dramatic as the crisis of May 1958 is how disengaged the population seemed to be. There was more excitement a month later about the World Cup, where France reached the semi-final for the first time. One of the complaints of the more engaged proponents of Algérie française was that, instead of offering the French a noble cause to defend in Algeria, de Gaulle was betraying his own vision of grandeur: a civilization of heroism was being replaced by one of fridges.[47] There was something in this. Exhausted by war, sickened by the political merry-go-round of the Fourth Republic and keen to profit from the material benefits offered by economic growth, the majority of the French were – for the moment at least – ready to enjoy their fridges, their televisions, their washing machines and their holidays, live their heroism vicariously through de Gaulle and allow him to govern as he wished.

DE GAULLE AT WORK

The centre of power under de Gaulle was the Elysée Palace, which had been the official residence of French presidents since 1871. Originally an eighteenth-century mansion belonging to Madame de Pompadour, it was where Napoleon had taken residence during the Hundred Days. He had also signed his final abdication there. In popular folklore the Elysée was famous for the fact that President Félix Faure had expired there in 1899 in the arms of his mistress – 'in full exercise of his functions', as the official communiqué put it. 'One might have wished for better' was de Gaulle's comment on these historical associations.[48] The Elysée was also situated in a quarter of Paris with which he felt no affinity: 'That of money, of the well-to-do, of luxury stores. There is nothing to recall our great glories, nor the people.' It was so different from the austere grandeur of the seventh arrondissement where de Gaulle had been brought up. He toyed with the idea of moving the Presidency to the Château de Vincennes in eastern Paris, but he was easily talked out of this impracticable notion.[49]

De Gaulle put up with the Elysée but treated it like a soldier posted to a garrison. It was never his home. Vincent Auriol had commissioned the well-known interior designers André Arbus and Jules Leleu to modernize the decor of the Elysée but the frugal de Gaulle, happy to spend state money on the Trianon in order to impress foreign dignitaries, was otherwise obsessive about not wasting public money, especially on himself.[50] After a few years, his aide de camp Bonneval was so appalled by the 'dilapidation' of the armchair in the General's office that he intervened to insist on the ordering of a new set of Louis XV or Directory furniture.[51] Because the new importance of the Presidential role meant a large increase in the personnel working at the Elysée, the former private apartments diminished in size. What had been the dining room of the Auriols now became the meeting place of the Council of Ministers. In what remained of the small private apartments – a bedroom, two modest sitting rooms and a small dining room – de Gaulle made no changes except to install a television and a separate electricity meter so that he could pay for his personal consumption out of his own pocket. He also reinstated (at personal expense) a chapel that Auriol had transformed into offices. This meant that if in Paris at weekends he could attend Mass in private. When in 1974 Valéry Giscard d'Estaing, the newly elected President, decided that he too would live in the Palace (de Gaulle's immediate successor Pompidou chose not to), his wife was shocked by the dowdiness of the furnishings.[52]

De Gaulle set up his office on the first floor overlooking the garden. Never an early riser, he would arrive from his private apartments at around 9.00. As throughout his life, he followed a meticulously regular routine starting with a reading of the French press, which was guaranteed to work him up into a rage; he also skimmed the *Daily Telegraph*, the *Frankfurter Allgemeine Zeitung* and the *New York Herald Tribune*.[53] The rest of the morning was spent working through diplomatic telegrams, prefects' reports and briefing papers for afternoon meetings. Most documents would be annotated in his barely legible hand. He never used the telephone unless it was unavoidable. When Lyndon Johnson suggested that the two presidents should have regular telephone contact, de Gaulle responded: 'One can write, one can telephone, but do you believe that the telephone can bring that human contact you are talking about?'[54] Unless there was an official reception, lunch took place at the Elysée with a few advisers or specially invited guests. De Gaulle was so obsessive about punctuality that anyone arriving even one minute late might find their place had been removed from the table. Official audiences were scheduled in the afternoon.

De Gaulle's offices were directly connected with those of his *directeur de cabinet* and the Secretary General of the Elysée. The former was in charge of the General's relations with 'the nation' – organizing his visits around the country or his 'audiences' – and the latter was in charge of all relations with 'the state' – that is to say with the Prime Minister (situated across the river at the Hôtel Matignon) and all the other government ministers. Along with the *directeur* of his military *cabinet* and the Secretary General for African Affairs (Foccart), these were known as the 'big four'. Each had a twenty-minute meeting with de Gaulle at the end of the day.

The most important were Foccart (as we have seen) and the Secretary General. The latter had regular access to de Gaulle and might see him several times a day.

The first Secretary General was Geoffroy de Courcel between 1958 and 1962; and the second Etienne Burin des Roziers between 1962 and 1967. Both of them had been with de Gaulle during the war. This made both of them 'historic' Gaullists, although neither had joined the RPF, something the General clearly did not hold against them. But it would be wrong to think that de Gaulle surrounded himself only with former 'companions'. Jobs were found for other historic Gaullists like Guichard and Lefranc, but over time the proportion of those with Gaullist backgrounds working at the Elysée diminished. Bernard Tricot, who became the third Elysée Secretary General in 1967, had no Gaullist past. He was appointed because de Gaulle, having used him as an adviser during the Algerian War, had come to appreciate his competence and discretion.

The Secretariat and the *cabinets* were staffed also by 'technical advisers' (*conseillers techniques* and *chargés de mission*) with specific areas of expertise (economy, education, diplomacy, the press). Most of these advisers were in post for about four years before they moved on. This group was popularly dubbed the 'entourage', but de Gaulle preferred to call them the *Maison* (Household). Under Coty the *Maison* had numbered about ten; under de Gaulle it was usually around forty-five. They were mostly young civil servants who had graduated from one of the Grandes Ecoles. Over the years there was an increasing proportion of graduates (11 per cent in 1959 and 20 per cent in 1966) from the Ecole Nationale d'Administration (ENA), that training school for civil servants set up by de Gaulle's government at the Liberation. Few *conseillers* had any previous Gaullist affiliations and they were recruited for their technical competence. Since the first two secretary generals were themselves products of the French diplomatic corps, there was a cultural homogeneity about the entire Household. Its guiding ethos was that of service to the state, a principle to which, as we have seen, de Gaulle ascribed almost sacred status. Although suspicious of the conformity of France's administrative elites, the General simultaneously felt a kind of veneration for them. He was indifferent to the political backgrounds of those who served him. The criterion was expertise, loyalty and discretion: Gaullist *compagnonage* was never political cronyism.

Although the Elysée *conseillers* were always presented to de Gaulle on appointment – and usually subjected to a quick grilling so that he was satisfied about their competence – they rarely saw him unless summoned to brief him personally on a particular issue. Otherwise their role was to draft regular notes and syntheses, ideally not more than two pages. These were sent to the Secretary General who selected which ones should be passed on to de Gaulle. Often the *conseillers* had no idea what happened to their efforts except when sometimes a note was returned with the words at the top '*Vu par le Général*' or stamped with a little Cross of Lorraine. Sometimes if they were lucky – or unlucky – there might be some handwritten annotations with corrections of grammar and style, occasionally a comment or a reprimand, sometimes even a joke. One of the economic *conseillers* had written in one note that de Gaulle 'risks being interrogated about . . .' and this came back with an injunction in the margin: 'Learn [twice underlined] that General de Gaulle never risks anything and never allows himself to be interrogated.'55 At least this showed that the document had been read. Otherwise, as one *conseiller* put it, they 'savoured the combination of their importance and their insignificance'.56 De Gaulle himself described the Household in his *Memoirs* as working 'methodically and away from any agitation'.57 One of the Elysée *conseillers* expressed the same idea slightly more negatively when recalling the 'glacial universe' of the Elysée: 'It was a universe somewhat cut off from life . . . The most useful thing I could do . . . was to receive as many representatives of civil society as possible . . . and then to pass on the information to the General in the form of short notes so that he did not find himself cut off from the real world.'58 De Gaulle of course believed that his regional visits were putting him in contact with the 'real' world, but it was the world as he wanted to see it, blurred through his thick glasses.

Despite their frustrations, the 'entourage', whether or not 'Gaullist', developed bonds of loyalty and even affection for the remote leader on the first floor whom they met so rarely. They knew that they were working for de Gaulle – and only for de Gaulle – and if they ever forgot they were sharply reminded. When Tricot told de Gaulle that he had submitted a particular document to the Prime Minister, he was subjected to a tirade: 'I do not need any intermediary with the Prime Minister. Your task is to help me, not to negotiate with the Prime Minister.'59

De Gaulle usually saw his Prime Minister once a week for a private meeting, and also briefly before the weekly Council of Ministers. Otherwise, given de Gaulle's phobia about the telephone, communication was by letter. There was a lot ministers were not told. When Peyrefitte told Pompidou that he had picked up a sense of what de Gaulle was going to say at his press conference of January 1963 – the one vetoing British entry to the Common Market – Pompidou's 'eyes opened like saucers'.60 De Gaulle received his Foreign Minister once a week, his Minister of Defence once a month, and others more infrequently. Although often cavalier about his own constitution, the General was in other respects meticulous about observing certain proprieties. He never gave instructions to a minister behind the back of the

Prime Minister without afterwards informing him. But the relationship between Matignon and the Elysée was inevitably difficult. Pompidou wrote on one occasion to Burin des Roziers to complain that Elysée *conseillers* were directly contacting his own ministers over his head: 'I beg you to calm the youthful impatience of your collaborators and understand how difficult is the situation of the General's Prime Minister.'[61]

The meetings of the Council of Ministers, every Wednesday, were formal and lugubrious. Except on special occasions, discussion was limited. Each minister was supposed only to report on his area. When in January 1960 Pinay, the Finance Minister, expressed an opinion on de Gaulle's foreign policies, as he would have expected to do in the Fourth Republic, he was rebuked by de Gaulle with the words: 'Since when does the Minister of Finance have views on foreign policy?' Pinay left the government soon afterwards. Foreign affairs were the remit of Couve, who was his master's voice. Couve would usually read out in a semi-audible monotone what any minister could have discovered from reading *Le Monde*. His interventions were so soporific that one day de Gaulle interrupted: 'Without asking him to bellow could the Minister for Foreign Affairs please speak up.' Malraux was accorded an indulgence de Gaulle allowed to no one else. He did not often speak but when he did his interventions enlivened the proceedings with their dazzling obscurity and historical panache. A discussion on policy towards Nasser's Egypt was the pretext for Malraux to embark on an historical fresco going back to the pharaohs followed by speculation about why the Nasserian revolution was more like France in 1788 than Russia in 1916.[62] De Gaulle would beam benignly and then gently bring the discussion back to earth – from the pharaohs to the present.

Under de Gaulle, the role of the Council of Ministers was not to discuss policy but to ratify policies already decided. The real business occurred beforehand in smaller inter-ministerial meetings (*conseils restreints*) which de Gaulle would convene to discuss a subject that was exercising him or where he felt that government was acting with insufficient vigour. These would be chaired by de Gaulle himself and attended by the ministers concerned, by the Prime Minister and sometimes by an Elysée *conseiller*. In these committees, de Gaulle could hardly have been more different from the solemn monarch of the Council of Ministers. Their minutes reveal him to be an attentive, open-minded chairman, listening, questioning, informing himself and then summing up crisply.

Those who had never encountered de Gaulle closely before, or saw only the public persona, were startled by his quickness of intelligence, his capacity for instant synthesis and his intellectual receptivity. A few weeks after taking up his position in Algiers, Delouvrier gave an account to the British

Consul in Algiers of his amazement at de Gaulle's 'remarkable memory and power of concentration':

[Delouvrier] told me that after his initial incognito tour of Algeria, he had made an oral report to the General. He had sorted out his impressions into a number of headings, and ran through them point by point, speaking for 25 minutes. The General listened without the slightest reaction, 'a trying experience, as you can imagine'. As soon as he had finished, however, the General went straight through the points in the order in which he had made them, giving his own comments and ideas, continuing without interruption for forty minutes ... He went on to say that there was never any discussion in conversation with de Gaulle. His interviews could best be described as the delivery by the General of a series of verbal short-arm jabs to see how his visitor would react. The General expected an intelligent and independent reaction, and if he failed to get it, he had no further regard for his caller.[63]

This side of de Gaulle, already familiar to those who had worked for him in London, contrasts completely with the image of someone ruling in Olympian solitude. Another witness reporting the same surprise as Delouvrier was Jean Mamert, a thirty-year-old civil servant with legal expertise who was summoned to give de Gaulle technical advice during the drafting of the constitution in 1958. Inevitably this junior official was trepidant when ushered into the presence of the General:

What amazed me, when I came out of our first meeting, is that I found the General quite different from what I had imagined ... Very simple, very relaxed, almost respectful ... After having listened to me, when he made his comments on what I had said, he took up exactly what I had said, word for word, almost to the last syllable! He had a fantastic memory ... One cannot exaggerate his capacity to listen. It is something that always amazed me.[64]

One of the economic *conseillers* at the Elysée remembered that at his first meeting, as de Gaulle peered intently at him through his thick glasses, he had 'the impression of being listened to with greater attention than had ever happened to me anywhere before'.[65] Nonetheless it needed strong nerves to stand up to de Gaulle in discussion. As Tricot recalled: 'It was necessary to choose the moment and the terrain well; one also had to dig in. Sometimes I felt the physical necessity to hold on to something.'[66] Even if de Gaulle's response was often 'no', a few days later an idea he had rejected would often reappear as his own. This was something that everyone working for de Gaulle in London had experienced.

The role of the Elysée *conseillers* was to provide de Gaulle with the technical knowledge he required to challenge his own government. An example of how this worked was the financial stabilization plan introduced by the government in 1963. The French economy had quickly recovered from the tough economic medicine administered by the Rueff Plan in 1958. With the stimulus provided by the lowering of tariffs as a result of the Treaty of Rome, the economy started to grow spectacularly, for the first time overtaking the growth rates of Germany. At the same time, prices started to rise.

On two occasions, Rueff wrote directly to de Gaulle to express his worries that measures needed to be taken to restrain inflation. This was consistent with Rueff's lifelong crusade for price stability and also the result of a more personal animus against the Governor of the Bank of France who he felt was pursuing a lax credit policy.[67] But Rueff was not the only person to be worried. Maxime Lévêque, the Elysée *conseiller* on the economy, bombarded de Gaulle with notes in 1962–3 warning against what he called the 'general inflationist tendency' and the 'exaggeratedly "expansionist" policy' of the government.[68] Pompidou, and his Minister of Finance Valéry Giscard d'Estaing, were more relaxed about the situation and feared the economic consequences of a more restrictive policy.

Deciding to intervene, de Gaulle summoned four inter-ministerial meetings in the spring of 1963 to discuss the issue, which resulted in a set of measures to tackle inflation. Further encouraged by Lévêque, de Gaulle felt these had not gone far enough. He returned to the matter in the autumn. Three more meetings were called, and an even more rigorous stabilization plan was introduced.[69] De Gaulle wrote to Pompidou in the most solemn terms to insist that the 'deep and permanent causes of inflation' must be eradicated: 'This is an issue I consider essential.'[70] Pompidou was intensely irritated by this, having assumed de Gaulle would not try to interfere in the running of the economy. He told Peyrefitte: 'The General is getting upset because Madame de Gaulle says to him "Charles, prices are rising."' He railed against de Gaulle's 'occult technical advisers who are inciting him against me and my government'; on another occasion he moaned: 'the General should not interfere in this. I see Rueff's hand behind it. He is profiting from the General's naivety in this area and pushing him like a rhinoceros in the porcelain shop.'[71] Rueff's influence should not be exaggerated. At one of the committees to reform the credit system, de Gaulle commented that 'we are not going to demolish a system to bend to the injunctions of M. Rueff'.[72] Probably the influence of the Elysée advisers was more important.

The stabilization plan was widely criticized in the press for being too deflationary. Probably the plan did no major harm, but the affair casts interesting light on how government operated under de Gaulle. Whether or not 'occult advisers' were stirring him up, as Pompidou suspected, they certainly provided de Gaulle with the ammunition he needed to impose his will on the government. Their real influence depended on whether the General had decided fully to take up the cause. There were counter-examples to the stabilization plan. The Elysée *conseiller* on education, Jacques Narbonne, worrying that the rapid expansion of France's university student population was unsustainable, had started to send de Gaulle increasingly alarmist notes arguing that it was necessary to impose a more restrictive policy of university selection. De Gaulle was receptive to this view but in the end did not force the issue. Pompidou and the Minister of Education – who took up Pompidou's lament against 'occult advisers' – were firmly set against. Pompidou, as an alumnus of the Ecole Normale Supérieure, saw himself as an expert on higher education. He was wedded to the principle that any student with the baccalaureate had an automatic right to higher education. De Gaulle did not feel strongly enough – or was not sure enough of his ground – to press the point. Policies were thus a balance of influence between Matignon and the Elysée – except on defence and foreign policy where de Gaulle was entirely dominant.[73]

GAULLIST MODERNIZATION

De Gaulle's decisive personal intervention to impose the financial stabiliza-tion plan belies the often repeated claim that he was uninterested in economics. Indeed he was intermittently obsessed by it. He always denied having ever said – as was often alleged – 'the supply train looks after itself' ('*l'intendance suivra*'). But the phrase did correspond to his idea that the role of the leader was not to get involved in the details of policy execution even if one can at times find him intervening in matters ranging from the price of milk and meat to the restructuring of the coal industry.[74] Since his two most direct personal interventions were the Rueff Plan of 1958 and the stabilization plan of 1963, it might seem that his instincts inclined to price stability over growth, fiscal orthodoxy over expansion. The reality is more complicated.

De Gaulle's sacralization of the state makes it impossible to pigeonhole him as a liberal in the style of Rueff. He remarked to Peyrefitte one day: 'The state must oversee the market.'[75] Pompidou, whose instincts as a for-mer banker were more laissez-faire, complained that de Gaulle is 'so voluntaristic that he cannot bear the idea that economic activity does not obey either his will or the Plan'.[76] There was truth in this. De Gaulle became obsessed after his return to power with enhancing the place of the Plan in French economic policy. The Planning Commissariat, somewhat offhandedly founded by de Gaulle in place in 1945, had remained. The first Plan (1946–52) had prioritized investment during post-war reconstruction. Targets were set through consultation between civil servants, business and trade unions according to a model of 'indicative' planning. The Plan had played an important role in allocating resources for reconstruction. A second Plan, for the period 1954–7, covered schools and hospitals. In this way the Planning Commissariat, established to address a specific post-war crisis, had become a permanent fixture of French economic policy. But its status was anomalous and contested. The civil servants of the Planning Commissariat benefited from the lack of political stability under the Fourth Republic: their Plans provided an element of continuity. Even so 'planners' felt themselves to be somewhat on the margins of the French administration, achieving their aims almost by default. There was supposed to be a Conseil Supérieur du Plan chaired by the Prime Minister, but this fell into abeyance and had not met since 1953.

De Gaulle decided to change this. As the Commissariat started to draft its new Plan in 1961, he decided to resuscitate the Conseil Supérieur du Plan and chair it himself.[77] So enthusiastic did he become about it that he developed the idea that the recommendations of the Plan should be made obligatory and given the force of law. Since this would have been quite impossible in a free market economy, de Gaulle's economic advisers – and Debré – became alarmed. At the last moment they managed to persuade him to change his 1961 speech on the subject.[78] In the end he employed a somewhat vaguer formulation, in classically ambiguous Gaullist style, calling for the Plan to be an 'ardent obligation'. He wanted to create a 'mystique of the Plan' but was stopped from going any further.[79]

All this makes de Gaulle's ideas on economics difficult to pin down: he combined a voluntaristic sensibility with an instinctive fear of inflation, whose effects he had first witnessed in Poland as a young soldier. The experience had marked him deeply as he recalled on more than one occasion: 'It was horrible . . . Housewives queuing at 4 in the morning to buy bread before the price went up . . . Utter despair everywhere.'[80] The economic content of 'Gaullism' remained fluid. This provided an opening for a highly motivated group of publicists, managers, economists and civil servants (*fonctionnaires*) who had a clear agenda regarding the need to 'modernize' the French economy. De Gaulle was their opportunity, and it was they who wrote some of the script of 'Gaullism' in this period.

Since Colbert, minister of Louis XIV, France has had a cult of the allegedly disinterested public servant working for the state. The nineteenth-century socialist thinker Saint-Simon developed an entire philosophy around the idea of a society governed harmoniously by an elite. The French word *fonctionnaire* is imbued with an almost sacred aura inadequately conveyed by the British translation 'civil servant'. After 1945, the spirit was embodied by a generation of *haut fonctionnaires*, mostly in their early thirties, passionate about the need to overcome the economic weaknesses they blamed for the defeat of 1940. These reformers had had different trajectories during the war – some had been involved with the Resistance, some with the Free French, some with the Vichy regime – but they all shared a missionary zeal for economic renewal. Their inspiration was Keynesianism; their mantra 'modernization'; and their instrument the Plan. Their *bêtes noires* were 'liberal' economists like Jacques Rueff and conservative politicians like Pinay, whom they saw as serving the interests of a backward-looking France of peasants and rentiers.[81] Some worked in the Planning Commissariat, others in European institutions, others in the Finance Ministry. For this reason, it is not quite accurate to call them outsiders, but they developed a group identity around the idea that France's elites were not fully converted to the gospel of economic growth and modernization. Viewing the Finance Ministry as an enemy citadel defending narrow monetary orthodoxy, they developed a self-image as 'conspirators of modernization'.[82] But they were very public conspirators, spreading their ideas through lectures to future generations of *fonctionnaires* at ENA or in articles in magazines like *L'Express*. One emblematic figure was the economist Jean Fourastié, a pioneer of Keynesian national accounting who had worked on the Planning Commissariat and later became famous for inventing the phrase the 'the Thirty Glorious Years'. Fourastié wrote best-selling books on the way that technology harnessed to economic growth could transform the world.

The politics of this generation of *fonctionnaires* was broadly left of centre, but they preferred to see themselves as apolitically working for a notion of the public good. Those of a more liberal and internationalist sensibility saw 'Europe' as the route to modernization; the more statist preferred to prioritize 'planning'. The former looked to Monnet as their inspiration; the latter to Mendès France, the only Fourth Republic politician to catch their imagination. Many of them had populated the brains trusts and *cabinets* of Mendès France's brief moment in power. What attracted them to him was not only that he spoke the same kind of language but that he was determined to overcome vested interests blocking growth and economic modernization. They were not instinctively Gaullist, even if many admired the de Gaulle of the war. His rhetoric of 'grandeur' seemed anachronistic, and the means by which he returned to power in 1958 aroused suspicion. Nonetheless it soon became clear that his return opened up possibilities for them.

One feature of de Gaulle's first government was the relatively large number of posts given in his governments to non-political 'experts' and civil servants over elected politicians. In January 1959, there were eight 'experts' to twenty politicians; a year later the ratio was almost equal.[83] When Pinay resigned he was replaced not by a politician but by the former Governor of the Bank of France, Wilfrid Baumgartner. This particular moment seemed like a symbolic revenge for the 'modernizers'. When Pinay had become premier in 1952 he demoted one of the most charismatic representatives of the modernizers, the civil servant François Bloch-Lainé, because he viewed him as too dirigiste.[84] As a sign of how things had changed, de Gaulle tried to tempt Bloch-Lainé into becoming his Minister of Finance. Bloch-Lainé was too committed to the left – and too shocked by the way de Gaulle had returned to power – to be willing to cross this particular Rubicon. Nonetheless he viewed de Gaulle with cautious sympathy, and de Gaulle did not hold Bloch-Lainé's refusal against him. He declared that he is 'one of us' – meaning that they shared the same belief in the possibility of the state to effect economic change.

Soon after de Gaulle's return to power the Socialist (and one-time member of the Free French) André Philip had written an article warning that:

> The danger of President de Gaulle is the orientation towards an authoritarian technocratic socialism; he risks grouping around him the experts and top administrators who are both efficient and authoritarian, and to find himself being used as a form of propaganda by which the masses are made to adopt the decisions taken by those who know best.[85]

Although 'authoritarian technocratic socialism' is not really a description of what occurred, the diagnosis of the importance that experts would take was astute. A notable feature of government under de Gaulle was the setting up of *ad hoc* commissions or para-political organisms operating outside the more bureaucratic routines of the traditional administration. One of these was given responsibility for scientific research – a particular obsession of de Gaulle's – and another for regional development (DATAR). These offered posts and opportunities to the modernizers. Paul Delouvrier, who had started his career in the Planning Commissariat, was never entirely at ease in the job de Gaulle gave him in Algeria. But in the mid-1960s he found a new role in a quasi-governmental organization responsible for overseeing the development of the Paris region. In this role Delouvrier was the architect of the urbanization plans which led to the building of a ring of new cities around Paris. The almost messianic zeal of the modernizers can be seen in the kind of language used by one of de Gaulle's Elysée *conseillers*, Jean Méo, who was passionate about reforming the structures of retail distribution in France. He wanted to begin by removing the huge, picturesque but inefficient Les Halles food market from the centre of Paris. Les Halles was in his eyes the 'quintessence of all the feudalisms ... A monstrous abscess at the heart of the capital'. With de Gaulle's support he felt he was 'taking on an economic Bastille', cutting out the most 'spectacular cancer in the country'.[86]

None of this seems integral to 'Gaullism' as it existed before 1958, but it is easy to see why de Gaulle would be receptive to such influences. From the 1920s, he had had a fascination with the modern – with Taylorism, with machines – which he saw as both a threat and an opportunity. It fitted into the way that he had framed the conflict with the army in Algeria as one between forward-looking modernizers and backward-looking soldiers fighting yesterday's war.[87] Again and again in his speeches and press conferences de Gaulle celebrated scientific progress, economic and social reforms and the modernization of the armed forces. The 1962 introduction to the Fourth Plan proposed its goals as the modernization of the army and 'giving to research the material power capable of assuring full participation of the French spirit in the great scientific and technical enterprise of the century'.[88] Or as de Gaulle put it more pithily in a speech two years earlier, France needed to 'embrace her era'.[89] The General also shared with the modernizers an impatience with vested interests – what he called 'feudalities' – blocking social and economic forces which needed the state to liberate them. A phrase much used at the time to characterize these dynamic social elements was *les forces vives* (vital forces), an elusive concept, not easy to translate into English, but implying the productive as opposed to the parasitic elements of society. It was out of this convergence between modernizers, *forces vives* and de Gaulle that the Gaullism of the 1960s was shaped.[90] Nothing better illustrates this than the quiet revolution taking place in the French countryside during the 1960s.

THE END OF THE PEASANTRY

The RPF had never paid much attention to agriculture. De Gaulle does not seem to have had any particular views apart from a desire to squeeze the best possible deal for French farmers out of Europe. One of the riskiest measures politically of the Rueff Plan was ending the indexation of agricultural prices. In normal circumstances this would have represented electoral suicide when 30 per cent of the population in 1962 still worked on the land. There were periodic protests against the government in the countryside in 1959 and 1960. The representative body of the farmers, the

FNSEA (Fédération Nationale des Syndicats d'Exploitants Agricoles), wanted higher agricultural prices to stem rural depopulation. The *fronde* in the countryside found support among rank-and-file Gaullists in parliament. In March 1960, a majority of *députés* signed a motion calling for parliament to be convened in a special session to discuss the agricultural crisis. The constitution stipulated that the government was required to grant such a request, but de Gaulle had no intention of doing so.[91] As he grumbled privately: 'The peasants are never happy. Either it is raining too much, or it is too dry, or too cold ... We are always having to feel sorry for them.'[92] Whenever farming organizations agitated for higher prices, de Gaulle exhorted Debré to be firm.[93] The idea that the government was indifferent to the sufferings of the peasantry was the origin of the first accusations that Gaullism had been hijacked by inhuman technocracy.

Not all representatives of agriculture were resistant to change. In the mid-1950s, a new generation of young farmers emerged to challenge the FNSEA. Led by Michel Debatisse, a charismatic young farmer from the Massif Central, they created a rival organization called the CNJA (Centre National des Jeunes Agriculteurs). It argued that instead of resisting the rural exodus, and protecting inefficient farmers, it was necessary to modernize French agriculture. These farmers presented themselves as 'entrepreneurs' running businesses – the *forces vives* of agriculture – not 'peasants' preserving a lifestyle. One of the Elysée *conseillers* seized this opportunity. He briefed de Gaulle in 1960: 'The effort to renovate French agriculture cannot be accomplished by the farmers alone against the government, nor by the State alone without the collaboration of the peasants themselves.'[94] He was even able to persuade de Gaulle to receive Debatisse, despite the General's dislike of meeting representatives of sectional interests. As another adviser later put it: 'We said to ourselves that there was no point in putting poultice on a wooden leg and that we needed to get to the root of the problem. Why have the good luck of de Gaulle being there, if the opportunity was not used to solve these problems?'[95] At the same time, the leaders of the CNJA quickly realized that in the Fifth Republic it was 'better to have two well-placed civil servants than 25 *députés*'.[96]

The result was a bold agricultural 'orientation bill' supported by the CNJA and opposed by the FNSEA. It put in place regional agencies (*sociétés d'aménagement foncier et d'établissement rural* – SAFER) to buy up land when it came on to the market and then sell or lease it to qualified farmers in order to replace the existing patchwork of tiny plots with more economically viable units. When the law came up for discussion in parliament in April, de Gaulle felt the matter important enough to write to

Debré from America, where he was on a state visit, stressing that he must be 'accommodating in form but immovable on the content' of the bill.[97]

The following year, more disturbances erupted in the countryside. Farmers blocked roads with their tractors and cut electricity wires; in Brittany they even occupied the *sous-préfecture* of Morlaix. This was one of the most violent episodes of rural protest in twentieth-century France. But what was significant – not everyone realized it at the time – was that the demonstrators were protesting not because they objected to the new law to modernize the countryside but because it was not being applied fast enough. The ineffectual Minister of Agriculture was dismissed in August 1961 and de Gaulle replaced him with one of those effective administrators of the type he appreciated. This was Edgard Pisani, whose role in the Resistance had led to his being appointed in 1944 the youngest *sous-préfet* in France. Pisani had gone on to rise in the prefectural ranks until he decided to enter politics. His political affinities were on the centre left, and he did not initially see himself as a Gaullist – he had voted in parliament against the five-year defence programme in 1960 – but he saw de Gaulle as an opportunity. Having accepted the post, Pisani was immediately treated to a mini-lecture from de Gaulle on how he should conceive his role: 'You are the Minister of Agriculture, not the Minister of the *agriculteurs* [farmers].'

Pisani introduced a second agricultural law in 1962 which accelerated the reforms of the first one, and the French countryside entered a period of rapid change. Between 1958 and 1968 the numbers working in French agriculture fell by about 150,000 every year. This decline had started in the Fourth Republic, and would have continued whether or not de Gaulle had come to power. But the Fifth Republic accelerated the process, and de Gaulle embraced it. Looking back on this in his *Memoirs* he wrote:

> How, being the person I was, could I not be moved and worried, to see the fading away of this rural world whose occupations had never changed and were structured by tradition; this country of unaltering villages, old churches, solid families, of the eternal cycles of ploughing, sowing and reaping; this country of ancestral legends, singing and dancing, of regional dialects, customs and local markets; this ancient France whose nature, activity and genius had made it essentially rural?

This elegiac homage to the bucolic life, which would not have seemed out of place in a speech by Marshal Pétain, reads more like a literary exercise than the expression of a heartfelt conviction. But it was followed by a paragraph about the need for change:

The time is now past when agriculture was about subsistence, where the peasant, never changing what he grew on his tiny plot of land, cultivated primarily what he needed just to feed himself and his family . . . Machines have done away with that, upsetting the old equilibrium, imposing higher yields, accumulating surpluses, creating new products and at the same time new desires . . . Thus it is the market which dictates the laws of agriculture: specialization, selection, sales.[98]

Whatever de Gaulle's lament for the 'ancestral legends' of the countryside, his roots were urban. When he bought a country residence, it was in an area of bleak landscapes where, as he liked to tell visitors, no habitations – no farms – could be seen. De Gaulle's ruthless existential nationalism allowed for little nostalgia about France's rural past. As he had said in a speech in June 1960 on the need to accept change in Algeria: 'It is entirely natural to feel nostalgia for the Empire, as one can regret the gentle light of oil lamps, the splendour of sailing ships . . . But there is no value in a policy that does not take account of realities.'[99]

25
Half-Time, 1965

INTERPRETING GAULLISM

By 1965, de Gaulle had been in power for seven years, but commentators, journalists and politicians remained perplexed about the nature of 'Gaullism' and the regime he had created. This was true even of the Communist Party, usually certain about everything. In May 1958, the Party's line was that de Gaulle was a 'fascist'. Maurice Thorez made contingency plans to escape abroad to avoid arrest. Once it became clear that de Gaulle had no intention either of banning political parties or of arresting his opponents, the Communists could no longer sustain the 'fascist' argument. Instead they denounced a 'regime of personal power' which 'opened the way to fascism'. This was also implausible – after all, France had a free press – and they settled finally on the idea that Gaullism was the reactionary instrument of 'monopoly capitalism' (Pompidou's previous banking career came in useful here). Other Marxists tried to develop a more sophisticated approach, arguing that Gaullism represented the dynamic elements of French capitalism opposed to the backward-looking protectionist and rentier interests clinging on to Algeria.[1] The Communist Party viewed this theory as heresy because it implied that Gaullism had a progressive side.

The Communists were not the only ones to have made comparisons with fascism. This was also the theme of an ephemeral review, 14 juillet, founded during the crisis of May 1958. It published contributions from an extraordinary constellation of French intellectuals including André Breton, Marguerite Duras and Maurice Blanchot. The editorial of the first issue declared: 'We cannot predict the rhythm of the process by which the current regime must end up purely and simply in fascism. But from today, without any risk of error, we can state that the regime of de Gaulle is in contemporary France the necessary step to the installation of Fascism.'[2] The second issue, after the outcome of the September 1958 referendum approving the constitution of the new Republic had become known, was no less alarmist: 'We declare the government of de Gaulle to be an illegal government of usurpation. We do not recognize the results of the referendum . . . Our relations with the pseudo Fifth Republic can only be analogous to those of the French with the government of Marshal Pétain: resistance to oppression.'[3]

The review *14 juillet* folded after only three issues when its apocalyptic predictions proved unfounded. But that did not make it any clearer what de Gaulle's return to power really signified. The most renowned political commentators of the day penned innumerable articles analysing a regime that did not fit into their analytical categories or correspond exactly to any precedents. At various times, comparisons were made with the Consulate of Napoleon, the Orleanist monarchy of the 1830s and the parliamentary Empire of the 1860s. Some saw Gaullism as a modernizing technocracy, others as a new avatar of Maurrassianism. This last idea was advanced by Raymond Aron in a much discussed article in *Le Figaro* in 1964. He noted the similarities between de Gaulle and Maurras: the obsession with the state and national independence; he also compared de Gaulle's refrain that the 'real' France was united behind him while only the superficial France of politicians was against him with Maurras's famous distinction between the *pays légal* and the *pays réel*. For a conservative liberal like Aron the comparison with Maurras was negative, but the comparison was also taken up mischievously in *Le Monde* by a former Maurassian, Gilbert Comte, who noted approvingly, 'since our master Maurras no one has given such a rude shock to the Republic.'[4] The most popular line was to compare Gaullism to Bonapartism: a form of rule that combined popular sovereignty, charismatic leadership and authoritarianism; a foreign policy that combined nationalism with progressive rhetoric; and an ideology that claimed to straddle the left–right divide and appeal to the 'people' over the elites.

France's two most prolific political commentators, the jurist Georges Vedel and the political scientist Maurice Duverger, were unable to develop a consistent point of view. Neither wanted to go back to the Fourth Republic, and each was an advocate of a presidential regime somewhat on the lines of the United States. The problem was that the Fifth Republic was constitutionally neither fish nor fowl. It was a hybrid between a presidential system and a parliamentary one and did not fit the models of political science textbooks and lectures.[5] The only consensus was that de Gaulle had invented something whose nature would become clear only once he had gone. Duverger entitled one of his articles, 'A Man Has Replaced the State'.[6] Another commentator compared de Gaulle to an 'old Prospero' who had 'dissipated all the invisible spirits around' but whose departure would probably leave 'a great institutional void into which the spirits of the storm will throw themselves'.[7]

Only the extreme right had no doubt what it thought of de Gaulle. Former Vichyites and unrepentant supporters of Algérie française – often one and the same – poured out their bile in publications whose only raison d'être was hatred of de Gaulle. They lived in a parallel universe of rancour, hatred and conspiracy, endlessly revisiting the 'treason' of 1940, the 'bloodbath' of 1944 and the 'betrayal' of Algeria. On the other hand, many on the left who admired the 'rebellion' of 1940, supported the 'purges' of 1944 and welcomed the 'independence' of Algeria were hardly less ferocious in their opposition. This was true for example of Jean-Paul Sartre's journal Les Temps modernes whose commitment to Algerian independence did not incline it to give de Gaulle any quarter. Sartre wrote: 'The herring barrel will always smell of fish; the Gaullist regime in all its manifestations will smell until the end of the arbitrariness and violence that gave birth to it.'[8] He never changed that view.

Sartre, the most famous intellectual in France – probably in the world – was violent in his anti-Gaullism, but his views were not unusual on the left. Hubert Beuve-Méry, editor of Le Monde, was a barometer of bien pensant progressive opinion. To preserve his independence, Beuve-Méry made a point of never attending de Gaulle's press conferences – but he devoted long editorials to each one. In these articles the incorruptibly austere editor of France's most respected newspaper offered a running commentary on the actions of France's unpredictable President.[9] Unlike Sartre, Beuve-Méry had cautiously supported de Gaulle's return to power. He had also advocated a 'yes' in the referendum on the constitution despite mutterings from his editorial staff. Although fascinated by de Gaulle, he became progressively more critical: of the incomprehensible twists and turns of de Gaulle's Algerian policy, of the wilder aspirations of his foreign policy, and of his style of government. After the referendum of 1962 on the reform of the constitution, Beuve-Méry's analysis was bleak: 'a divided and disorientated population, institutions in ruins . . . a kind of "scorched earth" where only factions will be left to fight in a cemetery of lost freedoms'.[10] By 1965, his hostility had ratcheted up in intensity: 'Does not an exclusive tête-à-tête between the people and its leader conform to the famous principle of ein Volk, ein Führer, which is the principle of totalitarian nationalism?'[11]

The only significant intellectual to support de Gaulle was François Mauriac. Since the Liberation, Mauriac had become an icon for French progressives not only because of his role in the Resistance but because of his opposition to the abuses of French colonialism. Through his weekly column in *L'Express*, he won an audience beyond the usual readership of his novels. He had become the conscience of the Catholic left as well as being admired by Socialists disgusted by their own party's complicity in torture in Algeria during the 1950s. After a moment of hesitation, Mauriac rallied to de Gaulle in May 1958. He rapidly moved from cautious support to unconditional adulation. This made him increasingly uneasy about writing in a publication where every editorial by Servan-Schreiber was an anti-Gaullist diatribe. Mauriac finally broke with *L'Express* in 1961 and moved his column to *Le Figaro*, the newspaper of bourgeois conservative opinion. Here his Gaullism sat as uneasily as it had in *L'Express* because the newspaper's readers had their own reservations about de Gaulle: most were nostalgic for *Algérie française*, many opposed de Gaulle's anti-Americanism because they were anti-Communist, and some harboured residual admiration for Pétain. Mauriac answered critics who accused him of unreasoning worship of de Gaulle by reminding them that he had opposed de Gaulle during the RPF period, but this alibi was a diminishing asset as the tone of Mauriac's Gaullism became quasi-mystical. After de Gaulle's speech in Barricades Week, he wrote: 'As a Christian I feel confirmed in my certainty: Charles de Gaulle is not a man of destiny, he is the man of divine grace [*homme de la grâce*]'.[12] In 1964, Mauriac published a biography of de Gaulle so hagiographical that even his admirers were embarrassed. By this point, Mauriac's Gaullism only served to discredit him in the eyes of those progressives who had revered him. Like Malraux some years earlier, Mauriac had moved from being a leftist intellectual who had rallied to de Gaulle to being a Gaullist who could no longer be viewed as a leftist intellectual.[13]

Although most left-wing intellectuals opposed de Gaulle, some began to find it less easy to pigeonhole him than they had initially thought. One of these was the hugely respected journalist Jean Daniel, a star reporter of *L'Express* until he went on to found his own periodical, *Le Nouvel Observateur*, in 1964. Daniel had a *pied noir* background, and although committed to Algerian independence he had (like his friend Albert Camus) more sensitivity to the problem of Algeria than some of his colleagues. Daniel also had many connections in the Third World. This led him to write a controversial article for *Le Monde* in 1964 exploring the paradox that de Gaulle, despised by the French left, was becoming a hero in the Third World because of his willingness to stand up to America: 'Fidel Castro's only real competitor in popularity with the youth of Latin America is de Gaulle.'[14] Another leftist intellectual who found himself uneasy with the knee-jerk anti-Gaullism of his milieu was Jean-Marie Domenach, editor of the left Catholic *Esprit*. In 1958 Domenach had imagined himself joining a new *maquis* to resist de Gaulle's return to power, but gradually he began to revise his view. De Gaulle's Algerian policy, his support for 'cooperation' with the Third World, his distancing from America were all issues which made Domenach cautiously sympathetic. But for him the problem was that 'de Gaulle has never understood his own destiny', refusing to break fully with his caste and his political origins.[15]

Symptomatic of the problem of responding to de Gaulle was the evolution of the Club Jean Moulin. This was an organization created in May 1958 by a group of former resisters at the moment when France seemed to be on the verge of a coup. One of its founders, the art dealer Daniel Cordier, had been parachuted into France in July 1942 to serve as an aide to Jean Moulin; another, the civil servant Stéphane Hessel, had worked for the BCRA. They had been Gaullist during the war but Mendésist in the 1950s because they disapproved of the RPF. In 1958 they were ready to embark on a new 'resistance' to fight the new Gaullist 'fascism' – even if they found it difficult to put their hands upon many guns. When it was clear that France had not become fascist, the Club mutated into a think tank reflecting on how to preserve democratic and republican values while rejecting the presidential authoritarianism of the Fifth Republic.[16] Gradually their criticisms of Gaullism became more nuanced. One member, George Suffert, wrote: 'If Gaullism is not just a conservative phenomenon, it is because it reflects in its own way, at the level of politics, some of the mutations of French politics.'[17] Or as he later put it drolly in his memoirs: 'The paradox was that we were living fine under the de Gaulle regime and as time went on we no longer knew the reasons why we wanted to change it.'[18]

Even Servan-Schreiber, whose opposition to de Gaulle was unconditional, recognized that once de Gaulle's constitutional reform had received popular approval in 1962, the left would have to change its stance. When de Gaulle's seven-year term as President came to an end in 1965, there would be – like it or not – a Presidential election by universal suffrage. This was a challenge the left had to accept. As *L'Express* put it: 'We want to go forward beyond Gaullism and not backwards.' To this end, in September 1963 *L'Express* launched a campaign to find 'Mr X' – a presidential candidate who had the best chance of beating de Gaulle if he chose to stand or of beating another Gaullist if he did not. The most obvious candidate would have been Pierre Mendès France, but he refused any compromise with de Gaulle's institutions. Mendès's style of government during his brief exercise of power had anticipated aspects of de Gaulle's style of government and yet he remained attached to the traditional principles of parliamentary republicanism. As one historian has neatly observed, Mendès France and de Gaulle were more like each other than they wanted to admit, almost symmetrical opposites: de Gaulle an authoritarian temperament dominated by a republican super-ego, Mendès France a republican temperament dominated by an authoritarian super-ego.[19]

After some months of suspense *L'Express* revealed that 'Mr X' would be the respected Socialist politician Gaston Defferre. The intention was that Defferre's name would rally the votes of both Socialists and the pro-European Catholic centre. What no one yet knew was whether de Gaulle would stand again. In his press conference of September 1964 he was asked a question about his health, five months after his prostate operation. He batted the question away: 'It is not bad at all but do not worry, one day I will not fail to die.'[20]

BUSINESS AS USUAL

As the election year opened, de Gaulle was giving nothing away about his intentions. For the moment it was business as usual. As tradition demanded, on 1 January he received major office holders (*corps constitués*) and dignitaries to offer them New Year wishes. In the Fourth Republic this ritual lasted several days – it gave the President something to occupy his time – but de Gaulle liked to get it over with in a day. He started with his bleary-eyed ministers who were sadistically summoned, after their New Year's revels, for 8.30 in the morning. Next came the presidents of the Assembly and Senate. Since the President of the Senate, Gaston Monnerville, had never been pardoned for his act of *lèse-majesté* in 1962 denouncing de Gaulle's alleged *forfaiture*, he was represented by a deputy. Finally, at the end of the day de Gaulle received the diplomatic corps.

On 19 and 20 January, de Gaulle had talks with Erhard at Rambouillet. In the evening, they watched a film of the General's triumphal visit to Germany in 1962. In their discussions, de Gaulle as usual attacked the MLF, but since the plan had been quietly shelved Erhard let this pass. Although the meeting covered no new ground, the atmosphere was more cordial than the last time the two men had met.[21] Three days later de Gaulle gave to Pierson Dixon a sense of what he was really thinking about the Germans at this time. Dixon, whose posting in Paris was about to end, had come to take his leave. Having so long been predicting de Gaulle's demise, he had changed his tune. He now believed de Gaulle was in an 'unchallengeable position': 'This one man, by a clever mixture of diplomatic gesture, threat and veto, but with no significant military or economic power, has done more than anyone to alter the balance of Western policies in the last two years.'[22]

For their valedictory meeting de Gaulle seemed in confiding mood, although Dixon warned London to guard against the possibility that he was setting a trap. When Dixon permitted himself to suggest that the General's assertions of national independence might prove contagious and revive the demons of German nationalism, de Gaulle evaded the point: 'It was right to make a clear distinction between French emphasis on national independence and the German brand of nationalism. France threatened no one. German nationalism was quite different, was dangerous, and certainly needed to be watched carefully.' De Gaulle was pessimistic about the chances of political cooperation between the Six since just getting the Germans and French to agree on how the German question might be settled with the Soviet Union would be difficult: 'It would be excellent, said the General with a smile, if the Germans would agree with the French approach . . . but he had no confidence in their doing so.' De Gaulle went on to 'ridicule' any idea of a common defence policy. Only the French would have the atomic bomb and the Germans 'must never be allowed to have . . . any real say in nuclear questions'. As for Monnet's ideas about integrated Europe, de Gaulle was scornful about this 'theoretician' and 'utopian'. The European Economic Community was a 'convenient commercial arrangement' and he did not fear that its institutions would develop 'a momentum of their own on supranational lines'. If, however, there was any danger of majority voting where France might find herself outvoted, 'she would leave the community and that would be an end of it.' 'How long, how long, does he think the Germans will stand for it?' minuted one British official in response to these comments.[23]

At the end of the month, de Gaulle spent a week secluded in Colombey preparing his next press conference, interrupted only by a visit to London to attend the funeral of Winston Churchill. The highlight of the press conference, which took place on 4 February, was de Gaulle's attack on the international monetary system which had been put in place by the Bretton Woods agreement of 1944. Bretton Woods had made the dollar a reserve currency, the only currency convertible into gold. This allowed American governments to run balance of payments deficits with the rest of the world knowing that their creditors would always be ready to hold dollars. As American balance of payment deficits – fuelled by military spending abroad – grew larger, the day loomed when the dollar holdings of foreign central banks might exceed American gold reserves. The system relied on the willingness of America's allies to hold their reserves in dollars – which they might not continue do if they felt that the dollar was no longer as 'good as gold'.

The situation gave considerable financial leverage to the Americans.

Holding huge amounts of dollars, America's creditors lent these back to America. In effect America's creditors were financing the penetration of their economies by American capital. This became an issue of public concern in France when in 1963 the Chrysler company purchased a controlling interest in the French car firm Simca. The following year, a French company (with the non-French-sounding name of Bull) specializing in the manufacture of office calculators found itself in need of capital and the American company General Electric offered to buy a 20 per cent stake. The French government tried to block this but the deal went ahead. Since Bull was the only possible French competitor to IBM, this was seen as a blow to French independence.

These were the issues raised by de Gaulle in his press conference. The worries he expressed about the international financial system were widely shared. Alarm bells about the resilience of the international monetary system had already been sounded by the Yale economist Robert Tiffin in 1960. But Tiffin was certainly not a supporter of the solution proposed by de Gaulle: a return to the gold standard. In making this proposal, de Gaulle had clearly been influenced by Rueff, who had been peddling the idea since the 1930s. But what Rueff saw as an economic problem – the Americans exporting inflation to the world by printing dollars – de Gaulle saw as a political one – America using her financial power to extend the tentacles of her influence abroad. Few economists took the idea of returning to the gold standard seriously and de Gaulle was widely ridiculed. The sensible part of his analysis about the structural problems of the international financial system was masked by the anti-American impulse which inspired it. Shortly before the press conference the French government had announced that it was converting part of its dollar reserves into gold.[24] De Gaulle dramatized this decision by refusing to allow the Americans to move the newly converted gold to the vaults of the Federal Reserve Bank. Instead he sent a special Air France plane to pick up the cargo from New York.

Attacking the dollar touched a nerve in the United States, causing more outrage than all de Gaulle's previous anti-American broadsides. There were demands in the American popular press to boycott French goods and 'French fries'. Alphand, who was coming to the end of his stint as Ambassador, noted: 'The public think that the evil General wants by satanic methods to attacks their wallets. Nothing counts here more than the dollar. Our best and most Francophile friends . . . have abandoned us in this quarrel.'[25] None of this perturbed de Gaulle in the slightest. Receiving Alphand in early May he seemed pleased with himself: 'It can't be easy being French Ambassador in Washington at the moment!'[26] He told Foccart the day after his press conference:

I will tell you one thing. A press conference by de Gaulle is noticed by the entire world . . . You can say what you want, and the Johnsons, the Wilsons, the Saragats can speak if they want to. Even if M. Kosygin started to give press conferences that would not have much impact, while if I speak it makes a mark. I can assure you that internationally everyone listens to me.[27]

If de Gaulle's comments on the dollar caused alarm across the Atlantic, the German government was worried by another part of the press conference. It had taken place exactly twenty years after the Yalta conference and de Gaulle evoked this anniversary to throw out some disquieting comments on Germany. Divided Germany, he said, was a chronically unsettling factor in the life of Europe – but it was a problem that the Europeans needed to solve themselves. He went on: 'Europe, the mother of modern civilization, must establish herself all the way from the Atlantic to the Urals, and live in a state of harmony and cooperation with a view to developing her immense resources, and so as to play, together with her daughter America, her worthy role in relation to the two billion people who so badly need her help.'[28] This was not the first time de Gaulle had used the phrase 'Europe from the Atlantic to the Urals' and no one ever quite knew what he meant by it. But if these words meant anything at all, it was that de Gaulle was thinking of a rapprochement with the Soviet Union as the first step towards a solution of the problem of Germany. There were other signs that this was what he had in mind. On 23 March, he gave a reception in honour of the Russian Ambassador, Vinogradov, who was leaving Paris after a long posting in the capital. In his toast, de Gaulle celebrated the 'century-old sympathy and natural affinity' of the two countries.[29] At the end of April, the Soviet Foreign Minister Gromyko held cordial talks with de Gaulle in Paris.

All this alarmed the Germans. In June, de Gaulle was in Bonn for two days of tetchy talks with Erhard. At a dinner in honour of the eighty-nine-year-old Adenauer, de Gaulle extemporized one of those pieces of virtuoso rhetoric of which he was such a master: 'We Europeans are the builders of cathedrals . . . Well, the cathedral we are building today, I mean in Western Europe, has a foundation, and that foundation is the reconciliation of Germany and France.'[30] But his recent remarks had sounded a different note. Even Adenauer was concerned, but when raising the matter with de Gaulle he received the sibylline reassurance that France's feelers to the Soviet Union were 'only an overture for a future, to the extent that there is a future'.[31]

African affairs continued to absorb much of de Gaulle's energy. In the first six months of the year, he found time to receive the President of the Central African Republic three times, and also the Presidents of Niger, Haute Volta, Chad, Madagascar, Togo, Gabon, Côte d'Ivoire and

Cameroon. Foccart was always at hand to brief de Gaulle in advance, and to debrief him afterwards. Foccart's main preoccupation in 1965 was the former Belgian Congo.[32] The country was still recovering from the civil war which had followed independence. In 1964, the Congolese President, in a spirit of national reconciliation, had invited the former secessionist leader Tshombe to head a unity government. Since Tshombe had been supported by the French during the civil war, Foccart saw an opportunity to bring the Congo into France's orbit and strike a blow against the United States and Belgium. The Quai d'Orsay doubted whether Tshombe would last, but Foccart would not be deflected.

Tshombe saw de Gaulle in Paris on 28 May, and following the meeting Foccart did all he could to poison the General's mind against the Quai. De Gaulle asked his opinion of the French Ambassador in the Congo. Foccart replied: 'An intelligent man who is not one of our friends and who did not at the start play the Tshombe card. If he did not play it is because it was not the Quai's card either and he was only obeying.'[33] This was music to de Gaulle's ears. He immediately rang Pompidou in Foccart's presence: '"I have explained everything to Foccart [in truth it seems to have been more the other way around] . . . He will tell you what I want. In broad terms, we must aid Tshombe, that is a necessity. We must put an end to all reticence.' Couve was then rung with the same message: 'You have to end all this resistance organized by the Belgians and the Americans which is unconsciously echoed on our side [meaning the Quai d'Orsay].' Foccart purred contentedly in his journal: 'I sensed that Couve was not terribly happy.'[34] This was only a pyrrhic victory for Foccart. A few months later Tshombe was ousted. In November General Mobutu seized power and Tshombe fled the country again. De Gaulle commented to Foccart: 'It is the revenge of the Belgians. Let us wait till Tshombe comes back' – but he never did.[35]

Foccart and de Gaulle also spent time discussing French domestic politics. Foccart's other area of responsibility, apart from Africa, was to watch over the UNR (whose MPs de Gaulle treated with the same condescending majesty as he did African heads of state). Municipal elections, due to take place in March, offered a test of the government's popularity. Although de Gaulle affected to be above the fray, he displayed an extraordinary interest in the details of electoral politics. This had already been the case during the RPF period when Claude Mauriac had been astonished, even a little dismayed, by how de Gaulle, like the most seasoned politician, 'enters into the tiniest details of organization, knows every name for places to fill'.[36] This was no less true when de Gaulle was President. After one discussion Foccart noted: 'As always he affects a complete lack of interest but in truth the issue much preoccupies him.' One night they embarked on a detailed discussion of a Marseilles constituency, until de Gaulle, suddenly realizing he had become too carried away, ended abruptly: 'this is nothing to do with me; it is no concern of mine.'[37] As always he was torn between what Pompidou called his 'unitary utopia' and the truth that he ruled through a party. His dream of a charismatic communion between people and guide had no place for party.

The first round of the municipal elections was disappointing. When the results were announced de Gaulle was in a furious mood: 'I have been much too implicated. You have little by little dragged me into this business . . . There you all are worrying about electoral questions, just thinking of political parties. But that is not the future; the future is the authority of the President.'[38] This was a typical example of Gaullist bad faith and Foccart had to ride the storm.

None of this gave Foccart any clue to de Gaulle's own intentions regarding the presidential election at the end of the year. No one was more exercised about this than Pompidou, who was the obvious Gaullist candidate if de Gaulle decided not to stand. Pompidou remarked to Peyrefitte in the previous year that he thought de Gaulle was 'dying to stand again' but 'since with him one is never sure of anything, one must prepare for other eventualities.'[39] May 1965 saw the publication of a hagiographical biography of Pompidou which had clearly been authorized by its subject. Pompidou's position was delicate. He knew that too naked a display of ambition might be the best way to provoke de Gaulle to stand. He could only wait – and hope.

If Pompidou secretly hoped that de Gaulle might not stand, so too did Yvonne de Gaulle for entirely different reasons. She hated living in the gilded prison of the Elysée and yearned for the domesticity of Colombey. Soon after moving into the palace she wrote to a friend: 'The house lacks gaiety! But after all it is just the 23rd place we have lived in.'[40] Sometimes she would look round and say half apologetically to visitors, 'You know none of this is ours.'[41] She told a niece that to retain the illusion of normality she would sometimes wash de Gaulle's socks in the basin.[42] As 'first lady' Yvonne de Gaulle ferociously guarded her privacy. She never once spoke in public and amazingly no recording of her voice exists. But she performed her role dutifully if unenthusiastically. In 1965, she was present for fifty-two of the seventy-five official banquets or meals. Her favourite subjects of conversation were children (at dinners she was provided in advance with a file card containing the family details of the person sitting next to her), flowers and travel.[43] Otherwise she had a minimalist view of her role. When Georges Pompidou became President, Yvonne de Gaulle's only piece of advice for his wife was: 'Wear a hat.'[44] The one part of the role she enjoyed were the trips abroad. If possible, she tried to visit a centre for children with learning difficulties. Otherwise her intense shyness made her a difficult guest to entertain. When the de Gaulles were put up at Birch Grove Dorothy Macmillan was frustrated by the difficulties of looking after Yvonne: 'She will not go to the hunt, nor the cripple crafts school nor even . . . the Pavilion at Brighton.'[45]

Yvonne de Gaulle treasured her time at Colombey – as did de Gaulle himself. La Boisserie was the only property they had ever owned. 'C'est ma demeure,' as he wrote laconically in his *Memoirs*.[46] In Paris before the war he had lived in various rented apartments when not stationed abroad; for visits to Paris after the war he had lodged at the Hôtel La Pérouse before entering the Elysée in 1959. La Boisserie, purchased in 1934, was the one pole of stability in his life. After he had become President, he and his wife would normally spend at least every other weekend there, and the summer holidays in August. No longer taking the long drive, they would travel there by helicopter, landing at Saint-Dizier about forty minutes' drive away. As President, de Gaulle needed always to be accompanied by an aide de camp who would live in the house with the de Gaulles as a member of the family. But the couple came to find this too much of an intrusion, and from 1960 the aide would be lodged near by at Chaumont and join the de Gaulles only for Sunday Mass and lunch.

The main contact with the Elysée was by telephone. In the 1950s a telephone had been installed in a sort of cupboard under the entrance staircase. Neither de Gaulle nor his wife liked to speak on the phone more than necessary. At the beginning this was de Gaulle's only form of communication with the Elysée and his *directeur de cabinet* was instructed to ring him each day at precisely 12.30 p.m. and otherwise never to disturb him except in cases of extreme emergency – as during Barricades Week in Algiers in January 1961 or when the coup took place in the Congo in August 1963. Since the telephone was an open and unprotected line, de Gaulle had to accept in 1961 the installation of a coded teleprinter in the house for use by the aide de camp.

It was difficult for the de Gaulles to escape the gaze of reporters and photographers lurking in the locality when they were in residence. The two domestic staff – cook and *gouvernante* – had the strictest instruction never to speak to any journalists. Yvonne de Gaulle was extremely upset when Augustine, who had been cook for three years, gave an interview to a magazine after leaving their employment. Her successor Honorine Manzoni waited until 1997 before publishing her memoirs, in which she revealed to the world that de Gaulle had a particular liking for *pot au feu* and rabbit.

La Boisserie was above all the domain of the de Gaulle family: five grandchildren, numerous nephews and nieces. Philippe and Elisabeth, the two surviving children, would often visit with their families. De Gaulle's brother-in-law Jacques Vendroux and his family were also quite regular visitors, as was de Gaulle's elder sister and only surviving sibling Marie-Agnès. She was a garrulous chatterbox with opinions on everything. This annoyed Yvonne de Gaulle, who did not believe that politics should be discussed *en famille*. But de Gaulle, who certainly did not believe that women should have political opinions, always displayed a gruff affection towards his sister. Above all he was a solicitously devoted grandfather, and among his nieces and nephews he was especially close to Geneviève (the daughter of his brother Jacques) and to his nephew François (son of Jacques), a priest who served as a missionary in Africa. De Gaulle had developed a close bond with Geneviève after her return in April 1945 from the Ravensbrück concentration camp where she had been deported for Resistance activities. For a month she lodged with de Gaulle and his wife at the Neuilly villa where they were living during his period as head of the provisional government. They had long and intimate conversations about her experiences in the camp, and she had found it easier to talk about this to her uncle than to her own father.[47]

Desperate to escape the gilded cage of the Elysée, in April 1965 Yvonne de Gaulle went to Foccart to plead the case against her husband's standing again: 'People need to know how to give up, Heads of State as much as artists. You become too old little by little, and you don't notice, and no one tells you ... You don't finish well; you finish badly. I don't want that to happen to the General.'[48] A week later she tried the same line with Peyrefitte, who had no more idea than anyone else what de Gaulle was intending.[49] He amused himself by noting the many occasions when the General seemed to be projecting himself into a post-1965 future.[50] All this was an endless source of speculation and gossip.

EUROPEAN CRISIS

In the summer of 1965, de Gaulle provoked a major European crisis that risked alienating the French farmers whose votes would be important in the presidential election. Despite his occasional tirades – public and private – against European supranationality, he ensured that France squeezed every possible economic benefit out of Europe through the Common Agricultural Policy. This was an area where French and German interests continued to diverge. France, as a major agricultural producer, wanted a protected

European market; Germany, as an agricultural importer, wanted to buy on world markets where prices were lower. The CAP set prices and imposed tariffs against imports from outside the Community so that each community producer was guaranteed to undercut external competition. The receipts from these tariffs were paid into a European fund which was redistributed to support farmers. Since Germany was the biggest food importer, it paid the largest share of the import levies. In other words, levies paid by Germany on food imports were subsidizing French agriculture.

By December 1963, agreement was reached in Brussels on levels of prices and tariffs for 85 per cent of agricultural production. It still remained to decide cereal prices. De Gaulle played no direct role in any of these discussions but kept up the pressure through occasional public threats. In October 1964, he issued a formal ultimatum to this effect: 'France would cease to participate in the European Economic Community if the Common Agricultural Market is not organized as it has been agreed that it would be organized.'[51] In private he told Peyrefitte: 'We have lived for many centuries without a Common Market. We could live several centuries more without a Common Market.'[52] In the end, after a marathon negotiating session at Brussels, an agreement was reached on grain in December 1964. In these negotiations France again enjoyed the support of the European Commission, one of those supranational institutions de Gaulle supposedly deplored. This has led some historians to argue that de Gaulle's opposition to supranationalism was merely posturing, that the reality of French economic advantage trumped the rhetoric of national independence.[53] This puts the case too strongly. De Gaulle was certainly not indifferent to French economic interests – he wanted grain *and* grandeur – and he had seen that the European Community could serve them. But he had not fully grasped that a by-product of France's success in defending her agriculture was incrementally to increase the ambitions of the Commission. This became clear in the spring of 1965 when the President of the European Commission, the German Walter Hallstein, fatefully overplayed his hand.

For the CAP to be fully operational, it remained to settle how its financial mechanisms would work. The Commission proposed in March 1965 that the income from import levies should go directly into the Community budget. It accompanied this suggestion with a proposed amendment of the Treaty of Rome which would have modified the voting rules of the Council of European Ministers, making it harder for member states to challenge budgetary decisions reached by the Commission. This would have significantly increased the power of the Commission at the expense of national governments. This bold move may have been prompted by the judgement that once France had fully achieved all her objectives on the CAP it would be more difficult to force the issue again. The Commission's proposal sparked all de Gaulle's latent suspicions of the European Community. Technically the formal deadline for an agreement on the working of the financial arrangements of the CAP was fixed for 30 June. Surprisingly it was Couve de Murville who raised the stakes by proposing to de Gaulle that France threaten a boycott of the Community's institutions until France obtained satisfaction on the agricultural issues.[54]

Presumably Couve had expected that as in the past a last-minute compromise would be reached. But the 30 June deadline passed with no deal. It was not that France's European partners were enthusiastic about the Commission's plans, but each had objectives that militated against immediate compromise. Nor did it help that Franco-German relations had become so strained over the last year. De Gaulle had no fund of goodwill on which to draw from Ehrhard. After the passing of the June deadline, the General announced that until further notice France would be boycotting the Community institutions. France's permanent representative in Brussels was summoned back to Paris. This was the beginning of the 'empty chair' policy, plunging the Community into the worst crisis in its short history. Although the Commission partially backtracked by offering a compromise, de Gaulle decided to push his opportunity further and use the crisis to challenge a clause of the Treaty of Rome which stipulated that from January 1966 the Council of Ministers would be able to take decisions by a majority vote. Whether or not de Gaulle would have challenged this clause anyway when the time came, the Commission had given him a pretext to act.

This was the kind of crisis de Gaulle enjoyed. He ticked off Peyrefitte for issuing an emollient communiqué after a French Council of Ministers meeting in July: 'You let people think that things were going to be sorted out. That is not the tone to use. On the contrary people need to be frightened. That is the best way of bringing our adversaries to heel.' After the next meeting he told Peyrefitte to keep a 'terrifying silence'.[55] As often with de Gaulle, these threats contained a degree of bluff. Although he recalled France's representative from Brussels, a deputy remained in place; although the French government announced that it was not ready to approve the European Community budget for 1966, this was done after Couve had assured de Gaulle that there was an emergency procedure to agree a new budget *in extremis*; although de Gaulle said publicly that he wanted a renegotiation of the Treaty of Rome, he gave signals that he was ready to accept a meeting of European foreign ministers to find a solution.[56]

In the end a compromise was reached in January 1966 in a meeting of foreign ministers at Luxembourg. According to the so-called 'Luxembourg compromise' no decision could be taken by a majority of the Council of

Ministers if any member state claimed that its national interests were being threatened. In that case, the other member states were required to find an acceptable solution within a reasonable period of time. The so-called compromise was really a fudge because it was not clear what would happen if no compromise could be reached. But this was a decisive brake on the process of European integration. De Gaulle had got both grain and grandeur.

In terms of French domestic politics the 'empty chair' crisis was a high-risk tactic if de Gaulle intended to stand in the Presidential election. It antagonized French farmers who believed that he was sacrificing a favourable agricultural deal to his wider anti-European agenda. But still no one knew if he was planning to stand.

TELEVISION ELECTION

By the summer of 1965, the candidature of Gaston Defferre, announced too early, had run out of steam. The plan to field a joint candidate of the Socialists and the Catholic Centre – in effect a resuscitation of the Fourth Republic's Third Force – foundered on the historical division between Socialists and the Catholics over the place of religion in the education system. Defferre withdrew his candidature. This was the signal, on 9 September, for François Mitterrand to announce that he would stand as the candidate of the left.

Mitterrand had long been one of de Gaulle's most implacable opponents. His anti-Gaullism had deep roots stretching back to a first disastrous meeting in Algiers in December 1943. According to Mitterrand, de Gaulle's opening conversational gambit had been to reprimand him for having arrived on a British plane.[57] There were deeper reasons for this frostiness. Having initially flirted with the Vichy regime – to the extent of being decorated by it – Mitterrand had moved into the Resistance during 1942, setting up an important Resistance movement of escaped prisoners of war. But he was one of those former Vichyites who had tried to square his former allegiances with his new ones by supporting Giraud over de Gaulle. Another ingredient in the mix was the existence of a second Resistance movement of escaped prisoners of war, run by de Gaulle's nephew Michel Cailliau, who had never compromised himself by supporting Vichy. De Gaulle was warned by Cailliau that Mitterrand was a recently converted Vichyite and not to be trusted. With all this baggage it is hardly surprising that the first encounter between de Gaulle and Mitterrand was not a success.

In the Fourth Republic Mitterrand had been a key figure of the centrist UDSR. He was a minister in several governments and had the regime not collapsed in 1958 he would have stood a good chance of becoming premier very soon. When President Coty had approached de Gaulle indirectly on 5 May 1958 to sound out his attitude if he were invited to form a government, it was because he feared that the only alternative might be Mitterrand, whom he did not trust. So de Gaulle's return had directly blocked the way for Mitterrand.[58] At the meeting in the Hôtel La Pérouse on 31 May where de Gaulle had met the leaders of the political parties to assure them that democracy would be safe in his hands, Mitterrand was the only one to refuse his support. He wrote later: 'I saw them all bowing and scraping in front of him ... De Gaulle was playing the master of ceremonies ... offering them this and that ... with a mixture of indifference and contempt.' Instead Mitterrand got up and announced: 'We risk entering into the era of South American Republics and pronunciamentos ... After the generals, it will be the rule of the colonels ... After all, General, you are mortal.' A furious de Gaulle replied: 'So you want me dead then.' On the next day, in parliament Mitterrand made his position public: 'When on 10 September 1944 General de Gaulle appeared before the National Assembly which was born out of the fighting of the external and internal Resistance, he had as his two companions: honour and the fatherland. Today his companions, even if he did not choose them, are coup and sedition.'

Over the next two years Mitterrand's career reached a low point as a result of the so-called Observatoire Affair, in which he was apparently the victim of an assassination attempt that he escaped only by clambering over the wall of the Luxembourg Gardens. A few days later, however, it turned out that Mitterrand had known about this in advance and might even have helped to stage it. The matter might have been forgotten but for the tenacity of Michel Debré, who pushed for Mitterrand to be stripped of his parliamentary immunity and came near to destroying him politically. Once Mitterrand had weathered this storm, he became de Gaulle's most ferocious opponent in parliament, playing on the theme of de Gaulle as a neo-Bonapartist dictator. This was the theme of his infamous pamphlet in 1964 denouncing the Fifth Republic as a 'permanent coup d'état'. As well as his anti-Gaullist past, Mitterrand, who had few settled political convictions, was a convinced European and Atlanticist. In short, he managed to condense in his person almost every strand of anti-Gaullism. But the visceral natural of his hostility to de Gaulle was ultimately existential. He was an ambitious and talented political loner who could never have accepted a political career in the shadow of anyone else. He was going to succeed on his terms or not at all. As he put it some years later: 'There are so many people who can summarize 30 years of their life with a "De Gaulle and me". I will not fall into this trap. I have seen and felt France without needing anyone else.'[59]

Mitterrand's brilliance as a debater and polemicist won him as many admirers as his murky past and overt ambition won him enemies. Although he had not been seen as a figure of the left in the Fourth Republic, he had reacquired a political virginity in the Fifth. For this reason, both the Socialist and Communist Parties agreed to back him. Mitterrand's candidature, located on the left, offered a different political configuration from the Third Force centrist alliance sought by Defferre. This paved the way for an almost unknown young Catholic politician, Jean Lecanuet, to announce that he too would stand in the election to represent the centre. Three other candidates declared themselves, including the lawyer Jean-Marie Tixier-Vignancour for the extreme right. Tixier-Vignancour had held a minor post in the early days of the Vichy regime and had defended several members of the OAS in the 1960s. The stage was now set for the first Presidential election by universal suffrage since 1848.

Still de Gaulle would not reveal his hand, to the increasing frustration of Pompidou, who told Peyrefitte on 13 October that his 'silence to me on the subject is becoming more and more discourteous'.[60] Foccart was especially frustrated because it would fall to him to prepare the campaign – but first he needed to know the name of the candidate. On 19 October, he presented de Gaulle with two possible posters for the campaign, but de Gaulle refused to look at them and would only refer to the 'Gaullist who will stand'. A week later, on 27 October, de Gaulle told his Council of Ministers that he would announce his decision publicly in the following week. Half his ministers believed he was planning not to stand, and the other half believed the opposite.[61] For the recording of the speech at 6.00 p.m. on 4 November only a tiny group were present including Peyrefitte and Foccart but not Pompidou. The blinds were pulled down to prevent those present signalling de Gaulle's intentions through a window. They were not released from the room until five minutes before the speech was televised. Peyrefitte immediately rushed over to the Hôtel Matignon where Pompidou's team was watching in tense silence. When it was over, Pompidou got up and left without saying a word. Since the theme of the speech, in a nutshell, was that without de Gaulle France would fall back into chaos and disaster, its implications were insulting both to what Pompidou had achieved as Prime Minister and to what he might have been able to achieve as President.

Waiting until the last moment was de Gaulle's tactic for wrongfooting his opponents and forcing them to reveal their hand in advance. But haunted by the fear of the 'shipwreck' of old age, and always prone to moments of melancholy, he had genuinely wondered whether he should not give up at the moment when his place in history seemed assured. As he had said to Peyreffite almost a year earlier, 'it is better to leave five years too early than a minute too late'[62] – but when would that minute come? In the end, de Gaulle's craving for power and his messianic sense of his own indispensability prevailed over his doubts.

The one-month presidential election campaign was the first in French history in which the methods of modern marketing played a role.[63] In the previous year, Foccart had been approached by a young advertising executive, Michel Bongrand, who had studied Kennedy's election in 1960. Believing that its techniques could be applied to France, he sent a 100-page proposal to Foccart. It is not known whether Foccart passed this on to de Gaulle. Since Bongrand was best known for having launched the James Bond brand in France it seems unlikely that de Gaulle would have been receptive. Instead Bongrand was hired by Lecanuet. He set about marketing Lecanuet as a kind of French Kennedy. A campaign film was presented on a large screen at Lecanuet's meetings where Lecanuet scarves were also on sale. Much play was made of Lecanuet's youth, his photogenic smile and the fact that he was relatively unknown. On his first television appearance Lecanuet opened with the words: 'My name is Jean Lecanuet. I am forty-five years old.' He then presented his background and family: 'I am not a hero of legend but a man among other men sharing your preoccupations and your worries.' It was easy to decode this message.

The campaign was dominated by television. Each candidate was given two hours of television airtime. Though, as we have seen, a pioneer in the use of television, de Gaulle failed to predict its huge impact on the election. He was convinced that the public would soon tire of listening every night to a political speech. The other candidates took time to hone their television skills since they had never previously had a chance to appear on the medium. Tixier-Vignancour, more used to pleading in court, was coached by another right-wing politician, Jean-Marie Le Pen. Mitterrand was initially stiff and ill at ease, and some viewers were put off by his wolfish smile, but his opening line struck a chord: 'The General poses problems which concerned our fathers while I am posing problems which will concern our children.' Mitterrand became more relaxed and experimented with a new format in which he was asked easy questions by a female journalist. In the end, what mattered for de Gaulle's opponents was less the quality of their performances than the fact that they were seen on television at all. A Le Monde journalist commented that it was as if the television station had been taken over by a gang of rebels. Television rentals soared.

Still de Gaulle refused to descend into the arena. He intended to speak only once on the eve of the election since the French knew him perfectly well. As he said to Peyrefitte: 'You are presumably not asking me to appear before the cameras and say: "My name is Charles de Gaulle."' As the polls began to look worrying, de Gaulle was reluctantly prevailed upon to make an extra television speech on 30 November, six days before the poll. Even the loyal Foccart judged it a disaster. De Gaulle looked stiff and awkward, his suit seemed creased. Concentrating on the past, he gave no reasons why the French should elect him for the future. He appeared so old that some worried electors rang up the Elysée to enquire after his health. Not mentioning any of his opponents by name, de Gaulle denigrated them as 'champions of decadence' who represented the 'old parties'. The implication was that only he was competent to deal with the problems of a 'difficult and dangerous world' although he did not say what he intended to do. His second television intervention on the eve of polling was only marginally better. The broadcast was so boring that it is still an effort to watch it today. It was as if de Gaulle, the consummate performer, could not see why he needed to make the case for a self-evident truth: no one else could ensure the salvation of France.

On the Sunday evening of polling, de Gaulle was in Colombey. The results were as bad as the polls had predicted. Although having the largest number of votes, with only 44.6 per cent de Gaulle was far short of the overall majority. He would be forced into a run-off with the second-placed candidate François Mitterrand (31.7 per cent). The surprise was that the previously unknown Lecanuet had scored 15.5 per cent; Tixier-Vignancour came fourth with 5.2 per cent. In the evening Pompidou, Peyrefitte and Joxe gathered nervously at the Matignon to decide how to deal with de Gaulle. Pompidou rang in the presence of the other two. He gave de Gaulle a reassuring interpretation of the result, but there was complete silence at the other end of the line. Pompidou was reduced to asking anxiously: 'Are you still there? Can you hear me?' In the end he passed the receiver to Peyrefitte who at least managed to get de Gaulle to speak but not to confirm that he would not withdrew his candidature: 'I don't see how the 56 per cent who did not vote for me today are going to change their minds in two weeks.' Peyrefitte laboriously tried to explain the logic of the system: 'In the first round one elects, in the second one eliminates.' At the end of the conversation, they had no idea what de Gaulle was planning. Later that evening Burin des Roziers rang to say that de Gaulle seemed 'depressed to a degree you cannot imagine'.[64]

After another day confined in Colombey, de Gaulle returned to Paris on Tuesday 7 December determined that he would fight on. It seems inconceivable that he had ever really contemplated anything else. His brother-in-law, visiting Colombey on Monday, had found him 'annoyed' but certainly not in the depression he had been in on Sunday evening.[65]

His advisers set about persuading him that he must change his approach and appear less detached from the ordinary concerns of the French. De Gaulle initially resisted: 'So you want me to talk to the French in pyjamas.'[66] In the end, he agreed to experiment with a new television format by doing three interviews with the pro-Gaullist journalist Michel Droit. The recording of the first session went so well that de Gaulle insisted on recording the next two immediately afterwards. The interviews were broadcast over three successive nights. The only cut suggested by his advisers was a phrase mocking Lecanuet's electors as 'choirboys who have stolen the communion wine'. De Gaulle agreed it was hardly politic to poke fun at the many Catholic centrists whose votes he needed in the second round.

The broadcasts were a great success. Sitting in an armchair opposite Droit, rather than alone in front of a table, de Gaulle offered the public a more relaxed image of himself. Droit succeeded in drawing him down from the 'summits' he liked to inhabit and getting him to discuss the ordinary problems of the French. De Gaulle expatiating on washing machines, fridges and vacuum cleaners was almost as startling as de Gaulle in pyjamas would have been. As always with the General, there were touches of theatricality as when he jumped out of his chair in exasperation at the suggestion he was not a good European: 'You need to take things as they are since politics must be based on realities. Of course you can jump up in your chair like a *cabri* [goat] crying "Europe, Europe, Europe" but that will lead nowhere and means nothing.'[67] This was one of those occasional archaisms which spiced up de Gaulle's speeches. Most people had no idea why he should have compared himself to a jumping goat; journalists rushed to their dictionaries to find out the origins of the phrase.[68] Curiously Mitterrand, trying to look Presidential, contrived to make it seem he was speaking from the Elysée, while de Gaulle appeared almost as his challenger.

An assortment of personalities and intellectuals, many of them former resisters, announced in the columns of *Le Monde* how they intended to vote. Emmanuel d'Astier de la Vigerie, who had pursued a post-war career as a Communist fellow-travelling journalist, announced that he would vote for de Gaulle in order to resist 'the hegemony of the United States'; while another former leftist resister, the novelist André Chamson, justified his vote for de Gaulle as a way of being faithful to the 'values of the Republic' and the ideals he had defended as a young supporter of the Popular Front. The writer Jean Guéhenno, also a former resister and former supporter of the Popular Front, took the contrary view that Gaullism was a 'variant of Pétainism' in its pursuit of a 'boastful and outdated' Maurassian policy of 'France alone'; and the art historian Jean Cassou, who had been in the same Resistance network as Agnès Humbert, whose reaction to de Gaulle in

1940 opened this book, opposed de Gaulle because he saw Gaullism as a new version of Bonapartism. The journalist Jean Cau, once close to Jean-Paul Sartre, said he would vote for de Gaulle because his opponents represented the spirit of the 'ex-Pétainist bourgeoisie' frightened of the idea of national independence: 'He is not of the left ... He is not that left we want to see born, but he is the person who will allow us to bury once and for all the old left.' Pierre Boutang, monarchist and former Pétainist, announced that he would vote for de Gaulle 'out of curiosity' and because, despite the betrayal over Algeria, he represented the Pétainist spirit. The economist Pierre Uri, close to Monnet, warned against being taken in by de Gaulle's phoney Third World progressivism, motivated by anti-Americanism rather than by any genuine desire to solve the real problems of developing countries. The leftist sociologist Edgar Morin announced he would abstain. He could not support the disparate ragbag of interests that had lined up behind Mitterrand, but he felt that the potentially progressive aspects of a 'Gaullian' vote risked being contradicted by the conservatism of Gaullism: 'I cannot totally dissociate the Gaullian personality from the Gaullist reality.'[69]

This range of positions reveals the extent to which the 'Gaullian personality' continued to defy pigeonholing, transcending normal political boundaries. In the end, however, the election proved the opposite about the 'Gaullist reality'. It was another blow to de Gaulle's idea that he enjoyed a mystical bond with the French straddling left and right. This had been true in moments of national crisis but in normal conditions the logic of the Fifth Republic was increased political bipolarization. In the second round of the election, de Gaulle scored 54.9 per cent of the vote to Mitterrand's 45.1 per cent. Whatever the success of de Gaulle's performances with Michel Droit, Mitterrand's result could have been statistically deduced from the results of the first round. He obtained the support of those who had supported the extreme right-winger Tixier. They would have voted for Caligula's horse rather than de Gaulle; and here Mitterrand's Vichyite past did him no harm. Most of Lecanuet's centrist voters ended up voting for de Gaulle since they were put off by the fact that Mitterrand was supported by the left. Although the background of the election had been the 'empty chair' crisis in Europe, there seems no evidence that it made much difference to the result even if it lost de Gaulle votes in the countryside.

De Gaulle's lofty way of dealing with the humiliation of having been forced into a run-off was to affect indifference. Replying to letters of congratulations, he always referred to his 'election' in quotation marks as if being elected had nothing to do with the reason why he was President. He wrote to his sister Marie-Agnès that the problem was that the French were not at the moment frightened of anything. As a result they were once again tempted by 'dispersion and facility'.[70] In his famous anti-Gaullist polemic describing the Fifth Republic as a permanent *coup d'état*, de Gaulle's 1965 nemesis François Mitterrand had written that he was one of those figures who 'only flourish in Misfortune and Disaster'.[71] The accusation was not entirely without foundation. The first stage of de Gaulle's extraordinary career had been made possible by the catastrophe of 1940, and its second stage by the Algerian crisis. His return to power in 1958 conformed to a recurrent pattern of French politics since that moment when Napoleon emerged in 1799 to save – or to bury, depending on one's view – the Revolution: the appeal to the providential saviour.[72] That tradition had been invoked successfully by Napoleon's nephew in 1848–51, unsuccessfully by General Boulanger in the 1880s, and most spectacularly in the twentieth century by Marshal Pétain in 1940. Although the recourse to the providential leader is seemingly the antithesis of the suspicion in French republican tradition of strong leaders, there have also been moments when republican politicians themselves succumbed to it as a way of extricating themselves from a crisis that the democratic system seemed incapable of resolving. One such moment was the republican cult of Clemenceau in 1917; another the appeal to Raymond Poincaré to save the franc in 1926. Up to a point the brief popularity of Pierre Mendès France in 1954–5 fitted into the same tradition.

But once the crisis is over the providential saviour is supposed to become redundant. De Gaulle's way of dealing with this was to deploy the inexhaustible repertoire of his Manichean rhetoric, warning that crisis was never far away: France's rank (*rang*) and grandeur were always threatened by decadence and mediocrity, her independence by servitude, her ambition by renunciation, the summits by the abyss, order and cohesion by disorder and division, unity and *rassemblement* by factions and clans. But this alarmist language had decreasing purchase in the prosperous France of the mid-1960s. It also undermined de Gaulle's own claim that he had for the first time since the Revolution provided France with stable and effective institutions. De Gaulle in 1965 had become a victim of his own success.

PART FIVE

Towards the End, 1966–1970

Glory does not respect old men! . . . I really believe that the Gods, when they cause the young to die, do it out of goodness and love. They make for them the choice of Achilles . . . The Duc de Saint-Simon . . . wrote of the Prince Eugène: 'It happens to great men that they live too long.'

De Gaulle to Pierre-Henry Rix in 1948,
in Pierre-Henry Rix, *Par le portillon de la Boisserie,* 101

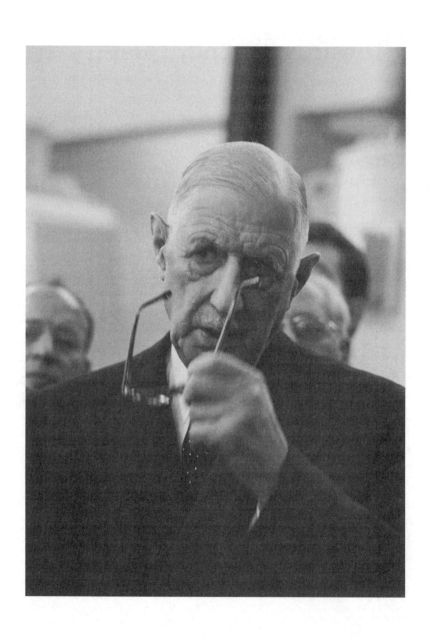

26

Upsetting the Applecart, 1966–1967

OLD MAN IN A HURRY

De Gaulle's re-election took place a month after his seventy-fifth birthday. He was now four years older than Pétain had been in 1925 – the year when, according to de Gaulle, he had 'died'. De Gaulle's youngest brother Pierre had died suddenly in December 1959 after a massive stroke which occurred while he was visiting the Elysée. Two years later de Gaulle wrote to the politician Louis Jacquinot whose own brother had just died: 'Losing a brother is not just to be deprived of a person one loved but also to see something of our youth disappear, that is something of oneself.'[1] After Pierre's death, Charles and his sister Marie-Agnès were the only survivors of the five children of Henri and Jeanne de Gaulle. One day in 1967, de Gaulle drew up a list of famous personalities who had continued to be productive in their old age. He included Goethe writing *Faust* at eighty, Verdi composing his *Te Deum* at eighty-five, Sophocles writing *Oedipus* at ninety, the Venetian Doge Dandolo taking Constantinople at ninety. Other names he noted were Titian, Monet, Chateaubriand, Hugo, Tolstoy, Bernard Shaw, Kant, Voltaire. At the end of his list, de Gaulle wrote: 'These are examples that one cites to oneself to reassure oneself about one's age.'[2] But de Gaulle was not reassured. He was haunted by the knowledge that his time was limited. This bestowed a somewhat frenetic quality on his policies after the re-election, as if this old man in a hurry was desperate to leave an indelible mark before it was too late.

The most dramatic initiative was the announcement on 7 March 1966 that France would withdraw from NATO and immediately end its participation in the integrated NATO command. In a subsequent letter to other NATO partners, de Gaulle made it clear that French troops in Germany would no longer be assigned to NATO, and that all foreign troops would be required to leave France by April 1967. Some weeks later de Gaulle found himself in conversation with his old Free French companion

René Pleven, at an Elysée reception. Pleven had broken with de Gaulle in 1947 and become a major player in Fourth Republic politics, since when the two men had had little contact. During their brief conversation, Pleven told de Gaulle that he opposed not so much de Gaulle's decision on NATO as the brutally sudden way he had announced it. De Gaulle was unrepentant:

> When one wants to do something, first one has to upset the applecart [*bousculer le pot de fleurs / kick the flowerpot over*]. Otherwise people will just say: 'it can be arranged; you must not do that.' If you give a big kick, the problem is posed and it has to be solved.[3]

Pleven, who had lived through similar Gaullist methods during the war – in Syria, in Saint-Pierre-et-Miquelon – should not have been surprised. The problem was that the effectiveness of this tactic wore off as de Gaulle's partners learnt that the most effective response was not to rise to the bait. Although Dean Rusk had sarcastically asked if removing troops from French soil included those in war cemeteries who had died for France, Johnson refused, in his words, to get into a 'pissing match' which would only serve 'to build de Gaulle up'. Another American official expressed the same idea more elegantly: 'De Gaulle is like a lightweight jujitsu artist. All his leverage comes from our over-exertion.'[4] To make the same impact as in the past, de Gaulle found himself having to kick more flowerpots over, and to kick them ever harder.

The shock of de Gaulle's decision to leave NATO lay above all in the timing and style of the announcement. Only two weeks earlier, the recently appointed French Ambassador in Washington, Charles Lucet, had assured the State Department that there was 'no sense of urgency' regarding NATO.[5] It is uncertain whether de Gaulle had always intended to leave NATO or whether he did so because he had been disappointed by the response to his Memorandum of September 1958. In 1963, he said of that famous document: 'I was looking for a way to leave NATO and get back our freedom . . . So I asked for the moon.'[6] This may be true, but it may not be. De Gaulle, who hated to admit defeat, possibly no longer knew himself what he had intended. If he had never taken the Memorandum seriously, it is surprising how often he returned to it between 1958 and 1962.[7] After that he seems to have given up on it, and his sights were clearly set on leaving NATO at some stage.

What did 'leaving NATO' mean? Originally de Gaulle seemed to object only to the system of integrated military command, not to the Atlantic Alliance itself. But on various occasions in 1965 he floated the idea that France might leave the Alliance entirely. In that case France would have replaced the multilateral Alliance signed in 1949 with a series of bilateral pacts with her partners.[8] No one knew how far he intended to go – or when. In January 1966, in a conversation with Manlio Brosio, Secretary General of NATO, he said that France planned to replace the 1949 Atlantic Alliance probably in the course of the year. This remark caused alarm and was followed by a series of corrective notes from Quai officials 'clarifying' exactly what de Gaulle had said – which no one quite agreed on.[9] Then de Gaulle told the American Ambassador the opposite of what he seemed to have told Brosio two weeks earlier: France would not leave the alliance but only NATO's integrated military command, and even that would not happen soon.[10]

The Quai d'Orsay prepared for various scenarios but had no more idea of de Gaulle's intentions than anyone else. One official wrote to Lucet: 'I have tried to keep you informed but I know no more. Let us wait for the press conference.'[11] The press conference in question, on 21 February, made matters no clearer. De Gaulle announced that 'without going back on her membership of the Atlantic Alliance' France would 'continue to modify successively its current dispositions'.[12] This seemed to suggest a progressive process of disengagement rather than a sudden break. It was on the strength of this that Lucet assured the State Department in good faith that nothing was imminent.

These cat-and-mouse tactics were vintage de Gaulle. He so enjoyed being – or playing at being – Machiavellian that he may well not have had much idea himself of what he was intending to do. Were de Gaulle's comments to Brosio about leaving the Alliance intended to cause such alarm that his allies would be relieved when he drew back from this extreme step? Did he have second thoughts about the Alliance when it dawned on him that this would deprive France of a justification for maintaining troops on German soil?[13] Was he still thinking of leaving the Alliance in due course but preferred to take one step at a time? No one knows the answer to these questions. Most probably de Gaulle's timing was linked to the fact that he had accepted an invitation to visit the Soviet Union later in the year. The break with NATO's military command offered the Soviet government concrete evidence that his intentions to shake up the Alliance were not just rhetorical.[14] Certainly de Gaulle's decision was part of a wider reorientation of foreign policy, whose next step was his visit to Moscow.

CONTAINING GERMANY

De Gaulle had always believed that the division of the world into two ideological blocs was contrary to the laws of history. Geopolitics would always trump ideology. He told Macmillan in December 1959 at a moment of extreme Cold War tension:

> I know you don't like long-term plans but I think the day will come when it will be possible to come to an arrangement with the Russians. They will become less Communist and more bourgeois . . . As for the Poles, they remain Poles, the Czechs Czechs, the Rumanians Rumanians, the Prussians Prussians [a revealing label] despite their bolshevism. One day, if war does not break out, all this will evolve towards peace . . . Or if there is war, it will be the end of everything.[15]

De Gaulle, influenced by the thinking of the 1930s 'nonconformists', believed that capitalism and socialism were only mirror images of each other, both manifestations of industrial mass society. As he put it to Khrushchev in 1960:

> You speak of the socialist and capitalist camps. I do understand the huge difference between these two systems. Nonetheless I must say to you that I attach less importance to it. We are all very dependent on technology. Our factories are not so different from yours. The conditions our workers experience are probably not so different conditions from yours. Material progress is growing everywhere . . . What will happen in the future? I don't know . . . But I think that with time the differences between capitalism and socialism are going to diminish. The experience of life has shown me that capitalism has gone through huge changes. In my youth a large part of the bourgeoisie lived off dividends. Today the most important industrialists live off their work. I think socialism is also evolving.[16]

For de Gaulle, the ending of the division of the world into two blocs was not only inevitable but also desirable. Only a multipolar world would permit Europe – and therefore France – to become a player in world politics again. As he put it in a speech in October 1966, the 'stifling rigidity' of two blocs 'paralyses and sterilizes the rest of the universe, placing it under a crushing hegemony'.[17] But between 1959 and 1962 Cold War tension over Berlin prevented any opening towards the Soviet Union. In these years, no one in the western camp had been less ready to compromise with Moscow than de Gaulle – which had helped him win the trust of Adenauer.

After the world had come to the brink of war over Cuba in 1962, there was a relaxing of international tension between the superpowers. This did not totally suit de Gaulle either. Any rapprochement between the United States and the Soviet Union above the heads of the European powers revived his 'Yalta complex'. He wanted détente – but détente carried out through the Europeans, not imposed on them by the great powers. He wrote to Adenauer in 1963 about the need for France and Germany to show 'great vigilance' regarding 'direct relationships that our Anglo-Saxon allies might be inclined to make with the east'.[18]

In 1964 the Rumanian Prime Minister Ion Maurer had expressed an interest in coming to Paris. His visit, which took place in July, was the first ever by a Communist Rumanian leader to any western capital. De Gaulle interpreted this to mean either that the Soviet Union was relaxing its grip on its eastern satellites or that it was no longer fully able to control them – although he knew that, before leaving for Paris, Maurer had travelled to Moscow to secure approval for the trip. After Maurer's visit, de Gaulle started receiving more signals that the Soviet Union would be interested in improving relations with France. He was cautiously receptive, although he told Alphand at the start of 1965: 'They will have to make their thinking clear ... It is not out of the question that one day some agreements could occur. But the Russians must give new and evident proof of their desire for détente and entente.'[19]

The path towards a diplomatic rapprochement was prepared by commercial agreements. Nineteen-sixty-four was a year of international negotiations over what technology should be adopted for colour television, a lucrative future market. The American government had approved its own system (NTSC – National Television System Committee) in 1954, and two years later a French engineer patented a different system named SECAM (later dubbed by the Americans the 'Supreme Effort Contra America'). The Germans were also working on their own system. For months, French and German industrialists had been discussing how to mesh their two systems to create a single European one. But at the beginning of 1965 the Soviets expressed interest in buying SECAM. De Gaulle, who hoped to steal a march on the Americans and the Germans, followed the issue with passionate interest. He sent Peyrefitte and two ministers to Moscow to extol the merits of the French system. An agreement was signed in March 1965. This was a small technological-diplomatic coup for France which caused some bitterness in Germany. The general view was that the French system performed least effectively. The Soviet leader Kosygin hinted that the Soviet decision to adopt SECAM had been taken for political reasons.[20] This paved the way for de Gaulle to accept a formal invitation to visit the Soviet Union in 1966 while evading any commitments in advance about what might emerge.[21] As he joked to Peyrefitte: 'We are not going to exchange colour television for recognition of East Germany.'[22]

Yet de Gaulle's opening to the Soviet Union *was* closely related to the problem of Germany. If de Gaulle has a justifiable reputation as one of the architects of Franco-German reconciliation, one must also remember that his suspicion of Germany was never far below the surface. Although he had occasionally dangled in front of the Germans the prospect of a nuclear partnership with France, his assumption was that the French would be in control. Once it was clear the Germans would not jeopardize their relations with America, de Gaulle became obsessed with the idea that Germany was trying, through the MLF, to inch her way towards nuclear power status. This could not be allowed.[23] 'For this warlike people', he told Peyrefitte, 'it would be a formidable temptation' – more dangerous, he added, than allowing them to occupy the Rhineland in 1936.[24] De Gaulle summarized his thinking on Germany in a paper for the government at the start of February 1966:

> She is no longer the polite and honest loser who is trying to win the good graces of her conqueror. The Germans can feel that elemental forces are being reborn and they are animated by new ambitions . . . They have now developed pretensions to have nuclear arms. They want to count in the western nuclear system, that is to say the American one . . . We will oppose this for our sakes, and for theirs. For them this pretension is contrary to what ought to be their essential objective, reunification. As for us, we have seen enough to know what the renaissance of the military strength of Germany means.[25]

When one finds de Gaulle a few months later worrying that a future economic association between the European Community and Austria might lead the way to an '*Anschluss*' it becomes clear – along with his reference to the Rhineland reoccupation – how suspiciously he was viewing Germany at this time.[26]

De Gaulle's turn to the Soviet Union was part of a long-term strategy to solve the 'problem' of Germany. The ultimate goal was that, in exchange for American disengagement from Europe, the Soviet Union would relax her hold on her eastern satellites, drop her support for Eastern Germany (GDR) and allow German reunification. In return, Germany would accept the eastern frontiers that had emerged out of the war – the Oder–Neisse Line – and renounce nuclear ambitions. The guarantors of this new European order would be the two continental European nuclear powers, the Soviet Union and France. De Gaulle portrayed himself as a visionary looking forward to the end of the Cold War, but this vision was very much the Europe of 1914 when the Franco-Russian alliance acted as a counterweight to this 'warlike people' at the centre of Europe – with the additional guarantee of nuclear weapons. When asked by Alphand in 1965 if he was not worried about a reunified Germany he replied:

Not if there is an agreement between East and West to make Germany respect her obligations. That agreement did not exist in 1936 [here again the memory of the 1930s]. And also atomic weapons have transformed the problem. None of us have any intention of helping Germany to become a nuclear power, or allowing her to become one.[27]

De Gaulle's idea of solving the German problem through reunification policed by a Franco-Soviet entente was obviously a long-term ambition. As he told an American senator in 1968: 'We want reunification to take place one day, but in the same way as the Jews used to say for 1800 years, "Next year in Jerusalem". This can last a very long time.'[28] And to the extent that he was serious about German reunification he envisaged it as taking the form of a kind of confederation rather than the reconstruction of a unitary state.[29]

De Gaulle saw his trip to the Soviet Union as a chance to test the water. Before he set off, he told his government that he wanted 'to see where the Soviets are going, and what they are ready to agree to; or at least where they are going and what they are not ready to agree to'.[30] His eleven-day visit to the Soviet Union in June was the longest he paid to any country during his period as President. He was treated with exceptional ceremony by the Soviet leadership, visiting Volgograd, Kiev and Leningrad, as well as spending three days in Moscow. On the day before returning home, he addressed the Russian population on television. Despite the warm reception, he remarked of his three long discussions with the Soviet leaders Brezhnev and Kosygin: 'I recited my lines and they recited theirs.'[31] From the first meeting, de Gaulle was adamant that he would never recognize the GDR: 'It is your creation and so an artificial state.' His interlocutors responded with the usual rhetoric about how the Federal Republic was a 'fascist' state. They ruled out German reunification under any circumstances. The only concrete result of the visit was the setting up of a commission to discuss economic cooperation between the two countries and the installation of a direct telephone hotline between the Elysée and the Kremlin.

De Gaulle's personal impressions of the Soviet Union were negative:

> The cooking is unimaginative and always the same, the champagne is very mediocre. Siberia is completely isolated and has no contact with Europe. There are lots of black students in the universities but they are all unhappy and have no contact with the Russians. In Leningrad, where I attended mass, there was a Lithuanian priest – a very good priest – but the churches are empty. Having said that, at least they did not subject me to an anti-religious museum.[32]

He put a more optimistic spin on the visit when he reported back to his government:

> The regime survives but is being transformed. It is becoming less ideological and more technocratic. The country is led by engineers not propagandists ... The differences of opinion on Germany were laid out but not insisted upon. Frankly the Russians do not give the impression of wanting war. But one must not tread on their toes. They are suspicious and really worried about the bellicosity of the US. They are thus pacific and worried.[33]

De Gaulle took a further opportunity to distance himself from the United States during a three-week autumn tour of the French Pacific where the French had tested their bombs since the loss of the Sahara testing sites. During the tour de Gaulle made a stop at Phnom Penh, capital of Cambodia. On 1 September, at the city's sports stadium, in front of a crowd of 100,000, he made his most spectacular denunciation so far of American intervention in Asia – just across the border from Vietnam. He described the war as one of 'national resistance' and, in a bravura rewriting of history, contrasted America's behaviour to that of France which had 'deliberately' taken the decision under his leadership to end the 132 years of her presence in Algeria although her forces 'dominated without contest'.[34]

This seemed like a radical escalation of de Gaulle's criticism of the Vietnam War. But things were not entirely as they seemed. The Phnom Penh speech was not just about upsetting the applecart. De Gaulle had informed the Americans in advance that he was intending to speak, and over the summer he had sent an envoy to Asia to see Ho Chi Minh. This did not displease the Americans, who wanted to open secret channels to the North Vietnamese. Johnson was careful not to make a fuss about de Gaulle's Phnom Penh speech. It won de Gaulle easy plaudits in the Third World, but he was also positioning France to play a possible role in brokering a peace.[35]

De Gaulle enjoyed his self-assumed position of moral superiority, but he also genuinely worried that the war in Vietnam was an obstacle to the policy of détente he was attempting to promote in Europe. Back in France, he received a visit from Kosygin at the end of the year. Both sides again simply recited their scripts as in Moscow. The truth was that the Soviets still viewed the world through Cold War lenses. They saw France as a possible weak link in the western bloc but were not really interested in moving beyond this to détente or to an agreement over Germany.[36]

Curiously, de Gaulle's policy of détente was proving more successful with the Germans than with the Russians. As he told Peyrefitte: 'It is essential to push Germany towards rapprochement with Russia. We have to disarm their reciprocal aggression. It is our game. It is the only one we have.'[37] The pro-American Ludwig Erhard, with whom de Gaulle had never got on, fell from power at the end of 1966. He was succeeded by a coalition headed by the Christian Democrat Kurt Kiesinger but which included Social Democrats. The new Foreign Minister, the Social Democrat Willy Brandt, former Mayor of West Berlin (and future inventor of *Ostpolitik*), was more receptive to the idea of détente than any of his predecessors. As a result, de Gaulle's meeting with Germany's new leaders in January 1967 was the most cordial he had had for nearly two years. The only major cloud on the horizon concerned Britain and the EEC. In November 1966, the Labour government of Harold Wilson had announced its desire to explore the possibility of another British application. De Gaulle, knowing that the Germans were likely to look on this more favourably than he did, laid his cards clearly on the table in his discussions with Kiesinger:

> The English have a permanent link with America and if the Americans give them up, the pound sterling will collapse along with the Commonwealth. If England enters into the Community, it will collapse because England will divide us . . . Of course one cannot say 'never' to them but 'one day perhaps'. In any case if our Community partners wanted to admit the English at any price, we would leave the Community.[38]

At the start of 1967, Wilson and his Foreign Secretary George Brown set off on a tour of European capitals to sound out the leaders of the Six, starting with Paris. De Gaulle was discouraging, but the British were not deterred and lodged a formal application in May. If the British went ahead anyway, it was because they believed they had learnt from the mistakes of their previous application. This time they did not attach any preconditions to their application and announced they were ready to accept the full terms of the Rome Treaty. De Gaulle's officials suggested that he nip the affair in the bud rather than allow protracted discussions. De Gaulle accepted this advice and announced at his press conference in May 1967 that Britain was not yet ready. But the British government refused to take the hint and retract its application. Harold Wilson was the first foreign leader to be put up officially at the newly restored Grand Trianon in June 1967 and was served lobster, *poularde de Bresse*, Château Lafite 1959 and Dom Ruinart champagne at the official luncheon.[39] Despite the grand surroundings and the show of French culinary grandeur, Wilson reported to Johnson that he had found de Gaulle in 'gloomy and apocalyptic mood' and that he appeared to be 'an old man obsessed in his fatalistic way by a sense of real impotence'.[40] The gloom was partly explained by the Middle East crisis which had broken out a few weeks earlier (see below) and de Gaulle was always susceptible to such moods, but Wilson drew the conclusion that French power might be waning and that the British should not abandon their efforts to join the Community. Over the coming months, the French tactic was to persuade their European partners that the British were not ready to play by the rules; the British tactic was to argue the opposite in the hope of isolating the French.[41] In the end this application was a non-event because de Gaulle had no intention of allowing it to succeed for the same reasons – commercial, economic and political – as in 1963, but he would have preferred to avoid a second veto which was likely to annoy France's European partners.

'THE ISRAELIS ARE OVERDOING IT' [EXAGERENT]

Although the rapprochement with Moscow had so far produced negligible results, de Gaulle saw one positive outcome so far: 'They consider that contacts with the West should go via France.'[42] The crisis that broke out in the Middle East in June between Israel and her Arab neighbours showed how wrong he was.

De Gaulle's had originally had considerable sympathy for Israel. In a conversation with Claude Guy in 1947 he remarked:

> In the Palestine business my preference goes to the Jews. The Arabs don't deserve to be helped: they are over-excitable. In 1930 when I went to Palestine for the first time, I remember having seen the orange trees cultivated by the Arabs: they were shrivelled, their fruits were bitter and small. The Jews on the other hand cultivated theirs remarkably successfully. These fanatical individualists, doubtless because they were working on what they had a sense of being the land of their birth, these former merchants from Poland and Germany, were ready to do the toughest work in the fields. During the war, when I returned to Palestine, the progress the Jews had made was amazing. That is why we need to help the Jews and we should hurry because anti-Semitism will reappear in its virulent form.[43]

De Gaulle had an unusually high personal regard for David Ben-Gurion, Israel's first Prime Minister, with whom he corresponded frequently. When Ben-Gurion visited Paris in June 1960, de Gaulle toasted him as the 'greatest statesman of this century' responsible for the 'remarkable resurrection, renaissance, pride and prosperity of Israel' – a formula going beyond the normal courtesies.[44]

But sentiment only went so far. De Gaulle's reaction to the 1967 crisis must be understood in the context of his attempt to extricate France from the unhealthily close relationship that had developed with Israel in the last years of the Fourth Republic as a result of the Algerian War.[45] Franco-Israeli collusion during the Suez crisis of 1956 was the most visible symbol of this situation. Although that crisis had turned into a Franco-British humiliation, French governments intensified military cooperation with Israel to the point of agreeing to nuclear cooperation. On returning to power, de Gaulle immediately put an end to any military nuclear cooperation – as with all other countries. The links between Israeli and French military personnel had become so embedded that a year later he felt obliged to reiterate the instruction.[46]

De Gaulle defined his policy a few months after coming to power as: 'Keep good relations with Israel but do not overdo it, so as to conciliate the Arabs.'[47] He declined an invitation to visit Israel while making clear that a visit from Ben-Gurion would be welcome. Under the pleasantries of this visit in June 1960, Ben-Gurion was under no illusion that things had changed. After the meeting Debré reported to de Gaulle that Ben-Gurion had told him he was 'profoundly saddened and worried' by what he had been told – especially regarding nuclear cooperation.[48] Even so France remained Israel's primary military supplier, and in 1961 de Gaulle authorized the sale of seventy-two fighter planes to Israel.

At the same time, once the Algerian War was over, de Gaulle also set about rebuilding bridges with the Arab states. He began receiving Arab leaders in Paris: King Hussein of Jordan in September 1963, the Syrian Vice-President in November 1964. While trying to hold the ring between Israel and her Arab neighbours, he became genuinely concerned that Israel harboured ambitions to expand her territories. In his *Memoirs* he recalled that, in a break during their talks in 1960, Ben-Gurion had told him that he hoped Israel could double her population from two to four million and 'revealed his intention to extend his frontiers as soon as the occasion presented itself'.[49] There is no official record of that conversation, and Ben-Gurion later remembered what was said in exactly opposite terms: that his two greatest hopes were for peace with his neighbours and an increase in population which he believed Israel's existing frontiers could contain. The future Israeli Prime Minister Simon Peres, who was present, noted Ben-Gurion's words in the same terms.[50]

Whether de Gaulle misunderstood wilfully or involuntarily, he had persuaded himself that the Israelis were fundamentally expansionist – and there was much in Ben-Gurion's previous policies to support this idea. Every time Ben-Gurion and his successors wrote to de Gaulle expressing fears about Israel's security, de Gaulle's response was to warn against any temptation to take armed action.[51] In private he was more forthright. He told Erhard in June 1965: 'We are being cautious regarding the Israelis. We are calming them and telling them not to overdo it [*exagérer*] . . . One must not be taken in by the Israelis who are very cunning, very skilful, and who exploit the tiniest things for their propaganda about the Arabs.'[52] Once de Gaulle had persuaded himself of something it was difficult to change his mind. His idea that the Israelis were *'exagèrent'* became a mantra.

Even taking account of all this, de Gaulle's reaction to the war of 1967 was a bombshell.[53] On 23 May, the crisis between Israel and Egypt escalated when Nasser closed the Straits of Tiran to Israeli shipping. For Israel, this was equivalent to an act of war. The French government had previously taken the same view. In March 1957 it had declared that if Israel forcibly resisted any violation of free navigation in the Straits this would be an act of legitimate defence. But the day after Nasser's announcement, de Gaulle told his government: 'France was then still scarred by the unfortunate Suez expedition and tended to espouse the Israeli cause with her eyes closed. Since then things have changed.'[54] The same day, de Gaulle met the Israeli Foreign Minister Abba Eban, on his way to Washington to solicit American support. In Eban's words, de Gaulle received him with 'grave courtesy'. Even before Eban had sat down, he said to him: 'Do not make war [*ne faites pas la guerre*].' Accompanying him to the door at the end of the meeting, he repeated the words solemnly: 'Above all do not attack. You would have to bear the consequences.'[55] It was a shock to Eban that de Gaulle did not regard the blockading of the Straits as a legitimate *casus belli* – though the response from the United States was not so different. The meeting revealed that de Gaulle had shifted to a higher gear in distancing France from Israel. At the same time, he was urging caution on the Arab states. On 1 June a Syrian representative was told:

> You, the Arabs, are many, and you are together. But you lack many things . . . If you want to destroy Israel your situation will be worse . . . Israel is a people. We French have not created it as a state; the Americans, the English and the Russians created it. But now it exists: it has organized itself and it works. We do not approve of all its excesses, and we do not approve of its raids against you . . . You have everything to gain by being patient. In many fields you are making great progress, but if you go to war, you will jeopardize most of it . . . But we have to negotiate, find a way, a solution . . . The Americans are biased against you, and the Soviets are biased in your favour, but do not bet on them going to war on your behalf.[56]

The next day King Faisal of Saudi Arabia was told: 'we are not committed to any side, neither to the Arabs nor to Israel. And we think every state has the right to live.'[57]

De Gaulle's preferred solution to the crisis was a meeting of the four great powers to broker a negotiated settlement. This was vetoed by the Soviet Union, which was inciting Nasser to hold firm. On 2 June, as tension escalated, the French government issued a communiqué, drafted personally by de Gaulle, declaring that France opposed the opening of hostilities by any power. On the next day, he announced an embargo on arms deliveries to all powers in the region. Since France was Israel's main arms supplier, this was not really an even-handed measure. Just before hostilities broke out, de Gaulle told Foccart: 'They are going to launch war ... I recognize that the Arabs are also unbearable, I recognize that the Arabs are threatening and that the Israelis feel suffocated ... [But] the Israelis will win, and after that everything will be different.'⁵⁸ This prediction was entirely accurate.

On 5 June, the Israeli air force launched a series of air raids on Egyptian airfields and destroyed the Egyptian air force in a day. The Israeli government did all it could to restrict the conflict to Egypt alone, but the Jordanian and Syrian governments both decided to join in, believing Egyptian propaganda that Israel was about to be defeated. Despite de Gaulle's public declaration regarding arms deliveries, on 7 June he did discreetly authorize the delivery of war matériel already paid for by Israel, including spare parts for Mirage jets. So during the short conflict Israel did not in fact lack the parts necessary for her air force.

After six days, a ceasefire was signed. The Arab states had been humiliated and Israel had seized territories from Jordan, Syria and Egypt in Sinai, the Golan Heights, Gaza and the West Bank. The Israeli government believed it had been betrayed by France, but once the war was over de Gaulle's official response was to refuse to take sides. On 14 June, France did not vote for a Soviet resolution at the United Nations Security Council condemning Israeli aggression but accepted a Soviet proposal for the General Assembly to debate the issue. During June and July, as foreign statesmen traipsed through Paris, de Gaulle's message to each was broadly similar, though with nuances.

Meeting the former American Vice-President Richard Nixon on 8 June, de Gaulle told him:

> Like you I think that a moderate settlement is necessary ... Those who will *exagérer* are the Israelis, and as you say, they should not do because they will not be able to resist in the long run against all the Arabs. But the Israelis are people who always *exagèrent*, and they have always done so; you only have to read the Psalms. The Arabs are no better. So with people who *exagèrent*, the great powers need to make them listen to reason. This needs the Russians; if not, nothing will be done.⁵⁹

To Kosygin a week later, de Gaulle's message was slightly different:

> You say to me that the aggressor must be punished and that Israel is the aggressor. It is true that Israel was the first to take up arms but there are

many who would say that they could not do otherwise, they were threatened, that they are a small country surrounded by Arabs ... I do not however think that we should let Israel *exagérer* and keep all her conquests. It might ... be possible after a long time and very difficult negotiations to reach a reasonable arrangement in the Middle East, if such a thing ever turns out to be possible. I mean by that a solution accepted by Israel and by the Arabs ... Israel would lose a part of what she has taken and keep some.[60]

Two days later, de Gaulle told Harold Wilson that 'Israel had been created by America, England and the Soviet Union; France had accepted it and it had taken root and flourished.' But France was now trying to improve her relations with the Arabs: 'There was no reason for the government of France – or he suggested that of the UK – to ruin their relations with the Arabs merely because public opinion felt some superficial sympathy for Israel because she was a small country with an unhappy history.'[61]

The more isolated de Gaulle found himself among his western allies, the more irritated he became, and the more extreme his private comments became about Israeli 'imperialism' and Israel's 'colonial war'.[62] Seeing Kiesinger in July he recalled yet again his conversation with Ben-Gurion about Israel's desire to extend her frontiers: 'They were looking for an opportunity and the Arabs stupidly gave it to them.'[63]

Historians are divided about Israel's responsibility for the Six Day War. Even Avi Shlaim, very critical of Israeli foreign policy, does not believe that Israel either planned or wanted this war. But the most recent study of the war's origins paints the picture of a hawkish Israeli military establishment which corresponds more closely to de Gaulle's suspicions.[64] Whatever the truth, nothing could shake de Gaulle's conviction that the Israelis were '*exagèrent*'. And his annoyance was exacerbated by the fact they had not listened to him – which he seemed to take as a kind of personal slight. Although he had started out hoping to play a mediating role – which the Israelis considered a betrayal in itself – he was moving closer to the Arab position. In the United Nations debate on 4 July, France backed a Yugoslav motion calling on Israel to withdraw from the territories she had occupied. This motion was otherwise supported only by the Soviet Union, her satellites and the Arab states.

The Middle East crisis had revealed the limits of French influence. De Gaulle's call for a four-power conference had been ignored before the crisis – and had no more success after it. During the war de Gaulle and Kosygin kept in touch through the special hotline set up after de Gaulle's visit to Russia.[65] This was just window-dressing. The Soviet leaders preferred to do their real business directly with the Americans. Johnson and Kosygin had two meetings on the subject at Glassboro in New Jersey on 23 and 25 June which showed how little account the Soviet government took of France.[66] Before the outbreak of war, when Abba Eban had mentioned to Johnson de Gaulle's idea of a four-power conference to solve the crisis, Johnson replied: 'The four Great Powers? Where the hell are the other two?'[67]

'VIVE LE QUÉBEC LIBRE'

During the Middle East crisis, many leading Gaullists, including prominent members of the government, were far from happy about the position de Gaulle had taken. The policy was de Gaulle's alone. Pompidou, speaking to a journalist before the meeting where de Gaulle informed his ministers that the closure of the Straits would not be considered a *casus belli*, had no inkling of what the policy of the government – supposedly *his* government – was going to be.[68] Two months later, another crisis, sparked by de Gaulle's visit to Quebec, caused equal consternation.

De Gaulle had shown little interest in French Canada before 1960. In August 1940, a broadcast from London to the French Canadians had met with little response. Conservative, Catholic Quebec was more sympathetic to Pétain than to de Gaulle, who therefore felt no sentimental debt to the French Canadians. It was during a state visit to Canada in 1960 that de Gaulle started to see potential in French Canada. He wrote excitedly to Debré from Canada that he had been struck by 'the vivacity of the senti-mental bonds which still exist between this part of Canada ... and the former motherland'.[69] On his return he told his brother-in-law that 'rising from the subconscious of the population was the hereditary love they felt for France.'[70] De Gaulle had picked up on a genuine new mood in Quebec politics. In 1960, after decades of political torpor, Quebec had elected a new Liberal government headed by Jean Lesage. The next decade in Que-bec was a period of rapid economic growth, accompanied by increasing political assertiveness. This 'Quiet Revolution', as it became known, also saw the emergence of a radical, although minuscule, independence move-ment. It is remarkable how quickly de Gaulle embraced the possibilities opened up by these developments.

At the start of 1961, de Gaulle welcomed a proposal that the province of Quebec should open an agency in Paris. He wrote to Courcel: 'The sim-ple fact that these relations might be disagreeable for the Ottawa government should not deflect us from setting them up.'[71] When Lesage visited Paris for the opening of the agency in October, the protocol surrounding his visit treated him as a head of state. Two years later, de Gaulle wrote to Burin des Roziers that he was ready to meet the Canadian Prime Minister Lester Pearson but that it was more important to establish special cooperation with French Canada, which will 'necessarily become a State and it is with this in view that we must act'.[72] In December 1966 he wrote: 'No question of sending a message to congratulate Canada on its centenary: it is not for us to congratulate the Canadians ... on the creation of a "State" founded on a past defeat of ours and on the integration of a part of the French people into a British ensemble. Besides, this ensemble is very precarious.'[73]

This was the moment at which de Gaulle was reinventing himself as a hero of the Third World, a posture which influenced his reading of the Canadian situation. He told Peyrefitte in 1963: 'We have given self-determination to the Algerians, so why could the English not do the same for the French of Canada?'[74] Frequently in private he complained that the French Canadians were living under an Anglo-American 'colonial' oppression.[75] The Quai d'Orsay was not enthusiastic about such remarks of course, but this was never an impediment for de Gaulle – quite the opposite. There was also a small clique of parliamentarians and officials – dubbed the 'Quebec Lobby' – and including René Saint-Légier, one of de Gaulle's Elysée *conseillers* – who encouraged the General down this path. Although it is clear where he was heading, he needed to find the moment to 'unveil our batteries', as he put it in October 1963.[76]

That moment came in 1967 with the opening in Montreal of the international Exhibition which was a symbol of Quebec's new dynamism. De Gaulle had been invited to visit the Exhibition by both the federal government in Ottawa and the provincial government of Quebec. Ottawa drew up the programme for a five-day visit, but de Gaulle substituted his own itinerary beginning with Quebec and ending with the federal capital, Ottawa. He made the journey across the Atlantic on the cruiser *Colbert*, allowing him to start the visit with a symbolically charged visit to Saint-Pierre-et-Miquelon. During the seven-day crossing de Gaulle wrote his speeches and also found time to read Malraux's recently published *Antimémoires*.

De Gaulle arrived in Quebec on 23 July. His first speech, hailing the 'passive resistance' by 'a fragment of our people' against forces threatening their cohesion, should have set alarm bells ringing.[77] The next day, he travelled in an open-top car along the 280-kilometre road on the north bank of the St Lawrence river which the first French settlers had dedicated to the King of France, dubbing it Le Chemin du Roy. The route was lined with cheering crowds, and de Gaulle stopped six times to address them. Montreal was the last stop on the journey. The official schedule programmed an appearance on the balcony of the Town Hall but no speech. De Gaulle had other ideas. He appeared on the balcony, raised his arms and spoke. Taking up the resistance theme he had broached in his first speech in Quebec, he opened: 'I am going to tell you a secret that you will not repeat. This evening and all along the journey I felt I was living an atmosphere similar to that of the Liberation.' But it was the end of the speech which caused the sensation: '*Vive Montréal, Vive le Québec* [long pause and then very deliberately with each word pronounced carefully], *Vive le Québec libre, Vive le Canada français, Vive la France.*' The crowd, momentarily stunned, and wondering if it had heard correctly, erupted into cheers, and roars of '*Vive de Gaulle*'.

Given how many Anglophone Canadians – and how few French Canadians – had died liberating France, de Gaulle's invocation of the Liberation analogy was at the very least in bad taste. The federal government made its displeasure public. De Gaulle cancelled the planned trip to Ottawa, cut short his visit and flew back to Paris on 27 July. There has been much speculation about whether he had uttered the incriminating phrase – '*Vive le Québec libre*' – calculatedly or in the emotion of the moment. There is no doubt about the answer. De Gaulle had said in private before leaving: 'If I am going there, it is not as a tourist. If I am going, it will be to make History.'[78] On the slow journey across the Atlantic, he asked one of his staff: 'What if I say *Vive le Québec libre*?' To the response 'Surely you are not going to do that?' de Gaulle answered: 'I think so. It will depend on the atmosphere.'[79] In the event, the 'atmosphere' was there. The speech was the logical culmination of all that de Gaulle had been saying over two days – and all he had been thinking over five years.

Back in France de Gaulle was not contrite. Receiving a telegram from the French Embassy in Ottawa worrying that it would take time for the wounds of the Ottawa government to heal, de Gaulle scrawled furiously: 'The question is not whether M. Pearson's "wound" heals. The question is whether the French people of Canada have the right to dispose of their own destiny.'[80] Immediately on his return he summoned Alain Peyrefitte and told him with satisfaction: 'I have upset the applecart.' He then moved on to a military metaphor: 'We have made a breakthrough. Now we need to occupy the terrain . . . This moment might be only fleeting. We need to give a strong push so that it becomes irreversible.'[81] Peyrefitte was told to go to French Canada to start negotiating cooperation agreements and regular meetings with Quebec representatives on the lines of those in the Franco-German Treaty. This was to be done behind the back of the Quai d'Orsay. Peyrefitte pointed out that Quebec was not a sovereign state, but de Gaulle would brook no objections just because Quebec was run by the English with their

French 'collaborators'.[82] In one of his evening meetings with Foccart soon after returning from Quebec, de Gaulle poured out all his bile:

> Do you think it mattered to me not going to Ottawa? . . . There would have been all those toasts to the Queen of England! I would rather die than go to Canada and toast the Queen of England . . . I was relieved when they offered me the pretext to leave . . . All that will give lots of copy to the worthless and supine press under the heel of the Americans, the Israelis and all the others.[83]

IMPASSE

Despite de Gaulle's bravado, when Hervé Alphand, now head of the Quai d'Orsay, reviewed the world in November 1967, wherever he looked – the Middle East, Vietnam, eastern Europe, the Soviet Union – his view was that 'everything has reached an impasse'.[84] France no longer even derived benefit from de Gaulle's recognition of Communist China, which had now entered the turbulence of the Cultural Revolution. There were demonstrations in 1967 in front of the French Embassy in Peking denouncing the 'tête de chien de Gaulle'.[85]

The limited results of de Gaulle's opening to eastern Europe were demonstrated during his visit to Poland in September 1967. The previous January he had seen the Polish Foreign Minister Adam Rapacki and pleaded eloquently for détente:

> We fear the future of Germany and that is the practical reason, for us, to come to an agreement, to have contacts with the Germans rather than abandon them. To abandon them would be to encourage them to seek adventure . . . It is not good to have this problem in the centre of Europe. We need to find a way forward; it will be long and difficult. This road will be a European arrangement, an agreement on Germany, with Germany, that she must be part of. As for her unity, it will not be a Reich, we want that no more than you, but a rapprochement, a conjunction, perhaps one day a confederation . . . I recognize that you cannot accept that if you are not sure of your frontiers . . . But you could be a bit more encouraging to them when they show good intentions . . . This will last a long time.[86]

Once in Poland in September 1967, de Gaulle put the same case to the Prime Minister Gomułka: 'With this division of the world it is difficult for a country like ours to maintain its independence; it is impossible for a country like yours to have its own.'[87] All this fell on deaf ears.

Since the Soviet Union had refused to cooperate with him over the

Middle East, de Gaulle felt disinclined to respect Soviet susceptibilities during his visit. His speeches made no mention of the Soviet Union and incited the Poles, in coded terms, to be faithful to their national traditions. In retaliation the Polish authorities did everything possible to blunt the impact of de Gaulle's visit. He had prepared a speech to be delivered to students at the University of Jagiellonian in Cracow with the provocative line: 'Under all foreign occupations the Jagiellonian University has remained the symbol, the guardian, the foyer of Polish culture and of universal culture.' But no student had the opportunity to hear these words. Peyrefitte, who was accompanying de Gaulle, described what happened:

> The official cortège dived into a small street which led not to the present campus of the university but the old one . . . Barriers held back the mass of people at each extremity of the street which was deserted. We crossed with difficulty through the enthusiastic crowd which tried to follow us but the police brutally stopped them. Our cars stopped outside the medieval university, now a museum, whose doors were closed except to us . . . In front of us were half a dozen professors in robes: the rector and the deans of the five faculties. No other professors. In the background lurked about thirty shadowy figures in gabardine raincoats. No students. The General raised his voice in this deserted hall as if addressing ten thousand students . . . Then we left down the same empty street in the other direction. The barriers opened again. There were even more students on this side than the other. They had not heard a word of the General's speech, nor the translation, but they gave him an ovation.[88]

On his return to France de Gaulle reported to the Council of Ministers: 'They hardly dare to remember that Poland is in Europe . . . It is not a national government; it is a Communist government linked to the Soviet Union.'[89] He put a brave face on it afterwards to Peyrefitte: 'I know these regimes are totalitarian. But I am sowing seeds which will perhaps flower in twenty or thirty years. I will not see them flower . . . The young Poles of today will shake off the Soviet yoke. It is written in the stars.'[90]

To the extent that de Gaulle's détente policy had any success it was not in ways that he could welcome. While French officials negotiated the details of France's departure from the integrated command, her NATO partners were debating how to meet the challenge posed by de Gaulle. One response was a report drafted by the Belgian Foreign Minister Pierre Harmel with the seemingly inoffensive title 'Future Tasks of the Alliance'. Its key idea was that NATO, founded as an anti-Soviet alliance, should be ready to explore détente with the east but that discussions should be pursued not by individual member states but by the Alliance as a whole. This was a way of reinvigorating NATO and 'Atlanticizing' the idea of détente where de Gaulle had wanted to Europeanize it.[91] Since France was still part of the Alliance – as opposed to the integrated NATO command – French representatives participated in the discussions. They succeeded in watering down the document but in the end they did not block its adoption in November 1967. One reason for this was that at the same moment de Gaulle was about to torpedo Britain's second application to the EEC in his press conference of 27 November 1967. His task was made easier by the fact that the British had been forced to devalue sterling a few days earlier, offering an easy pretext for his claim that for the moment Britain was not ready. But de Gaulle's European partners were not happy about the veto. There was a limit to how many battles even de Gaulle felt he could take on. In this case the price he paid was the Harmel Report.

Even in Africa, the showcase of de Gaulle's policy of 'cooperation', one senses, reading between the lines of Foccart's journal, that the General was beginning to feel his policies had reached an impasse. Foccart always worked to keep him focused on Africa, but his journal was peppered increasingly with comments like 'African issues are not exciting him much at the moment,' 'this did not seem to interest the General much,' 'the General was not paying much attention.'[92] After yet another request from Foccart to meet yet another African head of state, de Gaulle exploded:

> I have had enough of your Negroes. None of this is of any interest! Leave me in peace with your Negroes; I don't want to see another for two months, you understand. Not another one for two months. It is not so much that it takes up my time, although it is very boring, but it does not create a good image to the outside world; they only see Negroes at the Elysée. And I can tell you it is of no interest.[93]

In 1966 the Quai finally put an end to the independence of the Ministry of Cooperation. Foccart fought a rearguard action by warning de Gaulle against the Quai diplomats who 'go to cocktail parties ... and pick up gossip from other Ambassadors. That is not cooperation.'[94] But Foccart had lost that battle.

The problem was that the situation in Africa never settled down. Foccart's clientelist system of patronage was inherently unstable. After the coup in the Central African Republic in January 1966, Foccart remarked: 'I felt the General was fed up with these successive coups in Africa.'[95] In this case, Foccart had not intervened because he judged correctly that the new President, Bokassa, a fanatical admirer of de Gaulle and former Free French soldier, was completely reliable. De Gaulle commented: 'Yes, but he is also an idiot [couillon], and we will never be able to do anything with him.'[96]

Two years later, his view had not changed: 'I can't do anything, he is a lunatic.'[97] De Gaulle resigned himself to the situation, although he tried without success to stop Bokassa calling him 'Papa'. Foccart took the view that Bokassa might have been a lunatic but at least he was France's lunatic.

Nowhere was the instability greater than in Dahomey (Benin), where coups took place in 1963 and 1965. When in November 1967 Foccart tried to persuade de Gaulle to receive the current President Soglo and confer a decoration on him, de Gaulle exploded again: 'We give them a decoration, and after that they carry out a revolution, then they come on an official visit and we have to give them another decoration! It is crazy . . . Soglo will be reversed in his turn . . . His successor will come and it will all start again.'[98] His prediction could not have been more accurate. A month later, Soglo was overthrown. On this occasion, Foccart could not be reached because he was away hunting (not fishing, as when Youlou had been ousted from his position as President of Congo in 1963), and no decision to intervene was taken. When Foccart ordered an intervention on his return, de Gaulle furiously countermanded the order: 'Who is in charge here? You or me? . . . Leave me in peace with all this. Too bad for them if they are not capable of governing.'[99] A few months later, President Eyadéma of Togo was in Paris. Foccart wanted de Gaulle to receive him: 'Not another lunch! They are here the whole time . . . I told that one "be loyal to your President, don't carry out a coup d'état"; and so what does he do when he gets back home? A coup.' All Foccart could say in his defence was that at least he had waited six months before carrying out the coup. In this case de Gaulle gave in, and buckled down to yet another dinner.[100]

It was still possible to trigger de Gaulle's Fashoda complex when it came to countering the British or Americans. One such occasion presented itself with the outbreak of civil war in Nigeria. The eastern province of Biafra, the most economically dynamic region of the country, attempted to secede. The British supported the official Nigerian government. France declared an embargo on arms sales to either side and on 31 July 1967 a communiqué announced France's support for the Biafran cause in the name of a people's right to self-determination. Officially French aid to Biafra was only humanitarian, but arms were sent under this cover. France never went as far as recognition of Biafra, and official French policy was to support a negotiated settlement.[101] But in his private comments to Foccart, de Gaulle was quite clear about the reasons for the policy: 'We must dismantle these huge constructions created by the English such as Nigeria.'[102] At the end of the year Foccart downplayed information from the Quai that the rebellion was running out of steam. He assured de Gaulle the contrary was true.[103] De Gaulle took the view that neither side would win but that Biafra should be helped 'discreetly'. He was not happy when Foccart said that he was going to receive some Biafran representatives: 'That exposes me too much.'[104]

By the end of 1967, there seemed no other guiding principle to de Gaulle's foreign policy than sacred egoism. In Nigeria – and Canada – de Gaulle was unashamed about intervening in the affairs of other countries; at the same time, France refused to join the United Nations' condemnation of the apartheid regime in South Africa because this was interference in the internal affairs of another country. The real reason was that France needed access to the country's uranium and gold. On the same principle of non-interference – but more probably as a way of embarrassing the British – France abstained in the votes of the United Nations condemning Rhodesia, which had declared its independence in November 1965. Since the white minority had acted to avoid the installation of black majority rule, this sat oddly with de Gaulle's promotion of France as the herald of decolonization and the rights of the Third World.[105]

In private, de Gaulle's outbursts on foreign policy became wilder. One night he ranted to Foccart that eventually France should get back 'all these countries that England snatched from us ... One day we must get back the Channel Islands.'[106] In early 1968 he told an American journalist that 'only three peoples [were] under foreign oppression today – the French in Canada, the Arabs in Israel, and the Tibetans in China' (no mention of eastern Europe!). Charles Bohlen, the American Ambassador in Paris, was appalled when the comment was reported to him: 'Really, the old boy is going off his rocker.'[107] Bohlen believed that despite his unpredictability de Gaulle had 'always had a sense of measure, of timing, of place and appropriateness'; now he wondered if he had 'lost this sense of timing and of appropriateness ... his public utterances and indeed actions have more taken on a purely wilful and personal character'.[108] Many of de Gaulle's ministers were thinking the same. After the international outcry over Quebec, Pompidou had imposed a three-line whip on the government to greet de Gaulle at the airport on his return. One minister excused himself. As the others waited, there was a lot of muttering along the lines of 'he's off his head [cinglé],' 'this time he has gone too far.'[109] Pompidou was himself scathing in private about this act of 'gratuitous madness', that of 'a child playing with matches while he hides from the adults'. Couve's view was hardly different, although expressed in his characteristically muffled manner: 'The General's passion for Quebec can lead to nothing good. Our duty is to hold him back from going down this slope.'[110] How much longer could it go on?

27

Diminishing Returns

DE GAULLE AND POMPIDOU

On 2 August 1964 de Gaulle addressed the nation to mark the fiftieth anniversary of the outbreak of the First World War. There were many ways one might remember the war, and many lessons one might draw from it. The lesson that de Gaulle drew was simple: 'In an instant, the multiple political, social, religious quarrels and divisions of the country were wiped away.'[1] All his life, de Gaulle dreamt of such moments of national unity. His pursuit of what he called grandeur had the same domestic purpose: to overcome what he believed to be France's propensity to internal divisions. As he wrote on the first page of his *War Memoirs*: 'Only vast enterprises are capable of counterbalancing the ferments of dispersion which her people carries in her.' So far this policy had proved extremely successful. Despite the disappointing result of the Presidential election, in the second half of 1966 de Gaulle's popularity ratings reached levels surpassed only at the height of the Algerian War. Over 65 per cent of the population approved of him in this period, remarkable for someone who had been in power for over seven years. It was especially his foreign policy – leaving NATO and his criticisms of the United States – which was singled out for approval.[2]

For those on the left and centre who were pro-European and pro-Atlanticist, de Gaulle's policies represented all that was most retrograde – a kind of 'planetary Poujadism', as Mitterrand put it nicely in parliament.[3] The motion of censure presented by the opposition after the break with NATO won only 136 votes – far short of a majority. The truth was that de Gaulle's foreign policy had wrongfooted the left. As the political scientist Maurice Duverger wrote in *Le Monde*:

> In politics results count more than intentions ... It matters little that the motivations of the General are purely nationalistic, that they aspire to

realize a 'certain idea of France' ... that de Gaulle pursues a more or less mythical dream of grandeur, or even that he is trying to satisfy his personal rancour against the United States, if he has contributed in this way to reducing the domination of the largest power in the world over its allies turned satellites ... The General's actions are a bit like acts of isolated terrorism in the first phase of decolonization, destined to wake the consciousness of a people that has gone to sleep. Bombs of this kind are perhaps necessary to awaken Europe from the torpor in which it is plunged in regard to the United States.[4]

It was predictable that de Gaulle was able to win the approval of the Communist Party for his anti-American positions, but his appeal to the left went beyond the Communists. In May 1966, twenty-nine prominent left-wing journalists and intellectuals signed a manifesto supporting de Gaulle's foreign policy. They included Domenach, the editor of *Esprit*, who had been inching towards de Gaulle for several years, the Socialist André Philip, the former Trotskyist David Rousset. Their declared aim was to 'show the left that one can be Gaullist without a bad conscience while also giving Gaullism a left-wing conscience'.[5]

The main threat to de Gaulle's reputation in the first months of 1966 resulted from the fallout from a murky affair which occurred during the previous year's election campaign. Only several months later did it turn into a fully fledged political scandal. Everything started on 29 October 1965 when the Moroccan Mehdi Ben Barka, opposed to the policies of the Moroccan regime and living in exile since his expulsion from Morocco in 1963, was kidnapped outside a restaurant in central Paris. It later emerged that he had been taken to a villa outside Paris to be interrogated and probably murdered by the Moroccan secret services. His body was never found. It also turned out that the sinister Moroccan Minister of the Interior, Mohammed Oufkir, had been in Paris on the day of Ben Barka's disappearance. That a widely respected Third World activist should have been kidnapped on French soil by agents working for a foreign power was in itself shocking. But what turned a sordid settling of scores into a French scandal was the revelation that rogue elements of the French secret services had been implicated. One of these, Georges Figon, claimed to have witnessed Oufkir torturing Ben Barka. When Figon was himself found dead in January 1966 – supposedly as a result of suicide – all the elements of a major politico-espionage scandal were in place. The British Embassy reported that 'a James Bond story has suddenly come alive'.[6] For weeks, the story was headline news. Pages and pages of *Le Monde* were given over to ever more lurid revelations.

No one ever alleged that de Gaulle was involved, but the Ben Barka kidnapping seemed to vindicate those who accused some Gaullists of having an unsavoury predilection for shady undercover operations. This accusation had been made against the wartime BCRA, and it resurfaced during the Algerian War when the official police and intelligence services were rightly considered to be lukewarm about countering the activities of the OAS. This led some Gaullist activists to organize parallel intelligence operatives popularly known as Barbouzes (the 'bearded') who employed their own undercover methods against the OAS. One spectacular such operation was the kidnapping in March 1963 of Antoine Argoud, one of the most fanatical OAS leaders who had taken refuge in Germany. Captured in Munich, he was deposited, bound and gagged, in the boot of a car outside the Paris Prefecture of Police. Such episodes added a whiff of conspiratorial skulduggery to the image of Gaullism. Foccart was seen by many as the epitome of this dark side of Gaullism. He was rumoured, probably wrongly, to have been involved in the Ben Barka affair. This may have contributed to de Gaulle's occasional flashes of impatience with Foccart at this time. Foccart explained himself to de Gaulle, who seemed convinced – while discouraging him from indulging his passion for parachuting which seemed to give credence to his detractors.

Although de Gaulle accepted the unconventional methods of the Barbouzes as an unfortunate consequence of the impotence of the French state during the Algerian War, the idea of parallel secret services operating outside the orbit of the government was anathema to his sense of the authority of the state. He ordered that Oufkir be charged in a French court for his involvement in the affair, and instigated a reorganization of the French intelligence services. In these respects, de Gaulle's response to the affair could not be faulted. But he underestimated the sense of moral outrage that it had caused even among supporters like François Mauriac or the almost mystically Gaullist journalist Maurice Clavel, who broke publicly with de Gaulle as a result. When under criticism, de Gaulle always went on to the attack. In his February 1966 press conference, he dismissed the affair contemptuously as a 'vulgar and subaltern' business. It was on this occasion that he crushed one journalist who asked why he had been so slow to take the full measure of the scandal with the words: 'Put it down to my inexperience.' This raised laughs but showed that de Gaulle had not fully grasped the shock caused by the affair. In the end, however, even if de Gaulle had mishandled his response, the Ben Barka affair barely dented his overall popularity. It was one of those scandals adored by journalists but so complex that most ordinary mortals soon become too entangled in the thickets of conspiracy.

Apart from occasional interventions such as the price stabilization plan in 1963, de Gaulle had been happy to leave the day-to-day running of domestic policy to Georges Pompidou. One sign of Pompidou's growing authority was his insistence on reshuffling his government in 1966 after the Presidential election. His main purpose was to remove the Minister of Finance, the dangerously ambitious Valéry Giscard d'Estaing, even at the risk of converting a possible rival into a likely enemy. Leader of the Independent Republicans, a small parliamentary group on the centre right which supported the Gaullists while remaining organizationally distinct, Giscard owed his presence in the government to his reputation for technical brilliance, an unparalleled grasp of financial issues and an eloquence to match. He had been promoted to Minister of Finance at the exceptionally young age of thirty-six. De Gaulle, always impressed by intellectual virtuosity, had a certain *faiblesse* for this arrogantly confident young technocrat. But he did not feel strongly enough to interfere when Pompidou wanted to move him. Giscard was replaced by Michel Debré, who re-entered the government after four years.

De Gaulle continued to appreciate Pompidou's pragmatism, efficiency and ultra-competence. Pompidou hid a steely ruthlessness beneath his façade of geniality, looking out at the world through half-closed eyes, a cigarette always dangling from his lips. Despite enjoying the Parisian high life he retained something of the peasant shrewdness of his Auvergne roots – not someone to whom one would try to sell a sick cow, as the phrase went in his native Cantal. Pompidou worried about de Gaulle's *'grains de folie'* but recognized that they were inseparable from his peculiar genius. As he was in the habit of saying, 'the General is special.'

Nonetheless the relationship between the two men had subtly altered since that day when de Gaulle plucked Pompidou out of semi-obscurity to become Prime Minister. Unlike those crushed by de Gaulle's force of personality, Pompidou's awareness of de Gaulle's extraordinariness was always tinged by a touch of ironic distance. He was not by disposition a hero worshipper. And after 1965 a germ of resentment started to poison Pompidou's view of the General. He had been hurt by the cruel offhandedness with which de Gaulle had treated him as he dithered – or pretended to dither – about whether to stand in the Presidential election. Psychologically emancipated from the bond of obligation that had originally characterized their relationship, he developed a circle of aides whose first loyalty was to him. They had no links with the historic Gaullism of the war or with the RPF, and invested in Pompidou as their future. Pompidou had himself shed any sense of inferiority about his own lack of a Resistance past. His self-assurance was bolstered when Bernard Tricot

PLUNGING INTO THE CROWDS

54. Millau, 1961.

55. Oise, 1965.

56. Welcoming Konrad Adenauer to Colombey, the only foreign leader to be received there.

57. (*below*) De Gaulle, Harold Macmillan and their wives at Macmillan's home Birch Grove in November 1961. In contrast to Adenauer, no one is looking anyone else in the eye.

58. De Gaulle vetoing Britain's application to the European Economic Community,
14 January 1963.

59. (*above*) Mexico City,
March 1964.

60. (*right*) Moscow,
June 1966.

61. The stadium in Phnom Penh where he denounced American involvement in Vietnam, 1 September 1966.

62. Arriving in Quebec on 23 July 1967. He set off to Montreal to 'liberate' Quebec the next day.

63. The streets of Paris.

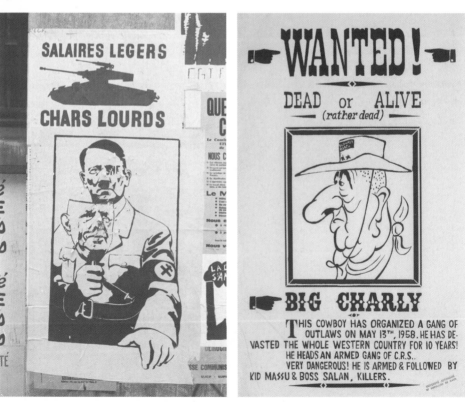

64–5. Anti-de Gaulle posters on the walls of Paris. On the left (de Gaulle as Hitler) the text reads: 'light [low] salaries, heavy tanks'.

MAY 1968

66. 29 May: de Gaulle returns to France after his secret helicopter visit to General Massu in Baden-Baden.

67. 30 May: pro-de Gaulle demonstration, Paris.

68. (*above*) 14 May 1969: the king in exile on Derrynane Beach, County Kerry, accompanied by his wife and aide de camp François Flohic, with a policeman walking behind.

69. 'De Gaulle is dead': French headlines on 10 November 1970.

became Secretary General of the Elysée in 1967. The two previous holders of this powerful post had longer Gaullist pedigrees than Pompidou, but Tricot had been 'Gaullist' for a shorter time than him. Pompidou once commented to Tricot: 'The main collaborator of the General is me; the Secretary General of the Elysée cannot have his own ideas.'[7] It is impossible to imagine Pompidou speaking to Burin des Roziers or Courcel so frankly.

Pompidou, twenty-one years younger than de Gaulle, was clearly emerging as his Dauphin. As he told one journalist off the record in September 1967: 'When people ask me if I am going to be President of the Republic one day, and I reply "I have no idea, I am prime minister" I am totally sincere . . . As for preparing myself to be the Head of State, I have in some sense been doing it for the last five years, but I cannot go any further since this would be improper and indecent towards the General, and obviously he would not like it.'[8] On de Gaulle's side, the existence of a dauphin was a reminder of his own mortality, and tinged his view of Pompidou with wary suspicion. This offered an opening to a that curious group who called themselves 'left Gaullists'.

ORPHANS OF GAULLISM

The left Gaullists were neither fish nor fowl – distrusted both by the left and by the Gaullists. Each had their own individual trajectory which had led them to de Gaulle at different moments. Some had been with him since the war; some had joined him during the RPF period and had been seduced by its nebulous social doctrines; some were former Mendésists who after 1958 transposed on to de Gaulle the hopes they had once invested in Mendès France. What united them was the conviction that the Gaullist movement cobbled together rapidly in 1958 to support de Gaulle – the UNR – was made up of opportunists and conservatives who were not 'authentic' Gaullists. The left Gaullists mostly favoured a 'liberal' policy on Algeria and wanted to save de Gaulle from becoming a prisoner of the army or the UNR.

In April 1959, the left Gaullists had formed themselves into an organization called the UDT (Union Démocratique du Travail). They had a newspaper, *Notre République*, which gave them a platform out of proportion to their minuscule numbers. Its two most prominent contributors were the jurist René Capitant and the economist Louis Vallon. Once the Algerian War was over, their central theme was the need to complete the 'mission' of Gaullism by giving it a social content. In their reading of history, de Gaulle had decolonized, he had reformed France's institutions, he had asserted national independence but it still remained to find that elusive third way between capitalism and socialism which had been promised by the RPF's 'association' policy. The left Gaullists survived because they were given discreet encouragement and funds by the Elysée. During the Algerian War de Gaulle had seen them as a useful weapon in parliament if the bulk of UNR *députés* followed Soustelle in support of *Algérie française*. A cartoon in *L'Express* in 1959 encapsulated this by showing de Gaulle with three miniature left Gaullists peeking out of his top pocket. The caption read: 'Look out – or I will release my left Gaullists.'[9]

After the end of the Algerian War, the left Gaullists were no longer needed for this purpose, but in anticipation of the elections of 1962 de Gaulle saw them as a possible counterweight in parliament to Giscard's Independent Republicans. He intervened to ensure that in a number of constituencies UNR candidates would not oppose UDT ones. Fourteen UDT *députés* were elected and the UNR was now officially dubbed the UNR-UDT. The left Gaullists were always hoping that de Gaulle would move more in their direction while not unaware that they were being used. One of them put their relationship to de Gaulle with a certain humour in a book revealingly entitled *Orphans of Gaullism*:

> The General tries not to forfeit any of the cards in his hand ... Let us suppose ... you decide to found a 'Gaullo-Communist Party' marrying the aims of the Third International and those of the French Employers Federation. Suppose, to pursue the example, that you ask for an audience with the General and that you have the undreamt-of chance of obtaining it. You find yourself in the presence of the President, affable and regretting that he sees so little of you and has so little time at his disposal. You outline your project and find your interlocutor a little patronizing, interested, but finally approving and very encouraging, ending the meeting in the most satisfactory possible manner by asking you to remain in contact with his *cabinet* and keep him informed of your project whose 'interest for the nation has not escaped him'.[10]

Since the left Gaullists had no significant electoral base, they counted only to the extent that de Gaulle was ready to back their ideas. After 1966 it looked as if he might at last be ready to take them out of his top pocket.

De Gaulle's dream of class reconciliation was one of his most deeply held convictions. Until 1962, his energies were absorbed by Algeria but once the war was over, he began dropping hints that he had not forgotten the policy of association. He told Peyrefitte in July 1962: 'The social consequences of capitalism are not acceptable. It crushes the weakest. It transforms men into wolves ... Collectivism is no better: it removes from people any desire to fight. It turns them into sheep. We need a third way – between wolves and sheep.'[11] At one of the first meetings of his government after the successful parliamentary elections of 1962, de Gaulle set out some of his future ambitions. Among these was what he called 'the integration' of the workers: 'There must no longer be a social question in France. I don't say that people will not always look out for their interests. They will always exist. But there must no longer be any question of social classes.'[12] Pompidou, who conceived of Gaullism as a non-ideological progressive, modernizing conservatism, had no time for this utopianism. On one occasion he commented: 'Capitant, Vallon and others . . . have stuffed the General's head with their nonsense . . . The left Gaullists trample over the economy like elephants in a china shop.'[13]

At the start of 1963 there was a major miners' strike which was badly mishandled by the government. De Gaulle had suffered a serious, if temporary, blip in his popularity. He drew the conclusion that the long-term solution was not just to pay the miners more but to change the entire relationship between workers and employers. When asked by Peyrefitte if he was thinking of what had been called the 'association of capital–labour' during the RPF period he replied: 'we need to go much further'.[14] The new word which now replaced 'association' was 'participation' – what Pompidou mocked as de Gaulle's new 'hobbyhorse'.[15] For the moment, however, the matter went no further because Pompidou was so obviously unsympathetic.

If at the beginning of 1966 de Gaulle started to push the idea more forcefully it was because he felt that the Presidential election had been a setback. He was looking for a way of relaunching Gaullism since 'modernization' seemed not to be a sufficiently mobilizing domestic theme. Pompidou's scepticism about de Gaulle's social ideas was now perceived by the General less as a reason to hold back than as a reason to accelerate the pace: 'participation' offered him an ideological pretext for his psychological dissatisfaction with Pompidou. It allowed him in his mind to blame Pompidou for the disappointment of the Presidential election, and his decision to embrace participation was as much a consequence of their growing estrangement as its cause.

But how to translate a vague aspiration into a practical policy? In 1965, during the debate in parliament on the budget, Louis Vallon had succeeded in inserting an amendment (Article 33) which required the government to implement measures to recognize the right of workers to share in the economic growth of their companies.[16] The government let this pass, and no one took the matter too seriously. Vallon himself seems not to have been entirely sure what to do next until he came across an article expounding the theory of 'pan-capitalism'. Its author, Marcel Loichot, was one of those engineer mystics, half crank half sage, who intermittently surface in French politics. Loichot, pleased that his ideas were finding an audience, now published an entire book on 'pan-capitalism' and set up his 'pan-capitalist union' whose ambition was nothing less than the 'intra- and inter-national reunification of the entire population of the globe'. Although Loichot wrapped his technocratic mysticism in graphs and inscrutable algebra, the central idea was quite modest: a part of company profits would be redistributed to workers in the form of shares. Loichot's ideas were plastered all over the *Nouvelle République* in January 1966. De Gaulle read his book and wrote to Loichot to say how 'very impressed' he had been: 'Perhaps you know that I have always been in search, although groping my way forward [*à tâtons*], for a practical means of effecting a change not in living conditions but in the condition of the worker.'[17]

When at the start of 1966, the government discussed how to implement the Vallon amendment Pompidou proposed setting up a commission to explore the idea. De Gaulle asked if Loichot would be a member; Pompidou replied that he would be asked to present his views. De Gaulle warned that the commission should not be a way of 'sweeping it into the long grass [*ne noyez pas le poisson*]' – which is exactly what it was.[18] The commission deliberated for some months, took advice from expert witnesses, found that neither unions nor employers were keen and a few months later produced a report burying the idea as impracticable. De Gaulle, who was still 'feeling his way', did not feel confident enough to push the matter further. Pompidou had won the first round – but de Gaulle had not given up. At his press conference in October 1966, having planted a question about Loichot, he launched into a long defence of participation. He promised – or threatened – that the government would revisit the issue after the parliamentary elections in March 1967 (the last elections had taken place in 1962).

De Gaulle's attitude to these elections as they approached was marked by his usual schizophrenia between what Pompidou sneeringly called his 'utopia of unanimity' and the truth that his government operated through a parliamentary majority. He ruminated to Peyrefitte in private on the lessons of the 1930s:

> The days are past when heads of government go down on their knees to scrabble together votes. We will show the parties who is boss. If ever the *députés* pass a vote of censure they will be sent back to explain themselves to their electors . . . If we have no majority in parliament we will do without one . . . This constitution was made to govern without a majority. I will call

on new men, technicians, specialists who are not compromised in political struggles but who are respected for their competence . . . In the end I would not be so unhappy to have a chance to demonstrate the resources that the Constitution gives me.[19]

Disconcerted by this outburst, Peyrefitte worried that de Gaulle was thinking of invoking Article 16. De Gaulle's reply was that Article 16 was for a real crisis and not suitable for such a situation. On the strength of this, Peyrefitte hinted in public that although de Gaulle would not resign if the parliamentary elections were unfavourable – since the source of executive power resided in him not in the parliament – he would never use Article 16 just because he was faced with a hostile parliament. De Gaulle dressed him down: 'One must never reveal one's batteries and *a fortiori* mine. Article 16 is my affair . . . One must let uncertainty hover over them. One must keep a terrifying silence . . . Leave them in cruel uncertainty.'[20] At the same time as nursing these startling ideas, de Gaulle publicly expressed on more than one occasion the idea that he needed a parliamentary majority to support his action. The alternative was 'plunging again, this time in graver conditions than ever, into the same upheavals of the old regime of parties'.[21] So much for the claim that the Fifth Republic had definitively solved the political problems of France! During the campaign de Gaulle appealed on television for a 'coherent and constant majority' in parliament' and he gave detailed instructions to Pompidou about which ministers should speak on television and what they should say.[22] So much for the 'arbiter' President above the fray!

Otherwise de Gaulle left the day-to-day running of the campaign to Pompidou. There was now a serious challenge from the left. Mitterrand, riding on the wave of his success in 1965, had succeeded in brokering a deal between the Communist and Socialist Parties. In the second round of the election the less well-placed candidate of the left in each constituency would stand down in favour of the other. This was a further step along the road to bringing the PCF in from the electoral ghetto where it had languished for so many years – and despite the paradox that its views on foreign policy were closer to de Gaulle's than to the Socialists'. To combat this threat from the left, Pompidou set about trying to negotiate unity on the other side. He created an Action Committee for the Fifth Republic to avoid splitting the conservative vote by reserving some seats to the allies of the UNR – such as Giscard's Republican Independents.[23]

Although de Gaulle pretended to be above these shabby deals of electoral politics, the subject often came up during his nightly conversations with Foccart, who was not taken in by his pretence of indifference and never ceased to be amazed by his detailed knowledge of each constituency, worthy of one of the old wheeler-dealer politicians of the Third Republic. De Gaulle affected to despise politics but he had always been fascinated by it. One night Foccart was reprimanded for the 'ridiculous' choice of candidate in Quimper: 'You forget one thing, that he is divorced ... He first married a rich Brazilian woman and then divorced her for the daughter of a banker, and you want to send him to Quimper where the priests rule the roost ... I don't deny his worth, but it is grotesque to send him to Quimper given his family situation.'[24] The committee set up by Pompidou drew up the lists of candidates, but each name had to be personally approved by de Gaulle.

The election results were a major disappointment. The Gaullists lost forty-three seats, and even with Giscard's small group of centrists could only just muster a majority in the new Assembly. There were several reasons for this. The financial stabilization programme of 1963 had caused a slight decrease in the rate of economic growth and a concomitant increase in unemployment. The transfer of votes between Socialists and Communists in the second round had operated effectively. And finally the Gaullists had lost some seats in the regions with a high concentration of repatriated *pieds noirs* who could not forgive the 'betrayal' of Algeria. But for the left Gaullists, the culprit was Pompidou for sabotaging their economic plans. Capitant publicly called for a new prime minister to be appointed. It was an open secret that de Gaulle planned to replace Pompidou after the election with Couve de Murville who, while not interested in these social issues, was more obedient. But Couve, who had never fought an election before, was defeated in the Paris constituency where he had stood. On the other hand Pompidou, who had also never stood for election before, was easily elected to a seat in his native Cantal. Even de Gaulle drew back from the provocation of replacing as Prime Minister someone who had just won an election by someone who had just lost one. So Pompidou remained in place, and Couve was kept on at the Quai d'Orsay.

To overcome the problems of its small majority, Pompidou's government asked parliament to grant it the power to legislate by ordinance for three months (as permitted under Article 38 of the constitution). The pretext was to allow the government to adopt a final raft of economic measures required by the Treaty of Rome. But de Gaulle also saw the opportunity to return to the question of participation. Sounding ever more like the nineteenth-century social Catholic thinker La Tour du Pin, de Gaulle took the view that the elections underlined the need to resolve the conditions of the working class. He told his government: 'We need a clear and attractive doctrine. The condition of the working class is more important than

the level of remuneration.' Even the ultra-loyal Debré felt moved to reply
that he did not understand what this might mean. De Gaulle was unabashed:
'The condition of the workers? It is largely about the dignity of the working class. When their dignity is recognized . . . the condition of the workers
improves. The question of the working class is, along with nuclear disarmament, one of the great questions of our time.'[25] This was to set the
bar very high indeed. The incredulity around the table was reminiscent of
that first meeting of the RPF when de Gaulle had launched the idea of
association to a small group of mystified followers.

The Elysée was in close contact with Loichot in the preparation of a
new law.[26] When Pompidou produced a draft plan, de Gaulle was unhappy
that it was so timid: 'I ask you therefore to review it, or to put it another
way, not appear more or less to contradict on Wednesday what I myself
said on Tuesday and consider to be essential.'[27] Despite this reprimand, the
result was a fairly anodyne law on profit sharing. Once again de Gaulle
had been thwarted.

Over the autumn, Foccart was subjected to regular tirades against Pompidou. These were embarrassing for him. Despite his devotion to de Gaulle,
he enjoyed good relations with Pompidou, and wanted them to remain
good in anticipation of the day when Pompidou took over. One evening
de Gaulle worked himself up into such a state of rage against Pompidou
that he forgot to leave in time for the start of the evening television news.
In this case de Gaulle's ire was also directed against parliament where there
had been an unfavourable vote. He complained that Pompidou was not
managing the parliamentary situation firmly enough. To Foccart's horror,
he mused about using Article 16 – which would certainly have caused a
constitutional crisis – or calling new parliamentary elections (which he
would almost certainly have lost): 'I will invoke Article 16 and we won't
need to worry about parliament any more . . . I don't want to be annoyed
by these people . . . Pompidou is finished. I will sack him, I want to change
him . . . He is always doing deals, he negotiates, he smooths things over . . .
He has no balls . . . I want no more of him.'[28] A month later he was back
on the same track of Pompidou being 'too soft [mollasson]'.[29] None of this
need be taken too literally. De Gaulle had always sounded off in this way –
but his increasing frustration with Pompidou was genuine.

The conclusion Pompidou had drawn from the election was that it was
urgent to transform the UNR into a modern political party rather than a
collection of MPs without real electoral roots and no identity except support for de Gaulle. He was preparing for a future where Gaullism could
exist without de Gaulle. To this end he organized a congress at Lille in
November 1967 to put the Gaullist parties on a new footing. This caused

a flurry among the left Gaullists who suspected that Pompidou was turning Gaullism into a vehicle for his future ambitions. Vallon and Capitant announced that they 'would not go to Lille'.[30] In the end, however, most left Gaullists attended the congress, which led to an overhaul of the party structures and the adoption of a new name. Pompidou had declared at Lille that the conference was not about '*après-Gaullisme*', but everyone knew that the opposite was true. The *Le Monde* correspondent rightly suggested that the congress had marked the burial of 'the old movement both sentimental and political . . . which only existed in relationship to a man'. The new word was not 'fidelity' but 'efficiency'.[31]

'NONE OF THIS AMUSES ME ANY MORE'

At his autumn press conference in 1967 de Gaulle ended with a flourish against those who were preparing '*après-Gaullisme*' while he was still around. But this implicit reprimand of Pompidou was buried in the furore caused by the rest of the press conference which proved to be the one of the most controversial of the General's career. De Gaulle found himself fighting on every front: unapologetically defending his *Québec libre* speech and announcing the formal veto of British entry to the Common Market. But this was as nothing compared to the fury unleashed by his defence of his Middle East policy. De Gaulle opened his remarks on this subject by referring to the Jews as an 'elite people, sure of themselves and domineering [*peuple d'élite, sûr de lui-même et dominateur*]'. The uproar caused by this remark overshadowed a passage which now seems more prophetic than shocking:

> Now on the territories she has taken, Israel is organizing an occupation that will be accompanied by oppression, repression and expulsions, and there is now developing against her a resistance which she will describe as terrorism . . . It is obvious that the conflict is not over and that there can be no solution except by international agreement.[32]

Raymond Aron was so outraged by de Gaulle's words as to be moved to publish a short book on *De Gaulle, Israel and the Jews* in which he accused de Gaulle of having 'knowingly, voluntarily, opened a new era of Jewish history and perhaps of anti-Semitism. Everything becomes possible again.' Aron did not however go as far as to accuse de Gaulle himself of anti-Semitism. He knew as well as anyone that throughout his career de Gaulle had been immune to the casual – or not so casual – anti-Semitism that was part of the culture of most French conservatives of his generation. The careers of Georges Boris, René Cassin, Mendès France, Aron himself and many others were evidence that de Gaulle was indifferent to the beliefs and backgrounds of those who were ready to support him. It is also true, however, that the suffering of the Jews in the Holocaust had never been central to his vision of the war – as was true of most people of his generation. And to have used such language to describe the Jewish *people* – whose experience of European history was surely more one of persecution than of 'domination' – was to exhume, whether consciously or not, clichés about Jews which were the stock in trade of anti-Semitic discourse in France at the end of the nineteenth century.

The explanation lies probably in de Gaulle's exasperation at the part played by some prominent French Jews in criticizing his Middle East policy. The idea that French Jews might see themselves as having a special loyalty to another country was anathema to de Gaulle's vision of patriotism. He told Léo Hamon, a prominent Jewish left Gaullist:

> My words were not addressed to men like you but since they have wounded you and those who are close to you I will take an opportunity soon . . . to repair the impression I have given. But how can a non-practising Jew like you be wounded . . . I was shocked by the declarations made by some French Jews, in particular the Rothschilds.[33]

De Gaulle realized his remarks had been badly judged. He lamely pretended that the comment about an 'elite' and 'domineering' people was not intended negatively and that he wished he could say the same of the French (but who would consider being called 'domineering' a compliment?).[34] In a meeting with the Chief Rabbi, Jacob Kaplan, and in a long letter to Ben-Gurion, de Gaulle insisted that he had not meant to be insulting – which was as close to an apology as he would ever get.[35]

All this suggested that de Gaulle was losing his touch. His foreign policy positions were causing more dissent than support; and his nebulous ideas on participation had failed to give Gaullism a new wind. After the *Québec libre* speech, Giscard, who had been gradually distancing himself from de Gaulle, denounced his 'solitary exercise of power'. The Gaullist magic seemed to be wearing off. Already in 1966, a British Embassy observer had remarked of de Gaulle's second press conference of the year:

> I suspect we are seeing the heyday of the press conference as a Gaullist technique . . . The performance is losing much of its novelty . . . The needle, when stuck in the groove of the old gramophone record, becomes blunted. The very artificiality of the occasion makes it increasingly unreal. The gallery becomes restive at the old actor's gestures. I think I detect a certain note of exasperation mixed with boredom.[36]

The ultra-loyal Foccart remarked of the press conference of May 1967 that two ministers nearly fell asleep – which he blamed on the heat. After the dramatic second press conference of 1967 Foccart admitted that 'even those of us listening attentively could not help ourselves succumbing to a certain somnolence'. He tentatively suggested to de Gaulle that perhaps the press conferences were sometimes 'too hard for ordinary mortals to follow'.[37] De Gaulle's television addresses had also started to seem stilted and outmoded. One result of the Presidential election of 1965 had been to introduce a breath of fresh air into the stuffy corridors of French television. The programme *Face à face* (based on an American TV show, *Meet the Press*) invited a politician to respond to questions from a panel of journalists; another programme, *Zoom*, used a magazine format to discuss social issues like racism, drugs, sexuality and so on. In contrast, de Gaulle's techniques of showmanship lost their novelty. De Gaulle's press adviser Gilbert Pérol tried to persuade him unsuccessfully that the grand press conferences had outlived their usefulness. Pérol concluded that de Gaulle continued the ritual only as an exercise of will to prove to himself that he remained as intellectually agile as the day he had entered the Elysée. These occasions were indeed an extraordinary feat of intellectual stamina for a man in his late seventies – they would have been for a man of any age – and there was no sign of any diminution of mental faculties. But Tricot wrote later that when he became Secretary General of the Elysée in 1967 de Gaulle 'was not quite the same' as he had been a few years earlier, that he tired more easily and that his attention would sometimes wander at the end of the day.[38]

At the start of 1968, Louis Joxe unburdened himself to the new British Ambassador Patrick Reilly:

> Joxe talked at length about the General. He said that he was still in good shape, but ageing. The success of his public appearances was based on his well-known tricks. He was becoming increasingly indifferent to many things and it was more and more difficult to talk to him. Joxe did not know who really did talk to him or who had any influence on him. He had a sort of crushing influence on the whole situation which cut off normal communication from the base to the summit in the French state. Not that de Gaulle sought deliberately to be an all-powerful dictator. It was just that he was there, overwhelmingly present. The men of Joxe's generation were being sacrificed. The years in which they might have held real power were slipping by without their being able to do so. Couve was simply an executant. 'We are all executants,' said Joxe: 'we do our jobs, but we have no opportunity for independent thought on major issues.'[39]

De Gaulle himself seemed increasingly prone to those bouts of melancholy which had periodically afflicted him throughout his life. One night he poured out his woes to Foccart:

In reality we are on the stage of a theatre where I have been keeping up the illusion since 1940. I am trying to give France the appearance of a solid, firm, confident and expanding country, while it is a worn-out [avachie] nation, which thinks only of its own comfort, which doesn't want any problems, which does not want to fight, which wants to upset no one, neither the Americans nor the English. The whole thing is a perpetual illusion. I am on the stage of a theatre, and I pretend to believe in it; I make people believe, or I think I do, that France is a great country, that France is determined and united, while it is nothing of the sort. France is worn out, she is made to be supine not made to fight. That is how things are, and I cannot do anything about it . . . I keep the theatre going as long as I can, and then, after me, have no illusion, things will go back to where they were.[40]

Such outbursts from de Gaulle were not new and they had always contained a performative element. But they were becoming more frequent. On many occasions in the early months of 1968, he expressed his sense of lassitude to visitors, in a detached and matter-of-fact manner different from his bouts of apocalyptic playacting. This was the impression he gave in April 1968 to the former Trotskyist David Rousset, a recent convert to the ranks of the left Gaullists. De Gaulle told him:

When it is about of institutions I am on ground that I am familiar with. When it is about developing the concept of a policy – I mean the concept, I feel at ease. It is when it comes to imagining and realizing the full articulation of the concept up to its execution that I feel ill at ease . . . and cannot see clearly . . . To realize a social policy I need popular support. I don't have it . . . I am the strategist. Matignon is in charge of tactics. Pompidou and Debré are mired in their immediate problems. So they hesitate on the great social policy . . . Capitalism, capitalist society, needs to be condemned. As does totalitarian communism.[41]

Jean-Marie Domenach, meeting de Gaulle a few weeks earlier, had a similar impression. He told de Gaulle that the young in France were much more interested in revolutionary events in South America than in anything going on in France. De Gaulle commented ruefully: 'I know, I know. They are right. It is really not very interesting.' Domenach launched into a long plea for de Gaulle to tackle the many social problems of contemporary France, and de Gaulle answered that there was so little he had the power to do: 'I left a bit sad. I saw a good man and a modest one. Quite the opposite of his image. Who would believe it? But seemingly weary, prisoner of a blocked system.'[42]

All this was summed up by what de Gaulle told his aide de camp Admiral Flohic in April 1968: 'None of this amuses me any more; there is no longer anything difficult or heroic to do.'[43]

Three weeks later, France exploded ...

28

Revolution, 1968

OLD MAN, YOUNG COUNTRY

Hitler? Never Heard of Him. This was the title of a much talked-about French documentary released in 1963. The film consisted of interviews with adolescents revealing how little they knew about history. The post-war baby-boom generation, who were becoming adolescents and young adults in the 1960s, did not dwell on the past. For those who were eighteen in 1968, the Algerian conflict had been the backdrop to their childhood, the Fourth Republic hardly a memory and the Occupation ancient history. De Gaulle, on the other hand, once heard to utter under his breath after a meeting, 'I have been saying it for a thousand years,' lived the history of France as an unbroken continuum between past and present. Between 1964 and 1966 he had given several speeches commemorating different anniversaries of the Great War, but French teenagers were less interested in this distant conflict than in the huge concert in the Place de la Nation in 1963 which heralded the arrival of pop music in France (in its French form *yé-yé*). To them, de Gaulle was a survivor of another age. Stalin, Roosevelt and Churchill were long gone; Eisenhower had given way to Kennedy in 1960, Adenauer to Erhard in 1963, Macmillan to Harold Wilson in 1964, Khrushchev to Kosygin in 1964. De Gaulle's only contemporaries in the Europe of the 1960s were Franco (b. 1892), the dictator of Spain, and Salazar (b. 1889), the dictator of Portugal.

A cartoon in the satirical newspaper *Le Canard enchaîné*, famous for its weekly chronicle parodying de Gaulle's Elysée as the court of the *ancien régime*, in its New Year issue in 1966 summed up with a mixture of affection and condescension how de Gaulle was viewed. It depicted de Gaulle riding on a donkey into 'Gaulilee'. Lying lasciviously on a beach was a scantily dressed Brigitte Bardot. At her side was Yvonne de Gaulle, her dress buttoned up to the neck, on her knees praying. In the France of the 1960s, 'Auntie [*Tante*] Yvonne' was the anti-Bardot: the symbol of all that seemed most prudish and narrow-minded in bourgeois Catholicism next to the symbol of sexual provocation, proto-feminism and youth. Yvonne de Gaulle, who did not lack a sense of humour, played up to her image. Once Bernard Tricot found himself next to her at a film showing in the Elysée. He looked up distractedly at the ceiling to see a cupid's private parts covered in gauze. Spotting his gaze Yvonne de Gaulle told him: 'Despite what you might think, I am not the one who added those ribbons.'[1] Yet there was truth in the caricatures of Yvonne. One day she excitedly bustled up to Peyrefitte after he had made some remarks on television about girls wearing miniskirts in mixed schools – an issue arousing much comment in the France of the 1960s: 'So it is true you are going to ban miniskirts?' Peyrefitte had to admit that this would not be possible: 'I saw a shadow of deep disappointment come over her.'[2]

Although there was no truth in the rumour that Yvonne de Gaulle intervened to prevent divorced men becoming government ministers – André Malraux for one was divorced and Palewski was not a model of conjugal rectitude – the de Gaulles would usually arrange a lunch to meet each of the new *conseillers* at the Elysée. Those subjected to this terrifying ritual had the impression they were being sized up for their morality as much as anything else. De Gaulle shared most of the conventional social values of his wife but was more open-minded. Claude Guy's journal records a revealing conversation between the two of them during the long years cooped up at Colombey out of power. Yvonne de Gaulle had expressed her outrage that the Pope should have received a 'sinner' like Eva Perón. De Gaulle took the matter lightly: 'The Church always soars above people's faults. It looks at all matters on the transcendental level. What counts for the Church is to lead the faithful to their salvation. That is why the Church treats these human matters with supreme indifference.' Yvonne de Gaulle was not to be deflected:

> Y: You can say what you want, but I think people take much too much interest in women of this kind! . . . Take Chateaubriand, for example . . . Take his 'friend' . . . You know that one who was ill.
>
> De G: [Quick as a flash] Mme de Beaumont? . . . [Impatient] What about her?
>
> Y: Well, the Pope asked Chateaubriand for news about that woman.
>
> De G: I call that excellent politics.
>
> Y: Well whatever you say I don't think it is right . . . She was not an honourable woman. Like Mme Pétain: when the Marshal went to Rome the Pope received her.
>
> De G: What was there to do? They were married in church. Her first husband the sculptor had died a while before.

Y: That does not alter the fact they had been living in sin. So I say that they should not have been married in Church.

De G: Yvonne, why do you always want the death of the sinner? What do I know? Perhaps they repented. One should after all give them a chance![3]

De Gaulle was not enthusiastic about the reforms of Vatican II. Although he agreed it was necessary for the Church to end its 'rejection of the modern world', he worried that Pope John XXIII had been too influenced by a Vatican group who wanted to revolutionize everything:

> There are always people who want to go so fast that they destroy everything . . . I am not sure that the Church was right to suppress processions . . . and the Latin service. It is always wrong to give the impression of denying oneself and being ashamed of what one is. How can you expect others to believe in you if you do not believe in yourself?[4]

During the Presidential campaign of 1965, Mitterrand had proposed that the contraceptive pill should be legalized. When it was suggested to de Gaulle that he might at least say he would not object if a bill along these lines were put forward in parliament, he would not countenance the idea: 'One must not reduce women to machines for making love! This goes against all that is most precious in women: fecundity. A woman is made to have children! If one tolerates the pill nothing will hold any more! Sex will invade everything . . . It is all very well to favour the emancipation of women but not their dissipation.'[5] There is nothing surprising about such views for a man of de Gaulle's background, but two years later, under pressure from his government, he allowed the legalization of contraceptives. He drew the line, however, at the state reimbursing those who bought them: 'We are not going to start reimbursing sex! One might as well reimburse people for buying cars.'[6]

The late 1950s and early 1960s were a period of extraordinary cultural and intellectual vitality in France. This was the heyday of the 'new novel' in literature, the 'new wave' in cinema, of thinkers like Roland Barthes, Michel Foucault, Jacques Lacan. While he was President, de Gaulle read two or three books a week – usually history, novels or poetry – and made a valiant attempt to keep up with contemporary literature. He always read the winners of the main literary prizes. In December 1963 he wrote to the twenty-three-year-old Jean-Marie Le Clézio who had just published his first novel *Le procès-verbal*. The novel's amnesiac young protagonist, Adam, is estranged from the world, not knowing who he is: possibly a deserter from the army, possibly someone who has escaped from a psychiatric ward. De Gaulle wrote to Le Clézio:

Your book drew me into another world, probably the true one, and like
Adam, I was able to traverse it in zigzags. As everything is just beginning for
you, the journey will have consequences. So much the better! For you have
a great talent. For me, who am at the end, you write that 'power and faith
impose humility'. For you, who have just passed by the first elm trees along
the road, I say the same about talent.[7]

One cannot imagine many other heads of state writing a letter of this kind
to a young writer.

Although he tried to keep up, even as a young man de Gaulle's tastes
had been conservative rather than avant-garde – Rostand not Proust. The
extraordinarily well-connected Ambassador Roland de Margerie was
amused one day to hear de Gaulle remarking with admiration that Margerie's daughter was related though her father to Edmond de Rostand while
not thinking it worthy of note that she was also related to Proust through
marriage to a cousin.[8] De Gaulle told his son that he did not like Proust's
'preciousness and contorted style, and his artificial milieu where the point
of existence was society dinners'.[9] One of the General's most admiring
early biographers, the Swiss writer Georges Cattaui, was also an admirer
and biographer of Proust – an unusual combination of heroes. When Cattaui sent de Gaulle his book on Proust, the General replied in terms so
elliptical that it remains unclear whether he had read Proust or not.

Before 1914, de Gaulle had little interest in the naturalist school of Zola.
He passionately admired Verlaine, but seems to have been indifferent to
Rimbaud. When he was on a tour of the north of France the Mayor of
Charleville presented him with a bust of Rimbaud who had been born in
the city, and later on the same tour the Mayor of Rethel presented him
with one of Verlaine who had taught in the city. De Gaulle joked privately
that he would put the two on the same mantelpiece: 'There is a God for
queers [*pédérastes*] after all.'[10] In the inter-war years, de Gaulle read the
modern classics by authors such as Bernanos, Mauriac and Malraux but
does not seem to have followed the avant-garde *Nouvelle Revue française*
of André Gide. Gide was not an author who counted for him; the opposite
would have been surprising. In his notebooks, however, de Gaulle records
an observation of Gide in his study of Dostoevsky that there 'is no work
of art in which the devil does not participate'. To that de Gaulle added:
'That is also true of action.'[11]

Of the immediate post-war literary stars, de Gaulle does not seem to
have rated Sartre: 'I am very ignorant of his writing. The little I have read
of it does not encourage me to go further. I don't say he has no talent but . . .'[12]
He was, however, a great admirer of Marguerite Yourcenar's *Memoirs*

of Hadrian, and when clearing out space in his library at Colombey in the mid-1960s he decided to keep the book on his shelves.[13] Much of de Gaulle's reading was of books that he had been sent by admiring writers who would usually receive a carefully chiselled letter where saying nothing with allusive eloquence was elevated to an art form. Unusually, Jacques Lacan, who sent de Gaulle a copy of his *Ecrits* in 1966 with an admiring dedication, did not get a reply – perhaps because even de Gaulle could not make enough sense of the text to pen a plausible reply or perhaps because he had no idea who Lacan was. His seventy-seven letters to the poet Pierre Jean Jouve are models of elliptical obscurity as mysterious as the poetry of Jouve itself. Hardly more comprehensible was de Gaulle's letter to Malraux, having read his *Antimémoires* while crossing the Atlantic on his way to Canada in July 1967, in which he claimed that he had found the 'book admirable in three dimensions'.[14] In his relationship to the cultural trends of the 1960s de Gaulle reminds one of the mysteriously haunting line by the symbolist poet Mallarmé: '*Calme bloc ici-bas chu d'un désastre obscur* [Calm block fallen down to earth from some obscure disaster]'. He was ill prepared to understand the intellectual origins of the extraordinary explosion that was about to burst upon France.

BACKGROUND TO REVOLUTION

At the end of 1967, de Gaulle had written to his son that 'politically, economically and socially the year is ending in calm'.[15] With hindsight this seems enormously complacent, but the complacency was almost universally shared. Even the ultra-leftist organization of young Communists (Jeunesse Communiste Révolutionnaire – JCR) saw no likelihood of any serious political upheavals over the coming months.[16] For de Gaulle, the month of May 1968 had even, to begin with, seemed a moment to celebrate. After the North Vietnamese Tet offensive at the start of the year, the American government finally accepted negotiations to find a way of ending the Vietnam War. Paris was chosen as the venue for the talks because de Gaulle's position during the war had won him the trust of the North Vietnamese. After all the setbacks of 1967, this was a signal success for French diplomacy. The talks opened at the Hôtel Majestic in Paris on 13 May, but this important event went almost unnoticed because on the same day France was plunged into revolution.

Youth rebellion was part of the history of western Europe in the late 1960s but Gaullist France had seemed immune. De Gaulle smugly told Erhard in 1966 that if there was 'so much long hair and so many young layabouts in England it is because the country has lost so much of its responsibility'.[17] But the problem was more complicated than this as de Gaulle well knew. The economic modernization of the 1960s, which he celebrated in speech after speech, was also bringing in its wake challenges to traditional cultural values. As he put in his television conversation with Michel Droit in the second round of the 1965 presidential election: 'France is like a household. The housewife wants a fridge, a washing machine, and even, if possible, a car. That is change. But at the same time, she does not want her husband out on the town (*bambocher*), her boys putting their feet on the table and her daughters coming home at all hours. That is order. The housewife wants progress but she does not want chaos (*pagaille*). Well, the same is true for France. She wants progress but not *la pagaille*' – or that is what he hoped.[18]

Quite apart from these new social and generational tensions the French university system was in crisis because of pressure on resources caused by the massive increase in student numbers in the 1960s – from about 215,000 in 1960 to about 500,000 in 1968 – owing to the combined effects of the post-war baby boom and the democratization of higher education. Not personally familiar with the university world, having himself been educated at Saint-Cyr, de Gaulle viewed it with a respectful wariness.[19] He had been scarred by an experience that occurred soon after he became President in January 1959. In conformity with a tradition dating back to the Third Republic, de Gaulle in his capacity as newly elected President attended the annual ball of the Ecole Normale Supérieure on 21 February 1959. The students were lined up to greet him. As he stretched out his hand to the first student, it was refused, and as he walked along the line he was rebuffed by each student in turn, one of them saying: 'I will not shake hands with your policies.' This was a carefully calculated stunt to express opposition to the way de Gaulle had come back to power six months earlier with army support. He left without saying a word and never referred to this humiliation even in private. Nor did he ever again take the risk of visiting a French educational institution.

During the first years of his Presidency de Gaulle was opposed by the student union UNEF for the slowness of his move to Algerian independence. Many of his private comments on the students in these years were dismissive. After a discussion on university reform in November 1963 he exclaimed: 'Why allow the universities to be invaded by students who have nothing to do there? They are clogging up the university system. They have no idea what they want except to benefit from the many advantages that the taxpayer grants them and to avoid the responsibilities of active life. They don't want to leave adolescence.'[20]

Despite these eruptions of irritation about a world that was foreign to him, de Gaulle was committed to the democratization of higher education in the interests of the economy, providing the process was tightly controlled. Under the influence of his education adviser, Jacques Narbonne, he had convened several *conseils restreints* to discuss the matter in 1963 and 1964. Before one of these he laid out his objective for Pompidou: 'A policy founded on the principle of democratization of secondary education ... and that of continuous orientation and selection directing pupils to an education that corresponds to their aptitudes and to the need of the national economy'.[21] Or as he put it more brutally to Narbonne: 'We must open the door but only to those who are worth it.'[22] In his view it was the role of educators to orient pupils in the right direction; the needs of the economy must trump the desires of students. It is hard to imagine a view more at odds with the mood of French students in the 1960s.

De Gaulle, as we have already seen, had had no luck with these ideas largely because of the opposition of Pompidou. As an alumnus of the ENS, Pompidou viewed education as his *domaine réservé* (he had few others).[23] When Alain Peyrefitte (also an alumnus of the ENS) was moved in 1967 from the Ministry of Information to that of Education, Pompidou suggested that he visit him once a month. Peyrefitte realized perfectly well that Pompidou wanted to keep an eye on him. He was warned: 'I know what one can and cannot do with the education system. It is not the General's world. And in fact he knows it.' The issue of selection was very much on the agenda again in the first half of 1968, but Pompidou made it clear to Peyrefitte that he remained as opposed as he had ever been. It was he said a 'hobbyhorse' of Narbonne: 'It is a delicate matter. I am liberal. I will not put French youth in barracks [*encasernerai*].'[24] The knowledge that the government was planning to introduce measures of selection was one ingredient of student dissatisfaction at the start of 1968.

Despite the belief of contemporary commentators that most of the French young were depoliticized, students had grievances which, while not conventionally 'political', could quickly become so. One source of resentment was the prohibition against male and female students visiting each other's halls of residence at night. This ban caused sporadic protests at several campuses. Older than the mass of the students, there was also a minority of highly politicized student leaders who had been radicalized by the Algerian War. These activists remembered the police brutality of the years 1960–62, of which the Charonne killings were the most notorious example. One popular slogan in 1968 denounced the French riot police – 'CRS = SS' – harking back to those dark days of protest during the Algerian War (though in fact that slogan had first been used in the insurrectionary strikes of 1947).

If the university system was a pressure cooker ready to explode, nowhere was this truer than at the soulless new university campus of Nanterre just outside Paris. Its buildings were still under construction and were inadequate for accommodating the flood of new students. Nanterre also harboured a small group of ultra-radical students, among whom was the truculent and articulate Franco-German sociology student Daniel Cohn-Bendit. De Gaulle's Minister of Youth and Sports, François Missoffe, had visited the campus in January 1968 to inaugurate the sports centre and swimming pool. He had been barracked by a number of students. Cohn-Bendit shouted out that Missoffe's recent report on the problems of youth had said nothing about sexual problems; Missoffe shouted back that if Cohn-Bendit had sexual problems he should jump into the new pool to cool off; Cohn-Bendit shouted back that Missoffe was a fascist because the construction of a sports centre was reminiscent of the Hitler Youth.[25] This was the first time that the name of Cohn-Bendit had come to public attention.

By the end of April, the sporadic disturbances at Nanterre were bringing the university to a standstill. The Dean decided to close the campus. This had the fatal consequence the next day, Friday 3 May, of driving the student activists to take their protest to the Sorbonne, in the heart of the Latin Quarter of Paris. Police were despatched to evacuate the Sorbonne and close it down. Students who had started out as bystanders found themselves sucked into the protests. The Latin Quarter witnessed its first night of violence. From this point, the 'events', as they soon came to be known, acquired their own momentum. Each demonstration called to protest against police violence, to demand the freeing of the arrested students and to get the Sorbonne reopened resulted in more police violence which provided the pretext for another demonstration.

The head of the Paris Police, Maurice Grimaud, had succeeded Maurice Papon in the previous year. Grimaud could not have been more different from his authoritarian predecessor, who had been in charge during the bloody events of October 1961 and the Charonne demonstration of February 1962. A man of liberal sympathies, who had once hoped to be a poet rather than a policeman, Grimaud felt considerable sympathy for the protesters. He was desperate to avoid police violence getting out of hand.[26] The slogan 'CRS = SS' could hardly have been less appropriate for him. But the rank and file of Paris police had learnt their trade under Papon and the brutality of their response to the first demonstrations was the main driver of protest in the first two weeks of May.[27]

The repression of a second demonstration on Monday 6 May was exceptionally violent. The next day, 25,000 students flooded across the Seine to the Champs-Elysées and then another night of violence followed in the Latin Quarter. The revolution of May '68 was under way.

ACT I: STUDENTS ON THE STREETS, 2–13 MAY

On 2 May, the day before the first night of violence, Pompidou had left France for a ten-day official visit to Afghanistan and Iran. The Minister of Justice, Louis Joxe, deputized for Pompidou in his absence but felt hampered in that he was playing only an interim role. He did not even feel that he had the authority to move into the Hôtel Matignon during Pompidou's absence. The two other key players in the first week of the crisis were Alain Peyrefitte, who had been Minister of Education since 1967, and an old Free French veteran and ultra-loyal Gaullist, Christian Fouchet, Minister of the Interior. Like Grimaud, Joxe was determined at all costs to avoid fatalities. He told Peyrefitte at the end of the first week: 'One thing is sure. I did not fire on the *pieds noirs* in Algiers and I am not going to fire on the students in Paris.'[28] Fouchet, despite his stern exterior as a Free French veteran, held the same view. De Gaulle was torn between thinking that the agitation of a few students was too trivial to require his intervention and irritation that the government was not acting more vigorously. As a result, the government oscillated haplessly between conciliation and firmness, while the student leaders pursued with great skill their tactics of provocation and escalation.[29]

At his nightly meeting with Foccart on 7 May, the third day of demonstrations, de Gaulle affected not to take the crisis seriously. But he had been worried enough to cancel his previous weekend in Colombey, summoning Fouchet, Joxe and Peyrefitte to the Elysée on Sunday morning (5 May). He took a tough line: 'When a child gets angry and oversteps the mark, the best way of calming him is to give him a smack.' The problem, Joxe replied, was that the demonstrators were 'neither quite children nor adults'.[30] Two days later, five Nobel prize winners, including the Gaullist François Mauriac, signed a petition protesting against police violence. An incensed de Gaulle shouted at Fouchet and Joxe: 'You seem terrorized in front of these children. Do not forget that a Minister of the Interior must know how, if necessary, to give the order to fire ... The state has a prerogative, that of striking down those who want to strike it down.' Neither Joxe nor Fouchet took this too seriously. As they left the room, Joxe said: 'He does not mean a word of it . . . He just wants to stiffen our resolve. But he knows perfectly well that this would be the best way of unleashing opinion against us and bringing the regime to its knees.'[31] De Gaulle did not press the point, but he did prevent his ministers offering any olive branch such as reopening the Sorbonne.

The week's events culminated on the night of Friday 10 May. At the end of another day of demonstrations, the students refused to disperse unless their two key demands were met: the freeing of students imprisoned after previous demonstrations and the reopening of the Sorbonne. Fraught negotiations went on late into the night between student leaders and the Rector of the Sorbonne. Meanwhile demonstrators started building barricades in the streets of the Latin Quarter. Foccart hurried over to the Ministry of the Interior to monitor the situation with Fouchet. They were joined by Debré, Joxe and Tricot. Foccart and Debré wanted the police to intervene at once; Joxe and Grimaud wanted to hold off as long as there was any prospect that negotiations might work. At 2 a.m. the police were ordered to destroy the barricades, which now numbered about fifty. The pitched battle that ensued was reported live through the night by the private radio stations Europe 1 and Radio Luxembourg. In the morning, Parisians woke up to scenes of devastation: burnt-out cars, felled trees, torn-up paving stones.

De Gaulle had gone to bed before the construction of the first barricade. Tricot woke him at 5 a.m. so that he would not hear the news first on the radio. At 6 a.m. de Gaulle summoned Joxe, Fouchet and the Minister of Defence, Pierre Messmer. He asked Messmer if the army should be sent in but was told that troops were not trained to deal with such a situation. To Joxe's comment 'Thank God there were no deaths,' de Gaulle said nothing.[32] During the day, de Gaulle saw Joxe, Fouchet and Grimaud individually. They were all in favour of defusing the crisis by announcing the reopening of the Sorbonne. De Gaulle refused. At the end of the afternoon he received Peyrefitte, who proposed a tactical retreat but not unconditional surrender: the Sorbonne would be reopened in return for assurances from student leaders that there would be no more demonstrations and proper controls governing entry to the Sorbonne. Peyrefitte left with the impression that de Gaulle was wavering. Everything waited upon the imminent return of Pompidou.

Throughout the week Pompidou was kept closely informed by his *directeur de cabinet* Michel Jobert. On 'barricades night' Pompidou telephoned Joxe to urge a tough line on the ground that 'the moment for concessions has not yet come'. Joxe suspected that Pompidou was reserving for himself the role of conciliator on his return.[33] Whether or not this was true, on the plane home Pompidou prepared a speech proposing concessions. Arriving at Orly airport on the evening of 11 May, he drove straight to the Hôtel Matignon where he told Joxe, Fouchet, Peyrefitte and Messmer that he had decided to reopen the Sorbonne. They were unanimous, given his reactions earlier in the day, that de Gaulle would never accept this. Pompidou replied: 'General de Gaulle no longer exists. Now it is I who need to be followed.'[34] Peyrefitte was worried that conceding the student demands, and asking nothing in return, risked 'setting off an avalanche'.[35] Like the others, he was sure de Gaulle would refuse. They were all the more amazed, turning on the radio just before midnight, to hear Pompidou announcing that the Sorbonne would be reopened and the imprisoned students released.

We have no idea why de Gaulle changed his mind. Pompidou merely tells us that as he was going to de Gaulle's office, Tricot told him that the General had 'evolved'; that the conversation was 'brief'; and that de Gaulle 'immediately' gave his agreement.[36] Some people believed retrospectively that this was a disastrous decision which caused the 'avalanche' Peyrefitte had predicted. De Gaulle himself came to believe this. He told Fouchet later that it had been a terrible mistake: 'It was not de Gaulle, it was Pétain.'[37] After the events were over, de Gaulle told Peyrefitte that Pompidou had blackmailed him into agreeing by threatening to resign.[38] There is no other evidence of this. Perhaps de Gaulle was trying to distance himself from a decision he subsequently believed to be wrong. The likeliest explanation for his volte-face is that he was won over by the eloquence and conviction of his Prime Minister whose fresh energy was a welcome contrast to the three exhausted ministers who had not slept properly for many nights.

Pompidou was wrong to believe that reopening the Sorbonne would end the movement. On Monday 13 May, the trade unions called a one-day strike of solidarity with the students. There were joint demonstrations of students and workers all over the country. At the end of the huge demonstration in Paris the students flooded into the Sorbonne, which was now 'occupied' day and night. That evening Foccart hosted a small dinner for de Gaulle's inner circle to celebrate the tenth anniversary of 13 May 1958 which had been the signal for de Gaulle's return to power. In the streets outside demonstrators were shouting: 'Ten years is enough,' 'De Gaulle to the museum'. Foccart comments wistfully: 'In the end, we spent more time talking about the present than evoking our memories of the past ... I had taken my little transistor radio to the table and we listened to the news ... with the same interest but in a different spirit from ten years earlier.'[39]

ACT II: DE GAULLE IN RUMANIA, 14–18 MAY

During the first week of the events, the Prime Minister had been absent in Afghanistan; during the second, the President was absent in Rumania. This trip had been long planned as part of de Gaulle's détente strategy. Rumania was the country in the eastern bloc which most consistently showed signs of wanting to distance itself from the Soviet Union. In the light of events in Paris, de Gaulle dithered over whether he should leave. Pompidou wanted him to go as a message to the world that the crisis was under control; Fouchet pleaded with him to stay and thought Pompidou was not unhappy to have de Gaulle out of the way. De Gaulle hesitated until the last moment. Before setting off, he told his ministers that he would address the nation on 24 May after his return.

Pompidou and his team now took full command, sidelining the Elysée entirely.[40] Although Fouchet remained in theory Minister of the Interior, his account of this period simply states: 'Here end, as far as I am concerned, the events of May 68.' Peyrefitte offered his resignation, but although for the moment Pompidou refused it, Peyrefitte no longer played any significant role. Pompidou himself, on the other hand, was everywhere. On 14 May, after de Gaulle's departure, he made a confident speech in parliament which won him many plaudits – but in fact the tide of protest was only just beginning.

Two days after the 13 May trade union strike in solidarity with the students, the workers at the Sud-Aviation aircraft factory near Nantes went on strike, and occupied their factory. The Renault factory at Cléon in Normandy followed suit on the next day, and by the end of the week at least a hundred factories had been occupied by their workers. Since workers in some factories started to go back to work as strikes started in others, the total number of strikers is difficult to calculate. But this was certainly the biggest social movement of its kind in French history, and at its peak on 25 May there were several million workers on strike. If some observers had been aware of the simmering crisis in the universities, no one – including the trade unions – had predicted this extraordinary social movement in the factories. Sparked by the government's indecisive response to the student protests, the strikes partly represented the sudden irruption into politics of the hundreds of thousands of new semi-skilled workers who had swelled the French labour force in the 1960s. Many of these were immigrants, or young men and women straight from the countryside; they had little in common with the traditional working class which formed the rank and file of the trade unions. Living in abysmal housing and working long hours with no trade unions to protect them, they were the workers who had made Gaullist economic modernization possible – but as its victims not its beneficiaries. The strikes revealed that they wanted not only better working conditions but also to be heard and to be noticed.[41]

This transformed the nature of the crisis. As one of de Gaulle's Elysée advisers observed when reflecting on the crisis many years later:

> It is not possible to avoid a workers' movement, but one cannot have at the same time a student movement; one must at all costs have them successively but not together, and the drama of 68 was that they arrived together, and joined together, and we were not able to prevent this tidal wave.[42]

This social tidal wave rapidly spread from the factories to almost every institution and professional group in France: writers and footballers, doctors and filmmakers, architects and lawyers. Grass-roots action committees sprang up like mushrooms to challenge authority and hierarchy. All over the country students occupied their faculty buildings. Even the bourgeois and respectable Ecole des Sciences Politiques in Paris was taken over by students, who erected a banner proclaiming 'No to the Gaullist dictatorship'. Students also took possession of the Odéon Theatre in Paris not far from the already occupied Sorbonne. The main lecture hall of the Sorbonne and the stage of Odéon were transformed into twenty-four-hour talking shops. The participants in these debates endlessly reinvented the world in a strange atmosphere of romantic lyricism where dogmatic Marxism coexisted with libertarian anarchism.

France exploded into slogans, tracts, debates, speeches and manifestos. Nothing better symbolized this strange dreamlike month than the endlessly inventive graffiti scribbled on every surface, and the posters plastered on every wall: 'It is forbidden to forbid,' 'Take your dreams for realities.' Suddenly everyone wanted to speak, and to be heard, in a country where it seemed that for a decade the only voice had been that of the ageing monarch in the Elysée. Having turned politics into theatre, de Gaulle's regime was confronted by a movement which turned theatre into politics. One famous slogan of '68 was 'Power is in the streets,' but it was also words that were in the street – and in Gaullist France words *were* power. One revealing symbol of this change was the role of the transistor radio in the unfolding of the events. During the abortive putsch of 1961 the conscripts in Algiers had been won over by listening to de Gaulle on their radios;

during the night of the barricades in 1968 the population of Paris followed the events minute by minute on transistors – but this time they had not tuned in to hear de Gaulle, who was soundly asleep.[43]

As France seemed to be grinding to a cacophonous halt, de Gaulle was pursuing his stately visit to Bucharest. His speeches repeated his familiar message that the countries of Europe should assert their independence of the two superpowers. When in his meeting with de Gaulle the party leader Ceauşescu insisted that his regime was not imposed by the Soviets, de Gaulle replied:

> I am not speaking about the regime. I am entirely determinist when it comes to regimes: there are circumstances, people, events, wars. I think that when a country keeps a regime for a long time that means it cannot do otherwise ... For Rumania, a regime like yours has a good side. It is useful but such a regime would be impossible in France or Britain.

The meeting produced few concrete results. As de Gaulle concluded: 'We have not learnt much about what the other is thinking.'[44] As always, the trip was a huge popular success. But there was something surreal about the French television news on 18 May leading with de Gaulle touring Rumania while the French 'troubles' were given only a brief mention followed by a long report on the prowess of French industry.[45] Three days later the ORTF, the state broadcasting company, went on strike because its journalists were no longer ready to play the role of lackeys of the government.

ACT III: PRISONER OF THE ELYSÉE, 19–28 MAY

De Gaulle's imperturbability was a mask. Briefed every night on the telephone by his Elysée staff, he was deeply anxious and sleeping badly. As the news became ever more alarming, he abruptly cut his Rumanian visit short by a day, returning to France on the evening of 18 May. The government was out in force to meet him at the airport. De Gaulle gave them an enthusiastic account of his trip – 'the Rumanians carry out selection and they have no trouble with their students' – and said that the anarchy ('*chienlit*') in France must come to an end. 'Reform yes, *chienlit* no' was the new mantra. The word *chienlit* – meaning literally 'shit in the bed' – was another of those colourful archaisms which most people had never heard until resuscitated by de Gaulle. The May '68 graffiti artists responded with posters of de Gaulle: 'He is the *chienlit*.' At the Council of Ministers on the next day de Gaulle fumed about the disorder – implicitly blaming Pompidou – and insisted that the police evacuate the Sorbonne and the Odéon by force. Grimaud reports in his memoirs a conversation between Fouchet and de Gaulle at the Elysée on the same day:

> Fouchet: General, you must realise that the police are traumatized.
> De Gaulle: 'Traumatized?' What does that mean? You need to give them some hard stuff [*gnôle*] to drink! That is what one always does for soldiers in the trenches.[46]

Despite this bluster, de Gaulle was talked out of the idea of a police assault on the Sorbonne but reiterated his order that the Odéon had to be evacuated within twenty-four hours.[47] Grimaud, who preferred students talking in the Odéon to fighting in the streets, was unhappy about this. In the end, de Gaulle agreed to leave it to Pompidou and Grimaud to decide the timing of the operation – which they discreetly shelved. For the first time since the start of the crisis, both the Prime Minister and the President were in France at the same time – and it was clearly the former who was in command. This was starkly revealed when de Gaulle tried to sack the Minister of Information, Georges Gorse, whom he felt was not up to the job. On 21 May, de Gaulle summoned the loyal Gaullist Alexandre Sanguinetti to the Elysée in total secrecy to let him know that he planned to name him Minister of Information. When Pompidou got wind of this the next day – from Foccart – he was furious that de Gaulle was trying to impose a minister on him behind his back. Sanguinetti spent the next three days unsure if he was going to be named. None of this added to the government's sense of direction. In the end Sanguinetti was not appointed – another indication that power had shifted from de Gaulle to Pompidou.[48]

On his return from Rumania, de Gaulle had been presented with a thick file of notes from his Elysée advisers suggesting how to deal with the crisis.[49] They seemed at a loss to know if anything would work. One possibility considered was the implementation of Article 16 but this was rejected as being likely to radicalize opinion further: 'The forces that have been released at present are on such a scale that it is hopeless to think they can be contained by tightening the lid.' Another possibility was a referendum on the reform of the university system. This too was rejected as being unlikely to interest the mass of the population or calm the social movement. Another possibility was a reshuffle of the government to replace the ministers responsible for social affairs, education and, especially, information: 'The ORTF is to the Fifth Republic what the Bastille was to Louis XVI.' Another idea was to call a referendum on the constitution. This too was rejected: 'It is not desirable to let it be believed that the institutions of the regime are threatened by the first upset caused by the students and trade unions.' If there was to be a referendum, it must be on a subject that would meet 'the confused but profound aspiration of the country for more autonomy from central power.' This was all very vague. The idea expressed in one note that 'the country is expecting a kind of miracle from de Gaulle' was itself indicative of the mind-set that the protesters of May '68 were challenging.

De Gaulle had decided what his 'miracle' solution would be. In a speech planned for 24 May he intended to announce a referendum. On the eve of his speech, he gave his diagnosis of the situation to the Council of Ministers. The troubles, in his view, were caused by a generation that had never known real hardship but was suffering from the effects of 'mechanical and technological civilization' (an old de Gaulle theme). Although this was a worldwide phenomenon, at least it was to be welcomed given that 'as always France was showing the way' (a typical de Gaulle touch). His judgement was that the protesters shared a 'general desire to participate' but did not want revolution: 'Everyone wants "to be involved", "to be consulted", to "participate".' Workers wanted to be involved in the running of their factories and electors in the running of their regions. This would be the subject of the referendum. If the answer was 'yes', measures on these lines would be introduced; if not, 'my task is over.' De Gaulle had resuscitated his hobbyhorse of participation and adapted it to the crisis. Although no one round the table seemed convinced, Pompidou ended the discussion: '*Mon Général*, we are faithful to your person and will remain so.'[50]

Although de Gaulle had his plan to resolve the crisis, he had also authorized Pompidou to start negotiations with the trade unions to end the strikes. Meanwhile – for ten days – Foccart had been working in his own way to solve the crisis. He began mobilizing his networks of former RPF activists. They set up Committees for the Defence of the Republic (CDRs) throughout France. Foccart also contacted former OAS activists whose hatred of long-haired anarchists surpassed even their hatred of de Gaulle. His plan was gather these disparate elements in a demonstration of support for de Gaulle which was tentatively scheduled for 30 May. De Gaulle did not discourage these efforts, about which Foccart kept him informed at their nightly meetings – and nor did Pompidou. There were thus three Gaullist strategies in play to end the crisis: de Gaulle's referendum, Pompidou's negotiations, Foccart's mobilization of the Gaullist base.

Of the three strategies, de Gaulle's fell flat at once. His speech on 24 May, announcing a referendum on participation, disappointed even his most loyal supporters. Listening at Matignon with his aides Pompidou's only comment was 'it could have been worse.'[51] De Gaulle seemed old and tired; his idea of participation seemed nebulous. Ironically he was not wrong that participation – or at least the sense that people wanted more control over their lives – was a major ingredient of the spirit of 1968. But who could believe that de Gaulle, whose style of government evinced contempt for those intermediary associations that were the necessary conduit of real participation, was the man to carry it out? Despite his use of the word 'participation' there was a cultural abyss between him and the protesters, whose celebration of individualism, personal freedom and self-expression was the antithesis of his austere patriotism, in which individualism was sublimated in the service of the nation. The events of May had many causes, but at some level they were a revolt against de Gaulle's style of rule and the values he represented in both his personal and his public life.

The night of de Gaulle's speech coincided with another big demonstration in Paris. The participants listened to him on their transistor radios, and greeted his words with derisive shouts of 'Adieu de Gaulle'. Afterwards the demonstration degenerated into the worst disturbances since the night of the barricades. For the first time violence erupted on the Right Bank. There was a half-hearted attempt to burn down the Bourse, barricades were erected again and a demonstrator was killed by a fragment of a police tear-gas grenade. De Gaulle's speech had seemingly made things worse. In reality, the violence was directed less against de Gaulle than against the government's attempt to refuse Daniel Cohn-Bendit (who was a German citizen) re-entry into France after he had left on a speaking tour abroad. De Gaulle seemed so irrelevant that he was no longer even the main target of the protesters' rage.

Meanwhile Pompidou was embarking on his plan to negotiate a deal between the trade unions and business leaders. His objective was to satisfy the material demands of the unions in order to separate them from the students. Public opinion, originally behind the students, was turning against them after the violence of the night of 24 May. In Lyons on the same night a policeman was knocked over and killed by a vehicle during a demonstration. This first fatality in the ranks of the police prompted a wave of shock. Pompidou, sensing that events might soon turn in favour of the government, insisted that the Minister of Finance, Debré, given his excitable temperament, should be excluded from the discussions with the unions. De Gaulle had no choice but to agree. Foccart found Debré in a state of 'absolutely indescribable rage', but managed to talk him out of resigning.[52] Pompidou's marathon negotiations started on the afternoon of Saturday 25 May and finished at 7 a.m. on Monday 27 May. They included a 35 per cent increase in the minimum wage and a 10 per cent hike in the average wage. But when Georges Séguy, leader of the largest trade union, the Communist CGT, arrived to present the agreement to the workers of the massive Renault plant of Billancourt outside Paris, he was shouted down. This alarming development suggested that the unions could no longer control their own rank and file.

At the Council of Ministers that afternoon Pompidou remained optimistic that with more concessions he could reach an agreement. De Gaulle, in an execrable mood, seemed slightly detached from the discussions. After Pompidou's report, he contented himself with the words: 'You have conducted the negotiations as well as possible and you are authorized to go on until you get an agreement.' 'Not a word of thanks,' remarked Pompidou bitterly as he returned to his team at Matignon.[53] Despite knowing that his speech had been a disaster, de Gaulle was still fixated on his referendum, which was scheduled for 16 June. He read out the draft text but the scepticism around the table was palpable. Messmer was bold enough to ask whether it would be possible to hold the referendum given that all printing presses and all public transport were on strike.[54] De Gaulle's only other intervention was to fulminate against the government's authorization of a meeting called by the student union UNEF at the Charléty stadium in the south of Paris. De Gaulle wanted it banned, but Grimaud and Pompidou both believed this would be unnecessarily provocative. Once again de Gaulle had to concede.

The Charléty meeting passed off on the evening of 27 May without incident. Its most significant moment was the appearance of Pierre Mendès France, who did not speak but was cheered by the crowd. The students of May '68 had little time for any politicians but Mendès was slightly different. He seemed untarnished by any implication in the Fifth Republic and still retained a legendary aura from the Fourth. His appearance at Charléty suggested that the events of May, having started in the universities and moved to the factories, were now entering a more conventionally political phase. Scenting that de Gaulle's days might be numbered, on Tuesday 28 May François Mitterrand, not to be outflanked by Mendès France, gave a press conference announcing that he was ready to form a provisional government of transition with Mendès France as his Prime Minister.

These developments led the Communist CGT to announce a big demonstration for 29 May calling for a 'people's government'. Throughout May, the Communists had been marginal to the events. The students despised them as a retrograde force who were as out of touch as de Gaulle: the Marxism of the students was inspired by Mao and Castro, not by the grey bureaucratic leaders of the PCF. In the factories the PCF had been taken by surprise when the strikes erupted and no union had been more accommodating than the Communist CGT in the negotiations conducted by the trade unions with Pompidou. Earlier in the month de Gaulle's brother-in-law, Jacques Vendroux, had been taken aside in parliament by the leader of the Communist Party, Waldeck Rochet, begging him to make sure that de Gaulle stayed in power.[55] The PCF had no desire for revolution and the purpose of its demonstration of 29 May was a show of strength to put itself into the frame if de Gaulle were to fall. A sense of *fin de régime* was hovering in the air.

During the tense days following his speech of 24 May, de Gaulle had little to do but morosely prowl the corridors of the Elysée. His advisers became increasingly alarmist. Foccart picked up rumours that explosives were being stocked in the Sorbonne, that an attack on the Elysée was planned, that the events were a plot masterminded by the CIA and Israeli secret services as revenge against de Gaulle's foreign policies. These luridly implausible fantasies give a sense of the mood in the Elysée. As he had done during the army putsch of 1961, Foccart prepared a helicopter to spirit de Gaulle away if the Palace were attacked.[56] De Gaulle continued to plan for a referendum in which no one else believed. On the evening of 27 May, the journalist Michel Droit was secretly summoned to the Elysée. It was his television interview with Droit that had helped de Gaulle bounce back after the first round of the 1965 election. Now he wanted to repeat the experiment to sell his referendum idea to the French people. Droit asked to return the next day with some ideas.[57]

On 28 May, all de Gaulle's visitors found him in a mood of apocalyptic despair. Arriving for his usual evening meeting, Foccart was told by the head of de Gaulle's military *cabinet*, General Lalande, who had just come out of his own interview, that he was worried about de Gaulle's state of mind. Foccart, a connoisseur of de Gaulle's moods, assured Lalande that there was nothing unusual about de Gaulle's affectations of despair. Once he had seen de Gaulle himself, Foccart was less sure. De Gaulle ruminated at length about the resemblance between May 1940 and May 1968, two moments, in his view, when France's elites had betrayed her. In 1940 he had been young but now he was not: 'I cannot struggle against the apathy and the desire of an entire people to let everything dissolve.' As he was coming out of his meeting, Foccart was stopped by Yvonne de Gaulle in a state of great agitation because that afternoon she had been insulted in the street by a man driving a Citroën DS: 'Can you imagine, M. Foccart, a Citroën DS, not just anyone.' Foccart worried that this was hardly likely to improve de Gaulle's state of mind.[58] That night Yvonne de Gaulle broke down at dinner and de Gaulle had their meal moved from the dining room to the salon next to his bedroom.[59]

When Droit returned to discuss the television programme, de Gaulle no longer seemed interested. Instead he launched into a long soliloquy as if Droit were not there: 'The French have never recovered from being beaten at Waterloo and Sedan. I was beaten at neither Waterloo nor Sedan. But that no longer seems to serve any purpose.' As Droit was leaving, Flohic pushed him out through a side door because Pompidou was arriving. He was told: 'Pompidou must not see you.' Pompidou's meeting was short. 'Are you sleeping?' de Gaulle asked. 'Yes, when I have the time.' 'You are lucky,' replied de Gaulle. Pompidou felt that he was close to an agreement with the unions; de Gaulle accused him of having been too optimistic throughout the crisis. The last visitor was Christian Fouchet, who was warned by Tricot as he went in that 'this is not one of his better days.' Fouchet was greeted with the words: 'Fouchet, you know that sometimes I think I am going to give it all up.' When he told Fouchet that the sound of grenades in the street was preventing him from sleeping, Fouchet suggested that he take the advice that Thiers had given to Louis-Philippe in 1848: move to Versailles. The General replied: 'I am not Louis-Philippe.'[60] After Fouchet had left de Gaulle retired for another sleepless night.

What none of these visitors knew was that earlier in the evening de Gaulle had rung his son-in-law, Alain de Boissieu, whose regiment was stationed at Mulhouse. Boissieu was told to be at the Elysée first thing the next morning. Yvonne de Gaulle had also rung up her brother and asked if he could drive their Elysée maid to her village. She had been granted a few days' leave – but Yvonne de Gaulle was not at liberty to say why. Despite his apocalyptic tirades, de Gaulle was clearly up to something – even if he was not sure what it was going to be.

DE GAULLE ESCAPES: 29 MAY

Wednesday 29 May 1968 was the most extraordinary day of de Gaulle's career. Most of the protagonists, believing they had lived through an historic day, wrote up their memories soon afterwards. This means that even if it is not possible to be sure what was going on in de Gaulle's head, we can at least reconstruct his actions in detail.

7.30 a.m: De Gaulle told his *directeur de cabinet*, Xavier de La Chevalerie, that he was exhausted and would take a day's rest in Colombey. The Council of Ministers due that afternoon would be postponed till the next day.

8.30 a.m.: De Gaulle summoned General Lalande, who had been so worried about him on the previous evening. Lalande was ordered to fly to Baden-Baden in Germany to see General Massu. Despite the tensions between the two men over Algeria, which had led to Massu's sacking in January 1960, Massu's deep personal loyalty to de Gaulle, dating back to his experience of the Free French (he was a Companion of the Liberation), had prevented him from following other army officers into open dissidence against de Gaulle. Their relations had recovered and Massu had been appointed in 1966 to command the French forces based in Germany, an important role as the French high command was renegotiating its relations with the German and American military in the wake of France's withdrawal from NATO. In sending Lalande to see Massu, de Gaulle wanted to know if the army could be relied upon if military action was required. After that Lalande was told to visit the army chiefs in Metz and Nancy and explore the same question. De Gaulle also instructed Lalande to take Philippe de Gaulle and his family to Baden-Baden with him. He added that he would rest in Colombey but would be back the next day.

9.00 a.m.: De Gaulle told Tricot to inform Pompidou that the Council of Ministers meeting would be postponed to the next day. When he heard this, Pompidou was terrified that de Gaulle was planning to relinquish power and bring the government down just as his negotiations were about to bear fruit. He rang Tricot several times insisting, 'I MUST see the General,' but without success. Whatever else de Gaulle was up to that day, one of his aims was to free himself of Pompidou.

9.30 a.m.: De Gaulle summoned Flohic, his aide de camp, and told him to be ready to leave soon with a bag packed. He was instructed to wear uniform. This might have alerted Flohic that their destination was not – or at least not *only* – Colombey, where de Gaulle's aides dressed in civilian clothing.[61]

10.15 a.m.: Boissieu arrived later than intended because fog had slowed his journey from Metz.[62] De Gaulle greeted him with the usual outpouring of gloom. Standing to attention, and addressing de Gaulle not as a father-in-law but as an officer speaking to his commander, Boissieu told de Gaulle that he could not give up. He assured him that he could rely on the loyalty of the army. This was presumably why Boissieu had been summoned in the first place. De Gaulle said that he needed to assure himself of this in person. To ensure total secrecy, they devised a plan by which Boissieu would head to Colombey and inform the household that de Gaulle would not be arriving that night. From the house Boissieu would ring Massu and summon him to a meeting with de Gaulle in Strasbourg. De Gaulle would then spend the night in either Mulhouse or Strasbourg, and go on to Colombey the next day. One idea was that he would address the nation from Colombey, Strasbourg or Mulhouse. At any rate, he would not be in Paris during the planned CGT demonstration: 'There is no point in attacking an empty Palace.' He also handed Boissieu a letter for Pompidou in case he could not continue to exercise his role as President. Boissieu refused to contemplate this idea and handed the letter back.

c. 11.00 a.m.: Emerging from his meeting with de Gaulle, Boissieu came upon Foccart. Having heard about the postponement of the Council of Ministers, Foccart, already worried by his meeting the night before, had rushed over to the Elysée. Boissieu had strict instructions that everyone – even Foccart – was to be told de Gaulle was going to Colombey.

c. 11.20 a.m.: De Gaulle finally agreed to speak to Pompidou on the phone. The conversation was, in Pompidou's words, 'short and strange'. The General told him not to worry. He needed to rest at Colombey but would be back the next day. The 'strange' part were his last words: 'I am old, you are young; you are the future. *Au revoir, je vous embrasse.*' As Pompidou observed, this was not de Gaulle's style. It sounded more like '*Adieu*' than '*Au revoir*'. When these words were later reported to Chaban-Delmas, he remarked: 'When the General "embraces" you you're the one who is fucked [*baisé*].'[63]

11.30 a.m.: De Gaulle left the Elysée by car, accompanied by his wife and Flohic. Since there was little traffic because petrol was in short supply, they were at the aerodrome of Issy in fifteen minutes. Helicopters were waiting for them. Loading the helicopters took a while because there was more baggage than for a normal visit to Colombey.[64] In the first helicopter were two pilots and Flohic. Seated behind were Madame de Gaulle and her husband. As they flew east, Madame de Gaulle pointed to the occupied factories below them with red flags flying. This was not liable to raise their spirits.

12.15 p.m.: Press agencies heard the news that de Gaulle had cancelled the Council of Ministers.

c. 12.30 p.m.: Boissieu arrived at Colombey. Unable to reach Massu because of a strike at the telephone exchange, he rang Saint-Dizier where de Gaulle was due to refuel on his journey east. He left a coded message to 'let the VIP know I have not been able to contact his correspondent'.

c. 12.45 p.m.: De Gaulle landed at Saint-Dizier for refuelling. The cryptic message sent by Boissieu did not get through to him. Since there was no message, once de Gaulle's helicopter was in the air he handed Flohic a scrawled note – the noise of the aircraft prevented them talking – instructing the pilot to head for Baden.[65]

c. 1.00 p.m.: At the Elysée there was consternation when it became known that de Gaulle had not arrived at Colombey. Pompidou almost physically manhandled Tricot, whom he believed was hiding the truth from him. In fact Tricot had no more idea than anyone else about de Gaulle's whereabouts. He tried to find General Lalande but discovered that he too had mysteriously vanished. The mood at the Elysée was not improved when Boissieu rang from Colombey to let Foccart know that de Gaulle was not heading for Colombey but that he was not allowed to say where he was going. Foccart was to tell Pompidou that it was 'for him to play now' and that an 'emissary' would arrive with instructions.

2.40 p.m.: De Gaulle's helicopter landed at the military airport of Baden. Flohic rang a startled Massu, who was taking his afternoon siesta, to say that they were about to arrive at his headquarters a short helicopter ride away. At that moment, two small planes landed at the airport. Their passengers were General Lalande, Philippe de Gaulle and Philippe's wife and children. Lalande was as surprised by the presence of Flohic and de Gaulle as Flohic was by the presence of Lalande and Philippe de Gaulle. Lalande went over to de Gaulle's helicopter to pay his respects. De Gaulle told him: 'I am going to see Massu. I will see you there. I will give you a letter for M. Pompidou.'[66]

c. 3.00 p.m.: The helicopter landed at the Massus' residence. De Gaulle and his wife got out for the first time since leaving Issy. De Gaulle was greeted by Massu and taken immediately to his office where the two men spent about fifty minutes talking alone. We only have Massu's account of the conversation. De Gaulle opened with the words 'It's all over [*Tout est foutu*].' This was followed by one of his tirades of despair. Massu believed for ever after that he had singlehandedly galvanized de Gaulle at a moment when he was about to give up. This may be true, or it may be that de Gaulle was putting on an act to test Massu's loyalty.[67] Their talk was interrupted for about thirty minutes by a short break when food was brought in. During the break Massu emerged from his office. Lalande reports him as saying: 'I told the General, who wants to take refuge in Germany, that this is impossible. It is madness. He cannot do it.'[68] While de Gaulle and Massu were talking, Flohic and Lalande were ensconced with Madame Massu and Yvonne de Gaulle. As Lalande reported, Madame de Gaulle poured out her woes: 'For a month my husband has not been sleeping, he listens to the radio, this cannot go on.'[69] Madame Massu, who harboured no warm feelings for the man who had sacked her husband in 1960, remarked perfidiously, 'One can't do 18 June again at the age of seventy-eight' – to black looks from Flohic.[70] During the break in his conversation with Massu, de Gaulle instructed that the German federal government's representative with the French forces should be informed of his presence on German soil. Since the official in question was away, de Gaulle told Flohic to contact the French Embassy in Bonn instead.[71]

4.00 p.m.: Meanwhile in Paris, the government had at last discovered de Gaulle's whereabouts. The CGT demonstration passed off peacefully. In Baden, de Gaulle emerged from his talks with Massu having decided not to stay. He dithered about where to go next and was still thinking of addressing the nation from Strasbourg. In the end, he decided to head straight for Colombey.

c. 4.30 p.m.: De Gaulle and his wife got back into their helicopter. Two hours later they were at Colombey. De Gaulle immediately rang Tricot and uttered to him the gnomic phrase that he had needed to '*se mettre d'accord avec ses arrières-pensées*', which Tricot interpreted to mean that he had always wanted to stay but needed to be persuaded that this was the best solution. His tone of voice suggested someone whose mood had completely changed since his gloom of the previous evening. De Gaulle also rang Pompidou to say that the government would meet the next day. Pompidou, who registered de Gaulle's new tone of firmness, was relieved, furious and wounded in equal measure. He drafted a letter of resignation which he resolved to hand over on the next day. That evening in Colombey, de Gaulle was in good humour. At dinner he recited some lines of poetry which he revealed were his own. He told Flohic that he had considered staying in Germany: 'Then I would have gone to Ireland, land of my MacCartan maternal ancestors, then much further. At any rate I would not have remained in France.'[72]

These were the events of 29 May 1968 as far as they can be accurately pieced together. Some details remain obscure. Thanks to Boissieu, we know that de Gaulle's decision to go to Baden had been taken at the last moment. But when had de Gaulle decided to see Massu himself? Since one of the first decisions he had taken that day was to send Lalande to see Massu, why did he need to do this himself (and indeed summoning Massu to Strasbourg as he originally intended would have made it impossible for Lalande to see him)? Was that decision taken only after de Gaulle had seen Boissieu? Was his original intention genuinely to go to Colombey? In that case, why had Flohic been told to wear uniform before de Gaulle had even seen Boissieu?

More difficult than reconstituting the events is interpreting what they meant. Was this de Gaulle's day of Varennes – as when Louis XVI escaped Paris to head for the French border and make contact with loyal troops? Was it the preparation for a new 18 June by which de Gaulle would address the French people and call them to resistance? Was it a repeat of 1946 when de Gaulle had renounced power? In piecing together the events we have the accounts of Tricot, Lalande, Boissieu, Flohic and Massu – each of whom saw de Gaulle at some point in the day. Boissieu's narrative is constructed to suggest that, after a short wobble, de Gaulle had master-minded the whole affair. He even claims that de Gaulle told him at their morning meeting, 'I want to plunge the French and the government into doubt and uncertainty so as to get control of the situation again.' At the other end of the spectrum, Massu awards himself the heroic role of having persuaded the desperate General not to give up. But each saw de Gaulle at only one point in the day – Boissieu in the morning and Massu in the afternoon – and their accounts reflect de Gaulle's mood only at the moment they saw him. Arriving tired and hungry at Baden, de Gaulle may well have been in a different frame of mind from when Boissieu had left him four hours earlier. The sober testimony of General Lalande, written up almost immediately, and with seemingly no axe to grind, supports much of what Massu claimed.

Three issues have excited much debate. First, de Gaulle's insistence that the German government be informed of his presence at Baden. Did this imply that he was planning to stay? More probably it should be interpreted as a formality which de Gaulle would have wished to observe however short his stay.[73] Secondly, there is the question of the luggage. Massu reports that several journeys were necessary to convey the suitcases into his residence. Philippe de Gaulle, on the other hand, suggests plausibly that there might have been a confusion in Massu's mind between the six bags of Philippe's wife and four children – who were intending to stay abroad for a period – and the luggage brought by de Gaulle. Flohic, who was used to travelling back and forth with de Gaulle to Colombey, claims there was more luggage than for a normal trip (but not as much as claimed by Massu), and Jeanne the maid said the same to de Gaulle's brother-in-law that morning. Given that it had possibly been de Gaulle's intention to spend the night in Strasbourg or Metz this does not necessarily suggest a plan to go abroad.

The third mystery is the letter to Pompidou. In the version of events that Boissieu wrote up for Pompidou on 6 June, he said that he had taken away de Gaulle's letter to Pompidou; in the account he gave to Foccart over the phone in October, he claimed to have given it back to de Gaulle. Lalande, on the other hand, implies that de Gaulle was still carrying a letter for Pompidou. If this is true, throughout the day de Gaulle had held on to his letter of resignation.

The truth is probably what de Gaulle himself said in his speech on the next day: 'In the last twenty-four hours I considered all eventualities without exception.'[74] He probably left for Baden with the intention of testing the loyalty of the army, and perhaps arrived there having decided to give up. But above all he had wanted to escape from the Elysée, free himself from his Prime Minister and make himself a central actor after several days of being sidelined by him – even if he remained unsure of what he intended to do.

DE GAULLE RETURNS, 30 MAY

On the morning of 30 May de Gaulle was back at the Elysée. Foccart rushed in to see him and found him quite transformed from two days earlier. De Gaulle said that he would be addressing the French people that evening. He agreed to Foccart's suggestion that the speech be given in the afternoon before the Gaullist demonstration planned by Foccart was due to take place. He then saw Pompidou, who was also impressed by de Gaulle's new sense of purpose. For the moment Pompidou decided not to present his own letter of resignation. De Gaulle read Pompidou the speech he intended to make and Pompidou insisted on one amendment: that de Gaulle announce he was dissolving parliament and calling new elections. De Gaulle was sceptical but, since Pompidou threatened to resign, he agreed.

The speech was delivered at 4.30 p.m. De Gaulle chose to speak on the radio instead of television. His intention was subliminally to recall the de Gaulle of the war, not the tired old man whom viewers had seen on television a week earlier. The speech lasted only four minutes, and de Gaulle's imperious tone could not have been more different from the rambling speculations of 24 May. He announced that the referendum would be postponed and parliament dissolved. In the event of any attempt to prevent elections taking place he threatened to employ any measures the constitution permitted (a veiled threat to use Article 16). He denounced the 'intimidation, intoxication and tyranny' exercised by a party 'which is a totalitarian enterprise'. This was a reference to the Communists, who he knew perfectly well had neither the desire nor the capacity to carry out a revolution. But de Gaulle was never more effective than when he had identified an enemy.

One comment that de Gaulle made during the crisis was that the situation was *insaisissable*, impossible to get a grip on, slipping through his fingers like sand. Power seemed to be disintegrating, but there was no identifiable enemy. After his return from Rumania, de Gaulle had received a note from one of his staff reporting that although after the night of the barricades a few students has taken up the cry 'To the Elysée' the slogan did not catch on: 'The theme most commonly expressed was that the Elysée was just a museum that does not concern the students and leaves them indifferent.[75] De Gaulle had said to Boissieu that no one would attack an empty palace, but so far no one had shown much interest in an inhabited palace either. Once the politicians had entered the fray on 27 May, and the Communists called a demonstration for 29 May, de Gaulle at last had a target. The timing of the speech was perfect. Public opinion had turned against the students; Pompidou had held his nerve and found a way of negotiating a solution; the unions were keen to find a deal; plans for a Gaullist demonstration on 30 May were under way. The new element was Pompidou's idea of dissolution, which meant that conservatives, traumatized by the disorder, were offered a chance to express themselves through the ballot box. For all these reasons, the crisis was probably close to a resolution. The importance of de Gaulle's flight to Baden was to put himself back at the centre of the stage, and add a touch of drama to a crisis that was already running out of steam.

The crowds were already gathering in the Place de la Concorde before de Gaulle spoke. His words were electrifying, but many of the thousands who joined the demonstration over the next two hours were presumably already on the way before he spoke. At its peak the demonstration covered the entire Champs-Elysées from the Etoile to the Place de la Concorde. Despite the often repeated figure of one million, the number of participants probably numbered about 400,000. This was still larger than any other demonstration during the events of May. Choosing the Champs-Elysées was a subliminal reminder of the Liberation parade of 26 August 1944, but also a ritual of purification and reappropriation. On 7 May students had marched up the Champs-Elysées and it was alleged that some demonstrators had desecrated – urinated on – the flame of remembrance under the vault of the Arc de Triomphe.

At the head of the demonstration were many grandees of Gaullism: Debré, Malraux, Joxe, Peyrefitte – and also the frail and ailing François Mauriac. But among the crowds there were more anti-Communist slogans than strictly Gaullist ones; there were also former supporters of *Algérie française* ready to bury the hatchet at least for a day for the higher cause of order.[76] The success of the demonstration spared France the arrival of President Bokassa, who had issued a proclamation that morning announcing that to 'save humanity and restore peace in the world' he would fly to France and offer de Gaulle his support. He was about to set off for Paris when news of the success of the demonstration dissuaded him.[77]

Although de Gaulle had yielded to Pompidou's insistence on parliamentary elections, on the next day Pompidou was forced to accept a major reshuffle of his government. No appointment can have been more disagreeable to swallow than the choice of his arch-enemy René Capitant, the apostle of participation, as Minister of Justice. Like many other left Gaullists, Capitant had been destabilized by the events of May. When the opposition presented a motion of censure against the Pompidou government on 19 May, he had announced that, as a Gaullist, he would have to vote with the opposition. In the end he drew back but resigned from the Gaullist parliamentary group. Some young left Gaullists had even joined the barricades, and during the 30 May demonstration a tiny group of them marched in the opposite direction from the mass of the demonstrators to proclaim their allegiance to de Gaulle the 'revolutionary'.[78] Bringing Capitant into the government was de Gaulle's way of signalling that the return to order would not necessarily be a return to the *status quo ante*. His signals to the right were even more spectacular. On the symbolically charged date of 18 June, which also happened to be a week before the elections, it was announced that all OAS officers still in prison were to be amnestied. As one newspaper commented: 'If Paris is worth a mass and political power is worth Salan, Salan himself is worth a few hundred thousand votes.'[79]

Although the consequences of the events of May '68 reverberated in French political life for years – indeed decades – the return to a semblance of normality was remarkably rapid. The process was accompanied by sporadic outbursts of violence more serious than anything that had occurred during the month of May itself. On 31 May, the government forcibly evacuated pickets from petrol depots. Petrol was now readily available again, and on the Whitsun weekend of 1 June there were traffic jams as the population of Paris headed out on holiday. By the end of the first week of June, public transport in Paris was back to normal. Violent battles between police and strikers outside Paris led to three deaths on 10–11 June. In response the capital witnessed its third – and last – night of barricades. This alarmed Foccart, who wanted to mobilize the Republican Defence Committees, but de Gaulle was rightly confident that this was the death agony of the May events, not the signal for a new explosion. He told Foccart that matters should now be left to the police. The students occupying the Sorbonne moved out on 13 June, and the next day the police dislodged the last occupants of the Odéon Theatre.

The short election campaign was uneventful. Anti-Communism played an important role. De Gaulle seemed back on good form when he did a new interview with Michel Droit on 7 June. There were two big themes. First, he returned repeatedly to the threat – the theme already of his speech on 30 May – of a 'totalitarian enterprise' represented by the Communists. He knew perfectly well that this was entirely imaginary but it was his means of rallying conservatives who had been traumatized by the collapse

of order over the last month. The second theme was his familiar one of the
threat to humanity posed by technocratic modern civilization and the need
to remedy it by 'participation'. In this way de Gaulle hoped to escape from
being cornered by the events of May into a position of purely reactionary
conservatism: 'if a revolution consists of fundamentally changing what
exists, and notably the dignity and conditions of the working class . . . I
am not at all upset to be called in that sense a revolutionary.' And for good
measure he listed all the revolutionary actions of his career from his combat against Vichy to 'the beginning of the Liberation of the French of
Canada'.[80]

As usual, de Gaulle kept a vigilant eye on the selection of every parliamentary candidate and the running of the campaign. He worried whether
Malraux, usually such a stirring orator, should be used during the campaign, telling Foccart: 'He seems rather tired these last days and I sometimes
have the impression he is taking drugs' (an entirely correct impression).[81]
As a special mark of favour, de Gaulle invited Foccart to join him in the
car which took him to the Mont-Valérien ceremony on 18 June. During
the drive, he gave Foccart his prediction of the result, showing that his
political antennae (as well as his bouts of irrational suspiciousness) were
as finely tuned as ever:

We will certainly win seats; the opposition will be eaten up by the others; the
Communists will suffer losses but they will maintain themselves. As for the
centrists, God knows how they are going to do. They have means behind them
which come, in the first instance, from the employers and from our traditional
enemies, as is normal, but also the Jews, and, I am certain, the Americans.[82]

In the end, the victory was a landslide greater than de Gaulle or anyone had
dreamt of. Major figures like Mendès France and Mitterrand were punished
for their attitude in the May crisis and lost their seats. After the second round,
the Gaullist party, which had rechristened itself Union pour la Défense de la
République (UDR), won 293 parliamentary seats, giving it a substantial
overall majority, something never previously achieved by any single party in
the history of French democracy. But whose victory was it?

29

The End, June 1968–November 1970

AMBIGUOUS VICTORY

In his bitter memoir of May '68 Pompidou recalled de Gaulle remarking to him after the first round of the elections: 'Pompidou, how can you explain why after such a victory we both feel so disenchanted?'[1] The explanation is not hard to find. On de Gaulle's side, there was the knowledge that the parliamentary victory was more Pompidou's than his; on Pompidou's, the knowledge that de Gaulle was aware of this and resented it.

Pompidou, exhausted by the events of May, was not keen to continue as Prime Minister. He had many reasons for wanting to withdraw. One was de Gaulle's continued obsession with the idea of participation, which had only been confirmed by the events of May. Two days after the election, de Gaulle mused at length to a sceptical Foccart on his desire to implement participation: 'We must do it now, it is the last great thing I have to accomplish, and the greatest service that I can give the country.'[2] Later that evening de Gaulle asked Pompidou point blank if he was now ready to carry out a policy of participation. Pompidou replied: 'I could reply if I knew what participation was.'[3] The prospect of having to wage continuous guerrilla war on this issue was not enticing.

Pompidou also wanted to create some distance and prepare himself in the wings to succeed de Gaulle, capitalizing on the reputation he had built during the May events. This was a plausible strategy – providing de Gaulle did not stay too long. In theory de Gaulle's mandate lasted until 1972 but many Gaullists expected he would decide to leave earlier. This is certainly what Yvonne de Gaulle hoped. Soon after the events of May, she launched into one of her pathetic pleas to Foccart that de Gaulle must go soon:

> The General is really very tired. Even for you, M. Foccart, he is on the stage. But I see him from the wings where there is no one else to see him . . . Apart from me, his son and his daughter all these others see him on the stage, including his

son and daughter-in-law, even his grandchildren. But even his grandchildren
see at moments how tired he is. This must not go on much longer.[4]

In the week following the election, Pompidou saw de Gaulle three times
and made it clear he felt he had served long enough. After each conversation Pompidou emerged unsure what de Gaulle wanted. While not pressing
him to stay, de Gaulle did not say that he wanted him to go either. In reality
de Gaulle was seething with rancour against Pompidou. During the election
he had raged to Foccart one night: 'Pompidou spoke on television and he
did not even mention my name. As if I did not exist'[5] – although in his long
television interview with Michel Droit on 7 June he had managed to talk
at length about May 1968 without once mentioning Pompidou's name. In
his nightly meetings with de Gaulle in the week after the elections, Foccart
got the impression that de Gaulle was keen to replace his Prime Minister
but wanted Pompidou to make the first move by formally resigning. On
the other hand, many of Pompidou's entourage, and Foccart too, were
urging him to stay.

On Friday night (5 July), Pompidou had a sleepless night and decided
to stay on. He was too late. On that same evening, de Gaulle had summoned Couve de Murville to the Elysée in total secrecy and offered him
the premiership. When on Saturday morning, Pompidou rang the Elysée
to say that he was after all ready to stay on, he was told that Couve had
accepted the post. That day Pompidou poured out his bile to Foccart about
having been tricked by de Gaulle and stabbed in the back by Couve. Tricot
described the relationship between the two men as a comedy of disappointed love in the vein of a play by Marivaux.[6] It still remained to decide
how Pompidou's departure should be presented. De Gaulle wanted a formal letter from Pompidou stating that he had decided to resign; in return
de Gaulle would write a stately latter thanking him for his service and
predicting a great future for him. Pompidou was not happy to play the role
of sacrificial victim. He remarked bitterly that Debré had received a letter
promising him that 'important tasks await you' – and then spent four years
in the political wilderness. Foccart found de Gaulle suspicious of Pompidou's motives:

> 'I wonder if it is really lassitude on Pompidou's part or if he is not playing
> some comedy and if this is not a tactic for the future . . . to prepare himself
> better for the future, to be in a more comfortable position. Because that is
> not something I could allow. Tactics exist, one must practise them, but it is
> for me to do, not for him to make the choice. And that is what I think is going
> on.' The General looked at me suspiciously as if I was somehow involved in
> the tactics he had condemned.[7]

In the end, Pompidou offered his resignation and de Gaulle wrote him a letter that satisfied Pompidou's *amour-propre*: 'I hope that you remain ready to accomplish whatever mission, and assume whatever mandate the nation might one day confer on you.' Honour was satisfied on both sides, but the slightest incident was liable to spark Pompidou's sense that de Gaulle had treated him with supreme ingratitude.

De Gaulle was not wrong to suspect Pompidou's motives. One reason Pompidou was keen to leave, as he told Foccart frankly, was that the cost of buying off the trade unions at the end of May would have serious economic consequences. Despite the stunning electoral success, the coming months would not be easy for the government. It made sense for Pompidou to keep himself in reserve and avoid association with what promised to be a rocky period. In fact the first serious challenge for the new government related not to the economy but to one of the pillars of de Gaulle's foreign policy: the rapprochement with Russia.

FOREIGN POLICY DISAPPOINTMENTS

For all the disappointments of his visits to Poland and Rumania, de Gaulle had remained optimistic about the longer-term validity of his détente policy. He told Flohic on one occasion: 'The upset that my policies are causing does not worry me at all. The Petite Entente is being reborn. That does not make the Russians happy. But once they have decided to play the good guys [*gracieux*] there is nothing they can do.'[8] The Petite Entente was the name given in the inter-war years to the alliance of Yugoslavia, Rumania and Czechoslovakia which the French government had encouraged as a bulwark against Germany, and as a way of isolating the Soviet Union. Since the 1950s, Yugoslavia had asserted her distance from the Soviet bloc; and in the 1960s Rumania had shown signs of wanting to pursue a more independent foreign policy. But in 1968 the real threat to Soviet authority came from Czechoslovakia. And the Soviets' response showed they were not necessarily ready to play the 'good guys' if their interests were threatened.

While France was plunged into her strange dreamlike revolution, on the other side of the Iron Curtain Czechoslovakia was experiencing her own revolutionary spring. In January, an internal crisis in the Czech Communist Party led to the appointment of the reforming Alexander Dubček as General Secretary. Dubček embarked on a series of liberalizing measures and, as the 'Prague Spring' acquired its own momentum, the Soviet leadership started to worry about the dangers of contagion in the rest of the eastern bloc. The events caused great excitement in the west. The journalist Jean-Marie Domenach rushed to Prague to witness them at first hand. On returning he tried to see de Gaulle, but we are told he was passed a message instead: 'They are going too fast and too far. The Russians will intervene. Then, as always, the Czechs will not fight, and night will fall over Prague again. There will be just a few students ready to commit suicide.'[9] If de Gaulle really uttered these words, it was one of those flashes of prophetic cynicism to which he was prone. But he was as surprised as anyone else when on the night of 20-21 August Soviet tanks rolled into Prague.

From Colombey, Couve de Murville and Debré, who had replaced Couve as Foreign Minister in the new government, concocted a communiqué with de Gaulle condemning the invasion. Two days later, in reply to an oral communication from the Soviet Ambassador in Paris, de Gaulle drafted a further statement condemning 'an action that infringes the principles of independence of states and non-intervention in their domestic policies'. He still held out the hope one day for a 'policy of détente, entente and European cooperation' but only once Soviet troops had withdrawn.[10] Hervé Alphand noted three days after the invasion: 'It is perhaps the end of a great effort to reunite the two worlds over and above ideology. The English press is making fun of the way that de Gaulle's grand design is now compromised. But what is the alternative except the Cold War?'[11] At his September press conference two weeks after the invasion, de Gaulle had no choice but to take a long view: 'What has occurred in Czechoslovakia, I mean the impulse [élan] of its people to obtain the beginnings of liberation ... demonstrates that our policy, momentarily impeded, conforms to the profound realities of Europe ... Taking account of the general aspiration towards progress and peace it is too late to succeed in the attempt to divide Europe into two opposing blocs.' He reaffirmed that France would not abandon her policy of working for 'the independence of peoples and the liberty of man ... for détente, entente and cooperation, that is to say for peace'.[12] These were the final words of what, although he did not know it, would de Gaulle's final press conference.

Despite this show of bravado, de Gaulle was deeply pessimistic after the Soviet invasion of Prague. Seeing two different American interlocutors in late September, he put the view that the Soviet occupation of Prague had to be seen in the wider context of the Soviets' insecurities about their geopolitical situation. His view was that as the Soviets became increasingly fearful about a future conflict with China, they were trying to ensure the security of their western flank: 'For if one day they find themselves at war with China, they fear that the Germans might fall on them; which is probably true.' In his view the operation against Czechoslovakia might be the prelude to some operation against Germany: 'You were perhaps expecting consoling and agreeable words; but our world is difficult and hard.'[13]

At a meeting with the German Chancellor Kiesinger in September de Gaulle expressed the same idea but also seemed to blame the Germans for causing the Soviet fears: 'All this happened because Franco-German cooperation did not function and because Germany wanted to pursue her own policy. It is clear that what is happening today is really about Russia and the Federal Republic. The Russian action is quite natural because they want to keep control over their Empire.' What de Gaulle seems to have meant by this was that the Germans had aroused legitimate grievances within the Soviet Union because they had still not accepted the post-1945 Oder–Neisse frontiers and still had nuclear ambitions (or so he persuaded himself). Blaming Germany for what had happened in Prague was de Gaulle's way of explaining the failure of détente that had been the linchpin of his foreign policy for the last three years. It reveals more about his fluctuating views of Germany than about the real reasons for the Soviet action. Nothing in the Soviet archives confirms his speculation that Moscow had been motivated by suspicion of Germany.[14]

One result of the Soviet move on Prague was what the American Embassy in Paris described as a noticeably 'improved atmosphere' in relations with France: 'This attitude is not due to any change of heart, but rather, we believe, to his [de Gaulle's] recognition that with the Soviets on the warpath this is not the time to be feuding with the United States.'[15] If de Gaulle had once considered the possibility of extricating France fully from the Atlantic Alliance in 1969, this was no longer on the agenda. There were also signs that he was seeking to build new bridges to the British, until this policy backfired spectacularly in the so-called 'Soames Affair' which blew up in March.

The origin of the Soames Affair was a request by the newly appointed British Ambassador, Christopher Soames (son-in-law of Churchill), for a private meeting with de Gaulle to explore ways of improving relations between the two countries. De Gaulle was encouraged to accept by his new Foreign Minister Debré. Instinctively more Anglophile than his predecessor, Debré was favourable to British entry into the EEC – not least because he thought Britain would be an ally in the opposition to supranationalism. The French were also worried by the sustained pressure the British were now exerting on the other five members of the Community to circumvent the French veto on British entry.[16] A meeting with Soames offered a way of undercutting this.

Soames and de Gaulle had a private and unofficial lunch at the Elysée on 4 February 1969. De Gaulle spoke impromptu and no official French record was kept. He speculated that it might be possible one day to amend the Treaty of Rome to make it a less supranational organization which Britain could more easily join. He also suggested that cooperation on political and defence issues – not currently in the remit of the Community – might be discussed at regular meetings of the four major European powers. When Soames asked how this could be compatible with NATO, de Gaulle said that one day Europe would need to take its own defence in hand. The second of these ideas was hardly novel for de Gaulle; and the first was rather nebulous. De Gaulle suggested further talks to explore these ideas.

What turned this anodyne meeting into a diplomatic incident were the reactions of the Foreign Office and the divergent interpretations of what had actually been said. The newly appointed British Foreign Secretary, Michael Stewart, was less pro-European than his predecessor George Brown. Like much of the Foreign Office he had an almost pathological suspicion of de Gaulle – not unreasonably given the events of the last few years. He suspected de Gaulle of setting a trap. Quite apart from this, it was quite natural that the British would see little point in starting bilateral negotiations with a leader who had never given them any favours – and would not be around much longer – behind the backs of other European leaders who had always been better disposed towards the British position.

Harold Wilson was seeing Kiesinger on 10 February and had to decide whether or not to brief him about the conversation. Since in their application to the Community the British had told the other countries that they were ready to accept all its rules, there was a danger that if the French leaked the news of the Soames conversation first, other countries might see the British as playing a double game. This was the trap the British feared walking into. In the end therefore Wilson decided to inform Kiesinger about the conversation. This in itself annoyed the French but what turned the affair into a fully fledged crisis was that on 21 February the Foreign Office took the extraordinary step of leaking the entire content of the conversation to *The Times* with a commentary giving it a more anti-American and anti-European spin than it really had. The French government was outraged by the Foreign Office's action, and Franco-British relations reached a new nadir.

The French had a genuine grievance. One British diplomat working in the Embassy at this time writes that it was 'without precedent in British history' for a government to leak to the press the content of a secret and unofficial conversation. But de Gaulle had not been quite as innocent – or had at least been less cautious – than the French protestations claimed. This was the view of Couve de Murville, who remembered later: 'He telephoned me immediately after his meeting with Soames. Something he had not done since 1959! He seemed a little sheepish.'[17]

POLITICAL MALAISE

De Gaulle's freedom of manoeuvre in foreign policy was constrained by the weakening of France's economic position since May. The increase in wages and government expenditure led to speculation against the franc on financial markets. The German government refused to agree a revaluation of the mark which would have helped the French out. As the run on the franc intensified, the French government was torn between two possible responses: a modest devaluation of 10 per cent accompanied by cuts in government expenditure, or a more massive devaluation to staunch the speculation once and for all. The problem with the former, favoured by Couve, was that it might not be enough to stop the speculation; the problem with the latter, favoured by Debré, was the shock it would inflict on the world monetary system.

After a Council of Ministers on 13 November, the government issued a communiqué reporting that de Gaulle had declared devaluation an 'absurdity'. The denial showed the subject had been discussed and only encouraged more speculation. Over the following week, the crisis reached a paroxysm. De Gaulle, railing in private against German speculators, told Foccart that devaluation was inevitable. The government met for four hours on the afternoon of Saturday 23 November to discuss the franc crisis. *Le Monde* announced with certainty that a devaluation of 10 per cent would be implemented before the end of the day. When the meeting was over none of the ministers present had the slightest idea what de Gaulle had decided.

As the world waited to hear the rate of devaluation, the Elysée issued a terse communiqué announcing: 'The existing parity of the franc will be maintained.' In taking this decision, de Gaulle had been encouraged by the economist Jean-Marcel Jeanneney, Minister of Social Affairs. Jeanneney brought in the French economist Raymond Barre, Vice-President of the European Commission, who assured de Gaulle that a planned international loan, vital for the support of the franc, would still be forthcoming if France decided not to devalue. Since a large part of this credit package was borne by America, keen to avoid any disruption to the international monetary system, there was an irony that de Gaulle's defiance of the markets was made possible only by American help – another reason perhaps for him to tone down his anti-American rhetoric at this time.[18]

De Gaulle's television speech announcing his decision to maintain the parity of the franc ended in characteristic vein: 'What is happening to our currency proves, once again, that life is a combat, that success requires an effort, that salvation requires victory.'[19] The arguments over devaluation were technical – and it was clearly a necessary measure that could not be indefinitely postponed – but de Gaulle had turned it into a test of leadership.[20] This was a typical reaction on his part but also an attempt to staunch a malaise that had been seeping into French politics since the massive Gaullist victory of June.

The elections had taken place in a mood of social panic and conservative reaction. Many of the newly elected Gaullist *députés* saw Pompidou as the man who had saved the situation. Although de Gaulle constantly came back in private to the idea that Pompidou had been too 'soft' in 1968, he was different from Pompidou in taking May '68 seriously – or at least in believing that it vindicated what he had long been saying about the need for social reforms. He remarked after the election: 'It is a PSF parliament [a reference to the right-wing League of the 1930s] which I will make carry out a PSU policy [the PSU was a small independent socialist party which embodied many of the ideas of 1968].'[21] The analysis had truth in it. There was much muttering in parliament against the reforms proposed by the new Minister of Education, Edgar Faure, to give greater autonomy and self-government to universities. De Gaulle himself was uneasy about the radicalism of Faure's proposals which he felt undermined the principle of authority in the university.[22] But he did not stand in Faure's way. There was also discontent in parliament about a further escalation of de Gaulle's anti-Israeli policy. At Christmas, as a reprisal for guerrilla raids launched from Lebanese territory, the Israelis had launched an attack on Beirut airport. De Gaulle announced a total embargo on the sale of military aircraft to Israel. This shocked even Gaullist loyalists like Debré.

Couve de Murville, a caricature of the soulless civil servant, did not have the political skills to calm the *fronde* of the Gaullist rank and file in parliament. Their king over the water was Pompidou, who was loudly cheered when he made his first appearance in the Chamber in June. The events of May had not only deepened the breach between de Gaulle and Pompidou but had also crystallized the emergence of a 'Pompidolism' as a distinct political sensibility. This was reflected in a divergence between de Gaulle's own electoral appeal and that of the Gaullist party. In the 1965 Presidential election de Gaulle had done well among traditional conservative voters, such as women and the old, but he had also attracted significant support from the working class; he performed less well among the peasantry and the professions. In the parliamentary elections of 1967, Gaullist support was socially narrower than de Gaulle's two years earlier: more successful with the professions and business, less so with the workers. The Gaullist landside of 1968 was achieved with a vote that deviated even more significantly from the social composition of de Gaulle's own electorate in 1965.

The rumbling psychodrama between Pompidou and de Gaulle took a strange new twist in the autumn of 1968. On 1 October, the body of Stephan Marcović, former bodyguard of the film star Alain Delon, was found in a dump outside Paris. The killer was never identified, but the police investigation discovered that Marcović had been in the habit of taking secret photographs at parties hosted by Delon, possibly with the intention of blackmailing the subjects. Among the celebrities rumoured to have attended these parties was Pompidou's wife, Claude. Once de Gaulle had been informed, he instructed Couve to tell Pompidou. Couve dragged his feet, and in the end Pompidou first heard the allegations from other sources. He was mortified that members of the government had known about these scurrilous rumours for some days without saying a word to him. No one found this situation more awkward than Foccart, who tried to remain close to both de Gaulle and Pompidou. From Foccart's account it seems that Couve had not been unhappy to see his predecessor (and possible future rival) in difficulty.

De Gaulle's view was that the Pompidous, while not guilty of any impropriety, had been imprudent. The Pompidous did enjoy mixing with figures from the Parisian beau monde – a world away from the austere lifestyle of the de Gaulles. De Gaulle commented to Foccart:

> She [Claude Pompidou] is rather a silly goose [bécasse]. Her head is turned by artists that she sees while not knowing anything about the lives they lead. Such people are always very dangerous because they have a court of louche people around them. You can easily get sucked into a world of receptions organized by artists. And then, unrespectable things take place, people take photos.[23]

De Gaulle agreed to see Pompidou, who emerged from their meeting half reassured about de Gaulle's attitude – although he later wrote that 'taking his leave of me, the General did not seem very satisfied about his own behaviour.'[24] At another meeting a few weeks later Pompidou arrived with a file of documents to disprove the allegations against him. De Gaulle consoled him that it was the fate of statesmen to be vilified; Pompidou replied that this was happening to his wife, not to him.

As the weeks went by Pompidou became ever more obsessed with the Marcović affair. Foccart, trying to act as mediator, could only watch in alarm as all his attempts at a rapprochement only seemed to make things worse. When planning who was to be invited to the December shoot at

Rambouillet, de Gaulle deleted Pompidou's name from the list: 'He has already been once; that is enough.' Foccart noted: 'I must say that this pained me and worried me about the future.'[25] Pompidou was rumoured to be keeping a little black notebook containing the names of those who had betrayed him.

The psychological estrangement caused by the Marcović affair emboldened Pompidou politically. During a visit to Rome on 17 January 1969, he made an off-the-cuff comment to a journalist confirming that in a future Presidential election he would be a candidate. Although Pompidou tried to pretend he had been taken unawares, de Gaulle was still enraged. He vented his fury to Foccart:

> He made a gaffe . . . He should have replied that the issue was not on the cards . . . If the interviewer had insisted, he should have said: 'One does not succeed General de Gaulle. Of course after General de Gaulle there will be elections for the Presidency of the Republic, but one does not succeed de Gaulle: one is elected President of the Republic after de Gaulle.'[26]

De Gaulle raised the stakes by having the Council of Ministers issue a terse communiqué to say that he intended to go on to the end of his mandate. This incited Pompidou to repeat his act of *lèse-majesté* more solemnly during a visit to Geneva on 13 February 1969 when he said that one day he expected to have a 'national destiny'. Gaullism seemed to be disintegrating in warring feudal baronies. This was not the ideal climate for de Gaulle to launch his long-awaited referendum: those Gaullists tempted to vote 'no' could do so in the knowledge that there would be a Gaullist candidate in the wings.

REFERENDUM

After the referendum had been lost and de Gaulle had left office, Malraux asked him: 'Why did you resign on a question as unimportant as regional reform?' 'For the absurdity of it' was de Gaulle's reply. There is no way of knowing if de Gaulle really said this, given Malraux's special relationship with historical truth. But it reinforces a commonly held idea that de Gaulle seized upon the referendum as an elegant way of leaving power. Nothing could be further from the truth. Originally the General had believed in the referendum – and expected to win it. In his eyes its purpose was partly psychological. He needed, as he told Fouchet, 'to feel that the nation was with me'.[27] But it would be wrong to think that the referendum was just a pretext to recreate the mystical bond between the leader and his people.

De Gaulle had genuinely convinced himself that it was his mission to introduce participation into French society, despite the fact that his way of exercising authority was the antithesis of participatory.

The problem with participation was that, like grandeur, its content was vague. More a posture than a policy, it was essentially what de Gaulle wanted it to be at any one time. In his interview with Michel Droit during the election campaign he had come back repeatedly to his favourite theme of industrial civilization, and the need for workers to 'participate'. But industrial relations was not in the remit of subjects that could, according to the constitution, be covered by referenda. De Gaulle therefore proposed two other reforms which preoccupied him. The first was a restructuring of the Senate, an idea he had first raised in his Bayeux speech of 1946. The idea was that instead of being a second legislative chamber, essentially composed of local notables and distinguished former parliamentarians, the Senate would become a consultative body representative of economic and social forces. This was an idea that had its roots in the corporatist thinking much in vogue in inter-war Europe. But it was also in tune with the thinking of progressive sociologists and economists in the 1960s who wanted decisions about economic policy to be taken in a more consensual and less statist way – on the model of the 'indicative planning' of France's Planning Commissariat. De Gaulle had wanted to introduce a reform of this kind in the 1958 constitution but had been dissuaded by Debré and others. On various occasions after the election of 1965, when he was looking to reinvigorate his domestic policies, he had mooted a possible referendum on this subject.[28]

De Gaulle had also been thinking for some time about regional reform. In a speech of March 1968 – before the events of May – he had declared that 'The multi-century effort of centralization which has long been necessary for France to realize and maintain her unity ... is no longer a necessity.'[29] During the events of May 1968 his Elysée advisers had proposed that both these sets of reforms could be combined and packaged under the general rubric of participation.[30] But this created an incoherent and messy bill which satisfied no one – and had little to do with participation as de Gaulle had previously defined it. And the truth was that while the proposed reform envisaged the creation of regional assemblies with powers of economic investment and infrastructure, this did not loosen the state's grip over regional financial resources. This reform was too little for those who wanted genuine regionalization, while the reform of the Senate was too much for the vested interests of the senators.

On 18 February 1969, the government announced that the referendum would take place on 24 April. Almost immediately de Gaulle had – or claimed to have – second thoughts about whether he had made the right decision. He told Foccart only two days later: 'The French only act when they are frightened; or they only get excited when they have something to defend. But regionalization means nothing to them; as for the Senate, they couldn't care at all.'[31] Three days later he wanted the referendum to be postponed. Foccart, who had never been enthusiastic, felt that it was too late to turn back:

> De G: This is a trap and I should not fall into it.
>
> Foccart: General, it would have been better not to set the trap but now that it is set . . .
>
> De G: That is no reason to jump into it and get caught.[32]

Gaullist 'barons' meeting for lunch on 26 February were appalled by the idea of retreating even if none believed in the referendum. Chaban-Delmas, a great rugby fan, offered an analogy:

> If we retreat, it will be the end of Gaullism. Gaullism is about being firm in the positions one adopts. Old father de Gaulle has gone for his 'thing' and he cannot now give it up . . . It would be like a rugby match where the spectators (the electors) are already in the stands; we go on to the pitch with the ball under our arms, and suddenly we are asked: 'are we going to play after all?'[33]

With de Gaulle one can never be sure if the doubts he expressed only two days after selecting the day of the referendum were genuine or just one of the games he liked to play to test his aides. Whatever the truth, after a week he agreed that there could be no going back: he would throw himself into the trap. Soon opinion polls began to indicate a serious possibility de Gaulle might lose. By the start of April, he was resigned to this eventuality and decided to seize the opportunity for an elegant departure. As the clock ticked, he performed the routines of being President for another month.

COUNTDOWN

On 1–2 March, de Gaulle received the newly elected President of the United States, Richard Nixon. This encounter could hardly have been more cordial. It was helped by the improvement of Franco-American relations since the Soviet invasion of Prague, but Nixon had always been an admirer of de Gaulle as a supreme exponent of *Realpolitik*. He imbibed de Gaulle's advice almost like a pupil receiving the wisdom of a master. De Gaulle's analysis of the world situation was familiar but delivered in a valedictory tone:

In London, Brussels, Bonn, Berlin and Rome you will have seen that there is no Europe. Perhaps it will exist one day but it does not exist today. There are European countries, more or less demolished by the war, of which two were defeated and two were victorious with you but suffered a lot of losses and destruction: Great Britain and France. There are also small countries like Belgium and Holland which are respectable but which do not have much weight. As for England, France, Germany and Italy, they are very different countries; they have always been different and are more so today than ever – by their languages, their centuries-old traditions. The United Kingdom is made for trade and open to the ocean; France and Germany are continental nations, also open to the sea but not in such an organic way as Britain . . . Germany's situation is very special: she is cut in two and watched suspiciously by Russia and her satellites, especially Poland. She has been weakened, not economically but politically. She is no longer an independent country. In fact, she wants to live under your protection without which it could not survive . . . England could have done without your protection but in the political, monetary and economic domain, since Churchill, she has preferred to follow your policies from which she hopes to profit. She has deliberately chosen to put herself under your general direction.

On Vietnam, he counselled Nixon to extricate himself as fast as possible:

If I speak to you frankly it is because I found myself in an analogous situation [in Algeria] – if not the same, because no situation is identical to another. I had to take an extremely cruel decision which was, in the end, the best . . . There were a million French there . . . Your situation is not the same: there are not a million Americans in Vietnam, which is not on your doorstep; we had been in Algeria for 130 years and we exercised direct administration over the country; that is not your case in Vietnam. And your country is so strong that settling this local situation will not really cause you such problems . . . You should get out of a situation which is bringing you nothing, which is dreadful and where there is no way out. Having your hands free after this would give you the advantage of being able to get on a better footing with the Soviet Union and see what can be done for better relations and cooperation . . . Naturally the Communists and the Communist system will not be crushed in Vietnam. But perhaps the Communist system gains in the world by being associated with the defence of the independence of peoples.[34]

On this visit, Nixon was accompanied by his main foreign policy adviser Henry Kissinger, who had his first and only opportunity to meet the man on whom he had written so perceptively when still an academic:

Somewhat awestruck, I approached the towering figure. Upon seeing me he dismissed the group around him and, without a word of greeting . . . welcomed me with this query: 'Why don't you get out of Vietnam?' I replied with some diffidence that a unilateral retreat would undermine American credibility. De Gaulle was not impressed, and asked where such a loss of credibility might occur. When I indicated the Middle East, his remoteness turned into melancholy and he remarked: 'How very odd. I thought it was precisely in the Middle East that your enemies were having the credibility problem.'

On the next day, after de Gaulle had outlined his vision of Europe to Nixon, Kissinger asked how de Gaulle would prevent Germany from dominating the Europe he had just described. His reply was: '*Par la guerre*.'[35]

On 13 March de Gaulle received the German Chancellor Kiesinger. This meeting was more amicable than their previous tetchy encounter. The two men discussed the important joint aeronautical project to produce Airbus which had been in gestation since 1960 between the British and French, and which the Germans had joined in 1967. Owing to rising costs the British government withdrew in 1968, but the French and Germans decided to continue. This meeting allowed de Gaulle to drop in some remarks against the perfidy of the British; and they agreed that Europe must not be seen as 'a single dish in which all the ingredients are mixed up'.[36]

As always, African affairs took up a large part of de Gaulle's time in these weeks before the referendum. There were problems with President Bokassa, who was behaving increasingly erratically; and France had also been obliged to send troops to Chad to prop up the government of President Tombalbaye. The Biafran secessionists were increasingly beleaguered, but Foccart and de Gaulle comforted themselves with the idea that victory might take ten years. They saw the British as the real problem. De Gaulle commented: 'It is always like that with them. It has been going on for 1000 years.'[37] The last head of state to be received by de Gaulle was President Mobutu on 27 March. De Gaulle had once had hopes for France in the former Belgian Congo, but these no longer seemed plausible. He was impressed by Mobutu, but told Foccart he was not convinced by Mobutu's denial that he was 'under the thumb of the Americans'.[38]

On 17 March there was a final half-hearted attempt to patch things up with Pompidou, who was invited to a private dinner at the Elysée. But Foccart, who was supposed to be there, had flu and cancelled; Debré, also suffering from flu, did attend. De Gaulle reported to Foccart afterwards: 'Madame Pompidou seems very ill. She has been very affected by these sordid stories. He was in good form but tense . . . It was not great.' On his side Pompidou reports that the evening was 'gloomy' with not a 'word from the heart'; Debré found it a 'sinister' occasion punctuated by long silences and a half-hearted attempt by de Gaulle to get Pompidou to go back on the public declarations he had made about being ready to stand as a future Gaullist candidate.[39]

De Gaulle went through the motions of defending the referendum in a final television interview with Michel Droit on 10 April. At the end he was explicit that he would leave office if the result were negative. But, as already noted, this argument of 'me or chaos' was less convincing with Pompidou in the wings. Pompidou also went through the motions of defending the referendum publicly to cover himself against accusations that he had sabotaged de Gaulle's chances. On 14 April, Giscard d'Estaing announced that he would be voting 'no'.

De Gaulle was already planning for his immediate post-referendum moves. He would listen to the results at Colombey on Sunday evening and if the result was as expected, he planned never to set foot in the Elysée again. He told Foccart: 'It is not a bad way to go. If the French do not want to listen to me, well, I will go, and afterwards people will see that I was right.'[40] No one looked forward to de Gaulle's likely departure from power more fervently than Yvonne de Gaulle – not only for the general reason that she had long yearned to be released from the Elysée but for the particular reason that she would be relieved from the obligation of having to receive Gaston Palewski, the President of the Constitutional Council, in the company of his new wife. In Palewski's career combining social snobbery and sexual promiscuity, the former had finally won out when in March 1969, at the age of sixty-eight, he married Violette de Talleyrand-Périgord, Duchess of Sagan. Yvonne de Gaulle, who had always disapproved of Palewski's career as a *coureur de femmes*, was not happy now to find herself required to give benediction to a union that both she and her husband considered absurd.[41] A week before the referendum, de Gaulle instructed his Elysée staff to start preparing for the removal of his archives. Foccart was terrified that if this became public it would deliver a final blow to prospects of victory. On Friday 25 April, de Gaulle gave his last television address, reiterating that he would leave power in the event of a negative vote. That evening he left for Colombey certain that he would never return.

On the morning of Sunday 27 April de Gaulle had Mass said in the salon of La Boisserie to avoid the crowds of onlookers at the church. He went to cast his vote in the afternoon. By the end of the evening it was known that the 'no' vote had scored 53.9 per cent. At midnight, the Elysée issued a communiqué de Gaulle had written several days earlier: 'I am ceasing to exercise my functions as President of the Republic. This decision takes effect today at midday.' Those were his last public words.

BURNISHING THE LEGEND

The first visitor at La Boisserie on the morning after was de Gaulle's brother-in-law Jacques Vendroux. He found de Gaulle seated at a table, playing patience, with Madame de Gaulle knitting at his side. For the first time ever, de Gaulle embraced Vendroux; and Vendroux for the first time in fifty years embraced his sister. 'We are a family that does not embrace,' he told Foccart two days later.[42] Pompidou, who announced his candidature immediately, wrote de Gaulle a carefully worded letter to seek his benediction. De Gaulle provided this in a reply on 28 April: 'It is completely natural and altogether normal that you stand.' But there was also a reproach and a threat: 'It would have been better if you had not announced this several weeks in advance, which lost some votes for the "yes", and will lose you some votes, and above all might cause you problems if you are elected.' He insisted that their exchange of letters remain secret and ended that 'it goes without saying' that he would take no part in the campaign.[43] This was the best Pompidou could have expected; it could certainly have been worse.

De Gaulle took his vow not to interfere to the extreme length of leaving France for the duration of the campaign. In complete secrecy, on 10 May he and his wife flew to Ireland where he had never been before.[44] He had been planning this trip for some weeks before the referendum. Why Ireland? Perhaps there was an element of family curiosity since on his great-grandmother's side de Gaulle had Irish ancestry. Perhaps there was the attraction of visiting this historic enemy of Britain. But what de Gaulle sought above all was isolation and remoteness. One of his aides, sent to find a suitable location, told France's Ambassador in Dublin that de Gaulle wanted somewhere 'wild and far from habitation with easy access to as deserted a beach as possible. Even better if it is next to a forest where one can take walks.'[45] The selected location, at Kenmare on the west coast of Ireland, fitted the bill perfectly. The couple lodged in the modest hotel of Heron's Cove near the village of Sneem. It was impossible to keep de Gaulle's presence secret and on several occasion photographers were able to thwart the vigilance of the police trying to protect him from prying eyes. On the windy beach of Derrynane, photographers took what have become famous pictures of de Gaulle, dressed in his huge overcoat, striding along the shore accompanied only by his wife, his aide Flohic and his chauffeur. De Gaulle deplored this intrusion, but these celebrated photographs added another touch to the myth – offering the world an image of de Gaulle as a kind of Lear in exile from the ingratitude of his kingdom.

The French Ambassador in Ireland, Emmanuel d'Harcourt, was a veteran of the Free French. He had not previously had much close contact with de Gaulle but saw him on several occasions during the visit. The notes he wrote after each encounter convey the General's characteristically fluctuating moods. Greeting de Gaulle on his arrival, he found him depressed and bitter, endlessly ruminating over the referendum defeat. In the two weeks they spent at Heron's Cove, the de Gaulles visited Derrynane House, birthplace of Daniel O'Connell where de Gaulle amazed everyone with his knowledge of O'Connell's life. His maternal grandmother had written a biography of him and de Gaulle had scribbled in a notebook in 1920 that 'this man was in himself an entire people'.[46] De Gaulle and his wife attended Mass at the church in Sneem and went on drives, but mostly they remained in the extensive grounds of the hotel. De Gaulle had brought along copies of Chateaubriand's *Mémoires d'outre-tombe* and Las Cases's *Mémorial de Saint-Hélène* as an inspiration for the writing of his new volume of memoirs, on which he began work immediately.

The bracing effect of the climate, the wild scenery and above all the fact that he was active again writing his *Memoirs* had a tonic effect. De Gaulle's gloom started to lift. When Harcourt saw him again after he had moved on 23 May to another location on the west coast, Cashel Bay in Connemara, he found him 'much better' than on the previous occasion, 'relaxed, less sad, less obsessed'. De Gaulle was in expansive mood, launching into the monologues he always enjoyed: 'The regret of my life is not to have built a monarchy, that there was no member of the Royal house for that. In reality I was a monarch for 10 years.' Getting into his stride, he suggested that the Common Market was not the way to build a real Europe: 'To make Europe one needs a federator, like Charlemagne, or like Napoleon and Hitler tried to be. And then one probably needs a war against someone to weld together the different elements. If France had had 100 million inhabitants perhaps she could have played this role.' He followed this alarming speculation with a few barbs against the 'fantasist [*fumiste*]' Monnet and the '*Boche*' Robert Schuman whose approach to Europe he deplored. Harcourt, not used to de Gaulle's provocations, was not quite sure how to take all this: 'Affable, supremely at ease . . . Courtesy of another age while also throwing in crudities of languages [*mots rudes*]. The man remains impenetrable.'[47] Finally the de Gaulles moved for a third time to a private property in County Kerry. Harcourt found de Gaulle in ever more spirited mood with lots of sallies against the English: 'Since Louis XV we have been opposed to them all over the world . . . If I had remained in power I would have helped the Walloons, the Jurassians, the Genevans, the Vaudois.'[48] Harcourt also drew de Gaulle out more generally on French history. On one occasion they had a

conversation about Louis XIV, whose methods of government Harcourt
ventured to criticize. De Gaulle disagreed: 'It was by these methods of government that he laid the bases of modern France, won the respect of the
rest of the world, a strong internal structure, grandeur.' Harcourt pressed
further, pointing out that by the end Louis had created a void around himself. De Gaulle replied: 'His succession was Louis XV's problem not his.'[49]
There was clearly a contemporary subtext here.

On 15 June Pompidou was elected President of the Republic. De Gaulle
sent a one-line message of congratulation, but in private he expressed
the view that France had chosen the route of 'mediocrity'. Any choice that
was not de Gaulle was by definition a choice for mediocrity. He wrote to
his sister: 'The French of today have not yet become a great enough people,
in their majority, to be able to sustain the affirmation of France that I have
practised in their name for thirty years.'[50]

Before returning to France, de Gaulle visited Dublin for the official stage
of his Irish journey. He was received by the virtually blind eighty-five-year-
old President Eamon de Valera. De Gaulle opened with a few words in
English and then disconcerted his interlocutor by asking: 'And now, M. le
Président, I would like you to explain Ireland to me.'[51] On the next day –
the symbolic date of 18 June – after de Gaulle had received members of
his ancestral MacCartan clan, Harcourt hosted a lunch for him at the
French Embassy. Before leaving, de Gaulle signed the visitors' book with
three maxims. The first was a line from the *Chanson de Roland*: '*Moult a
appris qui bien conut ahan* [He who has suffered has learnt a lot].' The
second was from Nietzsche: 'Nothing is worth anything, nothing occurs,
and yet everything happens, but this is a matter of indifference to me.' The
third was from St Augustine: 'You who have known me in this book, pray
for me.' The next day, de Gaulle attended a lunch held in his honour by
the Irish Prime Minister, Jack Lynch. De Gaulle in the toast at the end raised
his glass to 'Ireland as a whole [*Irlande toute entière*]'. This was not quite
as provocative as toasting 'united Ireland' but it was enough for the words
to be erased from the recording of the event.

If de Gaulle had delayed his departure from Ireland for a few days after
Pompidou's election, it was because he wanted to avoid being in France
on the anniversary of 18 June. Vowing never again to be present on French
soil for that anniversary, his actions were finely calculated to burnish his
legend and cause maximum discomfiture to his successors. He would be
the absent ghost – more disconcertingly present by his absence than his
presence. This caused some problems of protocol since the ceremonies at
Mont-Valérien were officially organized by the Order of the Liberation of
which de Gaulle was the first and only Grand Master. Each year he alone

had entered the crypt. The Chancellor of the Order of Liberation – the number-two position – was Hettier de Boislambert, who had been among the first people to join de Gaulle in 1940. De Gaulle told Boislambert that the ceremony should go ahead despite his absence. The situation in 1969 was complicated because Pompidou was only President-elect and therefore still a private citizen. The *ex officio* interim President was Alain Poher, President of the Senate. De Gaulle made it clear he did not want Poher to attend. Boislambert worried that he might try to do so and had police stationed to give false directions in case the Presidential car should be spotted on the road.

On 18 June of the following year, Pompidou was in power, raising thorny questions of protocol regarding the role he should play at the ceremony. In the end, Pompidou opted for as discreet a presence as possible. He arrived at Mont-Valérien but did not enter the crypt with Boislambert, because as he told him: 'De Gaulle is the only Grand Master of the Order. I am just M. Pompidou.'[52] For this second 18 June after his resignation, de Gaulle had elected to visit Spain, where he was keen to meet General Franco. The visit started on 3 June 1970 in Galicia because his wife wanted to go to Compostela. On 8 June they were in Madrid where a semi-senile Franco received de Gaulle for an hour at his private residence. In the afternoon there was a visit to the Prado which de Gaulle despatched in half an hour. 'Just the Goyas and Velázquez,' he stipulated, 'that will be enough.' The de Gaulles spent the rest of the holiday in two different Paradors in Andalusia where, apart from some visits to local sights, de Gaulle worked most of the time on his *Memoirs*. His decision to pay his respects to Franco shocked Mauriac and Malraux, both of whom had been committed to the defence of the Spanish Republic in the 1930s. This showed how little at some level they understood de Gaulle. Always entirely agnostic about the nature of a country's political regime, he had never cared one way or another about the fate of the Spanish Republic, except inasmuch as it affected France. What he had said to Ceauşescu about his indifference to the nature of the Rumanian regime in 1968 would have applied no less to Franco's Spain – and indeed to Mao's China, which he planned to visit in June 1971. Mao was one of the few twentieth-century titans he had never met.

Apart from these visits abroad de Gaulle spent all his time at Colombey. The de Gaulles lived the life of any retired couple. De Gaulle often watched television in the evenings, especially enjoying science-fiction films. He also liked to watch sports matches involving any French team, but Yvonne de Gaulle would call him into the room only when France was winning since she otherwise feared the effects on his health. They made a few entirely private trips – a visit to his parents' grave near Le Havre, another to the sites of the Verdun battles on 11 November. But always de Gaulle wanted to keep out of the public gaze. On the visit to Verdun they avoided eating in a restaurant and instead picnicked by the road as they had done many years earlier in the days of the RPF. De Gaulle never set foot in Paris again, apart from an incognito visit for the first communion of his granddaughter Anne.

The family was the centre of de Gaulle's life at Colombey. His bookish grandson Yves (b. 1951) remembered long discussions over literature during the summer holidays of 1970. These conversations revealed the range – and surprising eclecticism – of de Gaulle's literary culture. Although no fan of Zola, he recommended that Yves read some of the lesser-known novels – *L'argent*, *L'oeuvre*, *La faute de l'abbé Mouret* – and he recommended also a lesser-known work by Hugo, *Les travailleurs de la mer*. The two writers who are considered today to be France's greatest twentieth-century novelists, Proust and Céline, never came up in their conversations. Proust, as we have seen, was not a writer who interested de Gaulle (if he had read him); that Céline was not mentioned was presumably more because of his style than because of his wartime commitment to collaboration given that de Gaulle expressed to his grandson his admiration for the writing of both Robert Brasillach, whose death sentence for collaboration he had refused to commute in 1945, and Paul Morand, a celebrated inter-war writer who had rallied to Vichy and become after 1945 a visceral anti-Gaullist. Among non-French writers, de Gaulle sang the praises of Joseph Roth, Stefan Zweig, Arthur Schnitzler and Ernst Jünger. He commended Bulgakov's *The Master and Margarita* and Andrei Bely's 1931 novel *Petersburg*, of which he remarked that it was as good a book about a city as Joyce's *Ulysses* and Dos Passos's *Manhattan Transfer*. A conversation on Thomas Mann's *Magic Mountain* led de Gaulle to recall an episode that had tellingly stuck in his memory: 'Hans Castorp is deliciously enjoying the silence of the mountain when he is suddenly surprised by an unexpected snowstorm. He almost stops breathing and his certainties, the very sense of his existence, disappear. Time seems suspended and dilated – all this described with an extraordinary lyricism – and then he recovers himself, moves and escapes from death.'[53]

Apart from the family de Gaulle received a few visitors – Couve de Murville, Tricot, Jeanneney, Messmer – but no one who held any official positions under Pompidou. This ruled out visits from ultra-loyalists like Debré and Foccart who had continued to serve de Gaulle's successor. De Gaulle's constant mantra at this time was that 'nothing *they* do [the current government] has anything to do with me.' Of the few visits de Gaulle received, none left a more important trace than that of Malraux on 11 December 1969 because it gave rise, after the General's's death, to the publication of Malraux's evocative little masterpiece *Fallen Oaks*. In this book – whose title alludes to a couplet from Victor Hugo about the oaks being felled for the funeral pyre of Hercules – Malraux purports to give an account of his last conversation with de Gaulle. He presents it as the conversation of the Prince and the Poet – what Voltaire might have left for posterity if he had written up his conversations with Frederick the Great or Diderot his conversations with Catherine the Great. *Fallen Oaks* reads at times like a pastiche of Malraux by Malraux. The two men exchange elliptical and melancholy reflections on History, France and the World, but it is often impossible to work out who is talking. The words Malraux puts in de Gaulle's mouth often sound more like Malraux speaking and vice versa. If Malraux's record is 'true' it is only so in a poetic sense. Their forty-minute conversation cannot have been long enough to fill the 250 pages of the memoir. At one point Malraux has de Gaulle looking up at the stars and commenting on the 'insignificance of things' (a phrase used in the *War Memoirs*), but since Malraux left Colombey at about 3 p.m. it is unlikely that either of them can have seen any stars.

Nonetheless the elegiac tone of the book, and its brooding sense of melancholy, ring true, and resonate with other accounts of meetings with de Gaulle after his resignation. Day after day he savoured what Vendroux calls the 'bitter pleasure of ingratitude'.[54] He opened his conversation with Malraux: 'I had a contract with France . . . that contract is now broken . . . The French no longer have any national ambition . . . I amused them with flags.' Later he declared: 'I am the hero of *The Old Man and the Sea*: I have only brought in a skeleton.'[55] One can find such ruminations at many other moments of de Gaulle's career – but with the difference that in this case the end had definitely arrived. Since he had come to identify himself so totally with France, to reject de Gaulle was to reject France; and since France was what de Gaulle believed in most fundamentally, this rejection cast him into despair. As his wife said on the day he died: 'You know he has suffered so much for two years.'

What prevented de Gaulle succumbing to paralysing depression was his belief that he had one final mission to perform: writing a second set of memoirs to cover the years of his Presidency. He saw this as his political testament – like that of Richelieu – which would be an inspiration to future generations. He told Michel Droit, who visited to discuss publishing matters: 'I will be more to France than if I had left for the banal reason that my period of office had expired.'[56] The rapidity with which he now embarked upon the writing of the *Memoirs*, and the frenzy with which he pursued the task, was that of a man possessed.

De Gaulle had started writing in Ireland. He quickly decided on the architecture of the entire work, which was to be entitled *Memoirs of Hope*. Since he was addicted to the classical threefold division, there were to be, as with his *War Memoirs*, three volumes. The first *Renewal* (May 1958–June 1962), the second *The Effort* (July 1962–December 1965) and the third *The End* (January 1966–April 1969). His original hope was to write a volume a year, the first coming out in the autumn of 1970. Writing to one of his nephews in January 1970, de Gaulle seemed to envisage a slightly slower rhythm: 'God needs to grant me five years to get to the end.'[57] At the same time he also worked on a five-volume edition of his speeches which was published at monthly intervals between April and September 1970. Correcting the proofs over the spring of 1970, he displayed his habitual obsessive attention to detail. He had especially strong views on the position of the comma, systematically replacing commas in the text that had been corrected by the copy editor. This sucked up precious time from the writing of the *Memoirs*.[58]

De Gaulle usually wrote five hours a day, between 9 and 12 in the morning and between 4 and 6 in the afternoon.[59] Although his memory remained extraordinary, he relied upon a small team of former aides to provide the necessary documentation. Most closely involved was the diplomat Pierre-Louis Blanc, his last Elysée Press Secretary, who was a regular visitor to Colombey during the last eighteen months of de Gaulle's life. Apart from those already mentioned, most of the guests de Gaulle agreed to receive were there in connection with the writing of the *Memoirs*. Any others, apart from his beloved family, were an unwelcome distraction from his race against the clock. The first volume was finished by May 1970. In Spain de Gaulle was already correcting the proofs. The day before publication, Blanc spent the day at Colombey while de Gaulle signed 300 copies. Each dedication was calibrated carefully to register small nuances of appreciation or disapproval – from the warmest 'As a testimony of my faithful friendship' for those who had never wavered in their loyalty to the more curt 'En Souvenir' for those who had dropped off along the way, like Mendès France.

De Gaulle the showman had a final trick up his sleeve. It was announced that the first volume of the *Memoirs* was due to appear at the end of November but the true date was 7 October. This deception was planned like a military operation with hundreds of thousands of copies despatched secretly all over France so that they would be in bookshops on the morning of publication. The book was a huge popular success but the critical reception was not as enthusiastic as for the *War Memoirs*. Part of the problem was that the events de Gaulle was recounting did not have the same epic quality as those of the war. Macmillan, Eisenhower and Khrushchev do not excite the imagination like Churchill, Roosevelt and Stalin. But the Algerian War was hardly without drama, and if de Gaulle's account suffers from a certain flatness compared to his previous volumes, it is because he consciously set out to iron out the twists and turns – the putsch is just described as a 'melancholy conspiracy' – in order to tell an exemplary story of a far-seeing and benevolent France granting independence in the name of the eternal values which had always inspired her history.[60] Malraux remarked on de Gaulle's 'Roman simplification of events' – but this was accompanied by a slackening of dramatic tension. How de Gaulle would have dealt with the events after 1962 we do not know because he completed only two more chapters of the second volume which, tantalizingly, was to have ended with a dialogue between de Gaulle and leading figures from French history from Joan of Arc to Napoleon – but no drafts exist.

Although the critical reception of the first volume was lukewarm, de Gaulle, who always affected to despise the coalition of 'caucuses and scribblers' who he believed had always opposed him, cared more that the huge sales showed he had not been forgotten. Two days after publication, when Blanc arrived at Colombey to work on the next volume, he heard a sound he could not at first identify because he had never heard it before: de Gaulle whistling contentedly under his breath.[61]

Life at Colombey continued its tranquil course. De Gaulle, like many people of his age, was surrounded as much by the dead as by the living. In December 1969, Georges Catroux, whom de Gaulle had first encountered when they were both prisoners of war and who had then been an important member of the Free French whose style complemented that of de Gaulle himself, died at the age of ninety-two. An even greater shock was the death in September 1970 of François Mauriac, the twentieth-century French writer most admired by de Gaulle. Although Mauriac was much mocked for his almost religious devotion to de Gaulle after 1958, their relationship had been less smooth than that between de Gaulle and Malraux. Mauriac had opposed the RPF and, although de Gaulle did not usually hold this against people, in Mauriac's case it signified an independence of mind that showed he could not be fully counted upon. Mauriac was never invited to Colombey, and used to joke wryly that he was invited to the Elysée only for receptions with archbishops and cardinals. None of this reticence on de Gaulle's part was visible in the noble letter he penned to Mauriac's widow. If only de Gaulle could have found those words about Mauriac when he was alive, lamented Mauriac's passionately Gaullist son Jean.[62] November was often difficult psychologically for de Gaulle. Over the years his aides often observed a drop in his mood during the month. Perhaps it was an involuntary memory of that sad November in 1918 when he had returned like a 'living ghost' from captivity without having being able to play his full part in France's victory. Perhaps it was because his birthday on 22 November was a reminder of the passing of time.

November 1970 started without incident. On 2 November, All Saints' Day, de Gaulle and his wife went to pay their respects at the tomb of their daughter Anne. In leaving the little cemetery de Gaulle muttered: 'The gate is too narrow. As there will perhaps be some visitors when I am here, it will be necessary to drill a hole in the wall and make another one.'[63] On 6 November, he wrote to his sister: 'Like you, this week, I turn my mind and my prayers to those who have left us ... All is very calm here. I am continuing my great labour.' To his sister-in-law on the same day he wrote: 'Do please make vows and prayers for the great task I have undertaken and that is intended as much for our contemporaries as for future generations.'[64]

On Monday 9 November, de Gaulle worked all day interrupted as usual by two long walks round the grounds of La Boisserie. In the afternoon he met a young farmer who owned some neighbouring land. De Gaulle wanted to discuss plans he had to plant trees on a piece of new land he had acquired. He took tea with his wife at 5 p.m. and they returned to their activities. De Gaulle wrote a few family letters and scribbled a note to himself: 'What was the sequence of Ministers of Education between 1958 and Fouchet? How long did he remain Minister?' Then he started a game of patience. Suddenly, just before 7 p.m., he shouted out in pain and slumped on to the table. Yvonne called the doctor and the curé. By the time the doctor arrived, it was too late to do anything. De Gaulle received the last rites from the curé, and a few minutes later, at 7.25 p.m., he was dead. De Gaulle died of a ruptured aneurysm, exactly what had killed his brother Pierre and their father Henri.

Yvonne had de Gaulle's body laid out in the centre of the room, changed into his uniform and covered in a tricolour. On the table by its side were two candles, a crucifix and a cup of holy water. In his hands Yvonne placed the rosary he had been given by Pope John XXIII. Through the night, she sat alone in silent vigil over the body. From the early hours of the next morning, members of the family started to arrive. Just after 9.00 a.m. on 10 November 1970, the people of France awoke to hear the news that Charles de Gaulle was dead.

30

Myth, Legacy and Achievement

'IN THIRTY YEARS . . .'

De Gaulle never left anything to chance. In 1952 he had drawn up detailed instructions regarding his funeral. This document was entrusted to his son Philippe and to Georges Pompidou – a sign of how close the two men were at that time. De Gaulle had directed that he was to be buried at Colombey 'without the slightest public ceremony': 'My tomb will be the one in which my daughter already lies and where one day my wife will lie. Inscription: "Charles de Gaulle, 1890– . . . ". Nothing else.' He insisted that there was to be no public ceremony: no speeches in church or elsewhere. The only people authorized to attend the funeral would be his family, Companions of the Liberation and members of the municipal council of Colombey. The people of France could accompany his body to 'its last resting place' – but in silence. He was to be awarded no posthumous honours of any kind and any breach of this injunction would be 'a violation of my last wishes'.

When de Gaulle drafted this document the prospect of any return to power looked remote. His aim was to avoid his legend being annexed by the Fourth Republic. He had drawn up his will the day after the state funeral of de Lattre de Tassigny at the Invalides in January 1952 where all the dignitaries of the Republic had been in evidence to bask in the reflected glory. Although this danger of annexation had passed after de Gaulle's return to power in 1958, on several occasions he confirmed to his son that his wishes had not changed. In the late 1960s the new danger was an appropriation of de Gaulle's memory by Pompidou. There was an unseemly tussle between the de Gaulle family and the Elysée on the day after de Gaulle's death. De Gaulle's son Philippe was in Brest, where he was stationed at the naval base, when he was rung during the night with the news of his father's death. Passing through Paris on his way to Colombey he had rung the Elysée at 9 on the morning of 10 November but was unable to get through to President Pompidou. Later that day de Gaulle's faithful aide Pierre Lefranc rang the Elysée on Philippe's behalf to insist that it was for the family to publish the will. He was requested to ask the family to desist until Pompidou had read it out to the Council of Ministers. The family refused any delay and the document was published at almost exactly the same moment by the Elysée and the family to the annoyance of the latter, who believed that Pompidou was using the occasion to show the world that he was de Gaulle's legitimate heir.

The classical austerity of de Gaulle's instructions was his way of signalling that he belonged to no faction or party – but to all of France and to History. His wishes were not completely respected because the government organized a funeral Mass in Notre-Dame on the morning of 12 November, attended by thousands of dignitaries and over eighty foreign heads of state. But de Gaulle body's was not there and the real funeral took place at Colombey that same afternoon in the small church.

De Gaulle's death was one of the most intense moments of collective emotion in the history of modern France. One famous cartoon in *Le Figaro* showed a huge uprooted oak with a weeping Marianne at its side.

Hundreds of thousands of letters poured into Colombey. On the evening of the funeral tens of thousands of Parisians walked up the Champs-Elysées, in the pouring rain, to place flowers at the Arc de Triomphe. Among the thousands of testimonies let us quote that of Claude Lanzmann, recalling many years later his feelings when he had heard of de Gaulle's death: 'The disappearance of de Gaulle was a much harder blow than I

10 novembre 1970

would ever have expected, as if an entire wall of my life had been swallowed up with him ... De Gaulle was consubstantial with us; now he had gone our lives were affected by both an historic and an existential void.'[1] What gives this testimony a special poignancy is that it comes not from a Gaullist but from an enemy – a close friend of Jean-Paul Sartre and Simone de Beauvoir, who became editor of their journal *Temps modernes* which had opposed de Gaulle ferociously and uncompromisingly ever since its foundation in 1945. But whether one was an admirer or an enemy, de Gaulle had lived in the imagination of the French people for thirty years, and they had grown old with him. As one of those who walked up the Champs-Elysées that evening noted in his diary: 'Despite everything I opposed in the regime he set up (did I ever vote "yes" in one of his referenda?) – somewhere in the depth of my being I rediscovered that emotion I felt, the profound admiration I experienced as an adolescent when reading *The Call* [the first volume of his *Memoirs*] as I was just emerging from adolescence. The man made us all bigger.'[2]

There were few dissenting voices in this outpouring of national grief apart from the extreme right. From the other side of the political spectrum, the satirical ultra-leftist magazine *Hari-Kiri* carried on its front cover the headline: 'Tragic ball at Colombey: one dead' (this was a reference to a fire in a dancehall in the same month where 146 people had died). For this

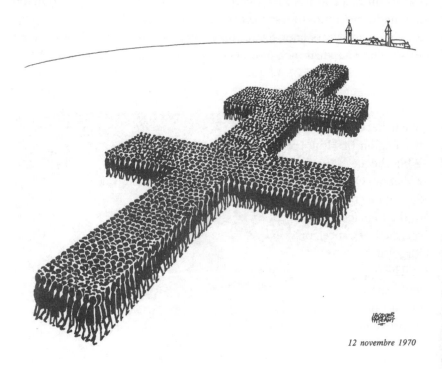

12 novembre 1970

impudence the government closed down the magazine which promptly renamed itself *Charlie Hebdo*.

After the outpouring of grief, life returned to normal. A few days after the decision, taken in the emotion of the moment, to rename the Place de l'Etoile the Place Charles de Gaulle, many municipal councillors went back on their vote. When the new name of the Place was inaugurated in December, there were anti-Gaullist demonstrations and the plaque had to be protected by the police to prevent it being defaced.[3] The faithful immediately set about tending the flame of Gaullist memory. Malraux's *Fallen Oaks* appeared a few months after de Gaulle's death; a National Association for Fidelity to the Memory of General de Gaulle was created by Pierre Lefranc in 1971. In that year also a 'pilgrimage' was organized to Colombey by the Order of Liberation. A public subscription campaign was launched to build a huge Cross of Lorraine at the top of a hill to the west of Colombey. This monument was inaugurated on 18 June 1972 by Pompidou, despite the reservations of some Gaullists who could not forgive the 'betrayal' of 1969. The press made much of Yvonne de Gaulle's supposedly frosty reception of Pompidou at the event.

Although she attended the ceremony, Yvonne de Gaulle was otherwise vigilant in her efforts to prevent some kind of religious cult growing up around the memory of her husband. Immediately after his death she had burnt almost all his personal effects, including his clothes and his mattress, and had refused to allow a mould of his face and hands to be made. She was persuaded by her son to keep only two *képis* and two uniforms – symbols of his official role, not his person. Her mantra otherwise was 'no relics'. The ceremony on 18 June 1972 was only one of three occasions in which she appeared publicly in any official capacity during the nine years between his funeral and her own death. She was discreetly present in 1975 when her son-in-law, Alain de Boissieu, received the Grand Cross of the Legion of Honour, and she no less discreetly met the head of the Bibliothèque Nationale to hand over the manuscripts of de Gaulle's *War Memoirs*. Otherwise she lived an entirely reclusive life at Colombey until September 1978 when she took up residence at the Convent of the Sisters of the Immaculate Conception of Notre Dame de Lourdes in Paris. There she died of cancer on 7 November 1979, almost unnoticed and largely forgotten.[4]

The opposite was true of the reputation of the General. The authorities had expected 40,000 people to turn out for the inauguration of the Cross of Lorraine in 1972; the actual number was nearer 25,000. This seemed to prove de Gaulle's gloomy prediction in his famous last conversation with Malraux: 'They will put up a huge Cross of Lorraine on a hill higher than all the others. Everyone will be able to see it. But as there won't be anyone there, no one will see it. It will incite the rabbits to resistance.' Whether or not de Gaulle really said this, it was entirely in the vein of his melancholy at that time. What he probably thought in reality was what he said to a government minister on the eve of his resignation: 'The French no longer want de Gaulle. But the myth, you will see the growth of the myth . . . in thirty years.'[5]

It is particularly striking how quickly the left started to invoke de Gaulle's memory. This too he had predicted in a conversation with the left Gaullist David Rousset in April 1968: 'The left does not forgive me for having carried out the policy it ought to have done and was not able to do . . . It will only pardon me after my death. After my death it will reclaim me. It will claim to be following my policies. But only after my death.'[6] He was correct. The first signs came from the Communist Party, whose implacable opposition to de Gaulle in the 1960s had always been tempered by grudging approval for aspects of his foreign policy. In the 1970s, as de Gaulle's successors – first Pompidou and then even more Giscard – embarked on a more Atlanticist and pro-European policy, the Communists began to see more good in de Gaulle and glided over those aspects of his domestic policy they had opposed.[7] One way of charting this reappraisal is to examine the way the Communists treated the events of 1940 – an embarrassing period in their history. Both the Gaullists and Communists built their political legitimacy on their role in the Resistance and were in competition to claim its legacy. The Communists therefore always ignored the anniversary of 18 June 1940 and instead celebrated 10 July 1940 when the Communist Party had allegedly made its own call to resistance. This was a largely fictitious event but necessary for the Communists to deal with the embarrassing fact that in 1940 they were not yet in the Resistance because of the Nazi–Soviet Pact. In 1976, for the first time, the Communist newspaper *L'Humanité* carried an article recalling 18 June (as well as 10 July): 'For the role he played, General de Gaulle is part of the patrimony of the French nation.' There were many more zigzags along the way – and the Party took a long time to let go of 10 July entirely – but in 1990 when France went into a kind of ceremonial frenzy for the fiftieth anniversary of 18 June the Communist Party newspapers carried fifteen pages on 'De Gaulle and Us'. Ten years later they had entirely forgotten 10 July.[8]

The non-Communist left moved towards de Gaulle a little later. In 1981, François Mitterrand was elected to the Presidency. Hating de Gaulle was the only consistent thread to his devious political trajectory. His first act on becoming President was to organize a public ceremony at the Panthéon where he laid a rose on three tombs including that of Jean Moulin. This was a clear attempt to reappropriate Moulin for the left, Mitterrand's response to de Gaulle's Pantheonization of Moulin seventeen years earlier. Otherwise Mitterrand performed his 'Gaullist' duties as President by attending the annual 18 June ceremony at Mont-Valérien. But when it came to celebrating the fortieth anniversary of the D-Day landings he managed the feat of avoiding any mention of de Gaulle's name – a not so subtle form of anti-Gaullism by omission.[9]

Attitudes among French Socialists changed in the mid-1980s when the Gaullist opposition, led by Jacques Chirac, looked as if it might win the parliamentary elections on a platform of economic liberalism inspired by Ronald Reagan and Margaret Thatcher. The French Socialists now resuscitated de Gaulle by contrasting his ambition to unite the French with the socially divisive policies of his proclaimed successors. The publication of Jean Lacouture's three-volume biography of de Gaulle between 1984 and 1986 was a crucial milestone in this rediscovery of de Gaulle by the left.

The final stage in the left's journey to de Gaulle came a few years later – this time as a way not of defending Mitterrand against Chirac but of venting disgust with the failures and corruption of the Mitterrand Presidency. The most remarkable example of this was the trajectory of the leftist intellectual Régis Debray. Debray had played no part in the events of 1968 because he was languishing in a Bolivian prison having gone to fight with Che Guevara. When Mitterrand won the election of 1981 Debray became one of his advisers on foreign affairs. Ten years later he had become completely disillusioned with Mitterrand and his 1990 book *Tomorrow de Gaulle* was his way of settling scores. He did not hold back: 'In my dreams I am on terms of easy familiarity with Louis XI, with Lenin, with Edison and Lincoln. But I quail before de Gaulle. He is the Great Other, the inaccessible absolute ... Napoleon was the great political myth of the nineteenth century; de Gaulle of the twentieth. The sublime, it seems, appears in France only once a century.' Mitterrand had called de Gaulle 'the last of the nineteenth-century great men', in the style of Metternich and Bismarck, but Debray proclaimed that on the contrary Mitterrand belonged to the nineteenth century while de Gaulle 'was really the first great man of the twenty-first century'. In contrast to the whiff of corruption around the Mitterrand court, Debray celebrated the Roman austerity of de Gaulle: 'It is so comforting to think that he was alive among us. For a long time to come, his name alone will serve as a giant India rubber to erase mediocrity.'[10] One former Maoist wrote in 1990: 'Nowadays, one no longer discusses de Gaulle, one contemplates his legend like a lost continent, that is, when one isn't dreaming of it.' When soon after de Gaulle's death Claude Mauriac commented to Malraux that it seemed to be among former anti-Gaullists that de Gaulle's greatness was being most widely recognized, Malraux replied: 'It wasn't the royalists but the republicans who created Joan of Arc.'[11]

From this point, the de Gaulle myth assumed unstoppable proportions. In 1990, the twentieth anniversary of de Gaulle's death, the fiftieth anniversary of his *Appel* and the hundredth anniversary of his birth offered the opportunity for a triple celebration. In that year the Fondation Charles de Gaulle organized a centennial conference whose seven published volumes run to a total of 4,000 pages. Twenty years later, on 18 June 2010, three television channels covered the anniversary celebrations live for several hours. Later in that year there was another bout of Gaullomania for the anniversary of de Gaulle's death; there were pilgrimages to his tomb at Colombey by many politicians including President Sarkozy. *Le Monde* ran a leader in November 2010 declaring that the French were still 'orphans of de Gaulle'.

GAULLIANS AND GAULLISTS

Ironically, at the same time as de Gaulle's myth was taking off, his narrative about French history – and his role in it – was progressively unravelling. This happened first in relation to the legend that de Gaulle had constructed around the war. After 1945 he had created the necessary myth that France had been a nation united in resistance – and united around him – with the collaborators being (in his words) only a small 'handful of *misérables*'. After 1968 this myth was challenged by a younger generation. One striking example was the famous documentary *The Sorrow and the Pity* by Marcel Ophuls which came out in 1969. While it is not quite true, as has often been claimed, that the film suddenly replaced the image of France as a nation of resisters with that of France as a nation of collaborators, it did offer an unprecedentedly dark picture of the Occupation in which there were a few heroes, a few villains and a lot of cowardly *attentistes*. In the four hours of the film de Gaulle was hardly mentioned. The film was iconoclastic enough for the government to refuse to allow it to be shown on television.

In the wake of *The Sorrow and the Pity*, popular memory of the war increasingly concentrated on the complicity of the Vichy government in the Final Solution. Jewish activists called upon the French government to make an official apology. These demands became vociferous during the second Presidency of Mitterrand (1988–94). But he refused to make the

apology on the grounds that since Vichy had not been a legitimate government it did not represent France. There was an irony that Mitterrand, an
historic anti-Gaullist, found himself implicitly subscribing to the official
Gaullist doctrine that the real 'France' during the war was in London. This
taboo was finally broken by Jacques Chirac, the first President of the Fifth
Republic too young to have taken part in the war. In a solemn declaration
in 1995 Chirac accepted the responsibility of 'France' for the fate of the
Jews. Thus it took a nominally Gaullist President – although one from the
Pompidou 'stable' – to undermine the foundation of the Gaullist interpreta-
tion of France's wartime history.

At the same time, another Gaullist myth was beginning to look increasingly unconvincing. One of de Gaulle's achievements had been to turn
France's defeat in Algeria into a kind of victory. Apart from the *pieds noirs*
the French seemed to be happy to buy into this. De Gaulle's narrative was
that France, although militarily victorious, had granted Algeria independence in accordance with her historic commitment to human rights. He
drew a line over the colonial past and offered the French a gleaming modern future. This was successful for two decades until memories of the
Algerian War began to surface in unpredictable ways. On the left, the
massacre of Algerians in Paris in October 1961 came to be seen as one of
the most terrible state crimes of post-war France. The fate of the Harkis
aroused increasing attention, and in September 2016 President Hollande
officially recognized the 'responsibility of the French government [de
Gaulle's government] in the abandonment of the Harkis'.[12]

From the other side of the political spectrum, the increasing French
obsession with the consequences of immigration, and with the presence of
large Muslim communities, has legitimated ways of thinking about the
Algerian conflict entirely at odds with de Gaulle's narrative. In 2015 the
recently elected extreme right-wing Mayor of Béziers, Robert Ménard,
debaptized the Rue du 19 Mai 1962, named after the date of the Evian
Accords, and renamed it instead Rue du Commandant Hélie Denoix de
Saint-Marc after one of the soldiers who had participated in the 1961 coup
against de Gaulle. This was a clearly anti-Gaullist gesture but others, proclaiming their loyalty to de Gaulle, have also reinterpreted the Algerian
War in their own way. One Gaullist wrote in the mid-1980s that one of de
Gaulle's achievements was to have predicted rightly that *Algérie française*
would cause the 'progressive invasion of the mainland by a non-European,
Berber-Arab and Muslim population'.[13] In 2015 a right-wing politician
claimed to be quoting de Gaulle when she asserted that France was
historically a 'white and Christian country'.[14] Thus for some conservatives
de Gaulle's achievement in Algeria has flipped from being a noble act

of decolonization to a prophetic – not to say racist – anticipation of the dangers of multiculturalism. In this case, at least the new slant might be closer to what de Gaulle really thought than to what he publicly proclaimed.

As the French become more 'Gaullian' they seemingly become less 'Gaullist'. But if the de Gaulle myth has not really been affected by the unravelling of the Gaullist 'story', that is because the myth transcends the person of de Gaulle himself and is vaguely linked to a nostalgia for the vanished *Trente Glorieuses* – that golden age before the French economy started down a slope of seemingly inexorable decline. The 1960s were a decade in which France was successful – indeed 'great', to use de Gaulle's word – not only economically but also culturally.[15] French intellectuals and artists did speak to the world, and de Gaulle's image bathes in the glow of that memory. 'De Gaulle's France' is the France of the Caravelle and the Citroën DS, of Jean-Paul Sartre and Claude Lévi-Strauss, of Brigitte Bardot and Jean-Luc Godard. In 2016, a right-wing journalist, Eric Zemmour, wrote a best-selling book apocalyptically entitled the *French Suicide*. It opened symbolically with de Gaulle's funeral on 12 November 1970. In Zemmour's noxious narrative, de Gaulle's death opened the floodgates to all the ills (as he sees them) of contemporary France – national decline, feminism, homosexuality, mass immigration.

THE LAST GREAT FRENCHMAN

As France shrinks de Gaulle seems to grow. If, then, de Gaulle is now widely viewed as 'the last great Frenchman', where does his greatness lie? Was he, as many have argued, a great visionary? François Furet, one of those many left-wing intellectuals so viscerally hostile to de Gaulle, wrote in 1963: 'What characterizes de Gaulle is not his ability to predict the future, it is his extraordinary capacity to be deceived by history yet to adapt to it. What makes him a great politician is not his strategy, it is his tactics.'[16] A similar line was adopted by Jean-François Revel, another liberal critic of de Gaulle, who wrote an excoriating pamphlet in 1959 deflating Gaullist triumphalism through a sarcastic dissection of the pomposities of de Gaulle's rhetoric. Thirty years later (1989), with de Gaulle long dead, Revel reissued his pamphlet with an introduction that was only partially repentant. He was now ready to accept that – as a man of action – de Gaulle was someone of a stature that France had rarely experienced in her history (he was implicitly comparing him to the temporizing Mitterrand). But contrary to the ambient hagiography, he still clung to the view that de Gaulle 'did not particularly understand the great problems of his era despite his reputation for being in advance of his time'. Revel viewed him as a man of the late nineteenth century, obsessed with the nation state, underestimating the importance of ideology and in particular the power of totalitarian Communism.[17] This remark seems in retrospect an ironic hostage to fortune since a year later the Soviet bloc had entirely disintegrated and the Cold War was a thing of the past. De Gaulle seems to have made that particular call more successfully than Revel.

Does that make de Gaulle a visionary? A comment sometimes made about de Gaulle is that it was never entirely clear if he was the man of the day-before-yesterday or the man of the day-after-tomorrow.[18] Debray's book in 1990 had no doubt that he was the latter. It is indeed astonishing how often de Gaulle was proved right. In the 1930s, his prediction about the future course of the Battle of France was more accurate than that of the French high command. Everything he did after June 1940 was built around his correct judgement that the Battle of France was only the start of a world war in which the Axis powers would be defeated. In the 1960s, commentators scoffed when he predicted the collapse of the Bretton Woods system but a few years later this had come to pass. For all the clumsiness of his remarks about Israel, his predictions about the corroding consequences for Israel of the occupation of the Palestinian territories seem prophetic. He was proved right about the Vietnam War – about America's inability to win it, about the future different varieties of Asian 'Communism', about the eventual conflict between China and Vietnam.

One can find other examples of de Gaulle's often startling lucidity about the future. For example, he predicted in a conversation with Peyrefitte in 1964 that Yugoslavia would not last: 'For that there needs to be a Yugoslav nation. There isn't. There are just bits of wood stuck together with a piece of string. That piece of string is Tito. When he is no longer there, the bits will fall apart.'[19] In another conversation in the same year he was equally prophetic about the future of Iraq: 'The Sunnis with the Shias and the Kurds. These are countries destined to be divided because they contain altogether different peoples who do not have the same religion, the same past.'[20] One might also mention his uncannily accurate prediction after the assassination of Kennedy that his widow Jacqueline would end her days married to a Greek shipowner. When reminded of this by Malraux in their last 'conversation' de Gaulle remarked – or so Malraux says – 'Did I really say that? I would rather have thought that she might marry Sartre. Or you.'[21]

But there was much that de Gaulle did not get right. His social ideas regarding class reconciliation and the challenges of industrial civilization – still celebrated by some 'left' Gaullists as one of his most important legacies – were as half-baked as they were generous: he oscillated between the two equally nebulous concepts of 'association' in the 1940s and 'participation' in the 1960s. His thinking on these matters was in the spirit of many social Catholics of his generation and of some 1930s' intellectuals. But there is no sign that he had any understanding of the massive structural changes that were affecting the French economy in the 1960s. As for his predictions about international relations, they were often proved wrong. In 1946–7, he was constantly predicting an imminent world war; he was slow to see potential for Franco-German reconciliation and his vision for the future of Germany in 1945–8 was stuck in the past (although not as much as has been claimed); he did not predict the end of Empire, and until 1950 he was still believing the French could win their war in Indo-China. But having learnt from his errors, de Gaulle showed a pragmatic capacity to adapt. He refused to hold on to impossible positions. Over Algeria, what is most striking is not that he predicted in 1958 what would happen in 1962 but the single-minded ruthlessness with which he pursued his objectives once he had decided to act.

It is de Gaulle's adaptability to circumstance that should inform our judgement on whether his ambitions for France in the world were absurdly over-inflated. Many commentators share the verdict of Lord Gladwyn: 'Undoubtedly the General's chief failing – and in the long run it was unfortunate – was to cast his country into a role which was beyond her power.'[22] Were de Gaulle's ambitions for his country delusions of grandeur inappropriate for France in the twentieth century? Accusations of 'madness' were, we have seen, common throughouth de Gaulle's career. And with someone who was regularly capable of referring to himself in the third person or saying (if half in jest) 'I have been saying it for a thousand years,' one is tempted to adapt to de Gaulle Jean Cocteau's quip about Victor Hugo, that he was a 'madman who believed he was Victor Hugo'. But de Gaulle was usually one step ahead of his critics, and anything they had said about the impossibility of his ambitions he had already said himself. One of his favourites phrases was 'I have always acted as if ...' – as if France was still in the war after June 1940, as if France could play a world role in the 1960s.

In the 1960s de Gaulle exhorted the French to believe in themselves as a 'great' nation – but *grandeur* was an attitude rather than a concrete goal. As de Gaulle put it famously in his *War Memoirs*: 'However difficult reality might be, perhaps I would be able to master it, to quote Chateaubriand's phrase, "by leading the French there through dreams".'[23] De Gaulle had few illusions about the decline in France's material power. As he said to Malraux: 'Of course the Spanish admire me. They like Don Quixote!' Or, when Malraux asked him which historical character he would compare himself to – Joan of Arc, Napoleon, Louis XIV? – de Gaulle replied: 'My only rival is Tintin! We are the small who refuse to allow ourselves to be cheated by the big. Only, no one notices the similarity because of my size.'[24] (A few years later he might have chosen Astérix, who had the further advantage of being French rather than Belgian.) On one occasion de Gaulle described his policy during the war as one of bluff, throwing dust in the Allies' eyes so that they might be blinded into thinking that France was great. This does not mean that grandeur was merely posturing: it was simply a question of using one's wits, like Tintin, and playing the cards one held to greatest effect. It was probably good for the world that de Gaulle did not have at his disposal the resources of Napoleon.

The tensions between restraint and hubris, reason and sentiment, classicism and romanticism, calculation and provocation, cunning and showmanship, *politique* and *mystique* (to use the Péguy terminology), Corneille and Chateaubriand, Descartes and Bergson, are a constant feature of de Gaulle's career. Or as Henry Kissinger once put it: 'De Gaulle's nationalism is in the tradition of Mazzini . . . His diplomacy is in the style of Bismarck.'[25] His bouts of pessimistic melancholy were a reflection of these two warring elements of his personality: the romantic *id* held in check by the classical *super-ego*, pessimism of the intellect and optimism of the will. For all his acts of provocation – from the occupation of Saint-Pierre-et-Miquelon in 1941 to the '*Vive le Québec libre*' speech in 1967 – de Gaulle usually knew when to draw back from the brink, whether breaking with the British during the war or leaving the Atlantic Alliance in the late 1960s. He denounced European supranationalism but was good at using it to further France's economic interests. There was something in Aron's observation: 'My own view is that de Gaulle does not himself take seriously half the arguments that he uses, and he take a solitary pleasure in the spectacle of the polemics he unleashes.'[26]

But it would be wrong to reduce de Gaulle's interventions to pure showmanship. He did not succeed in ending the Cold War, or reshaping the world order, or creating a 'political Europe', but many of the questions he posed and the issues he tried to address – how to create 'Europe', the problem of European defence, how to plan for a post-Cold War order – were genuine ones. It is true that his vision of the future of Europe looked more like the Europe of 1914 than the Europe in which we live today – but his intuition that a European project built by technocrats would have difficulty in creating a durable sense of common destiny and collective identity seems more compelling today than it did thirty years ago.

De Gaulle probably did overestimate the role that France could realistically play in the world, but his response would have been that it was better to err in that direction than the other. To 'create events' was part of the point; the ambition was what mattered. And despite Gladwyn's comment, de Gaulle *was* an extraordinary presence on the world stage in the 1960s. This was the view of the distinguished British diplomat Nicholas Henderson looking back thirty years later:

> It is difficult to exaggerate how overpowering for Western Europe in general and for the UK in particular was the looming presence at this time of de Gaulle . . . He had only to whisper over grain prices for Germany to shiver, over the MLF for the Atlantic to recede . . . He could make them dance to his tune by the merest threat. Nor did anyone else in the Western world look like countering him.[27]

Of course this was up to a point an ephemeral achievement even if some of de Gaulle's policies, contested at the time, are now universally accepted in France – for example the independent French nuclear deterrent. Since 2009, France has been back in NATO but the memory of Gaullist 'ambition' has left its trace, for example in the famous speech by the French Foreign Minister Dominique de Villepin to the United Nations in 2003 refusing any French participation in the Iraq War. Here de Gaulle seemed to be speaking from the grave.

But de Gaulle's most lasting achievement was not so much in the field of foreign policy as in the establishment of the constitution of the Fifth Republic in 1958. The constitution has been amended several times and operates in many respects differently from de Gaulle's intentions – but it is still in essence the regime that he created through his way of exercising power between 1958 and 1969. The constitution certainly has many dysfunctional characteristics, and the concentration of power in the hands of the President can have effects as deleterious as the instability of the Fourth Republic. But no political system is without flaws, and the Gaullist achievement was not so much to have produced the perfect constitution as to have created a consensus, for the first time in 150 years, around the nature of France's political institutions – despite regular talk about the need to create a Sixth Republic.[28] In an opinion poll organized in 1990 no action of de Gaulle secured a higher approval rating – 88 per cent – than the institution of the election of the President by universal suffrage.[29] Gaullism succeeded in becoming the synthesis of French political traditions, or as de Gaulle put it, reconciling the left to the state and the right to the nation, the left to authority and the right to democracy. The old argument about whether de Gaulle was a Bonapartist now has a rather fusty air about it. De Gaulle was no dictator, and despite the authoritarian style of his rule, he did voluntarily relinquish power in 1969. But he was a 'Bonapartist' in the sense that he sought to do what Bonapartism had sought to do but failed – to reconcile the Revolution and the monarchy, what de Gaulle had identified as his ambition to Macmillan in 1943.

What made it possible for de Gaulle to achieve this was the 'legitimacy' – to use his favourite word – he had acquired in the war. His role between 1940 and 1944 allowed him to transcend normal categories of left and right. He was for ever the 'man of 18 June'. In an opinion poll carried out in 2010, which showed that de Gaulle was the historical figure most admired by the French, it was the de Gaulle of the war who was above all remembered: 44 per cent associated him with the *Appel* of 18 June, 20 per cent with the founding of the Fifth Republic and only 4 per cent with decolonization.

Two moments present themselves to the French collective imagination regarding de Gaulle's role in the war: the first – June 1940 – is the image of a solitary figure – gaze fixed on the BBC microphone as if it was France; the second – August 1944 – is the image of the Liberator walking down the Champs-Elysées, watched by possibly one million people. As far as the first image is concerned, there was much more to de Gaulle than just a voice on the radio. De Gaulle himself would become exasperated at being reduced to just the speech of 18 June. Soon after his resignation in 1946 he exclaimed to Pleven one day over lunch:

> They make me laugh with their *Appel* of 18 June . . . What everyone seems to ignore is the incredible mixture of patience, of slow development, of obstinate creativity, of trick questions, the dizzying succession of calculation, negotiations, conflicts, trips that we had to carry out to accomplish our enterprise. Just take the example of Leclerc: they seem to think it quite natural that he disembarked in Normandy, liberated Strasbourg and Paris. No one seems to ask: 'where did he find the men and matériel? How is it that he was at just the right moment at the gates of Paris and then that he could fall on Alsace?'[30]

De Gaulle's exasperation was understandable. His achievement between 1940 and 1944 lay not just in the speeches from London but in the daily war of attrition he waged against his allies to prevent himself being subsumed by them. His more extreme interventions probably did him no good in the short term but overall they served the strategic purpose: with cunning, tactical skill and strategic vision, he leveraged his minuscule resources into securing for France a place among the victorious powers.

This takes us to the second image: de Gaulle on the Champs-Elysées in August 1944. One argument of anti-Gaullist Vichy apologists – and others – was that nothing de Gaulle did made any difference to the history of the war: that without de Gaulle France would have been liberated in 1944 by the Allies, and indeed that perhaps Vichy served the Allied cause better than de Gaulle had done by keeping North Africa out of German hands and thus making possible the American landings of 1942. Quite apart from the fact that this was an entirely unintended result of Vichy policy, it misses the point that de Gaulle's aim was not to help the Allies win the war – something that his exiguous resources would never have let him do – but to ensure that 'France' was an acknowledged partner in that victory, acquiring even a zone of occupation in Germany and a permanent seat on the United Nations Security Council.

Of course even if there had been no de Gaulle, the British would probably, for their own strategic reasons, have pushed for France to have a permanent seat on the Security Council and a zone of occupation in Germany. France had no more ardent defender at Yalta than Winston Churchill. But the assessment of de Gaulle's achievement cannot be reduced to a balance sheet of this kind: there is also a moral dimension to it. This was the theme of a spat that took place during the war between the two most famous French exiles in the United States, both of whom had reservations about de Gaulle: Antoine de Saint-Exupéry and Jacques Maritain. Saint-Exupéry, primarily remembered today as the author of the allegorical fable *The Little Prince*, was the best-known French writer in the United States. A fighter pilot in 1940, he had been plunged into despair by the defeat. His opposition to de Gaulle came out of disgust with the attitude of the French in 1940 and his refusal to accept the myth that de Gaulle was trying to create from the very beginning. As he put it pithily on another occasion: 'Tell the truth, General, we lost the war. Our allies will win it.'[31]

The American landings in North Africa in November 1942 ended Saint-Exupéry's crisis of confidence and for him the path of duty was now clear. In the *New York Times* that same month, when Darlan was still in place in North Africa, he published an 'Open Letter to the French Everywhere'. His theme was that the duty of the French was now to put aside all partisan squabbles, obey their military leaders Darlan and Giraud and unite for victory. This apolitical reading of France's situation provoked a long reply from Maritain headed 'Sometimes it is necessary to judge'. Maritain, as we have seen, had been himself reticent about de Gaulle between 1940 and 1942, and he was never a fully paid-up Gaullist. But in November 1942 he had no doubt where duty lay, and why de Gaulle had to be chosen over Darlan or Giraud:

> There are men who from the time of the armistice have endured the worst trials to continue that war by the side of the allies – I speak of the soldiers

of the Free French ... Their leader said no to the enemy from the first day; an act of that kind cannot be effaced. A sort of heroic chivalry has given back hope to the French.[32]

Now that the rancid arguments of Vichy apologists are long past, there cannot be a French citizen who does not recognize the truth of Maritain's statement and who does not feel justifiably prouder of their country as a result of what de Gaulle achieved between 1940 and 1944. He saved the honour of France.

Bibliographical Note

Full details of sources can be found in the Notes. This Bibliographical Note provides a summary of the most important sources used and a guide to further reading. The starting place for any biography of de Gaulle is now the de Gaulle archives at the Archives Nationales (AN). These have become open to researchers relatively recently (although many documents for the archives of the Fifth Republic require a *dérogation*). The first set of archives (Inventory: *Archives du général de Gaulle 1940–1958*, Centre Historique des Archives Nationales, 2003) cover the period 1940–58 but most of the material relates to the Free French period. The second set (Inventory: *Archives de la Présidence de la République. Général de Gaulle 1959–1969*, Archives Nationales, 2012) cover the period of the Presidency but also contain 200 *cartons* of personal correspondence covering the period 1945–69. For the wartime period another almost inexhaustible treasure trove are the documents collected by the Comité de la Deuxième Guerre Mondiale, and accessible at the Archives Nationales under the *cote* 72AJ. Especially useful are the many interviews that were carried out – many with members of the Free French – during the 1940s and 1950s.

Many, but by no means all, of the most interesting documents in the de Gaulle archives had already been published in thirteen volumes between 1980 and 1997 by de Gaulle's son Philippe in the collection *Lettres, notes et carnets*. These were reissued in 2000 in a three-volume edition with some further additions. The *Lettres, notes et carnets* also contain family letters from de Gaulle which are not in the de Gaulle archives; more such letters probably remain in the family. Other de Gaulle letters appear regularly for sale in auction, on eBay and from antiquarian booksellers (I cite such letters in Chapters 3, 6 and 30). But there are also probably some fakes circulating.

The other key published sources are de Gaulle's *Memoirs* of which the definitive Pléiade edition published the manuscript variants. The original publications of the three volumes of *War Memoirs* also contain a large number of documents from the archives which were not reproduced in the Pléiade edition. In addition there are the five volumes of de Gaulle speeches *Discours et messages* (Plon Poche, 1970) and the considerable body of his inter-war writings most of which are conveniently gathered together in *Le fil de l'épée et autres écrits* (Omnibus Plon, 1990).

Three invaluable tools when studying de Gaulle are Claire Andrieu, Philippe Braud and Guillaume Piketty (eds.), *Dictionnaire Charles de Gaulle* (Robert Laffont, 2006), Alain Larcan, *De Gaulle inventaire. La culture, l'esprit, la foi* (Bartillat, 2010 edn) – an exhaustive inventory (with commentary) of all de Gaulle's reading – and finally the seven volumes of the huge international conference held in Paris on the twentieth anniversary of de Gaulle's death: *De Gaulle en son siècle. Actes des journées internationales tenues à UNESCO Paris* (Documentation Française, 1991–2). The quality of the papers is variable.

The journal of the Fondation Charles de Gaulle, *Espoir*, also provides much information.

The *Documents diplomatiques français* are essential especially for the period of de Gaulle's Presidency. For the period 1944–54 they were edited by Georges-Henri Soutou and for the period since 1954 the editor has been Maurice Vaïsse. For an overview see Maurice Vaïsse, 'Les documents diplomatiques français: outil pour la recherche?', *La Revue pour l'histoire du CNRS* 14 (2006) at http://journals.openedition.org/histoire-cnrs/1836.

Diaries and Journals

The diary of the diplomat Hervé Alphand, *L'étonnement d'être. Journal 1939–1973* (Fayard, 1977) is remarkably useful because it is the only one covering (if intermittently) the entire period from 1941 to the end of de Gaulle's life. Claude Bouchinet-Serreulles, *Nous étions faits pour être libres. La Résistance avec de Gaulle et Jean Moulin* (Grasset, 2000) is excellent on the early Free French period; for the Algiers period see Henri Queuille, *Journal de Guerre Londres–Alger avril 1943–juillet 1944* (Plon, 1995). Claude Mauriac, *Un autre de Gaulle* (Hachette, 1970) is excellent for the immediate post-war and early RPF period, and Claude Guy, *En écoutant de Gaulle. Journal 1946–1949* (Grasset, 1996) for the first years of the RPF. Other diaries of interest are Louis Terrenoire, *Pourquoi l'échec. Du RPF à la traversée du désert* (Plon, 1981) and Pierre-Henri Rix, *Par le portillon de la Boisserie* (Nouvelles Editions Latines, 1974), which records conversations after 1947 about literature and history. Georges Pompidou, *Pour rétablir une vérité* (Flammarion, 1982) has interesting diary extracts, and can be supplemented by other material from Pompidou, *Lettres, notes et portraits 1928–1974* (Robert Laffont, 2012).

For the period of the Presidency the two most important diary sources are Alain Peyrefitte, *C'était de Gaulle* (Gallimard, 2000) and Jacques Foccart, *Foccart Parle. Entretiens avec Philippe Gaillard* (Fayard Jeune Afrique, 1995). There is some useful material also in Robert Buron, *Carnets politiques de la guerre d'Algérie* (Plon, 1965, 2002 edn).

Biographies

Three important biographies are the three-volume work by Jean Lacouture, *De Gaulle* (Seuil, 1984–6), Paul-Marie de la Gorce, *De Gaulle* (Perrin, 1999) and Eric Roussel, *De Gaulle* (Gallimard, 2002). The contributions of these works are discussed in the Introduction to this book. Only Lacouture is available in English in a rather abridged translation. Biographies of de Gaulle appear in France almost every year. One of the most recent and compact is Chantal Morelle, *De Gaulle. La passion de la France* (Armand Colin, 2015). Not surprisingly there have also been many biographies of de Gaulle by British and American writers. Among British biographers one of the most incisive was published in the middle of de Gaulle's Presidency, by the left-wing veteran journalist Alexander Werth who covered French politics for the *Manchester Guardian* over several decades: *De Gaulle* (Penguin, 1965). The biography by Bernard Ledwidge, *De Gaulle* (Weidenfeld & Nicolson, 1982) has some insights which come from the author's period on the British Embassy staff in Paris during the period of de Gaulle's Presidency. The two-volume biography by the Australian journalist Brian Crozier, *De Gaulle* (Scribner, 1973), was marred by the extreme Cold War positions of its author who viewed the de Gaulle of the 1960s almost as a Communist, and regrettably different from Franco, to whom Crozier devoted an admiring biography. The most recent English biography is Jonathan Fenby's extremely readable *The General: Charles de Gaulle and the France He Saved* (Simon & Schuster, 2010). Of American biographies, that by the journalist David Schoenbrun, *Les trois vies de Charles de Gaulle* (Julliard, 1965), although appearing in the middle of de Gaulle's Presidency, benefited from the author's own interviews with de Gaulle. There is also a pretty balanced American biography by Don Cook, for many years the *Los Angeles Times* correspondent in Paris: *Charles de Gaulle: A Biography* (Putman, 1984).

Personal Life

For the 'private de Gaulle' a good place to begin is the two-volume memoirs of de Gaulle's son Philippe de Gaulle, *Mémoires accessoires* (Plon 1997, 2000) and his two volumes of interviews *De Gaulle mon père. Entretiens avec Michel Tauriac* (Plon, 2003, 2004). The interviews need to be treated with caution regarding the 'public' de Gaulle since they settle many scores and refuse to countenance the idea that de Gaulle could ever be wrong: see 'Qui était Charles de Gaulle?', *Le Débat* 134 (March/April 2005). But the volumes of interviews do also contain fascinating information on the de Gaulle family that can be found nowhere else. Frédérique Neau-Dufour's *Yvonne de Gaulle* (Fayard, 2010) is now the best study of de Gaulle's wife.

Gaullism

For understanding 'Gaullism' Jean Touchard's pioneering *Le gaullisme* (Seuil, 1978) remains perceptive. Touchard was a lecturer at the FNSP and his books are almost all collections of the lectures he gave there. As a young man he worked in de Gaulle's *cabinet* in 1945. Anthony Hartley, *Gaullism: The Rise and Fall of a Political Movement* (Dutton, 1972) is another old book which is still worth consulting. The most recent overview of Gaullism is Serge Berstein's *Histoire du gaullisme* (Perrin, 2001). In a category of their own are the articles of Odille Rudelle collected in *République d'une jour, République de toujours* (Riveneuve, 2016). Rudelle made it almost her life's mission to situate de Gaulle in a liberal Catholic tradition: if she pushed the argument further than the evidence allowed, her work is a valuable corrective to the traditional view of de Gaulle as someone who started out as a Maurrassian nationalist. Nicolas Roussellier, *La force de gouverner. Le pouvoir exécutif en France, XIXe–XXIe siècles* (Gallimard, 2015) is an ambitious study of the idea and reality of executive power in France since the Revolution and has a lot to say about Gaullism along the way. The Italian Senator and political scientist Gaetano Quagliariello, *La religion gaulliste* (Perrin, 2006) offers an interesting study of the tension between party and charisma in the history of Gaullism. No one has surpassed the perceptions of the Franco-American political scientist Stanley Hoffmann whose many essays on de Gaulle and Gaullism are collected in *Decline or Renewal? France since the 1930s* (Viking, New York, 1974).

Before 18 June 1940

The proceedings of two colloquia of the Fondation Charles de Gaulle, *Charles de Gaulle. La jeunesse et la guerre 1890–1920* (Plon, 2001) and *Charles de Gaulle. Du militaire au politique 1920–1940* (Plon, 2004), contain many valuable contributions.

For the Great War see Historial de la Grande Guerre, *De Gaulle soldat 1914–1918* (Martelle Editions, 1999) and Frédérique Neau-Dufour, *La première guerre mondiale de Charles de Gaulle 1914–1918* (Tallandier, 2013).

Jacques Schapira and Henri Lerner, *Emile Mayer. Un prophète baillonné* (Editions Michalon, 1995) and Vincent Duclert (ed.), *Le Colonel Mayer de l'Affaire Dreyfus à de Gaulle. Un visionnaire en République* (Armand Colin, 2008) are excellent studies of the Colonel Mayer who mattered so much to de Gaulle in the inter-war years.

For the relationship with Pétain, Jean-Raymond Tournoux, *Pétain et de Gaulle* (Plon, 1964) remains essential. The best biography of Pétain is now Bénédicte Vergez-Chaignon, *Pétain* (Perrin, 2014) but it contains little about de Gaulle. Alain Larcan and Pierre Messmer, *Les écrits militaires de Charles de Gaulle* (PUF, 1985) offers an overview of de Gaulle's military thinking.

1940–1944

For the Free French the work of reference is Jean-Louis Crémieux-Brilhac, *La France libre. De l'Appel du 18 juin à la libération* (Gallimard, 1996). Although Crémieux-Brilhac was in the Free French as a young man, and his passion underlies his study, the book is a model of scientific research. It can be complemented by the articles in FDG, *De Gaulle chef de guerre. De l'Appel de Londres à la libération de Paris 1940–1944* (Plon, 2008). See also François Broche and Jean-François Muracciole, *Dictionnaire de la France libre* (Robert Laffont, 2010).

For the BCRA the definitive study is now Sébastien Albertelli, *Les services secrets du Général de Gaulle. Le BCRA 1940–1944* (Perrin, 2009). Jean-Luc Barré, *Devenir de Gaulle 1939–1943* (Perrin, 2009) was the first book to use the de Gaulle papers for the period. Daniel Cordier's massive three volumes on Jean Moulin, *Jean Moulin. L'inconnu du Panthéon* (J.-C. Lattès, 1989–93) are about much more than Moulin alone and contain a mass of documentation. The material is more accessibly presented in Cordier, *La République des catacombes* (Gallimard, 1999).

Eric Jennings, *La France libre fut africaine* (Perrin, 2014) reminds us of the importance of Africa for the Free French. See also Martin Thomas, *The French Empire at War 1940–1945* (Manchester University Press, 1998).

Guillaume Piketty, *Français en Résistance. Carnets de guerre, correspondance, journaux personnels* (Robert Laffont, 2009) is a priceless collection of various letters and private journals of some key Free French figures (Brosset, Pleven, Leclerc, etc.). Jean-François Murraciole, *Les Français libres. L'autre résistance* (Tallandier, 2010) is exhaustive on the backgrounds of the members of the Free French. Nicholas Atkin, *The Forgotten French* (Manchester University Press, 2003) is the best book on the life of the French (not just the Free French) in London during the war. Olivier Wieviorka, *Une histoire de la Résistance en Europe occidentale* (Perrin, 2017) allows one to compare the Free French with other exiled governments in London.

The period of the CFLN in Algiers is well covered by Crémieux-Brilhac, *La France libre* but there is also useful material in Arthur Layton Funk, *Charles de Gaulle: The Crucial Years 1943–44* (University of Oklahoma Press, 1959) and Yves Maxime Danan, *La vie politique à Alger de 1940 à 1944* (Paris, 1963). Chantal Morelle, *Louise Joxe. Diplomate dans l'âme* (André Versaille, 2008) is an important study of one of de Gaulle's key collaborators in Algiers – and indeed for the rest of his career.

Among other biographies of figures involved with the Free French in different ways are Jean-Christophe Notin, *Leclerc* (Perrin, 2005), Guillaume Piketty, *Pierre Brossolette. Un héros de la Résistance* (Odile Jacob, 1998), Henri Lerner, *Catroux* (Albin Michel, 1990), Sophie Davieau-Pousset, 'Maurice Dejean, diplomate atypique (1899–1982)' (unpublished PhD thesis, Ecole des Sciences Politiques, 2013), Philippe Oulmont, *Pierre Denis. Français libre et citoyen du monde* (Nouveau Monde, 2012), Jean-Louis Crémieux-Brilhac, *Georges Boris. Trente ans d'influence. Blum, de Gaulle, Mendès France* (Gallimard, 2010) and Raphaële Ulrich-Pier, *René Massigli (1888–1988). Une vie de diplomate* (Peter Lang, Brussels, 2006).

For the relations between Churchill and de Gaulle nothing has surpassed François Kersaudy, *Churchill and de Gaulle* (Fontana Press, 1990). A. B. Gaunson, *The Anglo-French Clash in Lebanon and Syria 1940–1945* (Macmillan, 1986) and Aviel Roshwald, *Estranged Bedfellows: Britain and France in the Middle East during the Second World War* (Oxford University Press, 1990) cover the conflicts between de Gaulle and the British in the Levant.

For the relationship with Roosevelt, see François Kersaudy, *De Gaulle et Roosevelt. Le duel au sommet* (Perrin, 2004) which can be supplemented by two excellent, more general accounts, Julian Hurstfield, *America and the French Nation 1938–1945* (University of North Carolina Press, 1986) and G. E. Maguire, *Anglo-American Policy towards the Free French* (Macmillan, 1995). Raoul Aglion, *Roosevelt and de Gaulle: Allies in Conflict: A Personal Memoir* (Free Press, 1988) is a memoir by one of de Gaulle's representatives in the United States. Kim Munholland, *Rock of Contention: Free French and Americans at War in New Caledonia 1940–1945* (Berghahn, 2005) is a detailed study of one major conflict between the Free French and the United States.

For the Free French and the Soviet Union, François Lévêque, 'Les relations franco-soviétiques pendant la deuxième guerre mondiale' (unpublished doctoral thesis, Paris 1, 1988) is exhaustive. There are several interesting articles relating to the Free French in the rest of the world in Sylvain Cornil-Frerrot and Philippe Oulmont, *Les Français libres et le monde* (Nouveau Monde, 2015).

Few leading participants in the Free French did not leave memoirs. Among the more interesting are Amiral Thierry d'Argenlieu, *Souvenirs de guerre. Juin 1940–janvier 1941* (Plon, 1973), Antoine Béthouart, *Cinq années d'espérance. Mémoires de guerre 1939–1945* (Plon, 1968), François Coulet, *Vertu des temps difficiles* (Plon, 1967), Claude Hettier de Boislambert, *Les feux de l'espoir* (Plon, 1978), Pierre Billotte, *Le temps des armes* (Plon, 1972), Georges Catroux, *Dans la bataille de la méditerranée 1940–1944* (Julliard, 1949), Pierre Denis (Rauzan), *Souvenirs de la France Libre* (Berger-Levrault, 1946), Colonel Passy, *Mémoires du chef des services secrets de la France libre* (Odile Jacob, 2001), Jacques Soustelle, *Envers et contre tout*, vol. I: *De Londres à Alger (1940–1942)* (Laffont, 1947), André Weil-Curiel, *Le temps de la honte* (Editions du Myrte, 1945).

1944–1958

For the period immediately preceding the Liberation and the early days of de Gaulle's provisional government, see the important collection of articles in FDG, *Le rétablissement de la légalité républicaine* (Complexe, Brussels, 1996). The foreign policy of the provisional government is covered by Pierre Gerbet and Jean Laloy, *Le relèvement: 1944–1949* (Imprimerie Nationale, 1991) and A. W. Deporte, *De Gaulle's Foreign Policy 1944–1946* (Oxford University Press, 1968).

For the development of de Gaulle's constitutional ideas see F. Decaumont (ed.), *Le discours de Bayeux. Hier et aujourd'hui* (Economica, 1990) and Jérôme Perrier, *Entre administration et politique. Michel Debré (1912–1948)* (Institut Université Varenne, 2013). Jean Charlot, *Le gaullisme d'opposition 1946–1958* (Fayard, 1983) remains irreplaceable for the RPF period but now needs to be supplemented by FDG, *De Gaulle et le Rassemblement du peuple français* (Armand Colin, 1998). *Gaullisme et Gaullistes dans la France de l'est sous la IVe République* (Presses Universitaires de Rennes, 2009) is less narrow than the title suggests.

There are interesting interviews with members of the RPF in FDG, *Témoignages*. *'Le temps du Rassemblement' (1946–1958)* (Nouveau Monde, 2005). For the RPF and the Empire see Frédéric Turpin, *De Gaulle, les gaullistes et l'Indochine* (Indes Savantes, 2005). For an analysis of de Gaulle's social thought in this period see Marc Sadoun, Jean-François Sirinelli and Robert Vandenbussche (eds.), *La politique sociale du général de Gaulle* (Centre d'Histoire de la Région du Nord et de l'Europe du Nord-Ouest, Villeneuve d'Ascq, 1990) and Patrick Guiol, *L'impasse sociale du gaullisme. Le RPF et l'action sociale* (FNSP, 1985). Jacques Soustelle, *Vingt-huit ans de Gaullisme* (Table Ronde, 1968) is bitter and unfair but not without interest for the RPF years. Olivier Guichard, *Mon général* (Grasset, 1990) is hard to classify. Part memoir and part biography, it is a subtle portrait of de Gaulle by one of his closest collaborators in this period.

1958

For the crisis of May 1958 Odile Rudelle, *Mai 1958: De Gaulle et la République* (Plon, 1988) is the essential starting point. Even if one does not accept all aspects of her interpretation, her presentation of the material is meticulous. Rudelle carried out numerous in-depth interviews with all the major actors of the crisis, the transcripts of which can be consulted at the Fondation National des Sciences Politiques. See also Christophe Nick, *Résurrection. Naissance de la Vème République, un coup d'état démocratique* (Fayard, 1998). There is also important material in Jean-Paul Thomas, Gilles le Béguec and Bernard Lachaise, *Mai 1958. Le retour du géneral de Gaulle* (Presses Universitaires de Rennes, 2010) which publishes the findings of an important colloquium on May 1958 and in Georgette Elgey, *Histoire de la IVe République. La fin. La République des tourmentes 1954–1959*, vol. III (Fayard, 2008). This forms the penultimate volume of Elgey's multi-volume history of the Fourth Republic and like all the other volumes it contains a mass of information from this historian-journalist's huge range of personal contacts. Michel Poniatowski, *Mémoires* (Plon, Le Rocher, 1997) (he was in Pflimlin's Cabinet) is also useful. For de Gaulle's six months as last premier of the Fourth Republic, Georgette Elgey, *Histoire de la 4e République*, vol. VI: *De Gaulle à Matignon* (Fayard, 2012), the last volume of her history of the Fourth Republic, is as always a mine of information. There are many useful articles in FDG, *L'avènement de la Vème République. Entre nouveauté et tradition* (Armand Colin, 1999). Bernard Lachaise, Gilles Le Béguec and Frédéric Turpin (eds.), *Georges Pompidou, directeur de cabinet du général de Gaulle. Juin 1958–janvier 1959* (Peter Lang, Brussels, 2006) covers the six months when to all intents and purposes Pompidou was Prime Minister of France. On the drafting of the constitution two sets of documents are essential: *Documents pour servir à l'histoire de l'élaboration de la Constitution du 4 octobre 1958*, vol. I (Documentation Française, 1987) and Didier Maus and Olivier Passelecq, *Témoignages sur l'écriture de la Constitution de 1958* (Documentation Française, 1997). For commentaries on the constitution see Didier Maus, Louis Favoreu and Jean-Luc Parodi, *L'écriture de la Constitution de 1958* (Economica, 1992). Brigitte Gaïti, *De Gaulle, prophète de la cinquième République (1946–1962)* (FNSP, 1998) is a bracing corrective to the idea that the new regime was a simple application of the ideas of the Bayeux speech.

On the Rueff–Pinay stabilization plan see Institut Charles de Gaulle, *1958. La faillite ou le miracle. Le plan de Gaulle–Rueff* (Economica, 1986).

Fifth Republic
Politics and Government

Pierre Viansson-Ponte's two-volume *Histoire de la République gaullienne* (Fayard, 1970–71) remains an excellent narrative introduction by a journalist who covered the politics of the period for *Le Monde*.

Eric Chiaradia, *L'entourage du Général de Gaulle juin 1958–avril 1969* (Publibook, 2011) offers an exhaustive prosopographical study of de Gaulle's advisers. See also Gilbert Pilleul, *'L'entourage' et de Gaulle* (Plon, 1979) and Serge Berstein, Pierre Birnbaum and Jean-Pierre Rioux (eds.), *De Gaulle et les élites* (La Découverte, 2008).

On the various Gaullist political movements, Jean Charlot, *L'UNR. Etude du pouvoir au sein d'un parti politique* (Armand Colin, 1967) and *Le phénomène gaulliste* (Fayard, 1970) were pioneering studies. They must now be supplemented by François Audigier, Bernard Lachaise and Sébastien Laurent, *Les gaullistes. Hommes et réseaux* (Nouveau Monde, 2013) and Jérôme Pozzi, *Les mouvements gaullistes. Partis associations et réseaux 1958–1976* (Presses Universitaires de Rennes, 2011).

Of the three secretaries general of the Elysée under de Gaulle, two left memoirs: Etienne Burin des Roziers, *Retour aux sources. 1962. L'année décisive* (Plon, 1986) and Bernard Tricot, *Les sentiers de la paix. Algérie 1958–1962* (Plon, 1972). On de Gaulle's prime ministers, Serge Berstein and Jean-François Sirinelli (eds.), *Michel Debré, Premier Ministre (1959–1962)* (PUF, 2005) provides a mine of information about Debré and can be complemented by Michel Debré, *Entretiens avec le Général de Gaulle 1961–1969* (Albin Michel, 1993) and by Debré's five volumes of memoirs, *Trois républiques pour une France* (Albin Michel, 1984–94). On Pompidou there is a biography by Eric Roussel, *Georges Pompidou* (J.-C. Lattès, 1984), and there have been several colloquia devoted to him: Gilles Le Béguec and Frédéric Turpin, *Georges Pompidou et les institutions de la Ve République* (Peter Lang, Brussels/Oxford, 2016) and Jean-Paul Cointet (ed.), *Un politique, Georges Pompidou* (PUF, 2001).

De Gaulle's relationship with Malraux has spawned a considerable literature of variable quality. There is an excellent debunking biography by Olivier Todd, *André Malraux. Une vie* (Gallimard, 2001). Janine Mossuz, *André Malraux et la*

Gaullisme (Armand Colin, 1970) is a study of Malraux and Gaullism, and Alexandre Duval-Stalla, *André Malraux – Charles de Gaulle, une histoire, deux légendes. Biographie croisée* (Gallimard, 2008) covers the relationship between the two men in not too starry-eyed a fashion.

The regime's use of propaganda, especially television, has spawned a considerable literature. The best studies are Jérôme Bourdon, *Histoire de la télévision sous de Gaulle* (Anthropos/INA, 1990), Aude Vassallo, *La télévision sous de Gaulle. Le contrôle gouvernementale de l'information (1958/1969)* (De Boeck, Brussels, 2005) and Riccardo Brizzi, *De Gaulle et les médias. L'homme du petit écran* (Presses Universitaires de Rennes, 2014).

On the political opposition to de Gaulle see Olivier Duhamel, *La gauche et la Ve République* (PUF, 1980) and Marc Lazar and Stéphane Courtois (eds.), *Cinquante ans d'une passion française. De Gaulle et les communistes* (Balland, 1991) which covers the relationship between de Gaulle and the Communists over the entire period since 1940.

One of the most illuminating ways to study de Gaulle in the Fifth Republic is through the writings of three personalities who were fascinated by him in different ways. First, Raymond Aron, *Mémoires* (Julliard, 1984) is almost as much about de Gaulle as about Aron and should be complemented by the three-volume collection of Aron's articles in *Le Figaro: Les articles de la politique internationale du Figaro de 1947 à 1977* (Fallois, 1990–97) with a useful commentary by Georges-Henri Soutou. Secondly, the five volumes of François Mauriac's *Bloc-notes* (Seuil, 1993), reissued with useful notes by Jean Touzot and an introduction by Jean Lacouture, provide a kind of running commentary on de Gaulle by the most celebrated writer-journalist of the period. Thirdly, Hubert Beuve-Méry, *Onze ans de règne 1958–1969* (Flammarion, 1974) is a collection of many of the editorials by the editor of *Le Monde*.

Foreign Policy

On this vast subject the standard work is Maurice Vaïsse, *La grandeur. Politique étrangère du général de Gaulle* (CRNS Editions, 2013) who was the first person to have access to the archives of the Quai. Since then, as editor of the *Documents Diplomatiques Français* (two volumes for each year), he has overseen the publication of the most important documents that he was the first historian to consult. These are a crucial source for the study of Gaullist foreign policy. For a much less favourable view of de Gaulle's foreign policy see Georges-Henri Soutou, *L'alliance incertaine. Les rapports politico-stratégiques franco-allemands 1954–1996* (Fayard, 1996). The memoirs of his father, the diplomat Jean-Marie Soutou, *Un diplomate engagé. Mémoires 1930–1979* (Fallois, 2011) offer a critical but perceptive viewpoint on de Gaulle's foreign policy. Philip G. Cerny, *The Politics of Grandeur: Ideological Aspects of de Gaulle's Foreign Policy* (Cambridge University Press, 1980) is now a bit dated but offers a stimulating interpretation. See also Christian Nuenlist, Anna Locher and Garret Martin (eds.), *Globalizing de Gaulle: International Perspectives on French Foreign Policies 1958–1969* (Lexington Books, Plymouth, 2010) and Jeffrey Glen Giauque, *Grand Designs and*

Visions of Unity: The Atlantic Powers and the Reorganization of Western Europe 1955–1963 (University of North Carolina Press, 2002).

De Gaulle's relations with the US have inevitably attracted a lot of attention. See Frédéric Bozo, *Deux stratégies pour l'Europe. De Gaulle, les Etats-Unis et l'Alliance Atlantique 1958–1969* (Plon, 1996), James Ellison, *The United States, Britain and the Transatlantic Crisis: Rising to the Gaullist Challenge* (Palgrave, 2007), Erin Mahan, *Kennedy, de Gaulle and Western Europe* (Palgrave, Basingstoke, 2002), Garret Joseph Martin, *General de Gaulle's Cold War: Challenging American Hegemony 1963–1968* (Berghahn, 2013) and Sebastien Reyn, 'Atlantis Lost: The American Experience with De Gaulle 1958–1969' (unpublished doctoral thesis, Leyden University, 2007, published under the same title by the University of Chicago Press, 2010).

On the Soviet Union (and not just for the Fifth Republic period) see Maurice Vaïsse (ed.), *De Gaulle et la Russie* (CNRS, 2006).

For de Gaulle and Britain see Peter Mangold, *The Almost Impossible Ally: Harold Macmillan and Charles de Gaulle* (I. B. Tauris, 1996) which also covers the wartime relationship of the two men. Piers Ludlow, *Dealing with Britain: The Six and the First UK Application to the EEC* (Cambridge University Press, 1997) is the definitive account of the first British attempt to join the Common Market.

For other specific aspects of de Gaulle's foreign policy see Pierre Journoud, *De Gaulle et le Vietnam 1945–1969. La réconciliation* (Tallandier, 2011), Maurice Vaïsse (ed.), *De Gaulle et l'Amérique latine* (Presses Universitaires de Rennes, 2014) and Samy Cohen, *De Gaulle, les gaullistes et Israël* (Alain Moreau, 1974).

Algeria

The most up-to-date collection of essays is Maurice Vaïsse, *De Gaulle et l'Algérie 1943–1969* (Armand Colin, 2006) and the most recent synthesis Benjamin Stora, *De Gaulle et l'Algérie* (Fayard, 2010). Matthew Connelly, *A Diplomatic Revolution: Algeria's Fight for Independence and the Origins of the Post-Cold War Era* (Oxford University Press, 2002) is a salutary reminder of the international context. Irwin Wall argues along the same lines in *France, the United States and the Algerian War* (University of California Press, 2001) but pushes his case too far. Other useful books covering de Gaulle and Algeria are Maurice Vaïsse, *Vers la paix en Algérie. Les négociations d'Evian dans les archives diplomatiques françaises. 15 janvier 1961–29 juin 1962* (Bruylant, Brussels, 2003), Chantal Morelle, *Comment de Gaulle et la FLN ont mis fin à la guerre d'Algérie* (André Versaille, 2012) and Maurice Vaïsse, *Comment de Gaulle fit échouer le putsch d'Alger* (André Versaille, 2011). Grey Anderson, 'The Civil War in France, 1958–1962' (unpublished PhD thesis, Yale University, 2016) is an excellent study of the army. For Debré's position see Association des Amis de Michel Debré, *Michel Debré et l'Algérie* (Champs Elysées, 2007).

Alain Dewerpe, *Charonne, 8 février 1962. Anthropologie historique d'un massacre d'état* (Gallimard, 2006) is a remarkable anthropological study of the Charonne massacre by the son of one of those who was killed.

Empire

On Foccart there are two excellent studies: Frédéric Turpin, *Jacques Foccart. Dans l'ombre du pouvoir* (CRNS, 2015) and Jean-Pierre Bat, *Le Syndrome Foccart. La politique française en Afrique de 1959 à nos jours* (Gallimard, 2012). See also Frédéric Turpin, *De Gaulle, Pompidou et Afrique (1958–1974). Coloniser et coopérer* (Indes Savantes, 2010), Pierre-Michel Durand, *L'Afrique et les relations franco-américaines des années soixante. Aux origines de l'obsession américaine* (L'Harmattan, 2007) and Philippe Oulmont and Maurice Vaïsse (eds.), *De Gaulle et la décolonisation de l'Afrique subsaharienne* (Karthala, 2014).

1968 and After

There is no study of de Gaulle in 1968, which is partly explained by the fact that he was in some sense entirely marginal to the events. Bernard Lachaise and Sabina Tricaud (eds.), *Georges Pompidou et Mai 1968* (Peter Lang, Brussels, 2009) covers Pompidou's handling of the crisis. Ludivine Bantigny, *1968. De grands soirs en petits matins* (Seuil, 2018) has quite a bit on the way that the regime and its police dealt with the crisis.

On de Gaulle after his 1969 resignation see François Flohic, *Souvenirs d'outre de Gaulle* (Plon, 1979), Pierre-Louis Blanc, *De Gaulle au soir de sa vie* (Fayard, 1990) and Jean Mauriac, *Mort du Général de Gaulle* (Grasset, 1972).

Memory and Legacy

The Ur text of Gaullist mythology is André Malraux, *Les chênes qu'on abat* (Gallimard, 1971). Sudhir Hazareesingh, *Le mythe gaullien* (Gallimard, 2010) is a superb study of the progressive creation of the Gaullist myth. Maurice Agulhon, *De Gaulle. Histoire, symbole, mythe* (Plon, 2000), is brilliant even if one is not quite sure reading it whether it is deconstructing the myth or buying into it. Philippe Oulmont (ed.), *Les 18 juin: combats et commémorations* (André Versaille, 2011) covers the way that 18 June was celebrated from its origins until the present day. Patrice Gueniffey, *Napoléon et de Gaulle. Deux héros français* (Perrin, 2017) has reflections on the two myths by the leading historian of Napoleon. To see what happened to Gaullism after 1970 – which has less and less to do with de Gaulle himself – see Andrew Knapp, *Gaullism since de Gaulle* (Aldershot, 1994) and Jean Mauriac, *L'après de Gaulle. Notes confidentielles 1969–1989* (Fayard, 2006).

Biographies

An asterisk indicates that they were one of the 1,061 Companions of the Order of the Liberation and is followed by the date that the honour was awarded.

Adenauer, Konrad (1876–1967). First Chancellor of West Germany from 1949. Played key role in reinserting West Germany into the community of nations through close relations with Fourth Republic politicians. Initially suspicious of de Gaulle in May 1958, but rapidly forged close personal bond with him after being invited to spend a night at Colombey in September 1958 – the only foreign leader accorded this privilege. The two men met fifteen times and exchanged forty letters. The relationship culminated in the signing of the Franco-German Treaty (January 1963) shortly before Adenauer's retirement. With no other foreign leader did de Gaulle develop a greater bond, and the relationship gave a symbolic force to Franco-German reconciliation that it not had before.

Alphand, Hervé (1907–94). Son of an ambassador. Financial Counsellor of French Embassy in Washington 1940–41. Arrived London September 1941, was put in charge of economic affairs for the French National Committee and then the CGLN. Pursued important diplomatic career after 1945 representing France at NATO's Permanent Council 1952–4. French Ambassador in USA on de Gaulle's return to power and kept in this post until 1965 at a difficult moment in Franco-American relations. Head of the Quai d'Orsay 1965–72. Cultivated and sophisticated figure whose lavish receptions helped blunt the asperities of the politics he was applying. Managed the feat of admiring de Gaulle and Monnet in equal measure.

Antoine, Jules Aristide (1891–1969). *Polytechnicien* who became business administrator. Rallied to de Gaulle 20 June 1940 and was appointed to head his *cabinet*. During de Gaulle's absence in Africa between September and December 1940 was one of the three figures delegated to run the FL. But his lack of tact, right-wing opinions and authoritarian style made him increasingly unpopular. Quickly sidelined from playing any significant role in the Free French.

Argenlieu, Georges Thierry d' (1889–1964) (*29/1/41). Born in Brest to naval family. Fought in navy during the First War. In 1920 entered Order of Carmelite Friars. Mobilized in 1938, taken prisoner and escaped to join de Gaulle in London in June 1940. Badly wounded during Dakar expedition. Named High Commissioner for the Pacific with the mission to protect French sovereignty in the region from American encroachments. One of the group accompanying de Gaulle to

Anfa January 1943, to Bayeux 14 June 1944 and to Paris 25 August 1944. Appointed by de Gaulle High Commissioner in Indo-China to restore French sovereignty. His high-handedness towards the nationalists helped scupper any chance of a deal. De Gaulle urged him not to resign and he was eventually sacked in March 1947. Devoted himself to his duties as Grand Chancellor of the Order of Liberation until ill health pushed him to return to his monastery in 1958. A Gaullist of the *première heure* who was often more Gaullist than de Gaulle.

Aron, Raymond (1905–83). Fellow student (and once close friend) of Jean-Paul Sartre at the ENS where Aron was top of his year in the *agrégation* of philosophy. In London during the war was the main contributor to the review *La France libre*. While not as anti-Gaullist as some contributors, wrote article in August 1943 on the 'Shadow of Bonaparte'. After the war combined brilliant university career with prolific journalism defending unfashionable liberal and Atlanticist ideas. Joined the RPF out of anti-Communism. In 1953 published *Opium of the Intellectuals* attacking sympathy of French intellectuals for Communism. Although France's leading liberal conservative commentator, advocated Algerian independence from 1956 at a time when even most on the left did not do so. Supported de Gaulle's return to power 1958 but became increasingly critical of his anti-Americanism. Wrote ferocious attack on the 1968 protesters. Later remarked wryly that he had been anti-Gaullist when he should have been Gaullist and Gaullist when he should have been anti-Gaullist.

Astier de la Vigerie, Emmanuel d' (1900–69) (*23/3/43). One of eight children of old aristocratic family. After starting career in the navy became in 1930s a littérateur, journalist and consumer of opium. The shock of defeat transformed him from a dilettante into a leader almost overnight. Founder of Libération-Sud, one of the most important resistance movements of the southern zone. The first Resistance leader from that zone to get to London (May 1942) where he was received by de Gaulle (whom he always referred to with respectful irreverence as 'the Symbol'). Two more visits to London followed. Appointed Commissioner of Interior in the CFLN November 1943. At a meeting with Churchill at Marrakesh in January 1944 persuaded him to arm the Resistance. Pursued post-war political career as Communist fellow-traveller until early 1960s. Supported de Gaulle in Presidential election of 1965. Became celebrated TV journalist. One of those flamboyant figures for whom de Gaulle had a certain indulgence and with whom he perhaps also felt a certain social affinity.

Auriol, Vincent (1884–1966). Inter-war Socialist politician close to Léon Blum whose Minister of Finance he was in 1936. After period in hiding arrived in London autumn 1943. As President of the Republic (1946–53) became suspicious of de Gaulle and worked behind the scenes to keep him out of power. But in 1958 his conviction that only de Gaulle stood between the Republic and a military coup played important role in persuading the Socialist Party to rally to him. Quickly moved into opposition to de Gaulle again and as an *ex officio* member of the Constitutional Council caused a minor stir by refusing to take his vote of office – but he no longer counted.

Bainville, Jacques (1879–1936). Brilliant journalist and best-selling royalist historian of the Action Française school. Famously described the Treaty of Versailles as 'too

harsh in its mild features, too mild in its harsh aspects'. Shared Maurras's opposition to romanticism, liberalism, democracy, internationalism and the French
Revolution, and his suspicion of Germany but seems to have been exempt from
his anti-Semitism. To the extent de Gaulle had some affinities with Action Française it was more as a Banvillian than a Maurrassian.

Barrès, Maurice (1862–1923). French novelist whose writing seduced generations
of French readers, including de Gaulle, from the 1880s. A major intellectual
inspiration of *fin de siècle* French nationalism and a convinced anti-Dreyfusard.
His syncretic and inclusive vision of French history resonated more profoundly
with de Gaulle than the narrower monarchist nationalism of Maurras. It was
fitting that the first propaganda biography of de Gaulle (published in Montreal
in 1941) was by Barrès's journalist son, Philippe.

Beuve-Méry, Hubert (1902–89). Leftist Catholic who was in the 1930s Prague correspondent of the respected newspaper *Le Temps*. Resigned after Munich. In 1945
became editor of the newly founded *Le Monde* (*Le Temps* having blotted its
copybook during the Occupation). While no Gaullist, he supported a neutralist
foreign policy position in the 1950s not so far from de Gaulle's views. Gave a
'conditional and provisional yes' to de Gaulle's return to power in 1958 and
supported him with decreasing enthusiasm until Algerian independence. Then
became implacable opponent of de Gaulle's domestic and international policies.
Austerely incorruptible figure, whose regular editorials responding to de Gaulle's
TV interventions and press conference were almost as eagerly awaited as de
Gaulle's own performances. He retired from running *Le Monde* after de Gaulle's
resignation – as if he had lost his necessary alter ego.

Bidault, Georges (1899–1983) (*27/8/44). Top in the history *agrégation* of 1925.
Taught history before becoming a left Catholic and anti-appeasement journalist
in 1930s. One of the Resistance leaders to cooperate most closely with Jean
Moulin and chosen by the Resistance movements to succeed him as President of
the CNR. Surprisingly appointed Foreign Minister in de Gaulle's government
1944–6. As leading member of the MRP was in most Third Force governments
from 1947 to 1953 usually as Foreign Minister where he played key role in
French–German reconciliation. His increasingly hardline commitment to the
French Empire marginalized him in his party and he did not hold office after
1953. Was one of the earliest politicians to rally to de Gaulle in 1958 believing
he would save *Algérie française*. After de Gaulle's September 1959 speech offering
self-determination to Algeria broke with him and became a vociferous opponent.
In March 1962 went into exile as head of a new farcical National Council of the
Resistance (CNR) – this time resisting the 'abandonment' of Algeria. Amnestied
along with other *Algérie française* ultras in May 1968 he returned to France.

Billotte, Pierre (1906–92) (*8/11/44). Son of a general killed in the Battle of France.
One of the 185 escaped prisoners of war who arrived in London in September
1941. Joined de Gaulle's military *cabinet* and became its head from May 1942.
Among the most anti-American of his advisers. Fought with Leclerc's 2nd
Armoured Division in Normandy in 1944. In 1946–50 headed the French military
delegation at the United Nations but resigned to join RPF in 1950 because he

opposed the government's Atlanticism. Elected RPF deputy 1952 but was one of those rebels who supported Pinay 1952. Although he was forgiven for this 'treachery' by de Gaulle after 1958, and was elected as a UDT-UNR deputy in 1962, he never held a significant ministerial post.

Bingen, Jacques (1908–44) (*31/3/44). Civil engineer from comfortable Jewish family (he was the brother-in-law of André Citroën). Arrived in London July 1940. Despite initial reservations about de Gaulle, worked for the merchant navy of the Free French. Eager to take more active role joined the BCRAM. Sent to France to offer support to Moulin in August 1943 and instead found himself having to act as de Gaulle's interim delegate in Moulin's place. Arrested May 1944 and swallowed cyanide to avoid speaking under torture. His remains were never found.

Bogomolov, Alexander (1900–68). Soviet diplomat. Official representative of Soviet government to Free French and then CFLN. Had none of the charm of the Soviet Ambassador to London, Maisky.

Boissieu, Alain de (1914–2006) (*18/1/46). Career soldier and tank expert in 1930s. One of the 185 escaped prisoners of war arriving in London in September 1941. With Free French forces in Tunisia, Normandy and Alsace. Married de Gaulle's daughter Elisabeth January 1946 and became part of de Gaulle's inner circle. Appointed brigadier general 1962. Was in the Citroën DS with de Gaulle during the OAS attack at Petit Clamart in August 1962. As military commander of French troops in Mulhouse was summoned by de Gaulle to see him on morning of 29 May 1968. Appointed Chancellor of the Legion of Honour 1975 but resigned in 1981 so as not to have to bestow the Grand Cross on the newly elected President François Mitterrand.

Bonneval, Gaston de (1911–98). Career soldier from impoverished aristocratic family with deep Catholic convictions. Deported to Mauthausen for Resistance activities. More dead than alive, appointed as an aide de camp to de Gaulle in October 1945 – and continued the role for twenty years. In May 1958, played an intermediary role between the Elysée and de Gaulle. Always a discreetly constant presence at de Gaulle's side until retiring in 1965. According to one (possibly apocryphal) story, at a reception at the Elysée Bonneval, at de Gaulle's side to brief him about the guests, whispered to him, when the filmmaker Jacques Tati appeared, that Tati's latest film was *Mon Oncle*. The General thanked Tati for his contributions to French culture, adding his pleasure at having met de Bonneval's uncle. Almost unique among de Gaulle's collaborators in not publishing his memoirs.

Boris, Georges (1888–1960). Left-wing journalist and economist in 1930s. Advised his friend Léon Blum on economics. Finding himself in London on 18 June 1940 was among the first to rally to de Gaulle. Initially kept a low profile because of his Jewishness and left-wing opinions. From 1942 became increasingly important as an organizer of Free French propaganda. Helped rally Blum to de Gaulle. At the Liberation tried unsuccessfully to nudge de Gaulle's economic ideas in a more socialist direction. Became key adviser to Pierre Mendès France in the 1950s. Although he opposed de Gaulle's return to power in 1958, never lost his admiration for the de Gaulle of 1940.

Bouchinet-Serreulles, Claude (1912–2000) (*30/3/44). Son of an industrialist, arriving in London in July 1940, Bouchinet (Serreulles in the Resistance) was introduced to de Gaulle by his school friend de Courcel. Served as ordonnance officer and general factotum from July 1940 to the end of 1942. Sent to France in June 1943 to support a beleaguered Moulin, he ended acting (with Bingen) as an interim replacement and worked effectively to maintain the CFLN's authority over a Resistance that was seeking to claw back its autonomy. Called back to London in March 1944 after he was blamed unfairly by rivals in the BCRA for a security lapse. After 1945 pursued a diplomatic career and then a business one. Although no longer involved in Gaullism, he was a discreet 'left' Gaullist for the rest of his life.

Brosset, Diego (1898–1944). (*20/11/44). Career soldier who telegraphed his support to de Gaulle from South America on hearing his broadcast of 26 June 1940. Arrived in London in January 1941. After six months on de Gaulle's General Staff was stationed in Syria with Free French troops in Syria. Commanded the 2nd Free French Division (DFL) in Tunisia in 1943. Joined the French Expeditionary Force in Italy in April 1944, and in August 1944 headed the 1st Free French Division (DFL) in Operation Anvil (the landings in southern France). Died in a jeep accident on 20 November 1944. One of the military heroes of the Free French whose recently published journal shows that he was as lucid about de Gaulle's faults as he was admiring of his virtues.

Brossolette, Pierre (1903–44) (*17/10/42). Agrégé d'histoire and graduate of Ecole Normale Supérieure. Socialist activist and journalist in 1930s. Opposed Munich Agreement. Involved with various Resistance organizations in the Occupied Zone from March 1941. In London April–May 1942. Argued in favour of bringing political figures from across the spectrum to London to increase de Gaulle's legitimacy. On mission to France June–September 1942 organized the arrival in London of the Socialist Philip and the rightist Charles Vallin. An article in September 1942 arguing for politicians of all political belief to sink their differences behind de Gaulle was viewed by some Socialists as a plea for fascism and has been seen by some others as offering a political vision of a future Gaullist Party. It was probably neither. Became one of the most powerful figures in the BCRA. On a mission to France with Passy in March 1943 to coordinate the Resistance movement in the northern zone clashed with Moulin. On another mission to France in February–March 1944 was arrested and committed suicide rather than reveal secrets under torture. One of the most forceful and controversial personalities of the Free French who did not suffer fools gladly.

Burin des Roziers, Etienne (1913–2012). From noble Auvergnat family. Entered public service in 1930s. An official at France's Washington Embassy, rallied to the Free French in April 1942. Became ordonnance officer to de Gaulle in 1943 and then adviser to him on foreign affairs. Pursued diplomatic career after 1946. Ambassador in Prague when de Gaulle returned to power, was appointed Secretary General of the Elysée 1962–7. Ambassador to Rome in 1967. Although not one of the original group around de Gaulle, nor ever in the RPF, his discretion, efficiency, loyalty and commitment to public service made him one of the people most trusted by de Gaulle.

Capitant, René (1901–70). Followed in his father's footsteps to become an eminent academic jurist. Involved in the Resistance movement Combat in 1941 whose leader Frenay was a former pupil. Seconded to the University of Algiers in 1941 he organized there a small Combat cell, almost the only Resistance presence in North Africa. After the American landings worked to bring Pétainist Algerian public opinion over to de Gaulle. Put in charge of education in CFLN. Influenced de Gaulle's developing constitutional ideas in 1945–6. Strong proponent of referendum and direct democracy. Elected to parliament in 1946 where he tried to organize a 'Union Gaulliste'. In the RPF was one of the so-called left Gaullists supporting the policy of 'association'. On de Gaulle's return to power was teaching in Tokyo. Returning to France in 1960 became one of the leading left Gaullists opposed to Pompidou. Elected to parliament in 1962. In May 1968 resigned his seat to avoid having to vote confidence in Pompidou government. After the events of May he was brought into the government by de Gaulle to give a left gloss to his government. De Gaulle good-humouredly indulged him while rarely listening to him.

Cassin, René (1880–1976) (*1/8/41). Respected jurist badly wounded in the First War. Delegate to the League of Nations and President of an important left-leaning organization of war veterans. Got on a boat from Saint-Jean-de-Luz to Plymouth on 24 June making him one of the earliest to rally to de Gaulle. Negotiated the technical details of the Agreement between de Gaulle and the British on 7 August 1940. Always trying to push de Gaulle in a more democratic and republican direction. Member of the Empire Defence Committee and then of the Conseil National. Played important role on the CFLN preparing the re-establishment of republican legality in France after Liberation. Helped draft the UN Declaration of Universal Rights in 1948. Despite some qualms, supported de Gaulle's return to power in 1958 but as a Jew opposed de Gaulle's stance on Israel in 1967. Awarded the Nobel Peace Prize in 1968; buried in Panthéon in 1987.

Catroux, Georges (1877–1969) (*23/6/41). Born in Limoges to a military family of republican convictions. Pursued a military career mainly in the colonies. Sacked by Vichy from his position as Governor General of Indo-China; arrived in London September 1940. As the most senior officer to join de Gaulle (five stars to de Gaulle's two) his decision to accept de Gaulle's authority was symbolically important. In 1941–2 was de Gaulle's main representative in the Middle East. In 1943 helped broker the deal between Giraud and de Gaulle. Joined RPF but resigned in 1952 because he found its views on the Empire too conservative. Sociable, worldly and charming, he was a key figure of the Free French. De Gaulle deplored his propensity to compromise while Catroux deplored de Gaulle's propensity to pick fights. The tensions were stoked by Catroux's ambitious wife.

Chaban-Delmas, Jacques (1915–2000) (*7/8/45). Graduate of Ecole des Sciences Politiques. Failing to get to London after defeat, made contact in December 1940 with Resistance network in northern France and with the BCRAM. Entered French administration to gather information for the Resistance. As the CFLN's Military Delegate in Paris (pseudonym Chaban) in the summer of 1944, played a key role in mediating between the impatience of the Resistance in Paris and the

caution of London and Algiers. Joined RPF and elected Mayor of Bordeaux in
October 1947. Served in several Fourth Republic governments. As Defence Minister in the Gaillard government worked behind the scenes on de Gaulle's
behalf. With de Gaulle back in power in 1958, got himself elected President of
the lower chamber against the General's own candidate but loyally served de
Gaulle's interests in parliament for ten years. Appointed Prime Minister by Pompidou in 1969 but his liberal views caused him to be replaced in 1972. His 1974
candidature as Gaullist candidate in Presidential election after the death of
Georges Pompidou failed disastrously. This handsome golden boy of Gaullism –
Alain Delon played him in the film *Is Paris Burning?* – who was also a tennis
player at international level, never overcame suspicions that he lacked political
weight.

Challe, Maurice (1905–79). Graduate of Saint-Cyr who joined air force in 1925.
Rallied to Resistance in November 1942. Appointed by de Gaulle to replace Salan
as army commander in Algeria in December 1958. After Barricades Week, where
de Gaulle felt he had been insufficiently firm, was kicked upstairs as commander
of NATO forces in Central Europe. Increasingly unhappy about de Gaulle's
Algerian policy and his anti-Atlanticism, he took early retirement in January
1961. Allowed himself to become reluctant leader of the April 1961 putsch against
de Gaulle. Gave himself up and was sentenced to fifteen years' imprisonment May
1961. Freed in December 1966; amnestied 1968.

Chauvel, Jean (1897–1979). Career diplomat who rallied to de Gaulle in Algiers in
March 1944. Appointed Secretary General (head) of the Quai d'Orsay in 1946.
When de Gaulle returned to power in 1958 he was Ambassador in London where
he remained until 1962. Although his career was hardly affected by his late rallying to de Gaulle, he felt unappreciated by him, and deplored his (un)diplomatic
style and his hostility to the British. A professional diplomat who served de Gaulle
while mistrusting him, he took revenge in his memoirs.

Cooper, Alfred Duff (1890–1954). British diplomat turned politician who resigned
from the Chamberlain government in protest against Munich. As Minister of
Information he was one of de Gaulle's supporters at Westminster. Sent by Churchill in December 1943 to represent the British government to the CFLN where,
in de Gaulle's words, 'placed between Churchill and myself he took on the task
of absorbing the shocks'. His success in this frustrating task led him to be
appointed Ambassador to France in 1945. Was a Francophile who had published a biography of Talleyrand, and de Gaulle respected and appreciated his
charm and culture as much as he could ever fully respect and appreciate the
qualities of any Englishman.

Cot, Pierre (1895–1972). Left-wing member of the Radical Party in inter-war years.
Controversial Minister of Aviation in Popular Front governments where his
nationalization of aircraft industries alienated the right. For this reason de Gaulle
refused his services in 1940 and sent him to support the Free French in the United
States. Became increasingly suspicious of what he considered de Gaulle's fascist
tendencies. Member of parliament throughout Fourth Republic as a Communist
fellow-traveller. Lost his seat in 1958 on de Gaulle's return to power. On a visit

to Moscow 1961 declared that France was under 'semi-military dictatorship'. The epitome of a left-wing tradition viewing de Gaulle as a fascist despite all evidence.

Coty, René (1882–1962). Lawyer and moderate centre-right politician. Elected to parliament for Le Havre 1923. Despite voting for Pétain in 1940, refused any involvement in Vichy regime. After thirteen rounds of voting, elected President of Fourth Republic 1953. Worried by the instability of the Fourth Republic was already hoping to effect de Gaulle's legal return to power before 1958. His message to parliament on 29 May 1958 was the key that unlocked the crisis and made de Gaulle's legal return possible. Continued to act formally as President with de Gaulle as his premier until the inauguration of the new Republic in January 1959. Did not support de Gaulle's constitutional reform of 1962 but died a few weeks after it had been approved.

Coulet, François (1906–84). Protestant from Montpellier who entered the diplomatic service in 1936. Posted to the Middle East, he rallied immediately to de Gaulle and joined his *cabinet* in 1941. Entrusted by de Gaulle with many key missions: sent to Corsica September 1943 to assert the authority of the CFLN in Corsica in September; accompanied de Gaulle to Bayeux on 16 June 1944 and was left behind as acting *Commissaire de la République*. Pursued diplomatic career after 1945 (Ambassador in Tehran and Belgrade). In 1960 sent by de Gaulle to shadow Paul Delouvrier in whom de Gaulle had started to lose confidence after Barricades Week. Described himself with pride as a 'fanatical' Gaullist.

Courcel, Geoffroy Chodron de (1912–92) (*18/7/43). Son of an officer and grandson of a diplomat. Joined diplomatic service. Educated at elite Lycée Stanislas. In 1937–8 attached to French Embassy in Warsaw. Appointed to de Gaulle's *cabinet* on 7 June 1940, was the only person to accompany the General to London ten days later. Close aide to de Gaulle in London until going to fight with Free French forces in North Africa in December 1941. From July 1943 *directeur adjoint* of de Gaulle's *cabinet* in Algiers. Returned to diplomatic service after 1945 and did not join RPF. In 1959–62, served as first Secretary General of the Elysée under de Gaulle. In 1962–72 served as French Ambassador in London. In some sense the first 'Gaullist' but always a discreet one: as affable as he was unflappable.

Couve de Murville, Maurice (1909–99). Despite the 'de Murville' added in the 1920s, hailed from a middle-class Protestant family. Proceeded effortlessly through France's elite educational institutions, graduating first in his class at the Inspection des Finances in 1930. In 1940–42 was senior official at the Finance Ministry under Vichy. Defected to Algiers after the American landings in North Africa. Initially intended to serve Giraud but soon rallied to de Gaulle becoming Finance Commissioner of the CFLN. Embarked on diplomatic career after 1945 (Ambassador in Cairo, Washington, Bonn). Plucked from the Bonn Embassy by de Gaulle in 1958 and made Foreign Minister, a post he held ten years, making him the longest-serving Foreign Minister since the eighteenth century. In June 1968 was appointed Prime Minister to replace Pompidou. After de Gaulle's resignation in April 1969 never held ministerial office again. Esteemed by de Gaulle for his loyalty, steely intelligence, mastery of technical detail and forensic negotiating skills. He rarely dropped his Protestant mask to reveal his intimate view of de

Gaulle's more extravagant initiatives. His unrevealing memoirs kept the mask intact.

Darlan, François (1881–1942). Head of French navy in 1940. Accepted armistice once he was sure the fleet would not be handed to Germany. Became ever more Anglophobe after the British attack at Mers-el-Kébir. While never previously associated with right-wing politics became pragmatically convinced of the need for collaboration. Acted as Pétain's deputy February 1941–April 1942. Met Hitler at Berchtesgaden on 11 May 1941 to push collaboration to a new level. Present in Algiers in November 1942, switched sides, signed an armistice with the Americans and was installed by them as the French leader in North Africa. Assassinated on 24 December 1942. Since his assassination served everyone's purposes it is impossible to know who was behind it. An opportunist, less clever than he imagined, who saw the world entirely through the distorting lenses of the French Navy.

Debré, Michel (1912–97). From a distinguished liberal conservative Jewish family (though Michel converted to Catholicism). After studying at Sciences Politiques entered Conseil d'Etat in 1934. Joined the Cabinet of Paul Reynaud in 1938. His experience of the weakness of the Third Republic made him a passionate advocate of state reform. In the Resistance played key role in selecting the personnel who would take over on behalf of the CFLN at the Liberation. Drafted into de Gaulle's *cabinet* in April 1945, he was the creator of the Ecole Nationale d'Administration to train France's future civil servants. Joined the RPF where his violent hostility to European supranationalism and opposition to the Fourth Republic drew him into de Gaulle's inner circle. After de Gaulle's return to power, played key role in drafting of new constitution. From January 1958 to March 1962 served as de Gaulle's first Prime Minister despite being forced to apply an Algerian policy of which he disapproved. After a period out of office returned to power as Minister of Finance in 1966 and was Foreign Minister in 1968–9. Following the failure of the Gaullist candidacy of Chaban-Delmas in 1974 assumed the mantle of a Gaullist Cassandra. As with Cassandra no one listened and at the Presidential election of 1981 he scored only 1.6 per cent of the vote. A great public servant who existed in a state of perpetual indignation which even the perpetually indignant de Gaulle found wearing while ruthlessly exploiting his loyalty.

Dejean, Maurice (1899–1982). Served in press service of France's Berlin Embassy in the 1930s. One of the first diplomats to join de Gaulle in London where he arrived in January 1941. Slightly suspicious of de Gaulle's politics but avoided involvement in the Muselier plot against him. Appointed Commissioner for Foreign Affairs September 1941 but sacked September 1942 for not supporting de Gaulle's anti-British line on Syria. Despite being briefly tempted by Giraudism rejoined de Gaulle's entourage in Algiers where he was in the pro-Soviet camp. Pursued diplomatic career after 1945 and was Ambassador in Moscow on de Gaulle's return to power. Remained in this post until falling victim to a KGB honey trap. On his recall to Paris in January 1964, de Gaulle allegedly greeted him with the words 'Alors, Dejean, on couche?' (So, Dejean, one gets laid?').

de Lattre de Tassigny, Jean (1889–1952) (*20/11/44). A year ahead of de Gaulle (and Juin) at Saint-Cyr. Accepted the armistice but, after trying to resist the German crossing of the demarcation line on 11 November 1942, was imprisoned by the Vichy regime. Escaped and arrived in Algiers to put himself at the service of de Gaulle. Commanded First French Army landings in Provence August 1944 and then the campaign into Germany 1945. Much resented by those officers like Larminat and Koenig who had joined de Gaulle at the start. Sent by de Gaulle to receive German capitulation in Berlin 8 May 1945. Flamboyant and vain – he was nicknamed 'le Roi Jean' – he was bitter not to be appointed by de Gaulle as commander of the occupying troops in Germany. Pursued military career after 1945 culminating in his appointment to lead the French army in Indo-China where he had considerable success. Deeply affected by the death of his officer son in Indo-China in May 1951 he soon afterwards died of cancer. De Gaulle wrote to their common contemporary Juin in 1952: 'De Lattre is dying. As a Frenchman, as a soldier, that causes me great sadness. We both knew well his defects. But overall his action weighed heavily in France's favour.' Promoted marshal on the day of his funeral.

Delbecque, Léon (1919–91). Born into working-class family in Tourcoing. Started working in textile factory aged fifteen. During the Occupation carried out sabotage and intelligence missions for the SOE's Buckmaster network. Became an RPF regional organizer in the Nord. Sent in 1957 by the Gaullist Minister of Defence, Chaban-Delmas, on an unofficial mission to organize opinion on de Gaulle's behalf. During the crisis of May 1958 helped to channel the street rising towards de Gaulle. Elected as UNR *député* to parliament 1958. An ardent supporter of French Algeria, quickly became disillusioned by de Gaulle's Algerian policies. Defected from the UNR and lost his seat at the elections of 1962. Testified for the defence at Salan's trial in 1962. Abandoned politics to pursue business career but remained close to Jacques Soustelle and later founded a newspaper defending apartheid.

Delestraint, Charles (1879–1945) (*17/11/45). Career soldier who specialized in tank warfare. Appointed brigadier general 1936. As commander of the 3rd Tank Brigade was de Gaulle's superior at Metz 1937–9. Shared his ideas on tanks and the two men had many conversations on the subject. In retirement after 1940 made contact with Resistance organizations while not playing active role in them. Was chosen by de Gaulle and Moulin to head the Resistance Secret Army in the summer of 1942. In London with Moulin in February 1943. Arrested in Paris on 9 June 1943 twelve days before Moulin. Executed in Dachau on 19 April 1945 ten days before the arrival of American troops.

Delouvrier, Paul (1914–95). A leading light of that generation of civil servant economists driven by a desire to modernize France after the trauma of defeat. Worked closely with Monnet in the development of economic planning after 1946. Despite lacking political experience was surprisingly appointed by de Gaulle as his civil representative in Algiers. Resigned in November 1960 after de Gaulle's speech on the 'Algerian Republic' – not because he disagreed but because he resented the fact that he had not been informed in advance. From 1961 was the government's chief planner for the Paris region and oversaw a programme of massive urban renewal (new satellite towns for hundreds of thousands of people). It was as a modernizer that Delouvrier's path crossed that of de Gaulle even if his real hero was Monnet.

Diethelm, André (1896–1954). Inspector of Finances in the *cabinet* of Georges Mandel in 1940. First met de Gaulle on 13 June 1940 at the meeting where Mandel persuaded de Gaulle not to resign despite his outrage at the growing defeatism of Reynaud's government. Reached London in August 1941 where his outstanding administrative abilities were invaluable on first the French National Committee (Commissioner of the Interior) and then the CFLN (successively Commissioner of Finances and then War) even if his political skills were less evident. Became a leading figure of the RPF and would certainly have played a major role in the Fifth Republic had he not died prematurely. The fact that de Gaulle emerged from the 'desert' in uniform to salute his coffin is a sign of the esteem in which he held him.

Dixon, Pierson (1904–65). British diplomat who was British Ambassador to Paris 1960–64 while also having responsibility for negotiating British entry to the European Community in Brussels in 1961–3 – too heavy a double burden for one man. Fascinated and exasperated by de Gaulle in equal measure. Wrote historical novels in his spare time and a life of Pauline Bonaparte in 1964.

Domenach, Jean-Marie (1922–97). Leading contributor to, and from 1957 editor of, the influential left Catholic journal *Esprit*. One of those left intellectuals torn between nostalgia for the de Gaulle of the Resistance, opposition to the de Gaulle of the Fifth Republic and fascination with his foreign policy at all times. In the end fascination trumped suspicion and he was one the twenty-nine signatories to a manifesto of left-wing personalities supporting de Gaulle's foreign policy in 1966.

Eboué, Félix (1884–1944) (*29/1/41). Of Guyanese origin, was appointed by the Popular Front as Governor of Guadeloupe, the first ever black governor of a French territory. In July 1940, as Governor of Chad, was the only imperial pro-consul announcing his willingness to rally to de Gaulle. Chad rallied on 26 August 1940. Member of Free French Empire Defence Council and played role in preparation of Brazzaville Conference of 1944 which did not go as far as he might have liked. An historic Gaullist among the first to be made a Companion of the Liberation.

Erhard, Ludwig (1897–1977). Adenauer's successor as Chancellor in the Federal Republic of Germany 1963–6. A believer in liberal economics and close ties with the United States, his relations with de Gaulle ranged from lukewarm to execrable.

Foccart, Jacques (1913–97). His father ran a banana business and he had little formal education. Founded his own import–export business before the war. In the Resistance ran a network linked to the BCRA. First met de Gaulle 1944. Played increasingly important role in RPF as organizer of it overseas branches and then as General Secretary from 1954 keeping the flame burning in the 'desert'. One of the key figures of the Gaullist entourage from this period until de Gaulle's death. From 1961 as Secretary General for African Affairs he saw de Gaulle almost every evening. Also in charge of Gaullist electoral affairs for which he created the notorious SAC which was viewed by opponent as a kind of dirty-tricks operation. For this, and because of his reputation as the inventor of the neo-colonialist France-Afrique, he was the target of rumours and press hostility. Continued in his African role under Pompidou; sacked by his successor Giscard; in 1995 President Chirac summoned him out of retirement as a special adviser – but Foccart's methods in Africa were out of date. In his heyday, however, no one was more trusted by de Gaulle and his reputation as a fixer in the shadows was hardly exaggerated.

Frenay, Henri (1903–88) (*24/3/43). Army officer whose Resistance movement Combat was the most important of the southern zone. Reluctantly accepted de Gaulle's symbolic authority over the Resistance from mid-1942 but fought hard for its autonomy. In the end neutralized when de Gaulle brought him into the CFLN in November 1943. Became a passionate European federalist after 1945 which provided further ammunition to his suspicion of de Gaulle. Supported de Gaulle in 1958 but called for a vote against him in 1965 election. Courageous, abrasive and somewhat charmless, he never really hit it off with de Gaulle and perfectly epitomized the suspicions of many Resistance leaders towards him.

Giraud, Henri (1879–1949). Graduated from Saint-Cyr 1900. Promoted general 1930. As Governor of Metz and Commander of the Third Army he first encountered (and disliked) de Gaulle in 1938 where he was his superior. Commander of the Seventh Army in 1940. Taken prisoner 18 May 1940 but escaped April 1942. This made him a patriotic hero who, as a supporter of the conservative policies of the Vichy regime, offered an alternative rallying point to de Gaulle. Installed in power in North Africa by the Americans after the death of Darlan. Reluctantly agreed to share the presidency of the CFLN with de Gaulle from 30 May 1943 but forced off the Committee in November 1943. Remained as titular Commander in Chief of the French Army in North Africa until losing even this post in April 1944. A courageous and reactionary soldier out of his depth as a political leader but was equally unimaginative in his military thinking.

Giscard d'Estaing, Valéry (1926–). Scion of an important liberal conservative family. Graduated from ENA and became Inspecteur des Finances. Entered parliament as member of the centre-right grouping of Pinay. Secretary of State for Finances in Debré government 1959–61 and then Minister of Finance 1962–6, appointed at the exceptionally young age of thirty-six. Supported *Algérie française* until the end. Founded his own parliamentary group, the Independent Republicans, which formed junior part of the 'Presidential majority' while being distinct from the Gaullists. Left the government 1966 and increasingly distanced himself from de Gaulle. On 17 August denounced the 'solitary exercise of power' after de Gaulle's Quebec speech. In 1969 refused to support de Gaulle's referendum. Minister of the Economy again under President Pompidou 1969–74 and then elected President himself in 1974. De Gaulle was for a while seduced by his brilliance and eloquence before becoming suspicious of his ambition.

Gouin, Félix (1884–1977). One of the Socialist MPs who refused to vote full powers to Pétain in 1940. Served as defence counsel to Blum in the Riom trial. Arrived in London in August 1942. Despite harbouring some suspicions of de Gaulle, rejected the anti-Gaullism of other French Socialists in London. Elected President of Consultative Assembly in Algiers where his parliamentary skills proved useful. De Gaulle's successor as head of the provisional government January–June 1946.

Served in several Fourth Republic governments. Unsuccessfully opposed de Gaulle's return to power and left politics in 1958.

Guichard, Olivier (1920–2003). Son of a naval officer and diplomat who worked in the *cabinet* of Admiral Darlan. A student in Paris during the war, joined the Resistance in 1943 and fought in the FFI at the Liberation. Met de Gaulle 1947 and became regional organizer of the RPF in the south-west. Succeeded Pompidou as head of de Gaulle's *cabinet* 1951. During the 'desert' was (with Foccart) the person who saw de Gaulle most regularly and kept him in touch with the political world. Played behind-the-scenes role in crisis of May 1958. Surprisingly not given major political role after de Gaulle became President. In 1963–7 headed quango (DATAR) to oversee regional development, town planning and economic 'modernization'. Returned to more political role after election to parliament in 1967: Minister for Industry 1976–8. Minister in all Pompidou governments and often talked of as a potential prime minister. Became increasingly disillusioned by the later drift of the Gaullist movements. One of the historic 'barons' of postwar Gaullism (the term probably derived from the fact that he was a descendant of a baron of the Empire).

Guy, Claude (1915–92). Born to an American mother. A law student in Paris when war broke out. Taken prisoner 1940. After escaping, made his way to London via the United States. Flew with Free French air force until being badly wounded. Became an aide de camp to de Gaulle in June 1944. Was in close proximity to him in the early years of the RPF but left de Gaulle's service in 1949 after committing an indiscretion and spent most of the rest of his career at the Quai d'Orsay. His devotion to de Gaulle was total and his journal of the period 1944–9 is the most invaluable document we have on life at Colombey in that period.

Harvey, Oliver (1893–1968). British diplomat. Although Spears described him as 'pale, correct, obviously hatched in the Chancery', as Anthony Eden's Private Secretary he was in fact one of de Gaulle's most passionate (if relatively junior) supporters in the Foreign Office during the war. British Ambassador in Paris 1948–54.

Hauck, Henry (1902–67). Teacher of history and Socialist activist before 1940. Working in the French Embassy (his wife was Welsh) in London June 1940, was one of the few Embassy staff to rally to de Gaulle. Worked at Carlton Gardens as an adviser on trade union issues. Despite feeling sometimes trapped as a left-wing hostage in the Free French, kept aloof from the anti-Gaullist Socialists in London. Helped push de Gaulle to the left in 1942. Worked for the ILO after the war.

Isorni, Jacques (1911–95). Called to the bar 1931. Although an admirer of Maurras was not involved in politics before 1946 and even defended Communists and resisters arrested by Vichy. Leapt to fame as the defence counsel of Brasillach in 1945 and then one of the team of lawyers defending Pétain. These experiences turned him into a visceral anti-Gaullist. Elected to parliament 1951. Voted against de Gaulle's return to power in 1958 on the grounds that the 'defender of Louis XVI cannot vote for Robespierre'. Supporter of *Algérie française* and defended Bastien-Thiry, the leader of the assassination attempt against de Gaulle in 1962.

Admirer of Salazar. Called for a vote for Mitterrand in 1965: anyone was preferable to de Gaulle.

Jebb, Gladwyn (1900–1996). British diplomat who first encountered de Gaulle in June 1940 when, from his relatively junior position, he had to deliver the news that the government wanted one of his broadcasts to be toned down. British Ambassador in Paris 1954–60. Created Lord Gladwyn in 1960 and sat as Liberal peer where he was an ardent pro-European federalist. For this and other reasons he was critical of de Gaulle while hugely admiring him. A Foreign Office grandee whom de Gaulle much esteemed. Almost all his predictions about de Gaulle proved wrong – starting with the one that he had no desire to come back to power in 1958.

Joxe, Louis (1901–91). *Agrégé d'histoire* and teacher of history at a lycée in Algiers from October 1940. One of a small group of de Gaulle supporters in Algiers. For his knowledge of the Algiers scene de Gaulle named him Secretary General of the CFLN June 1943. Held the same position in de Gaulle provisional government in Paris from August 1944. Did not join RPF. From 1947 to 1958 pursued distinguished diplomatic career (Ambassador in Moscow and Bonn, and then Secretary General of the Quai d'Orsay). From 1959 to 1969 continuously a minister in de Gaulle's government. Played key role in negotiating Algerian independence with FLN. During the events of 1968 acted as interim Prime Minister 4–10 June in Pompidou's absence in Iran. The epitome of the mandarin Gaullist.

Juin, Alphonse (1888–1967). Son of a gendarme from Bone (Algeria). Graduated top of his class from Saint-Cyr in the same year as de Gaulle (1910). Promoted general in 1938. One of the rising stars of the French army. Loyally served Vichy and took a few days to rally to the Americans after Operation Torch. Because he was likely to win the respect of the regular soldiers formerly faithful to Vichy, de Gaulle appointed him commander of the Expeditionary Force (CEF) to Italy August 1943. Won Battle of Garigliano. In 1944–7 served as Chief of General Staff. His public opposition to de Gaulle's Algerian policy led to his forced retirement in April 1962. Marshal of France 1952 but not a *Compagnon de la Libération*. As a contemporary of de Gaulle one of the few people who could *tutoie* him. Never a paid-up 'Gaullist' but accorded a state funeral by de Gaulle in 1967.

Kérillis, Henri de (1889–1958). Conservative parliamentarian and journalist who supported de Gaulle's ideas on tanks in the 1930s. The only conservative politician to vote against the Munich Agreement in September 1938. Arrived in London hoping to serve in the Free French air force but in the end went to America. From January 1942 was a leading journalist on the American-based pro-de Gaulle newspaper *Pour la victoire*. Progressively moved into opposition to de Gaulle during the latter's conflict with Roosevelt after November 1942. Broke publicly with him in March 1943 and entered into ever more extreme anti-Gaullism culminating in his semi-deranged 1945 pamphlet *De Gaulle dictateur*.

Koenig, Pierre (1898–1970) (*25/6/42). Career soldier. Fought in Norway 1940 and repatriated to London where he rallied to de Gaulle. Participated in the Dakar expedition. Promoted brigadier general in July 1941. The Battle of Bir Hakeim where his 1st Free French Brigade held off Rommel for several days in June 1942 was the most celebrated feat of arms so far of the Free French. In spring 1944 appointed as the military representative of the CFLN in London and commander of the FFI. Elected as RPF *député* in 1951. Not one of RPF defectors to Pinay but did serve in two Fourth Republic governments (including that of Mendès France). Resigned from each out of Gaullist orthodoxy but ended by being entirely trusted by no one and held no further important post after 1958.

Labarthe, André (1902–70). Had scientific training. Anti-fascist activist involved in Front Populaire and close to Pierre Cot. In July 1940 put in charge of Free French armaments and given a mission to rally scientists and engineers. Relieved of this post after two months having quarrelled with other members of de Gaulle's staff. In November 1940 founded the review *France libre*. Moved towards ever more strident anti-Gaullism – first at Muselier's side in 1941–2 and then Giraud's 1943. Went to United States in July 1943 from where he continued to attack de Gaulle until the end of the war. After 1945 became a journalist and scientific popularizer. Volatile, brilliant and unreliable schemer who may have been a Soviet agent.

Larminat, Edgard de (1895–1962) (*1/8/41). Career officer serving in the Middle East as lieutenant colonel in June 1940. Imprisoned after trying to persuade a group of soldiers to reject the armistice. Escaped 30 June and joined the Free French in Palestine. Played key role in winning over Congo-Brazzaville to de Gaulle. Appointed by de Gaulle to command French troops in Equatorial Africa. Promoted general July 1941. Participated in much of the fighting in Western Desert and Tunisia. Having started with extreme-right convictions came to embrace the revolutionary rhetoric of wartime Gaullism. Ardent advocate of purging Giraudists from the army in 1943. Cussed and perpetually spluttering with rage – his memoirs were entitled *Irreverent Chronicles* – he was one of those ultra-loyalist Gaullists ready to stand up to his idol. Held various military posts after 1945. Unique among Gaullists in his support of the EDC in 1952. In 1958 he refused to sign an appeal calling for the return of de Gaulle to power. Appointed to chair the Court of Military Justice to judge the putschist French officers, he committed suicide on 1 July 1962.

Leahy, William (1875–1959). Reactionary senior American naval commander whom Roosevelt appointed as Ambassador to the French government in Vichy January 1941–May 1942. In this role he fed Roosevelt's anti-Gaullist prejudices while over-estimating the regime's willingness to distance itself from Germany. Had been more successful in his previous role as Governor of Puerto Rico September 1939–November 1940.

Leclerc, Philippe (1902–47) (*6/3/41). Hidden behind this pseudonym to protect his family in France, Philippe de Hauteclocque was from an old aristocratic family. The most celebrated soldier of the Free French. Graduated from Saint-Cyr in 1924. Wounded and taken prisoner in 1940 but escaped and arrived in London in July. In August 1940 sent by de Gaulle to rally the Cameroons. In March 1941 captured Italian fort of Kufra in Libya. In 1942–3 fought in Fezzan Desert and Tunisia. Commander of 2nd Armoured Division participating in liberation of Paris in August 1944. In November 1944 liberated Strasbourg. In August 1945 sent to re-establish French authority in Indo-China. Killed in air crash 28 November 1947. Along with Moulin the figure about whom de Gaulle wrote most warmly in his *Memoirs*. Started the war as a captain and ended as a general. Marshal of France posthumously.

Lefranc, Pierre (1922–2012). Arrested for his role in anti-German student demonstration in Paris on Armstice Day 1940. Released after six months in prison and joined Resistance group *Liberté*. Making his way to North Africa via Spain spent a period in a Francoist prison. First met de Gaulle in Algeria on 30 May 1943. Became lifelong Gaullist. Joined RPF and was then one of the core circle of Gaullist faithful during the period of the 'desert'. Founded in May 1958 the 'Association to support the action of General de Gaulle'. In de Gaulle's *cabinet* at Matignon in May–December 1958. Helped created in 1968 the Committees for the Defence of the Republic to support de Gaulle during the 'events' of '68. After de Gaulle's death, founded in 1971 the Institut (later Fondation) Charles de Gaulle to keep de Gaulle's memory alive. An ultra-Gaullist who even looked remarkably like his hero in old age.

Leger, Alexis (1887–1975). Head of the Quai d'Orsay in 1940. Passed through London in June 1940 but refused to support de Gaulle whose political ambitions he suspected. From Washington was one those French exiles reinforcing American suspicion of de Gaulle who refused to meet him on his visit to the United States in July 1944. Stayed in America after the war (with long visits to France) where he pursued his other career as a poet under the name Saint-John Perse. De Gaulle did not write to congratulate him when he was awarded the Nobel Prize for Literature in 1960. When he commented to Alphand that Perse's poetry was incomprehensible Alphand replied cattily that he could understand it because he read the English translations.

Malraux, André (1901–76) (*17/11/45). Internationally celebrated novelist and adventurer who was in the 1930s one of the intellectuals most engaged in anti-fascist politics, bringing him close to the Communist Party. Retreated into private life during the Occupation until joining the Resistance in 1943. Although having shown no previous Gaullist affinity met de Gaulle in August 1945 and became an unconditional supporter. The admiration was reciprocal. One of the key figures of the RPF, responsible for propaganda. Briefly Minister of Information to de Gaulle in 1958 and then for ten years held the newly created post of Minister of Culture. Although an effective minister, his influence on wider policy was limited. He was an adornment to Gaullism and its choreographer. The mutual fascination between him and de Gaulle is hard to fathom – some Gaullists though it was metaphysical – but whether one views him as fraud or genius, or a bit of both, the book he published soon after de Gaulle's death is one of the summits of Gaullist mythology. Every word may be untrue but it has the stamp of poetic authenticity. Madame de Gaulle was not happy about his turbulent (heterosexual) private life.

Mandel, Georges (1885–1944). Right-hand man of Clemenceau in the Great War. Conservative politician in the inter-war years. As Minister of the Interior in the Reynaud government was one of the most ardent opponents of the armistice. Joined the *Massilia* to continue the struggle from Morocco and was arrested there

by the Vichy government. From prison wrote a precious letter of support to de
Gaulle on 20 August 1942. Murdered by the Vichy Milice on 7 July 1944. As an
implacably anti-German Jew he represented everything most hated by the ultra-
collaborators.

Margerie, Roland de (1899–1990). Son of an ambassador and nephew of the playwright Edmond Rostand. Joined Quai d'Orsay and was posted to Berlin (1922–33)
and London (1933–9). Opposed appeasement. In the *cabinet* of Reynaud in 1940
was in the anti-armistice camp which brought him close to de Gaulle. Vichy, wanting to sideline him, appointed him Consul to Shanghai. Passing through London
on his way decided out of a sense of duty to take up the post. Ignored a direct
appeal from de Gaulle in 1942 but did nothing to compromise himself and his
career did not suffer at the Liberation. On de Gaulle's return to power was Ambassador to the Vatican. De Gaulle offered absolution by appointing him to key post
of Bonn 1962–5. Never got over having made the 'wrong' choice in 1940.

Massigli, René (1888–1988). Senior French diplomat. Deputy Political Director at
the Quai d'Orsay in 1933. His opposition to appeasement increasingly marginalized him. Sacked by Vichy in August 1940. In contact with Resistance but put off
by the intransigence of de Gaulle's attack on Vichy, he finally made the leap to go
to London in January 1943. Appointed Commissioner for Foreign Affair by de
Gaulle, a post he held till the Liberation. As an Anglophile, suspicious of the Soviet
Union, was distrusted by the ultra-Gaullists. In September 1944 appointed Ambassador to London where he served till January 1955. His rallying to de Gaulle was
a major coup. De Gaulle appreciated his expertise and professionalism while suspicious of him as the incarnation of all that he deplored in career diplomats.

Massu, Jacques (1908–2002) (*14/7/41). Career soldier serving in Africa when the
armistice was signed. Joined the Free French immediately and fought in Africa,
Normandy and Germany. After 1945 served in Indo-China and participated in
the Suez operation. Sent to Algiers in command of 10th Parachute Division in
January 1957. Using systematic torture he defeated the FLN in the 'Battle of
Algiers'. As head of the Algiers Committee of Public Safety played key role in
channelling the *pied noir* rebellion of May 1958 towards de Gaulle. A newspaper
interview in January 1960 criticizing de Gaulle's announcement of self-
determination for Algeria led to him being sacked. But he never joined any anti-
Gaullist plots, was forgiven by de Gaulle and was appointed commander of
French forces in Germany in 1965. On 29 May 1968, at the height of the events
of 1968, de Gaulle flew to Massu's HQ in Baden-Baden. Massu for ever after
believed it was he who had persuaded de Gaulle not to resign. A classic Free
French *grognard* whose devotion to de Gaulle always trumped his disagreements
with him.

Mauriac, Claude (1914–96). As son of François was introduced into the literary
Tout-Paris from an early age. Married Marcel Proust's niece. Developed a literary
identity of his own as journalist, novelist, film critic. Through his friendship with
Guy entered de Gaulle's service in 1944 in charge of his correspondence. Although
sceptical about the RPF served as editor of the newspaper *Liberté de l'esprit*
which tried to rally intellectuals. Supported de Gaulle's return to power in 1958

but was pushed to the left by the events of May 1968 and became involved in many *gauchiste* causes in the 1970s. Supported Mitterrand in 1981. Being the son of François was both a blessing and a curse and gave him a hunger for heroes, who included at various times his own father, Proust (whom he did not know), Malraux, Genet, Foucault, Sartre – and de Gaulle. His greatest literary achievement were his ten volumes of journals, one of which is devoted to his period close to de Gaulle between 1944 and 1948.

Mauriac, François (1885–1970). France's most famous 'Catholic' novelist. Broke with his conservative milieu to oppose the Nationalist side in the Spanish Civil War. Under the occupation was one of the most important intellectuals involved in the Resistance. After 1945 developed a career as a brilliant polemic journalist attacking the abuses of colonialism and embodying the conscience of the Catholic left. A supporter of de Gaulle at the Liberation he did not back the RPF but rallied to de Gaulle after 1958 and became a fervent admirer leading to much ribald mockery from his former votaries on the left. But he was never an intimate in the same way as Malraux.

Mauriac, Jean (1924–). Younger son of François. Spent his career as journalist at AFP. Devoted to de Gaulle and acquired a kind of special journalistic status because of his accreditation to de Gaulle during his tours. Unlike his father and his brother nothing dimmed his complete devotion to de Gaulle.

Maurras, Charles (1868–1952). Stone-deaf ultra-conservative ideologue. Born in Martigues (Provence), his defence of France as the inheritor of classical Mediterranean civilization was key to his thinking. Came to prominence during the Dreyfus Affair by arguing that the captain who had forged the documents to convict Dreyfus had acted patriotically. His hugely influential newspaper and political movement Action Française unrelentingly attacked republican democracy, advocated the return of the monarchy and denounced the influence of the Jews in France. Although a lifelong Germanophobe, his opposition to democracy and socialism led him to support Vichy. He described Pétain's arrival in power as a 'divine surprise'. In 1945 he was condemned to life imprisonment, a decision he described as 'the revenge of Dreyfus'.

Mayer, Emile (1851–1938). Born into assimilated Jewish family in Nancy. Combined promising military career with one as journalist writing on military affairs. Marginalized himself in 1890s by articles contesting the prevailing belief in offensive warfare. Military career broken by three (anonymous) articles defending the innocence of Dreyfus. Reintegrated into the army when Dreyfus was rehabilitated but dismissed again in 1916 after censors seized a letter expressing heterodox opinions about the war. In inter-war years hosted a salon gathering together intellectuals, politicians and journalists. De Gaulle became a regular member. The salon brought him into contact with young nonconformist intellectuals and politicians. The two men did not always agree but Mayer was the nearest he ever had to a guru and mentor.

Mendès France, Pierre (1907–82). Elected youngest *député* in France 1932. On left wing of centrist Radical Party. Refusing the armistice, joined the *Massilia* June 1940. Arrested by Vichy authorities in Morocco as deserter. As a left-wing Jewish politician, represented everything Vichy abhorred. Escaped from prison June 1941; reached London February 1942. Fought in Free French air force and then became Finance Commissioner on CFLN November 1943. Resigned from de Gaulle's government in January 1945 because his ideas on monetary policy were rejected by de Gaulle. In the Fourth Republic increasingly criticized the economic wastefulness of the war in Indo-China. After Dien Bien Phu became Prime Minister and negotiated end to the war. Was too dominant a figure for the politicians of the Fourth Republic, and his government fell after nine months. In 1958 opposed de Gaulle's return to power and rejected the personalization of power represented by the new Republic. Remained a hero to many on the left but his intransigence excluded him from further political influence. His slogan 'To Govern is to Choose' could not have been more Gaullist – but he lacked the opportunistic cynicism necessary to be an effective politician and was left with only the hollow consolations of political virtue.

Michelet, Edmond (1899–1970). Active in Christian Democratic circles before the war. Issued a tract calling for resistance on 17 June 1940 citing the name of Péguy. Regional organizer for the Combat Resistance movement in 1941. Arrested and deported to Dachau. A founder of the MRP but left it for the RPF in 1947. A natural conciliator who tried to build bridges between his former Christian Democrat colleagues and de Gaulle. As de Gaulle's Minister of Justice from January 1959, clashed with the more hardline Debré on how to deal with the street opposition to de Gaulle's policies. As a sop to Debré, de Gaulle removed him in August 1961. Served as minister again in 1967–8. Lived his Gaullism as a kind of religious faith, believing that they shared the same social-Christian heritage.

Mitterrand, François (1916–96). From conservative bourgeois family active in extreme-right politics in 1930s. Initially worked for the Vichy regime (which decorated him) before moving into Resistance. His three encounters with de Gaulle between 1943 and 1945 were all frosty. Pursued career as centrist politician during Fourth Republic. Opposed de Gaulle's return to power in 1958 and penned radical attack on de Gaulle's 'permanent coup d'état' in 1964. Stood against de Gaulle at Presidential elections of 1965 and forced him into second round. At the peak of the events of May 1968 proposed to set up a provisional government to replace de Gaulle. This temporarily stalled his political career but he bounced back to take over the Socialist Party in 1971 and was elected President in 1981. A brilliantly unscrupulous political *condottiere* whose political career was guided by only one principle: hatred of Gaullism.

Mollet, Guy (1905–75). Teacher and trade unionist. In the Resistance movement OCM. Elected Socialist Mayor of Arras 1945. General Secretary of the Socialist Party 1945–69. Key figure in the Third Force coalitions that kept de Gaulle out of power in the Fourth Republic. As Prime Minister in 1956–7 condoned torture in Algeria making him hated by many Socialists. Played important role in rallying the Socialist Party to support de Gaulle's return in 1958. Had wrongly assumed de Gaulle's return to power would be a parenthesis. Opposed de Gaulle's constitutional reform 1962 and started to move the Socialist Party back towards an alliance with the Communists. Gave up the leadership of the almost moribund

PS in 1969 but remained Mayor of Arras until his death – probably the position he cared about most and the one he was least unsuccessful in.

Monnet, Jean (1888–1976). Son of cognac salesman from the Charente. In inter-war years became banker and financial adviser to many governments. In October 1938 negotiated the purchase of 500 American planes for the French air force. In 1939–40 helped coordinate Franco-British purchases from the United States. One of the inventors in June 1940 of the Franco-British Union proposal. Distrusting de Gaulle's ambition preferred to help the Allied war effort from the United States. Became close to many members of the Roosevelt administration. Sent by Roosevelt 1943 to bolster Giraud's position against the Gaullists. Having accepted the inevitability of de Gaulle was sent by him to Washington to secure American loans for the CFLN September 1943 to 1944. Persuaded de Gaulle to set up economic Planning Commissariat in January 1946. Having been founder of French planning became the architect and inspiration of the first European supranational institutions. As a convinced European federalist his vision of Europe could not have been more different from de Gaulle's. On one occasion when Eisenhower was singing Monnet's praises to de Gaulle the reply was: 'He makes good cognac. Unfortunately he does not find this enough to keep him occupied!'

Morton, Desmond (1891–1971). In 1920 worked in Secret Intelligence Service dealing with counter-Bolshevism. In the 1930s, as an opponent of appeasement, leaked intelligence information about Germany to Churchill (he lived only a mile away from Chartwell). Was appointed Churchill's Personal Assistant at 10 Downing Street in 1940. His personal link to Churchill caused irritation in Whitehall and his influence diminished as more normal bureaucratic procedures replaced Churchill's predilection for working through his own cronies. But Morton retained his brief of working with the foreign governments in exile, and in this capacity had many dealings with de Gaulle (although he did not technically represent a government). Tended to stoke Churchill's suspicions of de Gaulle.

Moulin, Jean (1899–1943) (*17/10/42). From an intensely republican family rose fast in the administration becoming the youngest Prefect of France. During the Popular Front, attached to the *cabinet* of Pierre Cot, played a role in smuggling arms to Spain. Prefect of Chartres in June 1940 he refused the German demand to sign a document dishonouring black French troops and attempted suicide. Sacked from his post by Vichy December 1940. Arrived in London October 1941 with information about the Resistance. Sent back to France as de Gaulle's delegate to the Resistance 2 January 1942–14 February 1943 where he pushed the Resistance to coordinate its activities and accept de Gaulle's authority. Back in London for five weeks, returned to France again on 20 March as de Gaulle's delegate for both zones with instruction to set up a National Resistance Council (CNR) including political parties. The CNR held its first meeting under Moulin's presidency on 27 May 1943. On 21 June Moulin was arrested and died from the effects of torture some time in early July.

Muselier, Emile (1882–1965) (*1/8/41). French Vice-Admiral who was forced into retirement in 1939 after a dispute with Darlan. Arrived in London in late June 1940 where he was the most senior officer to join de Gaulle. Feeling that he was

not given a status worthy of his rank – higher than de Gaulle's – he put himself
at the head of two plots against de Gaulle, the first in September 1941 and the
second in March 1942 which saw his effective exclusion from the Free French.
His unstable personality, ambition and predilection for scheming should not
overshadow his important role in building the Free French navy out of nothing.

Noël, Léon (1888–1987). Jurist and diplomat of bourgeois origins. Ambassador in
Warsaw 1935–40. One of the people sent to negotiate the armistice with Germany
by Pétain and then appointed by Vichy regime to represent its interests in the
Occupied Zone. Resigned in August 1940 but this brief Vichyiste flirtation weighed
on the rest of his career. Received absolution by being brought by de Gaulle into
the inner circle of the RPF despite the opposition of other Gaullists. Appointed
as first President of the newly created Constitutional Council in 1959 and had to
overcome a crisis of confidence regarding the constitutionality of de Gaulle's 1962
referendum. A man of bottomless pomposity and conservative opinions, he
appealed to the more conventional side of de Gaulle's personality.

Noguès, Charles (1876–1971). Commander of French forces in North Africa in June
1940. Although seeming originally to oppose the signing of an armistice, he
remained loyal to Pétain and refused a direct appeal from de Gaulle. Ordered
French troops to fire on the American invaders in November 1942. Took refuge
in Portugal in 1943. In 1947 was condemned *in absentia* to twenty years' hard
labour and loss of civil rights.

Palewski, Gaston (1901–84) (*17/1/46). From bourgeois Polish family established
in France since the nineteenth century. Studied at Sorbonne and for a year at
Oxford. In 1928–39 aide to Paul Reynaud and in this capacity first met de Gaulle
in 1934. In August 1940 arrived London. In February 1941–September 1942
fought with Free French forces in Africa. In September 1942 was recalled to
London to act as *directeur* of de Gaulle's *cabinet civil*. One of de Gaulle's closest
aides. Played leading role in RPF. In 1951–6 was an RPF *député* and in 1957–9
French Ambassador in Rome. In 1962–5 given responsibility for scientific research
in Pompidou government. Appointed President of Constitutional Council in 1965.
His *mondanité* and numerous amorous entanglements – including an affair with
Nancy Mitford – did not prevent his being a passionately devoted Gaullist.

Parodi, Alexandre (1901–79) (*27/8/44). Civil servant removed from his post at the
Ministry of Labour in September 1940. Joined the Resistance as did his younger
brother whose membership of the movement Liberation-Nord cost him his life.
Appointed in March 1944 to be de Gaulle Delegate to the Resistance – the post
once held by Moulin – and this made him a key figure during the Liberation of
Paris. As a senior official at the Ministry of Labour at the Liberation was one of
the architects of the post-war system of social security. Pursued diplomatic career
after 1947.

Passy (1911–98) (*20/5/43). Pseudonym of André Dewavrin. Captain in 1940 evacuated to London after the Narvik expedition. Decided to join de Gaulle and given
the role of running his intelligence service despite no previous expertise in this
area. A formidable organizer, he built it up – under its later name BCRA – into
one of the most important organisms of the Free French controlling a network

of agents in France. The unfounded rumours that he had belonged to the extreme-right pre-war terrorist organization the Cagoule arose because his powerful position made him a target for those wanting to attack de Gaulle. In August 1944 parachuted into France to fight with the Breton Resistance. In 1946 arrested for sequestering former BCRA funds to be used on de Gaulle's behalf in the event of a Communist rising. Nothing was proved and he was released after some months. But his career was broken and he turned to business activities. He resented the fact that de Gaulle had done nothing to help him during this murky affair.

Peyrefitte, Alain (1925–99). Graduate of the Ecole Normale Supérieure who started a career in the Ministry of Foreign Affairs but embarked on a political career being elected as Gaullist (UNR) *député* to parliament in November 1958. Came to de Gaulle's attention as one of the more intelligent young Gaullists. Used by him in 1962 to float an idea of partition of Algeria which he probably never had any intention of pursuing. As Minister of Information 1962–6 was dubbed by one British diplomat the 'Goebbels of the regime' – unfairly since he tried to nurse de Gaulle to a less dirigiste view of communication. As Minister of Education in 1968 was in the front line of the events before being entirely sidelined by Pompidou. The three volumes he published in the 1990s of de Gaulle's conversations and monologues are a major source for any study of the Fifth Republic.

Pflimlin, Pierre (1907–2000). Lawyer elected as MRP (Christian Democrat) *député* to parliament in 1945. Participated in several Fourth Republican governments from 1947 onwards. Developed liberal views on Algeria. His attempt to form a government in May 1958 sparked the rising in Algiers which brought de Gaulle back to power. Resigned to make way for de Gaulle on 26 May. Served in all his governments until resigning in May 1962 after de Gaulle's press conference attacking European supranationalism. Devoted himself to his activities as Mayor of Strasbourg. Wrote in his memoirs: 'From 1958 all my important decisions were taken in relation to General de Gaulle, the only great statesman I have met in my political life. I profoundly regret that . . . divergences on essential problems forced me to distance myself from him.'

Philip, André (1902–70). Academic Socialist economist. Elected to parliament 1936. One of the eighty MPs to vote against full powers to Pétain in July 1940. Joined Socialist Resistance circles. Arrived in London in July 1942 at a time when many Socialists were rallying to de Gaulle. His arrival was a considerable boost to de Gaulle's prestige. Appointed to head the Commission of the Interior. Sent on mission to Roosevelt in November 1942 which failed disastrously. Continued to serve de Gaulle until the Liberation but was not retained in his provisional government because his intelligence did not compensate for his legendary inefficiency. Opposed the RPF because he rejected de Gaulle's constitutional ideas and supported European integration. Opposed de Gaulle's return to power 1958. Gradually moved back towards Gaullism through support for decolonization and his foreign policies. One of the twenty-nine left personalities who signed a petition in de Gaulle's favour in 1966. His career had come full circle.

Pinay, Antoine (1891–1994). Son of a hat-maker. Started his career running small tanning business. Elected Mayor of Saint-Chamond (Loire) in 1929. Despite

discreet support for Vichy quickly resumed political career after 1945. Became
conservative Président du Conseil in March 1952 thanks to the defection of
twenty-seven RPF deputes. – leading de Gaulle to remark bitterly: 'I did not save
France to hand it over to M. Pinay.' During his nine months in power enjoyed
celebrity as the defender of the rentier. Rallied to de Gaulle in the crisis of 1958
after visiting him at Colombey (22 May). His popularity among conservatives was
useful to de Gaulle who appointed him Finance Minister in his first government
although the famous stabilization plan which bore his name was really that of
Jacques Rueff. Increasingly out of sympathy with the style of the new Republic
and with de Gaulle's anti-Atlanticism he was sacked in January 1960. Never
played a national politics role again but remained Mayor of Saint-Chamond until
1977 and played the role of conservative sage well into his nineties.

Pineau, Christian (1904–95) (*16/10/45). Son-in-law of the playwright Jean Girau-
doux. Became involved in trade union activity while working for the Bank of
France in 1930s. Through these contacts founded one of the most important
northern Resistance movements in November 1940. First major Resistance leader
to visit London in March 1942 from where he returned with the important Declaration to the Resistance (June 1942). Arrested and deported to Buchenwald
May 1943. On his return to France named minister in de Gaulle's provisional
government. Minister in several Fourth Republic governments including as Foreign Minister during the Suez Crisis. Did not accept the Fifth Republic and had
only a local political career after 1958.

Pleven, René (1901–93) (*20/5/43). From Republican family in conservative Brittany.
Pursued business career in 1930s with Anglo-Canadian Telephone Company.
Close to Jean Monnet who recruited him to the London-based Franco-British
purchasing commission in 1939. Unlike Monnet he decided to stay in London
with de Gaulle. His administrative competence, good contacts and perfect English
made him indispensable to de Gaulle. Sent to rally Chad to de Gaulle in August
1940. June–October 1941, sent on important mission to improve relations with
America. From autumn 1941 put in charge of the Free French economic portfolio and then of colonies. One of the architects of the Brazzaville Conference in
1944. As Minister of National Economy in de Gaulle's provisional government
clashed with Pierre Mendès France, rejecting Mendès France's currency reform.
Refused to follow de Gaulle into RPF and during the Fourth Republic (as a
member of the centrist UDSR) was many times a minister and twice Prime Minister where he supported and sponsored the EDC. The return of de Gaulle to
power ended his ministerial career. After de Gaulle's retirement enjoyed a brief
comeback as Minister of Justice in 1972. Although their paths diverged after
1945, there was no former 'companion' whose estrangement more upset de
Gaulle.

Pompidou, Georges (1911–74). Son of primary school teachers who ascended to the
summit of the French education system, the Ecole Normale Supérieure. Spent the
Occupation teaching and preparing his anthology of French poetry. Despite not
having any role in the Resistance was drafted into de Gaulle's *cabinet* in September 1944 and made his mark thanks to his outstandingly quick intelligence. From

1948 became de Gaulle's most trusted collaborator and head of his *cabinet*. After the formal dissolution of the RPF, started a successful career as a banker with Rothschild while remaining in touch with de Gaulle. As the head of de Gaulle's *cabinet* during his six months as Président du Conseil between May and December 1958 Pompidou was to all intents and purposes running the government. Although he returned to his banking career, de Gaulle continued to use him for confidential missions such as starting the talks with the FLN. Despite never having held elected office was appointed Prime Minister in April 1962. Serving in this role for the next six years he started to develop his own political identity and attract his own followers – an inevitable source of simmering tension with de Gaulle. His crucial role in keeping the government afloat in the events of May 1968 did not endear him to de Gaulle. After he was dismissed in June 1968, his increasing signals that he saw himself as de Gaulle's successor consummated the breach. Elected second President of the Fifth Republic in June 1969. Although there were periods when no one was more trusted by de Gaulle his 'Gaullism' – a non-ideological progressive, modernizing conservatism – was narrower than de Gaulle's, leading one leading Gaullist to dub him the 'Anti-de Gaulle'.

Queuille, Henri (1884–1970). A country doctor. Thirteen times Minister of Agriculture before 1940. Arrived in London in April 1943. Was given key responsibilities in the CFLN although his admiration for de Gaulle was tempered by suspicion of the genuineness of his democratic convictions. After 1946 resumed his political career and became a leading figure of the Third Force coalition which helped block de Gaulle including a period as premier for thirteen months between 1948 and 1949 where he adopted the principle that 'there is no problem that an absence of solution cannot eventually overcome.' Voted for de Gaulle in 1958 and then retired from politics.

Rémy (resistance pseudonym of Gilbert Renault) (1904–84) (*13/3/42). Action Française sympathizer who formed one of the most effective Resistance networks, Confrérie Notre-Dame. His propensity also to take his own political initiatives eventually exasperated the BCRA and he was forbidden to return to France after returning to London with the Communist leader Fernand Grenier in January 1943. After the war his best-selling memoirs turned him into the epitome of the dashing secret agent (he described how on one occasion he returned to London with an azalea for de Gaulle's wife). A key figure in the RPF he blotted his copybook with an article in April 1950 defending the idea that Pétain the 'shield' had been as important to France as de Gaulle the 'sword'. Reverted to increasingly right-wing views and de Gaulle had no further contact with him after 1958.

Reynaud, Paul (1878–1966). Leading inter-war conservative politician. Met de Gaulle in December 1934 and took up his ideas on tank reform. Opponent of Munich. In March 1940 became Prime Minister committed to prosecuting the war more vigorously than his predecessor Daladier. On 5 June 1940 appointed de Gaulle Under Secretary of State for Defence. Although opposed to the signing of an armistice in June, he resigned to give way to Pétain rather than taking the government abroad. Thus having failed to be the Clemenceau of 1940 he missed his chance to be Gaulle. Interned during the Occupation, he resumed a political career after 1945 in the Fourth Republic but supported de Gaulle's return to power in 1958 and presided over the consultative committee to review the drafting of the new constitution. Attached to parliamentarianism, he led the opposition to de Gaulle's constitutional referendum in 1962 and lost his seat at the elections. He wrote books attacking de Gaulle's anti-American foreign policy and supported Lecanuet at the 1965 Presidential election. To a letter he wrote to de Gaulle opposing his veto of British entry to the EEC, de Gaulle replied by sending an empty envelope to Reynaud on which he wrote: 'If away, forward to Waterloo, Belgium.'

Rueff, Jacques (1896–1978). Civil servant and economist who lost his post under Vichy. Ardent proponent of liberal economics – wrote a famous article in 1931 denouncing unemployment benefit as a cause of unemployment. His fear of inflation led him to cross swords with Keynes in the 1930s. Denounced the Bretton Woods agreement and remained a lifelong proponent of the gold standard. His ideas never changed. In 1958 was the main inspiration behind the financial stabilization plan introduced at the end of that year. He had never had any previous contact with de Gaulle but they shared the same obsessive fear of financial instability. Rueff was also behind de Gaulle's famous 1965 press conference calling for the return to the gold standard. But since de Gaulle also threw his weight behind *planification* he did not adopt all Rueff's ideas.

Salan, Raoul (1899–1984). The most decorated soldier in the French army. Loyal to Vichy at first but then ended the war fighting with de Lattre in southern France. Commander in chief of French troops in Indo-China and then in Algeria from 1956. A mysterious and taciturn man trusted by no one. Although the target of a right-wing assassination attempt in January 1957 by extremists who doubted his commitment to *Algérie française*, played key role in rallying the army to de Gaulle in May 1958. Removed from his Algerian command by de Gaulle at the end of 1958. In June 1960 moved back to Algeria in retirement and ever more strident opposition to de Gaulle. One of the leaders of the April 1961 putsch against him. Sentenced to life imprisonment for treason in April 1962. Released June 1968.

Schumann, Maurice (1911–98) (*13/7/45). A Jewish convert to Catholicism involved in left Catholic journalism in 1930s. Opposed Munich. One of the rare people to have heard the 18 June speech and joined de Gaulle at once. His gifts as broadcaster made him the best-known voice of the Free French on the BBC. One of the founders of the MRP after 1945 and despite anguished crisis of conscience decided not to join de Gaulle in the RPF. Supported de Gaulle's return to power in 1958 but resigned from the government in May 1962 after being in it for only three months because he disapproved of de Gaulle's jibe against Europe. But voted 'yes' in de Gaulle referendum of November 1962 and became a minister again in 1967. Constantly torn between his European convictions and his fidelity to de Gaulle, he always seemed, in the words of one commentator, 'to be personally bearing a piece of the true Cross – the Cross of Lorraine'. However it took the resignation of de Gaulle and the election of the more pro-European Pompidou in 1969 to give him the long-coveted prize of the Quai d'Orsay.

Soustelle, Jacques (1912–90). From Protestant family from Montpellier. In 1929 graduated top of his year at the Ecole Normale Supérieure. In 1934 became Deputy Director of the Musée de l'Homme. Organizer of anti-fascist intellectuals in 1930s. In July 1940 rallied to de Gaulle from Mexico, where he was working as an anthropologist. In 1940–42 organized Free French committees in Central and Latin America. In May 1942 took over Free French propaganda in London and in November 1943 was put in charge of merger of Gaullist and Giraudist intelligence services in Algiers. From 1947 put on hold career as academic anthropologist to become Secretary General of RPF. In 1951–8 was RPF *député* for Rhone. In 1955 appointed Governor General in Algeria and became passionate supporter of *Algérie française*. In 1958 became minister in Debré's government until he was sacked in February 1960 because of opposition to de Gaulle's Algerian policy. Went into exile April 1961 after failed putsch against de Gaulle. Amnestied in 1968 and returned to France. In 1983 was elected to Académie Française after a first unsuccessful attempt blocked by Gaullists. A passionate Gaullist in the 1940, he became no less passionately anti-Gaullist from 1960. After that his hatred never dimmed.

Spears, Edward Louis (1886–1974). Born to British parents in Paris. Changed his name from Spiers to more English sounding Spears in 1918 though always (falsely) denied Jewish origins. Joined army 1906. In 1914–18 acted as liaison first between French and British armies and then between British and French War Offices. Got to know most leading French politicians and generals including Pétain. In 1919 resigned his commission and went into business and politics. In 1931 elected Conservative MP for Carlisle. Became friend of Churchill, and passionate opponent of appeasement. Between 22 May and 17 June 1940 was Churchill's liaison with French government. Returned to London with de Gaulle on 17 June. Started as de Gaulle's most ardent supporter in London in early days of Free French. Quarrelled with him in July 1941 over Middle East and became his greatest enemy in London. From January 1942 to 1944, as British Minister to Lebanon and Syria, clashed with Free French and supported Arab nationalists. Defeated at 1945 election and pursued business interests in Africa. Wrote brilliant memoirs of both wars. A maverick who was never totally trusted by either the French or British. Anti-Semitism probably played a role in both cases.

Tardieu, André (1876–1945). Brilliant inter-war conservative politician who in the 1930s developed ideas on constitutional reform (referendum, greater power to the Presidency) which were rejected at the time but influenced de Gaulle later.

Terrenoire, Louis (1908–92). A Catholic journalist before 1940, he played a role in the Resistance before being arrested and deported to Dachau. Founding member of MRP, was one of those who, when forced to choose between it and the RPF, chose the RPF. Became its General Secretary in 1951. Minister of Information in 1960 and played key role in UNR.

Thorez, Maurice (1900–64). Leader of the French Communist Party 1930–64. Deserted from French army in 1940 and spent the war in the Soviet Union. De Gaulle allowed him to return to France in November 1944 where he played a key role in applying Stalin's policy that the duty of the Communist Party was, in the immediate term, to work with de Gaulle. Minister of State in de Gaulle's government 21 November 1944–20 January 1945. De Gaulle wrote of him subsequently that he had served the public interest: 'did he do this for politically tactical reasons? It is not for me to say. It was enough for me that France was served.'

Tixier, Adrien (1893–1946). Primary school teacher from the Limousin. Lost an arm in the Great War. French representative to the International Labour Organization in Geneva and then Washington. Although a Socialist by conviction agreed to be leader of the Free French delegation in Washington. A man of furious tempers exacerbated by the pain caused by his war wound, he was not the ideal diplomat. Served in the CFLN as Minister of Labour and in de Gaulle's provisional government as Minister of the Interior (he was the man in charge at the time of the Sétif massacre). Elected to parliament in November 1945 as a Socialist but died only two months later.

Tricot, Bernard (1920–2000). Son of a dentist. Before 1958 not a Gaullist but career civil servant. Through working as an adviser to the Mendès France government on Tunisia became convinced of necessity for decolonization. Taken on at Elysée in 1959 as adviser on Algerian affairs where he made no secret of his liberal opinions. Played increasingly important if discreet role in shaping de Gaulle's Algerian policy. Played key role in Si Salah affair. In 1967 became the third and last Secretary General of the Elysée and lived through the days of 1968 at de Gaulle's side. After de Gaulle's resignation his career suffered an eclipse because Pompidou did not feel he had backed him in Marcović affair. The epitome of the discreetly steely French civil servant who moved from being a Gaullist *de raison* to a Gaullist *de coeur*.

Vallon, Louis (1908–81). Son of Socialist primary school teacher. *Polytechnicien*. Socialist economic expert in 1930s. Joined leftist Resistance movement Libération-Nord 1941. Arrived London July 1942. Worked for BCRA. Served in de Gaulle's *cabinet* 1945–6. Joined RPF where he was a strong supporter of the policy of 'association'. After 1958 one of the leading left Gaullists. Elected to parliament in 1962. Became violently opposed to Georges Pompidou whom he saw as betraying the social policies of Gaullism. A maverick Gaullist for whom de Gaulle displayed weary indulgence.

Viénot, Pierre (1897–1944) (*23/10/44). Son of a provincial lawyer. Worked for Franco-German reconciliation and European unity in 1920s. Married in 1929 the daughter of the Luxemburg industrialist and proponent of European unity Emile Mayrisch. Elected to parliament as independent Socialist 1932. In 1936–7 Under Secretary of State for Foreign Affairs in the government of Léon Blum. Joined the Socialist resistance in the Occupation. Twice arrested. Arrived in London in April 1943. Once de Gaulle left for Algiers with Massigli became the London representative of the Algiers-based CFLN to the British government. During the furious arguments between de Gaulle and Churchill before D-Day he shuttled between the two men and was screamed at by both of them. The strain aggravated his poor health and he died of a heart attack on 20 July 1944. Posthumously made Companion of Liberation. De Gaulle commented of him in the 1960s: 'He was one of my best "companions" . . . A Socialist who was a bit naive, a bit of a ninny ... who believed in the great ideas of the nineteenth century, Humanity with a big H, Progress with a big P, Labour with a big L.'

Weygand, Maxime (1867–1965). Brilliant cavalry officer of uncertain parentage. Foch's Chief of Staff in the Great War. Chief of General Staff 1931–5. Appointed Commander in Chief by Reynaud *in extremis* on 17 May 1940 to save the situation but quickly came to the view that an armistice was necessary. Of profoundly reactionary political views he fully supported the domestic policies of the Vichy regime but wanted to restrict collaboration to a strict observance of the armistice terms. He was appointed Vichy's representative in North Africa where the British and Americans were continuously hoping he might switch sides and bring the army over to them. Despite the fact he never did this the Germans insisted he be recalled to France in November 1941. In November 1942 he was arrested and imprisoned in Germany. But de Gaulle who could never forgive him his responsibility for the armistice refused to allow him a state funeral at the Invalides in 1965 – an act of vindictiveness which shocked even some figures on the left.

Notes

Abbreviations

AN 3AG1: *Archives de Gaulle 1940–1944* (Archives Nationales)
AN 3AG4: *Archives Gouvernment Provisoire de la République française 1944-1946* (Archives Nationales)
AN 5AG1: *Archives de Gaulle (Présidence de la Cinquième République)* (Archives Nationales)
AN 72AJ: Archives of the Comité de la deuxième guerre mondiale
AN AP: Archives Nationales, Archives Privées
AP: Alain Peyrefitte, *C'était de Gaulle* (Gallimard, 2000)
CCC: Churchill College, Cambridge
DDF: *Documents diplomatiques français*. The references give the year followed by the volume for each year in brackets and finally the document number
De Gaulle, *Fil*: *Le fil de l'épée et autres écrits* (Omnibus Plon, 1990) [This volume contains in chronological order the four books written by de Gaulle before 1940 as well as other pre-war writings: DE = *Discorde chez l'ennemi*; FE = *Fil de l'épée*; AM = *Vers l'armée de métier*; FA = *France et son armée*]
DGESS: *De Gaulle en son siécle. Actes des journées internationales tenues à UNESCO Paris*, 7 vols (Documentation française, 1991–2)
DGM: Charles de Gaulle, *Mémoires* (Gallimard, 2000)
DMI: Charles de Gaulle, *Discours et messages. Pendant la Guerre (1940–1946)* (Plon Poche, 1970)
DMII: Charles de Gaulle, *Discours et messages. Dans l'attente (1946–1958)* (Plon Poche, 1970)
DMIII: Charles de Gaulle, *Discours et messages. Avec le renouveau (1958–1962)* (Plon Poche, 1970)
DMIV: Charles de Gaulle, *Discours et messages. Pour l'effort (1962–1965)* (Plon Poche, 1970)
DMV: Charles de Gaulle, *Discours et messages. Vers le terme (1966–1969)* (Plon Poche, 1970)
FI: Jacques Foccart, *Tous les soirs avec de Gaulle. Journal de l'Elysée I (1965–1967)* (Fayard/Jeune Afrique, 1997)
FII: Jacques Foccart, *Le Géneral en mai. Journal de l'Elysée II (1968–1969)* (Fayard/Jeune Afrique, 1998)

FDG: Fondation Charles de Gaulle
FNSP: Fondation Nationale des Sciences Politiques
FRUS: *Foreign Relations of the United States*
LNCI: Charles de Gaulle, *Lettres, notes et carnets 1901–1941* (Robert Laffont, 2010)
LNCII: Charles de Gaulle, *Lettres, notes et carnets 1941–1958* (Robert Laffont, 2010)
LNCIII: Charles de Gaulle, *Lettres, notes et carnets 1958–1970* (Robert Laffont, 2010)
MAE: Ministère des Affaires étrangères
MGD: Charles de Gaulle, *Mémoires de Guerre. Documents*, 3 vols (Plon, 1970)
RHA: *Revue historique des armées*
TNA: The National Archives

Introduction

1. Philippe Oulmont, 'Les voies "de Gaulle" en France. Le Général dans l'espace et la mémoire des communes', *Cahiers de la Fondation Charles de Gaulle* 17 (2009).   2. TNS Soffres (https://www.tns-sofres.com/publications/de-gaulle-40-ans-apres-sa-mort): 'De Gaulle, 40 ans après sa mort', 10/10.   3. Bernard Fauconnier, *L'être et le géant* (Régine Deforges, 1989); Benoît Duteurtre, *Le retour du Général* (Fayard, 2010); Jean-Yves Ferri, *De Gaulle à la plage* (Dargaud, 2007); Michel Tauriac, *Dictionnaire amoureux de De Gaulle* (Plon, 2010).   4. André Rossfelder, *Le onzième commandement* (Gallimard, 2000), 617, 621.   5. Gaston Palewski, 'De Gaulle et Malraux', *Revue des deux mondes* (12/74), 514.   6. DMII (10/3/52), 536.   7. Jean-Denis Bredin, *La Nef* 24–5 (10–12/65), 200.   8. Alain Decaux and Alain Peyrefitte, *1940–1945. De Gaulle. Celui qui a dit non* (TF1/Perrin, 1999), 12.   9. Pierre Nora, 'Gaullistes et Communistes', in Nora (ed.), *Les Lieux de mémoire*, vol. III: *Les France*, 1: *Conflits et partages* (Gallimard, 1992), 348–93 (357).   10. André Passeron, DGESSV 89.   11. Philippe de Gaulle, *De Gaulle mon père. Entretiens avec Michel Tauriac*, vol. I (Plon, 2003), 492–3.   12. Jean Lacouture, *De Gaulle* (Seuil, 1965); DGESSI 509.   13. Jean Lacouture, *De Gaulle*, vol. I: *Le rebelle* (Seuil, 1984), 122, 123.   14. DGESSI 532.   15. Lacouture, *Rebelle*, 364.   16. Ibid., 833.   17. Paul-Marie de La Gorce, 'Un journaliste "engagé et libre" ', *Espoir* 142 (3/05) (the whole issue is devoted to de La Gorce).   18. Paul-Marie de La Gorce, *De Gaulle* (Perrin, 1999).   19. DGESSVI 11. Or see De La Gorce, *De Gaulle*, 1146, describing the arrangements set up between de Gaulle's France and independent Algeria as 'a model to other countries that had resolved to transform their national economies and take them out of under-development'.   20. Louis Vallon, *L'anti-De Gaulle* (Seuil, 1969).   21. Eric Roussel, *De Gaulle* (Gallimard, 2002), 528–9.   22. Ibid., 84–5.   23. See the critique of Lacouture by Brigitte Gaïti, 'Jean Lacouture biographe', *Politix* 27 (1994), 76–93.   24. Odile Rudelle, *Mai 1958: De Gaulle et la République* (Plon, 1988). Rudelle's many articles which develop the same theme are collected in Rudelle, *République d'une jour, République de toujours* (Riveneuve,

2016), 354–637. **25.** Stanley Hoffmann, 'De Gaulle as Political Artist: The Will to Grandeur', in Hoffman, *Decline or Renewal? France since the 1930s* (Viking, New York, 1974), 216. **26.** Archives Groupe Jean Jaurès, Office Universitaire de Recherche Socialiste (OURS), 94PO3 (Henry Hauck, 16/6/42). **27.** Jean-Marie Domenach, *Beaucoup de gueule et peu de pouvoir. Journal d'un réfractaire 1944–1977* (Seuil, 2001), 157. **28.** Bernard Bruneteau, *Les paysans dans l'état. Le Gaullisme et le syndicalisme agricole sous la Vème République* (L'Harmattan, 1994), 43. **29.** For such an approach applied to the origins of the Fifth Republic see Brigitte Gaïti, *De Gaulle, prophète de la cinquième République (1946–1962)* (FNSP, 1998); and for such an approach applied to de Gaulle and the army after 1958 see Grey Anderson, 'The Civil War in France, 1958–1962' (unpublished PhD thesis, Yale University, 2016).

1. Beginnings, 1890–1908

1. DMI 3–4 (18/6/40). **2.** Claude Guiblin, *La passion d'agir* (Pensée universelle, 1993), 36. **3.** Léon Werth, *Déposition* (V. Hamy, 1992), 688. **4.** *Le Monde* 20/6/1980. **5.** Roger Langeron, *Paris, juin 1940* (Flammarion, 1946), 72 . **6.** Agnès Humbert, *Notre guerre* (Tallandier, 2004), 7–8. **7.** Ibid., 20–1. **8.** Werth, *Déposition*, 356. **9.** Claude Mauriac, *Un autre de Gaulle* (Hachette, 1970), 9. **10.** Pierre Lefranc, who demonstrated against the Occupation on 11 November 1940, believed the name must be a pseudonym (interview, 11/10). **11.** Romain Gary, *La promesse de l'aube* (Gallimard, 1960), 31–2. **12.** Sudhir Hazereesingh, *Le mythe gaullien* (Gallimard, 2010), 35–6. **13.** Maurice Garçon, *Journal 1939–1945* (Les Belles Lettres, 2015), 129. In the journal kept by Diego Brosset, one of the earliest officers to rally to de Gaulle, the name is at first regularly spelt wrongly: Guillaume Piketty, *Français en Résistance. Carnets de guerre, correspondance, journaux personnels* (Robert Laffont, 2009), 142 (29/6/40). **14.** LNCIII 649 (2/6/64). **15.** Philippe de Gaulle, *Mémoires accessoires*, vol. I: *1921–1946* (Plon, 1997), 9–42, has details on the family history. **16.** Jean-Raymond Tournoux, *Jamais dit* (Plon, 1971), 384–401. **17.** LNCII 911 (12/3/49). **18.** TNA CAB 66/26/25 ('Views of General de Gaulle'). **19.** AP 163 (19/5/62). **20.** Claude Guy, *En écoutant de Gaulle. Journal 1946–1949* (Grasset, 1996), 213; see also Edward Spears, *Two Men Who Saved France: Pétain and de Gaulle* (Eyre & Spottiswoode, 1966), 186, remembering that de Gaulle told him in September 1940 that his family was the 'second oldest in Paris'. **21.** LNCIII 1171 (9/11/70). **22.** Michel Marcq, 'La famille', in FDG, *Charles de Gaulle. La jeunesse et la guerre 1890–1920* (Plon, 2001), 21–8. **23.** LNCI 53 (3/1/09). **24.** Pierre Pierrard, 'Le Nord et Lille dans la vie de Charles de Gaulle', in FDG, *De Gaulle. Jeunesse*, 18. **25.** LNCI 100 (3/10/14). **26.** Jean-Claude Bonnal, *Charles de Gaulle en Périgord* (Editions du Roc de Burzac, Bayac, 1990). **27.** Jacques Vendroux, *Ces grandes années que j'ai vécues 1958–1970* (Plon, 1975), 98. **28.** They lived subsequently at 24 Avenue Dusquesne from 1892 to 1908, and 3 Place Saint-François-Xavier (today Place André Tardieu-Président Mithouard) after 1908. **29.** 'Le Maréchal Foch', in LNCI 712–13. **30.** DGM 5. **31.**

Guy, *En écoutant*, 70.   32. François Coulet, *Vertu des temps difficiles* (Plon, 1967), 165–6.   33. Guy, *En écoutant*, 168.   34. LNCIII 1150 (7/7/70).   35. She reported this to Paul Reynaud when they were both prisoners in Germany during the war. Paul Reynaud, *Carnets de captivité 1941–1945* (Fayard, 1997), 367.   36. See Rudelle, *République d'une jour, République de toujours*, 354–637.   37. Jean-Marie Mayeur, 'Charles de Gaulle et le catholicisme social', in Mayeur, *Catholicisme social et démocratie chrétienne* (Cerf, 1986), 255–6.   38. Jean Pouget, *Un certain capitaine de Gaulle* (Fayard, 1973), 28; Gérard Bardy, *Charles le Catholique. De Gaulle et l'Eglise* (Plon, 2011), 37.   39. Duclert in FDG, *De Gaulle. Jeunesse*, 107–18; Marcel Thomas, 'Une certaine idée de "l'Affaire" . . .' in ibid., 148–66.   40. De Gaulle, *Fil* (FA), 461–2.   41. Tournoux, *Jamais dit*, 394.   42. Unpublished letter of Jacques de Gaulle to his mother, 8/4/17, communicated to me by Claude Marmot of the FDG.   43. Marie-Agnès Cailliau de Gaulle, *Souvenirs personnels* (Paroles et Silence, 2006), 23–5.   44. De Gaulle, *Fil* (FE), 185.   45. Emmanuel d'Astier de la Vigerie, *Sept fois sept jours* (Gallimard, 1961), 137.   46. LNCI 15 (30/11/17).   47. Charles Péguy, *Oeuvres en prose complètes*, vol. II (Gallimard, 1988), 59; Eric Thiers, 'La révélation du 6 juin 1905', *Mil neuf cent* 19 (2001), 43–52.   48. LNCI 13.   49. Jean-Jacques Becker introduction to Henri Massis and Alfred de Tarde (Agathon), *Les jeunes gens d'aujourd'hui* (Imprimerie nationale, 1995), 38; Becker, '1905. Un Tournant', in Stéphane Audoin-Rouzeau and Becker (eds.), *Encyclopédie de la grande guerre 1914–1918* (Fayard, 2004), 151–6.   50. LNCI 826 (9/12/36), 918 (11/2/40); on Psichari see Frédérique Neau-Dufour, *Ernest Psichari. L'ordre et l'errance* (Cerf, 2001).   51. AP 784 (9/9/84). See also Alain Larcan, *De Gaulle inventaire. La culture, l'esprit, la foi* (Bartillat, 2010 edn), 368–94; Jean Bastaire, 'Péguy et de Gaulle', *Cahiers de l'Herne* (1973), 246–51.   52. Charles Péguy, *Oeuvres en prose complètes*, vol. III (Gallimard, 1992), 935.   53. Ibid., 929.   54. Ibid., II, 142.   55. De Gaulle, *Fil* (FA), 469–70.   56. Ibid., 470.   57. This was first pointed out by Alain Peyrefitte: AP 289 (n. 1). It came from Barrès's *Cahier* of 1920: '*donner de la France une certaine idée, c'est nous permettre de jouer un certain rôle*'. On Barrès and de Gaulle see Pierre Bernard, 'Un de Gaulle barrèsien ou un Barrès gaullien?' *Espoir* 72 (9/90), 5–8.   58. LNCII 1173 (23/12/54).   59. Lucy Shepard Crawford, *The Philosophy of Emile Boutroux* (Longmans, New York, 1924).   60. LNCI 279–80.   61. Cyrus Sulzberger, *The Last of the Giants* (Macmillan, 1970), 85–6.   62. LNCI 14 (31/8/07).   63. LNCI 44 (23/6/08).   64. The best treatment of de Gaulle and religion is FDG, *Charles de Gaulle. Chrétien, homme d'état* (Cerf, 2011). See also: Jean-Marie Mayeur, 'De Gaulle et l'Eglise catholique', DGESSI 436–41; Michel Brisacier, *La foi du général* (Nouvelle Cité, Montrouge, 1998); Laurent de Gaulle, *Une vie sous le regard de Dieu. La foi du général de Gaulle* (Toucan, 2009).   65. Jean Mauriac, *Le Général et le journaliste* (Fayard, 2008), 132 ('*toujours un peu absent: visage impassible*'); Mauriac, *Un autre de Gaulle*, 3/9/44 ('*correction un peu ennuyé*'); Jean d'Escrienne, *Le Général m'a dit 1966–1970* (Plon, 1973), 26.   66. The subject was discussed by Palewski, Malraux and Pompidou in 1951 with no one being sure what de Gaulle believed: Georges Pompidou, *Lettres, notes et portraits 1928–1974* (Robert Laffont, 2012), 225.   67. Jacques Prévotat, 'De Gaulle croyant et pratiquant', in FDG, *Charles de Gaulle. Chrétien*, 40–64.   68. Jean-Marie

Mayeur, 'De Gaulle as Politician and Christian', in Hugh Gough and John Horne (eds.), *De Gaulle and Twentieth-Century France* (Edward Arnold, 1994), 99. **69.** Guy, *En écoutant*, 166–7. **70.** LNCI 710. **71.** Pierre Lance, *Charles de Gaulle, ce chrétien nietzschéen* (Septième aurore, 1965). **72.** DMI 332 (14/7/43). **73.** David Schoenbrun, *The Three Lives of Charles de Gaulle* (Hamish Hamilton, 1966); Bardy, *Charles le Catholique*, 9. **74.** DMII (3/11/43). **75.** Maurice Agulhon, *De Gaulle. Histoire, symbole, mythe* (Plon, 2000), 30–34. **76.** De Gaulle, *Fil* (FA), 165. **77.** Larcan, *De Gaulle inventaire*, 196. **78.** DMII 360 (11/2/50). **79.** DMI 327 (27/6/43). **80.** DGM 88. **81.** LNCI 51; LNCIII 1185.

2. 'A Regret That Will Never Leave Me', 1908–1918

1. On de Gaulle and Germany in these years, Pierre Maillard, *De Gaulle et l'Allemagne. Le rêve inachevé* (Plon, 1990), 17–24; Jean-Paul Bled, 'L'image de l'Allemagne chez Charles de Gaulle avant juin 1940', *Etudes gaulliennes* 17 (1977). **2.** LNCI 45 (23/6/08). **3.** Coulet, *Vertu*, 108. **4.** Louis Joxe, *Victoires sur la nuit. Mémoires* (Flammarion, 1981), 144. **5.** DGM 573. **6.** Claude Roy, *Nous* (Gallimard, 1972), 65. **7.** Jules Maurin, 'De Gaulle saint cyrien', in FDG, *De Gaulle. Jeunesse*, 187–92. **8.** DGM 6. **9.** LNCI 522. **10.** 'Du patriotisme', LNCI 70–77. **11.** DGM 6. **12.** 'Notes d'un carnet personnel', LNCI 79. **13.** Ibid. **14.** On de Gaulle's war see especially FDG and Historial de la Grande Guerre, *De Gaulle soldat 1914–1918* (Martelle éditions, 1999); Frédérique Neau-Dufour, *La première guerre de Charles de Gaulle 1914–1918* (Tallandier, 2013); and also Charles de Gaulle, Jacques Vendroux and Gérard Boud'hors, *La génération du feu* (Plon, 1983); Jean d'Escrienne *Charles de Gaulle, officier* (Addim, 1991). **15.** LNCI 83–7. **16.** 'Le Baptême', LNCI 93–100. **17.** De Gaulle, *Fil* (FA), 481. **18.** 'Aux nouvelles recrues', LNCI 68. **19.** Unpublished letter of Jacques de Gaulle to his mother, 23/10/14 (communicated by Claude Marmot). **20.** 'Notes', LNCI 118 (11/12/14). **21.** LNCI 115 (7/12/14). **22.** 'Consignes', LNCI (17/1/15). **23.** Neau-Dufour, *Première guerre*, 113. **24.** 'Au 33 régiment', LNCI 153 (20/2/15). **25.** 'De la guerre', LNCI 341–2. **26.** LNCI 231 (23/12/15). **27.** LNCI 116 (7/12/14). **28.** LNCI 203 (23/11/15). **29.** LNCI 231 (23/12/15). On 31/12/15 he condemns the 'irremediable inferiority of our republican parliamentary regime', LNCI 237. **30.** LNCI 199 (18/11/15). **31.** LNCI 247 (15/1/16). **32.** LNCI 158 (2/5/15). **33.** LNCI 258 (14/2/16). **34.** LNCI 442 (8/12/18). **35.** Gérard Boud'hors, 'Le Capitaine de Gaulle et le 33 R.I. à Douaumont (fin février–début mars 1916)', RHA 179 (1990), 6–15. **36.** Frédérique Neau-Dufour, *Geneviève de Gaulle-Anthonioz* (Cerf, 2004), 118. **37.** LNCI 374. **38.** LNCI 345. **39.** Cédric Marty, 'Le corps au corps au prisme des indentités sociales', in François Bouloc, Rémy Cazals and André Loez (eds.), *Identités troublées 1914–1918* (Privat, 2011), 73–6. **40.** In general see François Cochet, 'Le capitaine de Gaulle et l'expérience de la captivité', in FDG, *De Gaulle. Jeunesse*, 222–38. **41.** LNCI 327 (21/3/17). **42.** LNCI 329 (22/4/17). **43.** LNCI 327 (21/3/17). **44.** Fernand Plessy, 'J'ai connu de Gaulle captif', in *De Gaulle soldat*, 187. **45.** LNCI 279. **46.** LNCI 328 (8/4/17). **47.**

LNCI 337 (19/12/17). **48.** Quoted in *En ce temps là. De Gaulle* 15 (n.d.) (BNF ref: 16-LN27-99335). **49.** Some of these are reproduced in the catalogue, Musée de l'Armée, *Churchill/De Gaulle* (Editions de la Matinière, 2015), 88–9. **50.** LNCI 266. **51.** LNCI 279. **52.** LNCI 334 (8/9/17). **53.** LNCI 325. **54.** LNCI 400–401. **55.** LNCI 384. **56.** LNCI 422 (1/9/18). **57.** LNCI 418 (1/8/18). **58.** LNCI 424 (4/10/18) **59.** De Gaulle, *Fil* (DE), 137. **60.** Lacouture, *Rebelle*, 97, has him working briefly in the Anilinfabrik chemical factory in Ludwigshafen but gives no source. Since POW officers were exempted from the requirement to work in enemy territory this seems unlikely: see Neau-Dufour, *Première guerre*, 295. **61.** LNCI 437 (1/12/18). **62.** Lacouture, *Rebelle*, 97. **63.** Bruno Cabanès, *La victoire endeuillée. La sortie de guerre des soldats français (1918–1920)* (Seuil, 2004). **64.** LNCI 673–85 (31/1/27). **65.** LNCI 427 (8/12/18).

3. Rebuilding a Career, 1919–1932

1. LNCI 421 (1/9/18). **2.** LNCI 447 (25/1/19). **3.** LNCI 449 (29/1/19). **4.** LNCI 455 (26/4/19). **5.** 'L'alliance franco-polonaise', LNCI 487. **6.** LNCI 456 (26/4/19). **7.** LNCI 462–3 (25/6/19). **8.** LNCI 460 (7/6/20). **9.** LNCI 467 (5/8/1919). **10.** LNCI 479. **11.** *En ce temps là. De Gaulle* 22 (n.d.), 89. On de Gaulle in Poland see Yves Faury, 'Le Capitaine de Gaulle en mission en Pologne 1919–1920', RHA 179 (1990), 16–25; Frédéric Guelton, 'Le Capitaine de Gaulle et la Pologne (1919–21)', in FDG, *De Gaulle. Jeunesse*, 242–60. **12.** LNCI 472 (18/11/19). **13.** This comes from de Gaulle's anonymous account 'La Bataille de la Vistule', published in the *Revue de Paris* in 1920 and republished in de Gaulle, *Fil*, 568–83 (570). **14.** 'Rapport sur l'organisation', LNCI 502–8. **15.** LNCI 500 (24/8/20). **16.** LNCI 597 (16/1/597). **17.** AP 1503 (6/9/67). **18.** LNCI 499 (3/7/19). **19.** LNCI 464 (17/7/19). **20.** Guy, *En écoutant*, 224. **21.** LNCI 276. **22.** De La Gorce, *De Gaulle*, 50. **23.** Guy, *En écoutant*, 95. **24.** LNCII 42–3 (9/3/42). **25.** LNCI 326 (18/3/17). Neau-Dufour, *Première guerre*, 241, 296 suggests that 'M-L' was Marie-Lucie, the eldest daughter of his maternal uncle Jules Maillot. But she had died of meningitis in occupied Lille, whereas he did have another cousin, Anne-Marie, who died as a result of a bombardment on 17 November 1917. **26.** In general see Frédérique Dufour, 'L'officier dans sa vie privée', in FDG, *Charles de Gaulle. Du militaire au politique 1920–1940* (Plon, 2004), 252–85. **27.** LNCI 464–5 (17/7/19). **28.** LNCI 492 (27/1/20). **29.** Philippe de Gaulle, *Mémoires* I, 78. **30.** Philippe de Gaulle, *De Gaulle mon père* I, 318–19. **31.** For this paragraph, see Frédérique Neau-Dufour, *Yvonne de Gaulle* (Fayard, 2010), 99–105. **32.** Ibid., 105. **33.** The ideas were trailed in 'La fatale querelle d'un chancelier et un militaire', *Revue militaire générale* 15/5/23, 15/6/23; 'L'envers d'un décor', *Revue militaire générale* 15/11/23, 15/12/23. **34.** De Gaulle, *Fil* (DCE), 12–13. **35.** Ibid., 126. **36.** Ibid. **37.** Ibid. **38.** De Gaulle, 'La défaite, question morale', in ibid., 645. **39.** Georges Loustaunau-Lacau, *Mémoires d'un Français rebelle (1914–1948)* (J. et D. Editions, Biarritz, 1994 edn), 60–61. **40.** Jean-Raymond Tournoux, *Pétain et de Gaulle* (Plon, 1964), 382–91, reproduces all de

824 NOTES

Gaulle's mark sheets from the Ecole. **41.** LNCI 604 (13/9/24). **42.** 'Doctrine a priori ou doctrine des circonstances', *Revue militaire française* 45 (1/3/1925), 306–28. It was mentioned in *Le Temps* 31/3/25, in article headed 'Le dogmatisme dans l'armée'. The manuscript, received by the *Revue militaire française* on 7/11/24, was analysed by Colonel Laure of Pétain's *cabinet* and Pétain noted of the article 'tres bonne étude', *En ce temps là. De Gaulle* 27 (n.d.), 110. De Gaulle's thinking on this subject was influenced by his reading of the *ancien régime* military theorist the Comte de Guibert, an admirer of Frederick the Great and proponent of the '*la doctrine du réel*'. **43.** LNCI 686 (3/3/27); note the scepticism of Claude Carré, 'Charles de Gaulle, professeur et conférencier', in FDG, *Du militaire*, 203–16. **44.** Jean-Raymond Tournoux, *Le tourment et la fatalité* (Plon, 1974), 21. **45.** Jacques Schapira and Henri Lerner, *Emile Mayer. Un prophète baillonné* (Editions Michalon, 1995); Vincent Duclert (ed.), *Le Colonel Mayer de l'Affaire Dreyfus à de Gaulle. Un visionnaire en République* (Armand Colin, 2008). **46.** Jean Auburtin, *Le Colonel de Gaulle* (Plon, 1965), 9. **47.** LNCI 779 (de Gaulle to Halévy, 5/6/35). **48.** LNCI 702 (16/1/28). Paul Bourget was an extremely successful novelist of the period. **49.** LNCI 704 (23/1/28). **50.** The entire Pétain correspondence on the manuscript is reproduced in 'La Correspondance de Gaulle–Pétain 1925–1938', *En ce temps là. De Gaulle* 15 (n.d.) (fifteen-page insert). **51.** LNCI 708 (20/6/29). **52.** 'Allocutions', LNCI 722. **53.** LNCI 690 (24/12/27). **54.** Joël Coignard, 'Le commandment du 19e BCP', in FDG, *Du militaire*, 33–42. **55.** Jacques Vendroux, *Cette chance que j'ai eu 1920–1957* (Plon, 1974), 48–52. **56.** Neau-Dufour, *Yvonne*, 113–29. **57.** LNCI 703 (18/1/28). **58.** Lacouture, *Rebelle*, 181–2. **59.** Chanoine Bourgeon in *En ce temps là. De Gaulle* 13 (n.d.), 31. **60.** LNCI 837 (10/2/48). **61.** Philippe de Gaulle, *Mémoires* I, 89. **62.** Neau-Dufour, *Yvonne*, 166. **63.** Ibid., 168. **64.** Philippe de Gaulle, *De Gaulle mon père* I, 510. **65.** LNCI 265 (6/9/16). **66.** LNCI 492 (27/1/20). **67.** LNCI 725 (26/11/29). **68.** J.-M. Marill, 'Le chef du bataillon de Gaulle au Levant (1929–1931)', RHA 179 (June 1990), 38–43; Pierre Fournié, 'Le séjour du commandant de Gaulle dans les Etats du Levant 1929–1931', in FDG, *Du militaire*, 42–59; Alexandre Najjar, *De Gaulle et le Liban. Vers l'orient compliqué*, vol. I: *1929–1931* (Ed. Terres du Liban, 2002); Isabelle Dasque, 'Le Commandant de Gaulle au Levant', in Clotilde de Fouchécour and Karim Emile Bitar (eds.), *Le cèdre et le chêne. De Gaulle et le Liban. Les Libanais et de Gaulle* (Guethner, 2015), 65–88. **69.** LNCI 727 (24/4/30). **70.** LNCI 726 (11/12/29). **71.** LNCI 725 (11/12/29). **72.** LNCI 732 (2/1/31). **73.** LNCI 730 (7/7/30). **74.** LNCI 726 (11/12/29). **75.** LNCI 728 (30/6/30). **76.** De Gaulle, *Fil* (FE), 154, 184–5. **77.** LNCI (2/11/29). **78.** LNCI 374. **79.** LNCI 432. **80.** LNCI 706 (21/12/28). **81.** Philippe de Gaulle, *De Gaulle mon père* I, 54. **82.** De Gaulle, *Fil* (FE), 146. **83.** LNCI 708 (20/6/29). **84.** Unpublished letter, 16/5/32.

4. Making a Mark, 1932–1939

1. LNCI 672 (21/1/27). **2.** LNCI 731 (7/9/30). **3.** Pétain to de Gaulle, 5/3/31, 12/3/31, in 'La Correspondance de Gaulle–Pétain 1925–1938'. **4.** Frédéric Guelton,

'Charles de Gaulle au Secrétariat général du conseil supérieur de la défense nationale 1931–1937', in FDG, *Du militaire*, 62–71. **5.** DGM 7. **6.** For drafts of the project see AN 3AG1/299 (7–10). **7.** 'Projet de Loi d'Organisation de la nation pour le temps de guerre', LNCI 817. **8.** Cpt. Gilbert Bodinier, 'De Gaulle, rédacteur au SGDN, commenté et corrigé par ses chefs hiérarchiques', RHA 1 (1980), 239–54; 2 (1981), 167–80. **9.** LNCI 743 (24/11/32). **10.** LNCI 747 (29/12/33). **11.** Alain Larcan and Pierre Messmer, *Les écrits militaires de Charles de Gaulle* (PUF, 1985) for an overview of de Gaulle's military thinking. **12.** LNCI 773 (17/4/35); 826 (9/12/36). **13.** See also LNCI 734 (1/10/31). **14.** 'Vers l'armée du métier', *Revue politique et parlementaire* 10/4/33, 10/5/33; *Etudes* (12/33); 'Forgeons une armée de métier', *Revue des vivants* 13/1/34. See dossier of press cuttings in AN 3AG1/299 Dr. 4. **15.** Jean-Nicolas Pasquay, 'Vers l'armée de métier et l'armée allemande avant la seconde guerre mondiale', in FCG, *Du militaire*, 144–70. **16.** Christopher S. Thompson, 'Prologue to Conflict: De Gaulle and the United States, from First Impressions through 1940', in Robert Paxton and Nicholas Wahl (eds.), *De Gaulle and the United States* (Berg, Oxford, 1994), 14–24. **17.** LNCI 774 (17/4/35). In his *Memoirs*, DGM 15, he acknowledges the influence of Liddell Hart, Fuller and Seeckt. **18.** De Gaulle, 'Rôle historique des places françaises', reprinted in de Gaulle, *Trois études* (Plon, 1973), 73–120. **19.** De Gaulle, 'Forgeons une armée de métier' (13/1/34), reprinted in *Articles et écrits* (Plon, 1975), 309. **20.** Those comments come in fact from his 1929 article 'Philosophie du recrutement', reprinted in *Fil*, 647–58, but they are in the spirit of *Vers l'armée de métier*. **21.** De Gaulle, *Fil* (AM), 325–6. **22.** LNCI 781 (28/6/35). **23.** LNCI 806 (27/10/36). **24.** Jean-Michel Royer, 'Le style, c'est l'homme', in *En ce temps là. De Gaulle* 16 (n.d.), 279–83. This issue also contains a facsimile of the corrections. **25.** Stéphane Giocanti, *Maurras. Le chaos et l'ordre* (Flammarion, 2006), 370. **26.** François-Georges Dreyfus, 'Aux sources de la pensée du Général', *Espoir* 56 (9/86), 6–19. **27.** Robert Aron, *Charles de Gaulle* (Librairie académique Perrin, 1965), 40–41. The meeting took place at the salon of Daniel Halévy. **28.** LNCI 884 (10/9/35). **29.** LNCI 760 (8/6/34). **30.** LNCI 319, 323. **31.** Nicolas Roussellier, *La force de gouverner* (Gallimard, 2015), 414–29. **32.** De Gaulle, *Fil* (AM), 326. In *Le fil de l'épée* de Gaulle invokes the century of the 'système Taylor', *Fil* (FE), 188; or see his reference to 'Taylorization' in his 1933 article on the 'Métier militaire' in *Fil*, 788. **33.** LNCI 449 (11/2/19). **34.** De Gaulle, *Fil* (AM), 363. **35.** De Gaulle, *Fil* (FE), 188. **36.** Jean-Pierre Guichard, 'Charles de Gaulle et Gustave le Bon', *Espoir* 113 (12/97), 31–41; Jean-Baptiste Decherf, 'De Gaulle et le jeu divin du héros. Une théorie de l'action', *Raisons politiques* 26 (5/2007), 217–34. **37.** LNCI 279. **38.** De Gaulle, *Fil* (FE), 146, 180, 181, 185. **39.** LNCI 665. **40.** DGM 17. **41.** Loustaunau-Lacau, *Mémoires*, 118. **42.** *Journal Officiel* 1935, 1040–42. **43.** Ibid., 1037; 1025. **44.** LNCI 779 (31/5/35). **45.** LNCI 775 (6/5/35). **46.** LNCI 800 (5/8/36). **47.** LNCI 795 (25/6/36). **48.** LNCI 802 (22/9/36). **49.** LNCI 863 (11/9/38). **50.** DGM 25. **51.** LNCI 836 (27/8/37). **52.** LNCI 828 (20/12/36). **53.** 'L'alliance franco-polonaise', LNCI 491. **54.** LNCI 866 (1/10/38). **55.** LNCI 866 (6/10/38). **56.** LNCI 850(24/3/38). **57.** Vendroux, *Cette chance*, 357. **58.** LNCI 846 (12/1/38). See also the letter to his son, LNCI

852 (30/4/38). **59.** LNCI 608 (5/25). **60.** LNCI 786 (16/12/35); Roussel, *De Gaulle*, 66. **61.** LNCI 827 (14/12/36). **62.** Francois Cochet, 'La société miltaire en France: réalité et perception par Charles de Gaulle (1919–1940)', in FDG, *Du militaire*, 18–31. **63.** LNCI 739 (23/5/32). **64.** LNCI 799 (5/8/36). **65.** LNCI 858-9 (18/8/38). **66.** LNCI 868 (7/10/38). **67.** See the excellent analysis by Philippe Ratte, 'De Gaulle historien', in FDG, *Du militaire*, 222–37. **68.** All the quotations in the last two paragraphs come from de Gaulle, *Fil* (FA), 331, 342–3, 384, 359, 421, 412, 422, 497–8. **69.** Joël Chambre, 'Le Colonel de Gaulle et son régiment. De la théorie à la pratique', *Cahiers de la FCDG* 11 (2002). **70.** AN 3AG1/2792 (21) (Dossiers Militaires). **71.** Neau-Dufour, *Yvonne*, 166. **72.** LNCI 840 (13/11/37). **73.** LNCI 866 (1/10/38), 874 (26/12/38). **74.** LNCI 838 (15/10/38). **75.** Chambre, 'Le Colonel de Gaulle', 162–3, 211–12. **76.** LNCI 772 (29/3/35). **77.** LNCI 849 (17/3/38). **78.** LNCI 690 (24/12/27). **79.** LNCI 872 (24/11/38).

5. The Battle of France, September 1939–June 1940

1. LNCI 864 (n.d.). **2.** LNCI 897 (12/10/39). **3.** Paul Gaujac, 'Le Colonel de Gaulle, commandant des chars de la Vème armée (septembre–mai 1940)', RHA 179 (June 1990), 57–71. **4.** LNCI 899 (22/10/39). **5.** LNCI 918 (11/2/40). **6.** LNCI 896 (8/9/39). **7.** In addition to Gaujac, 'Le Colonel', see Bruno Chaix, 'Charles de Gaulle et le débat doctrinal du début des années trente', in FDG, *Du militaire*, 91–101; de Gaulle's notes are in LNCI 893–6, 901–8. **8.** Gaujac, 'Le Colonel', 64 **9.** 'Note au sujet de l'emploi et de la constitution des unités des chars' (17/12/39), AN 3AG1/299 (2). **10.** De Gaulle, *Trois études*, 58–60. **11.** 'Note', LNCI 911–13 (12/1/40). **12.** LNCI 923 (21/2/40). **13.** AN 5AG1/1153 (letter from Rops, 11/9/44, reminding de Gaulle of this). **14.** LNCI 925 (14/4/39). **15.** Letter of 7/4/40 published January 2018 in catalogue of Autographe des Siècles, Lyons (une page ½ in-4°). **16.** Roland de Margerie, *Journal 1939–1940* (Grasset, 2010), 163; Paul de Villelume, *Journal d'un défaite* (Fayard, 1976), 305–6. **17.** LNCI 927 (3/5/40). **18.** TNA CAB 21/1323. **19.** François Bédarida, *La stratégie secrète du 'Drôle de guerre': le conseil suprême interallié* (FNSP, 1980), 482. **20.** LNCI 928 (8/5/40). **21.** For an overview of de Gaulle as commander of the DCR, Gérard Saint-Martin, 'Les combats de la 4e division cuirassée', in FDG, *Du militaire*, 181–97. **22.** LNCI 930 (15/5/40). **23.** LNCI 929 (15/5/40). **24.** DGM 36-7. **25.** Paul Huard, *Le Colonel de Gaulle et ses blindés. Laôn 15–20 mai 1940* (Plon, 1990). **26.** LNCI 930 (21/5/40). **27.** LNCI 932 (24/5/40). **28.** LNCI 932-3 (27/5/40). **29.** On Abbeville, Henri de Wailly, *De Gaulle sous le casque. Abbeville 1940* (Perrin, 1990). **30.** LNCI 935 (2/6/40). **31.** Roussel, *De Gaulle*, 80. **32.** Ibid., 83. **33.** Huard, *Le Colonel de Gaulle*, 296–8. **34.** Jean-Pierre Guichard, *Paul Reynaud. Un homme d'état dans la tourmente. Septembre 1939–juin 1940* (L'Harmattan, 2008). **35.** LNCI 936 (2/6/40). **36.** LNCI 938 (3/6/40). **37.** LNCI 939 (5/5/40). **38.** E. L. Spears, *Assignment to Catastrophe*, vol. II (Heinemann, 1954), 195. **39.** *The Times* 7/6/40; *Le Populaire* 8/6/40; *Action Française*

10/6/40. 40. Villelume, *Journal*, 393. 41. *The Private Diaries of Paul Baudouin* (Eyre & Spottiswoode, 1948), 130; Spears, *Assignment* II, 85. 42. LNCI 939–40 (7/6/40). 43. Villelume, *Journal*, 399. 44. Martin Gilbert, *Finest Hour. Winston Churchill 1939–1941* (Heinemann, 1983), 486–7; Spears, *Assignment* II, 120, was told the same; the French version does not report this: DDF 1940(1) 388 (Visite du Général de Gaulle à Londres). 45. Gilbert, *Finest Hour*, 487; Churchill's high opinion of de Gaulle was also communicated to him by the French Military Attaché Lelong: AN 3AG1/329 (Lelong dossier, 11/6/40). 46. DGM 54. 47. DGM 55–6; Bernard Destremau, *Weygand* (Perrin, 1989), 503–4. 48. Spears, *Assignment* II, 139, 145. 49. Gilbert, *Finest Hour*, 499–512. 50. Earl of Avon, *The Eden Memoirs. The Reckoning* (Cassell, 1965), 116. 51. Baudouin, *Diaries*, 152. 52. Guy, *En écoutant*, 488–9. 53. Jules Jeanneney, *Journal politique* (Armand Colin, 1972), 67. 54. *The Diplomatic Diaries of Oliver Harvey 1937–1940* (Collins, 1970), 387. 55. Guy, *En écoutant*, 88. 56. DDF 1940(1), *Les Armistices de juin*, 6. 57. LNCI 941 (14/6/40). Since the letter is dated 14 June it was presumably drafted in the small hours. 58. DGM 64. 59. Philippe de Gaulle, *De Gaulle mon père* I, 182 60. Winston Churchill, *The Second World War*, vol. II: *Their Finest Hour* (Cassell, 1949), 184. 61. John Colville, *The Fringes of Power: Downing Street Diaries 1939–1945* (Hodder, 1985), 160. 62. DGM 69. 63. DGM 71. In a similar vein he wrote to Robert Aron that the departure was 'without mystery . . . even without risk', LNCIII 624 (9/2/64). 64. Spears, *Assignment* II, 311–22. 65. CCC SPRS 8/13 (Spears Diary). 66. CCC SPRS 8/20 (letter to Churchill, 24/11/48). 67. AN 3AG1/320; CCC SPRS 8/13 (Spears Diary). 68. Spears, *Assignment* II, 323. 69. DGM 71, 73. 70. LNCI 304. 71. Jacques Soustelle, *Envers et contre tout*, vol. I: *De Londres à Alger (1940–1942)* (Laffont, 1947), 19–20. 72. Jean-Michel Royer, 'Le style, c'est l'homme'. 73. TNA CAB 65/7/66 (Peake. 14/7/42); he said the same to Spears in April 1941: St Antony's College, Oxford, Spears Papers, Box 1, File 5 (23/4/41). 74. Philippe de Gaulle, *De Gaulle mon père* I, 182–3. 75. DGM 69–70; and LNCII 349 (17/5/43). 76. De Gaulle, *Fil* (FE), 158. 77. Ibid., 171–2. 78. Ibid., 170. 79. LNCI 376.

6. Rebellion, 1940

1. DGM 73. 2. Gille Ragache, *Les Appels du 18 juin* (Larousse, 2010); François Delpla, *L'Appel du 18 juin 1940* (Grasset, 2000); Jean-Louis Crémieux-Brilhac, *L'Appel du 18 juin* (Armand Colin, 2010). 3. AN 5AG1/1556. 4. AN 3AG1/251 (110) (de Gaulle to Corbin, 17/6/40); LNCI 942 (de Gaulle to Colson, 17/6/40). 5. Jean Monnet, *Mémoires* (Fayard, 1976), 22. 6. Colville, *Fringes*, 164. 7. Ibid., 165. 8. There remains to this day some uncertainty about the exact details surrounding the speech. It has been suggested that, because no recording of it exists, it was broadcast live. But since we know that it was rebroadcast, and since de Gaulle claims to have arrived to speak at 6.00 p.m. and the speech went out at 10.00 p.m., we must assume it was recorded. If no recording survives, the reason can only be that no one at the BBC at the time realized it was important enough to

keep the disc.   9. There is what seems to be an earlier draft in CCC SPRS 1/134 (telegrams June–July 1940).   10. Philippe de Gaulle in his memoirs continues to insist against all evidence that de Gaulle did broadcast that day and even claims that he remembers de Gaulle coming back from the BBC that evening (*Mémoires* I, 139), but since in fact he by his own admission arrived in London the next day (*Mémoires* I, 180) this was impossible. The speech de Gaulle would have given is probably the one dated 2 July 1940 in TNA FO 371/24349 ('*Aussi longtemps que le gouvernement français combattra . . . le devoir consiste à combattre avec lui*'). Here he says that '*demain jeudi*' he will speak again: 19/6/40 was a Wednesday.   11. Alexander Cadogan, *The Diaries of Sir Alexander Cadogan* (Cassel, 1971), 304–5.   12. TNA FO 371/24349 (Strang minute, 19/6/40).   13. CCC SPRS 1/136/2; SPRS 1/131/1 (memo to Churchill, 20/6/40).   14. *Cadogan Diaries*, 305.   15. AN 3AG1/251 (114) (20/4/40 1 p.m. to Lelong); AN 3AG1/251 (116); Delpla, *Appel*, 238–9; Destremau, *Weygand*, 581, quoting a report from Lelong in the defence archive of the Service Historique des Armées (SHAT).   16. André Weil-Curiel, *Le temps de la honte* (Editions du Myrte, 1945), 225–8.   17. Philippe de Gaulle, *De Gaulle mon père* I, 181–90.   18. CCC SPRS 1/134/1 (memo to Churchill, 20/6/40).   19. LNCI 943 (23/6/40).   20. TNA FO 371/24349.   21. Cadogan, *Diaries*, 306.   22. AN 3AG1/257 (101); TNA PREM 3/174/2.   23. CCC SPRS 1/134 (Churchill to Ismay, 24/6/40).   24. Llewellyn Woodward, *British Foreign Policy in the Second World War*, vol. I (HMSO, 1970), 325–6.   25. DGM 271–2; LNCI 944–5 (24/6/40).   26. Cadogan, *Diaries*, 307 (25/6/40).   27. Lord Gladwyn, *The Memoirs of Lord Gladwyn* (Weidenfeld & Nicolson, 1972), 99–100.   28. DGM 273–4; AN 3AG1/257(106).   29. LNCI 947–8 (27/6/40).   30. René Cassin, *Les hommes partis de rien. Le reveil de la France abattue (1940–1941)* (Plon, 1975), 76.   31. DDF 1940(1) 428 (Cambon to Baudouin, 29/6/40).   32. MGDI 277–83.   33. Bernard Ledwidge, *De Gaulle* (Weidenfeld & Nicolson, 1982), 76.   34. DGM 83.   35. Nicholas Atkin, *The Forgotten French* (Manchester University Press, 2003).   36. Edward Spears, *Two Men Who Saved France: Pétain and de Gaulle* (Eyre & Spottiswoode, 1966), 165. See also Max Egremont, *Under Two Flags: The Life of Major-General Sir Edward Spears* (Weidenfeld & Nicolson, 1997), 198; CCC SPRS 1/135/1 (Spears to Churchill, 5/7/40).   37. AP 160 (19/5/62).   38. CCC SPRS 1/135.   39. Spears, *Two Men*, 158–9.   40. Daniel Cordier, *Alias Caracalla* (Gallimard, 2009), 107–8.   41. CCC SPRS 1/134 (Oswald Hotz to Churchill, July 1940).   42. Colonel Passy, *Mémoires du chef des services secrets de la France libre* (Odile Jacob, 2001), 61–2. The original edition was published in two volumes 1947–8. This new edition has an introduction by Jean-Louis Crémieux-Brilhac.   43. AN 72AJ/220 (8) (Maurice Schumann Témoignage).   44. Georges Boris, *Servir la République* (René Julliard, 1963), 295–6.   45. Robert Mengin, *De Gaulle à Londres vu par un Français libre* (Table Ronde, 1965), 61.   46. *Pierre Bourdan vous parle* (Editions Magnard, 1990), 29–30; see also Emile Delavenay, *Témoignage 1905–1991* (Edisud, 1992), 179.   47. CCC SPRS 134/2 (Colin Coote, 1/7/40).   48. Paul-Louis Bret, *Au feu des événements. Mémoires d'un journaliste. Londres, Alger 1929–1944* (Plon, 1959), 147.   49. Jean-François Muracciole, *Les Français libres. L'autre résistance* (Tallandier, 2010).   50. Claude Hettier de Boislambert, *Les feux de l'espoir* (Plon, 1978), 178.   51. Margerie, *Journal 1939–1940*, 375–94.   52. MGDI 270–71 (23/6/40); LNCI 946 (24/6/40).   53. Guillaume Piketty (ed.), *Français en Résistance. Carnets de guerre, correspondance, journaux personnels* (Robert Laffont, 2009), 934–7.   54. Cassin, *Hommes partis*, 88–116.   55. AN 3AG1/330 (Muselier dossier) (Spears to de Gaulle, 4/8/40); TNA FO 371/24349 (Committee on French Resistance, 8/7/40); Jean-Luc Barré, *Devenir de Gaulle 1939–1943* (Perrin, 2009), 166–72, has information from Muselier's naval records.   56. Hugh Dalton, *The Second World War Diary of Hugh Dalton 1940–1945* (Cape, 1986), 60.   57. CCC SPRS 1/134/1.   58. TNA FO 371/24340 (C8391/7328/17).   59. Charlotte Faucher, 'The "French Intellectual Consulate to Great Britain"? The Institut Français du Royaume-Uni, 1910–1959' (unpublished PhD thesis, Queen Mary University of London, 2016) is the definitive study of the French Institute in this period. See also Martyn Cornick, 'The First Bastion of the Resistance: The Free French in London, 1940–1', in Debra Kelly and Martyn Cornick (eds.), *A History of the French in London: Liberty, Equality, Opportunity* (Institute of Historical Research, 2013), 343–72.   60. DGM 100–102.   61. LNCI 1006 (19/8/40).   62. See the report in AN 3AG1251 (112), partly reproduced by Barré, *Devenir*, 132–4, who attributes it to Boislambert, but Patrick Girard, *De Gaulle, le mystère de Dakar* (Calmann-Lévy, 2010), 92–4, is probably correct to say that it was written by a British officer.   63. See Arthur Marder, *Operation 'Menace' and the Dudley North Affair* (Oxford University Press, 1976). For a vivid account by the British officer acting as liaison to de Gaulle on this trip see Duncan Grinnell-Milne, *The Triumph of Integrity: A Portrait of Charles de Gaulle* (Bodley Head, 1961).   64. CCC SPRS 5/36 ('Dakar Diary', 11/9/40).   65. Spears, *Two Men*, 189.   66. CCC SPRS 5/36 ('Dakar Diary', 19/9/40).   67. Gilbert, *Finest Hour*, 790.   68. AN 3AG1/251 (128) (notes by Courcel).   69. 'Carnets de route du Capitaine Desjardins (Michel Bréal) 1896–1977: Avec de Gaulle devant Dakar', *Espoir* 49 (12/84), 7–15; 51 (3/85), 14–27.   70. Marder, *Operation*, 137.   71. Michel Tauriac, *Vivre avec de Gaulle. Les derniers témoins racontent l'homme* (Plon, 2008), 138.   72. Amiral Thierry d'Argenlieu, *Souvenirs de guerre. Juin 1940–janvier 1941* (Plon, 1973), 182.   73. CCC SPRS 5/36 ('Dakar Diary', 24/9/40).   74. LNCI 1045–6 (28/9/40).   75. LNCI 1049–50 (1/10/40).   76. Martin Thomas, *The French Empire at War 1940–1945* (Manchester University Press, 1998); Eric Jennings, *La France libre fut africaine* (Perrin, 2014); on India see Akhila Yechury, '"La République Continue, Comme par le Passé": The Myths and Realities of the Resistance in French India', *Outre-Mers, Revue d'Histoire*, 103/388–9 (2015), 97–116.   77. LNCI 1044 (27/9/40), 1054 (9/10/40).   78. AN 3AG1 (162).   79. Coulet, *Vertu*, 88.   80. Lacouture, *Rebelle*, 447.   81. LNCI 1004 (17/8/40).   82. Colville, *Fringes*, 244; Cadogan, *Diaries*, 327 (17/9/40). See also CCC SPRS 1/134/3 (Spears to Morton, 23/8/40, on how to deal with Catroux).   83. Cassin, *Hommes partis*, 173–6.   84. LNCI 1022 (29/8/40), 1035 (18/9/40).   85. CCC SPRS 5/36 ('Dakar Diary', 19/9/40); LNCI 1039–40 (22/9/40).   86. Henri Lerner, *Catroux* (Albin Michel, 1990), 153–8.   87. Catroux, DGM 116. AP 331: '*Catroux s'est incliné devant mes deux étoiles, lui qui en avait cinq.*'   88. TNA PREM 11/4230.   89. MGDI 297–300.   90. LNCI 1065 (25/10/40).   91. TNA FO 371/24335 (Strang, 27/10/40).   92. Cadogan, *Diaries*,

335 (8/11/40).   **93.** It seems to have been Muselier who had the idea of adopting the Cross of Lorraine as the Free French symbol. For the history of the Order of the Liberation see *Cinquantenaire de l'Ordre de la Libération* (Musée de l'Ordre de la Libération, Paris, 1990).   **94.** AN 3AG1/251 (61).   **95.** MGDI 309–10 (2/11/40).   **96.** AN 3AG1/257 (197); Gilbert, *Finest Hour*, 865–7.   **97.** Schoenbrun, *The Three Lives of Charles de Gaulle*, 94–5.   **98.** LNCI 1063 (22/10/40).   **99.** LNCI 1062 (21/10/40).   **100.** Aurélie Luneau, *Je vous écris de France* (L'Iconoclaste, 2014); AN 3AG1/320 (1–42).   **101.** Robert Gildea, *Fighters in the Shadows: A New History of the French Resistance* (Faber & Faber, 2015), 63.   **102.** Alain Monchablon, 'La manifestation étudiante à l'Etoile du 11 novembre 1940', *Vingtième siècle* 110 (4–6/11), 67–81.   **103.** Christian Delporte, *La France dans les yeux. Une histoire de la communication politique de 1930 à nos jours* (Fayard, 2007).   **104.** Garçon, *Journal*, 564.   **105.** Philippe Foro, *L'antigaullisme. Réalités et représentations* (Honoré Champion, 2003), 158–61.   **106.** Aurélie Luneau, *Radio Londres 1940–1944. Les voix de la liberté* (Perrin, 2005), 90–94.

7. Survival, 1941

1. Claude Bouchinet-Serreulles, *Nous étions faits pour être libres. La Résistance avec de Gaulle et Jean Moulin* (Grasset, 2000), 123.   **2.** AN 3AG1/330 (Passy dossier, 24/10/40); AN 3AG1/251 (48) (61).   **3.** LNCI 1060 (20/10/40); Passy, *Mémoires*, 93–8.   **4.** Colville, *Fringes*, 326 (27/10/40); AN 3AG1/257 (182) (Somerville-Smith to Spears).   **5.** Gaston Palewski, *Mémoires d'action 1924–1974* (Plon, 1988), 137–78.   **6.** TNA FO 371/24344 (Conversation with Palewski, 12/11/40).   **7.** AN 72AJ/220 (Legentilhomme interview, 4/2/49).   **8.** Hervé Alphand, *L'étonnement d'être. Journal 1939–1973* (Fayard, 1977), 89.   **9.** Coulet, *Vertu*, 111; AN 72AJ/2320 (Bouchinet to Pleven, 21/8/41): '*De quelle carence d'individus nous souffrons*'.   **10.** Soustelle, *Envers et contre tout* I, 204.   **11.** De Gaulle, *Fil* (FE), 184.   **12.** Boislambert, *Les feux*, 186; Bouchinet-Serreulles, *Nous étions*, 165.   **13.** Passy, *Mémoires*, 352.   **14.** Joseph Zimet, 'Jacques Bingen, un condottiere pour la France libre?', in FDG, *De Gaulle chef de guerre. De l'Appel de Londres à la libération de Paris 1940–1944* (Plon, 2008), 276–99.   **15.** Sébastien Albertelli, *Les services secrets du Général de Gaulle. Le BCRA 1940–1944* (Perrin, 2009), 50.   **16.** Ibid., 32–5.   **17.** AN 3AG1/329 (Larminat dossier, 14/2/41).   **18.** AN 3AG1/327 (Catroux dossier, 23/2/41).   **19.** LNCI 1152 (17/2/41).   **20.** Neau-Dufour, *Yvonne*, 209.   **21.** Colville, *Fringes*, 388; Albertelli, *Services secrets*, 35–8.   **22.** Albertelli, *Service secrets*, 72, 209–17.   **23.** AN 3AG1/258 (609).   **24.** Jules Moch, *Rencontres avec … de Gaulle* (Plon, 1971), 65.   **25.** Boislambert, *Les feux*, 186.   **26.** The 'sticky' comment is quoted by Susan Raven in a well-documented article on de Gaulle in London, 'Our Guest and One-Time Friend', *Sunday Times Magazine* 5/5/68. For the sociability of the Free French in London see Debra Kelly, 'Mapping Free French London: Spaces, Places, Traces', in Kelly and Cornick (eds.), *A History*, 303–41, and André Gillois, *Histoire secrète des Français à Londres de 1940 à 1944* (Hachette, 1973). Gillois was the pseudonym of Maurice Diamant Berger who worked on the

Free French radio during the war. 27. Leo Amery, *The Empire at Bay: The Leo Amery Diaries 1929–1945* (Hutchinson, 1988), 672 (16/1/41), 674 (13/2/41). 28. James Stourton, *Kenneth Clark: Life, Art and Civilisation* (William Collins, 2016), 173. 29. *The Second World War Diary of Hugh Dalton 1940–1945* (Cape, 1986), 59. 121, 342. 30. Harold Nicolson, *Diaries and Letters 1939–1945* (Collins, 1967), 138, 147 31. Colville, *Fringes*, 159 (16/6/40). On Morton, Gill Bennett, *Churchill's Man of Mystery: Desmond Morton and the World of Intelligence* (Routledge, 2007). 32. LNCI 1142–4 (3/2/41). 33. AN 3AG1/275 (229). 34. TNA FO 371/28419 (12/2/41). 35. MGDI 344–8. 36. MGDI 371–2 (30:/41). 37. Paul Reynaud, *La France a sauvé l'Europe* (Flammarion, 1947), vol. II, 458–9; TNA FO 371/24336 (Catroux to Noguès and Weygand, 2/11 and 8/11/40). 38. MGDI 375; TNA PREM 3/120/10a (Colville to Hopkinson, 1/3/42); TNA FO 371/24336. 39. Cassin, *Hommes partis*, 246. 40. Jean-Louis Crémieux-Brilhac, *La France libre. De l'appel du 18 juin à la libération* (Gallimard, 1996), 181–4. 41. LNCI 1100 (note, 11/12/41). 42. Sophie Davieau-Pousset, 'Maurice Dejean, diplomate atypique (1899–1982)' (unpublished PhD thesis, Ecole des Sciences Politiques, 2013); Albertelli, *Services secrets*, 93–6. 43. AN 72AJ/220/III (Bouchinet interview); Bouchinet-Serreulles, *Nous étions*, 242–3. 44. LNCI 1083 (17/11/40). For the British reaction TNA FO 371/24336 (13/11/40). 45. Jean-Christophe Notin, *Leclerc* (Perrin, 2005), 130–31. 46. LNCI 1194 (29/4/41). 47. The two indispensable books are: A. B. Gaunson, *The Anglo-French Clash in Lebanon and Syria 1940–1945* (Macmillan, 1986) and Aviel Roshwald, *Estranged Bedfellows: Britain and France in the Middle East during the Second World War* (Oxford University Press, 1990). 48. MAE, *Guerre 1939–1945*, 36 (Service Politiques to Catroux, 24/3/41); Gaunson, *Anglo-French Clash*, 16–19. 49. AN 3AG1/263 (135) (31/3/41). 50. DGM 149. 51. AN 3AG1/263 (147) (25/4/41). 52. St Antony's College, Oxford, Killearn Papers, Box 4 (14/4/41). 53. LNCI 1201 (10/5/41). 54. Edward Spears, *The Fulfilment of a Mission: The Spears Mission to Syria and the Levant 1941–1944* (Cooper, 1977), 49–50. 55. TNA FO 954/8a/165 (14/5/41). 56. MGDI 408. 57. AN 3AG1/266 (199) (24/5/41). 58. MAE, *Guerre 1939–1945*, 36 (Catroux to de Gaulle, 4/4/41). 59. DGM 160. 60. DGM 161; LNCI 1201 (10/5/41). 61. Gaunson, *Anglo-French Clash*, 44. 62. DGM 165. 63. Georges Catroux, *Dans la bataille de la méditerranée 1940–1944* (Julliard, 1949), 150–54. 64. DGM 165. 65. Catroux, *Dans la bataille*, 164. 66. TNA PREM 3/422/6 (note, 15/7/41). 67. MGDI 442 (15/7/40). 68. MGDI 442–4. 69. Spears, *Fulfilment*, 127. 70. DGM 166–9; MGDI 447 (21/7/41). 71. Oliver Lyttelton *The Memoirs of Lord Chandos* (Bodley Head, 1962), 247–8; St Antony's College, Spears Papers, Box 1, File 5 (21/7/41); Spears, *Fulfilment*, 133–6. 72. St Antony's College, Spears Papers, Box 1, File 5 (21/7/41); St Antony's College, Killearn Papers, Box 4 (21/7/41); TNA PREM 3/422/6. 73. Gaunson, *Anglo-French Clash*, 61. 74. DGMI 453 (24/7/41). 75. Gaunson, *Anglo-French Clash*, 72. 76. DGM 159, 176–7. 77. Gaunson, *Anglo-French Clash*, 54; Roshwald, *Estranged Bedfellows*, 78–9. 78. MGDI 468 (12/8/41). 79. AN 72AJ/220 (Legentilhomme interview, 4/2/49). 80. Piketty, *Français en résistance*, 213. 81. St Antony's College, Spears Papers, Box 2, File 6 (Somerville-Smith, 23/5/41). 82. Spears, *Fulfilment*,

121. 83. St Antony's College, Killearn Papers, Box 4 (23/7/41). 84. MGDI 454–5 (25/7/41), 467 (10/8/41). 85. MGDI 468–9 (13/8/41). 86. TNA HS 6/311 (29/8/41). 87. St Antony's College, Spears Papers, Box 2a, File 1 (Somerville-Smith to Spears, 11/8/41). 88. AN 72AJ/2321 (28/8/41). 89. Bouchinet-Serreulles, *Nous étions*, 159. 90. TNA PREM 3/120/10b (31/8/41). 91. TNA FO 371/28584 (2/9/41). 92. TNA FO 371/28545 L7769 (3/9/40). 93. Jean-Louis Crémieux-Brilhac, *Prisonniers de la liberté. L'odysée des 218 évadés par l'URSS* (Gallimard, 2004). 94. Alphand, *Etonnement*, 88 95. TNA FO 371/2858 (Somerville-Smith, 24/89/41). 96. John Colville, *Footprints in Time* (Collins, 1976), 114–15. It has to be said that none of this is in Colville's contemporary diary of the event, so one can assume a certain poetic licence. 97. TNA FO 371/29545 (19/9/410); AN 3AG1/257 (266–8). For the British minute, TNA CAB 66/18/44; for the French one, LNCI 1290–93. 98. TNA FO 371/28214 (Mack to Law, 17/9/41). 99. François Kersaudy, *Churchill and de Gaulle* (Fontana Press, 1990), 163–9, is the best account of the crisis. 100. TNA FO 371/28545. 101. LNCI 1299–1307. 102. TNA FO 371/28584; Oliver Harvey, *The War Diaries of Oliver Harvey* (Collins, 1978), 46 (25/9/41). 103. Kersaudy, *Churchill and de Gaulle*, 166.

8. Inventing Gaullism

1. AN AP382/31 (Cassin Papers, 14/7/41). 2. AN 72AJ/2321 (Bingen Journal, 13/7/41). 3. LNCI 993. 4. LNCI 1169–70. 5. DGM 86. 6. AN AP382/31 (Cassin Papers, Cassin to Pleven, 9/7/41); Maritain wrote the same to Pleven, AN AP560/25Dr 2(a) (Pleven Papers, 26/8/41). 7. Jay Winter and Antoine Prost, *René Cassin* (Fayard, 2011), 153. 8. Weil-Curiel, *Le temps*, 318. 9. Philippe Oulmont, 'Le haut-commissaire de l'Afrique française libre (1940–1941)', in Philippe Oulmont (ed.), *Larminat. Un fidèle hors série* (Editions LBM, 2008), 102. 10. LNCI 459 (27/5/19). 11. For the sake of completeness, one should also mention a note addressed to the head of the military *cabinet* in 1942: 'We must immediately stop the wave of Israelites who are arriving here from Lisbon. Telephone Lisbon to say that we will examine every case individually and meanwhile refuse them without my personal authorization.' We know nothing about the context of this note, quoted by Eric Roussel, *Pierre Mendès France* (Gallimard, 2007), 141 (source AN 3AG1/372 Dr. 6), which may have been elicited by complaints that too many Jews were joining the Free French. 12. 'Bataille de la Vistule', reprinted in de Gaulle, *Fil*, 568. 13. Winter and Prost, *René Cassin*, 153; see also an unsigned note, 'Antisémitisme au Quartier Général' (30/12/41), AN AP382/30 (Cassin Papers). 14. Weil-Curiel, *Le temps*, 331. 15. AN 72AJ/2321 (13/7/41). 16. Coulet, *Vertu*, 80. 17. Albertelli, *Services secrets*, 91; Daniel Cordier, *Jean Moulin. L'inconnu du Panthéon*, vol. III (J.-C. Lattès, 1993), 671–2, provides other examples of Rémy's views. 18. Jean-Louis Crémieux-Brilhac, *Georges Boris. Trente ans d'influence. Blum, de Gaulle, Mendès France* (Gallimard, 2010), 140. 19. AN 3AG1/251 (53), 'Note sur les conditions nécessaires à la formation d'un gouvernement de la France Libre susceptible d'être reconnu par les gouvernements britanniques et américains'

(22/10/40). **20.** TNA FO 371/24344 (27/10/40). **21.** AN 3AG1/278 (224). **22.** Albertelli, *Services secrets*, 98. **23.** LNCI 1161 (2/3/41). **24.** LNCI 1248 (8/7/41). **25.** Colville, *Fringes*, 370 (13/12/40). **26.** DMI 77. **27.** TNA FO 371/28214. **28.** AN AP560/16 (Pleven Papers, note, 18/9/41; letter to Pleven, 13/9/41). **29.** DMI 144–7. **30.** DMI 153 (25/11/41). **31.** AN 72AJ/2321 Bingen (8/5/41). **32.** LNCI 979 (25/7/40); Raoul Aglion, *Roosevelt and de Gaulle: Allies in Conflict: A Personal Memoir* (Free Press, New York, 1988), 26. **33.** AN AJ72/220 (8) (Schumann interview). **34.** DMI 131. **35.** AN 3AG1/266 (132) (4/9/41). **36.** Maritain's letters in *Cahiers Jacques Maritain* 16–17 (4/88), 62–3 (21/11/41), 68–9 (21/3/42); de Gaulle's replies, LNCII 3–4 (7/1/42), 62 (24/4/42). **37.** Bouchinet-Serreulles, *Nous étions*, 194. **38.** AN 72AJ/520 (12/3/42). **39.** Alphand, *Etonnement*, 111. **40.** TNA HS 6/311; AN 3AG1/257 (492). **41.** The report is published integrally in Cordier, *L'inconnu du Panthéon* III, 1218–26. **42.** Tournoux, *Jamais dit*, 98; Gilberte Brossolette, *Il s'appelait Pierre Brossolette* (Albin Michel, 1976), 144. For the record, Jacques Baynac, *Présumé Jean Moulin (1940–1943)* (Grasset, 2007) is sceptical about Moulin's Gaullist 'conversion', but his account needs to treated with much caution. **43.** Cordier, *L'inconnu du Panthéon* III, 1267–9. **44.** TNA PREM 3/184/9 (30/10/41). **45.** Cordier, *L'inconnu du Panthéon* III, 1268. **46.** Ibid., 859–61. **47.** Christian Pineau, *La simple vérité* (Julliard, 1961), 157–9. **48.** Ibid., 185–9. **49.** DMI 189–90. **50.** Crémieux-Brilhac, *Georges Boris*, 138; Oulmont, 'Le haut-commissaire', 105–6. **51.** LNCI 89 (6/6/42). **52.** AN 3AG1/329 (Larminat dossier, 3/10/41). **53.** Oulmont, 'Le haut-commissaire', 105–6.

9. On the World Stage, September 1941–June 1942

1. MGDI 543–4 (2/8/41). **2.** François Lévêque, 'Les relations franco-soviétiques pendant la seconde guerre mondiale' (unpublished PhD thesis, University of Paris-I, 1992), 594. **3.** Ibid., 597. **4.** DGM 194. **5.** Lévêque, 'Relations franco-soviétiques', 593. **6.** DGM 196–7, 252–5; MGDI 620–25, 638, 639; AN 3AG1/3 (328) (Ismay dossier). **7.** AN 3AG1/328 (Ismay dossier); DGM 254–5; LNCI 1363 (31/12/41). **8.** TNA FO 371/32001 (Peake to Mack, 26/3/42). **9.** Passy, *Mémoires*, 196. **10.** Pierre Billotte, *Le temps des armes* (Plon, 1972), 189. **11.** LNCI 1359 (24/12/41). **12.** LNCI 960 (11/7/40), 978–80 (25/7/40), 996–8 (12/8/40). **13.** LNCI 1066–8 (26/10/40). **14.** St Antony's College, Spears Papers, Box 2, File 1 (Parr to Eden, 26/7/41). **15.** FRUS 1941 II 130 (18/3/41). **16.** AN 3AG1/329 (Kérillis dossier, 17/6/41). **17.** LNCI 1217 (28/5/41). **18.** LNCI 1335–56 (28/11/41). **19.** MGDI 501–3 (27/12/41). **20.** Richard Sinding, 'Le ralliement de Saint-Pierre-et-Miquelon à la France libre en 1941', *Guerres mondiales et conflits contemporains* 194 (1999), 162–72. **21.** TNA FO 371/31873 ('St Pierre et Miquelon, a Diary of Events'). **22.** LNCI 1360 (24/12/41). **23.** Mauriac, *Un autre de Gaulle*, 112. **24.** MGDI 523 (29/1/42). **25.** TNA FO 371/38173 (Z766); there is also a minute of this meeting in AN 3AG1/341 which differs from the British one and the version that de Gaulle sent to Muselier (LNCII 15–17). **26.** TNA FO

371/31873 (6/1/42). **27.** TNA FO 371/31873 Z643. **28.** TNA FO 371/31959 (this file covers the whole affair). **29.** MGDI 659 (18/3/42). **30.** LNCII 51 (19/3/42). **31.** Bouchinet-Serreulles, *Nous étions*, 190. **32.** TNA FO 892/133 (Peake to Eden, 23/3/42). **33.** TNA FO 371/32001/Z1743 (Peake to Mack, 27/3/42). **34.** TNA FO 371/31948; TNA PREM 3/120/10A. **35.** TNA ADM 199/616A (Peake to FO, 30/5/42). **36.** Peter Mangold, *Britain and the Defeated French: From Occupation to Liberation 1940–1944* (I. B. Tauris, 2012), 160. **37.** Martin Gilbert, *Road to Victory: Winston S. Churchill 1941–1945* (Guild Publishing, 1986), 248–9. **38.** Charles Robet, *Souvenirs d'un médecin de la France libre* (Sides, 1994), 85–7. **39.** On this crisis see: Kim Munholland, 'The Trials of the Free French in New Caledonia, 1940–1942', *French Historical Studies* 14/4 (1986), 547–79; Kim Munholland, *Rock of Contention: Free French and Americans at War in New Caledonia 1940–1945* (Berghahn, Oxford/New York, 2005); Thomas Vaisset, 'Maintenir et défendre la France libre aux Antipodes', in Sylvain Cornil-Frerrot and Philippe Oulmont (eds.), *Les Français libres et le monde* (Nouveau Monde, 2015), 74– 88. **40.** AN 3AG1/295 (de Gaulle to Tixier, 1/2/42). **41.** AN 3AG1/298 (de Gaulle to d'Argenlieu, 7/3/42). **42.** Roussy de Sales, *L'Amérique en guerre (Journal d'un Français aux Etats-Unis)* (La Jeune Parque, 1948), 269. **43.** Roussel, *De Gaulle*, 299–302. **44.** Martin Thomas, 'Imperial Backwater or Strategic Outpost? The British Takeover of Vichy Madagascar, 1942', *Historical Journal* 394 (12/96), 1049–74. **45.** AN 3AG1/328 (Churchill dossier, 16/12/41, 19/2/42); LNCII 25 (11/2/42). **46.** Bouchinet-Serreulles, *Nous étions*, 204; Pleven in Piketty, *Français en résistance*, 1023 ('Jamais l'avenir ne m'est apparu plus obscur'). **47.** MGDI 595–7. **48.** Crémieux-Brilhac, *France libre*, 305–6. **49.** Harvey, *War Diaries*, 125, 133 (18/6/42). **50.** TNA PREM 3/1/120/7. **51.** LNCII 78–9 (16/5/42). **52.** Lévêque, 'Relations franco-soviétiques', 626–7. **53.** Ibid., 645–6. **54.** MGDI 602– 3. **55.** TNA PREM 3/120/10B (27/4/42). **56.** TNA PREM 3/120/10B (23/4/42). **57.** TNA FO 371/32009 5/6 (Peake to Eden). **58.** TNA PREM 3/120/10a (Cairo to FO, 10/6/42). **59.** TNA FO 371/32009. **60.** Bouchinet-Serreulles, *Nous étions*, 192, 240. **61.** TNA FO 371/32001 (Mack 22/1/42). **62.** AN 72AJ/220 (Schumann interview). **63.** Amery, *The Empire*, 748. **64.** Neau-Dufour, *Yvonne*, 196–222; see http://www.itnsource.com/shotlist/BHC_RTV/1941/01/01/BGX408060358/?v=0&a=1. **65.** AN 72AJ 220/13. **66.** Annette Pleven (12/7/42) in Piketty, *Français en résistance*, 1026–7. **67.** Bouchinet-Serreulles, *Nous étions*, 183. **68.** Guillaume Piketty, *Pierre Brossolette. Un héros de la Résistance* (Odile Jacob, 1998), 218–19. **69.** Pineau, *Simple vérité*, 159 **70.** Pierre-Henri Teitgen, *'Faites entrer le témoin suivant'. 1945–1958. De la Résistance à la Ve République* (Ouest-France, Rennes, 1988), 159. **71.** Alphand, *Etonnement*, 114. **72.** Piketty, *Français en résistance*, 1026. **73.** TNA ADM 199/616A (Peake, 20/3/42). **74.** Nicolson, *Diaries*, 269. **75.** Coulet, *Vertu*, 107–13. **76.** AN 72AJ 220 (34) (interview with Madeleine Gex Le Verrier). **77.** Bouchinet-Serreulles, *Nous étions*, 253. **78.** Passy, *Mémoires*, 122. **79.** TNA FO 371/36064 (27/10/42). **80.** TNA FO 371/36013 (2/3/43). **81.** TNA FO 371/3207 (25/7/42). **82.** Mary Borden, *Journey Down a Dark Alley* (Hutchinson, 1946), 113–15. **83.** TNA PREM 3/182/6 (Macmillan memorandum, 3/1/44). **84.** Philippe Oulmont, 'Les

Free French et *Albion*', in Cornil-Frerrot and Oulmont, *Français libres*, 19–38. **85.** AN 72AJ 2320 (Bouchinet-Serreulles to Jacques Maritain, 8/4/41). **86.** AN 5AG1/1293 (André Weil-Curiel to de Gaulle, 27/12/47). **87.** FDG Papiers Barberot F26/46 ('Mes interminables ruminations sur de Gaulle'). **88.** Jean-Louis Crémieux-Brilhac, 'Pour Combattre avec de Gaulle', *La Marseillaise* 31/1/43. **89.** AN 3AG1/328 (14/9/41). **90.** Coulet, *Vertu*, 194. **91.** Piketty, *Français en résistance*, 1031 (29/8/42).

10. Fighting France, July–Ocober 1942

1. AN 72AJ2320 (Bouchinet-Serreulles to Garreau, 28/7/42). **2.** AN AP560/25 Dr. 2 (B) (Rauzan to Pleven, 10/9/41). **3.** Pineau, *Simple vérité*, 156–7. **4.** Maurice Chevance-Bertin, *Vingt mille heures d'angoisse* (Robert Laffont, 1990), 71–2; Jean-Pierre Lévy, *Mémoires d'un franc-tireur. Itinéraire d'un résistant* (Complexe, Brussels, 1998), 75. **5.** Madeleine Gex Le Verrier quoted in Julien Blanc, *Au commencement de La Résistance. Du côté du Musée de l'Homme 1940–1941* (Seuil, 2010), 366. For Gex Le Verrier's full account, see her *Une Française dans la tourmente* (Editions Emile-Paul Frères, 1945). **6.** Johanna Barasz, 'Un Vichyiste en Résistance, le Général de La Laurencie', *Vingtième siècle* 94 (4/6/2007), 167–81; Daniel Cordier, *La République des catacombes* (Gallimard, 1999), 162–3 quotes from the only contemporary document of the meeting. **7.** Albertelli, *Services secrets*, 194. **8.** AN 3AG1/327 (Giraud dossier, 14/8/42). **9.** Piketty, *Pierre Brossolette*, 183–90; his report of 8 May is reproduced in Passy, *Mémoires*, 246–7. **10.** D'Astier de la Vigerie, *Sept fois sept jours*, 83, 86. **11.** TNA PREM 3/184/9 ('Report on Opinion in France', 9/6/42). **12.** TNA PREM 3/184/9 (15/6/42). **13.** LNCII 107 (30/6/42). **14.** AN 3AG1/329 (Mandel dossier, 20/8/42). **15.** *L'oeuvre de Léon Blum (1940–1945)* (Albin Michel, 1955), 357–61 (5/4/42, 15/8/42). **16.** AN 72AJ220 (3c) (22/6/42). Reprinted in Boris, *Servir*, 298–303. **17.** *Cahiers Jacques Maritain*, 16–17 (4/88), 87–8. **18.** Thomas Rabino, *Le Réseau Carte. Histoire d'un réseau de la résistance antiallemand, antigaulliste, anticommuniste et anticollaborationiste* (Perrin, 2008). **19.** TNA HS 6/311 (10/7/42). Letter of de Gaulle to Eden, MGDII 341–2, TNA HS 6/311; Albertelli, *Services secrets*, 216, 222. **20.** TNA CAB 66/26 WP(42)285; CAB 66/27/29 WP(42)349. **21.** Harvey, *War Diaries*, 137–8 (4/7/42). **22.** Ibid., 166 (2/10/42). **23.** TNA FO 371/32027/Z5974 (reproduced in Cornil-Frerrot and Oulmont, *Français libres*, plates II–IV). **24.** Aglion, *Roosevelt and de Gaulle*, 116. **25.** Robert W. Hamblin, 'The Curious Case of Faulkner's "The De Gaulle Story"', *Faulkner Journal* 16/1 and 2 (Fall 2000/Spring 2001), 79–86; for the full scenario see Louis Daniel Brodsky and Robert W. Hamblin, *De Gaulle. Scénario William Faulkner* (Gallimard, 1989). **26.** TNA FO 954/8a/256; CAB 66/26 WP(42)285. **27.** MGDII 340–41. **28.** MGDII 343–5; Mark Clark, *Calculated Risk* (Harrap, 1951), 44–5; Ed Cray, *General of the Army: George C. Marshall, Soldier and Statesman* (Norton, New York, 1990), 334–5. **29.** The two aides present were Coulet (see FDG FAA20, Fonds Coulet) and Billotte (see Guillaume Piketty, 'Les voies douloureuses de la reconquête', in Cornil-Frerrot and Oulmont,

Français libres, 63). 30. MGDII 347 (de Gaulle to Tixier, 31/742). 31. TNA FO
371/3207 (Peake to Mack, 25/7/42). 32. TNA PREM 3/120/7 (Eden to Peake,
28/7/42); FO 954/8a/2828; LNCII 128–9 has minutes of this meeting. 33. Averell
Harriman, *Special Envoy to Churchill and Stalin 1941–1946* (Random House, 1975),
149–50; DGM 277. 34. Meir Zamir, 'An Intimate Alliance: The Joint Struggle of
General Edward Spears and Riad al-Sulh to Oust France from the Lebanon', *Middle
East Studies* 41/6 (2005), 811–32. 35. Gaunson, *Anglo-French Clash*, 147. 36.
LNCII 64 (4/5/42). 37. AN 3AG1/263 (16); Lord Casey, *Personal Experience
1939–1946* (Constable, 1962). 38. Brosset journal in Piketty, *Français en résistance*,
237–8. 39. Roshwald, *Estranged Bedfellows*, 111–17; Gaunson, *Anglo-French
Clash*, 97–9; AN 3AG1/263 (17) (meeting de Gaulle–Wilkie, 10/9/42). 40.
Bouchinet-Serreulles, *Nous étions*, 228. 41. MGDII 525 (5/2/42); LNCII 143
(28/8/43), 146–7 (1/9/42). 42. Bouchinet-Serreulles, *Nous étions*, 232–3. 43.
LNCII 154–5 (5/9/42). 44. MGDII 360–61 (27/8/42). 45. LNCII 174
(19/9/42). 46. DGM 296. 47. Harvey, *War Diaries*, 156 (14/9/42). 48. LNCII
182–8; TNA PREM 3/120/6. 49. TNA FO 371/31950 (6/10/42). 50. Harvey,
War Diaries, 164 (1/10/42). 51. TNA PREM 3/120/6 (Peake to Strang,
10/10/42). 52. AN 74AJ429 (de Gaulle to Catroux, 5/10/42). 53. 'Renouveau
politique en France', *La Marseillaise* 27/9/42. 54. Archives of Groupe Jean Jaurès,
Office Universitaire de Recherches Socialistes (OURS), 94APO3 (meetings of
26/9/42, 3/10/42). For Vallin's defence of his position see his article 'La dissidence
est à Vichy', *La Marseillaise* 4/10/42. 55. LNCII 131 (29/7/42). 56. AN
3AG1/269 (194) (de Gaulle to Guerin, 7/10/42). 57. Alphand, *Etonnement*,
124. 58. LNCII 189–94 (6/10/42); FRUS 1942 II (Europe) 541–8. 59. FRUS
1942 II (Europe) 544 (26/10/42).

11. Power Struggles, November 1942–November 1943

1. DMI 207–15. 2. Billotte, *Le temps*, 239. 3. TNA FO 371/31950. 4. MGDII
392. 5. Gilbert, *Road to Victory*, 252. 6. Soustelle, *Envers et contre tout* I, 454;
Bouchinet-Serreulles, *Nous étions*, 251. 7. TNA FO 371/31951 (Peake,
15/11/42). 8. Bouchinet-Serreulles, *Nous étions*, 255; LNCII 210–11
(14/11/42). 9. William I. Hitchcock, 'Pierre Boisson, French West Africa, and the
Postwar *Epuration*: A Case from the Aix Files', *French Historical Studies* 24/2
(Spring 2001), 305–41. 10. Jean-Christophe Notin, *Leclerc* (Perrin, 2005),
233. 11. Harvey, *War Diaries*, 191 (22/11). 12. MGDII 403–5; LNCII 216–
17. 13. MGDII 412–13 (de Gaulle to Tixier, 21/11/42). 14. Warren F. Kimball
(ed.), *Churchill and Roosevelt: The Complete Correspondence*, vol. II: *Alliance
Forged, November 1942–February 1944* (Princeton University Press, 1984), 7
(19/11/42). Gilbert, *Road to Victory*, 277. 15. FRUS 1942 II (Memorandum of
conversation by Undersecretary of State 20/11/42) 546–7; the first phrase was in
fact cut from the official record: see G. E. Maguire, *Anglo-American Policy towards
the Free French* (Macmillan, Basingstoke, 1995), 164; MGDII 408–12. 16. Robert
Sherwood, *The White House Papers of Harry L. Hopkins*, vol. II (Eyre &

Spottiswoode, 1949), 647.   17. TNA FO 954/8A/2885.   18. AN 3AG1/263 (27);
Roussel, *De Gaulle*, 326.   19. Kimball, *Churchill and Roosevelt* II, 22. Stalin
told Roosevelt that he completely approved: *My Dear Mr Stalin: The Complete
Correspondence between Franklin D. Roosevelt and Joseph V. Stalin* (Yale University
Press, New Haven/London, 2005), 103–4 (14/12/42).   20. LNCII (14/12/42).   21.
Christine Levisse-Touzé, *L'Afrique du Nord dans la guerre 1939–1945* (Albin Michel,
1998),   276–7; AN 72AJ/210/2 (interview François d'Astier de la Vigerie).
22. TNA FO 371/36047 (26/11/42).   23. TNA FO 317/31954 (Peake to Eden,
21/12/42).   24. Cadogan, *Diaries*, 498–9 (8/12/42).   25. Albertelli, *Services secrets*,
247–8.   26. Barré, *Devenir de Gaulle*, 373–83, speculates on this possibility.   27.
Cadogan, *Diaries*, 500 (27/12/42).   28. Alphand, *Etonnement*, 133.   29. LNCII
257–8 (11/1/43).   30. Cadogan, *Diaries*, 504.   31. Ibid., 505 (19/1/43).   32. Harold Macmillan, *War Diaries: Politics and War in the Mediterranean, January 1943
to May 1945* (Macmillan, 1984), 8–9; Robert Murphy, *Diplomat among Warriors*
(Doubleday, 1966) 165–6.   33. FRUS *The Conferences at Washington and Casablanca, 1941–1942* (President to Secretary of State 18/1/43) 816.   34. For the conference see DGMI 338–48; AN 72AJ/429 (memorandum drafted by Palewski,
29/1/43); Boislambert, *Les feux*, 379–86.   35. Sherwood, *Harry L. Hopkins*,
682–3.   36. FRUS *The Conferences at Washington and Casablanca, 1941–1942*
(Roosevelt–de Gaulle conversation) 694–5.   37. MGDII 441 (28/1/43); Boislambert, *Les feux*, 383, reports de Gaulle as saying he had met a '*homme d'Etat*' and
was appreciated by him.   38. Gilbert, *Road to Victory*, 305.   39. LNCII 266–8;
see also the letter he left with Pleven before departing, LNCII 264 (22/1/43).   40.
Harvey, *War Diaries*, 210.   41. Lord Moran, *Winston Churchill: The Struggle for
Survival* (Constable, 1966), 82.   42. MGDII 440 (26/1/43); AN 3AG1/251
(388).   43. Moran, *Winston Churchill*, 81–2.   44. Arthur Funk, 'The Anfa Memorandum: An Incident of the Anfa Conference', *Journal of Modern History* 26/3
(9/54), 246–54.   45. AN 3AG1/327 (Capitant dossier, 9/2/43).   46. LNCII 267
(23/1/43).   47. AN 3AG/251 (600).   48. AN 72AJ/220 (Billotte interview).   49.
AN 3AG1/251 (601); in a similar vein Bingen AN 3AG1/251 (603).   50. Raphaël
Ulrich-Pier, *René Massigli (1888–1988). Une vie de diplomate* (Peter Lang, Brussels,
2006), vol. I, 731.   51. Henri Queuille, *Journal de Guerre, Londres–Alger, avril
1943–juillet 1944* (Plon, 1995), 14, 19.   52. Pierre Laroque, *Au service de l'homme
et du droit. Souvenirs et reflexions* (Association pour l'étude de l'histoire de la securité
sociale, 1993), 136–9.   53. Jacques Beauce, 'Le 8 juin n'est pas une date complaisante', *La Marseillaise* 13/6/43.   54. René Vérard, *Jean Pierre-Bloch. Un Français
du monde entier* (Corsaire éditions, 1997), 154–5.   55. Reprinted in Raymond Aron,
Chroniques de guerre (Gallimard, 1990), 763–76.   56. Cordier, *République*,
243–54.   57. AN 72AJ/520 Gouin Papers, 'Rapport de Bremond [Boyer]'
(21/1/43).   58. LNCII 273 (10/2/43).   59. Cordier, *République*, 286–313.   60.
Passy, *Mémoires*, 363. The encounter is also reported by Frenay. There is no certainty
about the date: Cordier, *République*, 211, dates it to 16/11 ('*la veille de son départ*')
while Passy claims it occurred just after he arrived.   61. LNCII 288–9 (10/3/43);
AN 3AG1/329 (Churchill dossier).   62. AN 3AG1/279 (18) ('Bernard' and 'Lenoir'
to de Gaulle, 19/5/43); in general see Robert Belot, *La Résistance sans de Gaulle*.

Politique et gaullisme de guerre (Fayard, 2006), 329–52.   63. Francis-Louis Closon, *Le temps des passions. De Jean Moulin à la Libération 1943–1944* (Félin, 1998), 72–96, reproduces the entire report.   64. AN 72AJ/2321 ('Cléante' to Philip, 5/2/44). The issue is discussed by Cordier, *République*, 411–15, who also quotes a similar letter Bingen wrote to Philip on 4 May 1943. See AN 3AG1/279 (17) (note of Philip, 5/5/43) which shows that he took this on board.   65. Cordier, *République*, 413.   66. MGDII 477–9; see François-Yves Guillin, *Le Général Delestraint. Premier chef de l'armée secrète* (Plon, 1995), 200.   67. Catroux, *Dans la bataille*, 343–9.   68. TNA FO 954/8B/369 (conversation between Catroux and Eden, 29/1/43).   69. TNA FO 371/36047 (24/2/43).   70. Macmillan, *War Diaries*, 113. Peter Mangold, *The Almost Impossible Ally: Harold Macmillan and Charles de Gaulle* (I. B. Tauris, 1996) is a good overview of the relationship between the two men.   71. André Kaspi, *La mission de Jean Monnet à Alger* (Sorbonne, 1971).   72. Henri Giraud, *Un seul but, la victoire. Alger 1942–1944* (Julliard, 1949), 121–2.   73. AN 72AJ/429 (Catroux to de Gaulle, 19/3/43; de Gaulle to Catroux, 20/3/43).   74. LNCII 297–8 (19/3/43).   75. AN 3AG1/251 (691) (Marchal to de Gaulle, 29/3/43); MAE, *Guerre 1939–1945*, 1456 (23/3/43).   76. TNA FO 371/36047.   77. LNCII 314–19 (2/4/43).   78. Girard de la Charbonnières, *Le duel Giraud–de Gaulle* (Plon,1984) (Charbonnières was on Catroux's team); Macmillan, *War Diaries*, 57–8.   79. Charbonnières, *Le duel*, 100–101, 122–6.   80. TNA FO 954/8B/2950 (13/4/43).   81. René Bouscat, *De Gaulle–Giraud. Dossier d'une mission* (Argus, 1967), 93 (20/4/43).   82. Ibid., 116 (27/4/43).   83. LNCII 334 (26/4/43); Albertelli, *Services secrets*, 252; AN 3AG1/327 (Capitant dossier, 17/5/43).   84. MAE, *Guerre 1939–1945*, 1457 (Catroux to de Gaulle, 11/5/43); Eric Roussel, *Jean Monnet* (Fayard, 1996), 338.   85. TNA FO 371/36174; the rumour was also reported by Boislambert to Pleven, AN AP560/26.   86. Macmillan, *War Diaries*, 74.   87. Ibid., 68.   88. 'Extraits des notes du journal personnel de Léon Teyssot', in *Espoir* 59 (6/87), 34.   89. Macmillan, *War Diaries*, 84.   90. Ulrich-Pier, *René Massigli*, 768–9; AN 3AG1/329 (Massigli dossier, 4/5/43).   91. DMI 304–5 (4/5/43).   92. Soustelle, *Envers et contre tout*, vol. II: *D'Alger à Paris (1942–1944)* (Robert Laffont, 1950), 241.   93. AN 72AJ/429 (12/5/43).   94. Roussel, *Monnet*, 334–5.   95. MGDII 471–3 (6/5/43).   96. TNA FO 371/36039 (note, 18/1/43). After the war France kept control over the Fezzan until Libya became independent in 1951.   97. TNA PREM 3/442/19; Charbonnières, *Le duel*, 178–9.   98. Roussel, *De Gaulle*, 360.   99. TNA PREM 3/184/9 (21/5/43).   100. TNA FO 371/36047 (23/5/43).   101. Claude Paillat, *L'echiquier d'Alger*, vol. II: *De Gaulle joue et gagne* (Robert Laffont, 1967), 251. The source of this exchange is the generally well-informed journalist Claude Paillat, though the exact words of course cannot be authenticated.   102. DGM 366.   103. TNA FO 371/36178.   104. Macmillan, *War Diaries*, 97.   105. Ibid., 97–101; Catroux, *Dans la bataille*, 365–6.   106. Macmillan, *War Diaries*, 100–101.   107. AN 3AG1/252 (3); MGDII 488–9.   108. LNCII 355–6 (2/6/43); Charbonnières, *Le duel*, 212–13.   109. Macmillan, *War Diaries*, 107; Catroux, *Dans la bataille*, 369.   110. Kimball, *Churchill and Roosevelt* II, 231 (6/6/43).   111. LNCII 361 (9/6/43).   112. TNA FO 660/50 (11/6/43).   113. Macmillan, *War Diaries*, 122; TNA FO 371/36178 (14/6/43).

114. LNCII 364 (14/6/43). 115. Harvey, *War Diaries*, 268; Kimball, *Churchill and Roosevelt* II, 255–7 (17/6/43). 116. Macmillan, *War Diaries*, 128; AN 3AG1/263 (33); 3AG1/275 (190) (Eisenhower to de Gaulle). 117. TNA PREM 3/184/6 (24/6/43). 118. LNCII 368–70 (3/7/43); MGDII 505–6. 119. LNCII 367 (24/6/43). 120. André Gide, *Journal*, vol. II: *1926–1950* (Gallimard, 1997), 965. 121. Charbonniéres, *Le duel*, 204. 122. De Gaulle, *Fil* (FE), 183. 123. Macmillan, *War Diaries*, 136. 124. Roussel, *De Gaulle*, 370. 125. Ibid., 380 126. DMI 330–31. 127. LNCI 380 (3/8/40). 128. FRUS 1943 II 179–81 (31/7/43). 129. AN 3AG1/279 (340) (Coulet to de Gaulle, 22/9/43). 130. Queuille, *Journal*, gives a vote of 7:6; Crémieux-Brilhac, *La France libre*, 578–9, basing himself on the unpublished *carnet* of Georges, gives 6:3; General Legentilhomme implies in a letter to de Gaulle on the next day that de Gaulle had only 5 votes, AN 3AG1/251 (122). 131. DGM 409. 132. Macmillan, *War Diaries*, 230. 133. AN 3AG1/251 (130). 134. AN 3AG1/252 (9/11/43). 135. Queuille, *Journal*, 105–6; AN 3AG1/251 (158–6); Macmillan, *War Diaries*, 288–9. 136. TNA PREM 3/182/6 (memorandum on recognition, 3/1/44). 137. Alphand, *Etonnement*, 156.

12. Building a State in Exile, July 1943–May 1944

1. Kimball, *Churchill and Roosevelt* II, 334–5 2. Cordell Hull, *The Memoirs of Cordell Hull*, vol. II (Hodder & Stoughton, 1948), 1241. 3. FRUS 1943 II 173 (WSC to FDR, 21/7/43). 4. Arthur Layton Funk, *Charles de Gaulle: The Crucial Years 1943–44* (University of Oklahoma Press, 1959), 148–76. 5. Macmillan, *War Diaries*, 211 6. DGM 402 7. Soustelle, *Envers et contre tout* II, 265–6; Joxe, *Victoires*, 123–4. 8. Philippe de Gaulle, *De Gaulle mon père* II, 530. 9. John Julius Norwich (ed.), *The Duff Cooper Diaries* (Weidenfeld & Nicolson, 2005), 292. 10. Neau-Dufour, *Yvonne*, 222–6; René Cerf-Ferrière, *Assemblée Consultative vue de mon banc* (Editions réunies, 1974), 189–90. 11. Philippe de Gaulle, *De Gaulle mon père* I, 292. 12. Pierre Guillain de Bénouville, *Avant que la nuit ne vienne* (Le Grand Livre du Mois, 2002), 207. 13. Chantal Morelle, *Louise Joxe. Diplomate dans l'âme* (André Versaille, 2008). 14. Joxe, *Victoires*, 117; Armand Bérard, *Un ambassadeur se souvient. Au temps du danger allemand* (Plon, 1976), 491. 15. Colette Barbier, *Henri Hoppenot (25 octobre 1891–10 août 1977), diplomate* (Ministère des affaires étrangères, 1999). 16. Soustelle, *Envers et contre tout* II, 273–4; Ulrich-Pier, *René Massigli*, 865–71; MAE, *Guerre 1939–1945*, 1480 (Massigli to Vienot, 7/8/43). 17. AN 72AJ/220 (3) (Boris interview). 18. Joxe, *Victoires*, 152. 19. Jean Chauvel, *Commentaire. D'Alger à Berne (1944–1952)* (Fayard, 1972), 13–14. 20. General de Monsabert, *Notes de Guerre* (Editions Jean Curutchet, 1999), 134, 174. 21. AN 3AG1/328 (Juin dossier, 3/6/43). 22. Yves Maxin Danan, *La vie politique à Alger de 1940–1944* (Paris, 1963), 264–5; Cerf-Ferrière, *Assemblée*, 183–4. 23. Christian Girard, *Journal de guerre 1939–1945. Témoignage de l'aide de camp du général Leclerc de Hauteclocque* (L'Harmattan, 2000), 79, 112. 24. TNA PREM 3/120/10A (28/7/43). 25. Christian Chevandier and Gilles Morin

(eds.), *André Philip* (IGPDE, 2005), 437–48. **26.** Queuille, *Journal*, 86. **27.** LNCII 421. **28.** MGDII 600; Ulrich-Pier, *René Massigli*, 814. **29.** Raphaëlle Ulrich-Pier, *Correspondance Pierre Viénot–René Massigli. Londres–Alger, 1943–1944* (Armand Colin, 2012), 98 (16/11/44). **30.** TNA FO 660/37; Ulrich-Pier, *Correspondance*, 99–102. **31.** Queuille, *Journal*, 94, 108, 115, 130. **32.** Passy, *Mémoires*, 677. **33.** Charbonnières, *Le duel*, 277–9. **34.** TNA PREM 3/120/10A (16/10/43). **35.** Loïc Philip, *André Philip* (Beauchesne, 1988), 170–73. **36.** Chauvel, *Commentaire*, 21–2. **37.** AN 3AG1/279 (42) (The author was 'Sermoy', pseudonym of Jacques-Henri Simon of OCM.) **38.** Piketty, *Français en résistance*, 325–7. **39.** AN 72AJ/520 Dossier 2 (6/43); LNCII 364 (15/5/43). **40.** DMI 327–31. **41.** AN 72AJ/220 (3) (Boris interview). **42.** DMI 355–6, 411. **43.** Macmillan, *War Memoirs*, 281–2. Note also favourable references to Beveridge in *La Marseillaise*: Alain Chambery, 'Réforme sociale et production' 9/8/42 and 'Affranchir l'homme du besoin' 22/11/42. **44.** LNCII 381–2. **45.** Kimball, *Churchill and Roosevelt* II, 625–6. **46.** Roussel, *De Gaulle*, 411. **47.** AN 3AG1/279 (84) (Rapport mensuel Cléante, 4/44); AN 3AG1/279 (32). **48.** Laurent Ducerf, 'François de Menthon au Service du Général', in FDG, *De Gaulle chef de guerre*, 98–115. **49.** TNA FO 371/36178 (7/6/43). **50.** Philippe Buton, 'Les discussions entre de Gaulle et le Parti communiste français à l'automne 1943', in FDG, *De Gaulle chef de guerre*, 216–24. **51.** Robert Belot, *Aux frontières de la liberté* (Fayard, 1998), 232. **52.** Charles-Louis Foulon, *Le pouvoir en province. Les commissaires de la République* (Armand Colin, 1975), 57–8. **53.** Closon, *Le temps des passions*, 150–52 (His monthly reports are in AN 72AJ/1970.) **54.** Jean-Louis Crémieux-Brilhac, 'De Gaulle et la mort de Moulin', in J.-P. Azéma, *Jean Moulin face à l'histoire* (Flammarion, 2004), 195–207. **55.** Cordier, *République*, 562. **56.** Ibid., 497; Piketty, *Français en résistance*, 448–52. **57.** AN 3AG1/279 (21, 27, 28). **58.** LNCII 403 (1/10/43). **59.** AN 3AG1/279 (340). **60.** AN 3AG1/279 (68) (Luizet report, 23/10/43). **61.** MGDII 591–2. **62.** FRUS 1943 *Conferences at Cairo and Tehran* #238 (Minute of Meeting, 19/11/43). **63.** Christian Valensi, *Un témoin sur l'autre rive. Washington 1943–1949* (Comité pour l'histoire économique et financière de la France, 1994), 48–57; Roussel, *Monnet*, 407–8. **64.** AN AG3/1/262 (151–2). **65.** MAE, *Guerre 1939–1945*, 1488/159 (27/12/43). **66.** Ulrich-Pier, *René Massigli*, 875. **67.** AN 3AG1/260 (444) (22/9/43). **68.** Lévêque, 'Relations franco-soviétiques', 781–803; AN 3AG1260 (450) (Dejean, 3/11/43). **69.** TNA FO 954/8B/3084 (11/10/43). **70.** Kersaudy, *Churchill and de Gaulle*, 297. **71.** Harriman, *Special Envoy*, 231. **72.** Julie Le Gac, *Vaincre sans gloire. Le corps expéditionnaire français en Italie (novembre 1942–juillet 1944)* (Les Belles-Lettres/Ministère de la Défense-DMPA, 2013). **73.** AN 3AG1/275 (205, 210) (Larminat to de Gaulle). **74.** Harry C. Butcher, *My Three Years with Eisenhower: The Personal Diary of Captain Harry C. Butcher* (New York, 1946), 473; MGDII 67–76; TNA FO 660/188; AN 3AG1/328 (Eisenhower dossier, 29/12/44). **75.** Cooper, *Diaries*, 290; TNA PREM 3/181/3; Gilbert, *Road to Victory*, 644–7; Woodward, *British Foreign Policy*, vol. III (HMSO, 1971), 8–9. **76.** Gilbert, *Road to Victory*, 646. **77.** TNA FO 371/36036 Macmillan (21/10/43); Alphand, *Etonnement*, 175; TNA FO 371/41879. **78.** Queuille, *Journal*, 128 (14/2/44). **79.** AN

AP450/2 (Lecompte-Boinet Papers, 14/11/43). 80. AN 3AG1/266 (198) (Philip to de Gaulle, 5/10/43); (227) (Passy to de Gaulle, 9/11/43). 81. Soustelle, *Envers et contre tout* II, 293. 82. LNCII mission 488–9 (4/44). 83. DMI 406. 84. AN 3AG1/275 (215). 85. AN 3AG/1 (217–18) (7/3/44). 86. Claire Miot, 'Sortir l'armée des ombres. Soldats de l'Empire, combattants de la Libération, armée de la Nation: la première armée française, du débarquement en Provence à la capitulation allemande (1944–1945)' (unpublished PhD thesis, ENS Cachan, 2016), 61–5. 87. MAE, *Guerre 1939–1945*, 1464, 260–66 (Viénot to Massigli). 88. TNA FO 371/41879 (9/5/44). 89. Hillary Footitt and John Simmonds, *France 1943–1944* (Holmes & Meier, 1988), 19–28. 90. AN 3AG1/258 (469); MAE, *Guerre 1939–1945*, 1480 (4/4/44); Ulrich-Pier, *Correspondance*, 156–7. 91. AN 3AG1/258 (480); Roussel, *Monnet*, 418–19. 92. MAE, *Guerre 1939–1945*, 1481 (10/10/43, 19/5/44). 93. Lévêque, 'Relations franco-soviétiques', 914–16. 94. Alfred D. Chandler (ed.), *The Papers of Dwight D. Eisenhower: The War Years* III (Johns Hopkins University Press, Baltimore and London, 1970), 1691. 95. Kimball, *Churchill and Roosevelt* II, 145. 96. Woodward, *British Foreign Policy* III, 49. 97. Crémieux-Brilhac, *France libre*, 816–17. 98. Cooper, *Diaries*, 307. 99. Chandler, *Papers of Eisenhower* III, 1904.

13. Liberation, June–August 1944

1. MGDII 640. 2. Avon, *Reckoning*, 453. 3. Kimball, *Churchill and Roosevelt*, vol. III: *Alliance Declining, February 1944–April 1945* (Princeton University Press, 1984), 156 (1/6/44). 4. DGM 487–8; for the British record, Kersaudy, *Churchill and de Gaulle*, 341–2; the line about the false money is in Antoine Béthouart, *Cinq années d'espérance. Mémoires de guerre 1939–1945* (Plon, 1968), 242–3. 5. DGM 489. 6. Chandler, *Papers of Eisenhower* III, 1907. 7. Cadogan, *Diaries*, 635. 8. Harvey, *War Diaries*, 343 (9/6/44). 9. Cadogan, *Diaries*, 635. 10. R. Bruce Lockhart, *Comes the Reckoning* (Putman, 1947), 303–4. 11. DMI 431–2. 12. Kimball, *Churchill and Roosevelt* III, 171 (7/6/44). 13. Avon, *Reckoning*, 455–6; TNA FO 371/41879 (7/6/44). 14. MGDII 643. 15. Kimball, *Churchill and Roosevelt* III, 181 (12/6/44). 16. TNA FO 954/9a/206; 954/9a/3269. 17. MGDII 642–3. 18. Cadogan, *Diaries*, 635. 19. Guy, *En écoutant*, 398. 20. Ulrich-Pier, *Correspondance*, 158–60 (16/6/44). 21. TNA FO 954/18A/162; TNA CAB 120/867; Woodward, *British Foreign Policy* III, 61–2. 22. Henry L. Stimson and McGeorge Bundy, *On Active Service in Peace and War* (Harper & Brothers, New York, 1947), 549 (14/6/44). 23. René Hostache, 'Bayeux, 14 juin 1944: étape décisive sur la voie d'Alger', in FDG, *Le rétablissement de la légalité républicaine* (Complexe, Brussels, 1996), 231–4. 24. Harvey, *War Diaries*, 345 (14/6/44). 25. Boislambert, *Les feux*, 442. 26. Béthouart, *Cinq années*, 249. 27. LNCII 517. 28. Laroque, *Au service*, 184. 29. Coulet, *Vertu*, 230. 30. DGMI 494. 31. The film can be seen at http://www.ina.fr/video/AFE99000037. 32. TNA CAB 867 (15/6/44). 33. Coulet, *Vertu*, 227–51; see Coulet's letters to Boris and de Courcel in AN 3AG1/277 (272) and 3AG1/328 (Courcel dossier). 34. TNA FO 371/41880 (28/6/44). 35.

DGM 496–8. The comment comes from Alexander Werth, *De Gaulle: A Political Biography* (Penguin, 1965), 165. **36.** Aglion, *Roosevelt and de Gaulle*, 175; Francis Biddle, *In Brief Authority* (Doubleday, New York, 1962), 181–2. **37.** DGM 498–504. **38.** Kimball, *Churchill and Roosevelt* III, 369. **39.** FRUS 1944 III (10/7/44) 724–5. **40.** This is the version reported by Pierre Mendès France in Crémieux-Brilhac, *France libre*, 852. **41.** Aglion, *Roosevelt and de Gaulle*, 180. **42.** Woodward, *British Foreign Policy in the Second World War* III, 72–6. **43.** Roussel, *De Gaulle*, 438–9. **44.** AN 3AG1/252 (220); see also 3AG1/251 (214). **45.** François Rachline, *L.R. Les silences d'un résistant* (Albin Michel, 2015), 226, 259–61. **46.** Jean-Louis Crémieux-Brilhac, 'Quelle stratégie militaire pour quelle libération?', in Crémieux-Brilhac, *De Gaulle, la République et la France libre 1940–1945* (Perrin, 2014), 401–4. **47.** Miot, 'Sortir l'armée', 74–7. **48.** LNCII 538–9. **49.** Matthew Cobb, *Eleven Days in August: The Liberation of Paris in 1944* (Simon & Schuster, 2013), 36. **50.** AN 72AJ/1902 (17/8/44). **51.** TNA FO 954/9a/335; CCC (Cooper Archives) DUFC 15/1/31 (17/8/44). **52.** DGM 559. **53.** MGDII 703–5. **54.** DGM 568. **55.** DMI 467. **56.** AN AP450 (25/8/44). **57.** Charles Rist, *Une saison gâtée. Journal de guerre et de l'occupation* (Fayard, 1984), 432. **58.** Cobb, *Eleven Days*, 318–26. **59.** Berthe Auroy, *Jours de guerre* (Bayard, Montrouge, 2008), 335. **60.** DGM 573. **61.** LNCII 554 (27/8/44). **62.** René Courtin, *De la clandestinité au pouvoir. Journal de la Libération de Paris* (Editions de Paris, 1994), 48–9. **63.** Pasteur Vallery-Radot, *Mémoires d'un non-conformiste 1886–1966* (Grasset, 1966), 291. **64.** AN AP450/2 (27/8/44). **65.** Pierre Villon, *Résistant de la première heure* (Editions sociales, 1983), 116; also Maurice Kriegel-Valrimont, *La Libération. Les archives du COMAC* (Editions du Minuit, 1964), 228–9. **66.** AN AP450/2 (Lecompte-Boinet Papers, 1/9/44).

14. In Power, August 1944–May 1945

1. Teitgen, 'Faites entrer', 162. **2.** Laurent Douzou and Dominique Veillon, 'Les déplacements du General de Gaulle à travers la France', in FDG, *Rétablissement*, 656–7. **3.** Pierre Bertaux, *La libération de Toulouse et de sa région* (Hachette, 1973), 87–93. **4.** Serge Ravanel, *L'esprit de résistance* (Seuil, 1995). See also Ravanel, *Les valeurs de la résistance. Entretien avec Serge Ravenel* (Privat, Toulouse, 2004), 88–9. **5.** Lacouture, *De Gaulle*, vol. II: *Le politique* (Seuil, 1985), 49. **6.** Gildea, *Fighters in the Shadows*, 411–12. **7.** DGM 597, 600, 602. **8.** Teitgen, 'Faites entrer', 170. **9.** Mauriac, *Un autre de Gaulle*, 45. **10.** Bernard Lachaise, 'L'entourage de Charles de Gaulle, président du GPRF à Paris (25 août 1944–21 janvier 1946), *Histoire@Politique* 8 (2009/2). **11.** Mauriac, *Un autre de Gaulle*, 60. **12.** Indomitus, *Nous sommes les rebelles* (Collection Défense de la France, 1945); Pierre Hervé, *La Libération trahie* (Grasset, 1945). **13.** *Franc-Tireur* 24/9/44. **14.** LNCII 363; DGM 690–91. **15.** DGM 692–3. **16.** Mauriac, *Un autre de Gaulle*, 52. **17.** Jean-Luc Barré, *François Mauriac. Biographie intime*, vol. II: *1940–1970* (Fayard, 2010), 81–2. **18.** François Mauriac, *De Gaulle* (Grasset, 1964), 17–18. **19.** Lacouture, *De Gaulle* II, 19. **20.** Mauriac, *Un autre de Gaulle*,

77–8. **21.** Ibid., 97–9. **22.** Jacques Isorni, *Mémoires*, vol. I: *1911–1945* (Robert Laffont, 1984), 314–15. **23.** Mauriac, *Un autre de Gaulle*, 75. **24.** The fullest account is Alice Kaplan, *The Collaborator: The Trial and Execution of Robert Brasillach* (University of Chicago Press, 2000), who consulted the pardon file but wrote before the de Gaulle archives were open. According to the inventory of those archives there is a dossier of 'Notes sur l'affaire Brasillach', AN 3AG4/49 Dr. 13 – but that dossier is missing. **25.** DGM 1325. **26.** Mauriac, *Un autre de Gaulle*, 51. **27.** Although highly critical, the best overview of de Gaulle's foreign policy in 1944–6 is Pierre Gerbet and Jean Laloy, *Le relèvement: 1944–1949* (Imprimerie nationale, 1991). **28.** Alphand, *Etonnement*, 168–9; also a note by him in AN 3AG1/262 (307); Roussel, *Monnet*, 394–6. **29.** DMI 410 (18/3/44); Alphand note on western bloc, AN 3AG1/262 (316). **30.** LNCII 546 (10/8/44). **31.** DMI 410 (18/3/44). **32.** Raymond Poidevin, 'La politique allemande de la France en 1945', in Maurice Vaïsse (ed.), *8 mai 1945. La victoire en Europe* (Complexe, Brussels, 1985), 221–38. **33.** Ulrich-Pier, *René Massigli*, 894; AN 3AG1/254 (424). **34.** Jean-Rémy Bézias, *Georges Bidault et la politique étrangère de la France (1944–1948)* (L'Harmattan, 2006), 179. **35.** Roshwald, *Estranged Bedfellows*, 199. **36.** CCC DUFC 4/5 (21/5/45). **37.** Cooper, *Diaries*, 330. **38.** DGM 637. **39.** DGM 638–9. For the official record of the talks CCC DUFC 4/14. **40.** MGDIII 643–66; Lévêque, 'Relations franco-soviétiques', 1008–53; Georges Soutou, 'Le Général de Gaulle et l'URSS, 1943–1945: idéologie ou équilibre européen', *Revue d'histoire diplomatique* 4 (1994), 303–55; Jean Laloy, 'A Moscou: entre Staline et de Gaulle. Decembre 1944', *Revue des études slaves* 54/1–2 (1982), 137–52; see also the 'Dossier: comment a-t-on perçu le Traité franco-soviétique de décembre 1944?', in Maurice Vaïsse (ed.), *De Gaulle et la Russie* (CNRS Editions, 2006), 83–96; Roussel, *De Gaulle*, 465–78. **41.** Philippe Buton, 'L'entretien entre Maurice Thorez et Joseph Stalin du 19 novembre 1944', *Communisme* 45/46 (1996), 7–29. **42.** DGM, 650. **43.** Harvey, *War Diaries*, 368. **44.** AN AP549 (Jouve Papers, draft for memoirs). **45.** Harriman, *Special Envoy*, 377. The British diplomat John Balfour, also present, remembered de Gaulle remarking loudly: 'Do you think we will be able to get on with these people after the war?' The diplomat replied diplomatically, but de Gaulle, looking hard at Malenkov, a member of the Politburo to whom he had been talking earlier, added: 'When I see the looks of these future leaders of Russia whom I invited here to meet me tonight I very much doubt it.' Balfour's personal testimony to the British diplomat Bernard Ledwidge in Ledwidge, *De Gaulle*, 191. **46.** Soutou, 'Le Général de Gaulle', 338–40, compares the documents reproduced by de Gaulle with other French documents; and Lévêque, 'Relations franco-soviétiques', 1048–9, compares them with the Soviet ones. **47.** Jean Laloy, *Yalta: Yesterday, Today, Tomorrow* (Harper & Row, New York, 1988), 57. **48.** Guy, *En écoutant*, 141. **49.** Ibid. **50.** DGM 647. **51.** DGM 674. **52.** LNCII 644 (25/4/45). **53.** DGM 614; see also 725. **54.** MGDII 710–11 **55.** Piketty, *Français en résistance*, 693–5 (4/12/44, 10/1/45). **56.** Frank Gurley, 'Politique contre stratégie: la défense de Strasbourg en décembre 1944', *Guerres mondiales et conflits contemporains*, 166 (1992), 89–114. **57.** AN 3AG4/74 (Dossier 'Operation I Armée Française 1/45–4/5). **58.** DGM 732–6. **59.** Lord Alanbrooke, *War Diaries*

1939–1945 (Weidenfeld & Nicolson, 2001), 642. 60. CCC DUFC 15/1/34. 61. Kersaudy, *Churchill and de Gaulle*, 390–91. 62. Guy, *En écoutant*, 217. 63. FRUS 1945 IV #669. 64. Miot, 'Sortir l'armée', 606–10. 65. FRUS 1945 IV #698. 66. LNCII 675 (2/6/45). 67. FRUS 1945 IV #699. 68. FRUS 1945 IV #702. 69. DGM 767–8. 70. LNCII 581–4 (note of 12/10/44 prepared by Bidault but annotated by de Gaulle). 71. LNCII 586 (19/10/44). 72. François Kersaudy, 'Levant', in Institut du Temps Présent, *De Gaulle et la nation face aux problèmes de la défense (1945–1946)* (Plon, 1983), 251–2; also Kersaudy, *Churchill and de Gaulle*, 397–405. 73. Cooper, *Diaries*, 371. 74. DGM 780. 75. DGM 1342. 76. Kersaudy, 'Levant', 258. 77. AN 3AG1/279 (540). 78. Institut Charles de Gaulle, *Brazzaville. Janvier–février 1944* (Plon, 1988) was the first study but needs to be corrected by Martin Shipway, 'Brazzaville, entre mythe et non-dit', in FDG, *De Gaulle chef de guerre*, 392–404; Shipway, 'Les Français libres, la politique dite de "Brazzaville" et les perspectives d'avenir de l'union française vue de 1944–1946', in Cornil-Frerrot and Oulmont, *Français libres*, 231–45; and the first chapter of Shipway, *The Road to War: France and Vietnam 1944–1947* (Berghahn, Oxford, 1996). 79. DMI 492 (25/10/44). 80. Crémieux-Brilhac, *France libre*, 660–73. 81. Jean-Pierre Peyroulou, 'La politique algérienne du Général de Gaulle 1943–1946', in Maurice Vaïsse (ed.), *De Gaulle et l'Algérie 1943–1969* (Armand Colin, 2006), 28–37; and Roger Benmebarek, 'Le Général de Gaulle et les événements de mai 1945 dans le Constantinois', in ibid., 38–47. 82. Mauriac, *Un autre de Gaulle*, 112. 83. LNCII 656 (1/5/45). 84. Frédéric Turpin, *De Gaulle, les Gaullistes et l'Indochine* (Indes Savantes, 2005), 107; Shipway, *The Road to War*, 76–7. These two studies supersede Institut Charles de Gaulle, *De Gaulle et l'Indochine* (Plon, 1982) which tries unconvincingly to make a liberal case for de Gaulle's policy towards Indo-China. 85. Turpin, *De Gaulle*, 125–8. 86. LNCII 712–13 (16/9/45). 87. LNCII 729 (27/10/45). 88. LNCII 29/9/45. 89. Turpin, *De Gaulle*, 190 n. 97. 90. DGM 762–3. 91. Maurice Vaïsse, 'Remarques sur la capitulation à Reims (7 mai 1945)', in Vaïsse, *8 Mai 1945*, 43–65. 92. LNCII 691 (2/8/45). 93. Roussel, *De Gaulle*, 511. 94. This note is published by Rainer Hudemann in Henri Ménudier (ed.), *L'Allemagne occupée 1945–1949* (Institut d'Allemande, 1989), 169–75. See also Hudemann, 'Revanche ou partenariat? A propos des nouvelles orientations de la recherche sur la politique française à l'égard de l'Allemagne après 1945', in Gilbert Krebs and Gérard Schneilin (eds.), *L'Allemagne 1945–1955. De la capitulation à la division* (Institut d'Allemand, 1996), 127–52. 95. LNCII 719–24. 96. Rainer Hudemann, 'Le Général de Gaulle et la politique de reconstruction en zone française d'occupation en Allemagne après 1945', in DGESSV 313–24. 97. Harvey, *War Diaries*, 383. 98. DDF 1945(2) 59. 99. DDF 1945(2) 23. 100. Chauvel, *Commentaire*, 113–14. 101. De Gaulle, *Fil* (FA), 399. 102. René Girault, 'La France est-elle une grande puissance en 1945?', in Vaïsse, *8 mai 1945*, 195–218; Robert Frank, *La hantise du déclin. La France de 1914 à 2014* (Belin, 2014), 96–104. 103. DGM 782–3.

15. From Liberator to Saviour, May 1945–December 1946

1. LNCII 3 (7/1/42).   2. LNCII 23 (4/2/42).   3. LNCII 588 (annotation of a note by Pompidou, 23/10/44).   4. Philippe Viannay, *Du bon usage de la France. Résistance, journalism, Glénans* (Ramsay, 1988), 152.   5. AN 3AG1/276 (56).   6. AN 3AG1/276 (48) ('Rapport sur l'elaboration d'un programme du Comité de Libération Nationale').   7. Roussel, *Mendès France*, 141–55.   8. Pierre Mendès France, *Oeuvres complètes*, vol. II: *Une politique de l'économie 1943–1954* (Gallimard, 1985), 33–4; DMII 406–7 (18/3/44).   9. Mendès France, *Oeuvres* II, 48–9; AN 3AG1/268 (54).   10. AN 3AG4/1 Dossier 5 (3/3/45).   11. Crémieux-Brilhac, *Georges Boris*, 308–35.   12. Philippe Mioche, *Le Plan Monnet. Genèse et élaboration 1941–1947* (Publications de la Sorbonne, 1987), 82–4. On Monnet's skill in getting de Gaulle's support see Luc-André Brunet, *Forging Europe: Industrial Organisation in France 1940–1952* (Palgrave, 2017), 189–97.   13. AN 4AG/1 Dossier 5 (Vallon notes, 10/12/45, 19/12/45).   14. Macmillan, *War Diaries*, 289.   15. Roussellier, *La force de gouverner*, 26–68.   16. Ibid., 494.   17. Joxe, *Victoires*, 126.   18. DMIII 158 (17/11/59).   19. DGM 609.   20. FRUS 1943 II #148.   21. Michel Debré, *Mémoires. Trois républiques pour une France*, vol. I: *Combattre* (Albin Michel, 1984), 340–41.   22. Ibid., 314.   23. DGM 861   24. AN 3AG4/2.   25. Roussel, *De Gaulle*, 518.   26. The classic example is his speech of September 1959 over Algeria (see below p. 518).   27. Roussel, *De Gaulle*, 518.   28. Mauriac, *Un autre de Gaulle*, 130.   29. Jérôme Perrier, *Entre administration et politique. Michel Debré (1912–1948)* (Institut Université Varenne, 2013), 669–80; Debré, *Mémoires* I, 392–403.   30. Cooper, *Diaries*, 393.   31. DGM 859.   32. Cooper, *Diaries*, 395.   33. Roussel, *De Gaulle*, 522.   34. Perrier, *Entre administration et politique*, 687–8.   35. LNCII 771.   36. Guy, *En écoutant*, 57.   37. Moch, *Rencontres*, 124–6.   38. LNCII 778 (15/1/46), 783 (18/1/46). He said exactly the same thing at a committee meeting he chaired on Germany on 18 January: see Moch, *Rencontres*, 116–18.   39. Moch, *Rencontres*, 110–12.   40. Georgette Elgey, *La République des illusions 1945–1951* (Fayard, 1965), 85–6.   41. CCC DUFC 4/6 9 (letter to Eden, 2/2/46).   42. The most reliable account is that given a few hours afterwards by Teitgen as reported in Jean Charlot, *Le Gaullisme d'opposition 1946–1958* (Fayard, 1983), 18–27.   43. LNCII 779–80 (16/1/46).   44. LNCII 784 (21/1/46).   45. TNA FO 371/59956 (21/1/46).   46. LNCII 783 (21/1/45); Guy, *En écoutant*, 35.   47. AN 3AG4/1 Dr. 7 (20/1/46).   48. Guy, *En écoutant*, 42.   49. AN 3AG4/1 Dr. 7 (20/1/46).   50. Archives of Ministry of the Interior, AN F1a/3201.   51. Marcel Cachin, *Carnets 1906–1947*, vol. IV: *1935–1947* (CRNS Editions, 1997), 894.   52. AN 3AG4/98 (11/4/46); Guy, *En écoutant*, 55.   53. Mauriac, *Un autre de Gaulle*, 164.   54. Guy, *En écoutant*, 36.   55. Ibid., 38–9.   56. Alphand, *Etonnement*, 193–4.   57. Mauriac, *Un autre de Gaulle*, 167.   58. LNCII 791 (14/3/46).   59. DMII 10 (16/6/46).   60. Lacouture, *Politique*, 269.   61. For a critique of this idea see Gaïti, *De Gaulle, prophète de la cinquième République*, passim.   62. Guy, *En écoutant*, 79.   63. Gérard Conac, 'René Capitant et le référendum', in FDG, *Le discours d'Epinal. 'Rebâtir la République'* (Economica, 1997),

203–16.   64. Cassin, *Hommes partis*, 132–3; LNCII 854 (14/5/48).   65. Guy, *En écoutant*, 136.   66. F. Decaumont (ed.), *Le discours de Bayeux. Hier et aujourd'hui* (Economica, 1990).   67. AN 5AG1/1267 (Schumann, 12/6/46).   68. Odile Rudelle, 'L'accueil du discours dans l'opinion', in Decaumont, *Discours*, 65–86.   69. Guy, *En écoutant*, 146.   70. LNCII 800 (8/7/46); AN 5AG1/1247 (Pleven, 2/8/46, 8/10/46).   71. Bernard Lachaise, 'L'Union gaulliste en 1946', in Gilles Richard and Jacqueline Sainclivier, *La recomposition des droites* (Presses Universitaires de Rennes, 2004); on Capitant's visit Guy, *En écoutant*, 137–41.   72. AN 5AG1/1267 (Schumann dossier, 26/8/46).   73. Mauriac, *Un autre de Gaulle*, 237.   74. Guy, *En écoutant*, 186–7.   75. Ibid., 186.   76. Ibid., 201.   77. Ibid., 143, 195.   78. Ibid., 241–2.

16. The New Messiah, 1947–1955

1. Guy, *En écoutant*, 242–8.   2. Mauriac, *Un autre de Gaulle*, 266.   3. Guy, *En écoutant*, 117.   4. DMII 48 (30/3/47).   5. Mauriac, *Un autre de Gaulle*, 272.   6. Vendroux, *Cette chance*, 208; Vincent Auriol, *Journal du Septennat 1947–1954*, vol. I: *1947* (Armand Colin, 1970), 178; Jean-Raymond Tournoux, *La tragédie du Général* (Plon, 1967), 38.   7. Guy, *En écoutant*, 156–7; Philippe de Gaulle, *De Gaulle mon père* I, 458, also remembered the conversation.   8. Guy, *En écoutant*, 115   9. Ibid., 259–62.   10. LNCI 840 (13/11/37).   11. Larcan, *Inventaire*, 487–91; Jean Serroy, *De Gaulle et les écrivains* (Presses Universitaires de Grenoble, 1991), 69–97; Philippe Barthelet, 'Bernanos et de Gaulle', *Espoir* 72 (9/90), 19–21; Georges Bernanos, *Français, si vous saviez (1945–1948)* (Gallimard, 1950).   12. Patrick Guiol, *L'impasse sociale du gaullisme. Le RPF et l'action sociale* (FNSP, 1985); Jean-François Sirinelli, Marc Sadoun and Robert Vandenbussche, *La politique sociale du Général de Gaulle* (University Charles de Gaulle, Villeneuve d'Ascq, 1990).   13. DGM 681.   14. LNCII 877 (31/8/48).   15. Louis Vallon, *L'histoire s'avance masquée* (René Julliard, 1957),   16. Guy, *En écoutant*, 345.   17. Irwin Wall, *The United States and the Making of Postwar France 1944–1954* (Cambridge University Press, 1991), 80–4.   18. Guy, *En écoutant*, 329, 337.   19. DMII 143–5 (27/10/47).   20. DMII 147 (12/11/47).   21. Guy, *En écoutant*, 355.   22. Auriol, *Journal* I, 29; LNCII 810 (1/47).   23. Mauriac, *Un autre de Gaulle*, 252.   24. Vincent Auriol, *Journal du Septennat 1947–1954*, vol. II: *1948* (Armand Colin, 1974), 369.   25. Olivier Duhamel, '"La Trace et le sillon": l'UDSR et le RPF', in FDG, *De Gaulle et le Rassemblement du peuple français* (Armand Colin, 1998), 633–52.   26. AN 5AG1/1247 (Pleven dossier); AN AP560/16 (Pleven to de Gaulle, 21/3/48); Yves Beauvois, *Léon Noël. De Laval à de Gaulle via Pétain (1888–1987)* (Presses Universitaires du Septentrion, 2001), 276.   27. AN 5AG1/1267 (Maurice Schumann, 19/8/48).   28. Claude Michelet, *Mon père Edmond Michelet* (Presses de la Cité, 1971), 186.   29. Louis Terrenoire, *De Gaulle 1947–1954. Pourquoi l'échec. Du RPF à la traversée du desert* (Plon, 1981), 65–8; Michelet, *Mon père*, 189–90.   30. FRUS 1948 III 374 (14/1/48), 392 (17/3/48), 397 (8/5/48).   31. FRUS 1948 III 419 (12/10/48).   32. Terrenoire, *Pourquoi*, 84–5; Michelet, *Mon père*, 208–9.   33. LNCII 856 (15/5/48).   34. André Malraux, *Antimémoires* (Gallimard, 1967)

125–33. In general see Janine Mossuz, *André Malraux et la Gaullisme* (Armand Colin, 1970); Alexandre Duval-Stalla, *André Malraux – Charles de Gaulle, une histoire, deux légendes. Biographie croisée* (Gallimard, 2008). **35.** The diagnosis is made by Olivier Todd, *André Malraux. Une vie* (Gallimard, 2001). **36.** The remark was made to Todd, ibid., 17. **37.** See the October 1948 issue of *Esprit* entitled 'Interrogation à Malraux'. **38.** Georges Pompidou, *Pour rétablir une vérité* (Flammarion, 1982), 86. **39.** Ibid., 51. **40.** Charlot, *Gaullisme*, 153. **41.** AN 5AG1/1235 (Noël to de Gaulle, 8/7/48). **42.** Guy, *En écoutant*, 318. **43.** Pompidou, *Pour rétablir*, 88. **44.** Ibid., 102–3 (the letter was cut from subsequent editions). **45.** Pompidou, *Pour rétablir*, 69. **46.** Claude Mauriac, *Le temps immobile*, vol. II: *Les espaces imaginaires* (Grasset, 1975), 251 (5/6/52). Or see Pompidou's remark: 'I am a bit worn out by Charles's excessive severity. How to find a way of telling him that being so tough on other people one impoverishes oneself?' in Pompidou, *Lettres*, 214 (2/7/50). **47.** LNCII 826 (10/11/47). Or as he put the matter some years later, 'A programme? Never! Politics is about realities. Realities are always changing. One needs principles and objectives, not a programme': AP 446. **48.** Turpin, *De Gaulle*, 417. **49.** DMII 356 (11/2/50). **50.** DMII 521 (23/252), 616 (7/6/53). **51.** DMII 324 (25/9/49); 366 (6/3/50); 424 (7/1/51); 367 (16/3/51). **52.** Pompidou, *Pour rétablir*, 77. **53.** Christian Delporte, 'Les grands rassemblements', in FDG, *De Gaulle et le Rassemblement*, 146–63. **54.** Jean Garrigues, *Les hommes providentiels. Histoire d'un fascination française* (Seuil, 2012), 163–4. **55.** Delporte, 'Les grands rassemblements', 157. **56.** Vincent Auriol, *Journal du Septennat 1947–1954*, vol. VI: *1952* (Armand Colin, 1978), 46. **57.** Jean Galtier-Boissière, *Mon journal dans la grande pagaïe* (La Jeune Parque, 1950), 258. **58.** Pierre Debray, 'Bonpartisme, boulangisme et néo-gaullisme', *Esprit* (11/47), 889–97. **59.** Mauriac, *Un autre de Gaulle*, 196. **60.** This is the letter of 5/12/48 referred to in note 40. See Perrier, *Entre administration et politique*, 756–60. **61.** Mauriac, *Un autre de Gaulle*, 271. **62.** François Audigier, 'L'héritage de la Résistance pour les cadets gaullistes de la IVe République', in Bernard Lachaise (ed.), *Résistance et politique sous la IVe République* (Presses Universitaires de Bordeaux, 2004), 59–75. **63.** Bernard Marin, *De Gaulle de ma jeunesse* (Cercle d'Or, Sables d'Olonne, 1984), 20; Guiblin, *Passion d'agir*, 15,36; Jacques Dauer, *Le hussard du Général* (Table Ronde, 1994), 155. **64.** Jacques Baumel, *De Gaulle. L'exil intérieur* (Albin Michel, 2001), 182–3; Colonel F. Soulet, 'Témoignage', *Espoir* 18 (3/77), 50–52 has the story of a picnic under a tree in 1952. **65.** Charlot, *Gaullisme*, 179. **66.** Guy, *En écoutant*, 256. **67.** Ibid., 76. **68.** Neau-Dufour, *Yvonne*, 260–62. **69.** Baumel, *Exil*, 93. **70.** Mauriac, *Un autre de Gaulle*, 201; see also letter to Paul Guth, LNCIII 1003 (18/11/68): 'On comprend que la France est une terrible contrée. Mais à tout prendre, n'est-ce pas satisfaisant?' **71.** Guy, *En écoutant*, 207 (16/1/47). **72.** Terrenoire, *Pourquoi*, 126. **73.** André Astoux, *L'oubli* (J. C. Lattès, 1974), 388. **74.** Jacques Soustelle, *Vingt-huit ans de Gaullisme* (Table Ronde, 1968), 45–6. **75.** Terrenoire, *Pourquoi*, 163, 214. **76.** Frédérique Dufour, 'Colombey et la gaullisme sous la IVe République', in François Audigier and Frédéric Schwindt (eds.), *Gaullisme et Gaullistes dans la France de l'est sous la IVe République* (Presses Universitaires de Rennes, 2009), 353–71. **77.** DGM 873. **78.** Guy, *En écoutant*, 249–50. **79.**

Neau-Dufour, *Yvonne*, 310–14.   80. LNCII 837 (10/2/48).   81. Guy, *En écoutant*, 392.   82. LNCII, 855–6 (15/5/48).   83. Pompidou, *Pour rétablir*, 132.   84. DMII 293–4 (29/3/49), 372 (29/3/50).   85. Sudhir Hazareesingh, *Le mythe gaullien* (Gallimard, 2010), 96.   86. Rémy, *De Gaulle cet inconnu* (Raoul Solar, 1947), 30; Guy, *En écoutant*, 359. Rémy, *Dix ans avec de Gaulle (1940–1950)* (Editions France-Empire, 1971) gives his account.   87. Except by Domenach in *Esprit* (8/48), 224–7.   88. Pompidou, *Lettres*, 211–12.   89. Ibid., 221–2.   90. LNCII 1106 (26/1/53); Pompidou, *Pour rétablir*, 135.   91. Charlot, *Gaullisme*, 207–17.   92. Soustelle, *Vingt ans*, 68.   93. DMII 447.   94. Astoux, *L'Oubli*, 277–8.   95. Pompidou, *Pour rétablir*, 128.   96. Auriol, *Journal* VI, 17 (7/1/52). He said the same a few months earlier: Auriol, *Journal du Septennat 1947–1954*, vol. V: *1951* (Armand Colin, 1975), 476 (25/9/51).   97. Auriol, *Journal* VI, 49–50.   98. Charlot, *Gaullisme*, 259; Pompidou, *Lettres*, 230–32.   99. Auriol, *Journal* VI, 160–61.   100. Terrenoire, *Pourquoi*, 163–6.   101. DMII 537.   102. Pompidou, *Lettres*, 234–5.   103. LNCII 1075–9 (6/7/52).   104. Pompidou, *Lettres*, 235–6 (1/9/52).   105. AN 5AG1/1272 (Soustelle to de Gaulle, 11/5/52, 30/9/52).   106. Terrenoire, *Pourquoi*, 185–6; Frédéric Turpin, *Jacques Foccart. Dans l'ombre du pouvoir* (CRNS Editions, 2015), 81.   107. Pompidou, *Pour rétablir*, 137.   108. AN 5AG1/1131 (Bozel to de Gaulle, 12/11/51). Bozel, whose real name was Jean Richemond, is a rather forgotten figure of Gaullism. There are some memories of him in Jean-Louis Crémieux-Brilhac, *L'étrange victoire. De la défense de la République à la libération de la France* (Gallimard, 2016), 108–15.   109. AN 5AG1/1161 (Dronne to de Gaulle, 5/6/52, 10/6/52).   110. Pompidou, *Pour rétablir*, 137 (9/5/53).   111. DMII 609.   112. LNCII 1116–22 (13/6/53).

17. In the 'Desert', 1955–1958

1. Terrenoire, *Pourquoi*, 201.   2. *Foccart parle. Entretiens avec Philippe Gaillard*, vol. I (Fayard Jeune Afrique, 1995), 103.   3. Terrenoire, *Pourquoi*, 234–5.   4. Philippe Buton, 'La CED, l'Affaire Dreyfus de la Quatrième République?', *Vingtième siècle* 84/4 (2004), 43–59.   5. Terrenoire, *Pourquoi*, 219, 229.   6. DMII 622–3 (12/11/53).   7. LNCII 1156 (30/4/54).   8. Terrenoire, *Pourquoi*, 269.   9. Georgette Elgey and Jean-Marie Colombani, *La Cinquième ou la République des phratries* (Fayard, 1999), 29–30.   10. Frédéric Turpin, 'Printemps 1954. Echec à de Gaulle: un retour au pouvoir manqué', *Revue historique* 303/4 (10–12/01), 913–27; Terrenoire, *Pourquoi*, 270–71.   11. Astoux, *L'oubli*, 384.   12. DMII 647.   13. Terrenoire, *Pourquoi*, 284.   14. Ibid., 300–302; Tournoux, *Tragédie*, 178–9, was the first to publish an account of the meeting; Mendès France never commented on it but a private note of 1966 suggests he did not agree with de Gaulle's account of what was said: Roussel, *Mendès France*, 339.   15. Odille Rudelle, *Mai*, 76.   16. Garrigues, *Hommes providentiels*, 284–97.   17. DMII 662.   18. Cooper, *Diaries*, 292.   19. Pompidou, *Lettres*, 226.   20. Adrien Le Bihan, *De Gaulle écrivain* (Pluriel, 2010); Alan Pedley, *As Mighty as the Sword: A Study of the Writings of Charles de Gaulle* (Elm Bank, Exeter, 1996); Marius-François Guyard, 'Un écrivain nommé

Charles de Gaulle', in DGM, lxv–xcii. **21.** Terrenoire, *Pourquoi*, 198; Sulzberger, *Last of Giants*, 8. **22.** DGM 479–83; Crémieux-Brilhac, *France libre*, 730–33 gives the background to the affair. **23.** DGM 790. **24.** DGM 502. **25.** DGM 504. **26.** DGM 759–60. **27.** DGM 875. **28.** DGM 583. **29.** DGM 152. **30.** LNCII 975 (27/6/50). **31.** DGM 262. **32.** DGM 573. **33.** DGM 875. **34.** Hazareesingh, *Mythe*, 53–76. **35.** LNCII 929 (6/8/49). **36.** Guy, *En écoutant*, 335. **37.** Bernard Tricot, *Mémoires* (Quai Voltaire, 1994), 366. **38.** Guy, *En écoutant*, 335; Mauriac, *Un autre de Gaulle*, 253; Larcan, *Inventaire*, 234–53. **39.** DGM 874. **40.** LNCII 1166 (12/10/54). **41.** Garrigues, *Hommes providentiels*, 170. **42.** AN AP449 (Terrenoire unpublished journal, 9/1/55). **43.** Maxime Weygand, *En lisant les mémoires du Général de Gaulle* (Flammarion, 1955). **44.** Frenay, 'De Gaulle et la Résistance', *Preuves* 70 (12/56), 78–84. **45.** AN AP449 (Terrenoire unpublished journal, 18/10/55). **46.** Jean Mauriac, *Le Général et le journaliste* (Fayard, 2008), 129. **47.** Olivier Guichard, *Mon Général* (Grasset, 1990), 313. **48.** David Valence, 'Les cabinets des ministres Républicains sociaux (1953–1958)', *Espoir* 153 (12/2007), 119–27. **49.** Olivier Guichard, *Vingt ans en 1940* (Fayard, 1999), 11. **50.** See Turpin, *Jacques Foccart*. **51.** Philippe de Gaulle, *Mémoires accessoires*, vol. II: *1947–1979* (Plon, 2000). **52.** One might also mention their pets. There was a cat, Poussy, to which Madame de Gaulle was devoted, but they had less luck with their dog. It was an Alsatian which had been given to de Gaulle as a present when it was found as a puppy by one of the Free French soldiers who occupied Hitler's retreat at Berchtesgaden in 1945. But Hitler's puppy, which the de Gaulles called Vincam, grew up uncontrollably wild and had to be got rid of. Guy, *En écoutant*, 328. **53.** Ibid., 118. **54.** Ibid., 17. **55.** DGM 892. **56.** Mauriac, *Le Général*, 120. **57.** Georgette Elgey, *Histoire de la IVe République. La République des tourmentes 1954–1959*, vol. III: *La fin* (Fayard, 2008), 602; Robert Aron, *De Gaulle*, 44. These two visited together. **58.** Bernard Lachaise, 'Les visiteurs du Général de Gaulle au 5 rue de Solférino au temps de la "traversée du désert", septembre 1955–mai 1958', *Espoir* 131 (6/2002), 25–30. **59.** Robert Buron, *Carnets politiques de la guerre d'Algérie* (Plon, 1965, reprint 2002), 70. **60.** Domenach, *Beaucoup de gueule*, 101. **61.** Aron, *De Gaulle*, 46–7. **62.** Alphand, *Etonnement*, 281–3. **63.** The recipient of this tirade was Louis Terrenoire, Roussel, *De Gaulle*, 572, but others were told the same: see Tournoux, *Tragédie*, 209, 326. **64.** Comte de Paris and Général de Gaulle, *Dialogue sur la France. Correspondance et entretiens 1953–1970* (Fayard, 1994), 51, 55–6, 69. **65.** Pierre-Henry Rix, *Par le portillon de La Boisserie* (Nouvelles Editions Latines, 1974), 101–2. **66.** LNCII 1180. **67.** AN AP449 (Terrenoire unpublished journal, 15/10/55). **68.** LNCII 1183. **69.** Alain Larcan (ed.), *De Gaulle et la médecine* (Plon, 1995), 235–49. **70.** DMII 609–10. **71.** Terrenoire, *Pourquoi*, 202. **72.** LNCII 1206 (16/3/56). **73.** AN AP449 (Terrenoire unpublished journal, 18/10/56). **74.** LNCII 1231 (18/10/56). **75.** Paul Ely, *Mémoires*, vol. II: *Suez . . . le 13 mai* (Plon, 1968), 307–13, gives a sense of the complexity of army attitudes to de Gaulle. **76.** LNCII 1200 (12/1/56). **77.** LNCII 1238 (9/1/57). **78.** AN AP449 (Terrenoire unpublished journal, 19/6/57). **79.** DMII 682 (12/9/57). **80.** LNCII 1209 (5/5/56), 1252 (9/7/57). **81.** FDG, Baberot Papers F26/46 (Bollardière dossier). **82.** Pierre

Bas, *Secrets, manoeuvres, chocs et volte-face de Charles de Gaulle à Nicolas Sarkozy* (Editions Alexandre de Saint-Prix, 2012), 50. **83.** Garrigues, *Hommes providentiels*, 113. **84.** AN AP449 (Terrenoire unpublished journal, 19/1/56); Elgey, *La fin*, 615–17. **85.** Bernard Lachaise, 'L'état d'esprit des gaullistes de 1955 à 1958', in Jean-Paul Thomas, Gilles Le Béguec and Bernard Lachaise (eds.), *Mai 1958. Le retour du géneral de Gaulle* (Presses Universitaires de Rennes, 2010), 91–9 (98). **86.** LNCII 1266 (1/1/58). **87.** LNCII 1270 (10/2/58). **88.** Vendroux, *Ces grandes années*, 14.

18. The 18 Brumaire of Charles de Gaulle, February–June 1958

1. Patrice Gueniffey, *Le dix-huit Brumaire. L'épilogue de la Révolution française* (Gallimard, 2008). **2.** Guy, *En écoutant*, 46. **3.** LNCII 1116–17. **4.** LNCI 806 (27/10/36). **5.** George Suffert, 'L'exil', *Esprit* (12/57), 625–38, 877. **6.** Roussel, *De Gaulle*, 581–2. **7.** Maurice Vaïsse, 'Jacques Chaban-Delmas, ministre de la Défense nationale (novembre 1957–mai 1958)', in Bernard Lachaise, Gilles Le Béguec and Jean-François Sirinelli (eds.), *Jacques Chaban-Delmas en politique* (PUF, 2007). **8.** Archives of Fondation Nationale Sciences Politiques (FNSP), interview with Delbecque. This is one a whole series of interviews carried out by Rudelle for her important book on May 1958. They are a major source for the events of that month and after. See also Rudelle, *Mai 1958*, 107–9. **9.** Albert Camus, *Carnets*, vol. III: *Mars 1951–décembre 1959* (Gallimard, 1989), 216. According to another account of the meeting, reported by Camus orally, when the writer suggested the idea of giving the vote to all Algerians, de Gaulle replied, 'but that would send 50 *bougnoles* [a pejorative term for native Algerians] to parliament.' See Thierry Jacques Laurent, *Camus et de Gaulle* (L'Harmattan, 2012), 64–6. **10.** Elgey, *La fin*, 732 (Elgey interviewed Petit only a few months after this meeting). **11.** Raymond Triboulet, *Un Gaulliste de la IVe* (Plon, 1985), 300–301. **12.** TNA PREM 11/2339. **13.** Elgey, *La fin*, 732–3. **14.** FDG, Barberot Papers F26/6 (Jean Fournier, 26/3/58). **15.** Rudelle, *Mai*, 141. **16.** AN 5AG1/1156 (Delbecque to de Gaulle, 4/5/58). **17.** AN 3AG4/98 Dossier 1; *Foccart parle* I, 135; Olivier Guichard, *Un chemin tranquille* (Flammarion, 1975), 32–3. **18.** Anderson, 'Civil War in France', 124 n. 63. **19.** Christophe Nick, *Résurrection. Naissance de la Vème République, un coup d'état démocratique* (Fayard, 1998), 362–3. **20.** Ibid., 439, 452–4. **21.** Delbecque, FNSP interview 4, 11–15; Rudelle, *Mai*, 185–6. **22.** Rudelle, *Mai*, 170. **23.** DMIII 3–4. **24.** Michel Poniatowski, *Mémoires* (Plon, Le Rocher, 1997), 308. **25.** AN 5AG1/1281 (Triboulet dossier: letter to de Gaulle, 15/5/58). **26.** Delbecque, FNSP interview 4, 17–19. **27.** DMIII 4–11. **28.** TNA PREM 11/2339 (19/5/58). **29.** Nick, *Résurrection*, 756–810, publishes in entirety Vitasse's report of the mission. **30.** Ibid., Vitasse report 7. **31.** Poniatowski, *Mémoires*, 325. **32.** Elgey, *La fin*, 800. **33.** Crémieux-Brilhac, *Georges Boris*, 416–19. **34.** LNCII 1278 (23/5/58). **35.** Elgey, *La fin*, 808. **36.** LNCII 1279 (26/5/58). **37.** Pflimlin gave an account to Poniatowski immediately afterwards, *Mémoires*, 344–5; see also Pierre Pflimlin, *Mémoires d'un européen de la IVe à la*

Ve République (Fayard, 1991), 132–3. **38.** For the best analysis see Jean-Paul Thomas, 'De Léon Delbecque, acteur et témoin, au général Dulac: les "les feux verts" en question', in Thomas, Le Béguec and Lachaise, *Mai 1958. Le retour*, 121–42. **39.** Roger Miquel, *Opération Résurrection (le 13 mai en métropole)* (Editions France-Empire, 1975), 113–14. **40.** LNCII 1281 (28/5/58). **41.** Domenach, *Beaucoup de gueule*, 145–62, gives a good account of the mood, and in his 'Journal d'un débacle', *Esprit* (6/58), 126–9. **42.** Francis de Baecque, *René Coty, tel qu'en lui-même* (Editions STH, Nancy, 1990), 258–9. **43.** Nick, *Résurrection*, 723–9; Nicot's testimony is in Edmond Jouhaud, *Serons nous enfin compris?* (Albin Michel, 1983), 60–61; Lefranc refuted this accusation in *Le Monde* 18/6/84; *Foccart parle* I, 148–9; General Rancourt, cited by Roussel, *De Gaulle*, 599, also confirms what Nicot said. **44.** Raoul Salan, *Mémoires*, vol. III: *Fin d'un empire. Algérie française* (Presses de la Cité, 1972), 354; Nick, *Résurrection*, 724–5. **45.** LMCII 1282 (29/5/58). **46.** François Pernot, 'Mai 1958: l'armée de l'Air et l'opération Résurrection', RHA 2 (1998), 109–22. **47.** Nick, *Résurrection*, 722; Jacques Massu, *Le Torrent et la digue* (Plon, 1972), 143. **48.** See p. 32 of the Vitasse report in the Annex to Nick, *Résurrection*, and also Nick, 723 n. 1 **49.** Vitasse report in Nick, *Résurrection*, 36 (Vitasse seems to have wrongly dated this telegram in his report). **50.** Elgey, *De Gaulle*, 29 (This information comes from the journal of Gaston de Bonneval which Elgey had access to.) **51.** Georgette Elgey, *Histoire de la 4e République. La République des tourmentes 1954–1959*, vol. IV: *De Gaulle à Matignon* (Fayard, 2012), 45. **52.** Pierre Mendès France, *Oeuvres complètes*, vol. IV: *Pour une république moderne* (Gallimard, 1987), 424. **53.** Or as Bidault put it: 'today chamber music, tomorrow military music': Edgar Faure, *Mémoires*, vol. II: *Si tel doit être mon destin ce soir* (Plon, 1984), 687. **54.** Alexander Werth, *The De Gaulle Revolution* (Robert Hale, 1960), 173. **55.** FNSP (Delbecque interview, 27/6/86). **56.** Olivier Duhamel, *La gauche et la Ve République* (PUF, 1980), 44. **57.** TNA PREM 11/2339 (28/5/58). **58.** Moch, *Rencontres*, 287. **59.** Crémieux-Brilhac, *Georges Boris*, 416–21. **60.** FNSP (Delbecque interview, 28/5/78). **61.** Poniatowski, *Mémoires*, 306. **62.** *Foccart parle* I, 140–41. **63.** Nick, *Résurrection*, 592. **64.** Ibid., 516–17. **65.** DMIII 450. **66.** AP 198–200 (8/6/62).

19. Président du Conseil, June–December 1958

1. DMIII 21–3. **2.** On these precedents, Didier Maus, 'De la IVe à la Ve République, ruptures et continuités', in Maus, *Etudes sur la constitution de la Ve République* (Editions STH, 1990), 16–54. **3.** Wall, *The United States*, 133, 193. **4.** Keith Kyle, *Suez* (I. B. Tauris, 2001 edn), 466–7. **5.** Colette Barbier, 'The French Decision to Develop a Military Nuclear Programme in the 1950s', *Diplomacy and Statecraft* 4/1 (1993), 105–13; Bertrand Goldschmidt, 'La genèse et l'héritage', in Institut Charles de Gaulle, *L'aventure de la Bombe. De Gaulle et la dissuasion nucléaire (1958–1969)* (Plon, 1985), 24–37. **6.** Georges-Henri Soutou, 'Les accords de 1957 and 1958: vers une communauté stratégique nucléaire entre la France, l'Allemagne et l'Italie', *Matériaux pour l'histoire de notre temps* 31/1 (1993), 1–12. **7.** Maurice Vaïsse,

Conclusion to Vaïsse (ed.), *La France et l'opération de Suez de 1956* (Addim, 1997), 331–2. **8.** Sebastien Reyn, 'Atlantis Lost. The American Experience with De Gaulle 1958–1969' (unpublished PhD thesis, Leyden University, 2008), 199. **9.** Harold Macmillan, *The Macmillan Diaries: Prime Minister and After 1957–1966* (Macmillan, 2011), 74 (1/12/58). **10.** TNA PREM 11/2339 (Selwyn Lloyd to Jebb, 11/6/58). **11.** Bastien François, *Naissance d'une constitution. La cinquième république 1958–1962* (Presses de Sciences Po, 1996), 28–9. Janot gave another version in Didier Maus and Olivier Passelecq, *Témoignages sur l'écriture de la constitution de 1958* (Documentation Française, 1997), 11–12. **12.** Pierre Lefranc, *Avec qui vous savez. Vingt-cinq ans avec de Gaulle* (Plon, 1979), 125. **13.** Bernard Lachaise, Gilles Le Béguec and Frédéric Turpin (eds.), *Georges Pompidou, directeur de cabinet du général de Gaulle. Juin 1958–Janvier 1959* (Peter Lang, Brussels, 2006). **14.** Jean-Yves Perrot, 'L'entourage du général de Gaulle: Une figure exemplaire: René Brouillet', in Isabelle Chave and Nicole Even (eds.), *Charles de Gaulle. Archives et histoire* (Publications des Archives Nationales, 2016), 1–16. **15.** Elgey, *De Gaulle*, 104–5. **16.** FNSP Rudelle interview with the *préfet* Jean Lenoir (15/5/81). **17.** Jean El Mouhoub Amrouche, *Journal 1928–1962* (Non Lieu, 2009), 316–19. **18.** Michael Kettle, *De Gaulle and Algeria 1940–1960* (Quartet Books, 1993), 239. **19.** Elgey, *De Gaulle*, 171–3. **20.** AP 1032. **21.** Pierre Viansson-Ponté, *Lettre ouverte aux hommes politiques* (Albin Michel, 1976), 18. **22.** LNCIII 7 (6/6/58), 9 (11/6/58), 13 (19/6/58), 16 (21/6/58), 28 (22/7/58), 50 (13/9/58). **23.** LNCIII 42 (11/8/58). **24.** Pflimlin, *Mémoires*, 147. **25.** *Documents pour servir à l'histoire de l'élaboration de la constitution du 4 octobre 1958* (Documentation Française, 1987), I, 245–9. **26.** Roger Belin, *Lorsqu'une république chasse l'autre (1958–1962)* (Michalon, 1999), 59. **27.** Pflimlin, *Mémoires*, 149; see also *Documents pour servir* II, 301 (Comité consultative constitutionnel séance du 8 août). **28.** Jérôme Perrier, *Michel Debré* (Ellipses, 2010), 211. **29.** Didier Maus, 'Guy Mollet et l'élaboration de la constitution 1958', in Bernard Ménager et al. (eds.), *Guy Mollet. Un camarade en république* (Presses Universitaires de Lille, 1987), 359–65; Janot, 'Note pour le Général de Gaulle, 16 June 1958', in *Documents pour servir* I, 257–8. On arbitration see Didier Maus, 'L'institution présidentielle dans l'écriture de la constitution de 1958', in Maus, Louis Favoreu and Jean-Luc Parodi, *L'écriture de la constitution de 1958* (Economica, 1992), 262–76. **30.** Gaetano Quagliariello, *La religion gaulliste* (Perrin, 2006), 345. **31.** Elgey, *De Gaulle*, 104. **32.** Preface to Léo Hamon, *De Gaulle dans la République* (Plon, 1958), xl. **33.** *Documents pour servir* I, 449. **34.** Belin, *Lorsqu'une république*, 64–5. **35.** François, *Naissance*, 19. **36.** Raymond Aron, 'La Vème République, ou l'Empire parlementaire', *Preuves* 93 (10/58), 3–11. **37.** DMIII 56 (23/10/58). **38.** Bernard Lachaise, Gilles Le Béguec and Frédéric Turpin (eds.), *Les élections législatives de novembre 1958: une rupture?* (Presses Universitaires de Bordeaux, 2011), 15. This is the most recent study of the elections which rather downplays the idea that they represented a major rupture. **39.** Raymond Aron, 'Charles de Gaulle et la chambre introuvable', *Preuves* 95 (1/59), 3–12; see Mauriac on the danger of this *chambre introuvable* trying to be 'more Gaullist than de Gaulle': François Mauriac, *Bloc-notes*, vol. II: *1958–1960* (Seuil, 1993), 168–72 (24/11, 30/11/58). **40.** For the best overview see Maurice

Vaïsse, ' "Hisser les couleurs": rupture et continuité dans la politique étrangère de la France en 1958', in FDG, *L'avènement de la Vème république. Entre nouveauté et tradition* (Armand Colin, 1999). For the reactions of the British and Americans see in the same volume Charles Cogan, 222–35, and Anne Deighton, 265–76. 41. Kettle, *De Gaulle*, 254. 42. FRUS 1958–60 VII 145. 43. DDF 1958(1) 459. 44. DDF 1958(2) 16 (5/7/58); FRUS 1958–60 VII (Pt 2) 58. 45. Raymond Poidevin, 'De Gaulle et Europe en 1958', in DGESSV 79–87. 46. Kettle, *De Gaulle*, 256–7. 47. LNCIII 53–4. 48. FRUS 1958 VII #177 (18/12/58). 49. Klaus-Jürgen Müller, *Adenauer and de Gaulle* (Oxford, 1992). (Tagesbruche: 20/5/58: 287–9.) 50. Hans-Peter Schwarz, 'La République fédérale allemande et la crise de mai à septembre 1958 en France', in FDG, *Avènement*, 245–64. 51. LNCIII 57 (17/9/58). 52. Vendroux, *Ces grandes années*, 26. 53. There is a brief summary of the conversation in DDF 1958(2) 155; Roussel, *De Gaulle*, 616–18, publishes an account written by Adenauer immediately after it; Hans-Peter Schwarz, *Konrad Adenauer: A German Politician and Statesman in a Period of War, Revolution and Reconstruction*, vol. II: *The Statesman 1952–1967* (Berghahn, Oxford, 1991), has extracts from Adenauer's report to the President, 365–6. 54. Macmillan, *Diaries*, 164. 55. Schwarz, *Konrad Adenauer*, 369 56. DDF 1958(2) 370 (26/11/58). 57. Gladwyn, *Memoirs*, 316. 58. Institut Charles de Gaulle, *1958. La faillite ou le miracle. Le plan de Gaulle–Rueff* (Economica, 1986); Elgey, *De Gaulle*, 327–44. 59. Elgey, *De Gaulle*, 337. 60. Jacques Rueff, *Combats pour un ordre financier* (Plon, 1972), 153–4. 61. Jean Méo, 'Témoignage sur les questions économiques et financières', in Lachaise, Le Béguec and Turpin, *Georges Pompidou*, 115. 62. Jacques Rueff, *De l'aube au crépuscule. Autobiographie* (Plon, 1977), 234. 63. *Entretiens avec Roger Goetze, haut fonctionnaire des finances. Rivoli, Alger, Rivoli. 1937–1958* (Comité pour l'histoire économique et financière de la France, 1997), 342. 64. Ibid., 351. 65. Jean Aubry, 'Témoignage sur les questions économiques et sociales', in Lachaise, Le Béguec and Turpin, *Georges Pompidou*, 125. 66. Gilbert Meynier, *Histoire intérieure du FLN 1954–1962* (Fayard, 2002), 616–18. On these negotiations, Elgey, *De Gaulle*, 184–7, 212–15; the Algerian writer Jean Amrouche, who was involved, left a 'Note sur les contacts de Gaulle–FLN', Amrouche, *Journal*, 381–9. 67. AN 5AG1/1712 (19/9/58). 68. Herrick Chapman, *France's Long Reconstruction: In Search of the Modern Republic* (Harvard University Press, 2018), 278–88. 69. Matthew Connelly, *A Diplomatic Revolution: Algeria's Fight for Independence and the Origins of the Post-Cold War Era* (Oxford University Press, 2002), 182. 70. LNCIII 78 (24/10/58). 71. LNCIII 58 (de Gaulle to Salan, 18/9/58). 72. LNCIII 67 (de Gaulle to Salan, 9/10/58). 73. LNCIII 66–7 (9/10/58). 74. LNCIII 92. 75. AN 5AG1/1713 ('Reflexions sur l'Algérie', 13/12/58).

20. 'This Affair Which Absorbs and Paralyses Us', 1958–1962

1. TNA FO 371/153916/WF1052/35G (18/11/1960). 2. TNA PREM 11/3338 (Shuckburgh). 3. LNCIII 319 (22/1/61). 4. Buron, *Carnets politiques*, 100

(22/6/58), 119 (10/3/60), 129 (10/2/61).   **5.** DGM 917–19.   **6.** The only historian who unconvincingly argues the contrary is Irwin Wall, *France, the United States and the Algerian War* (University of California Press, 2001).   **7.** Stephen Tyre, 'From *Algérie française* to *France musulmane*: Jacques Soustelle and the Realities and Myths of "Integration", 1955–1962', *French History* 20/3 (9/06), 276–96.   **8.** Jacques Soustelle, *L'espérance trahie (1958–1961)* (Paris, 1962), 31–2. On the two occasions when Sérigny met de Gaulle in 1958 he could not get a word of support for integration out of him: see Alain de Sérigny, *Echos d'Alger II* (Presse de la Cité, 1974), 298–9, 331–3.   **9.** Alain de Sérigny, *La révolution du 13 mai* (Plon, 1958), 9.   **10.** Raymond Dronne, *La révolution d'Alger* (Editions France-Empire, 1958), 229. For a cooler analysis of this event see Malika Rahal, 'Les manifestations de mai 1958 en Algérie', in Thomas, Le Béguec and Lachaise, *Mai 1958*, 39–58.   **11.** AN 5AG1/1272 (Soustelle to de Gaulle, 17/5/58).   **12.** AP 65–6. The same idea was expressed even more crudely in de Gaulle's remark to the Gaullist *député* Dronne: 'Voulez-vous etre bougnoulisés', Tournoux, *Tragédie*, 307–8. Tournoux never gives his sources but he is usually well informed.   **13.** Soustelle, *L'espérance*, 22–3.   **14.** Patrick Weil, *Qu'est-ce qu'un Français? Histoire de la nationalité française depuis la Révolution* (Gallimard, 2004), 220–21.   **15.** AN 5AG1/1700.   **16.** AN 5AG1/1272 (Soustelle to de Gaulle, 16/10/58).   **17.** Jacques Frémeaux, 'De Gaulle, l'Algérie et les élites impossibles', in Serge Berstein, Pierre Birnbaum and Jean-Pierre Rioux (eds.), *De Gaulle et les élites* (La Découverte, 2008), 145–69.   **18.** FNSP interview (26/6/80).   **19.** AN 5AG1/1157 Delouvrier file (22/12/58).   **20.** LNCIII 101 (18/12/58).   **21.** FNSP interview (21/1/81).   **22.** For Debré's position, Chantal Morelle, 'Michel Debré et l'Algérie. Quelle Algérie française?', in Serge Berstein and Jean-François Sirinelli (eds.), *Michel Debré, Premier Ministre (1959– 1962)* (PUF, 2005), 449–67.   **23.** FNSP interview (26/6/80).   **24.** Bernard Tricot, *Les sentiers de la paix. Algérie 1958–1962* (Plon, 1972), 29–32.   **25.** FNSP interview (undated).   **26.** LNCIII 120 (17/1/59).   **27.** Roussel, *De Gaulle*, 625.   **28.** Belin, *Lorsqu'une république*, 84.   **29.** LNCIII 142 (24/4/59); also LNCIII (1/7/59).   **30.** Tricot, *Sentiers*, 104–6.   **31.** Michel Debré, *Entretiens avec le Général de Gaulle. 1961–1969* (Albin Michel, 1993), 18–19.   **32.** Belin, *Lorsqu'une république*, 85–6.   **33.** Maurice Vaïsse, *Comment de Gaulle fit échouer le putsch d'Alger* (André Versaille, 2011), 134.   **34.** FNSP, Archives Debré 2DE/12 ('Crise dans l'armée', 26/9/59).   **35.** Samy Cohen, *La défaite des généraux. Le pouvoir politique et l'armée sous la Ve République* (Fayard, 1994), 84. For the best discussion of the army's position see Anderson, 'Civil War in France', 40–109.   **36.** André Bach, 'Une armée en fronde', in FDG, *Avènement*, 105–18.   **37.** For an excellent analysis of the international context see Connelly, *Diplomatic Revolution*.   **38.** DDF 1959(2) 79 (21/8/59).   **39.** DDF 1959(2) 108 (2/9/59).   **40.** DMIII 128–34.   **41.** Most recently Benjamin Stora, *De Gaulle et l'Algérie* (Fayard, 2010).   **42.** Jean-Marie Domenach, 'Une barrière a sauté', *Esprit* (10/59), 392–4; Claude Bourdet, 'Le bon engrenage', *France observateur* 24/9/59.   **43.** Raymond Aron, 'De la politique de grandeur', *Preuves* 105 (11/59), 3–12.   **44.** LNCIII 184–5 (26/10/59).   **45.** Vendroux, *Ces grandes années*, 59.   **46.** LNCIII 171–2 (30/9/59).   **47.** Roselyne Chenu, *Paul Delouvrier ou la passion d'agir. Entretiens* (Seuil, 1994), 208–9.   **48.**

FNSP, Delouvrier Papers F2DV3 DR 1 sdr a (Synthèse hebdomadaire de renseignements). **49.** Belin, *Lorsqu'une république*, 88–91; Soustelle, *L'espérance*, 142;
LNCIII 212 (25/1/60). **50.** Michel Debré, *Mémoires. Trois républiques pour une
France*, vol. III: *Gouverner* (Albin Michel, 1988), 235. **51.** Merry and Serge Bromb-
erger, Georgette Elgey and Jean-François Chauvel, *Barricades et colonels, 24 janvier
1960* (Fayard, 1960), 360–68. **52.** FNSP, Archives Debré 2DE29 Dr. 2 (note,
28/1/60). **53.** General Ely, unpublished 'Journal de Marche', 28/1/60 (communicated to me by Maurice Vaïsse). **54.** Riccardo Brizzi, *De Gaulle et les médias.
L'homme du petite écran* (Presses Universitaires de Rennes, 2014), 154–7. Some 45
per cent of the content uses the first person. **55.** DMIII 176–80. **56.** LNCIII
218–19 (14/2/60). **57.** Raymond Aron, 'Un seul homme, un homme seul', *Preuves*
109 (3/60), 3–12. **58.** Soustelle, *L'espérance*, 160. **59.** *Paroles d'officers. 1950–
1990. Des Saint-Cyriens témoignent* (Promotion Extrême-Orient, 1991); Vaïsse,
Comment de Gaulle fit échouer le putsch, 127–8, publishes notes taken from the
press attaché to the Army Minister. **60.** Louis Terrenoire, *De Gaulle et l'Algérie*
(Fayard, 1964), 178–9; Tricot, *Sentiers*, 159–63. **61.** LNCIII 222–3 (7/3/60). **62.**
Tricot, *Sentiers*, 174–7. **63.** FNSP, Archives Debré 2DE ('Discussion avec l'émissaire
(MB) des dirigeants de l'organisation extérieure de la rébellion', 25/6/60). **64.** This
was the view of Pierre Racine in his note 'Le Malentendu de Melun', reproduced in
Rheda Malek, *L'Algérie à Evian. Histoire des négociations secrètes 1956–1962* (Seuil,
1995), 387–93. **65.** Debré, *Entretiens*, 19–20. **66.** Roussel, *De Gaulle*, 665. **67.**
For an overview see Guy Pervillé, 'L'Affaire Si Salah (1960): histoire et mémoire', in
Vaïsse, *De Gaulle et l'Algérie*, 146–62. **68.** Mauriac, *Le Journaliste*, 161. **69.** Paul
Isoart, 'Le conseil exécutif de la Communauté', in Charles-Robert Ageron and Marc
Michel (eds.), *L'Afrique noire française. L'heure des indépendances* (CNRS Editions,
2010), 237–68. **70.** Frédéric Turpin, *De Gaulle, Pompidou et Afrique (1958–1974).
Coloniser et coopérer* (Indes Savantes, 2010), 42. **71.** Ibid., 49. **72.** Alphand,
Etonnement, 308. **73.** FNSP, Archives Debré 2DE29 (26/9/59). **74.** AN
5AG1/1731 (note for de Gaulle, 14/9/60). On the work of these commissions see
5AG1/1731–2. **75.** AN 5AG1/1781 (note, 25/8/60). **76.** DMIII 256–8
(5/9/60). **77.** LNCIII 269 (14/10/60). **78.** Raymond Aron, 'La Presomption',
Preuves 117 (11/60), 3–10. **79.** *Le Monde* 29/9/60: 'Ce règne avait deux ans'. See
also Jean-Jacques Servan-Schreiber, 'Sérénité', and Pierre Mendès France, 'De Gaulle
Immobile', both in *Express* 8/9/60; Domenach, 'La nature des choses', *Esprit*
(10/60). **80.** Domenach, 'Prisonnier sur parole', *Express* 27/10/60; Jean-Michel
Bloch, 'Le moral de la nation', *Esprit* (8/60). **81.** Cited in Dominique Borne, 'Michel
Debré et la Justice', in Association des Amis de Michel Debré (ed.), *Michel Debré et
l'Algérie* (Editions Champs Elysées, 2007), 222. **82.** FNSP, Archives Debré 2DE/29
(26/9/60). **83.** Pompidou, *Lettres*, 308–12. **84.** FNSP, Archives Debré 2DE29
(26/9/60). **85.** DMIII 277–8. **86.** FNSP, Archives Debré 2DE29 (20/11/60). **87.**
LNCIII 276. **88.** FNSP, Racine interview with Rudelle 11/77. **89.** LNCIII 279–
81 (5/12/60). **90.** LNCIII 333 (18/2/61). **91.** Pompidou, *Lettres*, 319–38, 341–
2. **92.** DMII 309. **93.** Jules Roy, *Les années de déchirement. Journal 1925–1965*
(Albin Michel, 1998), 385, 388. **94.** Maurice Vaïsse, *Comment de Gaulle fit échouer
le putsch* is the most up-to-date account. **95.** Belin, *Lorsqu'une république*,

110. 96. Morelle, *Joxe*, 620–25. 97. Constantin Melnik, *De Gaulle, les services secrets et l'Algérie* (Nouveau Monde, 2010), 75–7. 98. Pierre Viansson-Ponté, *Histoire de la République gaullienne*, vol. I: *La fin d'une époque* (Fayard, 1970), 356. 99. *Foccart parle* I, 352. 100. Buron, *Carnets*, 159. 101. Léon Noël, *De Gaulle et les débuts de la Ve République* (Plon, 1976), 143. 102. DMIII 392–6. 103. Vaïsse, *Comment de Gaulle fit échouer le putsch*, 296. 104. LNCIII, 357 (27/4/61). 105. On Evian, see Maurice Vaïsse, *Vers la paix en Algérie. Les négociations d'Evian dans les archives diplomatiques françaises. 15 janvier 1961–29 juin 1962* (Bruylant, Brussels, 2003); Chantal Morelle, *Comment de Gaulle et la FLN ont mis fin à la guerre d'Algérie* (André Versaille, 2012), 123–49. 106. Morelle, *Comment de Gaulle*, 123. 107. Jean Morin, *De Gaulle et l'Algérie. Mon témoignage, 1960–1962* (Albin Michel, 1999), 179–86. 108. AP 92. 109. FNSP, Archives Debré 2DE30 Dr 2 (2/8/61, 21/8/61). 110. Belin, *Lorsqu'une république*, 125; Terrenoire, reported in Roussel, *De Gaulle*, 693, recorded the remarks with a slight variation. 111. DMIII 365 (5/9/61). 112. Debré, *Mémoires* III, 297. 113. FNSP, Archives Debré 2DE20 (11–16/9/61). 114. François Mauriac, *Bloc-notes*, vol. III: *1961–1964* (Seuil, 1993), 83 (18/11/61); Debré wrote a furious letter of protest to de Gaulle on this subject: FNSP, Archives Debré 2DE30 (27/11/61). 115. LNCIII 423 (3/11/61). 116. AP 99–103 (8/1/2/61). 117. 'Appel à la nation', *Esprit* (11/61), 607–10. 118. Belin, *Lorsqu'une république*, 129; Debré was no more sentimental: see his note to de Gaulle on 3/11/61, FNSP, Archives Debré 2DE30. 119. Roussel, *De Gaulle*, 697. 120. The best account is Alain Dewerpe, *Charonne 8 février 1962. Anthropologie historique d'un massacre d'état* (Gallimard, 2006). 121. Belin, *Lorsqu'une république*, 37; Roussel, *De Gaulle*, 703. 122. LNCIII 457 (13/2/62). 123. Dewerpe, *Charonne*, 260–61. 124. Ibid., 280–81. 125. DMIII 409. 126. Buron, *Carnets*, 187. 127. Ibid., 228–9. 128. AN 5AG1/1795. 129. LNCIII 461–2 (18/2/62). 130. AN 5AG1/1795. 131. Bernard Lefort, *Souvenirs et secrets des années gaulliennes* (Albin Michel, 1999), 69. 132. Belin, *Lorsqu'une république*, 139–40; Buron, *Carnets*, 244–5. 133. Roussel, *De Gaulle*, 705. 134. AP 141; Pflimlin, *Mémoires*, 204–5, has the same but dates it 24 April. 135. AP 268 (23/11/62). 136. Gilbert Pilleul (ed.), *'L'entourage' et de Gaulle* (Plon, 1979), 309. 137. Vaïsse, *Comment de Gaulle fit échouer le putsch*, 258. 138. AP 209 (25/7/62). 139. AN 5AG1/511 (26/7/62). 140. AP 1035 (7/5/63). 141. LNCIII 221. 142. Tournoux, *Tragédie*, 402.

21. Turning Point, 1962

1. TNA FO 371/163845. 2. Guy Mollet, *13 mai 1958–13 mai 1962* (Plon, 1962). 3. Pflimlin, *Mémoires*, 220. 4. AP 116. 5. LNCI III 236 (13/5/60); FNSP, Archives Debré 2DE29 (20/10/59). 6. FNSP, Archives Debré 2DE29 (3/8/59); 2DE29 (7/5/60). 7. FNSP, Archives Debré 2DE30 (13/8/61). 8. FNSP, Archives Debré 2DE30 (30/9/61). 9. Jean Charlot, *L'Union pour la nouvelle république* (Armand Colin, 1967), 85–91. 10. DMIII 264 (5/9/60). 11. Anderson, 'Civil War in France', 322 n. 158. 12. FNSP, Archives Debré 2DE30 (30/9/61). 13.

Debré, *Entretiens*, 48–61 (9/1/62). **14.** Pompidou, *Lettres*, 302–3 (16/1/60). **15.** In general see J.-P. Cointet et al. (ed.), *Une politique. Georges Pompidou* (PUF, 2001). **16.** Roussel, *De Gaulle*, 713. **17.** AP 117. **18.** AP 131–3. **19.** DMIV 435–7. **20.** Pflimlin, *Mémoires*, 213–14. **21.** AP 188. **22.** AP 716. **23.** *Le procès de Raoul Salan. Compte rendu sténographique* (Editions Albin Michel, 1962), 189. **24.** LNCIII 78 (24/10/58). **25.** *Procès*, 224. **26.** Ibid., 179. **27.** Ibid., 286. **28.** Ibid., 230–33. **29.** Pflimlin, *Mémoires*, 189–93. **30.** Jacques Isorni, *Lui qui les juge* (Flammarion, 1961). **31.** *Procès*, 184. **32.** Anne-Marie Duranton-Crabol, *L'OAS. La peur et la violence* (André Versaille, 2012), 80; P. Heduy, 'Nous avons choisi la Résistance', *Esprit publique* (1/62). **33.** Vaïsse, *Comment de Gaulle fit échouer le putsch*, 310–12 **34.** Pompidou, *Lettres*, 355. **35.** Ibid., 476–7. **36.** Ibid., 356–7. **37.** AP 185. **38.** AN 5AG1/1120 (20/12/62). **39.** Jean Foyer, 'La justice face aux activistes de l'OAS', in Alain Larcan (ed.), *Charles de Gaulle et la justice* (Editions Cujas, 2003), 230. **40.** Pompidou, *Lettres*, 476–7. **41.** AN 5AG1/1204 (Larminat to de Gaulle, 30/6/62). **42.** Alain Larcan, 'Interrogations sur un suicide. Essai de patho-biographie', in Oulmont (ed.), *Larminat. Un fidèle*, 292–308. **43.** AN 98AJ/4 (non coté). **44.** On Petit-Clamart, Jean-Noël Jeanneney, *Un attentat. Petit-Clamart, 22 août 1962* (Seuil, 2016). **45.** AP 225. **46.** Pflimlin, *Mémoires*, 188; DMIII 323–4; see also LNCIII 371 (4/6/61). **47.** DMIII 445–6. **48.** AN 5AG1/1686 **49.** Noël, *De Gaulle et les débuts*, 206–7. **50.** Yves Beauvois, *Léon Noël. De Laval à de Gaulle via Pétain (1888–1987)* (Presses Universitaires du Septentrion, 2001), 396. **51.** Ibid., 339. **52.** Ibid., 402–3. **53.** Todd Shepard, *The Invention of Decolonization: The Algerian War and the Remaking of France* (Cornell University Press, Ithaca, 2006), 112. **54.** Viansson-Ponté, *République gaullienne* I, 71. **55.** DMIV 40. **56.** LNCIII 680. **57.** DMIV 172. **58.** Pierre Viansson-Ponté, *Histoire de la République gaullienne*, vol. II: *Les temps des orphelins* (Fayard, 1971), 115–16. **59.** François Mitterrand, *Le coup d'état permanent* (Plon, 1964), 86, 122. **60.** DMIV 43–6 (7/11/62). **61.** AP 277–8. **62.** TNA FO 371/169107.

22. The Pursuit of Grandeur, 1959–1963

1. FRUS 1958–60 VII (Part 2) #160 (14/3/60). **2.** See above p. 30. **3.** AP 296 (23/4/63) **4.** AP 306 (10/9/62). **5.** DDF 1966(2) 364 (31/12/65). **6.** DMIII 238 (31/5/60). **7.** LNCIII 1005 (29/11/68). On law of the species DMIII 140 (31/5/60), 233 (3/11/59). **8.** AP 496 (23/5/62). **9.** DMIII 233–7 (31/3/60) **10.** DMIII 262 (5/9/60). **11.** DMIII 106 (18/6/59). **12.** DMV 274 (31/12/67). **13.** AP 293 (13/2/63). **14.** AP 683 (22/3/64). **15.** AP 300 (9/5/62). **16.** The essential starting point is Maurice Vaïsse, *La grandeur. Politique étrangère du général de Gaulle* (CRNS Editions, 2013). **17.** Carolyne Davidson, 'Dealing with de Gaulle: The United States and France', in Christian Nuenlist, Anna Locher and Garret Martin (eds.), *Globalizing de Gaulle. International Perspectives on French Foreign Policies 1958–1969* (Lexington Books, Plymouth, 2010), 115; LNCIII 43 (13/8/58); DDF 1958(2) 5, 56. **18.** Georges-Henri Soutou, *L'alliance incertaine. Les rapports* *politico-stratégiques franco-allemands 1954–1996* (Fayard, 1996), 126–30.   **19.** AP 173 (22/8/62).   **20.** DDF 1967(1) 347.   **21.** AP 375 (23/1/63).   **22.** Pompidou, *Pour rétablir*, 63.   **23.** AP 292 (24/1/63).   **24.** Henri Froment-Meurice, *Vu du Quai. Mémoires 1945–1983* (Fayard, 1998), 290.   **25.** These were Soutou, Froment-Meurice and Jean Laloy.   **26.** Alphand, *Etonnement*, 328.   **27.** Jean-Marie Soutou, *Un diplomate engagé. Mémoires 1930–1979* (Fallois, 2011), 217–18.   **28.** Etienne Burin des Roziers, *Retour aux sources. 1962. L'année décisive* (Plon, 1986), 140–41.   **29.** Roland de Margerie, *Mémoires inédites. Tous mes adieux sont faits*, vol. V (McNally Jackson, New York, 2013), 47–9.   **30.** DGM 1064–5.   **31.** Macmillan has a description of one shoot in his unpublished diaries (Bodleian Library), 15/12/62; there are others in FII 391; Vendroux, *Ces grandes années*, 81.   **32.** Karine McGrath, *Un président chez le roi. De Gaulle à Trianon* (Gallimard/Château de Versailles, 2016).   **33.** Vaïsse, *Grandeur*, 304.   **34.** TNA PREM 11/4811 (19/12/62).   **35.** TNA FO 371/177875/RF1051/34 (19/10/64).   **36.** Reyn, 'Atlantis Lost', 18 n. 4.   **37.** Mangold, *Almost Impossible Ally*, 89.   **38.** Frédéric Bozo, *Deux stratégies pour l'Europe. De Gaulle, les Etats-Unis et l'Alliance Atlantique 1958–1969* (Plon, 1996), 37–40.   **39.** FRUS 1958–60 VII(2) #79 (12/12/58).   **40.** Alphand, *Etonnement*, 316.   **41.** LNCIII 148–50 (25/5/59), 173 (6/10/59).   **42.** FRUS 1958–60 VII(2) #111 (5/5/59).   **43.** LNCIII 259–60 (9/8/60).   **44.** FRUS 1958–60 VII(2) #200 (27/9/60).   **45.** FRUS 1958–1960 VII(2) #27 (26/6/58).   **46.** Vernon A. Walters, *Silent Missions* (Doubleday, 1978), 490.   **47.** Piers Ludlow, 'From Words to Actions', in Nuenlist, Locher and Martin, *Globalizing de Gaulle*, 68–9.   **48.** Vaïsse, *Grandeur*, 176–8; DDF 1959(1) 174, 371.   **49.** LNCIII 134–5 (11/3/59), 143 (25/4/59), 418–19 (21/10/61).   **50.** FRUS 1958–60 VII(2) #131 (2/9/59): 255; see also DDF 1959(2) 108.   **51.** François Seydoux, *Mémoires d'outre-Rhin* (Grasset, 1975), 225.   **52.** Marc Trachtenberg, *A Constructed Peace: The Making of the European Settlement 1945–1963* (Princeton University Press, 1999), 336–7, argues that at least in the period 1959–61 he did; Vaïsse, *Grandeur*, 238–9, is sceptical, as is Maillard, *De Gaulle et l'Allemagne*, 192.   **53.** LNCIII 255–6 (30/7/60).   **54.** DMIII 236–7 (31/5/60).   **55.** LNCIII 256–7 (1/8/60).   **56.** Schwarz, *Adenauer*, 466–70.   **57.** Soutou, *Alliance*, 209–24.   **58.** LNCIII 267 (30/9/60).   **59.** LNCIII 265 (29/9/60).   **60.** DDF 1961(1) 59 (entretien de Gaulle–Adenauer, 9/2/61).   **61.** LNCIII 358 (27/4/61), 381 (17/7/61).   **62.** Vaïsse, *Grandeur*, 184.   **63.** Soutou, *Alliance*, 192.   **64.** Soutou, *Un diplomate*, 228. In general see Jeffrey Glen Giauque, *Grand Designs and Visions of Unity: The Atlantic Powers and the Reorganization of Western Europe 1955–1963* (University of North Carolina Press, Chapel Hill, 2002), 127–57; Jean-Marie Soutou, 'Le Général de Gaulle et le Plan Fouchet d'union politique européenne: un projet stratégique', in Anne Deighton and Alan S. Milward (eds.), *Widening, Deepening and Acceleration: The European Economic Community 1957–1963* (Bruylant, Brussels, 1999), 55–7.   **65.** LNCIII 457–8 (16/2/62).   **66.** LNCIII 493 (26/7/62).   **67.** Henry Kissinger, *Diplomacy* (Simon & Schuster, New York, 1994), 602. Kissinger put this argument at the time in 'The Illusionist: Why We Misread de Gaulle', *Harper's Magazine* 230/1378 (3/65), 69–77.   **68.** LNCIII 321–5 (1/61).   **69.** Reyn, 'Atlantis Lost', 162–3, 236.   **70.** Frank Costigliola, 'Kennedy, de Gaulle and the Challenge of Consultation', in Paxton and Wahl, *De Gaulle*,

170. 71. George W. Ball, *The Past Has Another Pattern: Memoirs* (Norton, New York, 1982), 96. 72. DDF 1961(1) 59 (entretien Adenauer–de Gaulle, 9/2/61). 73. TNA PREM 11/3319 (28/4/61). 74. DGM 1103–4. 75. FRUS 1961–3 XIII #107 (1/6/61). 76. AN 5AG1/723 (2/1/62). 77. LNCIII 445–56 (11/1/62). 78. LNCIII 256 (1/8/60); see also letter to Adenauer, 341 (9/3/61). 79. Vaïsse, *Grandeur*, 252. 80. LNCIII 498–9 (10/9/62). 81. Schwarz, *Adenauer*, 625. 82. FNSP, Archives Couve de Murville MCM7 (note on conversation with Charles Hargroves, 10/9/62). 83. FRUS 1958–60 VII(2) #194. 84. Macmillan, *Diaries*, 277–9. 85. Walters, *Silent Missions*, 83. 86. Mangold, *Impossible Ally*, 93. 87. DMIV 195 (7/4/60). 88. DGM 1093, 1391. 89. AN 5AG1/1273 Spears dr. 90. DGM 1087. 91. AP 377–8. 92. On the supposed nuclear deal Vaïsse, 'De Gaulle et l'élargissement du marché commun, 1961–1963', in Deighton and Milward, *Widening, Deepening and Acceleration*, 199–209. 93. Peter Hennessy, *Having it So Good: Britain in the Fifties* (Penguin, 2007), 607, from TNA PREM 11/2998 ('Points discussed with General de Gaulle'). 94. DDF 1961(1) 109, which records that this was a 'strictly private conversation' and not in any way a 'negotiation'. 95. DDF 1961(1) 42; TNA PREM 11/3325. 96. Macmillan, unpublished diaries, 29/1/61. 97. TNA PREM 11/3338; DDF 1961(2) 192. 98. Macmillan, unpublished diaries, 29/11/61. 99. DDF 1961(2) 211 (9/12/61). 100. LNCIII 433 (12/12/61). 101. DDF 1962(1) 172 (2/6/62); TNA PREM 11/3775. 102. DDF 1962(1) 168 (note, 1/6/62). 103. Harold Macmillan, *At the End of the Day 1961–1963* (Macmillan, 1973), 120. 104. AN 5AG1/647. 105. Piers Ludlow, *Dealing with Britain: The Six and the First UK Application to the EEC* (Cambridge University Press, 1997). 106. Douglas Brinkley, *Dean Acheson: The Cold War Years 1953–71* (Yale University Press, New Haven/London, 1992), 164–8. In general, Maurice Vaïsse, 'Une hirondelle ne fait pas le printemps', in Vaïsse, *L'Europe et la crise de Cuba* (Armand Colin, 1998), 89–109; DDF 1962(2) 112. 107. LNCIII 505 (26/10/62). 108. DDF 1962(2) 201; TNA PREM 11/4230. 109. Macmillan, *Diaries*, 526. 110. AP 342–4 (19/12/62). 111. Macmillan, *Diaries*, 521. 112. Respectively Trachtenberg, *A Constructed Peace*, 360–69; Soutou, *Alliance*, 236–7; Vaïsse, *Grandeur*, 154–7. Trachtenberg believes historians have given too much credence to de Gaulle's remarks to Peyrefitte and not enough to the diplomatic documents. But the remarks reported by Peyrefitte on this affair were not off-the-cuff *boutades* but reports of what de Gaulle said in the Council of Ministers, and have surely no less validity than the false trails he allowed his diplomats to leave. 113. Macmillan, *Diaries*, 527. 114. AP 348–9 (3/1/63). 115. TNA FO 371/177864 (12/3/64). 116. Edgard Pisani, *Le général indivis* (Albin Michel, 1974), 99–110. 117. DMIV 70 (14/1/63). 118. AP 360. 119. DDF 1962(2) 201 (meeting at the Quai d'Orsay, 16–17/12/62). 120. James Ellison, *The United States, Britain and the Transatlantic Crisis: Rising to the Gaullist Challenge* (Palgrave, 2007), 13. 121. DDF 1963(1) 41. 122. Vaïsse, *Grandeur*, 255–61. 123. Frank Costigliola, 'Kennedy, de Gaulle', 186. 124. Dean Rusk, *As I Saw It: A Secretary of State's Memoirs* (I. B. Tauris, 1991), 240. 125. Costigliola, 'Kennedy, de Gaulle', 191. 126. C. L. Sulzberger, *An Age of Mediocrity: Memoirs and Diaries 1963–1972* (Macmillan, New York, 1973), 301–8.

23. Going Global, 1963–1964

1. Macmillan, unpublished diaries, 4/2/63.　2. Ellison, *The United States*, 13.　3. TNA PREM 11/4811 (Dixon to Home, 17/7/63).　4. TNA PREM 11/4811 (Pierson Dixon to FO, 19/9/63).　5. TNA FO 371/169108/CF1012/2 (1/2/63).　6. James Ellison, 'Britain, de Gaulle's NATO Polices, and Anglo-French Rivalry, 1963–1967', in Nuenlist, Locher and Martin, *Globalizing de Gaulle*, 138 (12/5/64).　7. Ellison, *The United States*, 14.　8. Memorandum for the President, 29 January 1963, JFK Library, Papers of President Kennedy, President's Office Files, Countries, Box 116A (I am grateful to James Ellison for supplying this document).　9. FRUS 1964–8 XII #27 (3/64).　10. Reyn, 'Atlantis Lost', 69.　11. FNSP, Archives Couve de Murville MCM8 (17/12/65).　12. AP 674–9.　13. Raymond Aron, *La Coexistence (mars 1955–février 1965)* (Fallois, 1993), 1036–9 ('Le Grand Débat', 27/5/62).　14. AP 1353–9.　15. For an overview see Bruno Tertrais, ' "*Destruction assuré*": The Origins and Development of French Nuclear Strategy 1945–1981', in Henry Sokolski (ed.), *Getting MAD: Nuclear Mutual Assured Destruction, its Origins and Practice* (Strategic Studies Institute, Carlisle, PA, 2004), 51–122　16. Pierre Gallois, *Le sablier du siècle* (L'Age d'Homme, 1999), 372–3.　17. LNCIII 444 (11/1/62).　18. DMIII 139 (3/11/59).　19. LNCIII 604 (9/12/63).　20. LNCIII 603 (9/12/63).　21. Jean Lacouture, *De Gaulle*, vol. III: *Le souverain* (Seuil, 1986), 452.　22. FRUS 1961–3 VIII #125 (22/1/63).　23. LNCIII 589 (27/10/63).　24. AP 342.　25. Soutou, *Alliance*, 272–5, and Vaïsse, *Grandeur*, 573–4, interpret this affair differently.　26. LNCIII 657 (13/7/64).　27. AP 622 (21/8/63).　28. DMIV 159 (31/12/63).　29. DMIV 183–7 (31/1/64).　30. AP 323 (6/6/62).　31. *Cahiers de la Fondation Charles de Gaulle* (1995), 'L'établissment de relations diplomatiques entre la France et la Chine populaire'.　32. AP 1088 (8/1/64).　33. DDF 1964(1) 26 (15/1/64), 35 (18/1/64).　34. Alphand, *Etonnement*, 422 (3/2/64).　35. DGM 1105. The American record is rather less explicit than this: 'He considered Southeast Asia a bad terrain militarily, politically and psychologically to fight a war', FRUS 1961–3 XIII #230. See also DDF 1961(1) 265.　36. AP 1075 (29/8/63), 1993 (22/1/64).　37. Pierre Journoud, *De Gaulle et le Vietnam 1945–1969. La réconciliation* (Taillandier, 2011).　38. FRUS 1964–8(1) #202 (6/6/64).　39. DDF 1966(2) 363 (31/12/65).　40. AP 1104 (28/4/65).　41. In general see Maurice Vaïsse (ed.), *De Gaulle et l'Amérique latine* (Presses Universitaires de Rennes, 2014).　42. LNCIII 665 (18/9/64).　43. AP 1/63.　44. TNA FO 371/177874 (23/10/64).　45. Matthieu Trouvé, 'L'ambition et les contraintes', in Vaïsse, *De Gaulle et l'Amérique latine*, 115–29.　46. Roussel, *De Gaulle*, 766.　47. Luc Capdevila, 'Les aléas d'une captation d'image', in Vaïsse, *De Gaulle et l'Amérique latine*, 129–45.　48. Soutou, *Un diplomate*, 400.　49. Turpin, *De Gaulle, Pompidou*, 62.　50. FNSP, Archives Debré 2DE30 (13/8/61).　51. *Foccart parle* I, 479 (note, 5/7/61). Also note to Alphand, LNCIII 323–4.　52. LNCIII 216 (2/2/60).　53. Pierre-Michel Durand, *L'Afrique et les relations franco-américaines des années soixante. Aux orgines de l'obsession américaine* (L'Harmattan, 2007), 113–31.　54. DMIII 283 (20/12/60).　55. DMIII 424 (26/3/62); AP 405 (30/1/63).　56. Anne Liskenne, *L'Algérie indépendante. L'ambassade de Jean Marcel Jeanneney (juillet 1962–janvier 1963)* (Armand Colin, 2015), 50–51.　57. Jeffrey

Byrne, ' "*Je ne vous ai pas compris*": De Gaulle's Decade of Negotiation with the Algerian FLN, 1958–1969', in Nuenlist, Locher and Martin, *Globalizing de Gaulle*, 225–49 (226); Byrne, 'Négociation perpetuelle', in Vaïsse, *De Gaulle et l'Algérie*, 299–312. 58. Charles-Robert Ageron, 'La politique française de coopération avec l'Algérie', in DGESSVI 216 n. 4. 59. AP 1306 (29/5/63). This was said when Boumédienne became number two in the regime in May 1963. Two years later he took full power. 60. Jean-Pierre Bat, *Le syndrome Foccart. La politique française en Afrique de 1959 à nos jours* (Gallimard, 2012), 162–4. 61. LNCIII 471 (2/4/62); FI 552 (10/2/67). In general see André Lewin, 'La decolonisation de la Guinée, un échec', in Philippe Oulmont and Maurice Vaïsse (eds.), *De Gaulle et la décolonisation de l'Afrique subsaharienne* (Karthala, 2014), 119–53. 62. FI 552 (10/2/67). 63. FI 359 (11/2/66). 64. In general see Bat, *Syndrome Foccart*, 83–150. 65. LNCIII 626 (18/2/64). 66. Bat, *Syndrome Foccart*, 244. 67. FII 231. 68. *Foccart parle* I, 276–7. 69. FI 727 (3/10/67). 70. FI 425 (26/5/66). 71. FI 90 (4/3/65). 72. Durand, *Afrique*, 229–62; Charles and Alice Darlington, *African Betrayal* (David McKay, New York, 1968). 73. AP 1071; *Foccart parle* I, 213. 74. FI 105 (25/3/65). 75. *Foccart parle* I, 214; FI 106. 76. FI 106 (26/3/65). 77. FI 48 (18/1/65). 78. Omar Bongo, *Blanc comme nègre* (Grasset, 2001), 67. 79. FI 221 (21/9/65). 80. FI 105 (26/3/65). 81. Bodleian Library, Reilly Papers MS.Eng. c6925 (Draft Memoirs), 138–40 (my thanks to James Ellison for passing on this source). 82. Jean-Pierre Bat, *La fabrique des 'Barbouzes'. Histoire des réseaux Foccart en Afrique* (Nouveau Monde, 2015), 342–50. 83. Soutou, *Un diplomate*, 341–9. 84. AP 1056 (23/7/62). 85. Durand, *Afrique*, 443–4.

24. Modernizing Monarch, 1959–1964

1. Nicolas Mariot, *Bains de foule. Les voyages présidentiels en province, 1888–2002* (Belin, 2006), 42–3. 2. AP 155–6 (19/5/62). 3. André Passeron, *De Gaulle parle* (Plon, 1962), 550–58; AP 510–15. 4. Pierre Viansson-Ponté, *The King and his Court* (Houghton Mifflin, 1965), 38. 5. Hazareesingh, *Mythe*, 127. 6. AN 5AG1/177. 7. Jean-Paul Ollivier, *Le Tour de France du Général* (Julliard, 1985), 141. 8. Pisani, *Le général indivis*, 117. 9. AP 513. 10. Comte de Paris and de Gaulle, *Dialogue sur la France*, 137–8, 200–201. 11. AP 202, 1137. 12. LNCIII 371 (4/6/61). 13. AP 1137. 14. One telling detail: all newly elected presidents of the Republic since 1879 have had a commemorative medal struck with their portrait on one side and the effigy of the the Republic on the other. De Gaulle however chose on the reverse side of the medal to have a Cross of Lorraine. 15. Gérard Namer, *Batailles pour mémoire. La commémoration en France de 1945 à nos jours* (Papyrus, 1983); Danielle Tartakowsky, 'Des 18 juin de souveraineté quand même 1945–1957', in Philippe Oulmont (ed.), *Les 18 juin. Combats et commémorations* (André Versaille, 2011), 156–74. 16. Sudhir Hazareesingh, 'Les 18 juin sous la Vème République', in Oulmont, *Les 18 juin*, 183–207. 17. DGM 1119. 18. Henry Rousso, *Le syndrome de Vichy* (Seuil, 1987), 95–110. 19. See Jérôme Bourdon, *Histoire de la télévision sous de Gaulle* (Anthropos/INA, 1990); Aude Vassallo,

La télévision sous de Gaulle. Le contrôle gouvernemental de l'information (1958/1969) (De Boeck, Brussels, 2005); Brizzi, *De Gaulle et les médias*. For a loyal Gaullist account of the workings of the system by the ORTF's Director of Information see Edouard Sablier, *La télé du Général* (Editions du Rocher, 2001). 20. Christian Delporte, *La France dans les yeux. Une histoire de la communication politique de 1930 à nos jours* (Fayard, 2007), 86–7. 21. Marcel Bleustein-Blanchet, *Mémoires d'un lion* (Perrin, 1988), 218–19. He rather overplayed the reality in his memoirs, claiming wrongly that de Gaulle was in uniform and wearing a képi. 22. Brizzi, *De Gaulle*, 125–6. 23. DMIII 295–6. 24. AN 5AG1/1555. 25. AP 510 (5/62). 26. Jean-François Revel, *Le style du Général. Essai sur Charles de Gaulle (mai 1958–juin 1959)* (Julliard, 1959). 27. DMIII (13/6/58). 28. DGM 1133. 29. AP 223, 518, 573. 30. Delporte, *La France dans les yeux*, 102. 31. DGM 1134. 32. Vassallo, *La télévision*, 263–7. 33. AP 501; also 496–501, 768–78. 34. LNCIII 539 (18/2/63), 541 (3/3/63), 546 (3/4/63), 579 (2/9/63). 35. LNCIII 649 (29/5/64). 36. Guy, *En écoutant*, 354–5. 37. Brizzi, *De Gaulle*, 128–31. 38. Fauvet, 'Pour un régime d'opinion', *Le Monde* 24/2/66. 39. Raymond Aron, 'Le secret du général' (25/1/63), in Aron, *La Coexistence*, 1135. 40. Ibid. 41. AP 131–3 (18/4/62); also 472 (14/4/63). 42. Mauriac, *Un autre de Gaulle*, 201. 43. 'De Gaulle 44, de Gaulle 59', *L'Express* 26/3/59; 'Charles de Gaulle', *L'Express* 29/10/59; 'Notre haute cour', *L'Express* 2/6/60; 'Technique du coup d'état', *L'Express* 27/9/62. 44. Michel Winock, *Journal politique. La république gaullienne 1958–1981* (Thierry Marchaisse, 2015), 103. 45. Georges Vedel (ed.), *La dépolitisation. Mythe ou réalité* (Armand Colin, 1962). 46. Ibid., 29, 51. 47. For example Philippe Ariès's article 'Une ville "ennemie"' (10/5/61), reprinted in Ariès, *Le présent quotidien 1955–1966* (Seuil, 1997), 222–3. 48. AP 320. 49. AP 85; *Foccart parle* I, 411. 50. See articles 'Elysée' and 'Vie quotidienne à l'Elysée' in Claire Andrieu, Philippe Braude and Guillaume Piketty (eds.), *Dictionnaire Charles de Gaulle* (Robert Laffont, 2006), 427–9, 1156–7. 51. AN AP 569/53 (Lefranc Papers), 'Notes aux membres du cabinet'. 52. Neau-Dufour, *Yvonne*, 361–2. 53. Pierre-Louis Blanc, *De Gaulle au soir de sa vie* (Fayard, 1990), 155. 54. Vaïsse, *Grandeur*, 290. 55. Jean Méo, *Une fidélité gaulliste à l'épreuve du pouvoir. De Chirac à de Gaulle* (Lavauzelle, 2008), 149. 56. FDG, *De Gaulle et le service de l'état. Des collaborateurs du général témoignent* (Plon, 1977), 95. 57. DGM 1139. 58. Méo, *Une fidélité*, 115–16. 59. FDG, *De Gaulle et le service*, 112–13; Jacques Narbonne, de Gaulle's education adviser, was reprimanded for the same: Narbonne, *De Gaulle et l'éducation nationale. Un rencontre manqué* (Denoël, 1994), 128. 60. AP 345–6 (20/12/62). 61. Pompidou, *Lettres*, 377–8 (17/5/65). 62. AP 1488 (13/4/66). 63. Kettle, *De Gaulle and Algeria*, 307. 64. *Archives Constitutionnelles de la Ve république*, vol. V: *Témoignages 1958–1995* (Documentation Française, 2011), 124–5. 65. Jean-Maxime Lévêque, *En première ligne* (Albin Michel, 1986), 72. 66. Bernard Tricot, *Mémoires* (Quai Voltaire, 1994), 216. 67. AN 5AG1/2366. 68. AN 5AG1/2394. 69. The minutes are in AN 5AG1/2346. 70. LNCIII 591 (5/11/63). Or see LNCIII (30/10/63). 71. AP 521 (28/8/62), 529 (9/1/63), 538 (28/2/63). 72. AN 5AG1/2346 (7/12/63). 73. This is the theme of Narbonne, *De Gaulle et l'éducation*. 74. LNCIII 546 (26/3/63, 6/4/63), 818 (4/5/66), 731 (24/7/65), 776

(31/1/66). 75. AP 527. 76. AP 932. 77. AN 5AG1/2359. 78. Lévêque, *En première ligne*, 87. 79. AP 528–31. 80. Guy, *En écoutant*, 161. 81. On this generation see Gaïti, *De Gaulle prophète*, 263–309; Delphine Dulong, *Moderniser la politique. Aux origines de la Vème République* (L'Harmattan,1997). 82. Pierre Grémion, *Modernisation et progressisme. Fin d'une époque 1968–1981* (Editions Esprit, 2005), 239. 83. David Valence, ' "Une prise en main rigoureuse de l'appareil d'état?" Le pouvoir gaulliste face aux hauts fonctionnaires (1958–1962)', *Histoire@ Politique* 12 (2010/3); Luc Rouban, 'Le Gaullisme des haut fonctionnaires (1958–1974)', *Vingtième siécle* 116 (10–12/12). 84. On the complex relationship between the proponents of these ideas and the Finance Ministry see Laure Quennouëlle-Corre, *La direction du Trésor 1947–1967. L'état-banquier et la croissance* (Comité pour l'histoire économique et financière de la France, 2000). 85. Marc Olivier Baruch, 'Les élites d'état dans la modernisation', in Berstein, Birnbaum and Rioux, *De Gaulle et les élites*, 102–3. 86. Méo, *Une fidelité gaulliste*, 158. 87. Anderson, 'Civil War in France', 40–109. 88. Ibid., 46. 89. DMIII 242 (14/6/60); also slightly differently LNCIII 220–21 (2/60). 90. Brigitte Gaïti, ' "Syndicat des anciens" contre "forces vives" de la nation. Le renouvellement politique de 1958', in Michel Offerlé, *La profession politique XIX–XXè siècles* (Belin, 1999), 279–306. 91. LNCIII 225–6 (18/3/60). 92. AP 954 (27/3/63). 93. LNCIII 623 (6/2/64); 665 (19/9/64). 94. AN 5AG1/2424 (Méo note, 3/60). 95. Bruneteau, *Les paysans*, 43. 96. Gordon Wright, *Rural Revolution in France: The Peasantry in the Twentieth Century* (Stanford University Press, 1964), 162. 97. LNCIII 234 (30/4/60). 98. DGM 1016–17. 99. DMIII 241–6 (14/6/60).

25. Half-Time, 1965

1. Serge Mallet, *Gaullisme et la gauche* (Seuil, 1965). 2. 'Résistance', *14 juillet* 1 (1958). 3. This was a special one-page issue 'avant le n.2'. 4. Gilbert Comte, 'De Gaulle et la République', *Le Monde* 2–3/12/62. 5. Georges Vedel, 'Haute et basse politique dans la Constitution de 1958', *Preuves* 107 (1/60), 17–22; 'De l'arbitrage à la mystique', *Preuves* 112 (6/60), 16–24. 6. 'Un homme a remplacé l'état', *Le Nef* (5/59). 7. François Fontaine, 'Le vide politique et le mythe du vieux chef', *Preuves* 97 (5/59), 49–53. 8. 'La constitution du mépris', *L'Express* 11/9/58, reprinted in Jean-Paul Sartre, *Situations*, vol. V (Gallimard, 1965), 113–14. 9. Jean-Noël Jean-neney and Jacques Julliard, *Le monde de Beuve-Méry ou le métier d'Alceste* (Seuil, 1979). 10. Beuve-Méry, *Onze ans de règne 1958–1969* (Flammarion, 1974), 71–3 (26/10/62). 11. Ibid., 111–13 (18/12/65). 12. François Mauriac, *Bloc-notes*, vol. II: *1958–1960* (Seuil, 1993), 378 (30/1/60). 13. Michel Winock, 'Mauriac politique', *Esprit* (12/67), 1004–14. 14. Daniel, 'Le mythe gaulliste dans le tiers monde', *Le Monde* 5/2/64. 15. Jean-Marie Domenach, 'C'est toujours Munich', *Témoignage chrétien* 1/6/62; Domenach, 'Donnons congé aux fantômes', *Témoignage chrétien* 3/10/63. 16. Claire Andrieu, *Pour l'amour de la république. Le Club Jean Moulin 1958–1970* (Fayard, 2002). 17. Dulong, *Moderniser*, 229. 18. Georges Suffert, *Mémoires d'un ours* (Ed. de Fallois, 1995), 129. 19. Alain Slama in Robert Frank and Eric Roussel, *Deux passions françaises. Pierre Mendès France et Charles de*

Gaulle (CRNS Editions, 2014), 33.   20. De Gaulle chose not to include this in the published version of his speeches but it can be heard on the recording of the press conference: http://www.ina.fr/video/I00012523.   21. DDF 1965(1) 35 (21/1/65).   22. TNA FO 371/182932 (1/1/65); FO 371/182937 (5/2/65).   23. TNA FO 371/182949 (29/1/65).   24. LNCIII 689–90 (6/1/65).   25. Alphand, *Etonnement*, 447; DDF 1965(1) 185 (22/4/65).   26. Ibid., 451.   27. FI 63 (5/2/65).   28. DMIV 355.   29. DMIV 363 (23/3/6).   30. LNCIII 723.   31. DDF 1965(1) 275 (entretien de Gaulle–Adenauer).   32. Durand, *L'Afrique*, 266–331; Bat, *Syndrome Foccart*, 281–9.   33. FI 159 (28/5/58).   34. FI 159–61 (28/5/58).   35. *Foccart parle* I, 311.   36. Mauriac, *Un autre de Gaulle*, 310. Examples in LNCII 1001 (1/2/51), 1011 (25/4/51).   37. FI 85 (26/65).   38. FI 96 (16/3/65).   39. AP 1162–3 (12/1164).   40. Neau-Dufour, *Yvonne*, 358.   41. François Bloch-Lainé, *Ce que je crois* (Grasset, 1995), 113.   42. Neau-Dufour, *Yvonne*, 358–9.   43. Ibid., 364–73.   44. Ibid., 399.   45. Mangold, *Impossible Ally*, 163.   46. DGM 873.   47. Neau-Dufour, *Geneviève de Gaulle*, 114–19.   48. FI 116–17 (3/4/64).   49. AP 1155–6 (13/6/64).   50. AP 742 (17/6/64), 1146 (8/2/64), 1167 (11/2/65).   51. Vaïsse, *Grandeur*, 552.   52. AP 863 (28/10/64).   53. Andrew Moravcsik, 'De Gaulle between Grain and Grandeur: The Political Economy of French EC Policy, 1958–1970', *Journal of Cold War Studies* 2/2 (Spring 2000), 3–43, and 2/3 (Fall 2000), 4–68.   54. Vaïsse, *Grandeur*, 555.   55. AP 889 (13/7/65), 891 (21/7/65).   56. Ludlow, 'From Words to Actions', 93. The best account of the crisis is Piers Ludlow, *The European Community and the Crises of the 1960s: Negotiating the Gaullist Challenge* (Routledge, 2006).   57. François Mitterrand, *Ma part de verité. De la rupture à l'unité* (Fayard, 1969), 22.   58. AN 5AG1/1174 (Ganeval), Report of meeting between Ganeval and Foccart.   59. François Mitterrand, *La paille et le grain* (Flammarion, 1975), 26.   60. AP 1181 (13/10/65).   61. AP 1184 (20/10/65).   62. AP 1166 (14/11/64).   63. François Audigier, 'De Gaulle victime puis acteur de la modernisation de la communication politique', *Espoir* 150 (3/07), 25–51; Delporte, *La France dans les yeux*, 121–61.   64. AP 1205 (5/12/65).   65. Vendroux, *Ces grandes années*, 242.   66. AP 1208 (8/12/65).   67. DMIV 446 (14/12/65).   68. Lefort, *Souvenirs*, 135.   69. All articles from *Le Monde*: Astier de la Vigerie, 'Pour de Gaulle', 2/12/65; André Chamson, 'Pour défendre la république', 19–20/12/65; Jean Guehénno, 'Une certaine idée de la France', 19–20/12/65; Jean Cassou, 'Contre le Bonapartisme', 18/12/65; Jean Cau, 'Le seul choix d'avenir', 9/12/65; Pierre Boutang, 'Par curiosité', 17/12/65; Pierre Uri, 'Eclaircissements', 17/12/65; Edgard Morin, 'La contradiction', 19–20/12/65.   70. LNCIII 760 (29/12/65).   71. Mitterrand, *Coup d'état*, 36.   72. Garrigues, *Les hommes providentiels.*

26. Upsetting the Applecart, 1966–1967

1. LNCIII 404 (19/9/61).   2. LNCIII 1184.   3. FI 424 (25/5/66).   4. Garrett Martin, *General de Gaulle's Cold War: Challenging American Hegemony 1963–1968* (Berghahn, New York/Oxford, 2013), 117.   5. FRUS 1964–8 XII #53.   6. AP 360 (14/1/63).   7. Soutou, *Alliance*, 129–30, believes it was meant seriously.   8.

Alphand, *Etonnement*, 452; LNCIII 697 contains a note (23/2/65) on the drafting of a bilateral treaty with America to replace NATO. **9.** DDF 1966(1) 49 (21/1/66), 58 (25/2/66), 60 (26/1/66). **10.** FRUS 1964–8 XIII (7/3/66). **11.** Frédéric Bozo, 'Chronique d'une décision annoncée: le retrait de l'organisation militaire (1965–1967)', in Maurice Vaïsse, Pierre Mélandri and Frédéric Bozo (eds.), *La France et l'OTAN 1949–1996* (Complexe, Brussels, 1996), 331–58 (338). **12.** DMV 21. **13.** Soutou, *Alliance*, 291–2. **14.** Mikhail Narinsky, 'Le retrait de la France de l'organisation militaire de l'OTAN, vu de Moscou', in Vaïsse, *De Gaulle et la Russie*, 163–70 (166). **15.** DDF 1959(2) 295 (VIII 21/12/59). **16.** Roussel, *De Gaulle*, 663. **17.** DMIV 113 (28/10/66). **18.** LNCIII 575 (23/8/63). **19.** Alphand, *Etonnement*, 445. **20.** AP 983–5; Olivier Chantiaux, *De Gaulle et la diplomatie par l'image* (INA Editions, Bry-sur Marne, 2010). **21.** DDF 1966(1) 279 (29/4/66). **22.** AP 912. **23.** DDF 1965(2) 117 (de Gaulle to Ball, 1/8/65); LNCIII 657 (13/7/64). **24.** AP 1356. **25.** LNCIII 778–9 (4/2/66). **26.** LNCIII 842 (18/11/66). **27.** Alphand, *Etonnement*, 445. **28.** DDF 1968(1) 390 (19/11/68). **29.** AP 1416 (5/12/66). DDF 1967(1) 47 (27/1/67) ('*Ce sera un rapprochement, une conjonction, peut-être un jour une confédération*'). **30.** AP 1405 (15/6/66). **31.** Lefort, *Souvenirs*, 152. **32.** Roussel, *De Gaulle*, 801. **33.** AP 1407. **34.** DMV 81–2. **35.** Journoud, *De Gaulle et le Vietnam*, 246–60. **36.** Narinsky, 'Le retrait', 170. **37.** AP 1416 (5/12/66). **38.** DDF 1967(1) 19 (13/1/67). **39.** McGrath, *De Gaulle à Trianon*, 78–9. **40.** Ellison, *The United States*, 165. **41.** Helen Parr, 'Saving the Community: The French Response to Britain's Second EEC Application in 1967', *Cold War History* 6/4 (2006), 425–54. **42.** AP 1407. **43.** Guy, *En écoutant*, 254. **44.** Vaïsse, *Grandeur*, 619, notes that the French minutes do not actually have these words which are cited by one of Ben-Gurion's biographers. **45.** The fullest account is Samy Cohen, *De Gaulle, les Gaullistes et Israël* (Alain Moreau, 1974); the most up to date is Vaïsse, *Grandeur*, 615–47. **46.** LNCIII (31/7/59); AN 5AG1/511 (note, 24/5/63). **47.** DDF 1959(1) 106. **48.** AN 5AG1/788 (Debré note, 15/6/60). **49.** DGM 1114. **50.** Barnavi DGESSVI, 417–29; Cohen, *De Gaulle, les Gaullistes et Israel*, 86–7, quotes from the diary of Peres. **51.** LNCIII 557 (11/6/63); LNCIII 716 (14/5/65). **52.** DDF 1965(1) 274 (12/6/65). **53.** For an overview see Jean-Pierre Filiu, 'France and the June 1967 War', in Roger Louis and Avi Shlaim, *The 1967 Arab–Israeli War: Origins and Consequences* (Cambridge University Press, 2012), 247–63. **54.** AP 1489 (24/5/67); LNCII 896 (4/6/67). **55.** Abba Eban, *An Autobiography* (Weidenfeld & Nicolson, 1977), 341–4. **56.** DDF 1967(1) 238 (1/6/67). **57.** DDF 1967(1) 243 (2/6/67). **58.** FI 649 (5/6/67). **59.** DDF 1967(1) 275 (8/6/67). **60.** DDF 1967(1) 312 (16/6/67). **61.** TNA FCO 17/28 (18/6/67). **62.** LNCIII 910 (7/8/67); 661 (18/6/67). **63.** DDF 1967(2) 27 (12/7/67). **64.** Avi Shlaim, *The Iron Wall: Israel and the Arab World* (Allen Lane, 2000), 236–4; Avi Shlaim, 'Israel: Poor Little Samson', in Roger Louis and Avi Shlaim, *The 1967 Arab–Israeli War: Origins and Consequences* (Cambridge University Press, 2012), reiterates this position. For the most recent analysis, more critical of Israel, see Guy Laron, *The Six Day War: The Breaking of the Middle East* (Yale University Press, New Haven/London, 2017). **65.** DDF 1967(1) 258 (5/6/67), 267 (6/6/67). **66.** DDF 1967(1) 334, 335

(Lucet to Couve, 26/6/67). See Maurice Vaïsse, 'Les crises de Cuba et du Prochain Orient', in Vaïsse, *De Gaulle et la Russie*, 151–63. **67.** Eban, *Autobiography*, 437–8. **68.** Sulzberger, *Age of Mediocrity*, 344–5. **69.** FNSP, Archives Debré 2DE29. **70.** Vendroux, *Ces grandes années*, 93. **71.** LNCIII 318 (21/1/61). **72.** LNCIII 579 (4/9/63). **73.** LNCIII 845 (9/12/66). **74.** AP 1518 (24/4/63). **75.** AP 1521, 1528. **76.** AP 1530. **77.** DMV 202–4. **78.** AP 1543. **79.** AP 1551. **80.** LNCIII 908 (28/7/67). **81.** AP 1552–3. **82.** AP 1568 **83.** FI 686. **84.** Alphand, *Etonnement*, 494. **85.** DDF 1967(1) 53 (31/167). **86.** DDF 1967(1) 47 (27/1/67). **87.** DDF 1967(2) 111 (11/9/67). **88.** AP 60–61. **89.** AP 1510. **90.** AP 61. **91.** Martin, *General de Gaulle's Cold War*, 159–67; Ellison, *The United States*, 174–83. **92.** FI 304 (13/12/65), 547 (27/1/67). **93.** FII 427 (8/11/68). **94.** FI 502 (4/11/66). **95.** FI 314 (1/1/66). **96.** FI 323 (10/1/66). **97.** FII 14 (5/1/68). **98.** FI 765–6 (10/11/67). **99.** FI 790–91 (19/12/67). **100.** FII 67–8 (18/4/68). **101.** Vaïsse, *Grandeur*, 496–500. **102.** FI 694 (28/8/67); also 664 (20/6/67). **103.** FI 787 (14/12/67). **104.** FII 25 (23/1/68), 53 (2/4/68). **105.** Vaïsse, 'L'ONU, une tribune pour la politique gaullienne?', in *8e Conférence internationale des éditeurs de documents diplomatiques* (Ministère des Affaires étrangères, 2008), 169–75; Joanna Warson, 'A Transnational Decolonisation: Britain, France and the Rhodesian Problem', in Tony Chafer and Alexander Keese (ed.), *Francophone Africa at Fifty* (Manchester University Press, 2013), 171–85. **106.** FII 92 (6/5/68). **107.** Sulzberger, *Age of Mediocrity*, 404 (23/1/68). **108.** FRUS 1964–8 XII 74 (27/7/67). **109.** Alphand, *Etonnement*, 493. **110.** AP 1538 (10/11/65), 1562 (31/8/67).

27. Diminishing Returns

1. DMIV 246. **2.** Jean Charlot, *Les Français et de Gaulle* (Plon, 1971), 45–6. **3.** Quoted in *Le Monde* 19/4/66. **4.** Maurice Duverger, 'La gauche et l'OTAN', *Le Monde* 31/3/66. **5.** *Le Monde* 11/5/66; Domenach, 'A propos d'un manifeste sur la politique éxtérieure', *Esprit* (5/66), 1234–7. **6.** TNA FO 371/189100 (17/1/66). **7.** Eric Chiaradia, *L'entourage du Général de Gaulle, juin 1958–avril 1969* (Publibook, 2011), 449. **8.** Lefort, *Souvenirs*, 209. **9.** *L'Express* 23/4/59. **10.** Jacques Dauer and Michel Rodet, *Les orphelins du gaullisme* (Julliard, 1962), 202–3. **11.** AP 524 (11/7/62). **12.** AP 446 (12/12/62). **13.** AP 448 (13/12/62). **14.** AP 1000 (30/4/63). **15.** AP 1002 (20/8/63). **16.** Jean-Claude Casanova, 'L'amendement Vallon', *Revue française de science politique* 17/1 (1967), 97–109. **17.** LNCIII 809 (11/4/66). **18.** AP 1291–4. **19.** AP 1300–302 (10/9/66). **20.** AP 1307 (19/2/67). **21.** DMIV 126 (28/10/66). **22.** DMIV 153 (9/2/67), 159 (4/3/67); LNCIII 869–70 (12/2/67). **23.** Jean-Paul Cointet, Bernard Lachaise and Sabrina Tricaud, *Georges Pompidou et les élections (1962–1974)* (PIE Peter Lang, Brussels, 2008), 65–117. **24.** FI 511 (16/11/66). **25.** AP 1434. **26.** AN 5AG1/2760. **27.** LNCIII 893 (13/5/67). **28.** FI 734–40 (13/10/67). **29.** FI (9/11/67). **30.** 'Nous n'irons pas à Lille', *Notre République* 10/11/67. **31.** *Le Monde* 28/11/67. **32.** DMV 252–4 (27/11/67). **33.** Roussel, *De Gaulle*, 847. **34.** Jean d'Escrienne, *Le général* *m'a dit 1966–1970* (Plon, 1973), 148.   **35.** LNCIII 942–5 (30/12/67); Daniel Amson, *De Gaulle et Israel* (PUF, 1991), 111–13; Tournoux, *Le Tourment*, 205–9. See also his exchange with the Gaullist Louis Hamon in AN 5AG1/1185.   **36.** TNA FO 371/189100.   **37.** FI 636 (16/5/67), 746–7 (20/10/67), 778 (27/11/67).   **38.** Tricot, *Mémoires*, 253.   **39.** Bodleian Library, Reilly Papers MS.Eng.c6926, 'Unpublished memoirs', 165–6.   **40.** FI 690 (23/8/67).   **41.** Bibliothèque de Documentation Internationale Contemporaine (BDIC), Fonds Rousset, Delta 1880/112/5 (25/4/68).   **42.** Domenach, *Beaucoup de gueule*, 266.   **43.** François Flohic, *Souvenirs d'Outre-Gaulle* (Plon, 1979), 172 (28/4/68); similar comment in Lefort, *Souvenirs*, 234.

28. Revolution, 1968

1. Tricot, *Mémoires*, 227.   **2.** AP 1458 (6/9/62).   **3.** Guy, *En écoutant*, 364–5.   **4.** AP 7994–6 (5/6/63).   **5.** AP 1198–9 (24/11/65).   **6.** AP 1458 (6/9/67)   **7.** LNCIII 602 (9/12/63).   **8.** Margerie, *Mémoires inédites* V, 179.   **9.** Philippe de Gaulle, *De Gaulle mon père* I, 363.   **10.** AP 514.   **11.** LNCIII 1177.   **12.** Rix, *Par le portillon*, 145.   **13.** Information provided by Yves de Gaulle (interview 16/12/15).   **14.** LNCIII 908 (18/7/67).   **15.** LNCIII 939 (17/12/67).   **16.** Ludivine Bantigny, *1968. De grands soirs en petits matins* (Seuil, 2018), 38. This is the most recent, and now the best, book on 1968.   **17.** DDF 1966(2) 157.   **18.** DMIV 455 (14/12/65).   **19.** Didier Fischer, 'De Gaulle et la jeunesse étudiante de l'UNEF dans les années soixante', in FDG, *Charles de Gaulle et la jeunesse* (Plon, 2005), 324–42.   **20.** AP 15966 (20/11/63).   **21.** LNCIII 630 (3/3/64).   **22.** LNCIII 649 (5/6/64).   **23.** Sabrina Tricaud, 'L'éducation, un "domaine réservé" pour Georges Pompidou 1962–1968', in Bruno Poucet and David Valence (eds.), *La Loi Edgar Faure. Réformer l'université après 1968* (Presses Universitaires de Rennes, 2016), 51–8.   **24.** AP 1604 (21/4/67).   **25.** Hervé Hamon and Patrick Rotman, *Génération*, vol. I: *Les années de rêve* (Seuil, 1987), 40. On Missoffe, Laurent Besse, 'Un ministre et les jeunes: François Missoffe, 1966–1968', *Histoire@Politique* 4 (2008/1), 11–11.   **26.** Philippe Nivet, 'Maurice Grimaud et Mai 1968', *Histoire@Politique* 27 (2015/3), 18–32.   **27.** Bantigny, *1968*, 153–79.   **28.** AP 1707 (9/5/68).   **29.** Mathias Bernard, 'L'état en mai 68', in Xavier Vigna and Jean Vigreux (eds), *Mai–juin 1968. Huit semaines qui ébranlèrent la France* (Editions Universitaires de Dijon, Dijon, 2010), 131–44.   **30.** AP 1680–82 (5/5/68).   **31.** AP 1693 (8/5/68).   **32.** AP 1711 (11/5/68).   **33.** Ibid.   **34.** Jean Mauriac, *L'après de Gaulle. Notes confidentielles 1968–1989* (Fayard, 2006), 384; in another version of the conversation Joxe reported him as saying, 'The General no longer exists, de Gaulle is dead,' cited in Roussel, *De Gaulle*, 863.   **35.** AP 1719 (11/5/68).   **36.** Pompidou, *Pour rétablir*, 180.   **37.** Christian Fouchet, *Mémoires d'hier et de demain*, vol. II: *Les lauriers sont coupés* (Plon, 1973), 44.   **38.** AP 1783 (2/6/68).   **39.** FII 106.   **40.** In general, see Bernard Lachaise and Sabrina Tricaud (eds.), *Georges Pompidou et Mai 1968* (Peter Lang, Brussels, 2009).   **41.** Xavier Vigna, *L'insubordination ouvrière dans les années 68. Essai d'histoire politique des usines* (Presses Universitaires de Rennes, 2011).   **42.** Bernard Ducamin quoted in Bantigny, *1968*, 181–12.   **43.** Emmanuel Laurentin,

'Le transistor', in Michelle Zancarini-Fournel and Philippe Artières (eds.), *68. Une histoire collective (1962–1981)* (La Découverte, 2008), 285–90.   **44.** DDF 1968(1) 295, 330.   **45.** Michel Droit, *Les feux du crépuscule. Journal 1968–1970* (Plon, 1977), 27.   **46.** Maurice Grimaud, *En mai fais ce qu'il te plaît* (Stock, 1977), 210.   **47.** LNCIII 977.   **48.** FII 130–32.   **49.** AN 5AG1/2227 ('Documents de réflexion pour M. Tricot pour son retour de Roumanie. 18/5/68 au soir').   **50.** AP 1743–51; Jean-Raymond Tournoux, *Le mois du mai du général* (Plon, 1969), 117–37.   **51.** Edouard Balladur, *L'arbre de mai* (Marcel Jullian, 1979), 224.   **52.** FII 131.   **53.** Balladur, *Arbre*, 291.   **54.** AP 1756–61 (27/5/68).   **55.** Vendroux, *Ces grandes années*, 316–17.   **56.** FII 134–5.   **57.** Droit, *Les feux*, 33–8.   **58.** Lalande quoted in Roussel, *De Gaulle*, 870–71; FII 141–4.   **59.** Lacouture, *Souverain*, 696.   **60.** Droit, *Les feux*, 40–41; Pompidou, *Pour rétablir*, 186–7; Fouchet, *Lauriers*, 19–27.   **61.** Flohic, *Souvenirs*, 176.   **62.** Boissieu gave many versions: Alain de Boissieu, *Pour servir le Général 1946–1970* (Plon, 1982), 176–94; to Foccart in FPII 173–7, 397–401 (5/6/68, 22/10/68); in a memorandum for Pompidou (6/6/68), reproduced in *Espoir* 115 (4/98), 73–85; and an interview in the same issue of *Espoir*, 69–72; a letter to Pompidou (23/7/68).   **63.** Pompidou, *Pour rétablir*, 189; Claude Mauriac, *Les espaces imaginaires* (Grasset, 1973), 262–3.   **64.** Flohic, *Souvenirs*, 176.   **65.** Ibid., 177–8.   **66.** Roussel, *De Gaulle*, 875.   **67.** Jacques Massu, *Baden 68. Souvenirs d'une fidelité gaulliste* (Plon, 1983).   **68.** Roussel, *De Gaulle*, 876.   **69.** Ibid.   **70.** Flohic, *Souvenirs*, 181.   **71.** Massu, *Baden*, 89; Flohic, *Souvenirs*, 181.   **72.** Flohic, *Souvenirs*, 182.   **73.** The latter is the view of François Goguel, 'Charles de Gaulle du 24 au 29 mai 1968', *Espoir* 115 (4/98), 87–105, which argues forcibly for the Boissieu line.   **74.** DMV 319.   **75.** AN 5AG1/2101 (18/5/68).   **76.** Jacques Belle, *Le 30 mai 1968. La guerre civile n'aura pas lieu* (Economica, 2012), 45–64; Frank Georgi, ' "Le pouvoir est dans la rue". 30 mai. La "manifestation gaulliste" des Champs Elysées', *Vingtième siècle* 48 (1995), 46–60.   **77.** DDF 1968(2) 320, 322.   **78.** François Audigier, 'Les gaullistes de gauche en mai–juin 1968: la fin d'une certaine ambiguïté?', in Bruno Benoit et al., *A chacun son mai? Le tour de France de mai–juin 1968* (Presses Universitaires de Rennes, 2011), 327–41; Audigier, 'Le malaise des jeunes gaullistes en mai 1968', *Vingtième siècle* 70 (2001), 71–88; for the memoirs of a left Gaullist in 1968, Olivier Germain-Thomas, *Les rats capitaines* (Hallier, 1978).   **79.** Anderson, 'Civil War in France', 8.   **80.** DMV 324–36.   **81.** FII 205 (18/6/68).   **82.** FII 207 (18/6/68).

29. The End, June 1968–November 1970

1. Pompidou, *Pour rétablir*, 199.   **2.** FII 250.   **3.** Pompidou, *Pour rétablir*, 200.   **4.** FII 263.   **5.** FII 169 (4/6/68).   **6.** Lachaise and Tricaud, *Pompidou et Mai 1968*, 184–6; Pompidou, *Pour rétablir*, 199–204; FII 245–95.   **7.** FII 275.   **8.** Flohic, *Souvenirs*, 146   **9.** Lacouture, *Souverain*, 547.   **10.** LNCIII 991 (24/8/68).   **11.** Alphand, *Etonnement*, 513.   **12.** DMV 364–5 (9/9/68).   **13.** DDF 1968(2) 230 (20/9/68); also DDF 1968(2) 236 (23/9/68).   **14.** MAE, 'Secrétariat général Entretiens et Messages', 1956–71, 231QO/34. I owe the comment on the Soviet archives to Professor Robert Service. **15.** FRUS 1964–6 XII 83 (10/10/68). **16.** DDF 1969(1) 97 (3/3/69). **17.** Couve de Murville quoted in Roussel, *De Gaulle*, 904; a similar remark by Couve is quoted in Vaïsse, *Grandeur*, 612, who gives a balanced account of the crisis, 607–12; Ledwidge, *De Gaulle*, 363–7, is interesting because he was in the Embassy at the time. **18.** Reyn, 'Atlantic Lost', 653–60. **19.** DMV 387 (24/11/68). **20.** Brigitte Gaïti, 'La décision à l'épreuve du pouvoir. Le Général de Gaulle entre mai 1968 et avril 1969', *Politix* 82 (2008), 39–67. **21.** F. Bon, 'Le référendum du 27 avril: suicide politique ou nécessité stratégique?', *Revue française de science politique* 20/2 (1970), 209. **22.** FII 358; in general see Poucet and Valence, *La Loi Edgar Faure*. **23.** FII 414. **24.** Pompidou, *Pour rétablir*, 256. **25.** FII 466. **26.** FII 555–6. **27.** Fouchet, *Lauriers*, 48. **28.** DMV 33 (23/4/66). **29.** DMV 294 (24/3/68). **30.** AN 5AG1/1691 (15/5/68). **31.** FII 610. **32.** FII 617. **33.** FII 621. **34.** DDF 1969(1) 181–4. **35.** Kissinger, *Diplomacy*, 604. **36.** AN 5AG1/164 (13–14/3/69). **37.** FII 674. **38.** FII 664. **39.** FII 650; Pompidou, *Pour rétablir*, 268; Debré, *Entretiens*, 181. **40.** FII 679. **41.** FII 685, 715. **42.** Vendroux, *Ces grandes années*, 344; FII 755. **43.** Pompidou, *Pour rétablir*, 282–3. **44.** The fullest account is by Flohic, 'With de Gaulle in Ireland', in Pierre Joannon (ed.), *De Gaulle and Ireland* (Institute of Public Administration, Dublin, 1991), 98–117. **45.** Harcourt quoted in Roussel, *De Gaulle*, 910. **46.** LNCI 497. **47.** Roussel, *De Gaullle*, 915. **48.** Ibid., 916. **49.** Jean Mauriac, *Mort du Général de Gaulle* (Grasset, 1972), 63–4. **50.** LNCIII 1060. **51.** Roussel, *De Gaulle*, 916. **52.** Mauriac, *Après de Gaulle*, 55. **53.** Yves de Gaulle, *Un autre regard sur mon grand-père, Charles de Gaulle* (Plon, 2016); conversation with Yves de Gaulle (16/12/15). For the record there is one mention by de Gaulle of Céline in an unpublished letter (27/9/39) to an unknown correspondent addressed only by his first name 'Antoine' bemoaning the fact that a debate at the literary Club du Faubourg on Céline's anti-Semitic writings had focused on the writer's style and not his ideology (in catalogue of the Lyons bookshop Autographes des Siècles, August 2015). It should be noted also that de Gaulle's admiration for Morand's prose had not been enough to stop him successfully blocking his entry to the Académie Française in 1968, and then, when Morand was elected in 1969, breaking with the tradition by which newly elected academicians were received by the President. To Peyrefitte in 1963 he described Morand's conduct during the war as 'unpardonable': AP 779. **54.** Vendroux, *Ces grandes années*, 20. **55.** André Malraux, *Les chênes qu'on abat* (Gallimard, 1971), 79. **56.** Droit, *Les feux*, 127. **57.** LNCIII 1115 (9/1/70). **58.** Pierre-Louis Blanc, *De Gaulle au soir de sa vie* (Fayard, 1990), 265–6. **59.** Droit, *Les feux*, 188. **60.** 'Stanley Hoffmann, 'Last Strains and Last Will: De Gaulle's *Memoirs of Hope*', in Hoffman, *Decline or Renewal?*, 254–80. **61.** Blanc, *De Gaulle au soir*, 309. **62.** LNCIII 1157 (1/9/70). **63.** Mauriac, *Mort du Général*, 144. **64.** LNCIII 1170.

30. Myth, Legacy and Achievement

1. *Temps Modernes* 661 (11–12/2010). **2.** Winock, *Journal politique*, 240–41. **3.** Hazareesingh, *Mythe*, 152–3. **4.** Neau-Dufour, *Yvonne*, 440–507. **5.** To Jean de

Lipowski, quoted by Lacouture, *Souverain*, 755. **6.** BDIC, Fonds Rousset, Delta 1880/112/5. **7.** Francois Hincker, 'Le courant gaulliste dans la nation française', *Cahiers du Communisme* 12 (12/74), 60–69. **8.** Stéphane Courtois and Marc Lazar (eds.), *50 ans d'un passion française* (Balland, 1991). **9.** Julian Jackson, 'Les 18 juin de Pompidou à Sarkozy', in Oulmont, *Les 18 juin*, 208–31. **10.** Régis Debray, *Charles de Gaulle, Futurist of the Nation* (Verso, 1994), 4, 13, 52, 87. **11.** Claude Mauriac, *Et comme l'espérance est violente* (Grasset, 1976). **12.** *Le Monde* 27/9/2016. **13.** Guiblin, *Passion d'agir*, 181. **14.** Nadine Morano, http://www.lemonde.fr/les-decodeurs/article/2015/10/01/les-races-morano-et-de-gaulle-pour-clore-la-polemique_4780347_4355770.html. **15.** Marcel Gauchet, *Comprendre le malheur français* (Stock, 2016), 65–99. **16.** François Furet, 'Le "cinéma" du Général' (21/2/63) in *Penser le XXe siècle* (Bouquins, 2007), 50–53. On Furet's anti-gaullism see Christophe Prochasson, *Les chemins de la mélancolie. François Furet* (Stock, 2013), 370–87. **17.** Jean-François Revel, *Le style du Général* (Complexe, Brussels, 1988), 54–6. **18.** It seems impossible to establish who invented this phrase, which is often quoted with variants – for example http://www.jeuneafrique.com/58398/archives-thematique/de-gaulle-le-visionnaire. One biographer, Jonathan Fenby, *The General: Charles de Gaulle and the France He Saved* (Simon & Schuster, 2010), 3, attributes it to Malraux, but I have found the remark nowhere in Malraux's writings even if he did say it. **19.** AP 805 (1/7/64). **20.** AP 411–12. **21.** Malraux, *Chênes*, 119. **22.** Quoted in *Espoir* (6/83), 18. **23.** DGM 120. This was a slight misquotation of Chateaubriand who had in fact written: 'Je voulais moi, occuper les Français à la gloire, les attacher en haut, essayer de les mener à la realité par des songes.' **24.** Malraux, *Chênes*, 36. **25.** Kissinger, 'The Illusionist', 73. **26.** Aron, 'Le secret du général', in Aron, *La Coexistence*, 1136. **27.** Nicholas Henderson, *The Private Office* (Weidenfeld & Nicholson, 1987), 94–5. **28.** Bastien François, *La 6eme République. Pourquoi, comment?* (Les Petits Matins, 2015). **29.** DGESS-VIII, 73. **30.** Guy, *En écoutant*, 85–6 (26/6/46). **31.** Antoine de Saint-Exupéry, *Ecrits de guerre 1939–1944* (Gallimard, 1982), 259. **32.** Maritain's reply published in the newspaper *Pour la victoire*, 12/12/42, is reproduced in ibid., 275–81.

Index